International Directory of
COMPANY
HISTORIES

International Directory of

COMPANY

HISTORIES

VOLUME 12

Editor
Tina Grant

ST. JAMES PRESS

An ITP Information/Reference Group Company

I(T)P
―――――――――
Changing the Way the World Learns

NEW YORK • LONDON • BONN • BOSTON • DETROIT • MADRID
MELBOURNE • MEXICO CITY • PARIS • SINGAPORE • TOKYO
TORONTO • WASHINGTON • ALBANY NY ◦ BELMONT CA • CINCINNATI OH

STAFF

Tina Grant, *Editor*

Laura Berger, Joann Cerrito, David Collins, Nicolet V. Elert, Miranda Ferrara,
Paula Kepos, Janice Jorgensen, Margaret Mazurkiewicz, Mike Tyrkus, *Contributing Editors*

 The paper used in this publication meets the minimum
requirements of American National Standard for Information Sciences—
Permanence Paper for Printed Library Materials, ANSI Z39.48-1984.

Library of Congress Catalog Number: 89-190943

British Library Cataloguing in Publication Data

International directory of company histories. Vol. 12
I. Tina Grant
338.7409

ISBN 1-55862-327-2

Printed in the United States of America
Published simultaneously in the United Kingdom

I(T)P™

The trademark **ITP** is used under license.

Cover photograph of the International Trade Center, Budapest

10 9 8 7 6 5 4 3 2 1

CONTENTS _____

Company Histories

PREFACE

International Directory of Company Histories provides detailed information on the development of the world's largest and most influential companies. To date, *Company Histories* has covered more than 2000 companies in twelve volumes.

Inclusion Criteria

Most companies chosen for inclusion in *Company Histories* have achieved a minimum of US$200 million in annual sales and are leading influences in their industries or geographical locations. State-owned companies that are important in their industries and that may operate much like public or private companies also are included. Wholly owned subsidiaries are presented if they meet the requirements for inclusion.

St. James Press does not endorse any of the companies or products mentioned in this book. Companies that appear in *Company Histories* were selected without reference to their wishes and have in no way endorsed their entries. The companies were given the opportunity to participate in the compilation of the articles by providing information or reading their entries for factual accuracy, and we are indebted to many of them for their comments and corrections. We also thank them for allowing the use of their logos for identification purposes.

Entry Format

Each entry in this volume begins with a company's legal name, the address of its headquarters, its telephone number and fax number, and a statement of public, private, state, or parent ownership. A company with a legal name in both English and the language of its headquarters country is listed by the English name, with the native-language name in parentheses.

Also provided are the company's earliest incorporation date, the number of employees, and the most recent sales figures available. Sales figures are given in local currencies with equivalents in U.S. dollars. For some private companies, sales figures are estimates. The entry lists the exchanges on which a company's stock is traded, as well as the company's principal Standard Industrial Classification codes. American spelling is used, and the word ''billion'' is used in its American sense of one thousand million.

Sources

The histories were compiled from publicly accessible sources such as general and academic periodicals, books, annual reports, and material supplied by the companies themselves. *Company Histories* is intended for reference use by students, business people, librarians, historians, economists, investors, job candidates, and others who want to learn more about the historical development of the world's most important companies.

Cumulative Indexes

An Index to Companies and Persons provides access to companies and individuals discussed in the text. Beginning with Volume 7, an Index to Industries allows researchers to locate companies by their principal industry.

A.B.	Aktiebolaget (Sweden)
A.G.	Aktiengesellschaft (Germany, Switzerland)
A.S.	Atieselskab (Denmark)
A.S.	Aksjeselskap (Denmark, Norway)
A.Ş.	Anomin Şirket (Turkey)
B.V.	Besloten Vennootschap met beperkte, Aansprakelijkheid (The Netherlands)
Co.	Company (United Kingdom, United States)
Corp.	Corporation (United States)
G.I.E.	Groupement d'Intérêt Economique (France)
GmbH	Gesellschaft mit beschränkter Haftung (Germany)
H.B.	Handelsbolaget (Sweden)
Inc.	Incorporated (United States)
KGaA	Kommanditgesellschaft auf Aktien (Germany)
K.K.	Kabushiki Kaisha (Japan)
LLC	Limited Liability Company (Middle East)
Ltd.	Limited (Canada, Japan, United Kingdom, United States)
N.V.	Naamloze Vennootschap (The Netherlands)
OY	Osakeyhtiöt (Finland)
PLC	Public Limited Company (United Kingdom)
PTY.	Proprietary (Australia, Hong Kong, South Africa)
S.A.	Société Anonyme (Belgium, France, Switzerland)
SpA	Società per Azioni (Italy)

ABBREVIATIONS FOR CURRENCY _____

DA	Algerian dinar	Dfl	Netherlands florin
A$	Australian dollar	NZ$	New Zealand dollar
Sch	Austrian schilling	N	Nigerian naira
BFr	Belgian franc	NKr	Norwegian krone
Cr	Brazilian cruzado	RO	Omani rial
C$	Canadian dollar	P	Philippine peso
DKr	Danish krone	Esc	Portuguese escudo
E£	Egyptian pound	SRls	Saudi Arabian riyal
Fmk	Finnish markka	S$	Singapore dollar
FFr	French franc	R	South African rand
DM	German mark	W	South Korean won
HK$	Hong Kong dollar	Pta	Spanish peseta
Rs	Indian rupee	SKr	Swedish krona
Rp	Indonesian rupiah	SFr	Swiss franc
IR£	Irish pound	NT$	Taiwanese dollar
L	Italian lira	B	Thai baht
¥	Japanese yen	£	United Kingdom pound
W	Korean won	$	United States dollar
KD	Kuwaiti dinar	B	Venezuelan bolivar
LuxFr	Luxembourgian franc	K	Zambian kwacha
M$	Malaysian ringgit		

International Directory of
COMPANY
HISTORIES

A.L. Pharma Inc.

One Executive Drive
P.O. Box 1399
Fort Lee, New Jersey 07024
U.S.A.
(201) 947-7774
Fax: (201) 947-5541

Public Company
Incorporated: 1975 as A.L. Laboratories Inc.
Employees: 2,700
Sales: $469.3 million
Stock Exchanges: New York
SICs: 2834 Pharmaceutical Preparations; 2833 Medicinals
and Botanicals

Known as A.L. Laboratories Inc. until October 1994, A.L. Pharma Inc. is an international pharmaceutical company involved in manufacturing and marketing specialty generic and branded pharmaceuticals for people, as well as animal health products. Beginning as a subsidiary of a Norwegian pharmaceutical company, A.L. Pharma initially focused on producing animal feed antibiotics, particularly bacitracin, then increasingly became involved in manufacturing and marketing human pharmaceuticals. By the mid-1990s, A.L. Pharma's U.S. and international presence in the human pharmaceutical and animal products markets had increased considerably from the company's modest beginnings, positioning it as one of the emerging companies in the global pharmaceutical market.

A.L. Laboratories was formed in 1975 as a wholly owned subsidiary of Apothekernes Laboratorium A.S., a Norwegian manufacturer and marketer of pharmaceutical and health products for humans and animals. Founded in 1903, Apothekernes Laboratorium had been involved for years in the manufacture of bacitracin, an antibiotic for animal feed use. Initially, when Apothekernes Laboratorium began manufacturing bacitracin at its production facility in Oslo during the early 1950s, the substance was marketed as a pharmaceutical grade bulk antibiotic. Shortly thereafter, the applications for bacitracin broadened, and by the late 1950s Apothekernes Laboratorium began marketing the product as an animal feed additive. Bacitracin became the mainstay product for the newly-formed A.L. Laboratories when it established its headquarters in Englewood, New Jersey, in 1975.

Instrumental in the formation of A.L. Laboratories was I. Roy Cohen, who, along with Einer W. Sissener, would figure prominently in the company's history for roughly the next 20 years. Under Cohen's and Sissener's stewardship, A. L. Laboratories would experience dramatic growth, evolving into a well-rounded pharmaceutical company that, like its progenitor Apothekernes Laboratorium, would enjoy considerable presence in the pharmaceutical markets for both humans and animals. Initially, however, Cohen, who served as A.L. Laboratories' president, steered the company toward further growth in the bacitracin field; with annual revenues totaling $6 million shortly after formation, the full development of the company into other segments of the pharmaceutical market would take time.

The expansion of A.L. Laboratories' size and scope was facilitated by its relationship with Apothekernes Laboratorium. With its parent company's backing, A.L. Laboratories received more favorable terms on bank credit than competitor companies of commensurate size. This was an invaluable asset during the company's formative years, particularly when it came to acquiring other companies.

An important step toward increasing the company's U.S. and European presence in the bacitracin field was taken in 1979, when A.L. Laboratories acquired the chemical and fermentation businesses of Dawe's Laboratories, Inc. Located in Chicago Heights, Illinois, these facilities included chemical, fermentation, and blending installations that provided A.L. Laboratories with its entry into organic chemical production and augmented its bacitracin manufacturing capabilities. Ground was broken the following year for a multi-million dollar expansion of the Chicago Heights facilities that, as Cohen related to *Chemical Marketing Reporter* at the time, would "greatly increase antibiotic production capacity [and] multiply our output of feed grade bacitracin." With the bacitracin manufactured at these facilities, A.L. Laboratories marketed its primary product, "Bacitracin-MD," a feed supplement, used for disease prevention, growth promotion, and feed efficiency in the poultry and swine industries.

Prior to the expansion of A.L. Laboratories' Chicago Heights facilities, many of the products marketed as animal feed antibiotics were found to cause pernicious side effects. The FDA, responding to the complaints by meat and poultry producers, stepped in and began closely scrutinizing the production of animal feed antibiotics. Excluded from these charges of product inferiority was A.L. Laboratories' Bacitracin-MD, a product meat and poultry producers favored because it did not develop tissue residues in animals. Demand for Bacitracin-MD, and its companion product, "Solu-tracin 50", consequently shot up, providing a boost to A.L. Laboratories' business and creating a need for increased production, a need the expansion of the Chicago Heights facilities was designed to meet.

With business steadily growing, A.L. Laboratories entered the early 1980s propelled by the increasing popularity of bacitracin. By 1983, the company's Bacitracin-MD had been renamed as BMD. That year, A.L. Laboratories completed a major transaction, perhaps the most pivotal purchase in the company's early history, when it acquired a Danish health concern named A/S Dumex. Based in Copenhagen, Dumex was a manufacturer of branded pharmaceuticals, fermentation antibiotics, and nutritional beverage products, which the company sold in more than 40 countries. Included in the deal were manufacturing facilities that, along with Dumex' product line, complemented A.L. Laboratories' business in the United States and in Norway and gave the company access to important markets in Africa and Asia, where historically it had maintained only a nominal presence.

The following year, A.L. Laboratories became a publicly-held corporation, as Apothekernes Laboratorium gradually began to cede a part of its stake in its formerly wholly owned U.S. subsidiary. The year of A.L. Laboratories' initial public offering also marked the first full year that the company's 1983 acquisition of Dumex contributed to annual revenue. For the year, A.L. Laboratories generated $85.9 million and posted $4.3 million in net income, a laudable increase in nine years time. However, shortly thereafter, expectations would run high, leading A.L. Laboratories' management, still led by Cohen, to set goals of financial growth that dwarfed the company's record of growth during its first decade.

Generally, this desire to become a much larger company meant that A.L. Laboratories would increasingly become involved in the manufacture and marketing of pharmaceuticals for humans and pursue less aggressively its interests in the animal antibiotic market. This new business strategy was manifested in 1987, when A.L. Laboratories acquired Baltimore, Maryland-based Barre-National from Revco D.S. Inc. for $95 million. The largest U.S. manufacturer of generic cold medicines, Barre-National manufactured more than 200 prescription and over-the-counter drugs, giving A.L. Laboratories a substantial stake in the pharmaceutical market. But, the greatest asset the acquisition gave the company was Barre-National's commanding lead in the liquid (as opposed to tablets or capsules) generic drug market. In this expanding niche of the more broadly defined pharmaceutical market, Barre-National controlled 40 percent of the U.S. market, an entirely new market for A.L. Laboratories that represented the company's future.

Before being acquired by A.L. Laboratories, Barre-National had produced $45 million in annual revenues; by the end of 1988, the first full year under A.L. Laboratories' corporate umbrella, Barre-National's revenues jumped to $65 million, pushing A.L. Laboratories' revenue total for the year to $236.4 million. The growth of Barre-National (which, like Dumex, operated as a subsidiary of A.L. Laboratories) and the initial success recorded in the company's new market validated the decision by A.L. Laboratories' management to seek expansion through the manufacture and marketing of liquid generics, which promised to increase in popularity in the coming years. From 1989 to 1994, the liquid generics market was projected to nearly triple in dollar volume to reach $400 million, a substantial portion of which A.L. Laboratories expected to garner through Barre-National's tight grip on the market. Moreover, there was a relative paucity of competition in the field; only 12 percent of branded (non-generic) liquid pharmaceuticals had generic counterparts, while 25 percent of the branded pharmaceutical tablet and capsule products competed against generic equivalents. With these encouraging signs pointing toward potentially dramatic growth, Cohen gave the rest of the company's management a formidable goal: by the end of the 1990s, Cohen expected A.L. Laboratories to be a $1 billion company.

In late 1989, pharmaceutical sales composed 65 percent of the company's business, while animal health products contributed 20 percent. Although A.L. Laboratories had shifted its focus to pharmaceuticals for human use, the company still held an enviable position in the animal antibiotic industry, which continued to suffer from allegations that many of the products contained harmful residues. A.L. Laboratories had avoided these charges and earned a profitable reputation as one of the few reliable animal antibiotic manufacturers. Barre-National, by now in its second full year under A.L. Laboratories management, continued to grow, contributing $85 million, or 30 percent, to its parent company's revenue total. Shortly after Cohen made his prediction that A.L. Laboratories would reach the $1 billion plateau by the end of the decade, the company recorded $266.2 million in revenue. Although still a long way from the target figure, Cohen had plans to help A.L. Laboratories achieve the goal.

The most expeditious path was through the acquisition of pharmaceutical and animal antibiotic companies, a course of action for which Cohen prepared. Also during this time, Cohen, then in his late 60s, began looking for a suitable replacement for himself. This would be the first change in leadership in the company's history. After months of discussions in 1990, a suitable replacement was found in Richard P. Storm, an executive with 30 years of experience in the pharmaceutical industry. Of British and Norwegian descent, Storm was born in Argentina, where he later worked for Pfizer Inc., spending 19 years at the Argentinean operations of the giant pharmaceutical company. After leaving Pfizer, Storm moved to the United States in 1980 to join Abbott Laboratories, where he spent another four years before joining Rorer Group, a Fort Washington, Pennsylvania-based pharmaceutical manufacturer.

Selected as A.L. Laboratories' president and chief executive officer in January 1991, Storm left his position as executive vice-president at Rorer Group and immediately set himself to the task of achieving his new company's financial goal. The year of A.L. Laboratories predicted ascension to the $1 billion level had been formally pushed back to 2000, but Storm, nevertheless, approached its fulfillment with a sense of urgency. Several months before Storm assumed stewardship of A.L. Laboratories, the company had purchased NMC Laboratories Inc., a Glendale, New York-based manufacturer and marketer of prescription creams and ointments. The acquisition of NMC added $14 million to A.L. Laboratories annual revenue total, but, by the time Storm came aboard, Cohen had much more to offer his protégé.

In the months leading up to Storm's selection, Cohen had arranged the financing to launch a series of acquisitions, obtaining $220 million from a consortium of 11 European banks led by Union Bank of Norway. Accordingly, Cohen not only handed Storm the reins of the company in January 1991, but also a considerably fattened corporate wallet. Storm took both, clearly elated by the opportunity before him. In an article for the *Business Journal of New Jersey,* Storm related, "It has been my objective to be a CEO of a NYSE-listed company. This is a major move; hopefully, the last in my career." To the *New York Times* Storm succinctly related that becoming chief executive of A.L. Laboratories "fulfills all my ambitions."

Six months later, however, Storm was gone, leaving without explanation at the end of July 1991. In response to Storm's departure, company officials stated that his background at large pharmaceutical companies did not conform to A.L. Laboratories entrepreneurial style. To fill the void left by Storm's exit, the company created a three-member office of the chief executive comprising Jeffrey E. Smith, A.L. Laboratories' chief financial officer since 1984, Cohen, and Sissener, who had been and continued to be the board's chairperson.

Two months after Storm left, A.L. Laboratories acquired the entire feed additive line of Solvay Animal Health Inc., a $12 million company that fleshed out A.L. Laboratories' animal health product line. The following year, in 1992, a story of significant importance to A.L. Laboratories appeared in the *Wall Street Journal,* announcing the possibility that the company was intending to combine some or all of its businesses with Apothekernes Laboratorium, which by this point held a less than 40 percent stake in the company. Actually, talk of somehow combining the complementary businesses of Apothekernes Laboratorium and A.L. Laboratories first began in the mid-1980s, but by the early 1990s these discussions had become much more purposeful and explicit. After several years of negotiations, it was agreed in October 1994 that A.L. Laboratories would purchase the pharmaceutical, animal health, aquatic animal health, and bulk antibiotics businesses of its former parent, Apothekernes Laboratorium.

Beyond the material assets gained, the acquisition also led to a name change for A.L. Laboratories to A.L. Pharma Inc., which the company's management felt better reflected the scope of the company's operations and its greater interest in pharmaceuticals. Bolstered by the addition of Apothekernes Laboratorium's valuable assets, A.L. Pharma entered the mid-1990s with Sissener at the helm, serving as both the chairperson and chief executive officer. Commenting on the acquisition, Sissener stated, "The objective of the combination is to create an entity that will be in a stronger position to compete on a worldwide basis in specialized human pharmaceutical and animal health products." With this expectation, A.L. Pharma plotted its course beyond the mid-1990s, intent on eclipsing the $1 billion mark.

Principal Subsidiaries: Barre Parent Corp.; Barre-National, Inc.; G.F. Reilly Co.; ParMed Pharmaceuticals, Inc.; Biomed, Inc.; NMC Laboratories, Inc.; Able Acquisitions, Inc.

Further Reading:

"A.L. Laboratories Buys Danish Drug Concern," *Chemical Marketing Reporter,* September 12, 1983, p. 9.
"A.L. Laboratories Buys Dawe's Laboratories; Vitamin Line Is Included," *Chemical Marketing Reporter,* October 22, 1979, p. 4.
"A.L. Laboratories Inc.," *Wall Street Journal,* April 13, 1992, p. B4.
"A.L. Laboratories Inc.," *Drug and Cosmetic Industry,* August 1991, p. 62.
"A.L. Laboratories Inc.," *Fortune,* December 5, 1988, p. 140.
"A.L. Laboratories Inc.," *Wall Street Journal,* October 2, 1987, p. 32.
"A.L. Labs Completes Acquisition," *Wall Street Journal,* October 4, 1994, p. A8.
"A.L. Laboratories Picks Richard Storm for Two Top Posts," *Wall Street Journal,* January 15, 1991, p. B10.
"Bacitracin, Other Drugs Expanded with New Plant," *Chemical Marketing Reporter,* July 28, 1980, p. 5.
Byrne, Harlan S., "A.L. Laboratories Inc.: It Steers Clear of Generic Drug Troubles," *Barron's,* November 20, 1989, p. 58.
Cuff, Daniel F., "Chief Executive Named for A.L. Laboratories," *New York Times,* January 15, 1991, p. D4.
Peaff, George Jr., "Super CEOs," *Business Journal of New Jersey,* April 1991, pp. 24–5.
"Skin Deep," *Business Journal of New Jersey,* October 1990, p. 16.
"Storm Resigns as Head of Drug Maker A.L. Labs," *Wall Street Journal,* July 31, 1991, p. B4.

—Jeffrey L. Covell

Ace Hardware Corporation

2200 Kensington Court
Oak Brook, Illinois 60521
U.S.A.
(708) 990-6600
Fax: (708) 573-4894

Private Company
Incorporated: 1928
Employees: 3,900
Sales: $2.32 billion
SICs: 5072 Hardware

Ace Hardware Corporation is a dealer-owned cooperative that pools buying and promotions for more than 5,000 local hardware, home center, and lumber stores in all fifty of the United States as well as 57 countries and territories. Ace's emphasis on service and modern retailing techniques has helped locally owned and operated Ace retail stores confront intense competition from such home improvement powerhouses as Home Depot and Builders Square. In 1993 the retail support company surpassed $2 billion in sales, a 7.9 percent increase over the previous year.

The organization was founded in the early 1920s, when Richard Hesse, Frank Burke, Oscar Fisher, E. Gunnard Linquist, and William Stauber united to form a purchasing and advertising partnership among their Chicago-area hardware stores. Their combined buying power enabled the store owners to negotiate lower prices on merchandise purchased from wholesalers. The partners adopted the Ace name in 1927 and incorporated the following year. Within two years, Ace evolved into a wholesaling organization, purchasing direct from manufacturers and storing merchandise in its own Chicago warehouse. This move further reduced costs by cutting out the "middlemen" wholesalers, thereby giving Ace members the choice of a competitive edge (they could reduce retail prices) or fatter margins (they could maintain their prices and enjoy higher profits). Frank Burke served briefly as president of the organization, and was succeeded by Richard Hesse in 1930. Hesse served in that capacity over four decades, until the end of 1973.

For its first half-century of operation, Ace was essentially a conventional wholesale group, and its profits were shared by its shareholders. The group's low-cost purchasing and distribution quickly attracted new members and some franchisees. During its early years, use of the Ace name was recommended but optional; it would later be mandatory for new affiliates. President Hesse expanded services to associates, including a semi-annual dealer convention featuring the products and promotions available through the wholesaler. Those meetings continued through the 1990s. By the mid-1930s, the organization had 41 dealer/members and sales of more than $650,000. The expanding roster of affiliates necessitated a doubling of warehouse capacity during that decade.

The postwar era saw the dawn of America's "do-it-yourself" (DIY) revolution. Industry analysts have attributed the spectacular growth of this market to several factors. The generally high cost of new homes drove consumers into widely available, but sometimes neglected, existing homes. The high charges exacted by repairmen and contractors impelled homeowners to attempt home repair and improvement projects on their own. The emergence of new tools and products that were easy to use furthered the trend. Finally, some observers of the DIY movement have credited the more intangible, but undoubtedly strong, sense of satisfaction attained by consumers who completed a project themselves while saving money at the same time.

On the strength of growing DIY sales, Ace's nationwide revenues increased to $25 million by the end of the 1950s. The organization opened its first distribution centers beyond the bounds of Chicago in 1969. A California facility served the expanding West Coast membership, and an Atlanta warehouse promoted growth in the south. These were the first of 14 retail support centers across the country by 1994.

Before he retired in 1973, co-founder and long-time president Richard Hesse sold Ace to its member-dealers, thereby forming a dealer-owned hardware cooperative. Purchase of a minimum stake in Ace was required for membership, and dealers contributed a percentage of their co-op purchases to a national advertising fund. Under this new scheme, Ace's profits were returned to its dealer-owners through cash or stock rebates at year's end. The company opened its fourth distribution center in Toledo, Ohio, and moved its expanded corporate headquarters to Oak Brook, Illinois, a western suburb of Chicago, that same year. By 1976, when ownership of Ace had passed completely to its dealers, the organization's sales volume had reached $382 million. Since then, Ace's board of directors has been made up of dealers.

Arthur Krausman succeeded Hesse as president in January 1974 and advanced to chairman of the board in 1980. During the ensuing years, Ace's member services expanded to include training and education, merchandising, computerized inventory control, insurance, and store layout. The continuous addition of new members during the 1970s necessitated the establishment of new warehouses and distribution centers. By the end of the decade, the organization added five facilities in the Midwest and Southeast. This diffusion of distribution points helped save freight costs, since many manufacturers were willing to ship freight-paid within a given distance. The company achieved national penetration in 1978, when it signed on members in the eastern United States. Ace's growth coincided with a six-fold increase in the DIY market, from just under $6 billion in 1970, to $35 billion in 1980, to more than $100 billion by the end of the 1980s. Traditional hardware stores like those owned by Ace members soon found their competition growing too, as mass merchandisers like the ''category killer'' Home Depot, Inc., began to get in on the profitable trend. Even supermarketers, discounters, and drug stores began carrying profitable hardware lines during the decade.

While drugstores and grocery stores were overtaken by the chain store revolution in the 1970s, the hardware segment continued to be dominated by independents through the mid-1980s. By 1984, 85 percent of the 23,500 retail hardware stores in the United States were affiliated with co-ops, and those groups held the top share, 48 percent, of annual hardware sales. Some observers credited this phenomenon to dealer-owned cooperatives (or ''voluntary chains,'' as they were termed by the National Retail Hardware Association). Others credited the personalized service offered by independent retailers. In a 1980 interview with *Hardware Age,* Ace Chairman Krausman credited the flexibility, inventory depth, and advertising of independent operators with their success.

By 1984, Ace's national advertising budget topped $10 million, most of which was spent on television spots. Ace capitalized on its members' reputation for having knowledgeable personnel with the slogan ''Ace is the place with the helpful hardware man.'' (This was later modified to the gender-neutral ''helpful hardware folks.'') Television spots often featured celebrities, including singer Connie Stevens and actress Suzanne Somers in the 1970s and 1980s, and football commentator John Madden in the 1990s. The company continued to emphasize service in advertisements that showcased ''helpful'' Ace dealers around the country through the middle of the decade. Ace sales more than doubled during the 1980s, from $801 million in 1983 to more than $2 billion in 1993.

Following a trend that began in retail foods, Ace introduced a line of private label products in the early 1990s. Private label products enable retailers to offer their customers a consistently low-priced product while generating higher profit margins for themselves. One of Ace's first private label goods was paint, which it began manufacturing in 1984 in a state of the art facility in Illinois. (Until that time, Ace paint had been manufactured by the Valspar Corp., beginning in the 1930s.) Although paint is generally considered a low-growth commodity, it is a do-it-yourself mainstay. Low brand loyalty and high price sensitivity made it an ideal private label product. By the early 1990s, Ace's paint division was expanding faster than the rest of the paint industry, and had become the foundation of a private label program of nearly 7,000 items. From 1988 to 1993, private label sales grew at an average annual rate of 12.9 percent, to $350 million. The group planned to transform its private label into a national brand through extensive promotions in the mid-1990s. A second paint manufacturing facility opened in 1995 in Chicago Heights, Illinois.

While Ace manufactured many of its own paints, the company also purchased some paints (particularly aerosols) from other producers, including Sherwin-Williams, DAP, and ITW Devcon. The company became involved in a product labeling suit with the Attorney General of the state of California for neglecting to warn consumers that several of Sherwin-Williams' paints contained toluene, a known carcinogen. Although Sherwin-Williams' settlement cost it more than $1 million, Ace was simply required to add appropriate warnings on its toluene-based paints.

In October 1994, the Ace officers and board of directors launched a strategic plan known as ''The New Age of Ace,'' an acceleration of a previous strategic process called ''Ace 2000.'' They laid out four primary objectives to be achieved by the year 2000: improved retail performance, more efficient operations, international growth, and a faster pace for new store openings. Ace hoped to increase its wholesale sales to $5 billion by the end of the 1990s. The vast majority of that growth, or $4.2 billion, was expected to come from existing dealers. A key aspect of Ace's plan involved incentives for dealers to meet certain standards or risk losing full retail support from the corporation. These requirements included relinquishing connections with any other buying organizations, making at least 80 percent of merchandise purchases through Ace (including and especially Ace paint), using Ace signage, and participating with vendors on special purchases. By late 1994, about 1,500 of Ace's 5,000 dealers did not comply with these minimum requirements. One Ace executive noted that this list of noncompliant retailers would gradually be reduced, as they either joined the majority of dealers or dropped from the organization.

As part of its plan to improve retail performance, Ace also announced that it would open three of its own stores in the Chicago area to test retail concepts. Results would be shared with all Ace retailers. Although the company assured its members that it was not planning to acquire or build a significant number of group-owned stores, this aspect of ''Ace 2000'' disturbed some dealers, according to a December 1994 article in *Do-It-Yourself Retailing.* In fact, the strategic plan called for dealers themselves to generate nearly $500 million in new sales and open 1,000 new stores in underserved markets by the turn of the century. Ace planned to deploy consultants to help retailers identify potential new store sites.

Ace's strategic plan also called for improvements in its warehousing operation through technological advances and increased cooperation with vendors. Goals included vendor consolidation; enhanced electronic data interchange between vendors, warehouses, and retailers; and the expansion of vendor-managed inventory systems to control up to one-fourth of inventory.

The company planned to quadruple its international sales to $400 million by 2000, with a special focus on South America. The passage of the North American Free Trade Agreement (NAFTA) in 1994 prompted Ace to plan a paint plant in Texas, in order to meet anticipated demand from the 70 Mexican Ace stores that were open by that time, and the 26 more that were expected to open soon. Overseas sales had increased by nearly one-third overall from 1992 to 1993, and by more than 60 percent in Mexico alone. Other areas of concentration include the Middle East, Eastern Europe, Latin America, and the Pacific Rim. According to *Do-It-Yourself Retailing,* Ace hoped to ''evolve from being only an exporter to becoming a true world trading company'' by offering international affiliates the services enjoyed by dealers in the United States. Licensing could play an important role in the organization's overseas expansion.

The promulgation of the goals of Ace 2000 and The New Age of Ace exemplify two fundamental changes in the organization and the retail hardware industry. First, by the 1990s Ace had clearly expanded its expectations of and responsibilities to its affiliates. Second, it demonstrated the organization's determination to survive and grow in the face of increasingly intense competition from what one industry journal called "the big boxes," or mass home improvement merchants. As CEO Roger Peterson, who retired in May 1995, told *Do-It-Yourself Retailing* in December 1994, "Such growth is necessary if Ace is to remain a major player in the hardware industry, capitalize on the Ace name and reputation, and establish footholds in markets before competition gains a strangle hold."

Although Ace had clearly mapped out an independent future, the possibility of a coalition of hardware co-ops to compete with "the big boxes" had not been ruled out by Ace management. At a dealer forum in October 1993, Peterson acknowledged that he had met with leaders from the other leading home improvement cooperatives, including Cotter & Company, SERVISTAR, Hardware Wholesalers Inc., and Coast to Coast. He noted that while they consulted on issues including freight consolidation and insurance, joint purchasing and pricing agreements were, of course, off limits.

Further Reading:

"California Labeling-Suit Settlement Tops $1 Million," *Hardware Age,* May 1994, p. 17.

Cory, Jim, "On the Road," *Hardware Age,* April 1994, p. 73.

Davis, Jo Ellen, "Hardware Wars: The Big Boys Might Lose This One," *Business Week,* October 14, 1985, pp. 84–86.

Goldman, Tamara, "Nailing Down the Home Improvement Market," *Marketing Communications,* October 1988, pp. 49–52.

"Hardware Supplement—Hardware Sales: Healthy but Not Spectacular," *Discount Merchandiser,* August 1987, pp. 79–96.

Holtzman, M. Jay, "New Blood, Old Values," *Hardware Age,* October 1980, pp. 95–101.

"Home Improvement Booms in 1993," *Chain Store Age Executive,* August 1994, pp. 14A-16A.

Jensen, Christopher A., "The New Age of Ace," *Do-It-Yourself Retailing,* December 1994, pp. 57–58.

Pellet, Jennifer, "No Paint, No Gain," *Discount Merchandiser,* March 1992, pp. 74–75.

Reda, Susan, "DIYers Daunted by Paint Choices," *Stores,* August 1994, pp. 52–53.

Uihlein, Reven, "Co-Ops Stave off Hard Times for Hardware," *Advertising Age,* August 30, 1984, pp. 16–17.

—April Dougal Gasbarre

ADT Security Systems, Inc.

Security Systems

300 Interplace Parkway
Parsippany, New Jersey 07054
U.S.A.
(201) 316-1000
Fax: (201) 316-1330

Wholly Owned Subsidiary of ADT Ltd.
Incorporated: 1901
Employees: 12,000
Sales: $937 million
Stock Exchanges: New York London Frankfort Toronto
SICs: 7382 Security Systems Services

ADT Security Systems, Inc. is the principal subsidiary of ADT Ltd., which is comprised of a security division (68 percent of sales), a vehicle auction business (25 percent), and miscellaneous holdings. ADT Security Systems provides various security- and safety-related services, but its main source of revenue is electronic monitoring of its installed base of security systems. With operations primarily in the United States and Europe, ADT led the fragmented security industry going into the mid-1990s. Its systems protected more than 25 million people in 1994.

ADT's roots reach back to 1874, when the American District Telegraph Company (ADTC) was founded in Baltimore to deliver telegraph messages. The telegraph was the speediest means of communication known at the time. When a customer wanted to send a message by telegraph, he would write the communiqué and carry it to a local district telegraph agency. (Other customers had call boxes installed in their home or place of business which they could use to electronically summon a courier to come and get their message.) At the district telegraph agency, the message was reformatted for swift transmission over the telegraph lines to another agency, which would decode the memorandum and dispatch one of its uniformed messenger boys to deliver it.

The ADTC messenger boy system epitomized the intriguing slice of Americana that was the telegraph system. ADTC maintained rigid standards for its messengers, who attained nearly legendary status in some cities. Paramount among requirements were speed and dependability. According to company annals, one rule stated that "messengers on foot may not take more than one-and-one-half minutes per block." ADTC also required

the boys to be in and out of a building in less than two minutes. Some superintendents kept the boys in line by writing regularly to their parents, informing them of their offspring's performance. Worse yet, the racing messengers would reportedly be chased by children on occasion, who jeered "ADT . . . all day trotters."

ADTC was created by merging 57 district telegraph agencies from different cities into a single, consolidated operation. The resultant organization made it possible for the different agencies to benefit from various economies of scale. Importantly, an improved call box allowed customers in some cities to send different signals that would let the agency know their specific need before the messenger was even dispatched. The result of the new system was that customers were suddenly able to signal their need for the police, a doctor, the fire department, or even a wagon or coach.

Thus, the seeds of ADT security had been planted. By the late 1800s, in fact, a jingle had been written to promote ADTC's services: "A trusty guardian of property . . . day or night protection constantly . . . that's the system, value, and service of ADT." "Way back, they used to have runners," explained ADT Operations Supervisor Dave Roersma in the April 28, 1986 *Grand Rapids Business Journal.* Roersma related: "They'd get signals from different buildings. If somebody had a fire, they'd send a signal down and a runner would grab the message and run down to the fire department. They even used bicycles for a while."

ADT's advanced call boxes were installed only in ADT's more populous districts, while traditional messenger services continued to account for about three-quarters of the company's sales through the end of the nineteenth century. By the early 1900s, however, local telephone systems were rapidly displacing the labor-intensive messenger services. To combat telephone competition, ADT scrambled to convert the majority of its messenger systems to electronic signaling in a span of only ten years. The successful transition was partly a result of ADT becoming a subsidiary of Western Union in 1901. Western Union dominated the telegraph industry and was able to help finance ADT's widespread conversion to electronic signaling.

The supremacy of the telegraph system quickly waned after the turn of the century. Emerging communications giant American Telephone and Telegraph Company (AT&T) bought out Western Union, along with ADT, in 1909. Under the auspices of AT&T, ADT's messenger operations were jettisoned, and the company became focused entirely on the signalling business. AT&T took a particular interest in ADT, placing it under the direct leadership of former AT&T President Theodore N. Vail. Vail steered ADT toward an emphasis on security services. Benefitting from AT&T's renowned research and development labs, ADT leapfrogged its potential competitors throughout the 1920s and 1930s with ongoing advancements in theft and fire alarm systems.

A manpower shortage during World War II generated a need for automated alarm systems that were less dependent on humans to signal for help. In response, ADT developed several landmark systems that were considered extremely advanced at the time. Chief among its breakthroughs were the ADT Teletherm (an automatic fire detection system) and ADT Telewave (and automated intrusion detection system). ADT experienced strong growth during the postwar U.S. economic expansion of the 1950s and 1960s. In addition to assuming a leadership role in the U.S. security systems industry, ADT began expanding internationally, particularly in the United Kingdom.

ADT broke away from AT&T in 1968 and became a publicly traded company on the New York Stock Exchange. By that time, computer technology was already emerging that would radically change the complexion of communication and security related industries within a few decades. Specifically, semiconductor components began to be incorporated in security and communications equipment, a development that allowed ADT to begin building components and systems that were smaller, less expensive, and more capable. ADT introduced its first solid-state device in the early 1970s and subsequently developed the first multiplex detection and alarm system, which could simultaneously send multiple messages, or signals, on the same radio frequency or wire.

The advanced semiconductor equipment during the 1970s was significant in that it vastly broadened the potential market for all types of security systems. Prior to the 1970s, security and fire detection systems were purchased almost entirely by businesses or only very wealthy individuals. As the cost of new technology began to fall during the 1970s, though, it became clear to ADT that small businesses and middle-income homeowners would soon be added to the industry's expanding target market. By the late 1970s, in fact, many insurance companies were offering discounted premiums to homeowners who installed security systems.

To take advantage of surging demand, ADT continued to innovate throughout the 1970s and early 1980s. Importantly, ADT launched the first ''central station'' in the mid-1970s. Central station monitoring represented a major improvement over traditional, locally based fire and intruder systems. From a central station, ADT was able to monitor a large base of customers' premises electronically, round-the-clock, every day of the year. A single monitoring station would eventually be used to protect thousands of homes in a multi-state area. Integrated into ADT's central monitoring systems during the early 1980s were a variety of new components and services, including: Unimode, a fire detection system; CentraScan, a patented computer-based comprehensive security system; and Safe-Watch, an advanced residential surveillance system.

ADT continued to benefit from improved technology during the 1980s as its base of both commercial and residential customers expanded. The company also prospered as a result of rising crime rates, particularly in major metropolitan areas. By the late 1980s, ADT was serving virtually every Fortune 500 company in some capacity. Furthermore, even though the industry was highly fragmented, ADT's five-plus percent market share was estimated to be at least as great as the combined share of its next three largest North American competitors.

Much of ADT's growth during the 1980s was attributable to residential markets. As consumers became more concerned about crime, and as technology costs dropped, sales of home security systems surged. Instead of tailoring commercial equip-

ment to residential applications, ADT began developing entire product lines specifically for home use. The systems were designed to perform a variety of functions, such as tracking an intruder's movements inside the home, monitoring the home through the telephone, detecting broken pipes, and even noting whether a customer's freezer had stopped operating. A typical basic residential ADT system in the mid-1980s could be installed for under $1,000, with monitoring fees usually running less than $250 annually.

In 1987, ADT, Inc. was acquired by Hawley Group Limited of the United Kingdom. Hawley was a group of diversified companies active in service and other industries, including the electronic security industry. It had begun building its North American security company holdings in 1981 with the purchase of Electro-Protective Corporation of America in 1981. Between 1982 and 1985, Hawley purchased an assemblage of small security service businesses throughout North America. Its crowning acquisition was ADT. In fact, after the buyout, Hawley changed its name to ADT Limited, and broke its operations into two divisions, the largest of which became ADT Security Systems, Inc.

As a result of the merger with ADT, Inc. and several of Hawley's complementary subsidiaries, ADT Security Systems' sales bolted to about $800 million by the late 1980s. Furthermore, ADT purchased Britannia Security Group PLC, an industry leader in the United Kingdom, in 1990. That purchase, combined with other security company holdings in England purchased by Hawley during the 1980s, helped to boost ADT's aggregate sales to $880 million. Despite general economic malaise in both the United States and Britain, as well as major financial setbacks related to other of ADT Limited's holdings, ADT Security Systems, Inc. continued to perform admirably during the early 1990s.

New product introductions were an important contributor to ADT's expansion during the early 1990s. ADT introduced its popular FOCUS system, which allowed commercial customers to more specifically designate protection zones that could be independently monitored. For example, a perimeter area could be monitored while offices inside the perimeter were left open to employees. ADT also bolstered its line of video surveillance equipment and introduced a slew of home security devices.

By the early 1990s, ADT was offering a full line of advanced security services and systems for the massive upper-middle and middle-income residential market. In most cases, ADT retained ownership of the installed system. The customer paid a one-time installation fee and also agreed to pay an annual service charge for monitoring and maintenance. As new products and services were introduced, ADT expected to make money through system upgrades. The systems, like those designed for commercial use, were commonly configured to detect movement, break-ins, fire, smoke, flooding, and other hazards. ADT could respond by phoning the police, notifying the homeowner, and/or dispatching ADT security personnel to the home.

Besides new products, ADT's growth during the early 1990s was largely a consequence of its newfound emphasis on the booming residential market. After the 1987 acquisition, ADT implemented an aggressive program of consolidation and growth centered on the home security market. The company cut its number of central monitoring stations from 162 to just 30 in North America and Europe, while at the same time significantly boosting monitoring capacity and geographic coverage. The end result was reduced operating costs and system prices. Lower prices, in turn, translated into a larger base of potential customers, particularly homeowners in lower income, high-crime areas.

During the early 1990s, sales of security services and systems to the commercial sector stagnated, squelching sales and income growth in that segment; ADT's base of business customers (customers to which ADT continued to provide monitoring services) wavered around the 385,000 mark. In contrast, residential sales exploded. As a result of savvy marketing and proliferating homeowner concerns about security, ADT boosted its base of residential customers to a record 265,000 by 1991. By 1993, moreover, that base had multiplied to 477,000, representing a leading four percent share of the North American home security market.

As residential sales surged, ADT Security Systems' revenues rose from $880 million in 1991 to $901 million in 1992, and then to a record $937 million during 1993. Net income jumped similarly, to about $150 million in 1993. Adding to ADT's revenues were sales from its related electronic article surveillance business, which featured systems used to tag articles in inventory, such as retail clothing. The tags had to be removed by a special device to avoid setting off an alarm, which was usually located at the facility's exit. Electronic article surveillance equipment registered five percent, or about $44 million, of ADT's sales in 1993.

From a group of 57 telegraph service companies, ADT Security Systems had blossomed into a nearly $1 billion security systems company by the mid-1990s. The subsidiary employed a work force of more than 12,000 and generated more than 20 percent of its revenues from operations outside North America. Steady gains in residential sales and an uptick in commercial markets suggested continued growth in the short term. Likewise, increasing concern about crime in the United States, combined with decreasing technology costs, suggested a bright long term future for the industry leader.

Further Reading:

A Brief History of the World Leader in Security for Home and Business, Parsippany, N.J.: ADT Security Systems, 1994.
''ADT Security Welcomes Wendell Thomas To Winston-Salem,'' *Winston-Salem Journal,* April 7, 1992.
''ADT Reports Sales and Operating Income Increases for 1992,'' *PR Newswire,* March 11, 1993.
Fast, Doug, ''Security Systems—Just Like Having Clint Eastwood Around,'' *Grand Rapids Business Journal,* April 28, 1986, p. 5.
Poler, Donna, ''ADT Security Systems Introduces the Focus R 55 Commercial Security System,'' *Business Wire,* June 4, 1991.

—Dave Mote

AMC Entertainment Inc.

106 W. 14th Street
Kansas City, Missouri 64105
U.S.A.
(816) 221-4000
Fax: (816) 421-5744

Public Company
Incorporated: 1968
Employees: 8,000
Sales: $587 million
Stock Exchanges: American
SICs: 7832 Motion Picture Theaters Except Drive-In; 7833
   Drive-In Motion Picture Theaters

AMC Entertainment Inc., through its American Multi-Cinema, Inc. subsidiary, is one of the largest motion picture exhibitors in the United States in terms of number of theater screens operated. In 1994, AMC was running 236 theaters with 1,603 screens in 22 states. An industry leader in the development and operation of multi-screen cinemas, AMC was generating annual ticket sales of nearly $400 million going into the mid-1990s.

AMC was incorporated by Stanley H. Durwood in 1968, but the business was actually started by Durwood's father in 1920. The elder Durwood had previously been a struggling actor working for a traveling tent show. In 1920, he bailed out of his acting career and leased a movie theater in downtown Kansas City. Also in 1920, Durwood's wife gave birth to Stanley, who would grow the start-up business into a small theater empire before the end of the century. During the 1920s and 1930s, Durwood was successful enough to open a few more theaters in the Kansas City area. He was also did well enough to help send Stanley to Harvard during the early 1940s.

Stanley Durwood graduated from Harvard in 1943 with a Bachelor of Arts degree. He joined the U.S. Air Force after college and served during World War II, eventually attaining the rank of lieutenant. After the war, Stanley returned to Kansas City and joined the family business—Durwood Theaters. During the 1950s, Stanley, along with his father and younger brother and sister, slowly expanded the business into a chain of ten local movie houses and drive-in theaters. It was during this period that Stanley contrived an ingenious idea for a new kind of cinema—a single complex with multiple theater screens. Although he was never able to realize his vision while his

father was in control of the operation, he kept the idea alive in his mind.

Stanley's father died in 1960, and Stanley and his siblings continued to run the business, with Stanley in charge of operations. By the time Stanley took control of the business, the theater industry was rapidly evolving into a regional, and even national, industry. Because they owned only ten theaters, the Durwoods were under pressure from larger operators with more and bigger complexes. The market reach of such operations was often much greater, so they were usually able to lasso the choice releases, leaving the Durwoods to choose from the less popular motion pictures.

"I had to beg and plead for an Abbott and Costello picture," Durwood recalled in the March 25, 1994 *Kansas City Business Journal.* When Durwood finally got the comedy from the movie distributors, he hated it, but it was a big-name film, and his theaters were packed. Durwood noted, "I thought, what a crummy picture. Now if I could get two crummy pictures in here, I could double my gross and the rent would be the same." Seeking to boost attendance without increasing operating costs, Durwood believed that his multi-screen concept could be the solution.

In 1963, Durwood realized his vision when he built the first multiscreen theater. The concept was unheard of at the time and seemed extravagant; critics wondered why anyone would need two different screens. But the multiscreen theater, located in a suburban shopping mall, was a success. Durwood quickly began to reconfigure some of his existing facilities into multiple screen, or "multiplex," cinemas. In 1965, Durwood bought out his brother's and sister's ownership interests. Then, in 1968, he incorporated the business as American Multi-Cinema Inc. (the name was shortened in 1983 to AMC). At the time of incorporation, AMC consisted of a local chain of 12 theaters with a total of 22 screens. AMC boosted that figure in 1969 when it opened its first six-screen theater.

The 1970s were generally good to the movie theater industry. As Hollywood continued to churn out strings of blockbusters, the U.S. economy surged in the waning years of the post-World War II population and economic boom. Although total annual U.S. movie attendance remained at about one billion, many theater owners were able to boost profits through ticket price increases, concessions, and reduced operating expenses. AMC took advantage of industry gains during the 1970s, but was also able to consistently strengthen its competitive position in relation to its peers. It achieved those market share gains mostly through construction of new multi-screen cinemas, many of which were adjoined to, or located near, shopping malls.

Despite AMC's success, many of the company's competitors sat on the sidelines during the popularization of multiplex theaters, failing to recognize the long-term nature of the trend. A few competitors, particularly General Cinemas, also built some multi-screen theaters. But Durwood led the charge. During the 1970s and early 1980s, in fact, AMC's theaters were built with an average of more than five screens per theater. In contrast, the industry average was about half that amount. The AMC chain included more than 500 screens in theaters scattered mostly around the Midwest by 1981. And AMC's most rampant period of growth was yet to come.

The success of AMC's multi-screen concept was rooted in Durwood's penchant for efficiency. One prominent studio executive even referred to Durwood as the ''father of modern theater exhibition'' and the ''inventor of professional theater management.'' Despite its novelty, the multiplex philosophy was relatively straightforward. By putting several screens under one roof, AMC was effectively combining several separate theater facilities. The chief benefit was that the theaters were able to share infrastructure and employees, thus spreading costs over a higher revenue base. For example, by staggering starting times of the movies, one (or a few) employees could staff the box office, while twice as many workers would be needed at two separate theaters. Likewise, only one or two concession stands were needed, parking area requirements were minimized, and costs related to air-conditioning, the lobby, and other infrastructure elements were significantly reduced.

A corollary benefit of multi-cinema theaters, which Durwood especially recognized when he began building complexes with more than two or three screens, was increased market reach. By offering different types of movies, one facility could simultaneously appeal to several segments of the movie-going population. In addition, AMC could maximize profits on selected features by extending the run of movies that turned out to be very popular. Finally, multiple screens complemented other AMC technical and marketing innovations during the 1970s and 1980s. For example, AMC was credited with introducing automated projection systems. In the 1990s, AMC became the first theater to offer frequent movie-goer incentives through its MovieWatcher promotional.

AMC's most rampant growth spurt occurred during the 1980s. Although annual movie attendance throughout the decade remained near the one billion mark, the theater industry in general succeeded in steadily boosting ticket prices faster than inflation, thus increasing margins. More importantly, AMC continued to parlay its multi-screen concept into a competitive advantage and was able to significantly boost its share of box office receipts. During 1982 and 1983, AMC increased its total number of screens by more than 200, to about 700. Still eager to speed up expansion, the 63-year-old Durwood took his company public in 1983. Until that year, the company had been 100 percent owned by Durwood and his family. He reluctantly sold about 12 percent of AMC's stock in 1983 in a bid to raise expansion capital.

Figures released during 1983 showed that AMC had earned $10 million on revenues of $200 million, and that the company had increased its profits at an average rate of 22 percent since 1978. Encouraged by healthy returns, Durwood earmarked $70 million for new construction, including at least 200 new screens by 1985. By the end of 1984, AMC had boosted the number past the 800 mark, making it the third largest theater company in North America behind General Cinema and United Artists. By 1985, AMC was operating more than 900 screens, and, by 1986, AMC's total number of theater complexes had bolted past 200 with more than 1,100 screens in the United States. Furthermore, Durwood stepped up expansion in western Europe, Australia,

and Singapore. By 1990, he planned to be operating 2,500 screens in the United States and 1,500 more overseas.

AMC's strategy represented a slight departure from, or perhaps an amplification of, the growth tactics it had utilized in the past. Instead of building complexes with five or six screens, most of its new facilities during the early and mid-1980s housed eight to 12 screens. Furthermore, Durwood was targeting smaller cities in sunbelt states, especially Florida, Texas, and California. However, to achieve the stellar growth, Durwood was forced to take on a massive load of debt. By 1986, long-term debt had risen to $157 million, making up more than half of the previous year's revenues. By the end of 1988, moreover, AMC's debt had reached a hefty $380 million. Durwood and his executives remained undeterred. ''We are purposely leveraged,'' Durwood maintained in the September 22, 1986 *Forbes*. He hoped to pay the debt off in the long term from strong profit gains.

The success of AMC's multi-screen theaters did not go unobserved by industry leaders during the 1980s, as evidenced by industry statistics. Although the number of new theater complexes effectively stagnated and box office attendance declined slightly, the number of movie screens in the United States steadily surged from about 15 million in 1982 to about 20 million in 1986, and then to nearly 23 million by the early 1990s. AMC's major competitors had finally discovered the benefits of a large-scale multi-screen strategy. Still, AMC lead the industry in multiplexing. By the early 1990s, its complexes were sporting more than 6.5 screens on average, while the industry average had jumped to only 4.5.

As the U.S. theater industry expanded unchecked during the mid- and late 1980s, some critics feared that the market was becoming increasingly overbuilt as theater demand was declining. AMC's holdings, alone, had reached 1,500 screens by 1988, and a lot more construction was on the design boards. Furthermore, several of its competitors were hurriedly adding more screens to their existing complexes in what became a trend to 'add value' to their theaters. In AMC's case, critics also cited a lack of a market presence in key metropolitan areas like New York, Chicago, and Boston. Moreover, some observers felt that AMC, unlike other theater industry leaders, had made a mistake by not diversifying into movie-related industries during the 1980s.

The criticism about AMC's lack of diversification was prompted by the fact that the theater industry had felt increasing pressure from an onslaught of other movie medium since the 1970s. Indeed, home videos and cable television, particularly, had been vying for consumer entertainment dollars. In response, AMC's competitors had diversified out of the theater business. United Artists, the industry leader, had invested heavily in cable television and telecommunications. Similarly, General Cinemas had become active in soft-drink and retail industries. However, to AMC's delight, the movie industry continued to raise ticket and concession prices throughout the 1980s. AMC boosted both its ticket and concession revenues during 1988 and 1989 to bring its gross sales to more than $456 million during 1989. Part of that growth was attributable to specific blockbuster releases that buoyed earnings during the period.

Despite record sales during the late 1980s, AMC was having financial trouble that intensified during the early 1990s. Notwithstanding a history of extremely sound management of its theaters—Durwood himself was known for always flying coach class, buying his suits off the rack, and driving an economical Honda Civic—AMC had let is operating costs escalate during its rapid expansion. Furthermore, the company's cash flow was being devoured by a crushing debt load. AMC lost money every year between 1988 and 1992, with the exception of one year in which it gleaned $567,000 in earnings from its operations. To combat slumping profits, AMC reigned in its growth efforts beginning in the late 1980s and concentrated on whipping existing operations into shape. The company added a string of new theaters in 1988, bringing its total number of screens to nearly 1,700. But then it stopped expanding and started slashing costs.

Of its 276 theaters, AMC closed 40 of the least profitable, reducing its total number of screens to about 1,600 by 1994. It also cut its work force by about 1,000. As it scrambled to meet its debt obligations, industry revenues picked up. Although AMC's sales wavered barely above the $400 million mark, its operating costs declined and the company posted a $1.3 million net profit in 1993. Although the company was more than $300 million in debt, analysts were optimistic, and it appeared as though Durwood's long-term strategy might pay off after all.

Having overseen a period of great expansion, Stanley Durwood and his son, Edward D. Durwood, chief executive and president, respectively, remained in charge of AMC going in the early 1990s but installed a new operations team in 1992. They appointed Philip M. Singleton as chief operating officer. A former Marine Corp. captain and fighter pilot, Singleton had been with AMC since 1974. He was joined by Peter C. Brown, who was appointed chief financial officer and had been with AMC since 1979. The Durwoods were looking to their new management team for help in pursuing a different business strategy for the remainder of the decade. That stratagem essentially consisted of renewed expansion efforts combined with a greater emphasis on operating efficiency.

In the mid-1990s, founder Stanley Durwood had no intention of slowing AMC Entertainment's pace. In fact, the 74-year-old chief executive was laying new plans for the mid- and late 1990s to begin building a string of vast complexes with as many as 25 screens under the same roof. Management's optimism was fueled by a surge in sales during 1994 (fiscal year ended March 31) to a record $587 million, about $15 million of which was retained as earnings—the record year was partly the result of blockbuster hits including "Jurassic Park" and "The Firm." While critics continued to comment on AMC's lack of diversification into other movie medium, such as cable television, the Durwoods, who still owned more than 80 percent of the company, remained committed to the concept that had helped them build one of the largest theater companies in the world—multiscreen cinemas. "How many times are we [the theater industry] going to be worried about television," Durwood quipped in the September 10, 1984 Forbes.

Principal Subsidiaries: American Multi-Cinema, Inc.

Further Reading:

Bacha, Sarah Mills, "Movie Theater with 24 Screens Part of Project," Columbus Dispatch, August 10, 1994, p. G1.
Block, A. B., "What Makes Stanley Borrow? Stan Durwood's AMC Entertainment is Loaded with Debt and Costly Leases. So Why Does the Stock Sell for 27 Times Earnings?," Forbes, September 22, 1986.
Butcher, Lola, "AMC Needs to Recapitalize to Pay $23 Million Debt," Kansas City Business Journal, June 26, 1992, p. 8.
Butcher, Lola, "AMC's New Management Team Cuts Costs, Prepare for Growth," Kansas City Business Journal, December 11, 1992, p. 4.
Cardenas, Gina, "Movie Theater Economics," New Miami, September 1993, p. 18.
Carroll, John, "AMC Slows Its Expansion; Cuts Affect Architectural Firm," Kansas City Business Journal, October 19, 1987, p. 3.
Ginsberg, Steve, "Picture This: An AMC Multiplex Theater at 1000 Van Noss," San Francisco Business Times, August 12, 1994, p. 1.
Gold, Howard, "Screen Gem?," Forbes, September 10, 1984, p. 194.
Harris, Kathryn, "AMC Theater Empire Playing Real-Life Drama," Los Angeles Times, March 27, 1988, Sec. 4, p. 1.
Henderson, Barry, "AMC Bets on Theater Allure Over Couch," Kansas City Business Journal, March 25, 1994, p. 3.
Kaberline, Brian, "Ta Da! AMC May Show First Profit in 5 Years," Kansas City Business Journal, March 29, 1991, p. 1.

—Dave Mote

AmSouth Bancorporation

P.O. Box 11007
Birmingham, Alabama 35288
U.S.A.
(205) 320-7151
Fax: (205) 326-4072

Public Company
Incorporated: 1972
Employees: 5,300
Total Assets: $17.1 billion
Stock Exchanges: New York
SICs: 6021 National Commercial Banks; 6712 Bank Holding
    Companies

AmSouth Bancorporation is one of the largest bank holding companies in the southern United States. AmSouth is based in Alabama and is primarily active in that state and Florida, but it also operates some of its more than 300 banking offices in Tennessee and Georgia. AmSouth continued to grow rapidly going into the mid-1990s by acquiring other banks.

AmSouth Bancorporation was incorporated in 1972 to take advantage of new state and federal laws related to the banking industry. Indeed, during the early 1970s Alabama began to deregulate its banking sector, making it easier for holding companies to merge with or acquire other banks. Similarly, during the mid-1960s and early 1970s, Congress had eliminated several federal banking industry restrictions and created a variety of favorable tax incentives for specific banking activities. By moving to a holding company format, companies like the newly formed AmSouth Bancorporation were able to take advantage of deregulation and to participate in a number of non-banking-related financial markets.

Because of regulatory changes, several holding companies were formed in Alabama during the 1970s. The owners and managers of most of those holding companies hoped to establish regional or state-wide dominance by adding new banks to their portfolios. Specifically, many of them hoped to improve the performance of the institutions that they acquired and also benefit from various economies of scale. AmSouth Bancorporation, like other holding companies formed at the time, was structured as a corporation with its founding bank (Birmingham-based AmSouth) as its major subsidiary. Throughout the 1970s, AmSouth engaged in an aggressive growth and acquisition campaign that would make it the largest bank in Alabama by the end of the decade.

The man chosen to direct AmSouth's rampant expansion during the 1970s, and into the 1990s, was John W. Woods. Woods was born in 1931 into a military family, and in the 1950s he tried to join the Marines but was rejected because he was color blind. He did, however, pass the entrance test for the Air Force, where he served as a pilot for two years. Woods credited his military experience with giving him the confidence and personal strength that later helped him to build one of the most successful banks in the United States. "There are tough moments in everybody's career," Woods related in the November 13, 1991 *American Banker,* "and every time there's been a tough moment, I think about that Air Force training and think, by golly, I can whip this, too."

Immediately after leaving the service, Woods accepted an entry level position at New York-based Chemical Bank, where he had a successful career and eventually earned the title of vice-president in charge of Chemical's southern division. Woods spent several years traveling to banks throughout the Southeast, selling correspondent banking and loan syndication services. AmSouth hired Woods away from Chemical in 1969, and although he had only 12 years in the banking industry, he was named president of AmSouth's lead Birmingham bank. Three years later Woods was chosen to lead the newly formed holding company, AmSouth Bancorporation.

Under Woods's direction, AmSouth expanded rapidly during the 1970s and early 1980s by purchasing competitors and integrating their assets and branches into the AmSouth banking chain. By the early 1980s, AmSouth had become the largest banking chain in Alabama with nearly 20 percent of all state bank deposits. Besides simply increasing AmSouth's asset base, Woods and his fellow executives achieved success by improving the financial performance of their acquisitions. Not only did the banks that they purchased benefit from improved management, they profited from having AmSouth's well-known and respected name attached to their branches. In fact, an integral aspect of Woods strategy was to focus on expanding into areas where the AmSouth name was already established. Finally, the bought-out banks enjoyed access to a larger base of lending capital, as well as centralized, efficient administrative operations.

Although AmSouth Bancorporation was created in 1972, the history of its banking chain actually dates back long before the start of the nineteenth century. AmSouth's immediate predecessor, the First National Bank of Alabama, was founded in the late 1800s, and AmSouth eventually acquired a patchwork of Alabama financial institutions with similarly rich histories. In 1983, AmSouth absorbed the Commercial National Bank (CNB) of Anniston. E. Guice Potter, CNB's president, stayed with AmSouth, assuming the title of president of the newly named AmSouth Bank in Anniston. Potter's father had gone to work at CNB in 1926, just six years after it was established. Potter, who had succeeded his father as president of CNB in 1974, stayed with AmSouth until his retirement in 1994.

As AmSouth continued to purchase Alabama banks and to increase its existing operations, the holding company flourished. Although Woods was at the helm of the swelling operation, the company's success was also attributable to savvy AmSouth executives like William L. Marks. Marks joined AmSouth's acquisition and turn-around team in 1977. The 33-year-old Marks was hired away from Wachovia Bank and Trust Co. and named president of AmSouth's new American National Bank subsidiary. Similar to other AmSouth acquisitions, the bank suffered from a troubled loan portfolio, poor marketing strategy, and generally weak management. But it had a lot of potential.

Marks went to work revitalizing the bank and integrating it into the AmSouth empire. Within three years, the subsidiary made more money than it had in its entire 16-year history. "We decided what needed to be done and turned it around," recalled Marks in the March 12, 1990 *New Orleans City Business.* During the next 13 years, Marks would be moved around to several other new AmSouth banks. He consistently boosted productivity and profits at his posts, and, like his fellow regional managers, contributed significantly to the holding company's success. Marks was hired away in the early 1990s by Whitney National Bank, a struggling New Orleans institution. Interestingly, the 107-year-old Whitney had hired its first out-of-state chief executive from AmSouth Bancorporation's predecessor in 1930.

By 1984, AmSouth had blossomed into a dominant Alabama financial institution with nearly $5 billion in assets and more than $45 million in annual net income. Although that growth was impressive, it turned out to be mere preparation for the explosive expansion that AmSouth would conduct during the next decade. In fact, a turn of events in 1985 set the stage for what would become a major evolution in the banking industry. In that year, Congress effectively gave the okay for holding companies to engage in interstate banking. That meant that AmSouth could begin expanding outside of Alabama (and that AmSouth could potentially become a takeover target for larger out-of-state holding companies).

By increasing its Alabama holdings, AmSouth managed to swell its total asset base to nearly $7 billion by the end of 1986. Then, in 1987, AmSouth launched a major expansion into the Florida panhandle with its purchase of First Mutual Savings Association, a major regional thrift institution. Within the year, AmSouth had assembled a subsidiary bank with nearly $1 billion in assets. Unfortunately, that investment soon soured when the Florida real estate market collapsed, and AmSouth's Florida subsidiary was devastated as more than 40 percent of its total loans were eventually classified as nonperforming.

Although AmSouth also ventured into Tennessee in the late 1980s and considered other investment opportunities in Florida and Georgia, the company slowed its growth plans and focused on weathering a severe banking industry downturn. Indeed, in the late 1980s, the U.S. banking industry was trounced by the collapse of real estate and construction markets, as well as general U.S. economic malaise. As the number of nonperforming bank loans soared, many banks and thrifts were forced into bankruptcy. Although AmSouth was pressured, its tradition of sound management and making high quality loans paid off, allowing it to sustain meager profit growth during the late 1980s and early 1990s.

One of AmSouth's investments in Alabama that didn't fare so well during the late 1980s was its loan to the Birmingham Turf

Club, a venture initiated for the purpose of bringing horse racing to Birmingham. AmSouth had loaned $17 million to the organization and was eventually forced to write off the entire amount. Marks defended the loan decision on the basis that the venture would have brought more than 1,000 jobs to the Birmingham area. Nevertheless, AmSouth's local image was tarnished by the whole affair. Moreover, a string of fiscal problems and executive turmoil punctuated the AmSouth story between 1987 and 1992, before the banking industry, in general, began to recover.

Despite its losses in the 1987 Florida debacle, that acquisition boosted AmSouth's holdings to nearly $9 billion by 1989. Over the following three years, AmSouth's portfolio grew to about $10 billion. AmSouth's profit growth slowed during the period. Net income actually declined from $73 million in 1986 to $66 million in 1987, and then buoyed up around the $80 million mark until 1991. Spurred by recovering markets and improving loan portfolios in 1992, AmSouth enjoyed a net income surge to $108. Encouraged by improving margins and markets, AmSouth regained its vigor for growth and renewed its aggressive expansion strategy. Simultaneously, AmSouth was undergoing a three-year restructuring that it began in 1991. The intent was to slash operating costs by developing scrupulous performance standards for all of its subsidiaries and branches.

AmSouth elected to focus on the central and west Florida banking markets for expansion during the early 1990s. It started by acquiring First National Bank of Clearwater for about $90 million, and then snapped up an Orlando entity, Orange Bank, for about $50 million. Orange was the largest independent bank in the county, with 20 branches and $376 million in assets. AmSouth soon added nearby Mid-State Federal Savings Bank for about $100 million. After tagging St. Petersburg First Federal to its portfolio, AmSouth's Florida assets had suddenly surged to nearly $2 billion. During the same period, AmSouth boosted its holdings in Tennessee, where it would have 21 offices by 1994, and Georgia, where it would operate seven.

AmSouth's growth during the early 1990s was representative of a dynamic trend of consolidation within the U.S. banking industry that had been occurring since interstate banking began in the 1980s. Indeed, as smaller banks continued to face greater competitive pressures from less-regulated, non-bank financial institutions, the percentage of U.S. assets held by commercial banks had dropped from about 37 percent in the late 1970s to 25 percent by the early 1990s. To combat competitive threats, banks began merging to achieve economies of scale. The number of independent banking entities in the United States plunged from about 13,000 in 1983 to less than 10,000 by 1990. Meanwhile, the number of multi-bank holding companies grew from about 300 to around 1,000. Augmenting the consolidation trend was the fact that computers and electronic banking devices were increasingly making it easier for banks to operate across broad regions.

As a result of its acquisition activity, AmSouth's assets and income surged in 1993 to a $12.5 billion and $147 million, respectively. Furthermore, it was acquiring new banks and expanding existing subsidiaries at a rapid pace. Importantly, in 1993, AmSouth announced an agreement to purchase Fortune Bancorp. of Clearwater Florida. With 46 offices, Fortune was a major-league financial institution and gave AmSouth a commanding presence in central Florida.

By 1994, AmSouth would have at least 125 banking offices in Florida and more than $6 billion in assets. With its other operations, including about 150 Alabama offices, its total asset base would rise past the $17 billion mark by early 1995. Furthermore, the company's profits continued to be augmented by its emphasis on fee-based income activities, particularly trust services, mutual funds, and mortgage retail services. In a 1993 article for the *Orlando Business Journal,* banking analyst Sam Beebe suggested that AmSouth was "going to be very competitive" well into the 1990s.

After nearly 25 years of service at AmSouth, Woods was formulating plans for his retirement in 1995—he planned to actually leave his post in 1996. Reminiscent of his early years in the service, Woods was an avid military history buff and was looking forward to doing a lot more reading in that area. In addition, he planned to spend more time at his 700-acre cattle-breeding farm near Birmingham. "Its kind of my entrepreneurial outlet," Woods explained in the November 13, 1991 *American Banker,* noting that "on the farm, if I make a bad decision I pay for it pretty quickly." Until then, Woods was staying focused on AmSouth's strategy of continued acquisition and expansion throughout the 1990s.

Principal Subsidiaries: Amsouth Bank N.A.; AmSouth Bank of Florida; AmSouth Bank of Tennessee.

Further Reading:

Beall, Pat, "The New Bank on the Block: AmSouth Pick Orange Bank and Breaks with Age-Old Tradition," *Orlando Business Journal,* April 30, 1993, p. 13.

Burger, Frederick, "AmSouth's Potter with Retire January 1," *Anniston Star,* December 24, 1993, p. 1.

Campbell, Harvey E., "AmSouth Bancorporation to Acquire Fortune Bancorp," *PR Newswire,* September 13, 1993.

Cline, Kenneth, "AmSouth's John Woods Sees Smooth Flying Ahead," *American Banker,* November 13, 1991, p. 1.

Finn, Kathy, "CEO Aims High," *New Orleans City Business,* March 12, 1990, p. 1.

Underwood, Jim, "C. Dowd Ritter Elected President and COO of AmSouth," *PR Newswire,* August 18, 1994.

Underwood, Jim, "Dan L. Hendley to Resign as President and Chief Operating Officer of AmSouth Bank N.A.," *Business Wire,* August 10, 1990.

Weaver, Danielle, "AmSouth Wins Fortune, May Stop Now," *Orlando Business Journal,* September 17, 1993, p. 6.

Werner, Lisa, "AmSouth to Expand into Central Florida with December 9 Merger of Mid-State Federal Savings Bank," *PR Newswire,* December 8, 1993.

—Dave Mote

Anschutz Corp.

555 17th Street
Denver, Colorado 80202
U.S.A.
(303) 298-1000
Fax: (303) 298-8881

Private Company
Incorporated: 1958
Employees: 24,500
Sales: $2.80 billion
SICs: 1382 Oil & Gas Exploration Services; 4011 Railroads
   Line-Haul Operating; 4213 Trucking except Local

Anschutz Corp., originally funded by the oil and gas holdings of
Fred Anschutz, has since become a holding company for the
diversified interests of Fred's son, Philip F. Anschutz. Philip,
consistently shunning publicity, quietly became a billionaire in
the 1980s through his company's various activities, including
further oil and gas exploration ventures. He and the company
became better known in the late 1980s and early 1990s for
acquiring railroad lines, including the small Rio Grande Railroad and a railroad giant, Southern Pacific Rail Corp., which the
Anschutz Corp. struggled to turn around but profited from
through stock sales. Meanwhile, the company has ventured,
with less fanfare, into stock investments, real estate, and art.

Fred Anschutz purchased land in Wyoming in the late 1950s,
the worth of which was thought to be limited to range for cattle.
He later discovered it was rich with oil. Philip Anschutz bought
his father out in 1961. Anschutz Corp. bolstered its oil holdings
and wealth further with the 1970s purchase of another oil-rich
piece of real estate on the Wyoming-Utah border, known as
Anschutz Ranch East. The land happened to be sitting atop one
of the largest reserves of oil and gas in the United States. In
1982 the company sold a half-interest in the mineral rights on
the ranch to the Mobil Oil Corp. for $500 million. Amoco has
since operated the drilling operations there, paying the Anschutz Corp. a 17 percent royalty.

The Anschutz Corp. used this oil and gas wealth to venture into
the stock market, downtown real estate (primarily in Denver),
and, ultimately, the railroad industry. In the stock arena, *Forbes*
reported that the company had gained more than $100 million
through the purchase of stocks in ITT and Pennwalt in the
1980s, but such investments were not always so successful,

as shown by the company's involvement with Ideal Basic
Industries.

At the time one of the largest companies in Colorado and a
leading producer of cement and potash in the United States,
Ideal was reeling from the recession of the early 1980s when
Anschutz Corp. bought about 10 percent of Ideal's outstanding
stock in July 1983, then increased its share to nearly 25 percent
about a year later—an investment totaling $61.5 million. The
company reasoned that eventually, once the economy turned
around, the investment would pay off. Ideal's problems were
compounded shortly thereafter, however, when they spent $347
million to purchase a cement plant in Mobile, Alabama, which it
turned out they could not use because the limestone Ideal mined
in Alabama was incompatible with the Mobile plant's operation. The plant sat idle from 1984 to 1988. Ideal subsequently
underwent a restructuring to avoid bankruptcy proceedings in
late 1986. The *Denver Post* estimated that Anschutz Corp.
faced a post-restructuring loss on its Ideal investment of between $15 million and $49.8 million, although the actual loss
has never been reported. In 1989 the *Wall Street Journal* reported that Ideal was one of the ten worst stock performers of
the 1980s, losing 92.43 percent of its value with a December 8,
1989, closing of $1.75.

The first major Anschutz Corp. venture into real estate began
when it secured a 30 percent interest in all projects developed
by the Oxford-AnsCo Development Co.—a subsidiary of a
leading Canadian development company, Oxford Properties
Inc.—for $1 million and downtown property owned by An-
schutz in Denver and Colorado Springs. By the early 1980s, the
company had developed several major skyscrapers in Denver,
including the 56-story Republic Tower and the 39-story Anaconda Tower, worth an estimated $250 million. The relation-
ship with Oxford-AnsCo soured when Anschutz gained the vast
real estate holdings of the Denver & Rio Grande Railroad in
1984 and wanted to begin to develop real estate on its own
rather than through the Oxford partnership. Late in 1984, the
partnership was dissolved and the holdings divided between
Anschutz and Oxford, with Anschutz keeping the Anaconda
Tower (where the company's offices are still located), Denver's
Fairmont Hotel, and a half-block of undeveloped land in
Denver.

Anschutz's first foray into the railroad business began with the
1984 purchase of the Denver & Rio Grande Railroad, commonly known as the Rio Grande, a small railroad that then
consisted of more than 3,400 miles of track from Missouri to
Utah. Anschutz Corp. purchased the Rio Grande's parent, Rio
Grande Industries, Inc., for $500 million, $90 million of which
was in cash and the remainder in loans. This heavy debt load,
coupled with competition from the Union Pacific line and
several lost coal-hauling accounts, led to an approximate revenue loss of 20 percent over the first four years under Anschutz
and a net loss of $1.8 million over an 11-month period in 1987
and 1988.

The Rio Grande's small size and its position as a bridge carrier
(providing connections between other rail lines) led Anschutz to
pursue the acquisition of the railroad giant Southern Pacific
(SP) in an attempt to save the much smaller Rio Grande. With
20,000 miles of track thoroughly covering the West Coast and a

line through the southern United States to the Mississippi River, the SP was even more attractive to Anschutz for its connections to the Rio Grande lines in Kansas City and Ogden, Utah, making for a synergistic coupling.

Anschutz had to overcome a major hurdle to achieve its object of solidifying its railroad holdings. Santa Fe Industries Inc. had purchased Southern Pacific in 1983 with the intention of merging SP with the Atchison, Topeka & Santa Fe Railway (known as the Santa Fe), one of SP's main competitors. The proposed merger elicited immediate opposition from government officials and Santa Fe's competition, and with the added impetus of pressure from Philip Anschutz, whom *Forbes* called "politically influential," the Interstate Commerce Commission in 1987 blocked the Santa Fe-SP merger as anticompetitive. Robert Krebs, the chairman of Santa Fe Industries, was forced to sell one of his lines and chose SP, which he felt was the weaker of the two.

Anschutz Corp. closed the deal for Southern Pacific in the fall of 1988. Similar to many other takeovers of the 1980s, Anschutz engineered a highly leveraged purchase in which Rio Grande Industries paid Santa Fe Industries just over $1 billion in cash, most of it borrowed, for SP, assuming more than $700 million in SP debt. After the deal, Anschutz controlled 71 percent of the Rio Grande, while Morgan Stanley as a minority partner controlled the remaining 19 percent through its purchase of $111 million in Rio Grande common stock. As William P. Barrett noted in *Forbes,* "Beyond the original cash stake in the Rio Grande, Anschutz put not a penny more into the deal," thereby making the company's president the first individual to own a major railroad in decades.

In the initial years after the purchase, Anschutz Corp. struggled to overcome the huge debt load, which had led to $100 million-plus interest payments each year, as well as the decline in SP's traditional accounts in auto parts, lumber, and food; increased competition from Union Pacific and Santa Fe; and more rigorous safety inspections in California, where SP trains were involved in two chemical spills in July 1991. Amid speculation that he would be better off breaking up SP and selling it piecemeal (Krebs of the Santa Fe still coveted much of the SP line and approached Anschutz about a deal several times without success), Anschutz told *Forbes:* "I said in my original ICC filing that we would turn this railroad around; I'm in it for the long haul."

To reduce the debt load, Anschutz Corp. sold large portions of Southern Pacific's vast real estate holdings, more than $1 billion worth by the end of 1991 and nearly $400 million in 1992 alone. Anschutz also began to improve the quality of its service through heavy expenditures to maintain its track and hiring a quality expert, Kent Sterett, from its competitor Union Pacific. As trade between the United States and Mexico increased in the early 1990s, SP seemed best positioned to profit from it with its six Mexican gateways in California, Texas, and Arizona. Anschutz's strategy appeared to be working as an operating loss of $347.7 million in 1991 had been reduced to $24.6 million in 1992. But in 1993, SP slid back to a loss of $149 million. Contributing to the loss was $14 million incurred from the settlement of a class-action lawsuit stemming from one of the 1991 derailments that had contaminated the Sacramento River with weed killer.

In the summer of 1993, Anschutz turned to a railroad company veteran, Edward Moyers, to assist in turning SP around. Moyers had retired after a very successful four-year stint at Illinois Central, where he cut its operating ratio (operating expenses as a percentage of revenues) from 98 percent to 71 percent. Anschutz hired Moyers as chief executive, and Moyers immediately focused on Southern Pacific's operating ratio, which stood at 96.5 percent in 1993. The hiring enabled Anschutz to embark on a new and surprising strategy for a company that preferred to keep its dealings private: taking SP public.

In another effort to reduce the debt load, 30 million shares were offered in August 1993. Although the initial offering price was estimated at $20 per share, the actual price of the shares as issued was $13.50. Still, that the offering was successful at all was attributed by many to the hiring of Moyers. Investor interest in Southern Pacific increased in the several months that followed, so that by February 1994, when a second stock offering of 25 million shares was initiated, they sold for $19.75 per share. Following these sales, Anschutz owned 41 percent of the shares outstanding.

Moyers started a multi-pronged strategy for revitalizing Southern Pacific. First, he planned to cut costs by reducing the employee ranks through a buyout program and a reorganization. In his first year, he reduced the labor force by more than 3,000 to about 19,000 jobs. Second, Moyers focused on service to SP's customers, putting pressure on his subordinates to improve the operations. This initiative saved a lucrative Georgia-Pacific account by increasing on-time Georgia-Pacific deliveries from zero to 80 percent in three months. Overall, on-time deliveries were up by more than 50 percent in his first year. Moyers also sought to bolster Southern Pacific's equipment through the purchase of new locomotives, the rebuilding of existing locomotives, and better maintenance of both trains and track. Such improvements would lead to a more efficient operation, from which the savings could be passed on to SP customers, thus improving SP's competitive position.

Another strategy emerged in late 1993 involving real estate and harkened back to Anschutz Corp.'s ongoing interest in real estate development. Rather than simply selling Southern Pacific land to raise cash, SP would invest in its land by becoming a developer. In a deal that S. David Steele, vice-president for corporate real estate, said would make SP "a major player in the Sacramento real estate market," Anschutz and the mayor of Sacramento announced a downtown redevelopment venture called "Railyards" that would include offices, residences, stores, a hotel, and four parks, would double Sacramento's downtown area by the year 2020, and would cost $1 billion. About a year later, Philip Anschutz was involved in the planning of another downtown development, this time in his base city of Denver. Anschutz Corp. and Comsat, owners of the National Basketball Association's Denver Nuggets, developed a proposal for a $130 million sports and entertainment center that would include a new basketball and hockey arena and film and television studios. The center would be built on land to be purchased from Southern Pacific.

Meanwhile, the energy exploration side of Anschutz Corp. announced in late 1993 that it was forming Anschutz Exploration Corp. as an association of exploration consultants under the leadership of president John A. Masters, who had retired in 1992 after 20 years with Canadian Hunter and several major discoveries to his credit. The goal of the new company was to find cost-effective ways to drill for oil and gas in the lower 48 states at a time when the industry had largely abandoned such efforts as unprofitable. Anschutz Exploration intended to use the latest technology, such as electron microscopes, enlist local experts, and encourage innovative exploration techniques to achieve its goals. The full infrastructure of Anschutz Corp., including land, operations, finance, legal, and engineering, was to be made available to the new subsidiary.

Early 1994 saw another petroleum development with the agreement between Anschutz Corp. and subsidiaries of Chevron Corp. and Texaco Inc. to build the 130-mile Pacific Pipeline between Bakersfield, California, and Los Angeles under the newly formed Pacific Pipeline Systems Inc. The crude oil pipeline, to cost $150 million, would complete a route from the offshore oil rigs of Santa Barbara to the refineries in the Los Angeles area. According to the terms of the agreement, Anschutz owned 85 percent of Pacific Pipeline, Chevron 10 percent, and Texaco 5 percent.

The Anschutz Corp. also owned the highly respected Anschutz Collection of American West art, featuring more than 500 paintings by nearly 200 artists, including George Catlin, Asher Durand, Robert Henri, Thomas Moran, Georgia O'Keeffe, Jackson Pollock, Frederic Remington, and Charles Russell. Philip Anschutz, passionate about the American West, built the collection starting in the early 1960s and decided in the mid-1970s to allow others to enjoy the works of art through traveling exhibits.

Although Anschutz Corp. has steadily reduced its stake in the railroad business through the Southern Pacific stock sales, the mid-1990s still found the future of Anschutz tied closely to Southern Pacific. With Moyers's retirement from Southern Pacific early in 1995 for health reasons, the hiring of Jerry Davis (who had been executive vice-president and CEO with CSX Transportation Co.) to replace him, and rumors of further railroad consolidation (involving combinations of SP, Santa Fe, Burlington Northern, and Union Pacific), SP faced an uncertain future. Nonetheless, Anschutz Corp. had already recouped many times over its initial $90 million investment in its railroad empire. Henry Dubroff of the *Denver Post* estimated that through its SP stock sales, Anschutz "pocketed $350 million to $400 million in cash, before taxes." The company seemed well positioned to move into other investments—the nascent Anschutz Exploration Corp., the downtown redevelopment proposals, and perhaps some new, not yet public, areas of investment.

Principal Subsidiaries: Anschutz Exploration Corp.; Pacific Pipeline Systems Inc. (85%); Rio Grande Industries; Southern Pacific Rail Corp. (32%).

Further Reading:

"A Cowboy's Dream," *Financial Executive,* March/April 1993, pp. 32–33.

"Anschutz Teams up on Pipeline," *Rocky Mountain News,* March 11, 1994, p. 49A.

Barrett, William P., "Working over the Railroad," *Forbes,* October 31, 1988, pp. 51–54.

Berman, Phyllis, and Roula Khalaf, "I Might Be a Seller, I Might Be a Buyer," *Forbes,* February 3, 1992, pp. 86–87.

Burke, Jack, "With Alameda Corridor Deal in Hand, Southern Pacific Prepares to Sell 25 Million More Shares," *Traffic World,* December 20, 1993, pp. 26–27.

Curtis, Carol E., "Take a Ride on the Rio Grande," *Forbes,* May 20, 1985, pp. 106–107.

Delsohn, Gary, "Anschutz, Oxford Divvy up 4 Downtown Office Towers," *Denver Post,* p. 1A.

Dubroff, Henry, "Anschutz's Ride on Southern Pacific Has Been a Profitable One," *Denver Post,* November 13, 1994, p. 1H.

Machan, Dan, "The Man Who Won't Let Go," *Forbes,* August 1, 1994, pp. 64–65.

Mahoney, Michelle, "Southern Pacific Going Public," *Denver Post,* May 14, 1993, p. 1C.

Petzet, G. Alan, "Lucrative Discoveries Still Lurk in U.S., Exploration Group Says," *Oil & Gas Journal,* November 15, 1993, p. 73.

"Philip Frederick Anschutz," *Forbes 400,* October 17, 1994, p. 124.

Pitts, Gail L., "Ideal Restructuring Costly for Anschutz," *Denver Post,* August 2, 1986, p. 1D, 6D.

——, "Oilman to Buy $40 Million in Ideal Stock," *Denver Post,* July 30, 1983, p. 1H.

Weaver, Nancy, "Denver's Billionaires: Low-Key Anschutz Built His Empire Quietly," *Denver Post,* October 9, 1983, pp. 1A–17A.

—David E. Salamie

Arbor Drugs Inc.

3331 W. Big Beaver Road
Troy, Michigan 48084
U.S.A.
(810) 643-9420
Fax: (810) 637-1634

Public Company
Incorporated: 1974
Employees: 5,200
Sales: $618.56 million
Stock Exchanges: NASDAQ
SICs: 5912 Drug Stores and Proprietary Stores

With 160 stores across Michigan, Arbor Drugs is the second largest drugstore chain in Michigan and the fifteenth largest in the United States. The company has posted an impressive record of growth since its president, Eugene Applebaum, opened his first drugstore in Detroit in 1963. This performance has garnered the company a place among the *Forbes* ranking of the 200 Best Small Companies, as well as the *Drugstore News* award for "Small Chain Drugstore of the Year" in 1993. An emphasis on pharmacy, customer service, and convenience was the formula responsible for Arbor Drugs's success.

Eugene Applebaum, the founder and president of Arbor Drugs, opened his first drugstore in 1963 shortly after graduating from pharmacy college. Called Civic Drugs, the small store was located in the somewhat rundown east side of Dearborn, Michigan, a suburb of Detroit. "I loved pharmacy and I loved the business side. I also liked fast nickels and dimes," Applebaum said in a 1993 *Forbes* interview. By 1974 he had purchased five more stores in the greater Detroit area and decided it was time to incorporate. He named his new corporation "Arbor Drugs" after his Ann Arbor-based store and began to create an image for his new chain of drugstores.

Applebaum made the decision early on in the growth of his chain that Arbor would focus on prescription drugs and personal care products. During the 1970s and early 1980s a number of drugstore chain executives had begun to worry that traditional drugstore items, like cosmetics and personal care products, were increasingly being sold by large discount stores. Since most drugstores could not compete on price with these discounters, chain managers felt that they too must diversify or face obsolescence. Drugstores began to experiment with such diverse goods and services as dry cleaning, electronic equipment, and video rental. Arbor's main competitor in Michigan, Perry Drugs, even ventured into the auto care business, introducing an extended line of automotive products and services with very limited success.

Instead, Applebaum decided to stick with more traditional drugstore items. In the 1960s, at his original Civic Drugs store, Applebaum had experimented with selling records and learned that such fashion-driven markets could be wildly unpredictable. When a Beatles record would be released, the store would sell out, "But we were always stuck with too many Montavani," Applebaum joked in a 1993 interview in *Drug Topics.* "We learned and we never mix mascara with motor oil. Arbor has never strayed from its traditional drugstore format, which emphasizes convenience and health care."

By early 1981, Arbor had grown to 19 stores, and later that year the company acquired 11 former Cunnigham Drugs locations for a total of 30 Arbor Drug units. Over the course of the next five years the drugstore chain acquired 22 more stores and began its transformation from a small local chain to a major regional presence. In 1986 Applebaum decided that the time was right to take his company public in order to finance further expansion. In preparation for this step Applebaum made one of the few mistakes of his executive career. He opened three stores in the Carolinas in order to impress investors with the geographical diversity of his chain. "Stock analysts asked good questions, like how we'd service the stores, but I didn't take them as good questions," Applebaum admitted in *Forbes.* The analysts were right, and Arbor was quickly forced to retreat from these out-of-state ventures. With good investment from stockholders, Arbor Drugs was able to increase its rate of expansion and add 10 to 15 new Arbor stores a year in Michigan through the 1980s. By 1994, the Arbor chain owned and operated 154 stores.

The 1980s were a period of expansion for drugstore chains in general as many small independents found they simply could not compete with the big chains. Even during recessionary periods during the early 1980s and 1990s, the large drugstore chains continued to grow. Analysts ranked the industry as a whole among the top 10 percent as a good investment risk in the early 1990s. In Michigan, independent drugstores held a larger share of the market through the 1970s and 1980s than in other parts of the country, but during the 1980s both Arbor and its main competitor Perry Drugs continued to buy out the smaller companies at a rapid rate. At the beginning of the decade independents controlled well over half of the market in Michigan, but this share had dropped to only 43 percent by the early 1990s.

Arbor Drugs's expansion was accomplished through both acquisitions and new store openings. Major acquisitions included the Cunnigham chain in 1981, the Sentry chain in 1986, and the M&R chain in 1994. Toward the end of the 1980s, as Arbor's profits and assets grew, the company was also able to finance and build an increasing number of freestanding stores. This allowed the chain to expand without relying on retail mall real estate developers or acquisitions. The bulk of Arbor's acquisitions and new stores were located in southeastern Michigan, particularly in the Detroit area, where rival Perry Drugs had a relatively weak presence. In 1986, Arbor controlled only 13.5 percent of the greater Detroit market, but by 1992 this share had grown to 27.6 percent, surpassing Perry by .1 percentage points. This market share would continue to grow into the mid 1990s.

Part of Arbor's strength lay in the company's willingness and ability to expand into neighborhoods that were considered questionable by other large chains. In the early 1990s, for example, Arbor became the first large retailer of any sort in over 20 years to open an outlet in depressed Ecorse, south of Detroit. In 1993 the company opened an outlet in Hamtramck, a largely Polish community in the Detroit area, and promptly hired a Polish-speaking pharmacist to run its pharmacy department.

Large drugstore chains like Arbor Drugs could offer price advantages over their smaller, independent counterparts, not only because of their high volumes but also because of their access to insurance company prescription payment plans, which frequently excluded independent drugstores. Under pharmacist Applebaum, one of Arbor's main policies was to promote its prescription pharmacy services. As Arbor grew into a large chain in the 1980s, management decided to emphasize pharmacy service by placing the prescription counter in all stores to the center rear at the end of a wide aisle, so that it would be clearly visible from the entrance of the store. The pharmacy enclosure was also open, not glassed in as it was in rival Perry stores, so that the pharmacist would appear more accessible to the public.

Even more significantly, as early as 1979 Arbor was one of the first chains to computerize its pharmacy system so that prescriptions could be filled and refilled more quickly. By 1989, Arbor had extended this service by linking all of its stores in one network, allowing prescriptions to be filled from any store in the chain. Computerization also allowed the chain to keep track of billing for the increasingly large pool of drug insurance plans that were introduced during the 1980s. Beginning in the late 1980s, Arbor undertook a series of major advertising campaigns to promote its pharmacy services. These campaigns were a huge success, and by 1994 an independent polling organization reported that Arbor pharmacies were the preferred prescription centers in southeastern Michigan. The proportion of Arbor's sales provided by pharmacy jumped from 35 percent in the mid 1980s to almost 50 percent by 1994, at a time when the drugstore industry average was only 33 percent.

Under Applebaum's leadership Arbor Drugs seemed to lead a charmed existence. Sales grew impressively, but steadily enough not to alarm investors about over-expansion. When the company went public in 1986 it was earning net income of $5.3 million. By 1992 this figure had more than doubled to $15 million. Total sales soared from $150 million to almost $500 million in the same period. Even more significantly, sales at Arbor stores averaged a hefty $471 per square foot, 80 percent above the drugstore industry average. Income from pharmacy also kept growing, vindicating Applebaum's insistence on promoting this aspect of his business. Arbor made it onto the *Forbes* list of the 200 Best Small Companies in 1988 and was named Drugstore of the Year by both industry magazines. In 1990 Applebaum was named "Strategic Manager of

the Year" by the Planning Forum, and a 1992 poll by *Corporate Detroit Magazine* found that Applebaum was one of the most admired CEOs in metro Detroit. It began to look like Arbor Drugs could do no wrong.

Arbor Drugs's corporate honeymoon ended in 1993, however. The year opened with a new Democratic government in Washington promising major health care insurance reforms. Investors reacted by scrambling out of drugstore stocks for fear that government-regulated insurance would pay less for prescription drugs. Between January 4 and February 25, Arbor stock lost 25 percent of its value, which had reached a high of $23.75 in the first quarter of 1993. As it became clear that health care reform, if it ever materialized, would entail a far less dramatic change than investors feared, Arbor stock gradually recovered to about $20 a share.

But then, on July 7, Arbor was forced to disclose that, "after a routine audit," Blue Cross Blue Shield of Michigan was claiming that Arbor had overcharged the insurance company for prescriptions since 1988. As of July 1993 the total claim amounted to $17 million, which Blue Cross then demanded in payment from the drugstore chain. Wall Street responded quickly, and within one day the price for Arbor stock plummeted by 25 percent to only $15.50. To make matters worse, the U.S. Attorney's office launched an investigation to determine whether the charges involved criminal misconduct, while the federal government began its own audit to see whether Arbor had overcharged the federal Medicaid program. What had been a sterling rise to the top of the drugstore industry was suddenly marred by a serious blemish.

Arbor Drugs quickly denied any wrongdoing, saying that the dispute with Blue Cross Blue Shield arose from differences of opinion about how the reimbursement formula should be calculated. The main point of contention involved what could be included in the pharmacy's "cost" for acquiring the medication. Although neither side would release any details about the disagreement, analysts speculated that such gray areas as warehousing, the cost of vials, and the cost of labelling were probably among the disputed items. After months of negotiation the two parties reached a settlement in which Arbor agreed to pay Blue Cross Blue Shield a one-time fee of $15 million and to alter its billing procedures in the future. The following year the company agreed to pay the federal and state governments a total of $7 million in settlement of the Medicaid claims, and all criminal and civil charges against Arbor Drugs were dropped. With the dispute settled, investor confidence in Arbor Drugs was restored, but only at the high cost of $23 million—almost as much as the company's entire combined net income for the two years prior to the controversy.

Despite the difficult challenges it faced in 1993, Arbor Drugs's long-term success appeared to be just beginning. Although the company was forced to swallow a bitter pill with the billing dispute of 1993, sales and income exclusive of the settlements continued to rise. By 1994, the 154 Arbor Drugs stores posted sales totalling $618 million, at an average of $4.1 million per store, which was 37 percent above the industry average. As the average age of the American population continued to increase, analysts predicted that pharmaceutical sales would reach record numbers. Arbor Drugs, with its emphasis on prescription drugs, appeared well-positioned to benefit from the graying of America into the twenty-first century.

Further Reading:

Brookman, Faye, "Arbor Drugs," *Stores,* April 1994, pp. 16–19.
Brookman, Faye, "Arbor Drugs: Pharmacy Chain of the Year," *Drug Topics,* April 19, 1993, pp. 12–14.
Deck, Cecilia, "Arbor Stock Tumbles in Blues Dispute," *Detroit Free Press,* July 8, 1993, p. 1G.
"Putting a Nettlesome Issue to Rest," *Drugstore News,* June 27, 1994, p. 4.
Sullivan, R. Lee, "A Simple Prescription," *Discount Merchandiser,* September 1990, pp. 26–31.
Weinberg, Neil, "Innocent Victim," *Forbes,* September 13, 1993, p. 50.

—Hilary Gopnik

Banta Corporation

225 Main Street
Box 8003
Menasha, Wisconsin 54952-8003
U.S.A.
(414) 751-7777
Fax: (414) 751-7790

Public Company
Incorporated: 1901
Employees: 4,900
Sales: $811 million
Stock Exchanges: NASDAQ
SICs: 2732 Book Printing; 2759 Commercial Printing, Not
    Elsewhere Classified; 2672 Coated & Laminated Paper,
    Not Elsewhere Classified

Banta Corporation, one of the nation's largest graphic arts and printing companies, literally started in a small-town Wisconsin dining room in 1886. From its humble beginnings, Banta grew to become a technologically-advanced, multi-faceted reproducer of a wide variety of information, from small-run periodicals to popular educational games like "Trivial Pursuit" to CD-ROMs and on-line documentation. By the mid-1990s, Banta had acquired a diverse array of printing and graphics companies, reported sales of $811 million, and was poised for expansion into overseas markets.

In the 1880s, company founder George Banta was a traveling agent for Phoenix Fire Insurance, based in Menasha, Wisconsin, some 80 miles north of Milwaukee. Banta was also a printing buff and, much to the distress of his new bride, Nellie, he brought a printing press into the only room in their house big enough to accommodate it. Two years, one house, and one baby later, Nellie Banta insisted on evicting the press to a shed built in the backyard. George bought a noisy gasoline engine to run the press and also hired one full-time worker for the tiny operation whose main business consisted of printing his insurance forms.

After a fire in 1901 burned down the shed, Banta moved his equipment to a Main Street store front, added a platen job press, and incorporated the business as George Banta Printing Company, with the purpose of "engaging in the business of job and newspaper printing, bookbinding, and manufacture of books and pamphlets." Two years later the corporation was renamed

George Banta Publishing Company. The strain of running the shop along with his insurance job took its toll on George Banta, who had a history of malaria and lung problems. In 1904 his doctors ordered him west to recuperate. To save their business, Nellie decided to stay behind in Menasha and took over as manager. She proved a determined and effective entrepreneur. Meanwhile, George, who had been a Phi Delta Theta member at Indiana University and remained active in the fraternity's national organization, landed a contract to print the Phi Delta magazine, and in time also signed up a number of other fraternities and sororities.

George's educational contacts—his father was dean of the Indiana University law school—helped the company win orders for university catalogs and annuals, as well as some textbooks and magazines. Thus, Banta Publishing grew mainly as a specialist in book and periodical printing. Not that it turned away commercial customers; in its early days, it regularly printed large-volume promotional booklets for Quaker Oats. In 1910 Banta was ready for its own building, a two-story plant just across the Fox River. These facilities, vastly enlarged over the decades, remained the site of Banta Company's offices, the largest division of Banta Corporation, and a complex of printing facilities into the mid-1990s.

In 1911, 18-year-old George Banta Jr. dropped out of college and assumed charge of the office. The replacement of Nellie was somewhat brusque, wrote *Appleton Post-Crescent* contributor Kay Roberts, and while the "Founder's wife" reminisced that she "missed the five dollars a week she earned," she also maintained she had much to attend to at home and "left with few regrets." George Sr., while periodically bothered by health problems, continued to be a major sales contributor, and retained overall leadership as president until his death in 1935 at age 76. Nellie then assumed the presidency until she died in her 86th year in 1951.

The company grew nicely, with emphasis on the educational market. As a historical review in the 1990 annual report noted, Banta was emphatic on keeping "pace with [technological] change." But "rather than attempting to serve many markets, the company focused initially on ones in which it could build special strengths and capabilities." Even though the company consistently ranked among the top five U.S. printers in the 1980s and 1990s, Banta liked to concentrate on numerous niche businesses, and sought to be the leader or a strong contender in each market it entered.

By the time of World War I, Banta was printing 184 scholarly, technical, and educational journals. The war years brought a harsher climate which lasted into the early twenties, but then, as the decade progressed, Banta benefitted from an "explosion in education." By the end of the twenties, Banta found itself in the right place for an innovative concept. One of George Jr.'s brothers-in-law, Russell Sharp, wrote an elementary school workbook and turned to Banta to produce it. The company soon became the leader in printing workbooks as these softcover scholastic aids became a major educational tool from first grade right up through graduate school. Eventually this expertise helped make Banta a leader in softcover books for the professional market as well as for "trade" books (general-interest books sold through book stores).

Always technically progressive, Banta acquired its first web offset press in 1940. In the early days, the prevailing state of the art in paper, platemaking, ink, and other printing supplies limited the jobs considered suitable for offset. Banta became a pioneer in pushing development of improved supplies as well as speedier and higher-quality presses. As web offset developed into the printing method of choice for many applications, the expanding Banta Company established itself as a major player in the industry.

In 1946 Banta expanded beyond its home complex with the 42,000-square-foot Midway plant, built midway between downtown Menasha and nearby Appleton. Even as it kept expanding its printing business, the company contracted its name, dropping the ''Publishing'' to become George Banta Company, Inc. in 1954. The streamlined name also eliminated possible confusion about Banta's role: it did the production work for books and periodicals, while publishers (who create and market books) were its customers.

Banta, which did barely $3.5 million in business at the end of World War II and $10 million in the mid-1950s, attained $33 million sales by 1968. Family leadership had been interrupted in 1961 when John H. Wilterding, who had started at Banta in 1923, succeeded George Banta Jr. as president. However, on Wilterding's retirement in 1965, George Banta III, the son of George Jr., took over. Conglomeration had become the fashion throughout American enterprise, and the printing industry was no exception. George III related: ''We had many beautiful offers to sell out . . . but we decided to remain independent.'' Banta set out to prepare itself for the new order. In 1968 it brought in Menasha-born Kimberly Clark executive William H. Fieweger as president, with George Banta III as chairman, a post he retained until his retirement in 1983.

Within a year, the Banta-Fieweger team had the company's first long-range expansion plan ready, based on the recognition that the industry was ''becoming increasingly capital intensive'' and hence required ''larger economic units.'' The Banta plan aimed to: continue internal growth, ''notably from educational sources''; acquire selected small firms to promote expansion; and encourage technological advancement not just by buying new equipment, but by innovating new methods and directions. The acquisition program began in 1969 with the $2.4 million purchase of Daniels Packaging of Rhinelander, Wisconsin, which specialized in producing foil and flexible film wrap for food and other grocery products. Somewhat ironically, this first acquisition also became the first major unit disposed of by Banta; in 1989 the greatly expanded Daniels was sold for an after-tax gain of $9.6 million.

In 1970, Banta added periodicals printer Hart Press of Minnesota and Menasha neighbor Northwestern Engraving, which prepared color separations for printers (Banta was a major customer). These acquisitions along with internal growth boosted Banta sales volume above $50 million for the first time. In March of 1971 Banta was ready to go public, selling 455,000 shares (a 29 percent interest) at $12.50 per share. A series of stock splits has turned each of these original shares into nine current shares. By 1995, the share value had multiplied more than 25-fold.

Acquisitions continued through the 1970s and 1980s. Ling Products of Neenah, Wisconsin, acquired in 1973, made disposable products for the health and food service industries, such as examination gowns, table covers, and bibs. KCS Industries of Milwaukee, purchased in 1975, produced point-of-sale displays. And R. J. Carroll of Harrisonburg, Virginia, bought in 1976 and later named Banta Harrisonburg, provided Eastern production facilities for Banta's basic education-oriented business. Banta's most important acquisition came in 1988, under the leadership of chairman and CEO Harry W. Earle, when Minnesota-based Beddor Companies joined the fold. The move increased Banta's size by about two-thirds and put it into consumer catalogs and direct mail materials (thus serving the fastest growing segments of retail merchandising). It also added to Banta's soft-cover capacity through printer Viking Press of Minneapolis (no relation to the well-known New York publisher Viking). The merger pushed sales above the half-billion mark in 1989 and brought Banta into the *Fortune* 500. At the same time, Banta further streamlined its corporate name to Banta Corporation.

Acquisitions of ''high-quality'' companies remained high on the Banta agenda in the 1990s. Thus, in 1994, Banta added Danbury Printing and Litho of Connecticut, augmenting its capabilities in the direct marketing industry with a strategic manufacturing facility in the Northeast. Another 1994 acquisition was United Graphics of Kent, Washington, which gave Banta a second Western printing plant to complement its Utah facility, Bushman Press, acquired in 1991. Through the United Graphics purchase, Banta also added software giant Microsoft Corporation to its already broad roster of top-level computer industry customers.

All told, Banta has added 23 companies during the first quarter century of its acquisition policy. It expected acquisitions to contribute at least a third of future company growth, according to Donald D. Belcher, who came to Banta as president in the fall of 1994 from office supplier Avery Dennison and took over the chairmanship and CEO position from retiring Calvin Aurand, Jr. in 1995. Banta has succeeded at obtaining strong growth from companies once they have been acquired, which meshes into its overall plan for ''aggressive and profitable growth'' from internally developed new products and services.

Banta has organized its many acquisitions into several product groups that operate as largely autonomous enterprises, an approach the company believed would make them ''quicker, more nimble, and better able to respond to customer needs.'' The three largest groups in the 1990s, each with a little over one-fifth of total volume, were the Book, Catalog, and Direct Marketing units. The Banta Book Group handled both educational and general books, and also produced instructional games such as ''Trivial Pursuit,'' a game wildly popular in the mid-1980s.

The Publications Group, which accounted for about one-eighth of total volume, put out more than 500 educational, trade, religious, and fraternal magazines with circulation mostly in the 15,000-to-350,000 range. Niche-conscious Banta specialized in this type of periodical rather than large-scale consumer magazines ''because they are less subject to cyclical variation in number of advertising pages; also because regular planned growth is easier to achieve, since each new periodical adds only modestly to sales." Smaller groups were the Banta Digital Group, Information Services, and the more specialized KCS (signs, displays, etc.) and Ling (single-use products) units. One promising new product at KCS was U.S. postage stamps; it was among the first companies to win a contract when the government privatized some of its stamp printing in 1990.

Banta expected to stay strong in the 1990s, noted Belcher, by "investing ahead of the curve in new technologies." Between 1990 and 1994, Banta had reinvested $265 million in its operations, $87 million in 1994 alone. Such a figure represented around 10 percent of revenues, more than double the industry average. Capital acquired in the 1990s included a $20-million printing press whose wide web permitted the printing of 50 percent more pages across the web of paper while running at nearly 50 percent greater speed. In another plant, a new Xeikon full-color digital system printed entirely from digital information, requiring no film or plates. Other electronic and optical systems, often enhanced by proprietary software programs, sped prepress preparation and after-printing processing (e.g., addressing and distribution), enabling Banta to offer fast turnaround and highly customized service, such as catalogs or direct mail pieces with content tailored for specific recipients. Similarly, college texts could be custom-bound to match a professor's specific course curriculum.

Chairman Belcher expected Banta's core business to continue to be "imaging on paper," even as the design, production, and distribution processes which turn out these familiar print products are being "revolutionized by digital technologies." And he predicted that a broad array of non-print products, including CD-ROMs and "image archiving," would show proportionally faster growth than print. An example of the new kinds of jobs taken on by Banta was an electronic catalog for a major business-to-business cataloger that was essentially a CD-ROM version of its printed catalog. For computer industry customers, Banta not only printed instruction manuals but provided on-demand electronic printing, duplication of floppies diskettes and CD-ROMs, and assembly of software kits.

Though Banta had long expressed interest in the global market, foreign expansion had barely begun in the 1990s. In 1994, Banta established a software documentation unit in the Netherlands, which enabled domestic customers to download data for printing and distribution overseas. Similarly, chairperson Belcher explained, "we will have to go to the Far East," if only to meet requirements of domestic customers. In 1994, Banta had also set up KCS-Villanueva as a joint venture in Monterrey, Mexico, for producing in-store point-of-sale displays in Latin America.

Overall, the Banta formula has worked nicely. Since going public in 1971, the company has averaged annualized 13 percent sales and nearly 15 percent earnings growth. It earned $47 million ($2.33 per share) in 1994, and it has raised its dividend for 18 consecutive years. Revenues reached $811 million in 1994. As it moves ahead, Banta sees its industry's future based on capturing information digitally and then "repurposing" it into both print and digital formats. And it is intent on leveraging technology leadership to be in the forefront of this future.

Principal Subsidiaries: KCS Industries Inc.; Ling Products, Inc; The DI Group, Inc.; Danbury Printing & Litho, Inc.; United Graphics; KnowledgeSet Corporation; Banta Direct Marketing, Inc.; Banta Software Services International, Inc.

Further Reading:

Belcher, Donald D., Presentation on Banta Corporation to the New York Society of Security Analysts, company document, March 6, 1995.

Byrne, Harlan S., "Banta Corp. Acquisition Doubles Sales, Moves It into Fast-Growing Field," *Barron's,* May 29, 1989.

Roberts, Kay, "The Founder's Wife," *Appleton (Wisconsin) Post-Crescent,* February 4, 1979.

Stapel, Jeff, and Lorrie Potash, "Banta—90 Years of Growth," *Banta Company Magazine,* 1991, pp. 18–20.

—Henry R. Hecht

Bath Iron Works Corporation

700 Washington Street
Bath, Maine 04530-2574
U.S.A.
(207) 443-3311
Fax: (207) 442-1009

Private Company
Incorporated: 1884 as Bath Iron Works, Ltd.
Sales: $800 million
Employees: 9,000
SICs: 3731 Ship Building and Repairing; 8711 Engineering
    Services

For more than a century, Bath Iron Works Corporation (BIW) has been building ships, chiefly for the U.S. Navy. From its mile-long stretch of waterfront along the Kennebec River have come more oceangoing vessels than from any area of similar size in the world. In its busiest period, BIW built a quarter of the Navy's destroyers launched during World War II. The fourth largest shipyard in the United States and the largest private employer in Maine, BIW has not built a commercial vessel since 1984 and, with the end of the cold war and diminishing naval contracts, has sought to supplement its business, investigating, for example, the prospect of building large carriers to transport automobiles and trucks.

The history of Bath Iron Works is a vital chapter in Maine's seafaring history. Not more than a dozen miles away from the town of Bath, settlers established the first colony in New England—13 years before the landing of the *Mayflower*—and built the first oceangoing vessel made by Englishmen in America in order to take themselves home. But curiously, the company owes its origin to a soldier rather than a sailor. The scion of a prosperous Bath merchant family, Thomas Worcester Hyde was a Civil War army officer who rose to the rank of brigadier general in the Union Army at the age of 23. Hyde leased a local iron foundry after returning home and opened Bath Iron Works, Ltd. in 1884 as a family enterprise.

Starting with capital of just a little over $40,000, Hyde raised another $60,000, purchased a defunct iron works along the Bath riverfront, and equipped it to make steel ships, which were rarities at the time. Producing a wooden steamer in 1890, before obtaining his first naval contract, Hyde delivered to the Navy the first steel vessels built in Maine—two gunboats with auxil-

iary sails—in 1893. Two years later the Navy ordered two more such gunboats. During this time, BIW built other wooden steamers, lightships for the U.S. Bureau of Lighthouses, and private yachts as well. In 1894 Bath built the largest and most luxurious American-built yacht of its time, the *Eleanor,* for William A. Slater, at a cost of $300,000. The ship immediately embarked on a two-year, around-the-world voyage with a crew of 30. The company also built the 302-foot-long *Aphrodite* in 1898 for Colonel Oliver Payne.

But the Navy remained Bath's primary customer. Between 1899 and 1901 the company delivered five very light and high-speed torpedo boats to the Navy. These pioneering craft were the Navy's first of this type until World War II's PT boats. A cruiser, the *Cleveland,* was built in 1904, and BIW's only battleship, the *Georgia,* was completed in 1904.

However, the hull of the *Georgia* was barely able to clear the riverbed in Bath, and as battleships graduated into the larger Dreadnought class, it became clear that Bath would have to confine itself to building smaller ships. BIW's scout cruiser *Chester,* completed in 1908, was the first turbine-propelled ship in the Navy and its fastest vessel, except for torpedo boats. In a race against two other ships of this type, it averaged 25.8 knots over 24 hours.

In 1909 BIW built its first two torpedo boat destroyers. This new type of craft was designed to counter the smaller torpedo boat, yet carry its basic weapon. The name was soon shortened to simply "destroyer," and by 1912 BIW was the Navy's chief specialist for this kind of light, fast warship, which would become the most versatile of modern naval vessels. The destroyer has served as an escort ship on convoy duty and performed many other essential functions, but its chief mandate—especially since World War II—has been to detect, hunt down, and destroy submarines.

BIW briefly came under the control of Charles Schwab's U.S. Shipbuilding Trust between 1902 and 1905, and when this enterprise failed it was sold to John S. Hyde, the late general's younger son, for $275,000. Hyde died in 1917 while the shipyard was awash in World War I orders, and his heirs promptly sold out to a banking syndicate for $3 million. However, the investors awarded themselves big dividends during the fat war years, leaving BIW no margin for coping with the inevitable postwar bust. The naval disarmament treaty of 1921 sealed the company's doom. BIW went into receivership in 1924 and shut down operations the following year. In 1927 the idle facilities were slated for conversion to the task of turning out paper pie plates.

Nevertheless, the shipyard was saved from this fate by its former works manager, William S. "Pete" Newell. He leased it for $17,000 a year, established the Bath Iron Works Corp. with $125,000 in borrowed capital, successfully bid on three fishing trawlers, and won an order for a 240-foot yacht. Between 1928 and 1937 BIW built and delivered 18 trawlers. The company also constructed seven Coast Guard cutters designated for combating rumrunners during the Prohibition years. And in 1931 BIW won the contract for the *Dewey* and *Farragut,* the first destroyers authorized by the Navy since 1918.

Building yachts for captains of industry proved a profitable sideline. For J.P. Morgan II, BIW built the 343-foot-long *Corsair IV,* which was launched in 1930. Although the Great Depression largely ended Bath's yachtbuilding operations, in 1936 Harold S. Vanderbilt commissioned the company to build a racer to defend the America's Cup. The resulting *Ranger* was the last of the J class sloops to defend the cup, defeating the *Endeavor II* in four straight 1937 races.

In 1936 BIW offered stock to the public, for the first time, on the New York Curb Exchange (later the American Stock Exchange). This action placed the company on a sounder financial basis, enabling Newell to pay off the company's outstanding first mortgage bonds and to augment its working capital. By the time BIW was registered on the New York Stock Exchange in 1940, it had paid off all its bank loans.

During World War II, BIW employment peaked at 12,000 (1,600 of whom were women) in 1943, compared to 300 a decade earlier. Between Pearl Harbor and the war's end, BIW built 82 destroyers—one-fourth of the total ordered by the Navy—launching one on an average of every 17 days. Only eight of the ships were sunk during the war. Bath also established, jointly with Todd Shipyard Corp., a facility in South Portland to build 30 British cargo ships. This yard, which turned out Liberty ships for the U.S. Maritime Commission, was closed after the war.

Following a familiar pattern, employment sank to 350 in 1947. But BIW had already begun work on the first of 32 trawlers commissioned by the French government. Moreover, the company soon received new orders for destroyers from the Navy as well as contracts for frigates, ocean escorts, and LST's (landing ships, tank). Yachtbuilding also resumed. John R. Newell succeeded his father as the company's president in 1950.

By 1968, however, the company was beset by managerial and economic problems. That year the parent holding company, Bath Industries Inc., merged with Congoleum-Nairn Inc., a manufacturer of flooring materials. Troubles continued, with BIW losing out on major naval contracts and incurring losses on others because its fixed prices did not allow for the rapidly rising inflation of the early 1970s. In 1974 the shipyard lost $10 million.

The following year the parent company (now called Congoleum Corp.) brought in John R. Sullivan, Jr., a chemical engineer, to run the yard. Although Sullivan had never seen a shipyard, he set about putting Bath construction on a sounder basis. Sullivan made the yard's modular construction system, which had been adopted from Japanese practice, effective at BIW for the first time. Bath was the first U.S. shipyard to employ this technique, which involved building a hull out of modules constructed indoors and fitted there with electrical wiring, plumbing, ventilation, and hydraulic equipment. These modules were then hauled outdoors by crane and welded together. By 1981, Bath's safety record, once one of the worst in the industry, had become one of the best.

By this time BIW had built 13 of 24 FFG 7-class guided-missile frigates for the Navy, completing each in less than two years. The project was 99 weeks ahead of schedule and $44 million under budget. Bath's operations were comfortably profitable,

and there was a backlog of $800 million in military orders. In early 1980 Congoleum went private in a leveraged buyout. Several insurance companies joined the company's management in borrowing heavily to buy all the outstanding publicly held stock for about $450 million. Prudential secured 29 percent of the company, with Aetna, Travelers, and Connecticut General investing as well.

A *Forbes* article published in September 1984 indicated that this move was paying off. BIW's frigates were still coming in ahead of schedule and under budget, and the company's earnings for the past five years were estimated at about 15 percent on sales of about $400 million annually. In 1982 Bath won a contract to build the *Thomas S. Gates,* the first of eight Ticonderoga-class Aegis cruisers it was to build through 1991. More good news came on April 2, 1985, when Bath won an order worth about $322 million to build the *Arleigh Burke,* first of the DDG 51 Aegis destroyer class. By mid-1986, BIW had a $1.4 billion backlog in naval orders, including these Aegis-class cruisers and destroyers.

On this prosperous note, Congoleum's investors were ready to cash in, but before doing so management determined to make BIW even more attractive by putting a lid on labor costs. However, this initiative met with protest, as BIW workers walked out for 14 weeks in 1985. Labor and management eventually agreed to a wage freeze, with bonuses equivalent to an increase of three percent over three years.

In another leveraged buyout, announced August 21, 1986, the closely held New York investment firm of Gibbons, Green, Van Amerongen Ltd. bought BIW for an estimated $500 million. BIW then became a subsidiary of the new Bath Holding Corp., which itself became a subsidiary of the Fulcrum II Limited Partnership, the managing partners of which were Edward Gibbons, Todd Goodwin, and Louis van Amerongen.

By late 1992 BIW had a backlog of $2 billion worth of orders carried through 1997; in 1994, the backlog of 14 Burke-class destroyers extended through the year 2000. Aware, however, of impending defense cuts in the wake of the cold war, company managers began looking for ways to solicit civilian work. Bath had not built a civilian craft since 1985 and had "no contingency plan whatsoever," according to its president, Duane D. "Buzz" Fitzgerald, who sent a four-man team to Holland to "benchmark" ten shipyards there.

Fitzgerald replaced William Haggett as BIW's chief executive officer in September 1991, when Haggett opted to resign his posts as CEO and chairperson. A BIW official for 23 years, Haggett announced at a news conference that year that he had violated business ethics, admitting that he had ordered the photocopying of a government document, inadvertently left behind at the BIW shipyard by Navy officials. Although the document, which had included cost reviews of work performed by Bath and its chief competitor, Ingalls Shipbuilding of Pascagoula, Mississippi, had reportedly not been used to BIW's advantage, Haggett and two BIW vice-presidents involved in the photocopying resigned in 1991.

Under the leadership of Buzz Fitzgerald, BIW continued to be a major supplier to the Pentagon. The company was asked to build three $850 million Burke-class Aegis destroyers for the

Navy in June 1994. Moreover, in an effort to diversify, BIW joined with American Automar Inc. and Great American Lines Inc. in 1993 to develop carriers of automobiles and other vehicles that could also meet military needs. Also participating in the $14 million project were a giant Japanese shipbuilder and the Canadian ship-designing subsidiary of a Finnish group. This program received a $5 million federal grant and was being coordinated by a special Pentagon agency intended to foster ties between shipyards, carriers, university research centers, and the federal government. According to a 1994 Bath press release, the company was "on course to be competitive in the world commercial shipbuilding market by 1997."

Further Reading:

Biesada, Alexandra, "Strategic Benchmarking," *Financial World,* September 29, 1992, pp. 30–31.

Buell, Barbara, "Bath: A Tight Ship that Could Spring a Leak," *Business Week,* May 20, 1985, pp. 88–90.

"City of Ships," *American Heritage,* September 1991, pp. 28–30.

DeMott, John S., "Bath's Fighting Company," *Time,* October 12, 1981, p. 82.

Eskew, Garrett Laidlaw, *Cradle of Ships,* New York: G.P. Putnam's Sons, 1958.

Frank, Allen Dodds, "The Bath Money Works," *Forbes,* September 10, 1984, pp. 58–62.

Lewis, Diane, "Bath Shipyard Accord Reflects Fight to Remain Competitive," *Boston Globe,* September 5, 1994, pp. 1, 5.

Payne, Seth, "A Yard Sale Worth $600 Million?" *Business Week,* June 23, 1986, p. 47.

Ricks, Thomas E., "Navy Allocates Ship Contracts in Policy Shift," *Wall Street Journal,* June 9, 1994, p. A16.

Shorrock, Tim, "Maine Yard Gets US Aid In Designing Cargo Vessels," *Journal of Commerce,* December 16, 1993, pp. 1A, 10A.

Stevens, David Weld, "Floating the Navy the Bath Way," *Fortune,* October 6, 1981, pp. 160–63.

"Vote of Merger Plan," *Wall Street Journal,* September 9, 1968, p. 22.

Williams, John D., and Jan Wong, "Congoleum Sells Bath Iron Works Unit in Buyout Valued at About $500 Million," *Wall Street Journal,* August 22, 1986, p. 4.

—Robert Halasz

BayBank

BayBanks, Inc.

175 Federal Street
Boston, Massachusetts 02110
U.S.A.
(617) 482-1040

Public Company
Incorporated: 1928 as Old Colony Trust
Total Assets: $10.2 billion
Employees: 5,571
Stock Exchanges: NASDAQ
SICs: 6712 Bank Holding Companies; 6022 State
  Commercial Banks;
6211 Security Brokers & Dealers; 6162 Mortgage Bankers &
Correspondents

BayBanks, Inc., is one of the largest and most successful bank holding companies in New England. Located in Boston, Bay-Banks is the undisputed leader in providing consumer financial services across the state of Massachusetts. The firm operates an extensive network of retail banking outlets, with more than 200 full-service banking offices and more than 1,000 Automated Teller Machines (ATMs). This is the seventh largest network of ATMs in the United States and rivals the ATM networks of such huge banks as CitiCorp. BayBanks offers more than 160 banking products and financial services and is the official investment broker for a number of mutual funds. The company is also at the forefront of offering innovative services to its customers, including a banking catalog and a 24-hour customer service center.

Baybanks, Inc., was founded in 1928 when the management of a large Massachusetts business trust, already holding a significant amount of stock in nine state banks, decided to reorganize and establish itself as Old Colony Trust. For the first two years of its existence, Old Colony Trust was very successful. The high-flying stock market and seemingly unending opportunities for the banking industry contributed to the firm's growing asset base. As the bank prospered, it implemented an acquisition program and began to purchase interests in a number of small banks throughout the state of Massachusetts.

When the stock market crashed in October 1929, the entire banking industry was hit hard by the ensuing worldwide economic depression, and when Franklin Delano Roosevelt's reorganization of the banking industry was initiated during the early years of his administration, many banks were unable to keep their doors open to the public. Management at Old Colony Trust, however, shrewdly and cautiously steered the bank through the worst years of the Depression. By the mid-1930s, Old Colony was able to reinvigorate its acquisition program with the purchase of a few smaller banks. A well-planned strategy of mergers with small banks and additional acquisitions throughout the latter part of the decade helped to expand the firm's investment holdings.

During the 1940s, Old Colony prospered by expanding its customer base and by making numerous acquisitions. By 1944, the company had grown large enough to necessitate a comprehensive reorganization. Management also decided at this time to change the name from Old Colony Trust to Baystate Corporation, in order to reflect the widening scope of operations and services the firm provided throughout the state of Massachusetts. In the 1950s and 1960s, Baystate engaged in an aggressive acquisitions strategy and bought more than 40 banks. Baystate had grown to become one of the larger regional banks in New England, with extensive holdings and investments in small and medium-sized banks.

In 1974 Baystate hired William M. Crozier, Jr., as chairman and chief executive officer of the bank. Crozier had extensive experience in the financial industry, and was instructed by the bank's board of directors to use whatever measures he thought necessary to improve the performance of the firm and prepare it for the future. Under Crozier's supervision, it was determined that the bank's holdings were a rather unwieldy and disorganized collection of banking concerns. As a result, management merged and consolidated all of Baystate's investments into 12 banks. This move was aimed at centralizing operations to improve efficiency and establishing a unified image that customers could readily identify. In 1976 the bank's name was changed from Baystate to BayBanks, Inc., a title which was assumed by all of BayBanks' operations.

BayBanks had grown into a firm with more than $2 billion in assets, and Crozier filed notice with the Federal Reserve that five of its state-chartered bank subsidiaries were withdrawing from the Federal Reserve System. Crozier cited the reasons for leaving the system as the increasing expenses associated with holding idle reserve requirements with the Federal Reserve and the disadvantage in head-to-head competition with other banks due to the costs involved in carrying the deposits. Thirteen state-chartered banks had already left the system, all of them citing the reserve requirement as the reason. The Baybanks subsidiaries that withdrew from the system nonetheless continued as members of the Federal Deposit Insurance Corporation. Crozier's move helped BayBanks save nearly $1.5 million.

During the late 1970s BayBanks also introduced a number of innovative customer services. In June 1977 the firm brought out the BayBanks Card and, during the same period, the X-Press 24 hour automated teller machine (ATM) network. Within a few months, X-Press 24 was the preferred automated teller machine network throughout New England. In 1978 and 1979, the bank implemented a strategy that emphasized business product development, including cash management services, lending specialties, a full-service money desk, and an international department. This strategy, overseen by Crozier, was designed to improve the company's competitiveness.

During the 1980s, management at BayBanks formulated an aggressive strategy to expand the firm's commitment to customer service. BayBanks entered an agreement with Bank of Boston to implement a shared network of automated teller machines in supermarkets throughout Massachusetts, under a joint venture called CombiNet. Installed in early 1984, by the end of its first year CombiNet operated nearly 300 terminals. By this time assets at BayBanks had grown to $4.3 billion, and, with its eight subsidiary banks operating in the state of Massachusetts, the firm had developed the largest retail banking system in New England. Bank of Boston was already widely known as New England's largest banking organization with over $18 billion in assets. When combined, the two banks counted over one million ATM cardholders. For BayBanks, however, this joint venture in the ATM market was only the beginning. In 1986 BayBanks purchased the part of the Cirrus national automated teller network that already operated in the firm's statewide financial institutions, branches, and other locations. By the end of fiscal 1986, BayBanks reported $5.7 billion in assets, and had grown to become the fifth-largest bank holding company in Massachusetts. Continuing its expansion strategy, BayBanks purchased 10 branches from Northeast Savings during the same year. Northeast Savings, a savings and loan with more than $5.4 billion in assets, represented the company's first acquisition in Connecticut.

As the bank devoted more and more resources toward the development of its automated teller network, unforeseen obstacles began to arise. In 1986 BayBanks filed an anti-trust suit against New England Network, Inc., operator of the Yankee 24 network of automated teller machines. Yankee 24 implemented a ''sub-switching'' fee that would have been levied on numerous automated teller machine transactions. The fee, amounting to four cents, would have raised costs enormously for BayBanks when it processed transactions from ATMs for banks that belonged to both Yankee 24 and BayBanks' own X-Press 24 ATM network. Although the fee seemed minimal, the bank argued that the millions of ATM transactions would add up rapidly. In 1988 New England Network, Inc., finally relented and agreed to withdraw the fee. Terms of the settlement did not involve any financial payment, but BayBanks was clearly the victor—the bank's 87 million ATM transactions were freed from what could have amounted to a very costly levy.

In the early 1990s, Baybanks used its network of ATM machines to dominate the retail market in New England. With more than 1,250 automated teller machines in the region, BayBanks significantly increased its share of the retail market to 27 percent, an increase of five points in approximately five years. In 1990, one in four Massachusetts citizens owned a checking account from BayBanks or one of its affiliates. More than eight out of every ten customers held a BayBanks ATM card, and the BayBanks network had developed into the single most utilized system in the entire United States. The company's ATM network was found not only at branch offices, but also at supermarkets and transit stations. The bank prided itself on the capabilities of its ATM network, which included a customer's ability to receive cash after a deposit irrespective of the previous account balance, a fast-cash button that dispensed $100, the ability to

withdraw money despite a system failure, the ability to determine the most recent ATM transaction, and the ability to determine whether or not a check had cleared. In 1991 the company added new functions to its ATMs, including such unusual features as loan modeling and interest rate information, and also initiated plans to provide screens with wheelchair accessibility for disabled customers. With approximately $9.9 billion in assets, BayBanks was handling more than 230,000 ATM transactions per month. BayBanks' ATM network in New England was the banking equivalent of McDonald's ubiquitous golden arches.

In 1992 BayBanks continued its highly successful strategy of marrying sophisticated technology to mass marketing. The company introduced check-image statements, providing customers with miniaturized copies of all their checks rather than the actual checks in monthly statements. In 1993 BayBanks continued to expand the capabilities of its automated teller machine services by providing customers with the ability to apply for credit, bank by telephone at special ATM locations, and purchase postage stamps at selected ATM sites. BayBanks' ATM cardholders also had point-of-sale debit capabilities at more than 5,000 Mobile gas stations and nearly 200 supermarkets throughout the greater Boston area. Best of all, the company's cardholders could access more than 7,000 ATMs nationwide. BayBanks' market penetration was nothing short of astonishing. In eastern Massachusetts, 31.2 percent of all households had at least one account with BayBanks; in the entire state of Massachusetts, the figure was over 25 percent. Within one suburban Boston county, the number of households that had at least one account with BayBanks was an unbelievable 41 percent. BayBanks' automated teller machines could be found in airports, strip malls, universities, colleges, supermarkets, and stand-alone sites.

BayBanks derives 80 percent of its revenues from its retail business, while its closest rivals—Fleet Financial Corporation, Bank of Boston, and Shawmut National Corporation—have only been able to capture 15 percent of the retail market. Even though BayBanks is ranked as the United States's 67th largest commercial bank in terms of assets, it operates the seventh largest network of automated teller machines in the country. The bank's closest rival in the ATM market is Chemical Banking Corporation, a holding company 14 times the size of BayBanks and with nearly $150 billion in assets. BayBanks' spending on technological development ranges between $20 to $30 million annually, and untold millions are set aside for regional New England television and billboard advertisements.

Much of the recent success of the company is also tied to its emphasis on customer service. BayBanks has saturated the greater Boston metropolitan area with a 53-page catalogue of services and products that include such items as 24-hour toll-free customer service telephone numbers and various designs for checkbooks. In 1993 bank employees fielded five million customer service calls, handled nearly 40 percent of the bank's consumer loans, and opened approximately 15 percent of all new personal savings and checking accounts. In one instance, when a customer urgently needed travelers checks for an overseas trip, a BayBanks employee drove to the airport to deliver them personally. The company is also in the process of devising a highly detailed strategy to provide more comprehensive services to customers in Boston's large academic community, including Tufts, Brandeis, the Massachusetts Institute of Technology, and Harvard.

Principal Subsidiaries: BayBank Systems, Inc.; BayBanks Associates, Inc.; BayBanks Brokerage Services, Inc.; BayBanks Credit Corp.; BayBanks Finance & Leasing Co., Inc.; BayBanks Investment Management, Inc.; BayBanks Mortgage Corp.

Further Reading:

Barthel, Matt, "BayBanks Growing Electronically," *American Banker,* September 13, 1991, p. 11.

Chaney, Dale, "BayBanks' ATM Card Forms Bedrock of Its Winning Mass-Market Strategy," *American Banker's Management Strategies,* May 24, 1994, pp. 9–12A.

Gullo, Karen, "BayBanks to Offer Check-Image Statement," *American Banker,* January 17, 1992, p. 3.

Iida, Jeanne, "BayBanks Keeps up Pressure on Rivals with an Unswerving Focus on Service," *American Banker,* February 25, 1994, p. 4.

Layne, Richard, "BayBanks Gets Retail Edge with ATMs," *American Banker,* March 7, 1990, p. 7.

Spitzer, Bruce, *Historic Profile: BayBanks, Inc.,* Boston: BayBanks, Inc., 1995.

Tyson, David O., "Boston Banks to Share Supermarket Network," *American Banker,* November 22, 1983, p. 3.

Weinstein, Michael, "Yankee 24 Agrees to Drop Fee In Settlement of BayBanks Suit," *American Banker,* March 28, 1988, p. 5.

—Thomas Derdak

The original comfort shoe.™

Birkenstock Footprint Sandals, Inc.

8171 Redwood Boulevard
Novato, California 94945
U.S.A.
(415) 892-4400
Fax: (415) 899-1324

Private Company
Founded: 1967
Employees: 135
Sales: $60 million
SICs: 3149 Footwear Except Rubber Not Elsewhere
Classified; 3100 Leather & Leather Products

Birkenstock Footprint Sandals, Inc. is a shoe distributor best known for its clunky, comfortable orthopedic sandals. The Birkenstock family of Germany has a long history in the shoe-making trade. Throughout the first half of the twentieth century, the company marketed orthopedic shoe inserts. In the 1960s, Birkenstock used the principles behind these appliances to create a homey-looking sandal, designed with comfort foremost in mind. After these shoes were introduced to the United States they gained popularity with "hippies" and academics before reaching a mass market in the 1990s.

Birkenstock traces its roots to the late 18th century, when a German cobbler named Johann Adam Birkenstock, who was born in 1754, was first registered as a "subject and shoemaker" in the church archives of Langenbergheim, a town in the duchy of Hesse, Germany. By the end of the 19th century, Konrad Birkenstock, a descendant, owned two shoe stores in Frankfort, the capital of Hesse. These stores would become the foundation of the modern Birkenstock businesses.

Konrad Birkenstock had the inspiration that would form the basis for his family's business for the next hundred years. At the time, shoes were made with flat soles, despite the fact that the bottom of the human foot is curved. Birkenstock realized that a sole curved to complement the shape of the foot would be more comfortable than a flat surface. In 1897, he designed the first contoured shoe last, a tool used in shoe-making, to help his cobblers make customized footwear for patrons.

On the strength of this innovation, Konrad Birkenstock began to spread the word of his new kind of shoe. He gave frequent talks to other leading members of the shoemaker's guild, explaining

his fully contoured shoe. Birkenstock traveled throughout Germany promoting his new idea, and licensed other cobblers to produce shoes made with his technique. By the start of the twentieth century, he had moved beyond the borders of his native country, traveling to Austria and Switzerland as well.

By 1902, however, the popularity of custom-made shoes had begun to wane, as factory-manufactured footwear began to be more widely distributed. Adapting the essence of his idea for this new and growing market, Konrad Birkenstock developed flexible, contoured arch supports, which could be inserted into mass-produced shoes to make them more comfortable. Birkenstock's arch supports, which bent to accommodate the foot, differed from the other supports on the market, which were made of unyielding metal. With the rise of mass-produced shoes, the Birkenstock family business moved away from the crafting of custom-designed shoes to concentrate on the production of shoe inserts.

In 1908, Birkenstock pushed forward with the foot support when he developed his own substance, and built molding presses to manufacture the flexible orthopedic insert. Four years later, the firm continued its technological innovation when it created a new method for using rubber, a material just beginning to be developed, in shoe inserts. In 1913, Konrad Birkenstock's son Carl joined the family firm, insuring that continuity in the company's activities would be possible. In the wake of Carl's arrival, Konrad Birkenstock committed the bulk of his family's considerable assets to research and the development of rubber as a material for foot supports.

In the same year that Birkenstock undertook these efforts, Germany entered World War I. The company's contribution to the war effort was the design and manufacture of orthopedic shoes to be worn by wounded soldiers in a large military hospital in Frankfort. As a result of these activities, Birkenstock's products came to the attention of the doctor in charge of the hospital, who praised his efforts and encouraged him to market his orthopedic inserts more widely. In 1915, Carl Birkenstock began to travel throughout Germany, introducing the family's products to new buyers.

Two years after the end of World War I, a second Birkenstock brother, Heinrich, entered the family business. Though Germany's economy suffered following the war, the Birkenstock business thrived. The family opened a branch in Vienna, the capital of Austria, in 1923, and soon expanded its distribution to countries across Europe, selling orthopedic inserts in Austria, Switzerland, France, Italy, Belgium, Czechoslovakia, Holland, Luxembourg, Denmark, Sweden, and Norway. To accommodate this expanded customer base, Birkenstock opened a larger factory in the town of Friedberg, in Hesse. When demand for the Birkenstock product necessitated even greater manufacturing capacity, the company added night-shifts at the factory.

The late 1920s and early 1930s saw the company make many changes and additions to its product line. In 1926 and again in 1935, Birkenstock expanded its line of footbeds, adding different widths to better fit the foot and to accommodate fashionable shoes. In 1937, Birkenstock further altered the footbed, adding a "ring," which it patented, that allowed the insert to be easily adjusted to fit each foot. By 1928, Birkenstock's success had attracted the notice of its competitors, and other companies began to market non-metallic arch supports. For the first time, the company had competition for its products.

With the start of the 1930s, Birkenstock expanded its education and promotion efforts beyond people who made shoes to the public itself. The company published 70,000 copies of ''The Foot and its Treatment,'' a heavily-illustrated pamphlet of 50 pages, in an effort to inform customers about the company's theories of orthopedics. Two years later, in 1932, Birkenstock stepped up its education efforts when it began to offer training seminars and lectures to orthotic appliance sellers in most European countries. These sessions lasted a week, and included more than 5,000 people in the mid-1930s.

Germany's defeat in World War II changed but did not seriously disrupt Birkenstock's development. With the coming of peace in 1945, the company transferred its operations from the Frankfort area in Hesse, to the town of Bad Honnef on the Rhine. Innovation and education continued apace; in 1946 the company introduced a toe-free insert and in 1947 it began to distribute a pamphlet for shoe sellers titled ''Footorthotics System Birkenstock,'' with 112 pages and 55 illustrations. In 1950, Konrad Birkenstock, the creator of the flexible footbed and the company's driving force for half a century, died at the age of 77.

The decade following Konrad Birkenstock's death saw a number of changes in the venerable company. In 1956, Birkenstock introduced an insole made of shaped foam that was created through thermoplastic compression. Two years earlier, in 1954, a new generation of Birkenstocks had joined the family firm, when Karl Birkenstock, Carl Birkenstock's son, came aboard. Although his father envisioned the company's future exclusively in terms of orthopedic shoe inserts, the younger Birkenstock had more ambitious plans. He hoped to create a shoe that provided all of the benefits of walking barefoot. To do this, he experimented, combining his grandfather's techniques of flexible, contoured arch support, with his own understanding of how the foot works and moves.

Within a decade of Karl Birkenstock's arrival at the family firm, the company had re-entered the shoe business. In 1964, it began to manufacture a shoe whose design was based on the shape and function of the human foot. The new Birkenstock shoe was built from the inside out, starting with an orthopedically-based footbed, which gave firm support to the bottom of the foot. The company's goal was to make the wearer feel that he or she was walking on a surface that would yield, such as wet sand. In order to accomplish this, Birkenstock designed a footbed made of cork, latex, and jute, which absorbed shocks to the foot. The company also added a raised toe bar, to facilitate the instinctive gripping motion of the toes, and a heel cup, to cradle the heel and better distribute the body's weight. In 1965, Karl Birkenstock attached this sole to two simple leather straps to create a clunky, but comfortable, orthopedic sandal.

One year after Birkenstock began to market its new sandals, the shoes came to the attention of Margot Fraser, a German-born dress designer who had emigrated to the United States. While vacationing at a German spa, workers suggested that she try Birkenstock sandals to ease her chronic foot problems. Several months later, her foot pain had greatly improved. Fraser was

hooked, and she believed that other American women would also want an alternative to the uncomfortable high-fashion shoes typically marketed to women. She spread the word about Birkenstock sandals to her friends, bringing them shoes from Germany. Finally, along with her husband, a cookware importer, Fraser arranged with Karl Birkenstock to market his sandals in the United States.

When Fraser approached the owners of shoe stores about selling Birkenstock sandals in their stores, she was universally rebuffed. Repeatedly, shoe sellers assured her that no American woman would ever wear shoes that ugly, regardless of how comfortable they might be. Seeking alternate marketing channels, Fraser turned to the health food industry. ''We had to sell to people with a different vision,'' Fraser later recounted to *People* magazine. ''It was very tough at first,'' she told the *New York Times.* ''But it was when I went to a health fair, and people there wanted them that I got a start. They were interested in fitness.'' At a trade show, Fraser sold her first pair of sandals to a woman who was limping among the booths, holding her high-heeled shoes in her hands. After trying the Birkenstock sandals, this woman began wearing them constantly, and also bought several pairs to sell in her health food store.

Fraser set up business in her home in Santa Cruz, California, using her garage as a warehouse. Sales of the sandals through health food stores increased, and the shoes gained a reputation for their comfort. In addition, Fraser sold the shoes through the mail. Throughout her early years in business, Fraser was unable to convince the German Birkenstock company to make her its sole American distributor. Instead, she bought shoes directly from the factory, often in lots of 20 pairs, and had them shipped parcel post to her house.

In 1971, Fraser moved her business out of her house, leasing a small office on top of a San Rafael, California, health food store for $25 a month. At that time, she incorporated her company under the name Birkenstock Footprint Sandals, Inc., and formally became the sole American distributor of Birkenstock products. Fraser hired a part-time bookkeeper and packer. ''We made enough money to survive,'' she later told the *Sacramento Bee.* ''We were pinching out pennies, but we managed.'' By the end of that year, the company had sold 10,000 pairs of shoes to the American market, promoting the product through home-made fliers, small ads in health food publications, and booths at trade fairs and shoe shows. Often, the shoes were first bought by the owners of health food stores, who had to stand behind a cash register all day. With their recommendation, the popularity of the shoes spread through word of mouth.

While Fraser was working to sell Birkenstock products in the United States, the German parent firm was furthering its efforts to develop its line. In 1966, the company introduced a special paper, on which a customer's footprint could be marked, for a better fitting shoe. In the following year, Birkenstock developed and began to use ''Birko-Cork,'' a natural thermo-pliable product for use in footbeds. Two years later, the company also began to sell insoles that massaged the feet, called ''Nappy-Fit.''

During the 1970s the popularity of Birkenstock footwear exploded, as the shoes became associated with the Bohemian lifestyle popular with young people. In the United States, sales of Birkenstock sandals grew dramatically, and the company introduced a number of new styles. In 1970, a sandal called "Roma," with a strap that encircled the heel, was sent to stores. In the following year, "Arizona," designed by Fraser with two classic wide straps, was introduced. Overall, there were 12 different varieties of the basic Birkenstock shoe, all sold in natural earth tones.

In Germany, the Birkenstock company expanded its production facilities in order to meet the new demand. The company leased a factory in the town of St. Katharinen that housed punching presses to cut out the leather pieces for its shoes in 1974. Two years later, Birkenstock introduced "Birko Foam," yet another new material for use in its shoes, and in 1978, the company began to use superelastic light material to make new specially contoured soles.

At the start of the 1980s, Birkenstock modernized its production processes further, installing computerized last-making machinery to make the molds for shoes. Two years later, Birkenstock introduced its first significant variation on the basic sandal, the thong-sandal, which it began to sell in five different styles. In the next two years, the company received nearly 40 different design protection rights from the German Patent Office for its products, including two developed for the thong sandal. In 1984 Birkenstock opened a larger warehouse for its products.

Despite the innovation of the thong sandal, sales of Birkenstock shoes began to wane in the early 1980s, as fashions shifted away from the functional and down-to-earth. "We were struggling with the image . . . that we were a hippie shoe," Fraser later told *Forbes.* "We wanted to change that." In 1989, her company ditched its old, chunky logo, replacing it with something sleeker. In addition, the company joined with Birkenstock's German designers to increase the number of styles and colors offered to customers. Gradually, the number of Birkenstock sandal styles available grew to 125, with colors such as mango, moss, fuchsia, and cognac. In addition, Birkenstock sandals for children were introduced, under the name BirkiKids.

In 1990, Birkenstock's American branch began to sell its shoes through a glossy mail-order catalogue, which it updated every six months. Soon other catalogue merchants, such as L.L. Bean and the Sharper Image, were marketing the company's wares. By the early 1990s, popularity of Birkenstock sandals was once again soaring, as the baby boomers aged and comfort became chic. In 1992, Birkenstock's American arm purchased a large warehouse to distribute its products, which were shipped from Germany to Houston in containers, and then moved by rail to Novato, California. This facility used a mile of conveyor belts and a computerized bar-code inventory system to control stock after a $1 million renovation. From this warehouse, shoes were sent to more than 100 Birkenstock specialty stores, large department stores, and other vendors. As Birkenstock moved into the mid-1990s, the company's niche in the functional shoe market appeared secure. With more than 100 years of experience in cradling feet, the enterprise run by descendants of Johann Birkenstock seemed assured of a comfortable future.

Further Reading:

Chan, Gilbert, "Step By Step," *Sacramento Bee,* May 2, 1994, p. C1.
"Deja Vu Shoe," *People,* August 26, 1991.
Magiera, Marcy, "Woodstock's Kids Slip into Birkenstocks," *Advertising Age,* August 24, 1992, p. 12.
Patterson, Cecily, "From Woodstock to Wall Street," *Forbes,* November 11, 1991, p. 214.
Stengel, Richard, "Be It Ever So Birkenstock," *New York Times,* August 30, 1992.

—Elizabeth Rourke

bloomingdale's

Bloomingdale's Inc.

1000 3rd Avenue
New York, New York 10022
U.S.A.
(212) 705-2000
Fax: (212) 705-2001

Division of Federated Department Stores, Inc.
Incorporated: 1872
Employees: 10,800
Sales: $1.1 billion
Stock Exchanges: New York
SICs: 5311 Department Stores

Bloomingdale's Inc. operates 15 premier department stores in nine U.S. states, bringing in a total of approximately $1.1 billion in annual revenues. Famous for its glamorous flagship store in uptown Manhattan, Bloomingdale's traditionally caters to an upscale, trendy crowd. In the 1970s and 1980s, the store's flashy merchandise displays and intensely theatrical atmosphere made it a major tourist attraction in New York City, second only to the Statue of Liberty. Bloomingdale's fell on hard times in the early 1990s, when Campeau Corp. bought its parent company, Federated Department Stores for $6.6 billion. Federated filed for Chapter 11 bankruptcy in 1991. After undergoing a number of management changes, Bloomingdale's emerged as a more subdued and less theatrical merchandiser with a focus on customer service and shopping ease.

According to a Dun and Bradstreet report, Bloomingdale's history can be indirectly traced to mid-nineteenth century France, when the wife of Napoleon III invented the hoopskirt to hide her pregnancy from the French aristocracy. Across the Atlantic, Benjamin Bloomingdale, a New York entrepreneur, sensed that a major fashion trend had begun in France and opened Bloomingdale's Hoopskirt and Ladies' Notions Shop on Manhattan's upper East Side. His sons Lymen and Joseph ran the store while Benjamin peddled the highly fashionable hoopskirts to dressmakers and merchants across the eastern states.

At that time, the East Side was a working class neighborhood, full of shanty towns, garbage dumps, and stockyards. In spite of it's humble location, Bloomingdale's attempted to position itself as a vanguard of fashion for New York socialites. In 1872, as the popularity of the hoopskirt was declining, Lymen and Joseph opened Bloomingdale's East Side Bazaar and offered a

variety of ladies' "skirts corsets and fancy goods," and "gent's furnishings." The move was a bold one at the time because most respectable retail stores specialized in only one trade. Even bolder was the decision to remain in the upper East Side. Most of their customers (and all of their competitors) were located on the borough's tonier West Side. Nevertheless, the Bloomingdale brothers set up shop in a small, ordinary-looking row house near Third Avenue and 56th Street. Their store was a harbinger of things to come.

It seems the brothers were aware that their neighborhood was undergoing a major transformation. The Metropolitan Museum of Art had recently opened on the East Side, St. Patrick's Cathedral was erected a few blocks from Bloomingdale's, and Central Park and the New York City subway system were being developed. Within three years after the store's opening, wealthy families began moving into the upper East Side, building elegant brownstones that surrounded the new park. Bloomingdale's, a pioneer of the department stores that would dominate the twentieth century retail market, was there to greet them, offering ladies a dazzling assortment of high-end women's fashions.

In 1886, the brothers opened a new store with large plate glass display windows and spacious merchandising areas at Third Avenue and 59th Street. The two had a flair for dramatic presentation of merchandise, which continues to be a Bloomingdale's trademark to this day. Instead of "stuffing [windows] with an assortment of the goods they sold—as was common practice—they designed each window as a dramatic tableau," noted one writer. "Only a couple of their products served as props on a theatrical mise-en-scene." Many of these products were European imports, which greatly added to the store's elegant image.

By the turn of the century, the department store was becoming a mainstay of the urban retail industry. Bloomingdale's growth skyrocketed, offering customers everything from ladies' stockings at 10 cents a pair, to $10 men's wool suits and $149 upright pianos. The store's growth was facilitated by its convenient location at a hub of New York City's horse-drawn trolley system. In 1902, Lymen Bloomingdale's son, Samuel J., capitalized on the store's location by adopting the advertising slogan, "All Cars Transfer to Bloomingdale's," and commissioned artist Robert F. Oucault, creator of the famed Buster Brown Shoe drawings, to create a series of paintings around the theme. The campaign was the largest of its era, with the slogan appearing on everything from billboards to over 5,000 beach umbrellas offered free to street vendors and delivery cart drivers.

When Lymen Bloomingdale died in 1905, Bloomingdale's was handling a volume of $5 million per year. Hard times hit shortly after, as the whims of the upper class shifted once again and a popular shopping area sprang up further downtown, on Sixth Avenue between 14th and 23rd Street. Samuel J. Bloomingdale took over as president, and kept the business from declining drastically. When player pianos were invented, Bloomingdale's sensed another hot trend, and became the largest player piano distributor in the nation, adding an annual average of $2.5 million to its coffers. In 1913, the 58th Street Station of the Lexington Avenue subway was constructed in Bloomingdale's basement (further supporting the "All Cars Transfer to Bloomingdale's" message) and business picked up again.

By 1929, sales were $25 million. The following year, Bloomingdale's merged with Federated Department Stores, uniting it with three retail giants: Wm. Filene's of Boston, Abraham and Straus of Brooklyn, New York, and F. & R. Lazarus of Columbus, Ohio. Samuel Bloomingdale stayed on as honorary chairman of Bloomingdale's board and later went on to serve as director of Federated. In 1931, the Bloomingdale's building, which had grown by spurts and starts to engulf the entire block, was completely redesigned by architects Starret and Van Vleck in the Art Deco style. The store weathered the economic hardships of the Great Depression and World War II, and in 1947 entered into a new era of fashion merchandising.

"Exclusivity, excitement and sophistication," were the images Bloomingdale's sought to create when it hired prominent fashion designers Claire McCardell, Adele Simpson, and Pauline Tirgere to create an exclusive "Bloomingdale's Collection" in 1947. The collection was launched with an enormous media event entitled, "Women of the Year, 1947," and paved the road for further, far more elaborate events in the future. That year, Bloomingdale's also instituted its "model rooms," which showcased the talents of designers and artists such as architect Frank Ghery and filmmaker Federico Fellini while at the same time promoting special merchandise that tied in with the theme. Both campaigns were successful. Components of the original "Bloomingdale's Collection" are now part of the Metropolitan Museum of Art, and—more importantly for business—when Bloomingdale's inaugurated its first branch store in Fresh Meadows, New York, in 1949, over 25,000 people came through the store on opening day.

A decade later, Bloomingdale's expanded on these two concepts and introduced "Casa Bella," a 1960 promotional campaign that featured in-store cultural exhibits highlighting home furnishings and products from Italy. The following year, the store captured the media's attention by creating the first "designer shopping bag" to promote its "Esprit de France" exhibit. The design by artist Joseph Kinigstein was a reproduction of French tarot cards in dramatic shades of red, black, and white.

In 1962, Marvin S. Traub became merchandising manager at the store. A "constant traveler in search of the unusual," Traub made the store his museum. "The new direction in merchandising was both to seek and to create," says company material. "Buyers covered the globe to find exclusive and one-of-a-kind items. When they couldn't find what they wanted, they had it made." Traub made an institution of Bloomingdale's international fairs, which highlighted products from countries such as China, Mexico, and France, and inaugurated an era marked by even higher glamour and extensive in-store displays.

In 1969, Traub was appointed president of the company. Bloomingdale's volume was outgrowing its flagship store and, in addition to "generating excitement" with its merchandising, management focused on managing space and expanding business through opening branch stores. That year, two more branch stores opened in Garden City, Long Island, and Jenkintown, Pennsylvania. Bloomingdale's also launched a chain of home furnishing stores on the East Coast, offering products from the flagship's home furnishings department.

By the time Bloomingdale's celebrated its 100th anniversary in 1972, its flagship store had estimated sales of $100 million a year. In-store displays became so elaborate that retail analysts coined the term "retailing as theater" to describe them. Model rooms became even more showy, typified by a 1971 display called "The Cave," a multi-level structure wrapped completely in white polyurethane. According to a survey at the time, over 60 percent of its customers lived and worked in the luxury high-rise apartment and office towers nearby. Bloomingdale's catered to the neighborhood's young, affluent crowd by capitalizing on the popular trends of the day, be they pet rocks or glacial ice cubes. To maintain its prestigious image, Bloomingdale's launched fashion designers such as Ralph Lauren, Perry Ellis, and Norma Kamali, and opened in-store boutiques for well known designer labels such as Yves St. Laurent and Calvin Klein.

"On Saturdays, Bloomingdale's is the biggest party in town," Traub told the *New York Times* on the store's 100th anniversary, "It is a place where the young make dates for the night. We are proud that more and more people call us 'Bloomie's.'" Bloomingdale's capitalized on this close relationship with the young and trendy by stamping the name "Bloomie's" on ladies' panties as part of its launch for intimate apparel in 1973. As word of the store's incredible atmosphere spread, Bloomingdale's became a major tourist destination, and anything stamped with the name "Bloomie's" was considered a hot souvenir. The store's cachet was secured when the Queen of England visited the store in 1976.

Sales continued to grow in the late 1970s, fueled in part by the 1978 launch of the Bloomingdale's By Mail catalog. In its first decade of operation, annual catalog sales grew at a rate of 25 percent by catering to high-income households across the United States where no Bloomingdale's stores existed. The Bloomingdale's chain continued to expand, however, and by 1981 12 stores had been built along the East Coast, in Florida, and in California. Sales volume was $566 million in 1981, and leapt to $647 million in 1982.

The retail market boomed in the early 1980s, growing 31 percent between 1980 and 1985. During that time, Bloomingdale's sales increased a 48 percent, as new branch stores opened in Florida, Texas, and Pennsylvania. In the mid-1980s Bloomingdale's By Mail sales grew so quickly that the catalog ran into severe inventory problems. But Bloomingdale's image in the public eye remained untarnished. It held exclusive distribution rights to the Giorgio Beverly Hills fragrance line, the best-selling fragrance of the decade, and continued to dazzle customers with its merchandising. As the *Los Angeles Times* said, "If you wanted to be really with it, you *had* to go to Bloomingdale's."

In 1987, the Campeau Corporation paid $6.6 billion in a much publicized hostile takeover of Federated Department Stores. Allegedly Campeau's chairman Robert Campeau and his family were shopping at Bloomingdale's Boca Raton store and, as the story goes, "They liked it. They liked it so much, in fact, that Campeau bought Federated, thereby acquiring ... Bloomingdale's.'' Total takeover costs were $8.8 billion, a figure which caused some Wall Street analysts to question the new company's financial health. Campeau immediately streamlined operations throughout Federated, eliminating upper management positions in a move to cut $50 to $60 million from operating expenses. A large portion of the cuts were from Bloomingdale's operating budget, including the elimination of 245 jobs. Campeau then announced plans to open 17 to 18 new Bloomingdale's branches in the United States and his native Canada by 1993.

The following years were tumultuous for Bloomingdale's. According to Traub's book, *Like No Other Store,* Campeau projected Bloomingdale's earnings to grow from $128 million to $178 million in two years. Traub described those projections as ''wild,'' and added, ''No banker, ever, and I repeat, ever came to Bloomingdale's to ask if I thought we could deliver those numbers.'' The new budget cuts overburdened the store, and while it was still considered a posh place to shop, Bloomingdale's atmosphere began to reflect the tensions in upper management. A new branch which opened in Chicago experienced slow growth. Both the Bloomingdale's catalog and its stores had inventory problems. Customer service, which had been notoriously poor to begin with, began to lessen.

In an attempt to improve inventory levels, Bloomingdale's By Mail's order fulfillment center was moved from Virginia to Connecticut. According to *Catalog Age,* the transition was difficult. Customer satisfaction was low and sales were slipping. The company mailed 27 different books per year, and in the years between 1987 and 1989 experienced a 100 percent employee turnover.

In 1989, Campeau decided to put Bloomingdale's up for sale, and Traub attempted unsuccessfully to buy the store. In January 1990, Federated filed for Chapter 11 bankruptcy protection from its creditors. Federated's management, believing that Campeau ''drove the company'' into bankruptcy, ousted him from his position. At Bloomingdale's, Traub was asked to find a replacement for himself. In early 1991, after many disputes and discussions, Traub resigned and was replaced by Michael Gould, former president and chief executive of Giorgio Beverly Hills and Robinson's Department Stores in Los Angeles. Perhaps in honor of Traub, Bloomingdale's staged ''Tempo d'Italia,'' its largest international promotion ever, complete with gala party and an award-winning documentary that is now at the Metropolitan Museum of Art.

The story of Traub's departure and Gould's commencement as chairman is perhaps illustrative of the transformation Bloomingdale's was about to undergo. On that day in New York City,

pom pom girls and a marching band bid farewell to Traub as he exited the first floor, while the new chairman and chief executive officer quietly escorted designer Calvin Klein through the store's third floor bridge apparel department, discussing proposed changes in sportswear merchandising and the Calvin Klein boutique.

Under Gould, Bloomingdale's atmosphere was more subdued, or as the *Los Angeles Times* put it, ''more comfortable and less arrogant.'' Gould's proposed changes included less glamorous merchandising and more attention to customer service. He redesigned elements of the flagship store, creating wider aisles, grouping departments with related goods together, and improving inventory levels. All stores offered a wider array of ''bridge'' products and moderately priced designer brands. To maintain Bloomingdale's exclusive image, Gould established an ''Only at Bloomingdale's'' fashion collection.

In 1992, after two years in court, Federated pulled itself out of bankruptcy. In August of that year, Bloomingdale's opened its 15th store at the Mall of America in Bloomington, Minnesota, and announced its plans to open four stores in southern California. Catalog operations improved and began to show a small profit. 1992 sales increased five percent over the previous year to $1.201 billion, with earnings of $54 million.

As it neared its 125th anniversary, Bloomingdale's was once again undergoing a major transformation. As Gould said, ''We're in a transition from being a merchandising organization, which focuses just on the merchandise, to being a marketing organization, which focuses on the customer.'' This attention to customer service was perhaps also a reflection of changing customer demands. As the retail boom of the 1980s settled into leaner years, customer interests settled too. 1993 sales increased slightly over 1992 to $1.216 billion, a sign that change was slow, but coming. Gould's management style attracted less publicity than his predecessor's, but given the economic conditions of the 1990s, that style might be the ticket to keep Bloomingdale's at the forefront of the retail industry.

Further Reading:

Barmesh, Isadore, ''Bloomingdale's Sheds Its Frantic Past,'' *New York Times,* December 20, 1992, p. F5.

Moin, David, ''Room at the Top,'' *Women's Wear Daily,* February 16, 1993, p. 18.

——, ''Traub Talks Back, *Women's Wear Daily,* November 1, 1993, p. 4.

Perlman, Jeff, ''Bloomie's Bounces Back,'' *Catalog Age,* May 1990, p. 1.

Traub, Marvin, *Like No Other Store,* New York: Times Books, 1993.

—Maura Troester

BLOUNT

Blount, Inc.

4520 Executive Park Drive
Montgomery, Alabama 36116
U.S.A.
(334) 244-4000

Public Company
Incorporated: 1949 as Blount Brothers Construction
   Company
Employees: 4,700
Sales: $487.3 million
SICs: 3425 Saw Blades & Handsaws; 3482 Small Arms
   Ammunition; 3523 Farm Machinery & Equipment; 1541
   Industrial Buildings and Warehouses

By means of a well-conceived expansion strategy and timely acquisitions, Blount, Inc. has grown into one of the leading manufacturing firms based in the United States. The company's three main businesses include outdoor products, industrial and power equipment, and sporting equipment. Its product line ranges from specialty riding mowers and log loading machinery to small arms ammunition and telescopic rifle sights. With major manufacturing facilities spread throughout the United States, Canada, and Brazil, and with an ever-expanding distribution and sales network in Europe, company sales and earnings are on the rise.

By the time Winton and Houston Blount returned to their hometown of Union Springs, Alabama, after World War II, the family sand and gravel business had almost completely deteriorated. Winton and Houston's father had died during the war, and along with him the driving force behind the company. But the two brothers were determined to rebuild it, and within a few weeks they had purchased Army surplus equipment to use for sand and gravel projects. Winton, ever on the lookout for opportunities and bargains, decided rather impulsively to purchase four D-7 Caterpillar tractors a short time later. When Houston asked his brother why he had purchased the tractor's, Winton replied that they were going into the contracting business.

The first contracts the brothers landed were for constructing fish ponds in and around Union Springs. By the summer of 1946, the two siblings were doing subcontract work for the Alabama Highway. Although neither Winton nor Houston had any prior experience in constructing highways, they worked on numerous highways, roads, and bridges throughout Mississippi and Ala-

bama during the late 1940s. Their first big break came in 1949 with a $1 million contract to build the superstructure for a viaduct in Birmingham, Alabama. By 1951, the brothers had constructed their first building, followed shortly by a few gymnasiums. In the same year, the company, known as Blount Brothers Construction Company, procured a very lucrative contract to build a 500,000-square-foot plant used by Sperry to manufacture missile components for the U.S. Navy.

In 1952, the company won a contract that significantly altered the way it conducted business. A highly technical project, the contract was for building segments of a wind tunnel for the U.S. Air Force at the Arnold Engineering Development Center, near Tullahoma, Tennessee. Winton and Houston soon discovered that highly technical projects were not only more profitable, but that there was less competition for such contracts. As a result, they started to concentrate on complex construction-type projects, some of which were one-of-a-kind buildings. Soon after the Air Force project, the company constructed an atomic energy facility at Oak Ridge, Tennessee, and took on other increasingly complex projects.

By the middle of the decade, the Blount brothers were not only deeply involved in the construction industry, but also in the materials business, including gravel and sand, as well as asphalt and concrete pipe production. At this time, Houston Blount decided that he wanted to devote his attention exclusively to the materials operation. Thus, the two brothers organized all their plants in the materials business and formed the Vulcan Materials Company. Houston resigned from Blount Brothers Construction to become president and chief executive officer of the new firm.

Under Winton's strong leadership, Blount Brothers Construction continued to grow. The company was awarded major contracts by the Air Force to build Bomark and Nike nuclear missile bases in California, Massachusetts, Michigan, and Minnesota. In 1958, Blount Brothers constructed the first intercontinental missile facility in Wyoming. It was the first time the firm was asked to build a site under the "principle of concurrency," meaning that the design and testing of the missile was carried out as the facility itself was being designed and constructed; each testing of the missile resulted in a change of building specifications on the job site. Shortly afterwards, the company was contracted by the U.S. Navy to build an "indoor ocean" so that ship models could be tested under the most stringent conditions. The company also constructed the launching facilities at Cape Canaveral for the Mercury, Gemini, and Apollo space programs, as well as the world's biggest rocket test silo. Other projects during the late 1950s involved the construction of nuclear reactors, a cyclotron, the Atlanta airport, and numerous dams and river locks.

By 1962, Blount Brothers was growing so rapidly that it passed the $100 million mark for construction contracts. In the same year, the construction industry's trade publication, *Engineering News-Record,* ranked Blount as the thirty-third largest construction company in the United States. However, although Blount benefitted from the federal government's practice of awarding lump-sum contracts to the lowest bidder that could provide high-quality work, another government policy of using public work funds to regulate the economy began to create extreme cycles within the construction industry as a whole. As a consequence of this latter policy, management at Blount decided to decrease its reliance on government contracts and seek more work in the private or corporate sector.

In order to capture a significant share of the contracts in private industry, the company started a business development department and opened satellite offices in Boston, Chicago, and Houston. Initially, Blount was forced to accept small jobs, but these soon grew into larger and larger contracts. In 1967, management decided to embark upon an aggressive acquisitions program to accelerate its entry into private sector construction. The first acquisition was the Benjamin F. Shaw Company, a leader in the manufacture and installation of piping for chemical, paper, and power plants, as well as for oil refineries.

Winton Blount resigned from his position as president and chairperson in 1968 to accept the nomination as Postmaster General of the U.S. in Richard Nixon's new Cabinet. During his leave of absence, Austin Paddock, the administrative vice-president of United States Steel Company, was chosen to replace Winton. When Winton Blount left the company, he insisted that it no longer bid for government contracts while he was postmaster. Since over 50 percent of the company's construction contracts were still with the government, this meant the elimination of a huge amount of business at one stroke; at the same time, it also meant that the firm would devote itself to getting all of its contracts from private industry.

To compensate for the elimination of federal contracts, Blount continued its acquisition program. The most important acquisition during this time involved the purchase J.P. Burroughs & Sons, an agribusiness firm based in Saginaw, Michigan. Buying Burroughs, a public company listed on the American Stock Exchange, allowed privately-owned Blount to acquire all of the Burroughs shareholders. This move had been anticipated for years by management and led to Blount's listing on the American Stock Exchange in July 1972. In addition, the acquisition introduced the company, now known as Blount, Inc., to the field of agribusiness, which involved the manufacture of seed cleaners, roller mills, grain dryers, and bucket elevators.

When Winton Blount returned to the company in 1974 and assumed his former position as president and chairperson, he decided that it was time to determine the future direction of the firm. Taking advice from both Blount management and his brother Houston, Winton decided that the company would not become a conglomerate with operations in a variety of unrelated fields, but rather focus solely on the construction and agribusiness industries. Since the company was already well established in the construction industry, Winton immediately turned his attention to expanding its agribusiness operations. In 1976, Blount, Inc. purchased Modern Farm Systems, a manufacturer and distributor of grain bins and metal farm buildings. With facilities in Iowa, Indiana, Mississippi, Nebraska, and Pennsylvania, the acquisition enabled Blount, Inc. to quickly set up a comprehensive system to process, handle, and store grain.

In order to develop its agribusiness operations, Blount Inc. purchased York Foundry & Engine Work in 1977. Located in York, Nebraska, the company manufactured and distributed such items as bucket elevators and belt conveyors used to handle feeds, fertilizers, grains, and various other bulk materials. Another acquisition during the same year involved Redex Industries of Elm Creek, Nebraska, another manufacturer of materials handling equipment. The third purchase of that year was Mix-Mill Manufacturing Company of Bluffton, Indiana, a maker of different types of farm equipment used to process feed for cattle, poultry, and hogs. These acquisitions, in combination with increased grain production during the mid-1970s, led to record sales for the company; by 1979, Blount's agribusiness operations made up 45 percent of its operating income.

While Blount's agribusiness revenues were beginning to rise, management decided to expand its construction operations overseas due to a decline in the U.S. market. Offices were opened in the Middle East, and within a short period Blount had secured major contracts with Saudi Arabia and Iran; two of the largest contracts included a $150 million agreement for construction in Tabuk, Saudi Arabia, and a collaborative effort with the French firm Bouygues involving a $3.5 billion contract for constructing the University of Riyadh in Saudi Arabia. On the domestic front, Blount purchased Fred J. Early Jr. Company, a prominent contracting firm located in San Francisco, in order to extend its operations west of the Rocky Mountains. Additional acquisitions such as the R.S. Noonan Company, a process engineering firm, and Hoad Engineers, which provided consulting engineering services, gave Blount the opportunity to enter the utility, paper, chemical, cement, and petrochemical fields. In a risky undertaking, for $61 million management also decided to acquire the Washington Steel Company, a manufacturer of specialty steels. This purchase added a third major product line to Blount's well-established construction and agribusiness operations.

In 1980, Blount reported revenues of just over $554 million; by the end of fiscal 1982 revenues had increased dramatically to $788 million. The cash flow from the construction project in Saudi Arabia was a boon for the company, as was the performance of Washington Steel, and the burgeoning success of its agribusiness expansion into such countries as Mexico, West Germany, China, Venezuela, Nigeria, and Egypt. Revenues for 1984 were a hefty $847 million and earnings a record $24.3 million. Yet at the pinnacle of its success, trouble started to brew. Blount's foreign construction contracts began to decrease, and the farm machine business market suddenly tumbled into a worldwide depression. Anticipating these difficulties, Winton Blount began to implement a diversification strategy. Slowly beginning to sell off all the company's agribusiness holdings, in 1985, he purchased Omark Industries, a chainsaw and materials handling equipment manufacturer for the pulpwood and timber industry, and a leading producer of gun care equipment. In addition, Blount also bought W&E Environmental Systems, a Swiss-based resources recovery firm specializing in turning garbage into energy. These acquisitions, and the continued success of its projects in Saudi Arabia, helped push revenues past the $1 billion mark in 1986.

In 1987, although he remained the board's chairperson, Winton Blount decided to decrease the time he spent in managing the day-to-day operations of the company. He promoted his son, Winton Blount III to the position of vice-chairperson and gave him the primary responsibility of supervising the company's construction business. Having previously been the head of

Blount's international construction operations, Blount III seemed a natural choice. Yet from the very beginning of the younger Blount's tenure, the company's performance began to suffer. Washington Steel Corporation was sold off, in spite of its turning a profit during one of the most difficult periods in the steel industry. A $100 million, 80 megawatts co-generation project located in Pennsylvania landed in court following a dispute between Blount and Schuykill Energy Resources. Problems with the company's handling of a $150 million office complex for AT&T in Chicago also gave rise to litigation. Other construction projects in which the company lost control or entered into contract terms that were unfavorable led to declining revenues and profitability. The younger Blount was asked to vacate his position as vice-chairperson, and his father returned to turn the company around. By the end of fiscal 1990, however, revenues had dropped from over $1 billion to $683 million; revenues for the construction operations alone declined from over $600 million to $348 million.

The early 1990s were a period of disruption and realignment for the company. William R. Van Sant, president and chief executive officer of Blount from December 1990 to October 1992, suddenly resigned, creating a large gap in management. Van Sant had helped the company shift its focus to a more diversified mixture of manufacturing equipment and construction operations. John M. Panettiere, a management expert with considerable experience in the auto industry, was appointed president and chief operating officer, and he immediately began to help Winton Blount iron out the company's problems. One of their first decisions was to sell the resource recovery operation and not seek any additional contracts in the waste-to-energy busi-

ness. Their second decision involved a stronger commitment to manufacturing, including outdoor products, such as saw chains and specialty riding mowers; industrial and power equipment, such as industrial tractors and equipment for timber harvesting and loading; and sporting equipment, such as small arms ammunition, gun scopes, and gun care equipment. The company's overall realignment worked. In 1993, revenues increased to over $691 million from a 1992 figure of $637 million.

In early 1994, management decided to sell almost all of its construction business to Caddell Construction Company, headed by one of Blount's former employees. This decision opened the way for the company to eliminate the substantial operating losses its construction business experienced in the late 1980s and early 1990s. Although revenues dropped sharply as a result of this move, Blount was able to focus entirely on its three remaining divisions of outdoor products, sports equipment, and industrial equipment. Finally rid of the lingering effects of a worldwide slowdown in the construction industry, Blount's prospects for the future appeared much brighter.

Further Reading:

Blount, Winton M., *The Blount Story: American Enterprise at Its Best,* New York: Newcomen Society in North America, 1980.
Hussey, Allan F., "Profit Builder," *Barrons,* May 16, 1983, pp. 61–62.
Cook, James, "Moving the Mail," *Forbes,* September 9, 1985, pp. 62–63.
"Blount Sells Construction Units to Caddell Construction," *Engineering News Record,* February 7, 1994, p. 13.

—Thomas Derdak

Boston Chicken, Inc.

14103 Denver West Parkway
P.O. Box 4086
Golden, Colorado 80401-4086
U.S.A.
(303) 278-9500
Fax: (303) 384-5339

Public Company
Incorporated: 1985
Employees: 19,000
Sales: $383.7 million
Stock Exchanges: NASDAQ
SICs: 6794 Patent Owners and Lessors; 5812 Eating Places

Boston Chicken, Inc. operates and franchises food service stores, under the names Boston Chicken and Boston Market, specializing in providing convenient, quick, and complete meals that feature home-style meals, side dishes, and other traditional foods. The company was operating 534 stores at the end of 1994 and planned to open approximately 1,000 more by 1997. Boston Chicken's short history is characterized by inventiveness and rampant growth.

Boston Chicken was started in 1985 by two young friends eager to launch their own enterprise. Arthur Cores was a 33-year-old graduate of Northeastern University. With a degree in business, he had worked for several years as the manager of a gourmet grocery store and as a manager for top-notch catering companies. Cores' friend, Steven (Kip) Kolow, was 29 and had experience working in real estate. One day in 1985, they decided to come up with a simple business plan.

Cores' experience in the gourmet food industry lead him to believe that a market existed for fast, high-quality, home-style food. "I saw the trend in gourmet shops that people wanted to buy plain, simple, everyday foods," Cores recalled in the August 6, 1990 *Boston Business Journal.* Building from that insight, the two devised a plan for a restaurant called Boston Chicken. Their concept was simple: provide consumers with an alternative to both the existing fast food offerings and the hassle of having to go home and prepare a fresh meal.

Cores and Kolow borrowed recipes for chicken soup and oatmeal cookies from their grandmothers, and Cores also concocted some of his own dishes, based on traditional side dishes such as mashed potatoes and squash. To their array of vegetable and salad sides they added sweet corn bread. Their various side dishes would complement the centerpiece of every meal; marinated chicken roasted in brick-fired rotisseries. The two men rented a small, vacated store in Newton, Massachusetts, and opened their doors to business in December 1985.

Not long after it opened, Boston Chicken was a smash. Customers began flocking to the take-out chicken store and telling their friends about their discovery. Soon, people were literally lined up at the small store waiting for their orders. During the late 1980s, articles appearing in the *Boston Globe* raved about Boston Chicken, attracting customers from all over the Boston area. Growing sales kept Cores and Kolow busy between 1986 and 1989. In fact, they had several offers from individuals in the business community interested either in buying the store or partnering with the two entrepreneurs to expand the concept.

Then, the founders of Boston Chicken were approached by George Naddaff, a local businessman with a knack for growing start-up businesses. Naddaff had opened the first Kentucky Fried Chicken stores in the Boston area and had increased his holdings of that franchise to 19 stores within three years. He had also started his own chain of child care centers, which he eventually took public, and had founded a chain of business brokerage offices. Naddaff headed a venture capital company, Business Expansion Capital Corp., that found resources for start-up companies that could be replicated—companies like Boston Chicken.

One evening early in 1989, Naddaff's wife sent him to the Boston Chicken take-out store in Newtonville to pick up dinner. When he saw the long line stretching outside the restaurant, he became fascinated. Naddaff bought dinner and left, but he kept coming back for weeks to watch Kolow and Cores feed the non-stop dinner crowds. Finally, he approached the owners one night and asked them if they would be interested in selling their concept, recipes, and methods of operation. "I'd been watching them for several weeks and they were right on the money," Naddaff declared in the *Boston Business Journal* article.

Cores and Kolow had turned down previous suitors because they were concerned about losing control of their creation to someone who might inadvertently destroy it. However, they trusted Naddaff and believed that he could help Boston Chicken successfully flower into a chain. They eventually cut a deal with Naddaff, and New Boston Chicken Inc. was established in March 1989. Cores and Kolow effectively sold their rights to Boston Chicken but retained ownership of the original restaurant. Kolow continued to manage the restaurant, while Cores joined the newly formed corporation as head of product development.

To make sure that the Boston Chicken concept could be successfully replicated, Naddaff got a group of private investors to contribute $1.1 million for two new stores. Both were immediate hits, and Naddaff quickly began gathering more capital. By the middle of 1990, he had expanded the New Boston Chicken chain to a total of 13 restaurants, ten of which had been opened after the start of the year. Furthermore, an additional 15 or more stores were expected to open by the beginning of 1991 in Massachusetts, Connecticut, and New York. Naddaff expected the combined sales to top $7 million annually in 1990. But sales topped projections, jumping past $8.2 million and then rising to nearly $21 million in 1991.

By 1991, individual stores were bringing in $800,000 annually, on average, about 80 percent of which was attributable to take-out business. A major appeal was price. For $5 to $7, a person could buy a relatively healthy, freshly cooked, home-style meal. The same plate would cost $10 to $15 in a nice sit-down restaurant and would take more than one hour to prepare at home. Although growth capital was scarce, New Boston Chicken planned to expand the popular concept internationally to more than 400 stores within four years. Naddaff was even working to have a chicken bred specifically for his chain.

However, in 1991, Boston Chicken caught the eye of another chain-store capitalist—Saad J. Nadhir. Nadhir was an executive with Blockbuster Video at the time. He was driving around Newton, Massachusetts, when he, just like Naddaff a few years earlier, noticed a long line of customers waiting outside of a Boston Chicken outlet. Nadhir brought his colleague, Scott Beck, over to take a look at the restaurant and both were intrigued. They checked out Naddaff and the chain and determined that it had potential. They also believed that they had a better chance than Naddaff to exploit that potential.

Beck, in particular, was in a better position to grow the Boston Chicken chain. Although he was in his early 30s at the time, he had already established himself as a savvy corporate contender. While in his 20s, Beck had talked his father and a family friend into buying several Blockbuster Video stores, and he had spent the next several years whipping the outlets into shape and opening a string of new stores. By the late 1980s, Beck, with the help of his partner Nadhir, had increased his 106-store, midwest operation into the largest blockbuster chain in the United States. He cashed out in 1989, at the age of 31, selling his stake to Blockbuster for $120 million.

Beck and Nadhir bought a controlling interest in Boston Chicken from Naddaff in March 1992. They shortened the chain's name to Boston Chicken, Inc., moved the headquarters to Beck's native suburban Chicago, and immediately began assembling a staff comprised largely of young executives formerly of Blockbuster. Importantly, they hired 43-year-old Jeff Shearer as a key strategist. Shearer had served as a partner in their Blockbuster franchise and had been a general manager with the Bennigan's restaurant organization in the early 1980s. They also recruited restaurant veterans Alan Palmieri, Warren Ellish, and Eddie Palms.

Six months after taking control of Boston Chicken, Beck and company were overseeing a chain of 53 restaurants in ten states. They were planning to open at least 30 just in the Chicago area over the next 12 months. Planning to retain Boston Chicken's basic strategy of providing fast, fresh, high-quality food, they also made several operational and organizational changes. As they had done at Blockbuster, they would target key markets and try to take advantage of name recognition rather than spreading their resources too thinly over large regions. Beginning by establishing a national buying and distribution network designed to complement their ambitious expansion plans, Beck

and his team meticulously tweaked in-store operational elements, such as food display techniques.

By the end of 1992, Boston Chicken had 83 stores operating in its chain and several new outlets under construction. Total restaurant sales rose to nearly $43 million that year as Boston Chicken, Inc.'s revenue from its franchised and owned outlets increased to about $8.3 million. The company's basic strategy for growth in 1992 and into 1993 was to find well-heeled, experienced restaurateurs in key regional markets who were willing to expand the chain in their area. The degree of financing provided by Boston Chicken varied among the developers. The overall expansion effort would be directed from a centralized, streamlined headquarters office where Beck and his team were based.

Representative of the 'area developers' that Boston Chicken recruited to expand its chain was New York's Donald Cepiel. Cepiel started his fast-food industry career at the age of 16, peeling potatoes at a McDonald's restaurant. By 1993, the 43-year-old entrepreneur owned 21 Burger King outlets, among other holdings. He purchased the rights to Boston Chicken in 1991 and had built three outlets by mid-1993. Interestingly, in October 1993, Cepiel purchased the same site on which the McDonald's that first employed him had once stood. He began building a new Boston Chicken there and planned to open two more in the area during 1994.

Although Boston Chicken experienced surprisingly strong growth during 1991 and 1992, that expansion was a mere prelude to the explosive gains that Beck and team would achieve in 1993 and 1994. During 1993, in fact, the chain nearly tripled in size to 217 stores. Aggregate restaurant sales rose to $154 million, and Boston Chicken, Inc.'s revenues jumped five-fold to $43 million. To accumulate capital for even more growth, Boston Chicken went public in November 1993. Enthused investors bought heavily as Boston Chicken's stock price soared.

While Boston Chicken's rampant growth was largely the result of the ingenious concept devised in 1985 by Cores and Kolow, it was also the result of the savvy operational strategy created by Beck and his experienced management team. Indeed, they had carefully engineered systems for all aspects of the company's activities, from selecting real estate and constructing stores to tracking customer preferences and preparing food. For example, the company had developed a system by which a store could be completely built and operational within less than 75 days after the start of construction.

One of the chain's most impressive elements was its advanced computer systems. During the early 1990s, the company developed its own software at a cost of about $10 million. The software was used to drive a company-wide system that integrated all of Boston Chicken's operations, gathering and processing reams of data. For example, the system would alert store managers to put out more of a certain side dish based on how many had been rung up at the register—the system would even alter its advice according to the seasons and the established preferences of that store's customer base. Boston Chicken's store computers could also make up worker schedules, automatically reorder food and supplies from vendors, and update the store's financial results on an hourly basis. "I've never seen systems as impressive and sophisticated as Boston Chicken has," said stock analyst Michael Moe in the October 9, 1994 *Denver Post.*

Boston Chicken continued to use its advanced processes and systems to grow during 1994. By mid-1994, in fact, the company was employing 16,500 workers and operating a total of 330 stores, and the chain was expanding at a rate of one new store every business day. As its operations expanded, the company began looking for a new facility to house its burgeoning headquarters. Not surprisingly, Boston Chicken moved its offices to Golden, Colorado, in August 1994, where Beck had moved his family a few years earlier in an effort to improve their quality of life. There, the company opened a 42,000-square-foot, $10 million 'support center'; designed to accommodate future growth, the center housed about 140 employees when it opened.

Boston Chicken posted huge gains during the remainder of 1994, ending the year with 534 stores in its chain and continuing to add about one store each day and to hire 100 new workers every week. As annual restaurant sales rose past the $100 million mark in 1994, and the company posted strong earnings, Boston Chicken continued to seek new funds for expansion into the mid-1990s. In fact, management announced its intent to grow the chain at a rate of more than 325 stores annually at least through the end of the decade; the organization already had about 1,000 nonrefundable commitments from potential outlet operators who wanted a piece of the action. "They have the most aggressive expansion program ever undertaken in the restaurant industry," surmised analyst Mike Mueller in the April 10, 1994 *Restaurant Business.*

Further Reading:

Conner, Chance, and Jeffrey Leib, "Ruffling the Competition: New Blockbuster Boston Chicken Sets High Goals," *Denver Post,* May 29, 1994, p. G1.

Davis, Jessica, "Boston Chicken Hatches its Expansion Strategy," *Philadelphia Business Journal,* November 11, 1994, p. 7.

Romeo, Peter, "What's So Special About Boston Chicken?" *Restaurant Business,* April 10, 1994, p. 92.

Heimlich, Cheryl Kane, "Chicken Wars: One Down, but Another Far From Out," *South Florida Business Journal,* July 29, 1994, p. A1.

Kane, Tim, "Region's Burger King Back to Site Where He Started," *Capital District Business Review,* October 4, 1993, p. 4.

Parker, Penny, "Chicken Goes High-Tech: Restaurant Chain's Goal: Roast Competition with On-Line Help," *Denver Post,* October 9, 1994, p. H1.

Pearlstein, Steven, "Boston Chicken: Hot Stuff," *Washington Post,* July 4, 1994, p. A9.

Warner, Fara, "America, Meet the New Age Chicken," *Adweek's Marketing Week,* May 13, 1991, p. 22.

Witt, Louise, "Investors Flock to Boston Chicken," *Boston Business Journal,* August 6, 1990, p. 1.

—Dave Mote

Boston Edison Company

800 Boylston Street
Boston, Massachusetts 02199-2599
U.S.A.
(617) 424-2000
Fax: (617) 424-2605

Public Company
Incorporated: 1886 as Edison Electric Illuminating Company
   of Boston
Employees: 4,026
Sales: $1.55 billion
Stock Exchanges: New York
SICs: 4911 Electric Services

Boston Edison Company is a regulated public utility that provides electricity to the Boston area. Its activities include the generation, purchase, transmission, distribution, and sale of electric power. The area served by Boston Edison covers a total of about 590 square miles, all within 30 miles of Boston, and includes approximately 40 cities and towns. The population of the company's service area is approximately 1.5 million. About 86 percent of Boston Edison's revenue comes from retail electric sales. The rest is derived primarily from wholesale sales to other utilities and municipal electric departments. The company's facilities include the Pilgrim Nuclear Power Station in Plymouth, Massachusetts, and non-nuclear generating plants in South Boston and Everett, Massachusetts. These facilities generate electricity for a total of about 651,000 Boston Edison customers.

The Edison Electric Illuminating Company of Boston was established in 1886. From the beginning, the company established a reputation for innovation in its industry, which was itself in its infancy. Among the key figures in the formation of Boston Edison were electric industry pioneers Edward H. Johnson and Henry Villard. Financier J. P. Morgan, who had invested in many of the country's earliest electric operations, was also involved. The company set up its first station in a two-story building that formerly served as a livery stable and tenement house. Early in 1886, Boston Edison began providing electricity for its first customer, the Bijou Theater, which a few years earlier had become the first electrically lighted theater in the United States, using electricity from an isolated power plant.

By 1887 there was already fierce competition for the Boston area's electrical market, with thirteen companies in operation. That year Boston Edison opened a second generating station, installed an underground network to replace its overhead power lines, and hired Charles L. Edgar as a station manager. Edgar eventually became one of the electric industry's most important figures, serving as president of Boston Edison from 1900 to 1932.

During the 1890s, Boston Edison vied with another company, Boston Electric Light Co., for dominance in Greater Boston. Negotiations for a merger took place around the turn of the century, but plans for uniting the two companies were shot down by some of Boston Edison's directors, including Edgar. Boston Edison effectively put an end to the territorial battle by purchasing a third rival, Suburban Light and Power Company, in 1901. Boston Electric Light Co. was finally merged into Boston Edison in 1902, and the company became the area's sole provider of electric power.

The period between the turn of the century and the Depression was one of immense territorial growth, as well as tremendous advances in marketing and engineering, for Boston Edison. In 1903 alone, six neighboring power companies were acquired, including Milton Light & Power Company, Framingham Electric Company, and Somerville Electric Light Company. As the company increased its geographical range, it continued adding generating capacity at its existing plants. This enabled the company to meet the increasing power needs of Bostonians as well as those of its new customers outside of the city. Electricity also became less expensive, with the price per kilowatt-hour in Boston dropping by half between 1886 and 1909.

In the early part of the century Boston Edison launched several successful marketing campaigns to spur the use of electricity, some of which involved demonstrations of electrical appliances. The company also staged exhibits around the area, such as the "Farm of Edison Light and Power" and the "Colonial House of Edison Light." In 1911 Boston Edison became active in the development of electric vehicles. Although electric cars eventually lost the battle against the internal combustion engine, the company's efforts were not entirely wasted. Before World War I, many private fleets of electric vehicles, mostly used for delivery, were in operation around Boston.

In 1912 Boston Edison invested heavily in its employees, establishing an Employee Loan Fund, an Accident Prevention Committee, and a Medical Department. In addition, the company built a large recreational and technical complex containing a library, dining room, tennis courts, auditorium, pool tables, and many other amenities. The onset of World War I placed an entirely new set of demands on the nation's utility companies. Although restrictions were placed on lighting and other uses of electricity in order to conserve fuel, the needs of military manufacturing increased the overall demand for electrical power, improving Boston Edison's balance sheet.

With the continued increase in the use of electrical appliances and the growth of manufacturing in the 1920s, the demand for electrical power expanded precipitously. In 1923 Boston Edison launched its own radio station, WTAT, which it operated out of the back of an REO Speedwagon. WTAT was the first station to be operated by an electric utility company, and may have been the first portable radio station in the United States. The following year, the company added WEEI, a more powerful station which stayed in one place. WEEI became a fixture on New England's radio dials, providing a full range of music, sports, and news programming.

Meanwhile, the company continued to expand its generating capacity. A major expansion of its L Street Station, acquired in the Boston Electric merger, was completed in 1920. In 1925 operations began at the company's new Edgar Station in Weymouth. This facility was the first ''high-pressure'' central station in the world. The following year, the company was awarded the Charles A. Coffin award, one of the industry's most prestigious, in recognition of its many technological and marketing innovations.

The onset of the Depression in 1929 brought about a reduction in the use of industrial energy, which was reflected in a reduction in Boston Edison's revenues over the next several years. Offsetting the decline, however, was a rise in residential use of electricity, as more and more electrical devices made their way into American homes. The company continued to devise creative marketing and promotional ideas through the 1930s, including the ''Friendly Kitchen,'' an ongoing demonstration of electric cooking techniques. The further expansion of the WEEI radio station provided still more promotional opportunities.

In 1932 Edgar died, and Walter C. Baylies took his place as company president. By the middle of the 1930s, the Depression had caused even residential use of electricity to level off. During this period, the company was unable to begin any major construction projects, and some employees were forced to take wage cuts. In 1937 the company's name was officially changed from Edison Electric Illuminating Company of Boston to the less cumbersome Boston Edison Company. The following year, Edison's workers joined the wave of unionization sweeping the country. The United Brotherhood of Edison Workers was made the official collective bargaining representative of company employees.

As the 1940s began, mobilization for World War II began to increase the demand for power. Around this time, Edison president Frank D. Comerford, who had succeeded Baylies in 1935, announced plans for a large new generating station to be built on the Mystic River in Everett, Massachusetts. The first of Mystic Station's three units went into service in 1943. When Comerford died suddenly in 1941, James V. Toner was chosen as his successor. By the end of the war, Boston Edison's geographic expansion had ended, but growth continued as a result of rising consumption among its customers. The company's power plants were generating more than two billion kilowatt-hours of electricity a year. That total was double the amount generated ten years earlier, despite the fact that the company's service area and population had remained relatively stable during that period.

The boom years that followed World War II created a bigger demand than ever for electricity, with the proliferation of washing machines, refrigerators, vacuum cleaners, and other household appliances. Boston Edison sold and actively promoted the use of electrical appliances, selling 861 electric ranges in 1950 alone. The widespread introduction of television also increased company revenues, accounting for an estimated $1.5 million in sales for 1950. During this period, Boston Edison met increased demand by adding capacity to its existing facilities. Many of the company's technological advances at this time were in the areas of transmission and distribution. New cable technology allowed more power to reach customers more efficiently.

In 1952 the company reorganized its corporate structure. Two new operating organizations were formed: the Engineering and Construction Organization, headed by John T. Ward; and the Steam and Electric Operations Organization, led by Hugo Wellington. By the mid-1950s, demand in the suburbs of Boston had increased so much that six new substations had to be built in 1955 alone. A wave of new industrial and commercial development, particularly along Route 128, made Greater Boston a leading center of high-technology manufacturing in the late 1950s, and Boston Edison prospered. Its largest customer, and the area's biggest employer, was Raytheon Corporation. Other major users of Boston Edison power located along that corridor were Singer Sewing Machine Co. and Union Carbide.

The development of computer technology in the 1950s and 1960s enabled Boston Edison to run its operations at new levels of efficiency. The company installed its first computer, an IBM machine used for accounting, in 1954. In 1959 Boston Edison became the first utility company in New England to install a mainframe (a Univac II), and over the next few years computers became an integral part of every major phase of the company's operations. As its customer base in the outlying areas grew in the late 1950s and early 1960s, the company began establishing service centers to provide technical support in those areas.

In November 1965 a huge blackout struck the entire Northeast; in its wake, most utilities changed the way they operated. Boston Edison installed special jet engine backup generators and changed its switching and communications systems to reduce the likelihood of system failure. The blackout also prompted greater coordination between the various utility networks in the region. Boston Edison joined several interutility organizations over the next several years, including the Eastern Massachusetts and Vermont Energy Control in 1967; the Rhode Island-Eastern Massachusetts-Vermont Energy Control in 1969; and the New England Power Pool in 1971. Each of these networks served to centralize, to various degrees, the dispatching and transmission of electricity, thereby maximizing efficiency over a larger area.

In late 1967, Boston Edison began construction on the Pilgrim Station, a nuclear generating facility in Plymouth, Massachusetts. By 1969, company revenues had passed the $200 million mark. Commercial and residential electricity sales each made up about one third of that total, while industrial sales, sales to other utilities, sales of steam, and street lighting made up the rest. The company's customer base of 583,000 was not much bigger than it had been a decade earlier, but those customers were using more than twice as much power as their 1958 counterparts. As the 1970s began, Boston Edison benefitted from a rush of commercial development around the Boston area. Among the construction projects that added significantly to the area's power demands were the Marriott Motor Hotel, a

Christian Science Church office complex, and the John Hancock Building.

The 1970s were a turbulent decade for the entire energy industry, including Boston Edison. The longest strike in company history, lasting nearly three months, took place in 1971. In December 1972 the Pilgrim Station went into operation. The following year, the OPEC oil embargo caused huge increases in fuel prices, with devastating effects on companies like Boston Edison that used large amounts of oil. In response, the company ended its tradition of actively promoting the use of electricity, and by 1974 it had closed the last of its appliance stores. Rising energy prices, combined with a growing public awareness of environmental issues, resulted in decreased energy use by the middle of the decade, and plans for another nuclear facility were dropped. Nevertheless, new, more efficient technology enabled the company to thrive financially despite these pressures. The Edgar generating facility was retired in 1977, placing most of the burden on the new Pilgrim plant.

During the 1980s Boston Edison was plagued by regulatory problems, primarily concerning the Pilgrim plant. In 1982 the Nuclear Regulatory Commission (NRC) hit the company with the largest fine it had ever imposed, $550,000, for a litany of management and physical problems at the facility. Boston Edison spent $300 million on upgrades at the plant, but malfunctions continued to plague Pilgrim, which was the source of 40 percent of the company's power by this time. In 1986 the NRC called Pilgrim one of the six worst-managed nuclear plants in the United States, and Boston Edison was forced to shut the plant down to make wholesale improvements. Leadership of the company changed, with Bernard Reznicek replacing Stephen Sweeney as president. Reznicek received permission to restart Pilgrim in 1989 under a plan whereby the company would be rewarded or punished financially based on the plant's performance.

Meanwhile, Boston Edison sought to gear itself for the future. In December 1982 the company launched its IMPACT 2000 initiative, which sought to coordinate the company's conservation, environmental, technological, public relations, and load management goals into a single coherent package. Among the program's results were the conversion of both the Mystic and New Boston stations to dual fuel capability (the ability to burn both oil and gas), and the installation of scrubbers on the company's generating stations.

In 1991 Boston Edison experienced further problems with the NRC, when the Yankee Rowe nuclear reactor in Rowe, Massa-chusetts—which was ten percent owned by Boston Edison—was forced to close for safety reasons. Nevertheless, the company's financial performance was strong during the early 1990s. With Pilgrim back in operation, Boston Edison was able to improve its position as the second highest-cost electricity producer in Massachusetts in 1987 to the status of second-lowest in 1992. Its financial performance improved accordingly, from a $16 million deficit in 1989 to a profit of $107 million in 1992. As the 1990s progressed, Boston Edison continued to seek savings through improved technology. Among its breakthroughs were the 1993 development of "smart" meters capable of communicating information directly to the company, eliminating the need for meter readers, and the automation of over-the-counter bill payment. Reznicek resigned as chairman and CEO of Boston Edison in 1994 to become dean of Creighton University's business school. He was succeeded by Thomas May, the company's president.

Principal Subsidiaries: Harbor Electric Energy Co.; Boston Energy Technology Group; REZ-TEK International Corp.; Coneco Corporation.

Further Reading:

"Boston Edison Automates Over-the-Counter Payments," *Electrical World,* July 1993, p. 13.

"Boston Edison Reorganizes," *Electrical World,* March 17, 1952, p. 29.

Campanella, Frank W., "Big Commercial Demand Sparks Boston Edison," *Barron's,* September 14, 1970, p. 28.

Cavanaugh, H. A., "Having 'Created the Future' at Boston Edison, Reznicek Returns to Omaha," *Electrical World,* August 1994, pp. 9–10.

"Earnings Growth Plus Good Yield," *Financial World,* January 12, 1972, p. 7.

"It Electrified the Proper Bostonians," *Electrical World,* June 25, 1951, pp. 11–12.

Kripalani, Manjeet, "Who Needs Meter Readers?" *Forbes,* August 30, 1993, pp. 46–48.

"Low-Cost Facilities Help Fuel Boston Edison Gains," *Barron's,* June 30, 1969, pp. 29–30.

Sicilia, David B., *Boston Edison Centennial 1886–1986: History of the Boston Edison Company,* Boston: Boston Edison Company, 1986.

Smith, William D., "Construction Plans for Nuclear Plants Canceled by Utility," *New York Times,* June 29, 1974, p. 1.

Therrien, Lois, "Boston Edison Gets the Work: Fix the Nuke or Fold It," *Business Week,* June 30, 1986, pp. 39–40.

Wald, Matthew L., "A-Plant to Close Over Safety Issue," *New York Times,* October 2, 1991, p. A1.

—Robert R. Jacobson

Bradlees Discount Department Store Company

1 Bradlees Circle
Braintree, Massachusetts 02184
U.S.A.
(617) 380-8000

Public Company
Incorporated: 1961
Employees: 16,000
Sales: $1.83 billion
SICs: 311 Department Stores

The Bradlees Discount Department Store Company is a leading discount retailer in the Northeast. The company operates 136 department stores in nine states stretching from Maine to Virginia. Founded in Connecticut, Bradlees allied itself early on with a grocery store chain, and it remained a subsidiary of this company up until the early 1990s. After a leveraged buyout, the company went public independently, and subsequently embarked on a program of cost-cutting and new store openings.

Bradlees got its start in the late 1950s. The company was conceived by three businessmen in Connecticut, who envisioned a store that offered a wide variety of goods at discount prices. Because the three met to discuss their idea for the new store at the Bradley International Airport, outside of Hartford, they chose to call their store "Bradlees."

The first Bradlees opened in New London, Connecticut, in 1958. Rather than having all of its merchandise owned by one vendor, it was comprised of a group of departments, each of which was run by a different licensee. In 1961, just three years after its founding, the fledgling enterprise was acquired by Stop & Shop, a New England grocery store chain.

With its purchase by Stop & Shop, Bradlees received a much-need infusion of capital. In the early 1960s, the company gradually moved from a licensee operation to direct ownership of its various departments, by letting its arrangements with its licensees expire. In the next years of the decade, Bradlees grew rapidly, as the discount department store industry came of age. By 1968, the company boasted 52 stores, which produced annual revenues of $139 million.

Throughout the 1970s, Bradlees continued to expand the number of stores it operated around the Northeast. The company also altered the nature and content of its merchandise, in an effort to position itself as a retailer of high-quality, low-cost goods. Bradlees increased the amount of clothing and accessories that it sold. In addition, in response to greater consumer interest in do-it-yourself home improvements, the company began to devote a larger quantity of display space to hardware and housewares.

Throughout this time, Bradlees also spent money to upgrade its facilities. Renovations focused on increasing the amount of space devoted to sales in each of its outlets, and to modernizing fixtures, such as racks and shelves. In 1978 the company also announced that it would open six to ten discount stores devoted exclusively to women's sportswear in junior and misses' sizes.

By the end of the 1970s, Bradlees' overall sales had risen to $634 million. The company entered the following decade poised for greater growth in a highly competitive discount retailing environment, dominated by giants such as Wal-Mart and Kmart. Despite this competition, Bradlees' sales rose steadily throughout the early 1980s. In 1981 the company recorded $720 million in revenues, and in the following year, this figure rose more than 20 percent to $871.2 million.

With this strong revenue growth, Bradlees sought to meet the challenge of its mammoth competitors by expanding its geographic scope. In December 1982, the company announced that it had purchased 13 Memco stores located in the greater Washington, D.C., area, from the Lucky Stores company. Six months later, Bradlees stated that it intended to open 20 new stores in 1983. In October, the company took a significant step toward meeting this goal, when it simultaneously inaugurated operations at 10 Bradlees outlets in the Washington area. At that time, the company also launched an advertising campaign that sought to blur the traditional distinction between discount stores and more upscale department stores. At the end of 1983, Bradlees reported operating profits of $80.5 million. This figure rose to $85.2 million over the following year, as sales increased by nearly 20 percent, to $1.4 billion. During 1984, Bradlees announced that it would continue to expand its number of stores, adding six to eight new outlets.

Bradlees continued its policy of expansion through acquisition in the mid-1980s. In March 1985, the company announced that it would move into another area of the Northeast, opening three new outlets in the Philadelphia area. Three months later, the company made public its acquisition of 18 stores in the Jefferson Ward discount chain, which Bradlees purchased from Montgomery Ward. These outlets, which made up Montgomery Ward's northern division, were located in the Philadelphia area.

Despite this aggressive expansion, Bradlees lost market share throughout 1985. This posed a serious problem for its corporate parent, Stop & Shop, since this company had diversified into a number of different retail chains which had lost money in the mid-1980s, and Stop & Shop was looking to Bradlees, its stronger property, to compensate for red ink in other parts of its operation. In the middle of 1986, Stop & Shop removed Bradlees' president. By the end of that year, the company's sales had risen again, to reach $1.9 billion, up from $1.6 billion a year before.

In 1987 Bradlees announced that it would open 11 new stores and remodel 13 old ones in the course of that year. This policy was in keeping with Stop & Shop's overall reliance on its successful Bradlees subsidiary to contribute a larger portion of the company's revenue.

In the late 1980s, Bradlees built on its presence in the Philadelphia area by moving into the New Jersey market. The company bought a chain of stores from the Two Guys company, which, combined with its Jefferson Ward operations, made it a significant retail player in the nation's fourth-largest market. With this move, Bradlees' stores spanned the East Coast from Maine to Virginia, without any major gaps in coverage.

To support its operations in the Philadelphia/New Jersey area, Bradlees purchased a 530,000-square-foot distribution center in Edison, New Jersey. This warehouse facility was designed to increase the efficiency with which the company supplied its stores in the overall region.

In the late 1980s, Bradlees' corporate parent, the Stop & Shop company, became the target of a hostile takeover bid by the Dart Group Corporation. In January 1988, Stop & Shop began to take evasive maneuvers to avoid becoming a subsidiary of another, larger conglomerate. The result of these efforts was a leveraged buy-out, which took place in June 1988. After the company's stockholders approved the deal, Stop & Shop's outstanding stock was purchased for $44 a share, and the company became a privately held enterprise.

As a result of the financial turmoil of its parent company, Bradlees streamlined its operations, drawing back somewhat from its far-flung geographic reach. The company sold the leases to 37 of its stores located in its southern division, made up of outlets in North Carolina, Virginia, and Maryland, to the Hechinger's chain. This move allowed Stop & Shop to pay off some of the $1.2 billion debt it acquired in the leveraged buyout, and to focus Bradlees' attention more exclusively on markets in the Northeast.

In 1989 Bradlees brought in a new management team and set out to remake its operations for the 1990s. The company undertook a sweeping examination of its businesses, and made a number of changes. In April 1989, Bradlees unrolled a new advertising campaign in Massachusetts, Connecticut, and Pennsylvania. In this push, "Mrs. B," the old Bradlees' spokesperson, was replaced by a series of Bradlees shoppers who delivered monologues about what drew them to the store. These ads had been designed with the input of focus groups and surveys to allow the store to reach out to customers.

In addition, Bradlees instituted a program of certified values, which were indicated with black and gold signs throughout the store. In this program, the company offered low prices on certain items all the time, instead of relying on periodic sales to bring customers into the store.

Bradlees also began to modernize and automate many of its operations. The company began to test bar-code scanning at cash registers in one of its Massachusetts stores, which promised to allow for a greater degree of precision in tracking inventory and sales. In addition, Bradlees installed on-line credit verification, for faster processing of sales. The company also started implementing computerized scheduling, which it planned to have fully rolled out by the end of 1989. All told, Bradlees spent $34 million modernizing its retail systems.

While upgrading its machines, Bradlees also took steps to enhance the performance of its workers. The company instituted customer service training in all stores for all employees, in an effort to improve crucial interpersonal skills. In addition, Bradlees tried to involve local managers more thoroughly in decisions about merchandise choice, display, and store layout. To remove a layer of bureaucracy and centralize its operations, the company also closed its New York buying office in early 1989.

Bradlees opened only one new store during this year, in Meriden, Connecticut, but this outlet, inaugurated in June, represented a new prototype. It featured a redesigned children's furniture department, and boutique-like selling areas, clearly marked with special signs.

In addition to this new store, Bradlees redesigned nine existing stores in 1989. Using wider aisles, brighter lighting, and more vivid styling, Bradlees sought to update its selling environment for the 1990s. The company put the emphasis in these new stores on clothing and other "soft" items for the home, while still incorporating harder, more functional items. As a result of this revamping, Bradlees reported sales of $1.8 billion over the course of 1990. This figure rose by 2.2 percent in the next year.

In the early 1990s, Stop & Shop's managers decided to undo the leveraged buyout that had made the company a privately held concern, saddling it with cumbersome debts. In November 1991, the company decided to go public again, raising funds to pay off debts through an initial public offering of stock. Rather than present Stop & Shop to the market as one company, however, it was decided to separate out the grocer and Bradlees, which accounted for more than a third of the parent company's sales, and present the two companies separately. In this way, Bradlees would be able to update and expand independently of its longtime corporate partner.

Accordingly, Bradlees put in motion the steps necessary to become a separate public company. This process culminated when Bradlees sold 11 million shares on the New York Stock Exchange, commencing on July 1, 1992.

After this move, Bradlees continued to experience strong sales in the Christmas season of 1992. This momentum was not maintained, however, in 1993, as consumers remained cautious in spending their money, and bad weather hit the Northeast. In addition, Bradlees faced stiff competition from other discount retailers.

In an effort to counter these factors, the company embarked on a program of cost cutting. In November 1993, the company reorganized its merchandising operations. The company also changed the way its planning and allocation division worked, and also made changes in the way its stores were managed. In January 1994, Bradlees cut its payroll, reducing its management staff by 280 employees.

Despite its smaller staff, Bradlees planned to expand its profits by opening new stores, primarily in the heavily congested corridor between Boston and Philadelphia, with an emphasis on New York City. In the fall of 1994, the company opened 10 new stores, including four that opened in October in New Jersey. These stores were located in sites that had formerly housed Pace Membership Club stores, so they had a large, open warehouse format. The company took this opportunity to experiment with a store format that was larger than its traditional outlet. "The assortment is similar," the company's chairman told *DM*, "but the extra square footage allowed us to present the merchandise better and to give greater space allocation to those departments with high sales potential." The company took advantage of the warehouse space by keeping layouts open and incorporating skylights into its design.

Bradlees also opened six new stores in the first week of November. Among those outlets was a New York flagship store on Union Square in Manhattan. Formerly the site of a Mays department store, this outlet featured six floors of selling space, making it the largest Bradlees outlet ever. To fill these floors, Bradlees arranged ladies' accessories and apparel on the first floor, children's clothing and toys in the basement, more clothing on the second and third floors, hardware on the fourth floor, and electronics on the fifth floor, along with an Italian restaurant that looked out over Union Square Park. A top floor of the building was used for offices and storage. To draw customers up to the higher floors of the store, Bradlees planned escalators between individual floors, and several banks of elevators. The elevators located at the front of the store were encased in glass, to make an appealing display, as well.

One of the major challenges of doing business in Manhattan, in addition to the high price of real estate, was the difficulty of resupplying the store with new merchandise, given the congestion of city streets. "In your wildest dreams, you can't imagine the difficulties we face with distribution at this store," Bradlees' chairman told *DM*. The company was forced to supplement its regular fleet of 45-foot trailers with smaller, 26-foot trailers in order to bring goods into Manhattan. As a result of these efforts, Bradlees hoped that its Manhattan store would contribute sales of $50 million a year.

Building on this high-profile New York presence, Bradlees planned to open other stores in the region in Brooklyn and Staten Island. In addition, the company planned to seek further growth in New Jersey, Pennsylvania, and Massachusetts. After its strong effort to reduce costs, followed by a wave of new store openings, Bradlees looked to a new chief executive officer to further rejuvenate the company, and steer it into the future. With three decades of experience in discount retailing in the northeast, the company appeared to be in solid shape as it moved into the late 1990s.

Further Reading:

Chanil, Debra, and Roach, Loretta, "Bradlees Concentrates on Consumer Needs," *Discount Merchandiser,* July 1993, pp. 54–57.

Gelfand, Michael, "Bradlees: Fashion-Forward in Apparel," *Discount Merchandiser,* October 1992, pp. 28–29, 84.

Johnson, Jay L., "Bradlees' 'Customer Friendly' Renovation," *Discount Merchandiser,* April 1991, pp. 24–31.

Mammarella, James, "NYC Landmark One of Six New Bradlees," *Discount Store News,* November 21, 1994.

"News/Trends: Stop & Shop IPO," *Discount Merchandiser,* November 1991, pp. 10–13.

Pellet, Jennifer, "Ad Campaign to Reposition Bradlees," *Discount Merchandiser,* July 1989, pp. 48–52.

——, "Bradlees Flexes Its Muscles in Manhattan and Beyond," *Discount Merchandiser,* November 1994, pp. 24–27.

"Trends: Bradlees' New Look for 1994," *Discount Merchandiser,* December 1993, p. 12, 16.

—Elizabeth Rourke

Butler Manufacturing Co.

P.O. Box 419917
Kansas City, Missouri 64141
U.S.A.
(816) 968-3000
Fax: (816) 968-3265

Public Company
Incorporated: 1901
Employees: 3,500
Sales: $692 million
Stock Exchanges: NASDAQ
SICs: 1542 Nonresidential Construction, Not Elsewhere
   Classified; 2452 Prefabricated Wood Buildings; 3448
   Prefabricated Metal Buildings; 3523 Farm Machinery &
   Equipment

Butler Manufacturing Co. is a leading supplier of building systems, specialty components, grain storage systems, and construction services for the nonresidential construction market. The company garnered revenues of about $692 million in 1994 from both domestic and international sales and employed about 3,500 workers.

Emanuel Norquist along with brothers Charles and Newton Butler founded Butler Manufacturing Co., in Kansas City, in 1901. A few years earlier, Charles and Emanuel had worked together on building an improved livestock watering tank, and, during the early 1900s, along with Newton Butler, the men designed and built several agricultural products, particularly grain storage bins. The company enjoyed success selling such merchandise locally, and, by 1908, Butler's headquarters included a staff of 14—six women and eight men. Sales boomed throughout the 1910s and 1920s.

Although Butler would become famous for its grain storage bins, or "Butler bins," during the early and mid-1900s, the company began branching out into new sideline businesses early in the century. For example, in 1909, the company erected its first metal building, an all steel garage. That simple structure would help to lay the foundation for what would eventually become Butler's bread-and-butter business. Other major ventures included metal farm implements and oil field equipment.

Among the company's most interesting early endeavors was the Butler Aircraft Corp. Butler's founders started that subsidiary in

the wake of the airplane craze prompted by Lindbergh's famed transatlantic flight in 1927. In 1929, in fact, more licenses were issued for planes than at any time in U.S. history. Butler designed and built the Blackhawk, a biplane typical of the many aircraft being produced across the nation at the time. The ship stood nine feet tall and 24 feet long, boasted a top speed of 130 miles per hour, and could travel 650 miles on a single tank of gas.

Drawing on expertise and materials it had garnered from its metal bin and building operations to construct the plane, Butler fashioned a three-building factory to manufacture the Blackhawks, which were priced at $7,995 each. Unfortunately, the Great Depression quashed Butler's airplane division after only 11 of its Blackhawks had been produced. Like other manufacturers at the time, Butler suffered during the Depression years as sales and profits declined dramatically.

Butler survived the 1930s, buoyed mainly by its oil equipment operations. Although it was the largest manufacturer of grain bins, Butler's farm equipment segment actually contributed the least revenue of its five divisions. The grain bin industry was susceptible to the cyclicality of the overall agriculture business; when crop yields were high more storage was needed, and when yields were low, demand for new bins would plummet. Butler's bin sales had languished during much of the early and mid-1930s. However, that would soon change, as a result of an incident that would be highlighted in company annals throughout the century.

1938 turned out to be a very good year for crops, and 1939 was even better. As bumper crops were harvested, the nation's storage capacity was stressed. The U.S. Department of Agriculture (USDA), realizing the urgency of the situation, announced in July 1939 that it would accept bids on 30,666 steel storage bins. Incredibly, USDA officials required that all bids be submitted within 30 days and that the bins had to be delivered by the manufacturer within 60 days of receiving an order.

Butler's two plants in Kansas City and Minneapolis were already operating at full capacity, so Butler executives were split over whether or not to bid for the government work. They knew that failure to fulfill the contract terms could spell ruin for the company. Determined to capture a portion of the massive government job, nevertheless, managers embarked on a tenacious search for an abandoned plant that they could convert to build the bins. They found an acceptable, though dilapidated, plant in Galesburg, Illinois. As Butler scrambled to reclaim the facility, it also began preparing a bid to supply 14,500 bins, or about half of the entire contract.

Butler's bid was hand carried to Washington and opened on August 2, 1939. Butler, the low bidder, was awarded the job. "What occurred in Galesburg and throughout the company in the 60 days following that first contract is the stuff of legends," according to company archives. Indeed, Butler's work force launched a production campaign still unrivaled in its long history, churning out grain storage bins at an average rate of almost 250 per day. All 14,500 bins were delivered one day ahead of schedule. Furthermore, another 6,000 units that had been ordered in mid-contract were shipped 15 days later.

Butler used the government contract in 1939 as an opportunity to add a new production facility to its organization. The Galesburg plant was converted for year-round use in 1940 and began manufacturing steel buildings following World War II. Butler had been manufacturing metal buildings since the early 1900s, but it manufactured it first "rigid-frame" building design in 1939. Demand for its popular single-story, rigid-frame structures flourished during the postwar U.S. economic boom.

In the 1950s, the company stepped up its efforts in the metal building market. The shift to the production of metal buildings reflected management's desire to reduce Butler's susceptibility to volatile agricultural markets. Management completely eliminated the grain bin operations in the Galesburg plant, for example, converting it solely to the manufacture of pre-engineered, non-residential structures. Butler's goal was to create two major markets for its products—agricultural and construction—that would provide a more stable pattern of income. The scheme proved effective, and, although both industries were cyclical, Butler's construction and agricultural markets were rarely down at the same time through the 1960s and 1970s.

During this time, demand surged for Butler's expanding lines of agricultural and building products. Sales flourished, earnings rose, and the company posted profits virtually every year between the late 1950s and early 1980s. Butler's fortunes changed in the early 1980s, however, for several reasons. Most importantly, the U.S. agricultural market tailspinned into a long-term slump. Butler posted a loss in 1983 of $7.5 million, its first loss in more than 30 years. Moreover, the industrial and commercial construction markets were still struggling to recover from an ugly downturn that began in the late 1970s and lingered into the early 1980s.

Discouraged by its setbacks in agricultural markets, Butler management decided to begin downplaying that side of their business. They held on to their sporadically profitable grain bin operations (the storage bin business generally followed four or five year cycles, meaning that Butler could usually generate extremely high profits about one year in five), but jettisoned most of its other agricultural operations, which had less long-term potential. By 1986, Butler's agricultural holdings represented less than 15 percent of its total assets, down from about 25 percent just three years earlier.

Butler's decision to focus on pre-engineered buildings and related specialty products was made at a opportune time. The commercial and industrial real estate industry boomed during the mid- and late 1980s, bolstering demand for Butler's innovative pre-engineered buildings. Its structures ranged from airplane hangars, churches, and football practice facilitates to large steel mills and small commercial and industrial buildings. The structures were usually made to order in one of Butler's several factories and then assembled on-site.

To supplant revenue losses in its waning agricultural division, Butler acquired several companies that manufactured products related to its building division, such as exterior wall panels, windows, and electrical systems. Sales from those acquisitions, combined with it core operations, allowed Butler to generate sales of more than $500 million annually by the mid-1980s.

Earnings, however, remained in the $10 million range following the 1983 loss, despite strengthening construction markets.

In 1986, in an effort to improve the company's performance, Butler's directors placed Robert West at the helm of the organization as chairperson and named Donald Pratt as president. Both men had been with Butler since the mid-1960s. West oversaw the divestment of some of Butler's excess baggage, while seeking to integrate the company's newer acquisitions into its core building business. Unfortunately, he had his hands full with the latter task. Indeed, Butler was finding that many of its related subsidiaries were failing to perform as expected and were dragging down overall company gains.

For example, in mid-1986, Butler acquired Inryco, a manufacturer of exterior wall panels and accessories. Management hoped to integrate Inryco's product line and facilities into its pre-engineered building operations, and the Inryco plant was relocated from Minnesota to Kentucky at a considerable cost. Only one year after the acquisition, however, West was having doubts as to whether Butler would be able to keep the new subsidiary. Productivity and equipment reliability problems were proving much more acute than originally thought, and Butler stood to lose from the venture.

Moreover, Butler had made other acquisitions that it had hoped would enhance its mainstay metal buildings, companies that would provide skylights, window walls, and exterior wall panels, and handle other parts of the construction process. But some of those additions also languished. Its Naturalite division, for instance, lost money and required a restructuring cost of about $4 million during the late 1980s.

West restructured or dispatched Butler's nonperforming divisions during the late 1980s and focused the company's efforts on its core metal building business. Despite stagnant earnings growth, its balance sheet was extremely healthy and the company enjoyed robust cash flow. Part of its financial health going into the early 1990s was attributable to West's strategy of plowing cash back into existing operations, rather than making risky acquisitions as the company had done in the past. In 1989, in fact, Butler surprised shareholders with a one-time $20-per-share dividend.

Although Butler had made significant progress in restructuring its operations and shoring up its balance sheet since the early 1980s, commercial and industrial construction markets flopped begainning in the early 1990s, thus stifling opportunities for growth and tempering sales and profits for the company. Earnings hovered below the $10 million mark before the company posted the third loss in its history in 1991. Nevertheless, markets slowly began to improve in 1993 and 1994, and earnings eventually recovered.

While it repositioned its market stance during the 1980s, Butler also focused on improving the safety of its operations. The company had established a reputation for taking care of its employees, so when it recorded more than 130 major injuries in 1979, ranging from wrenched backs to broken bones, management decided to take action. Butler hired a safety director and initiated a 16-point safety program at its Galesburg plant. In fact, the program so successful that it was implemented company-wide. By the early 1990s, Butler was leading the industry in safety with an injury rate of .32 per 100 workers, compared to the industry average of 4.5 per 100. An added bonus was that Butler paid about half the workers' compensation insurance rates that most of its competitors paid.

Going into the mid-1990s, Butler was realizing the benefits of its restructuring efforts during previous five years. In addition, construction markets continued to improve, thus boosting sales of Butler's metal structures, while orders for grain storage systems also increased. Similarly, Butler enjoyed success with some of its subsidiaries. Its wood structure business, for example, which was acquired during the mid-1980s, was performing well and promised to represent an increasingly larger proportion of company revenues.

More importantly, Butler was making solid gains overseas. Already active throughout the world with operations in Saudi Arabia and the United Kingdom, the company was also achieving strong growth in developing nations. Butler contracted with Wal-Mart to build stores in Mexico and South America, for example, and was engaged in a $6.7 million contract for an automobile plant in China in 1994; total sales to the Far East topped $28 million in 1994. Butler was also enjoying demand growth in Russia and other former Eastern Block countries. Foreign sales growth contributed significantly to Butler's 1994 revenue figure of $692 million and accounted for 15 percent of revenues. Operating earnings rose to $33 million in 1994, buoying Butler's stock price.

An interesting aside to the Butler story developed in the early 1990s and involved the old Butler Aircraft Corp. division of 60 years ago. Sometime after World War II, one of Butler's Blackhawk planes ended up in pieces in a barber's garage. LeRoy Brown, one of the barber's customers, purchased the pieces in the late 1960s for $250. Brown, a Pan American DC-10 pilot, spent 20 years restoring the plane. In 1980, Brown flew the plane for Butler executives, and the company purchased the aircraft in 1991. The plane, which Butler stored in a Kansas City hangar, continued to perform just as it had when the Butler brothers completed it in 1929.

Principal Subsidiaries: BUCON, Inc.; Buildings Division; Butler Real Estate Division; Butler Building Systems, Ltd.; Butler World Trade; Grain Systems Division; Lester Building Systems Division; Vistawall Architectural Products Division.

Further Reading:

Butcher, Lola, "Butler Steering for Smoother Road Through Economic Cycle," *Kansas City Business Journal,* December 14, 1987, p. 2.

Csir, Floyd J., "Connecticut Company to Buy Butler Manufacturing," *Parkersburg News,* November 6, 1993.

Cunningham, Norma, "Progress '92: Butler Plant Produces Array of Buildings," *Register-Mail (Kansas City),* September 14, 1992.

Gose, Joe, "Butler Manufacturing Establishes New Low in Lost-in-Time-Injury Rate," *Kansas City Business Journal,* January 22, 1993, p. 11.

Gose, Joe, "Butler Plane, 63, Can Still Fly," *Kansas City Business Journal,* July 2, 1993, p. 1.

Grossman, Steve, "Butler Builds for Wal-Mart in Argentina," *Kansas City Business Journal,* August 5, 1994, p. 3.

Grossman, Steve, "Butler Signs $6.7 million Deal with Chinese Carmaker," *Kansas City Business Journal,* July 29, 1994, p. 1.

Kaberline, Brian, "Butler Pre-Pays Debt, Impresses Market With Cash Flow," *Kansas City Business Journal,* September 10, 1990, p. 8.

Pulliam, John R., "Business Booming at Butler Manufacturing Plant Here," *Register-Mail (Kansas City),* September 20, 1994, p. C2.

Raine, Meredith, "Walker's Path Brings Changes," *Parkersburg News,* July 15, 1994, p. S10.

—Dave Mote

Caldor Inc.

20 Glover Ave.
Norwalk, Connecticut 06856-5620
U.S.A.
(203) 849-2000
Fax: (203) 849-2019

Public Company
Incorporated: 1951
Employees: 20,000
Sales: $2.4 billion
Stock Exchanges: New York
SICs: 5311 Department Stores

Caldor Inc. is a leading retailer of upscale discount goods in the northeastern United States. Through its chain of Caldor discount stores, the company sold nearly $2.5 billion worth of goods and employed a work force of more than 20,000 in 1994. Caldor expanded rapidly beginning in the early 1980s to become the fifth largest discount chain in the nation by the early 1990s. A discount industry pioneer, Caldor predates the start of both Kmart and Wal-Mart by more than a decade.

Caldor was launched in 1951 by husband and wife team Carl and Dorothy Bennett; they coined the name "Caldor" by combining both of their first names. Carl's brother, Harry, was also involved, handling Caldor's real estate dealings from its inception into the mid-1980s. The original enterprise consisted of a single tiny store for three years before a second small shop was added, marking the start of a chain expansion that would blanket the Northeast by the 1990s. The 1,400-square-foot addition was manned by a small, hard-working staff supervised by Carl.

Despite its early entrance into the retail discount store industry, Caldor faced stiff competition from both old and new competitors. For example, Sears, the largest retailer in the world at the time, operated a store across the street from Caldor's second outlet. In addition, Eugene Ferkhauf had started his chain of Korvette discount stores just a few years earlier. That venture became hugely successful and elevated Ferkhauf to star status in the industry. In fact, Korvette had served as an impetus for the Bennetts and even helped to pave the way for other discount retailers.

Carl Bennett and his crew were determined to see the fledgling Caldor chain become successful. Bennett carpooled to work in the early days with Luke Kirby, Jr., the fourth employee hired at the new store. Together, they would lug cases of motor oil and other goods into the store from the car and do whatever else was necessary to give the tiny store an advantage over its well-heeled competitors. "We'd run double-truck ads; customers would come and say, 'where's the rest of the store,' " Kirby recalled in the February 18, 1985 *Discount Store News,* stating that "If I had a brother I wouldn't have worked as hard as I did for Carl."

Impressed by Kirby's knack for sales, Bennett had hired him away from a good sales job in a liquor store chain. The 27-year-old Kirby knew that he was taking a huge risk by leaving his safe job—the chain was owned by Kirby's relatives—but he had a good feeling about Bennett and the new discount store concept. Kirby and Bennett worked well together. They were both savvy and aggressive entrepreneurs who loved to negotiate and take risks. As Bennett slowly expanded the chain during the 1960s and 1970s, Kirby managed the development of the company's hard goods mix, which accounted for the large majority of sales. His acute knowledge of Caldor's inventory and buying systems, combined with his knack for dealing with vendors, eventually earned him the title of vice-president of the company.

The 1960s and 1970s were good years for Caldor. The U.S. economy flourished in the wake of the massive postwar population and consumption boom, and the retail sector thrived. Discount stores, in particular, benefitted, as consumers began to recognize the cost benefits associated with economies of scale. By the 1970s, discount retailers like Caldor, Kmart, Wal-Mart, and Korvette were quickly stealing market share from more conventional retailers, such as department stores and specialty stores. The traditional mom-and-pop shop located in the town square was rapidly becoming a memory.

By 1981, Bennett and his team had built Caldor into a major regional discount retail powerhouse on the East Coast. The chain consisted of 63 stores, all of them much larger than the original 1,000-plus square foot outlets, and Caldor's revenues were approaching $700 million annually. By the early 1980s, however, the retail discount industry was becomingly increasingly competitive and, therefore, consolidated. That trend was intensified by a slowdown in consumer spending during the U.S. economic recession of the late 1970s and early 1980s.

Many of Caldor's competitors, including Korvette, were pushed out of the market or absorbed into larger retail chains during the late 1970s. In contrast to some of its debt-laden peers, however, Caldor was buoyed both by its regional dominance and by its healthy balance sheet, both of which reflected Bennett's management style. Unlike some other discount chains, Caldor had remained focused on a few key markets on the East Coast, where its name recognition had maximum impact. Bennett had also been careful to keep debt to a minimum, which reduced opportunities for expansion but helped to ensure solvency.

Attracted to the company's growth potential and low debt, Associated Dry Goods (ADG) made a bid for Caldor in 1981. ADG, a diversified conglomerate, was already active in the upscale retail sector through other retail holdings, such as its chain of Lord and Taylor stores, and it sought to round out its retail portfolio with a discount chain like Caldor. That year, ADG acquired Caldor, and, although Caldor lost its independence, Bennett was retained under a five-year management contract, as were several other executives, including Kirby.

Under the control and financial backing of ADG, Caldor expanded at a rate of more than 20 new stores annually between 1981 and 1985. It remained focused on the East Coast, opening outlets in New York, Connecticut, Massachusetts, and New Jersey, among other states. As the number of Caldor stores escalated to nearly 100 by 1986, sales surged to about $1.4 billion, or nearly double revenues before the ADG buyout. During the same period, ADG continued to expand through other retail holdings, such as Loehmann's, a department store retail chain.

While Caldor's growth during the early 1980s seemed impressive, ADG failed to profit from the acquisition as it had hoped, and Caldor became a drag on its bottom line. In fact, rapid expansion, the absence of a defined growth strategy for the chain, and ADG's general lack of expertise in discount retailing had resulted in mediocre profitability by the mid-1980s. Critics cited ADG's failure to market to young families. In addition, the chain's product mix had become unwieldy, and its signing and display techniques were considered poor in relation to its competition. Furthermore, Caldor's inventory and sales tracking systems had become obsolete compared to many of its technically advanced rivals.

Evidencing the continuing trend toward industry consolidation, May Department Stores Co. purchased ADG in 1987 in a stock swap valued at $2.7 billion. A major U.S. retail powerhouse headquartered in the Midwest, May Department Stores had a reputation as an aggressive, profitable retailer. Its major holdings included Famous Barr, a chain of upscale department stores, and Venture, a retail discount chain similar to Caldor in both size and market positioning. May named Don R. Clarke chief executive of Caldor and Marc Balmuth president, both of whom had formerly headed up May's successful Venture chain. Clarke replaced the short-term successor to Bennett, who had left Caldor when his contract expired in 1985; Bennett and his wife, Dorothy, subsequently started a real estate consulting firm in Stamford, Connecticut.

Clarke's first move at Caldor was to squelch the ambitious growth plans made by its former parent, ADG, which had planned to double Caldor's outlets to 200 by 1990 and to boost revenues past the $2 billion mark. Instead, May wanted to concentrate on improving the financial performance of the chain. During 1986, Clarke liquidated Caldor's bloated inventory—at a cost of $30 million—and began to reestablish a profitable mix of goods. Importantly, he initiated an emphasis on soft lines, particularly clothing, thus diminishing the chain's extreme concentration on hard goods. He also shaped up Caldor's advertising and promotional programs and developed a plan to renovate Caldor's older stores.

During 1988, Caldor added only three new stores, bringing its total to 119. Clarke and Balmuth remained focused on improving the performance of the chain and remodeling existing outlets. They reduced the number of managers in each store and used the payroll reductions to lower prices. Computerized sys-

tems were implemented to improve efficiency, and electronic scanning guns were installed at all of Caldor's registers. Changes achieved during the late 1980s significantly improved Caldor's performance. Caldor generated revenues of $1.6 billion in 1988, about $50 million of which were kept as earnings; May's aggregate sales during that year were $11.6 billion.

May had increased Caldor's earnings by more than 300 percent since 1986 and had gone a long way toward improving the competitiveness of the discounter. Still, Caldor's problems proved greater than May had anticipated, and income growth was slower than expected. A U.S. economic recession that started in the late 1980s, moreover, threatened to hinder Caldor's gains. Finally, the discount retail industry was becoming increasingly competitive as regional discounters saturated local markets. Discount giants Kmart and Wal-Mart, for instance, both began aggressively vying for market share in Caldor's traditional stomping grounds.

In light of proliferating competition and general disenchantment with its discount operations, May decided to sell its discount chains in 1989 and to focus its energies entirely on its department stores. In a $537 million leveraged buyout, an investment group named Odyssey Partners borrowed heavily to buy the 120-store Caldor chain. Clarke and Balmuth remained at the helm and continued to pursue a strategy of slow growth, while implementing new internal changes designed to add value to the company. They revamped Caldor's pricing system, for example, by instituting a two-tier pricing system that helped to reduce overall mark-ups by about two percent. They also stepped up their efforts to offer increasingly profitable soft lines, boosting sales of those items from 27 percent of revenues before the leveraged buyout to about 31 percent by 1990. Finally, Clarke and Balmuth made plans to increase the average size of the stores and changed the Caldor logo and color schemes.

Caldor flourished as an independent company. Despite the recession, revenues jumped more than five percent in both 1990 and 1991 before rising more than ten percent during 1992. Similarly, net earnings soared past $34 million in 1992. In fact, Caldor surpassed its $2 billion revenue goal in 1992. Furthermore, Odyssey Partners was able to reduce its large debt load in 1991 through a public stock offering. Clarke and Balmuth used those proceeds to launch an ambitious store remodeling plan that they had started in 1989, as well as to begin expanding the chain again. In 1992, in fact, Caldor outbid other retailers to take control of six New York City stores that were being dumped by Alexander's, another retailer.

During 1992, Caldor added a total of eight new stores to its chain, bringing its total to 136. Those additions represented the start of a plan to add a total of 60 new stores by 1995. To support its growth plans, Caldor constructed a 508,000-square-foot distribution facility in New York and began the installation of a major computer information support system, which went on line in 1993. Caldor tagged 14 new stores onto its portfolio during 1993 and completed 20 more renovations; by the end of 1994, more than 80 percent of Caldor's stores were newly constructed or recently renovated.

Caldor's improved appearance complemented its more competitive prices and new product mix. Indeed, as consumers became aware of the improvements, Caldor's sales and profits escalated. Revenues rose to a record $2.4 billion in 1993, and earnings hovered near a healthy $34 million. Despite hefty capital expenditures, improved earnings allowed Caldor to steadily shave its long term debt load from about $350 million in 1989 to $272 million by 1993. As a result of improvements, the company's stock price more than doubled between 1991 and 1994 to about $30 per share.

Going into 1995, Caldor was operating 158 stores in ten northeastern and mid-atlantic states. In its key geographic areas, it maintained a dominant role in the upscale end of the discount market, which included brand- and quality-conscious consumers. Clarke planned to step up expansion with the addition of 100 new stores by 1999, as well as to complete the renovation of all of its existing outlets. Caldor's steadily improving financial performance, combined with a strengthening retail sector in the mid-1990s, made those goals plausible.

Further Reading:

"Caldor Celebrates Successful Store Openings, Healthy Outlook," *Discount Store News,* November 5, 1990, p. 2.

"Caldor Opens Stores in Hamilton, Bristol," *Trentonian,* January 28, 1993.

Cooper, Jeanne Dugan, "Attn: K Mart Execs: Caldor Opens New Long Island Store," *Newsday,* July 27, 1990, p. 43.

Enrico, Dottie, "May Stores Puts Caldor on the Block," *Newsday,* June 28, 1989, p. 49.

Furman, Phyllis, "Caldor Runs to Fill the Big Store Void," *Crains New York Business,* October 4, 1993, p. 1.

Halverson, Richard, "Discount Pioneer Caldor Blazing Upscale Trail in the Northeast," *Discount Store News,* August 16, 1993, p. 88.

Jordan, Hope A., "Up Against the Malls," *Business Worcester,* December 25, 1989, p. 70.

Kamienski, Mark, "Competition, Tight Labor Market Alter Retailer's Strategy for Success," *Intercorp,* June 23, 1989, p. 18.

"Kirby, an Original, Retires from Caldor," *Discount Store News,* February 18, 1985, p. 3.

Lisanti, Tony, "Caldor Employs 'May-less' Look; Remodeling Key to Achieving Self-Sufficiency," *Discount Store News,* March 26, 1990, p. 1.

"Venture's Clarke Takes Helm at Caldor, Set to Fix Business," *Discount Store News,* November 10, 1986, p. 1.

—Dave Mote

CHANEL

Chanel

135 Avenue Charles de Gaulle
F-92521 Neuilly Sur Seine Cedex
France
Telephone: (1) 46434000
Fax: (1) 47476034
Telex: 630644

Private Company
Founded: 1924 as Parfums Chanel
Employees: 912
Sales: $450 million
SICs: 2844 Toilet Preparations

Chanel, worth an estimated $1.5 billion, is one of the largest companies in the $4 billion global perfume industry. Chanel started its success with the introduction of Chanel No. 5 perfume, which continued to be a top selling perfume into the 1990s. The company has since diversified its offerings beyond perfumes to include designer clothes and accessories, which are sold in department stores and Chanel boutiques around the world. The company boasts a rich history rife with intrigue, wealth, and scandal.

By the 1990s, the Wertheimer family of France had maintained controlling interest in Chanel for over 100 years. Chanel traces its roots back to 1870, when Ernest Wertheimer moved from Alsace, France, to Paris during the Franco-Prussian War. Shortly after his arrival he purchased an interest in a French theatrical makeup company called Bourjois. Bourjois successfully introduced dry rouge to the European market in the 1890s. The company grew rapidly, and by the early 1920s, Bourjois had begun making and distributing skin creams from his Rochester, New York, plant for cosmetic industry giant Helena Rubenstien. By the 1920s, Bourjois had become the largest cosmetics and fragrance manufacturer in France.

Though the Wertheimer family would control the finances of Chanel from its inception, the impetus and creative vision for the company came from Coco Chanel. Theophile Bader, founder of the successful French department store chain Galeries Lafayette, introduced Coco Chanel to Ernest Wertheimer's son, Pierre, in 1922. Coco Chanel sought financial help from Pierre Wertheimer to market a fragrance she had developed in 1921. An admirer of Coco Chanel, Pierre Wertheimer

wanted to help her succeed and, two years after their introduction, he founded Parfums Chanel to make and sell her upscale perfume, named Chanel No. 5. Pierre Wertheimer funded the venture and retained a 70 percent ownership share in the company. Coco Chanel got a modest 10 percent of the company and Bader received 20 percent.

During the 1920s and 1930s Parfums Chanel thrived. In addition to selling the famous Chanel No. 5 perfume, the company eventually introduced other fragrances. In 1929, Pierre Wertheimer introduced Soir de Paris, a fragrance aimed at the general public and marketed through the Bourjois company. Meanwhile, Coco Chanel operated a successful fashion studio near the Louvre museum in Paris. Under an agreement with the Wertheimers, she operated her design business as a separate company, but sold the clothes under the Chanel name. Although Parfums Chanel and Coco Chanel's design business flourished, the personal relationship between Coco Chanel and Pierre Wertheimer deteriorated.

The friction between Coco Chanel and the Wertheimer family stemmed from Coco Chanel's dissatisfaction with the terms of their original agreement. Coco Chanel resented what she viewed as an attempt by the Wertheimers to exploit her talents for their own gain. She felt she should have a larger than ten percent portion of the company, and she argued that she had unwittingly signed away the rights to her own name. The Wertheimers countered her grievances with an argument that reminded Coco Chanel that the Wertheimers had funded her venture in the first place, giving her the chance to take her creations to market, and had made her a relatively wealthy woman.

In 1935 Chanel hired a Parisian attorney, Rene de Chambrun, to renegotiate her agreement with the Wertheimers. But the Wertheimers successfully quashed those attempts. Furthermore, her fashion business sputtered during the late 1930s and at 56-years-of-age Coco Chanel closed it when the Nazis invaded France. Coco Chanel found a new way to fight the Wertheimers during World War II. In fact, the Wertheimers fled the country in 1940, eventually landing in the United States. With the powerful Wertheimer family gone, Coco Chanel went to work trying to use new occupation regulations to take control of the Parfums Chanel partnership. But the savvy Wertheimers stymied that move, too. In their absence, they found an Aryan proxy to run their businesses and keep Coco Chanel at bay.

During World War II, Coco Chanel stayed in Paris, moving into the Hotel Ritz with her new paramour, Hans Gunther von Dincklage, a member of the German information service. According to one of Coco Chanel's biographers, Edmonde Charles-Roux, she played a role in a secret peace mission near the end of the War. Charles-Roux contends that German intelligence sent Coco Chanel to visit Winston Churchill as part of a secret peace mission. Coco Chanel was arrested immediately after the Liberation of France and charged with abetting the Germans, but Churchill intervened on her behalf and she was released.

After her release, Coco Chanel immediately fled France for Switzerland. Meanwhile, Pierre Wertheimer returned to Paris to resume control of his family's holdings. Despite her absence, Coco Chanel continued her assault on her former admirer and began manufacturing her own line of perfumes. Feeling that Coco Chanel was infringing on Parfums Chanel's business, Pierre Wertheimer wanted to protect his legal rights, but wished to a avoid a court battle, and so, in 1947, he settled the dispute with Coco Chanel, giving her $400,000 and agreeing to pay her a two percent royalty on all Chanel products. He also gave her limited rights to sell her own perfumes from Switzerland.

Coco Chanel never made any more perfume after the agreement. She gave up the rights to her name in exchange for a monthly stipend from the Wertheimers. The settlement paid all of her monthly bills and kept Coco Chanel and her former lover, von Dincklage, living in relatively high style. It appeared as though aging Coco Chanel would drop out of the Chanel company saga.

At 70 years of age in 1954, Coco Chanel returned to Paris with the intent of restarting her fashion studio. She went to Pierre Wertheimer for advice and money, and he agreed to finance her plan. In return for his help, Wertheimer secured the rights to the Chanel name for all products that bore it, not just perfumes. Once more, Wertheimer's decision paid off from a business standpoint. Coco Chanel's fashion lines succeeded in their own right and had the net effect of boosting the perfume's image. In the late 1950s Wertheimer bought back the 20 percent of the company owned by Bader. Thus, when Coco Chanel died in 1971 at the age of 87, the Wertheimers owned the entire Parfums Chanel operation, including all rights to the Chanel name.

Pierre Wertheimer died six years before Coco Chanel passed away, putting an end to an intriguing and curious relationship of which Parfums Chanel was just one, albeit pivotal, dynamic. Coco Chanel's attorney, Rene de Chambrun, described the relationship as one based on a businessman's passion for a woman who felt exploited by him. "Pierre returned to Paris full of pride and excitement [after one of his horses won the 1956 English Derby]," Chambrun recalled in *Forbes*. "He rushed to Coco, expecting congratulations and praise. But she refused to kiss him. She resented him, you see, all her life."

Pierre Wertheimer's son, Jacques, took control of the Chanel operation in 1965. The 55-year-old Jacques was perhaps best known for his managment of the family's racing stables and horse breeding operations; Pierre Wertheimer had established one of the finest racing stables in the world in 1910, and Jacques became a renowned horse breeder. According to some critics, however, he did not direct as much attention on the operation of Chanel.

In 1974, Jacques's 25-year-old son Alain Wertheimer gained control of the company. While the press suggested that the move to new management involved animosity and family feuds, Chanel management maintained that control was ceded in a friendly and peaceable manner.

Chanel No. 5 was still a global perfume industry leader when Alain Wertheimer took the helm. But, with only four percent of the pivotal $875 million U.S. market, its dominance was fading. After years of mismanagement, Chanel had become viewed by many Americans as a second-rate fragrance that appealed to out-of-style women. Alain Wertheimer succeeded in turning Chanel around in the United States. He removed the perfume from drug store shelves in an effort to create a greater sense of scarcity and exclusivity. As the number of U.S. outlets carrying Chanel No. 5 plummeted from 18,000 to 12,000, Alain Wertheimer pumped millions into advertising Chanel's fragrances and cosmetics. His efforts increased profits.

In 1980, Alain Wertheimer stepped up efforts in Chanel's U.S. fashion operations. Attempts to parlay the Chanel fashion division into a profit center and promotional device for Chanel's fragrances succeeded. Chanel opened up more than 40 Chanel boutiques worldwide. By the late 1980s those shops sold everything from $200-per-ounce perfume and $225 ballerina slippers to $11,000 dresses and $2,000 leather handbags. Importantly, Alain Wertheimer refused to relinquish control of anything related to the family's Chanel operations. In fact, Chanel remains one of few companies in the cosmetic and apparel industry that does not license its fragrances, cosmetics, or apparel to other producers or distributors.

Part of Chanel's success during the 1980s (and throughout the 1900s for that matter) was its adherence to a conservative, proven image. Chanel designers and marketers were extremely careful to not tamper with the Chanel legend. While other perfumes had changed to follow short term trends, the Chanel fragrance remained classic and unchanged. Even the Chanel No. 5 bottle, with its traditional black-and-white label and simple lines, was considered a work of art by the company. "We introduce a new fragrance every 10 years, not every three minutes like many competitors," explained Chanel marketer Jean Hoehn Zimmerman in *Marketing News*. "We don't confuse the consumer. With Chanel, people know what to expect. And they keep coming back to us, at all ages, as they enter and leave the market."

As a result of Alain Wertheimer's efforts during the 1980s and early 1990s, the Chanel's performance improved significantly. Going into the 1990s, in fact, Chanel was considered a global leader in the fragrance industry and a top innovator in fragrance advertising and marketing. Chanel continued to spend more on advertising than almost any other perfume company and, as a result, was reaping the fattest profit margins in the industry. In addition, the company had continued to expand into new product lines, including Chanel watches retailing for as much as $7,000; additions to its popular shoe line; and other high-priced clothes, cosmetics, and accessories.

The Wertheimers would have been wealthy without their Chanel business. However, Chanel's success in the 1980s was credited with boosting the Wertheimer family's wealth to a new level. Alain Wertheimer moved his offices to New York in the late 1980s, reflecting Chanel's emphasis on the U.S. market. Although sales of high-end goods were hurt by the global recession of the early 1990s, demand began recovering in the mid 1990s and Chanel continued to expand its boutique chain and product line.

Further Reading:

Berkowitz, Harry, ''Not Everyone Shared Caged Fantasy: Does New Chanel Ad Evoke Freedom or the Same Old Constraining Attitudes?'' *Newsday,* August 30, 1992, sec. 1, p. 72.

Berman, Phyllis, and Zina Sawaya, ''The Billionaires behind Chanel,'' *Forbes,* April 3, 1989, p. 104.

Hunter, Catherine E., ''Scientist, Inventor, Futurist,'' *Drug & Cosmetic Industry,* May 1993, p. 20.

Johnson, Rebecca, ''Scent of a Woman,'' *ADWEEK Eastern Edition,* November 29, 1993, p. 30.

Kamen, Robin, ''Exec Suiting Up for Growth: Chanel to Open New Boutiques, Cater to Buyers,'' *Crains New York Business,* August 15, 1994, sec. 1, p. 13.

Oliver, Joyce Ann, ''She Innovates without Destroying a Legend,'' *Marketing News,* December 10, 1990, p. 10.

Swisher, Kara, ''Chanel Bucks the Trend Toward Tysons Corner,'' *Washington Post,* May 7, 1990, sec. E, p. 31.

—Dave Mote

CHEYENNE

Cheyenne Software, Inc.

3 Expressway Plaza
Roslyn Heights, New York 11577
U.S.A.
(516) 484-5110
Fax: (516) 484-1853

Public Company
Incorporated: 1983
Employees: 500
Sales: $97.74 million
Stock Exchanges: American
SICs: 7372 Prepackaged Software

Cheyennes Software, Inc. is engaged in the development, marketing, and support of software products for use in microcomputers. It is a leading U.S. provider of software for Local Area Network (LAN) systems, which link microcomputers and peripherals and allow them to share information. Following a rocky start, Cheyenne realized rampant growth during the late 1980s and early 1990s.

Cheyenne Software's history may be traced to 1983 and the New York investor Barry Rubenstein. Rubenstein, then in his late 30s, was having problems with a computer system that he had purchased at a local computer store. When he returned to the shop to complain, he met Frank Mena, a salesman at the store who also worked as a computer programmer. "We got to talking, and talking got to much more talking," Rubenstein recalled in the August 13, 1990 *Newsday.* "He said he wanted to get into his own business," Rubenstein noted.

Intrigued by the conversation, Rubenstein set about trying to come up with a solid business plan and money to back it. The well-connected Rubenstein was in a good position to find the start-up capital—at the time, he was working as an investment banker in New York for Prescott, Ball & Turben Inc., a Cleveland-based brokerage firm. Rubenstein contacted several potential investors and was able to round up $2.7 million in seed money. He and several friends and investors then started Cheyenne Software in 1983. Their plan was to develop and sell software for the emerging LAN market.

Cheyenne officially opened its doors for business in 1984. Rubenstein became chairperson of the newly formed Cheyenne and friend Eli Oxenhorn was named president. A software

industry veteran, Oxenhorn had served as head of software operations at Warner Communications for nine years and was eager to get involved in a start-up. Oxenhorn handled strategy and day-to-day operations, while Rubenstein concentrated primarily on finances and helping, in any way possible, to get the venture off the ground.

Cheyenne's first several years were largely spent in trying to develop marketable software products and to identify new opportunities. The first proprietary software program developed by the company was NetBack, which didn't actually reach the market until 1989. NetBack was a network utility (software program that supports a computer network) designed to back up, or copy and store, data. As Cheyenne worked to develop that and other LAN software products, the company continued to show annual losses throughout the mid-1980s, pouring millions of dollars into research and development.

In an effort to generate cash for its software development efforts, Oxenhorn decided to diversify into the booming microcomputer distribution business. To that end, during 1987 and 1988, Cheyenne completed the acquisitions of F.A. Computer Technologies, Inc. and Gates Distribution Company, both of which were engaged in the distribution of microcomputers, networking software, and computer peripheral equipment. Cheyenne combined them to form Gates/FA Distributing Inc., which Cheyenne took public in a 1989 stock offering. The move was also viewed as a potential complement to Cheyenne's software efforts, because Gates/FA would give Cheyenne a new marketing and distribution channel for its software.

About the same time that Cheyenne was assembling its Gates/FA subsidiary, the company suffered a setback involving some of the investors who had originally funded the venture. In 1987, *Barron's,* a major business periodical, published a lengthy article in which it lambasted Cheyenne's leading shareholders for playing "central roles" in transactions it called "highly questionable." *Barron's* based the piece on a 1986 report created by the President's Commission on Organized Crime. The report did, in fact, implicate major players related to Cheyenne in some shady dealings. At issue were the financial dealings of two of Cheyenne's top investors: Jackie Presser and Fred Dolin.

Jackie Presser, the head of the Teamsters Union, was awaiting trial at the time for a racketeering case. Fred Dolin happened to be the son of Nate Dolin, a Cleveland businessman who had recently lost an injunction by the Securities and Exchange Commission (SEC) against his company, Fortune Enterprises. The SEC effectively said that Nate Dolin was corrupt and that his company was a sham. Although neither Fred Dolin nor Presser ever had any direct involvement in Cheyenne—no one at Cheyenne had even met either man—the *Barron's* article implied that they were helping manage it. They did own a combined 13 percent share of Cheyenne, however, and the bad press was a setback for the struggling Cheyenne.

Nevertheless, Cheyenne continued to work toward its goal of becoming a major player in the emerging LAN industry, and the going was relatively slow. Although sales had surged following its buyout of Gates and F.A. Computer, profits remained elusive. In 1988 (fiscal year ended June 30), the company had sales of $55 million, but still lost money. And, although revenues rose to nearly $100 million the following year, Cheyenne continued to show losses. Furthermore, only $600,000 of its 1989 sales was attributable to software sales, the year in which NetBack was introduced, while the remainder came from the Gates/FA subsidiary. In fact, by 1989, after more than five years in business, Cheyenne had lost more than $7 million.

Cheyenne's financial performance during the 1980s may have appeared dismal to the casual observer. However, the company actually achieved significant gains during the period which were about to bear fruit. Indeed, throughout the decade Cheyenne had invested millions into developing top-of-the-line LAN support software. Cheyenne's staff, which numbered 30 in 1988 and grew to 40 in 1989, had labored in an old-fashioned, wood-and-brick building on the outskirts of Roslyn, New York. Finally, the group was ready to begin marketing two major proprietary programs that would add to its sole NetBack offering: Arcserve and Monitrix.

Cheyenne introduced both Arcserve and Monitrix in 1990, following the release of NetBack. Arcserve was a program used to back up other software programs and to ensure that data in the network system could not be lost. One of the Arcserve's chief functions was to automatically copy all of the information in the system so that mishaps, such as power failures and equipment malfunction, would not destroy or erase it. Monitrix was a system administration utility, which could be used to track, analyze, and report statistical information on the network. For example, data about a company's clients could be gathered from its network and output into customized reports.

Cheyenne was only one of many competitors vying for LAN software market share. Nevertheless, its products were immediately recognized by the marketplace as superior to many existing applications. Sales were brisk. In 1990, in fact, Cheyenne's software sales rose nearly 200 percent to $1.7 million, mostly as a result of Arcserve and Monitrix shipments. That figure still represented a relatively small portion of Cheyenne's total $168 million in 1990 sales, but management was convinced that the company was on the brink of huge gains from its software. They were right. Although Cheyenne posted a $2 million loss in 1990, the company boasted big profits throughout the remainder of early 1990s.

Oxenhorn was still running Cheyenne going into the early 1990s, while Rubenstein had left in 1987. But the man who received the most credit for Cheyenne's success during the early 1990s was software programmer ReiJane Huai. A native of Taiwan, Huai had already become known for his abilities in math and science before coming to the United States in 1984. He received his Masters in computer science from The State University of New York at Stony Brook in 1985. Huai immediately joined Cheyenne before serving a brief tenure with the acclaimed AT&T's Bell Laboratories. After his stint at Bell, the 25-year-old Huai returned to Cheyenne, where his talents were quickly recognized, and he assumed the lead role in Cheyenne's research and development arm. Besides being highly intelligent and capable, Huai was a self-described workaholic. "I work all the time," he explained in the *Newsday* article, adding that "this career is my life."

After five years of hard work, including many 16-hour days, Huai and his coworkers were finally able to enjoy the fruits of their labor during the early 1990s. Although NetBack had realized only moderate success, sales of Monitrix increased between 1991 and 1993. Shipments of Arcserve, moreover, exploded throughout the period, and that program became Cheyenne's flagship product. As software revenues soared, Cheyenne altered its business strategy. It began selling off its interests in Gates/FA in 1992, and by 1994 had effectively jettisoned the distributor. Although that move reduced Cheyenne's revenues, it didn't hamper profits. In fact, Cheyenne announced its first profit in 1991 of $3.3 million. Net income in 1992, moreover, sailed to nearly $8.2 million.

Although Cheyenne's prosperity following the introduction of its key software products was largely the result of its top-notch development and marketing efforts, it was also partially a consequence of timing. Indeed, during the late 1980s and early 1990s the computer networking industry grew dramatically. Companies were increasingly finding that they could network several microcomputers and peripherals together with a server, or main processor, to achieve the same computing environment previously created by mainframe computing systems. In addition to LANs, WANs (wide area networks) increased in popularity during the early 1990s, offering an entirely new realm of opportunity for companies like Cheyenne; similar to LANs, WANs tied together geographically separated groups of microcomputers.

In addition to Arcserve and Monitrix, Cheyenne introduced a string of new products during the early 1990s and continued to develop more. In 1992, Cheyenne began selling InnocuLAN and FAXserve. InnocuLAN was a software program designed to protect Novell networks—Novell was a popular networking system—against a host of different computer viruses (code designed to destroy data). FAXserve, on the other hand, allowed the network file server to send and receive facsimiles more easily than traditional fax systems. In addition to those new offerings, Cheyenne brought out an improved version of its core program, Arcserve, early in 1993. Cheyenne also purchased Applied Programming Technologies, Inc., an imaging company, hoping to parlay that purchase into new software products aimed at the imaging market.

Just as important to Cheyenne's success as new products during the early 1990s was the company's new marketing strategy. In the past, Cheyenne had marketed its software through "strategic partners" who paid royalties to Cheyenne for every program they sold to a third party. During the early 1990s, however, Cheyenne began to focus on selling its products to original equipment manufacturers (OEMs). For example, Cheyenne reached agreements with such hardware manufacturers as IBM and Hewlett-Packard to sell its software alongwith their computers, tape drives, storage devices, and other equipment. Such agreements vastly boosted Cheyenne's market reach at a relatively negligible marketing cost.

In 1990, Cheyenne entered into a major agreement with Tecmar, a producer of tape drives, and followed that contract with an arrangement in 1991 with Intel, a manufacturer of semiconductors. Subsequent OEM agreements were made with industry giants Hewlett-Packard, IBM, Compaq, Computer Associates, and nearly 15 other companies. By 1993, sales through OEMs were making up about 25 percent of company revenues. By that time, however, OEM gains were being rapidly overshadowed by Cheyenne's success at selling its software through independent distributors. Under those arrangements, Cheyenne agreed to let the distributors sell its products and provided technical training to the distributors, who also shared promotional costs. This distributor channel was particularly effective in reaching Cheyenne's growing European customer base in the mid-1990s.

As Cheyenne began to gain momentum going into the mid-1990s, it continued to release and develop new products. The company brought out a series of new ARCserve products tailored specifically for different market segments, such as Macintosh and Windows users. And it also introduced some completely new products. NOSS (Network Object Storage System), for example, was a program designed to help network administrators facilitate optical storage of corporate records, databases, spreadsheets, and other types of documents. Similarly, Optical Storage Manager was a high-tech storage system that integrated both magnetic and optical (laser) storage technologies to cut storage costs without reducing performance.

As Cheyenne rolled out new products, expanded overseas, and opened new marketing channels, company sales more than doubled in 1993 (fiscal year ended June 30) to $56.7 million, a significant increase after the falling revenues experienced following the sale of most of the Gates/FA subsidiary. More importantly, Cheyenne's net income reached a record $20.7 million, reflecting an increase of about 150 percent of 1992 profits. In 1994, moreover, revenues rose to $97.7 million as income jumped to an impressive $32.5 million. Enthused investors sent Cheyenne's stock price soaring. 1994 gains were largely a result of European expansion; European shipments increased from $4.2 million in 1991 to nearly $34 million in 1992. Cheyenne's sales were also surging in Canada and Asia.

In a move reflecting Huai's impact at Cheyenne, Oxenhorn stepped aside as president and chief executive of Cheyenne late in 1993, and Huai assumed both titles. Under his direction, Cheyenne continued to focus on improving its stance in the fast-growing LAN industry. However, Huai also revealed his intent to introduce a new dynamic to Cheyenne's strategy. "The main direction I'd like to see the company move in is communications," Huai stated in the February 28, 1994 *LI Business News.* "Research and design on communications products [for computers] are going to be an important part of our future," Huai

noted. Supporting that claim was the company's creation of Cheyenne Communications, a separate subsidiary created to explore opportunities related to computer communications software.

When Huai took the helm, Cheyenne was facing a string of challenges. The company had received some complaints of bugs in its Arcserve software, as well as criticism of its technical support by users that were having difficulty. In addition, some shareholders had filed lawsuits alleging that the company had failed to make legally required security disclosures. In response, the SEC began an informal inquiry into the company's stock volatility—the stock price had dropped from a high of $30 at the start of 1994, to $15 after reports of high inventory, and then to $6 one day after the company announced disappointing fourth quarter results in mid-1994.

Nevertheless, Cheyenne continued to post profit gains going into 1995 and to expand its operations. For example, Cheyenne Communications purchased Bit Software, Inc., a leading communications software firm. In December 1994, Cheyenne bought NETstor, Inc., a manufacturer of network memory storage products and related goods. Going into the mid-1990s, several factors suggested sustained expansion at Cheyenne, including: the growth of WANs and Cheyenne's related efforts in communications software; Cheyenne's pending acquisitions; new product introductions and programs still under development; and global growth of the networking industry.

Principal Subsidiaries: Cheyenne Communications, Inc.; Cheyenne Software International, Inc.

Further Reading:

Bernstein, James, "New Products Buoy Software Maker," *Newsday,* August 13, 1990, Sec. 3, p. 5.

Brandel, Mary, and Thomas Hoffman, "Cheyenne Growth Spurt Sputters," *Computerworld,* July 11, 1994, p. 32.

"Huai Leads Cheyenne to Greater Communication," *LI Business News,* February 28, 1994, p. 516.

Oxenhorn, Eli, "Cheyenne Names ReiJane Huai as President and CEO,"

Business Wire, October 8, 1993.

Rigney, Steve, "Cheyenne Goes After the Workgroup," *PC Magazine,* July 1994, p. N17.

Talley, Karen, "Cheyenne Software Draws Attention," *LI Business News,* March 25, 1991, p. 3.

—Dave Mote

Cifra, S.A. de C.V.

José Maria Castorena 470
Delegacion Cuajimalpa
05200 Mexico City, DF
Mexico
52-5-327-9211
Fax: 52-5-327-9259

Public Company
Incorporated: as Aurrera S.A.
Sales: $4.6 billion
Employees: 39,934
Stock Exchanges: Bolsa
SICs: 5310 Department Stores; 5411 Grocery Stores; 5812
    Eating Places

Cifra, S.A. de C.V. is Mexico's largest retailer, its second largest publicly owned company, and, according to a 1993 *Euromoney* survey, Latin America's best-run company. Among Mexican retailers Cifra was the first to be publicly owned, offer generic brands, and include clothing, food, and hardware within a single store. The Cifra empire was vast in the mid-1990s, including department stores, discount warehouse stores, supermarkets and hypermarkets, and restaurants. More than three-quarters were in the Mexico City area, which was the largest metropolitan area in Latin America and was Mexico's largest and fastest-growing region. In 1991 Cifra began greatly expanding its operations, forming joint ventures with Wal-Mart Stores, Inc., the largest retailer in the United States.

Cifra was founded in 1958 by Jerónimo Arango. The son of a Spanish immigrant to Mexico who prospered in the textile business, Arango spent his youth studying art and literature at several American universities and traveling in Spain, Mexico, and the United States. While in New York City he saw a crowd waiting patiently for the opportunity to enter E.J. Korvette, then a pioneering Fifth Avenue discount department store. Impressed by Korvette's success, he persuaded his father to lend him the equivalent in pesos of $240,000 so that he could organize a similar venture with his two brothers, Placido and Manuel. Called Aurrera Bolívar, this discount store was opened in downtown Mexico City in 1958.

Like the Korvette store, Aurrera Bolivar immediately drew the public, and—also like Korvette's—it attracted the hostility of established retailers, who felt threatened by competition engen-

dered by Aurrera Bolivar's low prices. In fact, the store was selling household goods and clothing at 20 percent below manufacturers's list prices, while established retailers were marking them up by 40 to 45 percent. Soon the brothers had to locate alternate sources of goods as far away as Guadalajara and Monterrey because the Arangos's suppliers were threatened with boycott by angry rivals. Nevertheless, Aurrera reportedly won sympathy by publicizing its competitors's tactics during its sponsorship of the popular television show "The 64,000 Peso Question." By 1965 eight Aurrera stores were in existence, drawing $16 million in sales. The company's first Superama supermarket opened in 1960 and the first Vip restaurant in 1964.

In 1965 Jewel Cos. of Chicago organized a joint venture with the Arango brothers to start new stores, and a year later Jewel acquired a 49 percent stake in the business for about U.S. $20 million. While Manuel and Placido Arango took their part of the money and left the business to establish other enterprises, Jerónimo studied modern retailing at Jewel headquarters in Chicago. In 1970 he opened the first of the firm's Bodega Aurrera discount warehouse stores and Suburbia department stores. Aurrera S.A. became publicly owned in 1976, the year it opened its first hypermarket, and was so successful that by 1981 Jewel's Mexican operations accounted for nearly one-third of its income. Jewel's stake had dropped to 41.7 percent of the outstanding shares by 1980 and would eventually fall to 36.1 percent.

Hard times came in 1982, when the peso collapsed because of huge foreign debt, touching off an inflationary crisis and a severe recession that lasted for years. But Arango was confident enough of the future to buy back Jewel's share in the business (which he renamed Cifra in 1984) from its successor, American Stores Co., for about $53.4 million. He kept all existing stores open and retained its employees, although they were expected to work longer hours and those who left were not replaced.

Cifra's emphasis on discounting helped sustain the company during these dark years. Located in the poorer neighborhoods of Mexico City, the Bodega Aurrera stores, for example, stocked all types of nonperishable goods to the ceiling and offered prices as low as half those of other retailers. By the end of 1989 Cifra was in its best financial shape ever. It had grown in sales by 20 percent or more in every year of the decade. Its sales in 1989 were about $550 million, and its stock more than tripled in value during the year.

In 1990 Cifra's sales grew by 26 percent, and between 1990 and 1991 its stock shot up almost fivefold. At the end of 1991 there were 38 Almacenes Aurrera self-service department stores, selling general merchandise, clothing, and supermarket items. The high-income Superama chain consisted of 34 freestanding community supermarkets. Next came the 29 Bodega Aurrera discount warehouse stores and the 29 Suburbia family-oriented department stores, selling discount clothing and dry goods. The Vips restaurant operations consisted of 59 cafeterias, 15 El Porton restaurants (initiated in 1978), and four more specialized restaurants. Gran Bazar was the name for Cifra's hypermarkets, and Sigla for its real estate interests in opening new shopping centers.

In May 1992 Cifra announced that it intended to invest $211 million to open 12 new stores during the year and another $68 million to renovate 78 existing ones. The restaurants were modernized to attract new and younger customers. In addition, an investment of $80 million was to be made in such technological developments as information and point-of-sale systems, satellite-based communications, and complex data-processing units. By this time, the implementation of a computerized inventory-control system had made the company the leader in the industry for inventory management. Its point-of-sale systems allowed it to collect, analyze, and make use of vast amounts of data concerning consumer preferences and the effects of price changes. Cifra's sales per square foot were almost twice as high in 1992 as those of its competitors, and its liquidity in cash and equivalents as well as its inventory turnover were the highest in the industry.

Cifra's growth remained impressive in 1992. Twenty-three units were built that year. Sales rose by 20.7 percent to $3.7 billion. Operating profits increased by 32 percent during 1992. As much as 31 percent of the company's earnings came from interest income on its considerable cash surplus. An investor buying $1 of Cifra B shares at the start of 1988 had seen his investment reach $39.46 at the end of 1992. Sales in fiscal 1993 rose to $4.6 billion and were the best per square foot in Mexico.

Cifra formed two joint ventures with Wal-Mart in 1991. One, Commercializadora Mexico-Americana, promoted trade between Mexico and the United States. The other, Club Aurrera, was directed at small businesses and their employees and was patterned on Wal-Mart's Sam's Club. In fact, after a short period of time the Club Aurrera stores renamed Sam's Club. The first Club Aurrera opened late in 1991 and three more were opened in 1992. This joint venture was serving many customers wishing to buy in quantity. Like Sam's Club, Club Aurrera members-only stores typically offered just one brand of an item stacked to the rafters in cartons. The customer base was expected to include restaurants, discos, and clubs.

In May 1992 the Cifra-Wal-Mart joint venture was expanded to oversee all the new Almacenes Aurrera, Superama, Bodega, and Gran Bazar stores. The rationale behind this move was that Wal-Mart's technology and marketing know-how would fuel Cifra's growth to otherwise unattainable levels. One analyst also noted that it precluded the prospect of Wal-Mart forming links with another Mexican retailer or opening stores in Mexico on its own.

By June 1994 there were three Almacenes Aurrera stores, 18 Bodega stores, three Superama Supermarkets, two Suburbia stores, 11 Vips restuarants, ten Sam's Clubs, and three Wal-Mart Supercenters. combination stores. Wal-Mart had built three Supercenters in 1993 and early 1994, one of which, with 244,000 square feet, became the largest Wal-Mart Supercenter in the world. And a revision of the agreement added the field of collaboration to Cifra's restaurant and clothing-store divisions, previously excluded.

Wal-Mart's expertise was considered especially important in the creation of regional distribution centers. Because Cifra had concentrated on the Mexico City metropolitan area, it was relatively inexperienced in the efficient delivery of supplies to other cities, including Guadalajara, León, and Monterrey to the north and west and Villahermosa and Mérida to the south and east. During this time, the collaboration between Cifra and Wal-Mart was managed primarily by Mexican nationals in Mexico. Wal-Mart was contributing a few dozen Mexican expatriates to help out, but their roles were shifting increasingly to Mexican citizens as skills were passed on to local personnel, according to Bob Martin, president and chief executive officer of Wal-Mart International.

A prototype Almacenes Aurrera was erected in the Mexico City suburb of Las Auguilas. Executed by Fitch Inc. of Worthington, Ohio, the store featured white walls and color codes for the major merchandise categories. New fixtures allowed more prominent opportunities for display and highlighting than in the past, with red—Aurrera's signature color—drawing attention to new merchandise, sales items, and other promotions. Free-standing archways in the back corners were intended to draw customers to the perimeter. The parqueteria, an outside bottle-return, bag-check, and security checkpoint standard in Mexico, was sheltered to shield shoppers from the elements.

The creation of the North American Free Trade Agreement (NAFTA) at the beginning of 1994 deepened the collaboration between Cifra and Wal-Mart. In January 1994 the joint venture was extended to include all future Suburbia stores and Vip restaurants. And in October 1994 Cifra and Wal-Mart announced a 50–50 joint venture with Dillard Department Stores, Inc. to build and operate Dillard stores in Mexico. The first Dillard store was expected to open in Monterrey in late 1995.

In late 1994 Cifra was reportedly planning to invest heavily in the expansion of its store and restaurant chains. By that time the Cifra empire, by itself and in combination with Wal-Mart, consisted of 35 Almacenes Aurrera, 58 Bodegas Aurrera, 36 Superamas, 33 Suburbias, 22 Sam's Clubs, and 11 Wal-Mart stores, in addition to 114 Vips cafeterias and restaurants.

The mid-1990s presented some challenges for Cifra. The company's financial reportings for 1993 proved disappointing to many analysts, and the company's stock was trading at about 28 times estimated 1994 earnings, although a cost-cutting campaign helped the company's operating profits to climb 23 percent during the first quarter of 1994. A blow was then dealt to all publicly traded Mexican companies in 1994, when the value of shares on the Bolsa stock exchange experienced a sharp drop. Mexican stocks ended the year down by 44 percent. Finally, the devaluation of the peso in December 1994 triggered a financial panic, and during the first half of January 1995 Mexican stocks dropped another 28 percent. Wal-Mart and Cifra announced during the month that plans to open 24 new stores in Mexico during 1995 were "temporarily on hold" due to the country's economic conditions. Cifra representatives noted, however, that this decision did not affect the long term growth strategy of the joint venture, nor did it change the level of commitment by both partners in the association. Moreover, analysts noted that one point in favor of Cifra's future was its lack of foreign-currency debt.

Principal Subsidiaries: Controladora de Tiendas de Descuento; Cifra-Mart; Wal-Mart Holding Company Mexico; Comercializadora Mexico-Americana.

Further Reading:

"Cifra: Aiming to Be a Mexican Wal-Mart," *Euromoney,* May 1993, pp. 107–108.

"Cifra, SA," *Latin Finance,* November 1992, pp. 33–34.

"Merger of Merchandising Magnates," *Business Mexico,* June 1994, pp. 22–24.

Millman, Joel, "The Merchant of Mexico," *Forbes,* August 5, 1991, pp. 80–81.

Moffett, Matt, "Mexican Retailers Jockey for Position, Hoping to Win Big as Nation Recovers," *Wall Street Journal,* August 26, 1991, p. A4.

Sandler, Linda, "Retailer Cifra Lights Up Mexican Stock Market, But Its Spectacular Run-Up Raises Caution Flag," *Wall Street Journal,* September 9, 1991, p. C6.

Torres, Craig, "Mexican Retailer Cifra, with a High Multiple and Disappointing Results, Falls into Disfavor," *Wall Street Journal,* February 23, 1994, p. C2.

—Robert Halasz

**CINCINNATI
MILACRON**

Cincinnati Milacron Inc.

4701 Marburg Ave.
Cincinnati, Ohio 45209
U.S.A.
(513) 841-8100
Fax: (513) 841-8008

Public Company
Incorporated: 1884 as Cincinnati Screw and Tap Co.
Employees: 7,885
Sales: $1.02 billion
Stock Exchanges: New York
SICs: 3541 Machine Tools, Metal Cutting Types; 3559
    Special Industry Machinery, Not Elsewhere Classified;
    3823 Process Control Instruments; 3291 Abrasive Products

With the acquisition of German-based Krupp Widia GmbH in late November 1994, Cincinnati Milacron, Inc. became the third-largest player in the metal-cutting tool market. Commenting on the Widia acquisition in *The Cincinnati Enquirer,* Milacron chairperson and CEO Daniel J. Meyer expressed his expectation that Cincinnati Milacron would become "a premier global player in the market for industrial consumable products," which, he asserted, would become the company's primary focus. Milacron's industrial products were expected to make up 40 percent of its forecasted 1995 revenue of $1.5 billion. In 1994, industrial products accounted for 31 percent of revenue, while Milacron's other core businesses, plastics machinery and machine tools, accounted for 35 percent and 34 percent, respectively.

Cincinnati Milacron traces its roots to 1874, when George Mueller inherited his father's machine shop on Vine Street in Cincinnati and asked his friend, Fred Holz, to be his partner. Initially, the men maintained the elder Mueller's focus on manufacturing parts for sewing machines and repairing small machines. Gradually, however, they began building specialized machinery, including a device that produced screws and the taps and dies that cut threads for them. By 1876, the business was largely centered on manufacturing the screw machine, and Mueller and Holz renamed their business The Cincinnati Screw and Tap Company.

Around 1878, when the small company needed a new milling machine for the tap making business and could not afford one, Holz put his machinist background to work and built one with an improved basic design. Soon, other shops began requesting machines, and by 1882, Cincinnati Screw and Tap found itself adding milling machines to its product line. In 1884, the company became incorporated to raise the capital it needed to produce the more costly machines and to finance a move to a larger facility near the Ohio riverfront.

In 1887, Frederick A. Geier, while doing business with the Cincinnati Screw and Tap Co., became excited about this innovative company's potential. Within three months, Geier, then 21 years old, had bought interest in the company. While Holz concentrated on the technology side of the business, Geier focused his energy in the areas of organization and sales. Believing that a company should focus primarily on one product, Geier favored the production of the milling machine over the company's screw and tap business. In early 1889, the stockholders approved the sale of the screw and tap business to a group of employees. Holz, Mueller, and Geier all stayed with the milling machine business, which became the Cincinnati Milling Machine Company, or the Mill, as employees would come to call it. Two years later, co-founder Mueller would sell his one-third interest in the company and retire.

Although the milling machine industry had long been controlled by companies in the eastern United States, the Mill found its niche by emphasizing quality. In 1889, Holz built a cutter grinder that would help shops and factories save money by sharpening cutting tools so they would last much longer. This gave the company a new product to sell with its millers and helped to build the Mill's machine tooling reputation with its customers.

As early as the next year, the Mill had its first export order to a Swedish company. This was the beginning of an export business that would continue to grow and would, in fact, help keep the company afloat during times when the U.S. economy was troubled.

One of those troubling times occurred in 1893, when a sharp recession hit, and factories and machine shops stopped placing orders for new equipment. Sales were almost nonexistent, credit was unavailable, and, moreover, the Mill had its capital tied up in building a new plant on Spring Grove Avenue. Nevertheless, the company worked its way out from the slump by taking a chance. When an order for a dozen milling machines came in from a bicycle maker in Indianapolis, who was short of cash and would need nine months to pay, Geier called the employees together and asked them what they wanted to do. The employees decided to take the order; the bicycle maker received his 12 machines and paid for them. The Mill survived and by 1895 was again prosperous. Reportedly, throughout the 1890s, bicycle makers purchased almost half the machine tools made by the company.

During the early 1900s, Holz sold his common stock to Geier and retired from the company. Geier, who had already held controlling interest in the company, was looking to move the company again, this time to a site where the Mill could be as self-reliant as possible with its own foundry and power plant. By 1907, land had been purchased in the nearby community of Oakley, financing had been secured for the move, and work on the foundry was begun. The foundry and power plant were completed in 1908, and, by 1911, the new complex was complete and operational. The new plant had more than six acres of floor space and was the world's largest milling machine factory. Geier's timing had been perfect. The motor car was just becoming popular, and the Mill was ready to provide the tools that the industrial world needed.

The onset of World War I in 1914 brought with it an initially sluggish market for the Mill. However, once the Allies realized the war was going to last for a while, they began to turn to America for machine tools to gear up for war production. In 1916, the U.S. government began their own war-readiness program, which put even heavier demands on American industry, particularly on the machine tool makers. Sales for the Mill were $1.4 million in 1914, and grew to $7 million in 1917, while its work force increased from 310 to 1,270.

By the time the armistice was signed in November 1918 and the postwar return to "normalcy" had begun, however, government contracts were being cancelled, and the Mill found itself with a sudden excess capacity. In 1919, in an attempt to temper the cyclical nature of the business, Geier announced a plan to build a warehouse for storing the milling machines produced by the company until a time when orders exceeded capacity. As Geier sought to keep his employees in work year-round, and for the highest possible wages (a strategy known as "work-spreading"), Mill employees remained generally disinterested in forming unions or becoming involved in strikes during the labor union wars of the early 1920s.

Still, the economic climate during this time remained ominous, and, early in 1921, Geier announced to his workers that the company had out-produced sales by 66 percent. Specifically, the Mill had 561 machines on hand, unsold. The policy of paying employees to make machines that weren't selling did not make business sense, and changes had to be made. Management salaries were cut, and a 15 percent wage reduction was initiated. Employment fell from an average of 1,004 in 1920 to 250 in 1921.

In the midst of this economic downswing, Geier's son, Frederick V. Geier, convinced management that the company should branch out into the production of centertype grinding machines, devices that used wheels to grind metal into round or cylindrical precision parts, such as pistons, valve stems, and bearings. This move, the younger Geier contended, would help absorb overhead and more fully utilize plant capacity. In September 1921, the company bought controlling interest in the Cincinnati Grinder Co. and the following year moved production of the grinding machine to Oakley. In addition, the Mill obtained the rights to key patents on centerless grinding, and formed a subsidiary, Cincinnati Grinders, Inc. With the success of these machines, in 1926, Cincinnati Milling became the nation's largest machine tool company.

When the Great Depression hit, the Mill was able to rely on its export trade to carry it through. Exports, one-fifth of all sales in 1929, grew to represent one-third of sales in 1932. During this time, the Mill continued to "spread" work, keeping as many employees on the payroll as possible. Management also worked closely with the Mutual Aid Committee, which was founded in 1916 as an employee insurance association and used as a relief organization for those hardest hit during the Depression.

Changes occurred at the Mill during this era. Traditionally, the company had used agents and distributors to sell machines to customers. In 1931, after providing sales training for graduates of its co-op program with the University of Cincinnati, the Mill put some of its own sales staff in the field and began direct selling. The company formed a wholly owned sales subsidiary and opened offices in Detroit, Chicago, and Cleveland.

Moreover, instead of guarding its resources and waiting for better days, the Mill continued to invest in research and development. During this time, the company introduced hydraulic-powered machines, broaching machines, able to make finer and more precise cuts, and the Dial Type milling machine, which, with its power speed and feed change features, became the industry standard. In 1932, the Mill agreed with Heald Machine Co. of Worcester, Massachusetts, to share engineering, research, and patents. Although both companies produced grinding machines, their machines were used in different applications and therefore complemented one another. A little over 20 years later, after years of working together, the Mill would purchase Heald outright.

In 1934, Frederick A. Geier died of a heart attack. A month later, his son, Frederick V. Geier, was elected president of the company. One of the younger Geier's first projects was to establish a subsidiary in Great Britain to make machines for world markets. In fact, as World War II began, Britain became one of the Mill's major customers, buying $16.5 million worth of machines in 1940.

Because of the increased number of military orders before the war, the machine tool industry was prepared to meet demand once the United States began mobilizing forces. With forethought, the Mill had decided to expand the company's capacity in 1938 and had also began a formal three-stage training program for workers. This training program became invaluable, as the Mill's work force escalated to a wartime peak of 8,561 employees.

Throughout the war, the Mill continued its emphasis on research and development. It began exploring the physics of metalcutting as well as ways to increase tool life. Out of this research, came the Mill's first synthetic cutting fluid, called Cimcool.

In 1943, Geier began meeting regularly with four other key executives in an effort to identify strategies for postwar growth. According the official company history, *Cincinnati Milacron 1884–1984: Finding Better Ways,* the four goals the committee agreed upon were: "to extend overseas manufacturing; to broaden machinery product lines; to enter the industrial consumables market; and to develop new technologies." These goals for growth and diversification brought with them the task of finding a way to finance new company endeavors. In February 1946, the Mill raised $3.8 million in new capital when it issued its first public stock offering.

The next ten years brought a variety of acquisitions and the development of new product ideas. Some of these new products included: grinding wheels, cutting fluids, and lathes. In 1955, the Mill expanded its move into chemicals, acquiring a company that, among other things, made additives for plastic. By 1957, the Mill was working with glass reinforced plastic components and had formed the Cimastra division to oversee production and sales of the materials. This division began selling molded plastics to different companies, including manufacturers of children's sleds, seats for bowling alleys, and cases for movie projectors.

The 1950s also bore witness to the Mill's expansion in Europe. The company increased its holdings in England by acquiring and expanding plants and foundries in Birmingham and nearby Cannock. In 1952, the Mill began building a machine tool factory in the Netherlands that was completed in 1954.

The electronic era at the Mill began in the late 1950s, as the company became involved with a new technology called numerical control. Using numerically coded instructions on punch cards, the technology allowed computers to control the movements of machine tools and thus had great potential in automating American industry. In 1955, the Mill received a contract from the U.S. Air Force for numerically controlled machines that could produce intricate aircraft parts at high speed. The company continued to improve on its use of the technology, and in, 1966, the Mill introduced a new generation of controls for its machines using miniaturized integrated circuits, rather than the cumbersome vacuum tubes and mechanical relays it had relied on. Using its expertise in both plastics and electronics, the company also began producing plastic circuit boards that were used in TV sets, radios, and eventually computers.

As the 1960s came to a close, Cincinnati Milling found it had become a far more diverse company than its name indicated. In May 1970, the stockholders approved a new name. Cincinnati Milacron capitalized on the continued use of Cincinnati—a name linked with machine tools—while also introducing a new word, Milacron, the roots of which meant "highest precision." Thus, despite the name change, company employees could logically continue to refer to their company as the Mill.

The 1970s became a time of streamlining and redirection for the Mill. Frederick V. Geier retired from his position as chair of the executive committee in 1976 and was given the honorary title of director emeritus. His cousin, Philip O. Geier, Jr., who had served as the Mill's president and then chairperson, also retired during this time, leaving James A.D. Geier in charge as chairperson. Under Jim Geier, the company began focusing its machine tool efforts on computer-controlled equipment, and perhaps more importantly, a corporate research department was set up to look into non-machine tool products. As an outgrowth of this research, the Mill moved into the plastics machinery business. With expertise in injection molding and extrusion, the Mill worked with E.I. du Pont Co. to perfect a reheat blow molding machine that would revolutionize the way soft drinks were packaged. A fourth molding process called reaction injection molding was also introduced by the Mill. By 1977, the Mill was the largest U.S. maker of plastics machinery.

Also in the 1970s, the Mill intensified its focus on electronically operated machines, venturing into the markets for minicomputers and semiconductors. While its efforts to manufacture and market minicomputers proved disappointing and short-lived,

the company had more success with semiconductors, specifically in the development and manufacture of the silicon wafers on which semiconductors were built. Demand for the Mill's silicon epitaxial wafer prompted the company to provide its semiconductor materials division with its own facility in 1979, and, by 1984, the Mill had become the world's largest supplier of this type of wafer. Also during the late 1970s, the Mill unveiled the first commercially available CNC industrial robot, which became integral to assembly lines at such companies as Ford, General Electric, and Volvo, among others.

In 1980, the Mill sold its profitable specialty chemical operations to the Thiokol Corporation, in order to focus more closely on its three more closely allied divisions: machine tools, plastics machinery, and industrial specialty products. During the 1980s, the company felt the effects of a severe economic recession that became second only to the Great Depression in terms of loss in the capital goods markets. In addition, the Japanese were giving U.S. machine tool builders some severe competition. The Mill began cost cutting measures including plant consolidations and early retirement plans. Worldwide employment fell by one-third, and, in 1983, the company reported its first annual loss.

In fact, the Mill reported losses in five of the next ten years. Increasingly tough competition and misdirected business turns took their toll on the Mill. Nevertheless, in 1986, in the Mill's plastic division, a campaign began that would help fine tune the company for the 1990s. Called Project Wolfpack, this product redevelopment effort utilized the teamwork of employees from different disciplines to cut product development cycles and cost. According to an April 1992 article in *The Cincinnati Enquirer,* each team was charged with improving the quality of Milacron's machines while removing up to 40 percent of the cost and 40 percent of the components. The teams worked together to consider the market needs, feasibility of design concepts to operate machines of the size range being considered, and the availability of the latest technology to perform functions required. Harold Faig, vice-president of the U.S. Plastics Machinery Division said in *The Cincinnati Post* in May 1991, "Our single goal is to offer the best quality, American-made machines with the widest range of features at a competitive price."

The success of the Wolfpack, as well as moves to abandon or sell several money-losing businesses such as robots and semiconductors, helped the Mill return to profitability in 1992. Aligned with the Wolfpack's goals, the Mill committed itself to simpler, lower-priced, globally competitive tools. In 1993, excess capacity in machine tool facilities caused the Mill to consolidate operations. In October 1994, the Mill's plastic machinery plants in Ohio were named among the *Industry Week* magazine's ranking of the ten best plants in America for their performance, production, and customer satisfaction.

With the Wolfpack as its foundation, Cincinnati Milacron became a secure player in the world market. Its acquisitions in the 1990s set the pace so that almost half its revenue was expected to come from outside the United States in 1995. Its divisions each roughly represented one-third of the business, which evened out the cyclical nature of the business identified so long ago. Due to a continued emphasis on research and development, more than 75 percent of the Mill's 1993 machinery sales consisted of products not sold five years ago. In 1993's report to shareholders, Daniel J. Meyer, chairperson and CEO, and Raymond E. Ross, president and COO, stated, ''For the longer term we believe that improved efficiencies in our U.S. machine tool operations . . . and in our European plastics machinery marketing organization, will help Milacron achieve good profit growth throughout the rest of the 1990s.''

Principal Subsidiaries: Cincinnati Milacron-Holdings Mexico SA de CV; Cincinnati Milacron-Mexican Sales SA de CV; Cincinnati Milacron Marketing Co.; Cincinnati Milacron Commercial Corp.; Cincinnati Milacron International Marketing Co.; COGE A.G.; Cincinnati Milacron Holding Gesellschaft GmbH; Cincinnati Milacron Austria Gesellschaft GmbH; Cincinnati Milacron Kunststoffmaschinen Europa GmbH; Ferromatik Milacron Maschinenbau GmbH; Cincinnati Milacron U.K. Holdings Co.; Cincinnati Milacron U.K. Ltd.; Cincinnati Milacron-Korea Corp.; Mandelli/Cincinnati Milacron Aerospace SRL (50%); Cincinnati Milacron Assurance Ltd.; Cincinnati Milacron BV; Cimcool Europe BV; Cimcool Industrial Products BV; Cincinnati Milacron-Canada Ltd.; Cincinnati Milacron-Herald Corp.; Cincinnati Milacron Resin Abrasives Inc.; Cincinnati Milacron SRL; Factory Power Co. (82.2%); Cincinnati Milacron-Sano Inc.; Valenite Inc.; Valenite-Modco International Inc.; Nippon Valenite-Modco KK; Valenite-Modco PTE. Ltd.; Valenite-Modco SARL; Valenite-Modco (U.K.) Ltd.; Valenite-Modco SRL; Valenite-Modco GmbH; Valenite-Modco Ltd.; Valenite de Mexico SA de CV; Valenite-Modco Industria E Comercio Ltda.

Further Reading:

Boehmer, Mike, ''Milacron to Build German Plant,'' *The Greater Cincinnati Business Record,* May 14, 1990, p. 1.
Boyer, Mike, ''Milacron, Hounded by Foreign Competition, Unleashes Wolves,'' *The Cincinnati Enquirer,* April 20, 1992, pp. 1D, 5D.
Boyer, Mike, ''Milacron to Acquire Krupp Widia,'' *The Cincinnati Enquirer,* November 30, 1994, p. 6B.
Cincinnati Milacron 1884–1984: Finding Better Ways, Cincinnati: Cincinnati Milacron, Inc., 1984, 218 p.
Rawe, Dick, ''Milacron Unveils Latest in Plastics Machines,'' *The Cincinnati Post,* May 29, 1991, p. 6A.
Rhodes, Gary, ''Milacron Wins National Award,'' *The Cincinnati Post,* October, 24, 1994, p. 1D.
Rhodes, Gary, ''Plastics Boosting Milacron,'' *The Cincinnati Post,* April 27, 1994, p. 6D.
Schiller, Zachary, ''One Takes The High-End Road, The Other Takes the Low,'' *Business Week,* May 18, 1992, pp. 100–101.
Smock, Doug, ''Milacron Places Its Bets on Electric Machines,'' *Plastics World,* July 1994, pp. 6–7.

—Jennifer Voskuhl Canipe

Colt's Manufacturing Company, Inc.

P.O. Box 1868
Hartford, Connecticut 06144-1868
U.S.A.
(203) 236-6311
Fax: (203) 244-1366

Private Company
Incorporated: 1855 as Colt's Patent Fire Arms
  Manufacturing Company
Employees: 925
Sales: $100 million
SICs: 3484 Small Arms

Colt's Manufacturing Company, Inc. is one of the world's most famous manufacturers of firearms. Weapons made by Colt have played a part in every war involving the United States since the middle of the 19th century, and the Colt revolver, invented by company founder Samuel Colt, is known widely as "the gun that won the West." In addition to its revolvers, the company makes a wide variety of other firearms, including pistols, shotguns, and machine guns. Its M16 line of combat weapons is used by military units all over the world. Founded in 1836, Colt's is one of the oldest companies in Connecticut. The company manufactured 145,000 guns in 1990, making it the seventh largest gun producer in the United States.

Samuel Colt's invention of the revolver represented a major improvement over the flintlock pistols that were the best available until the 1830s. Colt was only 18 years old when he applied for the patent for his revolver in 1832. When the patent was finally approved four years later, Colt immediately opened his first plant with the assistance and backing of his uncle, a successful local businessman. The company was called the Patent Arms Manufacturing Company and located in Paterson, New Jersey. Initially, three revolver models (pocket, belt, and holster) and two rifles (hammer-cocked and finger lever) were offered. Although the first generation of Colt guns performed well, the public apparently had doubts about such an unfamiliar concept in gun technology. Sales remained slow for several years, and Patent Arms Manufacturing Company was out of business by 1842.

When U.S. Dragoon forces and Texas Rangers began battling Indians in Texas in 1845, the Colt company was given its second chance at success. Using Colt firearms, the Rangers and

Dragoon fighters defeated the Indians. The U.S. War Department took notice of the superior performance of the Colt guns. As a result, the Army sent Captain Samuel Walker to collaborate with Colt on an improved design when war broke out with Mexico the following year. The Government immediately ordered 1,000 of the new revolver, known as the "Walker Colt." Since Colt did not have a factory at the time, he contracted with Eli Whitney, Jr., the famous inventor's son, for the use of his New Haven, Connecticut factory.

With the successful completion of the government order, Colt was able to set up a new factory of his own in his home town of Hartford, Connecticut. Colt guns quickly became the weapon of choice for such diverse groups as California miners and foreign statesmen. Even at this early stage, Colt demonstrated a genius for marketing and public relations, hiring military officers to promote his guns in other regions, and actively lobbying government officials. By 1851, Colt had set up a factory in England (the first American manufacturer to do so), and work had begun on a larger facility in Hartford. The new plant was completed in 1855, the same year the company was incorporated as Colt's Patent Fire Arms Manufacturing Company. Within two years, Colt's was making 150 guns a day, and Samuel Colt was a millionaire.

Samuel Colt died suddenly in 1862, but the company he founded continued to surge. Colt's widow, Elizabeth Jarvis Colt, and her family maintained control of the company through the rest of the 19th century. From 1865 to 1901, Colt's brother-in-law, Richard Jarvis, served as company president. The Civil War brought huge government purchases to Colt's. In 1867 the company began manufacturing the famous hand-cranked Gatling machine gun. The Colt single action Army Model, a six-shot .45 caliber revolver, was first produced in 1873. That gun gained a huge following almost immediately, and was the model that went down in history as "the gun that won the West."

Many additional models were added to the Colt line during the 1880s, including double-action revolvers, hammerless shotguns, pump action rifles, and revolvers with cylinders that swung out to make loading easier. In 1891, Colt's relationship with inventor John Browning began. The Colt-Browning machine gun, which became known as the "Peacemaker", was first produced in 1895. It eventually replaced the Gatling gun as the top Colt machine gun. Around the same time, Browning began developing a line of automatic pistols for Colt's, and he continued working on new guns for the company for a few more decades.

In 1901, Mrs. Colt sold the company to a group of outside investors based in New York and New England. She died four years later. Under its new management, the company continued to produce guns for the government in huge numbers. Browning developed the Colt 45 automatic pistol in 1911. One of the most popular guns of all time, the Colt 45 was the standard issue sidearm for American troops in both World Wars. It also saw action in later military conflicts, and was a huge success commercially as well. The U.S. Government alone purchased 2.5 million Colt 45 pistols over the years. When the United States entered into World War I in 1917, business boomed to its highest levels yet for Colt's. The company's Browning Automatic Rifle became a big seller to the government. During the war, Colt's workforce swelled to 10,000 people. The company's revenue tripled in the last three years of World War I, and profits soared accordingly.

With the end of the war, Colt's sought to diversify in order to keep production at a high level in the face of shrinking demand for weapons. Printing presses, commercial dishwashers, and plastics were among the products the company began manufacturing after the war. Browning's last invention, an anti-aircraft cannon, came in 1921. Two years later, the company established an electrical division that made, among other things, fuses. Meanwhile, Colt's continued selling guns wherever they were needed.

Like many manufacturing companies, Colt's was devastated by the 1929 stock market crash and the Great Depression that followed. Revolver sales dropped below their pre-World War I levels, and many workers were laid off. A series of events in the second half of the 1930s battered the company even further. In 1935 a bitter and sometimes violent strike took place at the Colt's armory, lasting 13 weeks. A flood in 1936 and a hurricane in 1938 filled the Colt's factory with mud and water and inflicted huge monetary losses on the company.

World War II brought with it huge new government orders for weapons, creating another boom period for Colt's. By 1942, the company's workforce had tripled to 15,000. Those employees worked three shifts, seven days a week at three plants. In spite of the large numbers of pistols and machine guns being turned out for the war effort, Colt's struggled to remain profitable during that last few years of the war. The 1941 unionization of Colt's employees had dramatically increased the company payroll. In addition, production techniques were becoming outmoded. The inexperience of the quickly growing workforce also contributed to efficiency problems. Amazingly, the company was losing money by the later stages of the war. Production was sagging due to ancient machinery, layoffs, and labor squabbles.

When World War II ended, Colt's government orders dried up, leaving the company's finances in shambles. Operating now under the name of Colt's Manufacturing Company, the company spent the postwar years frantically searching for ways to cut costs and improve manufacturing efficiency. The Korean War in the early 1950s provided a rush of business for Colt's, but the surge was only temporary. By the middle of the decade, the company was once again losing money. With losses mounting by the month, Colt's began actively looking for a prospective buyer for the company. In 1955 Colt's was purchased by Penn-Texas Corporation, a holding company controlled by Leopold Silberstein, and one of the first conglomerates.

For the rest of the 1950s, Colt's operated as a wholly owned subsidiary of Penn-Texas. Silberstein lost control of Penn-Texas in 1958, and a year later Penn-Texas changed its name to Fairbanks Whitney, following its acquisitions of two larger companies, Pratt & Whitney, a Connecticut manufacturer; and Fairbanks Morse Company, a diesel engine firm based in Chicago. A major overhaul of the parent company's management in 1964 resulted in yet another name change. Although Colt's represented only a small fraction of the conglomerate's busi-

ness, the name chosen was Colt Industries, and Colt's became the Firearms Division.

The escalation of the Vietnam conflict in the 1960s brought a new rush of business for the Firearms Division of Colt Industries. The M-16 rifle, developed by Colt in 1959, soon became the standard issue for U.S. armed forces. The first big government order for M-16s came in 1963, when the Air Force agreed to purchase 25,000 of the rifles. By 1966 the Division had 1,600 employees, nearly half of them engaged in putting together M-16s. The company delivered its one millionth M-16 rifle in 1969. That year, the Division was divided into two separate units, one for military production and one for small arms.

When Vietnam began winding down in the early 1970s, Colt was again faced with the pressures of adjusting for peacetime production. The company began to focus more attention on sporting guns, and in 1970, rifles and revolvers for sport generated $17 million in revenue. Around the same time, interest in classic Colt guns as collector's items began to climb. In order to capitalize on this emerging market, the company established its Custom Gun Shop in 1976. The Custom Gun Shop specialized in producing replicas of famous historic Colt guns, such as the ones presented by Samuel Colt to Czar Nicholas I of Russia and to the Sultan of Turkey in the 1850s. By the end of the 1970s, the Custom Gun Shop was generating annual sales of $3 million. For 1977, Colt's Firearms Division recorded $11 million in profit on sales of $77 million, trailing only Winchester, Remington, and Smith & Wesson in volume. Orders from the U.S. Government, however, dried up almost completely that year, and the Division's sales and profits lagged for the rest of the decade.

The slump at the Colt Firearms Division continued into the 1980s. Military demand was still depressed, and Colt was also continuing to lose ground to competitors in the law enforcement market, long one of its most important outlets. In 1982 and 1983 the company laid off 700 employees, half of its total workforce. Rumors of the Division's imminent demise began to circulate. Labor problems made matters even worse. In 1986 workers represented by the United Auto Workers (UAW) began a strike that eventually became the longest in Connecticut history. The company continued operating with replacement workers. Colt suffered a huge blow in 1988 when it lost out to FN Manufacturing Co., a subsidiary of a Belgian company, in the bidding for the U.S. Army contract to make M-16s, its bread-and-butter product. That year, parent Colt Industries went private, with ownership consolidated into the hands of Colt Holdings Inc., a newly created holding company. The Firearms Division was put up for sale soon after.

CF Holding Corporation, a group of private investors led by Shared Technologies Inc. chairman Anthony Autorino, purchased the Firearms Division in 1989 for about $100 million. The newly independent company was christened Colt's Manufacturing Company, Inc., the same name it had carried for a period after World War II. The company quickly resolved the lingering strike, reinstating striking workers and giving the UAW three seats on the board of directors. As part of the transaction, a Connecticut state pension fund paid $25 million for 47 percent ownership of Colt's. With new management intact and labor disputes under control for the time being, Colt's set out to win back some of its lost police business and stake out more ground in the sporting gun market.

Sales remained hard to come by in the early 1990s, however. Colt handguns had a difficult time finding a niche in a market flooded with cheap handguns and more sophisticated semi-automatic weapons. Colt products were considered either too expensive or too old-fashioned by many police departments and other potential buyers. Under the burden of a growing debt load, Colt's filed for Chapter 11 bankruptcy protection in 1992. While in bankruptcy, the company took measures to streamline its operations while updating its manufacturing equipment. Colt's suffered a setback in 1993 when the semi-automatic, military-styled Sporter—the company's best selling rifle—was banned in Connecticut, its home state.

In spite of that ban and potential bans in other states, Colt's was able to emerge from bankruptcy in 1994 when it was purchased by a partnership headed by the New York investment firm Zilkha & Company. The partnership acquired an 85 percent stake in Colt's. Whether Colt's new ownership can return the company to the exalted position it once held among gunmakers remains to be seen. Even during one of the most humble periods of its business history, the Colt name continues to evoke a sense of historical import and a great deal of respect among gun enthusiasts, regardless of the difficulties the company has encountered in recent times.

Further Reading:

Bryant, Adam, "Colt's in Bankruptcy Court Filing," *New York Times,* March 20, 1992, p. 1D.
——, "Colt's New Chief Likes to Fix Businesses," *New York Times,* May 15, 1992, p. 5D.
"Colt's Manufacturing is Officially Out of Chapter 11," *New York Times,* October 1, 1994, p. 19.
"Firm to Sell Firearms Unit to Some Private Investors," *Wall Street Journal,* November 29, 1989, p. 5B.
Grant, Ellsworth S., *The Colt Legacy,* Providence, R.I.: Mowbray Company, 1982.
Johnson, Kirk, "Crying Betrayal in Hartford, Colt Faces Uncertain Future," *New York Times,* June 12, 1993, p. 1.
Manges, Michelle, "Connecticut State Pension Fund Buys 47% Holding in a Firearms Company," *Wall Street Journal,* March 23, 1990, p. 14.
Verespej, Michael A., "Colt's New Rider," *Industry Week,* October 1, 1990, p. 14.
Wilson, R. L., *The Colt Heritage,* New York: Simon and Schuster, 1979.

—Robert R. Jacobson

Columbia TriStar Motion Pictures Companies

Sony Pictures Entertainment
10202 West Washington Boulevard
Culver City, California 90232-3195
U.S.A.
(310) 280-7128
Fax: (310) 280-1509

Division of Sony Corporation
Incorporated: 1924 as Columbia Pictures Corporation
Employees: 6,000
Sales: $3.18 billion
SICs: 7812 Motion Picture & Video Production

Columbia TriStar Motion Pictures Companies is part of Sony Pictures Entertainment Inc. (SPE), a global operation involved in motion picture production and distribution, television programming and syndication, home video distribution, and several other areas of the entertainment business. As the motion picture segment of SPE, Columbia TriStar held an average of 17 percent of the domestic box office market between 1990 and 1995, producing such popular films as *Sleepless in Seattle, A Few Good Men, Philadelphia,* and *In the Line of Fire.* Under the Sony Corporation corporate umbrella, Columbia TriStar Motion Picture Companies consisted of the popular film companies Columbia Pictures and TriStar Pictures; Sony Pictures Classics, a company specializing in acquiring, marketing, and distributing foreign and independent films; Triumph Films, specializing in films that further diversified SPE's motion picture roster; and Columbia TriStar Film Distributors International, which focused on the distribution of SPE's motion pictures.

The history of Columbia TriStar Motion Pictures may be traced through the founding of Columbia Pictures Entertainment Inc., which was incorporated in 1924 as Columbia Pictures Corporation. Hollywood in the 1920s was a booming entertainment factory. As the film industry began to realize its vast potential, ornate moviehouses were erected throughout American cities and towns, and cinema became the nation's new favorite pastime. Hollywood's production studios grew rapidly and opportunities for filmmakers abounded.

It was in this environment, in 1918, that independent producer Harry Cohn, his brother Jack, and their associate Joe Brandt started the CBC Film Sales Company with a $100,000 loan. By 1924 the little company on Hollywood's "Poverty Row" had made its presence known. The company changed its name to Columbia Pictures Corporation and began a period of growth that would rank it among the major studios within ten years.

Columbia was ruled somewhat autocratically by its brash founder, Harry Cohn, for more than 30 years. Cohn, the son of immigrant parents, began his career in film in 1918 as the secretary to Carl Laemmle, a founder of Universal Studios. By the mid-1920s Cohn had gained a reputation as one of the industry's toughest businessmen. He ran Columbia's Hollywood film production unit while his brother Jack and Joe Brandt handled financial matters in New York. In 1926 Columbia purchased a small lot on Gower Street that had two stages and a small office building; the move improved the company's status among the small motion picture studios.

Cohn slowly built Columbia during the 1920s by enticing talent from other studios to join his operation. He reduced costs in production by refining out-of-sequence shooting, in which scenes with high-priced stars were filmed one after another whether they followed one another in the narrative or not. Under this method, stars were not left idle on the payroll while scenes they were not needed for were shot. By the end of the decade Columbia was considered a major studio, although a lesser one. At the time, Hollywood was dominated by the "big five"—Warner Brothers, RKO, Twentieth Century Fox, MGM, and Paramount—and the "little three—Universal, United Artists, and Columbia.

By the late 1920s a power struggle had begun to develop between the New York and Hollywood operations of the company, culminating in an unsuccessful attempt by Jack Cohn and Joe Brandt to wrest control of the studio from Harry Cohn. In 1932 Joe Brandt resigned as company president and sold his shares in the company, leaving Harry Cohn to become the first executive in Hollywood to serve as production head and president at the same time. Jack Cohn stayed on as vice-president and treasurer, but the feud with his brother was never mended, and gradually Harry became virtually omnipotent at the studio.

In 1929, Columbia produced its first "talkie" feature film, *The Donovan Affair.* The film was directed by Frank Capra, the man who would prove to be Columbia's most valuable asset in the years to come, and met with both critical acclaim and financial success.

The Great Depression had different effects on different studios. Columbia, which did not have the theater holdings the Big Five had, didn't feel the impact of empty theater seats in the early 1930s. And when theater attendance picked up, Columbia found it had one very special asset—Frank Capra.

Capra's view of the world seemed to strike a chord with the average theater-goer during the difficult years of the Depression. His films glorified the common man, the unlikely hero who beat the odds. Films like *It Happened One Night, Mr. Deeds Goes to Town, You Can't Take it With You,* and *Mr. Smith Goes to Washington* firmly placed Capra and Columbia Pictures within the Hollywood establishment.

Throughout the late 1930s and the 1940s, Columbia made many "B" movies—lower budget films that often served as the supporting feature at a theater. About 70 percent of Columbia's annual roster of between 50 and 60 pictures were B movies, including the highly successful *Blondie, Boston Blackie,* and *Lone Wolf* series. The so-called "srewball comedy" became Columbia's standard fare during the era.

Columbia continued to pump out motion pictures throughout the war years. Between 1940 and 1946 revenues doubled and profits increased sixfold. After the war, however, cinema in the United States was faced with a serious crisis: television. As the number of small screens in American living rooms increased, the number of paid admissions to the big screens plummeted. Columbia was the first studio to react to the new medium. In 1948 the studio launched a TV subsidiary, Screen Gems, which began to produce TV shows in 1952. In addition to producing new programs like "Rin Tin Tin," "Captain Midnight," and "Father Knows Best," the Screen Gems subsidiary sold the rights to old Columbia films for television broadcast. Meanwhile, gimmicks like Cinemascope, which emphasized the largeness of the theater, were undertaken with limited success. Nevertheless, a number of big hits in the 1950s, including *From Here to Eternity, The Caine Mutiny,* and *On the Waterfront,* helped Columbia thrive.

In 1958 Harry Cohn died. Some 1,300 people attended his funeral, which was held on a Columbia soundstage. Over the years Cohn had become one of the most despised men in Hollywood, and it was quipped that the large congregation at the funeral had come not to bid farewell but to make sure he was actually dead. Cohn had cultivated his image as a tyrant, keeping a riding whip near his desk and occasionally cracking it for emphasis, and Columbia had the greatest creative turnover of any major studio due largely to Cohn's methods. Yet even Cohn's enemies acknowledged his knack for running a profitable studio.

Cohn was succeeded by Abe Schneider, who had come to Columbia in the late 1920s as an accountant. The company, like other Hollywood studios, struggled to turn a profit in the early 1960s. Theater attendance had dropped drastically since the golden era of the 1930s and 1940s, and without the success of the Screen Gems unit, Columbia would have been in serious trouble. Several box office hits in the early 1960s provided even bigger returns with television broadcast—in 1966 the rights to *The Bridge On the River Kwai* alone brought $2 million for two showings on ABC. *Lawrence of Arabia, Suddenly Last Summer,* and *The Guns of Navarone* promised big payoffs as well.

In 1966 a takeover attempt threatened Columbia's management. Maurice Clairmont, a well-known corporate raider, attempted to gain a controlling interest in the company; when he failed to do so on his own, he combined forces with the Banque de Paris et de Pays-Bas, which owned 20 percent of Columbia, to acquire a majority of shares and snatch control of the company from Abe Schneider. But the Communications Act of 1934 prohibited foreign ownership of more than one-fifth of an American company with broadcasting holdings, and Columbia's Screen Gems unit at the time held a number of TV stations. The Federal Communications Commission allowed the French bank to buy more shares but prohibited it from "any action looking toward

an assertion of control by it alone or in concert with any other person over Columbia," effectively thwarting Clairmont's efforts to oust Schneider.

Columbia had a string of film successes in the late 1960s including *Oliver!; Guess Who's Coming to Dinner; To Sir, With Love; Divorce American Style;* and *In Cold Blood.* In 1969 *Easy Rider,* starring Peter Fonda, Dennis Hopper, and Jack Nicholson, was made for $400,000 and grossed $25 million for the studio.

But the early 1970s were devoid of box office successes. By 1973 the company had to impose strict cost-cutting measures after losses of $82 million in three years. In July 1973, Alan J. Hirschfield took over as president and CEO of Columbia. Hirschfield had formerly been with the Wall Street investment-banking firm of Allen & Company, which had gained a substantial interest in Columbia.

In August of that year former talent agent David Begelman was brought in to head the motion picture division. Begelman oversaw a number of successful projects, including *Funny Lady, Shampoo, Tommy, The Deep,* and *Close Encounters of the Third Kind.* Begelman, however, brought disgrace to himself and embarrassment to Columbia in 1977 when it was discovered that he had misappropriated about $60,000 in corporate funds. His offenses included cashing a $10,000 check made out to actor Cliff Robertson. The board of directors suspended Begelman in July, and then in December reinstated him. Public outcry over his reinstatement compelled him to resign two months later, but not until after he had landed a lucrative three-year contract as an independent producer. Alan Hirschfield temporarily took over as head of the motion picture unit, but it was clear that his talents lay in finance, not motion picture production. By July 1978 Hirschfield was replaced by Francis T. Vincent, an attorney with no experience in film. The decision to replace Hirschfield was less obvious than the one to remove Begelman, but some speculated that some board members felt that Hirschfield had not shown appropriate gratitude to Begelman through public support in his moment of crisis; the company had, after all, jumped in net worth from $4 million to $130 million since Begelman joined Columbia (although at least some of the credit belonged to Hirschfield, who secured new forms of financing). Other speculation centered on Hirschfield's desire to merge with the toy manufacturer Mattel, a move which would have diluted the equity of Columbia's major shareholders.

As Columbia entered the 1980s, changes in the entertainment business provided new opportunities as well as new challenges. The early 1980s saw the significant development of cable TV and home videotape recorders. At first seen as a threat to the movies, these new outlets eventually bolstered demand for product.

In 1981 Columbia narrowly escaped a hostile bid from Las Vegas financier Kirk Kerkorian. The federal government reportedly frowned on the move because Kerkorian owned a controlling interest in MGM at the time, and his acquisition of Columbia would have violated antitrust statutes.

In 1982 Columbia Pictures was purchased by The Coca-Cola Company in a stock and cash deal worth some $700 million.

With Coca-Cola as a parent, Columbia changed in a number of ways. The studio used even more market research on film ideas than it had before. Columbia also benefited from the greater efficiencies that Coke's volume discounts on advertising could provide.

Also in 1982 Columbia joined CBS and Home Box Office to launch a new motion picture studio called TriStar Pictures. For five years the fledgling studio pumped out hits and expanded its holdings. TriStar earned hefty sums through the distribution of movies like *Rambo: First Blood Part II* and *The Natural.* In 1985 the company offered its shares to the public. Although response was at first lukewarm, 43 percent of TriStar was eventually sold to the public. The company began to branch out in late 1986 when it purchased the Loews theater chain for $295 million. It also took over video cassette distribution of its own films.

Management changes at the studio in the mid-1980s seemed to hinder Columbia's performance. The studio had changed leadership four times since Coca-Cola purchased it and hadn't had a major hit since *Ghostbusters* earned $200 million in 1984. To make matters worse, as president of the motion picture unit during 1986, British producer David Puttnam (best known for the Academy Award-winning *Chariots of Fire*) complained of overpriced talent and inflated egos and tried to buck Hollywood's well-established star system. As a well-intentioned outsider, Puttnam's attempt to inject a bit of reality into the glamour capital of the world proved a miserable failure for Columbia.

In 1987 The Coca-Cola Company board decided to merge Columbia with TriStar to form Columbia Pictures Entertainment, Inc. TriStar's Victor Kaufman became president and CEO of the new company. Also in 1987, Dawn Steel was brought in from Paramount to replace Puttnam. While Steel lured back Hollywood's top talent, the studio continued to struggle to find a hit. In 1988, Columbia's share of domestic box office receipts fell to a dismal 3.5 percent. In spite of the relatively solid performance of subsidiaries Columbia Pictures Television and Merv Griffin Enterprises, Columbia registered a $104 million loss for 1988. In 1989, Columbia released the highly successful *When Harry Met Sally,* but while prospects looked better, the company still struggled to find the cash flow to finance more productions.

Then, in late 1989, Columbia entered into an agreement with Sony USA, Inc., a subsidiary of Japan's Sony Corporation, for the purchase of all Columbia's outstanding stock. With the completion of that transaction in November 1989, Columbia joined the ranks of media and entertainment companies throughout the world that had combined to create huge enterprises. Under the leadership of newly appointed co-chairmen Peter Guber and Jon Peters, Columbia faced the challenges of the global media market of the 1990s on firmer footing. Sony assumed Columbia's $1 billion debt and by 1991 the studio was earning an operating profit, but continued to post a loss after taxes and other costs were taken into account.

The majority of Columbia's profits came from its television division which generated about $240 million in operating profits in 1992—almost double the amount generated by all the company's other divisions, according to industry analysts. They were quick to note, however, that the majority of this $240 million was earned by syndication of older television programs such as "Married . . . With Children" and "Who's the Boss?" From 1988 to 1991, not one of Columbia's new television series was successful; and this was after the company negotiated contracts totalling over $100 million with top name writers and producers. Sensing that the company might be facing an unprofitable future, Alan Levine, president of Sony Pictures Entertainment, stepped in and made some changes.

Levine's first move was to launch a third television production unit through acquiring a large portion of an independent company called New World Entertainment. He also made some executive changes, replacing Gary Liberthal, the president of Columbia Pictures Television, with Mel Harris, an executive with Paramount known for his ability to spice up ailing production companies. Levine also cut the amount paid to writers and producers to about $20 million, 50 percent less than what the company paid in 1991.

But as Columbia's television unit began slipping, both Columbia Pictures and TriStar began to enjoy some box office success. TriStar's *Terminator 2: Judgement Day* was the highest grossing film of the year in 1991, with over $200 million in box office receipts in the United States alone. The success of other films such as *The Prince of Tides, My Girl,* and *Boyz in the Hood,* provided Columbia and TriStar with a combined market share of 20 percent, the highest in the industry.

Sony also formed another subsidiary, Columbia TriStar Home Video, a video distribution operation which gave the company an entry into the lucrative video market. Within two years, Columbia TriStar Home Video captured the top position in the worldwide video market, fueled by the success of Columbia and TriStar's recent releases and supported by Sony's already strong international distribution system.

By 1993, although they remained Sony's leading motion picture companies, Columbia and TriStar had become fully assimilated into Sony Pictures Entertainment. Columbia's one-time subsidiary Merv Griffin Enterprises became an independent branch of Sony Pictures and Columbia Pictures Television Distribution also became an independent arm of Sony Pictures, handling the syndication of Castle Rock's smash television series "Seinfeld," as well as Columbia Television's "Designing Women" and "Married . . . With Children." Columbia TriStar International Television was also created in 1993 and began producing German versions of television series such as "Who's the Boss?" and "Married . . . With Children" for distribution on the RTL network.

Although Columbia had lost some of its independence with the Sony acquisition, it had gained the capital and the management resources necessary to reignite box office sales. In 1988, Columbia/TriStar posted a $104 million loss. A few years later, the duo held almost 20 percent of the film market and grossed $1.7 billion in box office receipts. Columbia TriStar Television and Columbia TriStar Television Distribution also seemed to profit from Sony's capable management and international marketing expertise.

Nevertheless, in the mid-1990s, Columbia and TriStar again struggled, as their box office share dropped by nearly half in 1994 and film production for 1995 slowed considerably. In addition, Gruber and Peters left the studio in early 1994. In November 1994 Sony, which had invested an estimated $8 billion in its Hollywood studios over the past five years, announced that it would take a loss of $3.2 billion on the value of its Hollywood studios, reducing their book value by $2.7 billion. During this time, industry analysts speculated that Sony might sell an interest in Columbia and TriStar.

Further Reading:

Grover, Ronald, ''Sonywood Babylon,'' *Business Week,* June 20, 1994, p. 40

Harris, Kathryn, ''Living Off Its Past,'' *Forbes,* April 13, 1992, p. 56.

Landler, Mark, and Ronald Grover, ''Sony's Heartaches in Hollywood,'' *Business Week,* December 5, 1994, p. 44.

Masters, Kim, ''Sony's Hollywood Headache,'' *Vanity Fair,* April 1994, pp. 126–31.

McClintick, David, *Indecent Exposure,* New York: William Morrow, 1982.

Stanley, Robert, *The Celluloid Empire: A History of the American Movie Industry,* New York: Hastings House, 1978.

Sterngold, James, ''Sony, Struggling, Takes a Huge Loss on Movie Studios,'' *New York Times,* November 18, 1994, p. A1.

——, ''Tortoise, Hare, and Corporate Japan,'' *New York Times,* November 21, 1994, p. D1.

Weinraub, Bernard, ''Turmoil and Indecision at Sony's Film Studios,'' *New York Times,* October 24, 1994, p. D1.

—Tom Tucker
—updated by Maura Troester

Commercial Federal Corporation

2120 S. 72nd Street
Omaha, Nebraska 68124
U.S.A.
(402) 554-9200

Public Company
Incorporated: 1887 as South Omaha Loan and Building
    Association
Total Assets: $5.8 billion
Employees: 1,201
Stock Exchanges: NASDAQ
SICs: 6035 Savings Institutions, Federally Chartered; 6162
    Mortgage Bankers and Loan Correspondents 6211 Security
    Brokers, Dealers and Flotation Companies 6411 Insurance
    Agents, Brokers and Service 6712 Offices of Bank
    Holding Companies

Commercial Federal Corporation is the largest financial institution based in Nebraska and is that state's largest business overall. Through an aggressive acquisition program, the company extended its operations to Colorado, Kansas, and Oklahoma during the 1980s. Following the period of economic malaise generally characterizing the savings and loan (thrift) industry as a whole in 1989 and 1990, Commercial Federal rebounded and was again expanding its operations in the mid-1990s. In 1992 Commercial Federal ranked seventh among public thrifts based on five-year average return on equity and tenth based on profits per employee. Moreover, the company was among the 17 largest thrift institutions in the nation in 1994.

The history of Commercial Federal may be traced to the 1880s, when a group of Omaha businessmen bought land just south of the city limits, near the new Union Stockyards then under construction. In 1887, only a year after the village was incorporated, the South Omaha Loan and Building Association was opened. It was a mutual (depositor-owned) savings association, with voting privileges for all who subscribed for five shares at $200 a share. Customers paid for their shares through a regular savings plan and, to encourage regular saving, were fined if they missed a monthly payment. Once payments and interest reached $200 a share, the saver could then exchange the five shares for $1,000. A customer whose payments had reached one quarter to one-third of the value of the shares could pledge them for a mortgage on a $2,000 home.

One of the savings and loan's early customers was an Irish immigrant named James J. Fitzgerald. In 1893 Fitzgerald was elected to the board of directors. Five years later he quit his job in a packing plant to become secretary-manager of the association at a salary of $60 a month. By 1910 the association was prosperous enough to establish an office in downtown Omaha and changed its name to the Commercial Savings and Loan Association. When South Omaha was annexed by Omaha in 1915, however, the association closed the downtown office and used the savings to purchase its own three-story office building.

By 1929 Commercial's assets had grown from the original $10,000 to $4 million. Under the impact of the Great Depression, however, assets fell to $2.1 million in 1935. During this bleak period, the thrift institution made every effort to avoid foreclosing on the property of its borrowers, in order to maintain good customer relations and because land sold after foreclosure typically resulted in a sharply reduced selling price. Commercial also refinanced mortgages at lower interest rates during this time, which meant smaller returns on its investments. Unlike some thrift institutions, Commercial did not go "on notice"—meaning the institution was not required to have the cash to pay for all withdrawals. Fitzgerald's younger son William F. Fitzgerald, who became a teller in 1933, later recalled that sometimes, when a customer would come in to withdraw his funds, "I would count the money very slowly to give them time to think.... Once they realized the cash was there and Commercial would be able to meet their withdrawal, they would decide to leave the money and let it continue to earn dividends."

Total assets did not begin to rise again until 1939, and by 1945 assets had again reached the 1929 level. By this time James Fitzgerald was the company's president, and William was serving as secretary-treasurer. Commercial, fifth in assets among the six Omaha savings and loan associations at the end of World War II, soon became the largest lender to veterans in Nebraska under the G.I. Bill. It was also aggressive in meeting the pent-up postwar demand for housing by financing tract developments. Commercial placed the first television ad in Omaha, promoting its sixty-fifth anniversary in 1952 widely, and in 1953 it opened a drive-in teller window—Nebraska's first. In 1959 Commercial got into data processing, signing up other savings-and-loans to help pay for a computer that more than met its own needs at the time.

Although James Fitzgerald retired in 1955, he continued to serve as board chairperson and went to the office nearly every day until his death the following year at the age of 87. William Fitzgerald became president in 1950, and his son, William A. Fitzgerald, joined the company in 1955. The younger William would rise in the corporate ranks, becoming president in 1974, chief executive officer in 1983, and board chairperson in 1994.

By 1960 Commercial had five locations, and a new home office was opened two years later, when assets reached $100 million. This three-story structure featured an 85-foot tower with carillon bells and served as the model for all later Commercial branches.

In 1967 the association moved outside the Omaha metropolitan area for the first time by merging with Allied Building and Loan of Norfolk. Soon Commercial had branches in other Nebraska communities as well, some started from scratch, others by merger with an established savings and loan institution. By the end of 1974 Commercial was the largest savings and loan association in Nebraska, with 15 offices and $516 million in assets. In 1979 it became the first such thrift in its market to sell mortgage-backed bonds. Two years later it was among the first savings and loans to offer checking accounts. Also in 1981 Commercial introduced automated teller machines and spun off its lending division into a separate mortgage-banking subsidiary. A full-service brokerage program was introduced in 1983.

Reincorporated in Nebraska on August 18, 1983, as Commercial Federal Savings & Loan Association, the company converted the next year from a depositor-owned federal mutual savings and loan to a publicly traded, investor-owned institution. A holding company, Commercial Federal Corporation, became the parent company of the savings and loan association. A national public offering of shares in Commercial Federal was completed before the end of 1984, with 1.76 million shares of common stock sold at $8.50 each.

Commercial Federal's business strategy in the 1980s was based on expansion, diversification, offering high-quality loans, and achieving economies of scale through computer technology. By early 1986 it was the largest depository financial institution in Nebraska, with assets in excess of $3 billion. On March 3, 1986, Commercial Federal opened its first depository institution outside the state, acquiring about $86 million in insured deposits of the insolvent Denver-based Sierra Federal Savings and Loan Association from the Federal Savings and Loan Insurance Corp. Fitzgerald told *American Banker* that the acquisition was "part of an overall plan for targeted expansion in the Midwest," which would mean expanding into "four additional states within the next four years."

The company already had loan mortgage banking offices in surrounding states, was offering discount stock brokerage services, and was adding a full range of insurance products. By early 1988 the company also had a subsidiary, Commercial Service Corp., which acted as a vehicle for insurance sales, real estate developments and the marketing of pooled real estate investments, and other projects.

In September 1984, even before the holding company was formed, Commercial Federal had purchased an 81.3 percent interest in Systems Marketing Inc., a firm that primarily leased IBM peripheral computer equipment to Fortune 500 companies. And it was active in the mortgage market, buying fixed-rate mortgage loans and securities with long-term Federal Home Loan Bank borrowings. By March 1986 the company had realized substantial gains from these investments, while avoiding direct loans to agriculture, despite its location in the nation's farm belt. Its rate of nonperforming loans was less than one percent, and its stock had risen from the original $8.50 a share to about $27.

Soon thereafter, Commercial Federal acquired two failed thrift institutions. The first, in August 1986, was Coronado Federal Savings and Loan Association of Kansas City, Kansas. One month later it bought Denver's Empire Savings, Building and Loan Association from bankrupt Baldwin-United Corp. for $45 million in cash. The purchase price, about 57 percent of Empire's regulatory net worth, was considered a bargain. To help pay for the acquisition, Commercial Federal issued $60 million of preferred stock to El Paso Electric Co. The company then moved into its fourth state—Oklahoma—when it acquired insolvent Territory Savings and Loan Association of Seminole, Oklahoma, in January 1988 for $4.2 million.

The fourth leg of the company's strategy—computer technology—was represented by several efforts. In 1985, for example, Commercial Federal became the first financial institution in the nation to introduce personal banking machines (PBMs) in branch offices. By April 1988 it had 68 branches and was providing at least one product or service to 54 percent of the households in its home market of Omaha. To better understand its customer base, the company had created a Marketing Customer Information File—a database of its account relationships. One objective of this database was to increase revenues by repackaging and repricing products for specific customer segments. And the paper records of the company's largest subsidiary, Commercial Federal Mortgage Corp., were transferred to a microfilm-based computer-assisted retrieval system. By 1994 the company credited its computer-driven automation with allowing each agent to service 850 loans, compared to an industry average of about 600.

However, Commercial Federal faced some major challenges beginning in 1989. With Denver's economy in a serious slump, Empire Savings became a liability rather than an asset. Part of the problem was attributed to federal regulators, who had imposed tighter capital restrictions, making it harder for Commercial Federal to mark down Empire's bad loans as goodwill. The objective of the regulators, Fitzgerald later said in a 1994 interview published in *American Banker,* "was to see how many writedowns they could take to finally find the bottom in the value of a financial institution. Whether or not you agreed with them, it didn't matter."

Suddenly Commercial Federal was facing the same abyss that had swallowed so many of the savings and loans during this time. "They had one foot in the grave," a banking analyst recalled of Commercial Federal in an *American Banker* article, noting that "on a tangible net worth basis, they were bankrupt." Company executives responded by shedding nonperforming assets—mostly commercial loans—and cutting costs. Over a 15-month period, they reduced assets from $6.8 billion to $4.8 billion, closed 20 branches, and laid off 400 employees. All lending was halted, and all assets were converted to mortgage-backed securities. The company's stock fell below $2 a share in 1990.

Commercial Federal emerged by issuing a capital plan that was approved by the Federal Office of Thrift Supervision in May 1990. By then the holding company had purchased Commercial Federal Savings and Loan's outstanding preferred stock, augmenting tangible capital by $61.4 million. The plan called for adding $70 million to its capital by mid-1991 and meeting the new federal capital guidelines about two years before the compliance deadline of December 31, 1994. Commercial Federal Savings and Loan Association converted its federal charter to a federal savings bank on July 30, 1990, changing its name to

Commercial Federal Bank, FSB (the initials standing for Federal Savings Bank).

During a six-month period in 1992, the parent company sold all $3.3 billion of its mortgage-backed securities to several investors. In addition, the company sold $950 million in loan servicing rights to Source One Mortgage Services Corp. of Detroit in a single transaction. Then it offered about $40 million in equity and a similar amount in subordinated notes to improve its capital position and, in Fitzgerald's words, "get the regulators off our backs."

Commercial Federal also began bolstering its thrift holdings again in 1993, acquiring 19 thrift branches in Oklahoma and Kansas to reach a total of 67. In October 1993 the company paid $18.2 million to the Federal Deposit Insurance Corp. for 12 offices and the $567.9 million of deposits of Heartland Federal Savings and Loan Association of Ponca City, Oklahoma. In June 1994 it acquired four branches and about $255.7 million of deposits of the bankrupt Franklin Federal Savings Association in Kansas from the Resolution Trust Corp., a federal bailout agency, for about $9 million. In July 1994 the company announced it had paid about $9 million for the two branch offices and $87.1 million of deposits of the Home Federal Savings & Loan of Ada, Oklahoma.

By 1993 Commercial Federal had recovered so well that it had become the subject of takeover talk. CAI Corp., a Dallas-based investor group with a stake of nearly ten percent in the company, campaigned for a sale, driving the stock price to over $23 a share in June. However, the offer was ultimately rejected. Over the course of the following year, the company's stock value ranged between $28 and $17.50 per share. Moreover, for fiscal 1994 (the year ended June 30), operating earnings had increased 20 percent and total assets had reached $5.52 billion on deposits of $3.36 billion. By the end of the calendar year, total assets had grown to $5.8 billion.

In April 1995 Commercial Federal announced that it had acquired the Provident Federal Savings Bank of Lincoln, Nebraska. In the transaction, Commercial Federal gained five offices in Lincoln with assets of around $95 million and deposits of $57 million. Also during this time, the company entered into an agreement to acquire Railroad Financial Corporation of Wichita, Kansas. In a press release, chairperson and CEO Fitzgerald noted that "the acquisitions will immediately strengthen our retail franchise and our future earnings potential."

A booming economy was helping the company, with unemployment below four percent in all four states where it maintained bank branches. "The goal now," company vice-president Stan Blakey told *American Banker*, "is to make yourself a little more profitable, to exceed the analysts' estimates by a little bit every quarter, and to do a little better than the rest of the guys out there."

Principal Subsidiaries: Commercial Federal Bank, FSB; Commercial Federal Insurance Corp.; Commercial Federal Investment Services, Inc.; Commercial Federal Mortgage Corp.

Further Reading:

Basch, Mark, "Commercial Federal Moves West with Deal for Failed Denver S&L," *American Banker,* March 4, 1986, pp. 2, 22.
Bennett, Andrea, "Nebraska Thrift Company Moves into Oklahoma," *American Banker,* February 2, 1988, p. 23.
1887-1987: Milestones & Reflections A Centennial Retrospective, Omaha: Commercial Federal Savings and Loan, 1987.
Engen, John R., "Omaha's Commercial Federal Corp. Breathing Easy After Brush with Disaster," *American Banker,* September 30, 1994, pp. 4–5.
Fraust, Bart, "Baldwin-United to Sell Empire Savings for $45 Million to Commercial Federal," September 16, 1986, pp. 7, 16.
Helzner, Jerry, "Canny Cornhusker," *Barron's,* June 23, 1986, p. 53.
Katz, Martin, "Marketing CIF," *Bank Systems & Equipment,* April 1988, pp. 62–65.
"Savings and Loan Creates Its Own Savings Plan," *Management Review,* March/April 1989, pp. 19–21.
Stieven, Joseph A., "Commercial Federal Corporation," *Wall Street Transcript,* July 21, 1986, p. 82569.

—Robert Halasz

ConAgra, Inc.

ConAgra Center
One Central Park Plaza
Omaha, Nebraska 68102
U.S.A.
(402) 595-4000
Fax: (402) 595-4595

Public Company
Incorporated: 1919 as Nebraska Consolidated Mills
    Company
Employees: 42,993
Sales: $21.5 billion
Stock Exchanges: New York
SICs: 2048 Prepared Feeds, Not Elsewhere Classified; 2879
    Agricultural Chemicals, Not Elsewhere Classified; 2041
    Flour & Other Grain Mill Products; 6211 Security Brokers
    & Dealers

In 1919 Alva Kinney brought four grain milling companies in south central Nebraska together to take advantage of increasing grain production in the Midwest, and the Nebraska Consolidated Mills Company was born. Seventy years and a name change later, ConAgra, Inc. is a diversified international company whose products range from agricultural supplies such as fertilizers, pesticides, and feeds to prepared gourmet dinners for a new age of consumers.

Officially formed on September 29, 1919, the Nebraska Consolidated Mills Company (NCM) was headquartered in Grand Island, Nebraska. At first Kinney concentrated on milling the bumper postwar wheat crops at his four Nebraska locations. But soon, to accommodate his growing business, Kinney added a mill in Omaha, in 1922, and moved the headquarters of the company there. He continued to run a profitable and relatively quiet company solely in Nebraska until he retired as president in 1936.

Kinney was succeeded by R. S. Dickinson. Initially, Dickinson followed his predecessor's simple but successful policy of milling grain in Nebraska. World War II and the postwar boom kept the demand for grain high and the milling business profitable.

During the early 1940s Dickinson began to use the company's profits to expand. Other successful milling operations, such as

General Mills and Pillsbury, were expanding both the number of plants and the number of products they offered, and NCM followed the same trend. In 1942 Dickinson opened a flour mill and animal feed mill in Alabama. He also promoted research into new types of prepared foods that used flour, which led to the development of Duncan Hines cake mixes, introduced in the early 1950s.

The Alabama expansion was profitable, but Dickinson found that it was more difficult to gain a foothold in the prepared-foods market. Cake mixes, though only a small proportion of the total flour market, accounted for as much as $140 million a year in retail sales by 1947. But the market was dominated by General Mills's Betty Crocker brand and by Pillsbury, each with one third of the market share, while Duncan Hines controlled only ten to 12 percent. Unable to increase its share of the highly-competitive cake mix market, NCM eventually decided to get out of prepared foods and use the money it raised to expand in basic commodities: grains and feeds. So, in 1956 the company sold its Duncan Hines brand to Proctor & Gamble.

The new president of Nebraska Consolidated Mills, J. Allan Mactier, used the proceeds from the sale to expand aggressively. In 1958, NCM built the first major grain processing plant in Puerto Rico through its subsidiary, Caribe Company. The $3 million plant processed flour, corn meal, and animal feeds at Catano in San Juan harbor. Production at the plant did not compete with the parent company's already-existing concerns; none of the flours and feeds produced there were exported to the mainland.

Caribe's foothold on the island led to further Puerto Rican expansion in new areas. A second subsidiary, Molinos de Puerto Rico, took over Caribe's animal feed business on the island while also developing Puerto Rico's virtually nonexistent beef industry as a market for its products. In Molino's first five years of operation, consumption of animal feeds in Puerto Rico increased from 136,516 tons, of which 100,314 were imported, to 249,267 tons, of which only 46,723 were imported. The company also profited from an increased demand for meat and milk on the island.

Elsewhere, however, flour millers faced shrinking profits as demand leveled off in both domestic and foreign markets. European grain production had recovered from the disruption of World War II, and prosperity at home in the 1950s and 1960s allowed consumers to buy more expensive food items, leading to lower flour consumption.

Large millers turned to diversification to offset declining profitability. Industry leaders General Mills and Pillsbury developed their consumer foods lines and introduced new types of convenience foods, while the third of the "Big Three" in flour milling, International Milling Company, Inc., diversified primarily into animal feeds. Nebraska Consolidated Mills, perhaps unwilling to compete again in packaged foods after its experience with Duncan Hines, also developed the animal feed end of its business. Throughout the 1960s and into the 1970s, the company developed mills and distribution centers for feed and flour in the Southeast and Northwest.

NCM also turned to another basic commodity: chicken. It developed poultry growing and processing complexes in Georgia,

Louisiana, and Alabama during the 1960s. In 1965 the company also began to expand into the European market by going into partnership with Bioter-Biona, S.A., a Spanish producer of animal feed and animal health products and breeder of pigs, chickens, and trout.

By 1971 Nebraska Consolidated Mills had outgrown its early base in Nebraska as well as its name. It chose a new name to reflect its new concerns: ConAgra, meaning "in partnership with the land." ConAgra was listed on the New York Stock Exchange in 1973.

The new name, however, did not necessarily mean continuing success. The early 1970s, in fact, brought the company to a low point. Many of its acquisitions during the expansion of the 1960s and early 1970s were only marginally profitable at best. In 1974 the company posted net losses and suspended dividends. Heavy losses in commodity speculations brought ConAgra to the brink of bankruptcy in 1975.

ConAgra's first high-profile chief executive, former Pillsbury executive Charles Harper, was named president in 1975 with a mandate to turn the ailing company around. Essential to Harper's turn-around plan were strict financial goals combined with a series of acquisitions that served to broaden's ConAgra's sales base. To reduce debt, Harper first sold nonessential operations. He then began to buy agricultural businesses at the low end of their profit cycles and turn them around. Harper originally intended to stick with ConAgra's emphasis on basic commodities rather than compete with the packaged-food giants. When he purchased Banquet Foods Corporation in 1980, he claimed that the acquisition was not an entry into prepared foods but a way to increase ConAgra's chicken capacity. ConAgra's chicken production did increase by a third, bringing the company from eighth to fifth place among chicken producers. Harper expanded into fish as well as poultry in the 1970s with investments in catfish aquaculture.

Another of Harper's acquisitions put ConAgra back in the forefront of the flour market. In 1982 ConAgra bought the Peavey Company, a Minneapolis-based flour miller and grain trader, giving it 16.3 percent of the nation's wheat-milling capacity and a system of grain exporting terminals. Political barriers to U.S. grain exports had depressed Peavey's profits, and the acquisition was not the early success story that Banquet was for ConAgra. By 1986, however, Peavey was posting a $16.4 million profit on sales of $1.2 billion, a promising upward trend.

Harper also kept to a commodity-oriented approach by diversifying into agricultural chemicals. ConAgra expanded into fertilizers, and in 1978 acquired United Agri Products, a distributor of herbicides and pesticides. Higher grain prices, Harper reasoned, would mean increased demand for such chemicals.

But, in an attempt to counter the cyclical profit pattern of basic agricultural commodities, Harper also entered areas that didn't mesh well with the company's traditional orientation: pet accessories, a Mexican restaurant chain, and a fabrics and crafts chain, among others.

In a dramatic change of direction during the 1980s, ConAgra decided on prepared foods as a better way to balance cyclical profits in the food industry. The company's stringent financial goals were being met: return on equity averaged 20 percent; annual growth in trend-line earnings were over 14 percent and long-term debt was held to below 35 percent of total capitalization. With the company on firmer financial ground, ConAgra began a series of acquisitions which would ultimately make it the nation's second largest food company.

ConAgra's moved into the prepared seafood market in 1981 with the purchase of Singleton Seafood, the largest shrimp processor in the country, and Sea-Alaska Products. In 1987 ConAgra bought Trident Seafoods and O'Donnell-Usen Fisheries, the producer of Taste O' Sea frozen seafood products, thus positioning the company to compete against the leading frozen seafood brands, Mrs. Paul's Kitchens, Gorton's, and Van de Kamp's.

In 1982, during a low in the poultry cycle, ConAgra moved to take first place in the chicken industry by forming Country Poultry, Inc. By the next year, Country Poultry was delivering more than a billion pounds of brand-name broilers to markets, making it the biggest poultry producer in the country. In 1986, the company formed ConAgra Turkey Company and in 1987 it acquired another poultry company, Longmont Foods, further strengthening its position in the field. But ConAgra's poultry concerns no longer focused on the basic bird Harper purchased Banquet for: Country Poultry introduced a number of higher-profit convenience poultry products, such as marinated chicken breasts, chicken hot dogs, and processed chicken for fast food restaurants.

ConAgra moved into another area of processed foods in 1983 when the company purchased Armour Food Company, a processor of red meats such as hot dogs, sausage, bacon, ham, and lunch meats. The acquisition also included Armour's line of frozen gourmet entrees, Dinner Classics, which complemented Banquet's line of frozen foods. As with many of his other acquisitions, Harper bought Armour in a down cycle for book value ($182 million). By waiting to complete the deal until Armour closed several plants, Harper painlessly eliminated about 40 percent of Armour's major union's members. Some Armour plants still have unions, but without a master contract labor costs were slashed. Harper then reorganized the company, emphasizing new marketing strategies (reintroducing the familiar Armour jingle to take advantage of consumer recognition) and refocusing product lines. The Dinner Classics line was hurt by price competition and the introduction of new brands of premium frozen dinners. Armour as a whole was still unprofitable through the early 1990s, but the Classics line has increased profits since the purchase.

In 1986, Harper increased ConAgra's presence in frozen foods by purchasing the Morton, Patio, and Chun King brands. And in 1987, the company expanded in red meats with its purchase of E.A. Miller, Inc., a western producer of beef products, and Monfort of Colorado, Inc. Almost a decade earlier, ConAgra had tried to purchase MBPXL Corp., the number-two beef packer in the country, only to be blocked at the last minute by the privately owned Cargill Inc. The Monfort deal, for $365 million in stock, made ConAgra the third-largest U.S. beef producer. Health-conscious consumers began eating less beef in the late 1980s and ConAgra responded by working to develop new, leaner beef products as it developed new poultry products. Another 1987 acquisition, 50 percent of Swift Independent Packing Company, a processor of beef, pork, and lamb, made ConAgra a leading meat processor as well. Harper rounded out his changes at ConAgra by developing the company's international trading position and by forming its own financial services subsidiary.

By the late 1980s, ConAgra had grown into a well diversified food company, better able to absorb the ups and downs of the industry. 1987 was a banner year for ConAgra's poultry division, which posted $130 million in operating profits due to a tremendous (and ultimately unsustainable) upswing in the poultry market. The poultry division's operating profits plummeted the following year to $20 million, but by then ConAgra's other divisions were strong enough to make up the difference. The company posted net earnings of $155 million, about 5 percent higher than the previous year.

In 1988 Harper boasted that ConAgra was probably the only food products company to "participate across the entire food chain." However, in the grocery store, the majority of its packaged food products were found in the frozen foods section, where it held the top market share in the country. In 1990, sensing that even greater diversification was necessary to ensure steady earnings growth, Harper led the purchase of Beatrice Co., which produced top brands such as Hunt's Tomato Paste and Butterball Turkey and had annual sales over $4 billion. The Beatrice purchase gave ConAgra a broader portfolio of products and provided a strong sales and distribution system in the "dry goods" segment. ConAgra paid $2.35 billion for the company and assumed a debt of about $1 billion in the process.

In the early 1990s ConAgra expanded at a rate of about 35 acquisitions and joint ventures a year. The company's international presence grew as it formed joint ventures in Japan, Thailand, France, Canada, Chile, and Australia. Key acquisitions included Australia Meat Holdings and the malt, wool, and 50 percent of the beef business of Elders Ltd., another Australian concern. On the home front, ConAgra made its first foray into the kosher foods business with the purchase of National Foods and also entered the private label consumer products market with the acquisition of Arrow Industries, a clothing manufacturer.

In 1991 the company enlarged its frozen foods market share further with the introduction of Healthy Choice, a low fat, low sodium, and low cholesterol line of frozen dinner entrees. Within two years, the brand had expanded to offer everything from healthy hot dogs to ice cream. By 1993 Healthy Choice posted sales of over $1 billion and was lauded as the "most successful new food brand introduction in two decades" by *Advertising Age*.

The company also reorganized some of its divisions in the early 1990s, creating ConAgra Grocery Products Companies to unite its Hunt-Wesson companies with its frozen food businesses and ConAgra Meat Products Companies to bring together its branded package meat business and its fresh red meat businesses. 1992 sales surpassed $20 billion for the first time, as the company posted its 12th consecutive year of record earnings.

In 1992 Harper resigned his post at ConAgra to become chairman and chief executive officer at RJR Nabisco Holdings Corp. Phil Fletcher, ConAgra's longtime president and chief operating officer, assumed Harper's post. In his first two years at the helm, Fletcher cut operating costs by enforcing stricter cost-control measures and fostering greater communication and cooperation between the company's six dozen individual units. Continuing Harper's acquisition strategy, ConAgra began expanding globally, with new ventures in China, Australia, Denmark, and Mexico. 1994 earnings reached $437 million on sales of $23.5 billion.

1994 marked ConAgra's 75th anniversary, and, as part of the company's celebration, $200,000 was donated to a museum in Grand Island, Nebraska, for the erection of a replica of the original Glade Mill, one of the four mills merged to create the company in 1919. In its 75 year history, ConAgra had transformed itself from a low-profile flour miller into an international food company with sales well over $20 billion. It gained its stature through a remarkable mix of conservative fiscal management and aggressive expansion through acquisitions and joint ventures. With its 60-plus operating units—selling everything from livestock feed to microwaveable dinners—ConAgra seemed well positioned to absorb the cyclical trends of the food industry. Building on the strengths of his predecessor, Fletcher was transforming ConAgra into a leaner, more efficient company, and given his track record, the company's future seemed in good hands.

Principal Subsidiaries: ConAgra Agri-Products Companies; ConAgra Diversified Products Companies; ConAgra Grocery Products Companies; ConAgra Meat Products Companies; ConAgra Red Meat Companies; ConAgra Poultry Company; ConAgra Trading and Processing Companies; ConAgra Broiler Co.; ConAgra Frozen Foods Co.; Beatrice Co.; Camerican International Inc.; Monfort Inc.; Country General Stores Co.; E.A. Miller Inc.; Decker Foods Co.; United Agri Products Cos.; General Spice Inc.; Agrichem Co.; Arrow Industries Inc.; Camerican International Inc.

Further Reading:

Burns, Greg, "How a New Boss Got ConAgra Cooking Again," *Business Week*, July 25, 1994, p. 72.

"ConAgra's Quantum Leap in Buying Beatrice Co.," *Mergers & Acquisitions,* September/October 1990, p. 54.

Henkoff, Ronald, "A Giant That Keeps Innovating," *Fortune*, December 16, 1991, p. 101.

—updated by Maura Troester

Crain Communications Inc

Crain Communications, Inc.

740 N. Rush Street
Chicago, Illinois 60611
U.S.A.
(312) 649-5200
Fax: (312) 649-5228

Private Company
Incorporated: 1916
Employees: 1,000
Sales: $160 million
SICs: 2721 Periodicals: Publishing & Printing

Crain Communications Inc. is an anomaly in the business world—a solid, innovative media conglomerate run with the values of a neighborhood grocery. This small, family operation quietly yet rigorously carved a place for itself among the nation's media titans. What was once a fledgling, two-publication company became an international empire of 1,000 employees headquartered in Chicago, with 15 offices in cities worldwide, including Denver, Detroit, London, Los Angeles, New York, Washington, D.C., Frankfurt, and Tokyo. Publishing primarily trade periodicals, as well as providing subscription, direct mail, and custom printing services, Crain's roster of 24 magazines and news weeklies includes industry heavy-hitters *Advertising Age, Automotive News, Business Insurance* and *Crain's Chicago Business.* Additionally, consumer and specialized Crain publications like *AutoWeek, Detroit Monthly, Euromarketing, Modern Healthcare, Rubber & Plastic News,* and *American Laundry Digest* produce respectable revenues in a growing number of niche markets worldwide. Rounding out Crain's holdings is a 100,000-watt Florida Keys radio station and new ventures into electronic media, such as on-line *Crain's Chicago Business* and *Crain's Small Business* information services and one-minute local news briefs broadcast on Chicago radio and television stations.

Gustavus Dedman Crain, Jr. (known as "G.D.") was born in Lawrenceburg, Kentucky, in 1885, the second of three boys. Raised in Louisville, G.D. delivered newspapers as a boy. After serving as editor of his high school newspaper, G.D. accepted a scholarship to Centre College in Danville, Kentucky, graduating in three years with a masters degree in English. Returning to Louisville, he signed on as a staff reporter with the *Times,* developing a powerful instinct for breaking news and frequently

scooping his rivals, the *Herald* and *Courier-Journal.* While writing for the *Times,* G.D. augmented his income by freelancing for other publications. He was soon writing, or "stringing" as it was called, for dozens of business papers. Quitting the *Times,* G.D. hired a small staff and started his own editorial service, churning out news and features on a daily basis. Yet something was still missing—despite the autonomy of running his own company and succeeding, G.D. longed to be on the other side—to receive the copy, edit it, and actually publish it. In 1916, 31-year-old G.D. put his experience to the test and founded two specialized periodicals, *Hospital Management (HM)* and *Class.* Later that year Crain moved the company, his wife Ailiene, and daughters Jane and Mary to Chicago, a burgeoning hub of the business world. Setting up shop at 608 S. Dearborn Street, in what is known as Printer's Row, Crain Publishing Company revolved around a simple premise: give readers what they want—factual, fairly-reported news written and edited in a professional manner—and they'd keep coming back. G.D.'s unbridled enthusiasm and energy became the cornerstone of Crain Publishing Company and its eventual successor, Crain Communications, Inc., while setting the course for a decades-long career in publishing.

Crain's first endeavor, the 36-page, 7-by-10-inch *Hospital Management,* debuted in February 1916. Directed to medical administrators, managers and decision-makers, *HM* covered the ever-expanding hospital field, competing with a St. Louis-based magazine called *Modern Hospital.* G.D.'s second venture, the smaller-formatted, 32-page *Class* was a business-to-business digest covering the industrial advertising and sales field. It was also a convenient way to advertise its sibling publication, *HM.* To devote himself to selling ads and editing copy for *Class,* G.D. hired sportswriter Matthew Foley as editor of *HM.* In 1919, G.D.'s older brother Kenneth relocated to Chicago, and soon became *HM*'s general manager. By 1922, Crain Publishing Co. was thriving. Yet the year also brought two disparate occurrences with long-reaching consequences: the first was the tragic death of G.D.'s wife, Ailiene, leaving his young daughters motherless; the second, the auspicious appearance of a young man named Sidney R. Bernstein. Under Foley's tutelage, Bernstein was given his first writing opportunity and named *HM*'s assistant editor, one of many titles he would hold over the next 71 years.

In 1927, *Class* (revamped in the early 1920s to *Class & Industrial Advertising*) was now *Class & Industrial Marketing (C&IM)* and grew from pocket-sized to a more accepted 8.5-by-11 inches. G.D., longtime friend Keith Evans, and other colleagues helped create the National Industrial Advertisers Association (NIAA), to address the collective and individual problems of industrial advertisers and marketers. In the months before Black Tuesday, October 29, 1929, G.D. finalized details for a newsweekly called *Advertising Age.* On January 11, 1930, without knowing the full extent of the nation's financial quandary, G.D. published the premiere issue of *Ad Age,* promoted as the "national newspaper of advertising." With no advance notice, 10,000 copies of the 12-page edition appeared on the desks of professionals selected from the Standard Advertising Register. Its premise was to print all news related to advertising and marketing, and moreover, to cover what the industry's bible, *Printer's Ink,* deemed unimportant. Many thought G.D. made a crucial mistake with the precipitous launch of *Ad Age*—

not only was *Printer's Ink* a well-established and respected business periodical, but the risks were phenomenal. Why publish another publication about marketing anyway? Yet G.D.'s passion would not be quelled, and years later he admitted he probably would have gone ahead with *Ad Age* despite even the worst financial forecasts (his risks paid off handsomely—*Printer's Ink* folded in 1967 and *Ad Age* has been considered the "publication of record" for decades). In the lean years of the Depression, the previously healthy *Class* and *HM* suffered losses and wavered in red ink. To the credit of Ellen Krebby, who was hired in 1921 to handle the office and accounting, G.D. never realized the tenuity of the company's financial status. In 1933, rather than sacrifice *C&IM* altogether, it became a special section of *Ad Age* until ad sales and circulation could recover.

Ad Age was not profitable until 1934, four years after its birth. In the interim, Sid Bernstein was named assistant to the publisher in October, 1931; the average number of pages grew to 16 and circulation cracked 9,000, an increase of nearly 1,400 from the previous year. G.D.'s younger brother, Murray, became *Ad Age*'s managing editor, and the three brothers made Crain Publishing Company a family affair. In January of 1935, tragedy struck when Matt Foley suffered a heart attack and died at the age of 44. Unable or unwilling to run *HM* without Foley's guidance and verve, G.D. sold it. Oddly enough, *HM* would return to Crain after its buyers neared bankruptcy. Though the medical magazine would be sold again in 1952, the company would once again delve into the medical field by purchasing *Modern Healthcare* from McGraw-Hill in 1976.

In June 1935, *C&IM* reemerged from *Ad Age* as *Industrial Marketing*, then underwent its final name change to *Business Marketing* (as it exists today) in 1936, its 20th anniversary. Amidst a flurry of retail and advertising agency growth in the area, Crain relocated north to 100 E. Ohio Street. This year was also pivotal for G.D. personally: while meeting with a sales executive of the National Broadcasting Company (NBC) in New York City, G.D. met a 25-year-old woman named Gertrude Ramsay, a secretary at NBC's offices in Rockefeller Center. After a whirlwind courtship, the two married and Gertrude was whisked off to Chicago. The company, meanwhile, known as Advertising Publications, Inc. (API), opened an office in Washington, D.C. in 1939, and G.D. relinquished his status as *Ad Age*'s editor-in-chief by appointing Bernstein (then director of research and promotion) to editor and moved Managing Editor Irwin Robinson to New York full-time in 1940. As the U.S. became embroiled in World War II, G.D. declared, "There are many essential services which advertising is called upon to perform in wartime," and set about fulfilling this obligation. On the homefront, Gertrude had given birth to sons Rance (1938) and Keith (1941).

In 1943, API implemented an unheard of concept—an employee profit-sharing plan—fully funded by the company and the first of many employee benefits programs. When World War II ended, G.D. and Sid rethought priorities in preparation for a postwar society. In a January 7, 1946 editorial, Bernstein announced "Advertising has emerged from the war with a new stature, new tasks and new duties. It will never again be confined only to the sale of goods and services." This year also marked *Ad Age*'s foray into agency profiles, breaking the industry's silence on billings. The 1950s brought the addition of a features section and the launch of the yearly "100 Leading National Advertisers" poll; by the end of the decade, circulation hit 48,400 with the purchase of rival *Advertising Agency*. Once more outgrowing its premises, API moved into a remodeled warehouse at 200 E. Illinois Street, its home until April 1962 when operations moved to 740 N. Rush Street.

New developments in the sixties included the debut of *Advertising Requirements* (later *Advertising & Sales Promotion* then *Promotion* before merging into *Ad Age* and shutting down in May 1974), and what many termed a changing of the guard in 1964. Nearing 80, G.D. stepped down as publisher of *Ad Age*, a post he held for 34 years, naming Sid president and publisher while assuming the newly-created position of chairperson. The next several years marked both growth and loss: a publication for college students, *Marketing Insights,* would fail after a few semesters, but *Business Insurance,* first published in October 1967, and the acquisition of *American Drycleaner, American Laundry Digest, American Co-Op* and *American Clean Car* substantially increased the company's holdings. To better represent its diversity, API became Crain Communications Inc. (CCI) and created an American Trade Magazines subsidiary with offices at 500 N. Dearborn Street, in Chicago.

As Rance and Keith grew up, curiosity in the family business gave way to genuine interest. Generally considered opposites, Rance and Keith familiarized themselves with CCI through years of Saturday office visits and nightly dinner conversations with their parents. Yet as Rance and Keith chose their divergent paths up the corporate ladder, each faced the daunting task of proving himself to be more than the boss's son. After studying at DePauw University in Indiana for two years (he received an honorary degree in 1987), Rance attended Northwestern University to study journalism, becoming sports editor of the *Daily Northwestern*. His tenure at Crain began as a cub reporter for the New York and Washington, D.C. bureaus of *Ad Age,* where his peers gave him little support and less chance of succeeding. But Rance persevered, doggedly tracking stories and proving both his mettle and writing skills. His management expertise and sagacity would prove paramount to the success of his greatest personal triumph, *Crain's Chicago Business,* as well as the continued prosperity of *Ad Age.* "*Ad Age* would have been bland and faceless had Rance not been there," commented Niles Howard, a former *Ad Age* reporter. Lou DeMarco, a former v-p and retired *Ad Age* publisher, concurred: "Rance's enthusiasm is limitless; you can't satisfy his hunger for new ideas."

In 1978, Rance channeled his energy in a new direction. After meeting Bob Gray, publisher of the *Houston Business Journal,* he decided a business weekly about the Chicago area "would be twice as successful" as the Houston endeavor. Marking the first public use of the Crain family name, *Crain's Chicago Business* seemed kissed by fate: the *Chicago Daily News* was going under and several staffers including Dan Miller, Sandy Presman and Joe Cappo jumped ship to *CCB*. The rest, as they say, is history—though not a smooth one. Just as Rance's drive and enthusiasm pushed *Ad Age* and *CCB* to the forefront, there were misfires as well. Neither *Thursday* (a jazzy, mid-week edition of *Ad Age*), *The Collector-Investor* nor *Crain's Illinois Business* generated sufficient interest, and *Crain's New York Business* has faced an uphill battle since its founding in 1985. Yet Rance has stated unequivocally that he'll never give up on *Crain's New York,* believing it will someday be to the New York area what *Crain's Chicago* is to the Midwest.

Just as Rance's newshound instincts propelled his career, Keith's abiding interest in cars was the backbone of his own. A car enthusiast since his teens, Keith attended Northwestern University then sold ads and worked on a variety of Crain publications before heading to the company's offices in Detroit to indulge his passion. In 1970, on Keith's behalf, Sid Bernstein bid on the downtrodden *Automotive News* (*AN*), a 46-year-old weekly tabloid based in Detroit. Keith was not only familiar with the internal workings of cars, but soon demonstrated an innate sense of how a trade magazine *about* vehicles should be written, edited and marketed. Publisher of *AN* at the age of 30, the often brash, always pertinacious, Keith won over Detroit's plutocracy and solidified a place among them. Keith's first *AN* issue came out on June 7, 1971; within six months, it was breaking even and eventually secured a 100 percent paid circulation. As the Detroit office boomed, Keith purchased Akron-based *Rubber & Plastics News* (*R&PN*) in 1976, stipulating that editor and publisher Ernie Zielasko and Lowell (Chris) Chrisman, vice-president of sales, come along. *R&PN*'s first issue under the CCI banner appeared in April, signifying an important venture into the Akron/Cleveland area.

In 1977, Keith led the company into virgin territory with the purchase of *AutoWeek,* CCI's first consumer periodical in 61 years of publishing. Overhauling the tabloid into a glossy magazine, *AutoWeek*'s circulation soared from 25,000 to nearly 280,000. Zielasko and Chrisman, the dynamic duo of *R&PN,* were also the driving force behind the formation of *Crain's Cleveland Business* in 1980, which overtook its competition, the *Northern OhioBusiness Journal,* to become the area's definitive newsweekly. In May 1981, Keith was named vice-chairman, overseeing CCI's daily activities with Rance. Taking over Keith's former duties as secretary-treasurer were his wife, Mary Kay as treasurer, and Rance's wife, Merilee, as company secretary (both women, along with Gertrude, Rance and Keith make up CCI's board of directors).

Gertrude Crain began her own pivotal role in the company when the boys were in high school. A graduate of secretarial school in Manhattan, Gertrude's business interests were put aside to raise her sons. Beginning part-time and progressing to full-time, Gertrude mastered a myriad of tasks that included representing the company at conventions worldwide, overseeing CCI's extensive benefits program, monitoring expense accounts, scouring accounts payable invoices, even signing checks. As the 1970s progressed, Gertrude, Rance and Keith confidently plied their trades and CCI hit several milestones. G.D.'s baby, *Ad Age,* commemorated its 40th anniversary and reached a circulation of 65,000, while the Crain think-tank developed *Pensions & Investments* in July 1973.

On November 7, 1973, G.D. was felled by a stroke. Though he recovered temporarily, the ebullient patriarch died December 15th at the age of 88. Despite their grief and loss, however, the family did not let G.D.'s death send the company into a tailspin. In January, Gertrude became chairman of the board; Keith assumed her former duties as secretary-treasurer; Sid was named chairman of the executive committee; and Rance be-

came president. Though Mrs. Crain has often downplayed her role at CCI, under her influence the company more than quadrupled its number of publications, generating revenues of $160 million in 1993, a steep climb from 1974's modest $10 million.

In October 1975, G.D. Crain was belatedly inducted into the American Advertising Federation's Hall of Fame. Fourteen years later, Sid Bernstein, known in the industry as "Mr. Advertising," was finally given his due as well, inducted into the Advertising Hall of Fame on March 28, 1989. Gertrude, meanwhile, was busy too—in 1986, at age 75, she rode shotgun with NASCAR racer Tim Richmond, hitting 185 mph; for her 77th birthday, she went parasailing in Key Largo. Yet Mrs. Crain has been recognized not only for her spirit of adventure, but by her peers as well: in 1987, she was inducted into *Working Woman*'s Hall of Fame; named Chicagoan of the Year by the Boys and Girls Club of Chicago; and selected as one of the Top 60 Women Business Owners by *Savvy* magazine; in 1988, she received Mundelein College's "Magnificat" medal; in 1992, she was inducted into the Junior Achievement Chicago Business Hall of Fame; and in 1993, she was honored with a lifetime achievement award from the Magazine Publishers of America. Mrs. Crain has also served on the board of directors for several organizations, including the International Advertising Association, the National Press Foundation, and the Advertising Council of New York.

Called "as near a perfect example of a specialist magazine as is possible to produce" by Eric Clark, a journalist from the United Kingdom in his book, *The Want Makers, Ad Age* celebrated its 60th anniversary by unveiling a spiffier look and new logo. Rance, after years of commuting, finally moved east to be near CCI's New York offices. On May 29, 1993, another Crain legend, 86-year-old Sid Bernstein, died. "Sid Bernstein has always served as the editorial conscience of our company," Rance said in a tribute published in *Ad Age* shortly after Sid's death. Yet CCI carried on, expanding in the memory of both G.D. and Sid. In 1994, in a joint venture with America On-Line, *Crain's Chicago* and *Crain's Small Business* were hooked up to Chicago On-Line. In the fall, CCI staffers laid the groundwork for a new magazine, *Franchise Buyer,* set to debut with a March/April issue in 1995.

With Gertrude Crain well past traditional retirement age, the industry has been rife with speculation about who will take the reins of CCI when the time comes. "If you ask my mother about succession plans," Keith has said with characteristic wit, "she'd probably wonder about how to replace Rance or me, because she plans to outlive both of us." Yet when Mrs. Crain does step down, will the company's atmosphere and direction be irrevocably altered? Will the *joie de vivre* be replaced by the pursuit of profits? Would the corporate headquarters be moved from Chicago to Detroit if Keith took over? Or to New York if Rance succeeded his mother? Though Rance and Keith have taken CCI's interests to new highs, many have openly found fault with the brothers' unusual brand of decision-making—like choosing ventures based on interest and convenience rather than profit. When Mrs. Crain was asked in a 1987 interview what the biggest problems facing CCI were in the near future, she quipped "Rance and Keith."

One thing is certain: Gertrude, Rance and Keith will always be united in perpetuating G.D.'s vision. Yet as Nancy Millman, who wrote a family profile for *Chicago* magazine in 1993, pointed out, "The last time a Chicago media empire passed to two brothers with very different personalities and interests, Marshall and Ted Field ended up selling the *Chicago Sun-Times* to Rupert Murdoch—a spot of history that isn't lost on the journalists at Crain." Regardless of who succeeds Gertrude Crain and when, Crain Communications Inc. will continue to ply its trade in the quirky, unpredictable manner its detractors and admirers have come to expect.

Principal Subsidiaries: Crain Associated Enterprises, Inc., Crain News Service, Crain Subscription Services, Crain's List Rental Service, Detroit Monthly Custom Printing.

Further Reading:

Bernstein, Jack, "PR—Aid to Management and Media," *Ad Age,* September 24, 1984, p. 20.

Bernstein, Sid, "A Little Book of Proven Truths," *Ad Age,* June 8, 1992, p. 19.

Conklin, Michele, "Rance and the Family Bible," *Madison Avenue,* November 1986, p. 19.

"Crain Adds Detroit and N.Y. Papers," *Ad Age,* May 24, 1984, p. 1.

"Crain Communications Inc.," *Ad Age,* July 20, 1992, p. 39.

Crain, Rance, "If You Can't Beat 'Em, Join 'Em," *Ad Age,* May 25, 1992, p. 28.

——, "New Course in Adopt-A-School," *Ad Age,* October 27, 1986, p. 58.

——, "New Worlds to Conquer," *Ad Age,* January 21, 1991, p. 34.

——, "The Conscience of Our Company," *Ad Age,* June 7, 1993, p. 22.

——, "The Daredevil of Publishing," *Ad Age,* July 19, 1993, p. 17.

——, "Wear-'Em Down School Prevails," *Ad Age,* February, 4, 1991, p. 24.

"Crain Receives Lifetime Achievement Award from Magazine Publishers," *Automotive News,* August 1989, p. 22.

"Crain's *Franchise Buyer* to Cover Burgeoning Industry," *Ad Age,* August 1, 1994, p. 2.

Danzig, Fred, "Sid Bernstein Leaves a Legacy of Ideals, Progress," *Ad Age,* June 7, 1993, p. 1.

——, "Triumphs and Failures: Six Decades of Marketing's Roller Coaster Ride," *Ad Age,* June 18, 1990, p. 50.

Goldsborough, Robert, *The Crain Adventure: The Making & Building of a Family Publishing Company,* Lincolnwood, Ill.: NTC Business Books, 1992.

"*Governing* Absorbs *City & State,*" *Ad Age,* January 24, 1994, p. 8.

Magiera, Marcy, "Two Shots . . . A Woman Screamed," *Ad Age,* May 4, 1992, p. 52.

McManus, Kevin, "Two Crains Running," *Forbes,* February 27, 1984, pp. 94–96.

"Media Moves: Crain Communications Inc.," *Ad Age,* November 11, 1993, p. 53.

Millman, Nancy, "Two Crains Running," *Chicago Magazine,* April 1993, p. 73.

"The 1987 *Working Woman* Hall of Fame," *Working Woman,* November 1987, p. 107.

Sanderfoot, Alan E., "Business Press Attacks Sequential Liability," *Folio,* January 1992, p. 30.

Silber, Tony, "Business Title Targets Detroit's Foreign Visitors," *Folio,* June 1991, p. 21.

Tannenbaum, Jeffrey, "Franchise-News Junkies," *Wall Street Journal,* September 28, 1994, p. B2.

Wilkinson, Stephan, "The Keeper (and Stoker) of the Company Flame," *Working Woman,* October 1987, p. 70.

—Taryn Benbow-Pfalzgraf

Culligan International Company

1 Culligan Parkway
Northbrook, Illinois 60062
U.S.A.
(708) 205-6000
Fax: (708) 205-6030

Wholly Owned Subsidiary of Astrum International
Incorporated: 1936 as Culligan Zeolite Company
Employees: 1,500
Sales: $190 million
SICs: 3589 Service Industry Machinery

Culligan International Company became known across the United States as the father of the soft water industry. "Hey Culligan Man!" was an advertising mantra nationally synonymous with conditioned water. Despite a flurry of changing ownership in the past decade, Culligan's basic operations have remained virtually unchanged since its heyday. In fact, in 1995 the company was still based in the same town whose streets were first used for solar drying its key product.

Emmett J. Culligan developed a novel process for manufacturing zeolite, the man-made mineral used in water softeners, in 1936, which involved the very early use of solar drying. With a lot of confidence and a little money, Culligan approached the city council of Northbrook, Illinois, that year and offered to lease a stretch of streets. The streets had been paved, but then left unused when a real estate project went under. Several miles of empty, paved streets were just what Culligan needed for drying his zeolite in large quantities, using the sun. The council leased him the streets for $50 and a company was born: Culligan Zeolite Company.

From the start, the company was a community endeavor. Culligan's first home was a shared blacksmith's shop behind the Northbrook Garage on Shermer Avenue, run by "Jock" McLachlan. As the operations grew, Culligan rented a brick garage building beside the blacksmith's shop and relocated the blacksmith's building to face Walters Avenue. The garage became the first manufacturing plant for portable exchange units. The office and laboratory stayed in the blacksmith's shop. Eventually, these buildings grew together, with more manufacturing space on the ground floor and offices added onto the second.

Through franchised dealers, Culligan soon launched a campaign for soft water in every home. In 1938, the first Culligan dealer started up business in Wheaton, Illinois. Growth was swift. The number of dealers bloomed to 150 by the beginning of World War II. While the war slowed growth—no new dealers were signed on during that time—Culligan's skills were called upon for the war effort and a facility was developed in San Bernardino, California. There, Culligan manufactured silica gel, a dehydrating material that protected metals from atmospheric corrosion. Silica gel was greatly in demand during the war and Culligan soon became one of the largest suppliers. The company was later given an award for its contributions to the war effort.

After the war, state-side expansion resumed. The dealer organization was growing again by 1946. Only a few years later, the Northbrook plant had become the largest producer of water softeners in the world. The San Bernardino facility had quickly converted and become—with its 34 acres of solar drying basins—the largest zeolite manufacturing plant in the world. Further plant facilities were purchased in Evanston, Illinois, not far from the Northbrook headquarters, and these were also expanding. In 1947, a two-story structure was added to the Northbrook home base.

A mere 15 years after Emmett Culligan approached the city council with $50 and an off-kilter idea, Northbrook proclaimed a "Culligan Day." On October 13, 1951, a square dance and barbecue gathered the town's residents together to celebrate Culligan's new half-million dollar plant on South Shermer Road. Soft water had become such a national mainstay that the old plant had suffered from eight major expansions. With the new facility, Culligan had more than 450,000 square feet of space to accommodate its sales growth.

The Culligan Zeolite Company became Culligan Incorporated in 1952. Over the decades, Culligan grew in scope, broadening its water-quality improvement offerings and branching out over the oceans. To reflect that expansion, the company's name was again changed in 1970 to Culligan International Company. Internationally, Culligan products were available through licensees in 85 countries.

In 1978, Culligan became part of Beatrice, a food products conglomerate. Beatrice later became a privately held company as a result of a buyout, and at that time a number of brands, including Culligan, were reorganized into E-II Holdings. E-II was purchased by American Brands, Incorporated, in 1988 for $1.1 billion. American Brands, a holding company with interests in tobacco, distilled spirits, and insurance, kept five of E-II's companies and sold the rest of E-II, including Culligan and Samsonite, to the Riklis Family Corporation. American Brands had owned Culligan for about six months before it sold E-II to Riklis. About three years later, Riklis issued junk bonds and E-II fell into bankruptcy. A struggle then ensued between financiers Carl C. Icahn, who purchased senior junk bonds, and Leon Black, who purchased junior junk bonds.

Throughout this time, Culligan remained quite profitable, keeping its recipe for success basically unchanged. It had endured the bankruptcy of E-II and was still doing business and making money. In fact, Culligan did not feel many effects after the change of ownership. While junk bonds were being swapped, Culligan quietly kept at its business. In the spring of 1993, Ametek Inc. and Icahn made a bid for E-II and Culligan, but the package ultimately went to Black. After the sale, E-II became Astrum International. Culligan remains a subsidiary of Astrum, a holding company whose core businesses include American Tourister and Samsonite luggage; McGregor, a line of men's tailored clothing; and Global Licensing, which licenses trademarks.

In the summer of 1994, Culligan was an official sponsor of the Goodwill Games, which took place in St. Petersburg. At the same time, the company provided a water purification system for a group of townhomes in that city, the first American-style housing development in the Commonwealth of Independent States (CIS), formerly the Soviet Union. Culligan warmed up for this event by supplying water treatment systems for both visitors and athletes at the Olympic games in Barcelona in 1992.

In the mid 1990s, Culligan's mainstay was still water treatment, and it still operated sales and distribution franchises. In fact, Culligan had changed very little over the years. From the beginning, it was one of the few water treatment companies that offered a complete water treatment line, from homes to corporations and commercial use. Most of its competitors provided either industrial or household water treatments, but not both. Culligan was able to offer that range because of its size, history, and fiscal stability. This provided Culligan with distinct advantages, because when one side of business was up, the other was often down. Company executives stated their intention to carry on the traditions begun by the company's founder in years to come.

Principal Subsidiaries: Everpure Corporation.

Further Reading:

''Culligan International,'' *New York Times,* June 15, 1994, p. D3.
''The Culligan Man Is Splashing into Supermarkets,'' *Beverage Industry,* October 1994, p. 19.
Elliott, Stuart, ''Culligan International,'' *New York Times,* October 7, 1994, p. C16.
McClenahen, John, ''Hey, Culligan Man,'' *Industry Week,* October 17, 1994, p. 21.
Oloroso, Arsenio, ''Desert Calls for Culligan Man: Firm Seeks to Provide Water to U.S. Troops,'' *Crain's Chicago Business,* September 3, 1990, p. 3.
Strom, Stephanie, ''Ametek and Icahn Join in Bid to Control E-II,'' *New York Times,* May 25, 1993, p. D5(L).

—Carol I. Keeley

Cummins Engine Co. Inc.

500 Jackson Street
Box 3005
Columbus, Indiana 47202-3005
U.S.A.
(812) 377-5000
Fax: (812) 377-3334

Public Company
Incorporated: 1919
Employees: 25,600
Sales: $4.74 billion
Stock Exchanges: New York Pacific
SICs: 3519 Internal Combustion Engines, Not Elsewhere
   Classified; 3621 Motors & Generators; 3694 Engine
   Electrical Equipment; 3714 Motor Vehicle Parts &
   Accessories

Cummins Engine Co. Inc., founded in 1919 by a chauffeur who worked on motors in his employer's garage, is the world's largest independent manufacturer of diesel engines. It is involved in the design, manufacture, and sale of diesel engines, components, and subsystems. While Cummins does not produce its own trucks, its engines are offered as options by every major U.S. truck manufacturer, even those that manufacture their own diesel engines and compete with Cummins. In addition to trucks, Cummins diesel engines are used for drilling rigs, boats, industrial locomotives, compressors, pumps, logging equipment, construction equipment, agricultural equipment, municipal and school buses, and a variety of other applications.

The company's founder and the man who adapted Rudolf Diesel's engine design for mobile use was Clessie L. Cummins, the chauffeur of a 1909 Packard touring car owned by Will G. Irwin, a wealthy industrialist and philanthropist in Columbus, Indiana. Cummins was regarded by Irwin as indispensable, since he was the only man who could keep the Packard in running condition. When shortly before World War I, Cummins demanded a pay hike to $85 a month, Irwin threatened to fire him. However, the two men reached a compromise. Cummins would accept a salary reduction if the family garage were equipped with tools so that he could do engine repair work. In 1917, Cummins began making wagon hub caps for the U.S. Army, while reading news about Germany's diesel-powered U-

boats. Most diesel engines at that time were large and smoky, and entirely impractical for any kind of transportation.

Cummins started working full-time on diesels in 1919 when he heard that Sears, Roebuck & Co., would buy 3-horsepower farm diesels made on a European patent. He persuaded Irwin to negotiate a contract with Sears and established Cummins Engine Co. Inc. The beginning was inauspicious; Sears said the engines were defective, and Irwin had to financially rescue his chauffeur. Neither Irwin nor Cummins was quitting, however. Irwin gave Cummins $10,000 to correct the initial defect, and eventually poured more than $2.5 million into the company.

The problem with diesel engines at that time was that engineers kept adding devices to them to give them more power. Cummins accepted only one common premise, that of "combustion ignition," or fuel oil in the cylinder bursting into flames to provide power, and systematically disposed of any other "add on" parts. He initially reduced engine horsepower, but ultimately got his diesel to run faster than other models. For ten years his experimental engines ripped the bottoms out of fishing boats or tore themselves to remnants, but Cummins still would not quit. His breakthrough was what he called "the Sneezer," a device that discharged every last particle of fuel oil into the cylinder to ensure that no oil was released as smoke. He also created a fuel injector experts described as "simpler than a fountain pen."

With his diesel at last perfected, he installed it in a Packard and drove the 792 miles from Columbus to New York City on $1.88 worth of heating oil without refueling. He then exhibited the car in the 1930 New York Automobile Show. When skeptics suggested he had used more fuel than he admitted, Cummins proved them wrong by driving across the country on $9.36 worth of fuel. He also entered a Duesenberg race car at the Indianapolis Motor Speedway and finished thirteenth while establishing a record speed for a diesel-powered car of 80.389 mph.

Cummins' fuel pump and injector were now regarded as the best in the industry, but truck manufacturers refused to use them and continued to manufacture gasoline engines, while trying to design their own diesel engines. Irwin came to Cummins' rescue by having the engines of delivery trucks used by his grocery chain of Purity Stores in California replaced by Cummins diesel engines. The truckers liked these new engines, which were powerful, fuel-efficient, and reliable. As these truckers recommended the engine to their colleagues, the business began to flourish.

Irwin's grand-nephew, J. Irwin Miller, a young man with a pronounced taste for Greek and Latin but no business training, was appointed as head of the company. Miller was an unlikely manager: he had stuttered as a child, was something of an outcast at school, and knew nothing about engines. But he had expected to inherit some facet of the family business, and he applied himself rigorously to the business at hand.

Miller replaced the chauffeur's hand tools with production equipment and constructed a full-scale plant. He then helped employees organize the Diesel Workers Union, and solicited business during the Great Depression by pointing out to cash-starved truckers that they would save money if they bought only those trucks that offered Cummins engines as options. Miller referred to this strategy—going to the users and not the suppliers—as a "back-door approach." Fortunately for the young company, the trucking business prospered in the 1930s due to improved roads and demand for point-to-point deliveries. Diesel engines for large trucks that needed maximum fuel efficiency were more and more in demand. In 1937 the young company turned its first profit. Selling engines to competitors was an uncertain way of doing business, but it worked and remained, however unorthodox, the Cummins approach. Miller, who was admired as a scholar and philanthropist, and who served as the first lay president of the National Council of Churches, later acknowledged, "We're in the business of selling engines to engine makers, which is surely not the smartest way to make a living."

The company was not just unorthodox in its marketing approach. It contributed five percent of its pre-tax profits each year to a number of charitable and social service projects. Years later, Cummins became one of the first companies in its industry to hire blacks for other than janitorial jobs. Miller helped beautify the company's hometown, Columbus, Indiana, with the creation of a unique endowment that paid the architect's fees for many public buildings. The fund helped draw some of the United States's finest architects to the Midwest town. In 1992, the Business Enterprise Trust recognized Miller's magnanimity and philanthropy when it awarded him its Lifetime Achievement Award. Miller's sense of justice and scholarly background helped him at times decide against prevailing business trends as well. For example, when asked why Cummins was resisting pressure to diversify, Miller told *Forbes,* "This may be counter to trends, but we believe that by diversifying you are liable to lose confidence in the value of a good product."

The company doubled its sales in five years and continued to double sales every five years into the 1960s. Sales in 1946 hit $20 million; a decade later they reached more than $100 million. Cummins' best-selling engine was a 2,590-pound diesel for trucks of 13 tons or more. In order to maintain the high demand for Cummins engines, the company had to stay ahead of the competition, which soon included Mack Trucks, Caterpillar, and GM's Detroit Diesel. In 1952 the company unveiled a turbo-diesel which used exhaust gases to turn a gas turbine supercharger. The device increased the horsepower of each Cummins engine by 50 percent without raising fuel consumption. That year Cummins demonstrated the engine at the Indianapolis Motor Speedway, where it malfunctioned. Miller was nonplussed. "We have progressed from failure to failure," he said, confidently predicting that the turbo-diesel would soon be perfected and marketed, which it was.

Cummins stayed way ahead of its competition in the 1950s by securing up to 60 percent of the heavy truck market in North America. Its in-line six-cylinder engines were renowned for their power and longevity. Cummins distributors, who handled nothing but Cummins engines and parts, were regarded as highly reputable because of their expertise with the single product line. Although it faced competition from Caterpillar and Euclid, Cummins also began selling engines for off-road construction. "We'll build the roads and then we'll run on them," said Miller.

However, the heavy truck market appeared to be saturated by 1960. To expand into alternative markets Cummins crafted a new line of V-6 and V-8 engines, based on an "oversquare" gasoline engine design. Since the diameter of the cylinder in oversquare engines is greater than the piston stroke, the engines produce more power at high speeds. Diesel engines had been long-stroke, but Cummins' engineers found the right combination of fuel and air to inject into the combustion chamber and make their engines workable.

The new engines, the Vim, a V-6 model with 200 horsepower, the Vine, a V-8 with 265 horsepower, and the Val, a V-6 with 120 horsepower, represented the first time Cummins attempted to penetrate the lighter truck market. At that time, 44 percent of trucks 13 tons and over had diesel engines, but fewer than 1 percent of the trucks from eight to 13 tons were diesel-powered. With heavier trucks representing just six percent of the market, and the lighter trucks 22 percent, management concluded that manufacturing smaller engines would raise revenues. But the lighter truck market proved difficult to enter. Gas was cheap and diesel engines, which at that time cost $1,000–$4,000 more than gasoline engines, were seen as economical only if the vehicles were driven approximately 4,000 hours per year.

In the early 1960s Cummins began a slow decline. Sales and profits fluctuated. A new line of engines with more than 300 horsepower, introduced by the company in 1962, failed to gain a dominant market share for more than two years. Management was criticized for being behind in both product development and market share.

Part of the problem was Cummins' policy of diversification. Beginning in the late 1950s Cummins started acquiring an interest in companies that produced diesel-related products. By the late 1960s it had become genuinely diversified, purchasing a ski manufacturer, a bank, and even an Irish cattle feeding outfit. Management had decided to make these acquisitions due to the slow growth of the diesel market. While Cummins' sales averaged 15 percent annual growth, the diesel market was projected to expand at half that rate. A number of new diesel competitors, such as GMC Division and Perkins, compounded the problem.

By 1967 Cummins' share of the crucial heavy-truck market had slipped to less than 45 percent. Earnings were off 78 percent. A strong truck market helped sales rebound in 1968, reaching a record of $365 million. Vigorous sales continued over the next few years, but earnings were erratic. Miller's hand-picked young successor, Henry Schacht, who joined the company after graduating from Harvard Business School and assumed the presidency just two years later, blamed surprisingly strong demand for the thin margins. Instead of preparing for an increased truck demand, Cummins had diverted resources to its non-diesel holdings. To catch up to the competition, Cummins operated its factories 24 hours a day, seven days a week, and paid a large amount in overtime wages. A two-month long strike only exacerbated the company's difficulties.

"We clearly left the door open to competitors," Schacht told *Forbes.* Demand exceeded supply, and customers went elsewhere. There was criticism that Cummins met the demands of only its biggest customers and that smaller consumers were forced to buy from the competition. Cummins' share of the large truck market reached a low point of less than 40 percent in the early 1970s. The company elected to sell its other holdings and concentrate on meeting the unexpectedly high diesel demand.

The main challenge was to devise a marketing strategy for engines that remained about five per cent more expensive than the competition's. The company refused to downgrade its product line. Management believed that the most significant problem for truckers who drove their vehicles 240,000 miles and more a year was downtime. So the company's response to its slipping market share was to make its engines more powerful, which in turn made them more reliable. In this way Cummins held on to its largest customers. Furthermore, the company expanded its overseas operations. It had a worldwide network of 3,000 service outlets, and a computerized analysis of 50,000 miles of major highways, allowing it to match the best engine to the customer's requirements. Its reputation helped it gain access to new markets. By the mid-1970s, 25 percent of the company's revenues came from overseas, and additional profits were being made in the agriculture, construction, and marine enterprises for which Cummins was designing extra-large engines of 1,200 horsepower.

Then Cummins made an apparent mistake and introduced a line of 450-horsepower engines. This was 50 percent more power than a truck needed to haul a loaded rig at 65 mph on a level highway. Cummins was marketing power in its engines, but the problem was the new 55 mile-per-hour speed limit. The company confronted this issue with an advertising campaign that stressed "reserve power." According to the ads, the new engines could easily maintain 55 mph even on uphill grades, so truckers would not have to lose more speed than they had to by law. Furthermore, constant speed and less shifting would actually increase fuel efficiency.

The new engines didn't sell very well at first, as the truck market in 1975 slumped 40 percent. The following year, however, the market rebounded, and Cummins took the lion's share. Sales reached $1 billion and earnings were $59 million. Cummins benefitted from the erratic enforcement of the 55 mph speed limit. Furthermore, the company outperformed its competitors by introducing a turbo-charged, slower-running version of its large-block engine, offering five percent better economy.

Nonetheless, management was increasingly concerned about the volatile truck market. While automating company plants in order to stay competitive within the truck engine industry, Cummins increased its profit from non-highway engines until they accounted for nearly 25 percent of revenues. This stabilized the company, for the demand for agricultural and construction equipment ran in cycles that were unrelated to the demand for truck engines. Cummins also established plants in Scotland and England to penetrate the European market while avoiding European tariffs. It faced new rivals, such as Renault in France and Iveco in Italy, which placed only their own engines in trucks they were manufacturing. But Cummins, which had faced a similar obstacle in the 1930s, was undeterred. New laws allowing trucks of up to 38,000 pounds on European highways, in addition to the escalating costs of fuel, persuaded the Cummins management that Europe was the new market for Cummins'

diesel engines. For Cummins, the European market grew slowly but steadily.

In the meantime, Cummins faced a Japanese incursion on the domestic market. These new competitors sought to establish a foothold in the United States by offering their diesel engines at 10 percent to 40 percent below Cummins' prices. Cummins met the challenge with his own price cuts, a strategy that helped prevent the new rivals from capturing a significant share of the market. In order to maintain profitability, Cummins' CEO, Schacht, instituted a program of austerity and restructuring. From 1979 to 1986, the company cut employment by 22 percent, set up flexible production methods that reduced inventory, increased productivity, and launched outsourcing programs. And although the company lost millions in the early 1980s, Schacht committed about $200 million annually to capital investments and improvements, and maintained Cummins' dividend.

In 1986 the company entered a period of continuous, comprehensive restructuring that embraced every aspect of the business. The adoption of an employee training and empowerment program known as JDIT-Kaizen helped transform the corporate culture. The acronym JDIT stood for the well-known catchphrase, "just do it." Kaizen was one of a number of Japanese management techniques that were in vogue at the time. It encouraged creativity at all levels, with the ultimate goal of continuous, gradual improvement. This management strategy may have helped ease labor relations at Cummins, which had earlier moved production to non-union factories in the southern United States to avoid labor disputes. In 1993, in fact, the independent Diesel Workers Union—representing workers at four Indiana plants—gave Cummins an overwhelming vote of confidence when it ratified an extraordinary eleven-year contract. Furthermore, a consolidation trimmed operations in the United Kingdom and shuttered two U.S. plants, reducing floor space for worldwide engine manufacturing and distribution by 19 percent.

Notwithstanding these efforts, Schacht and Cummins also made some significant missteps during the last half of the 1980s. Some industry observers criticized the company's downsizing efforts when a resurgence in demand compelled the company to pay overtime rates in order to keep up. In response to ever more stringent emission control regulations, the company hurried to beat its competitors in bringing a compliant engine to market. Although the new model met U.S. EPA standards, tests conducted after the engine's launch revealed significant shortcomings. At the same time, rival Detroit Diesel Inc. introduced an electronic engine that drew customers away in droves. Cummins' share declined steadily throughout the late 1980s and early 1990s, from over 60 percent in 1984, to 55 percent in 1988, 50.3 percent in 1989, and 40 percent in 1991, its lowest level in two decades. During this same period, the company lost over $300 million and recorded only one year of meager profitability.

In 1990, Schacht convinced Ford Motor Co., Tenneco Inc., and Kubota Ltd. to invest a combined total of $250 million in a 27 percent stake in Cummins. The CEO used the infusion of capital to pay down debt and expand European operations. When sales of long-haul trucks bounced back in the early 1990s, Cummins' long years of preparation paid off. In 1993, the company enjoyed its first fiscal-year profit since 1987. In 1994, after seeing the company through one of its most difficult periods, Schacht announced that he was stepping down as CEO. That year—Cummins' 75th in business—the company achieved record sales of $4.74 billion and, perhaps more importantly, record profits of $252.9 million. James A. Henderson succeeded Schacht as CEO, and Theodore M. Solso became president and chief operating officer. They inherited a company well-positioned to capture significant shares of the vital Japanese and European markets. Henderson became chairman and Solso became president in 1995.

Principal Subsidiaries: Cummins Natural Gas Engines, Inc.; Cummins Brasil S.A. (Brazil); Cummins S.A. (Mexico); China National Automotive Industry Corp.; Atlas Inc.; Cummins Electronics Company, Inc.; Diesel ReCon Company; Holset Engineering Company; Dampers, Iberica (Spain); Dampers, S.A., and Techniparts, S.A. (France); Holset KBB Kompressorenbau (Germany); Onan Corporation; Newage International Ltd. (England).

Further Reading:

Benway, Susan Duffy, "Geared Up for a Turn: Cummins Comes Through a Rough Patch," *Barrons,* September 22, 1986, pp. 13, 41.
Bergstrom, Robin Yale, "Old Measures, New Rules, *Production,* June 1994, pp. 62–64.
Cimini, Michael H., and Susan L. Behrmann, "Developments in Industrial Relations," *Monthly Labor Review,* July 1993, pp. 56–58.
Faltermeyer, Edmund, "Cummins Engine: A Long Term Bet Pays Off at Last," *Fortune,* August 23, 1993, pp. 79–80.
Gold, Jacqueline S., "The Twelve Labors: To Hell and Back with Henry Schacht of Cummins Engine," *Financial World,* June 9, 1992, pp. 60–61.
Henkoff, Ronald, "The Engine That Couldn't," *Fortune,* December 18, 1989, p. 124.
Kelly, Kevin, "Turning Cummins into the Engine Maker that Could: Why Kubota Hitched Its Tractor to Cummins," *Business Week,* July 30, 1990, pp. 20–21.
——, "Does Cummins Have the Oomph to Climb This Hill?," *Business Week,* November 4, 1991, pp. 66, 68.
——, "A CEO Who Kept His Eyes on the Horizon," *Business Week,* August 1, 1994, p. 32.
McManamy, Rob, "Market Focus: Columbus, Inc., the Town that Builds First Class," *ENR,* April 6, 1992, pp. 36C7–36C12.
Smith, Geoffrey N., "The Yankee Samurai," *Forbes,* July 14, 1986, pp. 82–83.
Taylor, David L., and Ruth Karin Ramsey, "Empowering Employees to 'Just Do It'," *Training & Development,* May 1993, pp. 71–76.
Townsend, Blaine, "The Corporate Responsibility Hall of Fame," *Business & Society Review,* Spring 1992, pp. 47–50.

—updated by April Dougal Gasbarre

Danskin, Inc.

111 West 40th Street
New York, New York 10018
U.S.A.
(212) 764-4630

Public Company
Incorporated: 1882
Employees: 1,797
Sales: $129.8 million
SICs: 2253 Knit Outerwear Mills; 2251 Women's Hosiery
   Except Socks; 2252 Hosiery Not Elsewhere Classified

Danskin, Inc., is a leading maker and marketer of women's athletic and fitness wear. The company sells clothing to be worn during dance and exercise, and also offers hosiery. Founded in the late 19th century, Danskin made its name as a vendor of tights, tutus, and leotards, which became the standard for dancers across the United States. With the fitness boom that began in the 1980s, Danskin expanded its line of products to meet the needs of a much wider segment of the population.

The company that became Danskin was founded in 1882 in New York City, when the Goodman family opened a small dry goods store, which sold tights and hosiery that it imported from Europe. The store soon became popular with dancers, and, sensing a market opportunity, the Goodmans began to manufacture goods specifically for dancers' needs. From this start, Danskin soon came to dominate the market for clothing worn while dancing. The Goodmans introduced the first knit tights and leotards, and also pioneered the production of such dance standards as fishnet stockings. The company also popularized the use of the colors "ballet pink" and "theatrical pink" for dancer's tights.

Throughout the late 19th century and the first half of the 20th century, Danskin dominated the market for dance wear in the United States. Over time, the company's goods and products became synonymous with dance clothing. In addition to its tights and leotards for dancers of all sorts, the company introduced similar products for gymnasts and figure skaters.

In the late 1960s, Danskin broke out of the relatively restricted market consisting of dancers, gymnasts, and skaters when it marketed its first product for wear on the street by the general population. This innovative adaptation of its traditional product line was the bodysuit. The company added snaps for convenience to a conventional leotard, and also updated its styling to make it more fashionable. In this way, Danskin hoped to market its products to a broader range of consumers.

Following this innovation, Danskin entered a new market in the mid-1970s. In 1976, the company began to market swimwear, another extension of its basic leotard line. Using new technology, Danskin invented a shiny, stretchy fabric that was a blend of nylon and spandex. The company used this fabric in a maillot bathing suit, which, like the leotard, fit the wearer's body like a second skin. By the end of the decade, Danskin boasted an 80 percent share of the bodywear market overall.

At the start of the 1980s, Danskin ceased to be a privately held firm, when the company was sold to International Playtex, Inc., on April 29, 1980. Danskin's new owner had itself been purchased and become a subsidiary of a conglomerate called Esmark, Inc., in 1975. Esmark was founded in 1972 to take over the assets of the Swift & Company meatpacking business and since the early 1970s had grown by purchasing companies in a wide variety of fields, which were divided into four loose groupings: food divisions, leather and chemicals, insurance and financial services, and petroleum and oil.

With the purchase of Playtex, Esmark moved into the consumer goods area, and this unit's subsequent purchase of Danskin strengthened its holdings in the knit goods and hosiery fields. Playtex had first entered the market for women's hosiery in August 1977, when the company bought Pennaco Hosiery, Inc., which marketed women's stockings under the brand name "Round the Clock." Playtex augmented its holdings in this field five months later, when it also acquired Virginia Maid Hosiery Mills, Inc.

In the early 1980s, Danskin saw the rapid expansion of another potential market for its products, as the popularity of aerobic exercise grew. As women flocked to dance and exercise classes, Danskin began to market a special line of athletic wear for use in fitness classes. The company's entry into the workout apparel market expanded its line of product offerings and its overall sales throughout the 1980s.

Four years after Danskin became a part of Esmark, the company's corporate parent itself was acquired by the Beatrice Companies, Inc., on August 7, 1984. Beatrice had grown through acquisitions into a wide-ranging and far-flung conglomeration of business interests, of which Esmark made up only a small part. As Beatrice moved into the mid-1980s, the company became caught up in the turmoil of the financial industry. By early 1986, efforts were underway to take Beatrice private in a leveraged buy-out, as clearly the company's various parts would have to be broken apart and sold off in order to pay off part of the debt taken on when the company went private. As part of this process, Beatrice announced in October 1985, that it would sell its knitwear operations, including Danksin.

Preparatory to this effort, Beatrice set aside Esmark's apparel units, which consisted of Danskin and the Pennaco Hosiery company, forming Esmark Apparel, Inc., on February 21, 1986. These operations recorded combined sales in 1985 of $100 million. Then, on April, 17, 1986, the leveraged buyout of Beatrice was completed, as the company's outstanding shares were purchased by the BCI Holdings Corporation for $6.2 billion. Two months later, Beatrice announced the successful sale of its knitwear operations to Eaglewood Partners. Eaglewood Partners was an investor group put together by a private New York investment banking firm, Hero & Company. Eaglewood announced that its managing partner, Byron A. Hero, would be put in charge of Esmark. Danskin's general manager, Barbara Khouri, became the company's president. With this move, Esmark, with two divisions, Danskin and Pennaco Hosiery, once again became a privately held company.

At the time of its purchase by Eaglewood, Esmark Apparel held the largest portion of the fragmented women's exercise clothing market. However, Hero maintained that the company had missed opportunities to seize an even larger portion of this field, because it had not moved aggressively enough into the burgeoning fitness market. The company had not introduced enough new products to meet the growing demand in this sector of the market, according to Hero.

In addition, Hero felt that as a company on the auction block for nine months Esmark had been relegated to second class status within the Beatrice organization, which had hampered Esmark's efforts to expand its product line more effectively. Therefore, Byron Hero planned to capitalize on the brand name recognition of Danskin and Pennaco, and to broaden the company's offerings of legwear and leotards. With Esmark as a privately held firm, Hero planned to reinvest the company's profits in expanding operations and market penetration. "The kinds of businesses that do well in the fashion industry are independently run and more sensitive to the market," Hero told the *Wall Street Journal.*

At the end of 1986, Esmark took its first steps toward expanding the company's line of goods, when it bought Dance France, Limited, another maker of dance apparel, from that company's French founder, Francois Greis. The operations of this company were merged into Danskin's pre-existing structure. In the following year, Danskin further expanded its product offerings, introducing Danskin-Plus, a line of large-sized bodywear, in the fall of 1987.

Esmark announced that it would promote this new line, as well as its other products, with a $5 million advertising campaign. This campaign was slated to build on the $3 million campaign, which featured the slogan "all the world's a stage," which Danskin had used to promote a line of short, tight-fitting dresses. This effort boosted sales of the company's adult streetwear by more than one-third in 1987. In addition, Danskin saw sales of its dancewear for children grow by 40 percent over the course of 1987. "It seems that every little girl wants to be a ballerina," Rose Peabody ("Podie") Lynch, Danskin's new president, told *Forbes.*

In September 1987, Esmark made another strategic acquisition which strengthened its presence in the dancewear market. At that time, the company bought Repetto France, a French manufacturer of dancewear, which specialized in ballet shoes and tutus. Esmark also enhanced its standing in the hosiery market when it acquired the right to distribute the Givenchy Hosiery line of products in foreign markets.

By the start of 1988, Esmark's Danskin division boasted a 98 percent consumer recognition rating in its core bodywear market, but its share of the market had shrunk to 35 percent, down from 80 percent at the start of the decade. Outside of its traditional dance product line, the company had become firmly identified in consumer's minds with Lycra-blend workout wear, a perception which held down sales of the company's non-dance-related clothing.

"We want to reposition Danskin products as young, vital and at the forefront of fashion," Lynch explained to *Forbes.* The company targeted women from the ages of 18 to 44, hoping to encourage customers to wear its clothes not just for workouts, but for everyday purposes as well. Surveys indicated that nearly half of Danskin's apparel buyers already saw the company's products in this versatile light, but Danskin hoped to increase this percentage even more. "Many of [our customers] like to exercise, but they all like to look good," Lynch maintained.

In addition to increasing sales, Danskin set out to hold down costs. The company reduced the work force at its York, Pennsylvania, knitting mill from 2,500 to 600. Eighty-five percent of the products Danskin sold were manufactured in York, and the other 15 percent were made in Taiwan and shipped to the United States. "Because of the weak dollar, we are bringing the concept of quality circles from Taiwan to our York plant to increase productivity," Lynch noted. All in all, as a result of these efforts, Danskin's sales had risen by 45 percent within two years of its sale by Beatrice.

Building on these gains, Danskin introduced a new line of tights made with Supplex nylon and Lycra in August 1989. Three months later, the company also rolled out Danskin Pro, a collection of athletic wear for women. This clothing was made for those participating in gymnastics, figure skating, track, volleyball, running, water sports, and other activities. To promote these products, Danskin recruited a group of female athletes, which it dubbed "Team Danskin," to serve as consultants, testers, and spokespersons. Among the members of "Team Danskin" were skater Katarina Witt and ballet dancer Darci Kistler.

Danskin continued its promotional efforts in 1990, when the company launched the "Danskin Women's Triathlon Series." This event was designed to meet the need for sports and fitness competitions among female non-career athletes. The triathlon started with events held in three cities, and soon spread to six locations, encompassing more than 10,000 first time participants.

At the end of 1990, Danskin announced that it would introduce a new line of footwear the following spring. Overall, the company planned to diversify its product line and to further enhance its marketing effort. These efforts began to bear fruit in March 1991, when Danskin introduced a line of headbands and pony tail holders that matched its activewear. One month later, the company announced that it had seen a 50 percent rise in sales for items in its Danskin Plus line, an early attempt by the company to reach out to new customers.

On July 2, 1992, Esmark Apparel changed its name to that of its most important operating unit, Danskin. Six days later, the company offered $3 million of stock to the public, in an effort to raise $36 million to fund further expansion. The company's initial public offering, however, was so successful that $39 million was raised.

While it sought capital in the market, Danskin outlined four strategies for further growth, which it had first elucidated in 1988. The first of these goals was to focus greater attention on expanding wholesale distribution of Danskin products. The company hoped to tailor its product lines to different segments of the market, defined as department stores, specialty shops, and sporting goods stores. Danskin hoped to hone marketing techniques that would push more Danskin goods onto the shelves of all of these retail outlets. In addition, Danskin planned to increase the number of retail stores selling its goods directly, by opening a chain of factory outlet stores, that would then be followed by more elaborate full-price stores.

To keep these stores supplied with as wide a range of merchandise as possible, Danskin plotted two strategies to broaden its product offerings. The company moved to license its brand names for use on products made by other manufacturers, and also moved to maximize its production capabilities, expanding the Danskin line of goods in every way possible, given the company's factory equipment. Finally, Danskin hoped to expand sales by increasing overseas marketing efforts.

Shortly after its first public stock offering, Danskin augmented its product offerings by adding a line of children's swimwear. At the end of the year, the company, led by president Mary Ann Domuracki and CEO Howard Cooley, announced that it would push further into the active wear market, building on its strength in the workout gear segment of the apparel industry.

In the spring of 1993, Danskin stepped up its licensing activities. The company purchased rights to the "Shape" label from the Imagination Factory, which it used to launch a line of goods for sale in chain stores and mass merchandisers. One month later, Danskin's Pennaco division licensed its Round-the-Clock hosiery brand name to Paul Lavitt Mills.

Late in April 1993, Danskin introduced a collection of sportswear for the fall, as the company continued its quest to add market share in the women's apparel field. Although Danskin's sales and earnings showed improvement throughout the first nine months of 1993, the company ran into difficulty in the last quarter of the year, its most important segment for sales. Bad weather forced the company's factory in York, Pennsylvania, to close for 22 days of production in the winter of 1993, and the company's southern hosiery mills, located in Memphis, Tennessee, and Grenada, Mississippi, were also affected.

Although sales of Danskin products increased for the seventh year in a row, Danskin's hosiery division lost $6 million over 1993, as the stocking industry suffered from severe overcapacity. In an effort to stem the losses in this area, Danskin sought to expand into other, stocking-related products, such as socks and tights, and also to add new brand names, such as Christian Dior, a license acquired during the year.

In its effort to expand overall distribution channels, Danskin opened 15 new factory stores, bringing the company's total to 32. In addition, Danskin signed leases for full-service retail outlets in Manhattan and in Miami's trendy South Beach neighborhood. In these stores, Danskin planned to stock clothing for dance, exercise, and sports in a fashion environment. The company hoped that these flagship stores would give other Danskin retailers ideas about how best to present the company's merchandise. In addition, Danskin continued its push into international markets, signing an agreement with a retailer in Australia to market its apparel there.

Although Danskin's initial year as a publicly held company proved a disappointment, the strength of its brand name, and its firm establishment in its niche of the apparel market boded well for the company as it moved into the late 1990s.

Principal Subsidiaries: Danpen, Inc.

Further Reading:

Cuff, Daniel F., and Stephen Phillips, "Suitor of Esmark Plans to Broaden Its Lines," *New York Times,* June 11, 1986.
Grieves, Robert T., "Stretching the Image," *Forbes,* April 18, 1988, p. 99.
Hasty, Susan E., "Congrats, Danskin," *Apparel Industry Magazine,* April 1994.

—Elizabeth Rourke

Dean Witter, Discover & Co.

Dean Witter, Discover & Co.

Two World Trade Center
New York, New York 10048
U.S.A.
(212) 392-2222
Fax: (212) 392-7562

Public Company
Founded: 1924
Employees: 27,000
Sales: $4.5 billion
Stock Exchanges: New York San Francisco
SICs: 6211 Securities Brokers and Dealers; 7389 Business
Services Not Elsewhere Classified

Dean Witter, Discover & Co. is engaged in providing securities brokerage and credit card services. The company is a leading U.S. provider of brokerage services for individuals, electronic transaction processing services, and consumer financing. The company is also the largest credit card issuer in the nation with 29 million accounts issued through its Discover credit card.

Dean Witter, Discover & Co. was formed in 1993. Prior to becoming a public company, Dean Witter was operating as a subsidiary of retail giant Sears, Roebuck & Co. Sears purchased Dean Witter in 1981 for about $600 million as part of its strategy to diversify out of the retail industry. At the time, Dean Witter—then an investment-only business named Dean Witter Reynolds—was the fifth largest brokerage house in the United States. Sears planned to make Dean Witter the nucleus of what would become a national financial services network.

The original Dean Witter brokerage house was founded in 1924 by Dean Witter, his brother Guy, and cousin Jean. The trio started Dean Witter & Co. as a West Coast securities firm dealing in municipal and corporate bonds. They set up shop in San Francisco and, in 1928, purchased a seat on the San Francisco Stock Exchange; that exchange was later incorporated into the Pacific Stock Exchange. The company enjoyed immense success during the explosive bull market of the 1920s. In 1929, in fact, Dean Witter opened a New York office and purchased a seat on the New York Stock Exchange.

Dean Witter survived the Depression-era securities industry shakeout and even managed to post profits every year during the 1930s and into the 1940s. The company also became known as

an innovator on Wall Street. For example, Dean Witter was one of the first securities firms to establish an account executive training program. The company grew rapidly during the 1950s and 1960s, establishing itself as a major U.S. brokerage house. Dean Witter died in 1969, and, the following year, Guy Witter retired, passing the top position to Jean Witter's son, William M. Witter, who became CEO of the operation. The company was taken public in 1972 with an offering of 1.5 million shares on the NYSE. In 1977, Dean Witter purchased InterCapital Inc., an investment management firm with $200 million in assets.

At the same time that Dean Witter was rising to prominence on Wall Street, another company was making its mark on the securities brokerage business. Reynolds & Co. was started in 1931 by Richard S. Reynolds Jr., Thomas F. Stanley, and Charles H. Babcock, all members of the Reynolds family. That company also went public in the early 1970s, becoming Reynolds Securities. In 1978, Reynolds and Witter joined forces in what was then the largest merger in the history of the U.S. securities industry and would remain the largest merger to date going into 1995. Both firms were industry leaders and neither had posted a loss since they had opened their doors. The resultant company, Dean Witter Reynolds, was the fifth largest broker in the United States.

By the late 1970s, Sears, the largest retailer in the world, was facing several challenges. Its retail store operations were increasingly under fire from new competitors, particularly from discount retailers and upscale department store chains. Likewise, its well-known catalog division was threatened by a new breed of specialty catalog retailers. In short, Sears retailing strategy had become obsolete and the company was floundering. In an effort to overcome its problems, Sears experimented with a variety of fixes. During the early 1980s, for example, it decided to diversify into new businesses, including financial services. Toward that end, Sears acquired Dean Witter Reynolds in 1981.

Sears hoped that Dean Witter would provide the foundation for a giant financial services network—the Sears Financial Services Group—that would be offered to consumers through the company's extensive chain of retail stores. The network would provide Sears customers with an easy way to purchase mutual funds, stocks, and insurance, and even allow them to obtain financing for homes and other purchases. To head Dean Witter, Sears chose Philip J. Purcell, a strategic planner at the Sears Chicago headquarters. Purcell moved to New York to run the operation from Dean Witter's office.

Sears decided early that Dean Witter should make a major shift in its strategy. Instead of serving both the retail and institutional sectors, it would shift its focus to the former, the individual consumer. Purcell believed that market would fuel growth in the financial services industry in the coming decade, and he felt that Sears offered the infrastructure to reach that group. Thus, the strategy was relatively synergistic: Sears would create a sort of financial services supermarket aimed at the broad middle consumer market. A combination of heavy foot traffic and general goodwill toward Sears would lead millions to entrust their money with Dean Witter and its affiliates. "A lot of people don't trust brokers, but they do trust Sears," explained John

Fallon, a Dean Witter account executive, in the December 14, 1987 *Crain's Chicago Business.*

Many critics regarded Sears's scheme as simplistic and illusory. "Do consumers really want to buy socks and stocks under the same roof?" they quipped. Similarly, stockholders wondered why Sears was involving itself with financial services, when its core business was being assaulted by Wal-Mart and other aggressive contenders. In response, Sears cited its success with Allstate, an insurance company that it had started in 1931. Sears enjoyed success with that operation and hoped to replay those gains with broader financial offerings. In addition to Dean Witter, in fact, Sears purchased Coldwell Banker, a provider of mortgage and brokerage services. Sears aimed to achieve a synergy between Allstate, Coldwell, and Dean Witter that would allow the three to benefit from their complementary offerings.

During the early 1980s, Sears used its retail store network to open new Dean Witter and Coldwell Banker offices in areas of the country in which they had been nonexistent or poorly represented. After establishing a base in the local Sears store, satellite offices were spun off in surrounding neighborhoods. Sears invested millions of dollars into the Dean Witter operation during the early 1980s, opening 280 new offices between 1981 and 1986. Indeed, in 1983, Sears announced its intent to at least double Dean Witter's chain of 350 outlets during the 1980s and to establish it as a leading securities firm for individual investors. Sears initiated similar growth plans for Coldwell Banker as well.

However, Sears's aggressive efforts to turn its financial services division into a star performer had achieved lackluster results by the mid-1980s. Critics of the strategy sounded off after the stock market crash of 1987, which seemed to expose weaknesses in the division. Indeed, after focusing on building Dean Witter's retail sales, the financial services division was facing the possibility of a long-term bear market during which retail sales growth would undoubtedly wane. Worse yet, Dean Witter's position in the traditional investment banking and underwriting sectors had deteriorated rapidly since 1981. Many of its top executives and managers had jumped ship after the transition to retailing. Not surprisingly, Dean Witter's rank in the corporate debt and equity underwriting market had slipped from tenth to 15th, and investment banking accounted for less than ten percent of Witter's revenues by 1987.

Sears financial group posted a loss of $37 million in 1987 on sales of about $3.5 billion, while Sears earned $1.35 billion from $44 billion in sales during that year. Nevertheless, some contended that Dean Witter's performance was not as bad as it seemed. In fact, the overall financial services operations had posted healthy profits of $80 million just one year earlier. Furthermore, much of the 1987 loss was attributable to the Discover Card, a credit card introduced the year before by Sears, which sought to enter the growing $200 billion industry. Sears had invested $200 million into the project during 1986, with the expectation of losing money in the short term.

Discover Card had been set up as a division of Dean Witter, which was still under Purcell's direction. The main appeal of the card for consumers was that it was free; most other cards at the time charged annual fees ranging from $10 to $50. In addition, the card offered cashback bonuses and interest-free cash advances. The card was distinguished from Visa and Mastercard in that Sears controlled its brand image, features, service level, and pricing. Even though many retailers were initially slow to accept the card, within two years the card boasted more than 22 million subscribers and was accepted at 740,000 merchant outlets.

Discover's growth dropped off significantly during the late 1980s as credit card competition intensified. According to some analysts, Discover's profitability failed to live up to Sears's original expectations, and the concept received a generally lukewarm reception from the Visa/Mastercard-dominated credit card market. Nevertheless, Sears poured more than $1 billion into the project, and Discover turned its first profit in 1988. Discover's account base continued to increase past 25 million by the early 1990s as the total number of dispensed cards topped 40 million. In fact, Discover became the largest single issuer of general purpose credit cards. Its profitability remained well below that of many of its peers, but its sheer size allowed Discover to generate earnings of about $174 million annually by 1991.

Like Discover, Dean Witter's other operations experienced some challenges during the late 1980s. Although Dean Witter had nearly doubled in size between 1981 and 1989, it appeared as though Sears had failed to achieve the financial services synergy for which it had hoped. Sears announced plans to close about 200 of Dean Witter's 650 outlets, primarily those located in its department stores. Viewed as a failed attempt to capitalize on the individual financial services market, the barely profitable Dean Witter was frowned upon by frustrated Sears stockholders. In the early 1990s, however, the fortune of Dean Witter and its Discover Card began to turn.

Falling interest rates in the early 1990s sent many investors scurrying to the stock market in search of higher returns. As a result, Dean Witter's sales skyrocketed. Much of its gains were attributable to Dean Witter's emphasis on mutual funds. The company had begun investing heavily in its mutual fund offerings in the early 1980s, speculating that the funds would become the investment vehicle of choice for its target market. That strategy began to pay off in the early 1990s. Importantly, Dean Witter introduced a new family of proprietary funds (funds managed in-house) in 1992, giving it a steady stream of cash in the form of management fees as well as up-front fees charged to enter the funds. As cash began to pour in, Witter's mutual fund assets increased to more than $50 billion by 1992.

To the surprise of its critics, Dean Witter staged a major comeback in the early 1990s. In 1990, Witter posted profits of $109 million while the average Wall Street brokerage house saw a loss of $162. In 1991, moreover, net income from Dean Witter and its Discover division rose to $171 million and $173 million, respectively, as combined sales soared to a record $3.35 billion. Then, in 1992, total net income surpassed $400 million from revenues of $3.7 billion. Although Witter's securities operations were enjoying healthy gains, its success was also the result of big advancements by Discover, which was finally beginning to bear fruit.

As its financial services division posted solid gains during the early 1990s, the performance of Sears's core retail operations waned. By 1992, the mismanaged retail giant was suffering under a massive $38 billion debt load. In an effort to pare its debt and refocus its energies on its core business, Sears announced its intentions to sell its financial services operations. Although they were going to lose their deep-pocketed parent, many Dean Witter managers welcomed the decision to spin-off the operation. Indeed, some of them felt that the Sears name wasn't helping their image; in 1992, Sears posted the worst performance in its 108-year history, a staggering $3.9 billion loss.

On February 22, 1993, Sears spun off 20 percent of Dean Witter and Discover into an independent, publicly traded company called Dean Witter, Discover & Co. The remaining 80 percent was spun off on June 30, 1993. During its first year of operation, Dean Witter Discover revenues rose more than 20 percent to $4.6 billion as net income reached $600 million. Moreover, the company's stock soared. Gains continued in 1994 as both credit card and securities operations continued to advance, causing many of Witter's competitors to adopt the operating strategies that they had once ridiculed. Going into the mid-1990s, Dean Witter, Discover & Co. remained the largest credit card issuer in the United States, was the third largest broker, and offered a variety of related financial and transaction processing services. In 1994, moreover, the company started a new credit card, Prime Option, aimed at the Mastercard/Visa segment of the market.

Principal Subsidiaries: Dean Witter Reynolds Inc.; NOVUS Credit Services Inc.

Further Reading:

Beldky, Gary, and Robert Reed, "Dean Witter Woes Spur Retrenchment," *Crain's Chicago Business,* December 14, 1987, p. 1.

Elstrom, Peter J. W., "What's Next for Split-Up Sears: Discover Loses Muscle in Card Battle," *Crain's Chicago Business,* October 5, 1992.

Gleason, Mark, "Consumers Discovered Gold with Sears' Bold Credit Card," *Cincinnati Business Courier,* October 12, 1992, p. 12.

Herr, Jeff, "Job Growth on Track Despite Sears Moves," *Arizona Business Gazette,* October 1, 1992, p. 1.

Lefton, Terry, "Amid Rate, Fee and Rebate Squabbles, Sears Finds it Costs to Discover," *Brandweek,* November 9, 1992, p. 34.

Parker, Marcia, "Debt, Credit Rating Crucial at Dean Witter," *Crain's New York Business,* October 5, 1992, p. 1.

Roberts, William L., "Dean Witter, Discover Spinoff May Become Major Competitor," *Philadelphia Business Journal,* February 1, 1993, p. 3.

Robinson, David, "Dean Witter's Retail Focus is Finally Paying Off," *Buffalo News,* September 20, 1992.

Waldstein, Peter D., "Sears Stores Cut Financial Outlets," *Crain's Chicago Business,* March 13, 1989, p. 1.

Willis, Gerri, "Dean Witter Laughs Last," *Crain's New York Business,* February 7, 1994, p. 1.

Zonana, Victor F., "Trying to Become Financial Supermarket," *Los Angeles Times,* September 30, 1992, p. D1.

—Dave Mote

arose, however, Congress passed the industry-renowned Public Utilities Regulatory Policies Act of 1978 (PURPA).

PURPA was created to encourage the production of power from alternative (non-oil or coal generated) sources. Utilities were required by this federal law to purchase power from new "qualifying facilities," if these facilities could produce the power at a cost equal to or less than those facilities that the utilities could build themselves. While the law was originally intended to reduce U.S. utilities' reliance on oil, it ultimately resulted in the creation of a healthy market for nonutility power generators (NUGs), like Destec. Under PURPA, Destec's facilities would have to meet at least one of two specified conditions: they would have to generate less than 80 megawatts of power, a small amount in comparison to some large utility generators, or, they would have to cogenerate. Destec's units would still be susceptible to federal price controls, but they would be free from stricter state price caps applied to the utility companies that would purchase Destec's power.

Although Dow created Destec in 1989, it had already been active in the cogeneration industry for several years. In fact, Dow was considered a pioneer in U.S. cogeneration. Dow's founder, Herbert H. Dow, generated electricity and steam from wood in the late 1880s. During the 1900s, Dow used the efficiency of cogeneration to supply power to its own factories, thus giving its products a strong cost advantage over competing goods. Dow didn't enter the cogeneration market until it formed Destec. However, Dow's early efforts at its own facilities were important in demonstrating that cogeneration was a reliable and cost-effective means of producing energy.

During this time, a company that would figure prominently in Destec's future was preparing for expansion. PSE, Inc., a pioneer in the cogeneration industry, was founded in 1969 by Albert Smith Jr. and Tom McMichael, and the company had remained private until the 1980s. In an effort to raise capital for expansion, PSE went public in 1986 and subsequently became engaged in several new cogeneration projects. However, its growth continued to be hampered by a lack of capital.

Following the passage of PURPA, PSE built CoGen Power in 1983, a cogeneration facility in Port Arthur, Texas, that had a production capacity of only five megawatts of electricity and 550,000 pounds of steam per hour. The small plant sold its steam to Chevron, while both the Great Lakes Carbon Corporation and the Gulf States Utilities Co. purchased the electricity. PSE's first project was the Salt Grass cogeneration unit it built at Dow's Texas division in 1969 (before PURPA). That successful experiment served as a stepping stone to a string of much larger facilities that PSE would construct throughout the 1980s and early 1990s. In 1985, CoGen Lyondell went on line in Channelview, Texas. That large cogeneration facility eventually had an electric capacity of 465 megawatts and 1.15 million pounds of steam per hour. As lessee of the plant, PSE supplied power to the giant Texas Utilities Electric Company, and Lyondell remained Destec's largest facility going into the mid-1990s.

In 1987, Dow opened its third power plant, as a result of the U.S. Treasury Department's Synfuels Corporation, which promoted alternative technology: the Louisiana Gasification Technology, Inc. (LGTI) facility in Plaquemine, Louisiana.

Destec Energy, Inc.

P.O. Box 4411
Houston, Texas 77210-4411
U.S.A.
(713) 735-4000
Fax: (713) 735-4201

Public Company
Incorporated: 1989
Employees: 610
Sales: $727 million
Stock Exchanges: New York
SICs: 4931 Electric and Other Services Combined

A subsidiary of The Dow Chemical Company, Destec Energy, Inc. is a leading U.S. independent power producer and a major player in the emerging independent power industry. Through its ownership interests in power generation and coal-gasification facilities, Destec's power production capacity in 1994 was about 2,400 megawatts of electricity and three million pounds per hour of steam. Destec has grown rapidly since its inception in 1989.

Dow's formation of Destec in 1989 reflected its desire to capitalize on growth occurring in the market for cogeneration and alternative energy provided by private companies. Cogeneration is a power production technology that provides the sequential generation of two or more useful forms of energy, such as electricity and steam, from a single fuel source, such as natural gas or coal. Destec's principal power production technologies are gas-fired cogeneration and coal gasification, the latter being a process in which coal is converted into syngas, an alternate energy source. Destec uses those technologies to generate three primary products: electricity, thermal energy, and syngas.

Strong demand growth in the 1980s and early 1990s for alternative power sources was largely the result of federal government initiatives. Between the 1930s and the late 1970s, production, transmission, and distribution of electric power was relegated exclusively to vertically integrated, monopolistic, government-regulated utilities. The industry was governed by the Public Utility Holding Company Act (PUHCA) of 1935, which essentially barred non-utilities from participating in the generation (and distribution) of power. When the oil crises of the late 1970s

Designed and built by Dow, LGTI was a coal-gasification facility capable of churning out enough syngas to fuel the production of 160 megawatts of electricity. LGTI was the first of two coal-gasification plants that Dow would open by the mid-1990s and was developed in part as an experiment, supported by the federal government, to determine the viability of the new process. Dow itself used the syngas supplied by LGTI.

In 1988, PSE helped to open the Corona cogeneration facility in Corona, California. PSE was a partner with several other investors in that project, which supplied electricity to a California utility and steam to a local food processing company. Early in 1989, PSE opened three more facilities in Kern, California, that were similar to Corona. PSE owned about 20 percent of those cogeneration plants, each of which could produce 48 megawatts of electricity and 100,000 pounds of steam per hour. They supplied electricity to Pacific Gas and Electric Company, a major utility, and steam to Occidental Petroleum Corporation.

By 1989, PSE owned or operated seven cogeneration plants, while Dow owned and operated one coal-gasification facility. The combined capacity of those units was over 500 megawatts of electricity and more than one million pounds of steam per hour. Dow believed that the industry offered excellent growth potential. Indeed, by 1989, independent power producers like PSE were already supplying about 20 percent of the nation's electricity. And energy analysts projected the figure to surpass 40 percent by the mid-1990s.

Signaling its commitment to the growing cogeneration industry, Dow created Destec as a separate subsidiary under which many of its energy operations were organized. The chief impetus behind the formation of Destec was Charles F. Goff, who had joined Dow in 1966 and had worked in a variety of manufacturing and management positions. In 1986, Goff was named manager of energy resources, and he became director of mergers and acquisitions in 1988. Experience at Dow convinced him that the company would benefit by creating a separate subsidiary to sell power to other companies. Dow took his advice and asked Goff to serve as president of the newly formed Destec.

Goff's first move at Destec, with Dow's help, was to acquire PSE, Inc., the independent power producer, which by this time was reporting about $230 million in annual sales but was still hampered by a lack of capital. Recognizing PSE's potential, Goff arranged for the acquisition of PSE late in 1989. In 1991, Destec conducted an initial public offering, in which about 28 percent of the outstanding shares in Destec were sold for $260 million.

Destec entered the 1990s as one of the largest companies in the fast-growing independent power industry. It was also among the companies best situated for growth. Destec benefited from a strong foothold in the chemical and petroleum markets for inexpensive power, and it had access to a reserve of expansion capital through its initial public offering. Furthermore, most of its existing cogeneration plants were engaged in long-term contracts that assured steady cash flow at least through 1994. Backed by those credentials, Goff and fellow executive Robert McFedries, Destec's chairperson, launched an aggressive growth initiative in 1990.

Destec participated in the construction and operation of two new cogeneration plants that came on line in 1990: the San Joaquin and Chalk Cliff facilities, both of which were located in California and supplied most of their output to Pacific Gas and Electric. In 1991 and 1992, Destec tagged three more cogeneration facilities onto its operating project list: Badger Creek, McKittrick, and Live Oak. All three of these cogeneration plants were 50 percent owned by Destec. Located in Bakersfield, California, they also supplied energy to Pacific Gas and Electric and sold the steam to various corporations. Like most of Destec's other California facilities, the three plants each had an electricity capacity of about 45 to 50 megawatts.

Also in 1992, Destec completed one of its largest projects, the Commonwealth Atlantic plant in Virginia. That facility was Destec's first to begin operating following the enactment of new federal laws that further diminished government requirements for independent power producers. In fact, the plant was not a cogenerator; it could produce 340 megawatts of electricity but no steam. Destec owned 50 percent of the facility. In 1993, Destec acquired a 50 percent interest in another plant, the Black Mountain facility, in Las Vegas.

By the end of 1993, Destec had interests in 14 different projects with a combined generating capacity of more than 1,300 megawatts of electricity and about two million pounds per hour of steam. It was also marketing about 425 megawatts of power cogenerated by Dow Chemical. Furthermore, Destec boasted owned reserves of over 100 billion cubic feet of natural gas. As Destec's capacity expanded, sales shot up to more than $500 million in 1991 and then to $673 million in 1993, despite a U.S. recession. Likewise, net income bounded to more than $80 million in 1991 and then to more than $100 million in 1993. Destec's future looked bright as it entered 1994. It had the equivalent of 1,200 megawatts of new facilities under construction and another 673 megawatts on the drawing board.

Part of Destec's success during the early 1990s was attributable to favorable markets. Since 1990 about 50 percent of all new power generation capacity in the U.S. had been supplied by independents, and the trend was expected to continue. But Destec's gains were also a corollary of savvy management strategies. For example, Destec differed from its industry peers in that it maintained a large engineering staff to design its facilities. Its integrated structure allowed it to profit where other companies couldn't. Furthermore, Destec's affiliation with Dow gave it access to Dow plant sites and global markets.

Despite its seemingly strong competitive position, however, Destec began to encounter some problems in 1994. Importantly, two ten-year power supply contracts with Texas's largest investor-owned utilities expired. In 1993, Destec garnered about one-third of its sales and nearly three-fourths of its profits from contracts related to the power it produced or marketed in Texas. One of those contracts, for power supplied by CoGen Lyondell, ran out April 30, 1994, leaving Destec without a long-term customer to buy the power. Furthermore, two other contracts for Destec's Texas power were set to expire December 31, 1994 and April 30, 1995. According to some analysts, the problem was exacerbated by a glut of power in the region, which some expected to significantly reduce any new contract rate that Destec might negotiate.

Mostly as a result of its looming Texas problems, Destec's stock price tumbled 23 percent during 1994. Although net income increased, worried investors registered their concerns on Wall Street. Goff therefore adopted a new strategy. He decided to deemphasize the company's vertical integration by downsizing its large engineering and design staff; those layoffs would come as part of a $9.5 million restructuring effort. Most important, Goff announced plans to emphasize global expansion, particularly into high-growth developing regions such as Latin America and Asia.

As Destec regrouped in 1994 and 1995, it sustained its aggressive growth program. The company brought two major plants under its wing in 1994, in which it had a 50 percent interest: Hartwell Energy Project, a 300 megawatt gas-fired plant in Georgia, and the Oyster Creek cogenerator in Texas, which had a capacity of 424 megawatts of electricity and 1.1 million pounds of steam per hour. In January 1995, the company brought on line Tiger Bay, a 212 megawatt gas-fired cogenerator, in which it held a 50 percent share. That year, Destec planned to open a new California cogenerator, Bear Mountain, which it owned in partnership with the Consolidated Natural Gas Company. Other Destec openings in 1995 were also expected to include a 262 megawatt-equivalent coal-gasification facility and a 123 megawatt cogeneration project, Michigan Power, in Ludington, Michigan.

Furthermore, Destec was in the process of developing seven more plants, scheduled to open in 1996 and 1997. Those facilities, combined with the new plants opened in 1994 and 1995, would bring the total electricity producing capacity of Destec's facilities to more than 5,000 megawatts and the steam producing capacity to nearly five million pounds per hour. Among the largest of those facilities was Terneuzen, a cogeneration plant in the Netherlands, scheduled for completion in 1997. That project represented Destec's first overseas venture. Despite minor setbacks in 1994, healthy long-term market projections combined with Destec's strong balance sheet suggested a long-term industry presence for the independent.

Further Reading:

Brown, Marvin L, Jr., "Goff Elected Chief Executive Officer of Destec Energy Inc.," *Business Wire,* August 12, 1992.

de Rouffignac, Ann, "S.A. Purchasing Electricity for Houston-Based Firm," *San Antonio Business Journal,* August 19, 1994, p. A6.

Duke, Keith D., "Destec Energy Reports Financial Results," *Business Wire,* January 26, 1994.

Kemezis, Paul, "Building a Business Independent Power Production: Cogeneration Aims Thrive at Dow, Air Products," *Chemical Week,* December 1, 1993, p. 31.

McNamara, Victoria, "Dow Expands Cogeneration Base," *Houston Business Journal,* November 6, 1989, p. 9.

Palmeri, Christopher, "Steady on the Tiller," *Forbes,* September 13, 1993, p. 190.

Putnam, Katherine K., "Transco, Destec Acquire Interests in Power Projects by Each Other," *PR Newswire,* September 10, 1992.

Salpukas, Agis, "In Power Industry: Changes Batter Independents," *New York Times,* March 17, 1995, p. C1.

—Dave Mote

The Dexter Corporation

One Elm Street
Windsor Locks, Connecticut 06096-2234
U.S.A.
(203) 627-9051
Fax: (203) 627-9713

Public Company
Incorporated: 1914 as Dexter Corporation
Employees: 4,800
Sales: $650 million
Stock Exchanges: New York
SICs: 2297 Nonwoven Fabrics; 2830 Drugs; 2891 Adhesives
& Sealants; 2860 Industrial Organic Chemicals; 2821
Plastics Materials & Resins; 3499 Fabricated Metal
Products, Not Elsewhere Classified; 2899 Chemical
Preparations, Not Elsewhere Classified

With a history that stretches back over two centuries, The Dexter Corporation is the oldest company listed on the New York Stock Exchange. Founded in 1767, the firm was owned and operated by members of the same family until 1988. Dexter originally comprised a saw and grist mill, then expanded into the manufacture of specialty papers. Having diversified and grown internationally in the latter half of the twentieth century, the company concentrated on the aerospace, automotive, electronics, food packaging, and medical markets in the early 1990s.

When Thomas Dexter, an educated scholar and a farmer, arrived in America in 1630, he came determined to make his fortune. By the time he died in 1677, he had amassed a significant farming estate. In the early 1700s, Seth Dexter, Thomas's great-great-grandson, settled in the area now known as Windsor Locks, Connecticut, and started a clothing business. In 1767, Seth's son, Seth II, a wealthy clothier, bought 160 acres of timberland and a saw mill, and founded the company today known as the Dexter Corporation. In 1784, with the help of his brother-in-law and business partner, Jabez Haskell, Seth II built a grist mill and annexed it to the company.

Soon Seth II's son, Charles Haskell Dexter, joined his father's business, and C. H., as he was known, began paper making experiments, where he successfully made wrapping paper from Manila rope by employing the waste power from the mill. The discovery yielded little or no remuneration at the time, but laid a foundation for future products. With his brother-in-law, Edwin Douglas, a noted engineer, C. H. Dexter reorganized the business under the name C. H. Dexter & Company in 1847. When Douglas left, Dexter continued to operate the company alone. C. H. made the company self-sustaining, while simultaneously helping to increase his hometown's water power and industrial versatility.

In 1867, C. H. Dexter brought his son, Edwin, and two sons-in-law into the business, changing its name to C. H. Dexter and Sons. One of the sons-in-law, Herbert R. Coffin, assumed supervision of the paper mill and made it a principal part of the company. In 1873 a fire severely devastated a large portion of the paper mill, but by 1875 a new mill, equipped with up-to-date machinery and a solid brick structure, was built and in operation. When Edwin Dexter died in 1886, Herbert R. Coffin assumed full control of the property and the business. He improved the company's products and distribution, which led to increased sales.

After Herbert Coffin's death, his two sons, Arthur and Herbert II, operated the business as a partnership. Following incorporation in July of 1914, Arthur D. Coffin became president and Herbert II became vice-president. In 1922, Arthur Coffin hired a young M.I.T. graduate, Fay Osborn, who played a principal part in the development of the porous long fiber tea bag paper which Dexter introduced in the 1930s. This same technology led to the development of the fibrous meat casing, as well as the stencil base tissue, and a general line of absorbent and filter paper still being produced and developed in the late twentieth century.

Innovation and experimentation led Dexter to the forefront of new paper products. Dexter marketed the first packaged sheet of toilet paper, which was sold with a wire loop so that it could be hung on a convenient hook or nail. The toilet paper came in two grades, but was discontinued in the early 1930s. The company also introduced the first catalogue cover paper, as well as the "electrolytic absorbent capacitor" paper, and patented a metal tarnish preventative tissue which sold extensively to the silverware manufacturers.

In 1936, when Arthur's son, Dexter, became president of the company, its main products were short fiber paper products, such as carbonizing tissue, lightweight air mail writing papers, and condenser tissues for the electrical industry. The company produced long fiber paper only on a limited basis. Under Dexter Coffin's administration, however, the company devoted 100 percent of its production to long fiber paper and webs for industrial uses.

By the time David L. Coffin became Dexter's president in 1958, the company had gained a reputation as being a stodgy old New England relic that was nearly stagnant. The company produced only paper products, opposed hiring from outside the Windsor Locks area, and prohibited borrowing from lending institutions. It lacked an organized sales force, and almost one-third of its personnel was 65 or older. To modernize the company's approach to business, David Coffin hired young professional managers and restructured the family-controlled executive board to include outsiders. He instituted strong cost controls, and trained and organized a sales force. (Coffin had himself started out as a salesman for the company in 1948.) He also established a plan for acquiring and divesting companies to achieve growth. Coffin's target was the field of specialty chemicals. In 1958 the Dexter Corporation acquired the assets of Standard Insulation Company, manufacturer of laminates, preimpregnated products, and closure materials. Dexter sold Standard, however, when the company decided to narrow its focus to the area of specialty formulators of industrial finishes. Dexter bought Chemical Coatings Company in 1961, Lacquer Products Company in 1962, and Midland Industrial Finishes Company in 1963.

In 1967, on its 200th birthday, the Dexter Corporation offered its shares to the public. With this new capital, the company embarked on a path of mergers and acquisitions. In November of 1967, the company merged with Hysol Corporation (currently a division of the company). In 1973 the company bought Puritan Chemical Company, maker of chemical specialties for the sanitation industry, for $6.9 million. Dexter purchased Howe and Brainbridge Inc. for $11.1 million in 1976, and acquired Mogul Corporation for $50 million in 1977. In 1981 Dexter purchased Fre Kote Inc., a plastics release agent firm, and merged it with the Hysol Division. In 1983 the company acquired Bethesda Research Labs and merged it with the GIBCO Corporation (formerly a wholly owned subsidiary) to form Life Technologies, Inc., whose major product is a DNA-based test to determine the presence of cancer in the cervix.

In 1985 the company launched a two-year restructuring program, New Directions, intended to stimulate productivity and ensure a healthy return on investments. The company became more centralized, divested its low-margin holdings, and sought new areas of investment in materials technology and development. Dexter targeted seven main business areas it planned to enter: specialty thermoplastics, high performance formulated chemicals, advanced composites, specialty materials for packaging, specialty industrial services, environmental services, and biotechnology supplies and products. To build on its existing business, Dexter acquired several businesses in the areas of advance composites, with applications in both the aerospace and housing industries (the tough plastics are used as frames and moldings for windows because they do not conduct heat), as well as specialty thermoplastics targeted for the automotive industry (the light-weight durable plastics replace metal parts in cars).

In 1985 Dexter's Hysol Division, producer of epoxies, Courtaulds PLC of Britain, a pioneer in the development of carbon fibers, and several other investors joined to form Hysol Grafil Composite Components Company (HGCC), a small custom molder of high-tech aerospace and defense parts. HGCC's biggest markets are the large aerospace engine manufacturers, such as General Electric Company. Dexter and Courtaulds shared a 50–50 investment in research, development, and marketing in the company. HGCC, one of only eight companies licensed to produce the aerospace resin patented and licensed by the National Aeronautics and Space Administration, was the first to sell this resin in liquid form.

The federal government selected Dexter to supply carbon fiber and resin to major defense contractors competing for contracts to manufacture the government's new LHX helicopter. The company currently supplies the industry with other products,

such as adhesives used in McDonnell Douglas AH-64 Apache helicopters.

The purchases of Research Polymers International (RPI), a leading manufacturer of thermoplastic polyolefin compounds, in September of 1986, and Rutland Plastics, a specialty plastics firm, in December of the same year, signaled Dexter's entrance into the high-performance thermoplastics market. Rutland, a leading manufacturer of plastics screen inks primarily for use with textiles, was one of only a few companies to serve the automotive market with specialty plastics. The company divided its thermoplastics businesses into two divisions in order to focus on different market segments. RPI/Dexter directed its attention to automotive plastics, while Dexter Plastics concentrated on the medical, appliance, and electrical markets. Plastics comprised 20 percent of Dexter's $650 million sales by the mid-1990s.

By 1988, the New Directions program had seen the divestment of about 13 businesses and the acquisition of 13 new interests. That year, the corporate restructuring culminated in a management shift the likes of which Dexter Corporation had never experienced. After over 220 years under the leadership of a descendant (by blood or marriage) of Thomas Dexter, K. Graham Walker was selected to succeed David L. Coffin as The Dexter Corporation's president and chief executive officer. Although it was a profound event in the company's history, the transition from family administration did not bring the immediate, drastic organizational change that some might have expected.

For two years, Walker essentially continued the strategy of his predecessor, watching for likely acquisition and divestment targets. Then, in 1990, the new leader announced a comprehensive restructuring that would extend from the roster of businesses to operations and even to the corporate culture. The three-year plan traded lagging (but often not losing) holdings for increasingly "upstream" businesses. In 1992 and 1993, the company completed the sales of its water management, composites, plastisols, and pultrusions businesses. New interests included a strategic joint venture with the Netherlands company Akzo Coatings International B.V. wherein Dexter traded its North American coil coatings business for its partner's aerospace coatings interests in the Americas. The two companies mutually financed a joint aerospace coatings venture in Europe. The 1993 acquisition of Vernicolor A.G., of Switzerland, helped better position Dexter in the European food packaging market. Overall, the restructuring reduced Dexter's operating divisions by half.

Internal aspects of the early 1990s restructuring included an analysis and revision of Dexter's executive pay plan by the Hay Group, pioneers in the field of compensation. They recommended linking incentives more closely to performance objectives. Workforce reductions eliminated 16 percent of the company's total payroll. An employee empowerment plan gave the remaining manufacturing personnel more training, as well as more control over their work environments. These changes in Dexter's corporate culture helped decrease rejects and accidents as well as overhead. The company included certification with the International Standards Organization as one of the qualifications for reaching its goal of becoming a "preferred supplier" to its increasingly global customers.

In the midst of the restructuring, Dexter endured a $7 million loss that was partially attributable to the multi-million settlement of environmental litigation regarding its Windsor Locks nonwoven fabrics plant. After declining slightly from 1992 to 1993, the company's annual revenues rose to $974.72 million and net income recovered somewhat to $38 million in 1994.

In the years following Dexter's reorganization, CEO Walker hoped to continuously improve financial performance through a variety of strategies. He planned to invest operational savings into increased research and development with a goal of originating the proprietary technology that could carve out a profitable niche for the company. Dexter would also continue to seek key niches in its chosen markets, promote synergy among divisions, and focus international growth on Europe and Asia. Other long-term goals included: boosting annual earnings per share, increasing profitability, and keeping long-term debt under 35 percent of capital.

Principal Subsidiaries: Dexter Aerospace Materials; Dexter Automotive Materials; Dexter Electronic Materials; Dexter Magnetic Materials; Dexter Nonwovens; Dexter Packaging Products; Dexter S.A.; Life Technologies, Inc.; D&S Plastics International (50%).

Further Reading:

Abelson, Reed, "Bags for the Tea of China," *Forbes,* May 10, 1993, p. 46.
Failla, Kathleen S., "Dexter, 220 Years Old, Embraces New Ventures," *Chemical Week,* May 13, 1987, pp. 42–44.
——, "Walker Charts a New Course at Dexter," *Chemical Week,* June 8, 1988, pp. 18–19.

—updated by April Dougal Gasbarre

Di Giorgio Corp.

2 Executive Drive
Somerset, New Jersey 088737
U.S.A.
(908) 469-4444
Fax: (908) 469-9151

Wholly Owned Subsidiary of DIG Holding Corp.
Incorporated: 1920 as Di Giorgio Fruit Co.
Sales: $782 million
Employees: 561
SICs: 5141 Groceries—General Line

Once a vast fruit-growing empire that owned almost 50 square miles of California and Florida farmland, the Di Giorgio Corp. became a conglomerate in the 1980s and, following a takeover and restructuring in the early 1990s, emerged as a distributor of food products. Di Giorgio distributes a variety of grocery products under the White Rose brand name, primarily to the tri-state region of New York, New Jersey, and Connecticut.

The founder of the company, Giuseppe Di Giorgio, was born in Cefalu, Sicily, in 1874. One of nine children born to a small-scale vineyard owner and lemon grower, he arrived in New York in 1888. After a few years working for a fruit jobber, the young man—now Joseph Di Giorgio—moved to Baltimore and became a middleman himself. Borrowing money from a bank, he founded the Baltimore Fruit Exchange in 1904. Eventually he was to have a controlling interest in the Baltimore, New York, and Pittsburgh fruit exchanges. In 1911 he bought the Earl Fruit Co., a well-established California shipper.

Di Giorgio became a grower in 1918, when he started to acquire land in Florida for growing citrus fruits. A year later he bought 5,845 acres of land north of Arvin in California's southern San Joaquin Valley for about $90 an acre. This was arid, saline scrubland, but its owner, who established the Di Giorgio Fruit Co. in 1920, obtained water by drilling wells hundreds of feet deep with powerful electric pumps and began to plant trees and vines to grow apricots, grapes, and peaches. By 1929 the company had the largest fruit-packing plant in the nation. A branch railway line serving Arvin was built to provide shipping facilities for Di Giorgio and other fruit growers. The end of prohibition in 1933 enabled Di Giorgio Fruit to expand grape production, and it took a sizable equity position in California wineries, including its own Del Vista Wine Co.

By 1946 Di Giorgio Fruit occupied about 33 square miles in the San Joaquin Valley and was the largest grape, plum, and pear grower in the world. It was also the second largest producer of wine in the United States. Other crops grown there included potatoes and asparagus. The company also held thousands more acres in the state, as far north as Marysville (north of Sacramento) and as far south as the Borrego Valley, near the Mexican border. In addition, the company held about 14 square miles of land in Florida and was the largest producer of citrus fruit in that state. Nongrowing income (about ten percent of the total) came from dividends from the fruit exchanges and minority interests in other fruit auction companies, returns as a packer, loader, and commission merchant, an Oregon lumber and box facility, and the winery. The corporation's annual revenue rose from $5,7 million in 1938 to $18.2 million in 1946. In the latter year, Joseph Di Giorgio and other family members owned 59 percent of the corporation's common stock and a controlling portion of the cumulative preferred stock.

However, this vast farm empire began to experience dramatic setbacks over the next 20 years. In the late 1930s and early 1940s the water table under the major portion of Di Giorgio's California properties sunk about 150 feet. To survive, the operation needed federal irrigation water but was disqualified by the U.S. Bureau of Reclamation, which restricted its services to individual recipients who owned less than 160 acres—a limit Joseph Di Giorgio referred to as a Bolshevist measure.

Labor unrest also played a part in Di Giorgio's struggles. The corporation withstood a 1947–50 strike aimed at union recognition for its farm workers, but in 1966 the company signed a contract with Cesar Chavez's United Farm Workers Organizing Committee. Prior to the settlement, civil rights activists had organized a boycott of Di Giorgio grapes and other products.

Joseph Di Giorgio died in 1951. Among his four nephews in high-level management, Robert Di Giorgio eventually came to the fore. A graduate of Lawrenceville School, Yale University, and Fordham Law School, Robert Di Giorgio's ambitions and management style contrasted sharply to those of his uncle. Under the leadership of Robert Di Giorgio, who became president in 1962, the corporation increased the nonagricultural portion of its business from 15 percent in 1955 to 87 percent in 1964 and to over 98 percent in 1967. "Fruit" was dropped from the company name in 1964, the year its annual report described Di Giorgio as a "publicly held, profit oriented processor, distributor and marketer of foods." The Florida citrus holdings were sold in 1972, and by 1976 Di Giorgio owned only 2,500 acres of farmland, in the Marysville area, which was soon sold in 1978. Another 6,000 acres of land in the Borrego Valley was retained for nonagricultural development.

During this time, the company began to diversify its interests, and by the late 1960s the Di Giorgio Corp. controlled 15 nonfarming subsidiaries. In the late 1950s Di Giorgio had acquired S&W Fine Foods, TreeSweet Products, and the White Rose food distribution business in greater New York. Serv-A-Portion, purchased in 1967, packaged packets of sugar, mustard, ketchup, and other condiments for use by fast-food businesses and institutional cafeterias. Los Angeles Drugs (LAD), acquired in 1968, distributed drugs, pharmaceuticals, and cosmetics in southern California. Peter Carando, Inc., also bought in 1968, processed Italian-style meats in New England. Acquired in 1969, Las Plumas Lumber Co. raised the company's stake in West Coast timber production.

Di Giorgio's activities also included land development for shopping centers, condominium apartments, recreational areas, and mobile home parks. Investments and directorships tied the company to such powerful California enterprises as the Bank of America, Pacific Gas and Electric, and Southern California Edison. Assets reached $82.9 million in 1965, while sales passed $100 million, ranking Di Giorgio ninth in rate of sales growth among the nation's 500 leading corporations. Robert Di Giorgio moved up from president to chairperson in 1971, while also remaining chief executive officer.

By this time the company's White Rose subsidiary was the largest independent wholesale-grocery distributor in the greater New York area. TreeSweet was processing and marketing citrus juices in Europe as well as the United States, while the Serv-A-Portion subsidiary marketed small containers of jams, jellies, and sugar in Europe. An international subsidiary bottled Sunland juice products in Belgium for distribution in European supermarkets and food stores, and DG Leisure Products was building and distributing campers and travel trailers made by Di Giorgio factories in California and Michigan. A California subsidiary was making machines used in peach canneries to extract pits. Precut housing components and wood chips were being exported to Japan from sawmills in the Pacific Northwest.

Like many other conglomerates of that era, Di Giorgio eventually proved to have taken on more than it could handle. After the national economy fell into recession in late 1973, the company suffered its first loss in 1974 since the 1930s, $3.1 million. Corporate earnings totaled $24.8 million in 1975, but $9.6 million was paid out in interest on the corporation's heavy debt, which included $70 million in long-term debt. Net earnings for the year came to only $630,000.

By 1979 Di Giorgio's annual sales were approaching $1 billion. However, a reviewer in the *New York Times* article described Di Giorgio as "an association of marketing men looking for something to sell," meaning that the company still lacked focus. "We went into a rush program of acquisitions," Robert Di Giorgio later conceded, observing that "when you do that, you make some very good ones and some bad ones. Fortunately, there were more good ones than bad ones, but we made some mistakes." These mistakes included money-losing units that manufactured plastic tableware and wrought-iron and aluminum furniture. As a result, the corporation sold off peripheral businesses, including the sawmills and recreational vehicles, reducing its subsidiaries from 28 to 18. Of the company's 1978 revenue of $897.1 million, 44 percent came from the corporation's building materials division, 32 percent from the food distribution division (which included drugs), 14 percent from the food processing division, and ten percent from automotive accessories.

Among the company's problems, according to some analysts, was uncertainty over its future course. In 1980, as Robert Di Giorgio approached his seventieth birthday, investors (disappointed with the corporation's overall earnings of only $11 million on sales of $1 billion) wondered if a successor would be able to rein in the 15 powerful divisional presidents. Allowed great autonomy under Di Giorgio, most of them had been owners of the acquired businesses they continued to manage. In some cases they had sold their businesses for Di Giorgio stock and had thus become large shareholders. Di Giorgio stepped down as chairperson in 1982 and was succeeded by Peter Scott, who also remained president. However, Di Giorgio remained to chair the board's executive committee.

In 1983 Di Giorgio's building materials sector opened two new facilities, a California plant for precut, preassembled lumber, and a Denver facility for extruding aluminum used in doors, windows, and panels. White Rose continued to be the company's most profitable unit, while Allied Distributing Co., a distributor of electronics products, was reported to have invested too heavily in the glutted video game market. Also during this time, a major luxury resort development in Borrego Springs overseen by Di Giorgio began operations.

A restructuring program was adopted in 1984, a year in which the corporation's stock fell 98 cents a share. Sun Aire, a California commuter airliner, was sold to Skywest Airlines. Also sold that year were TreeSweet, Allied, and real estate, other than Borrego Springs previously held for development. By August 1985 Di Giorgio's was profitable again, and its stock had rebounded from a low of under $10 a share in late 1984 to more than $16 a share. The following year the Los Angeles Drug Co. (LAD) was sold for about $40 million.

Would-be corporate raiders started putting Di Giorgio "in play" during 1986. First, Kane-Miller Corp. acquired a 9.4 percent stake in the company but then backed off and sold some of those shares. Later in the year, Mario Gabelli raised his holdings to 11.2 percent of the stock. Although Gabelli initially denied that he would attempt to take over Di Giorgio, he did remark that food companies were prone to buyouts because of undervalued assets and attractive cash flow. By September, the company's stock had risen to $25 a share.

By July 1987 Gabelli Group Inc. owned 28.6 percent of Di Giorgio's common stock, which had reached $31 a share. After two partnerships related to the Gabelli Group made an unsolicited $238 million leveraged buyout offer for Di Giorgio, the company management adopted a "poison pill" defense. Under this plan, each share was issued the right, in the event of a takeover or merger, to be exchanged for twice its value in the stock of the surviving company. In addition, shareholders not belonging to a person or group holding 30 percent of the common stock received the right to buy company shares at half price. In early 1988 Di Giorgio enacted a $70 million, $21-a-share buyback offer, ultimately buying about 41 percent of the outstanding shares.

To help pay for the buyback, the management sold five divisions, including Serv-A-Portion, the Belgium-based international food processing subsidiary, an aluminum products division, and the land development unit. These transactions brought in $122 million and left Di Giorgio to focus on two lines of business: food processing and distribution and building materials.

New Jersey native Arthur M. Goldberg became, in February 1989, the fourth investor in less than three years to buy more than five percent of Di Giorgio's stock and seek control. Goldberg had previously attempted to take over Di Giorgio in 1984 but had sold his stock when the price rose. A former trial lawyer and an active investor in medium-sized companies, Goldberg had a history of taking quick profits, sometimes in the form of "greenmail," the name given to a company buyback of a raider's shares at a premium price. Goldberg's investments reportedly had earned $80 million for himself and his partners. He denied being only interested in speculative profits, however, telling a *San Francisco Chronicle* reporter, "I've tried to always build companies, rather than tear them down. . . . In all the situations I've been in, all the stockholders have done very, very well."

Di Giorgio's management rejected a $30-a-share offer from Goldberg in June 1989. He owned 13 percent of the corporation's stock in August, when he made a tender offer of $32 a share to the stockholders, which was reduced to $30 a share in December. The bid, estimated to be worth $154 million, was managed by New York's Bankers Trust Co., which stood to gain as much as $10 million by providing a bridge loan, underwriting the subordinated debt, and handling the sale of some of Di Giorgio's units. By the end of the year Goldberg's DIG Acquisition Corp., a unit of Rose Partners L.P., in which he was the only general partner, held or had been tendered at least 75 percent of Di Giorgio's shares.

Goldberg took control of Di Giorgio in February 1990, becoming its chairperson, president, and chief executive officer. Also during this time, he became chairperson and chief executive officer of Bally Manufacturing Corp., the casino and health-club operator. Di Giorgio's headquarters were moved from San Francisco to Somerset, New Jersey, the base for Goldberg's investment partnerships. Of Di Giorgio's remaining five divisions, all except White Rose were sold by 1994.

Early that year a competitor, the Fleming Companies, Inc. of Oklahoma City, indicated that it had signed a letter of intent to sell most of the assets of its Royal Foods dairy and delicatessen products business in Woodbridge, New Jersey, to Di Giorgio. Terms were not disclosed. This operation had revenues of about $300 million in 1993, bringing Di Giorgio's combined annual revenue to about $1.1 billion.

Principal Subsidiaries: White Rose Corp.

Further Reading:

Beckett, Peter, "Goldberg Finishes Buying Di Giorgio," *San Francisco Chronicle,* February 10, 1990, p. B3.
Beckett, Peter, "The Man Who Wants to Control Di Giorgio," *San Francisco Chronicle,* March 6, 1989, pp. C1, C6.
Campanella, Frank W., "A Much Better Year," *Barron's,* August 5, 1985, pp. 39–40.
"Di Giorgio Seeking Its Niche," *New York Times,* April 19, 1979, pp. D2, D9.
Galarza, Ernesto, "Big Farm Strike, *Commonweal,* June 4, 1948, pp. 178–182.
Galarza, Ernesto, *Spiders in the House & Workers in the Field,* South Bend, Ind.: University of Notre Dame Press, 1970.
"Heir Apparent Difficulties at Di Giorgio," *Business Week,* October 27, 1980, pp. 172L-172M.
"Joseph Di Giorgio," *Fortune,* August 1946, pp. 97–103, 205–208.
"On the Rebound," *Barron's,* October 10, 1983, pp. 55, 57.
Pender, Kathleen, "Pursuing Di Giorgio, *San Francisco Chronicle,* February 10, 1989, pp. C1, C20.
Richards, Art, "Spotlight on Di Giorgio Corp.," *Journal of Commerce,* June 3, 1976, pp. 2, 5.
"Vast Di Giorgio Farm Empire Nearing End After Many Woes," *New York Times,* December 25, 1968, pp. 51–52.

—Robert Halasz

Dibrell Brothers, Incorporated

512 Bridge Street
Danville, Virginia 24543
U.S.A.
(804) 792-7511
Fax: (804) 791-0180

Public Company
Incorporated: 1904
Employees: 4,200
Sales: $919.1 million
Stock Exchanges: NASDAQ
SICs: 5159 Farm-Product Raw Materials, Not Elsewhere
    Classified; 5193 Flowers and Florists' Supplies

An international leader in two business lines, Dibrell Brothers, Incorporated purchases, processes, and sells leaf tobacco and operates as an importer, exporter, and distributor of fresh cut flowers. Tobacco and flowers together, the company operated in 24 countries throughout North America, Europe, the Middle East, the Far East, and South America, deriving 87 percent of its revenues from outside the United States.

Formed as a partnership in 1873, Dibrell Brothers entered the tobacco trade several decades before widespread consumption of leaf tobacco in the United States began. To be sure, tobacco represented one of the chief agricultural crops supporting the country's growth, beginning with its introduction into the American colonies in 1612, then underpinning the growth of the southern United States throughout the eighteenth and nineteenth centuries. However, domestic leaf tobacco consumption did not reach great proportions until cigarettes became a widely consumed product during the early 1900s. Before then, tobacco was most widely used to produce plug and twist tobacco, chewing tobacco, smoking tobacco, and cigars, the manufacturers of which constituted Dibrell Brothers' customers during its first several decades of existence.

Functioning as a tobacco merchant, Dibrell Brothers purchased raw tobacco from individual growers or at auctions, cured it, stored it, and then sold and transported the processed tobacco to manufacturers. Although many tobacco manufacturers first entered the industry as tobacco farmers then diversified into the manufacturing side of the business, most could not fulfill all their tobacco needs, a deficit tobacco merchants like Dibrell Brothers filled. This, then, was the company's role in the tobacco industry. Positioned between tobacco farmers and tobacco manufacturers, Dibrell Brothers served both, inextricably woven into the process of tobacco manufacture and consequently an indispensable part of the dramatic growth of the tobacco industry during the twentieth century.

Founded in Danville, Virginia, where the company headquarters remained a century later, Dibrell Brothers was located in the perfect place for a business of its type, on the border dividing Virginia and North Carolina, the principal and almost exclusive region of tobacco farming and manufacture in the United States. Not long after the company was formed, the manufacturing side of the tobacco industry—Dibrell Brothers' customer base—comprised only a handful of manufacturers. Accordingly, Dibrell Brothers' potential customers were a limited few, consisting primarily of the five principal manufacturers that dominated the 1870s and 1880s: Washington Duke Sons & Co., Allen & Ginter, Kinney Tobacco Co., William S. Kimball & Co., and Goodwin & Co.

These companies formed what was known as the "Tobacco Trust," an elite group of tobacco manufacturers that wielded overwhelming control of the industry and purchased nearly all of Dibrell Brothers' processed tobacco. In 1890, these companies joined together at the urging of Washington Duke Sons & Co.'s James Duke to form the American Tobacco Company, which held nearly every part of the industry until the U.S. Supreme Court issued a dissolution decree in 1911 that divided the tobacco giant into 16 independent corporations. During the period bridging the birth of the American Tobacco Company and its court-mandated dissolution, Dibrell Brothers was incorporated in 1904, formally beginning a corporate history that would see the former partnership evolve into the largest company of its kind in the United States.

Under the American Tobacco Company's 20-year reign, Dibrell Brothers prospered, supplying the huge company with the processed tobacco necessary for producing chewing tobacco and cigars.

During the 1920s and 1930s, domestic leaf tobacco consumption jumped nearly 43 percent, driven largely by the enormous 1,450 percent leap in cigarette production from 8.6 billion to 125.2 billion during the period. With the widespread popularity of cigarettes came the exponential growth of the tobacco industry and the prosperity of those companies involved in it, a prosperity Dibrell Brothers shared in. However, it was not until the 1970s, a century after its formation, that the company became a major player in the tobacco processing market.

By the early 1970s, Dibrell Brothers had enjoyed considerable success, having paid a dividend to its shareholders every year since 1925. In the decade to follow, the company began its ascent to the number one position in its industry. This transformation occurred as a result of Dibrell Brothers' geographic expansion, which, aside from increasing the physical and financial size of the company, helped insulate it from the usual risks involved in dealing with an agricultural commodity, including political unrest, inclement weather, and import/export restrictions.

During the 1970s, Dibrell Brothers enlarged the boundaries of its area of operations considerably. Expanding on its operations in Canada and the United States, the company also moved into Central and South America, the Far East, India, and Italy, where a joint venture in 1972 with Italian partners ceded Dibrell Brothers a minority interest in a company named Reditab S.p.A. and, more important, gave the company entry into the European Common Market. Following this initial burst of overseas expansion, the company relocated its international sales operations to Europe in 1980, a move that resulted in tax savings on the profits from sales of non-U.S. tobacco. In 1980, the United Nations decided to lift Zimbabwean tobacco sanctions, and Dibrell Brothers established a presence in Zimbabwe, adding a nominal presence in Africa to its expanding worldwide operations.

During this time, the company expanded in the United States as well, diversifying into businesses unrelated to tobacco. In 1967, the company acquired Richmond Cedar Works Manufacturing Co., a manufacturer of home ice cream freezers and decorative woodenware. Two years later, Dibrell Brothers purchased Dunning Industries, the largest manufacturer of wooden lamps in the country. Dibrell Brothers also moved into the restaurant business in 1973, when it launched a chain of steak houses in Kentucky and Tennessee called Kentucky Rib-Eye. By the end of the decade, there were eight restaurants in the chain, including operations in Indiana, and the subsidiary was renamed Briarpatch, Inc.

Such non-tobacco businesses generated $14 million in annual revenues in 1975, helping Dibrell Brothers post $227 million in aggregate revenues for the year. By this point, roughly five years into the company's concerted movement to diversify and expand abroad, its financial performance had improved dramatically. The revenue total in 1975 was more than twice that of four years earlier, when Dibrell Brothers generated $112 million. The company's net income recorded a commensurate leap, increasing from $1.3 million to $2.7 million, confirming management's belief that Dibrell Brothers' path to greater success was routed through global expansion and diversification.

Despite the irrefutable success of the company's entry into foreign tobacco markets, its attempts at diversification led to more prosaic financial results. With the exception of its freezer business, none of the company's diversification moves had proven particularly successful by the end of the 1970s, so the company began the 1980s by selling one of its non-tobacco businesses, its wooden lamp manufacturer, Dunning Industries. The company's two remaining non-tobacco subsidiaries, Briarpatch, Inc. and Richmond Cedar Works, contributed 4.6 percent of Dibrell Brothers' total sales and 3.6 percent of its operating profits in 1980; clearly diversification had not added greatly to the company's financial performance. Within the next ten years, both Briarpatch and Richmond Cedar Works would be divested as well, but the company's resounding success in tobacco offset the lackluster performance of its non-tobacco business ventures. In less than a decade, Dibrell Brothers had become a leading force in the tobacco processing industry.

By 1980, Dibrell Brothers was recognized as the second largest independent processor of leaf tobacco in the United States, a distinction almost entirely earned by its successes abroad. The previous decade's expansion had driven the proportion of the company's international sales upward so that they now repre-

sented 60 percent of Dibrell Brothers revenue volume. These foreign customers, primarily cigarette manufacturers, helped propel the company's sales growth, which proceeded at a less prolific rate than during the first half of the 1970s, but engendered an enviable record of net income growth nonetheless. From 1975 to 1981, Dibrell Brothers' sales recorded a respectable 6.6 percent increase, climbing from $227 million to $328 million, while the company's bottom line grew more robustly, soaring from $2.6 million to $5.4 million.

Encouraged by these results, the company's management made another overseas move in 1981, when Dibrell Brothers acquired Amsterdam-based B.V. Tabak Export & Import Compagnie (TEIC) for approximately $25 million. The acquisition was regarded by industry pundits as the most ambitious to date, and one that gave Dibrell Brothers many valuable overseas assets, assets that together generated as much profit as Dibrell Brothers' entire existing operations. Through the acquisition, Dibrell Brothers inherited TEIC's operations in Zimbabwe, West Germany, the Dominican Republic, and northern Brazil. The company also assumed ownership of TEIC's wholly-owned subsidiary, Verafumos Ltd., one of the leading producers and exporters of Brazilian tobacco.

The acquisition of TEIC added much, particularly the Brazilian properties, which a company spokesperson described at the time as providing a "quantum jump" in Dibrell Brothers' supply of Brazilian tobacco. However, following the purchase of TEIC, until the late 1980s, the company registered essentially flat financial growth. Sales fluctuated during this period, amounting to $327 million in 1984, then rising to $381 million the following year, and finally dipping to $308 million in 1987. The company's net income was similarly erratic, plunging from $5.7 million in 1984 to $647,000 the following year, then rebounding to $5 million in 1986. 1987 represented the nadir of Dibrell Brothers' 1980s revenue plunge, but by the following year a recovery was clearly on its way, as the company experienced a resurgence that would carry it into the early 1990s, a revitalization sparked by Dibrell Brothers' first overwhelming success with a non-tobacco business.

In 1987, Dibrell Brothers acquired a 54 percent interest in Florimex Verwaltungsgesellschaft mbH for $10.7 million, then purchased the remainder of the company over the next three years. Once Richmond Cedars Works was sold in 1990, Florimex, involved in the importation and distribution of fresh-cut flowers in Europe, North America, and Japan, would stand as Dibrell Brothers only non-tobacco property and one that greatly contributed to its recovery from the financial malaise afflicting the company in 1987. Dibrell Brothers lost $1 million on $308 million in sales in 1987, closed three of its five U.S. facilities, and then, with the addition of Florimex, reversed its fortunes and generated $12.7 million in net income in 1988 on sales of $555 million. Florimex was responsible for 70 percent of this increase in sales, buoying the company's financial prospects for the future and giving Dibrell Brothers a reliable source of income excluded from the cyclical tobacco market.

During the late 1980s, the tobacco market was undergoing more sweeping and defining changes than the usual market fluctuations. Throughout the world, but particularly in the United States, consumers were increasingly opting for low-priced generic cigarettes, a trend that intensified during the early 1990s and promised to reshape the tobacco industry. Dibrell Brothers stood well-positioned for the changes affecting the industry because for years it had imported a sizeable amount of inexpensive tobacco, thereby enabling it to benefit from the popularity of low-priced cigarettes. Moreover, the company had responded early to another trend affecting the tobacco industry: the popularity of the lighter "American blend" cigarette. Eastern Europeans, who previously smoked high-tar cigarettes, demonstrated a preference for lighter cigarettes in particular during the early 1990s, a predilection Dibrell Brothers' management had foreshadowed in 1988 by moving out of high-tar tobacco markets in countries such as the Dominican Republic and Indonesia.

Prepared as such for the changes that were taking place in the tobacco industry, Dibrell Brothers began demonstrating a vitality that few of its competitors could match. The company's stock tripled in value in 1991, driven by the profitability of Dibrell Brothers' Brazilian operations and the remarkable growth of Florimex, which doubled its annual revenue total between 1989 and 1993 to reach $360 million, or $42 million more than Dibrell Brothers generated when it acquired the fresh-cut flower concern. Sales eclipsed the $1 billion plateau in 1991, having nearly doubled in three years. However, shortly thereafter, the company's exponential spurt of growth screeched to a halt, arrested by a worldwide oversupply of tobacco.

To offset the effects of tobacco oversupply, Dibrell Brothers looked to increase the economies of scale involved in its tobacco processing operations; more volume meant lower processing costs and higher profit margins. This prompted the company to conduct negotiations with Standard Commercial Corp., a worldwide leaf tobacco processor, about the possibilities of a merger. In early 1993, the merger was announced, creating, once the shareholders of the two companies and the federal government gave their approval, a tobacco processing giant with more than $2.2 billion in annual revenues. Several months later, however, Standard Commercial backed out of the proposed merger, explaining to the *Wall Street Journal* that the merger was "not in the best interest of our shareholders."

Dibrell Brothers pursued Standard Commercial throughout 1993 and into 1994, but the Wilson, North Carolina-based company remained adamant in its refusal to merge. The difficulties caused by the oversupply of tobacco, meanwhile, had crippled Dibrell Brothers' financial performance, knocking the company off the $1 billion plateau. The company recorded $919 million in sales in 1994 and reported a loss of $9.1 million, a precipitous drop from the $38 million gain registered the year before.

In late 1994, however, Dibrell Brothers at last found an agreeable partner for a merger, buoying hopes that the company could reverse its retrogressive slide. In October, Dibrell Brothers and Monk-Austin Inc., a Farmville, North Carolina-based tobacco processor, agreed to merge, creating a $1.4 billion operation to be called DiMon Inc.

The addition of Monk-Austin's operations instilled Dibrell Brothers' management with hope for a recovery in the mid-1990s. By combining processing operations in Brazil, Africa, and the United States, where both companies maintained a presence, fixed costs were expected to decline and profits to rise. As the company entered the mid-1990s, its most immediate task was to conclude the merger and combine operations where appropriate, then begin building toward a more profitable future in the company's third century of business.

Principal Subsidiaries: Eastern Carolina Leaf Processors Inc.; Tobacco Export & Import Co. Inc.; Dibrell Brothers GmbH (Germany); Dibrell Brothers Tobacco Company, Inc.; Dibrell Brothers Tobacco Processing, Inc.; Dibrell Brothers of Canada Ltd.; Dibrell Brothers International S.A. (Switzerland); Dibrell Limited (England); Dibrell do Brasil Tabacos Ltda. (Brazil); Dibrell International B.V. (Holland); Felemenk Turk Tutun A.S. (Turkey); Rohtabakvergaetungs A.G. (Germany); Florimex Verwaltungsgesellschaft MbH (Germany); Baardse B.V. (Holland)

Further Reading:

Biesada, Alexandra, "Dibrell Brothers Shares Are Still Smokin'," *Financial World,* January 21, 1992, p. 13
Campanella, Frank W., "Steak Houses to Tobacco, Dibrell Finds Diversification a Boon," *Barron's,* February 2, 1976, p. 65.
"Dibrell and RJR Unit Reach a Settlement on Brazil Firm's Sale," *Wall Street Journal,* October 17, 1991, p. A9.
"Dibrell Bros. and Standard Commercial, Leaf-Tobacco Processors, Agree to Merge," *Wall Street Journal,* March 29, 1993, p. B3.
"Dibrell Brothers, Incorporated," *Barron's,* August 24, 1992, p. 44.
"Dibrell Brothers, Incorporated," *Barron's,* August 29, 1988, p. 39.
"Dibrell Brothers, Incorporated," *Barron's,* February 3, 1986, p. 67.
"Dibrell Brothers, Incorporated," *Wall Street Transcript,* October 12, 1981, p. 63,278.
"Moving Abroad," *Barron's,* July 12, 1982, p. 42.
Ruffenach, Glenn, "Dibrell Brothers and Monk-Austin Inc. Agree to Merger of Tobacco Merchants," *Wall Street Journal,* October 24, 1994, p. A5.
Schwartz, Jerry, "2 Big Tobacco Processors to Merge," *New York Times,* October 25, 1994, p. D4.
"Standard Commercial Corp.," *Wall Street Journal,* March 28, 1994, p. B4.
"Still Smoking," *Forbes,* January 4, 1993, p. 157.

—Jeffrey L. Covell

Dillon Companies Inc.

P.O. Box 1266
Hutchinson, Kansas 67504-1266
U.S.A.
(316) 663-6801
Fax: (316) 663-3631

Wholly Owned Subsidiary of The Kroger Co.
Incorporated: 1921 as J.S. Dillon and Sons Stores Company,
   Inc.
Employees: 44,000
Sales: $5.8 billion
SICs: 5411 Grocery Stores

Dillon Companies Inc. is one of the largest owners and operators of convenience stores in the United States. Dillon, which functions as an autonomous, wholly owned subsidiary of The Kroger Co., operated about 230 supermarkets and 940 convenience stores going into the mid-1990s. Conservative, intelligent management helped the company to grow steadily since its inception in the early 1900s.

Although Dillon Companies was officially founded in 1921, the organization's roots date back to 1913. It was during that year that John S. Dillon opened his J.S. Dillon Cash Store in Hutchinson, Kansas. Dillon was the son of a Presbyterian preacher, the father of seven sons and three daughters, and a carpenter by trade. He had opened his first business, a wagon and buggy repair shop, in the 1890s in Sterling, Kansas. His new dry goods and grocery business, with a tin roof and coal stove heat, proved an important learning experience. Most importantly, Dillon discovered that crediting customers, as was customary at the time, could lead to serious financial problems.

Dillon's second effort in Hutchinson represented his attempt to employ a new marketing concept—cash and carry. Other food stores at the time operated on a credit basis. Customers would buy their groceries on a charge account and pay later. As a result, the store owner was forced to continually carry a very large investment in inventory. In addition, most stores delivered the groceries to the customer's home. After his experience in Sterling, Dillon decided to make his J.S. Dillon Cash Store a cash and carry, meaning that customers had to pay cash and carry the food home themselves. He would attract business by passing the savings on to the customers in the form of lower food prices. Customers were slow to accept Dillon's concept.

But when they began to realize how much money they could save, the store caught on and became very popular. Dillon opened a second market in 1915. He managed the new shop himself and placed Ray E. Dillon, his 18-year-old son, in charge of the original store. The company was incorporated under the name Dillon Mercantile Co., Inc. in 1917.

In 1918, Ray left the business to serve in World War I, joining his brother, Clyde, in the renowned 35th Division. With his sons at war in France, John Dillon decided to sell his company to his investment partners. Soon after he sold it, though, the war ended and both brothers eventually returned to Hutchinson. John and Ray opened a new store together in 1919, called J. S. Dillon and Sons Store, and incorporated the venture as J.S. Dillon and Sons Stores Company, Inc. in 1921. It was in their first store that the Dillons established the basic principles upon which the company would be built during the twentieth century. In addition to the cash and carry concept, they placed a great emphasis on cleanliness, service, and value. Hanging in a conspicuous space on the wall in their early stores, in fact, was a sign which read ''Dillon Honesty, Economy, Efficiency, and Courteousness.''

The Dillons' first store was successful, and they began branching out during the mid- and late 1920s with new stores. Ray had attended a Super Market Institute meeting in Cincinnati in 1920 and was excited about opportunities for growth. ''I saw what others were doing and I was inspired to grow larger, faster,'' he recalled in the December 23, 1979 *Hutchinson News*. Also in the early 1920s, Ray met and married Stella Schmitt, whom a local business college had recommended in response to Ray's request for a bookkeeper. Clyde joined the operation as well, and he and Ray gradually assumed control of the business. John Dillon sold his interest in 1925 and retired.

Despite the Great Depression in 1929 and the succeeding lean years, Dillon sustained steady growth throughout the 1930s. To attain those gains, the Dillon brothers typically worked from 7:00 a.m. to 7:00 p.m., five days per week, and until 10:30 p.m. on Saturdays. In addition to hard work, innovation remained a Dillon hallmark, as Ray and Clyde introduced such novelties as public rest rooms and off-street customer parking. The Dillon brothers put great effort into pleasing their customers and finding new profit centers. For example, during the Depression years, Ray saw a need for what he termed ''a practical gift for business people to give at Christmas time.'' His answer to that need was a Dillon Store fruit basket. The fruit basket was a big success, and Dillon eventually developed a large base of customers who would purchase the baskets every year. Even as the company grew to corporate status, Ray considered the project ''his baby'' for several years. By the late 1970s, Dillon was selling 13,000 baskets every Christmas and had to develop an assembly line system every year to pack the gifts of fruit.

By the end of the 1930s, the Dillons were operating 24 stores in central Kansas. Part of Dillon's success during its early years was attributable to Ray's personnel policies. He took pride in hiring the ''right people'' for the job, and attributed the success of the company to its workers. In addition, he decided in the early 1920s that he wanted to hire employees that would stay with the company for the long haul. He studied the J.C. Penney employee benefit program, which was designed to encourage workers to stay with the company, and then labored to devise a system that would produce similar results at Dillon. The outcome of his effort was one of the first employee profit sharing plans. In fact, starting in 1922, Dillon began encouraging his workers to buy stock in the company. Some of those who followed his advice in the 1930s and 1940s eventually became millionaires, leaving huge estates to their survivors.

Importantly, the Dillons began to convert their stores to self-service food markets in the early 1940s, evidencing a nationwide trend. They also added centralized bakery operations, which served the entire Dillon chain. In 1941, Clyde Dillon was killed in a hunting accident in Colorado. Among Clyde's survivors was his son, Paul, who would join the executive ranks at Dillon in the 1970s.

Dillon's growth prospects during the 1940s were thwarted by World War II. Because of a shortage of materials, very little new construction was allowed. In addition, many of Dillon's employees were called away from their jobs for military service. Although Ray opened three new stores, he also closed down three others, and the company spent the 1940s reorganizing and positioning for future expansion. Ray remodeled most of the chain's stores and expanded his warehouse facilities. He also converted the remainder of the outlets to self-service stores, which resembled the modern system of food aisles and checkout cash registers.

By 1949, Dillon was still operating 24 stores in 14 different central Kansas towns. Its work force surged back to 800 following the return of U.S. forces. In 1946, Dillon's 25th anniversary, the company generated sales of $12.6 million.

The Dillons played catch-up during the postwar economic boom that took hold in the 1950s. Ray replaced six of the chain's existing stores with new units and added a total of five new stores during the early and mid-1950s. More importantly, he purchased the entire Wichita Division of the Kroger Company in 1957, which tagged 16 stores onto the Dillon portfolio and significantly broadened its regional presence. Dillon also bought out King Sooper, a small regional grocery store chain. Besides adding links to its chain during the 1950s, Dillon began experimenting for the first time with merchandise other than traditional grocery items, including health and beauty aids, housewares, books and magazines, and various soft goods. Likewise, Dillon lead the charge into the emerging frozen foods market by incorporating large freezer sections into its floor plans.

Although the company's founder, John S. Dillon, died in 1957, he had lived long enough to see the chain that bore his name grow into a multimillion-dollar venture. But only his sons and grandsons would watch the rampant expansion that followed. Following its 1957 acquisitions, in fact, Dillon expanded at an explosive pace. The company went public in December of 1957 to raise growth capital and by the late 1950s was operating a total of 40 supermarkets in 20 Kansas towns. During the 1960s, the company added many new stores, including several in northwestern Arkansas and northern Oklahoma. It also built a giant new distribution center in Hutchinson, which included new offices, warehouse space, and a frozen food warehouse. Reflecting its enduring emphasis on innovation, Dillon computerized its operations in the mid-1960s. It also became one of the

first Midwest grocers to implement a discount pricing policy during the late 1960s, and was among the first supermarket chains to adopt an environmental program aimed at reducing pollution and recycling waste.

Even more important to Dillon's growth during the 1960s and 1970s than its core supermarket business was its expansion into a variety of related businesses. Throughout the period, Dillon purchased a string of other companies that complemented its grocery operations. Reflecting its growing diversity, the organization changed its name from J.S. Dillon and Sons Company to Dillon Companies in 1968. One year later, Dillon joined the New York Stock Exchange. "There is no standing still," Ray Dillon declared at the time, according to company annals, noting that "you either grow or shrink."

By the end of the 1970s, Dillon Companies had become a multi-billion-dollar corporate conglomerate. Its core supermarket division, Dillon Stores, consisted of a chain of large grocery stores in Kansas, Oklahoma, and Arkansas. In addition to that operation, though, were a number of healthy subsidiaries. It continued to operate its King Sooper chain, for instance, which encompassed more than 30 stores in the mid-1970s. Dillon also bought City Market Inc., a chain of 16 grocery stores in the West, and Fry's Food Stores, a 28-store chain in Arizona. Dillon also owned Mr. D's Food Centers, which consisted of four ultra-modern supermarkets in Wyoming, and Gerbes Super Markets, Inc., an operator of ten supermarkets in Missouri.

Aside from supermarkets, Dillon also set its sights on the burgeoning convenience store industry during the 1970s. That move represented a major shift in the company's market focus. Indeed, by the 1980s, Dillon would be one of the largest operators of convenience stores in the nation, a status it achieved largely through acquiring other chains. During the 1970s, for instance, Dillon purchased Time Saver Stores, a 101-outlet chain of convenience stores in Louisiana. It also bought Quik Stop Markets, Inc., a 35-store chain of outlets in San Francisco, and the 54-store Kwik Shop, Inc. chain in the Midwest. Peripheral investment activities during the decade included controlling interests in Wells Aircraft, Jackson Ice Cream Co., Bohm-Allen Jewelry, and department store chain D.G. Calhoun.

After 64 years in the grocery business, most of it at the helm of Dillon Companies, Ray Dillon retired in 1979. The 82-year-old Dillon had previously relinquished daily operating activities to other senior executives, many of whom were Dillon family members. At the time of his departure, the company was ranked as the 33rd largest U.S. grocery store chain and was boasting about $2 billion in annual sales. The massive $2 billion mark contrasted with the $165,000 annual revenue of the first store that Ray Dillon had managed in the early 1920s. Indeed, Dillon had turned his one-shop operation into a corporate giant with more than 200 supermarkets, 300 convenience stores, and 18 department stores scattered throughout 11 states. An employee who had invested $100 in Dillon in 1957 would have seen the stock value rise to more than $1,500 by 1979. "It was a slow steady pull," remarked the energetic Dillon, before his departure, in the December 23, 1979 *Hutchinson News*. "We just kept grinding away."

After Ray Dillon's departure, son Ray E. (Ace) Dillon Jr. became the board chairperson. The younger Ray had already proved himself by leading the company as president for more than a decade. Richard W. Dillon, another son, became president, and Paul Dillon (son of cofounder Clyde Dillon) became senior vice-president. Under their direction, as the company had been for several years, Dillon continued to expand at a rapid pace. Between 1979 and 1982, in fact, Dillon added about 15 more supermarkets and 50 new convenience stores. It also diversified into a range of new ventures, including real estate, investments, and restaurants. By 1982, Dillon had bolstered its revenues to $2.8 billion, about $50 million of which was kept as earnings.

Dillon's unchecked growth through acquisition during the 1970s reflected a predominant grocery store industry trend toward consolidation. Partly because of advancements in distribution, food preservation, and electronic information technologies, companies were finding that they could achieve significant economies of scale by acquiring their competitors. Dillon, for example, succeeded by purchasing companies and allowing them to operate relatively autonomously. It benefitted from greater influence with its suppliers and, in some cases, by integrating some of its subsidiaries' activities such as reporting or warehousing into the larger Dillon organization. As the food industry became increasingly competitive during the late 1970s and early 1980s, consolidation intensified. It was not surprising, then, that supermarket powerhouse Kroger made a bid for Dillon Companies in 1982.

Kroger had been a major player in the U.S. grocery store industry since the early 1900s. The chain was founded in the 1880s by Barney Kroger, who started his company in a bright red wagon that he would haul around Cincinnati to sell tea and coffee. By the time Barney retired in 1928, he was a wealthy grocer with a chain that dwarfed the Dillon venture at the time. The chain expanded at a pace similar to that achieved by Dillon during the mid-1900s, making it the second largest grocer in the nation next to Safeway. After acquiring Dillon in 1982, the Kroger portfolio swelled to more than 1,200 food stores, 500 drug stores, and 33 manufacturing plants by the mid-1980s.

Although Kroger was known as an aggressive, bottom-line competitor, it also had a reputation for leaving its successful acquisitions alone. In fact, when Kroger bought out the Dillon chain, it promised the Dillon brothers that it would allow them to continue running the company with only minimal interference. Kroger lived up to that promise during the 1980s. Dillon Companies Inc. became an independent division of Kroger and sustained its fast expansion. The greatest difference effected by the acquisition was that Dillon suddenly had access to a larger pool of capital. Between 1982 and 1987, Dillon tagged 30 more supermarkets onto it chain. It also launched an initiative to renovate a large number of existing stores. Most notably, Dillon aggressively attacked the convenience store segment. It grew its number of convenience store outlets to more than 900 by the late 1980s, a three-fold increase since the late 1970s.

Dillon expanded during the late 1980s and early 1990s, though at a much slower pace than it had throughout the late 1970s and mid-1980s. A U.S. recession slowed overall expansion in the industry, and Dillon's access to capital was curbed. In fact, Kroger was forced to borrow $5.3 billion in 1988 as part of an effort to fend off a hostile takeover. Industry leader Safeway Stores was consumed in a similar takeover and was subsequently sold off in pieces, making Kroger the top player in the industry. By that time, Dillon was under the leadership of President David Dillon, a great grandson of John S. Dillon. David Dillon reigned in expansion plans during the remainder of the 1980s and into the 1990s.

Kroger restructured its finances during the early 1990s as the U.S. economy began to recover. Dillon began buying and building new stores and also continued to revamp existing outlets. By 1994, Dillon was operating 240 supermarkets through its various operating companies. Its Dillon Stores had ceased to be the largest revenue producer in its supermarket holdings. In fact, only about 20 Dillon stores were operating in the early 1990s. The original chain had been overcome by Dillon's 66-store King Sooper division, its 45 Fry's stores, and chain of 36 City Markets. Dillon's convenience stores had swelled to about 930 in number by 1994. The company had sold most of its peripheral holdings with the exception of a real estate company and two dairies. Although its financial statistics were not disclosed, Dillon's parent company posted record revenues in 1993 and was supporting Dillon's long-term growth strategy in the supermarket and convenience store markets.

Principal Subsidiaries: City Market; Dillon Food Stores; Fry's Food Stores; Gerbes Supermarkets; King Soopers Inc.; Kwik-Shop; Loaf 'N Jug; Mini-Mart; Quick Stop Markets; Sav-Mor; Time Savers Stores; Tom Thumb Food Stores; Turkey Hill Minit Markets.

Further Reading:

"Dillon Firm was Founded at Sterling," *The Hutchinson News,* December 23, 1979.
Dillon's 50 Golden Years: 1921–1971, Hutchinson, Kan.: Dillon Companies, Inc., 1971.
"Dillon's Keeps Policies that Made it a Leader," *Kansas Business News,* December 1987, p. 6.
Goodyear, Steve, "Fry's Food Stores Link Up with Motorola Codex," *Business Wire,* October 5, 1992.
Huttig, J.W., Jr., "New Kid on the Block," *Wichita Commerce,* March 1991, p. 14.
"Little Store Became Big Giant," *The Hutchinson News,* December 23, 1979.
Tate, Skip, "The Public File: The Kroger Co.," *Greater Cincinnati Business Record,* September 27, 1993, p. 14.
Vaughn, Doug, "Supermarket Shootout," *Denver Business,* February 1986, p. 47.

—Dave Mote

Dixon Ticonderoga Company

2600 Maitland Center Parkway
Suite 200
Maitland, Florida 32751
U.S.A.
(407) 875-9000
Fax: (407) 875-2574

Public Company
Incorporated: 1868 as Joseph Dixon Crucible Company
Employees: 1,250
Sales: $81.9 million
Stock Exchanges: American
SICs: 3952 Lead Pencils and Art Goods; 3951 Pens and
    Mechanical Pencils; 3295 Minerals and Earths, Ground or
    Otherwise Treated; 6552 Subdividers and Developers, Not
    Elsewhere Classified

The eleventh oldest company in the United States, Dixon Ticonderoga Company for many years was known predominately for its yellow and green pencils, but, after nearly two centuries of growth, Dixon's product line expanded substantially, comprising a diverse assortment of writing instruments and art supplies by the mid-1990s. With these products, as well as real estate holdings and graphite-related manufacturing operations predicating its business, Dixon represented one of the leading companies of its kind and the primary player in the history of the pencil in the United States.

For Joseph Dixon, the bustle of commerce along the waterfront in his native Marblehead, Massachusetts, provided the inspiration for his life-long work, an inspiration that was remarkable for two reasons: it came from a sight seen nearly every day by the residents of Marblehead and it came to Dixon when he was only 13 years old. Born in 1799, Dixon was the son of a local ship owner and, naturally, spent a considerable amount of time at the harbor watching ships arrive and depart from Marblehead's busy port. Bound for destinations along the eastern seaboard, to ports in Europe, and to as far away as the Orient, the ships left loaded with goods, the weight of which functioned as a ballast to keep the vessels upright. When ships returned without any goods, ship owners filled their hulls with sand or stones to give their ships the necessary ballast to counteract the weight of the ship's sails. Ship owners, like Dixon's father, who sailed between the Orient and Marblehead, used Ceylonese

graphite as ballast for their ships, then dumped the graphite once back home. This wasted substance, which generally was discarded in the bay, was the source of Dixon's inspiration, the common occurrence he noticed one fateful day in 1812 that led to the creation of Dixon Ticonderoga and America's dependence on the ubiquitous and indispensable pencil.

With the help of a local chemist named Francis Peabody and a cabinetmaker named Ebenezer Martin, Dixon was able to make a crude pencil, certainly not the first such writing instrument, but an item that was regarded nevertheless as somewhat of an oddity by Americans at the time. Pencils first appeared shortly after 1564, when a storm in Cumberland, England, uprooted a large tree and exposed a rich deposit of plumbago, or "black lead," the purest form of graphite yet discovered. Shepherds used chunks of this graphite to mark their sheep. These early versions—sticks of graphite known as "marking stones"—were considerably more primitive than Dixon's first attempts, but after several centuries of gradual improvements, pencils began to rival goose quills as the writing instruments of choice, the most noteworthy among the pencil's adherents being Napoleon Bonaparte, who reportedly became upset when his campaign to overrun Europe led to a paucity of graphite pencils. Accordingly, it was not so much the originality of Dixon's work with pencils, but his persistence in marketing the products that earned him the distinction as one of the pioneers of the U.S. pencil industry.

The same year in which Dixon's waterfront observations led him to make his first pencil, the War of 1812 broke out, stanching the flow of British graphite into America, but dwindling supply did not spark increased demand. Americans, in contrast to Europeans, still had not developed an affinity for pencils. That relationship would be engendered later, by another war; Dixon, meanwhile, moved on to other interests, maintaining through his teenage years his fascination with pencils while pursuing an education in printing, medicine, and chemistry.

Ten years after his first introduction to pencil fabrication, Dixon, age 23, married the daughter of the cabinetmaker who had helped him construct his first pencil. Together, Dixon and Hannah Martin began experimenting with different ways to make pencils, a process that accidentally led to considerable success with another product, one of several innovative successes credited to Dixon. Through their experimentation with graphite, the Dixons discovered the substance could be used as an effective stove polish, which they marketed, to widespread demand, as Dixon's Stove Polish. The product sold exceptionally well throughout the country, giving the couple sufficient profits to develop and refine their pencil business. The result of their labor and monetary investment were pencils they could produce and sell for ten cents apiece, but demand for their products still eluded them.

Dixon, however, did not go the route of a penniless entrepreneur selling his product to an unreceptive audience. Instead, he continued to find other, more marketable uses for graphite that met with considerable success. With the start of the Mexican-American War in 1846, iron and steel production in the United States increased substantially, and Dixon, producing a heat-resistant graphite crucible (a vessel used for melting iron and steel at high temperatures) shared in the profits spawned by increased military spending. He built a crucible factory in Jersey City, New Jersey, and opened the Joseph Dixon Crucible Company in 1847, which manufactured crucibles, stove polish, and, of course, pencils. Dixon's crucibles sold well, but as before his attempt to generate profits from producing pencils met with disappointing results. After his first year of business, Dixon pocketed $60,000 from the sale of crucibles and lost $5,000 from selling pencils, financial results indicative of his more than 20-year history in the pencil business and his almost begrudging success with other products.

The country's next war, the largest and deadliest of any before it, finally engendered Dixon's long-awaited dream, as more and more Americans began buying and using pencils. More easily carried than quills and ink, pencils became popular with Union and Confederate soldiers during the Civil War, and their use spread throughout the country. By 1866, Dixon had invented a wood planing machine that churned out 132 pencils per minute, enabling him to meet the rising demand for his four-inch long, cedar pencils. However, three years later, just as the pencil segment of the Joseph Dixon Crucible Company began to perform on an equal level with his stove polish and crucible segments, Dixon died, 57 years after his work with pencils had begun. In addition to his accomplishments with stove polish and graphite crucibles, Dixon had also designed a camera with a mirror—the precursor to the modern photographic view-finder—and had patented a double-crank steam engine. He had also invented a new method for tunneling underwater, developed a photolithography process used in printing banknotes that was designed to thwart counterfeiters, and attracted the prestigious company of fellow American inventors Robert Fulton, Samuel Morse, and Alexander Graham Bell. None of these achievements, however, ranked in Dixon's mind as equal to his life-long achievements with pencils.

After Dixon's death, his son-in-law took control of the company and presided over the first decade of genuine success in selling vast numbers of pencils. By 1872, the factory in Jersey City was making 86,000 pencils a day, which was roughly one-third of American consumption at the time. The following year, the company purchased the Ticonderoga, New York-based American Graphite Company. The addition of American Graphite and the city in which it was located (near a fort of the same name that passed between British and American control during the American Revolution) led to a brand name change in the company's pencils. Dixon pencils now became Dixon Ticonderoga pencils, although the company continued to be known as the Joseph Dixon Crucible Company. Leadership of the company devolved into receivership in 1883, when a bank president named Edward F.C. Young assumed control of the company, then was passed on to his son-in-law, George T. Smith.

By World War I, competition in the pencil market had intensified. European manufacturers had joined the fray, led by German and Japanese pencil producers, while in the United States, four pencil manufacturers, the "Big Four," battled for market share. Along with Eberhard Faber, American, and Eagle, Dixon was one of the four pencil manufacturers in the country that wielded overwhelming control over the market, together accounting for 90 percent of the pencil sales in the United States. Despite their enviable position, Dixon and the other three dominant pencil manufacturers began clamoring for increased tariffs in early 1920s to staunch the flow of cheaper German and Japanese pencils entering the United States. A decade later, as foreign competition mounted and the Great Depression tapered demand, the Big Four's market share slipped to 75 percent.

World War II resuscitated the American economy and along with it the demand for pencils. By 1942, despite shortages of graphite, clay, metal, and rubber, 1.5 billion pencils were being produced annually, and Dixon, as one of the largest in the industry, captured a lion's share of the booming market. After the war, demand slipped slightly to 1.3 billion pencils a year, but whatever the annual volume of demand, the industry's Big Four, almost exclusively, continued to supply it. By 1954, however, the Big Four's 30-year dominance of the industry had drawn the attention of federal officials and each was charged with violating the Sherman Antitrust Law. Together, Dixon, Eberhard Faber, American, and Eagle generated $15 million in annual sales, accounted for 50 percent of domestic sales and 75 percent of export sales, and controlled all aspects of pencil production, which, as the U.S. government alleged, included price-fixing. Each entered pleas of no defense, agreed in a consent decree to desist from further illegal practices, and paid a nominal $5,000 fine apiece.

Following the company's legal turmoil, Dixon began to feel pressure from the pencil industry's fifth largest competitor, Empire, which prompted Dixon to redesign the packaging of its products and effect a merger, in 1957, with the American Crayon Company. Based in Sandusky, Ohio, American Crayon manufactured "Old Faithful" pencils, Prang school and marking crayons, and Tempera colors and art materials, which were then added to the Dixon product line, giving the company a broader supply of graphite lead pencils and valuable connections with the nation's school system, one of American Crayon's primary customers.

While for Dixon the next two decades passed without any major developments, significant developments were occurring elsewhere that would result in a change in ownership for the venerable pencil and crucible manufacturer. Several years after Dixon merged with American Crayon, a series of events began unfolding in a small, family-owned bar and restaurant. The restaurant was Pala's Cafe in Wilmington, Delaware, run by Gino N. Pala, who left school in the eleventh grade and began working in his father's fruit market in 1944. Shortly after his twenty-first birthday, Pala began running the family restaurant and bar in Wilmington, which by the mid-1960s had become a meeting place for the city's lawyers and real estate developers. During this time, some of the executives who frequented Pala's Cafe began inviting Pala to join them in their investments. Pala, who had been running the cafe for roughly 20 years by this time and had profited from a furniture business he and his brother had opened in 1954, had the cash and began investing it with some of his customers. One customer with whom Pala became particularly involved with was David K. Brewster, a former deputy attorney general and securities commissioner of Delaware. In 1975, Pala and Brewster bought 20 percent of the shares in a company called Electric Hose & Rubber for $1.6 million, then initiated a proxy fight to gain control of the company. They lost the battle, but the company's management ended up buying the shares back for $2.4 million, giving each investor a healthy profit.

Pala and Brewster combined forces again in 1978, paying $1.5 million for a 51 percent stake in a failing real estate, restaurant, and bus company named Bryn Mawr Corporation. With $9 million of debt, Bryn Mawr needed much attention, so Pala ceded control of his restaurant to a younger brother, then moved to Florida and began selling off Bryn Mawr's assets. Several years and $25 million in assets later, Pala had revived Bryn Mawr, enabling the company to net $10 million in pretax profits. Pala and Brewster then began looking for another acquisition, and in 1981 found one: the Joseph Dixon Crucible Company.

Dixon had since become a lackluster performer, earning $1 million in 1981 on revenues of $64 million, then recording a $1 million loss the following year as revenues slipped to $57 million. After acquiring 13 percent of Dixon's stock, Pala and Brewster convinced the company' management to approve a merger between Bryn Mawr and Dixon, which was concluded in 1983. Concurrent with the merger, the Joseph Dixon Crucible Company became Dixon Ticonderoga Company, adding the brand name of its famous yellow and green pencils to its corporate title. Shortly thereafter, the company exited the crucible business entirely.

Once in control, Pala sold off some of the company's assets, consolidated operations, revamped some of the company's manufacturing plants, and by 1985 had paid off $5.4 million of debt. Under Pala's stewardship, Dixon prospered for the next three years, expanding the scope of its operations and the breadth of its product line along the way. In 1986, Dixon purchased David Kahn Inc., a manufacturer of writing instruments marketed under the Wearever brand name, then two years later acquired Ruwe Pencil and National Pen & Pencil. By 1988, the company's net income had eclipsed $3 million on revenues of nearly $80 million. However, shortly thereafter problems began to surface as the company's three-year period of financial growth turned into a retrogressive slide.

In an effort to explain Dixon's anemic financial performance, Pala later related to the *Orlando Business Journal* that "I hired guys that I thought could run the company, [but] they didn't know how to run a business," a imputation that was evident in the precipitous drop in Dixon's net income. The company lost $5 million in 1990, halfway through an injurious profit drought

that left Dixon without a profit in 1989, 1990, and 1991. To effect a recovery, Pala reorganized Dixon's sales, marketing, and customer service operations, closed down two inefficient manufacturing plants in Ontario and Sheloyville, Tennessee, and trimmed superfluous layers of the company's middle management. By virtue of such measures, Dixon once again returned to the black in 1992, when the company reported a modest yet reassuring $327,000 in net income.

After recording a meager $3,000 gain in net income in 1993, the company plotted its course for the mid-1990s and beyond, revitalized but yet to capitalize financially on the steps its management had taken to provide for a more profitable future. By reformulating the company's marketing strategy to embrace national office wholesalers and streamlining its manufacturing operations in the early 1990s, Pala and Dixon's management had repositioned the company for such a future and increased the likelihood that the product of Joseph Dixon's labors would enter its third century of business.

Principal Subsidiaries: Bryn Mawr Resorts, Inc.; Bryn Mawr Real Estate Co.; Bryn Mawr Water Co.; Bryn Mawr Sewer Co.; Bryn Mawr Ocean Resorts, Inc.; Bryn Fair Finance of Indian River City, Inc.; Dixon Ticonderoga, Inc.; Dixon Ticonderoga Co. de Mexico, S.A. de C.V.; Dixon U.K. Ltd.

Further Reading:

Bromfield, Jerome, "Everything Begins with a Pencil," *Kiwanis Magazine,* 1976, pp. 25–33.
"Growing Sharper, Dixon Ticonderoga Points to Earnings of $2 a Share This Year," *Barron's,* April 16, 1987, p. 64.
"Companies Involved in Largest Insider Purchases," *Insider's Chronicle,* March 4, 1991, p. 3.
Marcial, Gene G., "This Penmaker Has Written Itself a Hot New Script," *Business Week,* May 9, 1988, p. 134.
Meeks, Fleming, "Better than an M.B.A.," *Forbes,* June 26, 1989, p. 88–94.
Meeks, Fleming, "Easier Does It," *Forbes,* October 29, 1990, p. 10.
Perrault, Mike, "Pencil in Profits, Dixon Ticonderoga to Erase Losses," *Orlando Business Journal,* June 26, 1992, p. 1.
"Lowly Pencil Involved in Global Controversy," *Wall Street Journal,* October 19, 1990, p. B1.

—Jeffrey L. Covell

Dominion Textile Inc.

1950 Sherbrooke St. West
Montreal, Quebec, H3H 1E7
Canada
(514) 989-6000
Fax: (514) 989-6214

Public Company
Incorporated: 1905 as the Dominion Textile Company
    Limited
Employees: 8,700
Sales: C$1.33 billion
Stock Exchanges: Montreal Toronto
SICs: 2200 Textile Mill Products

Dominion Textile Inc. is one of Canada's largest textile companies and the world's largest manufacturers of denim. Dominion grew slowly throughout the twentieth century, first strengthening its role as a Canadian manufacturer before acquiring a number of companies in the United States, mostly in the 1970s and 1980s. By 1994 Dominion posted sales of C$1.33 billion and held strong market positions in denim, yarn, technical fabrics, apparel fabrics, and nonwovens.

The roots of Dominion Textile reach back to 1890 with the formation of the Dominion Cotton Mills Company. Eight small, struggling textile firms had banded together to pool their resources; each had suffered from the high costs and inefficiencies associated with producing a small number of many items. Dominion, like many other Canadian textile firms, grew to depend on the profitable trade to the Far East, which had become possible with the completion of the Canadian Pacific Railway in 1885. However, the Boxer Rebellion in China in 1900 disrupted trade to that lucrative market. In 1905, in a further effort to stave off financial ruin, a handful of companies again banded together. They were the Dominion Cotton Mills, Ltd. (which by that time had plants in Halifax and Windsor, Nova Scotia; Moncton, New Brunswick; Montreal, Magog, and Caoticook, Quebec; and Kingston and Branford, Ontario), the Montmorency Cotton Mills Company, the Montreal-based Merchants Cotton Company, and the Colonial Bleaching and Printing Company, also of Montreal, for a total of eleven plants. The new entity was called the Dominion Textile Company Limited.

Montreal financier David Yuile was the company's first president, but it was Charles B. Gordon, who became president in 1909, who dominated the early history of the company. One of the first battles the company weathered was brought on by security holders of the former Dominion Cotton Mills Company and Merchants Cotton Company who had refused to sell their stock in 1905. The case was heard by the Canadian high court, the Privy Council, which ruled in favor of Dominion.

With the advent of World War I, Gordon was put in charge of war-purchase missions in the United States by the British and Canadian governments; he was later knighted for his duties. Dominion's plants ran continuously to supply goods for the war. The plants' overuse during the war meant that in the years immediately following much of the company's resources were put into repairing and refurbishing its manufacturing facilities, which included the facility that it acquired in 1919 when it bought the Mount Royal Spinning Company of Montreal.

A stock offering in 1922 brought Dominion C$2,500,000 in new capital. A new entity, the Dominion Textile Co. Limited, sometimes called Domtex, took over the assets of the Dominion Textile Company. A series of technological upgrades (after the introduction of long-draft spinning and multiple loom sets) and acquisitions swiftly followed. In 1928 Dominion bought two American companies that made tire fabric: the Jenckes-Canadian Company became a subsidiary known as Drummondville Cotton Company Limited, and the Canadian Connecticut Cotton Mills became Sherbrooke Cotton Company Limited. (In 1934 Sherbrooke was converted into a sheeting-fabric manufacturing plant, and tire manufacture was concentrated in Drummondville.) In 1930 Dominion took over the management of Montreal Cotton Limited, a company in which it had an interest since 1908. In 1948 Dominion bought the last of Montreal Cotton's shares, and by 1953 it was completely folded back into Dominion.

As with many other industries, the onset of World War II put a spur to textile production, which had suffered during the Depression. A plant that had lain dormant from 1934 was reactivated in 1940, and Dominion made a range of products for military purposes, from camouflage nets to bootlaces. With an eye on the postwar economy, Dominion entered a joint venture in 1945 to make rayon with the Burlington Mills Corporation of North Carolina, called Dominion Burlington Mills Limited. In March 1952 Dominion bought Burlington's 50 percent share and the company's name was changed to Domil Limited (those plants became fully integrated with the company in 1966).

During the 1960s, Dominion built four new plants in Quebec and Ontario, where a popular new fabric, the polyester/cotton blend, was spun, woven, and finished. One print ad created during this time featured "the unwrinkable Molly Brown," a little girl whose clothing, made of Dominion's Truprest fabric, stayed smooth and wrinkle-free. Also during this time, Dominion acquired Penmans in Ontario, a company engaged in the manufacture of knitted leisurewear. This represented Dominion's first move outside the primary textile industry.

In November of 1969 the company's name was changed to Dominion Textile Limited. A string of acquisitions and divestitures followed, as the North American textile industry tried to come to terms with the flood of cheap imports from the Far East. In 1969 Dominion bought Fiberworld Limited and Jaro Manufacturing Co. Ltd. In 1972 it formed a joint venture—DHJ Canadian, Ltd.—with New York-based DHJ Industries, Inc. Three years later, Dominion bought DHJ Industries Inc., which consisted of eight plants in the United States as well as affiliates and distributors throughout the world. That purchase strengthened Dominion's hand in the international marketplace as the textile industry continued to rapidly shift out of North America.

The DHJ takeover was an unfriendly one. The financially troubled company (with $64 million in debt, $20 million from the first nine months of 1975 alone) was dominated by chairman and founder Herbert Haskell. Much of his family's holdings in the company were held as collateral for personal loans made by Chemical Bank of New York. When Haskell refused to sell to Dominion, Dominion went to his banker and negotiated a deal without him, purchasing DHJ for $9.2 million. Haskell sued and vowed to go into direct competition with Dominion, but he eventually settled. Dominion got a lot out of the deal, for DHJ owned one of the largest denim manufacturing facilities in the United States through its Swift Textiles, Inc. subsidiary and had sales of $191 million for the fiscal year ending June 1974.

In 1979 Dominion, which had been renamed Dominion Textile Inc., continued to try to move away from "commodity" fabrics, which were dominated by imports. In October of 1979, DHJ and Facemate Corporation of Chicopee, Massachusetts, formed a joint venture—DHJ-Facemate Corporation—and merged their interlining operations. In 1980 Dominion bought Linn-Corriher Corporation of Landis, North Carolina, which made cotton and synthetic yarns, for $25 million. In 1981 it acquired Mirafi, Inc., the civil-engineering fabrics division of the Hoescht Celanese Corp. of Somerville, New Jersey. Mirafi made plastic-based materials used in roadbeds and drainage systems. In 1988, Dominion acquired Wayn-Tex, a manufacturer of carpet backing, based in Virginia. Also that year, the company acquired the London-based Klopman International, Europe's largest producer and distributor of workwear fabrics.

Recession exacerbated the difficulties brought by the inexorable growth of cheap imports, and from 1982 to 1985 Dominion lost money. Dominion responded by paring down operations. In 1981 it sold its 50 percent interest in DHJ-Facemate. Between 1983 and 1986 Dominion closed 13 of its 26 plants. Most of these facilities were in Quebec, where the company had repeatedly locked horns with the aggressive union Centrale des Syndicats Democratiques. As opposed to the United States, where most textile workers were not unionized, most of the workers in Canada at that time were, and wages ran approximately 7 to 10 percent higher than in the United States. Canadian textile executives also complained of the difficulty in competing against U.S. makers when U.S. plants were flexible enough to run seven days a week if necessary; strict union rules prohibited such flexibility, they said.

In 1986 Dominion again tried to make an incursion across the border when it tried to purchase Avondale Mills, a denim and yarn maker in Sylacauga, Alabama. Dominion lost out to AM Acquisition, which had countered its $26-dollar-a-share bid with an offer of $28. Dominion was not daunted by the effort and simply went after a bigger prize. That prize was none other than its former joint-venture partner Burlington Mills of Greensboro, North Carolina, which by 1987 was the largest textile company in the United States, with fiscal year 1986 sales of $2.8 billion. Dominion's sales in fiscal 1986 were $671 million.

Burlington was vulnerable, having become dependent on selling commodity fabrics in a market that was dominated by overseas makers. Dominion teamed up with renowned New York raider Asher Edelman to try and win Burlington. Edelman first quietly gained control of 7.6 percent of Burlington stock. Edelman and Dominion then bid $1.51 billion for the company on April 24. Some suspected that Dominion was interested in only a handful of Burlington's plants and planned, if it won control of the venerable manufacturer, to sell off the rest. Burlington's denim plants contributed 25 percent of its revenues and were considered Dominion's real goal. Dominion was also eager to put down roots in the United States in an effort to get around the expected results of lower tariffs in negotiations that were then taking place between the United States and Canada. Dominion was fearful of being undercut by larger-volume, lower-cost facilities in the United States, where Dominion earned more than a quarter of its sales.

The struggle for control of Burlington raged for over seven weeks, with a series of offers and counteroffers made until Dominion made a final offer of $2.1 billion. Lawsuits were filed on both sides. In the end Dominion lost the battle—Burlington took itself private in a leveraged buyout—but won the war. Edelman and Dominion agreed to drop their hostile takeover attempt in exchange for $25 million and certain Burlington properties. Edelman and Dominion sold their 12 percent stake for a post-tax gain of $15.2 million. Further, Dominion snapped up several of Burlington's most desirable facilities: a denim plant in Erwin, North Carolina, which it bought for $205 million (the purchase contract included an agreement to drop all litigation from the takeover attempt); Klopman International, the largest producer in Europe of polyester- and cotton-blended fabrics for workwear, purchased for $90 million; as well as included Klopman International SpA (Italy), Burlington Industries Limited (Ireland), Burlington Deutschland GmbH, and Burlington AC. These moves seemed to say that Dominion would place the bulk of its future investments outside of Canada. After the purchase of Burlington's denim factories, Dominion became one of the world's largest denim manufacturers.

The acquisitions of the 1980s left the company in debt, and the recession that hit the apparel industry in 1989 meant that Dominion lost money in 1990 and 1991. Dominion restructured to bring focus to the company's sprawling assemblage of plants and subsidiaries, which made everything from electrical insulation to book bindings, bedding to upholstery. Plants were closed and divisions sold. Mirafi was sold off during this time, and Dominion merged its Caldwell towel division with the operations of New York-based C.S. Brooks Corporation. In 1992 it sold off its Wayn-Tex and Dominion Fabrics Co. divisions. Poly-Bond Inc., a wholly owned subsidiary, became the focus of its nonwovens efforts in North America, and heavy investments were made at its Waynesboro, Virginia, facilities.

Thus Dominion's emphasis was on denims, nonwoven fabrics, and commodity yarns. In 1990, Dominion had acquired Quebec-based Textiles Dionne, which specialized in cotton and synthetic yarns. The company acquired Nordlys S.A., a nonwovens manufacturer in Bailleul, France, and in 1991 completed construction on a modern new facility to house all of the operations. In 1992, another nonwovens plant was built in Malaysia. In further efforts to strengthen its core businesses, Dominion agreed in 1995 to sell DHJ Industries to Chargeurs Textiles of France. The company also restructured Dominion Specialty Yarns in Canada to focus on its most profitable product lines, and the Poly-Bond subsidiary entered into a joint venture with Corovin GmbH to produce new high-technology nonwovens.

The popularity of denim in the early 1990s (denim demand grew by 30 percent from 1990 through 1993) and a 20 percent drop in cotton prices helped Dominion's financial position. In 1994 sales were C$1.33 billion, with a net income of C$33.5 million, a turnaround from two years before when it had lost C$74.8 million. In 1994, the bulk of its business was derived from denim, which accounted for 39 percent of sales (C$518.3 million), yarns, which made up 21 percent (C$281.4 million), and technical fabrics, 17 percent (C$228.4 million). Apparel brought in 13 percent of sales (C$178.1 million).

Principal Subsidiaries: Swift Textiles, Inc.; Swift Textiles Canada; Swift Textiles (Far East) Ltd.; Dominion Yarn Corporation; Dominion Yarn Company; Dominion Specialty Yarns; Dominion Textile (USA) Inc.; Dominion Cotton Services; Intech-PEM Inc.; Vivatex; Dominion Textile International B.V.; Dominion Textile International (Asia) Pte. Ltd.; Nordly's S.A.; Klopman International S.r.l.; Klopman International Ltd.; Poly-Bond Inc.; Dominion Industrial Fabrics Company.

Further Reading:

"Dominion Textile Inc. Ends Bid for Avondale," *Wall Street Journal,* April 4, 1986, p. 4.
Foust, Dean, "Burlington Almost Invited Edelman to Attack," *Business Week,* May 1, 1987, p. 50.
——, "Dominion's Unraveling Bid," *Business Week,* June 1, 1987, p. 49.
"How Domtex Staged Its Coup at DHJ," *Business Week,* June 9, 1975, p. 26.
O'Connor, D'Arcy, "To Fade or Not to Fade," *Canadian Business,* June 1988, p. 45.
"Who's the Real Winner in Burlington Match," *Textile World,* June 1987, p. 23.

—C. L. Collins

Donnelly Corporation

414 E. 40th Street
Holland, Michigan 49423-5368
U.S.A.
(616) 786-7000
Fax: (616) 786-6034

Public Company
Incorporated: 1936 as Donnelly-Kelly Glass Company
Employees: 2,704
Sales: $337.26 million
Stock Exchanges: American
SICs: 3231 Products of Purchased Glass; 3211 Flat Glass

Founded in 1905 by Bernard P. Donnelly, Donnelly Corporation became one of the world's leading producers of interior rear-view mirrors for automobiles. Donnelly also manufactures a variety of other glass-related products for the worldwide auto market, including exterior mirrors, windows, and interior lighting systems. The company went public in 1988, but the Donnelly family maintained control over 93 percent of the voting stock, and Donnelly descendants have remained actively involved in company management. This family concern was perhaps best known for operating its business like a family. The company's longstanding participative management system has garnered numerous awards, and Donnelly has been named one of the ten best companies to work for in America.

The company known as Donnelly Corporation was founded in 1905 in Holland, Michigan, as a manufacturer of mirrors for the then-thriving Michigan furniture industry. Founded as the Kinsella Glass Company, the company was later renamed the Donnelly-Kelly Glass Company. Donnelly's main products in the early years were engraved mirrors for use on furniture as well as free-standing engraved wall mirrors. These "art" mirrors, featuring scenes from nature as well as ornate decorative motifs, became very popular for home furnishings through the early part of the century, and as a result Donnelly's business flourished. The engraving of the mirrors was done largely by hand, but the precision grinding and polishing that this craftsmanship required formed the basis for much of the glass technology that Donnelly would later develop. Being in business in Michigan during the 1920s meant watching the phenomenal growth of the American automobile industry. Although decorative mirrors remained the core of its business, Donnelly also

jumped on the automobile bandwagon and began production of rear windows for touring cars.

World War II marked a turning point for Donnelly. As America geared up for the war effort, the company converted its decorative mirror factory into a specialized lens and mirror production facility. These highly precise glass components were needed for military equipment ranging from aerial gunsights to submarine periscopes, and there were few manufacturers who could produce them with speed and accuracy. Donnelly scrambled to refit its factory with the necessary machinery to perform this task and to retrain its craftsmen to measure in microns instead of inches. Among the techniques developed by Donnelly during its wartime experience was the process of vacuum coating glass with a variety of materials to produce mirrors with varying degrees of reflectivity. This technology would prove invaluable during the company's later development of automobile mirrors.

When the war ended, Donnelly found itself with a great deal of new technology and experience, but in search of new markets for glass and mirror products. Not only had decorative mirrors gone out of fashion, but the furniture industry that Donnelly had supplied was moving south to find cheaper labor. The automobile industry in Michigan, however, was booming. Production could not keep up with the demand from product-hungry postwar consumers. Donnelly made the crucial decision to transform what had been a secondary market into a primary source of sales. The company began to manufacture interior and exterior prismatic mirrors for the automobile industry and soon became one of the leaders among automobile parts suppliers. Donnelly's experience in vacuum coating glass became one of its prime assets as the company developed a number of innovative applications in both the automotive and aircraft industries. By the mid 1950s, with new markets and products fully in place, management decided to change the company name to Donnelly Mirrors Inc. to better reflect this more specialized line.

The 1960s and 1970s constituted a period of major expansion for Donnelly in terms of both the range of products the company manufactured and the number of industries it supplied. One major innovation for the company during this period was the development of the encapsulated mirror, which was delivered to automotive manufacturers as a single unit mirror enclosed in a plastic frame. The plastic mirror housing was not only much safer than the previously standard metal frame, but was also much cheaper for automobile makers to install. Once Donnelly had the technology and equipment to produce the plastic molding, it was also able to expand its line to other plastic components and to provide customers with complete interior mirror assemblies, including the bracket used to attach the mirror to the car. This would mark the beginning of the company's expanded line of complete part assemblies.

By the mid 1970s, this new plastic molding technology allowed Donnelly to introduce one of the most important innovations in the car parts industry. Known as the modular window, this new product involved encapsulating window glass in a plastic frame that also incorporated attachment hardware and decorative trim. This new window not only greatly reduced labor costs at the automotive plants by reducing a four-step process to a single quick installation, but also substantially altered the design possibilities of new vehicles. The streamlined look that became so popular in vehicles through the 1980s was in large part made possible by the Donnelly modular window.

In addition to the major developments in product technology that Donnelly undertook during the 1960s and 1970s, the company also began to reach out to markets overseas. Anticipating the growth of the European and Japanese auto industries, Donnelly founded a wholly owned subsidiary, Donnelly Mirrors, Limited, in Naas, Ireland, to supply these expanding industries. The company also expanded its American markets by producing coated glass products for non-automotive applications, such as copy machines and fluorescent displays.

The 1980s were a demanding period for the American auto industry, as competition from abroad made serious inroads into the American car market. Donnelly survived this critical period by expanding its line of ready-to-install plastic and glass components as well as by increasing its already established relationship with foreign car manufacturers. As American auto manufacturers began to scramble to meet the quality and energy efficiency standards set by Japanese competitors, Donnelly's emphasis on product development and innovation made the company an increasingly attractive supplier.

Donnelly began to experiment with electronic lighting to provide low glare interior lighting in association with its rear-view mirrors. The company then branched out into producing integrated lighting systems including overhead, door, and visor lights. Like the modular window, which was proving increasingly successful for the company, these assemblies integrated a number of components that previously would have been installed separately by the manufacturers. The reduction in labor costs for the automakers was an important factor in increasing Donnelly's share of the auto parts market. In order to reflect the growing diversity in the company's product line—which by this time ranged from windows to liquid crystal displays (LCDs)—Donnelly Mirrors, Inc. was renamed Donnelly Corporation in 1984.

As Donnelly moved into the 1990s, the relationship between auto manufacturers and auto parts suppliers was undergoing a profound change. Not only were automakers increasingly looking to suppliers as partners in research and development, but they were also fostering more long-term cooperation and commitment between manufacturers and suppliers. Traditionally, American automakers had obtained lowest possible cost components by buying the same part from five or six suppliers, thereby encouraging cutthroat competition among auto parts manufacturers. As hard times during the 1980s forced many parts suppliers out of business, however, automakers were forced to substitute high-volume and long-term contracts for competition in order to reduce costs. While the early 1990s were lean years for Donnelly, and the auto industry in general, the company did benefit from several large contracts for complete mirror assemblies and modular windows from Honda, Ford, Mazda, and Chrysler. In order to meet these new large commitments, Donnelly undertook a costly overhaul of its production facilities, including construction of new plants in Michigan, Mexico, and France and of new production lines within older facilities.

During the 1980s and 1990s, Donnelly's extensive experience in coated glass products gave the company an entry into the then-booming electronics industry, as it began to produce electrically conductive coated glass products to be used in LCD applications. These new applications, including touch-sensitive computer screens, became a significant factor in overall sales. In the early 1990s, however, increased market demands for efficiency of operations prompted the company to restructure its non-automotive ventures. In 1992, Donnelly's display coatings business was transferred to Donnelly Applied Films Corp. (DAFC), a joint venture with Applied Films Laboratory Inc. in which Donnelly maintained a 50 percent share. Other non-automotive products were also transferred to, or developed in conjunction with, joint ventures operating independently from Donnelly's core automotive businesses.

One of the most promising new technologies developed by Donnelly in the 1980s was the electrochromic coating of automobile mirrors to allow them to adjust automatically to reduce glare. Donnelly, however, became embroiled in an ongoing legal dispute with Gentex Corporation about the patent rights to this technology. Gentex sued Donnelly in 1990 for patent infringement of its electrochromic mirrors. After a lengthy series of suits and countersuits, in 1993 the parties reached a settlement in which Donnelly agreed to pay Gentex $3.6 million in damages, which took a sizable bite out of net income for that year. Unfortunately, this did not lay the matter to rest, as Gentex promptly sued the company again, claiming that Donnelly had violated an injunction to stop work on certain aspects of this technology. In 1994 Donnelly responded with a countersuit claiming that "with every electrochromic mirror they produce" Gentex was infringing on patents owned by Donnelly. This dispute was still in litigation in the spring of 1995.

Above all else, Donnelly has gained a strong reputation in the world of business for its longstanding innovative approach to company management. Donnelly has earned numerous awards and citations over the years for its participative management system, and has been listed as one of the top ten best companies to work for in America. In 1952, when much of Michigan industry was settling down into long-term combative relationships with big unions and top-heavy management systems, Donnelly introduced a system of employee participation and bonuses called the Scanlon Plan. Developed by an MIT professor, Joseph Scanlon, the plan was based on the principle that if employees were informed about the reasons for company decisions, and could participate directly in the benefits of these decisions, employee satisfaction and productivity would increase. The core of the plan involved a set of weighted bonuses for all employees calculated as a percentage of the cost/sales ratio.

From the perspective of the 1990s, when Total Quality Management and employee satisfaction became buzzwords, the plan would not appear revolutionary. In the early 1950s, however, the idea of sharing increases in profits with workers was viewed as almost communistic by some in the auto business. John F. Donnelly, a former seminarian and then president of the company, was firmly committed not only to the management position that this type of plan would lead to increased productivity, but also to the philosophical belief that as the head of a company he was responsible for ensuring a decent and fair work environment. Donnelly Corporation management remained firmly committed to these ideals over the course of almost fifty years.

By the 1990s, what had started as a bonus plan for employees had evolved into a complete team approach to all decision making in the company. While a hierarchy of management teams was retained, with the executive team at the highest level and ultimately responsible for the operation of the company, decisions were made at each level using cooperative decision-making practices that included all members of the work force. In addition, a series of "equity" committees with elected representatives from all levels in the company were responsible for such issues as pay structure, benefit plans, and grievances. This constantly evolving system has made employee satisfaction among the highest in the country, while the constant questioning and feedback about work processes that the committee structure encourages has led to almost no waste in the Donnelly production line. One unexpected result of this participative management system was that when it became crucial for American car parts makers to forge ties with the Japanese auto industry, Donnelly's management style meshed very closely with that employed in Japan. An important contract with Honda in the mid 1980s was partly the result of these harmonious corporate cultures.

When World War II temporarily halted the manufacture of decorative mirrors at the Donnelly-Kelly Glass Company, the company had a respectable $1 million worth of annual sales. By 1965, with the company firmly entrenched in the automobile parts industry, sales had quadrupled to almost $4 million, but this still represented only a very small portion of the auto parts market. It was during the 1960s and 1970s that Donnelly's growth began in earnest, with sales mounting to almost $40 million by 1980. This dramatic increase was mainly due to the company's success at garnering an increasingly large portion of the auto interior mirror market, thanks to its plastic-cased "safety" mirrors and complete mirror assemblies. By 1976 Donnelly controlled 70 percent of the rear-view mirror market. By the early 1990s this figure rose to an impressive 90 percent.

The domination of the interior mirror market, in addition to strong growth in exterior mirrors and modular windows, created annual sales of some $337 million by 1994.

Traditionally the performance of auto parts suppliers has been almost entirely dependent on the state of the automobile manufacturing industry. When the auto industry went into a deep recession in the early 1980s and again in the early 1990s, Donnelly's sales flattened out and income dropped. By 1992, however, earnings had risen once again and Donnelly appeared to be well on its way to a strong recovery. Although sales did rise in 1994 and 1995, the very large expenditures involved in renovating and constructing new manufacturing facilities, as well as litigation expenses from the ongoing patent dispute with Gentex, caused net income to drop. In the first quarter of 1995 Donnelly recorded a net loss of $85,000, at a time when the auto industry as a whole was reporting soaring profits. However, Donnelly remained confident that these losses were temporary and were the result of the company's insistence on building towards long-term goals. Its long tradition of innovation, quality products, and solid management should help Donnelly to attain its goals well into the twenty-first century.

Principal Subsidiaries: Donnelly Mirrors, Ltd. (Ireland)

Further Reading:

Ewing, David W., and Pamela Banks, "Participative Management at Work—An Interview with John F. Donnelly," *Harvard Business Review,* January–February 1977, pp. 117–127.
Levering, Robert, and Milton Moskowitz, *The 100 Best Companies to Work for in America,* New York: Doubleday, 1993, pp. 102–107.
Magnet, Myron, "The New Golden Rule of Business: It's Love Thy Supplier," *Fortune,* February 21, 1994, pp. 5–10.
Moskal, Brian S., "Donnelly Manages for the Future," *Industry Week,* February 1, 1993, pp. 27–33.
Rescigno, Richard, "Greater Than the Whole: Auto Parts Suppliers Are Prospering, While the Big Three Lag," *Barron's,* August 12, 1991, pp. 8–9, 26–30.

—Hilary Gopnik

Doskocil Companies, Inc.

2601 N.W. Expressway, Suite 1000W
Oklahoma City, Oklahoma 73112
U.S.A.
(405) 879-5000
Fax: (405) 879-5573

Public Company
Incorporated: 1963
Employees: 3,500
Sales: $750 million
Stock Exchanges: NASDAQ
SICs: 2011 Meat Packing Plants; 2013 Sausages & Other
  Products

Doskocil Companies, Inc. is a leading U.S. manufacturer and distributor of processed meat products engaged with three primary markets: retail, wholesale foodservice, and delicatessen customers. With product lines ranging from bacon and boneless hams to sausage and Mexican foods, Doskocil is the number one supplier of meat toppings to the $30 billion-per-year U.S. pizza industry. In addition, the company markets its products under a variety of proprietary brand names, including Wilson Foods, Corn King, Wilson's Continental Deli, Fred's, Doskocil Foods, Jefferson Meats, Rotanelli's, Posada, American Favorite, and Butcher Boy.

Doskocil was founded in Kansas by Larry Doskocil. As the story goes, Doskocil stopped to have dinner one night in 1963 at a new local restaurant called Pizza Hut. While he was waiting for his pizza, he noticed that the owner of the establishment was making his own ingredients from fresh meat. The man, perturbed by the time-consuming process that was keeping him from a softball game, gladly accepted when Doskocil offered to cook a batch of meat-topping him. At the time, the 30-year-old Doskocil was already much involved in the meat business. He had earned his way through Bethany Nazarene College in Bethany, Oklahoma, by working in the meat department at the local Safeway supermarket, and later had served as a chef in the Army. After leaving the Service, he opened his own tiny meat company in Kansas. Doskocil's aspiration when he started his venture was to make his company a force in the brand-name sausage industry, a dream inspired by the successful J.C. Potter brand of sausage that he had sold at Safeway in Oklahoma.

Potter's sausage was very popular in Oklahoma, and Doskocil thought that he could produce a similar product in Kansas. "So I decided that I was going to become the J.C. Potter of Kansas," Doskocil recalled in the October 22, 1984 *Forbes*. He leased an abandoned chicken hatchery in 1961 and began producing sausage under the brand name Country Cousin. Doskocil sustained a exhausting schedule during the first few years, getting up at 5:00 a.m., making sausage until noon, and then loading it onto his truck and selling it until dark. He spent his evening hours slaughtering hogs for the next day's batch, and, during his first year in business, slept at his tiny manufacturing plant.

Doskocil soon became disenchanted with his fledgling shop. Growth was slow and it seemed like he was fighting an uphill battle in the sluggish sausage market. So he started looking for new opportunities, such as the one that presented itself at Pizza Hut. Shortly after the first delivery to the Pizza Hut owner, Doskocil knew that he had a winning idea on his hands. He began telephoning other pizza franchises, offering to supply them with pre-made meat toppings. Business boomed and Doskocil made his fortune.

During the late 1960s, 1970s, and early 1980s, Doskocil successfully developed his venture into a large corporation by focusing on the niche market for pizza toppings. His timing could not have been better. As demand for pizza soared, sales of Doskocil's toppings surged. In addition to expanding markets, Doskocil benefited from a pizza industry trend toward greater efficiency, and thus greater consumption of processed toppings.

Doskocil got his foot in the door with Pizza Hut, and was able to parlay that early gain into major contracts to supply other pizza industry giants like Godfather's Pizza, Domino's Pizza, and ShowBiz Pizza. As the popularity of pizza surpassed that of the hamburger in the United States, Doskocil enjoyed steady double-digit growth rates throughout the 1970s and early 1980s. Estimated sales in 1983 topped $100 million and net income was approaching $8 million. "We have a neat little niche here," Doskocil explained in the *Forbes* article. "We're very happy."

Doskocil's profitable market niche was undoubtedly important to its mid-1980s success, but Larry Doskocil's operating strategies were also integral to the company's gains. Indeed, Doskocil was competing in an industry dominated by meat processing giants like Hormel and Oscar Mayer. To fend off competitors, the company had to keep costs low and continually offer new and better products that fit its customer's changing demands. Doskocil was the first to introduce "crumbly" pizza toppings, for example. And it introduced several sizes of chunky toppings, which made it possible for pizza chains to successfully enter the deep dish market.

To create new products and to improve production efficiency, Doskocil had even formed a company, Reno Technologies, to design and manufacture custom food processing equipment. The division started out producing machines for Doskocil but eventually began building systems for other food processing companies. Doskocil's proprietary machines were just part of its carefully cloaked manufacturing operations during the 1970s and 1980s. Visitors were rarely allowed onto the company's premises, which were located about 40 miles north of Wichita.

And not even a small sign identified the 65-acre manufacturing complex before truckers complained in the early 1980s.

Doskocil's Reno Technologies division reflected the company's penchant for vertical integration, which Doskocil considered an important element of his low-cost strategy. For example, to fuel his factory Doskocil had purchased a natural gas transmission company and two wells. About the only part of the operation that he did not control was the raising of the cattle and hogs that Doskocil transformed into pizza toppings. Doskocil also kept costs low by avoiding union labor. Although he paid his workers union-equivalent wages, he managed to avoid the ugly labor disputes that had plagued many of his competitors, particularly Hormel.

As a result of innovation and low costs, Doskocil was able to dominate its market niche. And its supremacy was barely challenged. Hormel, for example, had attempted to challenge Doskocil in the late 1970s before discovering, to its chagrin, that it simply could not compete on a cost and quality basis. Then, Doskocil widened its lead by opening a high-tech production line capable of processing 10,000 pounds of meat per hour using 60 percent less energy than previous production lines. By the early 1980s Doskocil was churning out 70 percent of all precooked processed beef and pork toppings used by U.S. pizza chains, and it was expanding into markets for frozen and make-at-home pizzas.

After having grown his venture into a $100-million-plus company, the 52-year-old Doskocil was ready to move on by 1983 and let somebody else complete the company's transition from the entrepreneurial growth stage to a mature corporation. He turned down an offer from Pet Inc., a division of IC Industries, to buy Doskocil for $71 million. Instead, he sold a large interest in the company to Aeicor for $64 million. The deal was attractive to Doskocil because it allowed his company to remain independent, but matched it with some well-heeled partners that could finance future growth initiatives.

Doskocil entered the transaction based on advice given to him by the Bass brothers, a group of prominent financiers. They profited handsomely after the buyout as their $260,000 investment in Aeicor turned into a $11 million stake in Doskocil by 1984. Larry Doskocil kept a 30 percent share of the Doskocil stock, which was valued at more than $30 million. During the mid-1980s Doskocil continued to post gains in its core pizza toppings market, and to search for new growth opportunities. As a result of increased sales and new acquisitions, Doskocil' revenues surged past the $250 million by the late 1980s. Meanwhile, Larry Doskocil ceded his position as chief executive.

In 1988, the Doskocil organization changed radically. In what seemed like a major coup at the time, Doskocil bought out Wilson Foods, an Oklahoma-based firm founded in the mid-1800s and credited with such innovations as the boneless ham. When Doskocil bought it, Wilson was a $1.3 billion (in sales) manufacturer and distributor of processed pork products. Wilson had posted solid gains for more than a century before it ran into trouble in the early 1980s. Despite its recent checkered past, it had improved markedly by the late 1980s. Its sales were only one-fifth of Wilson's, but Doskocil was able to purchase the producer for $238 million. The acquisition saddled Doskocil

with debt, but management believed the purchase complemented its existing operations and competencies.

Wilson's problems during the early 1980s stemmed from its spin-off from LTV Corporation, a holding company. After being ranked as the 37th largest corporation in America in 1955, Wilson had been purchased by LTV. LTV owned the division until the early 1980s, when stagnant pork markets caused the troubled LTV to jettison the subsidiary. Before LTV dumped the company, though, it sold off some of Wilson's assets, kept the cash, and loaded Wilson with heavy debt. Wilson lost $37 million in 1981 before posting an encouraging gain of $17 million in 1982 on sales of $2.2 billion. By 1983, though, it was again losing money and staggering under its crushing debt load.

To escape insolvency, Wilson filed Chapter 11 bankruptcy late in 1983. Then, it immediately voided its union agreements and slashed wages for both hourly and salaried personnel. During the succeeding five years Wilson continued to cut costs, shed non-performing operations, and change its product mix. It focused on the fast food markets, for example, and increased efforts to penetrate supermarket delicatessen and fat-free markets. By 1987, Wilson had emerged from its bankruptcy and seemed relatively healthy. It lost nearly $17 million in 1986, but made its last Chapter 11 debt payment in 1987 and earned about $6 million in that year. Meanwhile, Wilson's former parent, LTV, languished and filed for bankruptcy in 1986.

Doskocil's hostile takeover of Wilson seemed like a good idea at first. Sales and profits were up early in 1989 and Doskocil's stock price surged. But the heavily leveraged enterprise started to buckle when the economy soured and processed meat markets began to slow. Doskocil floundered. In March of 1990 Doskocil management threw in the towel, filing for Chapter 11 bankruptcy protection from creditors. John T. Hanes, former head of the Wilson division, was appointed president and chief executive in 1991. He was joined by chief financial officer Ted Myers, a Harvard graduate skilled in financially restructuring corporations.

During the next few years, Hanes, Myers, and other of Doskocil's executives worked to revive the ailing meat processor. They dumped several of Wilson's and Doskocil's marginal enterprises, such as slaughtering operations and some processing plants. They also sold Reno Technologies. At the same time, Doskocil began a transition from a processor and distributor of commodity-type meat products to a producer of high-margin processed foods in which it had a competitive advantage.

Doskocil recorded a loss of nearly $27 million in 1992 before posting a 1993 deficit of $32 million. The 1993 loss, though, was mostly the result of a one-time charge against earnings for retirement benefits. So, after about three years of restructuring and refinancing, the company's financial condition had improved considerably. "They bought Wilson Foods and choked on it," observed analyst Jeffrey Wiegand in the March 19, 1994 *Press Enterprise.* "They have spent the last years getting rid of things they didn't want . . . debt is very manageable and they have good cash flow."

After reviving the defeated Doskocil, both Hanes and Myers left the company. R. Randolph Devening, a Harvard M.B.A., took over as president and chief executive. He had been credited with helping to develop Fleming Companies, Inc. from a $2.8 billion (revenues) company into a $19 billion diversified conglomerate. When Devening took control of Doskocil, it was generating about $650 million in annual revenues from its three processed foods divisions: Foodservice, Deli, and Retail.

Evidencing its intent to expand in the high-margin processed foods industry, Doskocil reached an agreement in 1994 to purchase International Multifoods Corporation's frozen foods division for about $135 million. Doskocil also continued to exit non-performing businesses, secure financing for continued expansion, and to streamline existing operations.

In the spring of 1995, Doskocil changed its name to Foodbrands America, Inc., to better reflect the company's operations as a broad-based food processor marketing high-profile, branded perishable and frozen foods. In April of that year, the company announced plans to sell the assets of its retail division to Thorn Apple Valley, Inc. for about $70 million in cash and assumption of debt. Regarding the sale, Devening noted, "While this divestiture reduces our revenue base, it enables the company to pay down a significant portion of its outstanding debt. We expect a substantial improvement in our earnings outlook given the solid profitability of the remaining operations."

Principal Subsidiaries: Doskocil Foods; Wilson Foods.

Further Reading:

Bork, Robert H. Jr., "On Top of Pizza," *Forbes,* October 22, 1984, p. 115.

Bynum, Bryant, "Doskocil Announces Appointment of Chairman, President and Chief Executive Officer," *Business Wire,* August 1, 1994.

Colodny, Mark M., "The Bass Brothers Lose One," *Fortune,* July 30, 1990, p. 243.

"Doskocil 'Savior' to Retire this Summer," *Hutchinson News,* July 8, 1993.

Fromson, Brett Duval, "Wilson Foods Corp.," *Fortune,* April 27, 1987, p. 110.

"Hanes to Retire as Doskocil Proxy," *Nation's Restaurant News,* November 15, 1993, p. 32.

McAuliffe, Don, "Multifoods' Frozen Food Division Sold," *Press Enterprise,* March 19, 1994, p. C1.

Peterson-Davis, Sara, "Doskocil Sells Reno Technologies," *Hutchinson News,* January 26, 1994.

Price, Margaret, " 'Reorganizing' Labor Costs," *Industry Week,* May 16, 1983, p. 21.

Williams, Monci Jo, "The Return of the Meatpackers," *Fortune,* May 2, 1983, p. 257.

—Dave Mote

Drackett Professional Products

8600 Governors Drive
Cincinnati, Ohio 45249
U.S.A.
(513) 677-3200
Fax: (513) 632-7449

Wholly Owned Division of S. C. Johnson
Incorporated: 1915 as P.W. Drackett & Sons Co.
Employees: 100
Sales: $570 million (est. 1993)
SICs: 2842 Polishes & Sanitation Goods

For over 70 years, Drackett Co. was a primary competitor in the homecare products market. Among its products were Drano drain cleaner, Windex glass cleaner, Vanish toilet bowl cleaner, Behold and Endust furniture polishing aids, Mr. Muscle oven cleaner, Scrubbee scouring pads, Renuzit air fresheners, and O-Cedar brooms and mops. The company became a subsidiary of Bristol-Myers Squibb in 1965 and was sold to S. C. Johnson & Son, Inc., in 1992. S. C. Johnson absorbed several of Drackett's products into its own lines, sold others, and consolidated operations. The only remaining vestige of the original company is S. C. Johnson's Drackett Professionals Division, which was still located in Cincinnati in 1995.

Company founder Phillip Drackett began his career as a pharmacist in Cleveland, but his personal interest in chemicals soon drew him from the end products to their components. At the age of 56, Drackett got out of the drug business entirely to start a bulk chemical brokerage with his wife, Sallie, in Cincinnati in 1910. When their sons, Phillip Jr. and Harry, joined the firm in 1915, the company was incorporated as P. W. Drackett & Sons Co. The company sold chemicals, including lye, ammonia, and epsom salt, under the "diamond D" trademark. But, like its Cincinnati neighbor and sometime competitor, Procter & Gamble Co., Drackett would make its fortune from the emerging revolution in American homemaking.

Drackett's first consumer product, Drano, was developed from lye, a corrosive cleaner made by leaching wood ashes. Lye had long been used to dissolve animal fat into soap, and its cleansing power was well known. Drano's creation and success can be attributed, in large part, to the installation of indoor plumbing in most American homes after World War I. According to Susan Strasser's *Never Done,* an examination of housekeeping in the

United States, indoor plumbing aroused a mixture of relief and apprehension in homemakers. While they no longer had to haul water and sewage to and from their homes, they now feared the specter of "sewer gas," clogged drains, and backups. Introduced in 1923, Drano helped alleviate this concern.

Crystal Drano was a combination of solid lye and bits of aluminum that produced a hot, fizzing reaction that promoters called "churning action" to melt and scrub away dirt, grease and hair. The Dracketts soon proved themselves savvy marketers as well as an astute product development team. Sallie Drackett devised the Drano name, with the macron above the "a" that ensured there would be no confusion about the product's intended use. Her drawing of a gooseneck pipe with a dotted line representing clear-flowing pipes remained the Drano symbol throughout the brand's history. For nearly fifty years, Drano was virtually the only chemical drain cleaner used in American households.

The company acknowledged its shift from industrial to consumer goods by changing its name from Drackett Chemical Co., which it had adopted in 1922, to just Drackett Co. in 1933, when it went public.

Based on Drano's commercial success, Drackett turned its attention toward the development of other consumer cleaning products. The company's Windex, introduced in 1935, was the first successful glass cleaner on the market. Before its launch, window washing was reserved for spring and fall cleaning—and in many middle-class homes, it was reserved for the servants. But as hired help disappeared from the average domestic landscape, physically demanding and time-consuming chores such as window cleaning fell to homemakers. Windex's blue formulation of water, its trademarked "ammonia-D," and additional chemicals that hastened evaporation were both effective and convenient. The pre-mixed product eliminated hauling buckets, the need for a squeegee, and streaks. Windex's convenience prompted women to clean windows and mirrors more often, thereby increasing sales. Both Windex and Drano captured and held more of their respective markets than all other competitors combined for decades.

In the late 1930s and early 1940s, Drackett diversified into soybean processing. The early 1930s had witnessed the development of new methods of processing soybeans into the edible byproducts of oil and meal. World War II's shortages drove increased demand for soybean oil, which was used in the food industry in margarine, shortening, salad oil, mayonnaise and other food products. Paint and varnish manufacturers also used it as a replacement for linseed oil, which was in short supply. Soybean meal was used as a high-protein livestock feed. Drackett's corporate research facility developed a soy-based textile it called Azlon. In 1943 the *Cincinnati Post* reported that the fiber could be used in "hats, hose, underwear [and] blankets." A dog treat called Charge was another moderately successful soy product.

These diversification efforts, along with continuously increasing sales of its core products, multiplied Drackett's sales dramatically from $3.5 million in 1941 to a peak of $27.7 million in 1948, for average annual increases of over 30 percent. Performance during the immediate postwar era was torrid, with a stock split in 1946 and profits that just fell short of $1 million in 1947. However, growth declined in the latter years of the decade, to $21.4 million sales and roughly $580,000 net in 1949.

Drackett added to its already strong national production and distribution network of plants in Ohio, California, and Pennsylvania with the construction of facilities in Indiana, Pennsylvania, and Texas. Over the course of the 1950s, the company enhanced the convenience of Windex with the introduction of a plastic sprayer bottle. The company integrated vertically with the acquisitions of Calmar Co. and Maclin Co., bottle and plastics manufacturers, in 1954. Drackett launched Twinkle brass and silver polishes around 1957. The 1958 acquisition of the Judson Dunaway Corp. gave Drackett control of Vanish, a toilet bowl disinfectant, and Delete stain remover.

Roger Drackett represented the third and final generation of the founding family to lead the company. He implemented a program of corporate rationalization that included the sale of the soybean business (which had suffered waning sales in the early 1950s) to concentrate capital investments in the company's core consumer goods. Drackett took its major brands international with the 1958 establishment of Drackett Co. of Canada, Ltd. Increased funding for research and development, plant modernization, acquisitions, and aggressive promotion generated another impressive growth spurt in the late 1950s and early 1960s, with the company's sales more than doubling from $19.5 million in 1958 to $49.7 million in 1963. This success resulted in Drackett's listing on the New York Stock Exchange.

In the early 1960s Drackett also acquired Martin-Marietta Corp.'s O-Cedar division for about $9.5 million. O-Cedar—described as "the biggest name in mops"—produced a comprehensive line of mops, brooms, polishes, waxes, and related products in the United States and Canada. At the time of the company's purchase, O'Cedar's annual sales were estimated at $14 million. By 1964 Drackett had distribution outlets for Drano and Windex in Germany, Australia, England and other common market countries. Drackett supported its products with comprehensive advertising campaigns in newspapers and magazines as well as on television. By the mid-1960s, the company's advertising budget was second only to its raw materials expenditures.

By the time it was acquired by Bristol-Myers in 1965, Drackett was earning more than $5 million annually on sales of $58.5 million. At the time, Bristol-Myers had sales of $265 million and profits of $23.1 million. With the support of its huge new parent's research and marketing expertise, Drackett introduced new products, extended several mainstays, and expanded global distribution via Bristol-Myers's established operations in the Middle and Far East.

Drackett used its new parent's clout to challenge some of its bigger rivals in the household cleaner market. With Endust, Drackett presented the most effective challenge ever experienced by S. C. Johnson's category-leading Pledge. Endust was promoted as a waxless dusting aid that would not leave an accumulation of wax on furniture. The pitch worked. Endust garnered market share from Pledge, and continued to threaten the leader's dominance of the market for decades. Endust even

carved out a new category, "dusting aid," as opposed to "furniture polish."

Drano got its first brand extension in over forty years with the 1966 introduction of Liquid Drano. Unlike the original, the new formula could be poured through standing water to unclog drains. Its much lower concentration of lye (2.4 percent compared to more than 50 percent), was also gentler on the new garbage disposals that were being installed in homes. Drackett also introduced an "all-purpose" version of Windex during the 1960s, but the product didn't catch on and was subsequently dropped. The company acquired and aggressively promoted Renuzit solid air freshener beginning in 1969. Bristol-Myers also transferred some of its food marketing operations to Drackett, including Nutrament supplements and the Weight-Watchers line, in the 1960s. (Weight-Watchers was divested in 1979.)

Roger Drackett relinquished the company's presidency to Nicholas Evans in 1969, but stayed on as chairman until 1972. The 1970s brought increased competition for both Windex and Drano. In 1969 Clorox acquired and heavily promoted Liquid Plumr drain cleaner. Drano's share of the market declined from over 90 percent to less than half, as Clorox brought out savvy brand extensions like Professional Strength Liquid Plumr. Windex fared better under assault from all-purpose cleaners introduced around the same time. Although products like Texize's Glass Plus, Miles Laboratories' S.O.S. Glass Works, and Procter & Gamble's Cinch knocked Windex's market share down to 40 percent, the Drackett brand was able to maintain its leadership.

The 1989 merger of Bristol-Myers and Squibb marked a turning point for Drackett's long-time parent. Bristol-Myers Squibb became the second-largest pharmaceutical company in the world, and concentrated ever more strongly on ethical and over-the-counter drugs, which constituted over half of annual sales by that time.

In 1992 Bristol-Myers Squibb announced that Drackett was on the auction block, spurring rumors that some of the country's biggest names in household products, including Clorox, Procter & Gamble, and S. C. Johnson were all bargaining. By the end of the year, Drackett's longtime rival S. C. Johnson won the bidding war with a $1.5 billion offer. The deal was Johnson's largest purchase ever, and had far-reaching effects. Before, Johnson's stable of brands included Pledge furniture polish, Glade air freshener, Raid bug spray, and Edge shaving gel. All were category leaders, but some analysts noted that they were up against lightweight competition. The Drackett purchase merged the number-one and number-five players in polishes and sanitation goods and took the privately held S. C. Johnson into more direct competition with "heavyweight" rivals Procter & Gamble and Clorox. In 1994 S. C. Johnson's Executive Vice President for North American Consumer Products, Richard Posey, told *Fortune* that the purchase took his company "from Triple A baseball to the majors." But for Drackett, the change in ownership heralded a move from the playing field to the bench.

The new parent kept Windex, which still commanded an estimated 40 percent of the nearly $200 million window cleaner segment, as well as Drano, which had relinquished its lead to Clorox's Liquid Plumr brand cleaner. Vanish, leader in the toilet-bowl cleaning category, was soon joined by Johnson's own Toilet Duck.

A combination of regulatory requirements and corporate priorities compelled the new owner to break up Drackett's family of brands, however. In 1993 O-Cedar was sold off to Vining Industries to form the world's largest stick goods supplier, with over one-third of that $500 million market. The Federal Trade Commission directed S. C. Johnson to divest Behold and Endust to prevent the creation of a furniture care monopoly. Renuzit, too, was sold off, so that Johnson could concentrate on its own line of Glade brand air fresheners.

Within six months of the Drackett acquisition, S. C. Johnson had transferred virtually all the division's production to its Waxdale, Wisconsin, plant near its Racine headquarters. Cincinnati newspapers documented the ever-shrinking workforce, "teary farewells," and "long good-byes" as the new owner consolidated operations to achieve the economies of scale enjoyed by its larger rivals. By 1995, only a "skeleton crew" remained to run the company's institutional products division.

Further Reading:

Cobleigh, Ira U., "The Drackett Company," *Commercial and Financial Chronicle,* January 2, 1964, p. 5.

"Drackett Earnings Gleam on Research, Promotion," *Barron's,* February 9, 1959, pp. 34–36.

"Examine Synthetic Apparel: Soybeans Made into Hats, Hose, Underwear, Blankets," *Cincinnati Post,* December 3, 1943, p. 34.

Fitzgerald, Kate, "How Johnson Will Gain with Drackett," *Advertising Age,* November 2, 1992, p. 13.

Freeman, Laurie, "Drackett Fights to Keep Household Edge," *Advertising Age,* February 27, 1989, p. 35.

Gallagher, Patricia, "Johnson to Relocate Drackett Units," *Cincinnati Enquirer,* January 5, 1993, p. B5.

Gopnik, Hilary, "Drano," *Encyclopedia of Consumer Brands, Vol. 2,* Janice Jorgensen, ed., Detroit: St. James Press, 1994, pp. 192–94.

Gopnik, Hilary and Donald McManus, "Windex," *Encyclopedia of Consumer Brands, Vol. 2,* Janice Jorgensen, ed., Detroit: St. James Press, 1994, pp. 575–78.

Henkoff, Ronald, "S. C. Johnson & Son: When to Take on the Giants," *Fortune,* May 30, 1994, pp. 111–14.

Hurley, Daniel, ed., *Cincinnati: The Queen City,* Cincinnati: Cincinnati Historical Society, 1988, p. 206.

Powell, Cheryl, "The Long Goodbye," *Cincinnati Enquirer*, August 5, 1993, p. D1.

"Recent Acquisition Adds Sparkle to Profits Picture at Drackett," *Barron's,* October 8, 1962, p. 20.

Rolland, Louis J., "Drackett Cleans Up," *Financial World,* August 5, 1964, p. 19.

Van Sant, Rick, "Teary Farewells at Drackett," *Cincinnati Post,* February 25, 1993, p. 1A.

—April Dougal Gasbarre

DREXEL HERITAGE®

Drexel Heritage Furnishings Inc.

101 N. Main Street
Drexel, North Carolina 28619
U.S.A.
(704) 433-3000
Fax: (704) 433-3349

Wholly Owned Subsidiary of Masco Corp.
Incorporated: 1903 as Drexel Furniture Co.
Employees: 5,000
Sales: $200 million
SICs: 2511 Wood Household Furniture; 2512 Upholstered Wood Household Furniture; 2521 Wood Office Furniture; 2522 Office Furniture, Except Wood 5023 Home Furnishings

Based in the foothills of North Carolina's Blue Ridge Mountains, Drexel Heritage Furnishings Inc. has been producing furniture for almost a century. A subsidiary since 1986 of Masco Corp., the world's largest furniture manufacturer, Drexel Heritage is also a retailer of home furnishing accessories.

The Drexel Furniture Co. was founded in 1903 in Drexel, about five miles east of Morganton, North Carolina. At the time this community consisted of little more than a railroad siding built to accommodate a sawmill and flour mill. Both enterprises were operated by Samuel Huffman, who with five Morganton businessmen founded the company. Their initial investment of $14,000 went towards erecting a factory and installing furniture-making machinery within.

Starting operations on a shoestring budget was typical of this era for the furniture industry of the Piedmont region, which relied on ample supplies of hardwood, water power potential, and low-cost and plentiful labor. Burke County, in which Drexel is located, was still about one-third untouched forest in 1903 and had not a single mile of decent road. The finished building, erected on the site of Huffman's sawmill, was accompanied by a second facility for the finishing and shipping department. Production began with about 50 workers making oak dressers, washstands, and chiffonniers. The Drexel plant burned down in late 1906 but was rebuilt with an insurance payment of $25,000.

A pioneer in the furniture industry later conceded that "North Carolina factories in those days were accused of selling lumber

and not furniture." During Drexel's earliest period its workers and managers had to learn the trade by trial and error, and the company had to entrust most of its sales to outside agents who designed and priced, in addition to selling, the furniture. Sometimes Drexel shipped furniture to these agents "kd" (knocked down, or in parts), so that it could be assembled elsewhere. Also called "selling in the white," this practice saved money on freight. Low costs enabled Piedmont companies like Drexel to undersell northern competition in their native area. By 1918 the plant had grown by 20,000 square feet, and the Blue Ridge Furniture Co. in neighboring Marion had been acquired by cash payment.

Between the two world wars Drexel and other Piedmont furniture manufacturers in North Carolina and Virginia expanded their markets beyond the South into national furniture markets. Styles offered by northern manufacturers were copied, and the quality of the products improved. Drexel's net worth had passed the $500,000 mark by the end of 1922, and in the following year a 1300 percent stock dividend was declared and a plant acquired in Morganton. In 1928, Drexel's sales were above $2 million and its total assets about $1.7 million. By the following year North Carolina led all states in the production of wooden furniture.

Suffering the effects of the Great Depression, however, net sales at Drexel fell to $1.3 million in 1935, and the company's cash balance fell alarmingly. During this period the company moved away from wholesale distribution, relying instead on retail stores and commission salesmen located throughout the country. National advertising eventually began in 1937.

In 1935 the last of Drexel's four principal founders died, and Samuel Huffman's son Robert O. Huffman was elected president. He delegated authority, declaring his managerial philosophy was to "get good men to the job and leave them alone to do it," Nevertheless, the younger Huffman would make several managerial decisions that would facilitate the company's fortunes. First, he opted to abandon the low end of the market in favor of issuing medium-priced quality furniture. In 1950, when Drexel's net sales reached $18.3 million, its share of the nation's wood household furniture sales had tripled since 1935 to 1.5 percent, an impressive result considering that furniture manufacturing was a highly fragmented field.

Moreover, the company's expansion in the early postwar years could be attributed largely to Huffman's 1947 decision to spend sizable amounts on advertising and his 1950 decision to develop a force of salaried salesmen to replace independent commission agents. By 1957 Drexel's product line included 1,200 different pieces. The aim was to sell 50 to 80 related pieces of living room, dining room, and bedroom furniture in a basic style. Pieces from such correlated groups accounted for 80 percent of sales in 1956. The company's furniture was sold directly to retailers at 50 percent of list price.

During this period the company attempted, in the words of its merchandising vice-president, "to cover every fast-selling style field in the country." In 1948 nearly three-fourths of the company's sales were in the traditional vein (an eighteenth-century inspired mahogany style), but in 1955 traditional accounted for only one-third of sales. Sales of French provincial quadrupled in this period to one-fifth of all sales, and contemporary styles doubled to 36 percent. Sales of early American and colonial pieces increased from four to ten percent. In 1957 the product line also consisted of Italian provincial (a more contemporary look than French provincial) and casual, which included "ranch-type" styles. During these years bedroom pieces replaced dining room furniture as the top-selling group, and Drexel became the nation's largest manufacturer of bedroom and dining room pieces in the middle- and upper-priced brackets.

By 1957 Drexel furniture was available in about 2,500 retail stores in all parts of the country. A standard franchise agreement stipulated that a representative part of the Drexel line would be kept in stock, displayed to specifications, and locally promoted and advertised. Drexel's policy was to franchise only stores with a reputation for selling quality goods. About half of the dealers accounted for more than 90 percent of total sales.

By 1957 Drexel had ten manufacturing facilities, including six end-product plants located within 30 miles of one another. In addition to the original Drexel plant, these facilities included five factories in Morganton, three producing furniture and the other two for storage, samples, jigs, and fixtures. One plant was acquired when Drexel bought the Table Rock Furniture Co. in 1951. Two Marion plants produced contemporary furniture, with a third supplying parts for the other two. A facility in Kingstree, South Carolina, provided commercial veneers and gumwood panels.

Drexel was employing about 2,300 hourly workers, all non-union, in 1957. In addition to wages for a 40-hour work week, they received an annual bonus under a company profit-sharing plan that amounted to between five and eight-and-a-half weeks pay a year. These workers, generally drawn from surrounding rural communities, traditionally worked one to each machine, with the operator usually pacing the machine and responsible for its performance. The average hourly wage in the southern furniture industry was $1.32 an hour in October 1956.

Through an exchange of common stock, Drexel acquired control in January 1957 of the Morganton Furniture Co., a producer of case goods (a trade term for wooden bedroom and dining room furniture) and Heritage Furniture, Inc. of High Point and Mocksville, a manufacturer of upholstered furniture. Heritage became a wholly owned subsidiary of what became Drexel Enterprises Inc., and Morganton a division of Heritage. Both acquired companies continued to operate autonomously, producing and selling their own regular brand lines. The purchase of Heritage in particular provided a dependable supply of high-quality upholstered furniture, which Drexel had never offered. Immediately following the merger, plans were being drawn up for a correlated line of bedroom, dining room, and living room furniture under the Heritage name.

The expanded company continued to enjoy robust sales growth into the following decade. A 1966 *Business Week* story ranked the firm third among U.S. furniture manufacturers, with annual sales of about $76 million. The article also listed Drexel as among the innovators in this traditionally low-tech industry. The company was cited for a process called conveyorized bleaching to reduce variations in natural wood and veneer skins in order to ensure permanence and uniformity of the finish. Conveyorized operations had also been adapted to upholstery, although two Drexel executives agreed that once the frame was made, upholstered furniture remained basically handcrafted.

By early 1968 Drexel was operating 16 plants and employing 6,300 people. Its product line had expanded to include institutional as well as residential products, including laboratory, library, dormitory, hospital, office, church, and hotel/motel furniture. The company's 65-year independent history came to a close on March 7, 1968, when Drexel Enterprises agreed to be acquired by U.S. Plywood-Champion Papers Inc. (later known as Champion International Corp.) for stock valued at $100 million. The agreement called for Drexel stockholders to receive nine-tenths of a share of U.S. Plywood-Champion Papers common stock and four-fifths of a share of $1.20 convertible preference stock for each of the 1.42 million shares of Drexel common stock.

A joint statement noted that the two companies served complementary markets, emphasizing their commitment "to broaden our separate product bases to provide a variety of furnishings and building materials for homes, institutional and educational facilities, hotels and commercial buildings." Karl B. Bendetsen, the newly elected chief executive officer of U.S. Plywood-Champion Papers expressed the rationale for the acquisition more succinctly, remarking, "our building materials create the space, and Drexel will help fill it."

Acquisition by a major building materials supplier—then the second largest manufacturer and distributor of forest products in the world—gave Drexel financial support for expansion. Additions had already been made to the High Point upholstery plant, the Hilderbran office and institutional furniture plant, and the Morganton chair and table factories. A new wood furniture factory was planned for Mocksville, North Carolina, while new automation machinery installed in the Whittier plant, which produced drawer sides and backs for other case goods factories, was said to make that facility one of the most efficient industry operations.

In 1971 U.S. Plywood-Champion Papers announced that the Drexel and Heritage lines would expand to include styles ranging from modern to Mediterranean in the upper-middle to high-end price ranges. Moreover, the company was engaged in organizing a full Drexel and Heritage unified retail system. Allen MacKenzie, president of the company's Furnishings Group, said U.S. Plywood would be able, within a few years, to supply an entire Drexel-Heritage retail system in-house, saving both retailer and consumer a considerable amount of money. This system, inaugurated the following year, consisted of distribution through Drexel Heritage stores (built or converted to the company's specifications), conventional stores (many of which installed galleries), and department stores. Sales through other retailers were cut drastically, and more business was conducted with fewer accounts.

Drexel Enterprises had sales exceeding $100 million in 1971. During 1975, in the wake of a nationwide recession, sales were only $86 million, but the company (eventually renamed Drexel Heritage Furnishings Inc.) remained profitable. Two years later, the Drexel Heritage unit was sold to Dominick International

Corp. for about $57 million, of which about $40 million was paid in cash and the remainder in preferred shares and subordinated notes, a sales price that amounted to book value plus $1 million.

Under Dominick International, Drexel's retail efforts advanced significantly. In 1983, there existed 70 Drexel Heritage stores and about 330 other outlets for its products, and the unit's management team had drafted a goal of opening 30 more Drexel Heritage stores. The product line was also expanded, following the 1982 acquisition of Frederick Edward Inc., a Morganton upholstery manufacturer.

Annual Drexel Heritage Furnishings Inc. sales were in excess of $200 million when Masco Corp. bought the company from Dominick International in 1986 for an undisclosed cash sum. Once a midsized maker of auto parts and plumbing products, Masco had engineered more than 100 friendly takeovers since 1957, turning the Michigan-based company into three interconnected conglomerates. Earlier in the year, Masco had acquired Henredon Furniture Industries Inc. During the next few years, counting Drexel and Henredon, Masco would bring ten furniture companies for about $1.5 billion.

According to one market analyst, "the move into furniture was absolutely brilliant, but the timing was wrong." A recessionary economic climate between 1989 and 1991 hurt the housing market and consequently hit furniture sales hard. In 1991 Masco's Home Furnishings Group earned only $80 million—six percent—on sales of $1.4 billion, and the company as a whole registered its third straight year of declining earnings.

Nevertheless, Drexel Heritage was making preparations to forge ahead into a new century. Between 1993 and 1994 its outdated showrooms were replaced by a new 100,000-square-foot edifice on Highway 68 in High Point, and construction of a 501,000-square-foot warehouse facility was underway on Causby Road near Morganton. In 1994 Drexel Heritage maintained 11 factories. Ten of these were in North Carolina: at Black Mountain, Drexel, High Point, Hildebran, Longview, Marion, Mocksville, Morganton, Shelby, and Whittier; and one in South Carolina, at Kingstree. Drexel and Heritage wood and upholstered furniture and home furnishings accessories were being offered by about 75 Drexel Heritage showcase stores (which generally sold Drexel Heritage products exclusively); about 150 galleries of 10,000 square feet or more within larger outlets; and about 250 other locations.

Principal Subsidiaries: Southern Dowel Co.

Further Reading:

"A Dealer Network for U.S. Plywood," *Business Week,* October 2, 1971, p. 59.

"Dominick International Buys Unit of Champion International Corporation," *Wall Street Journal,* August 17, 1977, p. 12.

Henkoff, Ronald, "Kinder, Gentler Takeover Artists," *Fortune,* June 18, 1990, p 91.

Koselka, Rita, "Resetting the Table," *Forbes,* March 16, 1992, pp. 66–67.

"Masco Corp. to Acquire Furniture Maker for Cash," *Wall Street Journal,* September 23, 1986, p. 48.

Reckert, Clare M., "U.S. Plywood Gets Furniture Maker," *New York Times,* March 8, 1968, p. 55.

Skinner, Wickham, and Rodgers, David C., *Manufacturing Policy in Furniture Industry,* Homewood, Ill.: Richard D. Irwin, Inc., 1968.

"Technology Restyles Furniture Business," *Business Week,* November 19, 1966, pp. 94–96.

Willatt, Norris, "Sitting Pretty," *Barron's,* April 23, 1968, p. 11.

—Robert Halasz

DrugEmporium™

Drug Emporium, Inc.

155 Hidden Ravines Dr.
Powell, Ohio 43605
U.S.A.
(614) 548-7080
Fax: (614) 888-3689

Public Company
Incorporated: 1977
Employees: 2,200
Sales: $749 million
Stock Exchanges: NASDAQ
SICs: 5912 Drug Stores & Proprietary Stores

Drug Emporium, Inc., is a chain of 235 deep-discount drug stores that has been credited with taking the concept nationwide. The foundations of the deep discount segment of the drug store industry have been traced to Depression-era shops offering closeouts and other cut-rate goods. Drug Emporium capitalized on the second period of strong growth experienced by the segment, during and after the recession of the 1970s.

Deep-discount drug stores sought to offer brand-name products at competitive prices to satisfy the demands of recession-weary consumers: these shoppers wanted quality and low prices, and were willing to sacrifice ambiance, convenience, and selection. Deep discounters kept overhead low by renting older and cheaper, but often larger, retail spaces than their traditional drug store counterparts. The stores featured very simple, usually hand-made signs and product displays, which were often just opened and stacked delivery cases. One observer noted that "The 'art' of deep discount seems to make a mockery of space management." In fact, these techniques portrayed efficiency to bargain-hunting customers, thereby adding to the stores' appeal. Deep discounters also kept labor costs low with lower-than-average hourly wages and lean, hands-on management. In 1984 *Chain Store Age Executive* noted that "Perhaps the most striking feature of the deep discounters is entrepreneurial ownership. It is nearly universal." One deep discounter noted that "The [traditional drug store] chains are just too top-heavy."

From the outset, deep discounters obtained merchandise directly from manufacturers. Their independence freed them to act quickly to obtain the best deals without having to wait for approval from chain headquarters. Buying stock in this way limited selection at deep discount drugstores and meant ever-

changing selection heavy on health and beauty aids (HBAs). Such deal-making required considerable experience, personal connections, and talent. Purchasers often settled for limited quantities in exchange for 12 percent to 20 percent discounts, and passed savings of 25 percent to 40 percent off suggested retail prices on to their customers. Deep discounters made up for their lean margins with high volume, however, garnering six to seven times the sales per square foot of their conventional counterparts.

Drug Emporium has been characterized as a pioneer of the discount drug concept. It was founded in 1977 in Ohio—known as "the cradle of deep discount drug retailing"—by Philip I. Wilber. Wilber had by that time advanced to vice-president and merchandising manager of Lane Drug Company in Toledo, Ohio. After a 22-year career with traditional chain drugstores, the executive decided to break out on his own. He observed that such deep discount drug stores as F & M Distributors in Detroit and Bernie Schulman's in Cleveland had found a profitable retail niche, and he hoped to emulate their success.

Using about $80,000 of his own money, $20,000 from his eldest son, Gary, and another $400,000 from 13 private investors, Wilber leased space in a Columbus, Ohio, strip shopping center and opened his first Drug Emporium in October 1977. He later characterized the move from Toledo to Columbus as "a lucky choice." Shortly thereafter the Toledo economy sagged due to the downturn in the automotive and glass industries while the Columbus economy, supported by state government and employment at the Ohio State University, held very steady."

Sales during those first months were depressingly slow, but with the support of his wife Cathy, son Gary, and colleagues in the industry, Wilber concentrated on providing top-notch service to the customers who tried the new concept. In a 1989 address to the Newcomen Society, the entrepreneur recalled January 18, 1978, as a turning point for the business. On that day the state experienced the worst snow storm in its history, and although the Wilbers dug out and made it to work, the patriarch recounted, "our hearts were low. To make things worse, the previous Friday we had used up our $500,000 capital and had borrowed $10,000 on our credit line to meet the payroll. I got on the phone to every radio and TV station and told them we were open. They had all discontinued their regular programming to talk about the storm, so we got a lot of free publicity. A few people started to trickle in in four-wheel drive vehicles . . . [to buy] . . . the 'Three C's,' cigarettes, condoms and Kotex. After ten days the streets were cleared and our business took off." Drug Emporium achieved profitability that April and broke even in its first year. This was a notable accomplishment: analysts noted that it usually took new stores 18 months to three years to turn a profit.

During the company's second year in business, Gary Wilber fine-tuned the retail concept, altering the store layout and product mix; his changes are credited with making a strong contribution to Drug Emporium's first decade of growth. Much of the chain's early expansion came through franchising, and in 1979 the company established a subsidiary, Drug Emporium Franchise Limited, to train and oversee new affiliates. Gary Wilber later told *Stores* magazine the reasoning behind franchising: "We didn't want to dilute or break our management continuity, and at the same time our goal was to get into as many cities as quickly as possible. Franchising enabled us to do that without the capital outlays. It would have taken many more years to hit the markets we did without the franchising program.''

Drug Emporium's first licensee opened in 1979 in Cincinnati and Wilber opened his second store in Columbus 1980. During the next few years franchises opened in Arizona, Dallas, Kansas City, Seattle, Tampa, Atlanta, San Diego, and Indianapolis. Wilber later noted, ''We were on a roll.''

A $6 million private stock offering in 1983 brought in funds to further this rapid growth. A reorganization merged the two family-owned stores with those of Atlanta franchisee Frank Shanower as well as the lead franchising operation to form Drug Emporium, Inc. The infusion of cash paid for new, company-owned stores in Atlanta and Columbus as well as investments in joint ventures. By 1983, the burgeoning chain had 27 franchised stores.

By 1984, the deep discount segment of drug retailing boasted about 150 stores and claimed two percent of the chain drug market. The deep discount drug store movement was concurrent with the expansion of super warehouse grocery stores, membership warehouse clubs, and other ''off-price'' concepts that featured brand name products at very competitive prices. The discounters' successes attracted the attention of conventional drug store chains as well as groceries and supermarkets. From 1985 to 1990, the number of deep discount drug stores nationwide more than doubled, from 313 to 700, to penetrate most large- and medium-sized markets.

When Drug Emporium raised $17.7 million in a 1988 initial public offering, it boasted 59 company-owned outlets and 78 franchised locations. The fresh cash flow was used primarily to pare down a $24.3 million debt to $3.3 million. During its first year as a public company, Drug Emporium's stock more than doubled and was split 2-for-1. Equally dramatic sales and earnings growth throughout the latter years of the decade disguised a plethora of underlying problems, both within Drug Emporium and in discount retailing in general. Sales increased 69 percent from $241 million in fiscal 1987 to $406.7 million in fiscal 1989, and earnings more than quintupled, from $1.5 million to $8 million, during that same period.

Drug Emporium was the single largest player in deep discount drugs during the late 1980s, but its dominance was both fleeting and deceptive. Competition had intensified dramatically during the mid-1980s, as an unprecedented multi-market price war among and between several classes of retailers emerged, especially in health and beauty aids. In the past, for example, supermarkets had concentrated on groceries while discounters emphasized HBAs. In the 1980s, however, each began to encroach on the other's traditional merchandise strengths: supermarkets began to aggressively promote HBAs, add pharmacies, and offer bulk packaging, while discounters strove to offer more grocery items and carry a more reliable selection of goods. Purchasing for discount chains continued at the individual store level, but corporate-level purchasing increased steadily. Although many discounters shifted their purchasing strategy, they maintained their low-price policies, thereby squeezing already-slim margins. Oversaturation in the market exacerbated these competitive pressures.

Chairman Philip Wilber set his sights on $1 billion in sales and 200 stores for fiscal 1991. Drug Emporium's financial growth came to an abrupt halt that year, however. Although sales increased by more than 25 percent from $487.9 million to $620 million, profits declined by almost 20 percent from $8.2 million to $6.6 million. Harlan S. Byrne, writing in *Barron's,* blamed the slowdown on a ''stepped up pace of spending for new stores.'' The company was striving to take advantage of a national real estate slump by buying up bargain properties, while simultaneously buying out many franchisees. During fiscal 1991 alone (ended February 27), company stores increased from 83 to 115, while franchised locations dropped from 112 to 102. Additions during that period included the acquisition of six stores from a struggling Washington, D.C., chain, increasing Drug Emporium's presence there to 14 locations. The chain stopped offering new franchises at this time as well, citing affiliates' general inability to raise capital for growth and expansion.

By the end of fiscal year 1992, Drug Emporium had lost $4.7 million. According to a June 1992 *Plain Dealer* article, ''inventory counting mistakes, overestimations of gross margins, restructuring charges and store closings'' were to blame. After fiscal 1993's net loss of $2.6 million, a ''frustrated'' board of directors ousted chairman Philip Wilber, reassigned Gary Wilber from CEO to vice-chairman and treasurer (he retired in April 1994), and demoted Robert E. Lyons III from president to senior vice-president of marketing and merchandising. Board member David Kriegel advanced to chairman and CEO, and took immediate steps to cut expenses, improve operations, and expand management responsibilities and lines of authority. Management accepted a five percent across-the-board pay cut to show fiscal leadership. In a December 1993 ''roundtable'' interview for *Discount Merchandiser,* Kriegel acknowledged the saturation of the market in discount drugs, and predicted ''dog-eat-dog'' competition. He closed 12 underperforming stores; centralized purchasing, accounting and marketing; implemented automated inventory control (including bar-coding and scanning); increased grocery offerings (including a private-label product line) and advertising support; and even offered home delivery in limited areas.

Drug Emporium launched a new store concept in Heath, Ohio, near the chain's headquarters in 1993. The location featured four primary departments: Health Care, Beauty Care, Cosmetics, and House & Home. The store had extra-wide aisles and ''Best Buys'' and ''Snack'' zones. A new, more upscale decor featured a purple, teal, and fuschia color scheme and neon signs.

Although some competing retailers saw the problems at Drug Emporium and other major discounters as signs that the deep discount drugstores were waning in popularity, the segment did maintain strong showings in certain markets. Drug Emporium, for example, continued to dominate the drugstore market in Atlanta. The chain had 235 stores at the end of fiscal 1994 (down from a 1993 peak of 252) and turned a profit of $1.3 million on sales of $749 million that year. After shoring up its franchise network, Drug Emporium indicated that it was once again ready to cautiously explore this avenue of growth.

Principal Subsidiaries: Cincinnati Drug Distributors, Inc.; Roemon Drug Distributors, Inc.; Centerline, Inc.; Barclay Farms, Inc.; Winter Fern Drug Distributors, Inc.

Further Reading:

Benway, Susan Duffy, "Feeling Some Pain: Competition Mounts for the Drugstore Chains," *Barron's,* Vol. 65, October 28, 1985, pp. 13, 31–32.

Brookman, Faye, "Deep-Discounters Ending up in Deeper Trouble," *Drug Topics,* Vol. 137, March, 8, 1993, pp. 74–79.

——, "Drug Emporium Unveils New Store Layout with Cross Aisles," *Drug Topics,* Vol. 137, July 5, 1993, p. 54.

Byrne, Harlan S., "Drug Emporium Inc.: Health and Beauty Are Its Prescription for Profits," *Barron's,* November 5, 1990, pp. 45–46.

"Deep Discount Drug Store Waters Run Still: Many Chains Adjust Strategies as Growth of Market Segment Slows," *Chain Store Age Executive,* Vol. 64, March 1988, pp. 102–09.

"Drug Emporium," *Business First—Columbus,* Vol. 5, July 10, 1989, p. 12.

Elson, Joel, "Deep Discount Drug Stores," *Supermarket News,* Vol. 40, February 5, 1990, pp. 1, 14–15.

Herold, June R., "In First Year, Drug Emporium Climbs Steadily," *Business First—Columbus,* Vol. 5, June 19, 1989, p. 3.

Keith, Bill, "Drug Emporium's Goal: Store No. 200 and $1 Billion in Sales," *Drug Topics,* June 4, 1990, pp. 54, 57.

Kriegel, David, "Presidents' Roundtable: A More Frugal Consumer," *Discount Merchandiser,* December 1993, p. 70.

Lochhead, Carolyn, "More Drug Chains Test Deep Discounting Waters," *Chain Store Age Executive,* Vol. 60, January 1984, pp. 29–31.

Reynolds, Mike, "Drug Emporium Takes Buy-Back Tack," *Stores,* Vol. 73, March 1991, pp. 50–51.

Snyder, Glenn, "Drugstores Raise the Ante," *Progressive Grocer,* Vol. 64, April 1985, pp. 101–02, 104–06, 109, 111.

——, "They've Had Their Day," *Progressive Grocer,* Vol. 73, February 1994, pp. 81–83.

Wilber, Philip I., *Drug Emporium, Inc.: Taking Care of Customers' Needs,* Princeton: The Newcomen Society of the United States, 1989.

—April Dougal Gasbarre

DSC COMMUNICATIONS CORPORATION

DSC Communications Corporation

1000 Coit Road
Plano, Texas 75075-5813
U.S.A.
(214) 519-3000
Fax: (214) 519-2203

Public Company
Incorporated: 1976 as Digital Switch Corporation
Employees: 4,041
Sales: $536.3 million
Stock Exchanges: NASDAQ
SICs: 3661 Telephone and Telegraph Apparatus; 3613
    Switchgear and Switchboard Apparatus

DSC Communications Corporation is a leading designer, developer, manufacturer, and marketer of digital switching, transmission, access, and private network system products for the worldwide telecommunications marketplace. Headquartered in Plano, Texas, just north of Dallas, DSC has facilities and customers throughout the United States and the world.

DSC, formerly Digital Switch Corporation, traces its history to 1976, when two engineers and two investors from the Washington, D.C. area joined forces. Their intent was to utilize emerging digital technology to create new switching systems for the local telephone companies's central offices.

The first five years of the company were chaotic. Among other things, the two original engineers left the brokerage firm that took Digital Switch public, John Muir & Company, soon went bankrupt; the records were in disarray; and the Securities and Exchange Commission accused some of the early officers of fraudulent stock sales. In an effort to right the company, the board of directors made several positive management changes. But by early 1981, it became increasingly obvious to the board that they needed a president with industry expertise.

Chosen for the post was James L. Donald. Donald brought with him an engineering degree, 18 years of experience at Texas Instruments and a record of having taken the Dallas-based switch manufacturing company Danray from $1 million to $100 million in sales. He also brought with him a handful of trusted colleagues. The challenges the new team faced were daunting. Within three months of his arrival at the Digital Switch offices

in northern Virginia, Donald replaced much of the board, began cleaning up the books, and moved the company to Dallas.

During this time, the Dallas area had become a major technology center. Collins Radio (later Rockwell Telecommunications) was a pioneer in communications product development and the linchpin of what became known as the Dallas area's "Telecom Corridor." The corridor also hosted such companies as Texas Instruments, EDS, and LTV. Here, Donald knew, Digital Switch could benefit from a highly skilled work force and a financial establishment that was friendly to high-tech ventures.

However, what the company needed at least as much as financial stability was a salable product. When Digital Switch relocated to Dallas in 1981, it had six employees, no orders, and no product. Nevertheless, Donald and his team had a plan: they would apply digital technology and distributed processing to switches, and their switches would serve not the increasingly saturated Class 5 local exchange central office switch market but the market for Class 4 tandems, the switches required by the new long-distance competitors to AT&T.

The possibility for the creation of these new companies, called Other Common Carriers (OCCs), first arose in the late 1960s. In what became known as the Carterphone decision, Thomas F. Carter of Dallas challenged the rules against attaching "foreign devices" to the AT&T network—and won. Then, during the early 1980s, federal antitrust action against AT&T resulted in a plan to split up the telephone monopoly. Local Bell companies were required to give equal access to any long-distance carrier selected by any individual customer. The long-distance market was ripe for expansion. AT&T had a heavy cost structure and was ill-prepared to compete with, for example, MCI and GTE Sprint. These smaller companies began building technologically superior, low-cost networks from the ground up. Digital Switch saw a great opportunity.

In one year of very hard work, the company completed the development of a large tandem switch—the first digital switch of its type and size, which it sold to MCI. The relationship with MCI was grounded in personal trust; in a previous management position, Digital Switch's Jim Donald had delivered on switching systems promises made to MCI's William McGowan. The relationship proved advantageous to both of the young companies. Digital Switch had a customer with an aggressive strategic plan and cash to advance for switch development; MCI had a vendor with cutting-edge technology and a willingness to extend favorable payment terms.

Digital Switch moved quickly to buttress its sales to MCI. Over the next year, it recruited a cadre of management personnel to handle financing, manufacturing, sales, and customer support for the new switch. It also reached out toward GTE Sprint and other long-distance companies. According to *Business Week,* the company's "sales jumped from zero in 1981 to $27.4 million," and the company "also reversed a 1981 loss of $3.4 million by showing a 1982 profit of $5.8 million." Digital Switch executives spoke of reaching a billion dollars in sales in 1990, and Donald noted that the only way the company could reach that goal was through diversification.

However, in August 1983, the Federal Communications Commission (FCC) handed down a ruling that stood to double the fees independent long-distance companies would have to pay for access to local-exchange companies. As a result, Digital Switch stood to lose projected equipment orders, and its stock was buffeted on Wall Street. Nevertheless, since the federal order would have stunted long-distance competition in the United States, the FCC later modified it in favor of the independent carriers. In the meantime, Digital Switch had broadened its product line with new switch-related products and had secured additional financing.

January 1, 1984 marked the beginning of a new era. On that date, AT&T was divested of the Bell operating companies. Although AT&T retained its equipment manufacturer, Western Electric Company, the probability of other equipment vendors' selling into the Bell companies greatly increased. In June of that year, Digital Switch took a major diversification step, acquiring a transmission equipment manufacturer called Granger Associates for approximately $350 million in stock. Granger, a California-based company that excelled in transmission technologies, had contracts with many local telephone companies, including some Bell companies. Granger gave Digital Switch an entry into the local exchange carrier market. More importantly, the Granger purchase filled out Digital Switch's product line and represented its first strategic growth through acquisition.

Also in 1984, Digital Switch decided to diversify into autodialers, small computer-based devices that automatically dialed the many digits OCC customers had to use to get onto the AT&T long-distance network. This decision turned out to be a serious mistake. Within months, the economic rationale for simulating equal access via the multi-digit codes disappeared as the FCC ruling on equal access to AT&T's network was revisited and put into effect.

Because Digital Switch had broadened its offerings of telecommunications equipment, the board agreed in the spring of 1985 to change the company's name to DSC Communications Corporation. The new name retained the initials of the original and enabled the company to make a break from its one-customer, one-product past. It was also in keeping with DSC's broader market focus on advanced telecommunications.

During this time, the company's tandem switch had captured well over half of the independent long-distance carrier market. Its largest customer was MCI, which built most of its core network around the more than $600 million worth of equipment that DSC had delivered by 1992. DSC then concluded sales agreements with US Sprint.

DSC also became the first manufacturer to sell into the Japanese public telephone network which, like the American market, was being opened to competition. The multimillion-dollar sale of digital switching equipment to Daini-Denden Incorporated (DDI) was DSC's first big international sale.

Despite these gains, the year proved very difficult for DSC. Among other problems, the company took a large charge against earnings, based on its reverses on autodialers. The company also faced a sharply diminished marketplace, as OCCs, which had not captured the predicted volume of AT&T business, consolidated or disappeared. One of the company's large customers refused to honor a switch purchase commitment,

which led DSC to restate earnings. Moreover, the company fell into technical noncompliance with certain of its loan covenants.

Not just in 1985 but over several years, despite strong growth and encouraging sales, DSC experienced large fluctuations in its share value. For example, after a three-for-one stock split in 1983, DSC shares dropped from $48 a share to $19 eight months later. One disgruntled shareowner told the *Wall Street Journal,* "It seems like the more good news this company has, the more its stock just keeps going down." The rapid drop in share value was not, however, limited to DSC. Many other high-tech stocks were also quite volatile. Nevertheless, DSC's business remained sound. The company's customer list grew, sales increased, and new product development proceeded smoothly.

DSC had ridden high on the growth of MCI and US Sprint and was doing well with its new Granger transmission products. Still, Donald predicted that its future would include wireless as well as wireline technologies and began seeking manufacturing agreements in the cellular communications industry.

In 1984, DSC established an exclusive manufacturing relationship with Motorola. The latter had developed a hand-held cellular phone and needed a switch that could accommodate the resultant calls. Demand for Motorola cellular products subsequently provided DSC with a steady source of profitable orders of cellular network equipment.

One of DSC's other successful product lines was digital cross-connect systems, which reduced the amount of equipment in a telephone company's central office, and efficiently and cost-effectively handled large volumes of calls. The company became a clear leader in these products; revenue from the cross-connects grew each year from 1985 through 1990.

Still, DSC continued to experience erratic and insufficient levels of profitability. The problems were in part related to the unstable nature of the market, the company's relatively small size, and its high leverage. DSC was forced to make up for low sales in any one quarter with high sales in subsequent quarters.

Continuing its program of diversification and new product development, the company returned to profitability, generated cash, and reduced its investment in noncash working capital in 1986. After installing its first and only Class 5 switch, the DSC DEX-5, at Rochester Telephone Corp., it determined to exit the central office market and redirect those resources toward the development of the company's first Intelligent Network (IN) product, the Signal Transfer Point (STP). With the STP, a high-capacity message switch, DSC became one of the first players in the burgeoning IN marketplace.

In 1987, DSC phased out certain older Granger products, concentrating more on sales of digital cross-connects and STPs as well as the development of new products. The company also reduced its long-term debt and broke ground on an assembly and shipping center.

In 1988, after AT&T announced a move to an all-digital standard, DSC discontinued its transmultiplexer business and began striving to make up for that revenue loss. It then delivered the first of its Signal Transfer Points in the United States. At its industry's major annual trade show, it also announced the DSC DEX MegaHub, a multi-functional product platform whose services and applications could be defined by customers.

1989 was a particularly active year for DSC. The company signed an expanded ten-year agreement with Motorola and extended its agreement with DDI Corporation of Japan. The first high-end DSC DEX ECS cross-connects were shipped, and management signed development agreements for a new Intelligent Network product, the Service Control Point (SCP). Finally, DSC began discussions to purchase Optilink Corporation.

The following year, DSC made the investment in Optilink, whose fiber optic Synchronous Optical Network (SONET)-based products would give DSC a new set of customers. During this time, however, the company also suffered through industry consolidations, a weak global economy, and perceived problems in manufacturing quality.

In 1991, two of the Regional Holding Companies, Bell Atlantic and Pacific Bell, experienced network failures, and in each case, a DSC STP was involved. Investigators soon found that a coding error in the DSC software had exacerbated other network flaws. The problem was easily corrected, and safeguards were built in that minimized the chances of such a failure recurring. Moreover, the FCC report on the event stated that the outages would have occurred with or without the STP's involvement. Still, DSC suffered enormous public relations damage, particularly in the investment community. Customers suspended their purchases, and share values plummeted.

For the first nine months of 1991, DSC posted a $100 million loss, including $55 million in write-downs and other charges. Although the company did not default on any bank lines or fall behind in its public debt payments, it was once again in technical default of its loan covenants.

In response, about 20 percent of DSC's work force was cut and capital spending was severely curtailed. In November 1991, DSC reorganized operations into four product divisions and a customer service division. Although rumors began to circulate that DSC was preparing to sell off all or part of its business, by the end of the year, DSC's fortunes began to turn upward, and the company remained intact.

DSC had taken its share of the blame for the 1991 summer network outages, and its customers—in particular Bell Atlantic and Pacific Bell—stood behind DSC, announcing major new purchases of DSC equipment early in 1992. Also that year, as the Bell companies lifted their spending constraints, Ameritech named DSC the lead vendor for its billion-dollar network upgrade program, which included DSC's fiber-based Litespan system.

In the early 1990s, MCI remained DSC's largest customer, with 15 percent of total sales, followed by Motorola, Bell Atlantic, and DDI. During this time, DSC moved cautiously, emphasizing sales in the more stable markets worldwide and enhancing its manufacturing, sales and distribution facilities in Canada, Puerto Rico, England, and Asia. Adopting greater manufacturing design flexibility, better inventory controls, and a total quality management program, the company regained profitability. Its gross profit margin increased from 30 percent to 43 percent in 1992.

The best news about DSC was the change in its financial picture. By the summer of 1992, the company had paid off its bank debt. At the end of 1992 and through 1993, it began to pay off its public debt, eliminating more than $70 million in outstanding debentures. By year-end 1993, DSC had progressed from being a company $280 million in debt with next to nothing in cash into a company with approximately $300 million in cash and less than $75 million in debt. While maintaining a strong focus on well-defined markets and growing into these markets in a careful and responsible manner, DSC had become a very profitable company.

Further Reading:

"Digital Switch Gains as Events Depressing Stock May Change, Including AccessCharge Ruling," *Wall Street Journal,* January 19, 1984, p. 61.

"Digital Switch's Profit Jump, Expansion Plan Fail to Lift High-Tech Cloud Among Investors," *Wall Street Journal,* April 30, 1984, p. 61.

"DSC Realigning Along 4 Core Product Lines," *Electronic News,* October 28, 1991, p. 5.

Goldman Sachs & Company, "DSC Communications," *Investment Research,* June 17, 1993.

"The Grand and Risky Goals of Upstart Digital Switch," *Business Week,* September 19, 1983, pp. 96B-96D.

"Phone Outages Expected to be Tied to Typing Mistake," *Wall Street Journal,* November 25, 1991, p. B4.

Salomon Brothers, "DSC Communications Corp.—A Texas-Sized Turnaround," *United States Equity Research,* October 15, 1992.

—Phyllis Guest

ECS S.A.

16. rue Washington
75399 Paris Cedex 08
France
1-49 53 33 33
Fax: 1-42 25 86 86

Wholly Owned Subsidiary of Societe Generale, SA
Incorporated: 1974
Employees: 1,035
Sales: FFr 10,75
SICs: 8323 Data Processing and Tabulating Services; 5087
    Service Establishment Equipment

As Europe's largest computer leasing company, ECS S.A. provides a wide range of computer-related services, from leasing to sales, installment, and maintenance of personal, mainframe, and minicomputers. While the company's emphasis was traditionally on IBM and IBM-compatible machines, ECS extended its expertise to other computer platforms by the 1990s. The company not only supervised hardware delivery and installation, but provided data processing assistance, user training, and hardware maintenance for multi-component computer systems. "Our role is to free companies from hardware-related constraints so that they can devote their undivided attention to data and applications," noted CEO Gilles Tugendhat in his 1991 letter to shareholders.

ECS (Europe Computer Systems) was founded in 1974, under the guidance of Jean-Louis Bouchard. Mr. Bouchard recognized that rapid growth in the computer industry would strain the budgets of increasingly computer-dependent companies. The costs of using and updating computer hardware, however, could be defrayed by the support of a third party, the computer lessor. ECS rose to the occasion, with special emphasis on IBM equipment, which set the standard for excellence in the information technology industry and also promised value in the second-hand market. In the late 1970s, IBM itself withdrew from the computer leasing business, giving ECS room to round up more of the market share.

By the mid-1980s, ECS had done just that, reporting a turnover of FFr 3,239 million ($324 million) and a net profit of FFr 42.3 million ($4.2 million) for 1985. Such figures marked a good point of departure for the company's new chairman, Gilles Tugendhat, who succeeded Jean-Louis Bouchard in December

1984. Indeed, by the end of 1986, ECS claimed 15 percent of the IBM market in France.

A strong home base served as a strategic ground for aggressive forays into international markets. Starting in 1984, ECS embarked on a major expansion program to establish a network of overseas subsidiaries in Italy, Japan, Belgium, West Germany, and the United Kingdom. Even though the company's late-1986 move into the United Kingdom came at a turbulent time in the computer industry, ECS projected a $50 million turnover in the first year for that market. Such optimism was justified; by May 1987, the company had already opened a second U.K. office at Birmingham's Aston Science Park. Other foreign subsidiaries also profited. ECS Japan, for example, had been created in 1986 to capitalize on the second largest market for operational leases on IBM equipment outside the United States. By November 1987, the Bank of Tokyo had acquired a five percent stake in the leasing company, promising future growth and stability in that key market. By 1990, ECS boasted an international sales network made up of 32 agencies or regional offices in France, 35 international offices, and 518 employees in 47 different cities, according to that year's annual report.

In its formative years, ECS's innovative rental programs were the backbone of its success. Such programs were particularly appealing to companies that wanted to fulfill their computer-related needs while eliminating the need for amortization. The purchase of equipment often forced organizations to exceed their financial means in order to accommodate their projected processing needs. Rental, on the other hand, permitted such companies to access the exact level of computing power they needed, without tying up capital. Moreover, rental programs permitted versatility by which ECS customers could stay on top of quickly evolving market trends and more easily seize state-of-the-art opportunities as they arose.

ECS employed numerous refinancing methods to maximize its financial credibility while minimizing its risk. Sale and lease-back agreements, for example, permitted ECS to bill customers for rent payments while making identical payments to finance companies, thus remaining a party, but not the sole issuer, of the rental contract. Lease contracts, on the other hand, permitted ECS to sign as an agent but not a party to the basic rental agreement; customers were billed directly by the finance companies for rent payments. By tailoring such techniques to the intricacies of each specific contract, ECS was able to free itself of liquidity, bad debt, and interest rate risks by transferring them to finance companies. Thus, ECS's financial savvy was as important as its technical computer expertise in distinguishing itself as a leader in the information processing industry.

Beginning in the mid-1980s, ECS adapted to the unprecedented growth of personal computers—and server-managed networks of such machines—for business applications where medium to large configurations had been used in the past. "The master/slave configurations inherited from centralized data processing will be replaced by client/server architectures in which micros and mainframes dialogue as equals," stated ECS's 1990 annual report. From 1987 to 1989, the microcomputer industry saw rates of growth approaching 30 percent, according to the market research firm IDC. Into the early 1990s, such growth continued at a healthy, but less astronomical rate of approximately 12.5 percent.

By 1988, the computer weekly *01 Informatique* had published a report which listed France's top 500 computing companies and ranked ECS in third place, after Compagnie des Machines Bull S.A. and market leader IBM France. ECS reported an increase of 122 percent in net profits to FFr 49 million for that year, according to *Les Echos* news source on March 8, 1989. In 1989, ECS Diffusion—the company division geared specifically toward microcomputer business—sold nearly 41,000 PCs in Europe. Then in 1990, that division grew by 67 percent, compared to the market average of 12.5 percent. Based on impressive turnover and profits in its main divisions, ECS planned to grow its business by about 20 percent per year from 1989 through the early 1990s, according to *Computergram* on May 15, 1989 (a projection that Antoine Colboc, managing director of ECS UK reaffirmed on May 2, 1991 in *Computer Weekly* magazine).

A key contributor to ECS's competitiveness was its move into software consulting and development in the late 1980s. In November 1987, the company set up a joint venture with software developer CCMC and founded its Proland subsidiary to provide standard software solutions. Proland's services catered primarily to small and medium-sized businesses and subsidiaries of large groups—clients that constituted the bulk market for IBM's mid-range computers, such as the 36 and 38 series and the AS/400, after its introduction in 1987. The company developed software programs specifically for those systems. Further development work in "native" AS/400 mode led to two key products in 1990: *Pluriel,* for personnel management, and *Réel,* for accounting management. Unfortunately, these products reached a market that was hardly accommodating.

The computer market of the early 1990s suffered the shock-waves of general economic malaise. With information technology accounting for a growing share of business expenditures, recessionary pressures of the late 1980s were felt more than ever before in computer-related industries. Growth of sales volume for suppliers in all categories (hardware, software, and services) hovered close to zero. In efforts to maintain their market shares, computer manufacturers engaged in an aggressive price war (one that showed no signs of abating as late as the mid-1990s). Rather than augmenting sales of their products, such price incentives merely encouraged consumers to buy more powerful computer configurations for their money. "The phenomenon illustrates a degree of maturity among users who are more interested in making the most of a given technical context," noted ECS's 1991 annual report. For lessors, the situation was exacerbated by re-entry into the 1990s leasing market of major manufacturers, especially IBM, which had discontinued such operations in the late 1970s.

Though ECS managed to hold high ground compared to its competitors, the company still felt the sting of the computer industry's lashing in the early 1990s. ECS suffered a loss in 1991, with performance falling 104.5 percent to a loss of FFr 7.1 million on a comparable basis (the net result was down 133.9 percent for a loss of FFr 23.8 million).

ECS's troubles were paralleled by the even greater woes of its main ally, IBM. That company, which had virtually dominated the computer industry through the mid-1980s, saw its market share plummet. Major strategic reorganization at IBM slowed down that erosion, but couldn't reverse it. "IBM has embarked on what could be accurately called a cultural and functional revolution on a scale commensurate with that of the organization, in other words, gigantic," noted ECS's 1991 annual report. IBM's initiatives included administrative downsizing, reorientation toward major original equipment manufacturer (OEM), and technological collaborations with other manufacturers such as Apple Computer, Inc. In addition, IBM continued to set industry standards with its products: AS/400 minicomputers (which claimed 23 percent of the market for intermediate systems in 1992, according to *Dataquest*); the OS/2 personal computer operating system (upgraded to a more powerful WARP version by 1994); and MVS standards for large systems. Still, the computer giant took it on the chin in the early 1990s, reporting 1992 losses of nearly $5 billion, the worst showing in its history.

Such challenges in the computer industry did reveal a bright side, though. As ECS pointed out in its 1991 annual report, "the recessionary climate and the resulting cost-cutting drives . . . [boosted] secondhand sales and [stimulated] interest in less costly third-party maintenance solutions." And in 1992, CEO Gilles Tugendhat conceded that lingering recession placed constraints on growth potential, but "presented new opportunities created by lower costs."

Along with other industry leaders, ECS stayed afloat in the turbulent market by trimming waste and consolidating operations. 1990 saw the consolidation of international branches, particularly in ECS's Italian operations; while setbacks in the company's German activities "served to remind us that procedures and expenditures must be constantly monitored," according to Tugendhat in his 1990 letter to shareholders. Inventory and stock management became key concerns as well. ECS informed *L'Usine Nouvelle* on February 13, 1992 that "savings of FFr 10 million per annum can be realized by reducing stock levels from six to three weeks."

To best realize such cost-cutting measures, ECS implemented a state-of-the-art, centralized management system for all its operations and constructed a central facility at the hub of its high-tech empire. Starting in 1987, the company forged ahead on its enhancement of the ECS Information System, a central administrative and management network in which FFr 65 million had been invested by 1990. The system comprised more than 2,000 programs and nine million lines of code, and connected more than 35 ECS branches throughout France. It streamlined everything from standard sales and financial management to company-specific brokerage, logistics, and accounting management of the installed base. In PC sales, for example, ECS Information System coordinated orders, billing, and commissions to sales agents.

ECS's efforts to centralize its operations brought about the 1990 construction of a new, 20,000 square meter center in Bussy-Saint-Georges, an investment of more than FFr 100 million ($20 million). By 1992, all technical and logistical activities of ECS on a European scale—from inventory management to testing, configuration, and logistics—were coordinated there. In 1992 alone, 60,000 PC configurations were shipped to European customers from Bussy, and more than 375,000 products passed through the plant (central processing units, peripherals, add-ons, software, application packages, etc.), according the 1992 ECS annual report. The site brought money-saving economies of scale and facilitated consolidation of inventory and standardization of international procedures and services. Through this common platform, "Bussy-Saint-Georges has become 'Bussy-upon-Europe'," according to the company report.

In preparation for the twenty-first century, ECS—like other leading leasing companies—moved toward broader diversification, to include microcomputer distribution, maintenance, and services as part-and-parcel of its main line of business. In 1991, the company introduced its ECS Plus package: an offer combining the sale and rental of full-service personal computer utilities in a single contract to simplify the upgrade of installations.

The company also kept close watch on new system trends in the computer industry to maintain its competitive edge. Users tended to move away from mainframe configurations toward increasingly powerful personal computers and server-managed PC networks. "From Multimedia to Electronic Data Interchange (EDI), local networks to databases, graphics interfaces to compression techniques," ECS's 1990 annual report noted, "all of the latest technologies are aimed in the same direction: the transparent circulation of information between companies, their employees, their customers and their suppliers."

By the mid-1990s, the "latest technologies" of 1990 had become commonplace. ECS continually refocused its development toward new applications and tools. "Content Applications," for example, represented enormous banks of data from which users would have information customarily "served" by machine. And as early as 1992, the company's annual report began outlining a new direction by which many different "content applications," would be linked together on a global information network. Whatever shape that "information highway" would take, ECS was positioning itself to travel in the fast lane—bringing together a broad range of financial, technical, and logistic competencies in the workplace, and in "cyberspace."

Principal Subsidiaries: ECS Diffusion; ECS Maintenance; ECS Technologies; Fortiori; Proland; ECS International Italia SpA (Italy); ECS International U.K. Ltd. (U.K.); ECS International Deutschland GmbH (Germany); ECS Japan K.K.; ECS International Belgium S.A./N.V. (Belgium); ECS Computer Suisse S.A. (Switzerland).

Further Reading:

Aryanpur, Arah, "UK: ECS Plans to Offer Complete Personal Computer Ordering, Supply and Maintenance Service," *Computer Weekly,* May 2, 1991.
"Bank of Tokyo Takes 5% of ECS Japan," *Computergram,* November 16, 1987.
"France: Computer Leasing Companies Report Poor Performance in 1989," *L'Usine Nouvelle,* May 11, 1990.
"France: Distribution Sector Affected by Computer Industry Crisis," *L'Usine Nouvelle,* February 13, 1992.
"France: ECS Hopes to Return to Black in 1992," *AGEFI,* June 18, 1992.
"France: Golden Age is Over for Computer Leasing Companies," *AGEFI,* August 2, 1990.
"French Computer Leasing Giant ECS is Trying to Break into the Competitive Mid-Range IBM Leasing Market in the UK," *Computing,* October 8, 1987.
"French Dealer ECS Plans to Break into Personal Computer Market," *Computer Weekly,* July 4, 1991.
Kornel, Amiel, "European Community Casts Watchful Eye on Pricing," *Computerworld Extra!,* December 3, 1986, p. 57.
"Leasing Companies Have Warned that IBM's Decision to Re-Sell Used Mainframes Has Knocked 30% Off Their Prices and Could Cause a Price War," *Computing,* November 19, 1987.

—Kerstan Cohen

Educational Testing Service

Rosedale Road
Princeton, New Jersey 08541
U.S.A.
(609) 921-9000
Fax: (609) 895-3044

Private Non-Profit Company
Incorporated: 1947
Employees: 2,650
Operating Revenues: $346 million
SICs: 8733 Noncommercial Research Organizations

Educational Testing Service is the world's largest administrator of standardized tests and a leader in educational research. The company develops, administers, and scores achievement, occupational and admissions tests, such as the Scholastic Aptitude Test (SAT), for The College Board, as well as for clients in education, government, and business. ETS has six regional offices and annually administers nine million exams in the United States and 180 other countries.

ETS was created in 1947 by three non-profit educational institutions, the American Council on Education, the Carnegie Foundation for the Advancement of Teaching (a part of the larger Carnegie Corporation), and The College Entrance Examination Board. Standardized tests had first been developed and distributed in the early 1930s. In 1930, the Cooperative Test Service of the American Council on Education began to conduct achievement tests at schools and colleges, administering 650 different exams. Six years later, the Educational Records Bureau began using the first test scoring machine, the IBM 805, to expedite the grading of standardized tests administered on a large scale by the Cooperative Test Service. In 1937, the Graduate Record Examinations (GRE) was introduced by the Carnegie Foundation, and the National Teacher Examinations followed shortly.

Although the president of Harvard University had publicly suggested a merger of the three test-giving services in 1937, the emphatic opposition of The College Board's associate secretary forestalled any further movement in this direction throughout the remainder of the 1930s. During World War II, the bulk of the standardized exams given by several test-giving bodies were administered to people enrolled in the military. In 1943, another Harvard administrator, Henry Chauncey, took an 18-month leave of absence from his job to run the Army-Navy College Qualifying Test, which was used to identify officer candidates. In 1945, Chauncey became director of The College Board's Princeton office.

In its pre-war incarnation, The College Board had had a relatively simple and straightforward mission, but its activities had been transformed and greatly expanded during the war years. Instead of simply testing candidates for admission to select colleges, the organization had taken on such diverse functions as making up exams for the State Department, for the military, and for other purposes.

This broadening of functions continued in the wake of the war, when the charitable Carnegie Foundation worked to transfer control of the GRE, which had started as an experiment but had grown to dwarf the rest of the Foundation, to The College Board. At the time of this proposal, The College Board was made up of 52 select member institutions. Absorbing the GRE necessitated a substantial restructuring of the organization, and again raised the issue of a consolidation of test-giving organizations. A committee was formed to examine various proposals, and it began meeting in the fall of 1946. In October, this body recommended the creation of one central test-giving organization.

By the end of 1946, the process of working out the actual details of a merger had begun in earnest among the three founding organizations of the tentatively-named Educational Testing Service (ETS). By June of 1947, difficulties such as the composition of a Board of Trustees had been resolved, and ETS was set up for a trial five-year period. Each of the member groups turned over its testing operations, and a portion of its assets. The Carnegie Foundation contributed the GRE, and the Pre-Engineering Inventory. The American Council on Education added the National Teacher Examinations, and the Cooperative Test Service, while The College Board turned over the Scholastic Aptitude Test (SAT), as well as the Law School Admission Test (LSAT), and several other programs. On December 19, 1947, the New York State Board of Regents chartered the new organization under the name Educational Testing Service.

The new organization set up operations in the old offices of The College Board at 20 Nassau Street in Princeton, New Jersey. Gradually, files, office equipment, and employees from the founding organizations of ETS arrived, until the organization had 212 employees. At the end of 1947, Chauncey was made president of the new organization, which had less than $2 million in initial capital. At the time, ETS elaborated a three-fold goal: to develop and administer tests, to conduct research, and to advise educational institutions.

Among the first clients of the newly-formed ETS were more than 50 colleges, the Association of American Medical Colleges, other foundations, the U.S. Atomic Energy Commission, the U.S. State Department, additional government agencies, the Pepsi-Cola Corporation, and other companies. The organization distributed a wide variety of tests for various assessment purposes. As the ranks of students at American colleges were swelled by soldiers returning from war and enrolling under the G.I. Bill, which promised a free college education to any soldier who had served in World War II, demand grew for ETS's services. In 1948, college admissions exams were taken by 75,000 students.

By 1950, ETS had begun to more fully understand and assess its role in society. In that year, Chauncey proposed in his annual report for ETS that a national census of abilities and talents be undertaken, in order to assist the military, and to strengthen educational and industrial planning. By 1954, ETS had already started to outgrow the building it had purchased on Nassau Street in Princeton, and Chauncey selected a new site for the organization, a 400 acre estate on Rosedale Road in Princeton, which had formerly served as a working farm as well as the Stony Brook Hunt Club.

Throughout the decade, the activities and number of tests administered by ETS continued to grow. In 1958, ETS began to release students' scores on the SAT to their high schools, so that they could in turn be passed on to the students. By the beginning of the 1960s, nearly 25 percent of all American high school students were taking the SAT. By 1962, 15 years after its inception, ETS had become not just a testing organization, but a more broadly-based educational entity.

In addition to expansion in the number of people taking ETS tests, the number of tests available also grew during the 1960s. The organization developed assessments to measure the abilities of people from secondary school right on through their professional career. Along with this growth in the number of tests given, the size and role of ETS expanded as well. On the occasion of the organization's 25th anniversary, ETS dedicated a $3 million conference center, named after Chauncey, its founding president, at its Princeton headquarters. During this time, ETS had also constructed a residence for its president on the Rosedale campus. This construction was made possible by the steady surge in growth ETS had experienced in the postwar years, as the organization's sales doubled every five years between 1948 and the early 1970s.

By the mid-1970s, ETS had become, in effect, the nation's leading testing organization. The organization's tools for measuring ability, particularly the SAT, the GRE, the LSAT, and other tests, had become a standard feature of American educational life. In 1976, the institution was cited as a hot growth company in American business by *Forbes* magazine. The revenues generated by ETS' activities continued to expand throughout the late 1970s. The company suffered its first serious threat at the end of that decade, when, in response to growing criticism of its monopolistic power, New York state passed the Educational Testing Act, a disclosure law, which required ETS to release certain test questions and graded answer sheets to students.

In the following year, 1980, ETS suffered its first small fiscal deficit. In response, the company reduced its staff and commissioned a strategic plan from a management consulting firm in 1982. Following the enactment of the truth in testing law, ETS suffered further criticism in the early 1980s, as outsiders asserted that its tests were culturally biased to favor white members of the upper middle class, and that they were poor predictors of actual performance.

ETS also took steps to protect its copyrighted materials from violation by entrepreneurs who offered courses to raise stu-

dent's scores on its exams. In 1982, students who had prepared for achievement tests by taking a Princeton Review course reported that they had already seen some of the questions on the test. This violation of test security, along with others, caused ETS to remove several questions from active use on its exams. In May of 1983, ETS sought and obtained an agreement with the Princeton Review that its workers would not retake the SAT again.

In response to concerns over the format and scope of standardized tests, The College Board undertook a revision of the exams in 1990. ETS announced that the old SAT and achievement tests would, in the future, be known as Scholastic Assessment Tests. The new SAT-I, which measured verbal and mathematical skills, included longer reading passages and more questions to determine how well students had understood them. In the math sections, students were required to work out some answers entirely on their own, with the use of a pocket calculator, rather than simply choosing from answers supplied to them. The SAT-II included a 20-minute essay. These changes, made at the direction of a committee headed by the president of Harvard, were designed to put a greater emphasis on problem solving.

Despite its somewhat embattled place in the culture of American education, ETS continued to thrive materially throughout the late 1980s. By 1990, it had solidified its place as by far the largest American private educational assessment service. The institution had a staff of nearly 3,000 employees, more than 270 clients, including the federal government, and gross revenues of nearly $300 million. Despite this impressive size, ETS sought, as it moved into the 1990s, to expand its activities even further. "Our traditional mission has been to place ourselves at the transitional points of education between high school and college, college and graduate school," ETS's president, Gregory Anrig, told *Time* magazine in 1990, adding that "now we are expanding into more and more programs that help kids to learn and teachers to teach more effectively."

Among the programs ETS began to offer at this time were educational tools making use of new technology. The company began to develop grammar school courses that used computers and interactive videos to foster critical-thinking skills. In addition, ETS used computers to re-configure the National Teachers Exam. This test was used in about two-thirds of the states to license teachers.

By 1991, ETS's gross revenues had grown to $311 million in revenues, of which 40 percent were derived from College Board activities. The company's roster of exams had ballooned to cover a wide variety of fields, from manicurists to shopping center managers. In addition, ETS had successfully expanded its geographic scope, offering tests in 170 foreign countries. By 1993, the company was administering nine million tests each year.

ETS continued to use new technology to update its tests throughout the early 1990s. In November 1993, the company introduced a computerized version of the GRE, which was slated to eventually replace the old paper-and-pencil version of the test. Rather than simply consisting of the old test on computer, the new exam was to be more adaptive, adjusting its level of difficulty to suit the aptitude of the student taking the test.

Students who answered questions correctly were given successively harder questions; students who answered incorrectly prompted the computer to offer easier problems. In this way, ETS hoped to make testing more personalized for each student, provide easier and more frequent scheduling, and immediately provide scores upon conclusion of the test.

ETS began to offer the computerized GRE at 170 testing centers located around the country. In addition, the company was developing computerized testing for nurses, teachers, and architects. With the use of computers, the time needed to take an exam was shortened, but critics worried that the computer itself would prove a barrier to people unfamiliar with the use of machines.

In March 1994, ETS ran into difficulty implementing another new testing program, when disabled students protested the limited number of dates available to them to take the new SAT-I test. After the U.S. Justice Department conducted an inquiry into the matter, ETS scheduled additional dates for disabled students to gain access to the exam. Later that year, ETS also encountered a snag in its admission of the new computerized GRE exam, when employees of a test preparation course who took the new test were able to memorize and later recreate a large portion of the exam after the fact. Presented with this evidence that the repetition of questions had compromised test security, ETS suspended administration of the computerized test for a week in December 1994, in order to tighten a variety of security measures.

One month later, ETS announced that it would reduce the number of times the GRE would be offered by computer, in an effort to limit opportunities for theft. The measure was taken in response to charges that some of the nearly half-million students who sat for the GRE each year were memorizing questions and using them to improve their scores when re-taking the test, or passing them on to their friends, who had not yet taken it. In an effort to prevent test preparation course employees from repeatedly trying to crack the test, ETS also filed suit against Kaplan Educational Centers, the largest such company, alleging copyright infringement and seeking to forbid its employees from retaking the test.

Despite such challenges, ETS remained an important part of American education in the 1990s. The company continued to design tests with input from educators and teachers and contributed policy and measurement research to help America meet its education goals.

Further Reading:

Celis, William, III, "Computer Admissions Test Found to Be Ripe for Abuse," *New York Times,* December 16, 1994.

Elson, John, "The Test That Everyone Fears," *Time,* November 12, 1990.

Honan, William, "Computer Admissions Test to Be Given Less Often," *New York Times,* January 4, 1995.

Owen, David, *None of the Above: Behind the Myth of Scholastic Aptitude,* Boston: Houghton Mifflin, 1985.

Nairn, Allan, *The Reign of ETS: The Corporation That Makes Up Minds,* New York: Ralph Nader, 1980.

Tabor, Mary B.W., "Disabled to Get an Extra Chance for S.A.T.s," *New York Times,* April 1, 1994.

Toch, Thomas, "A Stunning Second Lap," *U.S. News & World Report,* May 18, 1992.

Williams, Dennis A., "Testers V. Cram Courses," *Newsweek,* August 12, 1985.

Winerip, Michael, "No. 2 Pencil Fades as Graduate Exam Moves to Computer," *New York Times,* November 15, 1993.

—Elizabeth Rourke

El Paso Natural Gas Company

P.O. Box 1492
El Paso, Texas 79978
U.S.A.
(915) 541-2600
Fax: (915) 541-3062

Public Company
Incorporated: 1928
Employees: 2,500
Sales: $870 million
Stock Exchanges: New York
SICs: 4922 Natural Gas Transmission

El Paso Natural Gas Company owns and operates one of the largest natural gas transmission systems in North America. Its more than 17,000 miles of pipeline connected major gas supply regions throughout the American West and Mexico in the early 1990s and supplied about seven percent of U.S. natural gas demand. In 1992, El Paso was spun off from Burlington Resources, Inc., which had operated the company as a subsidiary since 1983.

Paul Kayser, a young Houston attorney, founded El Paso Natural Gas in 1928. In 1929, Kayser obtained a franchise from the El Paso City Council to sell natural gas to the city. He proposed construction of a 200-mile pipeline that linked El Paso with natural gas wells located near the city of Jal, New Mexico. After obtaining financing for the ambitious project, he immediately began hiring work crews and securing equipment and supplies.

Pipeline construction methods at the time were crude in comparison to techniques developed during the mid-1900s. The lines were built by hand and the men who worked on the lines had to be extremely tough. Difficulties related to building Kayser's pipeline were amplified by the fact that his pipes would cross some of the most difficult terrain in the southwestern United States. The pipeline had to cross 200 miles of rivers, mountains, and deserts and it had to be built to withstand all types of natural disasters. Although the work was tedious and time-consuming, Kayser's crews pioneered new methods of welding, ditching, and crossing unique terrain. The line was finished and put into service in 1930.

Unfortunately for Kayser and his fledgling start-up, the Great Depression began shortly after the building of the pipeline. El

Paso generated profits of $283,000 during the pipeline's first year of operation but the Depression-era economy threatened to quash the venture. Fortunately, the city of El Paso continued to buy Kayser's gas. The company was able to pay its debts and to expand its pipeline system during the early 1930s. The company built new lines extending to the copper mining areas of southern Arizona and northern Mexico and in 1934 extended service to Tucson and Phoenix, Arizona.

During the late 1930s, El Paso enjoyed steady growth. It built new pipeline systems extending throughout the oil- and gas-rich Permian Basin in south Texas and extended lines north and west to accommodate growing regional demand. By the late 1930s, the company was generating revenue of about $5 million annually and was beginning to post strong profit gains. Expansion slowed during World War II as the nation's labor and resources were steered toward the war effort. Following the war, El Paso benefitted from strong demand for natural gas in the growing southwestern United States. As the postwar economy and population boomed, cities throughout the region demanded energy sources to fuel growth and development.

El Paso experienced explosive growth in the late 1940s. Gains during that period were due in part to the completion of a 700-mile pipeline reaching from El Paso's Permian Basin operations to California. El Paso began supplying gas through a 26-inch pipeline and also began construction of new, larger pipelines aimed at the burgeoning California market. As a result of those efforts, El Paso's assets rose from about $23.5 million in 1945 to $285 million in 1950. Meanwhile, sales increased from $9 million to $41 million and net income climbed to a record $9 million in 1950.

During the early 1950s, El Paso continued to post steady gains as demand for its natural gas increased. It built or purchased pipes reaching as far north as Ignacio, a small town in southern Colorado, and continued its westward expansion, bolstering its feeder pipes going to California and increasing sales throughout Arizona and New Mexico. By 1955, El Paso captured nearly $30 million in profits annually from about $180 million in sales. By the early 1960s, those figures had risen to more than $40 million and $400 million, respectively.

El Paso's big gains during the late 1950s were partially attributed to its 1957 acquisition of part of the operations of Pacific Northwest Pipeline Corporation. The acquisition gave El Paso a presence in several western and northwestern states, with pipelines reaching as far as Washington and connecting to other companies' networks in Canada. In addition to geographic expansion, El Paso began to diversify during the 1950s into related oil and chemical businesses. It created El Paso Products Company as a subsidiary to manufacture chemicals from natural gas derivatives. Despite forays into other industries, El Paso remained focused on buying, transporting, and selling natural gas.

After 35 years of leadership, El Paso's founder left his chief executive duties during the early 1960s. The company's president, Howard Boyd, replaced Kayser. Kayser had transformed his company from a tiny start-up supplier with 200 miles of pipeline to a $500 million corporation with 20,000 miles of pipe delivering gas throughout the western United States. Throughout his reign, he remained committed to the pragmatic development of natural resources and sound business practices. "There is nothing more vital to our economy than the orderly, wise, and free use of our precious natural resources developed under practical, intelligent conservation policies," Kayser stated in 1954.

El Paso continued to grow at a rapid pace during the late 1960s and early 1970s. Although natural gas industry profits were generally cyclical, El Paso's overall sales and earnings grew during the period. By the early 1970s, El Paso operated one of the nation's largest pipeline systems. It stretched from northern Mexico to the northeast tip of Washington, with extensions throughout the Southwest and reaching into Wyoming, Idaho, and Oregon. Although federal regulators kept El Paso from operating its own pipes in specified regions, its lines connected with those of other operators to give El Paso access to markets in California, Kansas, Oklahoma, and Nevada.

Partly in an effort to minimize its exposure to cyclical gas markets, El Paso diversified during the late 1960s and 1970s. By 1974, non-gas operations contributed about one-third of El Paso's annual $1.3 billion in revenues. The company's largest non-gas division was its petrochemical business, which manufactured a variety of chemicals used in the growing synthetics industry. El Paso also became heavily involved in the fiber and textile industries, particularly nylon, rayon, and other synthetics. Other of El Paso's subsidiaries were involved with mining, gas and oil exploration, insurance, copper wire, and real estate development.

One of El Paso's most intriguing and promising ventures during the 1970s was a venture into liquefied natural gas. In 1969, El Paso reached what it termed a "historic agreement" with Sonatrach, an Algerian national oil and gas company. Under the arrangement, the Algerian company would deliver a billion cubic feet of natural gas in liquid form daily to El Paso Natural Gas. El Paso would then distribute the low-cost gas through its pipeline network. The ambitious project required the construction of a nine-ship fleet of special tankers to be owned and operated by El Paso, as well as the construction of storage terminals on the East Coast and in Algeria. El Paso moved 230 employees to Algeria for the project. Liquified gas deliveries commenced in 1978 and made a significant contribution to El Paso's bottom line.

Although El Paso's liquified gas venture represented an important success during the 1970s, its non-gas-related operations were generally less fruitful. El Paso jettisoned some of those operations and posted losses from major activities like chemical and fiber manufacturing. To make matters worse, El Paso was harmed by a Supreme Court decision in 1974. For several years, federal regulators had been trying to renege on their decision in the late 1950s to allow El Paso to acquire its northern operations. El Paso fought their efforts, but was defeated. In 1974, El Paso was forced to divest the holdings, effectively terminating its natural gas operations north of New Mexico and Arizona.

Despite some setbacks, El Paso managed to sustain long-term growth during the 1970s. Sales dipped following the 1974 divestiture but surged back up to $1.15 billion in 1975, rising to more than $2 billion in 1978. Earnings, however, fluctuated around $50 million to $60 million annually. El Paso's huge revenue gains during the late 1970s reflected turbulence in energy markets.

El Paso benefitted from the Natural Gas Policy Act which was passed in 1978. That act basically allowed El Paso to begin competing with other Texas companies for the purchase of natural gas reserves. El Paso greatly increased its reserves after the act was passed, building up a sizable reserve base near its Permian Basin pipeline operations as well as in other regions of the country. It simultaneously boosted its output capacity to meet the expected surge in demand during the 1980s.

As a result of strong natural gas markets and El Paso's increased output capacity, sales topped $2 billion in 1978, rose past $3 billion in 1980, and then increased to nearly $4 billion in 1981. In 1981, El Paso reported record earnings of $147 million. Unfortunately, El Paso's profit gains were short-lived. During the late 1970s and early 1980s, industry competitors had hustled to boost natural gas output capacity with expectations of strong demand. But a weak economy and a newfound emphasis on energy conservation slowed market growth. Supply outstripped demand in 1982 and natural gas prices dropped. Furthermore, El Paso's chemical businesses suffered major setbacks in 1982. Although El Paso's sales rose to $4.3 billion in 1982, its net income dropped to $53 million.

The El Paso Company, as it became known in the 1970s, ceased to exist as an independent corporation in 1983. The company was purchased by Burlington Northern Inc. and became a 100-percent-owned subsidiary. Burlington was a $9 billion conglomerate active in mineral development, timber and forest products, and rail carrier systems. Although El Paso was experiencing some problems at the time, Burlington viewed the company as an excellent complement to its existing mineral development operations.

The acquisition seemed like a good move, particularly in light of new federal legislation scheduled to take effect during the mid-1980s. The legislation had effectively deregulated certain aspects of the natural gas industry. Prior to the mid-1980s, El Paso, in accordance with the Natural Gas Act of 1938 and the Natural Gas Policy Act of 1978, was in the business of purchasing gas from other producers, transporting the gas, and then selling it to local distribution companies. Its business began to change in 1984. Federal legislation passed in 1984 had a tumultuous effect on prices, transportation, and contractual relationships between customers and suppliers. The net effect was that natural gas industries and markets became more competitive. As a result, El Paso shifted from merchant to distributor during the late 1980s and early 1990s. Rather than owning the natural gas it transported, it simply provided transportation services for a fee charged to the owners and/or buyers.

El Paso prospered under Burlington's management. Over the next few years, Burlington spun off or sold several of El Paso's nonperforming divisions and streamlined the company's natural gas operations. El Paso's conversion to transportation services, moreover, was well timed. During the late 1980s, gas prices remained suppressed. While many of Burlington's competitors went deep into debt buying up reserves, Burlington emphasized the service end of the industry through El Paso. Going into the early 1990s, El Paso was recognized as the low-cost provider of natural gas transportation services in its market.

In the early 1990s, Burlington changed its business strategy. After shunning the natural gas exploration and production business for several years, it decided to shift its focus to take advantage of a projected upturn in natural gas prices. During the early 1990s, Burlington sold most of its subsidiaries and reinvested the proceeds into natural gas reserves.

Burlington completed the spin-off of El Paso Natural Gas Company on June 30, 1992. William A. Wise was selected to act as president and chief executive of the again-independent El Paso. The 45-year-old Wise had been with El Paso since 1970, working as an attorney and then serving in various management positions. Wise was credited with helping the company make a transition to transport services during the late 1980s and with helping to make El Paso a low-cost industry leader. When El Paso regained its independence, its pipeline consisted of a 20,000 mile network connecting three oil producing regions in Texas, Oklahoma, and New Mexico to buyers primarily in California, Arizona, New Mexico, and Texas. Sales during 1993, its first full year of operation, topped $900 million, about $90 million of which was net income.

El Paso was in a relatively strong position in its industry going into the mid-1990s. It was the largest supplier of natural gas to the state of California and had successfully changed from mer-chant to transporter in compliance with new (1992) federal regulations. But it was also facing obstacles. Most notably, the California gas market was becoming glutted, dampening profits in El Paso's most important region. Nevertheless, investors were enthusiastic about El Paso's chances, as evidenced by a doubling of the company's stock price between 1992 and early 1994. El Paso was pinning its long-term hopes on the rapidly expanding Mexican market, to which it had unsurpassed access. It was also engaged in an ambitious effort to vastly increase its access to the northern California natural gas market.

Principal Subsidiaries: Mojave Pipeline Company; El Paso Gas Marketing; El Paso Field Services Company; El Paso Energy Development; El Paso Natural Gas Foundation.

Further Reading:

Graebner, Lynn, ''Mojave Pipeline Fate Is Near: Gas Project Hinges on Who Would Regulate It,'' *Business Journal-Sacramento,* December 20, 1993, p. 1.
Grunbaum, Rami, ''Gas Ignites Burlington Resources' Growth,'' *Puget Sound Business Journal,* July 17, 1992, p. 1.
Palmeri, Christopher, ''Pipeline Glut,'' *Forbes,* March 28, 1994, p. 71.
Prospectus: El Paso Natural Gas Company. New York: Morgan Stanley & Co., March 12, 1992.
Pulley, Mike, ''Mojave Makes Move; PG&E Cuts Its Staff,'' *Business Journal-Sacramento,* March 1, 1993, p. 1.

—Dave Mote

EMC²
THE STORAGE ARCHITECTS

EMC Corporation

171 South Street
Hopkinton, Massachusetts 01748-9103
U.S.A.
(508) 435-1000
Fax:

Public Company
Incorporated: 1979
Employees: 2,300
Sales: $349.1 million
SICs: 3572 Computer Storage Devices; 3674 Semiconductors
& Related Devices; 3672 Printed Circuit Boards

EMC Corporation is a leading supplier of data storage systems for mainframe computers. The company markets devices that use multiple inexpensive storage disks, linked together by special software, to allow large volumes of information to be retained and manipulated. EMC was started in the late 1970s, and grew rapidly through aggressive sales practices. In the mid-1980s, the company experienced some trouble with its technology, but regained a leading place in its industry in the 1990s through the early introduction of a new generation of computer memory technology. In 1994, EMC founder Richard J. Egan was named the "National, Master Entrepreneur of the Year," an award sponsored by Ernst & Young, *Inc.* magazine, and Merrill Lynch, for his lifetime achievement as an entrepreneur.

Egan began his career as an electrical engineering student at the Massachusetts Institute of Technology (MIT). While there, he worked on a team that helped to develop a guidance system for the Apollo lunar mission. The device designed by Egan's team helped the space capsule to return safely to earth after landing on the moon. After graduation from MIT, Egan founded a company called Cambridge Memories, later known as Cambex, which manufactured storage devices for computers. Under Egan's leadership, this company's revenues grew into the multi-millions.

After leaving Cambex, Egan worked as a technical consultant to other big computer firms, such as Honeywell. In 1979, he founded EMC. Like Cambex, EMC's main product was devices that allowed computers to store information. Egan created circuit boards that could be installed in popular computer models, in order to dramatically increase a pre-existing computer's memory. In this way, EMC's products were able to extend the life of mini-computers, allowing users to upgrade and keep on using old equipment, rather than having to buy a new machine.

Rather than put EMC's main emphasis on research and development, or engineering expertise, however, Egan focused the company's energy on sales. To fill out his staff, he recruited bright young college graduates who had played competitively on sports teams in school. In addition, to foster team spirit and competitiveness in his salesmen, Egan set up EMC's sales offices in a bullpen configuration. Different sales regions were designated by pennants, which indicated the relative standing of the regions. In the center of the room, a brass bell was hung. Anyone who gained an order of $10,000 or more got to ring the bell. In contrast, EMC also strove to keep costs down in its engineering and technical support divisions.

In the early 1980s, such decisions brought EMC rapid growth, and the company became the subject of a case study used by students at the Harvard Business School. The company's sales and profits continued to grow through the middle of the decade. By June 1985, however, EMC's continued success had attracted the unfavorable notice of a competitor, and the company was sued for patent infringement by the Digital Equipment Corporation (DEC) which also made memory boards. This suit was eventually settled in October 1987, when EMC was granted a license for the DEC technology in question, and in January 1989, EMC paid DEC $100,000 to settle the legal action.

Shortly after this suit was filed, EMC added to its product line again, as the company introduced new four- and eight-byte memory cards in July 1985. In August of that year, the company also augmented its offerings for the Hewlett-Packard 3000 computer.

In May 1986, EMC announced that it would offer stock to the public for the first time. The company planned to raise capital by selling 2.2 million shares. Five months later, the company announced that it had formed a new unit, Network Intelligence, Ltd., to develop software that would seek out and remove defects in local area network programs. At the end of the year, EMC reported record profits of $18.63 million.

EMC then expanded the market for its products, when Marubeni Electronics began to sell EMC memory boards for upgrading existing computers in Japan. In addition, EMC continued to introduce new products, announcing that it expected the bulk of its future growth to come from products designed to enhance the memory of large-scale and mid-range computers.

Toward this end, EMC introduced a new class of products, disk drives, in mid-1987. The company rolled out a disk drive and controller for use in IBM 9335-compatible machines in June of that year, and, two months later, introduced an optical disk subsystem for use in DEC VAX computers, which boosted the storage capacity of these machines, as well as a similar system for use with machines built by the Prime Computer company. Next, EMC augmented its line of disk drives for computers made by other companies yet again, when it rolled out a product designed to be used in Hewlett-Packard RISC-based Spectrum computers.

Pushed by these new products, EMC's sales took a giant leap in 1987, as sales gained 90 percent over the previous year, to reach

$127 million. Profits had grown to $24 million, and EMC was named the seventh hottest growing company in America by *Business Week* magazine. Over the course of early 1987, the company's stock hit a high of $29 a share.

By September 1987, however, EMC had hit a snag, as its new line of disk drives, which contained a small, inexpensive circuit board made by NEC Corporation, proved to be defective. When problems with the drives arose, EMC's response was to ship out new disk drives to customers through overnight mail. Because the replacement drives, which were much more expensive, were bulky and delicate instruments, they had to be delivered and installed by an EMC employee. In order to make this possible, the company was compelled to maintain inventories of the replacement drives at all of its 23 regional sales offices. In addition, its small staff of service representatives was severely taxed by the glut of problems.

As a result of these conditions, EMC's cost of doing business rose dramatically. The company's low-overhead philosophy, which had kept its investment in technical and service areas low, meant that the company was not well prepared to cope effectively with the crisis of its defective disk drives. By the end of April 1988, EMC's results had started to show the impact of this situation, as earnings over the previous three months dropped from $5.8 million to $1 million, despite the fact that sales rose by 57 percent. This reflected the fact that EMC felt compelled to keep shipping the problem drives, even after difficulties with the product had been identified, in order to keep up with sales targets.

EMC, which had experienced smooth sailing up until this point, came in for criticism as a result of these problems. The company's investors claimed that they had been kept in the dark and not notified early enough by EMC management about problems with the disk drives. "The company is in the doghouse," one financial analyst told *Business Week,* as the price of EMC's stock plummeted to $7 per share, half the level it had been in the wake of the stock market crash of 1987. "Their engineering and technical support is something they always skimped on," a competitor observed in *Business Week.*

In response to the difficulty with its disk drives, EMC's management made a number of changes. The company located two additional suppliers for the defective part made by NEC, and it also tried to beef up its engineering division. Responding to criticism that the company had focused on sales to the detriment of quality, Egan admitted that EMC should have tested the drives more thoroughly before shipping them out. In June 1988, EMC announced that it would raise the price of its products by five to 15 percent, due to the cost of the computer chips they housed. In addition, EMC brought in a new president and chief executive officer, Michael Ruettgers. "We had some serious quality and service problems," this executive later told the *New York Times,* adding "We were overwhelmed."

As EMC attempted to respond to the problems its rapid growth had engendered, the company continued to augment its product line. In October 1988, EMC brought out a new magnetic disk subsystem for use in DEC VAX machines. One month later, the company also introduced a solid state disk drive for use in IBM 3080 and 3090 model computers.

Despite the contribution of these new products, EMC's disk drive problems continued to plague the company, causing EMC to report a net loss for 1988 of $7.82 million. In January 1989, EMC responded to its falling financial returns by cutting costs, as the company reduced its staff by one-third, letting 60 people go. This move was part of a larger shake-up directed by EMC management in the company's sales and engineering operations.

Two months later, EMC introduced another new product, in an effort to shore up its sales. The company's latest disk drive offering was designed to be used with computers manufactured by the Wang company. Four months later, the company made a large sale, signing an agreement with Storage Technology to supply $100 million worth of EMC's solid state memory storage subsystems for resale. These products were designed to be used with IBM-compatible machines.

In October 1989, EMC also announced plans to market a new generation of memory boards that relied on a larger chip. This effort was part of the company's overall strategy of moving into new markets, with a new class of products. By the end of 1991, EMC was able to report improved financial results, as the company returned to profitability, with earnings of $2.7 million.

During this time, EMC's efforts to roll out new products started to bear fruit, as it announced the introduction of a new IBM-compatible disk system based on a 24-gigabyte computer chip, that used RAID technology. RAID, which stood for "redundant arrays of inexpensive disks," used a large number of small, commonly manufactured disk drives, such as the hard drive found in many personal computers. These separate memory cells were linked by special software to provide fast, reliable storage of very large quantities of data. This type of storage system contrasted with the product of EMC's main competitor, IBM, which relied on a single, complex, expensive disk drive for computer memory. With its RAID technology, EMC entered the field that would provide the bulk of its growth in the first half of the 1990s.

As EMC began to roll out its new line of products, the company's financial fortunes continued their improvement. At the end of 1990, EMC reported sales up 30 percent from the previous year, to $171 million, yielding earnings of $18.2 million. "EMC was on a roller coaster in the 1980s," one analyst told the *New York Times,* noting that "They're a more mature company today."

With that maturity, however, came further legal troubles. In November 1990, EMC lost a court battle with Cambex, Egan's first firm, over trade secrets involving add-in computer memory upgrade boards for use in the IBM 3080 model line. The company was ordered to pay Cambex $2 million. One month later, in December 1990, EMC announced that it would appeal this verdict.

In addition, in March 1991, EMC and two other computer companies were sued by the IBM Credit Corporation, the branch of IBM that leased large computers. IBM charged that EMC had misappropriated IBM Credit property by removing original parts and replacing them with others when it upgraded computers rented by IBM leasing customers. When customers returned the computers they had rented from IBM, they did not contain the same parts they had when IBM sent them out. EMC maintained that the suit was simple harassment over a practice that had long been permitted.

EMC continued to roll out new products for use with IBM computers. In March 1991, the company announced that it would incorporate software made by the Midrange Performance Group that performed minicomputer analysis. One month later, EMC also began shipping a new subsystem based on the IBM 9336 midrange disk drive.

EMC then completed an agreement with Sun Data that allowed this company to resell EMC memory products to its IBM AS/400 clients. EMC also launched a tape storage unit with a plug that made it compatible with IBM computers. By the end of 1991, these efforts had succeeded in pushing EMC's revenues even higher, as the company notched sales of $232 million, a rise of 35 percent. From these sales, EMC earned $11 million. This also represented a significant jump in net income of 47 percent. In response to these results, the price of the company's stock began to rise as well.

These gains continued in 1992, as EMC completed a $44 million two-year contract with Unisys to sell its new disk drives. The company also completed an alliance with Cambex, its former rival, to license technology for enhancing mainframe computer memory.

Overall, EMC enjoyed a strong lead in the race to implement RAID technology. Although one other competitor had announced an intention to enter the field, glitches in its technology had held up the marketing of its product, and EMC was able to enjoy a virtual monopoly. This circumstance allowed the company to make significant progress in stealing market share from IBM, which dominated the mainframe data storage market. "We've been unplugging IBM mainframe storage and installing EMC, and the choice is almost a no-brainer," one EMC customer told the *New York Times.*

In May 1992, EMC became embroiled in another legal dispute, after IBM released a statement to the press attacking EMC. The company sued IBM and IBM Credit for libel in the press release. At the time, EMC also announced that it was seeking an advertising agency to launch a $1.5 million campaign promoting its products.

One of EMC's primary advantages in competing with IBM was the small size of its products. In some cases, EMC storage devices took up one-seventh of the space of an IBM machine of equivalent capacity. In addition, EMC's practice of designing its own software linking together the parts of its storage devices, while relying on easily purchased parts from other manufacturers for its hardware, gave the company great flexibility. As advances in technology took place, it was easy for EMC to incorporate new products into its offerings. "We're riding a performance curve that is moving exponentially," an EMC software designer explained to the *New York Times.*

In the fall of 1992, EMC announced a new generation of disk storage products, predicting that this advance would power a dramatic increase in its revenues. The company's Symmetrix 5500 model, like earlier models, relied on RAID technology to store information quickly and reliably, backing up all data on more than one disk. EMC's new technology offered a 60 percent greater capacity than previous systems. The Symmetrix unit was designed to cost from $865,000 to $2.8 million. EMC completed 1992 with another big gain in sales, as revenues rose to $385 million, and profits more than doubled to reach $29 million.

Two months after rolling out its new Symmetrix line, EMC announced that it had clinched a $10 million contract with Delta Air Lines to install a Symmetrix system. By June 1993, EMC had sold more than 2,000 units of the Symmetrix system. Although EMC's memory system was more expensive than an equally large system produced by IBM, it could enable mainframe computers to perform some functions twice as fast. "We have a two-year lead over IBM today," EMC's chief executive, Michael Ruettgers told *Business Week.*

In August 1993, EMC, flush with the revenues generated by enormous sales of its Symmetrix system, began to purchase other computer companies. EMC bought Epoch Systems, Inc., as well as the Magna Computer Corporation, for about $118 million. At the end of that year, EMC reported that its revenue had reached $782 million, as income more than tripled to $127 million. On the basis of these results, EMC entered the *Fortune* 500 rankings for the first time.

Early in 1994, EMC acquired another company, purchasing the assets of Array Technology from Tandem Computers. As revenues and earnings continued to grow at a breakneck speed, EMC predicted that its sales would top $1 billion by the end of the year. Despite its somewhat rocky past, EMC appeared to be well-situated to thrive in its highly competitive industry in the coming years of the 1990s.

Principal Subsidiaries: Copernique, S.A. (France); EMC Asset Acquisition Corporation; EMC Computer Storage Systems France; EMC Computer Storage Systems Ltd., (Hong Kong); EMC Computer Systems K.K. (Japan); EMC Computer Systems Ltd. (United Kingdom); EMC Computer-Systems Deutschland GmbH (Germany); EMC International Holdings, Inc.; EMC Securities Corporation; EMC System Peripherals Canada, Inc.; Epoch Systems, Inc.; Magna Computer Corporation.

Further Reading:

Helm, Leslie, "How a Hot Company Overheated," *Business Week,* May 23, 1988, p. 126.
Verity, John W., "The Midgets, the Mammoth, and the Mainframes," *Business Week,* June 7, 1993, p. 31.
Wilke, John R., "Little EMC Challenges Leader IBM in Data-Storage," *Wall Street Journal,* July 9, 1992.

—Elizabeth Rourke

Engraph, Inc.

2635 Century Parkway, N.E.
Atlanta, Georgia 30345
U.S.A.
(404) 329-0332
Fax: (404) 320-7460

Wholly Owned Subsidiary of Sonoco Products Company
Incorporated: 1936 as the Herald Press, Inc.
Employees: 1,530
Sales: $235.4 million
SIC: 2679 Converted Paper Products Not Elsewhere
    Classified

Engraph, Inc., an innovative packaging company that converts paper, paperboard, and plastics into packaging material, is considered one of the leaders in its field. In the 1990s, its clients included some of the best-known national brands, including Hershey, Kodak, Coca-Cola, Pepsi, Wrigley, and Johnson & Johnson. Long an independent company, Engraph was purchased by Sonoco Products Corporation in 1993.

Engraph's roots lie in the Herald Publishing Company, a Charlotte, North Carolina-based commercial printer that was founded on April 1, 1933, when John H. Jordan leased a failing printing company. It was incorporated on July 6, 1936 as the Herald Press, Inc. As future chief executive T. J. Norman related to the *Charlotte Press,* "The company never should have made it. . . . We had worn out, antiquated equipment. There were too many printers in Charlotte. And we were in the depths of a Depression." But two developments kept the company afloat, claimed Norman. In 1938 the company began to produce and market paper and die-cut paper labels that were used by bakeries, candy manufacturers, and the textile industry. Second, rules were established by the Food and Drug Administration that required labels on bakery and food products with the name of the manufacturer and the products' weight. An important early client was snack-food maker the Lance Company, which needed labels for its cellophane packages. "From Lance, we grew," Norman said.

While on a visit to New York during World War II, Norman observed a process by which cellophane was printed on directly. "I said if too many people discover this the label business is going to be hurt." So he borrowed money and created the Package Products Company, Inc., to print flexible packaging

materials. Norman headed Package Products, which was incorporated in June of 1945, while continuing to work at Herald Press. The company's first flexographic printing press was delivered in early 1946, and, by trial and error, the company learned to use it. Although Package Products and the Herald Press were separate entities, they remained closely allied; for example, in 1951 Package Products moved to an addition to a Herald Press facility.

On November 1, 1955, the two firms merged, and T. J. Norman headed the new company, which was called the Package Products Company, Inc. The Herald Press became a wholly owned subsidiary that served as the commercial printing and sales division. Their combined sales at that time were slightly over $3 million. In 1956 the company went public, and profits and production both rose in the coming decade. Between the year it went public and 1968, sales rose some 420 percent, from $2.38 million to $10 million. The company continued to upgrade its flexible printing operations, so that in 1962 the company could say that it was producing 84 percent more with three presses than it had with four presses in 1956. But the Herald Press was sold in 1964 to a local competitor as the company found it best to focus of printing.

By the mid-1960s, Package Products focussed on printing on flexible packaging (which meant printing on materials such as cellophane, aluminum foil, and other plastic films and papers on rolls, sheets, or bags for the customer); labels (which involved printing, die-cutting, and embossing of pressure-sensitive, adhesive-applied and other labels); and the board specialty business (which included printing, cutting, folding, and gluing cardboard containers). Company clients included Swift, Armour, Holsum, Cannon, Fieldcrest, Chiquita Banana, and Gilette. The company had sales offices throughout the southeastern United States.

Package Products soon began to grow through the aggressive acquisition of other packaging concerns. It bought the Atlanta-based Imperial Packaging Corporation in December of 1970. Next was the Colonial Press, Inc., in February of 1972; in July of that year Package Products Company became Colonial Packaging Corporation. Also in 1972 the company bought Bliskin Supply Company, a printer of paperboard products, and Standard Cap & Seal, Inc. The buying spree continued through 1973. An acquisition that would prove crucial to its future success was that of Screen Art, Inc., of Knoxville, Tennessee. With that purchase came Creative Screen Print, Inc. Both companies used silkscreen methods to transfer images.

The growing company decided to reorganize and create a management company to contain the various parts of the company, and on October 1, 1973, the name of the company was changed to Engraph, Inc. Engraph sold off Imperial Packaging in 1976 and Container-Kraft, Inc. in 1982, but purchased the Morrill Press, Inc., in 1984. T. J. Norman retired in 1981. Norman had started working for Herald Publishing in 1933 for $2 a week, when he had got a job there because he had come to know the printer while working as business manager of his high school newspaper. The year Norman left, sales had reached more than $52 million.

Norman was succeeded by Leo Benatar. Benatar, who had formerly been a president at Mead Packaging, decided that Engraph's future was in niche packaging. "We decided we weren't going to be packagers to America," Benatar told *Fortune*. "We decided to look at what we did well and determine where there were growth opportunities and where the markets were very fragmented." In a further effort to position itself as a national company, Engraph moved its headquarters to Atlanta in June of 1982. It was reincorporated in Delaware in May of 1987.

Engraph bought Screen Graphics, Inc., in October of 1987 and Rixie Paper Products Inc., in November of 1988. Colonial was sold in March 1988 after proving itself to be a disappointing acquisition. Soon thereafter, in January of 1989, Engraph bought the Patton division of Alford Industries, Inc., for $23 million in cash. Patton made pressure-sensitive labels and on-package coupons. This business would also blossom in importance to Engraph. Patton brought with it over $40 million in revenues and broadened Engraph's client base in the health care and personal care segments of the industry. In July of 1990, Engraph created a joint venture with Ramallo Bros. Printing, Inc.—called Ramallo, Escribano & Co.—in Puerto Rico, where a number of health care and pharmaceutical companies had opened operations to take advantages of tax incentives there.

In 1990, Engraph restructured its operations, working to lower its costs, decentralize operations, and provide a quicker response time to customer orders. It also sold Package Products-Flexible in 1991, the core around which Engraph had originally grown, because it did not gel with the niche approach. That unit "was the root of the tree, but it was draining the company and took too much of our management time," Benatar said. In February of 1991 Engraph bought Graphics Resources, and the next year it purchased Polaris Packaging. Despite the recession that affected many segments of the economy, business continued to grow at Engraph, which in 1992 raised $235.4 million in sales, the best year in its history and a 14 percent increase over the previous year. Its net income was $10.2 million, an increase of 28 percent. The company's stock, which traded on NASDAQ, had risen 25 percent in the previous decade, and its sales had grown steadily since 1978.

Engraph was oriented around four sectors of the market: flexible packaging, labels and package inserts, screen-process printing, and paperboard cartons and specialties. Flexible-packaging printing was handled by Morrill Press and printed packages for candy, gum, and cookies. By this time Engraph was the largest manufacturer of candy wrappers in the world. Labels and package inserts were produced by six units: Patton, Graphic Resources, Inc., Screen Graphics, Inc., Package Products Specialty, Polaris Packaging Inc., and Ramallo, Escribano & Co. These units made Engraph one of the largest makers of pressure-sensitive labels in the United States. Customers were the

cosmetics, health care, and personal care companies that used labels on shampoo, cough medicine, and bubble packages. One particularly successful technique was to label the "clear" products that were popular in the early 1990s, including soft drinks like Clearly Canadian, so that it appeared the label was painted on. Other specialty areas included point-of-purchase advertising material, decals, posters, and metal signs; particularly important were coupons, popular with cigarette makers. Labels for the health care and personal care market brought in almost 20 percent of revenue.

Engraph's screen process printing business was centered on Screen Art, which created graphics for beverage vending machines, fountain dispensers, and delivery trucks. Engraph became a leader in applying large, colorful graphics to the sides of beverage delivery trucks, which turned them into traveling billboards. Its vending machine business represented 80 percent of the market. By 1992 Engraph also supplied all graphics materials to Coke, Pepsi, Dr. Pepper, and Seven-Up for their fountain machines in fast-food retailers. Engraph's paperboard cartons and specialties units were Standard Cap & Seal, Rixie Paper Products, and Package Products Specialties. They produced items such as the paperboard caps used by hotels to cover glasses in their guest bathrooms; Engraph held over 90 percent of this market.

Engraph's impressive growth and strong market position made it a desirable property in the acquisition market in the 1990s. In September of 1993 the Sonoco Products Company, an industrial packaging manufacturer based in Hartsville, South Carolina, acquired Engraph for approximately $300 million. Sonoco's revenues in 1992 were $1.84 billion. Engraph then became a wholly owned subsidiary of Sonoco. Sonoco's purchase of Engraph was seen as an effort to strengthen its position in the consumer products packaging market. There was virtually no overlap in the product lines of the two companies. With Sonoco's clout, Engraph stood poised to enter the international marketplace, especially following the 1994 acquisitions of Mexico City-based Print Art (which then became Engraph Mexico, and the English firm M. Harland & Sons Limited. If Engraph proves as adept at capturing world market share as it has domestic, the future of the company should be very bright indeed.

Further Reading:

Leibowitz, David S., "In Good Company," *FW,* July 23, 1991, p. 66.
Schwartz, Jerry, "Sonoco Acquiring Engraph," *New York Times,* September 14, 1993.
Smith, Faye McDonald, "Engraph Packages Hefty Sales Gains," *Business Atlanta,* March 1993, p. 46.
Solo, Sally, "Engraph," *Fortune,* April 5, 1993, p. 97.
Stilley, Dick, "The Hard Way: Engraph's T. J. Norman Joined Printing Firm at $2 a Week," *Charlotte Observer,* August 23, 1981, p. 5B.

—C. L. Collins

Etablissements Economiques du Casino Guichard, Perrachon et Cie, S.C.A.

B.P. 306, 24, rue de la Montat
Saint-Etienne Cedex 2, F-42008
France
77 45 31 31
Fax: 77 21 85 15

Public Company
Incorporated: 1898 as Societe des Magasins du Casino
Employees: 45,326
Sales: FFr 72.52 billion ($12.67 billion)
Stock Exchanges: Bourse (Paris)
SICs: 2013 Sausages and Other Prepared Meat Products;
    2051 Bread and Other Bakery Products; 5400 Food Stores;
    5812 Eating Places; 6531 Real Estate Agents and
    Managers

Etablissements Economiques de Casino Guichard, Perrachon et Cie, S.C.A., generally called Groupe Casino or simply Casino, is the second largest food retailer in France. The company's network of about 2,325 Petit Casino convenience stores was the largest in France at the end of 1993. The company also owned or operated, by that date, 108 Geant Casino and Geant Rallye hypermarkets (retail stores that are larger than supermarkets and sell nonfood as well as food items), 518 Casino supermarkets, 224 cafeterias, and two production plants. In addition, Casino owned and operated plants that processed meat, bottled wine, and turned out pastries and other confectionery goods. Etablissements Economiques de Casino Guichard, Perrachon et Cie was the holding company for more than 40 subsidiary companies, the majority of which were wholly owned.

The Casino philosophy stressed quality rather than low price. "Casino is perceived as the highest in quality, and the second highest for overall customer satisfaction," according to its chairman and chief executive officer, Antoine Guichard. "We are not in the discount game, we are in the quality game." Recognizing its need to advance technologically, however, Casino forged links with Great Britain's Argyll Group PLC and the Netherlands' Koninklijke Ahold N.V. in what came to be called the European Retail Alliance.

The origins of the company date back to about 1860, when a grocery store was opened in Saint-Etienne, a city about 30 miles south of Lyon. It was named for the nearby Casino Lyrique, which had been closed in 1858 by the city fathers for "licentious spectacles." In 1864 the founder of Casino, a Monsieur Brechard, took as a partner Jean-Claude Perrachon, and the business became a general store. Perrachon's nephew Geoffroy Guichard later became partner of what became the Etablissements Guichard-Perrachon. In 1898 Guichard created the Societe des Magasins du Casino and opened a second store in Veauche, about 12 miles to the south. To stock the stores it was necessary to build a warehouse in Saint-Etienne.

The father of eight children, Guichard was a paternalistic employer, and the company continues to give out scholarships to the descendants of his workers. Guichard also sponsored the city's museum of modern art and its soccer team, traditions the company maintains. In addition, Casino became manager of Saint-Etienne's museum of arts and industry in 1967.

Casino became a joint-stock company in 1900. Armed with an infusion of funds, it grew rapidly from this point. By the outbreak of World War I there were 215 branches, of which 56 were in Saint-Etienne alone. In 1919 a new factory replaced the existing facilities for making chocolate, confectioneries, and preserves. By 1922 warehouses also were located in Clermont-Ferrand, Lyon, Roanne, and Beaucaire, the latter to store wine. A soap factory and oil works were built in Marseille, and a perfume plant was opened in Saint-Etienne in 1922. Two more warehouses, at Chalon-sur-Saone and Avignon, opened in 1923. In 1934 a vast warehouse was established in Marseille to serve the entire southeast of France.

On the eve of World War II Casino was by far the biggest holding company in southeastern France. Yet its greatest period of expansion was not to begin until 1960, when it opened its first supermarket in Grenoble. A warehouse for fresh produce was opened in Rhone a Grigny the following year. Its first cafeteria was introduced in Saint-Etienne in 1967. Casino entered the Paris region in 1970 by creating a subsidiary with the acronym SOMACA to operate the supermarkets of Saint-Denis and Bagneux. In the same year it absorbed a similar business in southwestern France, l'Epargne, into a new subsidiary named SABIM Sable.

Hypermarkets under the name Geant Casino were established during the early 1970s, first in Marseille, then in Saint-Etienne, Frejus, Montpellier, Bordeaux, and Nantes. The one in Saint-Etienne covered 10,842 square meters (116,702 square feet). In the early 1980s it had 45 different departments, 2,000 parking places, and a staff of 470, and was accompanied by an auto service station, a cafeteria, and a gallery of shops. Casino entered a new field in 1977 with the creation of S.A. CARFUEL, a subsidiary for the distribution of petroleum products. Between 1978 and 1980 Casino established SOMABRI, in collaboration with the Belgian group G.B., to operate hobby-and-garden centers. The one opened in Saint-Etienne in 1980 was offering 27,000 products two years later.

By 1981 Casino also had established the restaurant chains SARL, Stefany, and Caf'Casino and had taken a half-interest in another, France Quick. SABIM operated slaughterhouses in

Sable and Saint-Maixent. The industrial complex of Pont-de-l'Ane produced chocolates, confectioneries, and preserves, 85 percent for Casino's retail needs. There was a meatpacking plant at Saint-Priest and one for roasting meat at Marseille that not only satisfied Casino's needs but also exported products overseas. Three great bottling plants were located in Beaucaire, Lyon, and Clermont-Ferrand, and Casino began exporting 2 million bottles of wine a year to other European Community countries. SAIC was a building society managing thousands of dwellings. Finally, a fleet of trucks transported goods from Casino's 11 great warehouses.

Groupe Casino's presence in the United States dates from 1975, when it created Casino USA Inc. as a California-based subsidiary. By 1984 it was operating four Petit Casino retail stores and eight Cafe Casino French restaurants. In March 1984 Casino USA bought a controlling interest in Thriftimart Inc., owner of 86 Smart & Final Iris Co. cash-and-carry warehouses, for more than $15 million worth of Class B stock. Casino intended to use Thriftimart outlets to distribute its lines of jelly, jam, and bottled water. At the time of the deal, Smart & Final Iris specialized in discount volume sales of food and hardware for bulk buyers and restaurants. Eventually, the deal had to be sweetened to avoid a lawsuit, so in the end Casino paid $116.7 million to acquire the company's Class A nonvoting shares of common stock as well.

The French parent saw a 10 percent increase in turnover in 1983 to FFr 157.9 million ($17.5 million), but this was accompanied by a decline of 2 percent in consolidated profits. However, Casino continued pursuing an aggressive acquisition program and in 1985 bought an 88 percent share of CEDIS, owner of hypermarkets, supermarkets, and smaller grocery stores. The transaction supplemented Casino's already strong presence in southern France and the Paris metropolitan area with CEDIS's base in eastern France, and added CEDIS's FFr 9 billion (about $977 million) in annual sales to Casino's FFr 23.5 billion (about $2.55 billion). Later in the year Casino entered into a joint venture with a subsidiary of the giant French oil company ELF-Aquitaine to create service stations, supermarkets, and fast-food outlets.

In 1986 Casino expanded further by acquiring a 46 percent interest in Paridoc and Giant supermarkets and a 99 percent interest in Etablissements Deloche, a wholesaler. In that year Groupe Casino was France's third largest food-distribution company, behind Leclerc and Carrefour. Its holdings in France consisted of 42 hypermarkets (16 under the Mammouth name of CEDIS) and 187 supermarkets, under the Casino, Suma, and Ravi names. In addition, there were 92 Smart & Final warehouses in the United States.

The company's activities in 1986 also included processed foods (12 percent of total sales) and restaurants and cafeterias (6 percent). The latter sector consisted of the restaurant chain Hippopotamus and the cafeteria chains O'Kitch and Quick, making Casino the largest food chain in France in number of meals served. Casino then sold Quick in 1993. American operations constituted another 6 percent of the company's volume, with food distribution accounting for the other 76 percent. Food processing declined to only 3 percent of revenues by 1993, while American revenues increased to nearly 8 percent of the total.

Casino's acquisitions were part of the consolidation of the food industry taking place throughout France. The American-style hypermarket first made its appearance in France in 1963. By 1986 there were 645 of these giant stores, accounting for one-fourth of the food dollar. Hypermarkets also saw a 10 percent annual gain in sales volume, compared to 2 percent for the industry as a whole. The big distributors expanded vertically as well as horizontally by absorbing suppliers.

In 1989 Casino stock reached a price level it would not attain again during the next four difficult years. Antoine Guichard announced in July 1990 that company employment would be cut by 1,450 before the end of 1992. Guichard explained that the company was being undercut by independent rivals offering lower prices because of their lower operating costs. He said the company would respond by renovating and remodeling its stores, and reorganizing the hypermarkets, supermarkets, and smaller food stores into separate and autonomous divisions. A new marketing division would be concerned with consumer relations, price, and the purchase and securing of provisions.

To cut its costs Casino sold its 172 service stations in December 1990 to Shell France and Agip France for FFr 660 million (about $131 million). However, Casino would continue to manage the stations under a 30-year contract. This transaction apparently was made to enable Casino to reduce its debt, which had grown to FFr 4.2 billion (about $840 million) after it had acquired La Ruche Meridionale, a supermarket company, earlier in the year.

In May 1989 Casino signed initial cooperation accords with Argyll Group PLC, owner of Safeway food stores in Great Britain, and Koninklijke Ahold N.V. of the Netherlands to form a combine. The accord called for the three food retailers to issue new shares that would give Argyll a 3.8 percent share in Ahold and a 3.4 percent stake in Casino, with Ahold and Casino in turn acquiring 1.5 percent of Argyll. The result was the European Retail Alliance (ERA), on which Antoine Guichard planned to base the company's future growth strategy. Looking toward the European Economic Union of 1993, Casino also bought 39 percent of an important Italian retailer, La Rinascente, in 1989.

In a 1991 interview for *Supermarket News,* Guichard envisioned a new kind of Casino store, based on an Argyll prototype, that would cover 35,000 to 40,000 square feet—more than three times the size of the typical French supermarket, but smaller than the hypermarkets. "There are about 20 . . . cities where we could open about 200 or even 300 superstores," he said. "And these would be more food-oriented than the hypermarket format—maybe 20 percent nonfood, but with no textiles." Guichard said the company was also studying Ahold test-concept stores, equipped with state-of-the-art electronics.

Guichard acknowledged that Casino was "not considered modern by our customers" and said the company would invest heavily to increase productivity. Casino planned to exploit its membership in ERA, through technology sharing, in order to dramatically restructure its distribution system and in-store MIS operations. Guichard added that the largest task would be to overhaul Casino's warehouse network by studying Argyll's more advanced operations in this field. Greater productivity, Guichard indicated, would allow Casino to eliminate about 30 percent of its warehouse space. He also said the entire computer system in warehousing and distribution would be changed to allow computerized price controls and automatic reordering from store to warehouse or from warehouse to vendor.

"The plan is to have the identical system, the same programming, working in all three companies," Guichard continued. "You will see identical computer systems in the stores of all three ERA partners, and you will even see the same cash registers and scanners." The three companies were to increase common purchases of meat, produce, flowers, and other goods. Elements of the training programs of the three companies would be shared, with Casino embarking on a campaign to teach its employees English. Guichard added that the partners were planning to create a joint ERA label to be marketed throughout Europe.

Casino moved into second place among French food distributors by acquiring rival Rallye S.A. in 1992, in exchange for new Casino shares representing more than 30 percent of the new ensemble. In so doing it acquired the 44 hypermarkets and 196 supermarkets of this Breton distributor. As a result sales increased to FFr 61.6 billion ($11.25 billion) in 1992 from FFr 40.6 billion in 1991, but profits fell from FFr 484 million to FFr 438 million ($80 million). Like other retailers, Casino was affected by stagnant consumer spending during a national economic recession that year. Rallye appeared to be a drag on the parent organization, its hypermarket sales falling 6 percent during the first four months of 1994 (while Casino's rose by 4.7 percent) and its supermarket sales dropping by 8 to 9 percent (while Casino's rose by 1 percent).

Through its subsidiary Casino USA, Groupe Casino had majority control of Smart & Final Inc., which operated 136 Smart & Final warehouse stores in the United States at the end of 1993. The number was scheduled to reach 149 by the end of 1994. More than half were leased from Casino Realty, with most of the rest subleased from Casino Realty or Casino USA. Among Smart & Final subsidiaries were Casino Frozen Foods Inc. and Casino American Food Services Inc. Under a joint venture with the Mexican retailer Central Detallista it was also to operate a chain of supermarkets in the southwestern United States and in Tijuana, Mexico, using the name Smart & Final. Two had opened by mid 1994, with a third scheduled for opening by the end of the year.

In order to accumulate money to remodel its French stores, Casino put Smart & Final Inc. up for sale in July 1993. Its Casino USA subsidiary held a 50.3 percent stake in the food chain, with a market value of about $178 million. The parent concern decided later that year not to sell, however, because in the words of Smart & Final's chairman, "Groupe Casino is convinced the long-term value . . . is far in excess of the amount it might realize in the current weak market." During the first four months of 1994 Smart & Final's sales rose by 14 percent.

During 1993 Casino turnover rose 2.7 percent to reach FFr 72.52 billion ($12.67 billion). Net profits increased 2.9 percent, to FFr 453.6 million ($79.25 million). These disappointing returns, representing percentage increases lower than the inflation rate, were attributed to stiff competition by "hard-discounters" in a difficult economic climate. Capital spending was scheduled to fall to FFr 1.85 billion ($323 million) from FFr 2.19 billion. To counter price competition, Groupe Casino began experimenting in 1994 with a new discounting concept called *l'As des Prix* (The Ace of Prices) being tested in the Lyon region. If successful, it would be adopted in 1995 and 1996 by the Super Rallye stores.

Principal Subsidiaries: Casino France; Casino USA Inc.; Unimas; Gem; Paradis; Pribas; Sodipra; Bonmets; Bladen; TPLM; Gelalp; Cogin; Nica; Soreso; Cladevi.

Further Reading:

Dowdell, Stephen, "Casino's Big Gamble," *Supermarket News,* April 1, 1991, pp. 1, 10–11.
Doyere, Josee, "Un [caddie] nomme desir," *Le Monde,* February 21, 1987, pp. 4–6.
Gardes, Gilbert, editor, *La ville des Saint-Etienne,* Grand encyclopedie du Forez et des communes de la Loire, Le Coteau: Editions Horvath, 1984, pp. 273–275, 298–305.

—Robert Halasz

Ethan Allen Interiors, Inc.

Ethan Allen Drive
P.O. Box 1966
Danbury, Connecticut 06813-1966
U.S.A.
(203) 743-8000
Fax: (203) 743-8298

Public Company
Incorporated: 1932 as Baumritter Corp.
Employees: 5,000
Sales: $437 million
Stock Exchanges: New York
SICs: 2273 Carpets and Rugs; 2511 Wood Household
Furniture; 2512 Upholstered Wood Household Furniture;
5231 Paint, Glass and Wallpaper Stores; 5712 Furniture
Stores; 5713 Floor Covering Stores; 5719 Miscellaneous
Home Furnishing Stores

Ethan Allen, Interiors, Inc. is the holding company for Ethan Allen, Inc., which manufactures and retails quality home furnishings, offering a full range of furniture and decorative accessories through 291 Ethan Allen Galleries (including 24 abroad), of which 58 were owned by the company itself in 1995. Ethan Allen products are available only through these dealers. In the early 1990s, Ethan Allen was North America's second largest furniture retailer and its eighth largest furniture manufacturer. In an industry characterized as highly fragmented, Ethan Allen maintained a national presence by branding its products and retail stores with the same name. The company was also distinguished by its vertical integration of operations, overseeing the design, manufacture, distribution, display, and marketing of Ethan Allen furnishings.

The history of Ethan Allen may be traced to the 1930s. In 1932, The Baumritter Corp., a housewares sales agency, was founded by two New Yorkers, Theodore Baumritter and his brother-in-law, Nathan S. Ancell. The worst year of the Great Depression was hardly an auspicious time for such an undertaking, and at the end of the year the partners were in the red by $3,000—more than they had put into the firm. According to a 1965 *Home Furnishings Daily* article, people out of work and struggling to make ends meet had little thought for the plaster gnomes, trellises, and garden swings manufactured by Baumritter.

"Looking back, I suppose 1935 was our crucial year," Ancell told Earl Lifshey in the interview for *Home Furnishings Daily.* Ancell continued, "we had managed to survive the depths of the Depression and began to make a little headway. But I could see no real future for the kind of drop-shipment jobbing business in which we were engaged. We were nothing but a middleman. I concluded—and Ted agreed completely—that if we were going to build our destiny we would have to control all the elements with which we were working."

Thus, in 1936, the partners bought a furniture factory, a bankrupt plant in Beecher Falls, Vermont, which a federal agency sold to them for $25,000. Ancell and Baumritter didn't realize at the time that the factory's machinery dated from 1917 and was belt-driven. Nevertheless, it wasn't long, Ancell continued, "before we fell hopelessly in love with Vermont and with what New England represents historically" and the partners remained committed to the idea of furniture manufacturing. Recognizing the market potential for Early American furniture, a style largely untapped in the industry, the partners put together a group of 28 pieces of Early American furniture, naming it for Ethan Allen, whose Green Mountain Boys fought to make Vermont the nation's fourteenth state. The furniture was first unveiled in 1939, but only to selected buyers who would be willing to display it properly in stores. This marked the beginning of the company's exclusive franchise policy.

Through their experiences, Ancell and Baumritter found that the typical furniture wholesale buyer focused primarily on price, while the typical customers, at the time, women, were more concerned with decorating techniques and customer service than price. The solution, they believed, was to offer correlated groupings of classic furniture from which a woman could select the specific pieces to solve her particular furnishing problem. Within the company's Early American decorating scheme, the customer could add to her furnishings and complete a room not just in a matter of months or a year, but several years later if she chose. By the mid-1960s, the Baumritter Corp. had a 1,600-piece line of Ethan Allen traditional Early American furniture: the biggest single group, by a very wide margin, of furniture made by any manufacturer in the world.

For Ancell, the company was selling "thoughts," not "things," an "environment—not furniture." He told Lifshey, "in this business we are dealing primarily with a series of very emotional products that are purchased and used in a very emotional manner primarily by the female of the species." Referring to the home as "the cornerstone and the hallmark of our civilization," Ancell suggested the female buyer looked for "protectiveness, for warmth, for orderliness" in her furnishings, and "it's at that point that she must have some place to go and some people with whom she can confidently talk and rely upon to safely guide and assist her in doing the job herself."

The policy of Baumritter Corp. was to reinvest every dollar of profit into the enterprise. By 1962 the company had 14 furniture factories in the East, and that year it acquired Kling Factories, Inc., which owned three furniture-making plants near Jamestown, New York. The Kling Colonial group of about 350 pieces and Viko line of about 150 steel-furniture pieces supplemented the Ethan Allen line. In addition to furniture, the company made lamps, painted wooden accessories, and decorative wall hangings.

By the mid-1960s there were around 700 Ethan Allen dealers in the United States, with others in Canada, Australia, France, Belgium, the Netherlands, and Switzerland. Baumritter management invoked a careful selection process before licensing a dealer for their furnishings. Potential store sites were carefully researched for sufficient levels of population, retail activity, average-income levels, and upper-income levels, and the prospective area would be studied not only on the ground but from the air. A dealer would be selected on the basis not only of financial considerations but understanding of the Ethan Allen program and willingness to dedicate himself to it. If selected, dealers then owned and operated the store themselves. The average store size at the time was 16,000 square feet, and about one-quarter of the dealers were accounting for three-quarters of sales volume.

In 1970 the company acquired the Volckman Furniture Manufacturing Co. of Morrison, Illinois, through an exchange of stock. This purchase added to the production of Ethan Allen upholstered living room furniture. Also in that year Ancell, the company's president, became chairperson, replacing Baumritter, who retired. In early 1972 the Baumritter Corp. changed its name to Ethan Allen Industries and moved its headquarters from New York City to Danbury, Connecticut.

That year, Ethan Allen began supplementing (and eventually phasing out) its regular franchised dealers with a network of 200 owner-managers of "showcase galleries." These outlets, concentrated in shopping centers of well-heeled suburban areas, were producing 72 percent of total sales volume, which rose to $70 million in 1971 from $43 million in 1965. The owner-managers invested $65,000 to $125,000 to build the stores but were not required to sign contracts with Ethan Allen or pay franchise fees and owned their inventory, unlike regular franchised dealers. By 1982 there were some 350 such galleries in the United States, of which 20 were owned by Ethan Allen itself.

In June 1972 Ancell announced plans to expand into furniture styles other than Early American, as well as into producing broadloom carpeting, oriental rugs, wallpaper, and draperies. Also during this time, the company, which had launched its first national print advertising campaign around 1951, developed its first series of nationwide television ads.

In 1979 Ethan Allen agreed to be acquired by Interco Inc., a St. Louis-based conglomerate. The transaction, which called for an exchange of stock originally valued at about $130 million and later at $150 million, was completed in 1980, with Ethan Allen continuing as an Interco subsidiary headed by Ancell. Over the next eight years annual sales grew from $230 million to $600 million.

Ancell was succeeded as president in 1985 and as chair and chief executive in 1988 by M. Farooq Kathwari, who had formed a joint venture with Ethan Allen to develop products in 1973 and had joined the company as a vice-president in 1980. Under Kathwari, Ethan Allen, Inc. became independent again, when a management group headed by Kathwari purchased the company from Interco for about $385 million in a leveraged

buyout in 1989. Ethan Allen was made a wholly owned subsidiary under a company incorporated as the Green Mountain Holding Corp., which would become Ethan Allen Interiors, Inc. in the early 1990s. Ethan Allen Interiors then went public, completing its first public offering in March 1993 by raising $156.9 million through the sale of common stock. A secondary public offering completed in November 1993 raised nearly $40 million. In July 1994, J.K. Castle controlled 11.9 percent of Ethan Allen's common stock, and Kathwari held 10.5 percent. Long-term debt came to $144.5 million.

The dynamic Kathwari was quick to change the direction of the company. At the time, the Ethan Allen network included over 100 retailers across the United States, and little consistency was maintained in store projection, interior display, merchandise mix, and advertising. Kathwari worked quickly to change that, coordinating efforts to ensure that the entrepreneurs invested in new product programs, storefront renovations, and advertising techniques.

Kathwari also focused on innovating Ethan Allen's product line. In a 1991 *New York Times* interview, he declared, "sixty percent of our individual items were created in the last two years. We started that process six years ago, when our research showed us that consumers no longer were buying Early American furniture as their predominant style." The new styles included American Impressions, introduced in 1991, which included straight-line pieces made of solid cherry inspired by Shaker furniture and the designs of Frank Lloyd Wright. This line soon became the fastest growing new product in the company's history.

A second contemporary line, American Dimensions, was introduced in 1992, accenting geometric shapes. After that came Country Crossings, featuring rustic-looking maple furniture; Legacy, based on Italian architecture styles; and the ultra-contemporary Radius, offering sleek styles recalling those of the 1960s. In addition, a choice of 2,000 fabrics was offered for upholstery. Seventy percent of the company's 1994 furniture revenues were expected to come from the new styles launched since 1991.

Perhaps more notably, Ethan Allen was transformed from strictly a furniture retailer into a total home furnishings source, offering textiles, wall decor, bedding, lamps, and other decorative items to its customers.

In addition, two factories were closed, others were retooled for new styles, and plants were added to produce such home furnishings as pillows, bedspreads, mirrors, and clocks. Quality control was improved and the company's 300 delivery vans were replaced by larger, less fuel-thirsty vehicles. Moreover, annual week-long courses for salespersons were given at "Ethan Allen College," established at company headquarters. And Kathwari cracked down on its dealers, many of whom had not been observing the requirement to sell Ethan Allen products exclusively.

An aggressive advertising campaign was launched in the fall of 1991 to attract younger customers conditioned to think of Ethan Allen as the choice of their parents. By mid-1992 only one-eighth of displayed Ethan Allen furniture was Early American. Classical yet contemporary storefronts began to replace the familiar white-column facades. Prices fell, with queen-size beds, for example, dropping from an average price of $1,000 to $700 or $800. The new approach was apparently paying off; in 1993 sales grew by 9.5 percent, and between July 1993 and April 1994 sales were up 20 percent in stores open a year or more. Moreover, for fiscal 1994, the company's net sales rose 13.8 percent to reach $437 million.

A new advertising campaign for 1994 featured nationwide television commercials with the theme ''Everyone's at home with Ethan Allen.'' In an interview, the company's vice-president of advertising remarked, ''The tag line invites a broader group of consumers to respond to our advertising, from older, empty-nesters to young people starting out. It says, 'Find your place within our spectrum of styles and price points'.'' The TV spots were to be supplemented with print ads and radio commercials featuring consumers varying widely in life styles and attitudes. A concurrent $45 million marketing program included a new logo, advertising, direct mail, merchandising, store displays, and signs. The target market was people between 25 and 54 with household incomes over $35,000.

These moves would, in part, help combat the heavy load of debt the company assumed in becoming an independent, which resulted in four years of red ink. In going public, Ethan Allen offered 48 percent of the common stock at $18 a share. By February 1994 the company's common stock was selling at $32 a share, but it had dipped as low as $19.50 during the year. At the close of 1994 the company turned its credit-card operations over to GE Capital Corp. under a long-term agreement.

In 1993 Ethan Allen owned 20 manufacturing plants, an assembly plant, three sawmills, eight distribution warehouses, and two home delivery centers. Ninety-two percent of its products were built in its own factories. The company offered a full range of home furnishings in what it considered the four most important style categories of the 1990s: formal, American country, casual contemporary, and classic elegance. Each collection included case goods such as bedroom and dining room furniture, upholstered furniture, and such accessories as carpeting, draperies, and lamps. A choice of 2,000 fabrics was available for upholstered furniture.

Principal Subsidiaries: Ethan Allen, Inc.

Further Reading:

Barmash, Isadore, ''New Lines and New Life for Furniture Maker,'' *New York Times,* October 6, 1991.
Elliott, Stuart, ''Advertising,'' *New York Times,* January 10, 1994, p. D7.
''Ethan Allen Breaks with Tradition,'' *Business Week,* June 10, 1972, p. 22.
''Ethan Allen Tries to Shed Its Colonial Past,'' *New York Times,* November 28, 1992, pp. 33, 41.
Lifshey, Earl, *The Baumritter Story,* New York: Baumritter Corp., 1965.
Marcial, Gene G., ''Fresh Looks and New Fans for Ethan Allen, *Business Week,* August 2, 1993, p. 78.
Power, William, ''Ethan Allen Sets Table in Bid to Slash Debt,'' *Wall Street Journal,* January 29, 1993, p. C2.
Roush, Chris, ''Rearranging the Furniture at Ethan Allen,'' *Business Week,* July 11, 1994, p. 102.
Singer, Penny, ''The Changing Face of Furniture Making,'' *New York Times,* November 6, 1994.
Stangenes, Sharon, ''A Revolutionary Look,'' *Chicago Tribune,* July 26, 1992, Sec. 15, p. 3.
''Tradition with a Twist,'' *Sales and Marketing Management,* April 1994, p. 24.

—Robert Halasz

The Eureka Company

1201 E. Bell Street
Bloomington, Illinois
U.S.A.
(309) 828-2367
Fax: (309) 823-5203

Division of Electrolux AB
Incorporated: 1910
Employees: 2,150
Sales: $390 million
SICs: 3635 Household Vacuum Cleaners

The Eureka Company is one of the oldest names in the vacuum cleaner industry and is widely acknowledged as one of its leaders, second to the Hoover Company since both companies were launched early in the twentieth century. Founded in 1909, Eureka was purchased in its 65th year by the Swedish company Electrolux AB and became a division of that company.

In 1909, real estate auctioneer Fred Wardell of Detroit, Michigan, acquired several patents for emerging vacuum cleaner technology and started up the Eureka Company. In 1910 he incorporated the company in Michigan. By 1913 Eureka's cleaners came in six different models with a multitude of attachments for walls, upholstery, and bare floors. The cleaners were sold to the public through two distributors, one handling accounts to the east of an imaginary line through Detroit, and the other handling accounts to the west.

From its headquarters in a 3.5-acre factory in downtown Detroit, Eureka manufactured 2,000 vacuum cleaners a day by 1919. Demand for the cleaners grew through the 1920s. Eureka advertised its cleaners nationally, and the company relied on an army of door-to-door salesmen who pitched the product's usefulness and efficiency to housewives throughout the country. Wardell was a fiery motivator who used tactics like betting his salesmen $2,000 to their $10 that they couldn't beat their quotas. Selling products this way was expensive—because of the cost of commissions ($22 on an $80 machine), the thousands of units tied up as demonstrators, and the fact that salesmen sometimes disappeared with customer's deposits or machines—but the ever-growing demand appeared to justify the cost. At times Eureka employed more than 3,000 door-to-door salesmen.

Eureka also used other modes of distribution. The company leased space in retail outlets but used its own salesmen to sell its cleaners, although customers were generally unaware that the salesmen represented Eureka and did not work for the retailer. The company also sold its products at utility-company retail outlets, which at that time sold a number of electric appliances. By the mid-1920s, Eureka held approximately one-third of the vacuum cleaner market. From 1919 through 1929, new sales averaged $7.88 million, and net profits averaged $1.09 million.

The Depression soon dampened Eureka's enthusiasm for its costly sales force. Like other companies, Eureka retreated from its dependence on door-to-door salesmen (who averaged 20 calls before they made one sale), and shifted its emphasis from selling *through* retailers to selling *to* them. From 1933 to 1936, sales averaged $2.68 million and profits were $251,000. Its expensive distribution system, unsuccessful new product introductions (Eureka also came out with a portable range, which flopped), and outdated factory exacerbated the effects of the collapse of consumer buying during the Depression. By 1937, the company was in the red, and from 1937 to 1939 its annual losses averaged $199,000.

Although the quality of Eureka cleaners was still respected, the company was floundering and Wardell had admittedly lost enthusiasm for running it. He persuaded Henry Burritt, the chief of sales for Nash-Kelvinator (the manufacturer of Kelvinator refrigerators), to take charge of the company. In 1939, Burritt took over and set about reorganizing Eureka's distribution system, shaking up top management, and redesigning the vacuum cleaner. In 1940, the company discontinued its use of door-to-door salesmen. Nevertheless, losses continued, with a $500,000 loss on almost $5 million in sales in 1941. Vacuum cleaners sales had fallen to about seven percent of the industry total.

From 1942 until the end of World War II, Eureka's factory produced only war materiel. During the war years Burritt and his managers focussed on how to take advantage of the surge in consumer spending that was expected to follow the war. The company decided to diversify its offerings of consumer appliances and decentralize operations. Burritt hoped to merge with another manufacturer whose products, distribution system, and production facilities would complement those of Eureka. Burritt was also eager to evacuate Eureka's outdated factory—and Detroit—because of what one vice-president called ''the contamination of the Detroit labor area,'' meaning the highly unionized workforce in that city. Also, a superhighway was set to be built through the center of Detroit and the middle of Eureka's plant. Burritt looked at dozens of the most obvious prospects, mainly manufacturers of other household appliances like refrigerators, but none were interested. He finally settled on Williams Oil-O-Matic Heating Corporation, a manufacturer of oil burners based in Bloomington, Illinois.

Oil-O-Matic had been founded by Walter W. Williams in 1918. Scarce coal supplies during World War I spurred Williams to invent—in his garage—a new type of oil burner, one that was designed to use crude oil or even used crank-case oil (as opposed to the water-white kerosene that was most often used). Oil-O-Matic had gone on to manufacture refrigerators (introduced in 1928), water heaters, and air conditioners (the Air-O-Matic came out on 1933). Before the war, the company could turn out 40,000 oil burners and 50,000 refrigerators annually. From 1942 through the end of the war, its plant made only products for the war, including parts for B-29 bombers and C-47 transport planes, and an automatic fire-control device. By 1945, Oil-O-Matic was not faring well; Williams had grown uninterested in his company and the company's stock, which once stood at $30 a share, was now selling for $7 a share.

In 1945, Eureka issued $1.76 million worth of common stock and used the proceeds to purchase 245,000 shares of Williams stock from Walter Williams for $1.39 million; the remaining 185,000 shares of Williams's stock were traded for Eureka common stock two-for one. Burritt, who knew nothing about oil burners, made it a condition of the merger that Williams's president, W. A. Matheson, would stay to run that division. The new Eureka-Williams Company came into existence June 4, 1945. The company used the $500,000 it had received in compensation for the condemnation of its Detroit plant to move to Bloomington, which was considered to have a much more "favorable" labor market than Detroit.

By 1946, the company was distributing its vacuum cleaners through 5,500 dealers, with 55 distributors, 12 of them company owned. By 1947, those numbers had increased to 8,500 dealers and 9,000 retailers. Burritt began to spend heavily on national advertising, a practice that had lapsed in the 1930s. The company had a net worth of over $6 million that year. In the fiscal year ending June 1947, sales totaled $21 million, with profits of $1 million. Oil burners accounted for approximately one third of sales and profits; however, there was almost no overlap in the production and distribution of the merged companies. In an attempt to broaden its array of consumer goods and enlarge its distribution network, Eureka-Williams bought the Chicago-based National Stamping & Electric Works in 1946 for $640,000. The company made electric toasters, irons, and other appliances under the "White Cross" label, with sales of $500,000 a year. The following year, it came out with a line of electric disposal units, the Dispos-O-Matic.

Even with wider distribution and national advertising, Eureka consistently ran behind Hoover. In vacuum cleaner circles a battle raged between the proponents of the canister-type cleaner and the upright models. Eureka sidestepped the issue by selling both, and an assortment of attachments, in the "Eureka Home Cleaning System," which in 1947 sold for the hefty sum of $144.95. This gimmick allowed Eureka to sell two cleaners per sale instead of one.

The problematic marriage of an oil-burner business with a vacuum cleaner company became more apparent over time. In 1952, oil-burner production was shifted to Sweden, where the product had been distributed for over 20 years. Burritt cited increased demand and high Swedish tariffs as reasons for this idiosyncratic move.

In 1953, Eureka-Williams was purchased by Henney Motor Company. Henney, based in Freeport, Illinois, was controlled by principal stockholder C. Russell Feldmann. The deal was reported to be worth $4 million, with Feldmann laying down only about $400,000 in cash while assuming Eureka-Williams' obligations. Eureka-Williams became a division of the Henney Motor Company.

Eureka celebrated its 50th anniversary year in 1959, the year in which Feldmann announced his intention to merge Eureka-Williams with National Union Electric Corporation, a heating and air-conditioning manufacturer of which Feldmann was both chairman and president. At the time of the merger Eureka-Williams was described as manufacturing vacuum cleaners, oil burners, school furniture, aircraft generators, hydraulic motors, starters and inverters, and thermal batteries at plants in Bloomington and Canastota, New York. Feldmann took Eureka private and it became a division of National Union.

Eureka-Williams fared well with National Union, playing the part of the steady and conservative manufacturer in a rather idiosyncratic company. Feldmann, an avid inventor and golfer, grew intrigued with the idea of an electric automobile and hatched a plan to build and market the cars through utility companies just like other electrical products. The car, whose top speed was 35 miles per hour, sold for $3,500. But of the one hundred cars manufactured, only 47 were sold. By 1971, Eureka-Williams accounted for 40 to 50 percent of National Union's sales and profits, and National Union reported that vacuum cleaner volume had climbed for the 12th consecutive year.

In June of 1974, Electrolux AB, the Swedish vacuum cleaner manufacturer, announced its bid for National Union. Electrolux had been unable to use its name in the United States since 1968 (when it sold its American Electrolux Co. subsidiary to Consolidated Foods Co.), and it was looking to re-enter the lucrative American market. National Union supported Electrolux's takeover of Eureka-Williams, whose name was changed backed to the Eureka Company.

Eureka's 75th anniversary year, 1984, was said by the company to be its best sales year ever. Eureka reported that sales had increased 211 percent over the previous decade, five times faster than the industry average. But the company continued to trail Hoover. In an attempt to cut production costs, Eureka began to move vacuum-cleaner production out of Bloomington, opening a plant to make uprights in El Paso, Texas, in 1983, and another in Juarez, Mexico, in 1984. In 1989, a major reorganization effort saw hundreds of employees laid off at its Bloomington facilities as recession rippled through the economy. In 1990, Eureka announced that it was moving production of upright cleaners completely to El Paso. The manufacture and assembly of canisters were consequently consolidated at its plant at Normal, Illinois, while headquarters and other manufacturing operations remained at Bloomington. Eureka reported that it spent $2.2 million restructuring its plants in Illinois.

In 1991 Eureka saw a loss in market share, especially to the third-place Royal brand. Some industry sources quoted in *HFD* blamed the drop on the company's late entry into the attached-tool upright market, which at that time held about 40 percent if the market. That experience prompted yet another round of reassignments, a visit from an executive at Electrolux to help streamline production, and another reorganization. Eureka seemed determined to take a more aggressive and proactive attitude toward product introduction and advertising, expanding its national advertising revenue by 300 percent. It also lowered prices.

An example of Eureka's efforts to create innovative products was the introduction of the Corvette Vac in 1993, a hand-held vacuum whose styling was designed to match that of the sports car. The Corvette name, on license from General Motors Corporation, was used to lure car owners who would be attracted to cleaning their car with it. The product was instantly successful. Eureka also introduced items at the high-end of the market to fill all categories of the home-cleaning market. Examples were wet/dry vacuums and rechargeable units.

By the mid-1990s, Eureka held steady at its perennial number two position in the vacuum cleaner market, but had rebounded from losses in market share in the early 1990s. The company claimed its highest sales ever in 1993. Eureka held about 20 percent of the $600-million full-sized cleaner market, as compared with Hoover's 35 percent. The company manufactured more than 100 different models of vacuum cleaners, for home as well as commercial use.

Further Reading:

"AB Electrolux Bid for National Union Nets 91 Percent of Shares," *Wall Street Journal,* July 2, 1974, p. 13.

"Another Merger," *Business Week,* May 19, 1945, p. 57.

"Board Backs Merger of Eureka Williams, National Union Electric," *Wall Street Journal,* May 9, 1960, p. 18.

"Canister, Upright, and Stick," *Barron's,* December 27, 1971, p. 11.

"Electrolux Plans Bid for National Electric," *Wall Street Journal,* June 20, 1974, p. 3.

"Eureka Celebrates 75," *Appliance,* April 1984, p. 9.

"Eureka Realigning Operations in Ill.," *HFD,* May 20, 1991, p. 86.

"Eureka Reinstates the Dealers," *Business Week,* August 31, 1946, p. 42.

"Eureka Takes 'Aggressive' Approach," *HFD,* January 10, 1994, p. 84.

"Eureka Williams," *Fortune,* December 1947, pp. 108–113.

"Financier Feldmann Sparks National Union," *Investor's Reader,* December 7, 1966, p. 18.

"Here's How to Increase Your Off-Peak Loads," *Electrical Merchandising Week,* March 28, 1960, p. 7.

"Holders Vote Sale of Eureka-Williams," *New York Times,* December 24, 1953, p. 21.

"To Make Oil Burners in Sweden," *New York Times,* April 8, 1952, p. 45.

Nellett, Michelle, "Going for Gold: Eureka Pursues Leadership Role with People-Driven, Product-Oriented Philosophy," *HFD,* October 10, 1994, p. 50.

"Small Electric Car Is Marketed," *Edison Electric Institute Bulletin,* April 1960, p. 123.

Troy, Terry, "Standing Upright: Eureka Prepares to Seize Back Lost Market Share with Attached-Tool Upright Vacuum Cleaner and New Marketing Strategy," *HFD,* January 13, 1993, p. 73.

—C. L. Collins

Exabyte Corporation

1685 38th Street
Boulder, Colorado 80301
U.S.A.
(303) 442-4333
Fax: (303) 442-4269

Public Company
Incorporated: 1985
Employees: 1,242
Sales: $382 million
Stock Exchanges: NASDAQ
SICs: 3572 Computer Storage Devices

Exabyte Corporation designs, develops, produces and sells tape subsystems for data storage applications. The company primarily makes a full range of eight-millimeter, four-millimeter, and quarter-inch minicartridge tape drives and tape libraries, as well data cartridges and media supplies. Exabyte also provides worldwide service and support for its full line of products. These products provide reliable compact data storage for discreet but fast growing segments of the computer industry, including mid-range systems, networks, workstations, and personal computers. Exabyte's products offer a range of storage applications for data acquisition and interchange, data and software distribution, automated storage management, and archiving.

In 1985, Exabyte was founded by Kelly Beavers, Juan Rodriguez and Harry Hinz, a camera buff who saw the possibilities of turning camcorder technology into an ultrafast, high-capacity data storage medium. Rodriguez had 20 years of computer experience at IBM and then as co-founder of Storage Technology, a producer of disk drives. Hinz and Beavers were fellow Storage Technology employees. The founders initially sought to produce and sell high-capacity, self-operating, eight-millimeter tape drives for use as data backups for mid-range computers. Before the creation of Exabyte, producing backup data was a laborious process, requiring the use of conventional tape technology and the presence of operators tediously changing reels or cartridges as they slowly filled with data. This process could take hours, sometimes days. With Exabyte's innovation, backup operations could be performed quickly and without the presence of manual operators. The company's success relied primarily on

the quickly changing computer industry and the increasing need to manage, store, and retrieve vast amounts of essential data.

The innovation of high speed backup systems was a relatively recent phenomenon. Early computers were designed for calculating rather than for storing and managing data, which was largely done on punch cards. Rapid advancements in computers rendered these machines obsolete, giving way to workstations, minicomputers, networks of personal computers, and supercomputers used for a host of academic, commercial, and scientific purposes. Central to these advancements were rapid innovations in the microprocessor, governing the speed and power of computer systems. Equally important were advancements in the ability of computers to collect, store, and retrieve huge quantities of data. The phenomenal growth in storage capacity, usually in the form of nonremovable disks, created a parallel need for efficient backup systems in case of data loss. While computer manufacturers had considerably increased disk drive capacities, innovations in tape backup systems lagged far behind. Exabyte was originally conceived for this purpose.

Exabyte's beginnings were not without difficulty. Rodriguez's reported run-ins with venture capitalists over product marketing, after only six months of testing the technology, almost torpedoed the company's chances. When the venture capitalists withdrew their backing, Exabyte had to fire all 11 of its employees. Enough local investors came forward, however, for the company to rehire them. After overcoming these obstacles, Exabyte's early success relied mostly on forging strategic partnerships to gain additional capital and manufacturing expertise. In 1986, the Japanese giant Sony Corp. agreed to produce mechanisms for the tape drives. Other agreements with Japan's Kubota to make tape drives and Solectron of Silicon Valley to produce circuit boards permitted Exabyte to limit its manufacturing role to final assembly, testing, and customization. The 1987 partnership with Kubota also brought in a large cash infusion which considerably boosted Exabyte's cash flow.

With the backing of these partnerships, Exabyte introduced in 1987 the EXB-8200 eight-millimeter tape drive to support minicomputers and networks of personal computers. The tape backup system packed 2.3 gigabytes of data onto a videocassette and sold for $2,055. As anticipated, the tape drive was self-operating and represented a breakthrough in adapting consumer video recording technology to the storage of computer data. Applying helical scan recording technology, which had been used in video products for 30 years, Exabyte produced a compact, relatively inexpensive eight-millimeter tape cartridge drive which could hold unprecedented amounts of data. Unlike other backup systems at the time, the tapes could also be conveniently removed and stored in a vault. The EXB-8200 was the world's first "eight-millimeter helical scan computer storage subsystem," reducing considerably both the labor and media cost for saving backup data. The product was also designed for other conventional data processing uses, including data acquisition, software distribution, archiving, and data interchange. In the realm of data acquisition, the EXB-8200 could record and archive seismic, satellite, telemetry and other scientific information. It also proved useful for medical and other imaging systems. In contrast to conventional tape drive technology, Exabyte's helical scan device employed relatively slow-moving tape using heads mounted on a rapidly rotating drum.

This method offered several advantages contributing to high recording density. The need for "tight tolerance" was considerably reduced as the tape drive used only one or two short tracks at a time, rather than multiple, lengthier tracks found in conventional parallel track recording. This method meant that recording tracks could be run closer together. In addition, the helical scan technology permitted the tape to run at a slower rate producing far less stress on the tape. In turn, less stress meant that thinner metal particle tape could be used to record at high densities.

In 1987, Peter Behrendt joined Exabyte as president, after more than 26 years at IBM, where, along with other positions, he directed its worldwide electric typewriter business and international marketing strategy for storage products. When Behrendt arrived at Exabyte, the company employed just 50 people and had sold only 69 tape drives worth $170,000. With Behrendt, sales tripled to $89 million in 1989 and then increased to $287 million in 1992, making Exabyte one of *Fortune* magazine's 100 fastest growing companies in America. In 1991, Behrendt became CEO. He then succeeded co-founder Juan Rodriguez as chairperson, after Rodriguez left in January 1992.

Several months later, in September 1992, eight complaints were filed against Exabyte in the U.S. District Court for Colorado, alleging that top officials hyped Exabyte's earnings potential in order to sell off large blocks of personal stockholdings before having to release bad news. The complaints came immediately after a 38 percent one-day drop in Exabyte's stock price following news that its 1992 third-quarter earnings would fall far below analysts' predictions. On January 21, 1993, the plaintiffs filed a consolidated amended complaint alleging primarily the same action. The District Court dismissed the consolidated complaint, however, after the plaintiffs failed to establish an actionable claim.

In 1990, Exabyte introduced the EXB-8500, the first in a series of second generation eight-millimeter tape subsystems, which included improved data recording capabilities, storage capacity, and retrieval and transfer speed. Exabyte produced its family of eight-millimeter drive subsystems with capacities ranging from 2.5 to ten gigabytes largely for the high end of the market. The products accounted for approximately 80 percent of total revenue from 1991 through 1993. In 1994, the company also introduced the Mammoth eight-millimeter cartridge tape subsystem, the industry's fastest, highest capacity tape drive. When shipped, the product would offer a major technological leap forward with a storage capacity of 20 gigabytes.

In addition, starting in 1992, Exabyte began a series of strategic acquisitions to move from focusing exclusively on eight-millimeter data storage products to providing a full range of eight-millimeter, four-millimeter, and quarter-inch tape solutions. In 1992, it entered the low to mid-range tape system market with the acquisition of R-Byte, a producer of four-millimeter cartridge subsystem tape products. In 1993, Exabyte purchased the Mass Storage Division of Everex Systems, Inc. which designed and produced quarter-inch minicartridge subsystems for the low-end and mid-range network and high-end personal computer market. The company then bolstered its position in the eight-millimeter market through the 1994 acquisition of German-based Grundig Data Scanner GmbH, adding helical-scan

tape component research and manufacturing capabilities. The production and distribution of automated tape libraries made Exabyte the leading supplier of this product in the world.

These strategic acquisitions considerably enhanced Exabyte's share of the tape drive market. In 1993 alone, the company announced nine new products spanning three tape drive technologies, as well as automated tape libraries. Between 1987 and 1993, the company's work force went from just 50 to more than 1,000. Moreover, Exabyte had also installed approximately 650,000 eight-millimeter tape drives throughout the world worth more than $1 billion. From a product line of one eight-millimeter tape drive subsystem with 2.5 gigabytes, by 1994 Exabyte was producing more than 30 distinct products in the eight- and four-millimeter, and quarter-inch formats, as well as library products that automatically stored between 50 gigabytes and 3.2 terabytes of data, a huge jump in storage capacity.

Exabyte's full range of products proved remarkably efficient and gained wide use among operators of personal computer networks, workstations, and mini and personal computers. Even before the advent of its second generation products and acquisitions, Exabyte counted among its customers IBM, Sun Microsystems, Motorola, NCR, Nixdorf, and Northern Telecom, to name a few. Since then, Exabyte added other customers including AT&T, Data General, Hewlett-Packard, Unisys, and many others. By 1990, the company had installed more than 100,000 tape subsystems to backup computers.

Exabyte produced its eight-millimeter and quarter-inch tape drives at its facility in Boulder, Colorado. The California firm, Solectron, manufactured Exabyte's four-millimeter products at its plant in Penang, Malaysia. The company's production strategy relied on "just-in-time" manufacturing techniques, which emphasized flexibility and continuous flow. Exabyte also customized its subsystems for selected customers. In 1993, the company acquired Tallgrass, a marketer of storage products, to sell and support Exabyte's full range of subsystems and tape libraries to distributors in North and South America. Exabyte also established a wholly owned subsidiary in the Netherlands and sales and technical support offices in Amsterdam, Frankfurt, Manchester, Paris, Singapore, and Tokyo to sell its products throughout Europe and Asia. In 1990, Exabyte established another subsidiary in Cumbernauld, Scotland, to provide repair services to European customers. The company later relocated these services in 1994 to a large facility in nearby Falkirk. In 1995, the company announced the opening of its Shanghai, China, office to meet the needs of the burgeoning Chinese market.

Since Exabyte went public in 1989, the storage market became highly competitive and subject to rapid technological innovation. A number of manufacturers with alternative technologies entered the market and competed for a limited number of customers. Many companies, some considerably larger than Exabyte, were also engaged in producing and commercializing data storage systems, including IBM, DEC, and Hewlett-Packard, which sought to incorporate their own storage systems in their computer products. The industry had also undergone consolidation. In 1992 and 1993, the industry experienced ten mergers and acquisitions, resulting in fewer but much larger multi-billion dollar competitors. This trend was attributed to the move toward single suppliers providing multiple products. In addition, these companies moved to restructure themselves and to form strategic alliances to adapt to changing market conditions and growing competition. While Exabyte appeared to have a lock on the market for eight-millimeter tape subsystems for data storage in the mid-1990s, some speculated that other companies would soon enter the lucrative market. At that time, Exabyte's competition came primarily from companies manufacturing and distributing four-millimeter products, which because of their lower cost and smaller size rivalled the eight-millimeter products at the low-end computer workstation market. Exabyte's four-millimeter products also competed directly with these offerings. In 1994, the company stated that "more than ever before, Exabyte is running a tough race for market leadership. While the company's expansion into new technology areas is designed to enhance its future growth prospects, it also means there are more fronts on which to fight the competition." Still, Exabyte's history of technological innovation and aggressive strategic acquisitions proved highly successful and seemed to have positioned the company well for the future.

Further Reading:

Alan Deutschman, "America's Fastest Growing Companies," *Fortune,* October 5, 1992, pp. 59–82.
Kathleen K. Wiegner, "Attention Packrats!" *Forbes,* May 14, 1990, p. 126.

—Bruce Montgomery

First Bank System Inc.

601 2nd. Avenue South
Minneapolis, Minnesota 55402
U.S.A.
(612) 973-1111
Fax: (612) 344-1029

Public Company
Incorporated: 1929 as First Bank Stock Investment Company
Employees: 12,300
Total Assets: $26.4 billion
Stock Exchanges: New York
SICs: 6712 Bank Holding Companies; 6021 National
  Commercial Banks; 6022 State Commercial Banks

First Bank System Inc. is one of the largest and most successful regional bank holding companies in the United States. Head-quartered in Minneapolis, Minnesota, First Bank System is made up of nine banks, four trust companies, and numerous other non-bank subsidiaries spread across a multi-state area, including Colorado, Illinois, Minnesota, Montana, North Dakota, South Dakota, and Wisconsin. The company operates almost 225 offices, of which 181 are banking locations and the remainder non-banking facilities. First Bank System's three core businesses involve retail and community banking (small businesses and consumers), commercial banking (middle market), and trust and financial investment services. First Bank System's non-banking activities are comprised of data processing, brokerage services, mortgage banking, and agricultural finance. The bank is also one of America's largest suppliers of Visa corporate cards, and ranks as the fifth largest merchant processor of Visa/Mastercards in the country.

In April of 1929, just one-half year before the great stock market crash, 85 banks located in the Ninth Federal Reserve district joined together in a loose confederation called First Bank Stock Investment Corporation. Since the Federal Deposit Insurance Company (FDIC) had not yet been created, the purpose of the confederation was to provide mutual financial support during difficult economic times. Although there was a great deal of speculation going on during this time in Wall Street brokerage houses, most banks throughout the country remained financially conservative and extremely cautious about using their assets for anything except the most stable investments.

Despite their fiscal conservatism, a number of banks were forced to close their doors during the 1920s. With the stock market crash of October 1929, and the onset of the Great Depression, conditions for the banking industry grew harsher and harsher. Many banks were forced to close during the years between 1929 and 1932. As the depression grew worse during the first few months of Franklin Roosevelt's presidency, he decided in early 1933 to close all the nation's banks for 10 days. The purpose of this dramatic decision was to make certain that only those banks with stable financial ledgers would be permitted to reopen their doors to the public. When the 10-day period was over, all First Bank Stock Investment Corporation subsidiaries were allowed by the federal government to reopen without any mandated reorganization. The conservative policies adhered to by First Bank management were so sound, in fact, that the holding company was able to start an acquisitions campaign that lasted through much of the 1930s.

During the 1940s, banks that belonged to the First Bank confederation largely operated independently of one another. Management at the individual banks were fiercely loyal to their own self-interests, and never hesitated to engage in extensive price cuts if they thought it might take a profitable customer away from another bank within the confederation. In fact, the competition among confederation banks was most intense in the Twin Cities of Minneapolis and St. Paul, Minnesota, where the largest individual banks in the First Bank system fought one another for customers. One cause of this counterproductive competition among the banks was the restrictive and antiquated branching legislation in Minnesota and other states in the region.

In 1954, the Bank Holding Company Act was passed by the U.S. Congress. This legislation gave the First Bank confederation and other bank holding companies throughout the nation the approval for already existing multi-state banking operations. Banks within the First Bank confederation were spread across a four-state area during this time, including Montana, South Dakota, North Dakota, and Minnesota. For the remainder of the 1950s, and throughout the decade of the 1960s, the banks of the confederation expanded their presence in these states by engaging in an aggressive acquisitions policy. By the 1970s, however, member banks of the confederation were operating so independently of one another that there was not only a lack of uniformity in services, but an overall lack of direction and centralized decision making.

During the late 1970s and early 1980s, the economy in the United States went into a tailspin, and the First Bank confederation was faced with the challenges of high inflation, uncertain interest rates, and growing competition from nonbank financial service companies. Confederation management recognized the need for more centralized control, and in 1982 began to prepare a comprehensive strategy for this purpose. In 1985, First Bank management made its first significant decision by selling 28 smaller, rural banks with little prospect for future growth. This decision resulted in the sale of 45 offices over a four-state region. Another major decision involved the 1988 merger of the large Minneapolis and St. Paul banks, and additional suburban banks in the Twin Cities area, into First Bank National Association. The increase in operational efficiency and reduction in service costs provided the bank with a greater opportunity to compete effectively in the entire Twin Cities metropolitan area.

Management at First Bank also purchased banks in the states of Washington and Colorado during this time, taking advantage of recent federal legislation that weakened many barriers to national banking.

More than the recession of the early 1980s led First Bank to reassess the adequacy and effectiveness of a loose confederation and hands-off management style. The farm crisis of the early to mid-1980s created credit quality problems for the regional banks affiliated with First Bank which were outside of the greater Twin Cities metropolitan area. Under the bank's own credit examination, its credit losses amounted to $424 million by 1986. This loss was compensated for by the $397 million in realized gains when the investment securities were sold. Yet when rising interest rates led to a substantial unrealized loss estimated at $640 million in the long-term bonds which had been bought to replace the securities recently sold, the company decided upon a hedging strategy to minimize the loss. Unfortunately, the hedging strategy failed, and the bonds were finally sold at a pre-tax loss of $506 million in 1988.

First Bank's emphasis on merchant banking, capital markets, and lending specializations had proved disastrous during the mid-1980s. With decreasing capital levels resulting from the securities and bond losses, rising noninterest costs, an increasing amount of nonperforming assets, and weakening profitability, the company announced a comprehensive reorganization strategy in late 1989. The strategy included a withdrawal from merchant banking and lending specializations, and a concentration on more basic banking services, such as merchant processing, credit cards, automated teller machines, and cash management. The company also began to capitalize upon and extend its geographic franchise. In 1989, First Bank recorded a restructuring expense of $37.5 million, while also reporting a $175 million provision for credit losses.

After a four month search, in January of 1990 the First Bank Board of Directors hired John F. (Jack) Grundhofer to act as chairman, president, and chief executive officer. Grundhofer, a former vice-chairman and senior executive officer at Wells Fargo, immediately initiated a massive cost-cutting strategy designed to bring the bank back to profitability. Grundhofer and his hand-chosen management team examined each line of the bank's business to determine whether or not it could remain competitive in the market. Grundhofer's first move was to stop lending to large corporations and concentrate more on retail banking, trusts and investments, and small and middle-range businesses. As a result, First Bank's portfolio of loans was drastically reduced. All the bank's national lending programs and its indirect auto loan programs were entirely eliminated, thus allowing the company to concentrate on expanding its regional commercial lending program and its direct consumer loan program. In general, First Bank's loan portfolio was gradually restructured to emphasize a larger number and more diverse mix of consumer loans.

The most important move that Grundhofer made, however, was to commit $150 million in First Bank funds to a cost-cutting technology program. When he arrived on the scene in the beginning of 1990, Grundhofer discovered that First Bank was mired in 1950s and 1960s technology. Over 45 banks under First Bank's umbrella had 47 different data processing centers,

715 different kinds of basic consumer deposit accounts, 16 loan processing centers, eight consumer loan centers, and 20 item processing centers. The bank also was without any centralized pricing structure for its products or services, and each bank within the system offered various kinds of products and services. The company's installment loan system was initially brought in during 1959 and was still in use. First Bank's customer information system dated back to 1964, without the benefit of any update since that time. The firm's DDA system dated from 1960, and its on-line savings system was more than 20 years old.

Within two years Grundhofer consolidated the bank's 47 data processing centers into one, and drastically reduced or eliminated all the other loan and processing centers. He implemented a fixed price structure for the bank's products and services, and standardized the products and services each of the banks offered within the First Bank system. As First Bank's efficiency ratio improved, more customers were attracted to the services provided by the bank. By 1992, a customer could walk into any of First Bank's affiliates in the Twin Cities area and get a cashier's check or automobile loan within 10 minutes. The bank also developed an extremely useful and very popular 48-hour turnaround on small business loans; for a $250,000 loan, the customer was asked to fill out a brief two-page application. Other processing capabilities that were improved by the bank's emphasis on technological development included a customer's ability to access information on their account in Colorado Springs, Colorado, even though their account is with a bank in Duluth, Minnesota. Finally, all of the bank's numerous customer service phone centers were consolidated into two locations.

When the cost-cutting technology program began to show financial rewards, Grundhofer decided to increase First Bank's asset base through an aggressive acquisitions program. First Bank purchased U.S. Bancorp's Oregon and Washington corporate trust operations in early 1993. Prior to this, it had purchased the California corporate trust subsidiary of Bankers Trust New York Corporation in 1992. The company acquired Colorado National Bank with over $3 billion in assets, and Boulevard Bancorp in Chicago with over $1.5 billion in assets. Perhaps the most important acquisition involved the purchase of the domestic corporate trust of J. P. Morgan & Company, one of the largest and most prestigious banks in the United States. In May of 1994, the company confirmed its acquisition of Metropolitan Financial Corporation for approximately $800 million. Metropolitan Financial, a Minneapolis, Minnesota-based bank with $5.7 billion in assets, operated a multi-state banking office network located in North Dakota, Iowa, Nebraska, Kansas, and Wyoming. The purchase of Metropolitan helped push First Bank's assets to $34.5 billion, ahead of the assets at First Fidelity Bancorp, the nation's 25th largest bank holding company.

In 1990 and 1991, the bank's capital restoration program involved a private placement of new common stock, which raised some $145 million from an investment partnership headed by Lazard Freres, and $30 million from the State Board of Administration of Florida. The bank also initiated a public offering of $114.5 million of preferred stock. These moves placed First Bank's capital ratio in the top percentile of regional banks in the United States.

Under Grundhofer's leadership, by the beginning of 1995 First Bank had grown into one of the largest and most successful of the regional banks. With its financial condition clearly improved, First Bank began to develop a community initiatives program that became a model for regional banks. First Bank's extensive community outreach program involved volunteerism, youth-employment projects, event sponsorships, and grants to nonprofit organizations. The company offered a comprehensive line of mortgage products and services to help low and moderate income families purchase their own homes. The bank also tailored loans for people with disabilities, provided customer assistance for non-English speaking peoples, and offered free accounts and services to individuals with low-income jobs. First Bank also extended credit to small businesses that fostered community development and rehabilitation by working closely with the Small Business Administration.

First Bank was growing by leaps and bounds in the 1990s as it positioned itself to become the largest regional bank in the upper Midwest. With an ever-increasing asset base, an aggressive acquisitions policy, high-tech banking equipment, and intelligent management, First Bank looked certain to reach its goal.

Further Reading:

Kapiloff, Howard, "Fourth-of-July Merger Fireworks," *American Banker,* July 5, 1994, p. 1.
Klinkerman, Steve, and Karen Gullo, "First Bank System to Purchase Morgan's Corporate Trust Unit," *American Banker,* January 5, 1993, p. 5.
Zack, Jeffrey, "Technology Gives First Bank's Grundhofer a Cost-Cutting Edge," *American Banker,* May 9, 1994, p. 1.

—Thomas Derdak

Fisher-Price®

Fisher-Price Inc.

636 Girard Ave.
East Aurora, New York 14052
U.S.A.
(716) 687-3000

Wholly Owned Subsidiary of Mattel Inc.
Incorporated: 1930
Employees: 4,200
Sales: $750 million
SICs: 3944 Games, Toys and Children's Vehicles; 2511
    Wood Household Furniture

Fisher-Price Inc. has dominated the infant and preschool toy market for over 60 years and has become known for the high quality and durability of its products. In fact, in 1990, a New Jersey research firm determined Fisher-Price to be among the top three brand names representing quality products among consumers, according to the *Buffalo News.* The company has extended its brand name to other related products, perhaps most notably in the juvenile furnishings market; six years after entering the juvenile furnishings market in 1984, Fisher-Price lead the category with its Fisher-Price high chair and car seat. Although its forays into toy markets for older children in the 1980s proved disappointing, the company successfully expanded its product lines in the 1990s to include a wider variety of toys for children from infants to age five, a category on which Fisher-Price planned continued focus.

Fisher-Price was founded in East Aurora, New York, in 1930, by Herman G. Fisher, Irving L. Price, and Helen M. Schelle. While Price and Schelle had worked in retail businesses that featured toys among their inventory, Fisher brought to the group his experience in the advertising and sales of games. All three proved adept at knowing what children liked and were committed to the idea that the public would appreciate high quality toys. Though the founders knew little about the actual manufacture of toys, they reasoned that popular products would have, according to the company's first catalog, "intrinsic play value, ingenuity, strong construction, good value for the money and action." Specifically, they observed, "children love best the gay, cheerful, friendly toys with amusing action, toys that do something new and surprising and funny!"

Such beliefs proved correct. From a frame and concrete-block house turned manufacturing headquarters in East Aurora, Fisher-Price manufactured 16 different toys during its first year

of operation. This line included Granny Doodle and Doctor Doodle, brightly colored wooden ducks that, when pulled, opened their beaks and quacked. During this time, Fisher-Price made its toys out of Ponderosa pine, a splinter-resistant wood. The wooden pieces were then joined by heavy steel parts and decorated with non-toxic lithographs and finishes, resulting in a uniquely durable and appealing product.

Withstanding the effects of the Great Depression, Fisher-Price reported losses during its first four years of business and eventually developed a healthy reputation and customer base. In the early 1950s, Fisher-Price augmented its line of wooden toys by fashioning new products from a popular new material, plastic.

During the period of increased consumerism following World War II, the toy industry grew and changed dramatically. Herman Fisher retired from his post as president of Fisher-Price in 1966 and was succeeded by Henry Coords, who had been recruited from AT&T's affiliate company Western Electric. Shortly thereafter, The Quaker Oats Company expressed interest in acquiring Fisher-Price, and in 1969, Quaker Oats purchased Herman Fisher's 67.4 percent voting stock and 14.1 percent nonvoting stock, along with Fisher-Price's additional outstanding shares, for $122 per share, the same amount paid Mr. Fisher. At the time of the purchase, Fisher-Price had sales above $30 million.

Also during this time, other cereal companies, including General Mills, General Foods Corp., and Nabisco, acquired toy companies. While some industry analysts speculated that cereal companies were purchasing toy manufacturers that would produce "premiums"—the small, inexpensive toys offered free inside cereal boxes—one toy company executive told *Advertising Age* that "the toy business is not really geared to premium offers. The merchandise is too expensive to be a successful premium item. It can't build business." Rather, some suggested, cereal and toy companies were merged, in part, to "piggyback" toy and cereal commercials. "It's a natural thing to form marriages of convenience with toys and cereals. They're aimed at the same market," one adman told *Advertising Age.*

The ad agency of Waring and LaRosa handled advertising for both Quaker Oats and Fisher-Price, and under Quaker Oats ownership, Fisher-Price's spending on advertising increased. In 1970, in what was then the largest advertising campaign in the company's history, Waring and LaRosa created a campaign emphasizing the quality and sturdiness of Fisher-Price toys. The estimated $1.25 million ad campaign declared Fisher-Price made toys to last a "whole childhood, and another childhood, and a childhood after that." Aimed at parents, the print ads ran in *Family Circle, Good Housekeeping, Ladies' Home Journal, Parents',* and *Women's Day.*

By 1976, Fisher-Price had diversified into three different businesses. While the majority of its business still lay in pre-school products for children 18 months through four years, the company also marketed a line of toys for children aged four to nine years and another line for infants. The newest additions to the company's toy lines were the 1974 introduction of dolls, the 1975 introduction of the Adventure Series, which included Adventure People for early grade school children, and the 1976 introduction of the Play Family Hospital for preschoolers.

As Fisher-Price entered new markets, it also expanded the scope of its advertising, offering commercial spots during children's television programming for the first time in 1976. Responding to criticism from such special interest groups as Action for Children's Television (ACT), concerned about advertising's potential for exploiting children, Fisher-Price president Henry Coords maintained that the ads would not exert high pressure and would be moderate in number. Fisher-Price continued advertising its toys on prime and daytime network television, as well as in women's service magazines, but also focused on reminding retailers in trade journals that Fisher-Price now serviced three distinct age groups. Though Fisher-Price consistently increased its ad budget, spending almost $2.15 million on network advertising in 1975, the company spent considerably less than did its top rivals. General Mills Fun Group, for example, spent $8.8 million on network advertising in 1975, while Mattel spent $6 million and Hasbro spent $4 million.

While Fisher-Price had turned its attention to its new markets in the 1970s, significant increases in the birth rate revived the stagnant preschool market, Fisher-Price's mainstay, in the mid-1980s. As toy giants such as Hasbro, Kenner Products, and Mattel expanded their presence in the preschool market, and other companies, including Matchbox Toys Ltd., Panosh Place, and Schaper Mfg. Co., entered the market with new lines ranging from baby exercise tapes to washable vinyl plush toys, Fisher-Price found its leading position in the preschool market threatened.

"In the face of major competition, Fisher-Price has become very aggressive in ad support for all its products," Fisher-Price's director of advertising Robert Moody told *Advertising Age,* reaffirming the company's commitment to "advertising of over 75 of the new and existing toys in its line on a year-round basis." To support its new plan, Fisher-Price increased its ad budget by 90 percent to $50 million in 1986. The company also afforded significant portions of its account to the advertising firms of J. Walter Thompson USA in Chicago and Backer & Spielvogel in New York. Funding for its new marketing expenditures came through reductions in overhead and controlling manufacturing costs.

With the help of ad support, Fisher-Price's new toy lines made 1986 a profitable year. An integral part of the company's product line during this time was represented by its Gummi Bear merchandise, toys based on a very popular Walt Disney Productions cartoon series featuring magical, Medieval bears. Gaining the license to use the trademarked Gummi Bear characters, Fisher-Price produced poseable figures, puzzles, stuffed animals, and other toys based on the cartoon. The Gummi Bear license, according to *Advertising Age,* was Fisher-Price's most profitable television license since that of the Sesame Street characters, which the company had obtained in the 1970s. Also during this time, Fisher-Price introduced a Toddler Kitchen, a Magic Vac (a toy vacuum cleaner that blew bubbles), and Puffalumps, ultra soft, silky stuffed animals. Puffalumps became the most successful new product in Fisher-Price's history, achieving sales of approximately $25 million in its first year.

As Fisher-Price revived its preschool line in 1986, it also pushed its fastest growing segment, an audiovisual toy division, created in 1982, which produced durable audiovisual products, simple in design, specifically for children. Among the division's most popular products were a phonograph, a tape recorder, and an AM-FM radio with a sing-along microphone. The company planned to increase its advertising support of the division by 40 percent in 1986, in response to an expected increase in the number of older children to whom the products would appeal.

In 1987, the company introduced the first video camcorder for children. Priced at around $200, the PXL 2000 Deluxe Camcorder System was well received at the American International Toy Fair in New York City, the annual showing of new products in the industry, and had sold out at retailers for the calendar year by late spring. Public response to the camcorder was bolstered by an aggressive $3 million ad campaign that featured 30-second television ads on network television and the Nickelodeon cable channel, as well as print ads in *Life, Newsweek, People, Sports Illustrated,* and *Time.* Unlike most toy ads, the camcorder print ads targeted men; J. Walter Thompson executive Matt Kurtz explained to *Advertising Age* that "most electronics purchases are made by fathers," and the magazines had been chosen because of their large male readership. The ad headline challenged readers to "Picture what your kid can do with the new PXL 2000," offering the camcorder as "a great way to turn on your kid's imagination."

While the camcorder met with initial success, Moody asserted in *Advertising Age* that "the camcorder shouldn't disguise what Fisher-Price is all about," which was toys for preschoolers. Nevertheless, Fisher-Price's offerings had expanded to include much more than preschool toys between 1984 and 1989, and the company now encompassed four main operating groups: the Infants Products Group, which included crib and playpen products as well as juvenile furnishings, accounting for 30 percent of the company's U.S. business; the Traditional Products Group, which included preschool toys, accounting for 60 percent of U.S. business; the Promotional Products Group, which included highly publicized toys like the Puffalumps and the PXL 2000 Deluxe Camcorder System, accounting for ten percent of sales; and International Business, which included sales in Canada and Europe, accounting for 25 percent of Fisher-Price's sales in 1987. As the company increased its efforts at expansion, management observed demographic trends indicating that the level of new births would remain static into the early 1990s and the number of older children would increase. Therefore, Fisher-Price's preparations for expansion into non-traditional products and products for older children was on target for future profits.

The company's expansion did not go as planned, however. According to some critics, as Fisher-Price entered the promotional products toy market in 1987, it shortchanged its preschool line, which had helped it grow steadily from 1930 to 1986. Though the first promotional products met with success and brought additional revenues to the company, by 1988 resources had to be shifted from the company's preschool, infant, and juvenile lines to support the failing promotional line, according to *Children's Business.* In the late 1980s, Fisher-Price began losing money, due largely to the failure of its promotional products (including a battery-powered sports car and a children's video camera), order cancellations because of some late merchandise deliveries, and intensified competition from Hasbro, Rubbermaid, and Mattel in the preschool market.

To combat these difficulties, Fisher-Price discontinued its line for older children and refocused its attention on its preschool line. In addition, newly appointed president Ronald Jackson and his management team began trying to turn the company around by cutting expenses. Toward that end, four of the company's 13 manufacturing plants and two distribution centers were closed, and the work force was reduced by more than 3,000. Production of some lines were moved overseas, while advertising and selling costs were reduced by $17 million, according to the *Business First-Buffalo.* The restructuring efforts had returned Fisher-Price to profitability by 1991.

Still, the company continued to struggle with the effects of its unsuccessful bid to market toys and furnishings for older children. Despite Fisher-Price's leading position in the market for preschool toys, industry analyst John G. Taylor suggested in the *Buffalo News* that "Fisher-Price is somewhat of an underdog in this competition. Fisher-Price doesn't have the financial resources that the other companies (Little Tikes and Playskool) have—they're owned by people with deep pockets."

In 1991, Quaker Oats decided to spin off Fisher-Price as an independent company, and, in the summer of that year, Fisher-Price began trading on the New York Stock Exchange. During this time, Mattel expressed an interest in acquiring the steadily improving Fisher-Price, but Quaker Oats had rejected the idea. In December 1993, however, Fisher-Price became a wholly-owned subsidiary of Mattel, making Mattel the leading toy company in the United States. Analysts referred to the deal as the most significant acquisition in the toy industry since Hasbro bought Tonka Corp. in 1991, as it allowed Mattel to challenge Hasbro's top position in the $17 billion toy industry.

Mattel and Fisher-Price fit together well. Mattel consolidated Fisher-Price's Mexican production, European sales offices, and media planning and buying with its own to make a "stronger, more focused entity," according to the *Buffalo News.* Journalist Frank Reysen told the paper that Mattel and Fisher-Price succeeded together because "neither is a hot-item type of company. They look to developing (toy) lines over the long term." Fisher-Price's infant and preschool lines became Mattel's second largest product category, after Barbie, making up an estimated one-fourth of Mattel's 1994 sales.

After several years of restructuring, Fisher-Price began to expand in 1994 with a new line of outdoor play yard toys. According to the *Buffalo News,* Fisher-Price saw "outdoor play yard toys as a means of increasing its sales without the risks associated with diversification outside the infant and preschool toy category." To support the new line, the company opened two new factories (the first such openings in 20 years), purchased additional equipment, added 300 production plant jobs and 50 white collar jobs, and began considering building a research and development center near its headquarters in East Aurora, New York. "We are going after market share, and we intend to grow," Fisher-Price president James A. Eskridge (who succeeded Ronald Jackson after the takeover) told the *Buffalo News.*

Though the outdoor playthings market was dominated by Rubbermaid subsidiary Little Tikes, Fisher-Price represented a challenge to competitors through lower manufacturing costs and sound merchant relations. Responding to the move, Little Tikes executive Kevin G. Curran remarked, "I wish them success, but Little Tikes invented this category 20 years ago, and we are going to defend it aggressively."

Fisher-Price's efficient operations and quality products garnered awards in the industry, including the title of 1993 Vendor of the Year, awarded by *Discount Store News.* Fisher-Price was the first toy manufacturer to ever win the vendor category of the award, the top award given manufacturers by the discount retailing chains. In addition, Fisher-Price ranked fifth in Total Research Corp.'s 1993 Equitrend survey of brand quality. Indeed, according to one stock analyst quoted in the *Buffalo News,* "the goodwill the toy maker has developed with consumers . . . was instrumental in the firm's rapid recovery after it suffered record losses in 1990 and early 1991."

Fisher-Price remained the leader in the $1 billion infant and preschool plaything market and was achieving sales records into the mid-1990s. The company's Little People playsets, Corn Popper, Bubble Mower, and other toys proved invaluable to parent Mattel, and the outdoor play toys also met with initial success. In addition, Fisher-Price was taking advantage of Mattel's global distribution and marketing network to bolster sales in Mexico, Italy, Germany, and Spain.

To increase exposure on retail shelves, Fisher-Price entered three new markets in 1994: games, dolls, and electronic learning toys. Unlike its expansion under Quaker Oats, Fisher-Price remained committed to marketing toward the age range with which it has had its greatest success. "We aren't getting outside of what we do best: toys for children zero to five years of age," Fisher-Price president James A. Eskridge told the *Buffalo News.* Eskridge noted, however, that continued focus on the preschool market did not preclude new product introductions, stating "we want to get into new aisles in the store and new play patterns" so that "you will see us all over the toy store."

Further Reading:

Baker, M. Sharon, "Quick, Decisive Moves Gave Fisher-Price a New Playground," *Business First-Buffalo,* May 11, 1992, p. 19.

Biltekoff, Judith A., "Fisher-Price Stuffs Ad Budget," *Advertising Age,* February 24, 1986, p. 62.

Colman, Gregory J., "Fisher-Price Leaves Home," *Children's Business,* August 1991, p. 8.

"Fisher-Price: Fighting to Recapture the Playpen," *Business Week Industrial Edition,* December 1990, p. 70.

Fitzgerald, Kate, "Fisher-Price Leads Pack: Back-To-Basics Is Key for Toy Fair," *Advertising Age,* February 8, 1988, p. 72.

Forkan, James P., "TV Use Is Key to Fisher-Price Profitability Plan," *Advertising Age,* March 15, 1976.

Jaffe, Thomas, "Fisher-Price Overpriced?" *Forbes,* August 19, 1991, p. 148.

Lefton, Terry, "How the Big Brands Rank," *Brandweek,* March 29, 1993, pp. 26–30.

Madore, James T., "Competitors Crowd Fisher-Price's Market," *Buffalo News,* February 20, 1994.

——, "Fisher-Price Poised for Major Expansion," *Buffalo News,* July 24, 1994, p. B13.

——, "They're Pulling Hair in the Playpen," *Buffalo News,* February 9, 1992.

O'Connor, John J., "Cereal Men Aren't Playing When They Enter Toy Marketing," *Advertising Age,* December 14, 1970, pp. 1, 74.

Stern, Sara E., "Youth Movement: Fisher-Price Turns on Kid Video," *Advertising Age,* October 5, 1987, p. 90.

—Sara Pendergast

Flowers Industries, Inc.

P.O. Box 1338
Thomasville, Georgia 31799
U.S.A.
(912) 226-9110
Fax: (912) 225-3808

Public Company
Incorporated: 1919
Employees: 8,000
Sales: $990 million
Stock Exchanges: New York
SICs: 2051 Bread, Cake & Related Products; 2037 Frozen
  Fruits & Vegetables

Flowers Industries, Inc., is a growing food company and one of the largest and most successful independent wholesale bakers in the United States. The company makes bread, rolls, snack cakes, doughnuts, and pies and packages frozen fruits and batter-dipped and breaded vegetables. Using highly efficient manufacturing technology and employing a sophisticated marketing strategy, the company has made its premium brands well known in kitchens and dining rooms throughout the country.

Flowers Baking Company was founded in 1919 in Thomasville, Georgia, by William Howard Flowers. A native of Blakely County, Georgia, Flowers attended school in Poughkeepsie, New York, before returning to his home state to marry. He moved his new family to Thomasville in 1909. In 1914 Flowers and his brother, Joseph Hampton Flowers, opened Flowers Ice Cream Company to cater to wealthy families from the North who vacationed in Thomasville.

Just before the First World War, Thomasville was a small, sleepy town known primarily as a popular winter resort. While the Flowers Ice Cream Company was moderately successful, the brothers soon discovered an even more promising opportunity in that Thomasville had no bakery. The town had to arrange for all of its bread to be shipped in from other locations, and there was no large bakery within 200 miles. Seizing the opportunity, William and Joseph opened a bakery in November 1919. The first modern bakery in the area, Flowers Baking Company was soon flourishing.

During the 1920s, Joseph remained in charge of the ice cream company while William directed the operations of the bakery,

which grew rapidly under his leadership. Soon local newspapers were lauding the bakery as having the most modern and sanitary machinery available, and noting that the company was able to produce thousands of loaves of bread each day. (They sold for nine cents a loaf.) In 1928 the company expanded its product line to include sweet rolls and cakes. By the end of the decade, as Flowers Baking Company garnered a reputation for high-quality baked goods, William Flowers began shipping the firm's products to customers throughout the region.

With the onset of the Great Depression in the 1930s, many businesses throughout the United States either collapsed or significantly scaled back their operations. Earnings for Flowers Baking Company fell precipitously; however, bread, being a staple, still sold at a brisk pace. In 1934, at the height of the Depression, Flowers Baking Company reported $90,000 in sales, counted 25 employees, and operated seven wholesale routes. During the same year, William Howard Flowers died, leaving his 20-year-old son Bill in charge of the bakery. Bill Flowers guided the company through its most difficult years. In 1937 he purchased a bakery located in Tallahassee, Florida, initiating a growth-through-acquisition strategy that served the company for many years.

When World War II began, Bill Flowers sought to join the U.S. Armed Services, but the federal government required him to remain at home and contribute his share to the war effort by running his bakeries at full capacity. Flowers' ovens proceeded to bake bread on a hectic schedule of 24 hours a day nearly seven days a week in order to meet the demand of American military bases in the Southeast. In 1942 Flowers Bakery joined the Quality Bakers of America, a baking industry cooperative. It was Quality Bakers that created the popular Little Miss Sunbeam trademark that member bakeries, like Flowers, could use to market their products. The trademark was an immediate hit with homemakers and helped Flowers Bakery sell large quantities of its bread. Like many other bakeries during the war, Flowers Bakery distributed small recipe pamphlets that showed how to cook healthy meals at a time when food rationing was common. The pamphlet included such culinary inventions as "Pigs in Clover," "Bologna Blitz," and "Peasant Sandwich."

In 1946 Flowers Bakery purchased a bakery in Jacksonville, Florida. In 1947 Bill's younger brother, Langdon S. Flowers, joined the company after serving in the U.S. Navy. Langdon Flowers sought to develop marketing strategies that would increase sales and foster growth. The Little Miss Sunbeam trademark became a prominent part of the Flowers Bakery marketing program, with the emblem adorning the uniforms of the company's sales force, loaves of bread, and delivery trucks. Little Miss Sunbeam became the company's highly popular "spokesgirl," and revenues skyrocketed. By the end of the 1940s, Flowers Bakery Company was ready to embark upon a period of enormous growth.

The Flowers Bakery Company expanded rapidly during the 1950s. In 1959 the baking industry introduced batter-whipped bread. According to company literature, batter-whipped bread was made by a new process that was "roughly comparable to what a housewife uses in preparing cake batter with an electric mixer." With a softer texture and no holes, the bread was immediately popular, and by the start of the new decade Flowers reported that 18 million loaves had been baked in its ovens.

In the early 1960s, annual sales for the company jumped to over $6 million, and employees numbered around 500. To inspire and honor its sales force, Flowers Bakery initiated annual award ceremonies such as the Outstanding Service award and Salesman of the Year award. The company arranged a televised ''Media Appreciation Day'' to strengthen its ties to local communities around Thomasville. In order to promote batter-whipped Sunbeam bread, the company conducted ''Miss Batterwhip'' contests across its entire marketing territory. During the mid-1960s, Flowers Bakery purchased bakeries in Panama City, Florida, and Opelika, Alabama. In 1965 the company opened a new bakery in Jacksonville, Florida, and two years later Flowers acquired the Atlanta Baking Company in Atlanta, Georgia. In 1968 the company changed its name to Flowers Industries, Inc., and went public, trading shares on the OTC exchange. One year later, the company was listed on the American Stock Exchange.

Entering the 1970s, Flowers was not only the pre-eminent bakery in the American Southeast, but also one of the fastest-growing companies in the United States. In 1970 the company had 2,600 employees and annual revenues of $54 million. Flowers' office staff had outgrown its small building in Thomasville, and in 1975 the company relocated its corporate headquarters to a new building on the outskirts of the city. More like a country estate than the home of a Fortune 500 company, the administrative offices were set among 15 acres of pine trees populated by quail, deer, and fox.

In 1976 Flowers entered the frozen food business by acquiring Stilwell Foods of Stilwell, Oklahoma, along with its subsidiary Rio Grande Foods of McAllen, Texas. Stilwell had a strong reputation for high-quality frozen foods, which included vegetables, fruits, desserts, and a variety of baked goods. Flowers aggressively pursued success in its new market, implementing a comprehensive capital expenditure program to retool Stilwell and Rio Grande production facilities, upgrade equipment and technology, improve cost-effectiveness, and promote more effective employee training methods.

The company also continued to grow its fresh baker business. In 1977 Flowers brought out a new line of variety breads called Nature's Own. These variety breads quickly became one of the best-selling variety breads in the southeastern United States. Besides Nature's Own, Flowers was selling many different kinds of bread, including Sunbeam Rye, Sunbeam Wheat, Sunbeam French, Hollywood Diet, Sunbeam Low Sodium, Sunbeam Batter-Whipped Enriched, and Sunbeam Thin-Sliced Sandwich.

During the 1970s and 1980s, Flowers purchased bakeries in Texas, Tennessee, West Virginia, and Kentucky, and other states, including such well-known regional companies as El Paso Baking Company in El Paso; Griffin Pie Company in London, Kentucky; Kralis Brothers' Foods in Mentone, Indiana; European Bakers, Ltd., in Tucker, Georgia; and Bunny Bread, Inc., in New Orleans. In 1983 Flowers introduced Cobblestone Mill, a premium brand of specialty breads, which soon developed into a diverse product line including sandwich buns and English muffins.

Also in 1983, William Flowers retired as Chairman of the Board after nearly 50 years of directing the company. For the next two years the company was run by Langdon Flowers, until he also retired. The position of CEO was filled by Amos R. McMullian, who had worked in a number of different positions at the company since 1963.

During the early 1990s, Flowers continued to grow. The company expanded its frozen bakery business and specialty bakery product line, while continuing to acquire firms that enhanced its traditional bakery business. In 1991 Flowers introduced Jubilee, a line of premium pastries and desserts. Also during the early 1990s, the company expanded its Our Special Touch product line for deli-bakery supermarkets and other in-store foodservice operations. Having discovered that Nature's Own brand of premium bread was one of the company's best sellers, management continued to add such new products as 100% Whole Grain and Light Sourdough to the product line.

In the mid-1990s, management at Flowers planned to continue its strategy of growth through acquisition while also expanding its extensive variety of breads, pastries, desserts, and frozen goods. To maintain its momentum in an extremely competitive industry, Flowers implemented a ''new generation'' of bakeries to help guarantee the highest quality control for its entire product line. With state-of-the-art computerized equipment, a well-trained staff of technicians, and an extremely efficient, high-technology operation, Flowers looked toward the future with a great deal of confidence.

Principal Subsidiaries: Atlanta Baking Company; Bunny Bread, Inc.; Colonial Cake Company; El Paso Baking Company, Inc.; European Bakers, Ltd.; Flowers Distributing Company of Birmingham, Inc.; Flowers Distributing Company of El Paso, Inc.; Flowers Snack Distributors, Inc.; Flowers Snack of Tennessee, Inc.; Flowers Specialty Baked Foods, Inc.; Griffin Pie Company, Inc.; Holsum Banking Company, Inc.; Huval Baking Company, Inc.; Kann's Bakery, Inc.; Kralis Brothers' Foods, Inc.; Mrs. Boehme's Holsum Bakery, Inc.; Richter's Bakery, Inc.; Schott's Bakery, Inc.; Stilwell Foods, Inc.; Table Pride, Inc.

Further Reading:

A Look Back At 75 Years: Flowers Industries, Inc., Flowers Industries, Inc.: 1994, pp. 1–32.

—Thomas Derdak

Follett Corporation

2233 West Street
River Grove, Illinois 60171-1895
U.S.A.
(708) 583-2000
Fax: (708) 452-9347

Private Company
Incorporated: 1894
Employees: 7,000
Sales: $700 million
SICs: 3575 Computer Terminals; 5192 Books, Periodicals &
   Newspapers; 5199 Contract Management of Book Stores;
   5942 Book Stores; 5943 Stationery Stores; 7372
   Prepackaged Software

The Follett Corporation is the oldest and largest company devoted entirely to serving the educational marketplace through its college bookstores, book and video distribution business, and its software products. Follett ranked 265 on the *Forbes* list of "The 500 Largest Private Companies in the U.S." in 1994, climbing 15 notches from the previous year. Headquartered in River Grove, Illinois, a suburb just west of Chicago, Follett had divisional offices in Crystal Lake, Elmhurst, McHenry, River Grove, and Chicago, Illinois, in 1995.

Follett family members were born and bred under the auspices of the printed word, a passion passed down through four generations from Follett's founder, Charles W. (known as "C.W.") Follett. The history of the Follett Corporation began in 1873, with a home-based bookstore located in Wheaton, Illinois. The homeowner and proprietor was Charles M. Barnes, a scholarly man who used his private library as his initial inventory.

Meanwhile, in 1901, 18-year-old C.W. Follett met and fell in love with Edythe Benepe, a Chicago reporter. Before the two could marry and begin a new life, however, Follett needed to find gainful employment in the Chicago area. During this time, Charles Barnes hired Follett for a week to help move his bookselling business to another location in Chicago. After his week was up, Follett stayed on and worked as a stock clerk and salesman, learning the book business from the inside out while working alongside Barnes's son, William.

Though Barnes's tiny bookstore had grown rapidly since its homespun beginning in Wheaton, it floundered in 1893 when the country was rocked by a recession. Needing capital, Barnes turned to his wife's family and gave up controlling interest. Subsequently, when William Barnes married Blanche Wilcox, her father invested in the company, making the Wilcox family large shareholders. By 1899, the Barnes bookselling enterprise had bounced back from losses during the recession with sales in excess of $237,000. In 1902, just a year after C.W. Follett had joined the company, Charles Barnes retired, leaving William and his father-in-law, John Wilcox, to mind the store. The business thrived under the direction of Wilcox and the younger Barnes until 1917, when William decided to relocate to New York to form a partnership with a gentleman named Noble. While the Barnes and Noble venture went on to make bookselling history, C.W. Follett was given an opportunity to pursue his own bookselling dreams.

When William Barnes left the company, Follett bought his shares and the bookstore was subsequently renamed J.W. Wilcox & Follett Company. In the preceding years, Follett had become head stock clerk and then made sales calls throughout the Midwest and beyond, so he was well-prepared for his new role. Wilcox died in 1923, and Follett purchased the Wilcox family's shares and shortened the company name to Wilcox & Follett.

C.W. and Edythe, now married, welcomed their first child in 1904, a son named Dwight. Three more sons soon followed: Garth, Robert, and Charles ("Laddie"). In the 1920s, Follett's four sons joined the business and pushed the company into new fields. Garth started a wholesale business to serve libraries, which later became known as Follett Library Resources; Robert began a business wholesaling college textbooks, out of which grew Follett Campus Resources and Follett College Stores; Dwight created an elementary textbook publishing operation. Charles "Laddie" Follett, the youngest son, worked within Wilcox & Follett's core business. For the remainder of the 1920s and into the 1930s, the company continued to grow and diversify its bookselling; even the Depression did little to stem its expansion.

Over the next two decades, the third generation of Folletts began joining the company, helping to fuel its continued growth. These family members included: Charles R. Follett, Sr., Garth's son, who built the company's library wholesaling business and eventually retired; Ross C. Follett, Laddie's son, who eventually headed up Follett Library Resources; Kent A. Follett, Laddie's eldest son, who would head up Follett Educational Services; and Richard A. Waichler, who married Dwight Follet's daughter Nancy and would eventually serve as vice-president of operations.

On December 19, 1952, C. W. Follett passed away at age 69, after 51 years in the book industry. Dwight Follett (C.W.'s eldest son) was tapped to succeed his father. During the 1950s, three new family members who would eventually converge in the executive suite joined the company.

Robert J.R. (known as "R.J.R.") Follett, Dwight's eldest child and only son, started his career as an editor for Follett Publishing Company in 1951 after graduating from Brown University and taking post-graduate courses at Columbia University. Like his grandfather before him, R.J.R. learned the business by holding a myriad of positions, including copywriter, designer, editor-in-chief, marketing manager, and salesman, eventually rising to the corporation's executive offices. P. Richard Litzsinger's association with the Folletts began with his 1954 marriage to Dona Lucy Follett (granddaughter of C.W. and daughter of Robert D.). After graduating from the University of Missouri with a double degree in accounting and finance and a three-year stint as an air force officer, Litzsinger began working at Follett in its retail stores division. Richard M. Traut joined the company in 1958, following his graduation from West Point and military service. While in the military, Traut married Charron, granddaughter of C.W. and daughter of Robert. Traut began his career with Follett in its textbook wholesaling division in 1958.

During this time, Follett created a corporate parent and distinct subsidiaries with officers for each, then relocated the entire operation to 1000 West Washington Boulevard in Chicago. At the time, the company was comprised of a retail division, a publishing company, and three wholesaling arms that dealt with colleges, elementary and high school (El-Hi) markets, and libraries. Follett's varied enterprises were only temporarily housed under one roof, however. Growth soon propelled several subsidiaries into the nearby suburbs.

Moreover, the company made publishing history by developing the first racially integrated textbooks as well as the first textbook program for educationally disadvantaged children. Another milestone, its ''JUST Beginning-to-Read'' series, featured small-formatted books with lively illustrations and straightforward prose (often retelling classic fairy tales). This series proved very popular with teachers and first-time readers.

By the 1960s, Follett's three young leaders were on the move. P. Richard Litzsinger was named Follett's retail stores supervisor in 1962; within four years he was president of Follett's college stores division. On the wholesale side of the business, Richard Traut was named assistant general manager in 1965. Traut would eventually take the reins of Follett Campus Resources as president in 1974. In 1968, R.J.R. Follett was named president of the publishing company, and continued his own writing and publishing efforts. In 1977, R.J.R. succeeded his father, Dwight Follett, as chairman of the board, and P. Richard Litzsinger was appointed president and CEO. This year also marked the founding of Apline Guild, an Oak Park-based publisher established by R.J.R. to produce business- and finance-related titles.

In 1977, Dwight Follett retired as president, and P. Richard Litzsinger was named president and chief executive officer. Dwight remained as chairperson until 1979, when he was succeeded by R.J.R. Follett. In 1982, Follett decided to sell its publishing division. ''In the future, there will be room only for large publishing companies covering a broad spectrum with strong sales support, or for small companies filling a specialized niche,'' Follett told *Publishers Weekly* in December 1982, shortly before the sale. ''Medium-sized companies are not going to be around.'' Rather than run aground as a well-intentioned, medium-sized publisher (1982 revenues exceeded $13 million), Follett Publishing Company—a leader in social studies texts and critically acclaimed children's books—was sold to the Esquire Education Group in 1983.

Using funds from its divestitures, Follett bought a chain of 35 college bookstores. With the acquisition of other bookstore management businesses, including Campus Services, Inc. and Brennan College Services, Follett became the country's largest operator of college bookstores.

The second generation of Litzsingers joined Follett in 1978, when Dick's son Mark arrived after completing his schooling at Texas Christian University. Beginning as a retail stores management trainee, the younger Litzsinger managed college bookstores at the University of Illinois at Champaign and Northwestern University before leaving retail to become director of corporate development. In 1989, Christopher Traut, Richard's son, came to Follett from Vanderbilt University and worked in the software division. In 1991, when Follett Collegiate Graphics was on the drawing board, Mark Litzsinger left his corporate post to head up the new division. Chris Traut then left Follett Software Company and replaced Mark as director of corporate development in 1992. Todd Litzsinger, Mark's brother, also worked for Follett, as midwestern regional marketing director for CAPCO, within the graphics division.

As the 1980s came to a close, Follett's college and El-Hi divisions continued to thrive by staying one step ahead of its competition. Using computers long before they were mainstream (starting in 1952 with an IBM punch-card sorting system), Follett eventually revolutionized the book industry with its software applications. The systems gave libraries and schools the ability to place and track orders and take inventory of their holdings with the touch of a button. In 1989, Follett introduced Tom-Tracks, a fully computerized college bookstore system for textbooks. By 1994, Follett had installed Tom-Tracks in over 500 other bookstores nationwide. Additionally, the company introduced FIRSTsystem (Follett Integrated Retail Systems Technology), a state-of-the-art, point-of-sale system for college bookstores that was fully integrated with an accounts payable system. 1989 also marked R.J.R. Follett's retirement as chairman. Richard M. Traut succeeded R.J.R., while P. Richard remained president and CEO.

As of 1995, after several incarnations and name changes, the Follett Corporation's six subsidiaries were: Follett Educational Services, Follett Library Resources, and Follett Software Company, all of which catered to elementary and secondary school markets; and Follett Campus Resources, Follett College Stores, and Follett Collegiate Graphics, all of which served colleges and universities across the country.

The company's retail largest division, Follett College Stores (FCS), located in Elmhurst, Illinois, was the country's largest operator of college bookstores. With more than 450 stores in 46 states and Canada, FCS's nearly seven decades of experience in the field met the needs of over 200,000 faculty members and upwards of three million students. Follett's stores carried not only textbooks and stationery supplies, but popular sidelines like computer software, clothing, and music.

Follett Campus Resources (FCR), the company's second-largest division, has been run by George Carr since 1994, when he succeeded Richard M. Traut, who became chairman. Located in River Grove, FCR served 3,000 U.S. college bookstores (450 of which were managed by its sister division, Follett College

Stores) in 1994, as both a wholesaler of new and used textbooks and as provider of software applications for college store management its automated textbook software system. FCR's used book services offered students discounted prices on their textbooks, and its retail systems helped college store managers operate more effectively and efficiently. FCR also produced the Follett Blue Book, the industry's premier wholesale pricing guide for more than 60 years, which featured over 90,000 available titles and was updated 11 times each year.

Follett Educational Services (FES), formerly Wilcox & Follett, was the oldest of the company's divisions, dating back to 1873, and was overseen by Kent A. Follett (grandson of C.W. Follett, son of Laddie). By 1994 FES had become the largest El-Hi provider of used textbooks and new workbooks in the industry, with more 23,000 customers nationwide. FES's state-of-the-art automated inventory and tracking system contained upwards of 20,000 titles and holdings in excess of two million books. With its "zero-defects policy," FES gave schools the chance to save money and be environmentally conscious at the same time. FES more than quadrupled in size over the past decade, to occupy a 65 percent share of the market.

Follett Library Resources (FLR), having serviced elementary and secondary school libraries for more than 50 years, entered both the high school and public library marketplace in the mid-1990s. Located in Crystal Lake, Illinois, and headed up by Ross C. Follett (the eldest son of Laddie), FLR was the largest distributor of books, videos, and CD-ROMs to elementary and high school libraries in the country. Supported by a growing selection of over 65,000 precatalogued titles available to its more than 45,000 clients (roughly 40 percent of the market), FLR delivered comprehensive processing and cataloguing services, automated bibliographic data, and a professional staff with the expertise to help school libraries select titles and build collections.

Follett Software Company (FSC), operated from offices in McHenry, Illinois, with Charles Follett, Jr. (son of Charles R. and great-grandson of C.W.) as president, was founded in 1985. With annual sales topping $21 million in 1994 (up from 1993's $16 million), FSC experienced incredible growth as a provider of automated management systems to 20,000 school and smaller public libraries. FSC's ongoing research produced trademarked DOS programs including AlliancePlus, CardMasterPlus, CirculationPlus, Sneak PreviewsPlus, and TextbookPlus, as well as MacCatalog and MacCirculation Plus for Macintosh computers.

Follett Collegiate Graphics (FCG), was founded in 1992 and run by Mark Litzsinger, P. Richard Litzsinger's son. Taking full advantage of a void in the production of customized anthologies after the departure of the industry leader, Kinko's, FCG secured a substantial share of the $250 million national anthology market, which accounted for ten to 15 percent of the college textbook market. While FCG's subsidiary CAPCO (Custom Academic Publishing Company) handled copyright clearance and centralized printing operations for anthologies, a software program called CAPNET monitored the assembly process and paid the appropriate royalties. CAPCO was a joint venture with BMI Systems Inc., a Canon dealership in Oklahoma City. With the anthology market expected to top $500 million by 1997, FCG was exploring several alternatives to traditionally printed materials, including multimedia applications.

Principal Subsidiaries: Follett Campus Resources; Follett College Stores; Follett Collegiate Graphics; Follett Educational Services; Follett Library Resources; Follett Software Company.

Further Reading:

Beiser, Karl, "CardMaster Plus," *Computers in Libraries,* May 1993, pp. 50–51.
Berss, Marcia, "A Family Affair," *Forbes,* March 27, 1995, p. 136
"Charles W. Follett" (obituary), *New York Times,* December 20, 1952, p. 17.
Christianson, Elin, review of *How to Keep Score in Business: Accounting and Financial Analysis for the Non-Accountant* by Robert Follett, *Library Journal,* August 1978, p. 1504.
"The 500 Largest Private Companies in the U.S.," *Forbes,* December 5, 1994, p. 208.
"General News: Follett Software Redesigns Products," *Online,* January 1994, p. 81.
"Leading Private Firms," *Crain's Chicago Business,* December 28, 1992, p. 5; December 26, 1994, p. 11.
"Management: Textbook Strategic System," *PC Week,* January 23, 1989, p. 48.
"Projected Sale of Baker & Taylor to Follett Corp. Called Off," *Publishers Weekly,* June 27, 1994, p. 13.
Review of *Your Wonderful Body* by R.J.R. Follett, *Booklist,* April 15, 1962, p. 578.
Richard, Ethel, review of *Your Wonderful Body* by R.J.R. Follett, *School Library Journal,* November 15, 1961, p. 4031.
Schmeltzer, John, "Used Books 101—A Course on Profit," *Chicago Tribune,* September 25, 1994.
St. Lifer, Evan, and Michael Rogers, "Follett Ready to Finalize Deal for Baker & Taylor," *Library Journal,* June 15, 1994, p. 12.
"Software News: Follett Introduces Library Applications for the Macintosh," *Online,* January 1993, pp. 68–70.
Unsworth, Tim, "Tales from Chicago," *Publishers Weekly,* October 14, 1988, p. 44.
"The Week: Esquire, Inc. to Acquire Follett Publishing Division," *Publishers Weekly,* December 24, 1982, pp. 18–19.

—Taryn Benbow-Pfalzgraf

Foundation Health Corporation

3400 Data Drive
Rancho Cordova, California 95670
U.S.A.
(916) 631-5000
Fax: (916) 631-5882

Public Company
Incorporated: 1978
Employees: 5,000
Sales: $1.52 billion
Stock Exchanges: New York
SICs: 8210 Life and Health Insurance; 8320 Health Care

Foundation Health Corporation is a leading U.S. provider of managed healthcare services for industry and government. Through its subsidiaries, Foundation served approximately 2.7 million Americans in 1993. The company also provides various insurance, workers compensation, and specialty services. Foundation emerged from financial distress in the late 1980s and expanded its operations rapidly into the 1990s.

Foundation Health Corporation was founded in 1978 by a group of California health industry executives eager to capitalize on changes taking place in the healthcare and health insurance market. Indeed, as the cost of medical care mushroomed during the 1970s and 1980s, demand surfaced for a new type of healthcare provider that could do a better job of containing costs. A popular alternative to traditional indemnity health insurance during that period became managed care organizations, particularly health maintenance organizations (HMOs). Although HMOs had existed since the 1930s, favorable federal legislation was passed in the 1970s (i.e. the Federal Health Maintenance Organization Act of 1973) that bolstered their viability.

HMOs typically arrange to provide medical services for members in exchange for subscription fees paid to the plan sponsor. Members receive services from physicians or hospitals that also have a contract with the sponsor. Although they serve the same basic function as traditional insurance plans, managed care plans differ because the plan sponsors play a greater role in administering and managing the services that the healthcare providers furnish. For this reason, some managed care plans are able to provide a less-expensive alternative to traditional indemnity insurance plans.

Foundation was formed, like many other managed care companies created in the 1970s and early 1980s, to operate as an HMO. Under the direction of President George Duebel, Foundation would act as a middleman by contracting with both healthcare providers and enrollees to deliver medical services. The enrollees would pay a set fee to Foundation that entitled them to services. Foundation would supervise the health care providers, thus allowing subscribers to benefit from reduced health care costs. Doctors that contracted with Foundation would benefit from a guaranteed base of patients.

Foundation, along with the rest of the managed care industry, realized healthy growth during the late 1970s and early and mid-1980s. During the 1970s, in fact, the HMO industry grew by more than 25 percent to encompass a full 4 percent of the U.S. population by 1980. The early and mid-1980s, however, constituted the period of fastest expansion for the industry. As the number of HMOs soared past 700 in 1987, enrollment swelled to include 15 percent of all Americans. Furthermore, HMO-like plans, such as preferred provider organizations, also proliferated, generating additional revenue and profit growth for Foundation and its peers.

Although Foundation benefited from generally positive industry trends during its first eight years of existence, its success also reflected the superior efforts of its entrepreneurial management team. Through an aggressive program of expansion and diversification, Duebel and company had grown Foundation into the second largest HMO in the Sacramento region—the largest was Kaiser Foundation Health Plan, part of Kaiser Permanente Corp., which was started in the 1930s and dominated the managed care industry.

By the mid-1980s, Foundation was serving more than 200,000 enrollees. Besides its California operations, the company was offering its plan to members in five other states. It had also created four subsidiaries in its effort to diversify. Foundation created PAC Insurance Services in 1982 to provide long-term care insurance and related services. In 1983, Foundation Services Inc. was formed to provide data processing and information management for corporations and state governments. In 1984 Los Lagos Corp was set up as a real estate holding and development company. Finally, Foundation Group Contract Furnishings & Equipment Inc. was created in 1987 to distribute office furniture and accessories.

To benefit from Foundation's rising strength in the local healthcare industry, Sutter Health purchased 30 percent of Foundation Health Corp. in a 1986 leveraged buyout (LBO). Sutter, with its Sacramento-based chain of six hospitals, hoped to benefit through a partnership with Foundation and one other provider that would allow it to eventually compete head-on with Kaiser. Foundation also benefited from the buyout; Sutter agreed in "sweetheart" contracts to treat Foundation's enrollees at cut-rate prices.

Entering the late 1980s, Kaiser appeared to be in an excellent position to continue, and even to accelerate, the impressive growth rate it had achieved since its inception. Healthcare costs were escalating at a record pace, thus increasing the importance of the cost-containment role of the managed care industry. In addition, Americans were becoming more amenable to the concept of HMOs. Nevertheless, Kaiser spiraled into an ugly decline beginning in 1986. In fact, a health insurance underwriting downcycle caught much of the HMO industry off guard in the late 1980s. Industry executives, many of whom were entrepreneurs with only average long-term management expertise, were generally ill-equipped to deal with the downturn. During 1987 and 1988 fewer than one-third of all U.S. HMOs even turned a profit. Enrollee growth practically stagnated and many HMOs filed for bankruptcy.

Foundation was no exception to the problems that beset the industry during the late 1980s, but its difficulties were exacerbated by several factors. Most notable was its parent organization's heavy debt load. Sutter had assumed $126 million in debt during the 1986 LBO, much of which was still burdening its balance sheet by 1988 and 1989. To meet its debt service, Sutter was intercepting cash flow from Foundation's already pinched operations. In addition, Foundation's ventures in the five states outside of California were either barely breaking even or losing money, as were its subsidiaries. Furthermore, Foundation was in danger of losing an immense, recently acquired military contract because of inadequate data processing systems.

After posting a loss in 1987, Foundation's net income plummeted to minus $49 million in 1988, partly as a result of a devaluation of its assets. The company was teetering on the edge of bankruptcy when, in 1988, its board of directors asked Duebel to resign his post and take a leave of absence. Duebel was given the job of evaluating Foundation's troubled subsidiaries and developing a strategy to improve their performance. Daniel D. Crowley was named president and CEO of the company in 1989. The 44-year-old Crowley had previously engineered the turnaround of Cleveland-based Blue Cross and Blue Shield Mutual of Northern Ohio, where he had taken the company from a $62 million loss to profits of $6 million in one year.

Under Crowley's direction, Foundation immediately embarked on an aggressive reorganization plan. It scrapped its ailing New Mexico and Washington subsidiaries, while its New Jersey division was seized by state regulators. Crowley brought in a new management team that whipped Foundation's operations into shape and jettisoned excess baggage from the overweight enterprise—70 managers were slashed from the payroll. In 1990, Crowley conducted a stock offering that brought in enough cash to all but eliminate its crushing load of debt. He also implemented smaller changes, such as biweekly breakfast meetings, called "the Breakfast of Champions," where employees were allowed to air their concerns.

Crowley's greatest contribution to the company from an operational standpoint was his relentless cost-cutting efforts. Besides dispatching unnecessary staff, he took back 60 company cars, eliminated cafeteria subsidies, took out several hundred phone lines, and began restricting long-distance calls. He also had automatic switches installed to turn off lights and air conditioners during nights and weekends, and he began personally checking employee expense accounts. Although some employees scoffed, shareholders applauded. "Crowley is definitely a take-charge kind of guy, and I'd have to say his track record is fairly impressive," observed healthcare consultant Hal O'Donnell in an August 1989 issue of *Business Journal-Sacra-*

mento. "He will make decisions, and they will not always be popular," O'Donnell noted.

Perhaps Foundation's most lucrative achievement after Crowley's arrival was its retention of an experimental $3 billion contract with the Federal Government. In the mid-1980s, Foundation had won a bid to provide managed care services for 850,000 military employees and retirees in California and Hawaii through CHAMPUS (Civilian Health and Medical Program of the Uniformed Services). The contract represented a massive infusion of cash into the struggling organization and an opportunity to immediately triple its customer base. Soon after Foundation began servicing the account, however, a massive backlog of medical claims accumulated as Foundation's data processing systems became overloaded. Doctors and health providers complained and the Department of Defense threatened to cancel the vital contract.

In a move that would not only save the CHAMPUS contract but would also provide much of the infrastructure necessary for Foundation's future expansion, Crowley hired Electronic Data Systems (EDS) to revamp its information systems. Working day and night, EDS and Foundation employees quickly turned the processing system around and created an operation capable of processing 1.5 million claims annually. "CHAMPUS was basically taking Foundation under," recalled Mark Fox, EDS regional director of public affairs, in a June 1990 issue of *Sacramento Bee,* adding, "They asked us to save the contract."

As debt payments and operating costs quickly declined, CHAMPUS revenues kicked in, and managed care markets began to recover, Foundation's sales and profits soared. Its receipts bolted to $822 million in 1989, to $978 million in 1990, and to a record $1.1 billion in 1991. Likewise, net income shot to $11.5 million in 1990 following three straight years of losses, and then to a whopping $29.4 million in 1991. "It all started to really gel for us," recalled Crowley in a January 1992 issue of *Sacramento Bee.* "It got to the point where we could begin to grow the company by strategic acquisitions."

By strategic acquisitions, Crowley was referring to the aggressive expansion strategy that Foundation had initiated in the late 1980s to extend its reach into related healthcare fields. Indeed, by the early 1990s Foundation had launched successful subsidiary operations designed to serve vision, dental, mental health, pharmaceutical, and life insurance markets. Several of the initiatives had been hugely successful. In 1992, in fact, Foundation boosted enrollment in all of its non-CHAMPUS plans from 292,000 to 767,000. Furthermore, its doctor enrollment increased from 5,000 to 7,550. Sales and net income ballooned during 1992 to $1.33 billion and $52.6, respectively, making it by far the best year in the company's history.

Also buoying the struggling managed care provider during its lean late-1980s years was its choice contracts with Sutter Health. Besides cutting the low-rate contracts with former CEO Duebel, Sutter had also provided infusions of cash into the ailing Foundation during the late 1980s and had worked to insure its survival. Sutter benefited by retaining an important source of patients. However, Crowley's management goals soon clashed with those of Sutter's president, Patrick Hays; both men wanted to turn their companies into leaders in their respective industries and were unwilling to compromise their independence for the partnership. When Sutter tried to raise the fees originally guaranteed by Foundation's contracts, a bitter feud erupted that was played out in full-page advertisements in local newspapers. Sutter began dumping its Foundation Healthcare stock in 1991, effectively terminating the partnership but leaving Foundation with a quality source of low-cost care for its members.

Low costs and membership gains continued to fuel Foundation's rapid rise into 1993—sales jumped to $1.5 billion and net income rose to $62 million. However, those gains cloaked a bombshell that shook up the giant managed care provider in July of 1993. To Crowley's surprise, the Department of Defense informed Foundation that it planned to transfer its CHAMPUS business to Aetna when the contract terminated in 1994. Foundation management was stunned. CHAMPUS had delivered nearly half of Foundation's revenues in 1993 and made up about one half of the company's total customer base. "I lost my breath," Crowley said (about the phone call informing him of the decision) in a March 1994 issue of *Financial World.* "I thought that he was joking or had made a mistake."

Foundation's stock price fell 35 percent the day after Crowley's phone call. By then, however, the company was already strategizing to overcome the dilemma. It began devising a plan to boost enrollment in its traditional HMOs and to place increased emphasis on the development of its specialty services. Revenues from its specialty operations had already soared from $16 million in 1989 to $86.7 million by 1993. At least two outside analysts in early 1994 expected that figure to swell to $546 million by 1995, representing over 30 percent of Foundation's sales. By mid-1994, in fact, Foundation had already replaced many of the customers that would be lost to CHAMPUS through stellar gains in non-CHAMPUS plans. With shareholder confidence restored, Foundation's stock price increased well past its June 1993 level.

As it prepared to enter 1995, Foundation was looking forward to healthy growth and increased profits. Besides political and market conditions that favored general growth in the managed care industry, Foundation Health Corporation's management had earned a reputation as one of the most adept in the industry. In addition, it remained committed to a single, underlying goal: Crowley asserted in a March 1994 issue of *Financial World,* "We think we can give the public a less expensive product and still increase our margins."

Principal Subsidiaries: Foundation Health, a California Health Plan; Foundation Health Federal Services, Inc.

Further Reading:

David, Gregory E., "Life After Death," *Financial World,* March 1, 1994.
Davis, Kurt, "A Bull by the Horns: New Foundation CEO Gets Serious," *Business Journal-Sacramento,* August 28, 1989, p. 1.
——, "Local HMOs Struggle for Footing in a Minefield: Losses Hit Foundation; Healthcare Takes a Hit," *Business Journal-Sacramento,* June 13, 1988, p. 1.
Elder, Jeffrey L., "Foundation Health Reports Record Earnings for Fiscal 1992 and Fourth Quarter," *Business Wire,* July 21, 1992.
Hicks, Larry, "Foundation Finds the Right Prescription," *Sacramento Bee,* January 5, 1992, p. H1.
——, "EDS to the Rescue: Data Processing Firm Helps Get Bills Paid," *Sacramento Bee,* June 4, 1990, p. C1.
Keaney, Edward B., *Stifel, Nicolaus & Company Incorporated; Foundation Health Corporation,* St. Louis: Stifel, Nicolaus & Company, Inc., April 29, 1994.
Kenkel, Paul J., "Improving Managed Care's Management," *Modern Healthcare,* May 14, 1990.
Olmos, David R., "Stock Sinks After Firm Loses U.S. Contract," *Los Angeles Times,* July 30, 1993, p. D2.
Pulley, Mike, "Foundation to Sell Its First Policies," *Business Journal-Sacramento,* October 25, 1993, p. 9.
——, "Health War Truce: Sutter, Foundation Back at the Table," *Business Journal-Sacramento,* December 7, 1992, p. 1.
——, "Foundation Plans to Set Up IPA for Outlying Physicians," *Business Journal-Sacramento,* March 2, 1992, p. 2.
Vignola, Margo, *United States Equity Research: Health Services; Foundation Health Corporation—Full Speed Ahead,* New York: Solomon Brothers, March 9, 1994.

—Dave Mote

Frank's Nursery & Crafts, Inc.

6501 E. Nevada Street
Detroit, Michigan 48234
U.S.A.
(313) 366-8400
Fax: (313) 366-8425

Wholly Owned Subsidiary of General Host Corporation
Incorporated: 1957 as Frank's Nursery Sales, Inc.
Employees:
Sales: $557.8 million
SICs: 5261 Retail Nurseries and Garden Goods

Frank's Nursery & Crafts, Inc. is one of the nation's largest retailers of lawn-and-garden, craft, and Christmas merchandise. With over 250 retail locations in 16 states, in such metropolitan markets as Detroit, Chicago, St. Louis, Philadelphia, New York, and Boston, Frank's has also launched the Frank's SuperCrafts store, a crafts store concept that it hoped to expand in new and existing markets. In fact, in the mid-1990s, as a subsidiary of the General Host Corporation, Frank's was seeking to become a truly national retailer with over 400 stores nationwide by the end of the century.

Frank's history may be traced to 1942, when Frank Sherr and his nephew Max Weinberg opened a food market, known as Frank's Market, on the northeast side of Detroit. Billing itself as "never closed and never undersold," the business thrived. Frank's Market began carrying seasonal plants, including Christmas trees, Easter plants, and flats of springtime annuals, in addition to their staples of fresh produce and other grocery items. In 1949 Sherr and Weinberg opened a greenhouse on a vacant lot across the street from the market to accommodate the growing number of annuals and perennials the market offered. According to Frank's lore, the inspiration for this focus on plants was a difficult customer who complained about the price of coffee beans but who then obligingly paid 79 cents for a potted geranium. The price—and the profit—on the geranium were much higher than those on the coffee, and Sherr and Weinberg realized that there was apparently money to be made selling flowers. Soon Frank's was selling fertilizer, trees, and other landscaping supplies.

The business thrived, and in 1957 the company—by then four stores strong—incorporated, becoming Frank's Nursery Sales, Inc. By 1965 Frank's owned 18 stores throughout

Michigan, and its sales were $11.35 million, with a net income of $509,000.

Since the lawn-and-garden business was highly cyclical in nature, with highest revenues during the growing season, the company sought to offset the regular drop in revenues during the winter months. Toward that end, Frank's diversified and began to sell craft and hobby supplies, a line that Frank's management believed would complement its gardening merchandise, since both appealed to customers interested in "do-it-yourself" projects. The first Frank's Trims, a store which sold only craft goods, was opened in 1966.

That year, Frank's Nursery Sales went public, gaining a listing on the American and Detroit stock exchanges. Frank's used the funds to expand and build new stores, particularly in the neighboring states of Indiana and Ohio. In 1973 Frank's opened its first four Illinois stores in suburban Chicago. The following year, Frank's moved into Minnesota when it purchased five garden centers in suburban Minneapolis from the Green Giant Company.

By the time of the company's 25th anniversary in 1974, 51 Frank's stores were in operation in five states, employing some 1,200 workers in high season. The company's sales had reached $37.2 million with a net profit of $1.13 million. Also during this time, Frank Sherr was succeeded by his son, I. William Sherr, who had previously served the company as executive vice-president and treasurer. Max Weinberg continued to serve as company president.

In 1980 the company's name was changed from Frank's Nursery Sales, Inc. to Frank's Nursery & Crafts, Inc., to emphasize the dual nature of the retail chain. Sales in 1980 reached $119.3 million on revenues rung up at 80 stores. Frank's continued to grow. In the 1980s Frank's stores were opened in Maryland, Pennsylvania, Delaware, Florida, Virginia, Missouri, New Jersey, Kentucky, and New York. During this time, much of Frank's expansion came by acquiring small regional chains such as Gaudio's in Philadelphia and Scott's Seaboard in Baltimore.

In 1983 Frank's Nursery & Crafts was purchased by General Host Corporation. General Host bought 96 percent of Frank's shares in a $19-a-share tender offer in March 1983; the value of the sale was thus approximately $42.4 million. Frank's at that time spanned 95 stores.

General Host was a large conglomerate comprised of an array of holdings. Since the 1970s, the company had actively acquired and divested companies as it continuously redefined itself. At the time it purchased Frank's, General Host's interests included meat packing, food service, and convenience stores; Frank's was the first lawn-and-garden company in its holdings. Upon its purchase of Frank's, however, General Host chairman and chief executive Harris J. Ashton began to see the potential profit in a national chain of garden supply/craft supply stores. Ashton's model was the Toys R Us retail chain, which through large volume purchases, low overhead, and low retail prices became one of the biggest success stories of the 1980s. Ashton felt that baby boomers would take an interest in gardening as they got older. He started to sell off his assets—including Hickory Farms of Ohio, Inc., All American Gourmet Co. frozen foods (maker of Budget Gourmet frozen entrees), and Hot Sam pretzel shops—to fund other acquisitions focusing on lawn-and-garden, craft, and Christmas merchandising.

At the time, Frank's stores were expensive to build, with each store costing over $1 million. A typical Frank's store was located on a three-acre site near a highly visible retail strip or shopping center. It covered 35,000 square feet, including an outside sales area. Ashton incorporated the wide aisles, shopping carts, and vast selection that had been component's of Toys R Us's success. Frank's also began to enclose their outdoor garden supply areas so that they could be used throughout the year.

In 1984 General Host sold off the profitable Van de Camp's Frozen Foods unit and Little General convenience stores, while bolstering its gardening centers through the acquisition of the East Coast-based merchandiser Flower Time, Inc. Flower Time was eventually merged into Frank's in 1989, and Frank's had become General Host's core business by the early 1990s.

In 1991 the first of Frank's stand-alone Christmas stores, Christmas by Frank's, opened. These stores were temporary installations placed in high-volume regional malls, allowing shoppers to purchase holiday decorations and gift wrap while they shopped for gifts. Indeed, Christmas decorations and crafts became increasingly important lines to Frank's, helping to compensate for the seasonal sales declines in gardening supplies.

In 1993 the company launched Frank's SuperCrafts, opening two stores in the Detroit area. Designed as "superstores," the SuperCrafts stores encompassed 20,000 square feet of retail space, allowing for a wider selection of craft supplies and home and holiday decorations, while incorporating in-store framing shops and floral arrangement services. Moreover, the stores featured hundreds of craft project displays, giving customers creative ideas and allowing them to see firsthand completed projects. In 1993, the company planned to open three more Frank's SuperCrafts stores.

During this time, Ashton took note of a major rival in the lawn and garden center business: the Sunbelt Nursery Group. In April 1993 General Host purchased Pier 1 Imports' 49.5 percent interest in Sunbelt, which consisted of over 100 lawn-and-garden centers under various names, including Wolfe Nursery

in Texas and Oklahoma, Tip Top Nursery in Arizona, and Nurseryland in California. Ashton stated that he wanted to open 25 more stores that year, perhaps in some areas where Sunbelt had outlets, hinting at a possible future merger.

Sales in 1992 grew to $558 million, a seven percent increase over the previous year, yet higher costs and interest on General Host's debt caused its profits to decline, from $8.7 million in 1991 to $2.9 million in 1992. By 1994, in fact, General Host's headlong expansion had come to an end, as a series of new stores proved unprofitable. In January, Frank's announced the closure of 26 stores, most of which were in the Nashville, Tennessee, area and in Florida. By September 1994, General Host had sold its interests in Sunbelt to another lawn and garden chain. Company officials announced that such sales and closings would save General Host $3.8 million annually; other cuts were to come in $25 million worth of inventory, all of which would help service General Host's $238 million in debt.

During this time, however, Frank's Christmas stores and SuperCrafts centers were thriving, exceeding sales expectations. Moreover, General Host implemented a line of proprietary lawn and garden products at its Frank's Nursery stores, which the company hoped would compete effectively with national brands. In a letter to shareholders, Ashton remained optimistic about the future of Frank's stores, expressing his conviction "that Frank's will retain its position as the best and largest lawn and garden chain in the United States and that this position is unassailable."

Further Reading:

Byrne, Harlan S. "General Host: It's Sown the Seeds of a Profit Revival," *Barron's,* May 24, 1993, p. 39.

"General Host Obtains 96% of Frank's Nursery," *The Wall Street Journal,* March 8, 1983, p. 53.

"General Host to Eliminate 26 Stores, Take Charge Totaling $13.6 Million," *The Wall Street Journal,* January 4, 1994, p. B4.

King, Resa, and Rebecca Aikman, "Blooming Madness or the Seeds of Success?" *Business Week,* April 22, 1985, p. 102.

"Lawn Product Retailer Posts Fiscal Fourth-Quarter Loss," *The Wall Street Journal,* April 11, 1994, p. A6.

Marcial, Gene G., "This Gardener's Thumb Is Finally Turning Green," *Business Week,* May 27, 1991, p. 100.

—Cheryl Collins

Fritz Companies, Inc.

706 Mission Street
San Francisco, California 94103
U.S.A.
(415) 904-8360
Fax: (415) 541-7813

Public Company
Incorporated: 1933
Employees: 4,968
Sales: $516 million
Stock Exchanges: NASDAQ
SICs: 4731 Freight Transportation Arrangement; 4226
    Special Warehousing & Storage, Not Elsewhere Classified

Fritz Companies is one of the largest firms in the integrated logistics field. Extending well beyond the company's original business of customs brokerage, integrated logistics comprises an array of services that supports the entire import and export process. These include air- and ocean-freight forwarding, warehousing, distribution, inventory tracking, insurance brokerage, shipment tracking, and numerous other capabilities. Integrated logistics differs substantially, and not merely semantically, from traditional transportation services: advances in information processing have allowed firms like Fritz to coordinate and harmonize logistical functions in truly revolutionary ways that have saved corporations millions of dollars.

Fritz Companies was founded in 1933, when Arthur Fritz became dissatisfied with his job at Harper Group (still located up the street from Fritz headquarters in downtown San Francisco, and still a major competitor). He decided to open his own four-man customs brokerage firm, i.e., a company that assists in clearing goods through customs by handling the paperwork and other duties. The company initially specialized in liquor and Chinese food products, and a significant portion of its business came from San Francisco's Chinatown merchants.

Over the next 30 years, Arthur Fritz expanded the company both functionally and geographically. In 1937 it began to offer ocean freight forwarding services, primarily selling cargo space. In 1942 the company's first branch offices were established in Los Angeles and New Orleans. In 1954 Fritz entered the fields of insurance services and duty drawback (that is, recovery of customs duties and taxes paid on imported goods that are later exported). In 1963 Fritz added warehousing and domestic distribution services to its menu of offerings. By 1965 Fritz had 475 employees and 750 clients, but was still a relatively small business. In the late 1960s, with annual sales of about $5 million, Fritz still couldn't afford its own computer.

Upon Arthur Fritz's retirement in 1971, the company was taken over by his daughter Sandra Davis and his sons Lynn and Arthur, Jr., with each acquiring a one-third stake. It was during the 1970s that Lynn, who had entered the business in 1965 while still in his early twenties, began to develop a broader vision for Fritz. He believed that as the world became more economically integrated, Fortune 1000 companies would require firms that could help them in all of the functions related to import/export, including transportation, warehousing, and transaction processing. These abilities would be expensive for each multinational to develop independently, especially compared with the cost of similar domestic services, since each firm would need to build its own staff and its own systems. Lynn Fritz foresaw that they would look for alternatives, and that companies that could manage all of their international logistics would be extremely well positioned.

Beginning in 1971, therefore, the company focused on two complementary objectives: becoming the information processing leader in the industry and targeting large national accounts that would require the use of international logistics services. In 1980 Fritz linked all of its offices by FAST (Fritz Automated System for Transportation), its on-line database network. FAST became one of the first systems that automatically linked into the United States Customs Service information database. In 1985 the on-line network was extended to its international offices, which by then included operations in the Far East. Throughout the 1980s, Fritz continued to expand its information capabilities, and as its technology improved, its roster of Fortune 1000 clients expanded as well. Between 1985 and 1989 the company's revenues increased significantly, and by 1989 they totaled $143 million.

In 1988 Lynn Fritz purchased his brother's and sister's share of the business in what one security analyst said "amounted to a leveraged buyout" (in which the buyer uses the assets of the company to collateralize the loans for taking it over). As sole owner of the company, Lynn Fritz was able to focus its operations more sharply. As Fritz entered the 1990s, the work of the past 20 years in developing advanced information systems and creating a worldwide network of operations begin to show huge dividends, and the company entered a period of rapid growth. In a major coup for Fritz in 1990, giant retailer Sears gave Fritz responsibility for all of its import logistics operation, allowing the company to eliminate about 100 clerical jobs. In the 1990s, many firms were restructuring their operations to enable them to compete in the emerging global economy, and outsourcing the logistics function became an attractive alternative. The list of blue-chip companies that turned over much or all of their international logistics function to Fritz included Boeing, Federal Express, McDonald's, Microsoft, and Polaroid.

Just what does international logistics entail, i.e., what exactly might Fritz do for one of its clients? Analyst J. G. Larkin of the Wall Street firm Alex Brown & Company offered an example in a 1993 report:

"Let's assume that Client A wants to source fabric from China and manufacture 10,000 shirts at a point on the Pacific Rim. That particular decision would be made by the client's purchasing department and then be relayed electronically to Fritz, which would arrange to have those T-shirts manufactured, packaged, and then brought via a local motor carrier in Asia to a warehouse, where that shipment of 10,000 shirts would be consolidated with shipments from other suppliers of Client A and many other clients bound for the United States. These shipments would be assembled into international steamship containers that would then be drayed to the Port of Hong Kong. For example, the container would be placed on a ship and transported to the West Coast of the United States. Once that container ship arrived at a port on the West Coast, Fritz would clear the goods through U.S. customs and arrange to have the container carrying the 10,000 shirts loaded on a stack train to be moved to Chicago.

"In Chicago, the stack train would be broken down into individual containers. The containers containing the 10,000 T-shirts along with various other shippers' products would be consolidated. The 10,000 T-shirts may be put on a less-than-truckload carrier's truck and then moved to the client's distribution center in Columbus, Ohio. Accordingly Fritz will have completely handled this complex, multimodal transportation transaction for Client A. Fritz arranged for various modes of transportation and various warehousing activities, and through its systems, allowed the customer the opportunity to track that bonded shipment as it proceeded through the logistics pipeline with full inventory control and on-time delivery schedule."

The automation platform that supported this transaction came from FLEX, the Fritz Logistics Expediting System (FLEX), which became substantially operational in 1991. Partly because of Fritz's leadership, by the 1990s computerized inventory systems were not unusual in the industry. FLEX, however, was more ambitious: a complete on-line tracking and management system that controlled all functions, from purchase order to delivery. It was FLEX that enabled the company—and its customers—to track the flow of goods through each step during the entire transportation process.

The attractiveness of Fritz's services were reflected in its results. In 1991 total revenues were up 25 percent to $202 million, and net income rose 21 percent to $5.4 million. The following year, revenues were up another 23 percent to $249 million, and earnings nearly doubled to $10.5 million. By that time, each year Fritz was growing substantially to offer better service to its clients. In 1992 alone, in Asia it added offices in Malaysia, the Philippines, Sri Lanka, Bangladesh, Thailand, and China; in South America, it acquired former local agents in Chile and Argentina; in Europe, it opened its first office in Belgium; and in the United States, it opened offices in San Diego and Kansas City. During the year Fritz also made an initial public offering, selling 28 percent of its shares, and was listed on the Nasdaq. According to the San Francisco *Chronicle,* the shares were oversubscribed by 800 percent, reflecting the enormous respect that the company commanded and the huge potential for its businesses.

In 1993 Fritz stepped up its expansion program to strengthen its worldwide capabilities. A primary focus was Latin America,

where Fritz opened offices in Brazil, Mexico, and Venezuela, which together represented 80 percent of the Latin American market. It also opened offices in Laredo and Austin in Texas as a conduit to the region. Domestic offices were established in Tampa, Orlando, and Phoenix, and the company strengthened its operations in the New York/New Jersey area. Beyond the Western Hemisphere, new offices were opened in the United Kingdom, the Commonwealth of Independent States, China, Korea, Sri Lanka, and Malaysia. The company also acquired a freight forwarder in Singapore, helping to double its business in this key hub for commerce and transportation. In total, 25 new offices were added in 14 countries. By the end of the year, the company served 20,000 clients with a staff of 3,140 in a network of 121 offices and affiliates and more than 500 business partners.

Results for the year demonstrated the huge expansion in service capabilities: revenues rose 37 percent to $342 million, while net income reached $14 million. Indeed, return on equity was nearly 55 percent, placing Fritz in the number one slot in profitability on the San Francisco *Chronicle*'s rankings of Bay Area companies for the year. The high return reflected Fritz's role as a service company, with relatively small investment in assets like real estate.

A particularly courageous move by Fritz was its entry into the former Soviet Union. The opportunity was vast, and the potential return appeared enormous. Moreover, it was a difficult place to ignore for a company that wanted to serve its clients in a truly international fashion. The market presented huge obstacles, though, including political instability, triple-digit inflation, poor infrastructure, inadequate legal protection, and large elements of corruption and outright thievery. Planning an operation in such an unpredictable political and economic atmosphere was enormously difficult. Indeed, in the middle of adopting an entry strategy in 1992, the U.S.S.R. became the Russian Federation, and suddenly such tightly centralized Moscow-based monopolies like the rail and transport ministries became the responsibility of 15 new nations and of increasingly independent local governments.

Fritz persevered, eventually opening a local, wholly owned subsidiary in 1993. Its staff initially consisted of a few Russian-speaking U.S. expatriates and one Russian staff member. Fritz brought in specialists from accounting to air-freight management to train the staff. Within a year, Fritz's operations had grown to 35 people in seven cities in five of the new republics. The company gained a great deal of hard-won experience in a market that frightened many Western businesses. Whether the effort and expense in penetrating these markets will ultimately be justified in high returns remained to be seen, but Fritz's mettle in taking up the challenge could not be denied.

During 1994 Fritz maintained its sterling performance. Revenues were up almost 51 percent to $516 million from $342 million a year earlier, and earnings rose 40 percent to $19.6 million from $14 million. The company continued its rapid expansion of offices and facilities. It acquired the Canadian international logistics firm Starber International, which had 500 employees and 50 service locations in Canada. The buyout was particularly noteworthy in light of the passage of the North American Free Trade Agreement, which lowered trade barriers throughout North America. Further expansion occurred in the United Kingdom and other European markets. Notably, Fritz took over I-DIKA Milan SRL, which not only strengthened Fritz's services in Italy, but also brought unusual expertise and relationships in the fashion industry. Thus, Fritz's growth comprised not only geographic expansion but strategic penetration of selected industries. In late 1994, Fritz took over Air Compak, a Rochester, New York-based global freight provider and third-party logistics provider with over 100 employees and offices throughout the United States, Canada, Europe, and Australia.

Fritz's heady expansion and stunning results made it a darling of Wall Street: between January 1994 and March 1995, the stock price soared from $26 to $65. While the stock was also helped by a secondary stock offering that had raised outstanding shares by 1.2 million, thus improving the equity's liquidity, the stock's performance was based on strong fundamentals and the potential for growth. Indeed, Fritz's share of the total logistics market was estimated in early 1994 at less than one percent, and while competition was becoming stiffer, there was still enormous opportunity in the business. In 1993 the company's diverse customer base included many of the Fortune 1000 multinational corporations, which sourced or distributed products globally. In addition, Fritz was also targeting medium-sized firmst for future growth. As Kant Rao, a professor of business logistics and transportation at the University of Pennsylvania, told *International Business,* "Fritz has built a reputation as a company that will go in and understand the problems of their customers." That capacity, coupled with the company's continuing commitment to information technology and its stable, superior management, appeared to ensure the company's success in the second half of the 1990s.

In May 1995, Fritz completed a merger with Intertrans Corporation, an international air freight forwarder based in Irving, Texas. Under the merger agreement, each outstanding share of Intertrans common stock was converted into .365 of a share of Fritz stock. Thereafter, Intertrans and Fritz's air freight division were combined and renamed Fritz Air Freight. Commenting on the merger, Fritz chairperson, president, and CEO Lynn C. Fritz observed, "Through this exciting transaction we are creating an even stronger company that is well-positioned to meet the increasingly complex logistical requirements of our customers worldwide."

Principal Subsidiaries: Air Compak International, Inc.; FCI Logistics, Inc.; Fritz Air Freight; Frontier Container Line, Inc.; Unlimited National, Inc.; TG International, Inc.; Dumanex N.V. (Belgium); Fritz Companies Nederlands B.V.; Fritz Companies France S.A.; Trace S.A. (France); Fritz Companies (U.K.) Limited; Fritz Companies Canada, Inc.; Fritz Chile S.A.; Fritz Companies Mexico S.A. de C.V.; Fritz Companies India (H.K.) Limited; Fritz China Services (H.K.) Limited; Fritz Air Freight (Taiwan) Co., Ltd.

Further Reading:

Bowman, Robert, "Decisions, Decisions," *World Trade,* October 1994, pp. 72–76.
Feller, Gordon, "O, Pioneer," *Profit,* July/August 1994, pp. 23–26.
Mencke, Carl, "Fritz Cos.: Pacing the Pack in Global Transportation," *Investor's Business Daily,* September 13, 1994.
Pelline, Jeff, "Logistics Firms Circle Globe," *San Francisco Chronicle,* January 17, 1994, p. B1.
Plotkin, Hal, "Profiting from Logistics," *International Business,* August 1993.

—Bob Schneider

Future Now, Inc.

8044 Montgomery Rd.
Cincinnati, Ohio 45236
U.S.A.
(513) 792-4500
Fax: (513) 771-5898

Public Company
Incorporated: 1976 as Cincinnati Word Processing
Employees: 1,500
Sales: $700 million
Stock Exchanges: NASDAQ
SICs: 7373 Computer Integrated Systems Design; 8243 Data
   Processing Schools

Future Now, Inc. is one of the largest computer resellers in the United States, supplying various computer support services through more than 25 offices in 19 states. In addition to providing direct sales to business, Future Now is also a leader in computer consulting services, and, after experiencing rapid growth in the late 1980s and early 1990s by acquiring other resellers and boosting its service offerings, has become a force in the fast-paced computer networking field.

The forerunner to Future Now, Inc. was Cincinnati Word Processing (CWP), a company formed in 1976 to sell and service Wang word processing equipment. It was generating about $1.5 million in annual sales when it caught the eye of Terry L. Theye in 1978. Theye, then a marketing executive at IBM, was eager to run his own enterprise, and bought CWP. During the remainder of the late 1970s and throughout the early 1980s, CWP posted slow but steady gains by offering a constantly changing mix of computer equipment and services. By 1985, Theye's Cincinnati-based CWP was generating about $3 million in annual revenue. The company was purchased in that year by Central Investment Corp., but Theye stayed at the helm.

CWP's stable growth during the 1980s was partially a result of increases in the overall demand for computer equipment and services. More importantly, it reflected Theye's ability to adapt to rapidly changing technology and markets. Notable was the emergence of a trend away from giant mainframe systems and turnkey devices to smaller workstations and personal computers (PCs). CWP started out selling and servicing dedicated word processing systems. The contraptions, though advanced at the

time, were soon made obsolete by less-expensive, more flexible desktop systems. Theye quickly changed his company's focus in response to the transition, and CWP began selling microcomputers.

Typical of other computer resellers at the time, CWP offered a complete package to its clients. Many companies were relatively computer illiterate in the early 1980s and wanted a knowledgeable company that could analyze their needs and propose a solution. Likewise, computer manufacturers and distributors needed intermediaries that could help buyers actually put their equipment to use. CWP, acting as an authorized dealer for different computer companies, would help its clients set up appropriate systems, including computers and all peripherals (such as video monitors, printers, and keyboards). Besides charging a mark-up on the equipment, CWP would profit from installation fees and by supplying ongoing service to its customers.

CWP enjoyed a healthy demand for its services during the early 1980s, and even into the middle part of the decade. But markets again began to shift. By the mid-1980s, computer users had become much more sophisticated. At the same time, computers were becoming more powerful and easier to use. A paradoxical corollary to the change was the gradual transition of computer hardware to a commodity-like good. Customers were increasingly able to purchase and set up their own systems, and they were more commonly buying their systems to accomplish specific tasks. Numerous new marketing channels opened up, such as discount warehouse stores and mail-order computer dealers, that offered little or no service. The end result for most independent dealers like CWP was that profit margins, particularly on equipment, were pinched.

Recognizing the need to adapt to new industry dynamics, Theye changed his business strategy to take advantage of what he viewed as emerging opportunities. In late 1980s, CWP management realized that the market for services was not necessarily drying up. Instead, user needs were changing. In the past, buyers were seeking advice related primarily to installing and using hardware. By the late 1980s, though, they needed more help with applications and software. For example, an increasing number of companies were looking for outside advice on how to interface multiple software packages on the same system. More specifically, they were interested in networking the PCs in their system to allow users to communicate with each other and to access peripherals and centralized information on servers.

CWP's answer to new market demands was a ''solution center'' approach to computer sales. That tactic entailed offering an array of equipment brands and showing customers how to hook up and smoothly integrate a multitude of different software packages. CWP eventually set up an actual solution center in its main Cincinnati office. There, computer systems and software were set up as they might be in a customer's office. Vendors, sales representatives, and customers used the center to come up with practical solutions to problems. In order to expand its market, CWP also began offering full lines of IBM, Apple, Hewlett-Packard, Zenith, and Compaq computers and peripherals, in addition to selling Wang equipment, which had been CWP's mainstay—at that time CWP was the largest independent Wang dealer in the United States, and was named dealer of the year by the company in 1987.

While to expanding product offerings and adjusting its service approach through the solution center concept, Theye and his fellow managers launched an aggressive initiative in the mid-1980s to grow through acquisition. Theye recognized that a major takeout was occurring amongst the horde of small independent dealers that had dominated the service and distribution market in the early 1980s. CWP believed that the only survivors would be those companies that could achieve economies of scale by purchasing competitors and establishing regional or nationwide networks. They also realized that service, rather than hardware, would drive profit growth. "They [independent resellers] basically had two choices," recalled Elliot Markowitz, editor of *Computer Reseller News,* in the August 1, 1993 *Cincinnati Inquirer.* "They could either sell out to a competitor or compete on the acquisition trail."

In 1988 CWP purchased two Cincinnati computer retail outlets from Donnellon McCarthy Inc. The stores, which were named Future-Now, boosted CWP's field sales staff to 24 and broadened its core Wang product line to include the brands mentioned above. The purchase also cemented CWP's status as one of the largest computer dealers in southern Ohio. CWP moved one of the stores to its 17,000-square-foot headquarters, and it retrained the staff to attune them with CWP's service orientation. Later that year, Theye and fellow managers, along with investment firm Reynolds DeWitt & Co., lead a management buyout of the company from Central Investment Corp. They jettisoned the obsolete CWP name in favor of Future Now Corp. The newly organized Future Now posted sales of about $20 million during 1988.

Throughout the remainder of the 1980s and during the early 1990s Future Now achieved stellar growth, mostly as a result of its acquisition efforts. Early in 1989, Future Now reached an agreement to purchase the Indianapolis franchise of Today's Computers Business Center (TCBC), the leading computer retailer in its geographic market. It also bought a sister Indianapolis business called Nitro Micro that sold computers and related supplies by mail order. Those purchases helped to boost Future Now's revenues to nearly $50 million in 1989, and its work force to about 150. Future Now reorganized and streamlined its new Indiana division, even adding a solution center in Indianapolis. Meanwhile, back in Cincinnati, Future Now's headquarters swelled to 28,000 square feet.

Future Now extended its reach into Kentucky with the acquisition of Paris Office Systems in Louisville in January of 1990. This increased the company's number of regional offices to four, located in Cincinnati, Columbus (Ohio), Indianapolis, and Louisville. In April of 1990, Theye stepped aside as president of Future Now, although he retained a seat on the company's board of directors and remained chief executive. He transferred the presidency and day-to-day operating control to Lewis E. Miller, the former vice-president of operations. Miller, also a former IBM employee, had joined Theye in the 1988 buyout of the company. By the end of 1990, Future Now employed about 180 people and captured revenues of about $90 million annually, while continuing to focus on its core commercial markets, including businesses and educational institutions.

Future Now's strong growth between 1988 and 1990 was a mere precursor to the explosive advances that would follow in

the early 1990s. In 1991, Future Now stepped up its aggressive acquisition program. It bought a small computer center in Dayton in April before spending $650,000 in July on Entre Computer Centers, a Virginia-based chain with an outlet in Louisville. In November, the company added three more companies to the Future Now fold: STKS, Inc, Kleine Company, and Multiple Connections. Those purchases, worth a total of about $2.5 million, broadened the company's sphere to Illinois and Iowa. In December, Future Now bought Micro Computer Center, Inc., for $2 million, giving it access to customers in Arkansas and Tennessee. Future Now's sales bolted to $139 million in 1991 as net income topped the $3 million mark.

Acquisitions continued in 1992. Future now picked up Evergreen Systems of Milwaukee for about $1 million in January. Then it completed a major purchase. Future Now had served as a reseller for products supplied by a company called Intelligent Electronics Corp. Intelligent Electronics was looking to get out of the service business, though, and focus instead on its hardware operations. So, in July, Intelligent sold its Computer Centers Division (CCD) to Future Now for about 30 percent of the purchaser's stock (valued at roughly $20 million). CCD represented a major addition to the company's holdings. The new division was expected to add $200 million in revenues, and would give Future Now nine different offices in cities across the United States, including Boston, Dallas, St. Louis, New York, and Los Angeles. As a result of the buyout, Future Now's 1992 revenues vaulted to $343 million, about $5.7 million of which was netted as income.

Future Now's national expansion drive during the early 1990s was complemented by its innovative operational strategy. Its tactics were relatively straight-forward. The company focused on the evolving computer services and consulting business (particularly related to networking), which it considered more profitable that the hardware distribution side of the business. It purchased smaller, often-ailing distributors as a way to expand its services into new geographic markets. The success of the strategy was reflected in the fact that by 1993 the percentage of its revenues attributable to services and consulting were about three times higher than the industry average for all computer resellers. Future Now also profited by relying on outside suppliers, such as Intelligent Electronics, rather than maintaining its own warehouses.

Future Now wowed observers again in 1993 by more than doubling its annual sales to $700 million. *Fortune* even ranked the company as the 27th fastest growing corporation in America. Big gains were primarily the result of a $12 million buyout of Basicomputer Corporation, a huge, Ohio-based reseller with offices strewn about the Midwest and East Coast. That purchase, combined with three smaller acquisitions valued at a total of about $3.5 million, boosted the corporation's work force to more than 1,800 by the end of 1993. Since 1988 Future Now had conducted 15 acquisitions, resulting in a national network with 30 regional offices. By 1994, Future Now had established itself as a leading national computer reseller and a leading provider of related services.

Unfortunately, Future Now's earnings—about $9 million in 1993—were not keeping pace with its sales. Management decided to pause during 1994 and reorganize its spreading enterprise, spending about $35 million on restructuring. Part of its reorganization entailed selling off its operations in five of its largest markets: New York City, Los Angeles, Boston, Baltimore, and San Francisco. The sale reduced the company's revenues by about $200 million in 1994, but brought $40 million in cash into its barren war chest. Future Now sold the concerns to its partner, Intelligent Electronics. Intelligent benefited from new distribution channels and Future Now profited by continuing to manage the offices for a fee. The cooperative effort reflected Future Now's intent to focus on its core competency, professional services, and Intelligent's ongoing penetration of the national hardware market.

After closing 23 branch offices and consolidating sales and management operations during 1994, Future Now planned to resume its acquisition drive in the mid-1990s. It also planned to spend an additional $15 million in restructuring as part of its ten-year plan to boost sales to $10 billion by the year 2005.

Principal Subsidiaries: Professional Services Group

Further Reading:

Boyer, Kerry, "Acquisition Helps Future Now Grow at Explosive Rate," *Greater Cincinnati Business Record,* May 31, 1993, p. 1.

——, "Future Now Takes a Breather from Acquisitions," *Greater Cincinnati Business Record,* November 22, 1993, p. 1.

Boyer, Mike, "Byte-to-Byte Growth: Computer Resell Firm Future Now Expands in Waves of Acquisitions," *Cincinnati Inquirer,* June 29, 1992, p. D1.

——, "Future Now Gobbles Up Rivals," *Cincinnati Inquirer,* August 1, 1993, p. D1.

Carlson, Alicia, "TCBC Founder Sells Computer Dealership to Ohio-Based Company," *Indianapolis Business Journal,* May 8, 1989, p. S3.

"Computer Services Industry," *Cincinnati Business Courier,* November 12, 1990, p. 22.

Fisher, Susan E, "Intelligent Electronics to Sell Company-Owned Stores," *PC Week,* February 24, 1992, p. 168.

Gee, Robin, "CWP Buys Future Now Stores; 1988 Sales May Reach $20 Million," *Cincinatti Business Courier,* February 8, 1988, p. 1B.

Harrington, Jeff, "Computer Firm's Future Goals May Come Early," *Cincinnati Business Courier,* June 26, 1989, p. 10B.

——, "Future Now Buys Indy Companies," *Cincinnati Business Courier,* May 8, 1989, p. 1.

McConnell, Bill, "Future Now Sells Baltimore Operations," *Daily Record,* November 4, 1994, p. 3.

Milstead, David, "Future Now Shifts Focus, Consolidates," *Cincinnati Business Courier,* December 12, 1994, p. 1.

Roethe, Jennifer, "For Success in Computers, the Future is Now," *Cincinnati Courier,* June 18, 1990, p. 9B.

—Dave Mote

G. D. Searle & Company

P.O. Box 5110
Chicago, Illinois 60680
U.S.A.
(708) 982-7000
Fax: (708) 470-1480

Wholly Owned Subsidiary of Monsanto Company
Incorporated: 1908
Employees: 10,500
Sales: $1.55 billion
SICs: 2834 Pharmaceutical Preparations

Chicago-based G. D. Searle & Company is a mid-sized pharmaceutical firm owned entirely by chemical producer Monsanto Company. Searle's best-known products include Dramamine, "the pill," and the intrauterine contraceptive (IUD). In addition to ethical pharmaceuticals, Searle's business interests include over-the-counter products, most notably NutraSweet brand sweetener. For the majority of its century-long history, the company was guided by four generations of the Searle family. Searle's innovative marketing and aggressive promotions, as well as its struggles to remain profitable, captured attention in the early 1990s.

The firm was named for Gideon D. Searle, who founded his namesake company in 1889 on the corner of Ohio and Wells streets in Chicago. Initially the small firm sold a wide variety of products, but soon reduced its product line to highly specialized and profitable items. In order to develop these goods, Searle's laboratory research concentrated on innovating drugs for the treatment of cardiovascular diseases, the central nervous system, and mental disorders. Son John G. Searle became president and chief executive officer of the company in 1936. In 1941 company headquarters were moved to Skokie, a northern Chicago suburb. One of the most successful products to emerge from Searle laboratories was the 1949 discovery of Dramamine, the first motion sickness pill. In 1966 Dramamine remained a leader in motion sickness medications; by the 1980s the drug had become a household staple.

The company's reputation as a manufacturer of quality drugs corresponded to its growing profits. Increasing sales by $1 million to $2 million annually, the company had sales of $37 million by 1960. Searle's former successes, however, offered no indication of the large profits to come with the introduction of one of the most revolutionary drugs of the decade—an oral contraceptive. Under the direction of Dr. Albert L. Raymond, head of Searle's research department since the 1930s, pioneering work with synthetic hormones in 1951 led to Searle's development of Enovid, the first contraceptive of its kind to reach the market. Within four years of the introduction of "the pill" in 1960, Searle's sales increased 135 percent to $87 million, with a 38 percent return on stockholder's equity. Moreover, almost half of the company's $73 million in total assets existed in cash and marketable securities, long-term debts were virtually non-existent, and Searle stock traded at 34 times earnings.

Notwithstanding three stock offerings between the years 1950 and 1966, the Searle family maintained a 46 percent share of their namesake enterprise. Upon John G. Searle's death in January of 1978, the family had become one of Chicago's wealthiest, with an estimated net worth of $250 million. John Searle's descendants were not only destined to become wealthy men, but his two sons would eventually assume positions of company leadership. Interestingly enough, however, in early 1963 a proposed merger between G. D. Searle and Abbott Laboratories, arranged by the two companies' presidents, was said to be inspired by John Searle's lack of confidence in his offsprings' business acumen. The golfing partners arrived at a tentative agreement over drinks in Chicago's exclusive Old Elm golf club. According to the arrangement, no plans were made to include top management positions for John Searle's sons.

The proposed merger never occurred. One explanation cited John Searle's realization that the amount of bickering on the golf course between him and Abbott's George Cain was an indication of how poorly they would get along as business partners. A more likely explanation pointed to the complications arising from the younger Searles's sizable holdings in the merged company. At any rate, John Searle went into semi-retirement during 1966 in the wake of the aborted merger; he assumed the title of chairman and his two sons moved into executive positions. William L. Searle became vice-president of marketing while his older brother, Daniel Searle, a Harvard Business School graduate, succeeded his father as president with the additional title of chief operating officer. Daniel now inherited the leadership of one of the most profitable pharmaceutical companies in the industry.

Yet even before the leadership had changed, a number of industry developments foreshadowed an era of growing problems. Competition from other manufacturers producing birth-control pills, including Upjohn and Johnson & Johnson, reduced Searle's share of the market. Furthermore, a concern about side effects associated with oral contraceptives slowed management's decision to increase production and prolonged the Food & Drug Administration's market approval of Searle's Ovulen, a second generation contraceptive. And finally, the increasing cost of research, coupled with its unpredictable results, meant that company scientists were unable to bring to fruition a new product line. By 1965 earnings decreased to $23.2 million, down from $24.2 million the previous year; while industry competitors posted net profit increases of 19.4 percent, Searle's dropped 4.4 percent.

It was under these circumstances that Daniel Searle initiated an ill-fated policy of acquisition. Purchasing a dozen small companies with a wide variety of products, including nuclear instrumentation, medical electronics, and veterinary and agricultural products, Searle diversified into unfamiliar waters. While industry competitors made similar purchases outside the business of ethical drugs, few companies were less fortunate in their choices. By 1977 Searle reported a $95 million write-off; sales had increased to $844 million, but return on equity dropped from 50 percent to 11 percent. The acquisitions outside the area of pharmaceuticals accounted for 57 percent of sales but only 13 percent of profits, and G. D. Searle's profitability decreased sharply.

In addition to a new generation of family executives, 1966 brought Dr. Raymond's tenure as director of the research department to an end. Dr. Thomas P. Carney, former director of research at Eli Lilly, succeeded Raymond as head of the Searle laboratories. Carney's background in both chemical engineering and organic chemistry, as well as his success in developing profitable agricultural chemicals for Lilly, promised to facilitate the development of new innovative drugs for Searle. Aldactone and Aldactazide, two diuretics used in the treatment of hypertension, and Flagyl, a drug to cure reproductive tract infections, awaited and received FDA approval.

By 1971 an estimated 80 percent of company profits resulted from sales of pharmaceuticals other than oral contraceptives. The previous years profits had actually risen 12 percent, but only on the company's ability to use its Puerto Rican operations as a tax shelter; while profits before taxes actually fell $5 million, Searle's tax bill was reduced by $9 million. Long-term debt was now reported at $49 million.

By 1973 sales of Aldactone and Aldactazide alone contributed 18 percent of annual revenues, surpassing sales generated from the birth control pill for the first time. Research at Searle laboratories, with expenditures increased 33 percent, led to the development of a new artificial sweetener. Discovered seven years earlier, aspartame's unique structure resulted from the combination of two naturally occurring amino acids. While the company awaited approval to market the product as a food additive, production was planned using the expertise of Ajinomoto, a Japanese company experienced in the manufacture of amino acids. With cyclamates removed from the market and questions circulating about the safety of saccharin, Searle's new product represented the possibility of a large market share. In addition to developing the sweetener, the company moved into new areas of birth control. A copper intrauterine contraceptive was introduced in England and awaited market approval in the United States.

The FDA approval of Aspartame's use as a table top sweetener, as well as a food additive in a number of items, resulted in a minor victory for Searle. Sugar prices had recently tripled and the market for low calorie products began expanding significantly. Furthermore, aspartame lacked the bitter after taste of saccharin and eliminated 95.5 percent of the calories of sugar. Yet several disadvantages in the new product caused industry analysts to remain cautious in their assessment of aspartame's future. The projected cost for the new sweetener was many times greater than that of saccharin, and its short shelf life—it

lost its sweetness after several months—precluded any speedy acceptance in the profitable soft drink market. Bottlers would resort to a more stable, less expensive product before they would turn to aspartame. Nevertheless, Searle persevered in the test marketing of Equal, the consumer brand name for its new product.

Despite such hopeful products emerging from Searle laboratories, many industry analysts remained skeptical about the company's future. Diluted earnings, resulting in part from the company's numerous acquisitions, aspartame's unclear future, and the expiration of a number of important patents all contributed to this attitude. Yet, apart from these problems, Searle management could never have been prepared for the series of blows dealt them in a televised hearing involving an FDA challenge to their reputation. A Senate subcommittee on health, headed by Edward Kennedy, sought to investigate allegations about questionable research surrounding the safety of both Aldactone and Flagyl. A 1972 article in the *Journal of the National Cancer Institute,* with the support of numerous subsequent independent studies, cited an increased incidence of lung tumors in mice treated with Flagyl. Similar cancer risks, not evident in Searle's research data, appeared in tests of Aldactone.

While conceding that "clerical errors" had occurred, Searle categorically denied any suppression of lab tests. The company did embark on a public relations campaign to improve its image of social responsibility. The price of company stock, however, dropped from around $25 to $15 per share as analysts estimated that sales of Flagyl, Aldactone, and Aldactazide would be reduced by half its previous volume. With a new strategy of public relations, Searle's problems were hardly over. In December of 1975, in an unprecedented move, the FDA suspended permission to market aspartame based on an audit of Searle's new drug applications filed since 1968.

The FDA actions resulted in more delays than actual damage. While labels warning about cancer risks appeared on the investigated products, sales for Aldactone and Aldactazide actually rose 24 percent on the last quarter of 1975; Flagyl's increased 12 percent. Aspartame remained under investigation, only to receive market approval seven years later. The $29 million already invested in its production was left in abeyance.

While the assault on Searle's corporate integrity marred the company's public image, internal problems threatened to disrupt its very operations. By 1977 money borrowed in the United States against the $420 million saved in the Puerto Rican tax shelter translated into an interest payment of $24 million; earnings from this same tax haven amounted to only $17 million. This, in turn, had some affect on overall company earnings so that shares gaining $1.56 in 1975 gained only $.57 in 1977.

To remedy the situation, an outsider was called in to assume control of the company. Donald H. Rumsfeld, a former congressman, presidential aide, and defense secretary, agreed to step in as president and chief executive officer, thus ending four generations of family management. Daniel Searle, who advanced to chairman, had met Rumsfeld 15 years earlier and supported him in his congressional election bid. Their friendship gave impetus to Rumsfeld's mid-life career change. While refusing to state he had given up public life for good, the accomplished politician rose to the challenge of correcting the company's numerous problems.

Searle's turnabout was almost immediate. By repatriating Puerto Rican dollars, bringing in new staff, selling unprofitable divisions, and announcing a massive write-off, Rumsfeld cleared the way for major changes in the company. An optical retailing business, under the name Vision Centers, represented a profitable new acquisition. In 1978 this retailer of eyeware contributed $91 million; a five year estimate placed contributions at $400 million. While long-term debt now stood at $350 million, Vision Center's profits were necessary to improve the company's performance.

By 1981 Searle reported the second-highest profit margin among 30 leading U.S. drug firms. Furthermore, an FDA announcement ended aspartame's years-old struggle to win market approval. Rumsfeld's revitalization of the research department through the infusion of $100 million promised a new line of pharmaceuticals from anti-ulcer medication to treatments for herpes. An aggressive policy of licensing and joint ventures generated income to supplement the research costs. Long term debt was reduced to $89 million as the renamed Pearle Vision Centers moved to the top of the optical retailing business.

In 1983 a 39 percent drop in earnings during the first quarter prompted a decision to sell the eyecare subsidiary. Ostensibly, income generated from the sale would help improve pharmaceutical research which had not produced an extremely lucrative "blockbuster" drug in several years. Drug research, however, did not bring the sought after profits; instead, industry analysts were surprised as sales of aspartame reached record breaking figures. As a tabletop sweetener and a food additive in cold cereals and dry drink mixes, sales between 1981 and 1982 increased from $13 million to $74 million. As the product was ready to enter into the immensely profitable soft drink market, Searle invested $25 million to expand production in the United States. Once Searle received the expanded FDA approval, carbonated drink companies lined up to secure contracts. By the end of 1983 virtually all major bottlers became Searle customers, and with the marketing plan to print the consumer name on all products using the sweetener, NutraSweet became a household name.

Despite this expansion after 17 years of testing, fears of aspartame's side effects were not completely dispelled. One study noted changes in behavior after large quantities of carbohydrates and aspartame had been ingested. Woodrow Monte, director of the Food Sciences & Nutrition Laboratory at Arizona State University, along with several consumer groups, challenged NutraSweet's safety by pointing to its production at high temperatures of methanol, a compound associated with poisoning. The FDA reasserted aspartame's safety by pointing to the existence of methanol in fruit juices.

While sales of aspartame reached $336 million in 1983, the continuing question of its safety was not the only issue to concern Searle management. The sweetener's patent was scheduled to expire in 1987; forthcoming competition threatened the sales figure. Even more disturbing was the lack of new pharmaceuticals. One observer facetiously predicted that the company, like its new campaign to sweeten sodas exclusively with Nutra-

Sweet as opposed to a combination with saccharin, was in danger of itself becoming 100 percent NutraSweet.

As sales of NutraSweet edged towards its maximum market potential the Searle family, still holding a 34 percent interest, announced its decision to liquidate part of its stake. Industry analysts, noting the timing of this announcement, predicted that the family could collect as much as $75 per share. Four months after the announcement, not one company had tendered an offer. The financial burden of running NutraSweet's huge operations, as well as an Internal Revenue Service investigation into allegedly deficient taxes paid by the Puerto Rican subsidiary, deterred potential suitors. Liability for the contested taxes was estimated at $381 million.

Only two months later, the announcement to withdraw the offer to sell Searle seemed to indicate a new effort to remain independent. The company purchased 7.5 million of the Searle family shares, reducing their holdings to 21 percent. Rumsfeld succeeded Daniel as chairman, which further solidified independent management. No sooner had these events taken place when Monsanto Co., a chemical firm, announced it planned to purchase Searle for an agreed-upon $2.7 billion. For Monsanto the acquisition represented an end to its long search for an ethical drug company that could generate the income necessary to boost its maturing agricultural chemical products. Monsanto also hoped to benefit from Searle's experienced marketing and sales staff, its biotechnological expertise, and the attractive market potential of new products like the antiulcer drug, Cytotec.

Along with Searle's attractive qualities, Monsanto also accepted the drug company's tax dispute liabilities. What the new parent company did not expect, however, was to become embroiled in a new controversy. Searle's Copper 7, the most widely used intrauterine contraceptive device (IUD), was suddenly accused of causing pelvic infections and infertility. Even more disturbing was a major business magazine's disclosure that the company distorted information surrounding the IUD's safety. The final version of the company's lab results did not state that some cells in the test monkeys developed "premalignant transformations," but only referred to cell modification. Similarly, Searle's human test results may not have accurately reported the rate of pelvic inflammatory disease developed by users. On January 3, 1986, facing 305 pending lawsuits out of a total 775 claims, Searle withdrew the Copper 7 from the market. While continuing to defend the product's safety, the company acted to preempt growing litigation costs; Searle's defense had already cost $1.5 million. The specter of events surrounding the Dalkon Shield, an IUD manufactured by A. H. Robins, undoubtedly expedited Searle's removal of the IUD from the market. Litigation costs surrounding alleged infections and ailments suffered by users of the Dalkon Shield eventually caused A. H. Robins to seek protection under Chapter 11 of the Bankruptcy Code.

The Copper 7 crisis continued to unfold in the late 1980s, as hundreds of new claims—including shareholders charging the company with failing to inform them of the IUD suits—were filed against Searle. Although a jury ordered Searle to pay $8.2 million for damages related to the Copper 7 IUD in 1988, the company appealed the decision.

Apparently undaunted by the ongoing litigation, Monsanto established a new strategy for Searle, combining research and development goals with performance objectives, and promoting those efforts with aggressive marketing initiatives. By the mid-1990s, the company planned to average one important new product introduction each year, annual sales of $3 billion, and a standing among the world's top 15 drug companies.

Launched in 1987, Searle's "Patient Promise" marketing program made it the first pharmaceutical firm in America to extend refunds on any of its products that proved ineffective. The program successfully promoted Searle's blood pressure treatment, Calan SR, to the leading position among such "calcium channel blockers." By 1990, the drug had captured one-fifth of that market in spite of competition from at least three similar medicines, and had become Searle's leading product. And according to an article published in *Forbes* magazine that year, Calan SR was the catalyst that changed Searle's financial losses into profits.

Searle countered burgeoning governmental and popular criticism of the U.S. pharmaceutical industry with a separate special public relations campaign. The company's "Rx Partners" program set up interviews wherein top executives of pharmaceutical firms could offer their perspectives on such divisive issues as pricing, marketing, and research and development.

Led by Sheldon G. Gilgore in the early 1990s, Searle underwent an admittedly "difficult" restructuring in 1992, as the company fought to achieve consistent profitability. The reorganization focused on three primary areas: rationalizing capacity; consolidating global research and development efforts; and a reduction of the administrative workforce by nearly 2,000 employees. Savings from this effort helped make possible a massive $305 million investment in research and development (20 percent of sales). Although Calan SR was still Searle's leading product, by this time it had lost its patent protection and was under competition from generics. Pinning its future on new patented drugs,

Searle launched three products in 1993: Daypro and Arthrotec, two nonsteroidal anti-inflammatory drugs (NSAIDs) specially-formulated for treatment of arthritis, and Ambien, an insomnia treatment. Daypro became Searle's first product to exceed over $100 million in sales within the first year of its American introduction. Heavy investment in research and development put several promising drugs in Searle's pipeline as well, including treatments for AIDS, cardiovascular disease, cancer, and septic shock.

Although these developments seemed to indicate Monsanto's continuing confidence in its pharmaceutical subsidiary, some business analysts speculated that an early 1990s industry shake-out that witnessed the merger of drug producers and distributors made Searle "ripe for divestiture."

Principal Subsidiaries: Akwell Industries, Inc.; Dental Health Services of Tampa, Inc.; G. D. Searle Inter-American Co.; LARO, Inc.; SCI Corp.; Searle Cardio-Pulmonary Systems, Inc.; Searle Chemicals, Inc.; Searle Food Resources, Inc. The company also lists subsidiaries in the following countries: Argentina, Australia, Bangladesh, Belgium, Bermuda, Brazil, Canada, Denmark, Finland, France, Greece, Hong Kong, India, Ireland, Japan, Korea, Malaysia, Mexico, The Netherlands, New Zealand, Norway, Pakistan, Panama, Philippines, Portugal, Puerto Rico, Singapore, South Africa, Spain, Sweden, Switzerland, Thailand, United Kingdom, Venezuela, and Zambia.

Further Reading:

Klimstra, Paul D., "Integrating R&D and Business Strategy," *Research-Technology Management,* January/February 1992, pp. 22–28.

Levine, Joshua, "Selling Hard Without Hype," *Forbes,* December 10, 1990, pp. 202, 204.

Ostrowski, Helen, "Pharmaceutical Giants Tell Their Story," *Public Relations Journal,* October 1993, p. 20.

—updated by April Dougal Gasbarre

G.I.E. Airbus Industrie

1 Rond Point Maurice Bellonte
31707 Blagnac Cedex
France
(61) 93 34 33
Fax: (61) 93 49 55

Private Consortium
Incorporated: December 1970
Employees: 1,300
Sales: $8.56 billion
SICs: 3720 Aircraft & Parts

G.I.E. Airbus Industrie is a consortium of European aircraft manufacturers formed in 1970. In a relatively short period of time and against formidable odds, Airbus grew to become the world's second-largest producer of commercial airliners, capturing about one-third of the global market in the process. Although Airbus does not publish financial statistics, it proudly reported its first-ever operating surplus in 1990. As the turn of the twenty-first century approached, the consortium set its sights on capturing 50 percent of the market for aircraft and parts. In 1994, for the first time in its history, Airbus had more new firm orders—125—than its competitor Boeing Company.

The impetus for Airbus Industrie's formation came in the post-World War II era, when the Boeing Company, McDonnell Douglas Corporation, and Lockheed Corporation, all American manufacturers, gained hegemony over the global market for commercial passenger aircraft. The last European jetliners to be produced in significant quantities were the French Caravelle and the BAC-111. When the production runs for these airplanes came to an end during the 1960s, France and Britain were faced with potentially high layoffs. European aerospace companies too small to shoulder the high investment costs of developing a new jetliner looked to pool their resources. British and French manufacturers attempted a mid-1960s merger, but political disagreements squashed their negotiations.

In May of 1969, however, the governments of France and West Germany concluded an agreement which cleared the way for the December 1970 formation of G.I.E. Airbus Industrie, a consortium headquartered and incorporated in France. The organization was characterized as a *groupement d'intérêt économique* (G.I.E., grouping of economic interests), a form of unlimited partnership commonly used by vinters and construction projects which involve several contractors. This uniquely French style of

industrial organization made success possible for Airbus Industrie because, as one official put it, "On other cooperative projects, like the Concorde, nothing could be done without unanimous agreement of all the partners. With the Airbus, they all had to be unanimous to stop us."

The founding consortium members were Aérospatiale of France and Deutsche Airbus (later renamed Daimler-Benz Aerospace Airbus, with 65 percent Messerschmitt-BölkowBlohm and 35 percent VFW-Fokker) of West Germany. Construcciones Aeronauticas S.A. (CASA) of Spain joined in 1971. As the catalyst of the group, Airbus Industrie provided research, development, and design as well as marketing and product support to its affiliates. Member companies, in turn, would procure, manufacture, and assemble components. For example, Deutsche Airbus manufactured most of the fuselages and vertical tails, CASA contributed horizontal tails, and Britain's Hawker-Siddeley (a subcontractor until 1979) made the wings. These parts were transported to Aérospatiale's assembly facilities in Toulouse where they were assembled with cockpits and center fuselages manufactured there.

At the time, the most popular medium-size American jetliners, the Boeing 727 and McDonnell-Douglas DC-9, were fitted with inefficient engines which consumed large quantities of fuel. The Airbus A300 was designed to compete with these jetliners by incorporating the latest avionic technology and the most efficient engines available. Britain's Rolls-Royce plc was selected to manufacture the A300's jet engines, but had to withdraw from the program when work on its RB.207 engine fell behind schedule. Airbus then turned to America's General Electric Company to supply an alternative engine, the CF6-50, which was built for use on McDonnell Douglas's DC-10. The choice of a new engine power plant forced a design change in the A300 which reduced its passenger capacity from 300 to 250. Although unplanned, it was a fortunate turn of events for Airbus: at that time many airline companies were struggling to avoid overcapacity caused by excessively large airplanes. Rather unexpectedly, the A300 had gained several competitive advantages.

The A300 made its maiden flight on October 28, 1972 (ahead of schedule) and entered regular service with Airbus's first customer, Air France, in May of 1974. Interest in the fuel-efficient A300 increased when the 1973 world oil crisis caused fuel prices to rise dramatically. By 1975 over 40 of these airplanes had been ordered.

At this time Henri Ziegler retired as the head of Airbus. He was succeeded by Bernard Lathière, who had previously served with the French Civil Aviation Authority. Lathière, known to airline executives around the world as "Monsieur Airbus," made aircraft sales his primary concern. The engineering and production coordination was largely handled by general manager Roger Béteille from his office at Airbus's final assembly plant in Toulouse. While Lathière was president of the consortium and maintained a high public profile, it was Roger Béteille who worked behind the scenes.

Lathière appointed George Warde, the former president of American Airlines, to promote Airbus sales in the United States. The American aircraft manufacturers (Boeing in particular) worked very hard to prevent Airbus from entering the American aircraft market. Warde was able, however, to reach an agreement with Eastern Airlines whereby Eastern would operate four A300s on a six-month trial basis and fund the $7 million crew training and maintenance costs. It was a risky and potentially costly gamble which paid off in 1978 when both Eastern and Pan American World Airways, Inc. decided to purchase the A300.

That July, Airbus Industrie announced the development of a new jetliner called the A310. This smaller and more efficient version of the A300 incorporated a unique fuel-saving feature. When the A310 is in flight, fuel is pumped from an aft tank into the main wing tanks to help maintain the airliner's center of gravity. On other aircraft a device called a "trim control" automatically adjusts the tail elevators in order to maintain level flight. However, excessive reliance on the trim control causes aerodynamic drag which wastes fuel. The A310s fuel pumping scheme has since been duplicated by other aircraft manufacturers and has become a regular feature of most modern aircraft designs. In addition, the A310s wings were redesigned to make it more efficient at distances of less than 1500 miles. This became a major selling point for Airbus, since three-quarters of all airline routes are distances of less than 1500 miles. The A310 made its inaugural flight in April of 1982 and entered service with Lufthansa a year later.

Britain became an official member of the Airbus consortium when, in January of 1979, Hawker-Siddeley became a part of the state-owned British Aerospace. The addition of British Aerospace established Airbus's capitalization ratio at 37.9 percent each for Aérospatiale and Deutsche Airbus, 20 percent for British Aerospace, and 4.2 percent for CASA of Spain. That May, Belairbus of Belgium and Fokker-VFW of the Netherlands joined as associate production affiliates. Fokker, which had become a subsidiary of West Germany's Vereinigte Flugtechnische Werke (VFW) in 1969, was sold back to public investors in 1980. VFW was subsequently acquired by Messerschmitt-Bölkow-Blohm, but Fokker continued to be associated with Airbus as a subcontractor.

Although Airbus had surpassed both McDonnell Douglas and Lockheed to rank second only to Boeing by 1980, it remained unable to achieve profitability, even with heavy government "launch-aid" or repayable loans. Upon his 1985 retirement, Lathière ended the tradition of having Frenchmen dominate all the highest managerial positions at Airbus by appointing a multinational troika. Jean Pierson, a Frenchman, was named chief executive officer; Johann Schaeffler, a German, was made responsible for production; and Robert Whitfield, a Briton, was placed in charge of managing the consortium's finances.

Roger Béteille, who had come to be known as "the father of Airbus," resigned his post due to ill health in March of 1984, just as many of his technological initiatives were coming to fruition. Just a year before, Airbus had developed altered versions of its two jetliners, the A300-600 and A310-300, with extended flight range. But the company's biggest coup came with the 1984 introduction of the A320, a twin-engine, medium-range craft that seated 150 and was designed to compete with Boeing's 737-300 and McDonnell Douglas's MD-80 for short-haul passenger markets. The new model featured "fly-by-wire" technology, an electronic signaling and control system that had been previously used on the Anglo-French Concorde supersonic airliner. Called "the most significant advance in the aviation

industry" in a 1990 edition of the *Far Eastern Economic Review*, fly-by-wire is a computerized automatic flight-control system (AFCS) that electronically executes the crew's commands to wing flaps, rudders, and elevators, thereby eliminating a number of formerly mechanical (and weighty) controls, including the pilot's control column and steering wheel. The weight loss helped make the A320 30 percent less expensive to operate than its competition. Although the absence of direct mechanical controls (the pilot uses a side-stick controller to input information to the AFCS) made many potential customers leery of the A320, Airbus claimed that it offered increased safety and improved maneuverability. The plane and its revolutionary guidance system soon made aviation history.

Even before its maiden commercial flight, Airbus received over 400 purchase commitments for the A320, making important inroads in the North American market in the process. Pan Am ordered 16 A320s in 1985, and the following year NWA, the holding company for Northwest Airlines, announced that it had ordered 10 A320s with an option to purchase an additional 90. Northwest's over $3 billion order made it Airbus's most important customer. This high demand soon made the plane the fastest-selling jetliner in history. By the end of the decade, fly-by-wire had become the standard for aviation controls.

Airbus's incursion on the North American market drew intensifying criticism from Boeing and McDonnell Douglas, who complained that the consortium's high level of subsidization gave it unfair technological and competitive advantages. Although both vowed that the A320 would not survive "more than four years in the market," neither had comparable innovations to unveil. Both met the Airbus challenge by developing a new generation of airliners which had the potential to be as much as 40 percent more efficient than the A320. These new aircraft, the 7J7 and MD-91, purported to use a revolutionary new engine called a "propfan" which combined the thrust of a jet engine with the efficiency of a high-speed propeller.

The proceeds of large orders for the A320 went a long way toward defraying Airbus's record of accrued losses, which were believed to amount to between $7 billion and $10 billion by the late 1980s. Financial statistics for Airbus are virtually impossible to find. Because of the nature of its industrial organization, Airbus Industrie is not required to publish an annual report. Different accounting methods and degrees of government involvement among the individual consortium members preclude the option of assembling data. A Boeing executive has said, "The Airbus partners aren't just hiding numbers; they don't know them."

If the consortium was a typical nationalized industry, its finances would be a matter of public record. But disclosure of Airbus's financial information has the potential to cause a great deal of opposition to the consortium in European political circles. The Airbus partners' member governments would like to prevent the consortium's economic performance from becoming a political issue; its becoming one might lead to its dissolution. Airbus is, after all, the European Community's only technically successful non-military industrial enterprise.

Stung by Airbus's encroachment on its largest industrial export category, the United States government joined the debate in the late 1980s. Trade officials voiced their concern that the extensive subsidies Airbus received from its member governments violated the principles of the General Agreements on Tariffs and Trade. A 1990 study by Gellman Research Associates, on behalf of the U.S. Commerce Department, cited in a 1991 *Aviation Week & Space Technology* article pegged previous and planned government contributions to Airbus at $12.5 billion, an amount that rivaled the initial cost of launching the consortium and exceeded the net worth of McDonnell Douglas and Boeing combined. Officials at Airbus countered that the American aircraft manufacturers benefit substantially and unfairly from government-funded aeronautic research, and that they had long enjoyed an effective monopoly over civil airline supply. In particular, they have complained that the Boeing Company subsidizes the development of new commercial airliners with proceeds from its profitable 747 program and lucrative defense contracts.

External criticism of Airbus was exacerbated by internal disagreements in the latter years of the decade. After losing nearly $300 million on its contracts with the consortium, member British Aerospace called for a reorganization of Airbus's financial and managerial structure. Spurred in part by an independent evaluation of Airbus's highly (and predictably) bureaucratic corporate operations, management was reorganized in 1988 through the trimming of the firm's supervisory board, the establishment of the positions of chief executive and finance director, and the creation of an executive board. Then, in 1989, a five-month strike at British Aerospace cost Airbus $250 million in lost production time.

In spite of these labor, organizational, and political dilemmas, Airbus continued to capture a growing share of the commercial aircraft market, winning contracts with Canadian Airlines International and Air Canada in the late 1980s. Airbus raised the competitive ante with the 1988 announcement that it would endeavor to build a complete line of commercial aircraft, from the small, short-range models it had traditionally manufactured to the medium- and long-range jetliners that had been dominated by Boeing. The move up was well-timed: to combat high levels of air traffic, airlines were increasingly purchasing larger-capacity planes.

By 1990, Airbus's 800-aircraft backlog positioned it with about one-third of the $40 billion global market for jet aircraft and gave it its first operating surplus. In 1991, the consortium demonstrated its growing liberation from launch aid with the flotation of its first international bond issue, the proceeds of which were used to finance development of a new "stretched" version of the highly successful A320. Governmental involvement was further lessened in 1992, when the German government gave automaker Daimler-Benz A.G. complete control of Deutsche Airbus with the sale of its 20 percent interest.

The introduction of the A330 and A340 planes helped fill out Airbus's product line. These modular aircraft shared the same basic fuselage, wing, and cockpit specifications, making possible time- and money-saving concurrent production. These large-capacity models also appealed to customers in the emerging Asian and Pacific Rim markets. In 1991, for example, Singapore Airlines canceled an order with McDonnell Douglas in favor of the new Airbus models, and in 1995 Gulf Air cancelled its Boeing 777 orders for the A340.

The expanded line won Airbus lucrative contracts with Northwest Airlines, Federal Express, American Airlines, and, in mid-1992, its biggest coup to date: a pivotal deal with United Airlines Inc. United, called "Boeing's best and oldest customer" in an *Aviation Week & Space Technology* article published that year, had previously designated Boeing as its exclusive supplier. The contract with Airbus capped a concerted North American marketing campaign that included product and technical support as well as innovative leasing programs. By 1992, practically every major U.S. airline was a customer of Airbus.

Having consistently held a 30 percent share of commercial aircraft over 100 seats throughout the early 1990s, Airbus confidently set its sights on capturing a leading share of the entire industry. Plans for the A3XX-100, a "mega-jumbo" jet capable of carrying 600 to 800 passengers, were expected to come to fruition after the turn of the century and firm up Airbus's strong position in the Far Eastern markets considered key to future growth.

Airbus's 125 orders in 1994 gave it over half of the market and the potential to become the world's largest manufacturer of commercial aircraft. But some analysts cautioned that Airbus faced several continuing challenges in the years to come. Rancor over trade issues, especially as they applied to GATT and relations between the United States and Europe, only intensified as Airbus chalked up success after success. Global recession, the after-effects of the Persian Gulf War, and ongoing price wars forced airlines to delay or even cancel many orders placed in the late 1980s and early 1990s. In 1992, for example, Northwest Airlines canceled its orders for over 70 Airbus planes and postponed delivery of another 44 craft.

Principal Subsidiaries: Airbus Industrie of North America, Inc.; Airbus Service Company.

Further Reading:
Banks, Howard, "Airbus Comes of Age," *Forbes,* February 23, 1987, pp. 36–37.
Bond, David F., "Airbus Subsidy Dispute Highlights Clash of U.S.-EC Industrial Cultures," *Aviation Week & Space Technology,* June 17, 1991, pp. 155–156.
Caplen, Brian, "Battle Is on Asia's Skies," *Asian Business,* January 1995, pp. 6–7.
Guttman, Robert J., "Aircraft Builders of the Future: Boeing & Airbus Go Head to Head," *Europe,* May 1993, pp. 9–13.
Lorrell, Mark A., *Multinational Development of Large Aircraft: The European Experience,* Santa Monica, Calif.: Rand Corporation: 1980.
McKenna, James T., "Northwest Cuts Airbus Orders in Survival Bid," *Aviation Week & Space Technology,* December 14/21, 1992, pp. 26–27.
Newhouse, John, *The Sporty Game,* New York: Knopf, 1982.
Ott, James, "Airbus Wins United A320 Order, Boosting U.S. Presence," *Aviation Week & Space Technology,* July 13, 1992, pp. 22–23.
"Plane Wars: A Paper Dart Against Boeing," *Economist,* June 11, 1994, p. 61.
Selwyn, Michael, "Airbus Industrie: Mega-Jumbo Plan for Asia," *Asian Business,* November 1991, p. 10.
Toy, Steward, "Zoom! Airbus Comes on Strong," *Business Week,* April 22, 1991, pp. 48–50.
Westlake, Michael, "Flying With No Pilot," *Far Eastern Economic Review,* July 5, 1990, p. 66.

—updated by April Dougal Gasbarre

General Electric Company

3135 Easton Turnpike
Fairfield, Connecticut 06431
U.S.A.
(203) 373-2211
Fax: (203) 373-2071

Public Company
Incorporated: 1892
Employees: 222,000
Sales: $60.1 billion
Stock Exchanges: New York Boston London Tokyo
SICs: 3511 Steam, Gas, & Hydraulic Turbines, & Turbine
   Generator Set Units; 3612 Power Distribution & Specialty
   Transformers; 6141 Personal Credit Institutions; 6159
   Miscellaneous Business Credit Institutions; 6411 Insurance
   Agents, Brokers, & Service

The history of General Electric is a significant part of the history of technology in America. GE has evolved from Thomas Edison's home laboratory into one of the largest companies in the world, following the evolution of electrical technology from the simplest early applications into the high-tech wizardry of the late twentieth century.

Thomas Edison established himself in the 1870s as an inventor after devising, at the age of 23, an improved stock ticker. He subsequently began research on an electric light as a replacement for gas light, the standard method of illumination at the time. In 1876 Edison moved into a laboratory in Menlo Park, New Jersey. Two years later, in 1878, Edison established, with the help of his friend Grosvenor Lowry, the Edison Electric Light Company with a capitalization of $300,000. Edison received half of the new company's shares on the agreement that he work on developing an incandescent lighting system. The major problem Edison and his team of specialists faced was finding an easy-to-produce filament that would resist the passage of electrical current in the bulb for a long time. He triumphed only a year after beginning research when he discovered that common sewing thread, once carbonized, worked in the laboratory. For practical applications, however, he switched to carbonized bamboo.

Developing an electrical lighting system for a whole community involved more than merely developing an electric bulb; the devices that generated, transmitted, and controlled electric power also had to be invented. Accordingly, Edison organized research into all of these areas and in 1879, the same year that he produced an electric bulb, he also constructed the first dynamo, or direct-current generator.

The first application of electric lighting was on the steam ship *Columbia* in 1880. In that same year, Edison constructed a three-mile-long trial electric railroad at his Menlo Park laboratory. The first individual system of electric lighting came in 1881, in a printing plant. However, the first full-scale public application of the Edison lighting system was actually made in London, at the Holborn Viaduct. The first system in the United States came soon after when Pearl Street Station was opened in New York City. Components of the system were manufactured by different companies, some of which were organized by Edison; lamps came from the parent company, dynamos from the Edison Machine Works, and switches from Bergmann & Company of New York. In 1886, the Edison Machine Works was moved from New Jersey to Schenectady, New York.

While these developments unfolded at Edison's company, the Thomson-Houston Company was formed from the American Electric Company, founded by Elihu Thomson and Edwin Houston, who held several patents for their development of arc lighting. Some of their electrical systems differed from Edison's through the use of alternating-current (AC) equipment, which can transmit over longer distances than DC systems. By the early 1890s the spread of electrification was threatened by the conflict between the two technologies and by patent deadlocks, which prevented further developments because of patent-infringement problems.

By 1889, Edison had consolidated all of his companies under the name of the Edison General Electric Company. Three years later, in 1892, this company was merged with the Thomson-Houston Electric Company to form the General Electric Company. Although this merger was the turning point in the electrification of the United States, it resulted in Edison's resignation from GE. He had been appointed to the board of directors but he attended only one board meeting, and sold all of his shares in 1894, although he remained a consultant to General Electric and continued to collect royalties on his patents. The president of the new company was Charles A. Coffin, a former shoe manufacturer who had been the leading figure at Thomson-Houston. Coffin remained president of General Electric until 1913, and was chairman thereafter until 1922.

In 1884, Frank Julian Sprague, an engineer who had worked on electric systems with Edison, resigned and formed the Sprague Electric Railway and Motor Company, which built the first large-scale electric streetcar system in the United States, in Richmond, Virginia. In 1889 Sprague's company was purchased by Edison's. In the meantime, the two other major electric-railway companies in the United States had merged with Thomson-Houston, so that by the time General Electric was formed, it was the major supplier of electrified railway systems in the United States.

One year after the formation of General Electric, the company won a bid for the construction of large AC motors in a textile mill in South Carolina. The motors were the largest manufactured by General Electric at the time and were so successful that orders soon began to flow in from other industries like cement, paper, and steel. In that same year, General Electric began its first venture into the field of power transmission with the opening of the Redlands-Mill Creek power line in California, and in 1894 the company constructed a massive power-transmission line at Niagara Falls. Meanwhile the company's electric-railroad ventures produced an elevated electric train surrounding the fairgrounds of the Chicago World's Fair in 1893. Electrification of existing rail lines began two years later.

By the turn of the century General Electric was manufacturing everything involved in the electrification of the United States: generators to produce electricity, transmission equipment to carry power, industrial electric motors, electric light bulbs, and electric locomotives. It is important to any understanding of the evolution of GE to realize that though it was diverse from the beginning, all of its enterprises centered on the electrification program. It is also worth noting that it operated in the virtual absence of competition. General Electric and the Westinghouse Electric Company had been competitors, but the companies entered into a patent pool in 1896.

In 1900 GE established the first industrial laboratory in the United States. Up to that point, research had been carried out in universities or in private laboratories similar to Edison's Menlo Park laboratory. Initially, the lab was set up in a barn behind the house of one of the researchers, but the lab was moved in 1900 to Schenectady, New York, after it was destroyed in a fire. The head of the research division was a professor from the Massachusetts Institute of Technology. The importance of research at General Electric cannot be underestimated, for GE has been awarded more patents over the years than any other company in the United States.

During the early decades of the twentieth century General Electric made further progress in its established fields, and also made its first major diversification. In 1903 General Electric bought the Stanley Electric Manufacturing Company of Pittsfield, Massachusetts, a manufacturer of transformers. Its founder, William Stanley, was the developer of the transformer.

By this time GE's first light bulbs were in obvious need of improvement. Edison's bamboo filament was replaced in 1904 by metalized carbon developed by the company's research lab. That filament, in turn, was replaced several years later by a tungsten-filament light bulb when William Coolidge, a GE researcher, discovered a process to render the durable metal more pliable. This light bulb was so rugged and well suited for use in automobiles, railroad cars, and street cars that it was still in use in the 1990s. In 1913, two other innovations came out of the GE labs: Irving Langmuir discovered that gas-filled bulbs were more efficient and reduced bulb blackening. To this day virtually all bulbs over 40 watts are gas filled.

The first high-vacuum, hot-cathode X-ray tube, known as the "Coolidge tube," was also developed in 1913. Coolidge's research into tungsten had played an important role in the development of the X-ray tube. The device, which combined a vacuum with a heated tungsten filament and tungsten target, has been the foundation of virtually all X-ray tubes produced ever since, and its development laid the foundation for medical technology operations at General Electric.

Perhaps GE's most important development in the early part of this century was its participation in the development of the high-speed steam turbine in conjunction with English, Swedish, and other inventors. Until this invention, all electricity (except hydroelectric) had been produced by generators that turned at no more than 100 rpm, which limited the amount of electricity a single unit could produce. An independent inventor had come up with a design for a very-high-speed steam turbine before the turn of the century, but it took five years of research before GE could construct a working model. By 1901, however, a 500-kilowatt, 1,200-rpm turbine generator was operating. Orders for the turbines followed almost immediately, and by 1903 a 5,000-kilowatt turbine was in use at Chicago's Commonwealth Edison power company.

Such rapid progress led to rapid obsolescence as well, and the Chicago units were replaced within six years. As a result, GE shops in Schenectady were soon overflowing with business. By 1910 the volume of the company's trade in turbine generators had tripled and GE had sold almost one million kilowatts of power capacity. At the same time, General Electric scientists were also researching the gas turbine. Their investigations eventually resulted in the first flight of an airplane equipped with a turbine-powered supercharger.

In the early days of electric power, electricity was produced only during evening hours, since electric lighting was not needed during the day and there were no other products to use electricity. GE, as the producer of both electricity-generating equipment and electricity-consuming devices, naturally sought to expand both ends of its markets. The first major expansion of the General Electric product line was made in the first decade of the twentieth century. Before the turn of the century, light bulbs and electric fans were GE's only consumer product. One of the first household appliances GE began to market was a toaster in 1905. The following year the company attempted to market an electric range. The unwieldy device consisted of a wooden table top equipped with electric griddles, pans, toasters, waffle irons, pots, and a coffee maker, each with its own retractable cord to go into any one of 30 plugs. The range was followed by a commercial electric refrigerator in 1911 and by an experimental household refrigerator six years later.

At the same time two other companies in the United States were producing electric devices for the home. The Pacific Electric Heating Company produced the first electric appliance to be readily accepted by the public: the Hotpoint iron. The Hughes Electric Heating Company produced and marketed an electric range. In 1918 all three companies were prospering, but to avoid competition with one another, they agreed upon a merger. The new company combined GE's heating-device section with Hughes and Pacific to form the Edison Electric Appliance Company, whose products bore either the GE or the Hotpoint label.

GE's first diversification outside electricity came with its establishment of a research staff to investigate plastics. This occurred primarily at the prompting of Charles P. Steinmetz, a brilliant mathematician who had been with the company since the 1890s. All of the initial work by this group was devoted to coatings, varnishes, insulation, and other products related to electrical wiring, so that even this diversification was tied in to electrification.

A more radical branching of GE's activities occurred in 1912, when Ernst Alexanderson, a GE employee, was approached by a radio pioneer looking for a way to expand the range of wireless sets into higher frequencies. Alexanderson worked for almost a decade on the project before he succeeded in creating electromagnetic waves that could span continents, instead of the short distances to which radios had been limited. In 1922, General Electric introduced its own radio station, WGY, in Schenectady. In 1919, at the request of the government, GE formed the Radio Corporation of America (RCA) to develop radio technology. GE withdrew from the venture in 1930, when antitrust considerations came to the fore. General Electric also operated two experimental shortwave stations that had a global range.

Other developments at General Electric contributed to the progress of the radio. Irving Langmuir had developed the electron tube. This tube, necessary for amplifying the signals in Alexanderson's radio unit, was capable of operating at very high power. Other important developments by scientists at General Electric included the world's first practical loudspeaker and a method for recording complex sound on film that is still in use today.

Developments continued apace at GE in the electric motor field. In 1913, the United States Navy commissioned General Electric to build the first ship to be powered by turbine motors rather than steam. In 1915 the first turbine-propelled battleship sailed forth, and within a few years, all of the navy's large ships were equipped with electric power. General Electric also owned several utility companies that generated electrical power, but in 1924 GE left the utilities business when the federal government brought antitrust action against the company.

During the Depression the company introduced a variety of consumer items like mixers, vacuum cleaners, air conditioners, and washing machines. GE also introduced the first affordable electric refrigerator in the late 1920s. It was designed by a Danish toolmaker, Christian Steenstrup, who later supervised mechanical research at the GE plant in Schenectady. And GE introduced its first electric dishwasher in 1932, the same year that consumer financing of personal appliances was introduced.

Also in 1932 the first Nobel Prize ever awarded to a scientist not affiliated with a university went to Irving Langmuir for his work at GE on surface chemistry, research that had grown out of his earlier work on electron tubes. The years that followed witnessed a steady stream of innovation in electronics from the GE labs. These included the photoelectric-relay principle, rectifier tubes that eliminated batteries from home receivers, the cathode-ray tube, and glass-to-metal seals for vacuum tubes. Many of these developments in electronics were crucial to the growth of radio broadcasting.

The broadcasting division of General Electric achieved a breakthrough in the late 1930s. The company had been developing a mode of transmission known as frequency modulation (FM) as an alternative to the prevailing amplitude modulation (AM). In 1939 a demonstration conducted for the Federal Communica-

tions Commission proved that FM had less static and noise. GE began broadcasting in FM the following year.

Of course, the light bulb was not forgotten in this broadening of research activity at General Electric. The world's first mercury-vapor lamp was introduced in 1934, followed four years later by the fluorescent lamp. The latter produced light using half the power of incandescent bulbs, with about twice the life span. Less than a year after the introduction of the fluorescent light, General Electric introduced the sealed-beam automotive headlight.

Even though production of convenience items for the consumer halted during World War II, the war proved profitable for General Electric, whose revenues quadrupled during the war. The president of General Electric at the time, Charles Wilson, joined the War Production Board in 1942. GE produced more than 50 different types of radar for the armed forces and over 1,500 marine power plants for the navy and merchant marine. The company, using technology developed by the Englishman Frank Whittle, also conducted research on jet engines for aircraft. The Bell XP-59, the first American jet aircraft, flew in 1942 powered by General Electric engines. By the end of the war this technology helped General Electric develop the nation's first turboprop engine.

When production of consumer goods resumed immediately after the war, GE promptly found itself in another antitrust battle. The government discovered that GE controlled 85 percent of the light bulb industry—55 percent through its own output and the other 30 percent through licensees. In 1949 the court forced GE to release its patents to other companies.

In this period the first true product diversifications came out of GE's research labs. In the 1940s a GE scientist discovered a way to produce large quantities of silicone, a material GE had been investigating for a long time. In 1947 GE opened a plant to produce silicones, which allowed the introduction of many products using silicone as a sealant or lubricant.

Meanwhile, as research innovation blossomed and postwar business boomed, the company began an employee relations policy known as ''Boulwarism,'' from Lemuel Boulware, the manager who established the policy. The policy, which eliminated much of the bargaining involved in labor-management relations, included the extension by GE to union leaders of a non-negotiable contract offer.

During the late 1940s General Electric embarked on a study of nuclear power and constructed a laboratory specifically for the task. Company scientists involved in an earlier attempt to separate U-235 from natural uranium were developing nuclear power plants for naval propulsion by 1946. In 1955 the navy launched the submarine *Seawolf,* the world's first nuclear-powered vessel, with a reactor developed by General Electric. And in 1957 the company received a license from the Atomic Energy Commission to operate a nuclear-power reactor, the first license granted in the United States for a privately-owned generating station. That same year GE's consumer-appliance operations got a big boost when an enormous manufacturing site, Appliance Park, in Louisville, Kentucky was completed. The flow of new GE products—hair dryers, skillets, electronic ovens, self-cleaning ovens, electric knives—continued.

Other innovations to come from GE labs during the 1950s included an automatic pilot for jet aircraft, Lexan polycarbonate resin, the first all-transistor radio, turbine engines for jet aircraft, gas turbines for electrical power generation, and a technique for fabricating diamonds.

Antitrust problems continued to vex the company throughout the postwar years. In 1961 the Justice Department indicted 29 companies, of which GE was the biggest, for price fixing on electrical equipment. All the defendants pleaded guilty. GE's fine was almost half a million dollars, damages it paid to utilities who had purchased price-fixed equipment came to at least $50 million, and three GE managers received jail sentences and several others were forced to leave the company.

During the 1960s and 1970s GE grew in all fields. In 1961 it opened a research center for aerospace projects, and by the end of the decade had more than 6,000 employees involved in 37 projects related to the moon landing. In the 1950s General Electric entered the computer business. This venture, however, proved to be such a drain on the company's profits that GE sold its computer business to Honeywell in 1971.

By the late 1960s, GE's management began to feel that the company had become too large for its existing structures to accommodate. Accordingly, the company instituted a massive organizational restructuring. Under this restructuring program, the number of distinct operating units within the company was cut from more than 200 to 43. Each new section operated in a particular market and was headed by a manager who reported to management just beneath the corporate policy board. The sections were classified into one of three categories—growth, stability, or no-growth—to facilitate divestment of unprofitable units.

When this reorganization was complete, General Electric made what was at the time the largest corporate purchase ever. In December of 1976 GE paid $2.2 billion for Utah International, a major coal, copper, uranium, and iron miner and a producer of natural gas and oil. The company did 80 percent of its business in foreign countries. Within a year Utah International was contributing 18 percent of GE's total earnings.

The divestiture of its computer business had left GE without any capacity for manufacturing integrated circuits and the high-technology products in which they are used. In 1975 a study of the company's status concluded that GE, one of the first American electrical companies, had fallen far behind in electronics. As a result, GE spent some $385 million to acquire firms in the field: Intersil, a semiconductor manufacturer; Calma, a producer of computer-graphics equipment; and four software producers. The company also spent more than $100 million to expand its microelectronics facilities.

Other fields in which GE excelled were in trouble by the mid 1970s, most notably nuclear power. As plant construction costs skyrocketed and environmental concerns grew, the company's nuclear-power division began to lose money. GE's management, however, was convinced that the problem was temporary and that sales would pick up in the future. When by 1980 General Electric had received no new orders for plants in five years, nuclear power began to look more and more like a prime candidate for divestment. GE eventually pulled out of all as-pects of the nuclear-power business except for providing service and fuel to existing plants and conducting research on nuclear energy.

Though General Electric's growth was tremendous during the 1970s and earnings tripled between 1971 and 1981, the company's stock performance was mediocre. GE had become so large and was involved in so many activities that some regarded its fortunes as capable only of following the fortunes of the country as a whole.

GE's economic problems were mirrored by its managerial re-shuffling. When John F. (Jack) Welch Jr. became president in 1981, General Electric entered a period of radical change. GE bought 338 businesses and product lines for $11.1 billion and sold 232 for $5.9 billion. But Welch's first order of business was to return much of the control of the company to the periphery. Although he decentralized management, he retained predecessor Reginald Jones's system of classifying divisions according to their performance. His goal was to make GE number one or two in every field of operation.

One branch of GE's operations that came into its own during this period was the General Electric Credit Corporation, founded in 1943. Between 1979 and 1984, its assets doubled, to $16 billion, due primarily to expansion into such markets as the leasing and selling of heavy industrial goods, inventories, real estate, and insurance. In addition, the leasing operations provided the parent company with tax shelters from accelerated depreciation on equipment developed by GE and then leased by the credit corporation.

Factory automation became a major activity at GE during the early 1980s. GE's acquisitions of Calma and Intersil were essential to this program. In addition, GE entered into an agreement with Japan's Hitachi to manufacture and market Hitachi's industrial robots in the United States. GE itself spent $300 million to robotize its locomotive plant in Erie, Pennsylvania. Two years later GE's aircraft-engine business also participated in an air force plant-modernization program and GE later manufactured the engines for the controversial B-1B bomber.

In 1986 General Electric made several extremely important purchases. The largest was the $6.4 billion purchase of the Radio Corporation of American (RCA), the company GE had helped to found in 1919. RCA's National Broadcasting Company (NBC), the leading American television network, brought GE into the broadcasting business in full force. Although both RCA and GE were heavily involved in consumer electronics, the match was regarded by industry analysts as beneficial, since GE had been shifting from manufacturing into service and high technology. After the merger, almost 80 percent of GE's earnings came from services and high technology, compared to 50 percent six years earlier. GE divested itself of RCA's famous David Sarnoff Research Center, since GE's labs made it redundant. In 1987 GE also sold its own and RCA's television-manufacturing businesses to the French company Thomson in exchange for Thomson's medical diagnostics business.

GE justified the merger by citing the need for size to compete effectively with large Japanese conglomerates. Critics, how-ever, claimed that GE was running from foreign competition by increasing its defense contracts (to almost 20 percent of its total business) and its service business, both of which are insulated from foreign competition.

In 1986 GE also purchased the Employers Reinsurance Corporation, a financial-services company, from Texaco, for $1.1 billion, and an 80 percent interest in Kidder Peabody and Company, an investment-banking firm, for $600 million, greatly broadening its financial services division. Although Employer's Reinsurance has contributed steadily to GE's bottom line since its purchase, Kidder Peabody lost $48 million in 1987, in part due to the settlement of insider trading charges. Kidder Peabody did come back in 1988 to contribute $46 million in earnings, but the acquisition still troubled some analysts.

General Electric's operations were divided into three business groups in the early 1990s: technology, service, and manufacturing. Its manufacturing operations, traditionally the core of the company, accounted for roughly one-third of the company's earnings. Still, GE continued to pour more than $1 billion annually into research and development of manufactured goods. Much of that investment was directed at energy conservation—more efficient light bulbs, jet engines, and electrical power transmission methods, for example.

In 1992 GE signaled its intent to step up overseas activity with the purchase of 50 percent of the European appliance business of Britain's General Electric Company (GEC). The two companies also made agreements related to their medical, power systems, and electrical distribution businesses. Welch said that his aim was to make GE the nation's largest company. To that end, General Electric continued to restructure its existing operations in an effort to become more competitive in all of its businesses. Most importantly, the company launched an aggressive campaign to become dominant in the growing financial services sector.

GE's aggressive initiatives related to financial services reflected the fact that the service sector represented more than three-quarters of the U.S. economy going into the mid 1990s. Furthermore, several service industries, including financial, were growing rapidly. GE's revenues from its giant NBC and GE Capital divisions, for example, rose more than 12 percent annually from about $14.3 billion in 1988 to more than $25 billion in 1994. Encouraged by those gains, GE's merger and acquisition activity intensified. For example, in 1994 the company offered a $2.2 billion bid for Kemper Corp., a diversified insurance and financial services company (It retracted the bid in 1995). GE's sales from services as a percentage of total revenues increased from 30 percent in 1988 to nearly 45 percent in 1994, and were expected to surpass 50 percent in 1996.

In contrast to its service businesses, GE's total manufacturing receipts remained stagnant at about $35 billion. Nevertheless, restructuring was paying off in the form of fat profit margins in many of its major product divisions. Importantly, GE made significant strides with its Aircraft Engine Group. Sales fell from $8 billion in 1991 to less than $6 billion in 1995, but profit margins rose past 18 percent after dipping to just 12 percent in 1993. Reflective of restructuring efforts in other GE divisions, the company accomplished the profit growth by slashing the engineering work force from 10,000 to 4,000 and reducing its overall Aircraft Engine Group payroll by about 50 percent, among other cost-cutting moves.

Despite a global economic downturn in the early 1990s, GE managed to keep aggregate sales from its technology, service, and manufacturing operations stable at about $60 billion annually. More importantly, net income surged steadily from $3.9 billion in 1989 to $5.9 billion in 1994, excluding losses in the latter year from Kidder, Peabody operations, which were discontinued. In 1994, in fact, General Electric was the most profitable of the largest 900 U.S. corporations, and was trailed by General Motors, Ford, and Exxon. Going into 1995, ongoing efforts by Welch to boost productivity, increase service sales, and expand internationally boded well for GE's long-term future.

Principal Subsidiaries: GE Aircraft Engine Group; GE Capital Corp.; Employers Reinsurance; National Broadcasting Company.

Further Reading:

Bongiorno, Lori, ''Hot Damn, What a Year!'' *Business Week,* March 6, 1995, pp. 98–100.

Farrell, John, ''GE Cuts Number in Layoff Plans,'' *Capital District Business Review,* October 31, 1994, p. 5.

Hammond, John Winthrop, *Men and Volts,* Philadelphia: Lippincott, 1941.

Pare, Terence P., ''GE as a Service Company,'' *Fortune,* April 18, 1994, p. 16.

Schatz, Ronald W., *The Electrical Workers: A History of Labor at General Electric and Westinghouse,* Urbana: University of Illinois Press, 1983.

Smart, Tim, ''Just Imagine if Times Were Good,'' *Business Week,* April 17, 1995, pp. 78–79.

Wise, George W. R., *Whitney, General Electric and the Origins of U.S. Industrial Research,* New York: Columbia University Press, 1985.

—updated by Dave Mote

GENERAL HOST CORPORATION

General Host Corporation

Metro Center
One Station Place
P.O. Box 10045
Stamford, Connecticut 06902
U.S.A.
(203) 357-9900
Fax: (203) 357-0148

Public Company
Incorporated: 1911 as General Baking Co.
Employees: 7,216
Sales: $568.6 million
Stock Exchanges: New York
SICs: 5261 Retail Nurseries, Lawn and Garden Supply
  Stores; 5947 Gift, Novelty and Souvenir Shops

General Host Corporation owns and operates Frank's Nursery & Crafts, Inc., a chain of specialty retail stores that sell craft and Christmas supplies as well as lawn and garden products. The company that became known as General Host, however, spent its first 50 years managing a group of bakeries. In the late 1960s, the company shifted course dramatically, looking for growth in several fields, but chiefly in food preparation and retailing. By the early 1990s General Host had discarded its earlier businesses and was focusing primarily on Frank's, the largest U.S. retail chain of its kind. Since 1970 General Host has been under the direction of Harris J. Ashton, the company's president, chairperson, and chief executive officer.

The history of General Host may be traced to 1911, when the General Baking Co. was incorporated in New York as an amalgamation of 19 former baking businesses covering many major cities between New Orleans and Boston. By 1930 the company owned 50 plants serving cities in 18 states. The production of bread, sold under the trade name of "Bond Bread," accounted for over 90 percent of its sales and production averaged nearly 1.5 million loaves per day. Cakes and pies were also manufactured under trade names. Net 1930 earnings of $8.1 million fell to $2.8 million in the Depression year of 1933.

Major expansion at General Banking did not take place until 1956, when the company bought a controlling interest in Van de Kamp's Holland Dutch Bakers, Inc. of Los Angeles, thereby stretching its operations to the West Coast. Besides Van de Kamp's bakeries in Los Angeles and Seattle, this company had

240 supermarket service and retail store units, four coffee shops, and a drive-in restaurant in California, in addition to 54 self-service retail stores, four supermarket outlets, and ten bakery shops in Washington. The acquisition added $22 million in annual sales to General Baking's $128 million from 40 bakeries. At the end of 1957 the company expanded its network to the Rocky Mountain states by acquiring Eddy Bakeries, Inc., of Helena, Montana.

By the early 1960s General Baking was earning less than one percent profit on its sales and suffering from increased competition from supermarkets, many of which had begun equipping their stores with their own bakeries. General Baking lost money in 1961 and 1965, and control passed to a Canadian firm, Denison Mines, Ltd., before the 1963 annual meeting.

In 1965, Goldfield Corp., an investment oriented mining concern, acquired 41 percent of General Baking's stock, which it raised to a majority share by June of the following year. Its chairperson, Richard C. Pistell, became chairperson of General Baking. The flamboyant Pistell, a rough-and-tumble former merchant seaman, shook the tranquil enterprise to its foundations.

One of Pistell's first moves was to address General Baking's loss of nearly $2 million in the first half of 1965 by closing 15 collectively unprofitable plants and distribution centers. The Bond Baking Co. division, previously run from headquarters, was made a separate entity with its own president. Eddy Bakeries, formerly a wholly owned subsidiary, was merged into General Baking as a division. In October 1966 General Baking acquired from Goldfield all outstanding stock of Yellowstone Park Co., Everglades Park Co., and five parcels of land in Arizona, Colorado, and New Mexico, together with related assets, for $6.4 million. These companies housed vacationers in motels and camps on park concessions. To better reflect the company's new activities, General Baking was renamed the General Host Corp. in 1967.

The late 1960s and early 1970s brought several challenges to General Host. First, in March 1968, a federal grand jury indicted seven baking concerns and eight of their officials on charges of illegally conspiring to fix bread prices in the Philadelphia area. Among these companies and officials were General Host, its president, and the regional manager of Bond Baking. As a result, General Host and the other bakeries agreed in 1971 to certify that each sealed bid for the sale of bakery products in the Philadelphia area had not involved collusive activity. In a similar case, four companies, including General Host, pleaded no contest in 1972 to a charge of fixing bread prices in the New York metropolitan region. Three of the four, including General Host, were fined $50,000 each.

During this time, General Host acquired Li'l General Stores Inc., operator of 377 convenience stores in seven states. The merger plan called for nine-tenths of a share of General Host stock to be exchanged for each Li'l General share. By then Goldfield's stake in General Host had been reduced to 17 percent. One month later Pistell made a much bigger deal, acquiring a one-eighth interest in Armour & Co., a diversified meat processor. This holding was expanded in subsequent months to between 53 and 57 percent of Armour's common stock, at a cost of $261 million in debentures, notes, a warrant, and carrying costs. By acquiring a majority interest in a company ten times its own size in sales and four times its assets, critics noted that General Host had taken on long-term debt of $207 million—far beyond its assets of $38 million.

Another problem for General Host was that a competing offer by Greyhound Corp. for Armour had secured that company a one-third interest, keeping General Host from authorizing a merger with Armour or a consolidation for tax purposes. Accordingly, General Host sold its Armour stock to Greyhound in May 1970 for $211 million, of which nearly $100 million was in not easily traded Greyhound warrants and convertible preferred stock. General Host reported a $67.3 million loss for 1969, including an extraordinary loss of $58.3 million, mainly from the Armour transactions. To fend off a possible challenge from unhappy shareholders, the managers had pushed through a series of far-reaching amendments to General Host's certificate of incorporation in October 1969, making it harder to oust them from office.

After the Armour fiasco, Pistell resigned, took a marquesa for his third wife, and left New York for an extended African safari. Harris J. Ashton, a corporate lawyer whom Pistell had made president of General Host, stepped up to become chairperson and chief executive officer as well. Like his predecessor, Ashton was not one to stand still. "I remember my mother always used sayings like 'never a lender nor a borrower be'," he told an interviewer for *New England Business* in 1987, "and I often tell her that I'd be broke if I followed that advice. You have to want to take risks and have confidence that you're going to extricate yourself if things go wrong."

Under Ashton, General Host acquired 86 percent of another meat processor, Cudahy Corp., in July 1971. Eventually the rest of Cudahy's stock was purchased, and the company, in February 1972, was merged into G.H. Holding Corp., a General Host subsidiary. The acquisition cost about $80 million. Hot Sam Co., a pretzel and snack-food retailing chain, also was purchased in 1971, for $2.2 million. Meanwhile, the company was disposing of virtually all of the Bond division, a process completed in 1972, on the ground that it did not indicate a potential for earning a reasonable rate of return on invested capital. And in January 1971 General Host exercised its option to acquire Goldfield's 17 percent stake in the corporation's common stock, an action that was challenged by Goldfield in court.

In January 1973 the Securities and Exchange Commission charged General Host with fraud in connection with its Armour transactions and of fraud and other violations of federal securities laws in its acquisition of Li'l General Stores and its Goldfield dealings. Under a settlement in December 1973, General Host agreed to be permanently enjoined from violating specific provisions of the securities laws and to be required in certain future acquisition efforts to follow procedural safeguards intended to ensure compliance with these laws, including the appointment of an "acquisition supervisor." Ashton was ordered to sell within five years 10,000 shares of General Host he had purchased in 1969 for $12 a share when the market price was $23.75, and to return the excess proceeds from this sale.

Despite such trials and tribulations, in 1973 General Host was being courted by two companies that were attracted to its

estimated $40 million in cash and marketable securities and about $80 million in net worth. In addition, the company had accumulated large tax credits for use in future years. General Host, however, fought the takeovers, accusing one suitor, Triumph American, Inc., of violating federal laws in its attempt to acquire the company and repelling a bid for control by Life Investors International Ltd.

For several years thereafter General Host kept a low profile. Net losses were reported in 1976, 1977, and 1978. The following year, however, the company began reporting healthy quarterly profits, accomplished largely by its cutting loose the subsidiaries that had lost money. By 1981 Ashton had lopped off about 15 businesses acquired since 1966 and had also cut the company's 1972 long-term debt of about $190 million by one-third. When a much smaller company, Clabir Corp., increased its existing stake in General Host stock to 24 percent in 1979 and began a takeover bid, Ashton countered by calling for redemption of General Host's convertible debentures. This move added 1.1 million shares to the 1.7 million outstanding and thereby reduced Clabir's share of the company. Clabir and its group of coinvestors sold their stock back to General Host in 1980 for $18 million.

In 1980 General Host attempted to acquire the Ponderosa System Inc., but the latter sought a temporary injunction preventing the takeover. General Host subsequently sold its 9.4 percent interest back to the steakhouse concern for about $7.3 million and promised not to buy Ponderosa stock for ten years. Concurrently, General Host began a tender offer for stock in Hickory Farms of Ohio Inc., in which it already held 45 percent. The nation's largest chain of specialty food stores, Hickory Farms was operating about 80 stores and franchising 450 more. Hickory Farms was fully acquired later in the year for about $41 million. In December the largest Hickory franchisee was purchased for an additional $11 million.

General Host's next mission was to unload Cudahy, which represented 51 percent of its sales of $762 million in 1979 but only 24 percent of its profits of $24.2 million. Unable to find a buyer, however, Ashton simply disposed of the subsidiary's meat operations, which has lost $2.5 million in 1980. Also sold were other Cudahy enterprises that had been spun off into General Host divisions and subsidiaries when the company was acquired in 1971: the Allied leather division, sold in 1978; Milk Specialties Co., sold in 1986, and American Salt Co., sold in 1988.

General Host next purchased Frank's Nursery & Crafts Inc., whose 95 stores sold lawn and garden supplies, plants, Christmas trees, and crafts. Purchased for $44.5 million, Frank's would eventually become General Host's core business, but at the time General Host remained essentially a food company. Its All American Gourmet Co. launched the popular Budget Gourmet frozen entrees during this time, and Hickory Farms, now with 1,300 stores, had become, according to a *Forbes* article, the premier gourmet food shop of middle America. One problem at Hickory Farms, however, was the seasonal nature of the business and revenues, since its products—chiefly gift boxes of cheese and beef sausage—were popular Christmas gifts, and the cumulative 1984 profit was practically nonexistent due to a weak Christmas season that year.

That year General Host sold Little General Stores (renamed in 1980) for $110 million and Van de Kamp's lucrative frozen-food division (dating from the 1960s) for $102.5 million. Also during this time, General Host acquired Flower Time, Inc., a Northeast chain, for about $27 million. Flower Time was merged into Frank's Nursery in 1989. To fend off corporate raiders eager to acquire General Host for its infusion of cash, the company in early 1985 adopted a "poison pill" defense that would make a takeover very expensive for any acquiring company.

By the spring of 1985 Ashton had decided to make the retailing of plants and flowers, rather than specialty foods, the center-piece of his company. Encouraged by a report that almost all Frank's Nursery shops made a profit of more than 18 percent on sales, Ashton foresaw supermarket-style outlets with shopping carts and wide aisles offering the public huge selection and competitive prices. An increase in common shares from 30 million to 100 million was authorized to raise capital. To accumulate even more, General Host sold the Hot Sam network of food stands for about $20 million in 1986.

The company's stock, as low as $2 a share in 1980, climbed to $25 in 1986. Still, the company suffered losses, which it attributed primarily to a mistake in Frank's Nursery's computerized accounts-payable system, which had understated the amount owed to suppliers. Nevertheless, Ashton remained committed to making Frank's the focus of General Host's operations. In 1987 Hickory Farms was sold for about $38 million, while General Host's remaining three-quarters share in All American Gourmet went for a whopping $96 million. An 80 percent interest in Calloway's Nursery Inc. was acquired by 1988 but was sold off three years later for $13.5 million. Ashton indicated his confidence in General Host's future by raising his personal stake in the company to more than eight percent by 1991.

By 1992 Frank's Nursery was General Host's core business. Serving customers out of 288 stores in 17 states, Frank's was a leading retailer of crafts, using its seasonal business in Christmas decorations and gifts to compensate for the lawn and garden trade's slack period. Trees, shrubs, roses, and plants accounted for about 24 percent of its 1993–94 sales; seeds, bulbs, accessories, and equipment for 26 percent; craft merchandise for 32 percent; Christmas items for 16 percent; and pet food and related supplies for two percent.

Despite the cash infusion of its recent sales, General Host remained burdened with debt, and during 1993 Ashton and his peers developed a plan to pare down General Host's long-term debt of $238 million by reducing costs. The plan included closing 26 unprofitable Frank's stores, mainly in Florida and the Nashville, Tennessee, area, freezing administrative salaries, implementing an inventory reduction program, and replacing the cash dividend with a stock dividend.

The company also opted to divest itself of its interests in the Sunbelt Nursery Group, Inc., of which it had acquired a 49.5 percent share from Pier 1 Imports Inc. in April 1993. The earnings of Sunbelt—which had more than 100 lawn-and-garden centers under the names of Nurseryland Garden Centers in California, Tip Top Nursery in Arizona, and Wolfe Nursery in Texas and Oklahoma—proved disappointing. So, in September 1994, General Host announced that it would sell its interests in the company to another lawn and garden chain for $4.2 million.

In the early 1990s, General Host began bolstering Frank's presence and product lines, creating the "Christmas by Frank's" boutique, which specialized in holiday merchandise, as well as opening two Frank's SuperCrafts superstores of 20,000 square feet apiece in the Detroit area. By the end of 1993, around 104 of the holiday boutiques were in operation, and sales from the superstores were exceeding expectations. At Frank's Nursery stores, General Host implemented a line of proprietary lawn and garden products, including weed and pest control products, which the company hoped would compete effectively with national brands.

After its restructurings, General Host moved into the mid-1990s seeking to strengthen its balance sheet and maintain its share of the market for lawn and garden and craft supplies. Ashton expressed optimism in a letter to the company's shareholders, published in the 1993 annual report, stating that "we are convinced that Frank's will retain its position as the best and largest lawn and garden chain in the United States and that this position is unassailable."

Principal Subsidiaries: AMS Industries, Inc.; Frank's Nursery & Crafts, Inc.; General Host Holding Corp.

Further Reading:

Byrne, Harlan S., "General Host," *Barron's,* May 24, 1993, pp. 39–40.
Curtis, Carol E., "Middle America's Gourmet," *Forbes,* March 14, 1983, pp. 90–92.
"General Host: Vertical Integration to Save a Subsidiary It Couldn't Sell," *Business Week,* January 19, 1981, pp. 103–104.
Ginsberg, Stanley, "No More Excuses," *Forbes,* April 11, 1981, pp. 78, 81.
"Growing—But Not by Bread Alone," *Business Week,* September 14, 1968, pp. 174, 176.
"It's All Done with Arithmetic," *Forbes,* February 15, 1970, pp. 22–23.
King, Rosa W., and Rebecca Aikman, "Blooming Madness or the Seeds of Success?" *Business Week,* April 22, 1985, p. 102.
Marcial, Gene G., "This Gardener's Thumb Is Finally Turning Green," *Business Week,* May 27, 1991, p. 100.
McGurrin, Lisa, "If You Really Want to Thrive, You've Got to Be a Self-Starter," *New England Business,* October 19, 1987, p. 72.
Nagle, James J., "General Baking Turns New Loaf, *New York Times,* May 29, 1966, p. 15.

—Robert Halasz

WIMPEY WORLDWIDE

George Wimpey PLC

27 Hammersmith Grove
London W6 7EN
England
81 748 2000
Fax: 81 741 4596

Public Company
Incorporated: 1919 as George Wimpey & Co. Ltd.
Employees: 11,590
Sales: £1.59 billion
Stock Exchanges: London
SICs: 1521 Family Housing Construction

George Wimpey PLC ranks among Great Britain's largest construction concerns. After emerging in 1993 from two consecutive years of losses, Wimpey concentrated its future efforts in three primary areas: residential housing in the United Kingdom and the United States, ongoing internationalization of its construction business, and capital investment in its minerals interests. Although the company has operations in 16 countries around the world, nearly 90 percent of its annual revenues came from the United Kingdom, United States, and Canada in 1993. The company's history was dominated by Sir Godfrey Way Mitchell, who led Wimpey from 1919 until 1973.

The firm was established by Walter Tomes and George Wimpey as a stone-working partnership in 1880. The young entrepreneurs initially took contracts for structural and decorative residential masonry, but by the late 1890s they had expanded into paving, specializing in laying the foundations for the horse-drawn streetcars of that era. Tomes sold out in 1893, leaving Wimpey with a sole proprietorship. Winning local public works contracts boosted the contractor's reputation in the 1890s. The company built the local town hall in 1896 and was contracted to lay the foundations for London's first ''electric tramway'' in the latter years of the decade. After the turn of the century, Wimpey won a prestigious contract to build the 140-acre White City complex. This series of pavilions and gardens built for the Franco-British Exhibition of 1908 featured an 80,000-seat stadium that also served as the site of that year's Olympic Games.

Four years of progressive illness culminated in George Wimpey's death in 1913 at the age of 58. Owing partly to the distractions and labor shortages of World War I, the founder's family put the business up for sale in 1919. With £500 for goodwill, £2,500 stock-in-trade, and an extra £100 to help the Wimpey heirs meet their last payroll, Godfrey Way Mitchell bought the firm and registered it as a private enterprise. In recognition of the fine reputation built during the company's first four decades, Mitchell retained the Wimpey name.

With £3,000 in working capital borrowed from his father, the 27-year-old Mitchell took his company back to its roots: paving. Mitchell built up a fleet of eleven steam rollers and took contracts for public and private paving jobs. In spite of severe economic recession in Britain in the early 1920s, Wimpey's annual revenues topped £137,000 by 1925. The company subcontracted for several housing developers during this period. Mitchell astutely observed that Wimpey stood to make higher profits (albeit at an increased risk) if it bought the land and built and sold homes itself instead of just contracting for the projects. The company's first residential development, Greenford Park Estate, was completed in 1928.

It seemed an inauspicious time to expand operations into such a capital-intensive venture: unemployment ran high in the 1920s, and in 1931, Britain followed the United States into the most serious economic depression in modern history. Although unemployment in the United Kingdom neared three million by 1933, Wimpey and its housing venture boomed. The company concentrated its early efforts on construction of inexpensive, accessible homes. Those in the Greenford Park development, for example, sold for £550. Buyers needed less than five percent (£25) down and received a £50 government subsidy as further incentive. Wimpey's emphasis on the low end of the residential market, with its high and relatively stable demand, would characterize its housing business for decades to come. The construction bonanza was credited with fueling one-third of Britain's re-employment from 1932 to 1935. In the decade before World War II, Wimpey built an average of 1,200 houses annually. The company continued to build roads throughout southern England during this period.

When Mitchell took Wimpey public in 1934, he set up a unique ownership scheme wherein the charitable Tudor Trust (later renamed Grove Charity Management) held about half of the firm's shares. By that time, the company's annual revenues neared £2 million—over 13 times its turnover of a decade before. In 1936 Wimpey won its first major civil engineering contract, an £800,000 government agreement to build the Team Valley Trading Estate in northeast England. The comprehensive job called for diverting a river as well as building railways, a viaduct, and other accouterments of an industrial park. By this time, the company was able to provide a full range of contracting services, from planning to marketing.

After Germany's 1938 invasion of Austria, the British government began issuing defense contracts in cautious preparation for a conflict that British diplomats tried in vain to avert. Wimpey's war-related government contracts started that year with immense underground concrete tanks used to store aviation fuel reserves. A second £4 million contract called for the construction of a Royal Ordnance Factory near Glasgow, but even this extensive project paled in comparison to Wimpey's later contributions to the war effort. In 1938 Wimpey began bidding on contracts to build airfields or ''aerodromes,'' as they are known in the United Kingdom. By the war's end, Wimpey had built nearly 100 of the facilities for the burgeoning Royal Air Force, which proved key to Britain's defense. Wimpey received so many government contracts during this time that some in the media speculated that the company was receiving preferential treatment and that Winston Churchill had a financial stake in it. In response, Mitchell himself requested a government investigation, which cleared the company of all charges and noted that Wimpey's efficiency won it the contracts. The company also built fortifications along Britain's eastern coastline in case of a German invasion. Although the RAF averted a ground invasion of Great Britain, intensive bombing forced Wimpey from its headquarters to a suburban, bomb-proof outpost on land owned by Mitchell. The Hammersmith complex was bombed shortly thereafter, and the company stayed in its "temporary" headquarters until a new office building was completed in 1949. In 1948 Mitchell was knighted "in recognition of his public services."

Mitchell laid the foundation for postwar growth by establishing local offices throughout Great Britain in the years immediately following the war. These satellites helped absorb the deluge of veteran workers and prompted diversification into coal mining, among other activities.

Demand for housing was especially high in the postwar era— nearly one-third of Britain's housing had been damaged in the bombing and practically no new homes had been built since 1939. A shortage of bricks drove Mitchell to seek out an economical, reliable, and efficient alternative method of construction. Wimpey architects and engineers based their "No-Fines" technique on a Norwegian idea. The concept employed concrete containing no fine aggregate (sand or stone), hence the name. Poured concrete walls formed the main structure upon which conventional interior and exterior finishes were then applied. Government housing contracts propelled the construction of tens of thousands of residences annually in the early 1950s, and after the government lifted restrictions on private home-building in 1954, Wimpey re-entered that market as well. The proliferation of automobiles brought many road building contracts. Other major projects in the immediate postwar era included a factory for Pirelli General Cable Works, the Queen Elizabeth II grandstand at Ascot, London Bridge House, and Heathrow Airport.

Wimpey became one of Britain's first contractors to expand overseas in 1946, when the company added offices in Cairo, Baghdad, and Singapore. Early international projects concentrated on roads and airfields, but the rapid expansion of the global automotive industry in the postwar era drove burgeoning demand for oil and petroleum products. Wimpey "mutually developed" with the oil industry, both at home and abroad. The company built oil fields, refineries, pipelines, and support systems in Kuwait, Borneo, Iraq, Syria, and New Guinea. Many of these early projects required the contractor to build its own roads out to the chosen sites. In Borneo, Wimpey built an entire town, complete with over 2,200 residences, a shopping center, swimming pools, hotels, and a power station. At first the company shipped laborers from the United Kingdom to its often-remote sites, but it gradually started training indigenous labor, subcontracting locally, and using local materials.

Wimpey naturally moved "downstream" in the petroleum industry, building numerous plants for the world's largest petrochemical firms. Contracts with chemical giant Union Carbide Corporation alone called for the construction of 15 plants in Sweden, Belgium, India, and Australia. Other major clients included Imperial Chemical Industries plc (ICI), Shell Oil Company, Conoco Inc., and, of course, British Petroleum Company PLC.

Oil industry projects often offered the foothold that Wimpey leveraged into other overseas contracts. For example, the company's expertise in petroleum took it to Jamaica in the mid-1950s, but construction of sugar processing plants, hotels, highways, schools, and offices soon established it as one the of the biggest contractors in the Caribbean. Political upheaval forced the closure of Wimpey's Cairo and Baghdad offices in the late 1950s, but by that time the company had launched operations in Canada and Australia that would prove vital contributors to overseas revenues. Wimpey's open-cast coal mine, launched in Australia in 1950, produced more than 1.5 million tons of coal in its first year alone. Over the years, operations "down under" expanded to three offices with the capacity to provide infrastructure, private and public housing, and general contracting.

Expansion into Canada was precipitated by a survey that indicated a "desperate need for construction and housing development expertise." Accordingly, Wimpey established an office in Toronto in 1955. The rapid pace of postwar suburbanization supported the company's expansion from residential construction into roads and highways as well as support systems like water mains and sewers. By 1970, Wimpey was building nearly 2,000 homes each year in the province of Ontario alone. Its high concentration of work in this region ranked Canada as the largest contributor to Wimpey's overseas revenues, at more than 30 percent.

Mitchell remained Wimpey's executive chairman until 1973. Geoffrey Foster's 1994 examination of Wimpey for *Management Today* noted the deep and lasting effects of Mitchell's tenure, characterizing him as a visionary, "patriarchal" leader whose influence was felt through the 1980s. Dick Gane, formerly chair of Canadian operations, led Wimpey from 1973 to 1976, when Reginald B. Smith advanced to the executive chair. A "life-long Wimpey man" and former chief estimator, Smith essentially carried on Mitchell's ideals as the company slogged through the difficult 1970s.

Wimpey's internationalization gave it something of a "split personality" during this decade. When the Organization of Petroleum Exporting Countries (OPEC) more than tripled oil prices after 1973's Yom Kippur War between Egypt and Israel, construction in the Middle East boomed, while most of the rest of the industrialized world went bust. Wimpey's activities there centered on Amman, the capital of Jordan, where the contractor built government offices, roads, and a stadium. Wimpey's overseas expansion earned it a Queen's Award for Export Achievement in 1977.

Although high oil prices meant a bonanza in the Middle East, they sparked astounding rates of inflation in the rest of the developed world. In the United Kingdom, wage freezes, strikes and 50 percent inflation characterized the middle years of the decade. When both the government and commercial interests lowered their capital expansion budgets, the company added remodeling of homes and historic buildings to take up the slack. In spite of the dramatic reduction in home-building, Wimpey was able to remain Britain's biggest private house-builder throughout the decade. The company also looked to joint ventures in continental Europe for new housing business.

A 1979 restructuring made Smith president, and nominally reorganized the company's numerous departments into four primary divisions: U.K. Construction, International and Engineering, Specialist Holdings, and Group Services. Wimpey had grown exponentially in the postwar era: by 1980, the company had 40,000 employees, and its annual revenues exceeded £1 billion. However, some critics noted that the company's management techniques had not developed to accommodate the company's expansion. Sir Clifford Chetwood, who took the Wimpey reins in the early 1980s, worked to create divisional autonomy and responsibility by transforming over a dozen British subsidiaries into three divisions: homes, construction or contracting, and minerals.

The housing and public works markets remained depressed through the 1980s, but the middle years of the decade saw another "boom" that helped mask any organizational shortcomings. The global recession of the late 1980s and early 1990s saw Wimpey slide from a pre-tax profit of nearly £145 million at a 1988 peak to £43 million (after exceptional items) in 1990. The company registered consecutive annual losses of £16 million in 1991 and £112 million in 1992. From 1989 to 1992, Chetwood had divested some nonessential businesses, reduced employment rolls in the United Kingdom by 30 percent, and reduced debt by 40 percent. The chief executive relinquished his office to a hand-picked successor, Joe Dwyer, at the end of 1992.

Dwyer intensified Chetwood's reorganization, coordinating all activities around business areas. Perhaps more importantly, Dwyer purged the top executive offices, bringing in a completely new, significantly younger, board of directors, some from outside Wimpey's ranks. These new managers brought new techniques to the somewhat dated company. For example, Richard Andrew, Wimpey's recently appointed director of the homes division, instituted market research to help guide that department's activities.

Dwyer also worked to change Wimpey's ownership structure. In 1993 he convinced the trustees of Grove Charity Management to reduce its stake in the contractor from over one-third to about five percent. Within a few months, Wimpey raised capital vital to fuel its continued growth with its first rights issue since going public in 1934. As Foster's 1994 article observed, "after three horrendous years, Wimpey found itself towards the close of 1993 with a strong balance sheet and a range of options such as it had not had in 50 years." The firm recorded a £25.5 million profit before taxes that year on revenues of £1.59 billion, and had reduced its debt another 80 percent, from £136.1 million in 1992 to £27.9 million. Management hoped that this positive financial position would place it in the vanguard of the global economic growth that was predicted for the latter years of the twentieth century.

Principal Subsidiaries: Wimpey Homes Holdings Ltd.; Wimpey France S.A.; George Wimpey Australia Pty Ltd.; Wimpey Leisure S.A. (Spain); George Wimpey Inc. (United States); George Wimpey Canada Ltd.; Wimpey Construction Ltd.; Grove Projects Ltd.; Wimpey Asphalt Ltd.; Wimpey Hobbs Ltd. (80%); Wimpey Minerals Inc. (United States); Wimpey Disposal Ltd.; Wimpey Property Holdings Ltd.; Wimpey Property Holdings B.V. (Netherlands); Wimpol Ltd.; Wimpey Environmental Ltd.; Wimpey Group Services Ltd.; Wimpey Fleming (Quarries) Ltd. (Ireland) (50%).

Further Reading:

Du Bois, Peter C., "U.K. Earnings Point to Mixed Revival," *Barron's,* Vol. 73, September 13, 1993, pp. 54–55.
Foster, Geoffrey, "Why the Whimpering Stopped," *Management Today,* February 1994, pp. 40–44.
White, Valerie, *Wimpey: The First Hundred Years,* London: Wimpey News, 1980.

—April Dougal Gasbarre

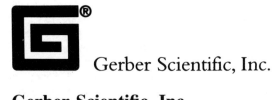

Gerber Scientific, Inc.

Gerber Scientific, Inc.

83 Gerber Road West
South Windsor, Connecticut 06074
U.S.A.
(203) 644-1551
Fax: (203) 643-7039

Public Company
Incorporated: 1948 as Gerber Scientific Instrument Company
Employees: 1,550
Sales: $254.4 million
SICs: 3559 Special Industry Machinery, Not Elsewhere
    Classified; 3861 Photographic Equipment & Supplies;
    3552 Textile Machinery; 3577 Computer Peripheral
    Equipment, Not Elsewhere Classified

Gerber Scientific, Inc. is a leading producer of machinery for use in manufacturing. The company's four main subsidiaries make devices that are used to produce apparel, graphic designs and printing, electronics, and optical devices, among other functions. Gerber was founded by one man, who came up with an innovative device while still in college. Although its product lines and areas of operation have expanded dramatically since the 1940s, the company remained committed to the spirit of inventiveness with which it was originally conceived.

Gerber was founded by H. Joseph Gerber in 1945. Gerber had emigrated to the United States from Vienna in 1940, at age 16, when he was forced to flee the Nazis. After arriving in Hartford, Connecticut, Gerber completed high school in two years. He then won a scholarship to Rensselaer Polytechnic Institute (RPI) in upstate New York, which he entered at age 19. As a junior at RPI, Gerber came up with a new kind of graphical numerical calculator, which he called a Gerber Variable Scale. This device looked like a slide rule, but used a triangular calibrated spring to make calculations.

In order to market his invention, Gerber formed the Gerber Scientific Instrument Company. While he was still in college, he turned to one of his former employers, who did a test sale of the new instrument, and then loaned Gerber $3,000 to start his own company. Gerber and his partner became equal owners of the new venture.

In 1946, Gerber graduated from RPI with a degree in aeronautical engineering. Two years later, on May 12, 1948, his fledgling enterprise was formally incorporated as the Gerber Scientific Instrument Company. The company's main product, the Gerber Variable Scale, rapidly became popular among engineers, scientists, and students. Two years after his company was founded, Gerber became the inspiration for a play entitled "Young Man in a Hurry," which was produced in New York and broadcast on television.

In its early years, Gerber Scientific was a one-product company, devoted to production and distribution of the variable scale. Over time, however, the company began to market additional engineering tools devised by Gerber. Gerber used his company as an outlet for what he called his "spirit of invention," as he told *Business Week*. All in all, Gerber turned out dozens of new tools designed to assist engineers in drafting and design. Among these were the Gerber GraphAnalogue, the Gerber Derivimeter, and the Gerber Equameter. These devices either converted graphs into digital information and equations, or converted equations into graphs. While they were original and clever ideas, however, the natural market for such tools was small, limited to a select group of drafting engineers and thus such innovations sometimes proved to be dead ends, financially speaking, for the company.

In 1961, Gerber Scientific sold stock to the public for the first time. Although the company had been in operation for more than 15 years, it sales had risen only to $738,000, despite the high degree of respect that Gerber had earned from his fellow engineers. In the first years after its public offering of stock, however, Gerber began to change the direction of his company. Using the expertise in basic drafting which it had long possessed, Gerber's company began to develop products with much broader uses. This new generation of Gerber inventions allowed for the automation of production processes, as well as design tasks.

The basis of these new machines was work that Gerber had initially performed on a contract for the Navy in the early 1960s. In response to this assignment, Gerber developed expertise in techniques to convert numbers to designs, and designs to numbers. In the mid-1960s, the company used this skill to develop a numerically controlled device that could automatically draw a precise engineering design on the basis of digital information. Gerber himself invented and patented this first truly digital drafting machine.

A Gerber customer, the International Business Machines Corporation, (IBM), which was trying to develop a computerized apparel design and production system, asked Gerber to convert this machine for clothing production by replacing the drafting pencil with a knife. With this change, the device could be programmed to cut fabric to a desired pattern automatically.

Although IBM later abandoned its apparel project in the face of the garment manufacturing industry's persistent refusal to automate, Gerber persisted in developing and perfecting the product, which he dubbed the "Gerbercutter." In addition, Gerber moved forward with another application of its designs-to-digits technology.

In response to a request from the RCA Company in 1964, Gerber modified its automatic drafting equipment a second time, replacing the pencil with a beam of light. This innovation allowed for the automatic production of printed circuitry, for use in electronic devices. The light produced a design on a photographic negative, which was used to make a master plate for printed circuit boards. In this way, Gerber provided for computer photoplotting, which also helped to automate manufacture of integrated circuits and better color television screens. With the technological innovation of its Gerber 400 photoplotter, Gerber dominated the printed circuit board industry in North America for the next two decades, as its device became a worldwide standard in the field.

By 1970, Gerber was also ready to introduce its first Gerbercutter. Although the machine represented a step forward in automation of the apparel industry, it was slow to win acceptance among garment manufacturers. The Gerbercutter was slow and awkward to use, and clothing makers were reluctant to invest in the new technology unless it could be guaranteed to cut costs, a difficult premise to prove. "The garment industry just was too sluggish to accept that kind of innovation," Gerber later told *Business Week.*

Despite weak demand, Gerber persisted in making changes to the Gerbercutter. For instance, in order to make the robotic cutting of limp fabrics more precise, Gerber invented a system of vacuum compression, which made flexible materials momentarily rigid, allowing identical cutting of a thick stack of fabric from top to bottom. Eventually, this technique made robotic cutting of pieces for luggage, shoes, furniture, and car and airplane parts possible.

Sales of the Gerbercutter remained sluggish in the early 1970s, but, by the middle of the decade, other companies had begun to introduce minicomputer systems that could be used for computerized design of apparel. In tandem with these machines, the Gerbercutter became a far more useful tool, since it could be programmed by the computerized design system. In 1976, sales of the $500,000 Gerbercutters began to grow dramatically, as large apparel makers turned to automated systems. Gerber began to receive large orders from companies such as Blue Bell, Inc., and the VF Corporation. The machine's new buyers liked its precision cutting, which led to more efficient use of fabric, and claimed that use of the Gerbercutter was able to reduce costs by five to ten percent.

In the same way that Gerber's fabric cutting device became most useful in conjunction with other machines, the company's photoplotting instruments were also most effective when linked to computer-aided design and manufacturing (CAD/CAM) systems. These systems used a minicomputer that allowed engineers to develop designs on a computer terminal, and then feed instructions to the photoplotter. In the mid-1970s, Gerber decided to enter the market for CAD/CAM systems, already dominated by half a dozen other firms, as well. In April 1978, the company introduced its first CAD/CAM product. Six months later, the Gerber Scientific Instrument Company changed its name to Gerber Scientific, Inc., to reflect the growing variety of the products that it made.

By 1979, sales of Gerber's CAD/CAM product had grown to $10 million. Sales of the Gerbercutter were also booming, as the company's backlog of orders rose to $13 million, up from $4.7 million just a year before. Overall, sales of this device had quadrupled over just three years, rising to account for one-third of the company's overall revenues. At the end of 1978, Gerber reported a 50 percent rise in its profits, as it announced an order for 14 new computerized cutting systems.

Despite these gains, Gerber's heavy outlays for research and development of new products, such as its CAD/CAM system, put a strain on the company's limited finances. In an effort to alleviate some of this pressure, the company raised funds by selling additional stock to the public in August 1979.

In order to position itself for further growth in the markets in which it competed, Gerber also undertook a restructuring of its corporate organization in April 1979. At that time, the company split its operations into three subsidiaries: Gerber Systems Technology, which produced CAD/CAM devices; the Gerber Scientific Instrument Company, which handled its traditional drafting products; and Gerber Garment Technology, which marketed the Gerbercutter and other tools for use in the apparel industry. "The banks recognize that we're structured now to grow," a Gerber executive explained to *Business Week.* The company ended 1979 with $45 million in sales.

Gerber's strong performance persisted in 1980. Demand for its products continued to grow, and halfway through the year, Gerber's backlog of unfilled orders had reached $35 million. Overall, the company's annual sales rose by 65 percent to $74.4 million, and earnings topped $5.8 million. In the following year, this figure rose to $8.8 million.

As it moved into the 1980s, Gerber began to expand its presence in foreign markets. In March 1981, the company formed Gerber Scientific France S.A.R.L., and in October of that year, it established Gerber Systems Technology International, Inc. This subsidiary was set up to take care of sales and customer service for the company's European clients. A month later, Gerber also founded Gerber Scientific Scandinavia, AB. Gerber held ten percent of the world market for CAD/CAM equipment by the end of 1981.

Gerber continued its international expansion in 1982, setting up a German subsidiary. Although Gerber introduced a new low-cost CAD/CAM system in 1982, called the Autograph system, which sold for under $100,000, the company's income dropped that year to $3.26 million.

In 1983, Gerber made its first acquisition of another company since the late 1960s, when it purchased Camsco, Inc., which it renamed Gerber Camsco. The company also continued to augment its international operations, founding Gerber Scientific Italy in March 1983. In May of that year, the company enhanced its capital-raising operations when it added the Gerber Venture Capital Corporation. In addition, the company undertook an effort to expand its technology into new applications, entering a joint venture to make an automated laser cutter for sheet metal.

This move was part of a major shift in one of Gerber's primary markets. Although constant innovations in its photoplotting equipment had allowed Gerber to maintain its standing as the industry leader in the printed circuit board field for nearly a quarter of a century, in the mid-1980s, the development of laser photoplotting caused a shake-up in the field. New companies and ideas arose to challenge Gerber's dominance. With the development of laser raster imaging, and the increased popularity of desktop computing, the number of potential clients for printed circuit board technology grew dramatically, and attempts were made to produce low-cost photoplotting systems, undercutting Gerber's hold on the market. In an attempt to respond to these challenges, Gerber made a strategic acquisition that brought it expertise in the new technology. The company purchased the Eocom division of American Hoechst in the spring of 1984. This company made laser imaging devices.

In the mid-1980s, Gerber also saw its dominance of the fabric-cutting field challenged. In 1986, the company filed a patent infringement suit against a French competitor, which had been founded in the early 1970s specifically to undercut Gerber's market share. The French firm modified Gerber's technology, offered its products at a lower price, and employed an aggressive sales force to seek out sales in the United States, winning 12 percent of the market. In 1994, however, Gerber finally won its long-running patent infringement suit against this company, and was awarded $5.7 million in damages.

In response to these challenges on its native ground, Gerber looked increasingly to foreign markets for further growth. After forming the Gerber Foreign Sales Corporation in December 1984, Gerber won an export license to ship its SABRE-5000 CAD/CAM system to China in late 1985. Despite this gain, the company's financial results in the mid-1980s were weak, as Gerber reported a loss of $1.364 million in 1984, and $790,000 in 1985.

Gerber added a Canadian subsidiary in March 1986, and then incorporated a Japanese arm a month later. In May 1986, GGT Canada, Limited, a subsidiary of Gerber Garment Technology, was created. That fall, Gerber formed GGT International Ptl. Ltd., to market the Gerbercutter in Australia. With these moves, the company hoped to shore up its flagging sales. Nevertheless, Gerber reduced its staff by more than one-third in late 1986.

Gerber's efforts to expand its worldwide presence in the market for apparel manufacturing equipment continued in 1987. In January of that year, the company formed GGT International (Far East) Limited, and three months later, it also established a New Zealand branch, called GGT International (NZ) Limited. In addition, Gerber launched its first mass market photoplotting device for use with a personal computer in March 1987, as the company attempted to catch up with changes in the printed circuit board industry.

At the end of 1987, Gerber also made an acquisition in the United States, purchasing the business and assets of Cambridge Robotic Systems, Inc., for $3 million. Nine months later, Gerber reorganized its foreign operations, transferring control of Gerber subsidiaries in six European countries from the parent company to Gerber Garment Technology. All of the European outposts were subsequently renamed.

At the same time, Gerber also formed GST Far East, Limited, a subsidiary of its systems technology unit. The company closed out the decade by entering the Mexican market, through the formation of GGT International de Mexico, S.A. de C.V.

At the start of the 1990s, Gerber marked its presence in another major market, when its optical division was formally incorporated as Gerber Optical, Inc., a wholly owned subsidiary of the company. In July 1990, Gerber also entered the Portuguese market.

During this time, a general recession in the economy produced a cutback in levels of factory output, and this, in turn, cut into demand for Gerber's manufacturing products. In response to these circumstances, Gerber adopted a policy of focusing on research and development to generate new products and keep sales levels high. Nevertheless, the company reported a drop in revenue in June 1992, of seven percent, to $261 million.

In mid-1992, Gerber reorganized its corporate structure yet again, combining two of its subsidiaries, the Gerber Scientific Instrument Company, and Gerber Systems Technology, Inc., into one entity, the Gerber Systems Corporation. Throughout the mid-1990s, Gerber worked to cut its costs, tighten its operations, and make the most of its assets, in an attempt to return to profitability in the changing marketplace. By 1993, those efforts had started to bear fruit, as the company once again began to report profits. Although its export operations, which contributed one-third of total revenues, remained weak, the company was able to introduce innovative new products to shore up its bottom line. In particular, Gerber rolled out new devices in its commercial graphics arm. With a long history of successful innovation behind it, Gerber appeared to be well-positioned for success in the late 1990s, despite its transitional difficulties in the previous decade. Founded in the spirit of inventiveness, the company's continued success appeared to depend on ongoing success in that endeavor.

Principal Subsidiaries: Gerber Systems Corporation; Gerber Garment Technology, Inc.; Gerber Scientific Products, Inc.; Gerber Optical, Inc.; Gerber Venture Capital Corporation; Gerber Foreign Sales Corporation.

Further Reading:

''Gerber Scientific: Finding Markets for Machines that Automate Output,'' *Business Week,* October 29, 1979, pp. 124–25.

Hanratty, Patrick J., ''The Selling of CAD/CAM,'' *Manufacturing Systems,* October 1992, p. 56.

Malait, Marie-Jo, et. al., ''Lectra's Computer-Aided Pattern for Success,'' *Business Week,* December 1, 1986, p. 128.

Ryan, David R., ''The Evolution of the Photoplotter,'' *Printed Circuit Design,* September 1989, p. 20.

—Elizabeth Rourke

During the 1870s, the brothers began "jobbing" other artists' products, such as the popular chromo-litho Currier and Ives prints. The company also jobbed imported German lithographed Christmas cards and oversaw production of the first American line of Christmas, New Year, and Valentine greeting cards, developed by L. Prang & Co., a Boston lithographer, in about 1866. Five years later, Prang had achieved sales of five million such cards a year, and the Gibson brothers were soon designing and making their own line of Christmas cards, Valentines, and Easter novelties.

In 1883, Robert Gibson, the business manager of the four, purchased his brothers' interest in the company, becoming the sole owner of the company until his death two years later. At that time, Robert's will dictated that the business was to be incorporated as The Gibson Art Company, with shares distributed equally to his four children: Charles, Arabella, William, and Edwin.

As Americans communicated with their loved ones overseas, World War I prompted an increase in greeting card popularity. During this time, many new companies entered the market, and competition led to the refining of printing processes, art techniques, and decorative finishing treatments. Gibson was credited with popularizing the "French Fold" card—one sheet of paper folded in half twice—which became the best-selling greeting card form and an industry standard.

In the 1930s Gibson began to focus on helping its retail customers market Gibson products. The company developed new merchandising methods and created display fixtures to help control inventory and improve retail sales. Gibson was the first in the industry to develop an electronic reorder system which allowed stores to maintain a profitable product mix.

The greeting card business weathered the Great Depression better than most industries, primarily because while most people couldn't afford expensive gifts on special occasions, they could still afford to give greeting cards. The period after World War II brought an improved economic climate as well as increasingly sophisticated printing, embossing, and finishing techniques, with better greeting cards produced each year.

In 1960 the company's name was changed to Gibson Greeting Cards, Inc., and by 1963, Gibson was reporting sales of more than $26 million, with net earnings of $1.8 million. As the country's third largest greeting card company, Gibson was involved in the production of conventional lines of greeting cards for all seasons, as well as foreign language cards, special designs of cards for supermarkets and discount stores, and a full line of gift wrappings. Gibson common stock was listed on the New York Stock Exchange in 1962.

Two years later, however, Gibson's private ownership ended when the company's assets were purchased by CIT Financial Corporation, as part of that company's plans to expand the scope of its operations. Later that year, CIT also acquired the Memphis-based Cleo Wrap Corporation, which bolstered Gibson's product line significantly. Under CIT's parentage, Gibson's product lines and facilities were enhanced, as CIT funded several plant expansions and continued to improve the company's production equipment.

Gibson Greetings, Inc.

2100 Section Road
Cincinnati, Ohio 45237
U.S.A.
(513) 841-6600
Fax: (513) 841-6739

Public Company
Incorporated: 1895 as The Gibson Art Company
Employees: 4,600
Sales: $546.2 million
Stock Exchanges: NASDAQ
SICs: 2771 Greeting Cards, 2679 Converted Paper Products, Not Elsewhere Classified

Gibson Greetings, Inc. is the nation's third largest greeting card manufacturer, ranking just behind Hallmark Cards, Inc. and American Greetings Corporation. In addition to greeting cards, Gibson also produces gift wraps and bags, boxed cards, calendars, party goods, and related items. Gibson is headquartered in Cincinnati, Ohio, while its gift wrap division, Cleo Inc., is based in Memphis, Tennessee. The company also has subsidiaries in Mexico and the United Kingdom.

Gibson Greeting's history can be traced to 1850, when George Gibson and his family emigrated to the United States from Scotland, where Gibson had operated a lithographic and copperplate engraving business. The family journeyed to the "land of opportunity" with a small French-made lithography press. While Gibson, his wife, and daughters eventually settled in St. Louis, one of Gibson's five sons found work with a canal system that led him to Cincinnati. His three brothers followed and decided they would go into business using the small press. In 1850, the Gibson brothers, Stephen, 34, Robert, 18, George, 14, and Samuel, 12, founded Gibson & Company, Lithographers.

Together, the brothers printed bonds, stock certificates, checks, business cards, and labels. From the start, the Gibsons preferred to produce their own goods for sale at retail stores, rather than hiring out their printing services for commercial purposes. Gibson & Co. sold such products as patriotically decorated stationery, Civil War prints, honor and reward cards for schools and Sunday schools, and Valentine novelties, which were marketed through stationery, novelty, and art stores.

In 1980, when the RCA Corporation acquired CIT, Gibson became a subsidiary of RCA. Two years later, however, a group of Gibson executives and The Wesray Corporation purchased Gibson from RCA. In 1983, Gibson's name was changed to Gibson Greetings, Inc. and it once again became a publicly owned company, trading shares on the NASDAQ exchange.

Like other industries during the 1980s, the paper products industry began to focus on improving production methods and materials in order to help conserve natural resources and preserve the environment. Gibson's gift wrap subsidiary, Cleo Inc., switched from the traditional solvent-based inks to safer water-based inks in 1986, and in 1989 Cleo began production of its first line of completely recyclable gift wrap, cards, and related products. The technology and research developed for the Cleo line was also implemented at Gibson, beginning with a line of recyclable cards made of recycled paper. In fact, Gibson became the first greeting card company to receive an endorsement from Renew America, a Washington-based non-profit environmental organization.

Gibson's international expansion began in the early 1990s, when the company formed Gibson Greetings International, Limited, a Delaware corporation, to market the company's products in the United Kingdom and other European countries. Gibson also formed Gibson de Mexico, S.A. de C.V., a Mexican corporation, which purchased the net assets of a Mexican manufacturer and marketer of greeting cards, to market the Gibson products in Mexico. Approximately two percent of Gibson's revenues in 1993 were from export sales and royalty income from foreign sources.

In the early and mid-1990s, Gibson's product lines consisted of traditional greeting cards for holidays and birthdays, as well as alternative cards intended for other more personal occasions. The company introduced its *Life As We Know It* line of cards in 1991 to enter the fast growing market for alternative cards. By 1993 Gibson had reshaped its alternative card line, making it easier for consumers to shop by dividing its new lines under the titles of *A Good Laugh,* for humorous cards, and *With Thoughts of You,* for non-humorous cards, including those designed with messages of love or encouragement, as well as blank cards for the sender to inscribe personally.

By 1994, Gibson was also the mass market leader in multicultural stationery products, focusing primarily on cards and gifts for the Hispanic, Jewish, and African-American populations. Specifically, Gibson's *The Family Collection* celebrated African-American family life, while another line of cards was introduced for marking Kwanzaa, an African-American celebration. A line of Chinese New Year cards was also launched during this time as was a Spanish card line called *Expresiones Por Gibson* for the Hispanic community. Gibson's Cleo subsidiary also marketed multicultural products, including gift wraps for Hanukkah and gift wraps featuring an African-American Santa Claus designed by Ardie and Gale Sayers.

Many of Gibson's products during this time incorporated well-known entertainment industry characters. Already maintaining a license to reproduce the *Sesame Street* characters and Disney's Mickey Mouse on cards and party favors, Gibson expanded its licenses in 1993, striking a deal to produce cards based on *MAD* magazine characters as well as an enhanced long-term agreement with Walt Disney Co. to reproduce its characters on cards, gift wraps, and other items. Gibson's licensed properties also included the movie *Jurassic Park,* the top selling video *Aladdin,* and the top-rated television shows *Home Improvement* and *The Simpsons.* Net sales associated with licensed properties accounted for approximately 14 percent of Gibson's overall 1993 sales. In 1994, Gibson licensed products based on the movie *The Lion King* and the World Cup soccer games which were viewed in more than 170 countries. Gibson's licenses, which in 1994 grew to almost 50, were mostly exclusive and generally for terms of one to four years with renewal options.

Gibson also maintained its commitment to servicing the retail outlets in which its products were sold. In 1993, the company's products were sold in more than 50,000 retail outlets worldwide, including supermarkets, deep discounters, mass merchandisers, variety stores, and drug stores. The company's five largest customers in 1993 accounted for approximately 35 percent of net sales, with Wal-Mart Stores, Inc., alone, accounting for more than ten percent of the company's net sales. Because of the value consumers placed on convenience, the company concentrated its distribution through one-stop-shopping outlets, using what it referred to as its "Store-Within-A-Store" concept. This original Gibson notion transformed retail space into a mini-store with a variety of "social expression" products, such as collectibles, picture frames, and other gift items, normally carried in traditional card and gift shops. Strategic alliances with more than 15 well-known quality manufacturers of social expression items helped Gibson ensure that shoppers could make all their gift purchases at a Gibson "Store-Within-A-Store." Gibson ordered and merchandised all such products at no cost to the retailer.

Gibson restructured its sales and service organizations in the 1990s, forming dedicated teams to serve its top 35 accounts. In addition, the company maintained a full-time staff of artists, writers, art directors, and creative planners who designed a majority of its products. The design of everyday products typically began approximately 12 months in advance of shipment, while design of seasonal products began approximately 18 months before the holiday date. In general, production increased throughout the year until late September, gearing up for the end-of-year holidays. A substantial portion of the company's shipments were typically concentrated in the latter half of year, requiring the company to carry large inventories.

In the spring of 1994, Gibson awarded Cleveland's W.B. Doner agency a contract to become the company's first outside advertising agency. The $5 million Gibson account included a first-ever major push into broadcast media. Industry analysts speculated that Gibson's focus on advertising may have been a response to competitive pressure from American Greetings, which had recently launched its own card outlet as well as Create-A-Card kiosks, a popular concept whereby shoppers designed and printed their own cards via a computer terminal. Moreover, competition intensified from industry leader Hallmark, which announced plans to extend its retail base by experimenting with several vertical retail outlets.

As Gibson moved into the mid-1990s, it experienced several financial and legal challenges. First, due to a change in product mix, pricing pressures, and customer discounts, Gibson's Cleo division operated at a loss in 1993. As a cost containment measure, Cleo moved its Bloomington, Indiana, gift tag operations to Reynosa, Mexico and McAllen, Texas.

Also during this time, Phar-Mor, Inc., a significant retailer of Gibson products, filed for Chapter 11 bankruptcy. As Phar-Mor had contributed 13 percent of Gibson's sales, Gibson's financial results that year reflected a 7.3 percent decrease in total revenues. Nevertheless, Gibson's revenues rebounded later in 1993, increasing 12.6 percent, which was attributed to a better market for domestic and international greeting cards as well as Gibson's acquisition of The Paper Factory of Wisconsin, Inc. The Paper Factory acquisition allowed Gibson to strengthen its position in the booming party products segment of the industry.

On July 1, 1994, the company announced that it had determined the year-end inventory of Cleo had been overstated by $8.8 million, resulting in an approximate 20 percent overstatement of previously reported 1993 consolidated net income. Five purported class action suits against Gibson were commenced by certain stockholders for violations of federal security laws. The Securities and Exchange Commission began conducting a private investigation to determine if the company or any of its officers engaged in conduct in violation of any rules or regulations of The Securities Exchange Act of 1934.

Additional legal issues ensued for Gibson in 1994. In October, the company sued its New York banks, Bankers Trust and its affiliate BT Securities Corp., for $73 million over losses resulting from derivatives purchases, then heralded as complex and risky investment vehicles. In November, Gibson and Bankers Trust reached an out-of-court settlement, which ended Gibson's exposure to losses of as much as $27.5 million. According to company officials, Gibson paid Banker's Trust $6.18 million, part of which would come from the $3.4 million Bankers Trust paid to Gibson in earnings on earlier derivative contracts.

With the bankruptcy of primary customers, a major earnings misstatement, and the derivative calamity, Gibson also experienced some public relations challenges. Faced with criticism from investors and Wall Street, Gibson began an effort to mend its wounded relations with hostile investors and frustrated industry analysts with a concentrated effort at "opening up." They invited industry analysts to visit their headquarters and made concerted efforts at improving communications at all levels.

Some industry watchers and investors such as Chicago's Harris Associates increased their holdings in Gibson during 1994. According to a November Forbes article, one Harris portfolio regarded it as "probably a reasonable assumption" that "earnings of this financially solid company have nowhere to go but up. In good years—most recently 1989, 1990, and 1991— Gibson earned over $2.50 a share, averaging more than eight percent on sales." In 1994, Gibson's stock was selling at $15, well below its $19-a-share book value.

Gibson announced in early 1995 that it expected to report a $35 million loss for fiscal 1994, more than half of which would be attributable to the Cleo gift wrap division. Gibson also lost money in its core greeting cards business, due to increased competition and the Chapter 11 filing of F&M Distributors, another major customer. Moreover, in January 1995, Hallmark announced that it planned to emphasize selling through mass merchandisers, Gibson's primary distribution channel. During this time, Gibson officials announced that the company would not pay a dividend in the first quarter of 1995 and expected to report a share loss of $2.20 for 1994.

With its financial outlook not likely to improve during the first two quarters of 1995, given the industry's seasonal, cyclical nature, Gibson appeared ripe for a takeover, according to some critics. In a February 11, 1995 article in The Cincinnati Enquirer, Jeff Stein, an analyst with McDonald & Co., asserted that the plummeting of Gibson's stock price "could be the final catalyst that may be needed to put the 'For Sale' sign up on this company. They've done nothing but disappoint the Street. . . . The financial health of the company appears very uncertain."

In response to its financial problems, Gibson stepped up efforts to reduce costs. The company eliminated 128 jobs in December 1994, and analysts believed that additional personnel cuts would be made in 1995. Furthermore, Gibson hired CS First Boston to help them devise strategies for the company's non-core assets, which some speculated might lead to the divestiture of Cleo. Seeking to offset the loss of some of its major customers, Gibson brought in two new accounts at Safeway Stores Inc. stores and The Vons Cos. stores.

Still, in February 1995, Wal-Mart, Gibson Greetings, Inc.'s largest customer, announced plans to phase out its Gibson merchandise. A Wal-Mart buyer, quoted in The Cincinnati Enquirer, remarked, "the chain will continue to stock gift wrap from Gibson's Cleo division but will phase the Gibson card line out." At the time, Gibson sold greeting cards to about 200 of Wal-Mart's 2,100-plus stores.

As Gibson readied itself for the 21st century, the company with the industry's hottest licensed properties, strategic alliances, and ethnic market leadership would have to overcome prior losses of customers and mismanagement of finances in order to reach its goal of becoming the leader in the social expression industry.

Principal Subsidiaries: Cleo Inc.; Gibson Greetings International Ltd; Gibson De Mexico S.A. de C.V.; Greetings USA. Inc.; Paper Factory of Wisconsin, Inc.

Further Reading:

Cebulski, Cathy, "Gibson's Cleo Introduces "Earth-Friendly" Products," *The Greater Cincinnati Business Record,* February 11, 1991, p. 2.

"Gibson Gets Right to Use Simpsons, Flintstones," *The Cincinnati Enquirer,* September 22, 1993, p. C1.

Henterly, Meghan, "On Gibson Wish List: Get Well," *The Cincinnati Enquirer,* October 16, 1994, p. E1.

Josten, Margaret, "Gibson Cashes in on Dinosaur Movie," *The Cincinnati Enquirer,* April 28, 1993, p. B5.

Kirk, Jim, "Gibson Sends Greetings," *ADWEEK,* June 6, 1994, p. 3.

Larkin, Patrick, "Gibson's Derivative Suit Ends," *The Cincinnati Post,* November 24, 1994, p. 1A.

——, "Gibson Unit Boss Resigns," *The Cincinnati Post,* November 29, 1994, p. 6B.

Olson, Thomas, "Gibson to Unwrap Earth-Friendly Products," *The Greater Cincinnati Business Record,* February 11, 1991, p. 1.

Phalon, Richard, "Valentine for Gibson," *Forbes,* November 21, 1994, p. 248.

Reese, Shelly, "Gibson Labels Talk of Chapter 11 False," *The Cincinnati Enquirer,* February 15, 1995, p. B6.

——, "Gibson Shares Take Nose Dive," *The Cincinnati Enquirer,* February 11, 1995, p. B7.

——, "Wal-Mart Will Say Good-Bye to Gibson Greetings," *The Cincinnati Enquirer,* February 14, 1995, p. B6.

Verna, Gigi, "Gibson Greetings Going MAD in '94," *The Greater Cincinnati Business Record,* May 10, 1993, p. 1.

——, "The Public File," *The Greater Cincinnati Business Record,* April 25, 1994, p. 28.

Wilson, William L., *Full Faith And Credit: The Story of CIT Financial Corporation 1908–1975,* New York: Random House, 1976.

—Jennifer Voskuhl Canipe

Goldstar Co., Ltd.

20 Youido-Dong
Yongdungpo-Gu
Seoul
Republic of Korea
2-787-3175
Fax: 2-787-3400

Chaebol Member
Founded: 1958
Employees: 33,000
Sales: $6 billion
SICs: 3579 Office Machines Not Elsewhere Classified; 3585
   Refrigeration & Heating Equipment; 3600 Electronic &
   Other Electrical Equipment; 3671 Electron Tubes

Goldstar Co., Ltd. is the largest manufacturer of electrical
appliances and consumer electronics in South Korea (Republic
of Korea). It led domestic production of major appliances like
televisions, refrigerators, and washing machines, and was also a
major global supplier of semiconductors and liquid-crystal displays in the mid-1990s. With approximately $6 billion in 1994
sales, Goldstar formed the primary division of the giant Lucky-
Goldstar *chaebol,* or business group.

Goldstar Co. was created in 1959 as part of the Lucky-Goldstar
chaebol. Chaebols are massive groups of interrelated companies that dominate South Korean industry. Rising to prominence after the Korean War, South Korean *chaebols* were
founded and operated by prominent, or ''royal,'' families. Different *chaebols* generally concentrated on separate markets,
such as those for chemicals or automobiles. Throughout the
middle 1900s, *chaebols* were characterized by hierarchical, centralized control, which was usually exerted by members of the
founding family. *Chaebols* traditionally had a central planning
division, or secretary's office, which was directly subordinate to
the *chaebol* chairman. The office would oversee all of the
group's activities and was responsible for strategic management. In the early 1990s, the four largest *chaebols*—Samsung,
Hyundai, Lucky-Goldstar, and Daewoo—accounted for nearly
half of Korea's total gross national product and about 40 percent
of the country's total exports.

Formed in 1947, Lucky-Goldstar was the third-largest *chaebol*
going into the 1990s. Formed by the Koo and Huh families, the
chaebol started out selling face creams and quickly grew to
become dominant in the national chemical manufacturing business. Like other *chaebols,* Lucky-Goldstar achieved strong
growth during the 1940s and 1950s through extremely hard
work. The chairmen and founders of the *chaebols,* in fact, were
known for working relentlessly—even putting in 16-hour days
for years on end without a vacation—to make their business
groups leaders in their respective industries. As Korea's economy surged during the 1960s and 1970s, Lucky-Goldstar and
other *chaebols* branched out into new industries, reflecting a
national economic strategy of boosting exports and focusing on
heavy industry. In 1958, Lucky-Goldstar became active in the
electronics industry with the formation of Goldstar Co.

Goldstar Co. represented Korea's first foray into the electronics
industry. The company started out assembling vacuum-tube
radios locally, many of which were exported. In 1959, in fact,
Goldstar became the first Korean company to build a radio. It
rapidly expanded during the 1960s, branching out into the
manufacture of appliances. It built the first Korean refrigerator
in 1965, for instance, and the first Korean television in 1966. It
subsequently began the manufacture of elevators and escalators,
air conditioners, electric typewriters, and other electronic
goods. Steady gains during the 1960s and 1970s were the result
of low-cost operations matched with manufacturing and product
innovations. Goldstar was the first Korean manufacturer to
establish a solid toehold in electronics export markets, for example, supplying televisions to various U.S. companies, such as
Sears and J.C. Penney. Those buyers sold the units under their
own brand names. Goldstar gradually earned a reputation as a
supplier of low-cost, high-quality electronic components and
appliances.

Goldstar's revenues continued to swell during the 1970s as it
extended its reach into new industries and marketing channels.
For example, it introduced its first product bearing the Goldstar
name brand in the United States in 1977. The success of that
19-inch black-and-white television prompted it to export several lines of low-cost electronics during the late 1970s and
1980s that were sold under the Goldstar label. Importantly,
Goldstar also began to advance into high-tech industry segments during the 1970s. For instance, it invested massive
amounts of capital to establish its own semiconductor manufacturing division. Its initial goal was to produce microchips for
use in its own electronic components. But Goldstar's long-term
strategy was to use the semiconductor division to position the
company to compete in the much more advanced electronics
and telecommunications industries that were emerging.

By 1980, the Lucky-Goldstar group was boasting sales of more
than $4 billion annually. Various chemical-related businesses
still accounted for the majority of that revenue. Encouraged by
the success of its electronics and appliance businesses, though,
the *chaebol* decided to shift its focus away from chemicals. To
that end, Lucky-Goldstar invested heavily in Goldstar Co. during the early and mid-1980s, boosting production capacity with
both domestic and foreign production facilities. Goldstar even
became the first Korean manufacturer to set up a manufacturing
plant in the United States. Built in 1983, its Huntsville, Alabama, television plant was churning out more than one million
color televisions and microwave ovens annually by the late
1980s. Goldstar augmented production efforts with a boost in

advertising expenditures from $2 million in 1983 to $12 million in 1984.

In addition to overseas efforts, Goldstar launched an aggressive growth program at home. It expanded production capacity for virtually every one of its major products during the early and mid-1980s and broadened its product lines to include a number of high-tech goods. Most notable was Goldstar's construction of a new factory south of Seoul, in Pyongtaek. The plant, which opened in 1984, represented Goldstar's intent to become a leading global supplier of VCRs, personal computers, facsimile machines, and other relatively high-tech consumer and business devices. In fact, the company publicly announced a goal of deriving a full 40 percent of its sales by the mid-1980s from high-margin, advanced technology products, rather than from its traditional core of relatively low-tech, low-priced commodity goods.

Summing up Goldstar's basic tactic during the 1980s was one of its advertising slogans: "Expensive electronics without the expense." The strategy seemed to benefit the *chaebol* during the decade. Goldstar established a solid presence in domestic and international markets for microwave ovens and televisions, as well as for refrigerators, washing machines, and other major appliances. As a result, Lucky-Goldstar's revenues rocketed more than five-fold to $22 billion between 1980 and 1989. Much of that gain was attributable to electronics, which was supplying more than 30 percent of Lucky-Goldstar's revenue by the end of the decade, while 25 percent came from chemicals and 33 percent from various trade and financial services companies.

Although Goldstar's sales gains during the 1980s may have seemed impressive to the casual observer, its financial performance began to wane in the mid-1980s and the company experienced a series of setbacks. Goldstar's woes were the result of a variety of factors, including shifting global economies, labor strife, and greater domestic competition. For example, Goldstar's dominance of Korea's domestic electronics industry, which it had enjoyed since the 1960s, was challenged by the Samsung *chaebol,* particularly beginning in the early 1980s. Samsung's electronics division surpassed Goldstar in both sales and profits by 1984 and continued to widen its lead throughout the decade. By the late 1980s, Goldstar's domestic market share had fallen from 45 percent early in the decade to just 36 percent.

Illustrative of Goldstar's difficulties during the 1980s was its reversals in the semiconductor business. In an effort to compete with rival Samsung, Goldstar had invested heavily to develop more sophisticated chip technology. Unfortunately, the semiconductors it developed had limited market applications and Goldstar had trouble mastering the production technology. The end result was that Goldstar was unable to achieve savings by producing its chips in-house, and it also failed to establish itself as a significant global chip manufacturer. Meanwhile, Samsung successfully transitioned into new semiconductor technology and eroded Goldstar's market share.

Adding to Goldstar's technology and competition woes in the 1980s were labor and economic setbacks. Because the Korean government restricted access to overseas financing sources, Goldstar was forced to fund much of its growth during the early and mid-1980s with loans from short-term domestic financiers. The unfortunate result by the late 1980s was that Goldstar was paying out more than 85 percent of its operating income to cover interest on its massive debt load. At the same time, Goldstar's primary export market, the United States, was maturing. Ongoing competition from Japanese producers exacerbated the export dilemma. To make matters worse, Goldstar lost much of its important low-cost labor advantage in the late 1980s when its workers rebelled. Frustrated union members went on strike, which ultimately cost the company $600 million between 1988 and 1990. They forced Goldstar to greatly boost wages, and as a result the company had to raise prices an average of eight percent.

But Goldstar's greatest problem by the end of the 1980s was that it was losing its reputation for quality. In 1990, for example, *Consumer Reports* ranked Goldstar's VCRs last in a comparison with 18 other brands. Part of Goldstar's quality problems stemmed from its reliance on outside suppliers—a faulty chip imported from Japan in 1987, for instance, nearly terminated Goldstar's American VCR operations. But it was also the result of Lucky-Goldstar's unwieldy organizational structure. By the late 1980s the *chaebol* was comprised of more than 30 different companies operating without cooperation. Research and development efforts were being duplicated in different divisions, and managers had lost touch with overall organizational objectives.

Quality and management problems, combined with a stronger won (the Korean currency unit), caused Goldstar's exports to the United States to crumble from $834 million in 1988 to just $535 million in 1990. That decline, along with plummeting domestic market share, caused Goldstar's net profit margins to drop by more than 100 percent during the period. The company was befuddled and had lost its focus. In 1984, for instance, management predicted that U.S. sales would top $1 billion by 1986. By 1990 that goal seemed like a foggy dream. Furthermore, Goldstar had fallen well short of its objective of generating 40 percent of its revenues from high-tech products—by 1990 only 12 percent of sales came from such goods.

The origin of many of Goldstar's problems in the late 1980s was the *chaebol* structure. Early in Lucky-Goldstar's history, the centralized, hierarchical structure of the *chaebol* had been an asset. The Koo family had made virtually all major decisions, and directives were regularly dispatched to executives from breakfast meetings over which the family presided. As the *chaebol* mushroomed in size, however, the authoritative nature of the organization became a liability. Importantly, the slow hierarchical decision-making process had become obsolete in the fast-moving global economy of the 1980s. Goldstar was still mostly family owned by the late 1980s and was run by the original founder's eldest son, Koo Cha-Kyung. "It would take days to make the most simple management decision because it [management] had to have the chops of everyone from the responsible manager right up to even the president at times," noted an industry analyst in the April 1991 *Business Korea*.

Recognizing the urgency of the situation, the 62-year-old Koo took drastic measures beginning in 1989 to turn the ailing Lucky-Goldstar around. Most importantly, he handed control of Goldstar to Lee Hun-Jo, a 27-year Lucky-Goldstar veteran. Koo cemented Lee's independence when, in 1991, he gave a written guarantee of autonomy to Lee in a public ceremony. In a remarkable departure from *chaebol* tradition, Lee was allowed to run the company as he liked and was only required to report to Koo twice each year. Lee quickly reorganized Goldstar into two major groups: consumer electronics; and personal computers and office equipment. Products that did not fit into those divisions were spun off, distributed to contractors, or absorbed by other Lucky-Goldstar electronics companies.

During the early 1990s Lee virtually transformed Goldstar from a lagging electronics producer to a leading, global high-tech contender. Lee, who spoke both English and Japanese fluently, integrated proven Western and Japanese management techniques. His efforts permeated Goldstar's management and work force. "You have to transform human beings," Lee explained in *Business Week* in 1994. "If you can't change your people, you can't change your organization. If you can't do that, you can't reach your goal." Lee jettisoned entire layers of management and successfully forged an amiable working relationship between top management and labor. He also upped promotional spending in an effort to woo former customers, and reasserted Goldstar's plan to assume a lead role in high-technology markets.

Largely as a result of Lee's efforts, Goldstar staged a major comeback during the early 1990s. Sales vaulted from $4 billion in 1990 to more than $6 billion in 1994, and net income rose to a record $120 million after slumping to around $12 million. More importantly, by 1994 Goldstar had regained its number one position in the South Korean market for color televisions, refrigerators, and washing machines, and it had suddenly resumed its contention for global semiconductor market share. Among the company's pivotal breakthroughs was a unique new refrigerator, introduced in the early 1990s, which was designed to keep Korea's national dish, Kimchi, fresh and odorless for a long time. Likewise, Goldstar was achieving marked gains overseas by focusing on emerging markets like Russia and Vietnam while at the same time increasing North American sales through overseas manufacturing and partnerships with U.S. companies. In fact, Goldstar's U.S. sales jumped 17 percent in 1994 to around $1.2 billion.

Going into the mid-1990s Goldstar continued to streamline its operations and push into new geographic and product markets. For example, it was investing heavily to develop technology related to advanced liquid-crystal displays, which were used in notebook computers, among other applications. To that end, Goldstar was building a $620-million factory in 1995 that would be capable of shipping one million of those units by 1997. Goldstar was also striving to establish a presence in the software industry, particularly in the gaming and interactive video segments. In 1994, Goldstar captured about 35 percent of its sales from home appliances, 25 percent from televisions, 13 percent from computer and office equipment, and the remainder from miscellaneous audio and video gear.

Principal Subsidiaries: Goldstar Electron Co. Ltd.; Goldstar Europe; Goldstar U.S. Inc.

Further Reading:

Clifford, Mark, "Electronic Leapfrog," *Far Eastern Economic Review,* November 1987, pp. 80–83.
Clifford, Mark, "Seoul-Mates Again," *Far Eastern Economic Review,* March 1990, pp. 46–47.
Crane, Geoff, "Ailing Goldstar Needs Strong Medicine," *Electronic Business,* August 20, 1990, pp. 67–69.
"Domestic Electronics Industry: Backbone of Korean Exports," *Business Korea,* October 1993, pp. 34–36.
"Lightening the Load at the Top," *Business Korea,* April 1991, pp. 26–28.
Nakarmi, Laxmi, "At Lucky-Goldstar, the Koos Loosen the Reins," *Business Week,* February 18, 1991, pp. 72–73.
Nakarmi, Laxmi, "Goldstar Is Burning Bright," *Business Week,* September 26, 1994, pp. 129–130.
Shin, Yoo Keun, Richard Steer, and Gerardo R. Ungson, *The Chaebol,* New York: Harper & Row, 1989.
Verespej, Michael A., "Can Goldstar Earn Its Gold Star," *Industry Week,* November 30, 1987, pp. 33–36.
"War of the Suds," *Business Korea,* January 1993, pp. 32–33.

—Dave Mote

Goody Products, Inc.

969 Newark Turnpike
Kearny, New Jersey 07032
U.S.A.
(201) 997-3000
Fax: (800) 631-0421

Wholly Owned Subsidiary of Newell Co.
Incorporated: 1933
Employees: 2,390
Sales: $218 million
SICs: 2844 Toilet Preparations; 3851 Ophthalmic Goods

Goody Products, Inc. is the leading producer of hair accessories for the American market. The company was founded in the early twentieth century by Henry Goodman, a recent immigrant, and grew through the decades, remaining in the control of Goodman's children and grandchildren. In the early 1980s, Goody sold stock to the public for the first time, and, in the mid-1990s, the company was acquired in whole by another company, becoming a subsidiary of the larger consumer products manufacturer Newell Co.

Goody was founded in 1907 by Henry Goodman, who had recently emigrated to the United States from the Ukraine with his family. Goodman first set out to be a grocer, and when that business failed, he set up shop as a peddler with a pushcart on the lower east side of Manhattan. Goodman soon recognized that the peddler next to him was doing much better than he was by selling ornamental combs for women's hair.

With his two sons, Abraham and Jacob, Goodman decided to enter the women's hair accessory business. Working out of their apartment, the family set up shop in a back room. Whenever the boarder who lived in the room was out for the evening, the three Goodmans used it as a workshop, drilling holes into blank combs they had purchased, and insetting them with rhinestones.

From these humble beginnings, the Goodman comb business grew and flourished. By the time Abraham and Jacob took over the family enterprise, H. Goodman & Sons had staked out a market in decorative combs not only on the lower east side, but also in jewelry stores up and down the east coast, from Hartford to Philadelphia.

The most logical place for Goodman & Sons to expand its distribution and sales was in variety stores, such as Woolworth's and Kresge's. However, throughout the 1910s, the company had no luck persuading buyers from these large national chains to carry their goods. Finally, the company got a lucky break in 1920. A buyer for the Kresge chain, Howard Patton, was in New York, and he wanted a jeweler to make him a set of rhinestone-studded dice. When the jeweler across the hall from the Goodman's turned Patton down, he went across the way to the Goodmans, who agreed to make up the dice, on the condition that Kresge begin to carry a full line of their products.

After this breakthrough, Goodman's sales rose rapidly throughout the 1920s, as hairstyles changed and women snapped up the company's products. With the profits that it made from its flourishing core business, Goodman purchased a 50 percent interest in the Foster Grant Company in 1929. Foster Grant was then a plastic molding concern that had fallen on hard financial times. In fact, the company was in such bad shape that, often, Goodman was forced to use its own funds to pay Foster Grant's workers.

In the wake of the stock market crash, and the Great Depression of the 1930s, Goodman's boom years came to an end, and the company's business slowed. In 1933, the company incorporated, under the name Goody Products, Inc. With the entry of the United States into World War II in 1941, and the conversion of the American economy to a wartime footing, Goody's fortunes sunk even lower. Because its products were considered nonessential, and raw materials were being carefully rationed to contribute to the war effort, Goody suffered from severe shortages of materials and manpower in the early 1940s.

By the end of World War II, the once thriving business of the 1920s was barely profitable. However, the company's subsidiary, Foster Grant, was doing well, having received contracts for defense work and experiencing an increased demand for its aviator sunglasses. Throughout the 1940s and 1950s, Goody's hair accessories company remained financially weak, while its Foster Grant unit thrived.

During this time, the market for consumer goods in America grew dramatically, as both the popularity and the demand for luxury goods in the postwar era expanded rapidly. Despite this growth, some of the small, privately-owned manufacturers in Goody's industry failed to invest in their businesses, and their products suffered. Goody did try to upgrade its equipment, borrowing money from banks and using its stock in the high-performing Foster Grant company as collateral for the loans it needed to build its market share. A new generation of Goodmans joined the business, as Leonard Goodman, the son and nephew of Abraham and Jacob Goodman, respectively, came on board.

Slowly, in painstaking steps, Goody developed new products and expanded its line of offerings. Still, the company's lack of funds for development hampered these efforts. "We were never out of debt on that stock," Leonard Goodman later explained to *Forbes*. "We were adding equipment in all buildings, borrowing as we went. At no time did we have a good balance sheet. Things were getting stretched tighter and tighter," Goodman recalled.

By the early 1970s, Goody's reliance on its Foster Grant stock to fund its further expansion had started to cause concern among the company's bankers. In 1970, another company, United Brands, purchased a large block of Foster Grant's stock after one of Foster Grant's founders died, and suddenly, Goody's control over the company seemed to be in doubt. Without effective control of Foster Grant, Goody's ownership of the company's stock was far less valuable, in the eyes of the firm's bankers.

The threat to Goody's finances became more serious as United Brands, headed by a well-known corporate raider, Eli Black, sought a greater stake in the company. "Our collateral was becoming less and less liquid," Goodman later recalled in *Forbes,* "We were really in serious danger." In September 1974, however, the company was saved, when Hurricane Fifi struck Honduras, devastating the banana plantations there owned by United Brands. In the face of this event, United Brands was forced to sell its holding in Foster Grant to another company, American Hoechst. At the time, Goody also divested itself of its holding in the company, reaping $24.6 million. For the first time in more than 30 years, Goody had a sizable sum of capital to invest in its business.

With this money, however, the company made several unwise investments, according to analysts. The company guaranteed loans for the Hebrew Arts School in New York City, an institution that had racked up $4 million in debt through costs associated with building and operating deficits. The company also lent its officers, directors, and associates a total of $1.3 million. In addition, Abraham Goodman, at that time in his 80s, involved the company in a Jacksonville, Florida, real estate project, that ended up losing hundreds of thousands of dollars a year.

As the 1970s came to a close, Goody's investments worsened. Deficits from the Florida real estate deal and the strong possibility of a default at the Hebrew Arts School left the company in a weak financial position. Faced with this predicament, Goody's owners, the two sons of its original founder, finally gave in and sold stock to the public. In July 1980, the company sold half a million shares, representing 24 percent of its outstanding stock, raising $4.4 million in the process.

With this money, for the first time in its history, Goody had the capability of investing sufficient funds to expand its market share. The company spent money on new machines to manufacture its products, as well as on new systems for its warehouses. Goody hoped to solidify its status as the lowest-cost, best-integrated supplier of hair accessories.

The company also sought to distribute a wider variety of hair accessories to retailers. In doing so, it offered higher profits than those reaped by many other hair care products. Goody accessories were 56 percent more profitable than shampoos, 68 percent more profitable than hair dyes, and 300 percent more profitable than hair sprays. Because of these high margins, Goody sought to persuade stores to give its products more display space than those of its competitors. The company's efficiency meant that many of its products provided more value for their price than competing accessories manufactured in

Japan, Hong Kong, and Korea. In fact, the company was successful in selling its goods in these markets, despite the generally low cost of manufacturing in the Far East.

By the start of 1982, Goody products held 60 percent of the market for hair accessories, more than twice the market share the company had held six years earlier. From sales of $123.2 million, Goody reaped $6.6 million in profits. These figures were the result of annual growth in sales and earnings of 20 percent since 1977.

At the start of the 1980s, Goody was producing 450 different hair care products. These included 75 new items, introduced as part of the company's Marvelle International Collection. This group of goods was designed to have a high-fashion look and to carry a higher price tag. These products, which were intended for sale in supermarkets, drug stores, variety stores, and other traditional Goody outlets, were the kind of merchandise ordinarily found in expensive boutiques and department stores.

To promote these new products, and to maintain the market share of its other, more traditional goods, Goody embarked upon an extensive advertising campaign in the early 1980s, a first in the hair accessory industry. The company spent $75,000 on television advertising and print promotions created by fashion photographer Richard Avedon. By the end of 1982, Goody's revenues had risen to $128 million, while its earnings shrank to $5.8 million.

Earnings continued to drop in the following year, decreasing to $5.1 million, while sales again grew to $129.4 million. In the following year, Goody embarked upon a program of expansion through acquisition of companies with compatible product lines. In October 1984, Goody bought Duray, Inc., for $3.2 million. This company, which manufactured cosmetics and travel accessories, was expected to help Goody capitalize on its own well-established network of distribution channels to enhance profits from sales of Duray products.

Also in 1984, Goody began to implement a new computer system to track raw materials and finished products. The company purchased new software and hardware in order to do so. At the end of that year, Goody reported revenues of $133.8 million and income of $5.4 million, as earnings rebounded slightly from the previous year.

In 1985, Goody made another acquisition, buying the sunglasses marketer Opti-Ray, Inc., for $20 million in cash. With this purchase and the Duray buy, Goody hoped to broaden its sales base significantly, generating higher sales and profits. Both of the company's new units were highly similar to Goody in their styles of operation. They had similar sales techniques, marketed to the same customer, and employed like warehousing and distribution processes. Nevertheless, integrating the new companies into the Goody operation promised to be challenging for the firm. "We have plenty to do over the next few years, fitting in these two acquisitions and expanding their operations," Goodman told *Barron's,* noting "We're going to have our plates full."

In addition to its core business in the hair accessory field, Goody had also branched out during this time to other related businesses. Through a subsidiary called J & PB Myers, the company made folding boxes and other packaging for cosmetics and pharmaceuticals. Goody also marketed an automated, computerized inventory, distribution, and shipping system through its Distribution Technologies division. In addition, the company continued to add to the hair care products it made. In 1985, for instance, Goody began offering hand-held mirrors and hair brushes. The company also introduced Little Miss Goody, a line of children's hair accessories.

The following year, Goody resumed its acquisition spree, purchasing the Ace Comb Company from the Beecham Group in July for $3.5 million. Soon thereafter, Goody also bought Pretty Neat Corp., a manufacturer of plastic cosmetic organizers, for $3.1 million. In making these acquisitions, Goody stuck to its program of buying companies whose products were sold in the same retail outlets as Goody's, and whose manufacturing processes were similar. Toward that end, the company divested itself of its carton manufacturing subsidiary, selling it to the Union Camp company in July 1987. By the end of that year, with the revenues contributed by its two new units, Goody's sales had risen 21 percent, to top $200 million, while earnings had increased by 70 percent.

By the start of the 1990s, Goody's steady success had caught the eye of outside investors, among them the Newell Co., a manufacturer of housewares and hardwares based in Beloit, Wisconsin. This company's goal was to acquire enough smaller consumer goods producers to become a serious supplier for large national retail chains such as Kmart and Wal-Mart. As part of that plan, the company bought stock in Goody, citing the hair accessory maker's strong presence in its market. "It fits the mold very well and has a strong staple product going into the mass merchandiser. Its core product has a 60 percent market share and was responsible for $150 million in sales last year," Newell's president, Daniel Ferguson, told *Financial Weekly.*

In September 1991, Newell increased its holding in Goody to 13.4 percent, expressing increased interest in the firm. However, since Goody had adopted a "poison pill," or plan to prevent outsiders from acquiring more than 15 percent of the company's shares, Newell did not press its interest in the company any further. "They don't want us . . .," Ferguson explained, "But we would still love to be allied with them in some way, even as an investor."

Four years later, in 1995, Newell got its wish, when the remaining shares of Goody stock were tendered to the midwestern manufacturer, and the company became a subsidiary of a larger conglomerate of consumer goods manufacturers. The enterprise that had started in the early years of the twentieth century on a pushcart on the lower east side of Manhattan would end the century as part of a much larger Midwestern firm, no longer a family business.

Principal Subsidiaries: Ace Comb Company, Inc.; Goody Canada, Limited; Opti-Ray, Inc.; Pretty Neat Corporation.

Further Reading:

Flax, Steven, "The Cost of Staying Private," *Forbes,* February 15, 1982, p. 102, 106.

Hackney, Holt, "Strategic Alliances," *FW,* October 29, 1991, pp. 20–22.

"Newell Shifts to Acquiring Stakes and Sharing its Expertise," *The Corporate Growth Report,* December 1991, p. 6.

Stephens, Charlotte S., "The Best of Both Worlds: A Mainframe- and Microcomputer-Based MRP-II System," *Production and Inventory Management Journal,* Third Quarter 1990, pp. 35–40.

Troxel, Thomas N., Jr., "Key Acquisitions," *Barron's,* April 1, 1985.

—Elizabeth Rourke

Grow Group, Inc.

Grow Group Inc.

200 Park Ave.
New York, New York 10166
U.S.A.
(212) 599-4400
Fax: (212) 286-0940

Public Company
Incorporated: 1950
Employees: 2,000
Sales: $400 million
Stock Exchanges: New York
SICs: 2842 Polishes & Sanitation Goods; 2851 Paints &
   Allied Products; 2891 Adhesives & Sealants

Grow Group Inc. is a leading manufacturer of architectural paints, high-performance specialty coatings, detergents, and cleaning/maintenance products for household, professional, industrial, institutional, and governmental use. Grow's operations are divided into two groups: coatings and chemicals, and consumer and professional products. The company's financial strength has been enhanced by its more than three dozen acquisitions since the 1970s.

Grow was founded in 1950 as a small, independent telecommunications company. The venture gained a moderate level of success during the 1950s and early 1960s, reaching sales of about $1.5 million in 1961. In 1961, Grow hired 42-year-old Russell Banks to help increase the company's fortunes. Banks used his many talents as experimenter, entrepreneur, manager, and deal maker to eventually turn the company into a major supplier of industrial coatings and maintenance supplies. Banks's leadership was not without problems, however. Banks's experimenting with new inventions had taken the company to the brink of insolvency before he turned its fortunes around.

A string of acquisitions during the 1960s and 1970s made Grow Chemical Corp., as it was formerly named, a major U.S. distributor of industrial coatings and chemicals by the mid-1970s. And Banks's knack for buying undervalued companies and turning them into performers earned him a reputation as a savvy deal maker and shrewd negotiator. Banks's most acclaimed deal during the 1970s was his acquisition of two paint companies from Celanese Corp. in 1976. The two divisions combined were two-thirds the size of Grow (by sales volume), and Grow was short on capital. Analysts doubted that Banks would be able to

pull off the exchange. Nevertheless, he leveraged the full amount, a feat lauded on Wall Street.

Although the Grow organization dates back only to the mid-1900s, the 1976 acquisitions demonstrate how the company's historical roots reach back much further through its different holdings. In fact, one of the divisions that Grow purchased from Celanese was Devoe & Raynolds Co. Devoe is America's oldest maker of paint and remained Grow's chief subsidiary into the mid-1990s. Devoe was started in 1754 by William Post, who opened a paint shop in New York City. The company prospered during the 1800s and 1900s by becoming a leading innovator and supplier in the industrial and commercial coatings industry. Like Grow, Devoe expanded through acquisition and merger. In 1928 and 1938, for instance, Devoe absorbed the varnish divisions of Peaslee-Gaulbert Co. and lacquer operations of Jones-Dabney Co.

Devoe is recognized for its advanced research and development efforts. Among the company's most notable inventions, in fact, is epoxy resin. Introduced in 1945, that discovery is credited as one of the most significant breakthroughs in coating technology during the twentieth century. "Epoxy resin is the backbone of all high-performance resins, giving them durability, hardness and adhesion," explained Gary Miller, Devoe & Raynolds president, in the *Courier Journal.* "Before epoxy resin, the coatings on chemical plants may have lasted a matter of months. After epoxy resin, the job lasted a matter of years." Devoe was bought by Celanese in 1964 before Grow acquired it in 1976. In the early 1990s Devoe & Raynolds and its sister company, Devoe Coatings, were supplying about 60 percent of Grow's total revenues.

Less than one year after finishing the leveraged buyout of Devoe, Banks conducted another coup that earned him praise on Wall Street. Grow was in deep debt and the stock market was extremely soft at the time—an ugly combination for a company seeking to make a public offering. But that is exactly what Banks proposed. At the time, *Forbes* described the proposition as "the equivalent of getting an oil tanker through the eye of a needle." To the surprise of observers, however, Banks persuaded two brokerage houses to underwrite a $5.6 million offering that brought much needed cash into Grow's coffers. As Grow's sales swelled to more than $200 million during the late 1970s, the company's stock price surged in the wake of investor enthusiasm.

As a result of sluggish activity in its core automobile and housing markets, Grow's profits and sales stagnated during the early 1980s, hovering around $240 million. Earnings began to recover in 1984, but Grow's pain during the downturn convinced Banks that the company should begin diversifying into other areas that offered more growth and would reduce the company's total dependence on coatings and chemicals. During the early 1980s, Banks began developing two pet projects, both of which were a distinct and perhaps odd departure from the paints and coatings business: Thermaljet and Enviro-Spray.

Thermaljet was a giant, stainless steel chicken cooker. Weighing in at 5,600 pounds and standing nearly nine feet tall, it was designed to cook 1,000 pounds of chicken parts at the same time on its 24 racks. The distinguishing feature of the Thermaljet, as its name implied, was its thermal jets, which sprayed hot water onto the chicken as part of a *foolproof* computer-controlled cooking process. The cooker recirculated the water and, unlike other machines, kept the water temperature just under the steaming point. The primary advantage of the contraption over existing industrial cookers was that it was less expensive to operate.

Banks's second project, Enviro-Spray, was more complementary to Grow's paint operations. It was a dispensing system billed as a marked improvement over conventional, polluting, aerosol spray cans. At the time, aerosol spray cans were ill-suited for food, pharmaceutical, agricultural, and other applications because of their petroleum-based propellant. Furthermore, they were apt to explode as a result of heat or puncture, making them much more expensive to insure for companies that produced or stored them. In contrast, Grow's propellant was a sort of pouch filled with carbon dioxide that forced the product out in a pure, rather than aerated, state.

Although in hindsight both inventions seemed like a stretch for Grow, investors and analysts were enthused at the time. In fact, Grow's stock price bolted by about 300 percent between 1982 and 1983, largely as a result of news concerning the products. At least one major stock analyst estimated that Thermaljet could eventually double Grow's earnings and that Enviro-Spray was poised to grab a significant share of the annual four-billion-unit U.S. and European aerosol market, which alone would double or triple the company's profits. *Forbes* declared in 1983 that Grow had "turned the corner under the unquestionably shrewd leadership of Banks."

During the mid-1980s, Grow focused its growth efforts on Thermaljet and Enviro-Spray, as opposed to seeking more acquisitions related to its core businesses. Unfortunately, both projects failed to bear fruit and were deemed a flop by observers. Banks finally jettisoned both experiments by spinning them off into a company called Grow Ventures, but not before they had lost about $22 million. "They were just needlessly throwing away money," assessed analyst Steven A. Larsen in *Crains New York Business*. But the failure of the two inventions was just a precursor to a string of bad luck that would plague Grow throughout the remainder of the decade.

In light of the failed poultry and aerosol ventures, Banks regained his appetite for acquisitions in the mid-1980s. His most important buy was Perrigo Co., the largest U.S. manufacturer of private-label health-care and beauty products, which he bought for $45 million. Perrigo was started by Luther Perrigo in 1887. Perrigo started out selling ointments and creams for farm animals and later began offering cold and cough remedies for people. During the 1900s, the company gradually moved into the sale of private-label health and beauty aids and grew to dominate the industry. Banks's Perrigo deal was praised as a great bargain by industry observers. The $100 million company was poised for strong growth and was considered much more valuable than the price Grow had paid for it.

Perrigo, combined with several other acquisitions, offered the potential for strong sales and profit gains. But those investments also saddled Grow with a tremendous debt load. Although Perrigo performed well and became a prominent feather in

Banks's cap, other late-1980s acquisitions—particularly Georgia-Pacific and Aqua Chem—became a serious drag on Grow's bottom line. By the late 1980s, Georgia-Pacific and Aqua Chem were more than nullifying gains in other Grow divisions. Despite a rise in sales to more than $500 million, earnings slumped from $7.6 million in 1986 to $1.3 million in 1987 as the company's stock price slid from $12.50 to around seven dollars by late 1987.

Environmental problems added to Grow's troubles during the late 1980s. For example, in 1981 Grow sold a marginal paint resin plant to U.S. Polymers Inc. and assumed that it had seen the last of the aging facility. In 1987, though, EPA investigators discovered that toxic materials had been dumped at the plant. Even though the dumping had occurred in 1969, two years before Grow assumed ownership of the facility, Grow was responsible for the $1 million clean up charge and was forced to seek remuneration from the plant's original owner through the courts.

As a result of its problems, Grow was losing money by the late 1980s. Grow lost $4.6 million in 1988. Desperate for cash to meet its burdensome debt load, Banks began looking for an investor that would purchase Grow and relieve its debt burden. Banks finally found a willing buyer in PPG Industries. Unfortunately, right before the deal was closed a fire broke out at one of Grow's Los Angeles warehouses. Hazardous gas clouds caused thousands of residents to evacuate. Scared off by a slew of lawsuits and Grow's expected $3 million loss for 1989, PPG backed out. Grow was left solve its own problems. "I wouldn't touch this company with a 10-foot pole," derided analyst Kenneth Hackel in 1989 in *Crains New York Business*. "If the bankers showed up at their door, they'd be in big trouble."

To stay afloat, Banks sold some parts of the company, closed down some marginal divisions, and consolidated the remainder of the company. Most importantly, he had to part with his prized Perrigo subsidiary for a meager $104 million. Banks's worst fears were realized when, two years after it was jettisoned, Perrigo's market value had lurched to $1.1 billion as a result of strong sales and earnings growth. "I could honestly say Perrigo was the best acquisition I ever made," Banks lamented in 1992 in *Forbes*. Although the Perrigo sell-off may have represented a missed opportunity for Grow, it did help the company slash its debt load from more than $155 million in the late 1980s to about $60 million by 1990.

In addition to getting cash from Perrigo, Banks was also able to find an investor. Venezuela-based chemical producer Corimon purchased 17 percent of Grow for $39 million in 1992. Furthermore, Banks sold Grow's U.S. paint division for a $10 million 1991 gain, and began to achieve a turn-around in several of Grow's previously marginal divisions. Meanwhile, its core Devoe operations continued to post profits and to benefit from a U.S. economic recovery during the early and mid-1990s. Grow posted its first profit in two years in 1990. The company lost money as a result of restructuring charges in 1991, but recorded steady gains in 1992, 1993, and 1994.

Having reestablished Grow's footings after the harrowing chain of events during the late 1980s and early 1990s, Banks resumed his acquisition efforts in 1994. He bought Sinclair Paint Company, a paint and coating manufacturer, for $51 million. Sinclair was founded by Frank Sinclair in 1928 as a single paint store in California. By 1993, its chain of 49 stores throughout the western United States was generating sales of $100 million and serving about 20 percent of the Los Angeles professional architectural market. Sinclair improved Grow's presence in the western United States and offered a sales channel for products in some of Grow's other divisions.

In addition to acquisitions, Grow expanded in the mid-1990s by improving existing operations and entering new markets. Its Devoe division branched out into consumer markets through mass retailers. Throughout its history it had only sold its paint and coating products through company-owned stores and independent dealers. And some observers doubted that consumers would be willing to pay the high price for Devoe's premium products. But Grow could no longer ignore the proliferating do-it-yourself market.

Grow seemed well poised for growth in the mid-1990s. Banks had restructured the company into two operating groups: the coatings and chemicals group, which included architectural paints, heavy-duty coatings, and automotive paint and coating products; and the consumer and professional products group. As markets strengthened and Grow's margins improved, its sales increased to more than $401 million in 1994 as profits surged to $14 million. Importantly, Grow's long-term debt had been slashed to a trifling $3.2 million by mid-1994. The company projected revenues of $500 million in 1995 (ended in June), a

figure that would equal its revenue peak of 1987. Meanwhile, the 75-year-old Banks showed no signs of slowing down.

Principal Subsidiaries: Ameritone Paint Company; Automotive Division; Devoe Coatings Company; Devoe & Raynolds Company; Grow Group Canada, Ltd.; Household & Professional Division; National Aerosol Products Company; Sinclair Paint Company; Zynolyte Products Company.

Further Reading:

Agovino, Theresa, "Grow Group Burns as PPG Backs Out," *Crains New York Business,* September 12, 1988, p. 2.
Benmour, Eric, "Devoe & Raynolds Moves to Increase Visibility," *Business First-Louisville,* January 1, 1990, p. 10.
Britt, Bill, "Toxic Real Estate—Buyers, Lenders Beware," *St. Louis Business Journal,* February 9, 1987, p. 1C.
Furman, Phyllis, "Grim Times at Grow Group," *Crains New York Business,* January 11, 1988, p. 3.
Hayes, John R., "The Golden Years," *Forbes,* October 26, 1992, p. 282.
Song, Kyung M., "Brushing Up on the Future," *Courier-Journal,* June 26, 1994, p. E1.
Temes, Judy, "Finally a Profit, but Grow May Have to Shrink Anyway," *Crains New York Business,* August 21, 1989, p. 2.
Wall, Jennifer R., "Grow Group Completes Acquisition of Sinclair Paint," *PR Newswire,* August 4, 1994.
Whisenhunt, Eric, "Wall Street's Loss, Perrigo Gain," *Michigan Business,* September 1988, p. 21.

—Dave Mote

Hannaford Bros. Co.

145 Pleasant Hill Road
Scarborough, Maine 04074
U.S.A.
(217) 883-2911
Fax: (207) 885-3165

Public Company
Incorporated: 1902
Employees: 17,000
Sales: $2.3 billion
Stock Exchanges: New York
SICs: 5411 Grocery Stores; 5141 Groceries, General Line

Hannaford Bros. Co. is the largest food retail chain in northern New England. Based in Maine, the company operates supermarkets in that state, as well as in parts of New Hampshire, Vermont, Massachusetts, and upstate New York. In addition to the company's 95 stores in those states, which operate under the names Shop 'n Save and Sun Foods, Hannaford Bros. has staked out new territory in the South with the 1994 purchase of the Wilson's Supermarkets chain, consisting of 21 stores in North and South Carolina. Aside from its retail operations, Hannaford Bros. sells on a wholesale basis to 19 supermarkets that it does not own.

Hannaford Bros. was founded in 1883 by brothers Howard, Arthur, and Edward Hannaford. The Hannafords were farmers in Cape Elizabeth, Maine, where they grew a variety of fruits and vegetables. They opened their first shop on the Portland, Maine, waterfront as an outlet for the produce they grew on the farm. Over time, Hannaford Bros. became a major produce wholesaler, operating out of their Portland warehouse. The company incorporated in 1902 and enjoyed steady growth during the first few decades of the new century.

The gradual shift from being primarily a wholesaler to primarily a retailer began in 1944, when the company opened its first supermarket. The move began to pick up steam in the early 1960s under the guidance of Walter F. Whittier, who had joined Hannaford Bros. in 1938 and was named president in 1960. Under Whittier, the company began to purchase equity interest in supermarket chains. The strategy was based on the knowledge that these equity partnerships yielded a much higher profit margin than did straight wholesale relationships. The linking of wholesale distributors with retailers in the grocery business was

revolutionary at the time, and Hannaford Bros. was at the forefront of this movement.

By the middle of the 1960s, Hannaford Bros. was distributing to about 100 stores, mostly located in Maine. Although that number remained fairly constant over the next several years, the size of the stores grew, as smaller units shut their doors and new, bigger locations were built. In 1966 the company bought the Sampson's supermarket chain for $4.5 million. Those stores had been Hannaford wholesale customers before the acquisition. Thirty percent of the Sampson stock was then immediately sold off to a group of investors involved in the stores' operation. This was typical of the equity partnership arrangement with Hannaford Bros.'s other stores, most of which operated under the Shop 'n Save name. By 1970 the company owned majority interest, usually between 51 percent and 70 percent, in 58 of the 103 stores it supplied. The rest were served strictly as wholesale customers, although Hannaford was also landlord to several of them. For 1970 the company returned a profit of $844,000 on sales of $124 million.

In 1971 James L. Moody, a twelve-year company veteran, became Hannaford's president, with Whittier continuing in his role as chairman and chief executive. Moody took over the CEO spot two years later. 1971 was a landmark year for the company in several other ways. Hannaford common stock was sold publicly for the first time that year, although a large portion of its stock remained in the hands of insiders. It also marked the first time that the company generated net earnings in excess of $1 million. The trend toward retailing continued into the mid-1970s. By 1974 Hannaford was the regional leader in both the wholesale and retail sale of groceries. Company officials attributed this success largely to the equity partnership system, which remained fairly unusual in the supermarket industry. By this time, the company had 58 equity partnership stores, which bought about 65 percent of their merchandise from Hannaford's distribution center; 16 wholly owned outlets; and 38 independent retail customers. Between those three types of stores, Hannaford was supplying about a quarter of all the food sold in Maine's supermarkets. Annual sales had reached $200 million by this time.

Around the same time, Hannaford began its push into the retail drugstore business. The company opened three Wellby Super Drug Stores in Maine in 1973, and several more Wellby openings followed during the next few years. Unlike its grocery outlets, all of these initial entrants into the pharmacy business were owned outright by Hannaford.

During the rest of the 1970s, Hannaford Bros. retreated somewhat from its equity partnership concept, choosing instead to purchase full interest in its retail operations. By 1981 the company had 73 stores in its stable, 52 of them wholly owned. The remaining 21 stores operated according to the company's well-established equity partnership pattern. The 1981 purchase of the outstanding equity in the Sampson chain accounted for a good part of that shift in balance. Hannaford also bought the outstanding equity in Progressive Distributors, a supplier of health and beauty aids and other general merchandise, during 1981. Progressive had been an equity partnership since 1967. As the growth in New England's population outpaced the national average, new Shop 'n Save and Sampson stores were opened throughout the region, and sales approached $500 million.

Hannaford continued to grow impressively in the 1980s. In keeping with its aggressive expansion program, the company sought innovative ways to stay ahead of the supermarket pack. Technology was one area in which Hannaford's progressive philosophy was apparent. The company had scanning capability in 18 stores by 1982, and its internally developed computer programs for inventory and other financial procedures was advanced enough to be coveted by other supermarket firms. Hannaford Trucking Company, a wholly owned subsidiary, was founded in 1982, giving the company more flexibility and control over its distribution system. In 1983 Hannaford opened its first superstore. Called Super Shop 'n Save, the outlet was the largest of its kind in the northern New England region. In addition to the usual supermarket products, the 42,000 square-foot unit included a pharmacy, hardware, automotive items, a plant department, and a bulk food area. The Super Store concept, the result of several years' planning and fine-tuning, was part of a national trend toward larger-format supermarkets. In 1984 Hugh G. Farrington, who had joined the company as a management trainee in 1968, was named president of Hannaford. Moody stayed on as chairman and CEO.

The expansion program continued during the second half of the 1980s. In 1986 Hannaford Bros. stock began trading on the New York Stock Exchange. Sales for that year totaled $910 million. By 1987 the company was operating 66 supermarkets under the names Shop 'n Save, Martin's, and Sun Foods. In addition, 36 Wellby Super drug stores were in business by that time. Sales at Hannaford broke the $1 billion barrier for the first time in fiscal 1987. Around this time, the company made its move into the upstate New York and Massachusetts markets. Plans for expansion into these areas included a Sun Foods super warehouse store in Lowell, Massachusetts, and New York stores to be located in Glens Falls, Plattsburg, Amsterdam, and Albany. Most of these new stores were either combination or super stores, selling general merchandise as well as groceries, as the trend toward larger facilities continued to gain momentum. At the same time, the company's home turf of Maine, New Hampshire, and Vermont remained an important part of the mix. In many of those states' markets, larger stores were built to take the place of small, outmoded locations.

As the 1980s drew to a close, Hannaford continued to thrive, despite a recession that dragged down much of New England's economy. For the entire decade, the company's profits had increased by an average of 18 percent annually, compared to 13 percent for the seven companies tracked by Standard and Poor's Food Chains index. The company's expansion into upstate New York continued, assisted by computerized marketing surveys that focused on areas where supermarket chains were sparse. By 1989 Hannaford's sales had grown to $1.52 billion, with a healthy $39 million in net earnings. Part of the company's success had to do with its adoption of a ''socio-technical system'' of management, based on Japanese factory management ideas. Under this system, decision-making is decentralized. Small groups including both managers and employees are given a great deal of autonomy in areas such as hiring, pay scales, and general rules.

In December 1990, Hannaford added eleven supermarkets to its collection at once by acquiring the Alexander's chain in Massachusetts and New Hampshire for $73 million. The deal also brought two free-standing drug stores and three free-standing bakery shops into the Hannaford fold. The early 1990s saw the rise of a new and potent type of competitor: the membership club. With the spread of wholesale clubs such as Sam's and BJ's into Hannaford's home-base states, the company faced more of a threat to its market share than ever before. To remain competitive, Hannaford introduced a number of institutional-size items and other club-style merchandise under the name Budget Values. In spite of the increased competition, Hannaford managed to boost its sales even further, reaching $2 billion for fiscal 1991 and keeping pace with the company timetable.

The Hannaford empire consisted of 129 stores by 1992. That year Farrington added CEO to his existing titles of president and chief operating officer, while Moody retained his chairmanship. As competition from the clubs and from Wal-Mart continued to heat up, Hannaford's management made the strategic decision to get out of the drug store business, where deep discounting was making it more and more difficult to turn a profit. In May 1992 Hannaford sold 34 of its 41 free-standing drug stores to the Rite Aid Corp. The sale of those Wellby outlets, which had generated less than five percent of Hannaford's total sales, enabled the company to concentrate its efforts more fully on its core supermarket business.

The ongoing recession and the elimination of revenue from the drug stores led to Hannaford's first decrease in annual sales in 1993, although the drop was small. Meanwhile the company managed to increase its earnings by 15 percent to $56.7 million. By the end of 1993, Hannaford was operating a total of 93 food stores, more than half of them in Maine. Fifty-seven of the company's stores were large combination stores offering a broad range of non-food merchandise, four were super-warehouse units, and the rest were conventional supermarkets. Among the company's new openings in 1993 were two combination food/drug stores in New York state; one in Concord, New Hampshire; and one in Farmington, Maine, that replaced a smaller unit. The Gloversville, New York, store was the first Hannaford store to go head-to-head with a Wal-Mart in the same shopping complex.

In 1994 Hannaford made its first foray out of the Northeast by acquiring Wilson's Supermarkets, based in Wilmington, North Carolina, for $120 million. Wilson's, a privately owned 20-store chain with units in both North and South Carolina, had expected sales of over $200 million in 1994. The deal also included five additional store sites (three already under construction) and several shopping centers. By September 1994, Hannaford had already opened a 21st Wilson's, located in Fayetteville, North Carolina. Day-to-day management of the Wilson's chain remained in the hands of the Wilson family, which had run the stores since the company's inception in 1919.

Hannaford's expansion into the South has opened up new horizons for the company. Now that it has broken free of its former regional constraints, the main challenge facing Hannaford Bros. in the coming years appears to be the ongoing competition from warehouse clubs and other large-scale stores whose sheer volume enables them to offer products at extremely low prices. Thus far, Hannaford has managed to hold its own in those markets where it competes directly with warehouse-type outlets. Its ability to continue competing effectively in that environment will play a large role in the company's future expansion plans.

Principal Subsidiaries: Analytical Services, Inc.; Cottle's Shop 'n Save, Inc.; Hannaford Properties, Inc.; Hannaford Trucking Co.; Plain Street Properties, Inc.; Progressive Distributors, Inc.; The Sampson Supermarkets, Inc.; Shop 'n Save Mass., Inc.; Shopping Center Properties, Inc.; Warehouse Properties, Inc.; Boney Wilson & Sons, Inc.

Further Reading:

Autry, Ret, "Hannaford Brothers," *Fortune,* November 19, 1990, p. 174.
Brumback, Nancy, "Hannaford Cites Recession, Competition for Tough Year," *Supermarket News,* May 25, 1992, p. 9.
Calkins, Jan, "Hannaford Gears for Expansion," *Supermarket News,* April 20, 1987, p. 2.
Campanella, Frank, "Warehouse Expansion, New Stores Enhance Hannaford Bros. Profits," *Barron's,* December 13, 1971, p. 34.
"Geography Lesson," *Forbes,* August 1, 1994, p. 120.
"Hannaford Expects $1 Billion Annual Sales in '80s," *Supermarket News,* May 10, 1982, p. 20.
"Hannaford's Home-Grown Savvy," *Dun's Review,* June 1974, p. 106.
Netzer, Baie, "How About a Grocer in the Northeast!?" *Money,* February 1992, p. 50.
Orgel, David, "Hannaford Moves South with Deal to Buy Wilson's" *Supermarket News,* June 27, 1994, p. 1.
Rosebaum, Clarence, "Hannaford Bros. Co. in the Vanguard of the Food Distribution Revolution," *Journal of Commerce,* December 7, 1971, p. 7.
Turcsik, Richard, "Hannaford Battling Club Assault," *Supermarket News,* November 4, 1991, p. 1.

—Robert R. Jacobson

Harcourt Brace and Co.

6277 Sea Harbor Drive
Orlando, Florida 32887
U.S.A.
(407) 345-2000
Fax: (407) 345-8388

Wholly Owned Subsidiary of Harcourt General, Inc.
Incorporated: 1919 as Harcourt, Brace and Company
Employees: 4,500
Sales: $919.5 billion
SICs: 2731 Book Publishing & Printing; 2721 Periodicals
Publishing & Printing

Harcourt Brace and Co. ranks among the world's largest publishers, with activities in educational, scientific, technical, medical, professional and trade segments of the industry. While the company's publishing endeavors are diverse, its greatest activity centers around elementary-, secondary-, and college-level textbooks. Harcourt Brace is recognized as one of the nation's leading publishers of elementary and secondary school textbooks, and ranks among America's top five publishers of college textbooks. A subsidiary, The Psychological Corporation, is believed to be the largest for-profit publisher of educational, psychological, clinical and professional tests. The company's BAR/BRI program was America's largest bar examination review program in the early 1990s. It is also the largest publisher of journals for the scientific and medical communities, offering about 240 scholarly journals each year. Although the majority of Harcourt Brace's activities are centered in the United States, the publisher also has operations in London, Tokyo, Sydney, Toronto, and Montreal.

The publishing firm was established at the close of World War I, when two former classmates from Columbia University, Alfred Harcourt and Donald C. Brace, left their positions at Henry Holt & Company and started their own trade publishing house in New York. The year was 1919, and the firm was known as Harcourt, Brace and Howe. Alfred Harcourt had served as acquisitions editor and salesman in his 15 years with Holt; Donald Brace worked in manufacturing and production. Will D. Howe, an author and editor, had headed the English department at Indiana University. He left the new firm less than a year after its founding, when the name was changed to Harcourt, Brace and Company.

Three months after its incorporation, Harcourt, Brace and Company published its first book, *Organizing for Work* by H.L. Gantt. In the months and years that followed, Harcourt, Brace and Company enjoyed one success after another. John Maynard Keynes's *The Economic Consequences of Peace* was considered a milestone in publishing history. Other notable works included Sinclair Lewis's *Free Air, Main Street*, and *Arrowsmith*, the latter winning a Pulitzer Prize. Lewis had followed his editor, Harcourt, from Henry Holt.

In its first decade, Harcourt, Brace and Company diversified into a number of genres, including religious works and college and high school textbooks. The house also published some of the nation's most outstanding trade books and authors. Throughout its history, Harcourt, Brace and Company would be recognized as an innovator in the publishing industry. In the 1920s the company offered women employees equal career opportunities, a practice virtually nonexistent in the trade at that time. This philosophy was attributed in part to Ellen Knowles Eayres, the firm's first employee, who later married Alfred Harcourt.

The head of the first children's book department, from 1946 to 1972, was Margaret McElderry. Well known and well liked, she is credited with the discovery of many famous children's authors, Joan Walsh Anglund and Eleanor Estes among them.

During World War II Harcourt, Brace and Company published *Men Must Act* by Lewis Mumford, an anti-fascist book. It was offered free, in an advertisement in *The New York Times*, to the first 500 New Yorkers to respond. The response was unexpected: all 500 copies were given away by noon, and it was estimated that another 2,000 people were turned away.

The house retained many famous authors throughout the years, but in 1955 several of them followed a well respected Harcourt editor, Robert Giroux, who left to become a partner in Farrar, Straus & Giroux. Among the more than 17 authors who left with him were T.S. Eliot, Flannery O'Connor, John Berryman, and Bernard Malamud.

In 1942 Alfred Harcourt resigned as president, leaving control of the company's operations in the hands of Donald Brace. In 1955, one year after Harcourt's death, William Jovanovich was elected president of Harcourt, Brace and Company. Donald Brace died in September of that year at the age of 74. William Jovanovich, a Colorado native, had joined the company in 1947 as a textbook salesman with a salary of $50 per week. Six years later he headed the school department, and in 1955 he was president of the company. While Jovanovich, at the time, was the youngest director with the company and owned no stock, he was the strong leader that the families of the two founders had sought.

Once at the helm, Jovanovich set a clear path for turning the company into a conglomerate. Two of his first goals were to take the company public and to merge with World Book Company, incorporated in 1905. Both moves were accomplished in 1960. Harcourt, Brace & World, Inc. was formed as a result, and took its position as the largest publisher of elementary, secondary, and college materials in the nation. The company would be lead by aggressive and determined Jovanovich until 1990. The company would diversify into dozens of publishing markets as well as into businesses totally unrelated to publishing by acquiring more than 40 companies.

In publishing, the late 1960s saw the acquisition of two educational filmstrip production companies; several farm and trade publications; and Academic Press, Inc., an international concern that published physical and applied science books and journals. Each year during the 1970s, except 1975, the company acquired at least one publishing or education-related firm.

In 1970 Jovanovich became chairman of the company, and its name was changed from Harcourt, Brace & World, Inc. to Harcourt Brace Jovanovich, Inc. (HBJ). Among the most notable acquisitions of the 1970s were The Psychological Corporation, in 1970, publishers of aptitude, diagnostic, achievement, and psychological tests; Beckley-Cardy Company, in 1972, a school supply house; Bay Area Review Course, Inc. and BRI Bar Review Institute, Inc. in 1974, the two being among the nation's best bar exam review courses; and Pyramid Communications, Inc. in 1974, renamed Jove Publications, Inc., a mass market paperback publisher of romance, inspirational, sports, and health books. Also in 1984 Drake-Beam & Associates, now Drake Beam Morin, Inc., an outplacement counseling firm, was acquired. By 1978 HBJ was publishing about 2,300 titles—from newsletters to romances—and 75 magazines, with revenues hovering around $360 million.

The 1970s were not without their drawbacks. In 1974 operations at four German publishing houses purchased in 1970 were terminated because of poor profits. Price controls affected profits at Academic Press for a number of years. Jove/HBJ, an experimental imprint, was failing, and it was sold in 1979. HBJ's trade division operated at a deficit beginning early in the decade. In 1977 HBJ lost $1.6 million on its general interest books alone.

In early 1978 Jovanovich cut the company's budget, firing six of the trade division's top personnel; he put himself in charge of hardcover adult and juvenile works. The discharge came several days after HBJ regrouped its operations and created an office of the president. Jovanovich claimed the firings had nothing to do with this reorganization.

Three executive vice-presidents were elected to fill the office of the president: Robert L. Edgell, Robert R. Hillebrecht, and Jack O. Snyder. HBJ was reorganized into five operational groups: university and scholarly publishing, school materials and assessment, periodicals and insurance, business publications and broadcasting, and popular enterprises. This latter group, headed by Hillebrecht, included the marine parks known as Sea World, an acquisition of 1976.

To acquire Sea World, Inc., HBJ had borrowed $46.7 million. Sea World was composed of three marine parks, located in San Diego, California; Cleveland, Ohio; and Orlando, Florida; and was considered some of the world's finest living museums. In 1977 Sea World helped push the company's gross sales to $281.7 million.

In 1980 Jovanovich told *The New York Times* that he was again looking for new acquisitions, and the decade would see HBJ's attention turned to theme parks, insurance, and more publishing. In 1980 HBJ purchased a commercial insurance broker for the dental profession. In 1982 HBJ bought three publishing concerns, acquiring business periodicals serving a number of specialized industries. Acquisitions made in 1984 and 1985 diversified HBJ into 11 new periodical markets. Also in 1985, HBJ acquired three insurance operations. The largest, purchased for $130 million, were Federal Home Life Insurance Company and PHF Life Insurance Company of Battle Creek, Michigan.

In 1982 HBJ announced that it would move its headquarters from New York City to Orlando, Florida, and the trade department to San Diego, California. *Business Week,* March 31, 1982, quoted Jovanovich as saying "We're moving because the continued profitability of publishing is in jeopardy." A projected annual savings in rent and operation expenses of $20 million topped Jovanovich's reasons for the move. "Too much time is spent lunching, and not enough is spent reading. Many of our writers don't live in New York anyway," Jovanovich noted.

HBJ planned to use the employee pension fund, which, the company stated, was "hugely overfunded," to finance the new corporate headquarters. The investment, according to Jovanovich, would yield a considerable return—15 percent of the building's cost in annual rent. In September 1983, the U.S. Labor Department prohibited the use of the fund, and HBJ was required to return all monies to the fund. The move, complete in 1984, included the construction of an eight story, 385,000 square-foot office building across from Sea World. The new HBJ headquarters cost the company $20 million. The move, as of 1986, cost HBJ a total of $35 million.

Once established in its new home, HBJ went on another theme park buying spree, spending a total of $67.7 million. In September 1984 HBJ bought Stars Hall of Fame in Orlando, which was soon converted to Places of Learning. The company acquired Florida Cypress Gardens, Inc., a botanical garden and entertainment park near Winter Haven, Florida, in 1985 through a $22.6 million stock trade. In December 1986 HBJ acquired Marineland Amusements Corporation in Rancho Palos Verdes, California.

Near the end of that year, HBJ made the biggest purchase in its history, the $500 million acquisition of the educational and professional publishing division of CBS Inc. The division's primary subsidiaries included W.B. Saunders, the world's largest publisher of medical and health science textbooks and materials; and Holt, Rinehart and Winston, Inc. (HRW), one of the nation's top textbook publishers. In an ironic twist, HRW was the evolutionary product of Henry Holt & Company—the firm from which Harcourt, Brace and Howe had started. The purchase made HBJ the largest publisher of elementary school and high school textbooks.

In 1987 Robert Maxwell, the chairman of British Printing and Communications Corporation (BPCC), set his sights on acquiring Harcourt Brace Jovanovich. Maxwell was looking for a U.S. publisher to add to his stable, and offered more than $2 billion for the company. HBJ was not interested. Takeover threats had prompted Jovanovich into action twice before in HBJ's history—once in 1978 by Marvin Josephson, and again in 1981 by Warner Communications. Neither the action nor the results in either case had been far reaching.

In a press release dated May 26, 1987, HBJ announced its plan to fight the BPPC proposal through a recapitalization distribution. The plan included a $40-per-share special dividend and the issuance of new preferred stock.

Within two days, Maxwell announced he had withdrawn his offer, but HBJ had paid a hefty price. To fend off the takeover, HBJ had more than tripled its debt, from $837 million to $2.9 billion, requiring bank loans for a substantial portion of that figure. The withdrawal of his offer notwithstanding, on June 1 Maxwell tried to block the reorganization plan. At the close of business June 2, more than 3.3 million HBJ shares had changed hands, with the price skyrocketing to $63.75. A number of companies, along with Maxwell's BPCC, opposed HBJ's reorganization. After an Orange County, Florida, judge ruled in HBJ's favor in late June, Maxwell withdrew.

In August 1987 HBJ began its attempt to cover the cost of the takeover defense by selling assets. Among the first to go were HBJ's two VHF television stations and three corporate jets, the sales of which brought in about $20 million. Two book clubs were next on the auction block. In November HBJ announced the sale of its 110 trade magazines and Beckley-Cardy for $334 million. The buyer was Edgell Communications Inc., a new, private corporation formed in part by Robert Edgell, a former HBJ executive.

By year's end HBJ had met its performing-asset sale requirement under its credit agreements. The company had sold more than $370 million in assets. Speculation continued, however, as did the rumors as to which property HBJ would sell next and to whom. On January 1, 1988, William Jovanovich announced that the HBJ theme parks were not for sale.

Several months later, HBJ eliminated 729 jobs from its theme park operations. While neither the HBJ publishing or insurance divisions were affected, the layoff included more than 343 positions at Florida-based theme parks, and 17 percent of the work force at Sea World in San Antonio, Texas.

On March 30, 1988, Ralph D. Caulo, age 53, was announced as HBJ's newly elected president and chief operating officer. Caulo, who joined HBJ in 1967 as a textbook sales manager, had served as an executive vice-president in Orlando, heading the school publishing division. William Jovanovich had been chief executive, president, and chairman since 1970. On December 17, 1988, at age 68, William Jovanovich resigned his position as president and chief executive officer of Harcourt Brace Jovanovich, retaining only his position as chairman.

During the late 1980s some analysts believed the company's financial situation to be anything but hopeful. Forced to sell revenue-generating assets to repay debt, HBJ had undermined its long-range solvency. William Jovanovich claimed that "HBJ could repay its obligations without now selling major assets."

In November 1989, HBJ sold all six of its theme parks and related land holdings to Anheuser-Busch Companies. The price was $1.1 billion, which went to retire the bank loans. The year also saw significant structural changes within HBJ operations. Elementary and secondary textbook divisions were divided. HBJ would now publish kindergarten through eighth grade textbooks, while subsidiary Holt, Rinehart and Winston (HRW) would publish those for grades seven through twelve. HBJ and HRW school department heads resigned, as did six executives in the elementary and secondary divisions. Ralph Caulo resigned as president, and Peter Jovanovich was elected in his place.

William Jovanovich's son, Peter William Jovanovich, was born in New York City in 1949, and had joined the HBJ trade department in 1980. Along with the leadership of the company his father had long enjoyed, Peter inherited HBJ's $1.6 billion debt. Wall Street analysts and institutional investors openly expressed concern regarding Jovanovich's ability to pull the company from its troubles. HBJ's operating loss for 1989 reached $242 million, with annual interest payments at $350.8 million. The firm's share price had plummeted from nearly $44 late in 1984 to around $3 by 1989.

The declining stock price was devastating for investors and employees alike. The company had eliminated its $74 million defined benefit pension plan in 1984 in favor of a $24 million employee stock ownership plan, or ESOP. The ESOP became employees' only source of retirement benefits, and the "extra" $50 million reverted to the company. In light of its plummeting market value, HBJ began offering a new defined contribution plan in 1989, but did not (and frankly could not) offer compensation to employees and retirees who had suffered significant losses.

In April 1990 HBJ confirmed its intentions to sell additional assets. Speculation by analysts targeted HBJ's professional publishing division, including W.B. Saunders as one possibility, estimating a sale price at around $600 million. Another option would be the company's insurance operations, which in 1989 had $456.3 million in revenues. Still other sources disclosed the possibility of a renewed interest in HBJ by BPCC chairman Robert Maxwell.

On May 29, 1990, William Jovanovich retired from his 36-year tenure as chairman of HBJ, naming John S. Herrington as his successor. The *New York Times,* May 30, 1990, quoted Roger Straus, chairman of Farrar, Straus & Giroux: "It is very sad. Bill was a great publisher in his time, but he went too far in resisting Maxwell. Now I suspect that he does not want to be there for the dismemberment." HBJ's 1990 annual report paid brief homage to its long-time leader, calling him "the soul of HBJ." A lawyer, Herrington had joined the board of directors in 1989 after serving as secretary of energy to U.S. President Ronald Reagan.

In September 1990 Vice-Chairman and Chief Operating Officer J. William Brandner, HBJ's second in command, resigned. HBJ announced that his departure was part of a budget cut that was expected to help curb operating expenses without hindering operations. In the same month, HBJ hired a spokesman—a first in its 71-year history. C. Anson Franklin had served as assistant energy secretary under Herrington and as assistant press secretary in the Reagan administration. Franklin's job, in addition to serving as liaison between the company, its shareholders, and the press, was to improve HBJ's community and company communications.

In spite of its serious financial difficulties, HBJ continued to publish great books. In 1990 HBJ's Octavio Paz was awarded the Nobel Prize for Literature. The poet, age 76, was the first Mexican writer to receive literature's highest recognition, awarded by the Swedish Academy of Letters. He is the author of *Convergences: Essay on Art and Literature*, and *One Earth, Four or Five Worlds: Reflections on Contemporary History*. That same year, HBJ's Charles Simic won the Pulitzer Prize for Poetry.

With the publisher's stock hovering at $1.25 per share, and its long-term debt at an astounding $1.76 billion, HBJ's board of directors decided to make the ultimate asset sale, seeking a merger partner in 1990. After negotiations with nine potential partners, HBJ entered negotiations with General Cinema Corporation and approved a merger in January 1991. Although its initial offer expired, General Cinema announced a revised merger plan in August 1991. The $1.5 billion deal, which culminated in November, made HBJ a wholly-owned subsidiary of General Cinema.

While some analysts criticized General Cinema's chairman, Richard A. Smith, for the acquisition, others believed that his company's cash hoard could be used to virtually eliminate HBJ's debilitating debt. Although its revenues had increased to $1.4 billion in 1991, HBJ suffered an $81 million loss that year due in part to $128 million debt payments. In 1992 alone, debt reduction cut annual interest payments by $250 million, thereby enabling HBJ to record a net profit of $107.98 million that year.

Mid-1992, Richard T. Morgan, former chief executive officer of Macmillan, Inc., replaced Peter Jovanovich as president and CEO of Harcourt Brace Jovanovich. General Cinema was renamed Harcourt General in 1993 to reflect both the spin-off of its theater business to shareholders, and the increased importance of its publishing business, which was renamed Harcourt Brace and Co. that year. By this time, Harcourt Brace contributed 26 percent of its parent's annual revenues and nearly 40 percent of operating earnings. Harcourt General's 1993 annual report suggested the company might make acquisitions to bolster its core publishing business, but also warned that a cyclical decline in textbook purchases could depress 1994 revenues and earnings.

Principal Subsidiaries: Academic Press, Canada Limited (Ontario); Academic Press, Inc.; AP Journals, Inc.; Books for Professionals, Inc.; Devices for Learning, Inc.; Foundation for Marine Animal Husbandry, Inc.; Grune & Stratton, Inc.; Harcourt Brace & Company Australia Pty. Limited (Australia); Harcourt Brace Export Educational Development Group, Inc.; Harcourt Brace Export Corporation; Harcourt Brace FSC, Inc. (U.S. Virgin Islands); Harcourt Brace International Corporation; Harcourt Brace Japan, Inc. (99.17 percent); Harcourt Brace Real Properties Corporation; Harcourt Brace General Insurance, Inc.; Holt, Rinehart and Winston Limited (England); Holt, Rinehart and Winston Publishing Asia Limited (99 percent) (Hong Kong); HRW and WBS Canada Corporation, Inc.; HRW Distributors, Inc.; Human Nature, Inc.; Innovation Research, Inc.; Johnson Reprint Company Limited (England); T & A D Poyser Limited (England); The Psychological Corporation Limited (England); Seminar Press Limited (England); AP Export Company, Inc.; Coronado Publishers, Inc.; Johnson Reprint Corporation (N.Y.); Learned & Tested, Inc., The Educational Company; Miller Accounting Publications, Inc.

Further Reading:

Fabrikant, Geraldine, "General Cinema's Big Bet on Harcourt Brace's Revival," *New York Times,* January 6, 1992, pp. D1, D9.

Montgomery, Leland, "General Cinema: The Value of Camouflage," *Financial World,* September 1, 1992, p. 17.

Tebbel, John, *A History of Book Publishing in the United States,* New York: R.R. Bowker Company, 1972–1981.

Vosti, Curtis, "The Haunting Side of ESOPs," *Pensions & Investments,* March 2, 1992, p. 30.

—Janie Pritchett
—updated by April Dougal Gasbarre

Hard Rock Cafe International, Inc.

5800 Kirkman Road
Orlando, Florida 32819
U.S.A.
(407) 351-6000
Fax: (407) 363-7128

Wholly Owned Subsidiary of Rank Organisation PLC
Incorporated: 1977 as Hard Rock International PLC
Employees: 1,500
Sales: $54 million
SICs: 5812 Eating Places

Without rival in the business of combining food, music, and entertainment, Hard Rock Cafe International Inc., owner of a majority of the Hard Rock Cafes dotting the globe, was created in the wake of a bitter dispute between the two founders of the original Hard Rock Cafe in London. Despite such animosity, however, Hard Rock Cafe International elevated the Hard Rock concept to new heights, creating one of the most unusual and successful chain of restaurants in the world. In 1988, Hard Rock gained notice as one of world's most influential companies in Milton Moskowitz's book *The Global Marketplace.*

The popularity of the Hard Rock Cafes grew exponentially from the inception of the first cafe in 1971 through the 1990s. The excitement generated by the first cafe, an opening that quickly drew queues of patrons eager to take part in the Hard Rock Cafe's carnival-like atmosphere, was duplicated with each additional opening of restaurants in other cities and other countries, becoming, if anything, more intense, as the restaurants themselves became grander and earned the reputation as popular gathering spots for celebrities.

As Moskowitz noted in *The Global Marketplace,* with Hard Rock, a successful formula had been created, one that worked irrespective of geographic boundaries and divergent cultures, with a Hard Rock Cafe performing as well in Australia as another Hard Rock Cafe in Iceland. This universal popularity of the Hard Rock concept represented a rare achievement in the global restaurant industry; large fast-food chains like McDonalds and Kentucky Fried Chicken operated successfully in many different locations, while traditional, full-service restaurants like Hard Rock Cafes seldom moved across international borders with any success. Hard Rock Cafes, accordingly, exemplified a singular breed of restaurants, an unusual success story achieved without benefit of any prodigious marketing effort.

Hard Rock Cafes, to a large degree, generated business merely by their existence.

The story of Hard Rock's growth took on a contentious flavor early, when two young mismatched Americans—the quintessential odd couple—created the Hard Rock concept in 1971. Isaac Tigrett and Peter Morton were both 22 years old when they opened the first Hard Rock in London. Tigrett, son of a wealthy Tennessee financier named John Burton Tigrett, had moved to England with his family at age 15, attended private school in Lugano, Switzerland, then later spent his days in London selling used Rolls-Royces to Americans. Morton came from a wealthy and venerable Chicago restaurant family, a heritage he tapped into when he opened The Great American Disaster, an American-style restaurant located in Chelsea, London. As a restaurateur, Morton was immediately successful, but his success with The Great American Disaster would be overshadowed by his later achievements, which emerged from his friendship with Tigrett, whom he met shortly after opening The Great American Disaster.

Outside of youth and family wealth, Tigrett and Morton had little in common. Morton was later described as aloof, reserved, and a "business-first businessman," personality traits that initially complemented then later butted against Tigrett's impulsive and quirky personality. A self-described "raving Marxist," Tigrett would become legendary for his flamboyance and recklessness, renowned for being an eccentric figure who played the principal role in many of the titillating stories composing Hard Rock Cafe lore. One such story put Tigrett behind Hard Rock's public address microphone after London had been devastated by an Irish Republican Army bombing, announcing to the cafe's patrons that anyone holding an Irish passport could eat and drink for free. Another described Tigrett stamping across the tables in the London Hard Rock shouting at patrons, "This is my restaurant! What are you doing here! Get out! This is my restaurant!"

Such incidents, as well as the storied sightings of celebrities at Hard Rock Cafes, added to the mystique and unpredictability of a visit to Tigrett's and Morton's establishment, creating invaluable marketing material for an organization that invested little time or money on traditional advertising. In fact, reports of celebrities seen imbibing or eating at a Hard Rock Cafe, coupled with Tigrett's fabled antics, began working to the two restaurateurs' advantage soon after they opened the London Hard Rock on June 14, 1971, primarily with money supplied by their parents. Located on Park Lane in London's fashionable Mayfair district, the Hard Rock Cafe contrasted sharply with the lavish hotels lining posh Park Lane, where strictly enforced dress codes were the norm, and hamburgers, milk shakes, and the music of the Rolling Stones most certainly were not.

The London Hard Rock Cafe opened just as the rock 'n' roll genre from which it took its name was emerging. The cafe would need the luminaries from rock's list of idiosyncratic entertainers to make its definitive leap from a popular London restaurant to the internationally recognized nexus of celebrities, celebrity-watchers, and celebrants the Hard Rock Cafe would later become, but initially it prospered as a welcomed alternative to the otherwise reserved atmosphere pervading Park Lane. The Hard Rock Cafe's menu diverged from typical Park Lane fare as well, offering customers a simple, decidedly American selection of food and drink that included hamburgers, barbecued ribs, milk shakes, sundaes, corn-on-the-cob, and apple pie, in addition to a wide variety of beer and hard liquor and suffusive rock 'n' roll.

It was not long before celebrities began patronizing the cafe; the rock group Led Zeppelin reportedly sent whisky bottles crashing against the Hard Rock's walls one evening, and Carole King wrote a musical tribute to Morton's and Tigrett's rock 'n' roll haven, replete with lyrical references to the increasingly popular Hard Rock Cafe. Eric Clapton's guitar found its way onto a hook on the cafe's wall, then Pete Townshend, of the rock group The Who, donated his guitar in riposte, along with a note that read, "Mine's as good as his." The two guitars became part of the cafe's growing rock memorabilia collection, while the magnetic power of the Hard Rock to attract celebrities also pulled in notable personages from outside the world of music; the Duke of Westminster stopped by, director Steven Spielberg ate lunch there every day during the filming of *Raiders of the Lost Ark,* and numerous other celebrities made widely reported visits to the raucous anomaly on Park Lane.

The publicized reports of who did what at the Hard Rock Cafe benefitted Morton and Tigrett commensurately. Soon, the London Hard Rock was the destination for tourists and local denizens, a site to pay homage to the famous and the peculiar. While the Hard Rock was a marketing boon, the swell of excitement it generated created one obstacle for Tigrett and Morton to hurdle: customers lingered, dawdled, and gawked, remaining for hours to take part in the paparazzi-filled days and nights, but they purchased little, engendering a debilitatively slow customer turnover rate that stunted profits. The solution Tigrett and Morton reached, however, was relatively simple; they turned up the volume of their music, increasing the decibel level in the cafe and, as a result, increasing the patron turnover rate. Louder music meant people talked less, ate and drank faster, and loitered less, a change that quintupled the cafe's turnover rate and lifted its profit performance to match its popularity. Tigrett and Morton also moved into merchandising during this time, offering shirts, hats, watches, and coffee mugs with the Hard Rock logo, items that contributed significantly to Hard Rock's bottom line.

However, as the restaurant became increasingly popular and successful, the relationship between Tigrett and Morton was also becoming increasingly strained. In 1974, Tigrett made an about-face in his personal life, when the former "raving Marxist" became a Hindu convert and devoted follower of spiritual leader, Sai Baba. Espousing a "Love All, Serve All" tenet, Tigrett moved in with Ringo Starr's ex-wife, Maureen Starkey, in 1976, then later married her, referring to her, in typical Tigrett bravado, as his greatest piece of rock memorabilia. By the end of the 1970s, however, Tigrett's all-inclusive doctrine of love excluded Morton, and the two partners went their separate ways, beginning with Morton's return to the United States in 1979.

A protracted separation ensued, during which the two former partners fought a battle over the legal rights to the Hard Rock name. Three years later, in 1982, the situation was resolved when Morton gained the rights to the Hard Rock name for all the world west of the Mississippi River, while all the world east of the Mississippi River was granted to Tigrett. There were exceptions to this demarcation line—Morton was given the rights to Chicago, while Tigrett was awarded Dallas—but from 1982 forward there would be two companies, Morton's Hard Rock America, Inc. and Tigrett's Hard Rock Cafe International, Inc., controlling the Hard Rock name and operating Hard Rock Cafes. What followed was a more truculent era in Hard Rock's history.

Morton's Hard Rock America beat Tigrett's Hard Rock Cafe International to the punch when it opened the first Hard Rock in the United States in 1982. Located in Los Angeles, Morton's Hard Rock was backed financially by Hard Rock devotee Steven Spielberg, Hollywood film studio magnate Barry Diller, actor Henry Winkler, and singers Willie Nelson and John Denver, who helped Morton transport the Hard Rock concept across international borders for the first time. But, while Morton first brought the concept to the United States, Tigrett was the first to realize immediate success with the concept, opening a Hard Rock in New York with the financial assistance of comedian Dan Aykroyd and actor Yul Brynner. Critics hailed Tigrett's New York Hard Rock as the first successful effort to incorporate the disparate elements that made the London Hard Rock the success that it was, and crowds flocked to the new venue. Inside the New York Hard Rock, Tigrett assembled the first guitar-shaped bar, the largest collection of rock 'n' roll memorabilia, and his "God Wall," a tribute to the inspirational forces that guided the lives of many people, featuring, among other things, a photograph of Sai Baba, a giant Krugerrand, and an enormous Quaalude.

After the opening of the New York Hard Rock, the two former partners continued to compete. Morton opened a Hard Rock in San Francisco in an old automobile showroom; Tigrett opened a Hard Rock in Stockholm in 1985 and then opened the largest Hard Rock up to that time in Dallas in 1986. While Tigrett and Morton built their respective empires, others joined the fray by appropriating the Hard Rock name and independently opening ersatz Hard Rock Cafes in Amsterdam, Bombay, Bangkok, and Manila. By the late 1980s, after nearly 20 years in existence, the Hard Rock concept had engendered a confusing mess. Of all the proprietors operating Hard Rock Cafes, both legitimate and illegitimate, those who knew each other did not like each other, in fact, did not even speak to each other, and those who did not know each other had every incentive to remain incognito. The restaurants themselves were flourishing, but behind the scenes a tempest was gathering force.

Then Robert Earl approached Tigrett with an offer of acquisition. The son of a British pop singer, Earl was several years younger than Tigrett and Morton. He had attended the University of Surrey, where he took courses in operating food and drink establishments. Thereafter he catered a rock concert attended by 250,000 fans in Lincoln, England, and completed apprenticeships at the Savoy and Grosvenor House before finding his niche in the restaurant industry. Earl's bent was attracting tourists, and to do so he rented banquet halls in London and converted them into venues for dinner shows with themes that appealed to the tastes of tourists. Staging medieval banquets, cockney evenings, and tributes to "Olde England," Earl quickly amassed a restaurant empire that totaled 70 restaurants by the time he merged his company, President Entertainments, in 1987 with Pleasurama PLC, a London-based leisure group. The transaction yielded Earl $63 million.

One of the first deals Earl completed for Pleasurama was the acquisition of Tigrett's half of the Hard Rock business. Tigrett had since taken his Hard Rock Cafe International public, selling a small portion of the company to London investors in 1984. Three years later, Drexel Burnham Lambert sold another parcel of the company to American investors, an ill-timed $40 million offering made prior to the stock market plunge in October 1987, which sent Tigrett's stock cascading downward. Less than a year later, in August 1988, Tigrett sold his Hard Rock holdings to Earl and Pleasurama for $100 million, ending his 17-year tenure as Hard Rock showman.

Tigrett went on to superintend the development of a pyramid-shaped sports arena in Memphis and the construction of a hospital for the poor in India, while Earl took the four Hard Rocks located in Tigrett's eastern sector and quickly sought to increase their number. Earl's corporate affiliation with Pleasurama, meanwhile, came to an end in 1989, when the leisure company was acquired by Mecca Leisure PLC, which, in turn, was swallowed by Rank Organisation, a British-based conglomerate, in 1990. By the time the dust had settled, there were 25 Hard Rocks dotting the globe, counting both Morton's and Earl's, the newest, largest, and most successful being the Orlando Hard Rock, which opened in 1990 and almost immediately began serving 5,000 customers a day.

The Orlando Hard Rock was Earl's, as were nine more Hard Rocks slated for construction in the coming years, and, during this time, Tigrett and Morton found themselves agreeing on one issue; neither could abide Earl. Tigrett condemned Earl for treating the Hard Rock concept like a cash cow to be duplicated again and again until its novelty was exhausted, while Morton and Earl had become adversaries during the course of their business relationship. Earl and Morton jointly owned Hard Rock Licensing Corporation, a company that controlled the exclusive rights to Hard Rock's lucrative trademarks and served as a proving ground for both Hard Rock owners' divergent views as to which direction the Hard Rock name should be taken. A running feud between the two had been ongoing essentially since Earl had spearheaded the acquisition of Tigrett's half of the Hard Rock empire in 1988, and as time progressed the animosity between the two had intensified.

Earl irrevocably aggravated tensions in 1991 when he opened Planet Hollywood in New York, one block away from the New York Hard Rock, with his own band of celebrity investors that included film producer Keith Barish, director John Hughes, and actors Arnold Schwarzenegger and Bruce Willis. Designed by Anton Furst (who designed the sets for the film *Batman*), Planet Hollywood was to the film world what the Hard Rock was to the world of rock 'n' roll, a restaurant that housed memorabilia from the film industry and provided customers with an opportunity to enjoy the glamour of Hollywood. Earl's new establishment, based on an idea originally put forth by Keith Barish in 1989 for a restaurant called Hollywood Cafe, angered Morton, who charged that Earl had illegally copied the Hard Rock concept. Earl flatly denied Morton's charge, stating to *New York* magazine, ''Planet Hollywood was carefully designed so there would be no accusation whatsoever of duplication. You'll find zero similarity.''

By the summer of 1992, however, less than a year after the New York Planet Hollywood had opened, Morton had found enough similarities between Planet Hollywood and Hard Rock Cafes to bring three lawsuits against Rank Organisation and Robert Earl. Earl responded later that year by announcing his intentions to leave Rank Organisation and pursue his Planet Hollywood-related business interests, which opened the door for a new leader of Tigrett's former Hard Rock holdings.

Stepping into the breach was Art Levitt, who was selected as the president and chief executive officer of Hard Rock Cafe International in early 1993. Levitt left Walt Disney Co., where he had blossomed under the tutelage of Walt Disney's chairperson Michael Eisner, to join Rank Organisation and steward the company's Hard Rock holdings and the theme-restaurants created by Earl, which were grouped under the Rank Leisure USA corporate umbrella. At Walt Disney, Levitt had enjoyed considerable success, gaining employment at the company in 1985 after he impressed Eisner with his fortitude while selling office furniture to the then newly named Walt Disney chairperson. Levitt rapidly rose from furniture salesman to vice-president of corporate projects at Walt Disney and eventually oversaw several Walt Disney projects in Orlando before taking over Earl's responsibilities at Rank Organisation.

When he assumed his new post, Levitt inherited 22 Hard Rock Cafes in 13 countries, almost all of which were vestiges of Earl's prolific years at Rank Leisure USA's helm. With these highly successful properties—the New York Hard Rock, for instance, ranked as the city's third largest tourist attraction, trailing only the Empire State Building and the Statue of Liberty—Levitt steered the Hard Rock concept into the mid-1990s. Ahead, was a future that promised to be as successful as the two decades before. Whether this future would prove as colorful as the past would be determined by Levitt, his successors, and the vagaries of Hard Rock Cafe life.

Further Reading:

Ball, Aimee Lee, ''Mr. Universe,'' *New York,* July 15, 1991, p. 38.
''CEO Is Named,'' *Travel Weekly,* February 18, 1993, p. F1.
Finkelstein, Alex, ''Hard Rock Cafe Sues Hard Hats Cafe,'' *Orlando Business Journal,* February 7, 1992, p. 3.
Giles, Jeff, ''No Fear of Frying,'' *Rolling Stone,* November 14, 1991, pp. 15, 18, 21.
''Hard Rock Cafe Plans to Open a Hotel/Casino in Las Vegas,'' *Travel Weekly,* June 13, 1991, p.1.
''Hard Rock Hotel to Headline in Vegas,'' *Restaurant/Hotel Design International,* October 1991, p. 14.
Hayes, Jack, ''Earl to Rank Leisure: Hasta La Vista Baby!,'' *Nation's Restaurant News,* December 14, 1992, p. 1.
''HRC's Morton Files New Suit to Block Chicago 'Knock-Off','' *Nation's Restaurant News,* June 29, 1992, p. 2.
Martin, Richard, ''Hard Rock Hits Planet Hollywood with Copycat Suit,'' *Nation's Restaurant News,* March 16, 1992, p. 3.
Middleton, Christopher, ''The Hard Rock with a Soft Sell,'' *Marketing,* April 25, 1991, p. 23.
Moskowitz, Milton, *The Global Marketplace,* New York: Macmillan Publishing, 1987, pp. 248–51.
O'Conner, Amy, ''The Man Who Puts the Rock in the Hard Rock Cafe,'' *Restaurants & Institutions,* February 15, 1994, p. 14.
''This Hard Rock Is Rolling,'' *Florida Trend,* January 1992, p. 18.
Zacharias, Beth, ''Art Levitt Rolls into Hard Rock,'' *Orlando Business Journal,* January 11, 1993, p. 3.

—Jeffrey L. Covell

The Hartz Mountain Corporation

700 Frank E. Rodgers Boulevard South
Harrison, New Jersey 07029
U.S.A.
(201) 481-4800
Fax: (201) 481-3305

Private Company
Incorporated: 1926 as Hartz Mountain Pet Foods
Employees: 4,500
Sales: $850 million
SICs: 2047 Dog and Cat Food; 2048 Prepared Feeds, Not
   Elsewhere Classified; 3199 Leather Goods, Not Elsewhere
   Classified; 3999 Manufacturing Industries, Not Elsewhere
   Classified

The product of a German immigrant's struggle to survive in a
new country, Hartz Mountain Corp. was started in 1926 as a
dealer in canaries, then grew to dominate the American pet
supply industry. By the 1990s, Hartz Mountain no longer sold
canaries imported from the Hartz Mountain region in Germany,
but sold nearly everything else a pet owner could desire. In their
distinctive orange packaging, Hartz Mountain pet toys, accessories, shampoos, and foods graced the shelves of retail outlets
throughout the United States and abroad, their presence a testa-
ment to the determination of the Hartzes to make their company
an unrivaled giant in the pet supply industry.

Devastated by soaring inflation and mounting unemployment,
Germany during the 1920s was a country in near economic ruin
headed toward political disaster. For a vast majority of Germans, the future looked bleak: each year the economic depression worsened, leaving many of the country's citizens destitute
and looking for relief from a faltering government. Some found
an answer to their myriad problems in a virulent, yet magnetic
political leader who promised to make Germany the greatest
nation in the world, while others looked for answers elsewhere.
One of those who chose to leave Germany and start life anew
elsewhere was a textile manufacturer named Max Stern. In
1926, Stern left Germany and immigrated to the United States,
ready to begin a career that would help create and define an
American industry. Stern carried with him the products of his
new trade: 2,100 canaries taken from the famous Hartz Mountain region in Germany.

Initially, Stern sold his canaries to small pet stores, but he soon
expanded the scale of his business when he began selling first to
mass retailers and later to supermarkets and department stores.
Stern's decision to broaden product exposure through mass
retailers was the first of several crucial steps that laid the
foundation for the pet supply empire that would follow. This
decision led the company to expand its distribution network to
accommodate the delivery of a greater number of birds, and also
prompted it to offer a diversified product line. The company's
distribution network took time to develop, but Stern broadened
his product line shortly after opening his business, when he
began selling bird food in addition to Hartz Mountain canaries
in 1930. By the beginning of America's own decade-long struggle with depressed economic conditions, Stern had established
the three distinctive attributes that would predicate the growth
of his company and lead to its dominance of the U.S. pet supply
industry.

Despite the harsh economic conditions during the 1930s and his
inability to speak English, Stern was able to secure several
contracts with mass retailers and, along with his brother, who
had remained in Germany to purchase the canaries that Stern
would sell in the United States, enjoyed considerable success
over the next several decades. By the end of the 1950s, Stern's
modest venture had become a formidable force in the pet supply
industry, thanks largely to the growth and sophistication of the
company's distribution network and the diverse assortment of
products that bore the Hartz Mountain name. The company by
this point sold birds, bird food, and bird accessories, products
that generated $18 million in sales by 1959, which Stern hoped
to use to fund further product diversification. Following a
family dispute in 1959, Stern bought out his brother's share in
the company for $8 million.

Thereafter, Stern soon found a new partner: his son, Leonard N.
Stern, who became involved in the family business during the
late 1950s when his father, in an effort to encourage his children
to enter the business, ceded partial interest in Hartz Mountain to
his three children. As a youth, Leonard Stern had sold merchandise door-to-door, then, at age 17, had entered New York
University's School of Commerce. Two-and-a-half years later
he was graduated *cum laude* and subsequently earned his Masters of Business Administration degree at night while working
days as a clerk.

At Hartz Mountain in the late 1950s, Leonard and his brother
Stanley purchased two failing companies involved in the fish
and fish supply business—Aquarium Supply Co. and Long Life
Fish Food Products—and created a new company named
Sternco Industries, which they then took public in 1962 after
achieving nearly the same success in the fish and fish supply
business as their father had in the bird and bird supply business.
Shortly after taking Sternco Industries public, Stanley Stern left
the company to pursue his interests in the real estate business.
Leonard bought out Stanley's shares and then turned his
attention to the growth of both Sternco Industries and Hartz
Mountain.

Although he would not become president and chief executive
officer of Hartz Mountain until 1971, Leonard Stern wielded
considerable control within the company during the 1960s. As
executive vice-president and chief operating officer, he spear-

headed several of its most defining marketing moves. He broadened the company's product line substantially to include dog and cat accessories (dog toys, cat litter, shampoos), which enabled the company to tap into the burgeoning growth of supermarkets at the time, yet purposely stayed away from entering into the dog and cat food business to avoid competition from entrenched pet food producers. Hartz Mountain was going to establish market dominance, both father and son had decided, and the fragmented pet supply and accessory industry provided the perfect arena in which their well-organized and diversified company could compete.

By the mid-1970s, Max and Leonard Stern were well on their way toward fulfilling their goal. Hartz Mountain by this point controlled roughly one-third of the nearly $900 million pet supply business through the company's 1,200 products, which ranged from birds, fish, hamsters and gerbils to pet food, pet health care products, and accessories. The company that was now regarded as one of the few giants in the industry bore little resemblance to the fledgling enterprise launched by Max Stern in the mid-1920s, and could no longer sell the company's original product because the importation of canaries was made illegal in 1972. Nevertheless, by this time, canaries represented only five percent of Hartz Mountain's sales, and racks of Hartz Mountain merchandise displayed in their distinctive orange packaging occupied pet supply departments in retail outlets across the nation, in many cases being the only pet products stores stocked. The company's distribution system, by now the industry's prototype after 50 years of improvement and solidification, left competitors with little territory that was not firmly held by Hartz Mountain, leading the business press to hail the Stern organization as the General Motors of the pet supply industry. Other accolades followed, and soon industry pundits were claiming Max and Leonard Stern had done to the pet supply industry what Kodak's George Eastman had done to the photography industry and what Henry Ford had done to the automobile industry.

Leonard Stern, by this point in full control of Hartz Mountain, had demonstrated his business acumen in other arenas as well. In addition to masterminding Hartz Mountain's rousing growth—the company recorded $135 million in sales in 1972, then nearly doubled the total five years later despite a nationwide economic recession—Stern had purchased sizable acreage in Secaucus and Meadowlands, New Jersey, during the mid-1960s, which by the following decade had risen enormously in value. With his real estate holdings Stern formed a private company he named Hartz Mountain Industries, then shortly thereafter began reorganizing the Stern family empire into distinct pieces. In order to rase the $40 million needed for the Meadowlands project, Stern took Hartz Mountain Pet Foods public in 1972. The following year Stern merged Hartz Mountain Pet Foods into Sternco Industries, the fish and fish supply company he and his brother had formed years earlier, to create Hartz Mountain Corp. Hartz Mountain stood atop its field, enjoying more than a 75 percent market share in many of its market niches and holding a nearly unassailable lead over its competitors.

During this time, Hartz Mountain faced several challenges. First, in the early 1970s, a magazine article was published claiming that the chemical used in Hartz flea collars was potentially harmful; the flea collar was the company's biggest seller and contributed roughly $15 million in annual sales at the time. Then, more serious allegations were levelled at Hartz Mountain, its executive personnel, and Leonard Stern. Specifically, accusations arose concerning the company's alleged violation of antitrust laws by exerting undue pressure on distributors to deal in Hartz Mountain products exclusively. Several lawsuits were brought by competitors and distributors against Hartz Mountain during the 1970s, charging that the company's far-reaching and well-developed distribution techniques were overly aggressive, forced distributors to handle Hartz Mountain products exclusively, and involved taking the products of competitors off the shelves and replacing them with Hartz Mountain products. Ultimately, these matters were settled, and, admitting no wrongdoing, Hartz Mountain paid court settlements and a $20,000 fine to the Federal Trade Commission.

By the end of the 1970s, Stern decided to take the company private and use the funds for developing his real estate interests. When Stern bought back the publicly-held shares in Hartz Mountain, he merged Hartz Mountain Corp. into Hartz Mountain Industries, the real estate and real estate development arm of the Stern empire. Despite the legal turmoil surrounding the company at the time, Hartz Mountain had relinquished little of its dominance in the pet supply industry and continued to exert overwhelming control in many of its markets. The 75 percent market share Hartz Mountain's pet supply business reached during the 1970s continued to fuel the company's growth throughout the 1980s, as Stern turned his attention elsewhere in a bid to broaden the scope of his business interests.

In 1985, he purchased the *Village Voice,* a well-known Manhattan weekly newspaper, from publisher Robert Murdoch for $55 million, then two years later launched another Manhattan weekly newspaper he christened *7 Days.* In the mid-1990s, the *L.A. Weekly* would also be added to Stern's publishing interests. In 1988, Stern formed the Harmon Publishing Company, a new division developed to oversee his real estate publications.

Also during this time, Stern formed Hartz Group Inc. to once again separate his real estate development and building operation business from his pet supply business. In the hierarchical reshuffling that followed, Hartz Group was made the parent company of Hartz Mountain Corp., and Harmon Publishing Company was organized as a division of Hartz Group. Structured as such, the conglomeration of Hartz-controlled businesses entered the 1990s cast in their separate roles.

In 1990, after failing to receive a suitable offer from bidders, Stern ceased publication of *7 Days,* which had proven to be a $10 million loser despite earning positive reviews and being nominated for a coveted National Magazine Award. Four years later, Harmon Publishing Company, which had acquired 60 publishing companies in its six years of business (all involved in publishing real estate magazines), was sold to United Advertising Periodicals for $108 million. With these business interests trimmed from his formidable corporate organization, Stern plotted his course for the mid-1990s and beyond, buoyed by the consistently strong performance of his pet supply business. The company continued as a largely family-run enterprise, with Stern's son Edward serving as executive vice-president of the Hartz Groups' pet supply operations, and another son,

Emmanuel, as executive vice-president of the real estate arm of Hartz's business.

Further Reading:

"American Home Products to Buy 2 Pet-Line Firms," *Wall Street Journal,* August 19, 1971, p. 13.

Blustein, Paul, "Hartz Owner Made a Prime Target of a Big Grand Jury Investigation," *Wall Street Journal,* January 17, 1983, p. 25.

——,"Will the Canaries Come Home to Roost?," *Forbes,* April 17, 1978, pp. 59–61.

Blustein, Paul, and Richard Greene, "The Public Be Damned? In 1979?," *Forbes,* April 2, 1979, pp. 38–40.

"Cages to Collars—Hartz Mountain Finds Pet Supplies Growth Business," *Barron's,* February 9, 1976.

"The Canaries That Laid Golden Eggs . . . ," *Forbes,* February 15, 1974, pp. 34–38.

"Developer Stern to Launch Newspaper in Manhattan," *Wall Street Journal,* July 30, 1987, p. 26.

Donaton, Scott, " '7 Days' Folds After Bidders Balk," *Advertising Age,* April 23, 1990, p. 16.

"Ex-Hartz Executive Convicted for Perjury Over Alleged Payoffs," *Wall Street Journal,* December 22, 1982, p. 7.

"Fido and His Friends," *Barron's,* March 22, 1965, p. 11.

Hammer, Alexander R., "A Billion Dollar Business Is Unleashed in Pet Sales," *New York Times,* April 7, 1968, p. F35.

"Hartz Mountain Corp. Votes to Go Private Despite Objections by Minority of Holders," *Wall Street Journal,* February 14, 1979, p. 14.

"Hartz Mountain May Go Private Via Cash Merger," *Wall Street Journal,* November 2, 1978, p. 20.

"Leonard Norman Stern," *Forbes,* October 26, 1987, p. 137.

"Leonard Stern Is Sued by Former Hartz Partner," *Wall Street Journal,* November 12, 1993, p. A5.

Mills, Joshua, "Harmon Publishing Sale to Link Ad Periodicals," *New York Times,* February 1, 1994, p. D7.

"One of the Family," *Barron's,* March 3, 1969, p. 11.

Robichaux, Mark, "Hartz Brings Back Insect Spray Some Pet Owners Fear Is Fatal," *Wall Street Journal,* September 6, 1989, p. B6.

"Two Hartz Ex-Aides Sentenced on Charges from Antitrust Suit," *Wall Street Journal,* May 24, 1984, p. 24.

—Jeffrey L. Covell

HECHINGER

Hechinger Company

3500 Pennsy Drive
Landover, Maryland 20785
U.S.A.
(301) 341-1000
Fax: (301) 925-3912

Public Company
Incorporated: 1959 as Hechinger Company
Employees: 20,000
Sales: $2.45 billion
Stock Exchanges: NASDAQ
SICs: 5251 Hardware Stores; 5211 Lumber and Other
   Building Materials; 5261 Retail Nurseries and Garden
   Stores; 5231 Paint, Glass and Wallpaper Stores

One of the leading retailers in the do-it-yourself industry, Hechinger Company is also one of the industry pioneers. The company sold home repair products in warehouse-size stores long before that retail format became the industry norm, and has expanded its presence from the Washington, D.C., area where it originated, to reach markets throughout the eastern half of the United States. Through two subsidiaries, Hechinger Stores Company and Home Quarters Warehouse, Inc., Hechinger operated 119 stores in 21 states and the District of Columbia in 1995.

The business that became a 119-store home hardware and garden giant began as a wrecking and salvage business in 1911, when the patriarch of the Hechinger family, Sidney L. Hechinger, a former civil engineer, began tearing down old buildings in Washington, D.C. Hechinger had an entrepreneurial approach to demolition. When Hechinger demolished a building, he demolished it piecemeal, removing anything of value from the structure to sell to customers directly from the demolition site. Hechinger removed nails from lumber, chiseled mortar from bricks, melted cast-iron pipe, and took anything else he could find to amass the Hechinger Company's first inventory.

Shortly after razing his first building, Hechinger began receiving requests from his customers for particular parts and specifically sized parts, requests he often was not able to meet with the limited inventory he had on hand. For Hechinger it was an early lesson in maintaining an inventory of sufficient breadth, a lesson which would lead to the enormously extensive inventor-

ies that underpinned the Hechinger Company's success. Hechinger's inventory grew as he began purchasing new materials in small quantities to compensate for what he lacked in second-hand materials.

New materials, of course, cost more, but to Hechinger's reported surprise, many of his customers opted for the higher-priced, new materials rather than the cheaper used materials and soon demand for the new outpaced demand for the old. As a result, Hechinger purchased more and more new materials, something that was much easier to do than tearing down buildings and gleaning pipes, bricks, nails, and whatever else from the resultant rubble. Nevertheless, Hechinger continued to sort through debris, selling the old and the new, for eight years after starting his business. During this period, his business had no permanent address; Hechinger moved from demolition site to demolition site, and his customers followed.

This all changed in 1919, when Hechinger opened his first store at Sixth and C Streets, near the nation's capitol in southwest Washington, D.C. With the opening of the first store, Hechinger formally entered the retail industry, a business that would employ and enrich three generations of Hechingers and lead to a proliferation of Hechinger Company stores throughout the century. To be sure, the opening of the Sixth and C Street store represented a genuine milestone in the company's history. But the first defining moment in the story of Hechinger Company's development occurred five years later, in 1924, when Sidney Hechinger pinpointed the type of clientele that would carry Hechinger stores to the top of their industry. Hechinger noticed that along with the expected building contractors who frequented his store, a considerable proportion of his customers were homeowners intent on refurbishing and remodeling their homes themselves. These customers represented what would later represent the do-it-yourself market, a niche of the larger building supply market that would expand enormously in the coming decades and fuel the Hechinger Company's growth.

From 1924 forward, Hechinger catered to the do-it-yourself customer exclusively, operating under a "no wholesale, no discount" business philosophy that spawned the Hechinger Company's trademark figures "Harry and Harriet Homeowner" and represented the distinctive quality separating the company's stores from the competition. Hechinger realized two chief advantages over his competitors. Oriented toward amateur, do-it-yourself customers, Hechinger Company stores were less intimidating to homeowners wishing to repair or remodel their residences themselves. Equally as important, however, were the economic benefits afforded by excluding particular types of customers from the company's customer base. Typically, home center stores like Hechinger sold not only to do-it-yourselfers but to building contractors and industrial/government customers as well, customers that added to a store's sales volume, but left it exposed to the capriciousness of the construction market. When construction activity waned, those stores catering to professional builders fell victim to the cyclical nature of the market they relied on for a percentage of their sales. Conversely, when economic conditions soured, the Hechinger Company's business usually picked up, since homeowners were more likely to fix their homes themselves rather than hiring expensive construction contractors during a recessive economic climate. Accordingly, throughout the company's history this emphasis on supplying homeowners with the materials required to complete home improvement and repair projects themselves would insulate Hechinger Company to a certain extent from deleterious economic cycles and distinguish it from competing home center stores.

With this distinctive quality established early in his company's history, Hechinger set himself to the task of increasing the number of Hechinger Company stores in the Washington area. By 1933, there were four such stores, with the fourth one opening that year. Despite the debilitative effects of the Great Depression, Hechinger was able to amass enough money to buy his own lumber yard in Falls Church, Virginia, eight years later, the same year in which the United States entered World War II. During the war, Hechinger's stores stocked approximately 5,000 items each, enabling him to gross roughly $1 million a year, but the first great spurt of growth in the do-it-yourself market was yet to come, and when it did the sagacity of Hechinger's decision in 1924 to cater exclusively to homeowners would begin to pay dividends.

During the two decades following the conclusion of World War II, the emergence of a suburban middle class sparked the emergence, then the growth, of a national do-it-yourself market. The economic expansion that swept across the country spurred industrial growth and increased personal income levels, inducing those with sufficient capital to become homeowners rather than home renters. Factory workers and corporate executives alike became weekend home renovators and repairers, taking their ladders and tools from garages to paint their homes or add a room, the materials for which were purchased from retail stores like Hechinger's that promoted themselves as home centers. The 1950s and 1960s were two decades of prodigious growth for both America and the do-it-yourself market, but Sidney Hechinger witnessed only half of this postwar economic resurgence, dying in 1958 after leading his company for 47 years. Behind him, Hechinger left a seven-store retail chain operating under the motto "Foundation to Roof, Rock-Bottom Prices" that, in the year of his death, generated $6.5 million in sales.

After Sidney Hechinger's death, leadership of Hechinger Company was assumed by Hechinger's son, John W. Hechinger, and his son-in-law, Richard England, who, after opening eight additional stores, took the company public in 1972. Once publicly held, Hechinger Company gained a new motto, "The World's Most Unusual Lumber Yard," and the financial means to launch a program of increased expansion, which touched off a decade of dramatic growth for the company that would be exceeded only by its performance during the following decade. Each year between 1972 and 1979 Hechinger Company increased its sales and net income totals, a record of growth that was made even more remarkable considering the economic environment in which it was achieved. The inflationary and recessive mid-1970s crippled many businesses, particularly retail concerns, yet during the worst years of the economic downturn Hechinger registered robust increases in its sales volume, recording a 20 percent increase in 1974 and an even more impressive 40 percent gain in 1975.

Perhaps more encouraging to the company's new management was how Hechinger's performance compared to its competitors. Hechinger was positioned in the recession-resistant home center industry. At rival home center stores, 1974 and 1975 represented bleak years, engendered largely by their reliance on business from professional builders. Two of the industry's largest members at the time, Lowe's Co. and Scotty's Inc., recorded losses attributable to the decline in construction activity caused by the recessive economic climate. At Scotty's, where sales to professional builders accounted for 23 percent of the company's revenues, sales dipped from $80 million in 1974 to $77.5 million in 1975. More precipitous was the decline in sales suffered by Lowe's, the industry's largest competitor. With 58 percent of its revenues derived from sales to professional builders, Lowe's exposure to fluctuations in the construction market was greater and so was its drop in sales, which fell from $362.5 million in 1974 to $340.9 million the following year. At Hechinger, meanwhile, sales climbed from $49.4 million to $69.1 million between 1974 and 1975, spurred by the increasing numbers of homeowners taking on their own remodeling and repair projects.

Against this backdrop of encouraging growth during a period of economic stagnation, Hechinger stores adopted a decidedly different look, taking on characteristics that would define the company's retail outlets during the 1990s. Hechinger stores that sold 5,000 products during the 1940s now sold 40,000 products and, consequently, were much larger than their predecessors. Averaging 60,000 square feet of selling space in the mid-1980s, the company's stores were early versions of the behemoth warehouse retail outlets that flourished during the late 1980s and into the 1990s. Further, each store represented a blueprint for another, as all Hechinger stores adopted the same design, layout, and inventory, enabling the company to realize internal management economies and giving it, in effect, a blueprint for success. More important to the company's growth was the extensive collection of products each of these large stores sold. The enormous breadth and depth of Hechinger's inventory created what company officials termed "category dominance," a vast selection of particular products that gave customers little need to shop elsewhere for home improvement and repair items. Someone looking for a hammer, for instance, could select from 62 different models displayed on the company's shelves, a diversity that led one Hechinger executive to note, "If it's for your home and garden and you can't find it at Hechinger, you don't need it."

By the beginning of the 1980s, the plans for rapid expansion that arose from the issuance of stock in 1972 had been largely realized. Hechinger, by 1980, comprised 27 stores selling lumber, paint, tools, garden supplies, and housewares, as well as a limited selection of toys and sporting goods. In 1980, U.S. consumers spent $31.1 billion refurbishing their homes, $9.4 billion of which was accounted for by the do-it-yourself market, a 47 percent increase from the previous year's total. Nearly commensurate growth would continue throughout the 1980s and fuel Hechinger's growth as well. The company generated $170.4 million in sales in 1980 and $6.8 million in net income; by the decade's conclusion Hechinger's sales total eclipsed $1 billion and it earned slightly less than $50 million, financial figures that would vault the company to the fore of the home center industry.

A major step toward achieving this remarkable record of growth during the decade was taken in 1982, when Hechinger announced it was opening a store in North Carolina. For years company officials had stated that Hechinger would not expand beyond a 200-mile radius around its distribution center in Landover, Maryland. More than 200 miles away from Landover and the company's delivery trucks, which were kept scurrying among Hechinger's stores to replenish massive inventories, could not make the trip in one day, a logistical problem the company's management wished to avoid. That all changed when Hechinger opened two stores, the company's 36th and 37th, in Charlotte, North Carolina, in early 1983, transforming it from being a metropolitan Washington, D.C. retailer into a mid-Atlantic retailer. The move into North Carolina also pitted Hechinger against industry giant Lowe's, which by this point was generating $1 billion a year in sales. Based in North Carolina, Lowe's had 51 stores in its home state, where Hechinger was relatively unknown, giving the battle between the industry's entrenched leader and its quickly ascending rival a determinative quality.

By this point, however, Hechinger had little to worry about. Confidence ran high at the quickly expanding retailer, its growth propelled by the growth of its aggregate retail space. From 1972 to the early 1980s, when Hechinger made its first steps outside the metropolitan Washington region, the company's retail and storage space increased from 506,000 square feet to over three million square feet, and the number of its stores rose from ten in 1972 to more than 40 (15 stores were opened in 1983 alone). With massive stores and enormous inventories, the company was attracting the lion's share of the do-it-yourself market wherever it maintained a sizable presence. In 1983, a typical Hechinger store averaged 500,000 customers a year, considerably more than the 120,000 averaged by competitors, a disparity that fueled optimism about the company's future along the mid-Atlantic seaboard.

By 1986, Hechinger had posted record profits every quarter since going public in 1972, which translated as an average 28 percent annual increase in profits. Sales that year reached $588.4 million, generated by stores that contained between 80,000 square feet and three acres of retail space. With John Hechinger, Jr. taking control of the company that year, the company planned to add ten to 14 stores per year to achieve annual sales growth of between 20 percent and 25 percent, as the company's management aimed their sights on reaching the $1 billion sales mark. Two years later, in 1988, two acquisitions helped the company achieve its financial goal. In December, Hechinger agreed to acquire the retail division and related real estate interests of Quakertown, Pennsylvania-based Triangle Building Supplies & Lumber Co. for approximately $27 million. The acquisition gave Hechinger six stores in Pennsylvania, which continued to operate under the Triangle name once the purchase was completed, but another acquisition completed earlier in the year provided a more substantial and longer lasting boost to Hechinger's business. The company purchased Home Quarters Warehouse, Inc. for $70.5 million, an acquisition that

experienced robust growth under Hechinger's management during the early 1990s.

With Triangle Building Center stores and Home Quarters stores complementing the company's flagship Hechinger stores, sales eclipsed $1 billion in 1989, then eclipsed $2 billion five years later. During this period, Hechinger faced mounting competition from a relative newcomer to the do-it-yourself market, Home Depot Inc., an Atlanta, Georgia-based retailer that quickly rose to the top of the industry. To combat Home Depot's incursion into Hechinger's territory, the company launched a prodigious expansion program in 1990 focused largely on increasing the number of its Home Quarters stores.

With 84 Hechinger stores at the time, the company planned to add 30 stores by 1992 to the subsidiary's 15-store chain, which as the decade progressed proved to be the engine driving the Hechinger empire. Between 1992 and 1993, Hechinger's Home Quarters Warehouse subsidiary's sales increased 42 percent; moreover, between 1990 and 1995 sales had grown at a compound annual rate of 46 percent. More impressive was the subsidiary's compounded annual rate of operating profits growth, which for the 1991 to 1994 period reached 41 percent. With the strong performance of its Home Quarters stores buoying its business, Hechinger recorded $2.09 billion in sales in 1993, a total reached despite the divestiture of its Triangle Building Centers division the year before.

In the 73 years between the founding of Sidney Hechinger's wrecking and salvage business in 1911 and the 119-store retail chain that described Hechinger Company in 1994, a do-it-yourself retail pioneer had emerged. Hechinger had developed a business philosophy and marketing strategies that many of its competitors copied during the increasingly competitive 1990s. Sidney Hechinger steered the company's marketing efforts toward the homeowner, establishing Hechinger Company's corporate focus. His son and grandson took the company to new heights by greatly increasing store and inventory size, making sure as they did so that Hechinger Company remained focused on the homeowner. As the company plotted its course beyond the mid-1990s and into the next century, these basic retailing strategies shaped its plans for the future.

Principal Subsidiaries: Home Quarters Warehouse, Inc.; Hechinger Stores Company.

Further Reading:

"Carpenter, Repair Thyself," *Forbes,* September 2, 1991, p. 232.
Gissen, Jay, "Nice Number, 40,000," *Forbes,* November 21, 1983, p. 292.
Glassman, James K., "A Family Affair," *Forbes,* September 29, 1980, p. 84.
Hartnett, Michael, "Hechinger Rolls Out Newest Home Project Store," *Stores,* August 1994, p. 78.
"Hechinger Co. Plans to Add 20 Stores within Two Years," *Wall Street Journal,* September 5, 1984, p. 25.
"Hechinger Company," *Wall Street Transcript,* May 16, 1983, p. 69,808.
"Hechinger Company," *Wall Street Transcript,* July 7, 1980, p. 58,454.
"Hechinger Focuses on Serious D-I-Yer with New Format," *Building Supply Home Centers,* May 1991, p. 46.

"Hechinger Plans Acquisition," *Wall Street Journal,* November 9, 1988, p. C6.

"Hechinger Plans Wide Expansion," *Baltimore Business Journal,* May 14, 1990, p. 6.

"Hechinger to Close Triangle Division," *Hardware Age,* June 1993, p. 30.

"Home Repair Gains Spur Expansion at Hechinger Co.," *New York Times,* April 13, 1981, p. D4.

Ichniowski, Tom, "Hechinger's: Nobody Does It Better in Do-It-Yourself," *Business Week,* May 5, 1986, p. 96.

"John Hechinger Takes the Reins," *Building Supply Home Centers,* March 1993, p. 69.

Kansas, Dave, "Hechinger's Refurbishing Effort Faces Additional Test," *Wall Street Journal,* December 23, 1992, p. B4.

"Kmart, Hechinger End Plan to Form Retailing Venture," *Wall Street Journal,* April 30, 1984, p. 20.

Shakin, Bernard, "Building Supply Chains," *Barron's,* October 27, 1975, p. 11.

Stocker, Susan J., "Hechinger Co. Remodels Itself," *Washington Business Journal,* March 11, 1991, p. 1.

—Jeffrey L. Covell

HITACHI

Hitachi Ltd.

6, Kanda-Surugadai 4-chome
Chiyoda-ku, Tokyo 101
Japan
(03) 3258 1111
Fax: (03) 3423 5480

Public Company
Incorporated: 1920
Employees: 330,637
Sales: ¥7.4 trillion (U.S. $71.85 billion)
Stock Exchanges: Amsterdam Frankfurt Hong Kong
    Luxembourg Nagoya New York Osaka Paris Tokyo
SICs: 3651 Household Audio & Video Equipment; 3613
    Generators, Motors, Power Transformers & Electrical
    Controls; 3621 Motors & Generators; 3563 Air & Gas
    Compressors; 3571 Electronic Computers; 3575 Computer
    Terminals; 3577 Computer Peripheral Equipment, Not
    Elsewhere Classified; 3632 Household Refrigerators &
    Freezers; 3661 Communication Equipment

Hitachi Ltd. is Japan's largest manufacturer of electrical machinery and a leading producer of semiconductors. According to *Business Week*, the company contributed two percent of Japan's gross national product in the early 1990s. The conglomerate's roster of over 20,000 products runs the gamut from the smallest, most powerful computer memory chips to massive nuclear and hydroelectric power plants, but its most familiar lines are consumer electronics. Often called the General Electric of Japan, Hitachi is one of the world's 30 largest conglomerates. Although the company's annual revenues were relatively stable in the early 1990s, its profits declined by over 71 percent from 1991 to 1994, as competition and weakening demand in the semiconductor market and consistent losses in consumer products prompted ongoing restructuring.

Hitachi's historical foundations can be traced back to 1910, when Namihei Odaira took his first engineering job with Kuhara Mining. The recent graduate of the Tokyo Institute of Science soon became frustrated with his company's reliance on technology imported from Europe and the United States. Odaira used his engineering skills to build small five-horsepower electric motors that rivaled the imports in quality and durability. His employer soon became his first, and—for a few years—only customer.

While Odaira's motors worked efficiently for the copper mine he had trouble selling them to other Japanese firms. It was not until the outbreak of World War I that he was able to gain some large customers. A major power company found that, because of the war, it could not obtain the three large turbines it had ordered from Germany and was forced to turn to Hitachi in the absence of a better alternative. Odaira made the most of his opportunity, delivering the 10,000 h.p. generators in five months. Impressed with his work, the power company soon ordered more equipment. Soon other corporations came to Odaira for help in improving their industrial capabilities.

Odaira incorporated his company in 1920 and named it for the town of Hitachi, where he had made his first sale. True to the company name, which means "rising sun," Odaira's success increased rapidly in the interwar era. In the 1920s Hitachi expanded its operations to meet the growing demand of Japan's burgeoning industrial economy. Through the acquisition of other companies, Hitachi became the nation's largest manufacturer of pumps, blowers, and other mechanical equipment. The company also became involved in metal working and began manufacturing copper cable and rolling stock. These developments served to consolidate Hitachi's ability to build and supply a major manufacturer without outside help. In 1924 it also built Japan's first electric locomotive.

The ascendancy of the Japanese military government in the 1930s forced some changes at Hitachi. Although Odaira struggled to maintain corporate independence, his company was nonetheless pressured into manufacturing war material, including radar and sonar equipment for the Imperial Navy. Odaira, however, was successful in preventing Hitachi from manufacturing actual weapons.

The Second World War and its aftermath devastated the company. Many of its factories were destroyed by Allied bombing raids, and after the war, American occupational forces tried to disband Hitachi altogether. Founder Odaira was removed from the company. Nevertheless, as a result of three years of negotiations, Hitachi was permitted to maintain all but 19 of its manufacturing plants. The cost of such a production shutdown proved prohibitive, but was compounded by a three month labor strike in 1950, which severely hindered Hitachi's reconstruction efforts. Only the Korean War saved the company from complete collapse. Hitachi and many other struggling Japanese industrial firms benefitted from defense contracts offered by the American military.

During the 1950s Chikara Kurata, who had succeeded Odaira as president of Hitachi, directed the company into an era of market expansion. Anticipating the future of electronic engineering, he established technology exchanges with General Electric and RCA. He also initiated a number of licensing agreements which allowed Hitachi to compete, through affiliates, in the worldwide market. In the 1960s the firm also began marketing consumer goods, introducing its own brand of household appliances and entertainment equipment.

Perhaps Hitachi's most important decision, however, was investing in computer research. In 1957 Hitachi built its first computer and entered into the high-tech age. During the 1960s Hitachi developed Japan's first on-line computer system, and emerged as the world's largest producer of analog computers, which are used in scientific research to compile complex statistical data.

Despite its technical advances, Hitachi and most other Japanese electronics companies still lagged behind U.S.-based International Business Machines Corporation (IBM). The Japanese Ministry of International Trade and Industry took direct action to narrow the gap and make Japan competitive. It funded a cooperative research and development effort which involved most of Japan's major technical firms. Hitachi benefitted greatly from this program, and ended its overseas policy of non-confrontation. From that point forward, the high-tech competition between America and Japan, and between IBM and Hitachi in particular, was under way. In the 1970s Hitachi developed and launched what were then known as "plug compatible mainframes." These "clones" cost less than but were compatible with IBM's machines, which set the industry standard.

Hitachi has long been recognized for its ability to adapt to changing economic conditions. Its flexibility was especially evident during the 1974 OPEC oil crisis that devastated Japan (which imports nearly 95 percent of its energy) and its industrial sector. Drastic cost-cutting measures were taken to keep the firm financially solvent, and company executives voluntarily took 15 percent pay-cuts. Following 1975, when the company had its first disappointing fiscal year, sales and profits at Hitachi began to increase dramatically.

Hitachi was working hard—many would say too hard—to transform itself into the IBM of Asia in the 1980s. In July of 1982, Hitachi and 11 of its employees were indicted on charges of commercial bribery and theft. Apparently some employees at Hitachi had been stealing confidential design secrets from IBM so as not to lose ground in the intense race for technological superiority. The FBI and the U.S. Justice Department arranged an operation which caught Hitachi employees paying for IBM documents.

Penalties for the offense were, on the surface, quite light. Hitachi was fined US$24,000 and only two employees were given jail sentences. The negative publicity caused by the scandal damaged Hitachi considerably, however. News of the trial appeared just as the company was beginning a full-scale marketing campaign for its products in the United States. Many American companies canceled their orders or refused to receive shipments. A civil suit brought by IBM won the American company at least US$24 million in annual royalty payments over the ensuing eight years and the right to examine Hitachi's new software releases for five of those years.

Hitachi recovered from this unfortunate set of circumstances, but soon faced other problems. Marketing had always been the company's weakest department, seriously hampering its competitiveness abroad. For many years, Hitachi's products were sold under competitors' names, thereby undermining the company's brand recognition. In 1986, profits dropped for the first time in a decade, down 29 percent from 1985 to US$884 million. Part of the decline could be attributed to external market factors: the strong yen made Hitachi's products comparatively more expensive; a global decline in semiconductor sales hamstrung that industry; and competition from low-cost manufacturers in Korea and Taiwan put a squeeze on profit margins. But Hitachi's sliding profits were also attributable to its concentration in mature and slow-growth markets. Its two largest sectors, industrial equipment and consumer products, were not all that promising: the conglomerate's large industrial customers had cut back on orders, and lackluster marketing efforts made Hitachi virtually indiscernible from the plethora of consumer electronics brands. The company was simply not positioned to enter into fast-growing markets.

To deal with these problems, Hitachi president Katsushige Mita sought to change the company's approach to its business. "We cannot live with tradition alone," he said. "I have to make Hitachi a more modern company." To this end, Mita reorganized Hitachi's operations and instituted new business strategies in the mid-1980s. Cost-cutting measures like increased automation helped reduce labor expenses and helped the corporation compete more effectively with its rivals in Southeast Asia. The transfer of production to other countries helped diffuse fluctuations in the exchange rate. The 1989 purchase of a controlling interest in National Advanced Systems (NAS), an American distributor of mainframe computers, helped shore up Hitachi's sales efforts in that important market. The subsidiary, renamed Hitachi Data Systems, hoped to challenge segment leaders IBM and Amdahl Corp. with machines that ran 20 percent faster than their competitors.

Increased investments in research and development helped the company stay in the technological vanguard, especially in semiconductors, consumer electronics, and computers. With the support of the Japanese government, Hitachi and its domestic competitors formed a research and development alliance known as the Very Large Scale Integration (VLSI) Project. The joint effort proved very fruitful, enabling Hitachi to stay one technological step ahead of its overseas competitors, continuously developing semiconductors with ever-higher memory capacity. By the early 1990s, Hitachi's R&D expenditures amounted to six percent of all corporate R&D spending in Japan. It also ranked as that country's top patent holder, and was even a contender for that standing in the United States.

However, technical superiority proved insufficient for the company; it also sought market share dominance. A 1985 memo leaked to the public revealed what American competitors had suspected: Hitachi was "dumping" its semiconductors on overseas markets. Dumping, selling goods in foreign markets at significantly lower prices than those set in domestic markets, is an anti-competitive practice. Once again, the company faced the wrath of the U.S. government.

An apparently contrite Hitachi charted a new, more cooperative course in the late 1980s. In 1988, it formed a trend-setting venture with Texas Instruments to jointly develop a 16-megabyte dynamic random access memory (DRAM) chip. In the early 1990s, Hitachi formed alliances with Hewlett-Packard, TRW, and even long-time rival IBM.

Still, Hitachi was unable to parlay its technological leadership into earnings growth: while the conglomerate's sales were essentially flat at around ¥7 trillion from 1991 to 1994, its profits dropped over 71 percent, from ¥230 billion to ¥65 billion. In 1990, President Mita announced a reorganization that focused, in part, on transforming the conservative corporate culture that some observers blamed for Hitachi's declining earnings. The leader shifted the company's primary emphasis from heavy industrial equipment to information systems. Organizational changes focused on the dismantling of a "plant profit center" scheme. Sometimes known as just "pc," this system integrated production, quality, and cost control as well as product design and planning within each factory. The new plan reorganized some divisions into autonomous operations and hoped thereby to emphasize consumer demands over production requirements. Pay freezes and cuts of up to 15 percent for white-collar workers were also instituted.

Although these efforts had yet to bear fruit, Mita (who had advanced to chairman) expressed his confidence that Hitachi would be well-prepared to capitalize on Japan's economic recovery and reverse its downward profits spiral in the middle and late 1990s.

Principal Subsidiaries: Babcock-Hitachi K.K.; Chuo Shoji, Ltd.; Hitachi Air Conditioning & Refrigeration Co., Ltd.; Hitachi America Ltd.; Hitachi Asia Pte. Ltd.; Hitachi Australia Ltd.; Hitachi Auto Systems Co., Ltd.; Hitachi Automotive Products (U.S.), Inc.; Hitachi Building Systems Engineering and Service Co., Ltd.; Hitachi Building Systems Sales (East) Co., Ltd.; Hitachi Cable, Ltd.; Hitachi Chemical Co., Ltd.; Hitachi Computer Products (Europe) S.A.; Hitachi Construction Machinery Co., Ltd.; Hitachi Consumer Products (America), Inc.; Hitachi Consumer Products (U.K.) Ltd.; Hitachi Consumer Products (S) Pte. Ltd.; Hitachi Credit Corporation; Hitachi Data Systems Holding Corp.; Hitachi Denshi, Ltd.; Hitachi Electronic Components Sales Co., Ltd.; Hitachi Electronic Devices (USA), Inc.; Hitachi Electronic Devices (Singapore) Pte. Ltd.; Hitachi Electronic Products (Malaysia) Sdn. Bhd.; Hitachi Electronics Engineering Co., Ltd.; Hitachi Electronics Service Co., Ltd.; Hitachi Engineering & Services Co., Ltd.; Hitachi Engineering Co., Ltd.; Hitachi Europe Ltd.; Hitachi Hokkai Semiconductor, Ltd.; Hitachi Home Electronics (America), Inc.; Hitachi Hometec, Ltd.; Hitachi Information Systems, Ltd.; Hitachi Keisho, Ltd.; Hitachi Kiden Kogyo, Ltd.; Hitachi Life Corporation; Hitachi Micro Devices, Ltd.; Hitachi Lighting, Ltd.; Hitachi Maxell, Ltd.; Hitachi Medical Corporation; Hitachi Metals, Ltd.; Hitachi Mizusawa Electronics Co., Ltd.; Hitachi Plant Engineering & Construction Co., Ltd.; Hitachi Printing Co., Ltd.; Hitachi Sales Corporation; Hitachi Seiko, Ltd.; Hitachi Semiconductor (America), Inc.; Hitachi Semiconductor (Europe) GmbH; Hitachi Semiconductor (Malaysia) Sdn Bhd.; Hitachi Service & Engineering (East) Ltd.; Hitachi Service & Engineering (West) Ltd.; Hitachi Setsubi Engineering Co., Ltd.; Hitachi Software Engineering Co., Ltd.; Hitachi Techno Engineering Co., Ltd.; Hitachi Telecom Technologies, Ltd.; Hitachi Tohbu Semiconductor, Ltd.; Hitachi Tokyo Electronics Co., Ltd.; Hitachi Transport System, Ltd.; Japan Servo Co., Ltd.; Nissei Sangyo Co., Ltd.; Taiwan Hitachi Co., Ltd. The company also lists operations in: Argentina, Austria, Belgium, Bermuda, Brazil, Canada, Chile, China, Costa Rica, Curaçao, Denmark, Finland, France, Germany, Greece, Hong Kong, Indonesia, Ireland, Italy, Luxembourg, Mexico, Morocco, Netherlands, Norway, Panama, Philippines, Singapore, Spain, Switzerland, Thailand, and Venezuela.

Further Reading:

Anchordoguy, Marie, *Computers, Inc.: Japan's Challenge to IBM,* Cambridge, Mass.: Harvard University Press, 1989.
Beauchamp, Marc, " 'We Have to Change,' " *Forbes,* September 22, 1986, pp. 84–92.
Gross, Neil, "Inside Hitachi," *Business Week,* September 28, 1992, pp. 92–98, 100.
Hara, Eijiro, "Hitachi: The Shackles of Past Glory, and Faith in Technology," *Tokyo Business Today,* March 1991, pp. 34–37.
Hof, Robert D., " 'The Japanese Threat in Mainframes Has Finally Arrived,' " *Business Week,* April 9, 1990, p. 24.
Imori, Takeo, "Hitachi: Too Little Too Late?" *Tokyo Business Today,* December 1992, pp. 12–13.
Mattera, Philip, *World Class Business: A Guide to the 100 Most Powerful Global Corporations,* New York: Henry Holt and Company, 1992.
Port, Otis, "What's Behind the Texas Instruments-Hitachi Deal," *Business Week,* January 16, 1989, pp. 93, 96.
Tsurumi, Yoshi, *Multinational Management: Business Strategy and Government Policy,* Cambridge, Mass.: Ballinger, 1977.
Sobel, Robert, *IBM vs. Japan: The Struggle for the Future,* Briarcliff Manor, N.Y.: Stein & Day, 1985.

—updated by April Dougal Gasbarre

CORPORATION

Holly Corporation

100 Crescent Court, #1600
Dallas, Texas 75201-6927
U.S.A.
(214) 871-3555
Fax: (214) 871-3560

Public Company
Incorporated: 1947
Employees: 531
Sales: $552 million
Stock Exchanges: American
SICs: 2911 Petroleum Refining

Holly Corporation is an independent oil refiner based in Dallas, Texas. Its chief product is gasoline. Through its two major subsidiaries, Navajo Refining Company and Montana Refining Company, it serves niche markets throughout the Southwest. Holly also produces jet fuel and operates an asphalt subsidiary. The company generated revenues of $552 million in 1994 and employed 530 workers. As Holly entered the mid 1990s, it had a refining capacity of approximately 70,000 barrels per day (bpd).

The United States had just embarked on its massive postwar economic expansion and demand for oil and energy products was booming when Holly was founded in 1947. Created to serve companies that were bringing the oil out of the ground, Holly took the raw crude and processed it into commercially useful material, particularly gasoline. As demand for gasoline and other refined products increased during the 1950s, Holly met with success.

During the 1960s, the oil industry suffered from flat prices, increased competition at home and abroad, and mismanaged federal energy policies. Between the early 1960s and the early 1970s, the number of companies in the U.S. oil and gas exploration business plummeted from about 30,000 to less than 13,000. Despite the turmoil, Holly kept its refineries profitable by following a relatively conservative course. While some other companies expanded rapidly, often incurring massive debt, Holly grew more slowly and focused its efforts on a few key, niche markets.

Holly's success during the 1960s and 1970s was largely attributable to its Navajo Refining Company. Located in Artesia, New Mexico, Navajo Refining was fed in part by West Texas's rich Permian basin. Because of its strategic location, the state-of-the art Navajo oil refinery enjoyed access to local crude supplies owned by other companies that were typically within 100 miles of the refinery. Holly developed a pipeline system to bring raw product in from southeast New Mexico and to ship refined product to east Texas. From Texas, the products could be piped to Holly's core Arizona markets, Phoenix and Tucson.

The oil industry began to emerge from its doldrums in the early 1970s. The Organization of Petroleum Exporting Countries (OPEC) in the Middle East began limiting its oil production to boost profits. As oil prices rose past a record $30 per barrel, domestic production and industry profit margins increased. Encouraged by booming sales, many of Holly's competitors launched aggressive growth programs. Leading competitors, including Tosco Corp. and Charter Oil Co., assumed large debt loads in an effort to expand capacity. Many developed large processing facilities that could quickly process large amounts of relatively inexpensive, low-quality heavy crude.

Holly resisted the temptation during the mid and late 1970s to take advantage of what it viewed as potentially short-term industry gains. Despite its access to outside capital, its directors elected to fund growth and improvements internally. Strong profit growth during the 1970s allowed it to make millions of dollars worth of internal improvements. Rather than developing its capacity to process low-grade crudes and oils, Holly focused on developing facilities that could deliver higher-grade, premium-priced light oils and less heavy crudes. In 1981, Holly installed a $25 million fluid catalytic "cracking" unit designed to boost output of higher-grade material.

In addition to improving its Navajo refinery, Holly steered its excess cash into other projects and assets during the late 1970s and early 1980s. It invested in reserves of oil and natural gas, land on which wells could be drilled in the future, and exploration and production operations. It also developed storage facilities for its products at pipeline termination points in Texas, Arizona, and New Mexico. Furthermore, Holly started manufacturing and supplying asphalt, mostly to contractors and government agencies for the purpose of constructing highways. Although it became slightly diversified in an effort to reduce its vulnerability to cyclical oil markets, Holly remained focused on its core refining business.

The oil industry slumped again in the early 1980s. Oil prices fell and domestic producers suffered. The wisdom of Holly's strategy during the 1970s boom years was made apparent during the 1980s. As many other oil refiners staggered under massive debt loads, Holly boasted a balance sheet with a long-term debt that was less than two percent of annual revenues. In addition, Holly had access to nearly $40 million in untapped revolving credit. Furthermore, Holly was well positioned to take advantage of increased demand for higher-value products. As its competitors scrambled to convert their refineries in the face of mounting debt, Holly was able to increase its market share and overcome many of the negative effects of falling prices.

Holly also managed to overcome another obstacle to success during the early 1980s. Historically, Holly had relied on the Tucson and Phoenix markets to supply about 30 percent of its total revenue. However, increased competition during the downturn of the early 1980s forced Holly to reduce its emphasis on those markets. Instead, it chose to turn its attention to less competitive niche markets in which it had a geographic advantage, including El Paso, Texas, and Albuquerque, New Mexico. Holly was also able to tap into the pipelines of major crude carriers, thus expanding its access to selected oil-producing regions that had little refining capacity and represented fast-growing markets.

Because of its savvy maneuvering, in 1982 Holly achieved record net income of $10.5 million from sales of $452 million. Its revenues dropped to about $445 million as net income plummeted to about $6.5 million in the wake of falling oil and fuel prices in 1983. Nevertheless, Holly's performance going into the mid 1980s was considered exemplary in comparison to most of its industry peers. Its refinery operated at 92 percent capacity in 1983, which compared to a 70 percent industry average, and had never posted an annual loss. Furthermore, by late 1984 Holly had virtually cleared itself of all long-term debt and was extremely well-positioned to take advantage of expected price recoveries in the mid and late 1980s.

By the mid 1980s, Holly had established itself as a major independent oil refining business in the Southwest. Its major products, which accounted for about 85 percent of production, included various grades of gasoline, diesel fuel, and jet fuel. Most of its diesel fuel was marketed to wholesalers, independent dealers, and railroads. Its jet fuel was sold to both military and commercial customers. In addition, it continued to increase asphalt sales as well as profits from the sale of carbon black oil and liquid petroleum gas (LPG) to petrochemical plants that processed the by-products. Nevertheless, its oil refinery operations still comprised more than 95 percent of Holly's revenues.

Although it was also still active in exploration and production through a subsidiary company in the early 1980s, Holly planned to jettison those operations so that it could focus on its more profitable refinery segments. Holly sold its exploration and production company in 1984 for $55.5 million in cash. The subsidiary included 1.4 million barrels of crude oil and 15.9 million cubic feet of natural gas reserves, as well as about 50,000 acres of land for potential drilling.

The sale, combined with improved operating results from its refinery business in fiscal 1985, resulted in a large influx of cash. Typical of the company's penchant for fiscal conservatism, Holly's directors chose to return the cash to its shareholders. "These people are to be commended," said securities analyst William Ainsworth in *Dallas-Fort Worth Business Journal.* "They don't want to buy some marginal refinery or something, so they're returning the cash they've accumulated to the shareholders. I think its refreshing."

Holly's very deliberate and profitable course during the 1970s and 1980s was the result of an acute management team. By the mid 1980s, the company was still primarily owned by the Norsworthy and Simmons families, who had purchased the operation in 1960. In fact, Lamar Norsworthy, who had become an executive officer in the company in 1971 at the age of 24, had played an influential role during the 1970s and 1980s and would remain president, CEO, and chairman of the board through the mid-1990s. Other executives that would help Norsworthy at the helm during the 1970s through the mid-1990s included Jack P. Reid, head of refining, and William J. Gray, who oversaw marketing and supply operations.

Although Holly was financially and managerially poised to take advantage of an oil price upturn in the late 1980s, it never had the opportunity. In fact, the oil market became glutted in 1986 and oil prices dropped. Prices remained suppressed throughout the end of the decade. Many of Holly's competitors suffered during the late 1980s as they scrambled to increase cash flow to meet burdensome debt obligations. In contrast, Holly managed to sustain its dominance of it niche markets despite increased competition. Although revenue growth stagnated, the company managed to post consecutive annual profits every year between 1985 and 1994.

At the same time that it jettisoned its non-refinery operations in 1984, Holly became active in another refinery operation, the Montana Refining Company (MRC). Initially a partner in the MRC, Holly eventually purchased the entire operation. MRC consisted of an oil refinery in Black Eagle, Montana, that had a related crude oil pipeline adjoining Great Falls. The operation represented approximately ten percent of Holly's total refining capacity by the early 1990s. The refinery complemented Holly's strategy of serving growing regions with little competition. Like Navajo, MRC supplied regional customers with gasoline, jet fuel, diesel, and asphalt.

Oil prices remained low through 1991 but began to recover in 1992 and 1993. Holly's 1990 sales were about $440 million, roughly equal to early 1980s levels. However, the company posted a net income of $24 million in 1990. Economic recovery bolstered demand during the early 1990s, causing Holly's total refinery output to increase from about 45,000 bpd in 1990 to nearly 65,000 bpd in 1993. Sales climbed as well, reaching about $630 million in 1993. Holly's 1993 gains, however, were largely the result of the temporary suspension of production by one of Holly's key competitors. But Holly also benefitted from the completion of a major $50 million expansion of its Navajo refinery from about 40,000 bpd to 60,000 bpd, which was completed in 1992.

By the early 1990s, Holly was operating two refineries and related pipelines, and eight storage terminals. It had expanded its core markets to include customers in Arizona, New Mexico, west Texas, northern Mexico, and Montana. In addition, it continued to run its asphalt operations and was also operating a jet fuel terminal in Mountain Home, Idaho, which supplied jet fuel to a nearby Air Force base. Gasolines accounted for about 55 percent of its total revenues in 1994 (up from 48 percent in 1990) and diesel fuels made up about 20 percent. Jet fuel represented approximately 15 percent of sales and the remainder of revenues were garnered from shipments of asphalt, LPG, and carbon black oil.

Despite industry improvements and additional production capacity in 1992, Holly suffered its worst year in a decade from a profit standpoint. Net income dropped to $2.8 million. Some investors voiced concern over the company's performance. However, management viewed the financial results as a necessary evil in accomplishing its long-term goals. The company still had little outstanding debt. It had completed its major capital improvements and had budgeted for major maintenance overhauls for both of its refineries in 1993 and 1994. Moreover, profitability recovered as net income surged into the $20 million range in both fiscal 1993 and 1994.

One of the company's chief long-term concerns going into the mid-1990s was increasing environmental regulation. Holly and its competitors had been forced to spend large sums of money trying to bring their facilities in line with stringent federal and state regulations governing output of wastes during the refining process. In addition, Holly, like many of its peers, had been served with charges of noncompliance by the Environmental Protection Agency that could potentially cost Holly millions of dollars. Holly quickly tried to conform with initiatives such as the Resource Conservation and Recovery Act and amendments to the Clean Air Act.

Although mounting environmental regulation was expected to have a detrimental effect on the industry as a whole, analysts expected Holly to benefit in the long-term in comparison to its peers. Indeed, the Clean Air Act was expected to result in the closure or slowdown of many West Coast refineries, which would likely reduce competition and open new markets to more remote companies like Holly. "The bottom line is the market is tough now," said securities analyst John Turo in the *Dallas Business Journal.* "But they have top quality management and the market will eventually turn." Industry gains, reflected in Holly's 1993 and 1994 balance sheets, corroborated Turo's appraisal.

Principal Subsidiaries: Montana Refining Company; Navajo Refining Company.

Further Reading:

Fraser, Bruce W., "Waiting for the Price War to End," *Financial World,* June 13, 1984, p. 32.
Golightly, Glen, "Oil Refiner Is Waiting Out Industry's Storm," *Dallas Business Journal,* March 27, 1992, sec. 1, p. 23.
Hughes, Ted, "Refining Firm to Share Big Cash Surplus," *Dallas-Fort Worth Business Journal,* September 23, 1985, p. 1A.
Teichholz, Henry A., "Holy Corp. Reports Fourth Quarter and Year End Results," *Business Wire,* September 25, 1992.

—Dave Mote

Homestake Mining Company

650 California Street
San Francisco, California 94108
U.S.A.
(415) 981-8150
Fax: (415) 397-5038

Public Company
Incorporated: 1877
Employees: 1,956
Sales: $705.5 million
Stock Exchanges: New York Basel Geneva Zurich Frankfurt
SICs: 1041 Gold Ores

Owner and operator of the oldest gold mine in the United States, Homestake Mining Company is an international gold mining company with substantial gold interests in Canada and Australia, as well as smaller interests in Chile. From the company's Homestake mine, which began producing gold in 1876, Homestake Mining built a mining empire that vaulted it past all competitors and ranked it as the premier gold producer in U.S. history.

In 1874, a U.S. Cavalry scouting party led by Lt. Col. George A. Custer inched its way through the deep valleys and steep ridges carved into the Black Hills of Dakota Territory, 15 years before the region became part of the country's fortieth state, South Dakota. The expedition begun that year set in motion a cavalcade of events that in a few years would lead to Custer's Last Stand at Little Bighorn, the massacre of Sioux at Wounded Knee, the financial ascension of the powerful and wealthy Hearst family, and the founding of Homestake Mining Company, the country's preeminent gold producer. These were the effects of one definitive moment when Custer's troops spotted traces of gold in the mountainous and sparsely populated Black Hills, an ill-fated moment for Custer and the Sioux and a propitious one for the Hearst family and all those enriched by Homestake Mining's formation.

For a populace already tantalized by the riches gold could bring, no formal declaration was required, and word of the new discovery quickly spread throughout the western territories. Within months, settlers were pouring into the area, scouring the countryside for further confirmation of gold's existence in the region. With their arrival, small yet burgeoning communities were established, such as Deadwood, the hotbed of entertain-

ment for miners and prospectors in the region, where Wild Bill Hickok and Calamity Jane met their end. As more settlers moved into the region, tensions between the Sioux and the region's new denizens mounted, touching off a war that led to Custer's death two years after his scouting party had discovered gold. Hostilities between the Sioux and U.S. forces did not end until the battle at Wounded Knee in 1890, by which time a more affirmative manifestation of the scouting party's discovery had already developed into a flourishing enterprise.

One fortune-seeker drawn by the news of gold in the Black Hills was a prospector named Moses Manuel, who in 1876 staked a claim that would become known as Homestake. Manuel's ownership of Homestake was fleeting, however, ending the following year when the mine was sold to a consortium of San Francisco investors led by George Hearst, father of publishing magnate William Randolph Hearst. Hearst and his backers paid Manuel $70,000 for the Homestake mine, and in return they received the largest gold mine in the United States: literally the mother lode of the Western Hemisphere. With the profits gleaned from his father's mine in southwest South Dakota, William Randolph Hearst would begin his meteoric rise, purchasing the *San Francisco Examiner* in 1887 and going on to build the world's largest publishing empire.

These were the effects of the frenzy for gold in South Dakota; lives were lost and fortunes were made, making for a quintessential chapter of life in the American frontier. Homestake Mining Company was incorporated in 1877. At the time, George Hearst and his syndicate likely had little idea of the magnitude of their purchase. The Homestake mine would eventually supply the United States with the bulk of its gold for over 100 years and would surpass competitors in becoming a prodigious force in the global gold industry.

The mining company enjoyed the lucrative years of gold mining's heyday during the first half of the twentieth century. The company prospered during this period, sending its miners deeper and deeper into the Homestake mine, where they located sizeable deposits of gold enveloped in tons of ore. In 1935, the company recovered enough gold to register $11.39 million in net income, a record that would stand for nearly 40 years. One year before Homestake mine established its net income benchmark, the price of gold, set by the U.S. Treasury Department at a fixed amount per ounce, was raised from $20.67 an ounce to $35 an ounce, welcome news for gold producers like Homestake Mining. However, the price of gold would remain at that price for roughly the next 40 years, fixed and unchanged as gold production costs rose.

As the years passed and production costs increased, the gap separating the cost to produce gold and the fixed price established by the government narrowed, coming inexorably together and threatening to make the country's largest gold mine a profitless hole in the ground. Homestake Mining's inability to increase or at least maintain its profit margin was a growing concern as the company entered the 1940s and America entered World War II.

America's entrance into World War II brought gold production to a halt, as miners and other workers were transferred to industries vital to the country's prosecution of the war. The

Homestake mine remained closed for three years, reopening again in 1945, which, as it turned out, benefited the company, as much of its competition dissolved during this time. For gold mining companies with smaller producing mines than Homestake Mining, the years before the war had been difficult enough. When the government called a halt to gold production, many decided against reopening after the respite, leaving Homestake Mining in a more favorable market position than before the war. Competition, however, was not the company's most worrisome problem; the upward march of gold production costs continued to hamper profits. To reduce production costs, the company installed automated hoisting equipment, introduced television monitoring and short-wave communication equipment, and sought to double each miner's productivity, but these were temporary solutions to a perpetual problem. By 1951, one ounce of gold cost Homestake Mining $22.18 to produce, a total that was creeping dangerously close to the fixed $35 per ounce price paid by the federal government.

In response, Homestake began a diversification program in 1953, purchasing over the next four years uranium properties in Utah, Wyoming, and New Mexico. By the mid-1960s, the mining of uranium was contributing more than half of the company's $4.9 million in net income, quickly supplanting gold as the company's greatest money earner. The Homestake mine, however, still represented the largest gold-producing property in the Western Hemisphere, making Homestake Mining the largest producer of gold by far in the United States. Although the Homestake mine had been expanded, reaching depths of 6,800 feet by the mid-1960s, its profitability had plunged as well, falling in the face of rising production costs and an industry-wide downturn. In the quarter century leading up to the mid-1960s, the number of gold mines in operation in the United States had plummeted precipitously from 9,000 to 600, while the cost of producing an ounce of gold had steadily risen from less than $20 to nearly $33. Operating income from the Homestake mine fell from $12.1 million in 1941 to $2 million in 1963, while dividends fell during the period from $4.50 a share to $1.60 a share.

To exacerbate matters, the amount of gold produced in 1963 represented the lowest peacetime level since 1884, further convincing Homestake Mining's management that the only viable solution lay in diversification away from gold production. In 1962, Homestake Mining entered into a joint venture with AMAX Gold to develop lead and zinc properties in southeast Missouri, then two years later entered into another joint venture to develop potash in Saskatchewan, Canada, which began production in 1968. The concerted movement toward diversification during the 1960s also brought Homestake Mining into Australia to produce and ship iron ore from Koolanooka, in western Australia, through its Homestake Iron Ore Company of Australia Ltd. subsidiary in 1966 and led to the formation of another subsidiary, Compania Madrigal, created to develop copper, lead, and zinc deposits in Peru in 1967. Also during this time, production began at Homestake's Buick lead and zinc mine in Missouri and silver production began at its Bulldog mine in Creede, Colorado, bolstering Homestake Mining's market presence in non-gold mining businesses.

After 20 years of diversification into uranium, lead, zinc, and copper, Homestake Mining had become a much different com-

pany, a transformation readily borne out it in its bottom line. By the early 1970s, uranium, lead, zinc, and silver production accounted for 75 percent of the company's profits, while the production of gold, formerly Homestake Mining's mainstay business, was increasingly becoming a break-even enterprise. The gold industry, however, was about to experience significant changes that would change the focus of Homestake Mining's business, redirecting it once again back to gold. During the 1970s, the price of gold was freed from its fixed price of $35 an ounce, at last removing the formidable barrier that forced Homestake Mining to diversify its business. In response, gold production was reinvigorated throughout the country and gold producers, such as Newmont Mining Corporation and Kennecott Corporation, began developing large gold properties, forcing Homestake Mining to either wait for the competition to catch up or supplement its existing gold properties.

The company's management chose the latter, deciding, as Homestake Mining's president and chief executive officer declared in a speech before the New York Society of Security Analysts, "to reestablish and confirm [the company's] reputation as the United States' preeminent gold miner." Beginning in 1978, Homestake Mining launched an aggressive exploration program to find new gold deposits, which resulted in the discovery of the McLaughlin gold mine in California in 1980, a symbolic discovery made in the first year of a decade that would see Homestake Mining move back into gold and away from uranium, lead, zinc, and silver.

The McLaughlin mine took five years and $280 million to develop, but, when it finally did begin producing gold in 1985, it added significantly to Homestake Mining's annual total of gold production, which tripled during the decade. The company's gold reserves tripled as well during the 1980s. Nevertheless, uranium, lead, zinc, and a relatively new business area for the company—oil and natural gas—continued to contribute significantly to the company's annual revenue total. During the mid-1980s, these non-gold businesses generated nearly half of the company's revenues, but by the end of the decade all would be divested, as Homestake Mining returned to its roots and became almost exclusively a gold producer and developer.

Homestake Mining had entered the oil business in 1980 through a joint venture with Hrubitz Oil Company. It then sought to strengthen and accelerate its position in the energy business with the 1984 acquisition of Felmont Oil Corporation. However, the company sold its interests in oil and natural gas in 1989, as it quickly began exiting its non-gold related businesses. Uranium mining was terminated in 1990, the same year Homestake Mining's lead and zinc properties, organized as part of The Doe Run Company in 1986, were sold to Fluor Corporation, creating a much more focused corporate organization.

In 1991, Homestake Mining recorded its first full-year loss in nearly 50 years, losing $262 million largely because of mining property write-downs, operational problems, and low gold prices. The following year, however, the company made the largest acquisition in its history when it purchased International Corona Corporation. With the acquisition of International Corona, Homestake Mining gained low-cost gold production properties, five million ounces of reserves, and gold development property in British Columbia. The write-down charges stemming from the acquisition totaled $176 million, $106 million of which was recorded in 1991, which accounted for a significant portion of the company's loss for the year.

Once acquired, International Corona was renamed Homestake Canada Inc., and then Homestake Mining initiated a corporate-wide restructuring program to ease the absorption of the unit into Homestake Mining's organization. Nearly 200 jobs were eliminated, administrative and exploration offices were closed, and upper management positions were changed during the restructuring process, as the company prepared for the mid-1990s and beyond.

With its enormous wealth of gold production properties, Homestake Mining entered the mid-1990s still holding tight to its venerable position as America's leading gold producer. Although the company's gold production costs were high compared to the rest of the industry, the addition of International Corona's low-cost gold production properties raised hopes that Homestake Mining would continue to outdistance its competition as it headed toward its third century of business, still producing gold from its coveted Homestake mine.

Principal Subsidiaries: Homestake Mining Company of California; Homestake Canada Inc.; Homestake Gold of Australia Limited; Homestake Nevada Corporation; Minera Homestake Chile, S.A.; Homestake Sulphur Company; Prime Resources Group, Inc.

Further Reading:

"Another Coin?," *Forbes,* March 1, 1965, p. 42.
Blackburn, Mark, "For Homestake, It's Okay to Be Dull," *New York Times,* January 27, 1980, p. F1.
"The Boom That Isn't," *Forbes,* June 15, 1972, p. 48.
Cook, James, "Nowhere to Go But Up," *Forbes,* November 12, 1990, p. 39.
"Gold Digs," *Newsweek,* May 25, 1964, p. 85.
"Gold from Lead," *Time,* March 11, 1966, p. 88.
"Gold Without Glitter," *Forbes,* December 1, 1962, p. 30.
"Homestake Mining Co.," *Wall Street Transcript,* August 5, 1985, p. 78,807.
"Homestake Mining Company," *Wall Street Transcript,* October 19, 1981, pp. 63,364.
"Homestake Mining Company," *Wall Street Transcript,* October 15, 1973, p. 34,675.
"Homestake Mining Corp.," *Wall Street Journal,* May 9, 1984, p. 44.
"Homestake Seeks Two Kinds of Gold," *Business Week,* April 23, 1984, p. 38.
"Homestake Winds Up with Red Ink in 1991," *American Metal Market,* February 24, 1992, p. 15.
Levine, Jonathan, "What's Pickens Really Panning for in Homestake?," *Business Week,* March 14, 1988, p. 42.
Loehwing, David A., "New Gold Rush," *Barron's,* June 18, 1973, p. 3.
"Luck vs. Judgment," *Forbes,* July 1, 1967, p. 49.
Palmer, Jay, "Golden Handcuff," *Barron's,* June 17, 1991, p. 16.
Sherman, Joseph V., "New Sourdoughs," *Barron's,* June 21, 1965, p. 3.
Viani, Laura, "Restructuring of Homestake to Save $25M," *American Metal Market,* August 24, 1992, p. 8.

—Jeffrey L. Covell

Honeywell

Honeywell Inc.

Honeywell Plaza
Minneapolis, Minnesota 55408
U.S.A.
(612) 951-1000
Fax: (612) 951-8494

Public Company
Incorporated: 1927 as Minneapolis-Honeywell Regulator Co.
Employees: 78,383
Sales: $7.15 billion
Stock Exchanges: New York London Paris Amsterdam
    Brussels Geneva Zurich Basel
SICs: 3822 Environmental Controls; 3669 Communications
    Equipment, Not Elsewhere Classified; 3812 Search &
    Navigation Equipment; 3823 Process Control Instruments

In 1883, when delivery men still toted coal into American basements, Albert Butz created a device to lift a furnace's damper when a home became too cold, letting fresh air fan the flames and warm the house. The "damper flapper," as the device was called, started a business that would become the backbone of Honeywell Inc., a multinational corporation that more than a 100 years later is not only a leading supplier of home, office, and industrial control systems, but also a major defense contractor and an integral part of America's space exploration program.

Despite its high-tech nature, Honeywell is most familiar to the public for its low-tech thermostats, especially the "Honeywell Round," Model T86, known in the 1950s for its snap-off plastic cover that could be painted to match the interior of a home. Thermostats are still a major part of Honeywell's business; today home and commercial accounts together make up a quarter of Honeywell sales. In the commercial arena, Honeywell designs computerized control systems that regulate heat and electricity flow for large buildings, and also manufactures its own switches, electronic parts, and motors for these systems. The company has also ventured into "smart" buildings that regulate themselves with packages that can link together a building's phone lines, control devices, and information systems.

While sales were on an upward trend in the mid-1990s, Honeywell's growth over the century has been far from smooth. The company fell upon hard times more than once in the years following its inception in 1885 and during the Depression of the 1930s. The longest and most difficult stretch in the company's history was its rocky marriage with the computer industry, one that ended in 1986 when it sold most of its computer assets to two foreign partners, Group Bull of France and Japan's NEC Corporation.

By the latter decades of the twentieth century, Honeywell was a powerful force in the public and private sectors. In the mid-1980s, the company had more than 35 divisions, 80 subsidiaries, and offices in all 50 states and around the world. In 1986 the company purchased the Sperry Aerospace Group, now incorporated into Honeywell's aerospace division. Honeywell consistently won military contracts in the millions of dollars, making torpedoes, guidance systems, and ammunition for the nation's defense; meanwhile, sales of its home, building, and industrial controls divisions reached $3 billion in 1987.

Honeywell traces its beginnings to 1885, the year that Al Butz invented the damper flapper. In 1886, the device was patented and the Butz Thermo-Electric Regulator Company formed to manufacture it. Butz, from Minneapolis, Minnesota, was more an idea man than a man of business, and the company does not seem to have prospered. In 1888, Butz sold the patent for the damper flapper to his patent attorneys, who founded the Consolidated Temperature Controlling Company the same year.

During its first years, the company went through financial difficulties and several name changes. It became the Electric Thermostat Company in 1892, the Electric Heat Regulator Company in 1893. In 1898, William Sweatt, a businessman who had joined the company in 1891, took over the company. He took charge of marketing the damper flapper, increasing advertising and even going door-to-door with his salesmen. This firsthand contact with customers prompted Sweatt to sell the wheelbarrow company he owned at the time and cast his entire future into the Electric Heat Regulator Company.

The damper flappers Sweatt sold remained basically the same until 1907, when a clock was added. Now the thermostat could automatically let a house cool at night and warm it in the morning. The clock also gave the thermostat a new look that would survive well into the 1930s. When consumers responding to his ads began to request the "Minneapolis" regulator, Sweatt changed the name of his product. He began calling the thermostat "The Minneapolis Regulator" in 1905; in 1909, "The Minneapolis" was put on the face of the thermostats and on the motors, and in 1912 Sweatt officially changed the name of the company to the Minneapolis Heat Regulator Company.

One year later, in 1913, Sweatt's son, Harold R. Sweatt, who had been elected to the board in 1909 at the age of 18, was elected vice-president. At the time, the company had fifty people and a motorcycle whose engine powered several machines. Sales hit $200,000 in 1914, the year that Sweatt's second son, Charles, joined the company. Sweatt stressed to his sons the importance of manufacturing thermostats, saying that it made no sense competing with their best customers by making furnaces.

As coal furnaces began to be replaced by sometimes dangerous oil burners, Minneapolis Heat Regulator made a circuit that stopped and started the burners. Early attempts failed to eliminate "puffs," as these explosions were called, but modifications on the circuit soon made it possible for the regulator to shut down the burner in case of a malfunction, and the Series 10 was born.

As the home heating market continued to expand, many companies began to manufacture products to compete with the Minneapolis Regulator. In the face of this competition, the company merged with the Wabash, Indiana-based Honeywell Heating Specialties Company in 1927. The two companies had been making complementary and competing products, including oil burner controls, clock thermostats, and regulators, and had even been involved in a legal suit over patents at the time of the merger.

The combination surprised the industry, and even the corporate heads themselves. But the merger made a lot of sense. Minneapolis Heat Regulator doubled its business and became a publicly held company, under yet another name: the Minneapolis-Honeywell Regulator Company. William Sweatt became chairman of the board in the new Minneapolis headquarters; Mark Honeywell, president; Harold Sweatt, vice-president and general manager; and Charles Sweatt, vice-president. The merger gave the business the resources to expand even after the 1929 stock market crash, and marked the start of a decade of acquisition and growth.

In 1931, Minneapolis-Honeywell bought Time-O-Stat Controls Corporation through an exchange of stock. Time-O-Stat was the result of a 1929 merger between four Wisconsin heating controls companies. The purchase brought the company several mercury switch patents and other controls technology. Minneapolis-Honeywell's next big acquisition marked a move to industrial accounts. In a chance train meeting, Willard Huff, Minneapolis-Honeywell treasurer, and Richard Brown, president of Brown Instrument Company, began discussing the similarities of their businesses. Brown's products measured the high temperatures inside industrial machines, while Minneapolis-Honeywell was a low temperature controls company. Within weeks, the firms were negotiating, and by the end of 1934, Minneapolis-Honeywell had purchased Brown's assets for $2.3 million.

Finally, in 1937, dissatisfied with the high costs of its own pneumatic control devices for larger buildings like schools and offices, Minneapolis-Honeywell bought the only two competing companies in the field: National Regulator Company and Bishop & Babcock Manufacturing Company. In the ten years since the 1927 merger with Honeywell, Minneapolis-Honeywell had tripled its employee ranks and its sales. Despite the Depression, the company had $16 million in sales and 3,000 employees.

Harold Sweatt had become president in 1934, following Mark Honeywell, who had succeeded William Sweatt. At the start of World War II, Sweatt headed a company with the experience and resources needed to develop precision instruments and controls for the military. In 1941, the army called upon a group of Minneapolis-Honeywell engineers who had worked on heat regulating systems to develop an automatic bomber pilot that gave precise readings of high-altitude coordinates. The company also produced a turbo regulator and an intricate fire control system. By war's end, Minneapolis-Honeywell was well on its way to becoming a major defense contractor.

After the war, Harold Sweatt held fast to his father's rule and kept moving in the direction of controls. He purchased two planes and turned them into flying laboratories for his aviation and research staffs. He also began buying companies related to the manufacture of control instruments. One such purchase came in 1950, when Sweatt bought the Micro Switch Division of the First Industrial Corporation of Freeport, Illinois. Micro switches are used in vending machines, industrial equipment, and even tanks and guided missile systems. Generally they need a small amount of physical force to activate the electronics. Two years after the purchase, Minneapolis-Honeywell was making 5,000 variations of micro switches.

About this time, Raytheon, a Massachusetts electronics firm, approached Minneapolis-Honeywell about teaming up to enter the computer business. After studying the issue for months, Minneapolis-Honeywell accepted Raytheon's offer in April of 1955. The companies formed Datamatic Corporation, a subsidiary owned jointly by the two companies. In 1957, the company installed its first line of mainframe computers. The Datamatic 1000 filled several rooms and weighed some 25 tons, and the first unit sold for $2 million. But Datamatic lacked the customer base that gave competitors like IBM an early edge. Raytheon wanted out, and that year the operation became Minneapolis-Honeywell's Datamatic division.

The company's aerospace divisions were also developing quickly. From the development of its first autopilot in 1941, Minneapolis-Honeywell was at the forefront of technology. By 1964, Minneapolis-Honeywell won a bid to make space vehicles designed to carry a variety of NASA equipment. Two were eventually launched, but the company decided expenses were too great to enter into the prime contract field. Still, the company was involved in every American space mission, and supplied digital flight control systems and display and performance monitors for the space shuttle. Also in 1964 the stockholders approved yet another name change, to Honeywell Inc.

While Honeywell ventured further into computers and aerospace technology, its international operations were also expanding. Between 1945 and 1965, Honeywell's overseas business in Great Britain, Canada, Japan, and the Netherlands had grown from almost nothing to account for 23 percent of sales and 20 percent of its work force; these percentages stayed roughly the same into the 1980s. In 1965, Honeywell's overseas operations consisted of 17 subsidiaries with 12,000 employees and revenues of more than $160 million.

Meanwhile, the computer division finally showed a profit in 1967, 12 years after it was established. But research and development costs continued to be enormous. In 1970, Honeywell shocked the business world by purchasing the large systems computer segment of General Electric. The purchase doubled its business and added 25,000 employees in a new subsidiary called Honeywell Information Systems (HIS). The move put Honeywell in second place in computers, behind only IBM. But in the end, the merger only pitted Honeywell against IBM, leading to a long, hard struggle and, eventually, disillusionment.

The early 1970s were a bumpy time for Honeywell. The company received a lot of negative publicity for its involvement with the war in Southeast Asia and for its investments in South Africa. One of the most vocal demonstrators was Charles Pillsbury, a dissident stockholder and heir to the flour empire, who in 1970 shouted the memorable question to Honeywell president James H. Binger, "How does it feel to be the Krupp of Minneapolis?," referring to the German industrialist who had helped re-arm Germany following World War I. But Binger, an outspoken and controversial leader, declared in 1971 that as long as the conflict in Southeast Asia continued, Honeywell would furnish support.

Within the corporation, the 1970s were marked by efforts to streamline business and cut out nonproductive assets. One of the divisions that dwindled during this period was the home smoke alarm business, which was finally cut in 1980. The market had become increasingly competitive; though well known for its fire protection products, the company discontinued its line. Honeywell's entry into microcomputers did turn a profit, doubling sales every year between 1976 and 1980. Unfortunately, however, HIS suffered nearly a 50 percent decline in operating profits between 1981 and 1982. Compounding the company's financial difficulties, anti-apartheid activists protested against the company's South African interests, and Native Americans claimed that land Honeywell held for defense experiments was sacred, and demanded Honeywell stop all activities there.

In 1982 Honeywell began a major corporate restructuring. James Renier, a Honeywell executive who had climbed the ranks, became president of the computer division. A total of 3,500 jobs were eliminated through layoffs, retirements, and transfers, earning Renier the nickname "Neutron Jim": "[A]ll the buildings were still there," one survivor explained to the *Wall Street Journal,* "it's just the people who were gone." Renier became president and CEO of Honeywell in 1986. Renier also redefined the corporate attitude toward IBM, resolving to live in an IBM world and begin marketing products that would work alongside IBM computers.

Once the computer division was whipped into some kind of shape, Honeywell decided in 1986 to sell the majority of it to Group Bull of France and Japan's NEC Corporation, creating a three-way joint venture. Honeywell retained 42.5 percent of the stock, but intended to sell all but 20 percent to its partners. The divestiture of its computer unit left Honeywell to concentrate on sales of thermostat systems, automation products, and aerospace and defense equipment.

In 1988, Honeywell suffered from a series of unusual charges related to the company's defense unit. Serious cost overruns in a number of contracts, many of them carryovers from the days when Unisys owned the unit, had to be absorbed by the company, resulting in a net loss of $434.9 million for the year. As a general slowdown in defense contracts combined with the Pentagon's waste-reduction measures created a tougher business

climate for defense contractors, James Renier looked to the company's commercial aerospace business to pick up the slack. By 1989 defense and aerospace accounted for almost half of Honeywell's sales and were contributing significantly to the bottom line. At the same time, automation systems were getting a boost from an upswing in capital investment.

The streamlined and focused Honeywell looked forward to reaping the rewards of its high-margin units. Honeywell had a solid foothold in the automation-systems market and continued to be a leader in heating controls and alarm systems. Buoyed by the 1987 acquisition of Sperry Aerospace Group for $1 billion, sales in its space and aviation unit leapt by 21 percent a year, despite a $435 million loss posted for the unit in 1988. Renier also streamlined operations, cutting 5,000 jobs, improving inventory turnaround time, and accelerating receivables collection. By 1991, although a recession had hit the company's major markets, operating margins had grown to 11 percent, and net income was about $331 million.

The recession continued through 1992, especially in the airline industry. But losses in Honeywell's Space and Aviation Unit were offset by record sales in its automation-systems unit. From a marketing perspective, the company began to successfully exploit growing societal concerns about environmental protection. Its most successful controls and automation systems were designed to help industries conserve energy, improve productivity, and meet emission standards set by the U.S. Clean Air Act.

Renier resigned as chairman and CEO in 1993, succeeded by Michael R. Bonsignore, who had been president and chief operating officer of the company. Despite its improved marketing focus and successful new line of building controls, Honeywell's 1993 sales were about $6 billion—$1 billion less than they were in 1988. Profits had declined dramatically, and a lawsuit further threatened the company's profitability, when a jury awarded Litton Industries a $1.2 billion judgment against Honeywell for patent infringement.

Under Bonsignore the company met its projected financial goals for 1994. Nevertheless, investor confidence began to erode as the company's long-term restructuring plan was perceived as a failure. Competitors Emerson Electric Co. and Rockwell International Corp. had nearly twice the operating margins of Honeywell, even in a sluggish market. Net income declined in 1994 to $279 million, although sales had increased 1.7 percent to $6.06 billion. Honeywell's stock prices slid as analysts complained that the company should have been more aggressive in trimming costs and accused management of supporting a "clubby, paternalistic culture that avoids tough decisions." Even a reversal of the $1.2 billion Litton judgment and a $600 million stock buyback did little to reverse Honeywell's slipping stock prices.

Despite these difficulties, Honeywell management remained confident in its restructuring plans and predicted double-digit growth in the near future. Their confidence was based on the fact that Honeywell remained a leader in technological development and continued to hold a respectable market share in both of its key divisions. But the company's future was tied to management's ability to deliver profits. Based on Honeywell's inconsistent financial record of the late 1980s and early 1990s, Bonsignore had a difficult task in front of him.

Principal Subsidiaries: Honeywell Federal Systems Inc.; Honeywell Finance Inc.; Honeywell Asia Pacific Inc. (Hong Kong); Honeywell Ltd. (Canada); Honeywell Europe S.A.; Tata Honeywell Ltd. (India; 50%); GoldStar-Honeywell Co., Ltd. (South Korea; 50%).

Further Reading:

Berss, Marcia, ''Under Control,'' *Forbes,* January 31, 1994, pp. 50–54.
The First 100 Years, Minneapolis: Honeywell Inc., 1985.
Kelly, Kevin, ''Not So Sweet Times at Honeywell,'' *Business Week,* February 20, 1995, p. 66.
Therrien, Lois, ''Honeywell Is Finally Tasting the Sweet Life,'' *Business Week,* June 3, 1991, p. 34.

—updated by Maura Troester

HOOVER

The Hoover Company

101 E. Maple Street
Canton, Ohio 44720
U.S.A
(216) 499-9200
Fax: (216) 996-5439

Wholly Owned Division of the Maytag Corporation
Incorporated: 1910 as Hoover Suction Sweeper Co.
Employees: 10,560
Sales: $1.5 billion
SICs: 3635 Household Vacuum Cleaners

A division of the Maytag Corporation, Hoover is probably best known for the line of vacuum cleaners it markets in the United States and Canada. However, the company also produces and sells high quality washers, dryers, dishwashers, and other products primarily in the United Kingdom and continental Europe. Maytag acquired The Hoover Company in 1989, providing Maytag an important foothold in the highly competitive international appliance market. In the mid-1990s, Hoover conducted business through two separate divisions, which reported separately to Maytag: Hoover North America, with headquarters in North Canton, Ohio, and Hoover Europe, with headquarters in Merthyr Tydfil, Wales. Manufacturing facilities in the United States, Canada, and Mexico were part of Hoover North America, while manufacturing facilities in the United Kingdom and Portugal were part of Hoover Europe.

The company's roots date to 1827, when Henry Hoover established a tannery near Canton, Ohio. More than 80 years later in 1908, W.H. Hoover and his son began selling vacuum cleaners from the family business after purchasing the rights to an electric suction sweeper invented the year before by Murray Spangler, an inventor by profession who was moonlighting as a janitor at a local department store. From a soap box, fan, sateen pillow case, and broom handle, Spangler assembled a crude machine to vacuum the dust that aggravated his asthma when he swept carpets with a broom. On realizing the product's sales potential, Spangler began a search for investors and found one in his cousin's husband, W.H. "Boss" Hoover. Hoover bought Spangler's patent in 1908, kept Spangler as a partner, and hired six employees to produce the machines in his tannery. Initially called the Electric Suction Sweeper Co., the company was incorporated in Ohio on December 6, 1910 under a new name, the Hoover Suction Sweeper Co.

Soon thereafter, Mr. Hoover began marketing the sweeper in stores throughout the country. His strategy relied on a small magazine ad, which ran in the *Saturday Evening Post,* offering a free ten-day trial period to those who wrote and requested it. Customers would then be directed to a nearby store that had agreed to stock the Hoover sweeper for the duration of the ad. Mr. Hoover's idea was to have selected stores distribute the machines to customers, allow the stores to keep the sales commissions, and then to invite them to become dealers for the company's product. This strategy proved remarkably effective, and the company eventually established a chain of 5,000 reputable dealers from coast to coast. Mr. Hoover's early success relied on door-to-door salesmen who represented each local store; that store, in turn, lent its name for a share of the sale. Hoover also stationed salesmen in dealer showrooms to give free product demonstrations.

Domestic sales aside, Hoover found new markets for the electric sweeper abroad. In 1911, he opened a Hoover plant in Canada and an office in England in 1919. By 1921, Hoover was selling the product worldwide, and by 1923 sales reached $23 million. Also during this time, Hoover began an engineering and development program to design better machines. In 1926, a breakthrough innovation with the "beater bar" utilized the memorable advertising slogan: "It beats as it sweeps as it cleans." The beater bar worked by thumping the carpet to loosen dirt which was then swept up into the bag by a bristle brush aided by strong suction. The company improved on the beater bar with the Quadraflex agitator, which doubled the brushing action and continued as a feature of Hoover vacuum cleaners into the 1990s. Hoover made numerous other innovations, including such convenience features as disposable paper bags, the vacuum cleaner headlight, and the self-mounted attached hose feature which was patented in 1936.

In 1942, the company turned its manufacturing facilities to the war effort, producing plastic helmet liners and parachutes for fragmentation bombs, as well as four components for the proximity fuse. With the end of the war came new changes for the company. Although Hoover had always prospered with door-to-door selling, changing times made it increasingly difficult to hire these salesmen. As housewives gained employment outside the home, they were no longer the promising sales prospects they had been. Moreover, the advent of the shopping center, greater mobility by automobile, and the explosion in commercial advertising via radio, television, magazines, and newspapers lured the public directly to retailers, undercutting the door-to-door sales system.

Hoover also met with heightened competition. When other companies, including General Electric, began selling through corner appliance stores, Hoover began to feel the pinch. Other companies, such as Electrolux, established Hoover-like sales forces, which also undercut profit margins. By the time Herbert Hoover, Jr. (no relation to the former U.S. president) succeeded his father, H.W., as chief executive in 1954, profits represented a mere three percent of sales, and the company's market share had fallen. As a result of declining market share, the company jettisoned door-to-door sales marketing, as well as its retail policy. Hoover then expanded its number of U.S. dealers to nearly 30,000. Under Herbert, Jr., the company also set up a subsidiary called Hoover Worldwide in New York to expand the company's management beyond Canton, Ohio.

In 1966, as a result of a proxy battle to oust Herbert Hoover, Jr., Felix N. Mansager became chief executive of the company. Mansager had started with Hoover in 1929 as a door-to-door salesman and rose to become sales manager of Hoover's North and South Dakota sales force. Realizing the obsolescence of door-to-door sales following World War II, he had abandoned the technique in favor of forming a cadre of dealer-supervisors to oversee and train retailers. The plan proved highly effective and was expanded nationwide. This accomplishment won him a position as Hoover's worldwide marketing vice-president in 1959.

While the balance sheet appeared respectable enough, the company suffered from declining market share, lagging domestic sales, and an exceedingly narrow product line. At the time, Hoover essentially produced only two products—vacuum cleaners in the United States and washing machines and vacuum cleaners in England. In the early 1950s, market share precipitously dropped to nine percent, and for almost a decade domestic sales barely budged from $51.7 million in 1953 to only $54.9 million in 1962. When compared to overseas volume, Hoover's domestic sales were anemic at best. In 1963, a full 55 percent of the company's $242 million in sales came from England, a consumer market considerably smaller than that of the United States. Another 20 percent came from its other overseas operations.

As executive vice-president, Mansager had moved to expand domestic growth through product diversification and acquisitions. With Herbert Hoover, Jr.'s consent, he had added new products, including toasters, irons, and hair dryers, putting the company in direct competition with the likes of Westinghouse and Sunbeam.

Mansager's rise to the top post represented the first time in 58 years that the company's management was dominated by non-family members. As the new chief executive, Mansager immediately announced a $20 million expansion of the North Canton plant. He also moved to address the imbalance between domestic and foreign sales through more product diversification and pushing stronger U.S. sales. As a result, by 1971, Hoover sold more than one-third of all vacuum cleaners in the United States, forcing competitors Westinghouse and General Electric to quit the floor-care market. The company also was selling many products in other markets, ranging from electric fondue pots to washing machines. This product diversification stemmed partly from Mansager's 1969 acquisition of Knapp-Monarch, a producer of small kitchen appliances. In 1971, stronger U.S. sales amounted to 37.8 percent of the total.

These promising developments were short-lived, however. In 1974, Hoover's earnings collapsed from $33 million to only $8.7 million, as a result of an overcrowded appliance market. Mansager then retired in 1975, eight months before reaching the mandatory retirement age of 65. His replacement by Merle Rawson heralded a more conservative direction for the company. In 1977, Rawson sold the small appliance unit to focus exclusively on Hoover's core products. He also moved Hoover Worldwide from New York back to North Canton, bringing with him only the remaining key personnel. By 1977, earnings had risen again, albeit not to earlier levels. Although Hoover's one-third share of the domestic vacuum cleaner market had barely moved since 1971, the company remained profitable enough. Its stock had already peaked years ago and now stood at around $11 per share.

In 1979, enticed by Hoover's low stock price, quality products, and its worldwide name, J.B. Fuqua, owner of the Atlanta-based conglomerate Fuqua Industries, targeted the company for a takeover bid. Fuqua's conglomerate specialized in making acquisitions, having purchased about 40 such firms in as many years. In building his conglomerate, with sales totaling $1.6 billion in such diverse areas as trucking, lawn mowers, and photo finishing, he preferred making quiet deals with major stockholders to launching hostile takeovers. What appeared to be an easy and lucrative acquisition, however, turned hostile when the small town family business resisted his overtures. Fuqua's strategy was to get a controlling share of Hoover stock directly from family members by offering $22 a share and then to acquire the rest by offering Fuqua stock and debentures.

Fuqua appeared assured of gaining a significant controlling interest, as Herbert was eager to sell his huge share of stock to Fuqua. On leaving the company, however, he had signed an agreement requiring him first to offer Hoover the option to match any buyout offer. Fuqua bet that the company would not borrow most of the needed $24.2 million and risk the lawsuits that would inevitably follow. He had miscalculated, however, and in the ensuing court battle initiated by Hoover, a federal judge ruled that Fuqua's bid by letter to family members rather than to stockholders constituted an illegal tender offer. Hoover's victory, however, came at a price. At $22 a share, Fuqua's bid was attractive to shareholders. When the deal fell through, angry stockholders filed three suits against management: two class action complaints charging that management improperly used company funds to block Fuqua's offer through purchase of Herbert's shares, and a third filed by family member Frank Hoover, who first opposed the buyout and now sought to force its acceptance. To appease litigious stockholders, Hoover promised to look for other buyers and to explore financial alternatives.

Nevertheless, just six years later in October 1985, Hoover received another unsolicited $40-a-share acquisition offer from the Chicago Pacific Corporation. Formed in June 1984, Chicago Pacific emerged from the bankruptcy reorganization of the Chicago, Rock Island & Pacific Railroad Company. In 1975, the railroad company (chartered in 1847) entered proceedings for reorganization under section 77 of the Federal Bankruptcy Act. On January 25, 1980, a federal district court ordered that the railroad begin liquidation of its rail assets. With more than $450 million in cash and huge tax credits from the sale, Chicago Pacific began searching for a substantial acquisition. After two failed efforts in 1984 to purchase Textron, Inc. and Scovill Inc., Chicago Pacific focused on Hoover, whose large domestic and overseas markets and its famous brand name made it an attractive target. Given the bid of $40 per share, Hoover's board rejected the offer, directing the company's management to seek other interested buyers to maximize value for shareholders. In

October, news of the move sent Hoover's stock up more than seven dollars in over-the-counter trading to around $43 per share. The tender offer was set to expire on November 1, but in last minute negotiations, Chicago Pacific signed a definitive agreement to acquire Hoover for $534.6 million. The key to the deal stemmed from Chicago Pacific's willingness to raise the bid to $43 a share, which Hoover's board of directors accepted. The agreement continued a trend on Wall Street that witnessed the takeover of several consumer product companies.

At the time of acquisition, Hoover's net income totaled more than $40 million, up from just $28 million in 1983. Its business consisted of producing and distributing electric vacuum cleaners and accessories, electric floor polishers, and other floor care appliances and supplies, as well as laundry equipment, including washers and dryers. Hoover also had subsidiaries in England, Canada, Mexico, Colombia, Australia, France, South Africa, and Portugal.

In January 1989, Chicago Pacific was acquired for $1 billion in a friendly buyout by the Maytag Corporation, a producer of microwave ovens, refrigerators, washers, dryers, and other appliances. The combined sales of the two corporations was expected to exceed $3 billion. Both companies made the deal for similar reasons. Chicago Pacific's efforts to evade a hostile take over by an investment group prompted it to look for a friendly buyer. Maytag also sought to avoid corporate raiders in the quickly consolidating international appliance market. As the fourth largest producer after General Electric, Whirlpool, and White Consolidated Industries, Maytag seemed an appealing acquisition. The purchase of Chicago Pacific not only would ward off corporate raiders by adding $500 million in debt to its balance sheet, but also would expand its markets overseas with the lucrative Hoover franchise. Maytag had no presence in the international market, while Hoover had 13 plants in eight countries that manufactured and distributed washers, dryers, refrigerators, dishwashers, and microwave ovens.

The acquisition gave Maytag the foothold in the international market that it needed. In 1991, Hoover reorganized its operations in the United Kingdom and Europe into Hoover Europe, which was responsible for all manufacturing and marketing throughout the region. To increase Hoover Europe's competitive position, $25 million in capital improvements were made to the plant in Wales, which began producing new washers and dishwashers. In 1993, Hoover also consolidated all vacuum cleaner production in Europe at its facility in Scotland, closing its manufacturing facilities in France. This restructuring of the company along pan-European lines produced a minor international row between France and Britain.

The French foreign minister, Roland Dumas, denounced the reorganization resulting in the loss of 600 jobs as a "serious incident." The French government then asked the European Commission to investigate whether the assistance offered by Britain to transfer the operations constituted a violation of EC rules. Accusations were also made that Britain was engaged in "social dumping"—attracting foreign investment through eroding workers' rights. In light of Europe's slow economic growth and rising unemployment, the free flow of capital and labor across international borders was a sensitive issue for nations experiencing job losses at home. To remain competitive in the fast emerging global business, Hoover found that it had to concentrate its production facilities in one European plant. The company also reasoned that Scotland would provide a more flexible work force—an important competitive advantage in many industries—than could be had in France.

In the mid-1990s, Hoover was the 68th most recognized brand name in the world. Its successful expansion into new markets during this time boded well for its future as a continued leader in floor care.

Further Reading:

"The Challenger from North Canton," *Forbes,* June 15, 1972, p. 60.

Crudele, John, "Hoover Accepts New Offer," *New York Times,* October 30, 1985, p. D1.

"Filling a Power Vacuum at Hoover," *Business Week,* October 21, 1967, pp. 84–88.

Gillman, R. W., "One Man's Theory Opens a New Door," *Nation's Business,* January 1970, pp. 84–85.

Greenhouse, Steven, "Hoover Rejects Takeover Bid," *New York Times,* October 16, 1985, p. D5.

Holt, Donald, "Fighting Off Fuqua Was an Unsettling Victory for Hoover," *Fortune,* October 22, 1979, pp. 139–140, 144.

"In the Nick of Time," *Forbes,* September 1, 1968, p. 46.

Salpukas, Agis, "A Chief is Elected By Chicago Pacific," *New York Times,* April 21, 1984, p. I31.

Siler, Julia Flynn, "$1 Billion Merger in Appliances," *New York Times,* October 25, 1988, p. D1.

—Bruce Montgomery

HOWMET CORPORATION

Howmet Corp.

475 Steamboat Road
Greenwich, Connecticut 06836-1960
U.S.A.
(203) 661-4600
Fax: (203) 622-4617

Wholly Owned Subsidiary of Pechiney International
Incorporated: 1903 as Howe Sound Co.
Employees: 8,000
Sales: $800 million
SICs: 3324 Steel Investment Foundries; 3479 Coating,
    Engraving & Allied Services; 3499 Fabricated Metal
    Products; 3511 Turbines & Turbine Generator Sets; 3542
    Machine Tools, Metal Forming Types; 5051 Metal
    Services Centers & Offices

Howmet Corporation, a wholly owned subsidiary of Pechiney
International, produces high-technology components used in
gas turbine engines for industrial use as well as for jet aircraft.
Specifically, the company casts complex superalloy, titanium,
and aluminum-alloy parts for such engines. Originally the
Howe Sound Co., a holder of North American mining securities, by the early 1960s Howmet had completely abandoned
mining for diversified manufacturing. The company was acquired by Pechiney in 1970, which later divided it into separate
subsidiaries. The Howmet unit engaged in the production of
aluminum and the fabrication of aluminum products was sold
in 1983.

The Howe Sound Co. was incorporated in Maine as a holding
company for buying the securities of mining companies. It was
named for a major copper strike along an inlet of the Pacific
coast of British Columbia. Mining operations began around
1906. By 1930 its subsidiary, Britannia Mining & Smelting Co.,
held properties that included 17 beach lots and 549 government-
granted mineral claims on Howe Sound, comprising 25,517
acres. Britannia also held 10 timber licenses comprising 5,600
acres adjacent to its mining claims, a hydroelectric development, and a mill with daily capacity of 5,000 tons of ore.
Through other subsidiaries it operated mines and a concentrating mill in Mexico.

In 1940 the company's largest investment still was in Canadian
properties producing copper, zinc, lead, silver, and gold. Torbit
Mining Co., a subsidiary of Britannia created in 1930, con-

trolled a property on Howe Sound 13 miles north of Alice Arm,
British Columbia. Howe's Mexican interests ranked second,
with a subsidiary, El Potosi Mining Co., and its subsidiaries
owning and operating about 400 acres of mining properties in
the state of Chihuahua, whose ores contained silver, zinc, and
lead. Through another subsidiary established in 1930, Chelan
Copper Mining Co., Howe also owned mining property at
Chelan, Washington, with ores containing copper, silver, and
gold. Active operations there began in 1938, when the company
completed a new milling plant at Holden, Washington. In all,
Howe's operating revenues in 1940 were a modest $11.6 mil-
lion and its total income $2.5 million.

At the end of 1949 Howe Sound Co. also operated another
subsidiary, Howe Sound Exploration Co. Located on the north
shore of Snow Lake in Manitoba, it milled gold and silver from
ore. Still another subsidiary, Calera Mining Co., was developing the Blackbird mine near Forney, Idaho, expected to yield
copper, cobalt, and gold. Between 1920 and 1950 Howe's
mines had produced more than 51 million tons of ore, recovering and selling 812,797 ounces of gold, 8,271,110 ounces
of silver, 407,147 tons of copper, 713,061 tons of zinc, and
951,862 tons of lead. The company had operating revenues of
$19.33 million in 1949 and a total income of $2.96 million.

The boom-and-bust nature of the mining industry was to lead to
a loss of nearly $10 million in 1957 and, consequently, a major
reconstruction of Howe Sound. During 1958 the company
merged with Haile Mines, Inc., a producer of tungsten concentrates, metallurgical-grade manganese nodules, and other materials. The transaction was on the basis of an exchange of one
Howe share for every two-and-a-half Haile shares. The merged
company was then incorporated in Delaware under the Howe
Sound name. By now the Manitoba and Washington mines and
one of the two Mexican mines had been shut down, but the
Blackbird mine was a major cobalt ore producer, and a refinery
near Garfield, Utah, was treating its concentrate. From Haile the
new company inherited a manganese mine near Henderson,
Nevada, and a tungsten mine near Henderson, North Carolina.
Howe also operated, among other properties, a copper-and-
brass rolling mill in Springdale, Connecticut, and a research
laboratory in Dover, New Jersey, and it inherited from Haile
four Pennsylvania factories, including an aluminum fabricating
plant and rolling mill near Lancaster that was to prove highly
profitable. Operating revenues in 1958 came to $60 million, but
total income was only $2.5 million.

Haile's president, William M. Weaver, Jr., became president of
the merged company. By 1962 he had almost totally recast
Howe from a mining to a manufacturing company. The Idaho
mine was abandoned and written off, the Nevada mine closed,
and the remaining Mexican mine sold. The Britannia and tungsten mines were shut down that year. "In 1962, less than 5
percent of our sales will be from mining," Weaver told a *New
York Times* reporter. "Manufacturing is not as risky as
mining." He said the company intended to concentrate its
future efforts in three main areas: dental and surgical products,
aluminum, and high-temperature alloys. But not all of Howe's
manufacturing was profitable, either; the Connecticut copper
rolling mill, bought for $18.5 million in 1958, eventually had to
be sold at a pretax loss of $5 million. By the spring of 1962
Howe's profits were down by more than half since the record

$6.6 million of 1959, and its stock had dropped from $29 to $15 a share.

A tennis game at Manhattan's exclusive River Club between Weaver and Yves H. Robert, an executive of an affiliate of the large French aluminum-making firm Pechiney, proved fateful for Howe Sound. A locker-room discussion revealed Robert's interest in Howe's aluminum mill, now the largest U.S. fabricator of the metal. In October of 1962 Pechiney made a tender offer for 40 percent of Howe's shares at $15 a share. By late 1964 the French company had invested $22 million in Howe and owned 46 percent of the stock.

In 1966 Howe started receiving its primary aluminum from Intalco Aluminum Corp., a company in which both Howe and a Pechiney subsidiary had taken a quarter stake. Howe's earnings were coming from superalloy products like blades and vanes for gas-turbine engines, aluminum sheet and strip, metal refractories for steel and other industries, and dental and medical products. Howe's sales had more than tripled in a decade, reaching $107.9 million in 1964—but income was only $2.5 million, and its aluminum operations were not profitable.

In 1965 Weaver was moved up to the post of chairman of the board, and John J. Burke, a 42-year-old aerospace executive, succeeded him as president. The company name was changed to Howmet Corp. because, in Burke's words, "we all got completely fed up explaining to people that we didn't make stereo sets, tape recorders, or any sort of hearing aid." In Burke's first full year, Howmet's stock scored the biggest gain in a losing year on the New York Stock Exchange, soaring from $20 to $48 a share. The quarterly dividend rate increased three times. These gains were realized by selling off unpromising parts of the diversified company and eschewing new acquisitions. In 1967 Howmet's sales reached $195 million, and its profit was $14 million. Its stock reached around $100 a share in 1968 before a split.

Burke, who also found time for scuba diving, motorcycle racing, and free-fall parachuting during his three-year tenure as president, moved to chairman in 1968 and was succeeded by Robert, the Pechiney executive whose tennis match with Weaver had changed Howe Sound's direction. In the same year Pechiney Enterprises, Inc., the company's U.S. subsidiary, decided to build jointly with Howmet a primary aluminum-reduction plant near Frederick, Maryland. The plant was to cost $190 million and have a capacity of 255,000 tons of aluminum a year, giving Howmet an additional source of the metal to support the planned expansion of its fabricating plants. Alumina, from which aluminum is made, would be supplied by Pechiney from abroad and shipped to Frederick from the nearby port of Baltimore.

Howmet had sales of $183.1 million and a net income of $8.9 million in 1969. It became a Pechiney subsidiary in 1970, when Pechiney Enterprises, its U.S. holding company, raised its stake in Howmet to 58 percent. Howmet then moved from New York to Pechiney's headquarters in Greenwich, Connecticut. The acquisition made Howmet, when the new Eastalco aluminum plant came on-line during the year, the nation's fourth largest producer of aluminum ingots and fabricated products. Its profitable medical, dental, and hospital products were placed into a

separate corporation called Howmedica, Inc., with 80 percent of its common stock distributed to Howmet's shareholders. Robert became chairman and chief executive officer of Howmedica, Andre Jacomet, a Pechiney executive, became president of Howmet, and Eugene Black, former World Bank president and chairman, succeeded Burke as chairman of Howmet. Pechiney raised its stake in Howmet to 69 percent in 1973 and 92 percent in 1975.

Effective at the start of 1976, Pechiney reorganized its U.S. operations. Howmet's aluminum business was placed under a subsidiary called Howmet Aluminum Corp. and its production of gas-turbine components into a subsidiary named Howmet Turbine Components Corp. Pechiney reportedly was prepared to sell a majority interest in the latter because of concerns by the U.S. government over full control by a foreign company of the sensitive military implications involved in the manufacture of components of gas-turbine engines. Howmet's work in this field had included precision castings for the engine powering the F-15 and F-16 airplanes. However, Howmet Turbine subsequently remained in the Pechiney portfolio.

In 1979 Howmet Aluminum opened the nation's first secondary-metals plant capable of producing high-quality aluminum from all-recycled materials. The $4-million factory, in Rockwell, Texas, had an initial capacity of 75 million pounds a year. And Howmet Turbine joined with Dow Chemical Co. the same year to create a joint venture intended to commercialize an electrolytic cell process for the production of titanium sponge. Dow and Howmet had been engaged jointly in research in this field since 1973.

Howmet Aluminum Corp. was sold to Alumax, Inc., an aluminum producer based in San Mateo, California, in 1983. Alumax in turn was half owned by Amax Inc. of Greenwich, Connecticut, and half owned by Japanese interests, with Mitsui & Co. holding a 45 percent stake. Alumax also took a quarter-interest in an aluminum smelter Pechiney had decided to build in Quebec.

Howmet was operating 22 facilities worldwide in 1985. Two years later it changed its name to Howmet Corp. to reflect its diversification of products. In 1987 the company was producing biomedical implants, industrial ceramic products, and large structural castings for the engines of a number of industries as well as for jet aircraft. The company also had begun repairing small-aircraft engine parts in 1982. By 1988 it was planning a similar facility dedicated to large engines, because, according to a Howmet executive, it was the only company in the repair business also making original turbine castings.

By mid-1990 Howmet was operating two U.S. plants refurbishing aircraft parts. The company purchased a site in North Haven, Connecticut, in August 1990 for still another repair plant. Howmet said this acquisition included a building where a facility was planned to coat and repair parts like blades and vanes for advanced jet engines.

Howmet installed its third chemical vapor-deposition production unit—the largest in the Western world, according to company officials—in 1990. This unit was capable of processing parts up to 40 inches in diameter and 50 inches in length. Coatings included aluminides, various metallics, carbides, nitrides, and oxides, in addition to fluoride-ion cleaning. Such coatings were being used for high-strength composites, superalloy hot-section turbine-engine components, and the cleaning of engine-run hardware. The company's Thermatech Coatings Division also was installing a low-temperature physical vapor-deposition unit capable of applying coatings to titanium hardware, tooling, and compressor section components. In addition this division expected to install a robotic air-plasma unit to help meet expected demand for thermal barrier coatings (TBCs). Production of engine parts in the 1990s was expected to employ TBC technology.

Howmet was also supplying the heat- and corrosion-resistant cobalt-, nickel-, and iron-based superalloys used in the casting operations needed to produce sophisticated components for jet-aircraft engines. In October 1991 the company announced it would consolidate its machining and alloy production activities. Its precision-machining facility in Whitehall, Michigan, was phased out and the work there merged with its facility in Winsted, Connecticut, while its alloy operations in Plymouth, Michigan, were phased out and merged with its facilities at Dover, New Jersey.

Howmet's Dover Castings Division was manufacturing high-technology airfoils for turbine engines. This division began rethinking its operations in 1988 by breaking up departments and reassembling them into decentralized cells. These cells rethought Dover's work processes and by so doing improved the inventory supply flow. A journal reported in 1993 that lead time was reduced 67 percent, work-in-progress inventory reduced 39 percent, scrap and rework reduced 30 percent, casting nonconformance improved 68 percent, and work-in-progress turns up 42 percent.

In December of 1993 Howmet established a joint venture with Rolls Royce named R-H Component Technologies, Inc. This 50–50 joint venture was to specialize in the refurbishment of certain aircraft parts, selling to North American markets. In 1994 Howmet joined a six-member consortium planning to develop a demonstrator automobile engine significantly lighter and more efficient than those in use, using high-temperature, high-strength materials. Named the Advanced Materials Engine Project Consortium, this body was planning a 1.5-liter, V8 overhead-cam reciprocating engine with four valves per head that would weigh only about 200 pounds. The valves would be fabricated from Howmet's gamma titanium aluminides.

An uncertain factor for Howmet in the mid-1990s was the proposed privatization of Pechiney CIF, in which the French government had held a majority share beginning in 1982. Sale of the company, initially planned for 1994, was put off because it lost FFr 800 million ($164.3 million) in 1993. Howmet represented only a small part of this giant diversified corporation, but it was thought the unit could share in layoffs and other cutbacks intended to improve the bottom line. Turbine operations accounted for somewhere between eight and 14 percent of Pechiney's sales in 1993.

In 1994 the Howmet structure consisted of 16 divisions devoted to such activities as making castings, coatings, alloys, ceramic products, insulators, and titanium ingots. The company operated ten facilities in nine states in the United States and three others in England, France, and Japan. Howmet Cercast (United States) and Howmet Cercast Canada were separate subsidiaries of Pechiney International.

Principal Subsidiaries: Howmet Sales, Inc.; Howmet Tempcraft, Inc.; Howmet, Ltd. (U.K.); Howmet S.A. (France); Komatsu-Howmet, Ltd. (Japan).

Further Reading:

Du Bois, Martin, ''Pechiney Emerges as Test of France's Will to Privatize,'' *Wall Street Journal,* August 17, 1994.

Buggs, Nandi, ''Howmet Opens New Facility in Texas,'' *Journal of Commerce,* November 14, 1979, p. 8.

''The Game That Two Could Play,'' *Forbes,* December 1, 1964, pp. 40–41.

Gampetro, Tony, ''Spotlight on Howmet Corp.,'' *Journal of Commerce,* November 14, 1969, pp. 3, 20.

Hawkins, Philip, ''Howmet Corp.'s Remarkable Performance Is Linked to Its Adventuresome President,'' *Wall Street Journal,* January 30, 1967, p. 24.

''Howmet to Join Machining, Alloy Work,'' *Defense News,* October 21, 1991, p. 37.

''Pechiney's Howmet Buys Site,'' *Wall Street Journal,* August 17, 1990, p. B10.

Regan, Bob, ''Pechiney Realigns U.S. Operations,'' *American Metal Market,* November 7, 1974, pp. 1, 20.

Smith, Kenneth, ''Personality: A Leader for a Transformation,'' *New York Times,* March 25, 1962, p. 3.

—Robert Halasz

HSBC Holdings plc

10 Lower Thames Street
London EC3R 6AE
United Kingdom
(071) 260 0500
Fax: (071) 260 0501

Public Company
Incorporated: 1865 as Hongkong and Shanghai Banking
    Company, Ltd.
Employees: 99,148
Sales: £2.58 billion
Stock Exchanges: London Hong Kong
SICs: 6711 Holding Companies; 6111 Financial Institutions;
    6012
Recognized Banks; 6411 Insurance Agents, Brokers, and
    Service

A significant force in international banking, HSBC Holdings
plc operates in some 60 countries and offers a comprehensive
financial service encompassing not only commercial and merchant banking but also capital markets, consumer finance, securities, investments, and insurance. Despite a high international
profile—the group's corporate customer base includes one-
third of the world's 200 biggest companies—HSBC Holdings'
principal asset remains its original one: Hongkong and Shanghai Banking Corporation, known colloquially as Hongkong-
Bank.

The history of HSBC may be traced through the Hongkong and
Shanghai Banking Corporation (HSBC). In the early 1860s,
Hong Kong's financial needs were served by European trading
houses called ''hongs.'' This system proved increasingly inadequate as the colony's bustling trade—primarily in tea, silk, and
opium—burgeoned. By 1864, the first proper banks had been
established, but as these were based in London or India and
controlled from abroad, there was a growing feeling that a local
bank was needed in the colony.

Dissatisfaction led to action when it was discovered that a group
of Bombay financiers intended to set up a Bank of China in
Hong Kong, and that this bank, chartered in London, was to
offer only a small proportion of its shares to China coast businesses. Thomas Sutherland, the Hong Kong Superintendent of
the Peninsula and Orient Steam Navigation Company, proposed
the foundation of a new bank modeled on ''sound Scottish

banking principles.'' The proposal was promptly taken up by
others of the Hong Kong business community; within days a
provisional committee—comprised of Britons, other Europeans, and Americans—was set up and the total capital of the
new venture set at HK$5 million. The move effectively
preempted the proposed Bank of China, whose representative,
when he arrived later in Hong Kong, could find no market for
his shares.

The Hongkong and Shanghai Banking Company, Ltd. opened
on March 3, 1865, with a second branch inaugurated in Shanghai one month later. A London office was opened later in the
year. The new bank was welcomed by both the foreign business
community and Chinese compradores—native businessmen
who acted as intermediaries with the Chinese community.
HongkongBank's timing could have been disastrous, coinciding
as it did with the international financial crisis of 1865–66, but
this event actually worked to the new bank's advantage, as it
recruited staff and customers from the banks that had failed.

Initially, the bank was established under the local Companies
Ordinance as the Hongkong and Shanghai Banking Company,
Ltd. Under the colonial law of the time, a bank had to incorporate either under a royal charter in compliance with the Colonial
Banking Regulations or else according to British banking legislation. However, the bank's founders objected to these options,
as they had particularly designed their enterprise as a local
concern. Eventually a deal was struck with the Treasury
whereby the renamed Hongkong and Shanghai Banking Corporation, under a unique ordinance, could retain Hong Kong
headquarters while complying with the Colonial Banking Regulations.

HongkongBank expanded rapidly throughout the nineteenth
century. By 1900, it had branches in Japan, Thailand, the
Philippines, Singapore, and the countries now known as Malay-
sia, Myanmar, Sri Lanka, and Vietnam. In some Asian cities,
HongkongBank was the first to usher in principles of modern
Western banking and was indeed Thailand's very first bank,
printing that country's first bank notes. In the United States and
Europe, HongkongBank branches opened in San Francisco in
1875, New York in 1880, Lyons in 1881, and Hamburg in 1889.
Except in New York, where a Canadian bank already operated,
HongkongBank was the first foreign bank in each of these
cities.

In Hong Kong, operations experienced a setback in the 1870s
when the bank made some unwise investments in local Hong
Kong industry—its reserves fell from HK$1 million to
HK$100,000—but the company soon regained its footing under
the leadership of a new chief manager, Thomas Jackson, who
brought the bank back to a renewed emphasis on its field of
expertise, trade finance. By the end of Jackson's reign, in 1902,
HongkongBank's paid-up capital stood at HK$10 million, and
its published reserves at HK$14.25 million, with additional
estimated inner reserves of HK$10 million.

The bank had, however, developed another lucrative role—that
of banker to governments. By the 1880s, HongkongBank was
operating in this capacity to the government of Hong Kong and
had acquired the Treasury Chest (the British government's military and foreign service) business for China and Japan. In

addition, the HongkongBank issued bank notes for Hong Kong and for the Straits Settlements (Singapore and Penang). Since these notes were not, at the time, legal tender, their popularity reflected the public's trust in HongkongBank. Perhaps the bank's greatest success was in mainland China: it financed that country's first public loan in 1874 and, by 1910, had become the foremost bank and clearing house for the national groups of the multinational China Consortium.

World War I proved a difficult time for the international bank both diplomatically and financially, as nationalistic fervor gripped the world. HongkongBank was censured by Britain for its ties with nations that were now enemies, and Germany was similarly dissatisfied—all the bank's German directors resigned. Business did improve to some extent after the war, with the bank opening new offices in Hankow, Bangkok, and Manila, but operations in an increasingly hostile China suffered; although the bank moved into Manchuria, its activities were limited to foreign trade activities. Furthermore, the rise of an indigenous Chinese banking industry curtailed the influence of HongkongBank. The bank also experienced disappointments in other Asian markets, incurring losses in the Philippines and the Malayan Peninsula, and found its branches in Java, Saigon, and Haiphong neglected in favor of Dutch and French colonial banks.

As hostilities mounted at the onset of World War II, HongkongBank just managed to ship its reserves (previously silver, now British sterling standard) to London before Japan invaded Hong Kong on December 8, 1941. During the war, most of the bank's European staff working in Asia were taken prisoner by the Japanese. Many were subsequently sent home, but some were held, including the bank's chief manager and his appointed successor, both of whom died during incarceration.

During this time, operations shifted to London, where the head office was moved. The London manager became chairperson and chief manager of the bank, and the London Advisory Committee took on the powers of the board of directors. When the war ended, HongkongBank was held liable for some HK$16 million in bank notes which it had issued under coercion during the occupation.

The bank soon recovered its losses, however, in the boom years after the war. Headquartered again in Hong Kong, HongkongBank was prominent in the effort to rebuild the colony after the war, providing financial aid to revitalize commerce and the economy. The bank also looked outward, establishing its presence even more firmly throughout Asia. However, as mainland China became increasingly volatile both politically and fiscally, HongkongBank began closing its branches in China soon after the war and by 1955 retained a presence only in Shanghai.

Nonetheless, the political situation in China also worked to the bank's advantage, as business in its home market of Hong Kong was boosted by unrest on the mainland. Refugees and industrialists pouring into the colony from China brought with them manufacturing skills and experience. HongkongBank was there to finance them, and thus played a significant part in helping to establish Hong Kong as one of the world's most prominent manufacturing centers.

HongkongBank also retained its interest in international operations, initiating a new policy of establishing or acquiring foreign subsidiaries incorporated in their country of operation. In 1959, HongkongBank purchased the Mercantile Bank of India, London, and China and the British Bank of the Middle East. The bank also consolidated an already strong position in Hong Kong with a friendly takeover of the extensive interests of the Hang Seng Bank in 1965.

HonkongBank's renewed interest in expansion was matched by a diversification in the banking services it provided. The bank formed a hire-purchase finance subsidiary, Wayfoong, in 1960, to deal with such operations as installment loans for consumer goods and financing motor vehicle purchases. This trend to offer a more comprehensive service continued, with the bank forming Wardley Ltd. in 1972, a subsidiary involved with merchant and investment banking, and the establishment of an insurance subsidiary, Carlingford.

In 1980, the bank acquired 51 percent of the New York-based Marine Midland Bank Inc. This was a highly significant move for the bank—the total assets of the acquisition represented 62 percent of the assets of HongkongBank—and a controversial one, sparking American fears (leading to congressional hearings) that the control of a major U.S. bank would move from the country. HongkongBank managed to placate these fears and indeed acquired the remaining interest in the American bank in 1987. Hongkong Bank of Canada was established in 1981, and, nine years later, HongkongBank acquired Lloyds Bank Canada. Moreover, the bank attempted to move cautiously back into China, as that country eased its economic restrictions on foreign financiers.

However, HongkongBank's expansionist policies were not always successful. Its acquisition of the U.S. Marine Midland, said initially to have boosted the bank's assets from HK$125.3 billion to HK$243 billion, soon proved a debacle. Ill-advised forays into real estate and Latin American lending led to significant losses, prompting the parent company in 1991 to completely overhaul its subsidiary—at a purported cost of $1.8 billion. Other high-profile failures of the 1980s include the bank's financing of an Australian tycoon, Alan Bond, who went bankrupt, and its support for London's ultimately unsuccessful Canary Wharf development, undertaken by the Canadian firm Olympia & York. Nevertheless, as Pete Engardio commented in *Business Week:* ''Booming Hong Kong provides HSBC with a cornucopia of cash.''

By 1991, HongkongBank had over 500 subsidiaries in 50 countries. In fact, its portfolio had become so expansive and complex that a new umbrella organization was formed. HSBC Holdings plc was incorporated in the United Kingdom, while its headquarters were established in Hong Kong. As a condition of its 1992 acquisition of Britain's Midland Bank plc, however, HSBC was required by the regulatory Bank of England to move its head office to London.

The acquisition of Midland was a coup, providing HSBC with the significant presence in Europe it had previously lacked. Variously described as a merger and a takeover, the amalgamation virtually doubled HSBC's assets and work force. The venerable Midland, the U.K.'s third largest bank, was not performing to standard at that time, being the least profitable of Britain's "big four" banks. However, the financial health and the international experience of the parent company began attracting larger corporate customers to Midland. In addition, many individuals were subsequently won over by the telephone banking service, First Direct, introduced by Midland just before the amalgamation and strongly backed by HSBC. HSBC's lead in technology—used, for example, to automate credit decisions and limit staff expenditure—also played a part in Midland's recovery.

As of 1994, HSBC ranked 10th in the financial world in terms of capitalization, 15th in assets, and among the top ten in profits. Its U.S. and Australian subsidiaries, which had experienced losses, were again returning profits. Future expansion in America, Europe, and Asia was planned. According to the *Investors' Chronicle,* the group's international success continued to be substantially fueled by the "phenomenal profitability of its Far East base [which] has given HSBC the strength necessary to pursue international expansion." Indeed, HongkongBank was so securely established in Hong Kong that it was known locally simply as "the Bank." Although the company faced some uncertainty regarding its future, as Britain was due to relinquish all control of the territory to China by 1997, HonkkongBank noted that it had received assurances from Peking that its future would be safeguarded. Optimistic for the company's future, chief executive John Bond commented: "In Chinese, 'threat' and 'opportunity' are the same character."

Principal Subsidiaries: British Bank of the Middle East; Carlingford Insurance Co. Ltd. (Hong Kong); Concord Leasing Inc.; Hang Seng Bank Ltd. (Hong Kong; 61%); Hongkong and Shanghai Banking Corporation Ltd. (Hong Kong); Hongkong Bank of Australia Ltd.; Hongkong Bank of Canada; James Capel & Co. Ltd.; Marine Midland Bank; Midland Bank plc; Samuel Montagu & Co. Ltd.; Wardley Ltd. (Hong Kong); Wayfoong Finance Ltd. (Hong Kong).

Further Reading:

Blanden, Michael, "After the Dust of Battle," *Banker,* August 1992, p. 36.
"Brief History: The Hongkong and Shanghai Banking Corporation Limited," Hong Kong: HSBC, 1991, 28 p.
Engardio, Pete, "Global Banker," *Business Week,* May 24, 1993, pp. 42–46.
"Far Eastern Promise and the Global Gamble," *Investors' Chronicle,* January 29, 1993.
"Greater than the Sum of His Parts," *Financial Times,* March 1, 1994.
Holmes, A. R., and Edwin Green, *Midland: 150 Years of Banking Business,* London: Batsford, 1986.
"HongkongBank's Global Gamble," *Economist,* March 21, 1992, pp. 107–08.
"Hong Kong/China Boom Spawns a Global Banking Colossus," *QL Stockmarket Letter,* July 1, 1993.
"HSBC Maps Strategy for US Market," *South China Morning Post,* January 14, 1993.
King, Frank H. H., *The History of The Hongkong and Shanghai Banking Corporation,* 4 vols., New York: Cambridge University Press.
"Loan Masters," *Economist,* August 28, 1993, pp. 65–66.
Vander Weyer, Martin, "Hongkong Officer Corps Builds a Global Empire," *Euromoney,* April, 1993, pp. 52–56.
"Waiting for the Griffin to Pull Its Weight," *Financial Times,* March 16, 1993.
"You Organise Your Bank around Your Customers," *Daily Telegraph,* March 22, 1993.

—Robin DuBlanc

The Hudson Bay Mining and Smelting Company, Limited

201 Portage Avenue
Suite 1906
Winnipeg, Manitoba R3B 3K6
Canada
(204) 949-4261
Fax: (204) 942-8177

Wholly Owned Subsidiary of Minorco
Incorporated: 1927
Employees: 2,064
Sales: C$449 million
SICs: 1300 Oil & Gas Extraction; 1000 Metal Mining

The Hudson Bay Mining and Smelting Company, Limited, is a major Canadian producer of copper and zinc which operates mines and metal processing facilities in remote areas of the province of Manitoba. The company has been removing metals from the ground for most of the twentieth century, and its efforts to industrialize western Manitoba have helped to foster development in the region. More than 23 mines have yielded ore to the Hudson Bay metal processing works over the last 60 years, as the company has engaged in aggressive geological exploration to support its metal refining activities.

Hudson Bay got its start in January 1915, when Tom Creighton, an early Canadian prospector, happened upon an outcropping of sulfide ore in an undeveloped area of Manitoba. In the previous decade, prospectors had discovered that an enormous greenstone belt stretched east from Manitoba into northern Saskatchewan. This geological structure contained numerous deposits of different metals mixed together, including zinc, copper, silver, and gold.

Suspecting that the outcropping he had found could signal a valuable deposit of copper and zinc, Creighton returned in the spring with a friend to confirm his discovery and stake the first claim. The two filed an official claim in September 1915, naming the body of ore they had found "Flin Flon," after a character in a dime store novel.

Over the next ten years, the rights to the Flin Flon stake were held by a number of different mining concerns, who did not take action to develop a mine. Finally, in 1925, the option to the site was acquired by a company associated with Harry Payne Whit-

ney in New York. Under the direction of Whitney, a sequence of metallurgical tests were performed on the ore deposit. Although the ore bodies were not found to be exceptionally rich, they were quite sizable. In December 1927, the decision was made to go ahead with mining operations, and the Hudson Bay Mining and Smelting Company, Limited, was formed to run the site.

In 1928 work began on the construction of what would become one of the largest industrial facilities in the world. The company planned an open pit mine, a vast metallurgical processing complex, and, to power these operations, the first major hydroelectric dam in northern Canada. In order to get at the mineral deposits, a lake overlying the ore was dammed and drained, and more than one million tons of mud and clay from the lake bed were removed. By October 1929, a dam had been constructed across the lake, and construction of other parts of the mine had also begun.

A dam was also built across the Churchill River, at Island Falls, Saskatchewan, to power the Hudson Bay hydro-electric plant. In addition, the company constructed a concentrator, a zinc recovery unit, and a copper smelter. Together, this enormous metallurgical complex at Flin Flon offered great economies of scale in smelting and refining. To bring the refined products of the Flin Flon mine to their ultimate users, the CN Railroad was also extended 140 kilometers, from The Pas, Manitoba, to Flin Flon.

Operations at Flin Flon began in late 1930, with ore removal from an open pit and refinement at the plant. In the ensuing decades, the metallurgical processing facility continued to operate 24 hours a day, 365 days a year, with only two interruptions ever taking place. On the strength of these operations, Hudson Bay opened a new region of Canada to further development.

From 1930 to 1935, more than two-thirds of the ore removed from Flin Flon came from the open pit, with the remainder coming from a shaft, named North Main. By 1936, however, the pit had reached its maximum depth. Exploration had revealed that the ore deposit was not contained in one large lens-shaped body, but was distributed in six distinct bodies, which angled downward to the south from the main area. In order to gain access to more of these deposits, a second shaft, South Main, was sunk in 1939. This site, one kilometer south of the North Main site, was designed to transport large quantities of ore faster than the older North facility.

Mining at Flin Flon continued throughout the 1940s. Early in the decade, Hudson Bay opened the first of many supplemental mines that the company would develop to feed its Flin Flon processing plant. Named Mandy, this facility operated for just a few years at the start of the decade before being exhausted. With the development of this ore source, Hudson Bay demonstrated its commitment to continued prospecting and the development of new small mineral deposits.

The company broke ground on five new mines during the 1950s. The Cuprus and Schist Lake sites, developed early in the decade, produced minerals for roughly a quarter of a century, shutting down in the mid-1970s. The Don Jon mine operated for several years in the middle of the decade, and the Birch

Lake and North Star shafts both yielded ore in the latter part of the decade.

In 1958 Hudson Bay inaugurated operations at a second major location, east of Flin Flon, called Snow Lake. At Chisel Lake, the company opened a zinc mine with two shafts, one to transport men and equipment, and another to bring materials to the surface. Underground, Hudson Bay used the cut-and-fill and the long-hole methods to remove zinc from the earth. Also at that time, the Coronation mine came on line. Coronation continued to produce ore into the mid-1960s.

Two years after Chisel Lake was opened, in 1960, Hudson Bay started a second mining operation at Snow Lake, the Stall Lake Mine, which produced high grade copper. The cut-and-fill method was used to remove ore in this location. For the next decade, all ore mined at Snow Lake was transported by rail to Flin Flon for processing. Beginning in the 1970s, however, Hudson Bay began to phase out the use of trains for this process, relying instead on trucks to move the products of all its mines except the South Main shaft.

The early 1970s brought a large number of new mines to the Hudson Bay operation. The Ghost Lake, Anderson, and Osborne operations came on line, as did the White Lake, Dickstone, and the short-lived Flexar mine. Ghost Lake and Anderson produced ore for nearly 20 years, while Osborne yielded minerals for roughly three-quarters of that time.

In 1979 Hudson Bay constructed a processing facility adjacent to its Stall Lake Mine at Snow Lake, thus diversifying its refining capabilities from its main Flin Flon site. The Stall Lake concentrator treated copper and zinc ores in separate facilities, producing 350 tons of copper and 100 tons of zinc concentrate each day. By locating this facility near its Snow Lake ore deposits, Hudson Bay was able to increase the total ore reserves available to it by making marginal mineral deposits profitable, since the cost of shipping them to be processed had been reduced. The products of the Snow Lake concentrator were shipped by rail to the Flin Flon metallurgical plant for further refining.

In the late 1970s, Hudson Bay also commenced mining operations at the Centennial and Westarm mines. In 1982 the company began to remove minerals from Trout Lake, located five kilometers north of Flin Flon. In order to remove the ore contained in deposits beneath the lake bed, the company dug a slanted tunnel to them, through which a 27-ton ore truck moved, bringing minerals to an area just below the surface, where they were crushed. As Hudson Bay was forced to dig deeper and deeper into the ground to retrieve ore, it became less economical to bring the minerals to the surface by truck, so a shaft was built to bring materials straight to the crusher.

With this new system, ore was removed from the ground by machines and subjected to an underground crusher, before being taken up to the surface on a conveyor belt. Further development of this facility included the construction of a secondary production shaft to transfer ore from the lowest levels of the mine to the crusher. Hudson Bay developed this project in partnership with an arm of the Manitoba government, another Canadian company, and a Finnish concern.

In 1983 Hudson Bay sealed off the main shaft of its first mine, North Main, at Flin Flon, as this original source of minerals began, after 60 years, to reach its final stages of depletion. By blocking the mine shaft at the 1170 foot level, the company made it possible for the remaining ore in the mine's pillars to be removed. This material was then moved by underground train to the South Main shaft and brought to the surface.

Also in 1983, Hudson Bay's corporate ownership underwent a reorganization. At this time, Hudson Bay and a half-owned subsidiary, Plateau Holdings, restructured their assets, forming the Inspiration Resources Corporation, based in New York. Hudson Bay then became a wholly owned subsidiary of this company. Inspiration held a wide range of natural resources properties, with operations in the agriculture, mining, base and precious metals, coal, construction, and equipment leasing industries. With the exception of Hudson Bay, all of Inspiration's holdings were located in the United States.

In the mid-1980s, Hudson Bay commenced mining at the Rod location, and at Spruce Point, part of the Snow Lake complex. The company also bought the Ruttan mining property, located in the town of Leaf Rapids, Manitoba. Construction of Leaf Rapids had begun in 1971, specifically for the purpose of making it possible for the Ruttan mine to run. The first families of the town had taken up residence by the end of that year, and the mine went into operation in the spring of 1973, under the direction of Sherritt Gordon Mines, Limited.

For the first six years, open pit methods were used at Ruttan while underground reserves were developed. During this time, because metal prices were low, the Ruttan mine operated at a loss. In 1979 the open pit was closed and the shaft mine came into full production. By the mid-1980s, however, the company that owned the property was looking for ways to shut down the mine and the town. After several years of negotiation, Hudson Bay purchased this property in 1987. In addition to mining ore, the company operated a concentrator at the sight, and began aggressive exploration for new copper reserves.

Also in the late 1980s, Hudson Bay entered into a joint venture, of which it owned 60 percent, to develop the Nanew Lake Mine, 70 kilometers south of the Flin Flon area. This property contained an ore body of nickel, a new product for Hudson Bay, which rested below Nanew Lake. In November 1988, Hudson Bay began mining operations at this site. Although the company's initial efforts were hampered by the unexpected presence of two bodies of water underground, necessitating the installation of pumps, by the fourth quarter of 1989 the mine was operating at full capacity.

The company removed nickel from Nanew Lake on two levels, using two different mining techniques, and brought it to the surface through a rectangular access shaft drilled on shore. Once extracted, nickel was processed in a mill at the mine site, and then trucked to a smelter in Thompson, or shipped on rail cars to a processing facility in Fort Saskatchewan.

These activities all took place at an environmentally sensitive location, since Nanew Lake itself was a clean body of water, used for sport and commercial fishing. In addition, wildlife in the area supported hunting, nearby forests were logged, and several Indian communities lived near the lake. In order to satisfy other users of the lake, the mining operation removed the natural fish population of Nanew Lake and replaced it with rainbow trout, a more valuable fish. Hudson Bay also established an environmental overview committee, with local citizens and government representatives, to address concerns about the mine.

In 1988 Hudson Bay also expanded its operations at Snow Lake yet again, when it inaugurated an open pit mine at the Chisel Lake site. This mine produced extremely high grade zinc ore, mixed with small quantities of lead, silver, and gold. Ore was taken from the pit by truck, crushed at Chisel Lake, and then processed at the Snow Lake mill. Within two years of opening the pit had reached a depth of nearly 250 feet.

In the same way that it had sought new resources at Snow Lake, Hudson Bay moved to further exploit its Flin Flon facilities in the late 1980s, opening a mine at Callinan, which was just one kilometer away from the Flin Flon metallurgy complex. This facility had three zones, designated North, East, and South. After purchasing the remaining interest in the Callinan project in 1989, Hudson Bay built two horizontal tunnels to reach the three ore zones from the pre-existing Flin Flon South Main shaft. In the lower tunnel, underground trains hauled ore 8000 feet from the lode to a crusher under the shaft. After being pulverized, materials were hauled to the surface in bins.

By the end of the 1980s, these activities had made Hudson Bay Canada's fourth-largest copper and zinc metal mining operation. The company mined 166 million pounds of refined zinc, 127 million pounds of refined copper, and 6.7 million pounds of nickel in 1989. In addition, it produced far smaller quantities of gold, silver, and cadmium.

In the 1990s, Hudson Bay was faced with the necessity of upgrading its somewhat antiquated facilities. By this time, its corporate parent had been transformed into Minorco. This entity, based in New York, approved plans to invest C$155 million in new smelting technology at the end of 1990. This money would be spent on the Flin Flon metal works, which badly needed modernization. With the changes to this facility, Hudson Bay hoped to move into compliance with new Manitoba environmental regulations and to improve its efficiency, increasing profits. Along with improvements to its smelter, Hudson Bay also planned to upgrade equipment at its Trout Lake Mine, installing a new shaft and ore hauling system.

In addition, Hudson Bay planned to spend C$17 million looking for new ore deposits to feed its processing plants, a prospect made somewhat easier by forest fires, which cleared vegetation from a large area, making mineral outcroppings easier to view. In addition, Hudson Bay brought in new executives to strengthen its operations.

In the early 1990s Hudson Bay closed two mines that had been exhausted of ore, and began to make plans to terminate operations at two more in Snow Lake. Late in 1992, the company announced that it could lay off as many as 600 employees as a result of these changes.

By the start of the following year, Hudson Bay had commenced construction of a new zinc plant, and the company announced in late January of that year that it would need additional ore reserves to feed this plant and its Flin Flon metallurgical facility. By 1994, Hudson Bay's exploration process had yielded two new mine sites, and development had commenced at Westarm, Flin Flon, and Photo Lake, near Snow Lake.

Principal Subsidiaries: Hudson Bay Exploration and Development.

Further Reading:

"Renaissance at Hudson Bay Mining and Smelting," *Canadian Mining Journal,* November 1990, pp. 14–17.

—Elizabeth Rourke

Hunt Manufacturing Company

230 South Broad Street
Philadelphia, Pennsylvania 19102
U.S.A.
(215) 656-0300
Fax: (215) 875-5252

Public Company
Incorporated: 1899 as the C. Howard Hunt Pen
    Manufacturing Company
Employees: 1,871
Sales: $234.9 million
SICs: 3951 Pens & Mechanical Pencils; 3579 Office
    Machines, Not Elsewhere Classified; 2521 Wood Office
    Furniture; 2899 Chemical Preparations, Not Elsewhere
    Classified

The Hunt Manufacturing Company is a leading producer and distributor of office supplies and arts and crafts products. The company started life making pens, and this one product grew into a line that includes more than 10,000 items. Owned and run by one family throughout almost all of its history, Hunt benefited from stability in its finances and management, which allowed it to embark upon a program of rapid expansion through acquisition of other companies in the late 1980s. Under this policy, the company's size has grown rapidly in the last decade.

Hunt traces its lineage to 1897, when the C. Howard Hunt Pen Manufacturing Company opened in Camden, New Jersey. Two years after this start, Hunt was turned over to new management and formally incorporated. In 1903, Hunt was purchased by George E. Bartol, whose family would retain control over the property throughout much of the twentieth century.

In 1915, Hunt introduced an innovative new product that would become a mainstay of its line: the Speedball ballpoint pen. This item marked the company's entry into the newly emerging ballpoint pen market, which was rapidly replacing the market for traditional ink pens. Bartol passed on the chairmanship of Hunt to his son, George E. Bartol, Jr., in 1921. Under the leadership of the younger Bartol, Hunt made its first major acquisition in 1925, when the company purchased the Boston Pencil Sharpener Company.

Hunt continued to manufacture pens and pencil sharpeners throughout the Great Depression, when many other businesses

failed, due to the essential nature of the products. In 1940, Hunt introduced pen points made of a non-stainless steel alloy, and this innovation helped the company to maintain its market share throughout the war years and the late 1940s. In 1957, a third generation of the Bartol family took the reins at Hunt, when George E. Bartol III became the company's president and chief executive officer.

Also that year, Hunt transferred its manufacturing operations from Camden, New Jersey, to Statesville, North Carolina. A second acquisition was made shortly thereafter, when the company purchased the Peterson Manufacturing Company, which produced parts for metal eyelets.

In 1962, the C. Howard Hunt Pen Manufacturing Company changed its name to the Hunt Manufacturing Company, reflecting the broadened scope of the company's activities. Also during this time, the company moved its headquarters from its long-time home in Camden to Philadelphia.

In the late 1960s, Hunt expanded its line of products from basic, functional office supplies to arts and crafts supplies as well. In 1966, the company bought the New Masters Company, which manufactured artists' paints. In addition, Hunt expanded its Statesville, North Carolina, manufacturing plant.

In 1969, George Bartol III took complete control of Hunt from his father, becoming chairman of the board. The following year, Hunt continued its move into the art supply field when it sought to acquire the Bienfang Paper Company, based in Metuchen, New Jersey. This company manufactured special papers for use by artists. The purchase was completed in 1971, the year that Hunt offered stock to the public for the first time. In 1972, Hunt purchased the Pariscraft line of arts and crafts supplies from Johnson & Johnson.

Hunt continued its aggressive move into the arts and crafts field during this time, adding the Art-Brite Chemical Company, also located in New Jersey, to its fold. Hunt's line of office products was enhanced as well, with the addition of Lit-Ning Industries. This company had operations in Florence, Kentucky, and Fresno, California, and Hunt paid around $2 million for the entire package.

In 1979, Hunt consolidated its operations, moving its Bienfang paper manufacturing activities to Statesville, North Carolina. With this transfer, Bienfang's operations became far more profitable, and by the end of the year, Hunt reported net income of $3.2 million, increasing its earnings for the eighth straight year since selling stock to the public.

In 1980, Hunt earned 55 percent of its sales, and two-thirds of its earnings, from the 2,000 different items it sold for use in an office environment. These products ranged in price from a 25 cent Bulldog paper clip, to a $250 computer workstation desk. Tools for arts and crafts contributed 38 percent of Hunt's sales and 30 percent of its earnings. The remainder of the company's returns was filled out by its metal stamping factory, which created parts for use in a wide variety of goods, including pens and pencils, lipsticks, fishing tackle, automobiles, and appliances.

Also in 1980, Hunt signed a contract with Conte S.A. of France, winning the right to become the sole American distributor of

Conte's high-priced artists' charcoals and pastel pencils and crayons. Hunt finalized this agreement, which would make strong contributions to its bottom line, in August 1980.

As Hunt moved into the 1980s, the company continued its long streak of profitability, as demand for its staple items continued strong. In March 1981, Hunt paid $13.9 million for two properties previously owned by CBS Inc., the X-Acto company, which made hobby knives, and the House of Miniatures company, which sold dollhouse miniatures through the mails. Both were located in Long Island City, New York. At the time of this purchase, Hunt took on $15 million in debt, in order to increase its holding in the hobby and leisure products industry even further, since it believed that this market showed strong potential for growth. These expectations were met when revenues rose 31 percent, to reach $54 million over the first eight months of 1981.

"Ten years ago, we set sales and earnings growth objectives of 25 percent a year, and we haven't missed them by much," Hunt vice-president, treasurer, and secretary Rudolph M. Peins, Jr., told *Barron's* in late 1981. Although demand for Hunt's goods had softened somewhat during that time, the company looked to newly invigorated sales in its arts and crafts division for further growth. A new line of craft kits, first introduced by Hunt in 1980, proved popular, as customers snapped up the $30 sets for painting, calligraphy, silk-screening, and several other craft projects. The following year, the company added ten new kits, some priced as high as $40, and laid plans to add six more in 1982.

Hunt also profited from increased sales of a new line of office furniture. The company's CommuniCore computer and word-processing workstations came in 12 different types and sizes, and cost between $40 and $250. In addition, Hunt successfully marketed a number of computer accessories, including swivel stands and storage holders.

Despite the importance of Hunt's new product offerings, the company's most important item remained the pencil sharpener. "As long as there's one person in an office using a pencil, that office will need a pencil sharpener, so sales are more a function of the number of offices in operation than the number of pencils in use," Peins explained to *Barron's*.

By the end of 1982, Hunt's sales had reached $78 million, contributing $4.8 million in income. At this time, the company's long-time leader, George E. Bartol III, was nearing retirement. Although he had four children, none were interested in following in his footsteps and taking over the family business. In order to ensure an orderly transition in Hunt's management, Bartol recruited a successor from outside his family and set out to prepare him to assume leadership of the company. Bartol's designated heir was Ronald J. Naples, who assumed the title of chief executive in the early 1980s.

In April 1982, Bartol retired as Hunt's chairman, and the 37-year-old Naples became the company's vice-chairman, assuming day-to-day control of Hunt. The purpose of this transition was to make it possible for Hunt to undertake a spurt of rapid growth. "A 61-year-old man probably wouldn't be as effective in a company committed to that kind of growth as someone who is under 40," Bartol told *Forbes*. To symbolize his departure

from intimate involvement with the affairs of the company, Bartol planned to move out of his large office at Hunt's company headquarters. "My role will be to provide advice and counsel. It's a tough role to play," Bartol noted.

Hunt's plan for rapid growth was based on further expansion in the market of peripheral equipment for computers. Demand for its main products, conventional office supplies, was not expected to exceed seven percent over the next decade, as many of Hunt's products had already saturated their markets. In addition, Hunt looked to rapid growth in the market for objects used during leisure time, such as the arts and crafts supplies Hunt produced. The company planned to expand its offerings in this area, primarily through further acquisitions of other companies.

In order to support further growth in Hunt's revenues, Bartol planned to liquidate some of his family's block of the company's stock, but not enough that an outside investor could threaten his ultimate control over the company. "We don't want management being sniped at by unfriendly acquirers if the company has a bad year because of investments or something beyond its control," Bartol asserted. Bartol's decision to retain his interest in Hunt, while relinquishing control over the company, reflected his confidence that his company was the soundest possible place to keep his money. "We are not going to sell because we don't think there's a better investment out there. This company's potential is terrific. We want to grow sales to $500 million and then maybe to $1 billion," he remarked in *Forbes*.

Toward that end, Hunt raised additional investment capital in 1983, when its stock began to be traded on the New York Stock Exchange. The company also divested its only branch that did not fall into the office products or arts and crafts fields: the Peterson Manufacturing Company. This property, which produced metal parts for other products, was sold in 1983.

The following year, Hunt made a move to expand its holdings in the computer supply field, when it offered $18 million for Innovative Concepts, a manufacturer of floppy disk parts, in August 1984. By September of that year, however, the deal had been called off. A month later, Hunt announced that it would seek immediate growth in its revenues not through this purchase, but through stepped up marketing efforts and new product introductions.

In April 1985, Hunt consolidated its operations further at its North Carolina manufacturing facility, when it moved its X-Acto operations to Statesville. Later that year, Hunt forged ahead with its quest for acquisitions, citing the need for sizable purchases to fuel its ambitious growth plans in a profile in *Mergers* magazine. In July 1985, the company announced that it would buy Bevis Custom Tables, a maker of low-priced office furniture based in Florence, Alabama, for $12 million. Hunt then changed that company's name to Bevis Custom Furniture. With the Bevis acquisition, Hunt doubled its sales of office products the following year, and the company was able to pay off more than half of the money it had borrowed to buy Bevis within 12 months. On July 30, 1985, Hunt also acquired Marketing Ventures Associates, Inc., for $1.1 million. With this move, the company brought the Executive Gallery, Inc., of Columbus, Ohio, into the Hunt corporate fold.

By the end of 1985, after a spurt of acquisitions, Hunt's revenues had surpassed $100 million for the first time. The following year, Hunt trimmed back its operations somewhat, selling off two divisions. Both the company's costly House of Miniatures mail-order operation and the Executive Gallery, Inc., purchased just the year before, were divested. The financial penalty Hunt paid for this move caused the company's earnings to drop for the first time in 18 years.

Also in 1986, Hunt augmented the product offerings of its Bienfang art papers unit, purchasing $5 million worth of machinery to manufacture half-inch foam board at its Statesville factory. With this equipment, the company was able to plate, heat treat, and die cast the foam boards, used for mounting art work and framing. "There's an art to manufacturing foam board," Peins explained to *Barron's,* adding that "It was a big step for us and there was a lot we had to teach ourselves."

In addition, Hunt strengthened its management team in 1986, appointing Robert B. Fritsch as chief operating officer. The following year, Fritsch became president and director of the board, and Naples took over Bartol's posts of chairman and CEO, as the company moved forward with its transfer of power from one generation to the next. By the end of 1986, Hunt's sales had risen to $136.7 million.

With its newly consolidated management structure, Hunt returned to the acquisitions track in 1987. At that time, the company expanded its product line by picking up the American and Canadian stapler product lines of Acco World Corporation for $13.4 million. By 1987, nearly 40 percent of the 10,000 items that the company offered had been introduced within the last five years. "If we're going to remain competitive, we've got to upgrade constantly," Peins told *Barron's.*

Hunt looked particularly to its expanded line of personal home computer workstations and modular mail rooms for further sales growth, as demand for these products grew rapidly. The company also hoped that the growing pool of retired people, driven by the aging of the baby boomers, would enhance demand for its leisure-time arts and crafts supplies.

Hunt also benefited in 1987 from the falling exchange rate of the dollar. This helped to push up sales of its products in foreign markets by nearly one-third; at the time, Hunt products were exported to 63 countries, including Canada, Japan, South America, and the Far East.

In the late 1980s, Hunt acquired the Data Products Division of the Amaray International Corporation for $5.4 million in cash, as well as three graphic arts businesses from Bunzl PLC for $37 million. The three companies—Seal Products, Inc., Ademco, Ltd., and parts of the Coated Specialties, Ltd. company—all marketed products for use in mounting and laminating artwork. Hunt also bought a distribution company in Germany.

As Hunt moved into the 1990s, it's search for suitable acquisitions with which to expand its business intensified. The company continued to add new products to its line, and in August 1993, it bought the Image Technologies Corporation, located in Cottage Grove, Wisconsin. By the end of 1993, Hunt's sales had grown to $256 million. With a nearly unblemished record of steady growth, and a strong financial footing, Hunt appeared to be assured of continued success as it moved into the late 1990s.

Principal Subsidiaries: Hunt Holdings, Inc.; Hunt X-Acto, Inc.; Bevis Custom Furniture, Inc.; Seal Products, Inc.; Hunt Europe, Limited (U.K.).

Further Reading:

Brown, Paul B., "The King Abdicates," *Forbes,* February 14, 1983, p. 88.
Gordon, Mitchell, "Hold Punchers to Pencil Sharpeners," *Barron's,* October 26, 1981, pp. 44, 49.
Leibowitz, David S., "Let's Hear It for Boring," *Financial World,* November 24, 1992, p. 84.
Werner, Thomas, "Crafty Acquisitor," *Barron's,* July 27, 1987. p. 37.

—Elizabeth Rourke

Idaho Power Company

P.O. Box 70
Boise, Idaho 83707
U.S.A.
(208) 388-2200
Fax: (208) 388-6910

Public Company
Incorporated: 1915
Employees: 1,609
Sales: $543.7 million
Stock Exchanges: New York Pacific
SICs: 4911 Electric Services

Providing power to southern Idaho for much of the twentieth century, Idaho Power Company propelled the progress of the territory and grew to become one of the leading utility companies in the United States. With 17 hydroelectric plants, part-ownership in three coal-fired generating plants, and a diesel-fired power facility, Idaho Power served more than 330,000 customers in a 20,000 square-mile service area, which consisted of southern Idaho, northern Nevada, and eastern Oregon.

Idaho Power Company was created as a regional utility company in 1915. Idaho Power was an amalgamation of the smaller local utilities that served Idaho's residential, industrial, and business customers. At one point there were 50 of these small predecessor power companies in Idaho, the oldest of which dated back to 1887. Shortly before the formation of Idaho Power these 50 were combined into five companies. On May 6, 1915, Idaho Power was incorporated and assumed ownership of the electric systems of Idaho-Oregon Light & Power Company, Idaho Railway, Light & Power Company, Idaho Power & Light Company, Southern Idaho Water Power Company, and Great Shoshone & Twin Falls Water Power Company. Fourteen months later, on August 1, 1916, Idaho Power commenced operations. Idaho Power's first year of operations brought $1.1 million in revenues and $558,000 in net earnings.

When Idaho Power began, hydroelectricity was a novel type of power that was particularly well suited for the Snake River, the largest river in Idaho Power's territory. Befitting its name, the Snake River cut a meandering 400-mile path through Idaho Power's territory, flowing from the corner of the Washington-Oregon border, then twisting into Wyoming, and dropping 2,500 feet during its circuitous route through Idaho.

With the companies Idaho Power had purchased upon incorporation, Idaho Power had acquired five hydroelectric developments along the Snake River and two additional plants along two of the Snake River's tributaries, the Malad and the Payette Rivers. In addition to these generating facilities the company leased two hydroelectric plants, giving it roughly 39,000 horsepower of generating capacity with which to feed through the company's 933 miles of transmission lines that linked together 57 substations. With this superstructure, Idaho Power served an estimated 150,000 people. The increase in the population in Idaho Power's territory would largely determine the company's growth throughout the century.

Even though Idaho Power operated as a monopoly in its territory, Idaho Power did not function without competitors. Idaho Power's business was dependent on nature and Idaho state's growth. Throughout its history, Idaho Power would fall victim to the whims of nature, an ungovernable reality of operating as a hydroelectric utility. Unusually dry weather drove costs up and decreased the utilities' ability to make power. Dry weather meant less snow on the mountain peaks of eastern Idaho and western Wyoming, less water run-off into the Snake River, and less hydroelectric energy produced at a greater cost. Nearly as uncontrollable as the weather was the growth of Idaho. Although any type of business inherently depends on the growth and economic vitality of its community, Idaho Power's dependence ran much deeper, Idaho's growth represented the chief dictate directing the company's growth. Idaho Power thus played the dual role of utility company and promoter of the quality of life in Idaho.

As the population of Idaho Power's territory grew, the company needed to generate more power. Idaho Power increased its generating capacity for the first three decades after its incorporation mainly by acquiring other utilities. Idaho Power acquired Thousands Springs Power Company in 1917. In 1928, the company acquired the utility operating property of Vale Power Company and Murtaugh Light & Power Company, the Salmon River Power & Light Company in 1935, the Nevada Power Company the following year, the Idaho properties of West Coast Power Company in 1944, the Jordan Valley Electric Cooperative in 1945, the Long Valley Power Cooperative in 1946, and the Malheur Cooperative Electric Association in 1949. As the company slowed its rate of acquisitions in 1950, Idaho Power's revenues had reached $14.7 million. Idaho Power recorded that it generated 1.5 billion kilowatt hours that year.

Perhaps more important to the long-term vitality of the company was that the growth recorded did not come at the expense of efficiency. Idaho Power employed two fewer people in 1968 than in 1950 (1,195 compared to 1,197), yet by the late 1960s the company conducted 4.5 times more business than in 1950. In the late 1960s Idaho Power brought in nearly $70 million in revenue and generated seven billion kilowatt hours. This enviable record of growth was aided by larger generating units and the beginning of plant automation, but one factor that greatly contributed to Idaho Power's substantial leap in power generation between 1950 and 1968 was an enormous construction project undertaken by the utility.

Though Idaho Power mainly had increased its generating capacity through acquisition before 1950, it had also constructed some new facilities. In Twin Falls in 1935, Idaho Power built a 10-megawatt plant. In 1955, however, Idaho Power embarked on the largest and most ambitious construction project of the company's history. Construction of the Hells Canyon Development would last 12 years, add three dams and plants to Idaho Power's growing superstructure, and dramatically increase its generating capacity. Located on a nearly inaccessible 40-mile stretch of the Snake River, Hells Canyon, the deepest gorge in North America, towered as high as a mile on either side of the river. The canyon's depth created myriad engineering and logistical problems for work crews attempting to harness the river's power. When the last dam was completed in 1967, however, the reward was well worth the labor. The addition of the Brownlee, Oxbow, and Hells Canyon dams quadrupled Idaho Power's generating capacity, raising it to 1.5 million kilowatts and prepared the utility to handle increased electrical demand in the future.

Initially, Idaho Power sold Utah Power & Light Company, a neighboring utility, the surplus energy generated by the Hells Canyon Development. Demand for electricity soon increased within Idaho Power's service territory, however, and the utility used all the power it generated. The demand for more power within Idaho Power's territory came with the increasing popularity of electric energy. During the construction of the Hells Canyon Development projects, new home builders installed electric heat apparatuses into their structures. In 1962, 17 percent of all new homes in Idaho Power's service area were outfitted with electric heat. As all three Hells Canyon dams operated to meet the utility's demand in 1968, nearly 54 percent of new homes contained electric heating systems. Demand for electricity was increasing in the late 1960s; 82 percent of all new apartment units installed electric heat, more than 60 percent of all new schools were installing electric heat, and two new college campuses were completely outfitted with electric heat. Idaho Power's management sought additional sources of power to meet increasing demand.

In addition to the increasing demand for household electricity, Idaho Power had to meet the increasing demand for industrial power. For years the mainstay industries in Idaho were potato farming, lumbering, and phosphate rock mining, but in the 1970s a new industry emerged in Idaho, attracted in large part by the relatively inexpensive hydroelectric power provided by Idaho Power. This new type of industrial customer was the electronics industry, lured by hydroelectric power rates that averaged roughly a third of those incurred by electronics manufacturers based in California's Silicon Valley.

As demand for Idaho Power's services grew so did its revenues. From 1965 to 1975, the utility's revenues more than doubled, rising from $52 million to more than $100 million, while per share profits increased 83 percent. In addition, by 1975, the company had paid a dividend every year since 1917. Complementing this solid financial performance, Idaho Power had added to its generating capacity in 1974 by opening the first of

three large coal-fired generating plants. Two more would be opened before the end of the decade, in addition to a new generating plant at the company's American Falls development in 1978 and the installation of a fifth hydro unit at Brownlee Dam two years later.

Nevertheless, the late 1970s would be primarily remembered as one of the most difficult times in the utility's history. A drought in 1977 brought with it the worst water conditions on record. As a result, Idaho Power, almost entirely dependent on adequate water supply to generate its power, incurred serious damages. The utility was forced to ask its customers to curtail usage and to replace its hydro power with expensive thermal power. By the following year, however, thanks to the return of water to the region, the company had rebounded well. In 1978, Idaho Power connected 11,140 new residential customers, the largest yearly gain in the company's history, and per share earnings climbed 35 percent.

As Idaho Power entered the 1990s, another severe drought negatively affected the company's financial performance. The drought lingered on throughout the early 1990s, compounding the debilitative effects of a concurrent nationwide recession that stifled Idaho's economic growth. The company's business and industrial customers, hurt from the poor economic conditions, curtailed usage. Idaho Power's financial performance languished as a result. Both the drought and the recession began to ebb by 1993 and Idaho Power recorded a resurgence, a 41 percent increase in the utility's net income from 1992 to 1993. Adding greatly to the optimism pervading the utility's management was the economic revival of Idaho Power's industrial customers, particularly the utility's electronics customers such as Hewlett-Packard, Micron Technology, Zilog, and American Microsystems.

As Idaho Power and its customers noted the improvements in the economy, Idaho Power gained license to protect itself against future power production cost fluctuations. In 1993 the Idaho Public Utilities Commission approved Idaho Power's request for a power cost adjustment (PCA), enabling the utility to adjust its power rates annually to reflect changes in power supply costs. By implementing this mechanism Idaho Power mitigated to a great extent its dependence on favorable water conditions, since a PCA allowed the utility to raise power rates when hydroelectric production declined and power costs rose.

The approval of Idaho Power's PCA fueled the company's optimism for the future, enabling Idaho Power's management to more accurately plot the company's future course. As the utility entered the mid-1990s, Idaho's population was expected to increase nearly 50 percent during the next 20 years. In addition, the future promised to bring more deregulation and with it a more competitive environment for Idaho Power. As one of the country's lowest cost producers of electricity, Idaho Power stood well-positioned as it entered the late 1990s.

Principal Subsidiaries: Idaho Energy Resources Co.; Idaho Utility Products Co.; IDACORP, INC.; Ida-West Energy Company.

Further Reading:

Ely, Owen, "Idaho Power Company," *The Commercial and Financial Chronicle,* September 28, 1967, p. 12.

"Idaho Power Company," *Wall Street Transcript,* November 8, 1982, p. 67,711.

"Idaho Power Company," *Wall Street Transcript,* May 21, 1979, p. 54,405

"Idaho Power Company," *Wall Street Transcript,* February 22, 1971, p. 23,275.

"Idaho Power Company," *Wall Street Transcript,* October 20, 1969, p. 18,267.

"Idaho Power Company," *Wall Street Transcript,* August 26, 1968, p. 14,189.

"Idaho Power Elects Carlsen to Added Post of Chairman," *Wall Street Journal,* May 7, 1971, p. 14.

"Idaho Power's O'Connor Gets Chairmanship as Well," *Wall Street Journal,* July 10, 1987, p. 10.

"What's So Special About Idaho Power?," *Financial World,* September 10, 1975, p. 14.

—Jeffrey L. Covell

IMPERIAL HOLLY CORPORATION

Imperial Holly Corporation

One Imperial Square, Suite 200
8016 Highway 90-A
Sugar Land, Texas 77478
U.S.A.
(713) 491-9181
Fax: (713) 242-6850

Public Company
Incorporated: 1924 as Imperial Sugar Company
Employees: 1,600
Sales: $660 million
Stock Exchanges: American
SICs: 2062 Cane Sugar Refining; 2063 Beet Sugar

One of the leading sugar producers in the United States, Imperial Holly Corporation refines raw cane sugar in Texas and processes beet sugar in California, Wyoming, Montana, and Texas. Imperial Holly traces its history back to 1843, when a sugar refinery was erected on a small sugar plantation in Sugar Land, Texas. The fledgling sugar enterprise grew as the nation grew, adopted the name Imperial Sugar Company during the early twentieth century, then merged in 1988 with Holly Sugar Company—a beet sugar producer with roots stretching back to 1905. Together, these two companies represented one of the largest and oldest sugar producers in the country.

In 1820, a rush of Anglo-American settlers began colonizing the vast region that 25 years later would become the state of Texas. Through the recruiting efforts of Moses and Stephen Austin, who promised to carry out their father's plan to populate the territory, Texas's population swelled enormously in the years following 1820, jumping from 7,000 in 1821 to 50,000 by 1836—by far exceeding Stephen Austin's promise to bring at least 300 families into the area. Texas became an independent republic in 1835, and its citizens voted the following year in favor of annexation by the United States. Statehood would be another nine years away, however, delayed as lawmakers debated whether or not to extend slavery into the new region. Another 60 years would pass before oil, the chief engine that would drive the state's economy, first erupted from a well near Beaumont, Texas. During the six decades that separated Texas's admittance to the Union and the discovery of oil, other agricultural and manufacturing industries fueled the region's growth, including the cultivation and processing of sugar cane.

Although the first sugar refinery in the United States began operations in 1689, sugar production did not become a major U.S. industry until the 1830s. Early settlers into Texas took up the trade upon their arrival. One such colonist was Samuel May Williams, who owned a sugar crop on Oakland Plantation in Southeast Texas in a community that later would be aptly named Sugar Land. Initially, the sugar cane was used to produce syrupy sweeteners, but by 1843—two years before Texas became a U.S. state—Williams and other neighboring farmers were harvesting sufficient sugar cane to warrant the construction of a commercial raw sugar mill. Completed that same year, the mill enabled the cooperative of sugar farmers to make granulated sugar. Imperial Sugar Company was spawned from this first mill, with the site Williams chose for Sugar Land's first sugar refinery serving as the site of Imperial Holly's sugar production over the next 150 years.

Before long, Williams's Oakland Plantation and the mill were sold to W. J. Kyle and B. F. Terry, under whose stewardship the property became known as Sugar Land Plantation, one of several sugar cane farms in a region referred to as the "sugar bowl." Kyle and Terry profited from their investment, as Sugar Land Plantation flourished in the years leading up to the Civil War, but the outbreak of the war signalled more prosaic growth for many of the sugar bowl's farmers. Once the war ended, sugar production in the region declined considerably and the number of sugar mills dropped to slightly more than a handful.

After the deaths of Kyle and Terry, Sugar Land Plantation and a majority of the other plantations in the area that had withstood the effects of the depressed agricultural climate were purchased by Edward H. Cunningham. Cunningham spent a considerable amount of money modernizing Sugar Land Plantation, investing more than a million dollars in machinery and construction projects by 1890. Slightly more than a decade later, however, Cunningham's holdings devolved into receivership and were stripped away from him by disgruntled and unpaid creditors. Sugar Land Plantation, along with the other properties formerly belonging to Cunningham, was acquired in 1906 by I. H. Kempner, his mother, and siblings, as well as W. T. Eldridge.

In the nearly 60 years since the first sugar mill was erected in Sugar Land, the property had passed through three sets of hands, and now, with the arrival of the new century, Kempner and Eldridge had become its fourth owners. There it would stay, remaining in the Kempner family for the next 80 years. I. H. Kempner and his descendants steered the company through its development from a small collection of sugar production properties to one of the largest sugar producers in the United States.

Kempner and Eldridge, like Cunningham, poured capital into their newly acquired properties, renovating the sugar production facilities and the community of Sugar Land itself. Toward the end of the nineteenth century Sugar Land was ignominiously branded "Hell Hole of the Brazos"—a swampy area populated by ex-convicts, drifters, professional gamblers, and deserters from ships sailing to and from the port of Galveston. Kempner and Eldridge sought to ameliorate this disreputable image of their town by draining the land and paving new gravel streets. In the process, Sugar Land became a company town, managed by the company, with company-owned stores—such as the Imperial Mercantile Company general store—catering to the residents. Later, churches, hospitals, and schools were constructed, additions that attracted more respectable Sugar Land denizens and gave Kempner and Eldridge a community upon which to build their sugar empire.

The sugar properties owned by Kempner and Eldridge were known as Sugarland Industries until 1924. At that time, Imperial Sugar Company—the predecessor to Imperial Holly Corporation—was incorporated to take over the properties owned by Sugarland Industries, including Sugar Land Feed Company and Imperial Mercantile Company. The name "Imperial" came from New York City's Hotel Imperial, one of the lavish hotels that graced the city's Herald Square in the 1890s. As a college student, Kempner had visited the hotel, been impressed by it, and decided to borrow its name as the name of his sugar company, co-opting the crown symbol from the hotel's stationery as well.

Imperial's sugar refinery by this point could produce 1.5 million pounds of sugar per day, a production capacity that required the importation of raw sugar from Cuba and the West Indies to keep the facility in operation throughout the year. Raw sugar was shipped to Galveston, unloaded in 300-pound burlap bags, then sent by rail to the refinery at Sugar Land, where granulated sugar was packaged in 25-, 50-, and 100-pound cloth bags bearing the Imperial brand name. By 1927, the company was producing slightly more than 300 million pounds of sugar per year and annual revenues had climbed to nearly $19 million. These results were encouraging, but the company would not eclipse these figures until the eve of World War II.

When the Great Depression descended on the country, stifling economic growth and forcing many businesses into bankruptcy, Imperial Sugar was not immune to its effects. The company's yearly sugar production and revenue totals both dropped substantially during the decade-long economic downturn. Revenues plunged from $18.8 million in 1927 to $6.3 million in 1932, while annual sugar production during the period fell from 219 million pounds to 165 million pounds—exceeding the magnitude of the recessive conditions following the Civil War. Moreover, the decline recorded between 1929 and 1932 did not represent the end of Imperial Sugar's financial woes. As the Depression dragged on into the mid-1930s, the company went into the red and was forced to cut its work force from 500 to 373. Imperial Sugar lost money every year between 1932 and 1937, recording its greatest loss in 1932, when the company showed nearly $300,000 in negative net income, down from the $750,000 gain it had posted in 1928.

Despite the losses, Imperial Sugar—through a wholly owned subsidiary named Fort Bend Utilities Company—spent $300,000 on a power plant, which supplied the sugar producer's energy needs. When the power plant was completed in 1937, the company was beginning to emerge from the effects of the Depression, generating $15.9 million in revenues that year and $19.7 million the following year, at last eclipsing the total recorded in 1927. Annual sugar production increased as well, climbing to nearly 400 million pounds in 1938, offering persuasive proof that the hard times were over.

After the war, the Eldridges sold their stake in Imperial Sugar and the Kempners became majority owners of the company,

which by the end of the 1940s was recording nearly one million dollars a year in net income. The production capacity of the refinery at Sugar Land by this time had been increased to two million pounds per day, and by a decade later reached 2.25 million pounds per day, as the company expanded to meet rising demand during the postwar economic boom period. During the 1950s, Imperial Sugar's financial performance fluctuated wildly, partly due to President Eisenhower's embargo against Cuba, then the company's principal source of raw sugar. The company's annual net income wavered between $395,000 and $1.2 million during the decade, which hinted at more difficult years to come.

Since the beginning of the century, the sugar industry had been subjected to federal regulation which, as time wore on, threatened to price sugar out of the U.S. market. During the 1960s and 1970s, as regulatory measures continued to inflate the price of domestic raw sugar, Imperial Sugar avoided much of the damage incurred by sugar producers located elsewhere. The migration of candy factories and bottlers into the Sun Belt during the period buoyed the company's business. By the end of the 1970s, however, the sugar industry had changed significantly and Imperial Sugar's position began to appear tenuous.

Sugar use experienced a precipitous decline during the 1970s, falling even as total sweetener consumption remained steady. From 1973 to 1983, Americans consumed 124 pounds of sweetener per person annually, yet sugar's share dropped from 107 pounds of the annual total to 71 pounds during the ten-year period. Corn sweeteners moved into the breach, increasing in usage by 130 percent. Exacerbating matters for sugar cane processors was the burgeoning popularity of artificial sweeteners such as saccharin and aspartame, as well as the rising price of domestic raw sugar. By the early 1980s, domestic raw sugar sold for 22 cents a pound, double the world market price. Imperial Sugar's management, now led by I. H. Kempner III, searched for a solution to the difficulties that lay ahead.

Imperial Sugar by this time was generating roughly $230 million a year in revenue, recording nearly $13 million a year in net income, and producing nearly a billion pounds of sugar annually. The totals were prodigious for a producer in the U.S. sugar industry, but they also reflected the uncertainties of a business derived exclusively from the refining of sugar cane. What the company lacked was a stake in those segments of the sugar market that were expanding, including companies that produced sugar from stock feed other than sugar cane. The realization of this need brought Imperial Sugar's management in contact with Holly Sugar Company, a producer that used sugar beets instead of sugar cane to make sugar. The resulting association between the two companies would alter Imperial Sugar's future dramatically.

In 1905, one year before Kempner and Eldridge acquired Sugar Land Plantation, the first Holly Sugar factory was constructed in Holly, Colorado, just in time for the sugar beet harvest that year. From the harvest the fledgling company produced 60,000 100-pound bags of sugar, enough to justify and help pay for the addition of a second factory in Swink, Colorado. Several years later, in 1911, expansion continued, this time across state borders into California, where Holly Sugar constructed a beet sugar factory in Huntington Beach. A year after the company extended the geographic scope of its business into Wyoming in 1915, a wealthy Colorado businessman named A. E. Carlton acquired the company and spearheaded its subsequent vigorous growth. Either through acquisition or plant construction, Holly Sugar added ten factories to its growing list of facilities between 1916 and 1931. As the company expanded its sugar beet operations, it also diversified into other business arenas, including livestock feeding operations and oil production and refining. By the mid-1980s, however, as Imperial Sugar was weighing its future moves in an increasingly volatile sugar market, Holly Sugar had been forced to close 12 beet sugar factories and divest its other business interests.

Imperial Sugar's management began actively courting Holly Sugar in 1987, convinced that the two companies would be more capable of competing in the sugar industry together than they would be apart. In October 1987, Imperial offered to pay Holly Sugar's stockholders $68 for each of Holly Sugar's 1.1 million outstanding shares, in addition to giving them one share in the combined company, which would cede a 23 percent stake in the merger to Holly Sugar's stockholders. Imperial Sugar's offer, however, was not the only one Holly Sugar's management had to consider.

Just prior to Imperial Sugar's attempt at effecting a merger between the two companies, a Melville, New York-based investment group named Plum Associates, led by Illinois businessman Peter R. Harvey, offered Holly Sugar a $94.3 million, two-stage takeover plan. Holly Sugar initially rebuffed Imperial Sugar's proposal, favoring instead Plum Associates' offer, but before two months had passed, Plum Associates cut its tender offer to $85 million. As a result, negotiations with Imperial Sugar resumed, leading to a definitive agreement between the two in December 1987 that stipulated Imperial Sugar would acquire Holly Sugar for $78.5 million plus cede a 25 percent stake in the merged company. The following April, Holly Sugar's shareholders approved the merger, joining together Holly Sugar's eight beet sugar processing facilities—four in

California, two in Wyoming, and one in each Montana and Texas—and Imperial Sugar's Sugar Land refinery, which created a new $660 million sugar concern named Imperial Holly Corporation.

After the merger, Imperial Holly's annual revenues initially rose to $717 million in 1990, but then the company recorded consecutive declines in 1991, 1992, and 1993. Entering the mid-1990s, Imperial Holly continued to suffer from external market forces that prevented the company from realizing the true benefits of the 1988 merger. The most damaging of these developments continued to be the depressed prices for refined sugar, which fell 11 percent between 1989 and 1994. More unexpected were losses resulting from adverse weather and disease in 1994, which froze beets in the Midwest and infected them in California, contributing to the $7.9 million loss the company recorded in 1994.

As Imperial Holly plotted its course beyond the mid-1990s, it looked forward to the return of more favorable market conditions. Despite the adverse conditions the company faced, however, it remained a formidable presence in the sugar industry, as a result of more than 150 years of development.

Principal Subsidiaries: Holly Sugar Co.; Fort Bend Utilities Co.; CSCO Inc.; Imperial Sweetener Distributors, Inc.

Further Reading:
Baldwin, William, "Bitter Taste," *Forbes,* November 7, 1983, p. 128.
"Imperial Sugar Agrees to Buy Holly for Cash and a Portion of Stock," *Wall Street Journal,* December 28, 1987, p. 24.
"Shareholders Approve Merger with Texas Sugar Concern," *Wall Street Journal,* April 27, 1988, p. 7.
"Sugar Processor Cuts Payout by Two-Thirds, Sets Layoffs," *Wall Street Journal,* October 29, 1993, p. B9A.
Totty, Michael, "Holly Sugar Receives Bid by Texas Firm," *Wall Street Journal,* October 13, 1987, p. 4.

—Jeffrey L. Covell

Ingalls Shipbuilding

Ingalls Shipbuilding, Inc.

P.O. Box 149
Pascagoula, Mississippi 39568-0149
U.S.A.
(601) 935-1122
Fax: (601) 935-1126

Wholly Owned Subsidiary of Litton Industries, Inc.
Incorporated: 1938
Employees: 13,000
Sales: $1.46 billion
SICs: 3731 Shipbuilding and Repairing

Ingalls Shipbuilding, a division of Litton Industries, is a leading supplier and servicer of marine vessels to the United States Navy and also builds ships for some allied navies. With approximately 14,000 employees, Ingalls was Mississippi's largest employer and one of the most financially healthy shipyards in the United States going into the mid-1990s. The company has played an important role in the U.S. defense industry since World War II.

Ingalls Shipbuilding was established in 1938 by the Ingalls Iron Works of Birmingham, Alabama. At the time, the iron works wanted to build a new shipyard to serve a growing market for cargo and passenger ships. As it needed a location with access to a deep water channel, a railroad, and a large and willing work force, company representatives approached the city of Pascagoula, Mississippi, about building the new shipyard on its river bank. City officials eagerly supported the proposal and even approved a $100,000 bond issue to help develop the site. Ingalls Shipbuilding was officially incorporated in 1938 and production of ships started within a year, thus initiating a legacy of shipbuilding innovation and success that would span the remainder of the twentieth century.

Ingalls Shipbuilding's first vessel was the SS *Exchequer,* a cargo ship launched on October 16, 1940. The ship was unique because it was the first one in the world to sport an all-welded steel hull. Prior to the SS *Exchequer,* ship hulls were created by overlapping steel plates and attaching them with rivets. In contrast, Ingalls welded the steel plates end-to-end, which resulted in a much more durable hull. The innovation, which became the global standard, is credited with revolutionizing ship design. During 1940 and 1941, Ingalls launched three more cargo ships, and the venture was considered an early success.

Ingalls's business changed radically with the onset of World War II, as the shipyard put its commercial operations on hold and shifted into high gear for the war effort. Indeed, throughout the early 1940s Ingalls operated around the clock building all types of ships for the U.S. military. As production surged and the traditional Ingalls work force was depleted as its young men went off to war, women were called on to replace them. Vera Anderson, for example, became the company's own version of "Rosie the Riveter," according to company annals, and even went on to become a national welding champion.

The first ship Ingalls completed for the war effort was the USS *Arthur Middleton,* a combat loaded transport launched in December 1941. Ingalls finished five more ships in 1942, including two aircraft carriers, before completing a total of 20 vessels during 1943. Throughout World War II, Ingalls built more than 60 ships ranging from submarine tenders and aircraft carriers to troopships and net layers. Many of those ships returned to Ingalls after the war and were converted into commercial cargo ships—Ingalls constructed, in 1945 alone, a total of 22 commercial cargo ships, many of which were converted war vessels.

By 1945, after fewer than seven years in business, Ingalls had been catapulted to the status of a prominent U.S. shipyard and was able to boast a seasoned work force and relatively large production capacity. During the late 1940s and 1950s, Ingalls parlayed that status into a string of contracts to build commercial ships. Besides building cargo ships, Ingalls launched a variety of vessels ranging from oil tankers and ice breakers to tow boats and passenger ships. In the late 1950s, in fact, Ingalls completed two of the largest luxury passenger ships ever built: the SS *Brasil* and the SS *Argentina.* In addition to building ships, Ingalls branched out during the 1950s into manufacturing off-shore oil rigs, rail cars, tunnels, mobile drilling platforms, and even a locomotive, among other commercial equipment.

Ingalls focused on the booming commercial sector during the 1950s, but it wisely stayed active in the military side of the business; although military contracts nearly halted after World War II, the Cold War was just beginning, and the Navy would call for increasingly more vessels in the mid-1900s. In the early 1950s, Ingalls converted segments of its commercial shipbuilding operations into highly sophisticated production facilities designed to build Navy combat ships. Before the end of the decade, the high-tech operation had built five innovative tank landing ships as well as eight dock landing ships. More importantly, Ingalls launched two newly designed destroyers in 1959: the USS *Morton* and the USS *Parsons.* Technology developed for those ships formed the foundation for Ingalls's core market of building major surface combatants during the next three decades.

Also during the 1950s, Ingalls entered the submarine business. Realizing the importance and potential of nuclear technology, Ingalls modified two of its shipways in 1955 to accommodate submarine construction. The company also established a nuclear power division to develop atomic submarine technology, having already gained experience in submarine construction when it produced the country's last conventionally powered submarine, the USS *Blueback,* which it launched in 1960. In 1961, though, Ingalls completed two groundbreaking, high-tech nuclear submarines: the USS *Sculpin* and the USS *Snook.* Ingalls would deliver ten more of the vessels during the 1960s and early 1970s and would overhaul and refuel nine others, thoroughly establishing its leadership role in the development of advanced defense-related technology.

By the time it launched its nuclear submarines, Ingalls had grown into the third largest shipbuilder in the country. In 1961, Litton Industries, Inc. purchased the company for $8 million along with $9 million in assumed debt. Litton was a diversified conglomerate with an emphasis on high-tech industries. Founded in 1954 by Charles "Tex" Thornton, Litton had expanded rapidly by developing its own technologies and acquiring other firms. Thornton hoped to integrate his patented electronic technologies into Ingalls's submarine and oil-drilling equipment operations.

Ingalls's first move under the Litton umbrella was to begin the construction of a new, ultra-modern shipyard that could produce complex ships faster and more efficiently. In a unique arrangement, the state of Mississippi partnered with Litton to finance the new shipyard. Dubbed the "shipyard of the future" by Litton, the facility was begun in 1968 on the river bank facing Ingalls's original facility in Pascagoula. Litton's plan for the new facility was to utilize "inverted modular" construction techniques, in which entire sections of the ship would be built—including piping, electrical systems, and ventilation—and then assembled and installed on land prior to completing the hull.

Traditional shipbuilding entailed striking the keel and building the hull, and then outfitting the ship from the inside, a relatively slow and costly procedure. Although the advantage of modular shipbuilding techniques had been known since before World War II, no U.S. builders had adopted modular methods because of the space and cost required to set up modular manufacturing facilities. The new Ingalls shipyard was, and would remain into the 1990s, the only completely new shipyard of any kind to be built in the United States since World War II, and Litton hoped to thereby help give Ingalls a competitive advantage in the industry.

Besides building a giant new shipyard, Ingalls launched nearly 50 new types of ships and submarines during the 1960s. In addition to several cargo and container ships and nuclear submarines, the company completed an exploratory fishing vessel and an amphibious assault ship, among other projects. In 1969 and 1970, Ingalls landed two pivotal contracts. The first was for the design and construction of a series of new-generation amphibious assault ships. The second was a contract to build 30 high-tech "multimission" destroyers. The assignments—two of the largest Navy contracts ever awarded—were an important win for Ingalls and its new shipyard. Besides keeping its production facilities busy, the contracts also helped the company develop expertise related to surface combat ships that would give Ingalls a technological edge for years to come.

However, the new Ingalls shipyard faced several challenges during its early years. Although its first vessel, the SS *Austral Envoy*, set sail in September 1972, four years after construction on the shipyard had begun, the modular system of ship construction took longer to implement than expected. During this time, Ingalls began to experience delays in their production

schedules and budget overruns. Litton posted a string of losses in the early 1970s, attributed in part to the struggles of Ingalls.

In 1973, Litton jettisoned its chief executive, Roy Ash, and brought in engineer Fred O'Green, who brought Litton into shape during the remainder of the decade by eliminating nonperforming divisions and streamlining operations at Ingalls. During the late 1970s, in fact, Ingalls got its new shipyard running like clockwork, and the facility began living up to its parent company's expectations. By 1975, Ingalls was delivering high-tech destroyers and assault ships at the rate of one every six weeks. The company delivered the last eight units of its two pivotal Navy contracts at the rate of one per month, setting a new peacetime production record. Between 1975 and 1980, in fact, Ingalls delivered 60 percent of all the ships supplied the U.S. Navy and had to scramble during the period to hire and train its work force, which swelled to a peak of 25,000 in 1977.

Ingalls entered the 1980s poised to take advantage of emerging industry trends. Through its major defense contracts of the mid-1970s, the company had positioned itself on the forefront of naval shipbuilding technology. For example, it was using advanced computer-aided design and computer-aided manufacturing techniques and had achieved a marked competitive advantage with its inverted modular shipyard. Ingalls was also starting to make strides in automating shipbuilding procedures, which would reduce its labor-related costs during the decade. All of these advantages, combined with increased defense spending by the federal government, would allow Ingalls to achieve record profitability during the 1980s.

Ingalls's first major victory of the 1980s was the delivery of USS *Ticonderoga* in December 1982. The giant surface missile cruiser was delivered well ahead of the date specified in the original contract. More importantly, the *Ticonderoga* was representative of a new generation of ultra high-tech naval surface vessels for which Ingalls's production facilities were eminently qualified to produce. The *Ticonderoga* was outfitted with the Aegis radar system, which was designed to revolutionize the Navy's ability to protect its battle groups from missile attacks. The *Ticonderoga* also gave Ingalls a chance to showcase its cutting-edge engineering team and manufacturing operations. During the 1980s, Ingalls was awarded contracts to build 19 of the 27 ships built in the Navy's Aegis program.

In addition to a throng of Aegis guided missile cruisers, Ingalls produced a number of other commercial and military vessels. Importantly, much of its work during the decade was building drilling rigs, including two that were semisubmersible, for the oil industry. The company also delivered four guided missile destroyers, a high-tech cement barge, and five amphibious assault ships. In 1985, Ingalls landed an important Navy contract to design and construct a new class of amphibious assault ships to be delivered in the early 1990s. In 1987, moreover, Ingalls was asked to build one of a new class of destroyers labeled the Arleigh Burke class. The program, which became one of the largest in U.S. military history, was created to form a new type of craft that would give the United States a decisive edge through the end of the century.

In addition to a string of new construction projects, Ingalls continued to benefit during the 1980s from a steady flow of repair and modernization work. More important modernization programs included the installation of vertical-launch missile systems on Naval surface ships and the 1987 restoration of the USS *Stark* after it was severely damaged in a Persian Gulf missile attack. As Ingalls's workload grew, so did its bottom line. By the late 1980s, Ingalls was posting consecutive annual profits of more than $100 million. Annual sales were topping $1 billion. Improved profitability was partly the result of increased productivity, as evidenced by Ingalls's work force shrinkage to less than 15,000 by the early 1990s.

The shipbuilding industry slumped during the late 1980s and early 1990s. U.S. economic malaise combined with huge cuts in military spending sent industry profits tumbling. More than 70 percent of the shipbuilders in the United States were forced out of business or acquired by larger competitors. Due largely to its technological expertise and reputation, Ingalls Shipbuilding managed to emerge from the melee relatively unscathed. New Navy contracts slowed during the early 1990s, but Ingalls succeeded in landing several significant jobs. Importantly, the Navy continued to seek the high-tech, large ships produced by Ingalls, focusing its cutbacks on submarines and support vessels. Ingalls entered the 1990s with more than $1 billion of contracts scheduled for delivery during the early part of the decade.

To augment its defense-related work, Ingalls began to renew its efforts to enter the commercial shipbuilding industry. The company also began focusing on international expansion, particularly in Israel, Venezuela, Germany, and the Middle East, among other locations. Still, Ingalls continued to secure new Navy contracts going into the mid-1990s by sustaining its high-tech orientation and by working to improve its productivity. Ingalls delivered six new ships in 1994: three Aegis destroyers and one amphibious assault ship for the U.S. Navy, and two guided missile corvettes supplied to the Israeli Navy. Ingalls generated annual revenues of about $1.5 billion between 1992 and 1994, and profits of about $130 million to $140 million annually.

Further Reading:

Bergstrom, Robin P., ''The Hour When the Ship Comes In,'' *Production,* August 1991, p. 44.
Deady, Tim, ''Litton Sailing Right Along on Military Shipbuilding,'' *Los Angeles Business Journal,* July 27, 1992, p. 6.
Ingalls Shipbuilding Record, Pascagoula, Miss.: Ingalls Shipbuilding, 1988.

—Dave Mote

Interstate Bakeries Corporation

12 East Armour Boulevard
P.O. Box 419627
Kansas City, Missouri 64141-6627
U.S.A.
(816) 561-6600

Public Company
Incorporated: 1924
Employees: 14,000
Sales: $1.14 billion
SICs: 2051 Bread, Cake, and Related Products; 6719
   Holding Companies

The Interstate Bakeries Corporation is the largest independent American baker, producing breads and cakes in more than 60 bakeries across the United States. The company distributes its products under a wide range of brand names, which include Sunbeam bread, Dolly Madison cakes, and through a subsidiary, Wonder Bread and Hostess cakes. Founded in the 1930s, the company grew by acquiring other bakers around the country. In the late 1970s, it was purchased by a failing computer leasing firm, whose financial difficulties troubled the company well into the 1980s. By the start of the 1990s, however, after more than a decade of modernization, Interstate had recovered fully enough to take the lead in its industry by buying out its largest competitor.

Interstate, a company based in Kansas City, Missouri, was founded in 1930 by baker Ralph Leroy Nafziger. Nafziger came from a family of bakers, and he produced wholesale bread loaves packaged in a distinctive country-gingham wrapper, which were resold in grocery stores. Seven years after its incorporation, Interstate merged with another, much better-established Kansas City baker, the Schulze Baking Company, Inc., which had been founded in 1893. This move was the first of a series of acquisitions and mergers that Interstate undertook over the course of the next several decades, as the bread baking industry changed from a highly fragmented field, made up of a large number of small, independent, local operations, to a more consolidated industry, with a few big producers of national brands.

Interstate's next acquisition came at the end of 1943, when the company bought the Supreme Baking Company of Los Angeles, whose plant it had previously rented. Seven years later, the company also bought the O'Rourke Baking Company of Buffalo, New York. With the purchases, Interstate sought to extend its geographic coverage into new areas.

Interstate's growth through acquisitions remained steady throughout the 1950s. In 1951, the company bought Mrs. Karl's Bakeries, located in Milwaukee. Three years later, the company moved aggressively into the cake baking industry, purchasing the Ambrosia Cake Company, the Remar Baking Company, and the Butter Cream Baking Company. Four years later, Interstate also acquired the Campbell-Sell Baking Company, based in Denver, Colorado. At the end of the decade, Interstate added to its cake franchise, when it purchased the Kingston Cake Bakery, in Kingston, Pennsylvania.

In 1960, the company strengthened its standing in the Midwest, when it acquired Cobb's Sunlit Bakery, of Green Bay, Wisconsin. Over the next two years, Interstate purchased the Schall Tasty Baking Company of Traverse City, Michigan, and the Sweetheart Bread Company. Other important acquisitions during the 1960s included Hart's Bakeries, Inc. After its long period of steady expansion, Interstate also undertook a consolidation of its operations, closing some plants. The company's Buffalo bakery, once owned by O'Rourke's Baking Company, was sold. In addition, Interstate closed its Butter Cream Baking Company plant and its Schall Tasty Baking Company factory. At the end of that year, the company's net sales reached $191 million, up from $124 million in 1959, through a period of steady growth.

Interstate began to expand again in the late 1960s. In March 1968, the company bought the Millbrook bread division of the National Biscuit Company. This division included seven bakeries, located in upstate New York, which produced bread, rolls, cakes, and doughnuts for distribution throughout the region. In addition, Interstate took possession of a fleet of about 700 delivery vehicles in the acquisition. This brought Interstate's overall total of motor delivery trucks to about 4,000.

In August 1968, Interstate moved outside the baking industry for the first time, acquiring a food processor, the Baker Canning Company, and its subsidiaries, Shawano Farms, Inc., and the Shawano Canning Company, companies that canned peas, beans, and corn at three canneries in Wisconsin. Its products were sold mainly to institutions and were distributed through six warehouse facilities.

By the end of the 1960s, Interstate was baking bread in 30 different cities throughout the United States, in a total of 36 different plants. The company's regional strengths were in the Midwest, the West, and upstate New York. On July 25, 1969, Interstate changed its name to the Interstate Brands Corporation, to reflect the broader scope of its activities, which now included canning as well as baking. The company had become the third largest wholesale baker in America. Its best known products were the Butternut and Blue Seal bread brands, and Dolly Madison cakes, which were distributed across the country. Interstate sold its canning operation in 1974 and resumed acquisition of properties that fit in with its core line of business, baking. In December of that year, Interstate bought Nolde Brothers, Inc., for $500,000.

Then, in 1975, Interstate became the object of an acquisition itself. The company's unwanted suitor was founded in 1961 as the Data Processing Financial and General Corporation, based in Hartsdale, New York, a suburb of White Plains, where the International Business Machines Corporation (IBM) was located. Data Processing, which changed its name to DPF, Inc. in 1971, leased IBM computers to other businesses throughout the 1960s. In 1970, IBM introduced a new computer model, and DPF's equipment instantly became obsolete. The company lost $43 million over the next five years, until it finally got back on its feet in 1974 and began to look for a company to acquire that would allow it to diversify its activities, since the computer leasing field no longer seemed tenable, as IBM continued to step up its pace of new product introductions.

In 1975, DPF decided that Interstate Brands would be a good business to buy. "We wanted a sober, solid, low-technology business," DPF's chairman later told *Forbes*. In June, DPF offered to buy 43 percent of the outstanding shares of Interstate. Immediately, the baker sued to block the acquisition, but its request was denied. Interstate Brands then, in turn, announced that it would purchase Farmbest Foods, a dairy products processor, from Philadelphia-based I.U. International Corporation. Interstate planned to issue a block of 375,000 shares of common stock to purchase Farmbest, which would have reduced the amount of stock DPF could control to only 37 percent of the total outstanding shares. DPF sued to block this move, and finally, after additional wrangling, DPF acquired Interstate for $37 million.

In the wake of this purchase, Interstate's headquarters were transferred to Hartsdale, New York. The company's new owners set out to wring greater profits out of its operations by upgrading facilities. "Almost nothing had been done here in terms of capital enhancement of the business for some years; some areas needed nothing more than a Band-Aid, while some needed major surgery," one DPF executive told *Barron's*. To modernize Interstate's plants, DPF embarked on a program that saw 17 factories closed and 19 new properties purchased during the last five years of the 1970s.

As part of this program, Interstate announced in 1976 that it would undertake the construction of a new $5 million bakery in Montana. The following year, the company shed the Nolde Brothers subsidiary and purchased the Silver Loaf Baking Company. Other acquisitions during this time included the Eddy Bakeries division of General Host and Mrs. Cubbison's Foods, Inc., a bread stuffing maker.

On February 27, 1979, DPF fully completed its merger with Interstate. Two years later, the acquiring firm sold what was left of its computer operations to a group of former managers and changed the entire company's name to Interstate Bakeries Corporation. Although Interstate earned a $50 million tax break from the collapse of the computer outfit, ultimately, the bakery operations were left with a heavy financial burden to bear.

By the start of the 1980s, Interstate was operating 36 different plants, selling bread and cakes in 30 different markets. Seventy percent of the company's revenues came from bread, and 30 percent from cakes. Although sales of white bread had grown stagnant, as people became more health conscious, sales of variety breads, such as Interstate's Pritikin diet bread and Sun-Maid raisin bread, which carried a higher price tag and had a longer shelf life, had benefited from this trend.

In addition, Interstate looked to benefit from the general recession gripping the economy, since a poor economy paradoxically meant good news for bakers. As one Interstate executive explained to *Barron's*, "Downturns in the economy always see people eating more bread than they might otherwise do." Interstate's cake business, which was supported through heavy advertising, offered higher profits than its bread sales, and was also relatively immune from the effects of a poor economy, since, some analysts noted, people tended to keep treating themselves to sweets when they couldn't afford more expensive luxuries.

With the separation of Interstate's computer business from the core baking operations, Dale Putnam, head of Interstate's bakery division, was named chief executive officer of Interstate in January 1982. Putnam moved Interstate headquarters back to Kansas City, its historical base of operations. The company then looked to focus all of its attention on baking, as well as on improvements in two areas: plant efficiency, and market penetration. Although the company had already spent $100 million upgrading its manufacturing facilities in the late 1970s, it planned to continue its efforts in this area, in hopes of increasing its profitability to a level consistent with that of its two largest competitors.

Despite these efforts, Interstate struggled in the early 1980s. The company was saddled with the financial consequences of DPF's failed computer business, the declining demand for white bread, its staple product, and stiff competition from other national bakers. A proposed merger with another independent baker, American Bakeries Company, never materialized, and Interstate was forced to close additional baking plants that were no longer profitable. In May 1983, Interstate closed out a four-year period of declining financial returns with a loss.

The bad news continued in 1984, as Interstate racked up $4.2 million in red ink. At that time, the company appointed a new president, Robert Hatch, a veteran of General Mills, who came on board just days before Interstate's bankers demanded payment on $36 million worth of loans. In an effort to get the company out of the shadow of its computer-leasing losses, Interstate took another $21 million write-off and cashed in its $37 million pension fund to pay off the banks. "We're trying to put our financial house in order," noted B.J. Hinkle, Interstate's chief financial officer, in *Barron's*. Termination of the pension plan, Hinkle reported, has "given us time to slow down a little bit and evaluate our product line." The pension plan was replaced by another retirement package.

Interstate next decided to emphasize strong brand marketing, rather than relying on price to differentiate its products from those of its competitors. The company therefore increased its spending on advertising by two-thirds. Interstate also attempted to sell its western operations to the Good Stuff Food Company of Los Angeles for $55.1 million, but this deal was ultimately abandoned.

As Interstate moved into the late 1980s, its efforts to recover appeared to be bearing fruit. Sales of white bread had stabilized, and the company also began to introduce new products, such as coffee cakes, pecan rolls, pudding pies, and a wider variety of breads. To keep manufacturing efficiency high, Interstate shut down five plants and spent $109 million to modernize 27 others.

In addition, in 1986, the company also made a series of acquisitions, in hopes of filling in marketing gaps. In May, it purchased the Purity Baking Company, of Decatur, Illinois, which made Sunbeam breads, and in December, Stewart Sandwiches of Utah was brought into the Interstate fold. Stewart Sandwiches sold frozen and refrigerated products, such as roast beef and turkey sandwiches.

Interstate reported $13.4 million in earnings for the year ended May 1987. Later that year, the company continued its string of acquisitions, purchasing Landshire Food Products, Inc. and Stewart of Northern California, Inc., the partner of its earlier acquisition. In addition, Interstate bought the Langedorf cake and cookie operations of the Good Stuff Food Company.

However, Interstate's most significant financial move during 1987 was its withdrawal from the financial markets through a leveraged buy-out. IBC Holdings Corporation (IBC) was formed to buy up all of Interstate's outstanding stock, and Interstate was taken private by its management, with the help of a group of investment banking houses, in September 1987.

Following this move, Interstate parent IBC made a major acquisition, purchasing the ten bakeries of the Merita/Cotton's Bakeries division of the American Bakeries Company for $132 million. Shortly after this purchase, the president of Merita, Charles A. Sullivan, moved over to take command of IBC, becoming president and CEO. With the contribution of the new Merita unit, and its own revitalized operations, IBC's sales grew strongly in the last years of the 1980s. The company reported sales of $855 million for 1988, which rose to $1.1 billion by May 1989.

In May 1991, IBC Holdings Corporation changed its name back to Interstate Bakeries Corporation, before the company once again went public, selling stock on the market in July 1991. Through this move, Interstate was able to raise $250 million to pay down its debts, which were holding down the company's profits, despite the company's increased efficiency and sales. With increased cash flow and reduced debt level, Interstate was able to decrease its expenditures on interest.

In the early 1990s, Interstate saw the popularity of its main product, bread, increase, as the federal government put forth new dietary guidelines. The company sought to take advantage of this new demand by decentralizing its operations, so that local facilities could run as efficiently as possible. "With 31 bakeries across the country, you can't run a business from Kansas City," Sullivan asserted.

By the mid-1990s, this strategy had succeeded so well that Interstate was in a position to make a major acquisition. In early January 1995, the company announced an agreement to buy one of its primary competitors, the Continental Baking Company, for $330 million and 16.9 million shares of Interstate stock. Continental, owned by Ralston Purina, produced the widely popular lines of Wonder and Wonder Lite breads, as well as the snack cakes, donuts, pies, muffins, and cookies marketed under the Hostess name. As Continental's plants were located in parts of the country not yet tapped by Interstate, the company could look forward to becoming a greater national presence. Moreover, Interstate had positioned itself to become the largest player in the baking industry, with anticipated annual revenues in excess of $3 billion. Thus, despite its checkered financial history of the last several decades, Interstate appeared to be well on its way to robust health in the coming years of the 1990s.

Principal Subsidiaries: Interstate Brands Corporation; Mrs. Cubbison's Food, Inc.; IBC Trucking Corporation.

Further Reading:

Rudolph, Barbara, "Out of the Computer and into the Oven," *Forbes,* March 15, 1982, p. 56.
Simon, Ruth, "Putting the Yeast Back into Profits," *Forbes,* February 9, 1987, pp. 62, 64.
Troxell, Thomas N., Jr., "Yeasty Return," *Barron's,* March 1, 1982.
Weiss, Gary, "Making Dough," *Barron's,* December 3, 1984, pp. 30–34.

—Elizabeth Rourke

J.B. Hunt Transport Services Inc.

P.O. Box 130
Lowell, Arkansas 72745
U.S.A.
(501) 820-8395
Fax: (501) 820-8395

Public Company
Incorporated: 1983 as J.B. Hunt Transport
Employees: 11,201
Sales: $1.02 billion
Stock Exchanges: NASDAQ
SICs: 4212 Local Trucking Without Storage; 4213 Trucking
Except Local

J.B. Hunt Transport Services, Inc. is the largest truckload carrier in the United States. Since the passage of the Motor Carrier Act of 1980, which essentially deregulated the trucking industry, the company has grown to become the nation's leader in providing irregular route trucking services—meaning that it picks up cargo and delivers it wherever the customer wants instead of relying on established routes—to businesses such as Wal-Mart, its largest customer. J.B. Hunt loads most its 17,000 trailers and 7,000 trucks with general commodities: its principal types of freight include foodstuffs, plastics and plastic products, general retail store merchandise, chemicals, paper and paper products, and manufacturing materials and supplies. While the familiar yellow and black J.B. Hunt logo is still most likely to be found on trucks travelling throughout the contiguous 48 states, the company has added new forms of transportation and extended its services to foreign markets, while increasing its capability to haul special kinds of freight. Among the company's many areas of growth initiated in the late 1980s, its foray into the intermodal service market was perhaps the most significant. Expected to generate nearly half of the company's total revenues by 1995, this hybrid form of transportation unified trucks, railroads, and sometimes cargo ships into one transportation system, so that shippers did not have to pack and unpack their cargo each time the mode of transit changed. J.B. Hunt has diversified into several other important areas of specialization as well, expanding its repertoire of services to include third party logistics management, hazardous waste and materials transportation, flatbed trailer services, and intrastate freight hauling. Through a joint venture with Mexico's largest transportation company and an alliance with Canada's largest railroad, J.B. Hunt has been able to offer its customers seamless service across both borders since the early 1990s. An industry leader in customer service, driver safety, and innovative technology, J.B. Hunt has become one of the ten largest trucking companies of any kind in the United States, surpassing the $1 billion mark in revenues for the first time in 1993.

Johnnie Bryan Hunt, the founder of the company that bears his name, reportedly carries a roll of $100 bills in his pocket and routinely offers them to people he meets who are in need: "I was hungry once," he explained to *Forbes* reporter Claire Poole, noting that "once you're hungry, you're different." The history of the former $1.50-a-day laborer turned millionaire is unique among the nation's top executives. Born during the Great Depression, Hunt was forced to quit school in the seventh grade to help support his brothers and sisters by working in an Arkansas sawmill. A budding 12-year-old entrepreneur, he began selling leftover shavings from the mill to poultry farmers for use as ground cover in their chicken coups. After a stint in the army, a brief career as a livestock auctioneer, and a failed livestock barn business, Hunt borrowed $10 from a friend, hitchhiked to Little Rock, and took a job as a truck driver, earning $40 a week while on the road every day of the week, including the day of his first child's birth. While driving through eastern Arkansas in the late 1950s, he saw that the farmers were burning their rice hulls, and—remembering his childhood experience at the sawmill—he realized that rice hulls could serve as litter for chicken coops. After coming up with a design to grind and package the hulls, he was able to sell enough shares to raise the $85,000 needed to build his packaging plant. While the company failed to make a profit in its first year, Hunt refused to listen to the naysayers and, by the late 1960s, was at the head of one of the largest rice hull operations of its kind.

In 1969, one of Hunt's customers complained about the service he was receiving from the trucking company that hauled his dressed chickens and encouraged Hunt to buy the trucker's five tractors and seven refrigerated trailers and take over the contract. J.B. Hunt Transport was born; the former driver was now an owner. As had been the case with his former ventures, though, the early years of his trucking business were not profitable. Looking for a way to expand his fledgling trucking company, Hunt tried to gain entrance into the dry goods segment of the industry, obtaining an authorization to do so from an Atlanta company in 1971. At that time, however, the strict Interstate Commerce Commission (ICC) regulations imposed heavy costs on those attempting to enter new markets.

Seven years later, on the brink of giving up his money-losing trucking business, Hunt listened to the advice of Paul Bergant, a Chicago lawyer, who later became the head of J.B. Hunt's marketing division and chief legal counsel. Bergant convinced Hunt that deregulation was imminent. Hunt followed Bergant's intuition and expanded his operations, purchasing a trucking company that added 24 trucks and ICC licenses covering 33 states to his business. Knowing that in a deregulated environment the high operating costs of his old-line competitors, who relied heavily on the expensive services of independent truck owner/operators, would no longer be protected by ICC barriers to competition, he looked for ways to increase the efficiency of his own operation. His strategy was simple: replace privately owned and operated rigs with his own nonunion drivers and equipment; lower fuel costs (which generally consumed 16 percent of trucking revenues) by offering monthly incentives to drivers who conserve fuel by driving 55 miles per hour; increase load ratio (the number of miles a truck runs loaded); and decrease driver turnover by offering higher wages and better working conditions.

Bergant's prophecy was fulfilled in 1980 with the passage of the Motor Carrier Act. Numerous route and commodity restrictions were lifted, and Hunt was in position to take full advantage. By the close of the following year, he had turned his previous losses into a $2 million profit on sales of $30 million. Encouraged by his success, he sold his rice hull business to Eli Lilly for $2.4 million and went public in 1983, selling 11 percent of his shares at an estimated $18.5 million. While other trucking companies were losing money, J.B. Hunt continued to expand its operation and set revenue records. Just four years after going public, the company had grown to become the nation's second largest truckload carrier and the largest publicly held truckload company.

Through the mid-1980s, having posted yearly profit margins that routinely exceeded ten percent—roughly twice that of its larger, unionized competitors such as Consolidated Freightways, Yellow Freight System, and Roadway Services—in the latter part of the decade, J.B. Hunt experienced contracting profit margins and slowed growth. Like its competitors, the company was set back by higher operating costs and declining tariffs in the Middle East, resulting in increased fuel costs. The most significant factor contributing to this decline, though, was the onset of an industry wide shortage in qualified drivers, which forced J.B. Hunt to keep many of its trucks parked.

In an attempt to combat the problem, Hunt constructed a strategy to recruit more drivers—and retain them. In 1990, the company increased the wages of its drivers with three years experience from 25 cents a mile to an unprecedented 28 cents a mile—four cents more than its competitors. J.B. Hunt also took the lead in improving the working conditions of its drivers, building 18 terminals equipped with showers, laundry services, and lunchrooms, by 1994. In addition to serving as homes away from home, the terminals facilitated "slipseating"—the practice of letting a tired driver turn over a load to a rested one. Such innovations helped J.B. Hunt's drivers to return home every two weeks, while drivers employed by its competitors were getting home an average of once every three weeks. In an attempt to attract more new drivers and cut down on accidents, the company also opened up a driving school in Lowell in 1988, offering its students free tuition and a job guaranteed upon graduation. While such capital expenditures increased operating costs in the short term, they later brought about significant decreases in driver turnover, which was down a record 20 percent in 1993, and accident costs decreased 30 percent that year.

In the mid-1990s, Hunt had no plans to relinquish control of his billion dollar company, but he began leaving the daily management duties to younger executives, such as Kirk Thompson, who was named the company's president and chief executive officer in 1987. Like his boss, Thompson did not follow the traditional path in gaining a place among the corporate elite. He dropped out of college to work in Hunt's accounting department and completed his accounting degree part-time, before being promoted to the top management position. Under Thompson's guidance, the company continued to lead the irregular route trucking industry in developing innovative technology and expanding into new markets.

Perhaps the most important among these developments was J.B. Hunt's refinement of intermodal transportation services. Formerly known as "piggybacking" since its inception in the mid-1950s, this hybrid form of transportation attempted to combine the cheaper fuel and labor of trains with the faster, more reliable service of trucks. The first major trucking company to cooperate with the arch rival railroads, J.B. Hunt began its intermodal division through a joint venture called "Quantum" with the Santa Fe Railway in 1989, enabling the trucking company to offer its customers door-to-door service in the California-to-Midwest corridor. Since that time, Hunt has built alliances with eight other railroads throughout North America, maintaining hauling agreements and 47 ramp locations with Burlington Northern, Canadian National, Conrail, Florida East Coast, Norfolk Southern, Santa Fe, Southern Pacific, Union Pacific, and Wisconsin Central. "Now we can walk in to a customer and lock in rates for several years because of the stability of the railroad's cost structure," explained Tom Williams, head of intermodal marketing, in a 1993 *Forbes* profile. "There's so much business out there," Williams noted, that "we're limited only by having enough equipment." To that end, Hunt invested heavily in the research and development of new containers that both attached to the base of a Hunt truck and stacked on a railway car—while having the capacity to carry 1,000 pounds more than average containers. In 1993, 7,500 of these multi-purpose containers were added to the Hunt fleet, and Hunt expected to have added them to the majority of its trucks by 1995. John Larkin, a trucking analyst at Alex, Brown & Sons, underscored the significance of these innovations for the rest of the trucking industry, suggesting in *Forbes* that Hunt "may be ready to redefine the industry by forging relationships with railroads" and "pioneering this new equipment." Accounting for roughly 30 percent of the company's total revenues in 1993, and expected to contribute one half of total revenues by the end of 1995 according to some predictions, intermodal services, indeed, promised to play a major role in the 1990s.

J.B. Hunt's intermodal services, most certainly, were not the only manifestation of the company's entrepreneurial spirit. In 1990, the company added a flatbed division to its repertoire, expanding its customer base to businesses, such as Reynolds Metals, that wished to ship materials too large for closed vans. Two years later, after negotiating an agreement with IBM, the company also began installing on-board laptop computers in its fleet, eliminating the countless hours its truckers spent looking for a phone or waiting on hold before contacting a fleet manager to find out about the next load. Tests conducted in 1993 on the new "smart communications" system known as "RoadRider," which linked its drivers via satellite or radio to the company headquarters in Lowell, showed that installation in 2,100 of its trucks—just over 12 percent of its total fleet—brought about a 60 percent reduction in the company's long-distance phone bill. Encouraged by the test results, J.B. Hunt and IBM began remarketing the new technology to other trucking companies in 1994. "Micromap," a new software program with the capability to evaluate more than 90 different assignment factors at a time, further simplified the logistics manager's responsibilities. Since its introduction into the system, the number of miles J.B. Hunt's trucks run empty decreased by ten percent, further cutting operating costs while enabling more drivers to return home on time.

Just as J.B. Hunt was in position to make the most of the government deregulation of the early 1980s, he prepared the company for the passage of another piece of legislation sure to affect the trucking industry: the North American Free Trade Agreement (NAFTA), which promised to relax trade restrictions between the United States and its neighboring countries of Canada and Mexico. In 1990, after having already acquired the requisite authority to haul freight in Ontario, Quebec, and British Columbia two years earlier, Hunt joined forces with the Mexican trucking firm Fletes Sotelo to form Hunt de Mexico. The bold move, like many of the company's throughout its history, initially puzzled some investors, who were well aware of the uncertainties, in terms of quality and on-time delivery, commonly associated with such international ventures. J.B. Hunt, however, implemented a plan to silence the critics: instead of relinquishing control of its trucks at the border, transferring freight to Mexican-owned and Mexican-driven trucks, Hunt de Mexico—like its J.B. Hunt counterparts in the United States—relied on the services of its own drivers, maintaining customs clearance all the way through to final destination. In 1992, Hunt de Mexico improved the efficiency of its operations by signing an agreement with Transportacion Maritima Mexican, Mexico's largest maritime steamship company. The following year—while J.B. Hunt was finalizing another intermodal agreement in Canada with Canadian National, the country's largest railroad—Congress passed NAFTA, confirming the company's remarkable foresight in matters of international expansion.

J.B. Hunt's commitment to intermodal development, technological innovation, and foreign market expansion—as well as its long-held devotion to customer service—enabled the company to surpass the $1 billion mark in sales in 1993, only ten years after going public. According to the annual report for that monumental year, its goal for the rest of the decade was no less than "to dominate the full-load, containerizable transportation business in North America and to enter and compete in the worldwide distribution business." In the three years since its 1990 ranking by *Business Month* magazine as the nation's 50th fastest growing company, J.B. Hunt Transport Services has watched its operating revenues increase more than 75 percent. While some analysts have suggested that the high costs of making the transition from a dry van, over-the-road truckload carrier to one offering intermodal and other lines of service,

may decrease profit margins in the mid-1990s, a 40 percent rise in net revenues for the third quarter of 1994 suggested that the company would continue to make progress towards achieving its expectations. Moreover, the colorful J.B. Hunt himself set an even more challenging goal for his company, promising to make 100 of his employees millionaires before his scheduled date of retirement at the age of 75. While such an ambitious statement may not fall within the boundaries of conventional business wisdom, it accurately reflected the unique entrepreneurial drive behind the bold decisions that brought the company to the top of the irregular route trucking industry. "I've developed a lot of things," Hunt explained to *Fortune*'s Sally Solo. "The reason is that if you went to college and you read the book about everything that's been taught of by man, you go back to the book whenever you have a problem. And when the book stops, you stop. But if you haven't read the book, you don't know where the borders are." With no "book" to follow, J.B. Hunt hoped to lead its competitors into the twenty-first century.

Principal Subsidiaries: J.B. Hunt Transport, Inc.; J.B. Hunt Logistics, Inc.; J.B. Hunt Special Commodities, Inc.; J.B. Hunt Flatbed; J.B. Hunt Transport of Texas; TMM/Hunt de Mexico (45%).

Further Reading:
Burke, Jack, "Hunt Cuts 1994 Container Purchases, Says Money, Not Quality Is the Reason," *Traffic World,* February 21, 1994, p. 9.
Donlan, Thomas G., "Another Arkansas Hero: J.B. Hunt Took Hold of Deregulation's Opportunities," *Barron's,* February 15, 1993, p. 10.
"The Fast 100," *Business Month,* May 1990, pp. 45–48.
"For Rail Intermodal, Santa Fe and J.B. Hunt Plan a Quantum Jump," *Railway Age,* January 1990, p. 17.
Jaffe, Thomas, "Hunt Country," *Forbes,* June 22, 1992, p. 244.
"J.B. Hunt Posts Record Results, Approves Stock-Buyback Plan," *Journal of Commerce and Commercial,* October 19, 1994, p. B3.
Harris, John, "Rough Road," *Forbes,* November 26, 1990, pp. 206–211.
Marcial, Gene G., "A Trucker Reroutes and Revs Up," *Business Week,* July 19, 1993, p. 80.
Mason, Todd, "Even Its Employees Are Becoming Millionaires," *Business Week,* May 26, 1986, pp. 98–102.
Poole, Claire, " 'Once You're Hungry, You're Different'," *Forbes,* October 19, 1992, pp. 44–46.
Scheer, Lisa, " 'We Want to Be a Federal Express,' " *Forbes,* December 12, 1988, pp. 71–75.
Schulz, John D., "Education Not Quick Profits, Goal of New Hunt de Mexico Venture," *Traffic World,* December 3, 1990, p. 19–21.
Solo, Sally, "Every Problem is an Opportunity," *Fortune,* November 16, 1993, p. 93.

—Jason Gallman

J. Crew Group Inc.

625 Sixth Avenue
New York, New York 10011
U.S.A.
(212) 886-8500
Fax: (212) 886-2666

Private Company
Incorporated: 1947 as Popular Merchandise, Inc.
Employees: 4,100
Sales: $466 million
SICs: 5961 Catalog & Mail Order Houses

J. Crew Group Inc. markets upscale men's and women's clothing through distinctive catalogs and a chain of stores. In the mid-1990s, the company was issuing 17 different catalogs each year and operating more than 30 retail stores and 25 factory outlet stores in the United States.

Popular Club Plan—the company from which J. Crew was launched—was founded in 1947 by Mitchell Cinadar and Saul Charles to sell low-priced women's clothing through in-home demonstrations. By the early 1980s, the owners of Popular Club Plan (which was by then under the direction of Mitchell Cinadar's son, Arthur) watched as catalog retailers of clothing, including Lands' End, Talbots, and L. L. Bean, reported booming sales. In an effort to duplicate the success of these companies, Popular Club Plan initiated its own catalog operation.

The company focused on leisurewear for upper-middle-class customers, aiming for a Ralph Lauren look at a much lower price. Accordingly, Popular Club situated its merchandise in the niche between Ralph Lauren, on the high end, and the Limited, on the lower end. In an effort to connote a "preppy" spirit, Popular Club Plan dubbed this operation "J. Crew." The first J. Crew catalog was mailed to customers in January 1983. Instrumental in orchestrating the J. Crew look was Arthur Cinadar's daughter Emily Cinadar (later Woods), who joined the company after graduating from college.

Over the next several years, J. Crew's catalog evolved a distinctive look featuring young, attractive models having fun in a variety of appealing settings. The pictures in the catalog appeared to be photographs from a house party of old friends, all of whom happened to be gorgeous and outfitted by J. Crew.

Their catalogs often showed the same garment in more than one picture, worn by different models and coordinated with other products. As a result, customers could get a sense of how the garment looked on the body, how it hung and draped, and how it could be used with various items of clothing. In addition, J. Crew included close-up shots of the fabrics from which its products were made, helping to validate its claims of quality.

J. Crew closely controlled the production of its catalog, selecting images from more than 8,000 rolls of film shot each year and having all catalog copy written in house. Catalogs with more than 100 glossy pages were mailed to customers 14 times a year. The company also maintained an in-house design staff to develop its products and carefully controlled the manufacturing process, hiring factories to produce garments to its specifications.

Throughout the mid-1980s, sales from J. Crew's catalog operations grew rapidly, as the catalog retailing industry as a whole experienced strong growth. During this time, J. Crew continued to refine its presentation and increase the number of people receiving its catalog. "Growth was explosive—25 to 30 percent a year," Cinadar later recollected in the *New York Times.* Annual sales grew from $3 million to more than $100 million over five years.

With the success of its first catalog operation, J. Crew launched a second catalog program in 1985. Dubbed "Clifford & Wills," this operation sold women's clothing that was more affordable than the J. Crew line. In 1986 Emily Cinadar was promoted to president of the J. Crew operation.

Despite the phenomenal success of J. Crew, and the prominent profile that the J. Crew catalog soon attained, internal management of the company was less than smooth. Both Cinadars, father and daughter, were reputed to be difficult to work with, and employee turnover was high. In 1987 the company suffered a setback when two high-level executives left to start their own catalog operation, Tweeds, which drew on the lessons learned and example established by the J. Crew operation. With a more European look, Tweeds was soon competing successfully with J. Crew.

Although J. Crew's sales continued to be strong throughout the fall season of 1988, when the company reaped annual sales of $100 million, by the end of the 1980s growth was beginning to slow in the catalog market as a whole. By 1989 rumors had begun to circulate in the apparel industry that J. Crew was in trouble and that the company might be up for sale.

Though these rumors were vociferously denied, it was clear that J. Crew would have to implement changes to sustain its vigorous growth. To begin with, the company undertook a number of steps to focus its attention on its most important and profitable units. In 1989 the company changed its name from Popular Merchandise, Inc.—a holdover from the 1940s, when the Popular Club Plan was the company's main business—to the J. Crew Group Inc. In February 1989, the company announced that the Popular Club Plan would be sold to International Epicure, a direct-marketing food company. With the proceeds from this sale, J. Crew planned to help finance a broadening of its J. Crew enterprises, and to compensate, in part, for the fact that its operations were less solidly financed than those of many of its catalog competitors.

J. Crew also planned to expand into retail. In opening stores, J. Crew hoped to capitalize on the strong brand identity it had established through its catalogs, and also to tap the significant number of customers that did not shop through catalogs (company research suggested that 60 percent of clothes buyers did not shop by mail, and that only 15 percent of apparel customers bought a significant number of items from catalogs).

To avoid compromising its existing catalog operations, J. Crew set up its new retail branch as a separate unit within the company. The Cinadars hired Arnold Cohen, who had previously worked for Gucci, to head a new management team that would be in charge of a chain of J. Crew stores. The start-up staff for this arm of the company, dubbed J. Crew Retail, numbered 22. In order to minimize cannibalization of its catalog operations, J. Crew planned to make 60 to 70 percent of the goods offered in its stores unavailable through its catalogs. In March 1989 the first J. Crew retail outlet opened, in the South Street Seaport in Manhattan. With four thousand square feet of selling space, this store was designed to appeal to the many members of the New York financial community who frequented the seaport. The company planned to open 45 stores in its first push into retail.

Five months after the opening of its first store, J. Crew added two new catalog lines: "Classics" and "Collections." "Collections" used more complicated designs and finer fabrics to create dressier and more expensive items, while "Classics" featured clothes that could be worn both to work and for leisure activities, and acted as a bridge between the products J. Crew had originally offered and its "Collections" items. With these lines, J. Crew hoped to further differentiate itself from its catalog competitors.

In the fall of 1989, J. Crew opened three new stores, each larger than the first, in Chestnut Hill, Massachusetts; San Francisco, California; and Costa Mesa, California. J. Crew chose these locations because they were in markets where catalog sales had historically been strong. Each of these openings was supported by print ads in local newspapers and magazines that featured images from the catalogs, with a line indicating the store's location. In November 1989, J. Crew also launched a national magazine advertising campaign. By the end of the year, this had helped to produce retail sales of nearly $10 million.

Despite 1989 revenues that were estimated at $320 million, J. Crew suffered a setback when its agreement to sell its Popular Club unit collapsed at the end that year. In addition, rumors circulated that the company's Clifford & Wills low-priced women's apparel catalog was doing badly. J. Crew began to delay payments to its suppliers and lay off staff members.

J. Crew embarked on an attempt to win greater sales from its existing catalog customers, noting that its expansion was limited by the relatively small segment of the population that served as its customer base, estimated at 7 to 10 percent of the population. J. Crew's target customer was young, educated, and affluent, with a median age of 32, some post-graduate education, and an annual household income above $62,000. "I don't know if there are 20 people left in the country who are prime J. Crew prospects who haven't seen the catalog 10 or 20 times," Cinadar went on. "So . . . I think most increases will come from increased sales per person." To bring this about, J. Crew broadened its line of merchandise even further, adding sleepwear, outerwear, working clothes, and versatile jackets. In this way, the company hoped to supplement its sales of low-priced items—such as its most offerings, t-shirts and socks—with higher-ticket purchases.

J. Crew saw revenues reach $400 million in 1990, but reported that its four existing stores had not yet started producing enough profits to cover their overheads. "We're working on improving merchandise selection and we're working on strengthening the visual image," J. Crew president Arnold Cohen told the *New York Times.* The next phase of store openings included outlets in Philadelphia, Cambridge, and Portland. The company scaled back its plans for opening retail stores from 45 stores to 30 or 35.

In early 1991 the company hired a director of new marketing development and began efforts to expand their sales across the Canadian border. In an effort to simplify the complications of doing business internationally, J. Crew "Canadianized" its catalogs, including information on the payment of taxes and duties, the Canadian Goods and Services Tax, and customs requirements.

In April 1991, J. Crew mailed 75,000 J. Crew catalogs and 60,000 Clifford & Wills catalogs to potential customers in Ontario. Response rates to this effort were slightly lower than in the United States, but each order, on average, was higher. Clifford & Wills received an especially warm response, and a second mailing of 120,000 copies of this catalog took place in September 1991. The company benefitted from the relative paucity of catalog retailers in Canada, which made its brochure stand out better, but also made collecting names of potential customers much more difficult.

In the following year, J. Crew intensified its push into international markets by hiring a new vice-president for international development. The company already mailed hundreds of catalogs to customers in Japan and Europe, most of whom had become acquainted with J. Crew while traveling or living in the United States. In early 1992, J. Crew conducted a feasibility study to explore avenues for marketing its goods to customers overseas on a larger scale.

Despite the economic recession at home, J. Crew racked up $70 million in retail sales in 1992, a strong increase from previous years. The company discovered that opening stores did not significantly hurt its catalog sales; in New York, in fact, opening a store increased catalog sales.

In addition, J. Crew moved aggressively into the Japanese market. In February 1993, the company completed an agreement with Japanese retailers Itochu and Renown, Inc., to open 46 stores there, with estimated annual sales of $68 million.

In March 1993 J. Crew began test-marketing a J. Crew catalog in France. In November of that year, the company signed an agreement with a French mail order firm, called 3 Suisses International, to launch a J. Crew catalog operation in France. Under the agreement, J. Crew's French partner would buy

J. Crew products directly from the company's manufacturing subcontractors around the world, so that French customers would receive exactly the same merchandise as American buyers. The French catalog was slated to be mailed less frequently than the American book, which was by this time being sent out 17 times a year, but the frequency was expected to increase over time. The agreement also included a retail component, giving the French company the right to open J. Crew stores in countries throughout Europe.

Principal Subsidiaries: Popular Club Plan; Clifford & Wills.

Further Reading:

Chevan, Harry, "J. Crew: Building on Its Brand," *Catalog Age,* September 1993, p. 7.

Graham, Judith, "Cataloger Tried Retail Units," *Advertising Age,* August 21, 1989.

Haggin, Jeff, and Bjorn Kartomten, "Product Photography: Glamour or Benefit?" *Catalog Age,* June 1989.

"J. Crew, CW Score High in Ontario," *Catalog Age,* October 1991, p. 8.

"J. Crew to Launch Catalog in France with 3 Suisses," *DNR,* November 30, 1993.

Kamen, Robin, "New Opportunity Seen Overseas by J. Crew's VP," *Crain's New York Business,* March 16, 1992.

Kleinfeld, N. R., "Even for J. Crew, the Mail-Order Boom Days Are Over," *New York Times,* September 2, 1990, p. 5.

Morgenson, Gretchen, "Storm Warnings," *Forbes,* December 11, 1989, pp. 140–48.

—Elizabeth Rourke

Jockey International, Inc.

2300 60th Street
Kenosha, Wisconsin 53140
U.S.A.
(414) 658-8111

Private Company
Incorporated: 1876 as S. T. Cooper & Sons
Employees: 5,000
Sales: $340 million
SICs: 2254 Knit Underwear Mills; 2322 Men's & Boy's
    Underwear & Nightwear; 2341 Women's & Children's
    Underwear; 2251 Women's Hosiery Except Socks

Jockey International, Inc. is one of the oldest and best-known American underwear manufacturers. The company markets a broad range of underwear for men, women, and children, along with related products. Privately-owned since its inception, Jockey began by making socks and branched out to make innovative designs in men's underwear, pioneering the marketing of the brief.

Jockey got its start in 1876, when Samuel T. Cooper purchased six hand-operated knitting machines. Along with his sons Charles, Henry, and Willis, he used this equipment to found S. T. Cooper & Sons, a hosiery manufacturer located in the small town of Ludington, Michigan. Cooper sold heavy wool socks to general stores, which in turn sold them to customers.

Cooper soon expanded its line from wool socks to men's underwear, adding union suits, the only men's underwear then manufactured. The union suit was a long-sleeved, long-legged knit garment that buttoned up the front. At the turn of the century, Cooper moved its operations from Ludington, Michigan, to the slightly larger town of Kenosha, Wisconsin, which became its headquarters. In addition Cooper changed its name to Cooper's Underwear Company. In 1910, Cooper's introduced a new design for its union suits which eliminated the need for buttons down their fronts. The "Kenosha Klosed Krotch" consisted of two overlapping pieces of fabric that could be drawn apart to create an opening. Cooper's patented this design innovation, and trademarked the "Kenosha" name.

In the following year, Cooper's undertook the first national advertising campaign for a line of men's underwear when it took out an ad in the *Saturday Evening Post.* The company hired

a well-known illustrator named Leyendecker for the magazine to produce a series of color renderings of Cooper's products. The first of these promotional spots ran in the May 6, 1911 edition of the journal. Three years later, a Leyendecker rendering of a "man on the bag" became a staple of the Cooper's brand identity.

With the entry of the United States into World War I, large numbers of men were inducted into the armed services for the first time in a generation. In the army, service men were given woven shorts to wear as underwear in the summer, as opposed to the long-johns typically worn in civilian life. After the war ended in 1918, many demobilized soldiers continued to prefer the greater comfort and convenience of boxer shorts, shunning the union suit. By the early 1920s, the more traditional kind of garment had fallen into disfavor. Despite this decline in popularity, Cooper's did not dramatically change its product offerings throughout the 1920s. In 1926, the company briefly changed its name to Cooper's, Inc., and two years later, Cooper's created an export department to facilitate the eventual marketing of its products outside the United States.

At the end of the decade, Cooper's introduced a new product line, a variation on the union suit called the "Jockey Singleton." This sleeveless, one-piece garment was made of Durene yarn, and came only to the knees. The company called the snug-fitting underwear "Jockey" to suggest athleticism and flexibility. Cooper's trademarked this name and the construction of the garment, and sold a high volume of this product throughout the 1930s. Three years after the introduction of the singleton, Cooper's rolled out another new product line when it began to sell knit pajamas. In 1934, Cooper's expanded its line of knit products once again, when it started marketing knit sports shirts to retailers.

In 1934, Cooper's made its most important innovation in underwear when it designed the brief. This idea came about after a senior vice-president of Cooper's saw a picture of men on the French Riviera wearing a new type of bathing suit. He saw this garment as a potential prototype for a new kind of men's support underwear. In September of 1934, Cooper's produced an experimental prototype, brief style #1001. In response to its introduction, competitors labeled the new underwear style a fad. On January 19, 1934, Marshall Field and Company, the premier Chicago department store, unveiled a window display featuring the new brief. On that day, Chicago was experiencing a severe blizzard, and the skimpy men's underwear in the window made a stark contrast to the wintry conditions outside. Under these circumstances, Marshall Field's managers gave the order to take the brief out of the window display. When the workers who were to carry out this order were delayed, however, the new underwear style stayed on display, and prompted an unexpected surge of demand for the product. More than 600 briefs were sold before noon, at a price of 50 cents a piece.

The brief's popularity remained strong in the following days. Over the next week, more than 12,000 of the new underwear style were sold. In its first three months of sales, Marshall Field's rang up more than 30,000 pairs of the red-hot item. With this runaway success, the brief garnered widespread attention in the underwear industry. In August of 1935, Cooper's Underwear Company received a patent on the construction principles of the Y-front brief from the U.S. Patent Office.

Building on the strength of its new underwear style, Cooper's introduced another new line in 1935, when it began to sell a Junior set of products for boys. The first items offered were a brief and an athletic shirt. Cooper's also became the first company to sell men's underwear in packages in that year. In 1936, Cooper's began to market its products outside the United States for the first time when it signed a contract for a Canadian firm to manufacture and sell its styles under license. In an effort to further enhance the sales of its brief, Cooper also unrolled an advertising campaign designed to point out the disadvantages of boxer shorts. Called the "stop squirming" promotion, this campaign went on to win awards in its field.

Following these efforts, Cooper's moved in 1937 to bring a greater degree of structure to the retail underwear business. In that year, the company introduced a model program for retailers to use in controlling their inventory of Cooper's underwear products, and also produced a manual called "New Era for Underwear Selling" that was designed to instruct retailers in the most effective marketing of Cooper's wares. In addition, the company began to offer special mannequins for use in displaying Cooper's products in stores.

Cooper's move toward greater retailing sophistication continued in February of 1938, when the company mounted an innovative display at the National Association of Retail Clothiers and Furnishers Convention in Chicago. The company presented the first underwear fashion show, which it called the "Cellophane Wedding." The display consisted of a male and female model, each dressed in evening clothes, as if for a wedding. The trick to the display, however, was that half of the man's coat and pants, and half of the woman's gown, were made of cellophane, displaying the couple's underwear underneath. The woman wore fashionable undergarments of the day, and the man wore a brief and a t-shirt. This fashion show caused a sensation at the convention, and pictures of the couple appeared in every major newspaper and magazine, winning Cooper's a bonanza of free publicity.

Also in 1938, Cooper's introduced another promotional device, the Jockey hip tape. This was used to insure a proper fit for underwear. The company received its second patent on the brief, this one for the "Classic," style #1007, with Y-front construction, on January 2, 1938.

In the following year, Cooper's enhanced its display systems for retailers when it designed a table-top dispenser for its products that customers could use themselves. In the late 1930s and early 1940s, Cooper's also employed a number of sports celebrities to endorse its products, including Babe Ruth, Yogi Berra, Bart Starr, and others. As the 1940s began, Cooper's also introduced a new trademark, the Jockey Boy statue, which it used to differentiate its products from those of its competitors.

To reinforce the consistent impression made by the Jockey Boy trademark, Cooper's introduced a slide and sound film on how to sell underwear in 1941. At the end of that year, the United States entered World War II, and Cooper's, like the rest of the country's industry, switched over to wartime production. The

company manufactured flare parachutes and underwear for the armed forces for the duration of the war.

At the cessation of hostilities, the American economy entered a period of rapid expansion. In order to help its market share grow, Cooper's began to use radio advertising to push its products in selected major cities in 1948. That year, the company also came up with a new way to make its briefs appealing to customers, when it began offering underwear made out of fabrics that had been decorated with novelty prints. These promotions went under the name "fancy pants." By 1953, Cooper's had expanded its "fancy pants" line by adding its most popular item, animal prints. Among the animal skin designs were leopard, tiger, and zebra.

Cooper's also expanded its line of non-underwear products in 1950, when it began to offer men's sportswear. Two years later, the company began to market products for women for the first time, introducing a feminine version of the Jockey short called the "Jockette." The company also stepped up its efforts to sell underwear for boys, taking out advertisements for its Jockey Junior line in *Parent's Magazine*. In a further promotional effort, Cooper's produced two new training tools for salespeople, how-to films entitled "All I Can Do" and "The Big Little Things."

Also in 1953, Cooper's introduced a new fabric which, like the design for the brief, had originated in France. Called "tricot," the French word for "knit," this material was originally made of pure silk thread, knitted into a soft, supple fabric. Cooper's adapted this substance for the American market, manufacturing tricot out of nylon. In addition, the company moved beyond basic white, offering products made of tricot in a full range of colors.

With the introduction of animal prints and colored tricot underwear, Cooper's moved away from the conception of underwear as a plain, functional item toward a conception of its product as a fashion item, with style and novelty value that extended beyond its basic utility. This process continued in 1954, when the company began to promote underwear as a gift item, packaging its products in a special Christmas box. This trend was expanded to a second holiday in the following year, when Cooper's introduced a special fashion brief as part of a Valentine's Day promotion.

In the following year, Cooper's again expanded the number of fabrics out of which its products were sewn when the company began to offer a line of woven boxer shorts. The company also took another step in its promotional efforts, when it began to advertise underwear on television, running spots on NBC's "Home Show." In addition to these advances, Cooper's notched yet another patent in its field after it developed a unisized hosiery package.

In 1957, Cooper's continued its promotional innovations when it proclaimed the first "National Long Underwear Week." In a further effort in this area, the company became a sponsor of the "Jack Parr Show" on NBC, which later became known as the "Tonight Show." Two years later, Cooper's scored another underwear fad when it introduced "Skants," smaller cut briefs with a no-fly front. In addition, the company extended its line of sportswear and also began to sell men's hosiery, returning to its original roots as a sock manufacturer.

In the 1960s, Cooper's continued to adjust the design of its products to keep pace with current trends in fashion. In general, the company's knit and woven underwear became shorter, tighter fitting, and were offered in more bright colors and patterns. Despite the broad variety of offerings, however, 97 percent of the company's sales still came from white underwear. In 1964, Cooper's rolled out "Life," a Lo Rise fashion underwear collection. At the same time, the company began to make its products out of Suprel, a trade name for a blend of polyester and combed cotton.

In the late 1960s, Cooper's returned to its earlier practice of using sports stars and other celebrities to endorse its products. The company's new line of golf sportswear, for instance, was promoted by Bert Yancey and Tom Weiskopf, and ads for Jockey brand products were run on the "Wide World of Sports" television program. For these efforts, Cooper's was named "Brand Names Manufacturer of the Year" in 1969.

Three years later, the Cooper's Underwear Company was purchased by Harry Wolf, who had previously worked as a consultant to the company. At that time, the company was renamed for its trademark, which Cooper's had promoted aggressively over the decades. On May 1, 1972, the company was re-incorporated under the new name Jockey International, Inc. In the following year, Jockey expanded its product line further by merging two similar categories of garment, the bathing suit and the brief, into a product called the "DP." In 1974, the company took another step away from strict utility and toward fashion when it hired a New York designer, Alexander Sheilds, to design its sportswear.

When Wolf died in 1978, ownership of Jockey was passed on to his three children. Within five years, Wolf's son sold his interest in the firm to his sisters, and Donna Wolf Steigerwaldt, who held a controlling interest in the company, became chair and chief executive officer of Jockey.

Jockey's promotional efforts received a big boost in 1980, when the company selected Jim Palmer, a handsome pitcher for the Baltimore Orioles and an experienced Jockey model, to be sole spokesperson. The image of Palmer wearing a Jockey "Elance" brief became so popular that it was manufactured and distributed as a poster. In 1982, Jockey stepped up its marketing of women's underwear, when it rolled out a new "Jockey for Her" line of cotton panties at a formal fashion show in New York. The company launched the line with three styles, and soon added fashion colors and stripes, and matching tops. Two years later, Jockey added a fourth style, the "French Cut" brief, and in 1985 a line of "Queen Size" underwear for taller and larger women.

Also in 1985, Jockey established its own in-house advertising agency to handle all of its promotional campaigns and marketing activities. In that year, the company began to feature "real people," such as a construction worker, an executive vice-president, and a mother, in its advertising, a strategy that won Jockey praise from women's groups.

Three years later, Jockey purchased Nantucket Mills, a hosiery manufacturer. Following this acquisition, the company began to market "Sheer & Comfortable," a collection of women's hosiery with four styles. This line was soon expanded to include "Sheerest Ever" and "Ultra Sheer" products. To promote its hosiery products, the company sponsored a nationwide "Legs Search" for real people to model its stockings.

Jockey continued to expand its line of product offerings in the 1990s, adding new styles and fabrics, as well as related products, such as socks. In 1993, the company's president bought out her sister's share of Jockey, and so became its sole owner. Under her direction, the company that got its start in the late nineteenth century seemed poised for continued success in the twenty-first.

Further Reading:

Backmann, Dave, "Jockey Park Dedicated: Time Capsule Buried During Ceremony," *Kenosha News,* May 22, 1993.
Hart, Elena, "Tommy Hilfiger Licenses Jockey for Underwear Line for '94," *DNR,* September 22, 1993, p. 2.
"In This Suit, Lawyers Will Argue about Briefs," *New York Times,* June 3, 1993, p. D4.

—Elizabeth Rourke

K & B Inc.

K & B Plaza, Lee Circle
New Orleans, Louisiana 70130-3999
U.S.A.
(504) 586-1234
Fax: (504) 585-4482

Private Company
Incorporated: 1905 as Katz and Besthoff, Ltd.
Employees: 4,500
Sales: $507.94 million
SICs: 5912 Drug Stores and Proprietary Stores; 2024 Ice
Cream, Bulk and Packaged; 6512 Operators of Non-
Residential Buildings; 7384 Photo Finishing Laboratory

K & B Inc. is a regional drug and convenience store chain
operating in six southern states with a home base in New
Orleans, Louisiana, where it was founded. Its outlets in 1994
numbered 177, with over 100 located in Louisiana. At that time,
among Louisiana-based businesses K & B ranked 22nd in size,
while nationally, among drugstore chains, it ranked 21st. Its rate
of growth was increasing with the region's economic recovery
from a deep recession caused by the oil industry's sudden slump
in the mid-1980s, and its prospects for future expansion were
considered excellent. Sensitive to changing market conditions,
K & B offers a wider range of general merchandise than most
drugstore chains and at some locations has other convenience-
store features, including drive-thru and 24-hour services. In
addition to its stores, K & B has two large distribution centers,
an ice cream manufacturing plant, and a photo processing
laboratory.

Following the typical pattern of many chain retail stores, K & B
evolved from a single store, opened in 1905 at 732 Canal Street,
in the heart of downtown New Orleans. It was the first venture
of a new partnership formed by Gustave David Katz and
Sydney J. Besthoff, Sr. under the incorporating name of Katz
and Besthoff, Ltd.

Katz was a native of New Orleans and a graduate of the Philadelphia College of Pharmacy. In 1896, after working briefly in a
drugstore located at Canal Street and Chartres Avenue, he
opened his own business at the corner of Jackson Street and St.
Charles Avenue, in an uptown, residential section of the city.
His store operated under the slogan "An uptown store with
downtown prices," and Katz, who had just turned twenty-five,

was quickly credited with being among the first to compete
aggressively with higher-volume downtown stores. Katz also
implemented a policy of double checking prescriptions, using
the telephone for calling them out and in, and making home
deliveries by bicycle.

Sydney J. Besthoff, Sr., from Memphis, Tennessee, who was
also a registered pharmacist and a successful drugstore owner,
first went to New Orleans to marry Florence Stich, a native of
the city. While there, he met briefly with Katz, then later
returned with plans to relocate in Louisiana. Katz had already
made up his mind to expand his operation into the downtown
area, thus he was very receptive to the idea of entering a
partnership with Besthoff when the latter came to consult with
him. Katz decided to sell his original store and give his full
attention to the new Katz and Besthoff enterprise. By arrangements made at the firm's first board of directors meeting on
November 2, 1905, his store's inventory was purchased and
transferred to the new drugstore.

The business was situated in the downtown shopping area, a
risky location that had proven disastrous for other drugstores
that had opened and closed there. Initially, the most dependable
patrons of the store, which sported the motto "Only the Best,"
were some of Katz's old customers. Then teenagers and young
adults started visiting the shop for late afternoon or evening
sodas or ice cream and friendly conversation. They insured a
summer clientele, providing important trade in a season when
prescription drug sales were light. Their parents soon followed
in their younger family members' footsteps.

Quite by accident, in 1908 the store also developed a highly
visible public-recognition emblem: a lavish purple wrapping for
items bought there. A large quantity of the paper had been
refused by a merchant who apparently found the color too
intense or gaudy, leaving the paper dealer with the problem of
unloading the consignment. Katz and Besthoff bought the shipment at a bargain price and began to use the paper in conjunction with newspaper ads announcing "If it's purple on the
outside, it's only the best from Katz and Besthoff." The purple
remained a distinct hallmark of K & B ever since.

The two partners contributed different but equally important
skills to the firm. Katz, named president in 1905, was an
excellent fiscal manager and careful organizer, while Besthoff,
secretary/treasurer, was a good public relations man and the
partnership's main innovator. Katz had instituted in his old store
what would become an important business policy for the new
company and one that would help it grow: customer credit
purchasing. However, it was Besthoff who pushed for expansion, convincing Katz that they should begin a retail chain.

In 1910, that expansion began. The partners opened a second
store, at 837 Canal Street, not far from the first. It was managed
by Edward L. Chapotel, who would later become a vice-president and the company's general manager. Like the first store,
the second was efficiently run, with special care taken in the
filling of prescriptions and in maintaining a clean and sanitary
soda fountain.

The chain was thus forged, and it continued to grow, slowly
at first, because operations were limited to downtown New
Orleans. The expansion in fact reflected the growth of the city,

and it was not until 1920 that the third Katz and Besthoff opened, at the corner of St. Charles and Louisiana Avenues. The fourth store, at Carroliton and Oak Streets, opened in 1923.

By that time, Sydney Besthoff, Jr. had already joined the company as a store manager. He had graduated from Newman College, and in 1921, when he started working for the firm, he was completing his degree in pharmacy at Tulane University. By 1924, he was a registered pharmacist, and, in 1926, when his father died of a heart attack, he succeeded the elder Besthoff both as Katz's principal partner and as the company's secretary/treasurer. With Chapotel, the new general manager, he aided Katz, the senior partner, in overseeing all phases of the business.

In 1928, stores five and six were opened. By that time, too, the firm, which had always made its own, in-house ice cream, had opened a small but modern, well-equipped ice cream plant and a laboratory for the manufacture of other proprietary products. Ten years later, in 1938, the company also began its own in-house developing and photo finishing laboratory, located on the third floor of the firm's drugstore at 1011 Canal Street. Under the management of William Leeper, Sydney J. Besthoff III, the grandson of the firm's co-founder, worked there between 1939 and 1941.

Gustave Katz, the remaining original partner, died in 1940, when the Katz and Besthoff chain consisted of fourteen stores and its supporting laboratories and processing plants. Katz had remained active in the business right up to his death. His heirs elected to sell his share of the business to Sydney J. Besthoff, Jr. and his family. Thereafter, the Besthoffs were the sole owners of the company, but during World War II, while Sydney Besthoff, Jr. served in the U.S. Army, the business was managed by two vice-presidents: Maurice Stich, the director, and Edward Chapotel, the general manager.

Major Sydney Besthoff, Jr. returned home in October 1945 to resume his position as the firm's senior officer. He was then joined by his cousins, Jac and Charles Stich, who witnessed the next phase of the business' expansion in the postwar boom. In 1947, Katz and Besthoff consolidated parts of its operation in a single building, located at 900 Camp Street. The new, four-floor facility housed the executive offices, originally quartered on the second floor of a Canal Street drugstore, plus a store with a soda fountain and cafeteria, a new ice cream plant, kitchen commissary, and printing, prescription, tobacco, and general merchandise departments.

Part of the firm's growing business resulted from its ice cream manufacturing and marketing. Although Katz and Besthoff had from the first made its own ice cream, its bulk packaging for home consumption was limited. The company had sold ice cream in "flat fifths," slim packages that fit in the small freezer compartments of old-style refrigerators, but after installing new equipment at the plant in the Camp Street building, the company began to make ice cream in much greater quantities, both quickly and economically. Aided by the increasing home use of bigger combination refrigerator-freezers and separate freezer units, the ice cream trade of the company prospered. The firm also began a home delivery service, making it easy for customers to get a special treat with just a telephone call. It was a product and service that caught on and held.

By 1955, during its 50th anniversary, the company had filled over ten million prescriptions. The chain at that time consisted of eighteen stores, still within New Orleans and its immediate suburbs. The drugstores ran golden-anniversary promotional sales and gave away prizes, including a brand new Ford sedan, and the company held a gala celebration at the Roosevelt Hotel, honoring its employees and its business achievements.

A new period of accelerated expansion began soon after 1962, when Sydney J. Besthoff III was made executive vice-president of the firm. While he had graduated from the Wharton School of Business at the University of Pennsylvania and had continued graduate study at Tulane University, he had also worked in the business for years, learning it from the ground up. When Besthoff took his new post, the chain had grown to 24 drugstores, but all were still in the New Orleans vicinity. In 1965, after he was made president and his father became chairman, Sydney J. Besthoff III instituted some forward-looking changes, including a policy of expansion beyond the New Orleans area. In 1968, Katz and Besthoff opened a drugstore about 30 miles away, in Slidell. Soon after that, it opened one in Baton Rogue, the state capital. Both tentative ventures were successful, convincing the firm's officers that it was worth a risk to open in other places, first within, then without the state.

In 1974, the executive offices of Katz and Besthoff moved into headquarters in K & B Plaza, at Lee Circle. The building, which won several design awards, had been planned by the world renowned architectural firm of Skidmore, Owings & Merrill and had been built to accommodate an art collection, begun there in 1977 by the Virlane Foundation. It would become the most important contemporary art collection in the city, free and open to the general public. Katz and Besthoff, furthering the development of culture in New Orleans, a year earlier had agreed to allow the Contemporary Arts Center to locate at its old 900 Camp Street site.

By 1975, Katz and Besthoff Inc. had filled nearly 50 million prescriptions. Its drugstores were also undergoing a timely facelift, wholly in keeping with changing times. The corner drugstore was becoming a relic, popular in the 1950s but not the 1970s, and the company reflected that change in a variety of ways. Most importantly, it phased out its soda fountains and added convenience-store shelves for beverages and foodstuffs. It had also opened its first distribution center, located in Metairie, moving its ice cream plant there and centralizing its stocking, shipping, and handling. The newer, streamlined, cash-and-carry drugstores no longer provided a place for customers to sit and talk, but the payback for patrons was realized in lower prices and more efficient and quicker service.

The new look was reflected in the company's new name, which, in 1977, changed from Katz and Besthoff, Inc. to K & B, Inc., and, for public relations, simply K & B. Since the business was rapidly expanding outside of New Orleans, the family names were quickly losing what had been a hometown recognition. By that time, too, Sydney Besthoff, Jr. had retired, and his son had become the firm's CEO.

K & B's expansion slowed when the great oil boom of the 1970s and early 1980s fizzled, and Louisiana went into an economic slump, but it did continue. In 1982, Sydney Besthoff died, in the same year that the company opened a second distribution center to facilitate growth; although it only opened one to two stores per year in the lean period following the oil bust, the company did increase its range of operation, finally to several out-of-state locations within a 400 mile radius of New Orleans.

As the State of Louisiana pulled out of its economic slump, K & B began a new period of growth, under the direction of James J. LeBlanc, who had been named president and chief operating officer on November 27, 1987. LeBlanc had been with K & B since 1975, working first as a pharmacist, then as a store manager, district supervisor, assistant operations director, and finally, in 1984, vice-president and operations director. A native of Paincourtville, Louisiana, LeBlanc was a graduate of Loyola University and the South School of Pharmacy. At the time of LeBlanc's promotion to president, K & B was operating 148 stores.

Under LeBlanc's tutelage, the company opened stores in Alabama and in Tennessee, where, in 1991, it bought out Osco, a small drugstore chain in Memphis. By then it was operating 170 units in six states: Louisiana (103 stores), Mississippi (25 stores), Alabama (20 stores), Florida (nine stores), Tennessee (seven stores), and Texas (six stores). It had also further streamlined its operations, downsizing its prototype store from close to 20,000 square feet to 12,000. And starting with a store located at Gentilly Boulevard and Elysian Fields Avenue in New Orleans, in 1991, it had begun 24-hour convenience service at select, high-volume locations. Its stores' merchandise inventories, reflecting K & B's new emphasis on its convenience-store service, carried an extensive array of items, including health aids, toiletries, cosmetics, household goods, tools, automotive supplies, foodstuffs, paperbacks, magazines, toys, school and office supplies, cameras, electronic items, greeting cards, and, where permitted, alcoholic beverages. In 1993, in the New Orleans K & B stores, prescription drug sales accounted for about 30 percent of K & B's annual sales, while the sale of health and beauty aids and general merchandise had grown to over 50 percent and would continue to account for a growing share of the business.

By 1994, K & B was employing nearly 2,000 full-time and 2,500 part-time workers, either in its home office or in one of its two distribution centers, 177 drugstores, separate camera center, ice cream plant, or superphoto laboratory. The company's new prototype stores were given a contemporary look, with wider aisles, better lighting, and a distinct exterior facade. The firm had also taken further steps to update both its customer services and computerized capabilities. For example, in 1993, at its Veterans Highway store in Metairie, the company had installed its first drive-thru prescription service. K & B had also expanded the use of fax equipment and inventory control computers to link individual stores with the company's distribution centers, ensuring accurate and efficient inventory control.

Reacting well to changing social and business trends, K & B was likely to have a bright future. Some have suggested that the key to such success would be in the company's response to the needs of two large consumer groups: senior citizens and women from middle and lower income households. Clearly, too, much of its expansion was likely to occur outside of Louisiana, in states where K & B had just begun to be a household name.

Further Reading:

Brookman, Faye, "K&B: Withstanding the Test of Time," *Stores,* November 1992, pp. 20–26.
"Katz & Besthoff Fetes 50 Years," *New Orleans Times-Picayune,* April 14, 1955.
"Katz and Besthoff Mark Twenty-Fifth Anniversary of Successful Business," *New Orleans Times-Picayune,* May 10, 1931.
Rosendale, Iris, "New Orleans Retail Scene as Diverse as the City," *Drug Topics,* August 17, 1992, pp. 89–90.

—John W. Fiero

Kaman Corp.

P.O. Box 1
Bloomfield, Connecticut 06002
U.S.A.
(203) 243-7100
Fax: (203) 243-6365

Public Company
Incorporated: 1945 as Kaman Aircraft
Employees: 5,239
Sales: $819.18 million
Stock Exchanges: NASDAQ
SICs: 3724 Aircraft Engines & Engine Parts; 3728 Aircraft
   Parts & Equipment; 3812 Search & Navigation
   Equipment; 5085 Industrial Supplies; Musical Instruments

Kaman Corp. develops and manufactures high-tech products
and provides technical services for government, industrial, and
commercial markets. Particularly well-known for its role in the
helicopter industry, it is also the largest independent distributor
of musical instruments in the United States. In addition, Kaman
supplies repair and replacement parts to nearly every heavy and
light industrial sector, and is a high-tech leader in the defense
industry. Kaman has a rich history that parallels a classic
American success story.

Kaman is the progeny of American paragon Charles H. Kaman,
an inventor, entrepreneur, musician, humanitarian, and visionary. He was born in 1919 and raised in Washington, D.C. His
father, a German immigrant, was a construction supervisor who
managed work on the Supreme Court building and Union Station. Kaman demonstrated an early interest in aviation design.
During the 1930s, he competed in the city's model airplane
design contests held at the local playground. He also showed an
enthusiasm for music. Kaman became an accomplished guitar
player as a teenager and even turned down an offer to play with
the Tommy Dorsey band for an alluring $75 per week.

Kaman continued to pursue his interest in aviation during college. For a contest held in Washington, D.C., he made a model
plane, which took more than 100 hours to build, was made of
balsa wood, covered with an ultra-thin film, and driven by a
rubber band. Kaman wound the propeller 1,500 times and asked
the judge to clock his warm-up flight. After setting an unofficial
record for time aloft, Kaman became determined to surpass
his own record. He decided to wind the propeller 3,500 times,

using an eggbeater. At about 3,000 turns the band snapped
and the plane imploded. Nevertheless, the episode cemented
his desire to become an innovator in the burgeoning aviation
field.

Kaman graduated magna cum laude with a Bachelor of Aeronautical Engineering degree in 1940 from Washington's Catho-
lic University. Although he had dreamed since childhood of
becoming a professional pilot, a severe infection following a
tonsillectomy that left him deaf in one ear made that an impossi-
bility. Instead of piloting flying machines, Kaman decided to
build them. After college, he accepted a position with aviation
pioneer United Aircraft (the forerunner to the United Technologies Corporation). He went to work in the company's helicopter
division, Hamilton Standard, which was marshalled by renowned inventor Igor Sikorsky. Kaman was told to help design
propellers.

The chief dilemma facing helicopter engineers during the industry's inception was stability and control. Engineers were challenged to figure out how to devise a machine that could be easily
maneuvered and landed, particularly in high winds. Aside from
stability and control, helicopters in the early 1940s suffered
from several problems. Vibration was a major obstacle. Because of the way in which the rotor was controlled from its hub,
the entire aircraft would vibrate, putting stress on the machine
that reduced its durability and dependability.

Kaman's contributions were quickly recognized at United, and
by 1943 he had become head of aerodynamics. Despite his
success at United, Kaman became frustrated by the company's
lack of attention to his ideas. Specifically, Kaman had suggested
an improvement that might increase the stability of United's
helicopters. He wanted to put flaps on the main rotor and scrap
the tail rotor altogether to improve control. On his own time,
Kaman built a homemade rig to test his theories. He fashioned
the contraption in his mother's garage using junk parts, including an engine from a 1933 Pontiac, the rear end of an old Dodge,
and a bathroom scale.

Kaman's initial designs failed. But after several weeks of experimenting he was able to build a device that incorporated his
revolutionary servo-flap rotor control system. The new design
significantly reduced vibration. It also required much less force
by the pilot to maneuver the aircraft, thus improving stability
and control. Excited by his discovery, Kaman approached the
manager of engineering at United and even demonstrated his
rotor blade test rig. "Charlie, we have our inventor at United
Aircraft," explained his supervisor. "His name is Igor
Sikorsky. We don't need another one."

Because United was not interested in his ideas, Kaman decided
to go to work for an employer that would put his theories into
practice, himself. With $2,000 and some rudimentary labora-
tory equipment, Kaman started a company that would become a
multi-million-dollar corporation, a leader in aviation technology, and among other credits, a guitar supplier to rock stars.
Kaman shaped his new enterprise around the contraption he
made in his mother's garage. He raised development funds by
holding weekend flying shows with his homemade aircraft, the
K-125, at Bradley Field, where he solicited observers to invest
in his idea.

Kaman was able to generate enough capital to build a new helicopter, the K-190, by 1948. It incorporated a dual-rotor system (but no tail rotor) and was touted as the most stable, easy-to-fly helicopter ever built. To reinforce his claim of stability, Kaman conducted a public relations coup in November of 1948 at Bradley Field. Ann Griffin, a young house wife with virtually no flying experience, jumped into the cockpit of the exotic contraption and flew it for ten minutes before an astonished audience. The stunt was widely publicized and resulted in an infusion of capital into Kaman's company. Most importantly, it helped Kaman to get his first helicopter orders.

Kaman, like many of his helicopter industry contemporaries, had grand visions for his flying machines. Many engineers believed that the helicopter would eventually replace the automobile as the vehicle of choice for families. Each family would have a helicopter in its back yard or on its roof. People would zip to work, to the grocery store, or even to vacation destinations in a matter of minutes or hours. Unfortunately, physical realities emerged that made the concept infeasible given twentieth century technology. Thus, Kaman determined that the immediate future of his company was in the commercial and defense markets.

Kaman achieved important technical breakthroughs during the late 1940s and 1950s. In 1951, for instance, he designed the world's first gas-turbine powered helicopter. The innovation became a major industry influence on the design of helicopter power systems through the mid 1990s. Despite technical advances, though, Kaman Aircraft realized spotty financial success. Kaman was unsuccessful at marketing his K-225 (successor to the K-125) as a crop duster. And, although descendants of the K-190 and K-225 models were purchased for use in search and rescue missions in the 1950s, his servo-flap design never found a mass market.

Kaman's helicopters, which became known as synchropters, had many advantages over other machines. Their chief drawback, however, was slowness. As the military increased its emphasis on speed during the 1950s and 1960s, synchropters lost favor to speedier designs that were more appropriate for battle. However, Kaman's machines still found demand in a variety of military applications that required improved control and stability (search and rescue operations and heavy lifting jobs, for example), particularly during the Korean War. In fact, the Husky performed more rescues than any other helicopter and was the first to perform with no loss of life or accidents attributed to the aircraft.

One of Kaman Aircraft's crowning achievements in the helicopter industry was its creation of the UH-2 utility helicopter. Kaman won the contract to design the machine in a contest. The project posed a formidable challenge because of the extremely demanding requirements set fourth by the Navy. It wanted a vehicle that could fly at night for several hundred miles with no external navigation. It also had to be able to pick up downed pilots at sea under icy conditions and then return to a different location. Because of the complexity of the instrumentation, Kaman found that the machine also had to have less than one-tenth of a G of vibration to make it difficult for the pilot to read the display panel. Kaman's UH-2 met the requirements and was introduced into service in 1963.

In addition to the UH-2, other successful Kaman helicopter designs included the H-43 Husky, which was used during Vietnam to rescue downed pilots, and the SH-2. The SH-2, an antisubmarine aircraft, was still being used by the Navy in the early 1990s. Throughout the 1950s and early 1960s, Kaman Aircraft's inventions relating to airplanes, rotors, drones, and other technologies made pivotal contributions to the field of aviation. Among its most notable contributions were the first servo-controlled rotor, gas-turbine helicopter, twin-turbine helicopter, all-composite rotor blade, and remotely controlled helicopter. Kaman also set numerous records related to time-to-climb, altitude, as well as other factors. In addition, Kaman designed the first helicopter (the H-43 Husky) to perform with no loss of life or accidents attributable to the aircraft.

Although Kaman managed to show a profit every year during the 1950s and early 1960s, its sales fluctuated because of its dependence on military contracts. In the early 1960s, John F. Kennedy's administration ordered 220 Seasprite helicopters from Kaman. Five days later, however, Kennedy was assassinated. President Johnson rescinded the order and Kaman's helicopter division was devastated.

However, the detrimental impact of the loss of the large Pentagon contract was diminished by Kaman's other operations. Since the late 1950s, Kaman had been trying to reduce its dependence on defense contracts, particularly related to helicopters. The board of directors determined that Kaman should have three basic elements to its business: defense, industrial, and commercial. Over time, they decided, each division would be built to approximate one-third of company sales. In the 1950s, Kaman began expanding into aerospace parts manufacturing, aerodynamics subcontracting, and advanced nuclear research, among other defense and industry-related activities. As a result of its diversification, Kaman continued to post profits throughout the 1960s and 1970s.

One of Kaman's most intriguing ventures away from the helicopter business involved musical instruments. Partly because of his own interest in playing the guitar, Kaman had long been interested in the music business. In the early 1960s, he set out to develop his own guitar. He sought help from Martin, a Pennsylvania-based manufacturer of acoustic guitars. Kaman was surprised at the primitive methods that Martin and other companies were still using to produce the instruments. He believed that he could improve both the guitars and the production process by incorporating modern manufacturing techniques and aerospace technology.

The owners of Martin refused to sell their company, so Kaman started his own operation. He drew on his knowledge of harmonics, which he gleaned from building helicopter rotors, to build a guitar with composites that still had a natural sound. "In a helicopter, you take vibration out," Kaman explained in the July 26, 1993 *Business Week*. "In a guitar you put it in." The end result of Kaman's early efforts was the Ovation guitar, a top industry seller distinguished by its round-back design. Kaman Music Corp. met with success during the late 1960s and particularly beginning in the 1970s by developing new products and acquiring other manufacturers. In 1974, Kaman's son, C. William Kaman II, started his career making guitars at Kaman Music Corp. He became president of that division in 1986.

Kaman continued to build its consumer and defense-related businesses throughout the 1960s and 1970s. In addition, it expanded into several industrial segments through merger and acquisition beginning in 1971. In that year, Kaman purchased three industrial distribution businesses, launching a buying spree that would make Kaman Corp. a Fortune 500 company by the 1980s. Kaman purchased more than 30 industrial companies during the 1970s and 1980s, making its Kaman Bearing and Supply subsidiary the third largest U.S. industrial distributor. By 1989, that division accounted for roughly half of Kaman Corp.'s revenues. Kaman Bearing and Supply had 156 offices in the United States and Canada and supplied over 750,000 different parts to every major industry.

Charles Kaman had success integrating the companies that he acquired into a cohesive whole. When appraising buyout candidates, Kaman looked for situations in which both companies stood to gain from each other's competencies. A musical instrument manufacturer, for example, might benefit from Kaman's marketing and distribution channels while Kaman would get access to new production facilities or patented processes or products. In addition, he applied years of experience in determining the integrity and substance of the candidate. ''After 45 years I just walk through and I've got it in about 10 minutes, maybe half-an-hour,'' Kaman told *Enterprise*. ''You can read it. . . . When we visit a military base I can tell you what the base commander is like by the attitude of the sentry at the guard house—are we greeted with smiles, does he know what's going on?''

At his home office Kaman set the leadership example that permeated his organization. Kaman was his company's major stockholder, but unlike most executives he had purchased all of his stock on the open market rather than receiving it as compensation, reflecting his faith in the company. In addition, he paid himself a relatively low salary compared with other chief executive officers of companies of similar size, and much of it was tied to the company's performance. Kaman believed in direct communication and candor and advocating empowering workers and recognizing their contributions. ''There's no politicking, no vying for power around here,'' stated Kaman in *Enterprise*. ''Its just straight-arrow stuff.'' Kaman Corp. was recognized for its acute management team and fruitful working environment.

Kaman continued to diversify into new markets and expand its defense, industrial, and consumer divisions during the 1970s and 1980s. Importantly, Kaman reopened its helicopter production line in 1981. It began manufacturing an updated version of its old Seasprite helicopter called the SH-2F, or LAMPS (Light Airborne Multi-purpose System) for the Navy, which wanted to use it as a submarine hunter and utility craft. The SH-2F had Kaman's original servo-flap system as well as a tail rotor. Renewed interest in the servo-flap design was partially a result of new technology and materials that made it more feasible for integration into new helicopters.

As Kaman expanded into new markets and revived old ones, its revenues continued to swell during the 1980s. Sales topped $380 million in 1983, about $6.4 million of which was net income. Receipts increased to $556 million by 1985 and then past $760 million in 1988 as net earnings rose past the $25

million mark. Likewise, Kaman's work force increased from 4,800 in the early 1980s to nearly 6,500 by 1989. Although sales of musical instruments languished, defense-related work boomed. Kaman continued to be a powerful influence in the high-tech defense arena. One of the company's projects in 1986, was an $8.5 million contract to build an electromagnetic coil gun, a high-tech cannon that used synchronized magnetic waves to fire projectiles at a rate of 2.5 miles per second.

Besides his lauded achievements in aviation and technology, Kaman was also well-known for another of his passions, breeding guide dogs for the blind. When a blind boyhood friend had his life improved by a guide dog, Kaman became interested in guide dogs. To improve blind people's access to the dogs, Kaman and his wife launched the Fieldco Guide Dog Foundation, a nonprofit foundation that breeds and trains dogs for the blind, in 1960.

Kaman handled his dog breeding operation in the same way he managed his business affairs. He applied rigorous breeding standards and was able to gradually weed out genetic defects, particularly susceptibility to certain disease strains, that have traditionally plagued guide dogs. The Kamans opened their own school in 1981 to match dogs with owners. The school provided dogs to recipients for $150 in the early 1990s, a mere fraction of the $17,500 training cost. In 1990, Fieldco launched an initiative to begin matching 100 teams (owner and dog) annually by the turn of the century.

Charles Kaman stepped aside as president of Kaman Corp. in 1990 at the age of 71, but remained chief executive and chairman of the board. He was succeeded by Harvey S. Levenson. Levenson took the reins just as the company was slipping into a downturn. After doubling its sales between 1980 and 1989, Kaman suffered setbacks primarily attributable to defense industry cutbacks. Several of its contracts ran out and new federal defense spending programs were capped in the wake of the post-cold-war military transition. Net earnings dropped to $8.7 million in 1989 and the rampant revenue growth achieved during much of the 1980s waned.

As defense dollars ebbed, Kaman adjusted to the new environment by restructuring and cutting its work force to about 5,300 employees by 1993. The company posted a disappointing loss in 1993, mostly as a result of restructuring costs, and total revenues remained below $800 million. Nevertheless, Kaman's strong performance in its industrial technologies, distribution, and music businesses had allowed it to remain profitable between 1990 and 1992. Furthermore, the company held a strong technological edge in its core markets and was solidly positioned for future growth. Virtually every mass-produced aircraft in the world already utilized Kaman parts, which secured its dominant market presence.

Kaman Music became the largest independent distributor of musical instruments in the United States with over 13,000 products when it acquired Hamer Guitars in the early 1990s, a $100 million guitar manufacturer. Boosting that segment's credibility was a long list of star performers that were using Kaman's guitars (and other equipment), including Glen Campbell, Richie Sambora of Bon Jovi, and Phil Collins. By 1993, in fact, music and consumer products comprised about 20 percent of Kaman's total sales. Industrial products and distribution activities represented about 43 percent and defense-related goods and services comprised the remainder of sales.

Kaman offset its defense-related losses by repositioning its helicopter products for use in commercial markets. In 1994, the company's breakthrough K-MAX helicopter was certified by the Federal Aviation Administration. The K-MAX was touted as an "aerial truck" and was designed specifically for repetitive heavy lifting. The K-MAX could lift three tons, more than its weight, and was particularly suited to logging in environmentally sensitive areas, fire fighting, construction, heavy equipment transportation, and a variety of specialty and industrial uses. The helicopter sold for $3.5 million or could be leased for $1 million per thousand hours of use. Kaman's latest helicopter represented the culmination of a lifetime of industry experience. "There's a whole goddamn lifetime of experience in there," Kaman said in *Business Week*.

Kaman Corp. entered the mid-1990s with a record of innovation and technological leadership rarely surpassed in American industry. Astute management, a strong balance sheet, a new emphasis on international expansion, and the slated introduction of several breakthrough products suggested a strong future for Kaman Corp.

Principal Subsidiaries: Kaman Aerospace Corporation; Kaman Diversified Technologies Corporation; Kaman Aerospace Corp.; Kaman Sciences Corp.; Kaman Instrumentation Corp.; Kamatics Corp.; Kaman Electromagnetics Corp.; Kaman Industrial Technologies Corporation; Kaman Music Corporation.

Further Reading:

Birchard, Bill, "The Art of Acquisition," *Enterprise,* Fall 1989, p. 9.

Gertzen, Ian, "Kaman Tightening Workforce," *Norwich Bulletin,* September 10, 1993, sec. 1, p. 1.

Kaman, Charles, Untitled, *Rotor Wing International,* May 1991.

Lehrer, Linda, "Charles Kaman, Who Founded His Own Fortune 500 Company, Now Takes Time Out to Raise and Train Dogs that Help the Blind," *Trump's Guiding Light,* September 1990.

North, Sterling, "A Defensive Move: Kaman Corp. Turns from Whirlybirds to Star Wars," *New England Business,* November 17, 1986, sec. 1, p. 53.

Rose, Peter, "Kaman Industries Goes High-Tech," *Idaho Business Review,* May 2, 1994, sec. A, p. 10.

Smart, Tim, "What Do Dogs, Guitars, and Choppers Have in Common?", *Business Week,* July 26, 1993.

Stuller, Jay, "The Taming of the Copter," *Air & Space,* December 1990, p. 92.

Valvo, Vincent Michael, "Kaman: Innovation and Ovation," *Intercorp,* May 29, 1987, sec. 1, p. 1.

—Dave Mote

Kia Motors Corp.

992-28, Shihung-Dong
Kuro-GU, Seoul 152-030
South Korea
82 2 7881114
Fax: 2 7840746

Public Company
Founded: 1944
Employees: 25,000
Sales: $6.8 billion
SICs: 3711 Motor Vehicles and Car Bodies; 3713 Truck and
Bus Bodies

Kia Motors Corp. is the second largest manufacturer of automobiles and trucks in South Korea. In addition to the core Korea market, Kia also exports vehicles to Europe, North America, and several Asian countries. The company entered the world's largest potential market, the United States, in 1992 with the formation of subsidiary Kia Motors America. Kia started out as one of Korea's giant *chaebols* (groups of companies), but was operating as an independent, publicly traded company in the early 1990s.

Kia was formed in 1944, shortly before North Korea invaded the South. The company would eventually succeed, first as a diversified manufacturer of bicycles and industrial products, and later as a manufacturer of trucks and automobiles. But during the late 1940s and 1950s commercial expansion was effectively thwarted by the Korean War. By the end of the war in 1953, in fact, South Korea's industrial base lay in ruins. Throughout the 1950s and early 1960s, Korea's recovery was slow. The Rhee (Rhee Syngman) government resorted to favoritism and corruption to maintain power and became increasingly authoritative. Student revolts in the 1960s forced Rhee Syngman into exile. The ruling party that finally emerged from the ensuing political fray was headed by military leader Park Chung-hee.

Park ruled Korea in characteristic military style. His regime during the 1960s and 1970s was marked by increasing centralization of power, both political and industrial. Importantly, though, his government was obsessed with economic growth and development. So while Park was widely criticized for his authoritarian style, his government is credited with laying the foundation for South Korea's economic renaissance. Between 1960 and 1980, in fact, South Korea's annual exports surged from a negligible $33 million to more than $17 billion. Kia Motors benefitted from the economic revolution, growing from a small bicycle manufacturer to a global supplier of automobiles. Kia started out producing steel tubing and bicycle parts before building its own line of bicycles in the 1950s. It eventually parlayed that know-how into its own line of motorcycles, and later turned to truck production.

A key dynamic influencing Kia's (and South Korea's) gains during the 1960s and 1970s was the *chaebol* (a business group consisting of large companies that are owned or managed by relatives of one or two 'royal' families). Park decided that the best way to develop South Korea's economy was to identify key industries and then select specific companies to serve those sectors. The government would work with the companies, providing protection and financial assistance as part of a series of five-year national economic growth plans. By concentrating power in the hands of a few giant, family-held companies, Park reasoned, impediments to success would be minimized and cost-efficiencies would result. The Kia *chaebol* was selected by Park to concentrate on trucks and various industrial goods such as machine tools. The company sold its first truck in 1962.

Kia grew quickly during the 1960s and 1970s through a combination of hard work and government assistance. Between 1962 and 1966, during the first of Park's five-year plans for the Korean vehicle industry, Kia acted much like an import processor. The company imported many of the parts used to build its trucks from foreign producers and assembled them locally. Kia was protected by the Motor Vehicle Industry Protection Law of 1962, which forbade the importation of already-assembled vehicles or major components. During Park's second phase (1967 to 1971), Kia increasingly developed its own parts using knowledge it gained from its outside suppliers. During the 1970s, Kia gradually weaned itself from extreme dependence on imports and started to develop proprietary technology that would eventually allow it to compete as an exporter of completed vehicles.

In accordance with Park's "Long-Term Plan for Motor Vehicle Industry Promotion" of 1973, Kia began manufacturing automobiles in 1974. Although that move represented new territory for the truck and tool manufacturer, another South Korean company—Hyundai—had preceded Kia's entry into the truck industry by about 15 years. In addition, Hyundai pioneered Korea's car industry with production of the Pony, Korea's first completely domestic passenger car, in 1968. Hyundai led Kia in automobile production throughout the 1970s and into the mid-1990s. But the two companies did not directly compete in their home country because the government set car prices according to engine size. Kia's domestic car and truck business proved successful and allowed Kia to become the second largest domestic vehicle manufacturer and the tenth largest *chaebol* in the country by the 1980s. Hyundai was ranked second, and its giant Hyundai Motors division eventually became one of the 200 largest companies in the world.

Despite Korea's economic gains, Park's government had many enemies. Park was assassinated in 1979. His successor, Chun Doo Hwan, was also a military leader. His economic goals were similar to those articulated by Park, and he sustained Park's basic long-term economic plan. For the 1980s, that scheme entailed Korea's transformation into an exporting, rather than importing, nation. To that end, Chun's government continued to support *chaebols* like Hyundai and Kia while blocking foreign competitors from entering the South Korean market on a significant scale.

In 1981 the Chun government decided that South Korea's automobile industry was growing too quickly. It chose to limit the number of domestic vehicle producers to the five in operation at that time, and to freeze the particular areas of production. Thus only three companies, including Kia, were allowed to manufacture cars, and only Kia was allowed to build light-weight trucks.

Chun's overall economic strategy was generally successful, despite citizens' growing displeasure with South Korea's authoritative, centralized political and economic structure. While Kia enjoyed a relative dearth of competition in its core domestic market, it also launched an aggressive and successful export campaign during the 1980s that penetrated Japan and Europe, among other regions. By the mid-1980s Kia was selling about 300,000 cars annually, mostly in South Korea. A major breakthrough for Kia occurred in 1987, when it started shipping automobiles to the largest single international car market, the United States. Kia reached an agreement to supply Ford with its Festiva model. The Festiva was a "microcar" aimed at the low-end buyer. Kia planned to ship about 70,000 units annually for Ford and a like number of the cars to other countries. Kia's sales topped US$2.4 billion in 1987 as its work force swelled to about 23,500.

Kia's arrangement with Ford reflected its strategy, first evident in the mid-1980s, to gradually assume Japan's role as the leading supplier of low-end economy cars. By the mid-1980s, in fact, it was clear to Kia executives that Japan was reducing its emphasis on low-priced cars and focusing on higher-priced, high-profit vehicles—Hyundai had also observed the trend, as evidenced by its 1986 jump into the North American car market. Kia planned to use its low-cost production advantages to fill the void. Kia's greatest edge in comparison to U.S., European, and Japanese automakers was labor. Indeed, until the late 1980s Kia paid its workers a mere fraction of what their foreign counterparts earned. The savings were mirrored in cars like the Festiva, which enjoyed steady demand as a result of its extremely low price. Over a period of about five years, Kia shipped 350,000 Festivas to Ford.

In addition to its low labor costs, Kia continued to benefit throughout the 1980s from rigid trade barriers imposed by its home country. Overseas producers had previously paid little attention to the restrictions because of the comparatively small size of the Korean market. By the late 1980s, however, foreign governments were pressuring South Korea to open its markets. The inequity was undeniable. In 1988, for instance, a total of 305 foreign cars were sold in South Korea. During the same year the country exported more than half a million automobiles, most of which were made by Hyundai and Kia. The government lifted some barriers in 1988 and 1989, but imposed less obvious restrictions. Nevertheless, foreign producers made inroads in the South Korean market during the early 1990s.

Besides proliferating domestic competition, Kia also suffered during the late 1980s and early 1990s from labor problems. Fed up with low pay and poor working conditions, South Korea's workers rebelled during the period. Union strikes forced many companies, including Kia, to significantly raise wages. The labor uprising was actually just one part of a much larger movement during the 1980s to dismantle South Korea's political and economic framework. Particularly since the mid-1980s, the government had been working to decentralize. A corollary of that effort was the diminished dominance of the *chaebols*. In the late 1980s the Chun government was voted out and replaced by a more liberal administration. Privatization and increased competition ensued. By the early 1990s Kia jettisoned its *chaebol* structure and became an independent, publicly traded company, although it continued to benefit from government ties and protected domestic markets.

Following a string of setbacks in the late 1980s and early 1990s, Kia experienced some major breakthroughs. One development was its 1992 introduction of the Sephia, a compact four-door sedan, to the domestic market. The car quickly became the best selling automobile in South Korea. The success of the car was a great relief to Kia, which was simultaneously preparing to enter the U.S. market with its own cars and dealers. Partly in preparation for that project, Kia invested heavily during the early 1990s to vastly expand its production capacity. By 1992 its debt load ballooned to more than US$2 billion—by 1994 the company's debt surged to a whopping $3.3 billion.

Kia bet heavily on its ability to market its Sephia and another new model, the Sportage, in international markets. The introduction was well-timed because car sales in many regions were booming in 1994. The big draw for Kia products was the low price. Kia claimed that products such as the Sephia were of comparable performance and quality to vehicles offered by other manufacturers, but at a much lower cost.

By the time Kia entered the United States with its own nameplate in 1993, it was already selling its cars in about 80 foreign countries and building a total of more than 500,000 cars annually. The company hoped to achieve unprecedented global growth during the mid- and late-1990s. Kia increased production capacity from 650,000 in 1993 to 930,000 in 1994 and planned to boost that figure to 1.5 million by 1997. Kia's global strategy was multi-faceted. In addition to European and U.S. operations, for example, it aggressively chased the blooming Chinese market. To that end, Kia opened the Yanbian Industrial Technology Training Institute in China to train expatriates in production techniques. Kia planned to eventually build a network along China's east coast.

Kia's U.S. foray in the mid-1990s was conducted through the newly formed Kia Motors America. Heading that division was automotive industry veteran Gregory Warner. Warner planned to bring Kia into the U.S. market slowly, starting with selected dealerships in California and expanding into 11 western states. His initial goal was to sell 30,000 to 50,000 units annually.

In 1994 Kia's diversified operations generated about $6.8 billion in revenues. Most of that amount was attributable to shipments of automobiles and related parts, although about 16 percent came from truck sales. The revenue figure marked a significant increase over revenues of $4.5 billion in 1993 and $2.5 billion in 1990. Kia's profitability, however, was extremely weak. Net income fluctuated around a paltry $20 million throughout the early 1990s before bobbing up to $27 million in 1994. Kia's stock plummeted in 1994. The company defended its stressed balance sheet by emphasizing anticipated profits from its popular new models. Kia entered the mid-1990s as the 20th largest car maker in the world and the 7th biggest corporation in South Korea.

Principal Subsidiaries: Kia Motors America

Further Reading:

Burstiner, March, "Kia Drives into Town with Nine Bay Area Dealerships," *San Francisco Business Times,* April 15, 1994, p. 3.

Darlin, Damon, "The Keep-it-Simple Strategy," *Forbes,* August 16, 1993, p. 98.

Harrison, Leah, "Dealers Hope Service, Low Cost Will Drive Kia Sales," *Puget Sound Business Journal,* November 19, 1993, p. 3.

Hart-Landensberg, Martin, *The Rush to Development: Economic Change and Political Struggle in South Korea,* New York: Monthly Review Press, 1993.

Luebke, Cathy, and Vince Maietta, "Kia Sephia isn't Too Good to Be True," *Business Journal,* May 27, 1994, p. 26.

Nakarmi, Laxmi, and Larry Armstrong, "Ford, Toyota, Volkswagen, Fiat, Kia . . . Kia?," *Business Week,* December 12, 1994, p. 58.

Nauman, Matt, "South Korea Import Tries to Crack Compact Car Market," *Knight-Ridder/Tribune Business News,* April 12, 1994.

Onishi, Norimitsu, "Korea's Kia Motors Enters U.S. Market with Sephia," *Knight-Ridder/Tribune Business,* September 22, 1993.

Shin, Yoo Keun, Richard Steer, and Gerardo R. Ungson, *The Chaebol,* New York: Harper & Row, 1989.

Whitehair, John, "Korea's Kia Arrives in Area," *San Bernadino County Sun,* August 6, 1994, p. B8.

—Dave Mote

Kimball International, Inc.

1600 Royal Street
Jasper, Indiana 47549
U.S.A.
(812) 482-1600
Fax: (812) 482-8803

Public Company
Incorporated: 1950 as the Jasper Corporation
Employees: 8,100
Sales: $822.48 million
Stock Exchanges: NASDAQ
SICs: 2511 Wood Household Furniture; 2512 Upholstered
    Household Furniture; 2517 Wood T.V. and Radio
    Cabinets; 2521 Wood Office Furniture; 2522 Office
    Furniture Except Wood

Kimball International, Inc. is a diversified manufacturer of consumer durable goods best known for its wide range of office, hospitality, healthcare, and home furnishings. The company achieved its first successes in the 1950s by specializing in the manufacture of television cabinets for a variety of original equipment manufacturers (OEMs). Over the years, Kimball has taken advantage of its control of several stages in the manufacturing process to broaden its line of wood cabinetry and furniture offerings to consumers and OEMs. A majority of its 1994 sales—$549 million of a total of $822.5 million—came from the furniture and cabinets segment of the company. Kimball received the majority of the remainder of its sales from its electronic contract assemblies and processed wood products segments. The company also continues to market Kimball pianos, a brand that dates its origins to 1857.

In 1950 a group of investors led by Arnold F. Habig took over the floundering Midwest Manufacturing Co. of Jasper, Indiana, an establishment with 30 employees and 25,000 square feet of production space. They soon realized that the company needed more than an infusion of capital. The group took charge of managing the small television and radio cabinet manufacturer, which they renamed the Jasper Corporation on May 23, 1950. With Habig acting as president and manager, the privately-owned company flourished, becoming a major supplier of television cabinets to electronics manufacturers. By 1955 the company's sales had grown to $4.6 million and it was employing 436 people.

During the 1950s, the Jasper Corporation took advantage of the booming market in televisions to increase its production capacity and to attain control of several of the stages in the manufacturing process, a strategy known as vertical integration. The company's first acquisition came at the pressure of its customers, who asked Jasper to diversify its manufacturing sites to ensure a steady supply of cabinets in case of accident. With this in mind, the company purchased the Borden Cabinet Corporation in Borden, Indiana, in 1952. The wisdom of diversification was made evident several years later, in 1962, when the Borden plant burned to the ground. Nevertheless, the plant was rebuilt on the same location within six months.

Jasper took its first step toward vertical integration in 1953 when it formed the Jasper-American Manufacturing Co. in Henderson, Kentucky. This company supplied flakeboard for Jasper's cabinets at a lower price than could be obtained elsewhere. Striving for efficiency, Jasper moved further in the direction of vertical integration in the years to come. The company acquired the Evansville Veneer and Lumber Co. in 1955 and formed the Lafayette Manufacturing Co. in 1959. These companies supplied high quality veneer and hardwood lumber and dimension wood parts, respectively. Such acquisitions allowed Jasper to tailor its supply of raw materials to fit its requirements, although the subsidiary companies were also able to produce goods for sale to other manufacturers. This efficient and diverse use of productive capacity fueled Jasper's sales, which grew to $14.6 million by 1959, and prompted management to consider the benefits of decreasing the company's reliance on the demands of consumer products manufacturers and becoming a consumer products manufacturer itself.

The Jasper Corporation made several major changes in 1959. Most notably, it purchased the W. W. Kimball Company of Melrose Park, Illinois. Acquisition of the Kimball Company, which had been manufacturing pianos since 1857, gave Jasper an established brand in a prestigious industry. Not coincidentally, Jasper already had the capacity to manufacture many of the raw materials that went into the construction of vertical and grand pianos. In the years to come, they would acquire companies involved in other steps in the manufacturing process of pianos as well. Also in 1959, Jasper formed a traffic division that provided transportation for raw materials between the company's growing number of plants and delivered Kimball products to retail dealers. In 1987 this division was renamed Kimball International Transit, Inc.; the outfit operated a fleet of trucks that carried the company's products and was also licensed to carry goods for other companies.

After purchasing the W. W. Kimball Company, the Jasper Corporation took several steps to expand and diversify the production of musical instruments under the Kimball name. Kimball Piano, as the division was named, moved its manufacturing facilities to West Baden, Indiana, and grew to include 300,000 square feet of floor space. The company's machine and equipment division fashioned advanced manufacturing processes for the plant, and over the years the company added a retail store—the Kimball Music Center—that sold Kimball and other musical products and offered piano lessons in its teaching studios. In 1961 it formed the Jasper Electronics Manufacturing Co. to produce Kimball electronic organs. Production facilities grew to 200,000 square feet in size, an expansion that made

Kimball a leading manufacturer of electronic organs and allowed it to develop expertise in the production of electronic components.

Jasper also expanded piano and organ production into European markets with the acquisition of the English company Herrburger Brooks P.L.C. in 1965. Merged in 1991 into Kimball Europe P.L.C., the unit makes and markets Herrburger Brooks brand piano components and office furniture for sale in the United Kingdom. Further expansion occurred in 1966, when Jasper purchased L. Bosendorfer Klavierfabrik, A.G., of Vienna, Austria, makers of fine concert grand pianos since 1828. With two facilities in Austria, the company produces a limited number of high-quality Bosendorfer brand pianos, some of which sell for as much as $100,000.

As sales of pianos and organs declined beginning in the 1960s, Jasper (and later Kimball International) changed the nature of its involvement in this business segment. The company phased out organ operations in 1983, though it retained and expanded its electronic assembly business in the renamed Kimball Electronics-Jasper manufacturing facilities. Both U.S. and European piano manufacturing plants have been made more efficient; U.S. facilities, for example, were converted to allow for the manufacture of products such as pool tables and jukebox cabinets for other companies. In addition, in 1988 the company expanded Kimco, S.A. de C.V., its Reynosa, Mexico, plant (established in 1973) to allow for lower-cost, up-to-date piano manufacturing. While the market for pianos continued to decrease into the 1990s, the company expected that gains in efficiency would allow this division to return to profitability after several years of losses.

By the late 1960s, Jasper Corporation had become highly efficient at manufacturing cabinetry and pianos, thanks in large part to Habig's efforts to achieve vertical integration and his ability to avoid debt by purchasing new companies outright. The company was capable of growing trees on its tree farms, processing lumber in its various sawmills, producing finished wood products in its veneer, laminate, and dimension lumber divisions, assembling a finished product in several assembly plants, and shipping its products via its own transport division. As the demand for television cabinets declined, the company took advantage of existing production capacity to manufacture office furniture out of its Borden, Indiana, plant beginning in 1970. Jasper also acquired an Alabama manufacturer of Victorian reproduction furniture in 1969; Jasper later renamed the company Kimball Furniture Reproductions, Inc. These new products became the center of the company's growth for the next two decades, propelling the company into the Fortune 500 and making it one of the largest employers in the state of Indiana.

In 1974 stockholders, primarily members of the founding Habig and Thyen families, voted to change the name of the company to Kimball International, Inc., in order to reflect the increasing recognition that the Kimball brand pianos and office furniture enjoyed in the marketplace and to recognize the company's international scope. Just two years later, Kimball became a publicly held company by offering 500,000 shares of Class B common stock.

In the late 1970s and early 1980s Kimball consolidated its position in the office furniture business through acquisition and reorganization. In November 1979 the company acquired design and manufacturing rights for a line of office furniture systems produced by Artec, which became a unit of Kimball International. The division, which operates a 200,000-square-foot plant in Jasper, Indiana, began producing the Cetra line of office furniture in 1988. This versatile system was designed for all levels of office use and became part of the Kimball Office Furniture line. In 1980, Kimball created the National Office Furniture division to manufacture economy-to-medium-priced furniture. This furniture was manufactured in two plants in Kentucky and Indiana. With two complete furniture lines—Kimball and National—Kimball International was able to manufacture and market to all segments of the wood office furniture market.

Kimball International grew quickly as a result of its strength in manufacturing and marketing office furniture: sales rose from $104.2 million in 1975 to $319.9 million in 1984. In 1988 net sales of $529.8 million placed the company on the *Fortune* 500 list of top companies in America. The company's organization came to reflect this vast growth, as manufacturing and marketing facilities were relocated and consolidated. Kimball's Jasper, Indiana, corporate headquarters were enlarged in 1985 and 1989, and a lavish corporate showroom was created in 1983 to display the entire line of office, hospitality, and healthcare furniture. Kimball restructured its corporate divisions as well in the early 1990s, grouping its many divisions and plants under office, lodging, home furniture, and, for European products, international groupings.

The Lodging Group was created in a 1992 merger of Kimball Healthcare Co., a manufacturer of beds, casegoods, and seating for long-term care facilities, and Kimball Hospitality Furniture, Inc., which produced beds, seating, tables, dressers, and other furniture for the lodging industry. The Lodging Group achieved particular success in the early 1990s. In recognition of the company's growing commitment to producing products for the hospitality industry, the company expanded its showroom in 1991. Kimball sales administrator Mike Paar told *Lodging Hospitality* magazine, ''The mock-up rooms [in the showroom] provide one-source shopping and enable the lodging operator or designer to take care of his or her entire furnishings needs under one roof.'' Kimball achieved more tangible recognition for its success in this business unit in 1993 when it was chosen to furnish the guest rooms—all 10,500 of them—for four new hotels in Las Vegas, Nevada.

While Kimball has earned its name and garnered the majority of its sales from furniture and cabinets, it also developed a strong presence with its electronic contract assemblies. Sales of electronic assemblies grew from three percent of Kimball's total sales in 1984 to 25 percent of sales in 1994, a leap from $9.3 million to $204.1 million in sales. Kimball supplies electronic components and assemblies to corporate customers in the computer, automotive, telecommunications, and home appliance industries. What had begun as a spin-off business from manufacturing organs had matured into a major income producer. The company reported in its 1994 annual report that it had manufactured over 11 million computer keyboards, while it expects its share of the antilock brake subassembly market to grow through its continued connection supplying control modules for the Kelsey-Hayes Company.

In addition to its electronic components business, Kimball also continues to manufacture television cabinets and stands for television manufacturers such as Mitsubishi, Thomson, Sony, and Toshiba. It also manufactures speaker cabinets for Thomson and Definitive Technologies. Through the 1980s and into the 1990s, Kimball also received between six and eight percent of total sales from sales of processed wood products. Though the divisions producing such wood products as veneer, lumber, and plywood exist mainly to supply Kimball's furniture making plants, outside sales reached $54 million in 1994. Kimball also receives a small portion of its sales from plastics and tooling operations, from its transport division, and from a transport repair division.

Kimball took a step toward further diversification in the production of furniture in 1992 when it acquired the Torrance, California-based Harpers, Inc., a manufacturer of metal office furniture. This acquisition gave Kimball an entrance into the largest segment of the office furniture market, estimated at $7.3 billion in 1992. Kimball immediately announced plans to move the company to Post Falls, Idaho, a small town just across the state line from Spokane, Washington. The Post Falls plant, at 461,000 square feet, is Kimball's largest and one of the largest in the inland Northwest. The plant began operations in 1994, manufacturing metal office furniture under the Harpers name.

Analysts cite several factors in explaining the steady rise of Kimball International. Most notable is the stability that family control has given the company. The majority of the Class A stock and six of seven senior executive officer positions remained in the hands of the founding Habig and Thyen families in the mid-1990s. In 1994 founder Arnold F. Habig acted as assistant to the chief executive officer; his son Thomas L. Habig served as chairman of the board; and another son, Douglas A. Habig, acted as president and chief executive officer. "Family control is a real asset," Indiana business expert Raymond H. Diggle, Jr., told *Indiana Business*. "It allows them to run the enterprise for cash flow and long-term return on equity. They don't have to be as concerned about short-term swings."

Another important component of the company's success, contends Kimball, is a corporate ethic that reflects an obligation to contribute to the communities—mostly small towns like that of Jasper, Indiana, where the company was founded—in which they base their operations. This community-minded ethic has led Kimball to pursue sustainable timberland development on its acreage in Indiana, Ohio, and Kentucky, to sponsor the Habig Foundation to award scholarships to the children of company employees, and to allow its employees to exert responsi-

bility and control over their jobs long before such a management philosophy became popular. With its sound financial base, its careful managerial philosophy, and its track record, Kimball seems poised to grow well into the twenty-first century.

Principal Subsidiaries: Kimball Office Furniture Sales; National Office Furniture Sales; Kimball Office Furniture Manufacturing; Artec Manufacturing; National Office Furniture Manufacturing; Kimball Upholstered Products; Harpers, Inc.; Kimball Lodging Group; Jasper Manufacturing Co.; Batesville American Manufacturing; Kimball Piano Group; Kimball Furniture Reproductions; The Jasper Corporation; Heritage Hills; Kimball Europe P.L.C.; L. Bosendorfer Klavierfabrik GmbH; Kimball Electronics Group; Kimco, S.A. de C.V.; Lafayette Manufacturing; Lafayette Sawmill; Dale Wood Manufacturing; Indiana Hardwoods; Indiana Hardwoods Sawmill; Greensburg Manufacturing; West Jefferson Wood Products; Jasper Laminates; Evansville Veneer and Lumber Co.; Jasper Plastics; ToolPro; Kimball International Transit, Inc.; Facilities/Technology Support Group.

Further Reading:

"Back on Key: Improving Piano Business Aids Results for Kimball," *Barron's,* December 24, 1984, p. 28.

Brooks, Nancy Rivera, and Michele Fuetsch, "Harpers, Citing High Business Costs, Will Move to Idaho," *Los Angeles Times,* August 26, 1992, p. D2.

"Easy Shopping at Kimball Showroom," *Lodging Hospitality,* January 1992, p. 70.

Hoffman, Marilyn, "Furniture Makers Target Multiplying Home Offices," *Christian Science Monitor,* April 5, 1994, p. 9.

Johnson, J. Douglas, "Knock on Wood," *Indiana Business,* December 1992, p. 8.

Jones, Grayden, "Furniture Company to Give Big Boost to Local Economy," *Spokesman-Review,* August 26, 1992.

"Kimball Furnishes Vegas Megahotels," *Lodging Hospitality,* January 1994, p. 44.

Mabert, Vincent A., John F. Muth, and Roger W. Schmenner, "Collapsing New Product Development Times: Six Case Studies," *Journal of Product Innovation Management,* Vol. 9, 1992, pp. 200–212.

Massey, Steve, "Hitting the Road: Behind the Scenes, Harpers Prepares for Life in Idaho," *Spokesman-Review,* May 8, 1994, p. E1.

——, "Greg Davis: Harpers Manager Knows What It's Like to Live in Small Town," *Spokesman-Review,* January 24, 1994.

Miller, Laura Novello, "Manufacturers Contribute Most to Indiana Employment Scene," *Indianapolis Business Journal,* May 23, 1994, p. B24.

Ripley, Richard, "Kimball Buys Property near Big Harpers Plant," *Journal of Business—Spokane,* July 7, 1994, p. 3.

Vaught, Martin, "Kimball International Subsidiary Announces Relocation," *PR Newswire,* August 25, 1992.

—Tom Pendergast

LADD Furniture, Inc.

One Plaza Center
Box HP-3
High Point, North Carolina 27261
U.S.A.
(910) 889-0333
Fax: (910) 888-6344

Public Company
Incorporated: 1981
Employees: 7,900
Sales: $592 million
Stock Exchanges: NASDAQ
SICs: 2511 Wood Household Furniture; 2512 Upholstered
   Wood Household Furniture; 2514 Metal Household
   Furniture; 2435 Hardwood Veneer and Plywood; 4213
   Trucking

LADD Furniture, Inc., one of the largest residential furniture manufacturers in the United States, designs, manufactures, and sells furniture through its ten furniture manufacturing subsidiaries. In the mid-1990s, LADD owned 26 manufacturing facilities, including nine in North Carolina, five in Virginia, and one in Mexico. The company also leased and maintained two retail stores in Kansas, as well as showrooms in nine cities, and transported some of its merchandise through its trucking subsidiary, LADD Transportation Inc.. In 1994, LADD products were reaching about 4,000 stores through independent sales representatives.

Although LADD was not created until 1981, the four furniture companies from which it was built (and whose initials made up the acronym LADD) go back much further. LADD's home base of High Point has long been regarded as the furniture capital of the South. In the late 1880s the first furniture factory in North Carolina was built at High Point, a town that offered excellent undepleted hardwood stands, year-round waterpower potential, rail transportation, and low-cost, dependable labor from neighboring rural areas. And for a region short of capital, the furniture industry was ideal, because the production process was relatively simple and required little investment. In 1902, 24 High Point factories were making furniture and related products.

Early in the twentieth century, High Point firms concentrated on producing inexpensive household furniture, which they sold only in the South. By 1921, however, High Point furniture

factories were capable of producing lines in the medium-price range that resembled goods from northern manufacturers and were considerably cheaper. That year the Southern Furniture Exposition Building opened in the heart of the city and became the third largest furniture mart in the United States. New plants moved into the area, and the population of High Point more than doubled in the 1920s.

Between 1969 and 1971 Sperry & Hutchinson Co., best known for its green trading stamps, acquired four furniture companies: David M. Lea & Co., American Furniture Co., Drew Furniture Co., and the Daystrom division of Schlumberger, Ltd. David M. Lea & Co., a privately held Richmond, Virginia, firm was 100 years old when it was purchased in August 1969. Lea got its start manufacturing packing boxes and had expanded into the furniture business, manufacturing low- and medium-priced bedroom and dining room furniture by the time it was acquired by Sperry & Hutchinson. Lea's sales came to $17.5 million in 1968, and the company had five plants in North Carolina, Virginia, and Tennessee.

American Furniture Co. and Drew Furniture Co., both of North Wilkesboro, North Carolina, were purchased in 1970 and merged into one unit called American Drew. The two affiliated firms made bedroom and dining room furniture in four plants in North Wilkesboro and had combined sales of about $15 million. The other company, Daystrom of South Boston, Virginia, got its start in 1934 making ashtrays but was mainly a producer of electronic instruments when it was sold in 1962 to Schlumberger, Ltd., a firm that provided services and equipment for oil drilling. By 1971, when Sperry & Hutchinson purchased it, the Daystrom division was manufacturing wood, metal, plastic, and plastic-laminate furniture for dining rooms and kitchens. Net sales for Daystrom were about $16 million in 1970.

David Lea, Daystrom, and American Drew were consolidated into a newly formed Sperry & Hutchinson furnishings division in 1974, with headquarters in Richmond, Virginia. This unit also included five more furniture companies acquired by Sperry & Hutchinson: Gunlocke Co., Homecrest Industries, Interlock Furniture, Paragon Design, and Pontiac Furniture Industries, along with its Bigelow-Sanford carpeting subsidiary and Buck Creek Industries, a synthetic-yarn processor. Gunlocke made commercial and industrial furniture; Homecrest, metal patio pieces; Pontiac, upholstered swivel rockers and recliners; and Interlock, modular wall systems. The furniture units accounted for $155 million of the division's record $344 million in revenues in 1976. By then American Drew, Daystrom, and Lea comprised a separate division, S&H Furniture, with headquarters in High Point.

In 1981, executives of S&H Furniture and other investors acquired the division in a leveraged buyout from Sperry & Hutchinson for $70.2 million, and a new entity, LADD Holding Co., was incorporated on August 14, 1981. The company's headquarters remained in High Point, and the separate product lines and sales and marketing offices of the companies remained unaffected. At the time, Lea had gained renown for its Walt Disney Magic Kingdom collection, and Daystrom for its dining room products. American Drew, believed to be the most profitable of the three, was respected for its excellent manufacturing facilities for case goods—the trade term for wooden bedroom and living room furniture. The company went public on May 28, 1983, under the name of LADD Furniture, Inc.

Every year through 1985 profits at LADD increased. The company's annual sales grew by 75 percent to $248 million in this period, and profits increased by an average 42 percent annually. At the end of 1985, LADD could boast debt of less than 20 percent of equity. During this time, about half of the company's sales were generated from case goods, mostly medium-priced bedroom pieces such as bureaus, vanities, and buffets. Such pieces, available in a variety of styles—colonial, traditional, country, and contemporary—were produced by the company's American Drew and Lea Industries units under such brand names as Cherry Grove, American Independence, and Vineyard Oaks.

In early 1984 LADD acquired Clayton-Marcus Co., a maker of upholstered furniture, for $14.7 million, and, by the close of the following year, about 40 percent of LADD's sales were coming from sofas, chairs, and other upholstered furniture, which were produced by the Clayton-Marcus subsidiary and by another recent acquisition, Barclay Furniture Co. The rest of the company's sales came from kitchen, dinette, and dining room furniture produced by its Daystrom division; plywood and similar products from its Lea Lumber & Plywood Co. subsidiary, and LADD Transportation, Inc.'s fleet of trucks, which delivered LADD furniture to distributors and served other manufacturers as well.

Company chairman Don A. Hunziker credited LADD's good standing to decentralized management and its diverse array of products, which allowed the company to react speedily to changing customer tastes. The company also increased its productivity by ordering data processing equipment and computer-controlled machine tools. In 1985 LADD's sales reached $248 million, a 75 percent increase in five years. Profits, $18.4 million in 1985, had averaged an increase of 42 percent a year.

By the end of the decade, LADD's stock was at a high of nearly $18 per share. Speculating that the company's stock was actually worth about $26 a share, given its increasing cash flow and low debt, Wall Street analysts suggested that the company was undervalued and that management might take the company private again. At this time LADD's customer base was broad and diversified, with its leading client in 1985 accounting for only eight percent of sales and its leading five for only 12 percent.

However, an aggressive acquisition program and an unfavorable industry climate brought on by economic recession presented LADD with several challenges in the late 1980s and early 1990s. Seeking to acquire other well-managed furniture makers capable of making an immediate contribution to aggregate profits, LADD had purchased the American Furniture Co. of Martinsville, Virginia, in 1986 for nearly $40 million, thereby moving up to fourth place among the nation's residential furniture makers. And on July 7, 1989, LADD acquired a "package" of six furniture businesses (Pennsylvania House, Inc., The Gunlocke Co., Brown Jordan Co., The Kittinger Co., The McGuire Furniture Co., and Charter Furniture Inc.) from Maytag Corp. for $201.1 million in cash and the assumption of a debt of $41.5 million. Gunlocke, McGuire, and Kittinger were

sold off, pursuant to LADD's pre-acquisition plan, while Charter was consolidated with LADD's American of Martinsville subsidiary.

However, the two remaining Maytag companies proved a drag on earnings during the subsequent recession, and reportedly fell far short of expectations. The company remained committed to expanding its holdings, purchasing the Fournier Furniture Corp. for $11 million in July 1992. However, no dividend was paid to shareholders that year, and one analyst even described the company as "a fallen angel that has bedeviled shareholders since its ill-timed, but strategically important acquisition." Indeed, LADD common stock, which peaked at nearly $25 a share in 1987, dropped to $4.50 a share in 1990.

Responding to adverse economic conditions, which included declining sales, particularly in the higher-priced furniture segment, LADD initiated a program designed to improve productivity and quality, as well as to reduce operating costs. The unprofitable lines of the American Furniture Co. of Martinsville were discontinued, while other manufacturing facilities were merged, reconfigured, and automated.

Despite disappointing earnings, largely attributed to such restructurings, investment analyst Wallace "Jerry" Epperson, known as "Mr. Furniture" for his wide contacts in the industry, pronounced himself bullish on the company in late 1993. "They allow you to participate in all the major sectors" of the industry, Epperson told a *Barron's* writer, referring to LADD's Fournier division in the ready-to-assemble field, American Drew in the middle sector, and Pennsylvania House for higher-priced traditional American furniture.

As LADD moved into the mid-1990s, its profit picture improved considerably. In the second quarter of 1994, the company posted sales of $153.2 million, its best quarterly record, with profits of $2.7 million. For the first nine months of 1994, LADD sales reached $445.4 million, an increase of 12 percent over the same 1993 period. Moreover, net earnings were $6.6 million, up 46 percent from the figure in the comparable 1993 period.

In January 1994, LADD acquired the Pilliod Cabinet Co., a High Point-based manufacturer of promotional-priced bedroom and occasional furniture, in a transaction valued at $54 million. The company, which was renamed Pilliod Furniture, Inc. following the acquisition, had annual sales of more than $85 million and factories in Ohio, Alabama, and South Carolina.

In the mid-1990s, LADD maintained a total of 12 operating subsidiaries. Lea Industries produced wood bedroom furniture in several styles, including colonial, traditional, and contemporary, and American Drew offered wood bedroom, dining room, and living room furniture in traditional, country, and contemporary styles. Daystrom manufactured kitchen, dinette, dining room, and bar furniture in contemporary styles incorporating metal, glass, and wicker, as well as wood, while Clayton-Marcus and Barclay Furniture were engaged in the production of upholstered household furniture. Pennsylvania House offered traditional and country style wooden and upholstered furniture in the upper-middle price range.

Following the consolidation and phasing out of some of American of Martinsville's residential furniture lines, that subsidiary focused on producing guest room furniture for the institutional market, including hotels, motels, colleges, and certain federal agencies. Fournier Furniture, bolstered by factory expansions and automation, produced ready-to-assemble furniture, while Brown Jordan was a design leader in outdoor furniture and accessories wrought from aluminum and iron. Finally, the company's Lea Lumber & Plywood subsidiary made cut-to-size plywood, veneer, and wood laminated parts, primarily for other manufacturers.

Beginning in the late 1980s, LADD also began focusing on developing its presence in the international market. LADD International was founded in 1992 to oversee international cross-marketing of products from all the LADD operating companies. The following year, LADD made shipments totaling more than $40 million to 51 countries, and management was exploring the possibility of entering into joint ventures with various overseas partners.

Principal Subsidiaries: American Drew, Inc.; Barclay Furniture Co.; Brown Jordan Co.; Clayton-Marcus Co., Inc.; Fournier Furniture, Inc.; LADD Transportation, Inc.; Pennsylvania House, Inc.; Pilliod Furniture, Inc.

Further Reading:

Bary, Andrew, "Comfy Again," *Barron's,* November 8, 1993, pp. 14–15.

Bary, Andrew, "Uncomfortable Seats," *Barron's,* August 1, 1994, p. 14.

Bugatch, Budd, "What the Analysts Say," *Washington Post,* November 15, 1993, Bus. Sec. p. 39.

Engardio, Pete, "What's Rearranging America's Furniture Industry," *Business Week,* September 29, 1986, pp. 86D–86F.

Gordon, Mitchell, "Not Knocking Wood," *Barron's,* January 20, 1986, pp. 48–49.

Marks, Robert, "S&H Sells Its Furniture Unit to Execs," *HFD,* September 7, 1981, pp. 1, 14.

"Sitting Pretty at LADD," *Business Week,* June 12, 1986, p. 96.

—Robert Halasz

Landmark Communications, Inc.

150 W. Brambleton Avenue
Norfolk, Virginia 23510
U.S.A.
(804) 446-2000
Fax: (804) 446-2489

Private Company
Incorporated: 1865
Employees: 4,400
Sales: $467 million
SICs: 2711 Newspaper Publishing & Printing; 2721
   Periodical Publishing & Printing; 2741 Photo Guide &
   Classified Advertising Publications; 2752 Commercial
   Printing, Lithographic; 2759 Broadcasting & Cable
   Programming; 4832 Radio Broadcasting; 4833 Television
   Broadcasting; 4841 Cable & Other Pay Television
   Services; 4899 Communication Services, Not Elsewhere
   Classified

Landmark Communications, Inc.'s diverse media holdings extend into virtually every vestige of American life, reaching more than 55 million homes in 50 states through radio, television, newspapers and magazines, as well homes in the United Kingdom and Scandanavia through its European cable television channel. According to *Advertising Age*'s 1994 edition of the "100 Leading Media Companies" in the United States, the Norfolk-based Landmark ranked 46th, climbing up a notch from 1993 with a six percent increase in total earnings. Though the bulk of Landmark's revenue came from its metropolitan newspapers (the *Virginian-Pilot* and *Ledger-Star*, Norfolk, Virginia; the *News & Record,* Greensboro, North Carolina; and the *Roanoke Times & World-News,* Roanoke, Virginia), television proceeds and recognition have steadily climbed since the launch of The Weather Channel and acquisition of The Travel Channel, KLAS-TV (Las Vegas), and WTVF (Nashville). Additionally, 75 community newspapers and specialty publications like *Antique Trader Weekly, The Antiques & Collectibles Price Guide, Military Trader,* and *Toy Trader* maintain a stable readership. Landmark has also continued to explore other media ventures, co-owning Trader Publishing Company (a producer of classified publications, primarily automobile, located in Norfolk) and Capital-Gazette Communications, Inc. in Annapolis (publisher of the *Washingtonian* magazine and newspapers, including the *Annapolis Capital*). Expansions in the mid-1990s included Pro-

motion Information Management, a business-to-business marketing service, and exploration of the Internet via InfiNet (a joint venture) and multimedia offerings on the Travel Channel. In 1994, Landmark launched *Travel,* based in London, with cable service throughout Great Britain and Scandanavia.

Landmark was founded by Samuel Leroy Slover, an enterprising gentleman immersed in the Virginia newspaper business for 55 years. A native of Tennessee, Slover migrated to Virginia in 1904, hoping to change his fortune. He had been the 20-year-old business manager of the financially troubled *Knoxville Journal.* Despite his efforts, the paper went bankrupt and Slover, then 22, assumed its liabilities ($36,400) as a debt of honor. After arriving in Virginia, Slover sold ads for a New York trade journal before approaching the well-connected Joseph Bryan, owner of the *Richmond Times,* for a loan to purchase a newspaper in neighboring Norfolk. Bryan, aghast, refused the young man. Slover, undaunted, asked to sell advertising for the *Times.* When he received a second rejection, Slover tried another tack: what if he sold ads, on a commission basis, to area merchants who were not current clients? With this proposition, Bryan had nothing to lose and everything to gain, so he accepted the offer and was soon rewarded with a multitude of new advertisers.

It was then Bryan's turn to make an offer to Slover—rescue a Newport newspaper from going under within one year and gain half interest in its ownership. Samuel took the challenge, triumphed, and was named publisher of the *Newport Times-Herald.* In 1909, relinquishing his title as publisher, Slover moved on to papers in Richmond, Petersburg and other cities in southeast Virginia.

During the next several decades, he dominated the state's newspaper trade, owning outright or controlling six of Virginia's biggest papers. His *modus operandi* was to swoop in and rescue an ailing paper, nurse it from red to black ink, then move on. Through Slover's machinations, small, struggling papers were often merged together to create large, healthier ones, usually resulting in hyphenated names like two of Landmark's backbone publications, *The Virginian-Pilot* and *The Ledger-Star.*

By centering his company, Norfolk Newspapers Inc., near a major military installation, Slover capitalized on the region's immense growth, not only with newspapers, but other media as well. In 1930, as the Depression deepened, Slover took a gamble and purchased Norfolk's WTAR-AM, Virginia's first radio station, for $10,000. Though many had little faith in the sensibility of an aural medium and even less in another experimental medium, television, Slover believed in both and was later responsible for bringing Virginia its second television station.

Throughout Slover's career, his exploits would prove both interesting and educational to his young nephew, Frank Batten, who joined the Slover household after the death of his father, Frank Batten, Sr., when the youngster was only two years old.

After serving in the merchant marines during World War II, Batten graduated from the University of Virginia in 1950 and received an MBA from Harvard in 1952. His initiation into the business world was fast and furious: he began as a reporter for the *Ledger-Star,* moved to the circulation and advertising departments of the *Ledger-Star* and *Virginian-Pilot,* progressed to vice-president in 1953, and was appointed publisher by Slover at the age of 27 in 1954. Having absorbed much under the tutelage of his uncle and mentor, Batten learned the ropes in record time—accelerating his pivotal role in Norfolk Newspapers Inc., the forerunner of Landmark Communications. While Batten settled into his role as publisher of two of the area's most prosperous newspapers, Slover, 81, slowed down and contemplated retirement. He also sought to share the fruits of his illustrious career, by liberally offering stock to his employees. With Batten at the helm a mere five years, Samuel L. Slover died in 1959, at age 86, leaving Batten a vast legacy.

Like his uncle before him, Batten's prescience would firmly move Landmark into the future: just as Slover had envisioned the many possibilities of radio and television, Batten had been studying an extension of traditional television called "cable" programming. Batten considered cable a medium with vast potential and decided to invest in its promise. Within a year of his initial interest, in 1964, Batten acquired two cable franchises—one in Roanoke Rapids, North Carolina, and a second in Beckley, West Virginia. These two stations were the cornerstone for the development of the TeleCable Corporation, of Greensboro, North Carolina, which would eventually operate 21 cable systems in 15 states, reaching 740,000 subscribers nationwide. TeleCable's success led to a bountiful opportunity for Landmark stockholders in 1984, when it was spun off into an independent corporation. In late 1994, an offer of more than $1 billion in stock was made by rival TCI (Tele-Communications Inc.), the largest cable-TV operator in the United States, to acquire TeleCable's assets. The deal was closed in January 1995.

In 1965, Batten further expanded the company by purchasing the *Greensboro Daily News, The Greensboro Record,* and a television station, WFMY-TV, all owned by the prominent Jeffress family. Landmark later combined the Greensboro papers into the Greensboro *News & Record,* which celebrated its centennial in 1990, and sold WFMY-TV. Two years after the Greensboro acquisitions, in 1967, Batten was named Landmark's chairman of the board. Within another two years, he was on the move again, this time acquiring the *Roanoke Times & World-News* in Virginia's third largest market (combined daily and Sunday circulation of over 240,000), bringing the Norfolk-based company's metro newspaper holdings to four. In the 1970s, Landmark also became home to community papers as well, including four dailies (*Carroll County Times, Citrus County Chronicle, News-Enterprise,* and *Los Alamos Monitor*); four tri-weeklies (*The Gazette, Lancaster News, Kentucky Standard,* and *Roane County News*); six semi-weeklies; 21 weeklies and 38 free "shoppers" available throughout the region and beyond.

In 1978, Landmark departed from its tradition of local and regional expansion by taking a leap to the West Coast, acquiring two television stations: KNTV in San Jose, for $24.5 million and KLAS-TV in Las Vegas, for $8 million. Though KNTV was later sold, KLAS, a CBS affiliate, became Las Vegas's top-ranked news station with 351,000 households, while another television acquisition, CBS-affiliate WTVF in Nashville, known as "NewsChannel 5" (purchased in 1992) delivered award-winning specials and highly-rated newscasts to 738,000 households. WTVF was also known for another distinction—

the hiring of a college student in 1974 who went on to conquer the media industry—Oprah Winfrey.

Three years later, still seeking opportunities to expand the company in both scope and value, Batten considered another leap—this one into the national broadcasting arena. In 1981, the Landmark think-tank developed what is probably regarded as the company's greatest achievement—a 24-hour cable weather service called "The Weather Channel." In less than 10 months, plans progressed from paper to programming reality. "The Weather Channel was the most challenging task we had undertaken," Batten admitted. "It was Landmark's first national venture, with all the complexities of marketing and distribution a national enterprise must consider." Despite jitters and numerous naysayers from within and outside the industry, Landmark was determined to live up to its name while also providing the quality of the major networks. On May 2, 1982, the Weather Channel (TWC) officially debuted, with the expressed purpose of becoming "the nation's primary source of weather information."

Part of TWC's success was its universalization of the weather. Because everyone was affected by Mother Nature—an uncontrollable force—viewers could at least tune in, be informed, and prepare, which constituted a form of control in itself. Subscribers also appreciated TWC's format and flow: "Viewers can find a constantly varied presentation of scientific information, friendly advice, and spontaneous philosophy," said Andrew Ross, in his 1991 book, *Strange Weather: Culture, Science and Technology in the Age of Limits.* Moreover, with programming Ross called "accessible, concrete displays of otherwise abstract weather events," viewers kept coming back for more, especially during catastrophic weather. Ratings skyrocketed during August 1991, as Hurricane Bob terrorized the coast; in March 1993 with the Northeast's unexpected blizzard; and again in December of the same year when snow once again threatened the East Coast.

TWC became a staple of contemporary programming, with what Batten termed "one of the most loyal consumer audiences in television." Numbers proved him correct: at any given moment in the mid-1990s 130,000 homes tuned in, while TWC programming was available to 56.7 million households that regularly watched its early morning and evening local forecasts, as well as a multitude of regular features (Boat & Beach Reports, Business Traveler's Reports, International Forecast, Michelin Drivers' Report, and Schoolday Forecast) and specials about weather-related health matters or seasonal hazards like hurricanes and tornados. TWC was available in 90 percent of all homes with cable television in 1995.

In 1990, Michael Eckert took over as president of what became Landmark's Video Networks and Enterprises Division. From 1991 through 1993, Paul FitzPatrick, formerly of C-Span, was The Weather Channel's president and chief operating officer. During that time, TWC's viewership increased from 48 to 56.7 million. By 1994, TWC's staff of 325 employees (65 as on-camera meteorologists or OCMs) used over $20 million worth of specialized equipment to ply their trade, including the state-of-the-art Weather STAR system, implemented in late 1993. The STAR system allowed TWC to insert local forecasts for the

United States's 750 weather zones, along with tags from local advertisers, into the channel's continuous transmission.

Once TWC was firmly into black ink, its skeptics and detractors were silenced; but just until Landmark's next national undertaking, The Travel Channel (TTC). Founded in 1987 by Trans World Airlines to help sell tickets and regarded as the bane of the cable industry for its blatant self-promotion, Landmark acquired a 97-percent share of TTC in 1992 for $50 million. Though TTC had never shown a profit and continued to lose $7 million annually, Landmark increased its stagnate viewership by 2.5 million during a concerted media campaign in 1993. Up to 20 million in 1994, Landmark hoped selling TWC and TTC as a team would bolster subscribers even more. Both the Travel and Weather channels have won the attention of their peers and received cable ACE awards; in 1991, the Weather Channel was given the industry's highest programming accolade, the Golden ACE.

As the 1990s advanced, Landmark initiated the first of several new ventures, each in different directions. Mid-May of 1992 marked the acquisition of the nine-year-old Summary Scan! (renamed Promotion Information Management [PIM] in 1993), a tracking service of print media promotions (in-store circulars, coupons, direct mail, etc.) for packaged-goods manufacturers. Purchased from the Chicago-based Advertising Checking Bureau, PIM maintained offices in both Chicago and Overland Park, Kansas, selling its findings to customers on a weekly or monthly basis.

This year was also pivotal for personnel, as John O. Wynne was named corporate CEO in addition to his duties as Landmark's president; and E. Roger Williams joined The Travel Channel as president (and later CEO) after leaving ESPN. In 1994, Douglas Fox, formerly vice-president of marketing for the Times-Mirror Newspaper Group, was named COO for Landmark.

In the fall of 1993, further demonstrating its progressive nature and support of the underdog, Landmark's TeleCable Corp. was one of six cable operators agreeing to carry the new Fox network's programming in the fall of 1993. In June of 1994, the company went online by forming a joint venture (70 percent ownership) with another Norfolk-based company, Wyvern Technologies Inc., to create InfiNet, a service bringing Virginia subscribers access to the Internet. In a related move in September, the Travel Channel and Gramercy Pictures teamed up on the Internet to publicize a new movie, offer prizes and promote TTC's programming. At the same time, the Weather Channel was in the news too: CEO Michael Eckert announced plans for international expansion, and was also one of seven agencies financing a study in Central and South America on the media habits (reading, viewing, consumption) of 5,800 subjects in 19 Latin American countries.

In February 1994, *Travel* began in London. In 1995, it served nearly one million cable households throughout the United Kingdom and all of Scandanavia. Despite national and international expansion, Landmark remained committed to its roots—the local and regional customers who have always been the foundation of the company. To continue meeting their needs, "Our managers must have room to grow and freedom to respond to their audiences and communities," chairman Batten explained. "I don't want the future of the papers and stations we own to be dependent on me or a corporate staff. Most of our enterprises are local. They should have roots and personalities reflecting their communities."

In May 1995, Landmark announced plans to expand further internationally by launching a new Travel Channel for Latin America, which would appeal, according to a press release, "not only to those who travel, but to those who are interested in learning about the world." The company expected the new channel, based in Miami, to be on the air by October 1995. Another announcement during this time concerned the formation of a joint venture between Landmark and Knight-Ridder, Inc. The new company, InfiNet, was formed to "help newspapers into the Internet access and electronic publishing businesses," according to a Landmark press release. A Landmark spokesperson noted that InfiNet would help "newspapers establish services on the World Wide Web without their making a capital investment and provides an immediate revenue stream to publishers as a share of access fees."

By keeping one foot planted firmly in the past (reflecting the values and philosophy espoused by Samuel Slover) and the other stepping into the future, Landmark hoped to maintain its edge, its on-going quest for quality and the loyalty of its constituents. "With competition heating up and technology changing fast, the media that succeed will be the ones that build competitive advantage," Batten declared. "We have undertaken a systematic effort to be the most productive media in our markets and the best in responding to customers." Current president and CEO John Wynne concurred: "all of us . . . are guided by this single mission: to pursue excellence in our products, our customer service and ourselves."

Principal Subsidiaries: News & Record; KLAS-TV; Landmark Community Newspapers, Inc.; Landmark Special Publications, Inc.; Promotion Information Management; *The Roanoke Times & World-News*; The Travel Channel; *The Virginian-Pilot & The Ledger-Star*; The Weather Channel; WTVF (TV).

Further Reading:

Davidson, Joe, "FTC Studies TCI's Proposed Purchase of TeleCable Corp.," *The Wall Street Journal,* October 18, 1994, p. A5.

"E.B. Jefress, 75, Dies," *The New York Times,* May 24, 1961, p. 41.

Eisenhart, Tom, "People to Watch," *Advertising Age,* April 8, 1991, p. 42.

Elliott, Stuart, "Defying the Skeptics, the Weather Channel Finds a Silver Lining in Mother Nature's Mood Swings," *The New York Times,* June 9, 1993, p. D19.

Elliott, Stuart, "Seven Agencies Help Finance Study," *The New York Times,* September 4, 1994, p. D15.

"Fates & Fortunes—John O. Wynne," *Broadcasting,* November 2, 1992, p. 77.

Garneau, George, "The Move to Alternative Delivery—A Success Story," *Editor & Publisher,* December 15, 1990, pp. 8–9.

Gersh, Debra, "Landmark Acquires Marcol," *Editor & Publisher,* August 19, 1989, pp. 13–14.

"In Brief—Landmark Adds Travel to Weather," *Broadcasting,* March 23, 1992, p. 97.

Kolbert, Elizabeth, "Conflict, Fury, Highs, Lows and Humidity," *The New York Times,* February, 14, 1993, p. 29, 38.

"Media Moves—E. Roger Williams," *Advertising Age,* March 30, 1992, p. 8.

Mehta, Stephanie N., "Small Fish Seek the Big as Internet Industry Consolidates," *The Wall Street Journal,* June 24, 1994, p. B3.

"100 Leading Media Companies," *Advertising Age,* June 30, 1986, p. S-45.

"100 Leading Media Companies," *Advertising Age,* August 8, 1994, p. S-2.

"Other Fields are Just as Green to Frank Batten," *Broadcasting,* July 19, 1982, p. 95.

Patsuris, Penelope, "Wild About the Weather," *TV Guide,* September 5, 1992, p. 24.

"Personals—John Wynne," *TV Digest,* October 26, 1992, p. 10.

"Program Notes—Weather Channel," *TV Digest,* October 11, 1992, p. 10.

"Promotion Information Management," *Advertising Age,* January 18, 1993, p. 38.

Robichaux, Mark, "If Snow is Forecast, the Tour of Tahiti Will be Irresistible," *The Wall Street Journal,* January 16, 1992, p. B3.

Robichaux, Mark, and Novak, Viveca, "TCI Expected to Get FTC Approval for its Bid to Acquire TeleCable Assets," *The Wall Street Journal,* December 6, 1994, p. A2, A8.

Ross, Andrew, *Strange Weather: Culture, Science and Technology in the Age of Limits,* London: Verso Press, 1991, pp. 237–46.

"Samuel L. Slover, Virginia Publisher," (obituary) *The New York Times,* November, 30, 1959, p. 31.

"Six Cable Operators Agree to Air New Fox Network," *The Wall Street Journal,* August 2, 1993, p.B3.

"Summary Scan! Sold," *Advertising Age,* May 18, 1992, p. 37.

"TWA Agreed to Sell . . . ," *TV Digest,* January 20, 1992, p. 4.

"The Weather Channel," *MediaWeek,* July 18, 1994, p. 6.

"The Weather Channel to Expand," *Adweek,* July 18, 1994, p. 12.

Williams, Debra Abe, "Taking a Safari on the Internet," *Advertising Age,* September 5, 1994, p. 14.

—Taryn Benbow-Pfalzgraf

Lane®

The Lane Co., Inc.

East Franklin Ave.
P.O. Box 151
Altavista, Virginia 24517
U.S.A.
(804) 369-5641
Fax: (804) 369-3677

Wholly Owned Subsidiary of Interco Inc.
Incorporated: 1912 as Standard Red Cedar Chest Co.
Employees: 6,000
Sales: $383 million
SICs: 2511 Wood Household Furniture;, 2512 Upholstered
   Wood Household Furniture; 2521 Wood Office Furniture

The Lane Co., Inc. is a leading U.S. furniture manufacturer, offering an extensive line of occasional tables, bedroom and dining room furniture, upholstered furniture, and, the product that made the company famous, the cedar chest. For 75 years the Lane family of Altavista, Virginia, ran the business, which became known for its sound management and enlightened labor policies. In 1987 The Lane Co., Inc. was acquired by Interco, Inc., a St. Louis-based conglomerate. Under the parentage of Interco, Lane was the second largest furniture company in Virginia during the early 1990s.

Holders of farms and a sawmill, and builders of many railway sections in the southeastern United States, the Lane family founded the town of Altavista in 1907 on the site where a section of the Virginian railroad was scheduled to cross the main line of the Southern Railway. Crucial to the town's development, in addition to its rail links, was its location on the Staunton River. The river's water power was vital not only to the future of Lane Co. but also to a cotton mill established by the Lanes.

In 1912 John Edward Lane bought a small packing-box plant in Altavista at a bankruptcy auction for $500. Placed in charge of the small, corrugated iron building, his son Edward Hudson Lane decided to convert the facility in order to make cedar chests. He ordered thousands of dollars of new machinery, and the venture was incorporated as The Standard Red Cedar Chest Co. The firm manufactured and sold hope chests for prospective brides, who used such chests to store linens and other items for setting up housekeeping, as well as keepsakes. In the words of one author, these chests were considered "as authentic a sym-

bol of romance as the wedding ring." Early production of about ten chests a day was sold through independent salesmen who also sold other goods on commission.

In its early days the business was run on a shoestring budget. Nearby buildings were purchased or rented as demand grew, with finished parts transferred from one building to another by means of a mule-drawn cart. Installation of a small sawmill to process the firm's own lumber saved only about five percent in manufacturing costs, but even this small amount gave Standard a crucial cost advantage over its competitors.

During these early years the firm's growth was restricted by elementary manufacturing methods, difficulty in securing financing, and a crude finished product. Ed Lane later recalled he was "one jump ahead of the sheriff most of the time." When a banker told him the company was insolvent, Lane asked him what that meant. "If you don't know what that means," the banker reportedly replied, "you probably would be better off to remain ignorant of its meaning. You might muddle through somehow." The elder John Lane never ceased to be amazed that the factory actually could sell all its production—which at the time of his death in 1930 came to between 250 and 300 chests a day.

Selling the product did not come easy, since multi-line commissioned salesmen could not give the Standard chests their undivided attention. At first Ed Lane had trouble finding reliable people to maintain production while he went out of town drumming up business, or to help manage sales while he attended to plant problems. Moreover, Lane also had to serve as his own advertising director. One early and particularly effective idea of his was a window display using small cedar trees and cedar logs and shavings as well as the company's cedar chests.

During World War I, when the federal government barred rail freight deemed nonessential, Standard Red Cedar Chest converted its plant to producing pine ammunition boxes. Experience in maintaining an assembly line led to the evolution of the first known moving conveyor assembly system in the furniture industry. After the war, the company shared in the remarkable growth of the southern furniture industry during the 1920s. Manufacturers in the Piedmont area, centered in northwestern North Carolina but also extending into southwestern Virginia, benefited from stands of high-grade hardwoods, plentiful water supplies, and a readily available low-wage labor force.

Standard changed its name to The Lane Co. in 1922 and began national advertising that year. The company also began an ambitious program of research and development, with the principal objectives being the utilization of wood waste and perfection of an aroma-tight cedar chest. Another vital objective was to develop a professional sales organization. By the 1930s the company also had its own salaried sales force. And, in 1925, the company hired its first staff designer. A complete design department was added after World War II.

Lane began producing miniature cedar chests in 1925. Five years later, the firm's sales manager converted these miniatures into a great promotional idea: the company invited young women about to graduate from high school to pick up a free miniature chest at their local furniture store. By 1984 more than

15 million prospective Lane customers had received these promotional gifts.

Another valuable promotional idea adopted in 1930 was the establishment of free insurance policies protecting the contents of the chests against damage from moths. To qualify, the consumer filled out and returned a card with information such as the name and age of the purchaser and owner, the price, whether the chest had been bought as a gift, and the dealer from whom it was purchased. The application cards thereby provided the company with useful marketing information.

By the onset of the Great Depression Lane knew all about "insolvency"; the company had barely avoided this fate in 1928, when New York banks unexpectedly called in a number of company notes at the annual peak of Lane's seasonal borrowing cycle. Henceforth the company would be debt-free, operating on a pay-as-you-go basis. As a result of stringent economies, Lane operated continuously through the Depression and maintained its unbroken tradition of paying a dividend each quarter. And Ed Lane was mindful of his father's advice on how to treat his workers; the elder Lane is said to have declared, "Son, I built railroads with a pick handle. You're going to have to handle your people with kid gloves, and your children will have to make them partners." Heeding these words, Ed Lane was an early convert to the creed of profit sharing, which he instituted in 1936.

During World War II The Lane Co. continued to make cedar chests, while also producing aircraft plywood and wood airplane tail assemblies, landing-craft parts, glider wings, and dogsleds. In 1946 the company bought a Smyrna, Tennessee, lumber and panel plant, in the heart of America's best cedar belt. The following year the company perfected a method for producing core particle board from wood waste, using newly available synthetic resin glues. This board, dubbed "Lanewood," was strong, uniform in size, and resistant to moisture and warping. Lanewood was an important forerunner in the development of particle board, which would later have applications in the furniture industry.

In 1951 Lane began the profitable sideline of making occasional tables. Diversification took a giant step in 1956, when Lane acquired Bald Knob Furniture Co. of Rocky Mount, Virginia, in order to produce case goods—the name given in the trade to wooden bedroom and dining-room furniture. In 1965 the company introduced such occasional furniture items as record cabinets and wall units, which became the focus of the company's Accents line. Two years later Lane added upholstered furniture to its line by acquiring the Hickory Chair Co. of Hickory, North Carolina, whose products included its famous James River Collection of authentic eighteenth-century reproductions.

The expansion program continued in 1969 with the acquisition of Clyde Pearson, Inc., of High Point, North Carolina, and the Hickory Tavern and Bruington Furniture companies of Hickory. Pearson and Hickory Tavern were manufacturers of upholstered furniture, while Bruington (later renamed HTB) offered an assortment of sectionals, modulars, sofas, love seats, chairs, and occasional tables. Action Industries of Tupelo, Mississippi, acquired in 1972, added rocker recliners to the Lane line, while Royal Development Co. of High Point, North Carolina, also

purchased that year, assured a dependable supply of chair mechanisms for Action recliners. Also in 1972 Hickory Tavern created Venture Furniture, a line of casual pieces, including rattan and wicker. In fact, by the mid-1980s the company's product line would grow to include some 2,500 pieces.

The Lane Co. went public in 1968 and essentially paid for these acquisitions with stock rather than cash. Management of the acquired companies, which became Lane divisions, remained autonomous, free to make design and production decisions. "We believe people who come closest to running their own business do the best job," explained Ed Lane's son Bernard Bell (B.B.) Lane, in a 1985 *Forbes* interview, adding, "we wouldn't someone who didn't want us—heart and soul." Sounding more like a philosopher than a manufacturer, B.B. Lane told the interviewer, "Christ was a carpenter, and, like him, we are searching for truth—in design and in the way we work with one another."

Under B.B. Lane, who became the company's president in 1976 and assumed the position of chairperson in 1981, a long-standing affiliation with the Bloomingdales department stores allowed Lane to show a line of reproductions authenticated by the Museum of American Folk Art and based on its handcrafted eighteenth- and nineteenth-century furniture collection. During this time, Lane also became the first wood furniture maker to adopt a computer-aided design and manufacturing (CAD/CAM) system. And in 1983 Lane introduced Italian Art Deco-style polyester-coated furniture before its competitors could adapt their production lines to the technically demanding process.

Between 1975 and 1985 Lane increased its earnings every year, except for recessionary 1982. In the fall of 1985 the company's equity was $162 million, and Lane stock reached $52 a share, up from $14 in 1982. During the first half of 1986, however, sales volume dropped by one percent and profits by eight percent, a decline attributed largely to the fact that lacquered furniture was rapidly going out of style and competition was increasing. During this time, Lane was reported to be cutting production of wood furniture and counting on recliners for growth.

Ironically, Lane's rock-solid finances made the company an attractive takeover candidate and eventually cost B.B. Lane his job. In 1980 the company paid corporate raider Victor Posner $550,000 in "greenmail" to look elsewhere for an acquisition, but in December 1986 Interco purchased the company for stock valued at around $487.5 million, or one share of Lane common stock for every 1.5 shares of Interco common stock. While the Lane family and company employees held 35 percent of the stock, B.B. Lane, who opposed the deal, personally held less than five percent. Several other family members also voted no, but the purchase was approved in April 1987 by a seven-to-two margin. R. Stuart Moore, Lane's president and a Korean War buddy of B.B. Lane, retained his job and was also elected an Interco vice-president.

While some institutional investors in Interco, a retailer and manufacturer of consumer products, thought the company was paying too high a price for Lane, the company, which in 1980 had acquired two other big furniture makers—Ethan Allen Inc.

(later sold) and Broyhill Furniture Industries Inc.—was determined to raise its stake in the industry.

By 1990 Interco was in deep financial trouble, having borrowed more than $1.6 billion to fight a takeover bid. Its furniture units—Lane and Broyhill—brought in more than half of company revenue but, like other furniture companies, they suffered in 1989 from a drop in housing starts. Because of its high level of debt, Interco fell into Chapter 11 bankruptcy even though its four operating businesses were making money. The company emerged from bankruptcy the following year, and, in August 1994, Interco announced a restructuring. Management planned to spin off its Florsheim shoe business and sell a 16 percent interest in its Converse shoe subsidiary, while continuing to own and operate Lane and Broyhill. This action was expected to reduce the company's debt from $579 million to about $435 million.

In 1994 Lane had six divisions: Lane, Lane Upholstery, Action Industries, Hickory Chair Co., Pearson, and Venture Furniture. The company maintained nine factories: two in Virginia, two in Mississippi, four in North Carolina, and one in Tennessee. The

company was operating out of modest offices in a warehouse renovated on the site of the original Standard Red Cedar Chest factory.

Further Reading:

Engardio, Pete, "What's Rearranging America's Furniture Industry," *Business Week,* September 29, 1986, pp. 86D–86F.

Fix, Janet L., "A Bundle of Sticks," *Forbes,* November 18, 1985, pp. 202–204.

Kilman, Scott, "Some of Interco's Shareholders Oppose Its $500 Million Accord to Buy Lane Co.," *Wall Street Journal,* April 1, 1987, p. 16.

"Lane Stockholders Approve Purchase by Interco—At Last," *HFD,* April 20, 1987, p. 36.

Ringer, Richard, "Interco Plans to Split Four Subsidiaries," *New York Times,* August 25, 1994, p. D3.

VandeWater, Judith, "Interco's Chief Says There Is a Way Out," *St. Louis Post-Dispatch,* March 4, 1990, p. E1, E8.

Zaslow, Jeffrey, "Lane Co. Agrees to Be Acquired by Interco Inc.," *Wall Street Journal,* December 19, 1986, p. 10.

—Robert Halasz

Leaseway Transportation Corp.

3700 Park East Drive
Beachwood, Ohio 44122
U.S.A.
(216) 765-5500
Fax: (216) 765-5077

Public Company
Incorporated: 1960
Employees: 8,500
Sales: $600 million
Stock Exchanges: NASDAQ
SICs: 4213 Trucking Except Local

Leaseway Transportation Corp. is a group of companies that provide physical distribution services to manufacturers, distributors, and retailers in the United States and Canada. Based in a suburb of Cleveland, Ohio, the firm evolved from a turn-of-the-century cartage service into a billion-dollar interstate trucking concern. A heavily leveraged buyout in late 1980s took the company private, brought on a massive debt load, and forced the company into Chapter 11 bankruptcy, from which it emerged in 1993.

Leaseway was founded around the turn of the twentieth century by Hugh O'Neill, who began distributing newspapers and other goods with a horse-drawn wagon. In 1912 O'Neill started the transition from "horse power" to "horsepower" and appropriately named his rapidly changing firm the Hugh O'Neill Auto Co. When the company won a contract to deliver a major local newspaper in 1921, O'Neill again renamed the business, this time to Superior Transfer. The second generation of O'Neills, brothers Francis and William, joined the company in the late 1920s. William has been credited with the development of long-term, all-inclusive leases combining vehicles, drivers, maintenance, and, later, logistical expertise. As contract carriers, O'Neill affiliates often sublimated their own corporate identities to suit customer needs. Since the 1930s, contract carriage has comprised the vast majority of the group's business.

At that time, the fledgling trucking industry was intensely competitive, with some truckers charging rates that were not sufficient to defray their operating costs. They forewent maintenance on their vehicles and drove long hours to compensate for the low prices. In 1935 the Federal Motor Carrier Act was ratified to bring stability to the motor carrier industry by setting rates and load limits. It also helped to establish the parameters of Leaseway's growth and expansion.

The new legislation limited individual trucking companies to eight contract customers, but the O'Neills (along with many other transport concerns) circumvented this rule by acquiring and creating separate firms. Each individual O'Neill affiliate could have eight contract clients. One of these subsidiaries, however, Anchor Motor Freight, Inc., sufficed with one: General Motors. The company's relationship with GM began in 1934 and evolved into the core of Leaseway's contract carrier trade. The family business grew rapidly over the next twenty-five years, with contracts to haul goods for such major manufacturers as Sears, Roebuck & Co., Whirlpool Corp., Montgomery Ward, and Standard Oil of Ohio.

After World War II, the field of transportation leasing grew rapidly. As many manufacturers decentralized, they looked increasingly to inter- and intra-state trucking to connect their activities; at the same time, the federal interstate highway system was being constructed and expanded. The O'Neills, led by Francis and William, embarked on an ambitious acquisition program. By the late 1950s, the family owned over 100 separate companies, and its annual revenues neared $20 million.

The O'Neill brothers took their family business public in 1960 as Leaseway Transportation Corp., with an initial capitalization of $2.25 million. Family members and close associates owned 90 percent of the company's stock during the early 1960s, a proportion that would steadily decline over the next two decades. In 1961 the new firm acquired 79 of the O'Neill affiliates and three years later it added 15 more of the family's properties (including Anchor Motor Freight, which contributed one-fifth of the corporation's annual revenues at its inclusion). As Chair and CEO, William O'Neill led Leaseway's dramatic growth from $25 million in annual revenues in 1961 to $475 million by the time he retired in 1975, acquiring 19 companies during that period. He also expanded leasing activities into Canada and Europe through several joint ventures. Leaseway earned a spot on the New York Stock Exchange in 1966. Within less than a decade of its incorporation, Leaseway had grown to rank second only to Consolidated Freightways among trucking firms. In 1975 William O'Neill was succeeded by his nephew Hugh O'Neill.

Just three years later, Hugh O'Neill resigned and was replaced by Robert A. Burgin, Jr. Although Leaseway's revenues had continued to rise during the last O'Neill's tenure, the competition grew even faster: by 1979, Leaseway ranked fourth among the largest highway transportation companies in the United States, after United Parcel Service, Consolidated Freightways, and Roadway Express. According to 1982 coverage in the *Plain Dealer,* Burgin was brought on to consolidate the 195 transportation-related companies that made up Leaseway in anticipation of the deregulation of the trucking industry that would occur during the early 1980s. O'Neill retained his seat on Leaseway's board of directors and remained a major stockholder.

Years of intense lobbying on the part of the trucking industry combined with the free-market ideals of the presidential administration under Ronald Reagan led to the 1980 repeal of many Interstate Commerce Commission rules governing shipping rates, the number of customers a given company could serve, and the size of individual loads. Although deregulation was hailed as a boon to Leaseway and the entire industry, rate cutting and other aggressive competitive measures, along with a recession in the early 1980s, sharply reduced profits. Leaseway consolidated many of its divisions around its two primary auto transport subsidiaries, Anchor Motor Freight and Leaseway Motorcar Transportation.

Deregulation also prompted Leaseway to hire marketing specialists and embark on an advertising campaign. The company also developed a multi-million dollar computer system called Route Assist, which analyzed orders, loads, destinations, and mileages, to develop more efficient transport strategies for all its customers. A satellite system was added at the end of the decade to help accommodate customers who required ''just-in-time'' deliveries.

In 1982 the firm launched a new subsidiary, Leaseway Express Inc., as a ''less-than-truckload'' common carrier. Based in Cincinnati, the non-union firm attempted to make what was traditionally an unprofitable segment of the industry pay off. The new venture boasted a greatly simplified rate structure based strictly on distance, rather than on an aggregation of rates based on formulas of distance, type of shipment, weight, and other considerations. Leaseway Express initially operated only in New York, Cleveland, Chicago, Philadelphia, Dallas–Ft. Worth, and Cincinnati, but expanded service to four more terminals in the eastern United States the following year. In spite of the parent company's high hopes for its new venture, Leaseway Express lost money in 1982 and 1983 and was sold to Thurston Motor Lines Inc. in 1985.

Leaseway's other endeavors fared no better during the 1980s. Although annual revenues grew steadily—and surpassed the $1 billion mark in 1983—Leaseway's profits declined from $45 million in 1981 and stayed low through 1984. Gerald C. McDonough, who had assumed the leadership of Leaseway in 1982, noted in the May 10, 1984, *Plain Dealer* that ''those of us in the secondary market positions are competing intensely with each other, but often, the net effect appears to be that we are swapping accounts in a market where demand has remained relatively flat.'' Still, McDonough maintained that Leaseway would benefit and grow as the result of deregulation.

In 1984 the CEO announced staff cuts and a plan to sell businesses that did not achieve 16 percent return on equity. Accordingly, he divested Leaseway Fleet Management Corp. to Dart & Kraft Financial Corp. Although Leaseway's profits jumped to more than $62 million in 1985, its stock continued to languish around the $30 mark, fueling stockholder discontent—especially among the O'Neills, who still controlled about 30 percent of the company's shares.

In April 1986, a family coalition of shareholders, led by Patrick J. and Hugh O'Neill, launched a proxy fight against Chairman McDonough. The O'Neills reasoned to the *Plain Dealer* that ''the company hasn't performed under him for four years, and consequently we feel the buck stops there.'' They demanded McDonough's resignation, and endorsed a slate of directors floated by the ''Committee to Revitalize Leaseway Transportation Corp.'' in the fast-approaching May board elections. Mc-

Donough, who enjoyed the support of the sitting board of directors, refused to step down. Although the two groups couldn't come to a compromise, they both announced that they would try to sell Leaseway in the new fiscal year.

Within weeks, McDonough and the Leaseway board won the closely fought proxy battle with the support of 56 percent of all shareholders and an overwhelming majority of the non-O'Neill vote. The still-influential O'Neills pushed for the quick divestment of Leaseway to beat an impending capital gains tax increase. If the sale was closed before January 1, 1987, they would avoid the new tax; if not, the O'Neills stood to lose about $10 million to the U.S. government.

Six months after the proxy battle, 40 of Leaseway's managers joined forces with Citicorp Capital Investors Ltd. to take the trucking firm private. Their $690 million leveraged buyout (LBO), which was announced in November 1986, offered shareholders $51 per share in cash, a slight premium over the going rate on the stock market. Complaining that the price was too low, the O'Neills and some other stockholders threatened to hold on to their shares. Finally, on December 24, the O'Neills sold 2.2 million shares (nearly all of their personal holdings) back to Leaseway for $48.12 per share to net well over $100 million. Regardless of the O'Neills' protests regarding the buyout offer, the LBO was later characterized as ''so over priced that it was doomed from the start,'' by Phyllis Berman of *Forbes* magazine. She noted that ''only one month after the ink was dry on the leveraged buyout documents (July 1987), Leaseway failed to make its initial projections.''

Even in the high-leverage trucking business and the freewheeling 1980s, Leaseway's buyout was universally denounced as over-leveraged. About $200 million of the $690 million buyout was generated through the sale of 13.25 percent unsecured bonds. Another $400 million was loaned by banks, led by the First National Bank of Boston. Citicorp Capital Investors raised the remaining equity. A recession that hit the auto industry especially hard during the late 1980s had devastating repercussions for Leaseway.

Asset sales, drastic reductions in capital spending, and a change in leadership did nothing to reverse Leaseway's declining fortunes. In 1988 Gerald McDonough turned the positions of Chair and CEO over to Richard A. Damsel, a former senior vice-president for finance and administration. Within a few months, Leaseway divested its Full-Service Leasing division, a significant portion of its contract and warehouse operations, and its Bulk Materials Group. Together, these represented $429 million, or one-third of its 1987 revenues. CEO Damsel made several unsuccessful attempts to wheedle lower interest rates out of bondholders, as Standard & Poor's relegated the debentures to ''junk bond'' status.

Leaseway was able to pay interest charges of $5 million per month throughout 1988 and 1989, but recorded successive losses of $46 million in the former year, and $18 million in the latter. Corporate leaders blamed excess capacity in its auto hauling and bulk truckload operations, as well as increased competitive pressures in its retail home delivery operations for the negative performance. Unfortunately, Leaseway had taken on its huge debt load at the same time that its two most important customers, General Motors Corp. and Sears, Roebuck & Co. (which together constituted about half of the shipper's business) were downsizing. Other clients, too, grew skittish: early in 1990, Ford Motor Co. pulled some of its business. CEO Damsel later acknowledged that Leaseway's image as a "troubled LBO" impeded the acquisition of new customers as well. This sluggish demand idled as much as 30 percent of Leaseway's fleet.

In February 1990, Leaseway missed a $12.75 million interest payment on its junk bonds. That October, amid continuing negotiations with its creditors, the company stopped paying on its remaining $140 million bank debt as well. In January 1991, Leaseway stopped paying interest to its senior lenders. Skipping its debt payments did not help Leaseway's bottom line, however: from January 1, 1990, through December 31, 1992, the firm lost a total of $253.8 million. Damsel staved off bankruptcy with on-again, off-again negotiations for years, until December 1992, when the company filed for protection from its creditors under Chapter 11.

Meanwhile, takeover artists like Carl Icahn were buying up the company's debt at rates as low as ten cents on the dollar. Icahn was one of five investors who owned about 80 percent of the company's unsecured debt by late 1992. The financier (who alone held 40 percent of the bonds) was later credited with bringing his fellow bondholders to the bargaining table. Icahn sold his bonds (for a reported profit of $35 to $45 million) before the restructuring was completed, but after it became apparent that the debt would be transformed into an equity position in Leaseway.

The reorganization only took ten months—after years of wrangling over the debt, both sides appeared ready to deal. The agreement rid Leaseway of $471.3 million in long-term debt and accrued interest by transferring substantially all of the company's stock to bondholders. The reorganized Leaseway was much smaller than the company that was taken private in 1986: its annual revenues had declined by more than half, from nearly $1.5 billion to $628 million. By its own admission, the firm's long-standing financial difficulties had reduced capital equipment expenditures, with the result that, on the average, its fleet was past "the mid-point of its expected useful life."

In spite of formidable challenges, Leaseway had strengths that gave its executives and employees reason to celebrate the company's emergence from bankruptcy with a barbecue at corporate headquarters. The firm's relationship with General Motors had remained intact for more than six decades, and the American auto industry was on an upswing, which could contribute to improving Leaseway's fortunes. In his last annual report—and Leaseway's "first"—CEO Damsel added "our reputation as a high-quality carrier, our industry expertise, our marketing strategy, and our improved financial condition" to the list of the company's strengths.

Late in 1994, Damsel announced that he would be resigning from Leaseway's chair and chief executive office. Darius W. Gaskins, Jr., a Leaseway board member, replaced Damsel as chairman in December 1994. Then, in March of the following year, Leaseway and Penske Truck Leasing Co., L.P. announced

a merger agreement under which Leaseway would be acquired for around $200 million by Penske subsidiary Penske Dedicated Logistics Corp. The merger was expected to be complete later that year.

Principal Subsidiaries: Anchor Motor Freight, Inc.; Appliance Transportation, Inc.; Atlas Service Co.; Automotive Transportation Systems, Inc.; Bejin Trucking Company; Better Home Deliveries, Inc.; Black Horse Carriers, Inc.; Charlton Transport (Quebec) Limited Consolidation Centers, Inc.; Custom Deliveries, Inc.; Dedicated Freight Systems, Inc.; Geo. McNeil Teaming Company; Gold Star Enterprises, Inc.; Gold Star, Inc.; Gross & Hecht Trucking, Inc.; Inter-City Trucking Service, Inc.; Leaseway Customized Transport, Inc.; Leaseway Deliveries, Inc.; Leaseway Finance Corp.; Leaseway Ltd.; Leaseway Motorcar Transport Company; Leaseway Multi-Transportation Services, Inc.; Leaseway National Service Corp.; Leaseway Personnel Corp.; Leaseway Purchasing Corp.; Leaseway Technology Corp.; Leaseway Transfer Pool, Inc.; Leaseway Trucking, Inc.; Logistics Partners Company; Logistics Resource, Inc.; Middlesex Leasing Corp.; Mountainside Transport, Inc.; Nu-Car Carriers, Inc.; Quest Partners Company; Savannah Service, Inc.; Signal Delivery Service, Inc.; Somerset Driver Corp.; Stam-Win, Inc.; Strategic Transportation, Inc.; TRM Transportation, Inc.; Terminal Personnel, Inc.; Transco Group, Inc.; Transco Service-Oakland, Inc.; Transco Service-Sacramento, Inc.; Transportation House, Inc.; Trident Export Corporation.

Further Reading:

Berman, Phyllis, "Staying Alive," *Forbes,* Vol. 147, June 24, 1991, p. 45.

Bryan, John E., "Horses to Horsepower, O'Neills Offer Transportation for Globe," *Plain Dealer,* December 20, 1965.

Cobleigh, Ira U., "Leaseway Transportation," *Commercial and Financial Chronicle,* Vol. 208, November 14, 1968, p. 1949.

Gerdel, Thomas W., "Crushing Debt Load Proves Major Burden to Leaseway," *Plain Dealer,* December 31, 1989, p. 1D.

——, "Leaseway Files for Reorganization," *Plain Dealer,* December 2, 1992, p. 1C.

——, "Leaseway Back from Chapter 11," *Plain Dealer,* September 15, 1993, p. 1E.

——, "Chief of Trucking Company Stepping Down," *Plain Dealer,* December 20, 1994, p. 5C.

Gleisser, Marcus, "O'Neills Began in Transportation," *Plain Dealer,* April 24, 1986, pp. 1–2E.

Kelly, Michael, "O'Neill Resigns from Leaseway," *Plain Dealer,* January 12, 1978, p. 6D.

Mahoney, Mike, "Battle Looms for Leaseway Control," *Plain Dealer,* April 24, 1986, pp. 1–2E.

——, "Leaseway on Rocky Road; Experts Wonder if Earnings Will Improve," *Plain Dealer,* April 25, 1986, pp. 10–11C.

——, "Leaseway Transportation Sold; O'Neills Will Hold Shares for Now," *Plain Dealer,* November 14, 1986, p. 1A.

Pallatto, John, "Leaseway Program Keeps Trucks on the Move," *PC Week,* Vol. 3, September 9, 1986, p. 41.

Thomas, Dana L., "Over the Hump: After Some Rough Going, the Trucking Industry Is Picking up Speed," *Barron's,* Vol. 44, June 8, 1964, pp. 3, 12, 14, 15–16.

"Trucker's Progress," *Forbes,* Vol. 102, November 15, 1968, p. 47.

—April Dougal Gasbarre

Lenox, Inc.

100 Lenox Drive
Lawrenceville, New Jersey 08648
U.S.A.
(609) 896-2800
Fax: (609) 896-3704

Wholly Owned Subsidiary of Brown-Forman Corporation
Incorporated: 1906
Sales: $310 million
Employees: 4,200
SICs: 3262 Vitreous China, Table & Kitchenware; 3229
  Pressed & Blown Glass

Lenox, Inc., is the oldest and most famous manufacturer of fine china in the United States. The company has filled orders for four American presidents, met the requirements of a desert prince who needed enough tableware to throw a banquet for 1,000 revelers, and sent a delegation around the world to sketch pheasants from various countries for a customer who wanted the images to decorate his service plates. Lenox china has become so famous and highly valued that it was selected by the New York Metropolitan Museum of Art for its 1989 exhibit on American porcelain, and it is the only American china ever shown at the renowned Ceramic Museum in Sevres, France.

The founder of Lenox, Inc., was Walter Scott Lenox, born in 1859 in Trenton, New Jersey. At that time, Trenton was a focal point for pottery and ceramics in the United States, and the young Lenox soon resolved to become a ceramicist. After a stint as an apprentice at the Willetts Manufacturing Company, he concentrated on problems of ceramic design and decoration. Lenox was recognized for his hard work and talent, and during his 20s he was hired by the well-known Ott and Brewer Company to serve as art director for its factory. By the time he reached the age of 30, Lenox had saved enough money to enter a partnership with Jonathan Coxon, Jr., and opened his own firm, the Ceramic Art Company, in 1889.

Lenox dreamed of producing china as good as or better than any other ceramics company in the world. During the 19th century, the nascent American ceramics and pottery industry produced unrefined wares due to their unsophisticated manufacturing techniques; as a result, wealthy Americans turned to famous, centuries-old European manufacturers for dinner service and tableware. Lenox's goal was thus formidable: he had to master the difficult techniques involved in making fine china, overcome American prejudices against domestic china, and, in addition, secure sufficient backing to finance his operations.

The Ceramic Art Company experienced severe financial hardship during the early years of its operation. Lenox and his partner hired talented craftsmen and spent large sums on materials, but the results were ever-increasing expenses and minimal profits. In 1894 Lenox purchased Coxon's interest in the Ceramic Art Company, and thereafter he ran the business alone. Lenox concentrated on producing a ware known as Belleck, a rich, thin, ivory-colored porcelain of extremely high quality manufactured in Belleck, Ireland, bringing two potters from Ireland to help him master the technique. But there were more disappointments in his attempts to produce a high-grade china than there were successes, and the company fell deeper and deeper in debt. At one point, in order to obtain financing for a new factory in Trenton, Lenox was forced to accept that the building would be so designed and constructed as to be quickly changed into a tenement building if his company went out of business. Undaunted, Lenox continued working toward his dream of creating high-quality American china.

In the early years of the new century, Lenox's health began to deteriorate. Gradually becoming paralyzed and blind, he redoubled his efforts. He continued to work at the factory on a daily basis, with his chauffeur carrying him to his desk, and began to monitor the production of porcelain with his hands as his eyesight deteriorated. Although Lenox still made all the decisions regarding production, he relied more and more on his assistant and secretary Harry Brown, who had been with Lenox since the early 1890s.

In 1906, with Brown's help, Lenox established Lenox, Inc. The company's first big break came when the firm filled an order from Shreve and Company, a retailer located in San Francisco, which was delivered just in time to be destroyed in the San Francisco earthquake of 1906. However, dug out of the ruins of Shreve's store was a glazed Lenox plate that looked as exquisite as it had on the day it was produced. The plate soon became the cornerstone of Lenox's marketing campaign.

Harry Brown approached Tiffany's in New York City with the surviving plate and other examples of Lenox china, and Tiffany's agreed to become Lenox's first account. Following their lead, stores from New York to Philadelphia began to sign on as customers. The company began to grow rapidly, and, by the time World War I began, Lenox was had gained wide respect as a manufacturer of quality china. In 1917 the company came to the attention of the White House, which was trying to fulfill a Congressional mandate of 1826 stipulating that everything used in the White House should be domestically produced. Until that time, however, presidents had been unable to find domestic china deemed suitable to serve honored guests at the White House table, and they remained dependent on foreign-made tableware. Woodrow Wilson broke this precedent by ordering a 1700-piece tableware set from Lenox at a cost of $16,000. (Subsequent orders for complete sets for the White House came from Franklin Delano Roosevelt in 1932, Harry Truman in 1951, and Ronald Reagan in 1981.) Thereafter, Lenox was recognized internationally as one of the world's premier manufacturers of fine china.

Walter Scott Lenox's health continued to deteriorate, but his company prospered, and when he died in January 1920 the firm was finally out of debt. Yet the battle for the American market continued, with European companies dominating both in revenues and design. Almost eight of every ten pieces of porcelain sold in the United States still originated in Europe.

After Lenox passed away, Harry Brown assumed the presidency of Lenox, Inc., and began to hammer away at the pre-eminent position that European ceramics held in America. During the 1930s, when the company was making significantly less than $1 million per year, Brown hired designer Frank Holmes. Breaking away from the elaborate style that European designers favored, Holmes began to create a new style in china that was soon described as "modern." With clean, simple lines, and uncomplicated decorative motifs set against a background of ivory, Holmes's modern style soon garnered a great deal of attention. By the end of the decade, the style was so successful that Lenox had captured 25 percent of the domestic market.

At the beginning of World War II, the company's revenues were just under the $1 million mark, and the war prevented the company from implementing any of its anticipated expansion plans. Fortunately for Lenox, however, the onset of the war led to the complete cessation of importing fine china from Europe. This situation encouraged numerous American firms to enter the market for fine china, and by the end of the war large amounts of capital were flowing into the domestic production of porcelain. As competition increased among American companies during the postwar period, new merchandising and sales methods were introduced to increase sales. Lenox itself used such mainstream methods as exhibits and displays, while also creating more unusual educational films about making Lenox china for distribution in schools and women's social clubs.

During the 1950s, Lenox broke away from the European system of selling china, which involved the purchase of an entire service set at significant cost. The result was that china represented an investment that was out of reach of the average family. Instead, Lenox began to offer five-piece complete place settings, three-piece-buffet/place settings, and individual pieces for sale. In addition, Lenox was the first company to develop a bridal registry, whereby women engaged to be married could register their choice of china at selected retail stores, and family and friends could purchase pieces from the registry as wedding gifts.

During the 1960s Lenox initiated an acquisitions program. The company's first purchase was America's oldest and best-known crystal glassblowing firm, Bryce Brothers, which was established in 1841 in Mt. Pleasant, Pennsylvania. Committed to maintaining Bryce Brothers' high standards of quality, Lenox produced crystal that became known for fine design and craftsmanship. Lenox's growing marketing sophistication also contributed to its line of crystal becoming the favorite choice of new brides across America. During the late 1960s, Lenox crystal was chosen by the vice-president of the United States for use at state occasions and by the State Department for use in its embassies and consulates. During the 1970s, Lenox continued its acquisition program by purchasing Hartmann Luggage, a manufacturer of quality luggage and leather accessories, and Athalon Products, Ltd., a highly regarded producer of nylon sports luggage.

In 1983 Lenox was acquired by Brown-Forman Corporation, a large conglomerate with most of its sales in the beverage industry. Brown-Forman's management was attempting to diversify its holdings at the time, and Lenox was a prime example of the new direction Brown-Forman wanted to chart. Management at Lenox, however, was not in favor of the acquisition, and a strong disagreement ensued. Brown-Forman finally convinced Lenox that it would not interfere with the production of its china, and Lenox was also assured that it would have some control over the marketing methods used to sell its products. An agreement was finalized and Lenox became a wholly owned subsidiary of Brown-Forman.

Lenox benefitted from the acquisition by Brown-Forman. The large conglomerate not only enabled its subsidiary to continue an aggressive acquisitions program, but also provided capital for the company to expand its facilities. In 1985 Lenox opened a new plant in Oxford, North Carolina, with state-of-the-art manufacturing techniques for the company's fine china gifts. In 1991 another new plant was opened in Kinston, North Carolina, to help the company maintain its competitiveness in the growing domestic bone china industry. That same year, Lenox acquired the Kirk Stieff Company, a producer of fine sterling; Dansk International Designs Ltd., the leader in consumer tabletop, houseware, and gift markets; and Dansk's subsidiary, Gorham Silver, the leading American manufacturer of sterling silver products. These acquisitions helped solidify Lenox's position as the pre-eminent fine china company in the United States and one of the world leaders in the industry.

Principal Subsidiaries: Hartmann Luggage; Athalon Products, Ltd.; Kirk Stieff Co.; Dansk International Designs Ltd.

Further Reading:

Lenox Fine China—The First Hundred Years, Lawrenceville, N.J.: Lenox, Inc., 1994, pp. 1–6.
The Story of Walter Scott Lenox, Lawrenceville, N.J.: Lenox, Inc., 1994, pp. 1–5.

—Thomas Derdak

LILLIAN VERNON

Lillian Vernon Corp.

543 Main Street
New Rochelle, New York 10801
U.S.A
(914) 576-6400
Fax: (914) 637-5740

Incorporated: 1951 as Vernon Specialties
Employees: 3,000
Stock Exchanges: American
Sales: $200 million
SICs: 5961 Mail Order Houses

The Lillian Vernon Corporation is a mail-order catalog company specializing in household, gardening, and decorative merchandise as well as gifts and children's products. Offering simple and practical merchandise, Lillian Vernon's catalogs have become a fixture in American pop culture, having gained mention on such television programs as *Northern Exposure, Roseanne,* and *Jeopardy.* Although the company went public in 1987, Lillian Vernon remained essentially a family-run company, with its founder Lillian Vernon acting as CEO, and her sons David and Fred Hochberg acting as vice-president of public affairs, and president and chief operating officer, respectively. Fred Hochberg left the company in 1992.

In 1994, Lillian Vernon's circulation of over 150 million encompassed five different catalogs: Lillian Vernon's original catalog, Welcome (targeted to people who had recently moved) Lilly's Kids, Christmas Memories, and sale catalogs. An additional catalog, Lillian Vernon's Kitchen, was introduced in February 1995, boosting circulation once again. Lillian Vernon purchased its products directly from companies in the United States as well as in Paris, London, Milan, and Hong Kong. It also maintained a wholesale division, Lillian Vernon Special Markets, which sells gifts and other products personalized with company names on logos. Although Lillian Vernon boasted Hillary Clinton, Tipper Gore, Frank Sinatra, and Loretta Lynn among its clientele, the majority (over 90 percent) of its customers were women with an average household income of $53,000. Over half worked outside the home and had children living at home.

Lillian Vernon Corporation was founded in 1951 under the name Vernon Specialties. The name was taken from founder Lillian Vernon's home in Mount Vernon, New York. At that time, Vernon was 22 years old, recently married, pregnant, and looking for a business she could run from her kitchen table. Using part of the $2,000 she and her husband had received as wedding gifts, Vernon took out a $495 advertisement in *Seventeen* magazine offering monogrammed leather handbags and belts for $2.99 and $1.99, each. The leather goods were purchased from Vernon's father, who ran a small leather factory. The 24-karat gold monograms were purchased from a distributor and hand-applied on the goods by Vernon herself.

Vernon received $32,000 worth of orders from her first ad. She then used her profits to buy ads in other popular women's magazines. Sales grew, and, within a few years, the company landed several contracts to manufacture custom-designed products for corporations, including Max Factor, Elizabeth Arden, Avon, and Revlon. In 1954, Vernon Specialties moved out of Vernon's kitchen and into three facilities in Mount Vernon in order to meet the growing demand for its products.

Two years later, in 1956, Vernon Specialties mailed its first catalog to the 125,000 customers who had responded to the company's magazine ads since 1951. The catalog had sixteen pages of black-and-white photos offering items such as signet rings, combs, cuff links, and blazer buttons—all of which could be personalized through the company's free monogramming service.

In fact, the key to Vernon Specialties' early success in the mail-order business was its offer of free monogramming, which continued as one of the features that distinguished the company from its competitors in the mid-1990s. Within a few years of its debut, the catalog was expanded by Vernon to include products for the home. She personally chose every product featured in her catalogs and had an "uncanny knack" for judging the needs and desires of middle-class housewives. Based on her own experiences, she knew that housewives required well-built products at reasonable prices. Although products were bought from a variety of manufacturers, most were customized under the Lillian Vernon name. As proof of the quality of its products Lillian Vernon offered a 100 percent money-back guarantee, which stated that "customers can return a product even ten years after it has been purchased."

Vernon Specialties' catalog was quite successful in its first decade, and sales continued to increase. In 1965, the company changed its name to Lillian Vernon Corporation. Sales were given an added boost in 1968, when Lillian Vernon introduced personalized Christmas ornaments in its catalogs. This product line would grow so popular that over 75 million ornaments would be sold by 1994. In 1970, the company's annual sales hit $1 million.

Sales continued to grow moderately throughout the 1970s. In 1978, as a response to the growing number of catalog customers interested in retailing Lillian Vernon products in their own stores, the company established its Provender wholesale division. Provender provided retailers with Lillian Vernon's own line of imported toiletries, fancy foods, and kitchen textiles, such as towels, aprons, and pot holders. Around that time, the company also opened The New Company, a wholesale manufacturer of brass products headquartered in Providence, Rhode Island.

In 1982, sales jumped again when the company introduced its first sale catalog offering overstocked merchandise at prices up to 75 percent off the original retail prices. Due largely to the success of its sale catalogs, Lillian Vernon posted record revenues of $75 million in 1983. The following year, Lillian Vernon introduced a line of private-label, exclusively designed home organization products in its catalog, a line that grew to represent 25 percent of business within ten years. In 1985, the company streamlined its operations by incorporating its Provender division into the main wholesale division.

The mail-order industry grew by leaps and bounds in the 1980s, with the number of people ordering merchandise by phone or mail increasing 70 percent between 1982 and 1992. Small, specialty catalogs like Lillian Vernon entered the market in full force, taking sales away from traditional mail-order giants like Sears and Montgomery Ward.

By 1987, Lillian Vernon was mailing out 80 million catalogs a year. The company went public that year, with an initial offering of 1.9 million shares on the American Stock Exchange. Proceeds for the offering were used to construct a state-of-the-art National Distribution Center in Virginia Beach, Virginia. That year, net income totaled $4.4 million on revenues of $115.5 million. The following year, net income grew to $6.9 million on revenues of $126 million.

Expansion continued with the 1989 addition of a computer center at the company's National Distribution Center. That year, Laura Zambano was named to the position of senior vice-president, general merchandise manager, taking over many of the merchandising responsibilities from Vernon. Also that year, the company opened its first outlet store near its Virginia Beach distribution center. The company made an attempt to further diversify its product offerings by introducing a high-end home furnishings catalog, which ultimately was incorporated into the company's other catalogs.

The following year, however, Lillian Vernon introduced the highly successful Lilly's Kids, catalogs specializing in toys, games, and personalized gifts for children. Sales hit $162 million, in 1991 with profits of $9.5 million. A new customer service center was opened in Virginia, as were two new outlet stores; one in a suburb of Washington, D.C. and the other in Williamsburg, Virginia.

Lillian Vernon was able to stay on top of the booming catalog industry by constantly introducing new products and by keeping prices reasonable. As the company entered its fourth decade, the average price of a product was $17 and the average customer order totaled $39. In 1992, the company declared its first quarterly dividend of $0.05 per share. That year, it also introduced its Christmas Memories catalog, specializing in Christmas ornaments and holiday decorations for the home. By 1992, Lillian Vernon was adding over 1,000 new products a year to its four catalogs and had three more outlet stores in Virginia and New York State.

In 1993, Lillian Vernon launched its Welcome catalog, offering home organization products and decorative accessories for people who had recently moved to new homes. 1993 net income totaled $12.8 million on revenues of $196.3 million.

Although the catalog/direct marketing industry boomed in the 1980s, cyclical downturns are inevitable. Company management regarded increased specialization and diversification of its catalogs as essential to success in this rapidly changing environment. In response to increased competition, Lillian Vernon began test-mailing its catalogs in Canada and also began investigating other foreign markets. The company offered products on television's QVC Shopping Network, and Vernon personally appeared on Joan Rivers' television shopping program in 1994.

In another effort to keep on top of trends in the direct marketing industry, Lillian Vernon became one of 39 catalogs to be featured on The Merchant, one of the first CD-ROM shopping discs.

As Lillian Vernon approached its fiftieth anniversary, the company seemed intent on expansion. It launched another specialized catalog in February 1995 offering cookwear, cutlery, table accessories, gourmet gifts, and small electric appliances. Two months later, it launched a special section in its core catalog featuring luggage and travel accessories. The company began selling its products through the Prodigy online service, and was also looking into further growth through acquisitions and expansion of its corporate gift, premium, incentive, and gift certificate markets.

Further Reading:

Byrne, Harlan S., "Lillian Vernon Corp.: Segmentation Builds Catalog Sales, *Barron's,* June 4, 1990, p. 58.
Coleman, Lisa, "I Went Out and Did It," *Forbes,* August 17, 1992, p. 102.
Garbato-Stankevich, Debby, "Lilly's Red-Hot Love Affair," *HFD: The Weekly Home Furnishings Newspaper,* June 21, 1993, p. 52.
Gattuso, Greg, "Lillian Vernon Looks to the Future," *Direct Marketing,* August 1994, p. 33.
Simon, Virginia, "A Marketing Maestro Orchestrates," *Target Marketing,* October 1992, p. 16.

—Maura Troester

⊖ Loews Corporation

Loews Corporation

667 Madison Avenue
New York, New York 10321-8087
U.S.A.
(212) 545-2000
Fax: (212) 545-2714

Public Company
Incorporated: 1969
Employees: 27,100
Sales: $13.5 billion
Stock Exchanges: New York
SICs: 6331 Fire, Marine & Casualty Insurance; 6311 Life
   Insurance; 2111 Cigarettes; 5094 Jewelry & Precious
   Stones; 7011 Hotels & Motels; 1381 Drilling Oil & Gas
   Wells

The Loews Corporation is a $13.5 billion conglomerate with
extensive interests in tobacco, insurance, watches, hotels, and
oil tankers. Major consumer brands include Bulova watches and
Newport cigarettes. In 1990, a *Financial World* analyst characterized Loews as "a closed-end fund or a holding company
disguised as an operating company." Run since the post-World
War II era by brothers Preston Robert (Bob) and Laurence
(Larry) Tisch, the company was amassed through "value investing." The Tisches earned a reputation for purchasing troubled firms, making them profitable, and selling them at a premium. Their major investments in the 1990s included the CBS
television network.

Although the Tisch's stake in the business has declined to about
one-fourth over the years, the Loews Corporation is still considered by many to be a family business. Bob is known for his
operational savvy, while elder brother Larry is considered the
financial genius. In the early 1990s, the brothers shared the titles
of co-chief executive officer and co-chairman. A number of
Tisch offspring have also become prominent members of the
company's management.

The Tisch family has tended not to supervise the day-to-day
operations of the corporation, however. Rather, the company
functions through a network of divisions which exercise a large
degree of autonomy and assume responsibility for performance.
Initiative and innovation are encouraged and rewarded. When
problems occur, however, they are brought quickly to Bob
Tisch's attention. Tisch boasted that there is no administrative

labyrinth in which to lose or hide operational defects. "Loews
is a big business run like a small business," Tisch has said. "I
hope we can keep it that way."

The Tisch brothers were given an early business education by
their father, Al, who owned a manufacturing plant in Manhattan. Bob and Larry were given the task of making phone sales to
retail stores and wholesale distributors. The two brothers also
helped operate a few summer camps their parents owned in
New Jersey. This "hands on" experience was coupled with
formal training. After a brief hiatus spent in the Army, Bob
graduated with a degree in economics from the University of
Michigan in 1948. Larry graduated cum laude from New York
University's School of Commerce at the age of 18, went on to
earn an MBA from the Wharton School in Philadelphia, and
later enrolled in Harvard's law school.

In 1946, Al and Sadye Tisch sold their summer camps and
purchased the Laurel-in-the-Pines Hotel in Lakewood, New
Jersey. The hotel business went well, and soon became more
than the parents could handle alone. Larry dropped out of
Harvard in order to help run the business and Bob soon followed. It wasn't long before the older couple decided to sign
over their share of the hotel (worth about $75,000 at the time) to
their sons and give them control of the operation.

The brothers soon began leasing two other small New Jersey
hotels and managed to turn a profit. Then, in 1952, they acquired two grand but old hotels in Atlantic City called the
Brighton and the Ambassador. They demolished one to build a
motel in its place, and quickly resold the other at a profit. Later,
the Tisches liquidated some of their New Jersey investments to
purchase their first two hotels in New York City. These early
transactions established the pattern that would characterize their
later business dealings, which grew increasingly diverse and
valuable.

In 1956, with only eight years' experience in the business, Bob
and Larry erected the $17 million Americana Hotel in Bal
Harbour, Florida, and paid for it in cash. Although it was
subsequently sold to Sheraton, it represented an important step
in the brothers' careers. With the Americana, they firmly established themselves among the major hotel operators, and later
acquired such prominent hotels in the United States as the Mark
Hopkins, The Drake, the Belmont Plaza, and the Regency.

In 1959 a major anti-trust ruling forced Metro-Goldwyn-Mayer
to relinquish ownership of Loew's Theaters. This decision created an opportunity for the Tisch brothers, allowing them to
move into a new business area. Six months before MGM was to
divest Loew's, Bob and Larry purchased a large stake in the
theater chain; by May of 1960 they had gained control of the
company.

The brothers did not enter into the theater business because they
knew about the motion picture industry. Nor did they purchase
Loew's because it was already a profitable operation on its own.
On the contrary, Loew's theaters were losing money. They were
large, multi-tiered movie houses with high ceilings and interiors
reminiscent of the industry's "golden age," by this time long
past. They played only one motion picture at a time and were
rarely filled to capacity. Television and the proliferation of films
coming out of Hollywood meant that theaters would have to

cater to various tastes simultaneously in order to secure larger audiences. The old Loew's theaters were not designed for this purpose.

The reason Bob and Larry Tisch purchased Loew's had to do with real estate. The Loew's theaters, though antiquated, were located on valuable city property. It was the opportunity to acquire this valuable property that prompted the brothers to purchase the company. Almost immediately they began liquidating the theaters, demolishing 50 of them in a matter of months and then selling the vacant lots to developers. This, of course, hastened the demise of the palatial movie house, but it was nonetheless a necessary business tactic. Loews (the apostrophe has since been eliminated) remains a prominent participant in the movie industry with theaters in 26 metropolitan areas. However, its 143 screens are located in only 61 facilities. There are often four screens in one building, each showing a different movie.

The long-established and well-recognized Loews name became the corporate title under which all Tisch operations (including hotels) were placed. The new Loews Corporation ran smoothly and efficiently, turning substantial profits every year. By 1968 the brothers again had the capital and the inclination to diversify and invest in a new business sector. This time they acquired Lorillard Industries, America's oldest tobacco manufacturer.

Lorillard, the maker of Kent and Newport cigarettes, had once been a major company with a large share of the tobacco market. However, managerial incompetence and discord had paralyzed the company, bringing it near collapse. Upon assuming control of Lorillard, the first thing Larry Tisch did was examine the firm's subsidiaries, particularly its candy and cat food divisions which were consuming a disproportionate amount of resources. The brothers discovered that the top executives spent 75 percent of their time on candy and cat food, which together made up only 5 percent of Lorillard's total business. Lorillard divested itself of these interests and of the executives who were so fond of them, then redirected the company toward its tobacco operations. Market share slippage was reversed, and Lorillard climbed back to the top ranks of America's tobacco market.

A similar scenario took place in 1974, when Loews acquired CNA Financial Corporation, a large insurance firm. The Chicago-based conglomerate had reported a $208 million deficit that year and was expected to lose more. Like Lorillard, its subsidiaries were draining the financial resources of the company. CNA's tangential interests were poorly managed and veritable "money pits." Moreover, there was considerable waste at the top of CNA's corporate structure.

When Loews took charge it divested unprofitable or distractive subsidiaries to concentrate on the worthwhile core businesses. The Tisch brothers then took aim at the wastefulness that plagued CNA's headquarters. Many executives were fired as Tisch austerity measures prevailed over past CNA lavishness. The 3,000-square-foot suite of the former chairman was rented out, as was the corporate dining room. The streamlining had a dramatic and positive effect. In 1975 CNA earned a $110 million profit, and remained financially sound over the next decade, achieving annual revenues of over $3 billion by the late 1980s.

Loews' next major turnaround target was the Bulova Watch Co. In 1979, the Tisch brothers bought 93 percent of the then-troubled firm for $38 million. At the time, Bulova's quality-control problems had contributed to its slip from the top of the watch market to the number-two spot. Not only had long-time rival Seiko Corporation won the market share battle, but Bulova was also threatened by Timex Enterprises Inc.'s introduction of competitively-priced entries. It looked to some observers as if Bulova had squandered its brand cachet; the name was simply not recognized by a new generation of consumers.

The Tisch brothers applied their proven method of managerial restructuring, but without total success. Bulova's problems went beyond personnel and corporate networks: the product itself needed to be revised. James Tisch, Larry's son, headed the operation and immediately introduced 600 new watch styles, complete with extended warranties. To deal with the image problem, an extensive advertising campaign was launched. The company recovered, but slowly. By 1984 it had cut its losses to $8 million (roughly half of its 1980 total), yet it was still not paying for itself. The company did not turn a profit until 1986. That year, Bob Tisch accepted an appointment as U.S. Postmaster General. Despite the concerns of those who felt his absence would weaken the company's performance, most analysts contended that Bob Tisch's move to Washington D.C. would help Loews, citing the advantages of both political and financial connections.

Late in 1985 Larry Tisch sold the company's namesake movie theaters and purchased a significant amount of CBS Inc. stock to help the company fight a takeover attempt by Ted Turner. Throughout 1986 Tisch increased Loews' share holdings in CBS to 24.8 percent and obtained a seat on the board of directors. He was elected president of CBS that September, much to the relief of stockholders and employees, who had grown frustrated and uneasy during the Turner takeover attempt.

Tisch's popularity was short-lived, however. Intending to operate CBS as if it were any other business, he took measures to alleviate waste and make CBS more cost-effective. Wage cuts and spending reductions, along with wholesale firings, caused a serious rift in the huge broadcasting firm. The news division, traditionally given considerable leeway in regard to fiscal accountability, was especially hard hit. Some wondered if Tisch would be able to mend CBS without sacrificing the people and principles that once made it the most respected of the three major American broadcasting networks. Eventually, Loews reduced its investment in CBS to 18 percent through sale of stock back to the company.

Bob Tisch's activities and interests outside Loews garnered attention as well. He was one of New York City's most vocal supporters and had been elected over 15 times to the chairmanship of New York's Convention and Visitors Bureau. In fact it was Bob Tisch and the Bureau's president, Charles Grillett, who came up with the idea of using an old jazz expression, the "big apple," to represent New York City. Later, Bob would represent the metropolis as its "official ambassador" (read lobbyist) in Washington, D.C. In 1990, he accepted the chairmanship of that city's Chamber of Commerce. In 1991, Bob

Tisch paid over $75 million to acquire half of the New York Giants professional football team.

Over the course of the 1980s, the Tisches had reduced their stake in Loews from 45 percent to 24 percent, prompting some analysts to speculate that they were preparing to dismantle their conglomerate. Instead, the company—which had amassed a $1.75 billion "war chest"—started investing in new ventures, most notably oil. By early 1990, Loews had spent $75 million on oil rigs and acquired Diamond M Offshore Inc., a Houston, Texas, drilling company. Loews amassed the world's largest fleet of offshore drilling rigs with the 1992 purchase of Odeco Drilling, Inc., which was merged with Diamond M. In spite of that status, Loews' drilling segment lost over $103 million in 1992, 1993, and 1994. The company's annual report for the latter year blamed regional overcapacity and reduced demand for the negative results.

While other large hotel companies struggled in the early 1990s, Loews thrived under the direction of Jonathan Mark Tisch. Tisch was praised for creative, ambitious, and often philanthropic promotions. His annual "Monopoly Power Breakfasts" featured celebrity contestants who played the famous Parker Brothers game competed on a customized board. Proceeds of the event went to charities. The upscale hotel chain's "Good Neighbor Policy" and its recycling programs earned it industry accolades as well. Following an industry wide trend, Loews Hotels lost $1.79 million in 1993, then reported a net profit of $17.02 million in 1994.

The Tisch's appeared to be continuing to apply their turnaround strategies to the Bulova division in the early 1990s. In 1995, they completed the divestment of that subsidiary's defense interests in order to concentrate on the core timepiece business. Although sales and profits declined as a result, this segment was able to stay in the black in the early 1990s.

Loews' two largest segments, cigarettes and insurance, were very vulnerable in the early 1990s. Price wars prompted the company to launch a bargain cigarette brand, Style, in 1992, then cut the retail price of its flagship Newport brand by 25 percent in 1994. In the decidedly anti-smoking climate that predominated then, cigarette manufacturers already faced with legislation that banned smoking from virtually all public places also encountered many lawsuits. As of fiscal 1994, Lorillard was a named defendant in 17 individual and class action suits brought by cigarette smokers, their estates and heirs, and even flight attendants who claimed to be victims of second-hand

smoke. Loews and Lorillard noted that, while losses in these cases would not hurt the company's long term performance, they could encourage more litigation.

When Loews subsidiary CNA Financial acquired The Continental Corporation in December 1994 for $1.1 billion, it became America's third-largest property and casualty insurer. It also took on Continental's liabilities regarding Fibreboard Corporation, a company that manufactured asbestos insulation products from 1928 to 1971. In 1993, Continental and its co-defendants reached a $2 billion settlement (of which Continental was responsible for $1.44 billion) to cover past and potential liabilities. Although the agreement had to be approved by a federal court—leaving open the possibility for even greater expense—Loews expressed confidence that the problem would not "have a material adverse impact on the equity of the Company."

Titular changes in the early 1990s seemed to indicate preparations for a changing of the guard at Loews. In the late 1980s, Bob had occupied the positions of president and chief operating officer, while Larry acted as chairman and CEO. But as the two brothers became septuagenarians, they consolidated their responsibilities, becoming co-chairmen and co-CEOs. James S. Tisch, a likely successor, advanced to president and chief operating officer, while Andrew H. Tisch led Lorillard.

Principal Subsidiaries: CNA Financial Corporation; Loews Hotels Holding Corporation; Lorillard Inc.; Bulova Corporation; Diamond Offshore Drilling, Inc.

Further Reading:

Dodds, Lynn Strongin, "Nothing to Fear," *Financial World,* September 30, 1986, p. 100.

Hager, Bruce, "Loews Sees the Future, and It's Oil," *Business Week,* March 19, 1990, pp. 126–127.

——, "Tisch the Younger Takes His Turn," *Business Week,* July 8, 1991, pp. 88–89.

Lesly, Elizabeth, "Loews Could Be Worth More Dead than Alive," *Business Week,* December 13, 1993, pp. 104–107.

"100 Leading Advertisers: Loews Corp./Mars Inc./Matsushita Electric Industrial Co.," *Advertising Age,* September 4, 1986, pp. 123–124.

Ozanian, Michael, "America's Most Undervalued Stock," *Financial World,* May 29, 1990, pp. 22–24.

Pesmen, Sandra, "Jonathan Tisch's Road Show," *Business Marketing,* February 1991, pp. 68–70.

—updated by April Dougal Gasbarre

The Longaberger Company

95 North Chestnut Street
Dresden, Ohio 43821-0073
U.S.A.
(614) 754-6300
Fax: (614) 754-2004

Private Company
Incorporated: 1973 as JW's Handwoven Baskets
Employees: 5,000
Sales: $300 million (est.)
SICs: 2499 Wood Products Nec; 3269 Pottery Products Nec

In less than twenty-five years, the Longaberger Company has grown from a basket-making sideline into a midwestern family empire. The company was founded in 1973 with two basket weavers, and by the early 1990s, hundreds of employees handwove millions of baskets for sale by tens of thousands of sales representatives each year. At that time, Longaberger enterprises included a basket plant, a purebred Angus breeding farm, four restaurants, eight retail shops, and a pottery-making operation. Founder Dave Longaberger was also planning for Longaberger Village, an entertainment/resort complex, to become another in a growing line of extraordinary successes. Using mottoes such as "Handmade to be handed down," the company has leveraged a strong sense of nostalgia and an appreciation for quality into a flourishing family legacy.

Born in the Ohio town of Dresden, about an hour northeast of Columbus, founder David W. Longaberger coped with a severe speech impediment and epilepsy, both of which hindered his academic career. He failed first grade once and fifth grade twice, and finally finished high school at the age of 20 at the insistence of his mother. Upon graduation, Longaberger briefly tried door-to-door sales and factory work, then settled into an eight-year stint driving sales and delivery routes for local bakeries.

Longaberger went into business for himself in 1963, when he and his wife bought an ice cream shop in Dresden, a town of less than 2,000 people. Within five years, they were able to purchase a local grocery store. The two businesses—known as "Popeye's," in reference to Longaberger's nickname—were so profitable that he began investigating other ventures in the early 1970s.

Longaberger took particular interest in the resurgent popularity of baskets as decorating elements. Longaberger's family had a basket weaving heritage dating back to 1896, when his paternal grandfather, John, moved to Dresden and started work at the Dresden Basket Factory. Until the mid-twentieth century, sturdy, utilitarian baskets such as those made at the small town plant were used to transport ceramics within pottery plants in the clay-rich region and by others for everyday chores like egg and vegetable gathering or shopping. Dave's father, JW (for John Wendell), began hand weaving at the basket factory in the late 1910s, and was able to purchase the plant for $1,900 during the Great Depression. He renamed it the Ohio Ware Basket Company, and involved all of his twelve children in some aspect of the business. In the postwar era, Ohio Ware suffered insurmountable competition from modern containers made of cardboard and plastic. In 1955 JW Longaberger closed up shop and went to work at a local paper mill.

The patriarch kept up his craft in the intervening decades, however, selling some baskets for $1.50 and giving others as gifts. So in 1972, when his son asked him to make a few for retail sale, JW agreed. Dave Longaberger soon found that customers would pay $10 and more for the high-quality hardwood baskets. He launched his third business in 1973, calling it JW's Handwoven Baskets for the man who died that spring at the age of 71. Dave hired two weavers to create each basket from thin strips of maple veneer. Promotional materials took pains to assert that "staples and glue are never used." The baskets were fitted with leather hinges, copper rivets, and sometimes maple lids, lightly stained, then initialed and dated by the weaver in a process that remained essentially unchanged throughout the company's history.

Despite his optimism and enterprise, a combination of sluggish retail sales and high startup costs found Longaberger deep in debt by the late 1970s. Instead of abandoning his product, he re-examined his sales method. He related the problem in a 1994 interview with *Columbus CEO* magazine: "I couldn't tell our story in the shops. I had baskets in a couple of shops, and I would go back on Friday and Saturday nights to see how they were doing. I'd watch the expressions on customers' faces as they picked up the baskets and think (about the sales clerk), 'Go on, tell them about Mom and Dad, tell them about the 12 kids, talk about the utilitarian purpose of the baskets, tell them about Dresden.' Well, the clerks didn't know all that, and they didn't really care." In 1978 a friend, Charlene Cuckovich, suggested direct sales. Selling the baskets at Tupperware-style home parties would give salespeople the opportunity to describe the craftsmanship and tradition represented by each basket, she reasoned. Home sales also focused the folksy pitch on the people who were most likely to become customers. Cuckovich became one of Longaberger's first sales consultants.

The new marketing scheme vastly improved sales—within a year, Longaberger had thirty associates and forty employees. In 1980 the entrepreneur agreed to purchase a veneer factory in nearby Hartville to accommodate his growing materials requirements. He even sold his thriving restaurant in order to raise the necessary capital. But before the purchasing agreement on the veneer factory was complete, the building, which was not insured for its replacement value, was destroyed by fire. Although Longaberger could have walked away from the deal, he instead sold his flourishing grocery store for $300,000, honored his commitment to purchase the property, and rebuilt.

Longaberger's under-capitalized business continued to founder in the mid-1980s. Longaberger later said wryly that "Banks almost put me out of business. The IRS [which negotiated a tax payment plan with the struggling entrepreneur] helped look for a way to keep me in." His perseverance finally began to pay off in increasing sales in the late 1980s, with the company selling 1.4 million baskets in 1987 alone. In spite of economic recession, the company began to record growth rates of almost 40 percent annually. In 1989 Longaberger's cash flow was strong enough to buy back his eatery, now known as the Longaberger Restaurant. In 1990 the company started production at a new plant and opened Popeye's Soda Shop. The addition of fabric liners, wood accessories, and plastic basket inserts added to both the fashion appeal and functionality of the baskets. That year also saw the launch of Woven Traditions Pottery and Dinnerware, a line of earthenware that capitalized on the burgeoning popularity of the hand-crafted baskets. The ceramics featured an embossed pattern that mimicked a basket weave, and, although not hand thrown, appropriated a hand-crafted image with marketing pitches like the following: "traditional pottery-making methods used for centuries," "our own secret [clay] recipe," and "handmade quality."

Upon achieving his own success, Longaberger made "stimulating a better quality of life for customers, associates, and employees" a corporate mission. He sought to manufacture quality products, adopt fair employment policies, support the community, and conserve the natural environment.

Longaberger's magnanimity was evident on the shop floor. In 1994 Vice-President of Corporate Affairs Mike Bennett told Columbus CEO that "Dave has an unwritten rule that 25 percent of the day should be dedicated to having fun," which keeps the atmosphere "very relaxed, very professional, [and] very creative." LTV, Longaberger Television, is one outgrowth of that corporate culture. This 70-monitor, closed-circuit network features company news, music videos, and employee interviews. Programming has even included the wedding of two employees who met at the plant. Employees work 35 hours a week, and their ample benefits plan includes tuition reimbursement. Some weavers, who are paid piece rates, made more than $40,000 per year in the early 1990s. Employees elect their front line supervisors. Weavers seeking a new challenge or break in the routine can apply to transfer into corporate landscaping and construction crews, one of four local Longaberger restaurants, the company museum, or recreation facilities. In 1993 the company's Weaver Request Program began offering a select few basket weavers the opportunity to travel around the country giving demonstrations of their craft at company sales meetings and events. The employee rolls include Dave's daughters, Tami Longaberger Kaido, president of marketing and sales, and Rachel Longaberger Schmidt, president of manufacturing and human resources, as well as seven of Dave's eleven siblings.

By the early 1990s, Longaberger's direct sales team numbered over 25,000 associates, mostly women, in all fifty states. The associates are also some of the company's best customers: a press release noted that some own more than 800 baskets.

According to Opportunity, a quarterly company publication, sales associates move up within the organization by bringing new consultants into the group and meeting sales targets. As they progress through the levels of branch advisor, regional advisor, and finally sales director, they cultivate their own sales organizations comprising hundreds of sales associates. Along with the increasing responsibility comes progressively greater rewards, with directors earning six figure incomes. Not surprisingly, Charlene Cuckovich became one of the company's first sales directors over the course of her career with Longaberger.

Exhibiting a combination of business acumen and altruism, Longaberger began revitalizing Dresden in 1988. The combination of public and private amenities helped make the village both a destination for hundreds of thousands of tourists every year and a more desirable place to live and work. Community investments included the Longaberger Fitness Center, the Swimming Center, the Senior Citizens Center, and an addition to the local public high school. The company designed Dresden's city landscaping—featuring Longaberger baskets, of course—maintained city parks, and even kept up some private property along the town's Main Street. The World's Largest Basket Park (certified by Guinness) featured a 23-foot-high hand-woven maple basket. A former bakery became the Longaberger Museum. Longaberger University, a nineteenth-century school, housed corporate training and education programs. Outside the town, Longaberger Farms bred Angus cattle and advocated agricultural education. The company even transformed its weaving plant into a tourist destination, offering "a full mezzanine view of hundreds of crafts people weaving baskets with a centuries-old method," according to a Longaberger press release.

The company's environmental programs include selective harvesting of the maple trees that go into its baskets, the use of water-based stains and recyclable plastics, and the pursuit of relationships with like-minded partners. Longaberger also makes contributions to programs like the International Center for the Preservation of Wild Animals.

Longaberger's philanthropy has won him and the company national recognition, including the Direct Selling Association's Vision for Tomorrow Award in 1990, the U.S. Department of the Interior's Take Pride in America Award in 1991, Inc. magazine's Socially Responsible Entrepreneur of the Year Award in 1992, and the Friend of Education Award and an honor from Childhelp USA in 1994. Longaberger was also named a Central Ohio Business Hall of Fame Laureate in 1994.

Dave Longaberger's confidence in the nostalgia market led him to take the phrase "company town" to a whole new level in 1994, when he announced plans to build Longaberger Village, an "educational theme park" just west of Dresden on a 625-acre campus. Longaberger Village's first phase, Main Street, promised to evoke a "typical" Midwest town of the 1920s. Plans for the complex included a reproduction of the Longaberger home, a soda shop, drug store, and barbershop, as well as gift shops, specialty shops, overnight accommodations, and Longaberger Characters who will "spin tales of the old days."

Dave Longaberger has boiled his company's success down to eighteen folksy "Principles of Management," including "You must always be looking on the bank for help and assurance no matter who you are,'' and ''The past is the present; the present is the future.'' His plans for the firm's future included venturing into furniture manufacturing and real estate, as well as perpetuating the eccentric charm, financial prosperity, and civic responsibility exemplified by the Longaberger Company for the past two decades.

Further Reading:

''Birth of a Basket Company,'' Dresden, Ohio: The Longaberger Company, [1993].

Nelton, Sharon, ''A Basket Maker with Vision,'' *Nation's Business,* July 1993, p. 14.

Ottolenghi-Barga, Carol, ''Dave Longaberger,'' *Columbus CEO,* October 1994, pp. 12–14.

—April Dougal Gasbarre

Lucasfilm Ltd.

P. O. Box 2009
San Rafael, California 94912-2009
U.S.A.
(415) 662-1800
Fax: (415) 662-2437

Private Company
Incorporated: 1971
Employees: 750
Sales: $250 million
SICs: 7812 Motion Picture and Video Production; 7822
    Motion Picture & Tape Distribution; 6794 Patent Owners
    & Lessors

The 16th largest motion picture producer in the United States, ranked by revenues, Lucasfilm Ltd. is a film and television production and distribution company developed by George Lucas, creator of the popular and profitable "Star Wars" and "Indiana Jones" film trilogies. By 1995, Lucasfilm consisted of three entities, each chaired by George Lucas himself: Lucasfilm Ltd., Lucas Digital Ltd., and LucasArts Entertainment Co. Lucasfilm Ltd. created Lucas's motion picture and television productions and administered the THX theater and home theater licensing and certification procedures. Lucas Digital Ltd. oversaw operations of Industrial Light and Magic (ILM)—the world's foremost visual effects production facility—and Skywalker Sound, one of the world's premier sound engineering facilities. Finally, LucasArts Entertainment Company produced multimedia and interactive computer entertainment and educational computer software, while also overseeing the licensing responsibilities for Lucasfilm stories and characters.

Company founder George Lucas was born in 1945 in Modesto, California, and was educated at the University of Southern California's film school. Having won a scholarship to observe Francis Ford Coppola direct the film *Finian's Rainbow,* Lucas would later recall in a *New York Times* interview that "Francis forced me to become a writer and to think about things other than abstract and documentary films." In 1970, Lucas wrote and directed his first feature film, *THX 1138,* the story of a future world in which people live in underground cities run by computers. Inspired by a short film he wrote while a student at USC, *THX 1138* was produced by Francis Ford Coppola's American Zoetrope. The following year, Lucas created his own

film company, Lucasfilm Ltd., with offices in Hollywood, across the street from Universal Studios.

In 1973, Lucas experienced his first commercial success with the film *American Graffiti,* a humorous look at one evening in the lives of some recent high school graduates in the early 1960s, which Lucas co-wrote and directed. In addition to receiving a Golden Globe award and awards from the New York Film Critics and the National Society of Film Critics, *American Graffiti* received five Academy Award nominations. Moreover, Lucas became known as one of the most popular directors in Hollywood, and his company began to expand. During this time, for example, Lucas founded Skywalker Sound, a full-service audio post production facility. He also created Industrial Light & Magic (ILM) to develop the use of computer graphics in film, focusing particularly on the striking visual effects that would be used in the upcoming film *Star Wars.*

Lucas wrote and directed the first *Star Wars* film in 1977. Made by Lucas and Lucasfilm for Twentieth Century Fox, the film reportedly incurred production costs of around $6.5 million. A fantasy/sci-fi tale featuring a young hero, a princess, a pilot, a villain, and a host of robots and creatures, *Star Wars* became a number one box-office attraction as well as an important part of American culture and film history. The film's characters also became the basis for a very profitable line of children's toy figures and other merchandise. In fact, profits from *Star Wars* allowed Lucas to fully finance subsequent films in the series and to retain a higher portion of the profits. Over the next six years, Lucas wrote and executive produced the *Star Wars* sequels *The Empire Strikes Back* (1980) and *The Return of the Jedi* (1983). Through 1995 all three films would maintain positions among the top 15 box-office attractions of all time and would continue to generate record toy sales.

In the early 1980s, a wholly owned subsidiary, LucasArts Entertainment Company, was added to Lucasfilm's holdings, providing, according to company literature, "an interactive element in George Lucas's vision of a state-of-the-art, multi-faceted entertainment company." LucasArts developed, in part, under the leadership of R. Douglas Norby, who joined Lucasfilm in 1985 after serving as chief financial officer at Syntex Corporation. As president and chief executive officer of LucasArts until 1992, Norby helped the subsidiary become a leading developer of entertaining and interactive multimedia computer software for schools, homes, and arcades. Such products combined Lucas' storytelling and character development strengths with the newest, most advanced technologies available. Early game efforts included *Maniac Mansion, Battlehawks 1942, Their Finest Hour: The Battle of Britain, Secret Weapons of the Luftwaffe, Loom,* and *The Secret of Monkey Island.* The company also produced software products based on the Star Wars and Indiana Jones series. *X-Wing* would become the best selling CD-ROM entertainment title of 1993, and in 1994 *Rebel Assault* became the best selling CD-ROM software of all time. Educational products, developed by the LucasArts Learning sub-unit, included *GTV: American History from a Geographic Perspective,* an interactive video disc and computer learning effort involving both the National Geographic Society and the California State Department of Education. Another program, *Life Story,* was developed in partnership with Apple Multimedia Lab and the Smithsonian Institution.

LucasArts was also charged with overseeing the licensing and design of toys and other products based on Lucasfilm ideas and characters. Comic books and novels extending the *Star Wars* and Indiana Jones universes were successful ventures for LucasArts. In 1991 *The New York Times* indicated that Lucas-Arts licensed *Star Wars* toys had grossed over $2.6 billion dollars around the world.

As Lucasfilm continued to profit, George Lucas gradually began to separate himself from traditional Hollywood. In 1981, he relinquished membership in the Academy of Motion Picture Arts and Sciences, the Writers Guild, and the Directors Guild and began moving his offices to Skywalker Ranch, a 3,000-acre secluded production facility located in San Rafael, 25 miles from San Francisco. Named for the *Star Wars* character Luke Skywalker, the ranch became the business and production hub of the Lucas financial empire. Discussing his intentions for the new ranch complex in an interview for the *New York Times,* Lucas said, ''As opposed to Hollywood, where the film makers support the corporate entity, Lucasfilm will support the overhead of the ranch. We'll make money out of the money by buying real estate, cable, satellite, solar energy—without buying anything we're ashamed of, like pesticides—and then the corporation will give us the money to make films.''

Despite their detachment from Hollywood, Lucas and Lucas-film continued to create widely successful films, producing a popular series of Indiana Jones movies, which were directed by Lucas's friend and colleague Steven Spielberg. The three movies, *Raiders of the Lost Ark* (1981), *Indiana Jones and the Temple of Doom* (1984), and *Indiana Jones and the Last Crusade* (1989) featured the adventures of Indiana Jones, an heroic archaeologist whose work brings him into contact with villains, dangerous situations, and romance. All three films achieved wide financial success.

Not all Lucasfilm productions achieved commercial success. Such motion pictures as *More American Graffiti* (1979), *Howard the Duck* (1986), *Labyrinth* (1986), and *Radioland Murders* (1994) met with disappointing ticket sales and critical reviews. Nevertheless, George Lucas remained a leader in his field; in 1992, he received the Academy of Motion Picture Arts and Sciences' prestigious Irving G. Thalberg award for pioneering work in film technology. Moreover, any losses the company incurred by its few commercial disappointments were offset by Lucasfilm's involvement in all aspects of movie production; ILM in particular began to thrive and gradually became the company's most profitable division.

Described by Lucasfilm as ''the largest and most advanced digital effects system in the entertainment industry,'' ILM not only mastered the traditional arts of blue screen photography, matte painting, and model construction, but also pioneered the development of motion control cameras, optical compositing, and other advances in special effects technology. Its use of computer graphics and digital imaging in feature films also involved developing such breakthrough techniques such Morfing, which allowed the seamless transformation of one object into another. ILM's film credits in the 1980s and 1990s included most of the *Star Trek* movies, *ET: The Extraterrestrial* (1982), *Cocoon* (1985), *Back to the Future* (1985), *Who Framed Roger Rabbit* (1988), *Ghost* (1990), *Terminator 2: Judgment Day* (1991), *Jurassic Park* (1993), *Schindler's List* (1993), *Forrest Gump* (1994), and many others. In fact, by the end of 1994, ILM had handled special effects for over 100 feature films, several of which won Academy Awards for best visual effects and technical achievement.

ILM also began working with Walt Disney Productions in 1985, developing over the years such theme park attractions as *Captain EO* (1986) for Disneyland, *Star Tours* simulator ride for Disneyland, *Body Wars* (1989) for Disneyworld's EPCOT Center, and *Space Race* (1991) a simulator ride for Showscan.

Skywalker Sound was also thriving during this time, with sound post production studios in Santa Monica, West Los Angeles, and at the Skywalker Ranch complex. At these facilities—which comprised sound and foley stages, mixing and editing studios, and screening rooms, all renowned for their technical sophistication and versatility—the sound was recorded for such popular films as *Jurassic Park, Mrs. Doubtfire,* and *Quiz Show.* Skywalker also undertook television commercial projects for such products as Pepsi, Listerine, the Jenny Craig diet plan, and Malaysian Air, among others.

In February 1993, Lucasfilm announced a reorganization, opting to spin off ILM and Skywalker Sound into units of a new company called Lucas Digital Ltd. Film producer Lindsley Parsons, Jr., a former manager of production at MGM/UA Entertainment, CBS Theatrical Films, and Paramount Pictures, was named president and CEO of Lucas Digital, while George Lucas served as the company's chairperson.

Two months later, Lucas Digital's ILM subunit teamed up with Silicon Graphics Inc., of Mountain View, California, to create The Joint Environment for Digital Imaging (the acronym Jedi referring to the heroic knights of the *Star Wars* trilogy). The joint effort was created to serve as a film production unit as well as a test lab for new technology in visual effects. The connection between Lucasfilm and Silicon Graphics was actually forged in the late 1980s, when Lucasfilm began using Silicon Graphics workstations to create their special effects. By working together, Lucasfilm gained greater access to Silicon Graphics's more advanced computer workstations, while Silicon Graphics gained access to Lucasfilm's proprietary software. The companies expected to revolutionize filmmaking through their use of computer graphics and reduce the costs of producing special effects by as much as 90 percent.

During this time, Lucasfilm also made a name for itself in the field of television production, performing its most notable work perhaps in 1993 through the television series *The Young Indiana Jones Chronicles.* Written and executive produced by George Lucas, the series won the Banff Award for Best Continuing Series, a Golden Globe nomination for best dramatic series, an Angel Award for Quality Programming, and ten Emmy Awards.

Another of Lucasfilm's activities involved its THX Group, which, according to Lucasfilm literature, was ''dedicated to ensuring excellence in film presentation.'' The commercial portion of the certification program, developed in 1982, involved certifying the quality of the listening environment in commercial theaters. THX certified theaters were required to meet Lucasfilm standards for such factors as speaker layout, acoustics, noise levels, and equalization of the signal. By 1995, Lucasfilm claimed over 770 certified installations in theaters and soundstages around the world.

The THX system also had applications in the home theater, a concept that was gaining popularity in the mid-1990s. Lucasfilm's home THX system certified equipment to ensure that it maintained the quality of film sound as it was transferred to the home. Specifically, home THX certification and licensing program controlled parameters that affected the clarity of dialogue, soundstaging (localizing sounds), surround sound diffusion, frequency response, and transparency. Such licensing was available to equipment manufacturers for certification of front and center speakers, surround speakers, subwoofers, amplifiers, preamplifiers, receivers, laser disc players, front video projection screens, and cords and interconnects.

In 1994, for the fourth year in a row, *Working Mother* magazine named Lucasfilm, Lucas Digital, and LucasArts Entertainment among the top one hundred workplaces for working mothers. The magazine praised the companies' child-care centers, flexible working hours, and profit sharing plans, as well as their reputation for equal treatment in pay. Moreover, the companies subsidized 100 percent of health care costs for the employee and 75 percent for the family. Not surprisingly, the three companies enjoyed a low turnover rate.

In the mid-1990s, George Lucas remained very involved in the arts and education, serving as chairperson of the George Lucas Educational Foundation as well as on the board of directors of the National Geographic Society Education Foundation, the Artists Rights Foundation, The Joseph Campbell Foundation, and The Film Foundation. He was also a member of the USC School of Cinema-Television Board of Councilors. Moreover,

Lucasfilm also remained poised for growth, announcing plans in 1994 to produce three more installments of the *Star Wars* series and one more installment of the Indiana Jones series. Plans were to film the three *Star Wars* films simultaneously and to released them biannually, beginning in 1997 or 1998. Steven Spielberg agreed at that time to direct the fourth Indiana Jones movie. With such projects underway, the companies that Lucas founded seemed well prepared for continued profitability.

Further Reading:

Champlin, Charles, *George Lucas: The Creative Impulse,* New York: Harry A. Abrams, Inc., 1992.

Fantel, Hans, "In the Action With 'Star Wars' Sound," *The New York Times,* May 3, 1992, p. 35.

Fisher, Lawrence M., "Lucasarts and Mattel In Joint Toy Venture," *The New York Times,* April 26, 1991, p. D4.

Fisher, Lawrence M., "Lucasfilm and Silicon Graphics Team Up," *The New York Times,* April 8, 1993, p. D3.

Fisher, Lawrence M., "Lucasfilm Subsidiary Loses Chief Executive," *The New York Times,* April 9, 1992, p. D4.

Gill, Eric, "Camp THX," *Audio Video Interiors,* September 1994, pp. 46–55.

Harmetz, Aljean, "But Can Hollywood Live Without George Lucas?" *The New York Times,* July 13, 1981, Sec. 3, p. 11.

Longsdorf, Amy, "George Lucas Interview," *Laserviews,* January/ February 1995, pp. 15+.

Moskowitz, Milton, and Carol Townsend, "Ninth Annual Survey of the 100 Best Companies for Working Mothers," *Working Mother Magazine,* October 1994, pp. 48+.

Pollock, Dale, *Skywalking: The Life and Films of George Lucas,* New York: Harmony Books, 1983.

Wilkinson, Scott, "The Force Is With Him," *Home Theater Technology,* October 1994, pp. 64–68.

—Terry W. Hughes

MAXXIM
M E D I C A L

Maxxim Medical Inc.

104 Industrial Boulevard
Sugar Land, Texas 77478
U.S.A.
(713) 240-2442
Fax: (713) 240-2557

Public Company
Incorporated: 1981 as Henley International Inc.
Employees: 2,300
Sales: $190 million
Stock Exchanges: New York
SICs: 3841 Surgical and Medical Instruments; 3842 Surgical
  Appliances and Supplies; 3845 Electromedical Equipment;
  2389 Apparel and Accessories, Not Elsewhere Classified

Maxxim Medical Inc. is a diversified manufacturer of specialty medical products, including disposable procedural trays, advanced diagnostic equipment, physical therapy products, and rehabilitation and fitness equipment. The company expanded briskly during the late 1980s and early 1990s by acquiring other companies and improving its existing operations.

Maxxim Medical is the offspring of a company started in the late 1970s, Henley International Inc. Henley was the creation of inventor and entrepreneur Ernest (Doc) Henley. A university professor and chemical engineer by training, Henley was known by his friends and associates as a thinker and tinkerer. Evidence of Henley's inventive nature came in the early 1970s after he took his son to a physical therapist for treatment of tennis elbow. Part of the therapy included a hot whirlpool. After observing the therapy, Henley became convinced that he could develop a significant improvement to traditional hot-water therapy.

Henley's idea stemmed from physics. He knew that the human body could tolerate higher temperatures if the heat emanated from a dry source. The problem was that air is a very inefficient way to transmit heat through the skin and into the tendons and muscles. In 1973, he came up with a solution to the dilemma, a tool he dubbed the Fluidotherapy device. Henley's invention used ground corn husks circulating inside a box where patients would stick their arms or legs. Like a whirlpool, the "corncob special," as therapists called it, increased blood circulation, thus stimulating healing and improving range of motion. Henley had experimented with glass beads and synthetics, but

finally choose corn husks. The corn husks made it possible to operate Henley's invention at temperatures as high as 120 degrees Fahrenheit, while whirlpools were generally limited to 105 degrees.

Henley patented his invention and spent several years during the mid-1970s perfecting it. He and his son, Davis Henley, started to market the product in 1979. Unfortunately, the start-up venture, incorporated as Henley International in 1981, lacked funds and made little headway. But, in 1982, Henley's efforts came to the attention of another Texas-based company called Intermedics. Intermedics was a leading manufacturer of pacemakers in the United States. The company's head of business development at the time, and the man that was most interested in the Henley venture, was Kenneth W. Davidson. The 35-year-old Davidson was a Canadian citizen. He had worked for medical industry giants Baxter and Merck as a salesman and marketing executive before joining Intermedics.

Davidson had met Doc Henley through his work at Intermedics and was impressed with his company's technology. Davidson even convinced Intermedics to grant Henley $500,000 in seed money to get the venture off the ground. In return, Intermedics got 30 percent of the company and Davidson got a seat on Henley International's board of directors. "At the time I didn't think that it was much of a perk," Davidson recalled about his appointment to the board in *Houston Business Journal.* "It was a three-employee company with one product."

Davidson and Doc Henley had a good business relationship. Davidson respected Henley's technological and creative intelligence, and Henley admired Davidson's business intuition and willingness to support his ideas. Davidson's interest in Henley International was cemented after he visited a physical therapy convention with Davis Henley. Davidson was intrigued by the contrast to the medical products conferences in which he had participated in the past. "When you walk in the door [of a typical medical convention] you see a bunch of little 10-foot booths of people trying to get someone to listen to their story, and a couple of 100-foot booths two stories high belonging to Baxter or Johnson & Johnson," Davidson told *Forbes.* "But when I first went to the APTA [American Physical Therapy Association] convention, I saw only 10-foot booths. Nobody owned the market."

Davidson felt challenged by the lack of market leadership in the physical therapy products industry. So, during the early 1980s he helped the company try to market the Fluidotherapy device. Meanwhile, Doc Henley continued to work on the research and development of new products for the business. Although the Fluidotherapy device never turned into a boon for Henley International, it carved out a profitable market niche. There was no statistical evidence to prove that it outperformed traditional whirlpool therapy, but most therapists and patients agreed that it was a preferable form of treatment. Furthermore, because it did not use liquids, there was no threat of bacteria transmission and, therefore, no cleanup required. The cornhusks were eventually replaced with synthetic pellets and the device was marketed as therapy for arthritis sufferers.

Davidson and the Henleys chose a good time to get into the physical therapy industry. An aging population and a steady increase in sports-related injuries were two factors driving market growth during the 1980s and 1990s. During the 1980s, in fact, the number of physical therapists in the United States rose about 50 percent, as did the number of accredited physical therapy training programs. As the scope and number of physical ailments proliferated, therapists sought new treatment methods and improved equipment. Henley International benefitted from the industry growth, and its sales increased to more than $5 million by the mid-1980s.

Encouraged by the success of Henley International, Davidson left his post at Intermedics in 1986 to run the venture. During the next few years, the company expanded rapidly by diversifying its product line to include a number of offerings geared for the growing physical therapy, home pain management, and disposable hospital products markets. Davidson's growth strategy was founded on two key assumptions: 1) demand would continue to rise for procedures and products that reduced health care costs and facilitated in-home care; and 2) an aging population and an increase in sports-related injuries would spur expansion of the physical therapy markets.

Henley International expanded through acquisition during the late 1980s. Davidson bought underperforming companies or divisions with products that complemented Henley International's products, cut their operating costs, and integrated their products into Henley International's marketing network. Among Henley International's more successful acquisitions was its buyout of a high-tech line of exercise/physical therapy equipment from LivingWell Inc. In addition, Henley International's research and development efforts spawned several new products that boosted profits. By the end of the 1980s, Henley International's research efforts had yielded 22 patents.

One of Henley International's more successful products was Chempad, a bandage-like pad that transmits drugs through the skin. The gauzy adhesive was used to transmit localized painkillers to aching muscles. The National Basketball Association began using Chempad soon after its release. Other Henley innovations included electrical transmitters that blocked chronic back pain, a device used to measure how much weight a person can repeatedly lift safely, and high-tech devices designed to prevent mistakes during laser surgery and to prepare patients for surgery faster.

As a result of six acquisitions and several new product introductions, Henley International's sales rose to $17 million in 1989, $685,000 of which was net income. By 1989, Henley International had had average annual growth of more than 50 percent since 1986. Moreover, income had nearly doubled to $1.2 million in 1990 as revenues increased to $27 million. The company's growth was expected to continue, if not accelerate, during the early 1990s. Henley had a host of new products waiting for federal approval and was engaged in several new acquisitions in the early 1990s. For example, in 1990 Davidson engineered the buyout of North Carolina-based White Knight Health Care, which boosted Henley International's 250-member work force by 100.

Despite Henley International's many acquisitions, Davidson had succeeded in keeping Henley International's debt burden low; in the early 1990s it was about $3 million. To raise addition

capital for expansion, Davidson took the company public in 1990 with a stock offering on the NASDAQ. Doc Henley remained the company's largest shareholder with a share of about 32 percent. That share, combined with interests held by Davidson and Henley's two sons, gave the foursome more than 50 percent ownership of Henley International. The company's worth was estimated at more than $15 million in 1990. Despite the fast expansion, Davidson considered Henley's gains conservative. "We've just been building slowly," he explained in *Houston Business Journal.*

Although Henley International's exploits were beginning to get noticed on Wall Street by the early 1990s, just as much attention was being focused on the company's unorthodox chief executive. Davidson's image was that of a corporate rebel with an eccentric flair. That perception was largely attributable to his status of aging rock-and-roller. With the exception of his long hair and drooping mustache, Davidson almost looked at home in his corporate suit and tie. But he appeared even more comfortable in his rock and roll garb—playing guitar, singing lead, and belting out tunes from the 1960s and 1970s with his group, Live Band. The band chose the name because "every club in Houston has a sign with 'Live Band' outside so people think we play all over the place," Davidson explained in the *New York Times.*

Live Band was comprised of a group of Henley executives, including chief operating officer Peter M. Graham. Graham and Davidson had played in a band together in Ontario during college and had performed their first impromptu concert at Henley International in 1985. Vice-president for marketing, Dan Lavelle, played drums, retail sales coordinator, Valerie Moulton, played the keyboard, and engineering manager, Norwood Brown, played guitar. Live Band played about 15 concerts per year in the early 1990s for its employees and customers, and for charity events. An 18-wheeler hauled the band's equipment and Saturday morning jam sessions were held at company headquarters in the music room, which was packed with $50,000 worth of instruments and lighting equipment. The band also played for workers at newly acquired companies as part of an effort to put the new employees at ease.

In addition to the rock band, Davidson spiced up the Henley International organization with an eclectic array of other pursuits and investments. The company sponsored a basketball team, and Davidson himself could sometimes be found shooting hoops with Henley International personnel. Davidson also started a Canadian Curling team, which was one of only nine in Texas. The company sponsored a Florida drag-racing team, as well, and Davidson had been known to sit behind the wheel. "It's a neat feeling to go from zero to 170 miles per hour in five seconds," Davidson remarked in *Houston Business Journal.* "It's a rush."

Henley International's growth during the early 1990s mirrored the acceleration of the company's drag car. Besides bringing numerous new products to market, Henley International added 12 companies to its roster between 1990 and early 1994 and built up a reservoir of more than 11,000 different healthcare-related products. Among its acquisitions during the early 1990s were three stand-outs: Argon Medical, Boundary Healthcare, and Sterile Design.

Henley purchased Argon Medical from drug industry giant Bristol-Myers Squibb in 1991. Argon was a leading provider in the fast-growing plastic catheter and disposable medical products industry, and the purchase added 350 workers to the Henley International payroll. In 1992, Henley International bought Boundary Healthcare, a top manufacturer of infection-control apparel worn by care givers in operating rooms. In 1993, the company acquired the Sterile Design division of Johnson & Johnson, making Henley International the largest producer of disposable surgical trays in the nation.

By 1993, Henley had evolved into more of a healthcare products company than a physical therapy company, with more than 80 percent of its sales coming from healthcare supplies and devices. Reflecting the organization's growth and product diversity, Davidson reorganized the company and changed its name to Maxxim Medical Inc. He organized Maxxim into four operating divisions, each of which bore the name of its chief subsidiary: Sterile Design; Boundary; Argon; and Henley. In December of 1993, Davidson moved Maxxim to the New York Stock Exchange and made a second successful stock offering.

As Maxxim's product base swelled, its sales and profits soared. Revenues rose to $130 million in 1993 as net income to $5.5 million. Only ten percent of its receipts were garnered overseas in 1993, but cross-border sales growth in 1994 reflected Davidson's new found emphasis on long-term international expansion. Maxxim had achieved its heady gains without taking on significant debt. Maxxim had less than $6 million of long-term debt going into 1994. Furthermore, Maxxim boasted a cash reserve of over $40 million that was earmarked for future acquisitions and overseas expansion.

Going into the mid-1990s, Davidson continued to pursue his goal of making Maxxim into a global leader in the manufacture and sale of healthcare-related products and supplies. As Maxxim continued to bring new products to market, Davidson focused on streamlining internal operations, acquiring more companies, and penetrating international markets. Medica B.V., Maxxim's fifth operating division, was purchased in January 1995. Medica was based in s'Hertogenbosh, Netherlands, and its 150 employees would represent European headquarters for Maxxim. Meanwhile, the company's founder, Doc Henley, spent some of his time tinkering in the company lab, but his primary occupation was teaching chemical engineering at the University of Houston. "He's just as likely to invent something on the beach as he is here," Davidson explained in *Houston Business Journal.* "But every once in a while he comes to board meetings and asks if there's any money in the bank."

Further Reading:

Graham, Peter M., "Henley International Reports Financial Results," *Business Wire,* June 6, 1990.

Koselka, Rita, "The Corncob Special," *Forbes,* October 15, 1990, p. 174.

McNamara, Victoria, "Henley International Buys Medical Manufacturing," *Houston Business Journal,* August 12, 1991, sec. 1, p. 15.

McNamara, Victoria, "Henley International: No Pains, Big Gains," *Houston Business Journal,* September 10, 1990, sec. 1, p. 1.

Palmeri, Christopher, "The Future's in the Tray," *Forbes,* November 22, 1993, p. 14.

Payne, Chris, "Maxxim Medical's Main Maverick: Kenneth Davidson Plays Rock, Races Cars, and Runs a Rapidly Growing Company," *Houston Business Journal,* May 23, 1994, p. 14.

Promice, Eva, "When Management Is Born to Be Wild," *The New York Times,* December 25, 1994.

—Dave Mote

MBNA Corporation

400 Christiana Road
Newark, Delaware 19713
U.S.A.
(302) 453-9930
Fax: (302) 456-8541

Public Company
Incorporated: 1982
Employees: 11,000
Total Assets: $9.67 billion
Stock Exchanges: New York
SICs: 6712 Bank Holding Companies; 6021 National
    Commercial Banks

Through its subsidiary MBNA America Bank, MBNA Corporation is the second-largest bank credit card lender and the leading issuer of affinity credit cards in the United States. The bank also offers individual loans and offered deposit products. MBNA has grown rapidly since its inception in the early 1980s, mostly by marketing its affinity cards to associations and financial institutions.

Charles Cawley founded MBNA in 1982. The small bank, based in a Newark, Delaware, supermarket, was formed as the credit-card subsidiary of MNC Financial, a regional bank holding company headquartered in Baltimore. The credit card industry was growing rapidly at the time and Cawley was eager to expand the enterprise. Rather than pursuing the same strategies as his competitors, though, Cawley was looking for a marketing strategy that would separate his product from the homogenous horde of credit card lenders that competed mostly on price.

In 1983 Cawley approached his alma mater, Georgetown University in Washington, D.C., about partnering with him. His idea was to get the Georgetown University Alumni Association to endorse a credit card that would be offered exclusively to its members and generate a royalty or percentage of all revenues derived from the cards. The enticement for cardholders was that their use of the card benefitted the alma mater, and that the card displayed their affiliation with Georgetown. The alumni association agreed to the project, and Cawley's first direct mailing effort was a hit. In addition to signing up an unusually large percentage of its prospects, MBNA benefitted from the overall credit quality of its new customers, who were generally catego-

rized as having relatively high income and education levels thereby resulting in lower delinquency in charge-off levels.

As a result of his success with Georgetown, Cawley was convinced that he was on to something. By issuing "affinity" cards and focusing on customer service, MBNA was adding value to an otherwise commodity-like service. He realized that if he could duplicate the results working with other groups, he could substantially increase MBNA's profit margins by capturing a more upscale and therefore less risky and higher spending segment of the market. Importantly, marketing costs per account could be greatly reduced because the response rate of direct sales efforts would be much higher than the industry average. Indeed, other credit card companies at the time often resorted to mass mailings targeted to broad groups identified by zip code or income level. In contrast, MBNA's prospects were motivated to review the credit card offer simply because of their affiliation with the group sponsoring the card.

Cawley next succeeded in getting the American Dental Association to sponsor an affinity card, and he followed that program with an affinity card for the Aircraft Owners and Pilots Association. Both efforts were successful. Throughout the mid-1980s Cawley aggressively approached new partners, focusing on various clubs and associations with an upscale membership. By 1985, in fact, MBNA was managing more than $1 billion in outstanding loans, compared to just $250 million going into 1983. MBNA's net income surged to $67 million in 1986 as outstanding credit vaulted to the $2 billion mark. Revenues and profits continued to surge as MBNA added affinity cards for major groups like the Sierra Club, Association of Trial Lawyers of America, the University of Texas, and National Education Association.

MBNA sustained its swift growth rate during the late mid- and late 1980s by scouting out upscale groups like college alumni associations and professional societies. After it selected an organization, it would offer future royalties in exchange for the group's membership list and permission to use its name and letterhead in direct-advertising efforts. By the early 1990s some groups were generating hundreds of thousands of dollars annually as a result of credit purchases under such agreements. For example, the Sierra Club arranged to receive one half of one percent of every charge made by its group members. MBNA had succeeded in signing up 45,000 of the environmental group's members by 1994, bringing more than $400,000 to the Club's coffers annually.

Although Cawley's strategy was unique for the early 1980s, by the mid-1980s other credit card companies were employing similar tactics. Nevertheless, MBNA continued to boost market share. Steady gains were largely the result of fruitful marketing programs. MBNA marketers regularly solicited prospective groups with phone calls and by attending trade shows. Once they had the accounts, they utilized aggressive telemarketing and direct mail techniques to constantly boost the sizes of the accounts. For example, the Penn State Alumni Association entered into an affinity card agreement during the mid-1980s with a local bank, which succeeded in signing 15,000 members to the card. MBNA took the account over in 1989 and proceeded to boost membership to more than 120,000 within four years.

MBNA maintained its high-quality customer base by relying on credit reports to identify the most affluent and responsible customers. The strength of its credit base was reflected in its extremely low percentage of uncollectible loans, which was well below the industry average. Once it got the customers, it focused on keeping them with good service. For example, MBNA was the first credit card issuer to offer 24 hour-a-day service to all of its customers, and its phones were answered by people rather than by machines. In addition, people, rather than computer software, also reviewed individual account applications.

As MBNA's accounts swelled, so did its profits. By 1987 MBNA was managing more than $3 billion in credit card loans and netting a healthy $75 million annually in income. Managed loans surpassed $4 billion and then $5 billion in 1988 and 1989, as profits ballooned to more than $100 million annually. By 1990, MBNA was managing about $8 billion in credit card loans and pulling down nearly $130 million in profit. Those figures reflected an annual growth rate of more than 17 percent between 1987 and 1990. MBNA had become the largest single issuer of gold MasterCards and the fourth biggest provider of premium Visa cards. Its gold cards, in fact, made up about 42 percent of its accounts and were responsible for nearly 60 percent of MBNA's outstanding loan balances. Going into 1991, MBNA was marketing affinity cards for about 1,400 groups, including 223 medical and 70 attorney associations.

MBNA's rampant growth during the late 1980s mimicked the gains of its corporate parent, MNC. MNC invested heavily in real estate during the period and enjoyed solid profits. Unfortunately, the commercial real estate market collapsed before the end of the decade. By 1990, MNC, swimming in red ink, was desperate for cash. After losing more than $240 million during the first three quarters of 1990, MNC put its crown jewel, MBNA, on the auction block. Several credit card companies inquired, including Sears's Discover Card unit, but they balked at the $1.1 billion price and waited to see if the desperate MNC would go lower. Instead, MNC spun off MBNA in January of 1991 in a public stock offering that raised about $955 million. The offering took place just two weeks before MNC's deadline to pay a $271 million debt.

Among the big winners of the MBNA spinoff was Alfred Lerner, a magnate with a personal worth estimated at $600 million at the time. Lerner was a major MNC stockholder. He had sold his bank, Equitable Bancorporation, to MNC in 1990 in exchange for MNC stock. Within weeks after the sale, however, MNC was drowning in real estate losses. Lerner was called in to run the bank, and he made the decision to sell MBNA. Shortly after the public stock offering, MBNA's stock price soared, and Lerner realized more than enough profit from his MBNA shares to offset his losses from his ownership in MNC. Lerner, who still owned about 10 percent of MBNA in the early 1990s, became CEO of the newly formed MBNA Corporation. But Cawley, as president, continued to run the company.

By the early 1990s, MBNA's work force had grown to more than 5,000. To house its thriving operations, MBNA developed new facilities, including several important new regional marketing centers in Atlanta, Dallas, Cleveland, and Maine. From those facilities, several hundred representatives would conduct direct-marketing campaigns throughout their region, and also provide service and information-processing functions.

The Northeast Regional Marketing Center in Camden, Maine, was representative of the marketing centers, and it also marked a tie to Cawley's past. Cawley's grandfather had once operated dress factories in Camden and adjacent Belfast, and Cawley was familiar with the area because he had summered nearby at his family's Lincolnville Beach estate. By the time the facility was completed in 1993, it was housing 250 people, and within two years MBNA had boosted that number to 600 and was planning further expansion in the area.

Despite the U.S. economic downturn of the late 1980s and early 1990s, MBNA continued to advance throughout the early 1990s. Managed loans nearly topped the $10 million mark in 1992 as MBNA's net income clambered to an impressive $170 million. By 1992, one-third of all U.S. doctors and about 20 percent of all attorneys were carrying MBNA credit cards, and their accounts were proving to be surprisingly profitable. Indeed, some analysts had questioned the wisdom of marketing credit cards to high-income individuals, few of whom would be expected to keep a running balance at high credit card interest rates. The average annual income of MBNA's cardholders in 1992 was an industry high of $54,000. But MBNA's typical customer kept a running balance (at an average interest rate of 17.3 percent) of $2,200, about 35 percent higher than the industry average. By 1995, the customers' average annual income had risen to $59,000 and they were carrying an average balance of $2,886 (at an average interest rate of 16.4 percent).

Furthermore, MBNA charged its customers annual card fees of $20 to $40. Despite a flurry of new competition in the credit card industry, though, MBNA's affinity strategy allowed it to continue to successfully charge fees while many competitors dropped fees or slashed interest rate charges. MBNA also profited by selling much of its receivables forward at a fixed rate, a practice that essentially allowed the company to finance its portfolio at relatively low interest rates. Although that strategy left MBNA vulnerable to rising short-term interest rates, it paid off big during the early 1990s when rates were depressed.

MBNA's strategy was to sell to people with a common interest. Besides the organizations and financial institutions that endorsed the company's products, MBNA began looking for ''created affinities.'' For instance, it began offering cards displaying family coats-of-arms, as well as cards picturing regional landmarks to people proud of their home towns or states. By the mid-1990s, it was marketing to fans of nearly 200 different professional sports organizations, including National Football League teams, motor sports fans, and teams in every other major sport.

Because of MBNA's efficient financing strategies, marketing tactics, and customer service, profits surged going into the mid-1990s. Managed loans jumped to $12.4 billion in 1993 as net income topped $200 million. By 1994, MBNA had issued more than 14 million cards and was partnering with more than 3,600 different organizations, including the Telephone Pioneers of America, American Legion, and more than 400 universities and colleges. Managed loans grew to nearly $19 billion by the end of 1994, and the credit quality of its accounts was still much better then the industry norm. MBNA began to augment its operations in 1993 with home equity loans offered through its subsidiary, MBNA Consumer Services, Inc. It also launched initiatives overseas: it started in the United Kingdom with an affinity card for members of the Rolls-Royce Enthusiasts' Club.

Principal Subsidiaries: MBNA America Bank, N.A.; MBNA Consumer Services, Inc.; MBNA International Bank Limited (United Kingdom); MBNA Marketing Systems, Inc.

Further Reading:

Berss, Marcia, "The Human Touch," *Forbes,* December 21, 1992, p. 218.
Bullard, Stan, "MBNA Eyes Huge Expansion," *Crain's Cleveland Business,* September 26, 1994, p. 1.
Hinden, Stan, "Recession Could Dim MNC's Shining Sale of Credit Card Firm," *Washington Post,* January 28, 1991, p. 27E.
Weber, Joseph, "How to Rope 'Em with Plastic," *Business Week,* September 26, 1994, p. 135.

—Dave Mote

McKesson Corporation

One Post Street
San Francisco, California 94104
U.S.A.
(415) 983-8300
Fax: (415) 983-7160

Public Company
Incorporated: 1928 as McKesson & Robbins
Employees: 14,500
Sales: $12.43 billion
Stock Exchanges: New York Pacific
SICs: 5122 Drugs, Proprietaries, and Sundries; 5047 Medical
and Hospital Equipment; 5199 Non-Durable Goods, Not
Elsewhere Classified; 2086 Bottled & Canned Soft Drinks;
3581 Automatic Vending Machines

With industry-leading operations in the United States, Canada,
and Mexico, McKesson Corporation is North America's largest
pharmaceutical wholesaler. The company also has interests in
bottled water and automotive care; its Sparkletts brand water
ranked second in this fast-growing beverage category in the
early 1990s, and its Armor All car-care products dominated
their market. Although these two segments contributed less than
four percent of McKesson's annual revenues, they added almost
one-third of operating profits. In spite of uncertainties that
troubled the health care industry in the 1990s, McKesson was
considered well-positioned to take advantage of virtually any
eventualities.

In 1833 John McKesson and a partner founded Olcott & Mc-
Kesson, a wholesale drug company in Manhattan. Twenty years
and another partner later, the firm changed its name to McKesson & Robbins. Yet this was just the beginning of the changes
experienced by McKesson. When John McKesson died in 1893,
the McKesson heirs left the company in order to form the New
York Quinine and Chemical Works.

In 1926, McKesson & Robbins was sold to Frank D. Coster.
The ownership transition plunged McKesson & Robbins into 13
years of disrepute attributed directly to its new owner and his
crime-prone family. Coster, whose real name was Philip Musica, was the son of a New York importer of Italian foods. The
Musica family had prospered in the import trade primarily by
bribing dock customs officials to falsify shipment weights.

When the Musica team was arrested in 1909, Philip paid a
$5,000 fine and served five months in prison for the crime.

The prison experience did not reform the criminal family, however, and they were again arrested in 1913 on similar charges.
This time, a hair importing business started after Philip left
prison had racked up $500,000 in bank debt based on virtually
nonexistent security. A bank investigation revealed that the
supposedly valuable hair pieces being used for collateral were
in fact only worthless ends and short pieces of hair. The Musica
family was caught trying to escape on a departing New Orleans
ship. Once again, Philip was the scapegoat for the family esca-
pades; he served three years in prison. When he was released in
1916 he worked for the District Attorney's office as an undercover agent named William Johnson.

During World War I Musica began a poultry business, but his
entanglement with the law was not over. After evading conviction for a 1920 murder, he changed his business interests from
poultry to pharmaceuticals, posing as president of Adelphi
Pharmaceutical Manufacturing Company in Brooklyn. In spite
of many "second chances," Musica appeared unable to avoid a
life of crime; his new venture, a partnership with Joseph
Brandino, was actually a front for a bootlegging concern.

When Adelphi failed, Musica changed his name to Frank D.
Coster. Hoping to put his criminal past behind him, Coster
managed to establish himself as a respectable businessman by
starting a hair tonic company that had a supposedly large
customer list. With this apparently firm collateral, Coster
seemed a viable acquirer when he offered to purchase McKesson & Robbins in 1926. In fact, for 13 years thereafter, Coster
was able to keep his identity a secret; he was even listed in
Who's Who in America, where he was described as a businessman as well as a "practicing physician" from 1912 to 1914.

Coster went on an acquisition spree when the Great Depression
weakened many competitors. In 1928 and 1929 alone, he added
wholesale drug companies in 42 cities to McKesson &
Robbins's American and Canadian operations. Five more were
acquired from 1930 to 1937.

Coster's true identity was revealed in 1938 when a treasurer at
McKesson & Robbins became concerned over the way the
profits were being handled. That curiosity soon led to an investigation that revealed a $3 million embezzlement scheme perpe-
trated by Coster. Some of the money was used to pay blackmail
fees to his former partner, Brandino, who had discovered
Coster's true identity and threatened to expose him. In 1939
Coster shot himself and Brandino was convicted of blackmail.

The company reorganized in the early 1940s and returned to
private ownership. Its operations were presumably closely held
during this period. However, the company's calm and relatively
quiet existence was intruded upon in 1967 when Foremost
Dairy of California implemented a hostile takeover. Acrimony
over the conduct of the buyout fostered an unhappy relationship
between the managers of the new "partners" for several years
after the merger. In fact, it was three years before McKesson
offices were even moved to San Francisco, the headquarters of
Foremost.

The new company formed by this merger, Foremost-McKesson, Inc. had no corporate strategy and appeared to be moving in several different directions at the same time. Rudolph Drews, head of the unified firm, was described by *Forbes* magazine as the "freewheeling" president who had acquired several diverse companies from "sporting goods to candy" after the merger with McKesson, and who was better at making acquisitions than managing them. In 1974 Drews was forced from the corporation after a day long board meeting; his management style was considered the cause for a "flattening" of earnings.

Drews' response, "I'll be back," after he was fired from Foremost-McKesson was no idle threat. Drews established his own corporate-merger consulting business and found an opportunity in 1976 to orchestrate a takeover bid of his former company. Drews' middleman for the corporate raid was Victor Posner, a Miami multimillionaire who saw his own opportunity to buy out Foremost-McKesson. William Morison, who had succeeded Drews as president of Foremost-McKesson, worked hard to prevent Sharon Steel, Posner's Pennsylvania firm, from acquiring his company's stock. Although Posner was able to obtain ten percent of Foremost-McKesson's equity, he soon found that the price of the stock could be measured in more than dollars and cents.

Morison's defense strategy focused on a negative public relations campaign that targeted Posner and Sharon Steel. Careful, well-publicized research revealed that Sharon Steel Corporation had overstated its earnings for 1975 by 45 percent in order to support its takeover offer. According to *Forbes,* Posner was "scourged coast to coast" for his tactics as a "corporate marauder." Having repulsed Posner and Drews' takeover attempt, Foremost-McKesson stockholders approved a charter change which prohibited any "unsuitable" party from acquiring over ten percent of the company's common stock. An unsuitable party was defined as any business that might jeopardize Foremost's liquor or drug licenses.

Although the takeover crisis only lasted a few months, Foremost-McKesson suffered long-term consequences. The company had lost valuable time in executing the turnaround plans devised by the new president William Morison. Morison was determined to make the company a more dynamic, streamlined operation. Up to this point, Foremost-McKesson had been viewed as two companies wedded together with no real direction or focus. Morison complained that "people on the East Coast think of us as McKesson the drug company, and people on the West coast think of us as Foremost the dairy company, and we don't think either one really fits anymore." Morison hoped not only to turn Foremost-McKesson around operationally, but also to create a new corporate image. In 1977, Executive Vice-President Thomas E. Drohan, compared the company to an elephant that, under the new direction of Morison, was now "off its knees and ambling noisily."

Morison had, in fact, worked to implement a reorganization in the midst of the 1976 battle to maintain autonomy. That year, Foremost-McKesson made two major acquisitions and sold or combined 11 of its less vital operations. Morison wanted to move the company away from its role of middleman as a wholesale distributor of pharmaceutical products, beverages and liquor, and emphasize production of proprietary products.

His objective was to streamline the company by selling its low profit operations and investing $200 million into new businesses by 1990. Although the battle with Posner sidelined many of these goals, Foremost's acquisitions of C.F. Mueller Company, the country's largest pasta marker, and Gentry International, a processor of onion and garlic, were two significant acquisitions made in 1976 that met the objectives set by Morison.

Over the course of the two years before Morison's retirement, he reorganized the company into four major operating groups: drugs and health care, wine and spirits, foods, and chemicals, as well as a small home-building division. This new strategic plan was the first of its kind for Foremost-McKesson, and it was one factor that placed the company in a more comfortable position for the future.

Thomas P. Drohan, who was elected president upon Morison's 1978 retirement, continued his predecessor's strategy. Drohan's defense against corporate raids was to maintain a prohibitively high stock price. His management style focused on productivity and efficiency. Specifically, he automated inventory and stock procedures, allowing Foremost to reduce personnel costs by a third.

Drohan also redefined the company's "middleman" role in the distribution chain by establishing data processing procedures that would be valuable to both suppliers and customers, placing Foremost-McKesson in the position of acting as part of the marketing teams. This business strategy has been characterized by one *Harvard Business Review* analyst as a "value-adding partnership." Over the course of the 1980s, independent druggists were faced with competition from powerful mass and discount drug chains. Foremost-McKesson's value-adding partnership offered these small businessmen—many of whom could not afford the computerized inventory controls that were a key to the national chains' success—the benefits of automated systems without the expense. These practices catapulted the company to the vanguard of wholesale practices and contributed to average annual profit increases of 20 percent, ten times the rate recorded before 1976.

Neil Harlan succeeded to the chairmanship of Foremost-McKesson in 1979. A former army captain, Harvard business professor, and McKinsey & Company director, Harlan soon initiated a second restructuring, selling the pieces of the company that did not fit its distribution image. In 1983 alone, Harlan divested over one-third of the conglomerate's holdings to focus on health care and retail products. Divisions sold included C.F. Mueller as well as Foremost Dairies and its food processing and residential construction subsidiaries.

Acquisitions made in the early part of the decade strengthened Foremost-McKesson's role as a major distributor of health care products. In 1982 the drug distribution business contributed $2.1 billion to the company's $4 billion in sales. Fueled by $90 million in acquisitions of distribution and distribution-related businesses, revenues increased steadily in the early 1980s. Harlan's aggressive consolidation helped make McKesson one of the leaders in wholesale distribution. His strategy was twofold; he believed that "any company that doesn't stick to what it does best is inviting trouble" and that "anybody who doesn't prepare [for a raider] is living in a dreamworld.'' A 1983 name change, to McKesson Corporation, reflected the declining influence of food operations.

Harlan, a popular leader, retired in 1986 and was succeeded by Thomas W. Field, Jr., formerly of American Stores Co., a national grocery chain. That same year, McKesson sold its poorly-performing chemical distribution division, McKesson Chemical, to Univar Corp. for $76 million. Proceeds of the sale funded acquisitions of additional drug and health care product distributors, software firms, and medical equipment distributors. The company also raised funds for capital investments through the public offering of shares amounting to about 15 percent of subsidiary Armor All Products Corp. and a similar stake in prescription reimbursement division PCS Health Systems Inc. in 1986. Part of the proceeds went toward a $115 million expenditure on increased automation and efficient new distribution hubs.

McKesson had acquired Armor All, the company that launched the automotive protective market, in 1979. After suffering five years of limited profits, Armor All took off in the late 1980s. Within four years of entering the Japanese market in 1984, the product had captured one-fourth of the market. By the late 1980s, Armor All had achieved $126 million in annual sales and held 90 percent of the U.S. auto protectant market. Hoping to parlay its complete dominance of this category into continuously-increasing sales, McKesson expanded Armor All's product line to include car waxes, detergents, and spray cleaners. By 1993, the products were offered in over 50 countries. McKesson's bottled water subsidiary also paid off during this period: from 1980 to 1990, the American market for bottled water grew by 250 percent, and McKesson's Sparklett's brand enjoyed a number-two ranking in that industry.

Although profits rose 33 percent and sales increased 46 percent over the course of CEO Field's term in office, he abruptly resigned in September 1989 amid difficulties related to McKesson's prescription reimbursement division, PCS Health Systems Inc. PCS managed pharmaceutical costs for the sponsors of corporate, government, and insurance health care plans by performing cost-benefit analyses of drugs and recommending the top candidates to their customers. Under pressure from insurance companies to cut costs, PCS had tried to reduce reimbursements to pharmacists and drug store chains. When major customers—including Rite Aid Corp. and Wal-Mart Stores—balked at the cuts, McKesson scrambled to keep both its constituencies satisfied. Neil Harlan came out of retirement to serve as McKesson's interim CEO. Harlan was able to rejoin the ranks of the retired by the end of the year, when Alan Seelenfreund, a 14-year veteran of McKesson, advanced to chairman and CEO.

Ironically, after causing such an uproar in the late 1980s, PCS evolved into a vital segment of McKesson's business in the early 1990s. During that time, PCS recorded sales and earnings increases of 50 percent annually, and although the company only contributed two percent of McKesson's annual sales, it brought in 20 percent of its profits. The parent company moved to transform PCS into what *Business Week* called ''a full-fledged medical-services-management company'' through the early 1994 acquisition of Integrated Medical Systems Inc., an electronic network designed to connect doctors, hospitals, medical laboratories, and pharmacies. While these two acquisitions improved PCS' operations, they also attracted the attention of an increasingly acquisitive pharmaceutical industry. In 1993, Merck & Co., then the world's largest ethical drug company, bought Medco Containment, a rival drug distributor, for $6.6 billion.

Merck's move prompted speculation that PCS and parent McKesson were the next logical takeover target. McKesson's stock increased by over 40 percent from July 1993 (when the Medco deal was announced) to February 1994. To a limited extent, that speculation became reality later that year, when McKesson agreed to sell PCS to Eli Lilly & Co. for $4 billion in cash.

McKesson used the sale as an opportunity to restructure its finances: the company gave shareholders $76 plus a ''new share in McKesson in exchange for each McKesson old share they held. The remaining $600 million in proceeds from the sale were reinvested in the company.

CEO Seelenfreund looked to McKesson's future in the company's annual report for 1993. He noted that ''In the competitive environment created by efforts to bring rising health care costs under control, the winners will be those organizations that have both the financial strength and the technological skills needed to improve the quality of care while cutting their own costs and those of their customers. McKesson is one of the few companies that possess both these strengths.''

Principal Subsidiaries: Millbrook Distribution Services Co.; Armor All Products Corp.; McKesson Service Merchandising Co.; McKesson Water Products Co.; Medis Health & Pharmaceutical Services Inc. (Canada).

Further Reading:

Byrne, Harlan S., ''McKesson Corp.: Big Drug Distributor Bounces Back From a Bummer Year,'' *Barrons,* June 25, 1990, pp. 51–52.
Hof, Robert, ''McKesson Dumps Another Asset: The Boss, *Business Week,* September 25, 1989, p. 47.
Johnston, Russell, ''Beyond Vertical Integration: The Rise of the Value-Adding Partnership,'' *Harvard Business Review,* July/August 1988, pp. 94–101.
Mitchell, Russell and Joseph Weber, ''And the Next Juicy Plum May Be McKesson?,'' *Business Week,* February 28, 1994, p. 36.
Schlax, Julie, ''Strategies: A Good Reason to Mess With Success,'' *Forbes,* September 19, 1988, pp. 95–96.

—updated by April Dougal Gasbarre

Merisel, Inc.

200 Continental Boulevard
El Segundo, California 90245-0984
U.S.A.
(310) 615-3080
Fax: (310) 615-6438

Public Company
Incorporated: 1980 as Softsel Computer Products
Employees: 2,500
Sales: $3.09 billion
Stock Exchanges: NASDAQ
SICs: 5045 Computers, Peripherals & Software

Merisel, Inc., is the world's largest publicly held distributor of computer hardware and software products. The company sells about 30,000 hardware and software products from 900 manufacturers to 65,000 resellers worldwide. About 70 percent of the company's revenues come from the United States and 30 percent from business overseas.

In 1980 the computer software industry was in its infancy. Programs were written primarily in one-person shops by computer junkies, who did it more for love than for money. Getting this software to the 1,200 or so owners of computer retail stores was, at best, a hit-or-miss affair. If the software writer went on vacation, for example, the factory was closed and shipments stopped. Deciding which software to buy was even trickier. Approximately 95 percent of personal computer software was being sold by retail dealers, but few were in a position to evaluate and select stock from the huge number of programs available.

While "distribution" can sound mundane, 33-year-old Robert Leff recognized exactly what the software business needed: a good middleman. A friend was selling computer software door-to-door, and Leff bought out his operation for $1,300. Leff retained his day job at Transaction Technology, a Citicorp subsidiary, and sold his software in the evenings and on weekends. The first month he grossed $5,000. A coworker, David Wagman, put up $10,000, and the two became equal partners in their new company, Softsel Computer Products.

By 1982, just a year and a half later, Softsel was generating $25 million annually, with its sales doubling every quarter. The company had a huge warehouse stocking more than a thousand software titles, ranging from VisiCalc, a pioneer spreadsheet application, to home video programs that have since been forgotten. Retail dealers phoned in their orders, which were then delivered by United Parcel Service. Leff and Wagman went far beyond simple distribution, however. They tested each of the 120 to 150 new programs that were arriving each month, making sure they performed as advertised and were easy to use. Then, with their heads of sales and product groups, the two executives would decide which programs had market potential. Softsel also sent out monthly bulletins to dealers, keeping them up to date on what was hot in the market and advising them of manufacturers' specials.

By the end of 1983 annual sales stood at $90 million and the number of dealer customers had grown to 8,000. Softsel carried 4,000 products and each month added 20 from the 300 new software programs being published. Meanwhile, Softsel was continuing to refine its support services. Its account representatives kept dealers fully informed of the strengths and weaknesses of specific programs and of sales trends, broken down by product sector and geographic region. When dealers had technical questions that Softsel's marketing staff couldn't answer, they were turned over to its technical department. The company invested substantial time in training each account representative, who would be able to suggest complementary products and evaluate the dealer's purchasing program.

The company had also begun publishing its Hot List, which each week cataloged the most popular computer programs. The list ranked Softsel's best-selling business, educational, and game software, as well as popular accessories, like joysticks. By 1985, the list had begun to be posted in thousands of computer stores, and soon consumers were using it as a guide to what to buy. Some critics called the list deceptive and even unfair, because it only tracked sales through Softsel and not through other channels; as a result, popular software that wasn't distributed by Merisel did not appear on the list. David Wagman, however, responded that the company had never represented the Hot List as anything but a record of Softsel's own sales. In retrospect, the controversy was a reflection of the scarcity of data about industry sales at that time: since few other tracking services were available, the computer industry used the only source available.

During the late 1980s the company continued to grow at a rapid rate, although more slowly than the phenomenal pace of its infant years. Sales reached $319 million in 1987 and $465 million in 1988, when the company went public. In 1989 the company took a major new direction by agreeing to acquire Microamerica, a large hardware distributor annual sales, through an exchange of stock. The companies' product lines complemented each other, as did their geographical market penetration, with Softsel established in Europe and to a certain extent in Australia, and Microamerica strong in Latin America.

Initially, however, the merger created substantial problems. While the companies made a good strategic fit, they were also two very different operations. Softsel's corporate culture reflected its Southern California environment, with its employees dressed in the Hawaiian-shirt look of Robert Leff, while Microamerica's people preferred the button-down look of the Northeast. Logistics also proved difficult. Following the merger in

1990, sales staff in scattered outposts resisted relocating to central locations in the Boston, New York, and Los Angeles areas. Softsel's mainframe didn't easily digest all of Microamerica's data, which meant costly mistakes and delays in customer deliveries. Scott Bye, the advertising district manager for Computer Reseller News, told *California Business* that "it was definitely a crazy time. . . . We were never quite certain where the offices were going to be or exactly what would happen day to day."

By 1991, though, the problems of the merger were largely behind Merisel (the company had changed its name in 1990 to better reflect its product mix). Sales for the year were up 33 percent to $1.59 billion—far above the computer industry's average increase of 13 percent. Net profits of $11 million weren't spectacular, but were substantially higher than the $635,000 recorded in 1990. The company had eliminated 200 jobs following the merger and now had about 1,300 employees. Costs were back under control, and top management was reorganized for greater efficiency. Focusing on overseas opportunities, the company created Merisel Europe, which allowed manufacturers to sell their products in the United Kingdom and continental Europe through just one distributor. Merisel Europe also installed software in its offices that allowed it to invoice in any language. By 1992, the company was supplying the products of 700 manufacturers to 50,000 customers worldwide. Approximately one-third of its business was generated overseas.

The company was also benefiting from industry trends. Many top computer makers were under pressure to increase profits, and they were searching for alternatives to traditional marketing methods, which had included costly direct sales forces and authorized dealerships. These manufacturers strengthened ties with Merisel to access different channels like value-added resellers (VARs), which were small, often one-person operations that provided value-added elements like configuration, technical service, or customized software. The VAR would determine the client's computer needs and then install a system, buying the components from a distributor like Merisel.

Since it was expanding its relationships with the top names in the industry, the company could increasingly supply a better, broader mix of products. In 1992 and 1993, Merisel concluded distribution agreements with companies including Apple, Compaq, Hewlett-Packard, and IBM, allowing the company to market parts or all of their product lines in designated locations throughout the world. Merisel was also one of the largest international distributors of software made by Microsoft, Lotus, Novell, and WordPerfect.

In addition, the company was benefiting from the increasing reliance of computer dealers on wholesale distributors like Merisel for credit and inventory management. In addition to filling orders efficiently, deliver merchandise quickly, and offer a wide range of technical and sales support, Merisel was able to maintain and build relationships in a competitive marketplace. The company was also concluding agreements with mass-market discount chains like Circuit City, Office Depot, and Montgomery Ward to supply them with computer products. It also entered the membership warehouse market, creating alliances with Sam's Wholesale Club and Boston-based B.J.'s Whole-

sale. The impact of these combined efforts was apparent in 1992 results: sales rose 41 percent to $2.2 billion, while net income increased 82 percent to $19.7 million. In 1993 the company recorded another impressive performance, as sales gained 38 percent to $3.1 billion, while net income increased 55 percent to $30.4 million.

In February 1994, Merisel further expanded its operations by buying ComputerLand's retail franchise and distribution division for $80 million. There were more than 200 ComputerLand franchise locations across the United States, and the division had installed the largest number of local area networks (LANs) in the country. With the purchase, Merisel acquired the right to refranchise the ComputerLand name in the United States. The company operated as a separate entity from offices in Pleasanton, California. For the fiscal year ending September 30, 1993, ComputerLand business generated approximately $1.1 billion in revenue.

By 1994, the breadth and depth of Merisel's offerings was truly remarkable. The company provided telemarketing services for companies like Compaq, IBM, and Microsoft, which included fielding inquiries from consumers, sending out literature, fulfilling orders, and conducting market research. In the merchandising field, Merisel was providing manufacturers with in-store services like returns processing, product replenishment, sales analysis, point-of-purchase display design and production, and demo loading. In the education and training area, it was teaching resellers and their customers about the most current technologies in UNIX, networks, systems, and connectivity. Its Softeach seminars, in which manufacturers conducted seminars on how to market their products, were attended by approximately 17,000 resellers in 1991.

Education was just a small part of Merisel's services to resellers, of course. Through its Dial-Up Sales Net, customers could use a computer with a modem to examine pricing, credit information, and product description and availability, and then place orders directly into Merisel's order processing system. Some of its largest customers could even directly access the company's mainframe for order processing and account information. The company also provided resellers with financial services, tools for inventory management, and direct fulfillment services (whereby Merisel shipped directly to the resellers' customers).

The company continued to record huge revenue and earnings increases in the first quarter of 1994, but profitability suffered in the spring and summer. For the first nine months of the year, sales were up 68 percent to $3.6 billion, but earnings shrank 24 percent to $14.1 million. Part of the contraction reflected the addition of the ComputerLand operations. Some analysts also believed that revenue growth in the core, non-ComputerLand businesses was slowing, and that the company faced operating losses in Europe. They also noted that Merisel had high levels of debt and that increased interest expense was hurting net margins. Wall Street's fears of a slowing computer industry under pricing pressure contributed to a drop in the company's stock price from a high of 22½ during the year to seven in December.

Nevertheless, it was important to keep the scale of the company's accomplishments and problems in perspective. In 15 years, what had started as one man, Robert Leff, going door-to-door with software under his arm had become a $5 billion company. (Leff was still co-chairman in 1995.) While some analysts questioned whether the company could maintain its sales growth and raise profitability, it nevertheless seemed certain that Merisel would continue to be one of the major players in the computer industry.

Further Reading:

"Back from Hell in a Handbasket Thanks to Better Cost Control and Management Delegation," *California Business,* June 1992, pp. 14–15.

Bellew, Patricia, "List of Top-Selling Computer Programs Draws Big Following—and Much Criticism," *Wall Street Journal,* June 24, 1985, p. 21.

Cole, Jeff, "Merisel Outlook for Sales Sends Shares Plunging," *Wall Street Journal,* June 9, 1994, p. B2.

Deady, Tim, "Merisel Bucks the Trend and Continues to Grow as Profits Look to Get Ready to Soar," *L.A. Business Journal,* December 13, 1993, p. 27.

Deady, Tim, "Merisel Gears Sales Operation to Changing Market," *Los Angeles Business Journal,* June 21, 1992, p. 11.

Glidewell, Richard, "Finally, the Heavy Hitters Are Offering Big Deals to Small VARs," *Systems Integration,* January 1992, p. 31.

Hayes, Thomas, "Parceling Out the Software," *New York Times,* December 14, 1983, p. D1.

Marken, G. A., "High-Tech: How It Maximizes Business Software Customer Contact," *Business Marketing,* August 1984, pp. 38–42.

Rowe, Jeff, "Softsel to Acquire Microamerica Inc. in Share Exchange," *Wall Street Journal,* November 30, 1989, p. B4.

Silverstein, Stuart, "Merisel Counts on Acquisition," *Los Angeles Times,* April 30, 1991, p. S17.

Veilleux, C. Thomas, "Merisel CPD Serving Sam's, B.J.'s," *HFD—The Weekly Home Furnishings Newspaper,* April 27, 1992, p. 143.

White, Todd, "Merisel Increases Market by Feeding Supply Chain," *Los Angeles Business Journal,* April 8, 1991, p. 34.

——, "Merisel Merrily Ignores PC Bad Times," *Los Angeles Business Journal,* February 24, 1992, p. 3.

——, "Merisel Sees Opportunities Abroad Despite Toughening Price Situation," *Los Angeles Business Journal,* July 20, 1992, p. 33.

Wiegner, Kathleen, "More than Middlemen," *Forbes,* May 10, 1982, p. 100.

—Bob Schneider

Miller Brewing Company

3939 West Highland Boulevard
Milwaukee, Wisconsin 53201
U.S.A.
(414) 931-2000
Fax: (414) 931-3735

Wholly Owned Subsidiary of Philip Morris, Inc.
Incorporated: 1888
Employees: 9,600
Sales: $4.2 billion
SICs: 2082 Malt Beverages

Between the establishment of the Miller Brewing Company in 1855 and the death of its founder in 1888, the firm's annual productive capacity increased from 300 barrels to 80,000 barrels of beer. This impressive growth has continued to the present day: Miller now operates six breweries, five can manufacturing plants, four distributorships, a glass bottle production facility, a label and fiberboard factory, and numerous gas wells. Beginning with a staff of 25, Miller now employs about 9,500 people. The company currently produces more than 40 million barrels of beer per year and is the second largest brewery in the United States.

The founder of the Miller Brewing Company, Frederick Miller, was born in Germany in 1824. As a young man he worked in the Royal Brewing Company at Sigmaringen, Hohenzollern. In 1850, at the age of 26, he emigrated to the United States. Miller wanted to start his own brewery and regarded Milwaukee as the most promising site, probably because of the large number of beer-drinking Germans living there.

In 1855 Miller bought the Plank Road Brewery from Charles Lorenz Best and his father. These two men had been slow to modernize their operation, but Miller's innovative techniques made him successful, indeed famous, in the brewing industry. The Bests had started a "cave-system" which provided storage for beer in a cool undisturbed place for several months after brewing. Yet these caves were small and in poor condition. Miller improved upon the Best's system: his caves were built of brick, totaled 600 feet of tunnel, and had a capacity of 12,000 barrels. Miller used these until 1906 when, due to the company's expansion and the availability of more modern technology, refrigerator facilities were built.

After his death, Miller's sons Ernest, Emil, and Frederick A., along with their brother-in-law Carl, assumed control of the operation which was incorporated as the Frederick Miller Brewing Company. By 1919 production had increased to 500,000 barrels, but it was halted shortly thereafter by the enactment of Prohibition. The company managed to survive by producing cereal beverages, soft drinks, and malt-related products.

Ernest Miller died in 1922 and was succeeded as president by his brother, Frederick A. Miller. Frederick A. remained president and chief executive until 1947 when his nephew, Frederick C., became head of the firm. Frederick C. instituted a program of expansion, and was instrumental in bringing major league baseball (the Braves) to Milwaukee, thus strengthening the relationship between the beer industry and the sporting world. The cultivation of this relationship led to increased sales for Miller. But tragedy struck when Frederick C. was killed in a plane crash in Milwaukee in 1954. At the time of his death, the Miller Brewing Company was ranked ninth among American brewers.

The expansion program initiated in 1947 was continued by Norman Klug, who became president following Miller's death. Under Klug's management, Miller purchased the A. Gettelman Company in 1961, and four years later bought the General Brewing Corporation of Azusa, California. That same year, the firm purchased a Carling O'Keefe brewery in Fort Worth, Texas. By this time Miller had formed a can manufacturing company in Milwaukee with the Carnation Corporation. The plant produced approximately 150 million beer cans a year.

Just before Klug's death, arrangements had been made for a diversified shipping firm, W. R. Grace, to acquire 53 percent of the brewing company. The Miller stock was owned at that time by Mrs. Lorraine Mulberger and her family, descendants of Frederick A. Miller. The Mulbergers were paid $36 million but Grace soon discovered that its purchase was significantly undervalued. Because of its cash reserves and growing importance within the industry, Miller was a prime acquisition target; in 1969 management at Grace decided to sell its interest in Miller to PepsiCo for $120 million. Yet suddenly, and without warning, Grace canceled the agreement and almost immediately sold its shares to Philip Morris for $130 million. PepsiCo filed suit in federal court to prevent this, but the suit failed.

Philip Morris purchased the remaining shares of Miller's stock from the De Rance Foundation of Milwaukee in 1970. In 1971 Miller extended its production activities in Fort Worth, obtained a tract of land in Delaware as a possible site for a new brewery, and also acquired Formosa Springs, a Canadian brewery. By 1972 Miller Brewing ranked seventh in the beer industry.

Under the Philip Morris management, Miller's marketing strategies and advertising campaigns became more important than ever before. Aiming to replace Anheuser-Busch as the nation's largest brewer, the company expanded its range of brands and penetrated all segments of the market. As a result, production rose from seven million barrels in 1973 to 31 million barrels in 1978.

Led by John Murphy, a Philip Morris executive trained as a lawyer and with notable marketing ability, the company began a thorough study of American beer drinking trends. Miller had been known previously as "The Champagne of Beers," and its advertising campaigns were directed to appeal to a specific group of white-collar consumers. Murphy revised this strategy and reoriented it toward the large blue-collar market with an emphasis on the work-reward relationship. Miller's new slogan was: "If you've got the time, we've got the beer." This slogan, and the marketing plan behind it, soon led to increased sales.

By 1985 reduced calorie beers accounted for 20.5 percent of all beer sales. Miller has the distinction of initiating this market with its Miller Lite, which still remains the number one product in this category. Rather than marketing Miller Lite as a diet beer, the company emphasized its lower calorie content and its unique flavor. Once again it was clever advertising that accounted for Miller's success. Television advertisements showed brawny men enjoying Miller Lite; the slogan proclaimed: "Everything you always wanted in a beer. And less." The Miller Lite allstars, included such personalities as Rodney Dangerfield and John Madden, have continued this approach in the beer's award-winning commercials. In 1986 the tagline emphasized the beer's uniqueness: "There's only one Lite beer. Miller Lite."

Miller's rivals soon responded with low calorie beers of their own, and the company tried to prevent brewers such as Schlitz and Heileman from using the world "Light." Fortunately for Miller's rivals—and for the English language—the U.S. Supreme Court ruled that Miller did not have exclusive rights to the word.

Shortly after the introduction of Miller Lite, the company began to market a domestically brewed version of Löwenbräu—a German beer with a 600-year old history—to which Miller owned the U.S. distribution rights. In an $11 million advertising campaign, Miller captured 10 percent of Anheuser-Busch's Michelob market. Anheuser-Busch promptly filed suit with the Federal Trade Commission accusing Miller of using deceptive packaging and advertising in order to convince consumers they were buying an imported beer. Later, when Anheuser-Busch introduced its "Natural Light" beer, Miller retaliated by pointing out that there was nothing natural about Anheuser-Busch's product.

Due to the phenomenal success of Miller Lite, Miller was in second place behind Anheuser-Busch by the early 1980s. But as Miller Lite sales were climbing, sales of Miller High Life began falling. Between 1981 and 1986, High Life sales dropped 60 percent. The decline was offset by Miller Lite and also by the introduction of Milwaukee's Best and Meister Brau, two lower-priced beers that grew to represent 16.9 percent of the company's output by 1988. Equally important in maintaining Miller's market share was the 1985 introduction of Miller Genuine Draft, one of the first premium unpasteurized beers to be made in the United States. Due to heavy advertising campaigns and a unique market position, production of Genuine Draft grew to 2.3 million barrels within the first two years.

Despite the success of Miller Lite and Genuine Draft, Miller was having a hard time capturing market share from Anheuser-Busch. In 1987, combined sales of Anheuser's Budweiser and Bud Light grew 23 percent while sales of all Miller products grew only 1 percent. Parent company Philip Morris began to grow nervous. Early in 1988, Miller's president and chief executive William Howell took an early retirement. He was replaced by Leonard J. Goldstein, a senior vice-president with considerable marketing expertise.

One of the first moves Goldstein made was to purchase the Jacob Leinenkeugle Brewing Company, a 120-year-old microbrewery that would provide Miller with a foothold in the growing "boutique beer" market. Although the 1989 beer market was sluggish, Miller increased its market to 21 percent, against Anheuser's 41 percent. The following year, Goldstein was named chairman, succeeded by Warren Dunn as president and chief executive. Under the two, Miller's market share continued to increase. By 1991, it had grown to 23 percent, or 43.5 million barrels. Yet Miller's goal of unseating Anheuser-Busch from the number one position remained far off. Although the company was firmly in second place—with a 13 percent lead over Coors—Anheuser-Busch prevailed as the undisputed market leader, with 45.7 percent of the market.

By 1993, many in the U.S. beer industry felt the domestic market was stagnant. With the exception of Genuine Draft, sales of all Miller beers fell in 1992 and income dropped 13.6 percent to $260 million. Coors and Anheuser both cut their workforce in early 1993; by December Miller had followed suit, eliminating 13 percent of its workforce through closing a manufacturing plant in Fulton, New York, and trimming 300 white collar jobs from its headquarter operations.

That year, in an attempt to compete with Anheuser-Busch in the international market, Miller paid $273 million for U.S. distribution rights and a 20 percent stake in Canada's Molson Breweries. Some analysts questioned the move, noting that although Molson was the leading brewer in Canada, its imports to the United States declined in the year preceding Miller's purchase. However, Miller fared better than its competitors in 1993, due to the purchase of Molson, heavy discounting of its Miller High Life brand, and aggressive marketing outside the United States, where sales of Miller Genuine Draft climbed 29 percent. As growing consumer interest in small "boutique brands" continued to threaten Miller sales, the company further protected itself by purchasing the domestic distribution rights to Fosters Lager and other imported beers. Although the domestic beer market remained static, the company continued to see its sales increase through the first half of 1994, fueled by the introduction of Ice House ice-brewed beer, and Lite Ice.

Under parent Philip Morris, Miller's focus in the 1990s was to dislodge Anheuser-Busch as America's largest brewery. Yet by the middle of the decade the company still had a long way to go. Miller sold approximately 41 million barrels of beer a year and had a 21 percent market share, compared with Anheuser-Busch's 67.8 million barrels and 36.6 percent market share. Miller's growth between 1985 and 1995 was slow but steady. Like Anheuser, Miller saw its market share increase as smaller breweries continued to lose ground. The competition between the two largest breweries in the United States continued.

Further Reading:

Baron, Stanley Wade, *Brewed in America: A History of Beer and Ale in the U.S.,* New York: Arno Press, 1972.

Heritage Born and Pledged Anew, Milwaukee: Miller Brewing Company, 1955.

Jabbonsky, Larry, "Consider it Dunn," *Beverage World,* September 1992, pp. 24–28.

O'Neal, Michael, "Can a Marketing Man Make it Miller Time Again?," *Business Week,* February 1, 1988, p. 26.

—updated by Maura Troester

▲ Mitsubishi Corporation

Mitsubishi Corporation

6-3, Marunouchi 2-chome
Chiyoda-ku, Tokyo 100
Japan
+81-3-3210-2121
Fax: +81-3-3210-8841

Public Company
Incorporated: 1918 as Mitsubishi Shoji
Employees: 13,959
Sales: ¥17.28 trillion ($169.38 billion)
Stock Exchanges: Tokyo Osaka Nagoya Kyoto Hiroshima
    Fukuoka Sapporo Niigata
SICs: 5084 Industrial Machinery and Equipment; 5044 Office
    Equipment; 5052 Coal and Other Minerals and Ores; 5172
    Petroleum and Petroleum Products Wholesalers, Except
    Bulk Stations and Terminals; 5153 Grain and Field Beans

Appearing on everything from automobiles to agricultural goods, the Mitsubishi Corporation's three diamond logo has become one of the most familiar symbols in the world. Mitsubishi Group companies are represented in virtually every country in the world, and the company has had a dominant presence in the development of eastern Asia since the 1870s. The firm is characterized as a *keiretsu* (banking conglomerate), a family of businesses linked through Japanese history and tradition, as well as cross-shareholdings, interlocking directorates, and personal contacts. This scheme provides Mitsubishi affiliates with common and well-known brand names, access to credit, and protection from hostile takeover. The Mitsubishi *keiretsu* is organized around Mitsubishi Corporation, the largest diversified trading company in the world; Mitsubishi Bank, Japan's fourth largest city bank; and Mitsubishi Heavy Industries, Japan's largest manufacturer of heavy machinery. The Mitsubishi *guruupu,* or group, includes such well-known affiliates as: Nikon Corp., Mitsubishi Motors, and Mitsubishi Estate Co.

Mitsubishi is the family business of the House of Iwasaki. Its founder, Yataro Iwasaki, was born in 1834, a peasant who purchased samurai status with the help of relatives. Despite his rural heritage, Iwasaki developed contacts with a number of urban administrators in the Tosa prefecture (or fiefdom). Later, as a Tosa official and member of the administrative class, Iwasaki established a number of personal relationships with influential politicians whose assistance and favoritism would later prove indispensable.

After the restoration of the Meiji emperor in 1868, the new government initiated a national program of industrial modernization. It established and operated several model corporations which were later sold to private investors. At this time, however, the only private interests with enough money to purchase these corporations were established companies run by Japan's richest families. Family companies such as Mitsui, Sumitomo, and Yasuda greatly expanded their financial interests when they took control of the government companies.

Yataro Iwasaki, however, was not from a rich family. Nevertheless, in 1870, during the first years of the Meiji government, he was able to purchase Tsukumo Shokai, the official Tosa shipping company. In 1873 he changed its name to Mitsubishi, which is Japanese for "three diamonds." Iwasaki was dedicated to an occupation as a merchant and to making Japanese shipping companies competitive with the large foreign lines.

Mitsubishi's greatest supporter in government, the Finance Minister Shigenobu Okuma, was a close friend of Iwasaki. He lobbied on behalf of Mitsubishi, designating the company for numerous subsidies and privileges. When the Japanese government launched a punitive military expedition against the island of Formosa (Taiwan) in 1874, Okuma saw to it that Mitsubishi was chosen to provide the ships. The government later offered direct subsidies to Mitsubishi *Shokai* (company) to ensure that Japan remained competitive in world shipping. With the active support and protection of the government, Mitsubishi, like Mitsui, Sumitomo and Yasuda, evolved into a *zaibatsu* (literally a "money clique").

By 1877, 80 percent of Japanese maritime traffic was controlled by the Mitsubishi Shokai. Iwasaki, however, had incurred some political and professional disfavor as a result of his privileged influence in government and trading practices. On numerous occasions Iwasaki was personally attacked in newspapers for his unscrupulous business practices. The other *zaibatsu,* particularly Mitsui, relied heavily on Mitsubishi for shipping and suffered greatly from its monopoly prices. Customers shipping freight on Shokai boats were obliged to use Mitsubishi warehouses and insure their goods with the Mitsubishi Maritime Insurance Company.

In 1880 Mitsui supported the creation of a rival shipping company called Tokyo Fuhansen. Within a year Mitsubishi had succeeded in driving Fuhansen out of business. However, after Count Okuma died in 1881, his political opponents joined Iwasaki's competitors with the common goal of breaking the Mitsubishi shipping monopoly. The following year Fuhansen was reorganized, merged with several other smaller shipping companies, and renamed Kyodo Unyu (United Transport). Kaoru Inoue, a political enemy of Okuma and close friend of Mitsui's Takashi Masuda, convinced the government to invest heavily in Kyodo Unyu. Thereafter, Mitsubishi and Kyodo Unyu engaged in an extremely costly and intense competition which drained both companies of virtually all their resources.

During the battle with Kyodo Unyu, Mitsubishi attempted to consolidate its operations by securing a guaranteed source of fuel. In 1881 the company purchased the Takashima coal mine.

Iwasaki also sent representatives to the northern island of Hokkaido to investigate its potential for coal mining. After gaining control of coal resources, Iwasaki turned his attention to gaining control of a ship supplier. Iwasaki reminded the government that the Russians had just completed a naval base at Vladivostok, while Japan's major shipyard at Nagasaki was barely able to handle minor repairs. Mitsubishi won a contract to lease and later purchase the bankrupt Nagasaki Shipyard from the government.

By 1885 the battle for supremacy in Japanese shipping was deadlocked. That year the director of Kyodo Unyu, Eiichi Shibusawa, invited the government to impose a regulatory monopoly on shipping. Suddenly it was learned that Yataro Iwasaki had acquired a controlling interest in Kyodo Unyu. In what may have been the world's first hostile takeover, Iwasaki secretly purchased a majority of his competitor's stock. He consolidated both companies into the Nihon Yusen Kaisha, or Japan Shipping Company, and denied managerial roles to both Masuda and Shibusawa who were stunned by their defeat. However, Iwasaki was unable to savor his victory; he died shortly afterward.

Iwasaki's associates, all of whom were samurai, were unable to assert themselves as independent managers until after Iwasaki died. Despite the fact that Mitsubishi was organized as a company, Iwasaki operated it as a family concern and exercised authoritarian control. His younger brother, Yanosuki Iwasaki, assumed the leadership of Mitsubishi Shokai and NYK in 1886.

The following year the Mitsubishi Shipbuilding Company became the first Japanese concern to manufacture a ship made of steel and equipped with a boiler. Japanese production of "black ships" for transportation and the military propelled Japan into a higher class of naval power. The major shipping companies, NYK and OSK (Osaka Shosen Kaisha), expanded their routes to China and Korea, and by 1899 to Europe, North America, India, and Australia.

NYK was a major beneficiary of the Sino-Japanese War (1894–1895), which opened several ports in continental Asia to increased Japanese trade. Like many of the other *zaibatsu,* Mitsubishi participated in Japan's colonization of Korea, Manchuria, and Taiwan. Mitsubishi, however, was primarily involved in establishing shipping links and developing an infrastructure in the colonial territories.

In 1893 Yanosuke Iwasaki initiated a reorganization of Mitsubishi and changed its name to Mitsubishi Goshi Kaisha. Three years later he diversified the company's operations by purchasing the Sado gold mine and Ikuno silver mine. He also purchased and developed a 110 acre swamp which later became some of the most expensive property in the Tokyo business district.

Koyata Iwasaki (who replaced Yanosuke as head of the company in 1916) continued the diversification program. Between 1917 and 1919 Mitsubishi established internal divisions for banking, mining, real estate, shipbuilding, and trading. As a victor in World War I, Japan was legitimized as a major world power with great influence in the Pacific. But this legitimization was owed to the *zaibatsu* (and not least Mitsubishi), which had built Japan into what it was.

In 1918 Mitsubishi was incorporated as a joint-stock company (totally owned by the Iwasaki family). At that time Mitsubishi Shoji Kaisha (Trading Company) was established as a separate business entity. Between 1917 and 1921 several more of the company's divisions were made independent public companies in order to attract investor capital. Mitsubishi Shipbuilding (later Mitsubishi Heavy Industries) was created in 1917, Mitsubishi Bank in 1919, and Mitsubishi Electric in 1921.

In the ensuing decade, nationalist political terrorists gained influence in the military and government. Political assassinations claimed the lives of many moderate and leftist figures. In 1932 terrorists murdered Takuma Dan, head of Mitsubishi's chief rival, Mitsui. Many of the *zaibatsu* tempered their growth during this period to avoid becoming targets of the militarists, who had seized power in Japan.

The militarists envisioned a regional economic regime for eastern Asia called the Greater East Asia Co-Prosperity Sphere. As part of this scheme, Japan would be responsible for industry and management, China for agriculture, Manchuria and Korea for mining and forestry, Indonesia for oil, and the Philippines for fishing. For this reason, the *zaibatsu* were essential partners to the militarists. They alone had the resources and expertise to implement such an ambitious development strategy. Mitsubishi in particular was involved in the most important fields: shipping, shipbuilding, mining, heavy manufacturing, electrical generation, warehousing, and trading.

After the Japanese invasion of China in 1937 Mitsubishi was required to provide the military and occupation forces with warships, aircraft, vehicles, weapons, and provisions. When Japan invaded the rest of eastern Asia and bombed Pearl Harbor in 1941, the uneasy partnership between the *zaibatsu* and the militarists became more important. Companies such as Mitsubishi continued to search for profit. They also comprised the military/industrial complex which perpetuated Japan's ability to make war.

While Mitsubishi Shipbuilding turned out warships, the aircraft division of Mitsubishi Heavy Industries manufactured over 18,000 warplanes, the most important of which was the "Zero." The simple technology of the Zero made it possible for thousands to be built quickly. Its vast numbers and ability to climb and accelerate made it one of the most formidable weapons of the war.

In 1945 Japan surrendered to American forces, which during the previous year had destroyed Japan's major cities, and with them Japan's major factories. What remained of Mitsubishi was left in ruins. The American occupation forces under General Douglas MacArthur formulated an industrial plan for the reconstruction of Japan which included the implementation of American-style anti-monopoly laws. As a result of the legislation, the *zaibatsu* were outlawed and use of their prewar logos was banned. Mitsubishi was divided into 139 independent companies. In addition, severe restrictions prevented the companies from coordinating business strategies and setting up cross ownership of stock.

The communist revolution in China during 1949 and the Korean War (1950–1952) significantly increased the strategic value of Japan as an industrial power and American ally. Many of the punitive laws imposed on Japan by the occupation authority were lifted. Subsequent legislation in Japan weakened the effect of the anti-monopoly laws. Starting in 1950 several of the former Mitsubishi *zaibatsu* companies had been allowed to reassemble. The surviving core of company interests readapted the Mitsubishi Shoji Kaisha name and the triple diamond logo. In 1953 the Mitsubishi Bank (called the Chiyoda Bank during the occupation) started to use its old name and began to coordinate the various former Mitsubishi companies. In 1954 Mitsubishi Shoji merged with three of its former component companies and started to re-establish its worldwide trading network.

A number of associated companies were created during the 1950s, including the Mitsubishi Gas Chemical Company and the Mitsubishi Petrochemical Company. The company's most important foreign associate, the Mitsubishi International Corporation (MIC), was established in the United States in 1954. MIC carefully observed industrial and consumer trends in the United States and played an important part in the formation of Mitsubishi's long-term international planning. MIC also served as a training ground for international representatives of Mitsubishi.

Japan's Ministry of International Trade and Industry (MITI) played an active role in maintaining a healthy balance of monopolistic competition between the new *zaibatsu*, Mitsui, Mitsubishi, Sumitomo and others. MITI is responsible for the excellent coordination of resources, planning and development which allowed Japanese companies to grow and perform successfully in the postwar period. With the new *zaibatsu* as its instrument, MITI prepared Japan for several decades of export-led growth.

As a result of the direction provided by MITI, Mitsubishi anticipated Japan's increasing demand for various mineral commodities. In the 1960's Royal Dutch Shell discovered a large deposit of natural gas in the sultanate of Brunei. At the time, demand for natural gas was increasing rapidly in Japan. Mitsubishi participated with the government of Brunei and Royal Dutch Shell in developing a system whereby natural gas can be compressed into a refrigerated liquid and shipped in specially designed tankers.

Next Mitsubishi turned its attention to the untapped mineral potential of Australia and Papua New Guinea. The company formed a subsidiary called Mitsubishi Australia to participate in a large coal mining project at Bowen Basin in Queensland. Beginning in 1971 raw materials were shipped from Australia to Japan where they were used to produce iron and steel.

In 1969 Mitsubishi helped to create a forestry company called Balikpapan Forest Industries at Sotek, Indonesia. In 1973 Mitsubishi formed a joint venture with the Mexican government to produce salt in Baja California, and with the Kenyan government to develop the tourist industry in that country. In the late 1970's Mitsubishi established a joint marketing agreement with the Chrysler Corporation to sell cars in the United States built by the Mitsubishi Motor Company.

In 1971 Mitsubishi Shoji Kaisha changed its name to Mitsubishi Corporation, an Anglicized name intended to reflect the company's growing internationalization. By this time, however, the amalgamation of the prewar Mitsubishi combine had ceased. Top level managers in the associated Mitsubishi companies

were reluctant to give up their independence (and possibly their jobs) by placing themselves under the direction of other managers. Consequently there are nearly thirty independent Mitsubishi companies whose directors belong to a monthly meeting group called the Kinyo-kai (Second Friday Conference) where their business strategies are formulated.

The *keiretsu* organizational scheme emerged from Mitsubishi's growth (and that of other Japanese conglomerates), which was accompanied by an accumulation of debt. Majority holdings of virtually all affiliates are maintained within the *keiretsu,* thereby preventing hostile takeover when share prices of a given member slip dangerously low. For example, when affiliate Akai Electric Co. encountered financial problems in the early 1980s, Mitsubishi Bank bailed it out. When Mitsubishi Heavy Industries' shipbuilding business slowed mid-decade, some of its employees were placed with other "three diamond" affiliates. The *keiretsu* also prevented Kuwait Petroleum Corp.'s threatened takeover of Mitsubishi Oil in 1984.

Takeo Kondo was named president of Mitsubishi in June of 1986. That year, after 18 years as Japan's leading trading firm, Mitsubishi fell to fifth place. A few months after assuming the corporation's leadership, Kondo presented a plan for reorganizing and reviewing its operations. In November, however, Kondo suddenly died. He was replaced by Shinroku Morohashi, a vice-president whom Kondo had charged to implement the restructuring plan. The "K-plan," as it became known, involved the divestiture of unprofitable operations, reorganization of staff, entry into newer, more promising fields such as high technology, and the introduction of more efficient administrative techniques.

Aggressive international acquisitions by Mitsubishi affiliates grabbed headlines in the late 1980s and helped it expand from its base in heavy industry. In 1985, for example, Mitsubishi Motors increased its cooperation with Chrysler Corp. through the creation of Diamond-Star Motors. In 1989 and 1990, Mitsubishi Estate Co. acquired a controlling interest in Rockefeller Center at a cost of nearly $1 billion. Around the same time, Mitsubishi Corp. boosted its chemicals interests with a controlling stake in Aristech Chemical Corp. of Pittsburgh. Other high-profile purchases included Eastman Kodak's Verbatim and California's Pebble Beach golf course. In 1990, the company's Mitsubishi Motors moved to form a joint venture with German automaker Daimler-Benz and acquired one-third of Netherlands-based Volvo the following year.

The group's fortunes, as well as the Japanese economy, declined in the late 1980s and early 1990s. Falling demand in Mitsubishi Corporation's vital fuels segment combined with a "strong-yen recession." In addition, many Japanese companies ceased to rely on the trading services provided by *sogo shosha,* or general trading companies like Mitsubishi Corp. In many cases they found it more cost effective to develop their own international networks. These factors combined to effect a steady revenue descent—from ¥19.73 trillion in 1991 to ¥17.28 trillion in 1994.

The 1992 appointment of British-born and Harvard-educated Minoru "Ben" Makihara as president of Mitsubishi Corp. was viewed by some observers as an attempt to improve the Japanese business's poor reputation in the United States. Perhaps not coincidentally, however, Makihara's father worked for Mitsubishi in London, and his wife was a great-granddaughter of the *keiretsu's* founder.

In the mid-1990s, operations of the Mitsubishi Corporation were divided into the following groups: metals (37 percent of annual revenues), machinery (including Information Systems and Services) (24.7 percent), foods (12.7 percent), fuels (11.4 percent), chemicals (7.3 percent), and textiles and general merchandise (6.9 percent). About 40 percent of its annual sales were made overseas.

Principal Subsidiaries: Asahi Glass Co., Ltd.; Dai Nippon Toryo Co., Ltd.; DC card Co., Ltd.; The Meiji Mutual Life Insurance Company; Mitsubishi Aluminum Co., Ltd.; Mitsubishi Atomic Power Industries, Inc.; The Mitsubishi Bank, Ltd.; Mitsubishi Cable Industries, Ltd.; Mitsubishi Construction Co., Ltd.; Mitsubishi Corporation; Mitsubsishi Electric Corporation; Mitsubishi Estate Co., Ltd.; Mitsubishi Gas Chemical Company, Inc.; Mitsubishi Heavy Industries, Ltd.; Mitsubishi Heavy Industries Air-Conditioning and Refrigeration Systems Corporation; Mitsubishi Kakoki Kaisha, Ltd.; Mitsubishi Kasei Corporation; Mitsubishi Liquified Petroleum Gas Co., Ltd.; Mitsu-bishi Materials Corporation; Mitsubishi Motors Corporation; Mitsubishi Nuclear Fuel Company, Ltd.; Mitsubishi Office Machinery Co., Ltd.; Mitsubishi Oil Co., Ltd.; Mitsubishi Ore Transport Co., Ltd.; Mitsubishi Paper Mills Limited; Mitsubishi Petrochemical Co., Ltd.; Mitsubishi Petroleum Development Co., Ltd.; Mitsubishi Plastics Industries Limited; Mitsubishi Precision Co., Ltd.; Mitsubishi Rayon Co., Ltd.; Mitsubishi Research Institute, Inc.; Mitsubishi Shindoh Co., Ltd.; Mitsubishi Space Software Co., Ltd.; Mitsubishi Steel Mfg. Co., Ltd.; The Mitsubishi Trust and Banking Corporation; Mitsubishi Warehouse & Transportation Co., Ltd.; Nikon Corporation; Nippon Yusen Kabushiki Kaisha; Shin Caterpillar Mitsubishi Ltd.; The Tokio Marine and Fire Insurance Co., Ltd.; Toyo Engineering Works, Ltd.

Further Reading:

Neff, Robert, ''Mighty Mitsubishi Is on the Move,'' *Business Week,* September 24, 1990, pp. 98–107.
Neff, Robert, ''The Harvard Man in Mitsubishi's Corner Office,'' *Business Week,* March 23, 1992, p. 50.
Wray, William D., *Mitsubishi and the N.Y.K. 1870–1914: Business Strategy in the Japanese Shipping Industry,* Boston: Harvard University Press, 1984.

—updated by April Dougal Gasbarre

⚭MOEN®

Moen Incorporated

25300 Al Moen Drive
North Olmsted, Ohio 44070
U.S.A.
(216) 962-2000
Fax: (216) 962-2770

Operating Unit of MasterBrand Industries Inc.
Incorporated: 1900 as Standard Screw Co.
Employees: 3,000
Sales: $600 million (est.)
SICs: 3432 Plumbing Fixtures Fittings & Trim; 3431
    Enameled Iron & Metal Sanitary Ware; 3089 Plastic
    Products, Nec; 2390 Miscellaneous Fabricated Textile
    Products

One of the world's largest manufacturers of faucets, sinks, and other plumbing products, Moen Incorporated ranks as the leading manufacturer of single-handle faucets, the top seller to the wholesale market, and the leading brand of faucet in the North American faucet market. Known for quality and style, Moen's faucets have been referred to as the "Cadillacs" of the industry. The firm is the leading subsidiary of MasterBrand Industries Inc., a group of residential hardware and home improvement companies. MasterBrand, in turn, is a subsidiary of American Brands, Inc., a conglomerate with interests in tobacco, distilled spirits, golf and leisure products group, and office products.

The firm and its products are named for Al Moen, inventor of the single-handle faucet. Trained as a mechanical engineer at the University of Washington, Al Moen was inspired to create the device after scalding his hands under a conventional two-handled faucet in the late 1930s. His first design was a double-valve faucet with a cam that controlled the mixture of hot and cold water from the two valves. In consultation with a major faucet manufacturer, however, the inventor became convinced that the cam design was inappropriate, and he went back to the drawing board. Throughout the early 1940s, Moen spent his spare time—and borrowed money—refining a cylindrical design with a piston action. He solicited several manufacturers for the faucet, but by the time Moen found a backer, World War II had begun and brass was being rationed, making production impossible.

After returning from wartime service in the Navy, Moen took his unique faucet idea to Ravenna Metal Products Corp., based in Seattle, Washington. The company sold its first single-handle mixing faucet in San Francisco in late 1947 for about $12. Moen's faucet was later named one of the 100 best-designed mass-produced products of modern times, and Al Moen was nominated to the U.S. Patent Office's Inventors' Hall of Fame. Over the course of his career, Moen obtained more than 75 patents in a variety of areas.

Ravenna Metal Products was acquired and absorbed by Chicago's Standard Screw Co. in 1956 and moved to Elyria, Ohio, a suburb of Cleveland. Standard Screw had been established in 1900 through the merger of Chicago Screw Co., Hartford Machine Screw Co., and Western Automatic Machine Screw Co. Standard Screw had sought a retail product to complement its lines of fasteners, precision parts, and automotive valves. For the next three decades, Moen operated as a division of Standard Screw.

Moen's sales increased steadily with the help of its new parent and through its own continuous innovation. By 1960, single-handle faucets (of which Moen was not the only manufacturer) comprised about five percent of the total faucet market. Moen catapulted to the lead of the single-handle segment during the 1960s on the strength of new faucet styles and technological innovations. Al Moen, who continued to lead the company's Engineering Department until 1982, was responsible for many of the innovations that drove that growth. These included the replaceable cartridge, a patented, washerless device that served as the basis of the manufacturer's lifetime limited warranty against leaks and drips. Company publications tout the mechanism, which features a self-contained assembly with no moving parts, as "the standard in performance by which other faucet systems are measured." Over the course of his career, Al Moen patented other key products in the company line, including the Flo Control Aerator, the Moentrol (a system to control shower pressure), the Swing'N Spray faucet with a sprayer head, a push button diverter, and a tub spout diverter.

By 1970, when Standard Screw was renamed Stanadyne, Inc., the Moen Division had grown to become the company's most important operation. Stanadyne's sales had increased from $49.1 million to more than $120 million over the course of the previous decade.

During the 1970s and early 1980s, Moen grew from a niche player among faucet manufacturers to the number-two marketer, behind Masco Corp. and its Delta, Epic, and Peerless brands. Despite competition from inexpensive Asian imports, the American faucet market enjoyed double-digit growth beginning in 1986.

During the late 1980s Moen experienced a corresponding double-digit growth in sales, which caught the attention of the investment community; in March 1988 Stanadyne was acquired through a leveraged buyout by the New York investment firm of Forstmann, Little & Co.. The new owners made Moen Stanadyne's primary focus by selling most of its other operating divisions, and Stanadyne assumed the name of its best-selling product in October 1989, becoming Moen Incorporated. In 1990, upon the conclusion of the Free Trade Agreement between Canada and the United States, Moen merged its U.S. and Canadian operations. Forstmann, Little sold Moen Inc. to MasterBrand for $982 million that same year.

MasterBrand appeared to be committed to Moen for the long term, supporting it with a $50 million infusion of capital. The money was spent on research and development, new manufacturing equipment, and facilities. During the early 1990s Moen shifted its sales focus from wholesale to include retail in response to economic and marketplace imperatives, which included economic recession and a corresponding decline in new housing construction, as well as growth in the home improvement market and the development of powerful new home improvement retail outlets like Home Depot, Builders Square, and Lowe's. The faucet maker assimilated several of MasterBrand's plumbing-related subsidiaries, expanded its product line, and launched aggressive new sales and marketing strategies.

The shift required a transformation of many of the manufacturer's processes. For example, Moen had to develop attractive packaging, speedier delivery, barcoding, and nationwide service. The company revamped its distribution, transportation, customer service, industrial engineering, information systems, and warehouse operations. The overhaul benefited Moen in many respects, not the least of which was improved productivity through automation.

During the late 1980s and early 1990s, Moen's product line diversified in both form and in function. Moen's faucets ranged from traditional cross-handled designs to sleek contemporary looks. Sinks made of Moenstone, "a high-tech, high-strength color-impregnated composite material," came in a wide variety of fashion colors and bowl configurations. The company also added specially designed faucets for the bar and laundry, as well as accessories like liquid soap dispensers and massage showerheads. The One-Touch faucet, a combination faucet and sprayer, and Riser spout, which lifted ten inches above the sink, combined practicality and fashion for the kitchen. The Monticello Collection of lavatory faucets, introduced in 1993, became the company's most successful product introduction of all time.

Between 1990 and 1994, Moen's sales nearly doubled. As it approached the turn of the 21st century, Moen counted competitive pricing, a strong reputation for quality, and good brand recognition among its strengths. Bruce Carbonari, president and CEO, pegged future growth on international sales, focusing corporate efforts on joint ventures in Asia, the Middle East, Mexico, and Central and South America. By the end of 1994, Moen had captured one percent of the competitive Japanese plumbing market. Carbonari expected increasing international sales to push his company over the $1 billion mark by the year 2000.

Principal Subsidiaries: Moen Inc. (Canada); Moen Japan K.K.; Moen de Mexico; HCG-Moen Corp. (Taiwan).

Further Reading:

Canedy, Dana, "Kitchen Sink, Too," *Plain Dealer,* August 17, 1994, p. 1C.

Gooley, Toby B., "Moen Catches the Retail Wave," *Traffic Management,* Vol. 33, October 1994, p. 40.

Lans, Maxine S., "Protecting Your Product's Shape," *Marketing News,* Vol. 28, March 14, 1994, p. 12.

Marsh, Simon, "Standard Screw Finds Diversification Rewarding," *Investment Dealers Digest,* March 31, 1969, p. 47.

Phillips, Lisa, "Faucet Sales Spout after Years in a Sink," *Advertising Age,* March 24, 1986, p. 34.

Sabath, Donald, "Stanadyne Renames Itself," *Plain Dealer,* October 4, 1989, p. 1C.

——, "Elyria Firm Will Be Acquired," *Plain Dealer,* July 21, 1990, p. 8C.

——, "New Moen Executive Sees Opportunities Overseas," *Plain Dealer,* December 6, 1994, p. 1C.

There's Only One Al Moen, Elyria, Ohio: Moen Incorporated, 1993.

—April Dougal Gasbarre

Nalco Chemical Corporation

One Nalco Center
Napierville, Illinois 60566-1024
U.S.A.
(708) 305-1000
Fax: (708) 305-2900

Public Company
Incorporated: 1928 as National Aluminate Corporation
Employees: 5,601
Sales: $1.35 billion
Stock Exchanges: New York
SICs: 2899 Chemicals & Chemical Preparations Not
   Elsewhere Classified; 2819 Industrial Inorganic Chemicals,
   Not Elsewhere Classified; 2860 Industrial Organic
   Chemicals; 2820 Plastics Materials & Synthetics; 5169
   Boiler Compounds & Chemicals; 7389 Water Treatment
   Equipment, Services & Supplies

With nearly one-fifth of the global market for water treatment chemicals, Nalco Chemical Company dominates that $3 billion industry. By making good on its corporate pledge to "find the customer need and fill it," Nalco expanded from a base in water treatment into the production and sale of specialty chemicals and devices used in pollution control, oil production and refining, steel making, energy conservation, paper-making, food production, and mining. In the increasingly regulated and efficiency-oriented 1990s, Nalco worked to provide its diverse industrial customers with the means to solve their problems. By the mid-1990s, water treatment products only constituted about one-third of annual sales, and the company ranked as one of the largest specialty chemical suppliers in the United States.

The merger that formed the National Aluminate Corporation came as the result of a natural synergy between the Chicago Chemical Company and the Aluminum Sales Corporation. The former company, organized in 1920 by Herbert A. Kern, had sold sodium aluminate to industrial plants for boiler feed-water treatment, while the latter, founded in 1922 by P. Wilson Evans, sold sodium aluminate to railroads for the treatment of water used in steam locomotives.

At its inception, Kern's Chicago Chemical Company marketed a water treatment product called Colline to industrial plants in the Chicago area. Unfortunately for the company, the chemical, while very effective on Chicago water, was not quite so effec-

tive on other water supplies. Kern found that water was not the same everywhere, and that treatments would therefore vary. He did, however, discover that the chemical compound sodium aluminate was more effective and more universally marketable than Colline. By 1922 Chicago Chemical Company began marketing Kern's Water Softener, KWS Sodium Aluminate. Kern contracted Evans' Aluminate Sales Corporation to supply the chemical for Chicago Chemical's water treatment business. Soon afterwards, however, the Chicago Chemical Company constructed a new plant in the Clearing Industrial District for the manufacture of sodium aluminate for both companies.

Nalco was formed in 1928 as the National Aluminate Corporation, the result of a merger between Chicago Chemical Company and Aluminate Sales Corporation, both of which manufactured and sold sodium aluminate, and some of the interests of the Aluminum Company of America (Alcoa), which held several patents on the manufacture of dry sodium aluminate. By 1929 the National Aluminate Corporation founded Visco Products Company to manufacture chemicals used in drilling oil wells. This company established National Aluminate within the oil industry. National's sales for the year 1929 totaled more than one million dollars.

In 1933 Emmett J. Culligan, then a chemist at National, persuaded Herbert Kern to allow the company to produce a water softening, gel-type chemical zeolite. Culligan was appointed manager of the new zeolite department at the Clearing Facility. The plant was ultimately forced to expand because of the large amount of space needed to manufacture the zeolite. Drying the material required several blocks of streets, leased from the Village of La Grange Park, Illinois. In 1935, after Emmett Culligan left National on friendly terms to start his own water softening company (now known as Culligan International), the company replaced the zeolites with more efficient synthetic ion exchange resins.

In 1937 the company constructed one of the first windowless, air-conditioned plants in the country, across the street from the old factory. National's sales for the year 1939, near the end of the Depression, had grown to more than $3.8 million. From the years 1940 through 1944 the company's sales grew rapidly. During World War II National Aluminate, which provided water treatment for steam locomotives, was classified as part of an essential war industry, thus keeping production at peak levels. Immediately after the war, when steam locomotives were replaced by diesel, National was forced to change its products and its market. The company developed combustion catalysts, coding system treatments, and fuel oil additives for diesel engines. In 1949 National Aluminate introduced a new diesel cooling system treatment in pellet form.

In the 1950s the company experienced a rapid expansion in both the domestic and international markets. In 1951 National incorporated its first foreign subsidiary, Nalco Italiana S.p.A., in Italy. By 1959 National had acquired several other foreign subsidiaries: Deutsche-Nalco-Chemie G.m.b.H. in Germany (1954); Nalco Espanola S.A. in Spain (1955); and Nalco Venezuela C.A. (1959).

Also in the 1950s, National added two new plants for catalyst production and oil field chemicals. To mark expansion into several new markets, National changed its railroad division's name to the transportation division. The company also penetrated the nuclear power field as a consultant on the land-based prototypes of the first atomic submarines, the first nuclear aircraft carrier, and the nation's first nuclear power plant at Shippingport, Pennsylvania.

In April of 1959, National Aluminate Corporation changed its name to Nalco Chemical Company. The name change signaled the company's expansion into new areas. By this time, Nalco manufactured a wide range of specialized chemicals in addition to sodium aluminate, the company's first product. By the end of the 1950s, its sales were approaching $50 million.

During the 1960s the company again expanded in size and scope. With its new polymer technology, Nalco maintained a solid position in the water treatment industry, and set standards in the areas of waste management and pollution control. In 1964 Nalco opened a new factory at Freeport, Texas, for the production of lead antiknock compounds for gasoline. The company employed a new electrolytic process recognized as a major achievement in chemical engineering technology. In October of that same year, Nalco's shares changed hands on the New York Stock Exchange.

Imperial Chemical Industries of the United Kingdom, or ICI, an important part of Nalco's development since the 1930s, was particularly instrumental in the company's growth in the second half of the 1960s. ICI and Nalco shared joint ventures in Katalco in the United States (1966), Nalfloc in Britain (1967), and Anikem in South Africa (1968). Katalco (which was subsequently sold) produced catalysts for the manufacture of synthetic natural gas, ammonia, and hydrogen. Anikem was the product of a merger between the operations of the Alexander Martin Company of Johannesburg, South Africa (acquired by Nalco in 1967) and part of the operations of another South African company. Nalco's sales for 1966 rose to $100 million, and increased to almost $160 million in 1969.

Because of increased business and growth opportunities, Nalco expanded and consolidated several of its domestic operations during the 1970s. The company established a separate Water Treatment Chemicals Group and a Pulp and Paper Chemicals Group within its Industrial division. The Transportation Chemicals Group's name was changed to Specialty Chemicals and became part of the Industrial division.

Nalco also sold or closed several of its operations during this period. The company sold its vegetation control business in 1974, and its Environmental Sciences Group in 1978. Industrial Bio-Test Laboratories, which was purchased in 1965 to conduct toxicological studies for governmental and industrial clients, discontinued operations in 1978 because of its inability to recover from a poor image following litigation and questions raised by two federal agencies regarding operation procedures.

Nalco's philosophy of consolidation and expansion continued into the 1980s. Worley H. Clark, elected president in 1982, emphasized acquisitions and new product development. To capture more of the world's markets, Nalco reorganized its International Division into three regions, including Nalco Europe, Nalco Pacific, and Nalco Latin America. Nalco also formed wholly-owned subsidiaries in Argentina, Ecuador, Japan, and

Hong Kong, and established a new affiliate, P.I. Nalco Perkasa, in Indonesia. The company also expanded its operations in Singapore and South Africa.

In 1984 the federal Environmental Protection Agency's restrictions on the use of lead antiknock compounds in gasoline (first announced in the late 1970s), in addition to the shrinking market for leaded gasoline, forced Nalco to discontinue its antiknock compound business. Production at the antiknock manufacturing plant in Texas was discontinued in 1985, and demolition and decontamination of the plant completed in 1988.

Nalco made several important acquisitions during the first half of the 1980s which allowed the company to penetrate new fields. In 1982 the company purchased Crescent Chemical, and in 1983 Nalco formed an Automotives Chemicals Group, both of which established the company in the automotive industry market. In June of 1985 Nalco also purchased the remaining 80 percent interest in Adco Products, a specialty chemicals manufacturer for the automotive, industrial, and construction industries, for $18 million in cash. In early 1986 the firm acquired Penray, a group of three companies which marketed a line of automotive chemicals to service professionals and automobile owners, for $15.6 million in cash.

Nalco's successes in the 1980s attracted much journalistic attention. In 1984 *Fortune* magazine named Nalco one of the thirteen "Corporate Stars of the Decade," based on the 21.5 percent return on shareholder's equity over the period of a decade. In 1985 *Forbes* magazine also commended Nalco's stock performance, with a five year return on shareholder's equity of 22.8 percent. A 1990 *Financial World* article attributed part of this success to the company's over 700 patents and its anti-licensing proclivity. This strategy helped Nalco cross the $1 billion annual sales mark in 1990 virtually debt-free.

In the aftermath of the accident at the Union Carbide plant in Bhopal, India, where a toxic gas leak killed 2,000 people and injured 15,000 in December of 1984, Nalco paid special attention to safety procedures. In August of 1985, for the first time in its history, Nalco opened its oldest and largest factory, the Clearing plant, for public inspection. Later in the decade, the company launched an internal safety program dubbed "PORT," for Plant Operations Review Teams. These groups were comprised of engineers and managers from various Nalco locations worldwide who made detailed inspections of physical plant, operations, and safety training and procedures, then made recommendations for improvements.

Nalco started the 1990s with a new president, 20-year company veteran E. J. Mooney. Although W. H. Clark relinquished Nalco's chief executive office as well in 1991, his status at the company and in the chemical industry did not diminish. He remained the industry's lead trade advisor to the American government, and made important contributions to the consideration of the North American Free Trade Agreement (NAFTA) and the inter-hemispheric General Agreement on Trade and Tariffs (GATT). The chemical industry acknowledged Clark's many contributions with the 1993 Chemical Industry Medal, and he retired in 1994.

Around this time, Nalco began to divest some of the divergent businesses acquired in the early 1980s, most notably the Penray

Companies and Day-Glo Color Corp. The proceeds of this asset sale were used to buttress international expansion in core businesses. In 1991, for example, the company bought the 50 percent interests of joint venture partner Imperial Chemical Industries plc in five overseas cooperatives.

Like many of its competitors in the recession-racked chemical markets of the early 1990s, Nalco utilized a variety of strategies to boost sales. The company's global team of about 2,200 sales representatives grew evermore attuned to increasing their customers' efficiency and helping them comply with stringent regulatory standards. In 1992, for example, Nalco developed a proprietary process to clean Mobil Oil Corp.'s crude oil tanks so that oil sludge previously categorized as hazardous waste could be recovered for other uses. The project thereby provided two benefits to Mobil at once: it eliminated the need to dispose of a hazardous waste and created a potential profit center.

Nalco further bolstered its sales through the use of new technology. In 1991, the company equipped 250 of its sales personnel with laptop computers on an experimental basis. The technology allowed its users to write contracts, close transactions, and place orders on-the-spot, with significantly fewer errors. Within six months, the leading-edge sales reps had chalked up $14 million in sales that could be directly credited to the hardware.

In 1994, Nalco formed a joint venture with Exxon Chemical Company that combined the partners' global chemicals businesses. Although some analysts doubted the short-term benefits of the enterprise, it did boost the company to the top position in the petrochemical industry segment, passing Petrolite, a long-time rival in that segment.

By the mid-1990s, Nalco had grown from a manufacturer of water treatment chemicals into one of the largest specialty chemicals companies in the United States. While the company had its share of disappointment in several markets, its plans for the remainder of the twentieth century included acquisitions and partnerships within its core competencies. By restructuring and bolstering its international holdings, Nalco Chemical Company planned to maintain and enhance its leading status.

Principal Subsidiaries: Aluminate Sales Corporation; Chicago Chemical Company; Board Chemistry, Inc.; East End Properties Corporation; Nalco Delaware; Nalco Foreign Sales Corporation (U.S. Virgin Islands); Nalco FT, Inc.; Visco Products Co.; Nalco International Sales Company; Nalco Leasing Corpo-

ration; Nalco Neighborhood Development Corporation; Nalco Resources Investment Company; Nalgreen Inc.; Oil Products & Chemical Company, Inc.; The Flox Company; Deutsche Nalco-Chemie, G.m.b.H. (Germany); Nalco Anadolu A.S. (Turkey); Nalco Applied Services of Europe B.V. (Netherlands); Nalco Argentina, S.A.; Nalco Australia Pty. Limited; Nalco Belgium N.V.; Nalco Canada, Inc.; Nalco Chemical A.B. (Sweden); Nalco Chemical B.V. (Holland); Nalco Chemical Company (Philippines) Inc.; Nalco Chemical Company (Thailand) Limited; Nalco Chemical Gesellschaft m.b.H. (Austria); Nalco Chemical (H.K.) Limited (Hong Kong); Nalco Chemii (Czechoslovakia); Nalco de Venezuela, C.A.; Nalco Espanola, S.A. (Spain); Nalco Europe B.V. (Netherlands); Nalco France; Nalco Italiana, S.p.A.; Nalco Limited (United Kingdom); Nalco Productos Quimicos de Chile S.A. (80 percent); Nalco Productos Quimicos de Chile Limitada (Brazil); Nalco Ecuador, S.A.; Nalco Egypt; Nalco GIAP-CHEM (Russia); Nalco Gulf Limited (Dubai); Nalco Hellas S.A. (Greece); Nalco Holdings Australia Pty. Limited; Nalco Investments Canada, Inc.; Nalco Investments Australia, Pty. Limited; Nalco Investments U.K. Limited; Nalco Japan Company, Ltd.; Nalco Kemiai Kft. (Hungary); Nalco Korea Co., Ltd. (South Korea); Nalco New Zealand, ltd.; Nalco Norge A/S (United Kingdom); Nalco Poland; Nalco Portuguesa (Q.I) Ltda.; Nalco South East Asia Pte. Limited (Singapore); Nalfleet, Inc. (United Kingdom); P.T. Nalco Perkasa (Indonesia); Taiwan Nalco Chemical Co., Ltd.; NCC Chemicals (Malaysia) SDN BHD; Quimica Nalco de Columbia S.A.; Suomen Nalco Oy (Finland); Nalco Saudi Company Ltd. (Saudi Arabia) (60 percent).

Further Reading:

Anderson, Earl, ''Chemical Industry Medalist W. H. Clark Speaks Out on Global Trade Issues,'' *Chemical & Engineering News,* October 11, 1993, pp. 11–14.

Baldo, Anthony, ''The Man Who Loves Patents,'' *Financial World,* May 29, 1990, pp. 58–59.

Davis, Gregory B., et. al., ''Crude Oil Tank-Cleaning Process Recovers Oil, Reduces Hazardous Wastes,'' *Oil-& Gas Journal,* December 13, 1993, pp. 35–39.

''Finding the Customer Need and Filling It:'' A History of Nalco Chemical Company, Napierville, Ill.: Nalco Chemical Company, 1990.

Gibson, W. David, ''Nalco Goes Back to Basics,'' *Chemical Business,* November 1992, pp. 11–14.

Hiatt, John T., ''Empowering the Global Sales Force,'' *International Business,* September 1994, pp. 16–20.

—updated by April Dougal Gasbarre

National Power PLC

Windmill Hill Business Park
Whitehill Way
Swindon
Wiltshire SN5 6PB
United Kingdom
(01793) 877777
Fax: (01793) 892781

Public Company
Incorporated: 1989
Employees: 5,097
Sales: £3.95 billion
Stock Exchanges: London New York
SICs: 4911 Electric Companies and Systems

National Power PLC is the largest of the three main electricity generating companies created from the break-up of the nationalized electricity industry in England and Wales. Carved out as a separate division of the Central Electricity Generating Board in 1989 as privatization loomed, National Power was incorporated as a public limited company (PLC) in 1990 and the majority of its shares were sold to the public a year later. National Power, Nuclear Electric, and PowerGen became the big three electricity generators in England and Wales. In the mid-1990s, National Power and PowerGen's market share was decreasing—and was expected to decline yet further—as the industry became more competitive. While National Power would likely continue to hold a significant niche in the home energy market, the company was also looking to allied ventures for new areas of growth, in particular the opportunities offered in international power markets.

Electricity was first harnessed for practical use in the United Kingdom in the late nineteenth century with the introduction of street lighting in 1881. By 1921 over 480 authorized but independent electricity suppliers had sprung up throughout England and Wales, creating a rather haphazard system operating at different voltages and frequencies. In recognition of the need for a more coherent, interlocking system, the Electricity (Supply) Act of 1926 created a central authority to encourage and facilitate a national transmission system; this "national grid" was achieved by the mid-1930s.

The state consolidated its control of the utility with the Electricity Act of 1947, which combined the distribution and supply activities of 505 separate bodies into 12 regional Area Boards,

at the same time assigning generating assets and liabilities to one government-controlled authority. A further Electricity Act, in 1957, created a statutory body, the Central Electricity Generating Board (CEGB), which dominated the whole of the electricity system in England and Wales; generator of virtually all the electricity in the two countries, the CEGB, as owner and operator of the transmission grid, supplied electricity to the Area Boards, which in turn distributed and sold within their regions.

This situation remained for 30 years, until 1987, when the government proposed to privatize the electricity industry. The proposal became the Electricity Act of 1989, and a new organizational scheme was unveiled. The CEGB was splintered into four divisions, destined to become successor companies: National Power, PowerGen, Nuclear Electric, and the National Grid Company (NGC). National Power and PowerGen were to share between them England and Wales's fossil-fueled power stations; Nuclear Electric was to take over nuclear power stations; and the NGC was to be awarded control of the national electricity distribution system. The 12 Area Boards were converted, virtually unchanged, into 12 Regional Electricity Companies (RECs), and these were given joint ownership of the NGC. The RECs' shares were the first to be sold to the public, at the end of 1990. The majority of National Power and PowerGen's shares were offered for sale the following year, though the government retained ownership of 40 percent of each of the new companies' shares.

In order to assess National Power's role within the electricity industry, it is helpful to understand how the system operates. The provision of electricity consists of four components: generation, transmission, distribution, and supply. In England and Wales in the 1990s, generation was the province of National Power, PowerGen, and Nuclear Electric, and an increasing number of independent generators and suppliers "imported" from France and Scotland. Transmission, the transfer of electricity via the national grid, was accomplished through overhead lines, underground cables, and NGC substations; distribution, or the delivery of electricity from the national grid to local distribution systems, was operated by the Regional Electricity Companies (RECs). Supply, a term distinct from distribution in the electricity industry, referred to the transaction whereby electricity is purchased from the generators and transmitted to customers. Under the terms of its license, National Power had the right to supply electricity directly to consumers, and in the mid-1990s was increasingly doing so, although its main customers were the RECs, who in turn sold the electricity on to the end users.

A new trading market was devised with the privatization scheme for bulk sales of electricity from generators to distributors: the pool. A rather complicated pricing procedure existed in the pool, according to which, each generating station offered a quote for each generating set for every half-hour of the day, based on the operating costs of that particular plant. The NGC arranged these quotes in a merit order—with the lowest price first—and made the decisions regarding which plant to call into operation based on the expected demand. The pool system was not relied upon exclusively, however, as the generators frequently agreed on contractual arrangements with distributors for a specified period of time as a means of mutual protection against fluctuations in the pool price.

National Power's position in the industry is a legacy of its comparative status it inherited with privatization. The undisputed leader of the industry, National Power provided nearly half the electricity supplied in England and Wales via its 40 power stations, boasting an aggregate Declared Net Capacity or Capability (DNC) of 29,486MW (a megawatt here defined as the generating capacity of a power station in any given half-hour). Its smaller rival PowerGen, in second place, had 18,764MW DNC. Nuclear Electric's figure was 8,357MW, the National Grid Company controlled 2,088MW, and British Nuclear Fuels PLC, the United Kingdom Atomic Energy Authority, and small independent generators together accounted for about 2,900MW. Another, though limited, source was provided by linkages with the Scottish and French electricity systems, with which import or export deals were sometimes agreed. National Power and PowerGen between them thus controlled some 78 percent of the electricity market in England and Wales, of which about 46 percent was held by National Power, with the majority of the rest controlled by Nuclear Electric.

Privatization of the utility was designed to promote a beneficial result through the free play of market forces. The introduction of competition in power generation, it was argued, would lead both to greater efficiency within the industry and to lower prices for the consumer. Within a few short years, however, concerns had arisen, as some critics of the scheme had predicted from the start. The creation of three big players holding such a significant majority of the electricity generating market was never likely to embody the purest form of free market operations.

In 1994, the industry watchdog, the Office of Electricity Regulation (Offer), became concerned about National Power and PowerGen's continuing dominance of the market. The market share of the big two had in fact declined since privatization, with National Power controlling some 33 percent and PowerGen holding less than 25 percent, but nonetheless rumors were rife that Offer would refer them to the Monopolies and Mergers Commission. After six months of deliberation, Offer stopped short of that proceeding, but the regulator did lay strictures on the two generating companies, requiring that they should use all reasonable endeavors to sell a specified amount of generating capacity—in the case of National Power 3,000–4,000MW, or 15 percent, of its total power output—and submit to price capping for a period of two years.

The demand to sell a portion of its holdings was expected to cause little hardship to National Power. Moreover, the issue of which plant to sell and when was up to the company's discretion, provided it complied with Offer's deadline of December 31, 1995. Thus the company would not be forced to make a disadvantageous sale. In preference to an outright sale, some speculated that National Power might arrange an asset exchange with a foreign power company. Another alternative under consideration was the demerger option, whereby a new company, designed to own and operate the capacity in question, could be created from a portion of National Power's capital holdings.

The required price caps, ironically, were likely to prove less burdensome to National Power and PowerGen than to the state-owned Nuclear Electric and to small independents, both existing and potential. While Offer's strictures caused the two largest players to lose around one-third of their market share, the companies retained their dominant position in the market. Na-

tional Power and PowerGen had, in effect, continued to control the establishment of pool prices, and this was unlikely to change to any significant degree. Residential customers, who purchased their electricity through the RECs, saw little change in their electricity bills, while most major industrial customers, who purchased straight from the pool, saw their prices fall 20 percent. While the potential for price hikes existed in long-term forecasts, given the costs of environmental clean-up, the company hoped to offset such increases with greater efficiency.

The government, apart from its concerns about fair competition and price, was especially eager to resolve any controversy or questions regarding National Power and PowerGen to clear the way for the sale of its remaining 40 percent share in each of the two companies. The sell-off to the public, in February 1995, raised a welcome £4 billion for the government, some £2.5 billion of which was attributable to National Power. Controversy dogged the two generators right to the end, however, as spiraling prices in the electricity pool, albeit over a period of only around a month, prompted Offer to delay publication of the share prospectus.

The electricity industry was slowly but dramatically changing in the 1990s. While plans were being laid to modernize and improve power generation, coal- and oil-fired plants remained the mainstay of the utility. Most of the stations National Power inherited after privatization were products of the 1960s and 1970s (with the notable exception of the 1980s-vintage Drax). British-mined coal remained, in 1995, the overwhelmingly dominant fuel source, but National Power, like others in the industry, was exploring a more diversified fuel base.

The company was slowly reducing the stockpiles of coal accumulated in the days of government ownership, when the CEGB bought more generously than necessary from the British Coal Corporation. Since privatization, National Power had already shut down some coal-fired plants. Some capability was made redundant by excess generating capacity, and more was jettisoned in favor of the trend toward combined cycle gas turbine plant (CCGT): the so-called "dash for gas." National Power's first CCGT plant, at Killingholme, South Humberside, was completed in 1993. One in North Wales followed in 1994, with another in Bedfordshire expected in 1995 and yet another, in Oxfordshire, in 1996. Moreover, a fifth CCGT plant was in the early planning stages. More closures of coal-fired plant were likely as the new CCGT stations came online.

Linked economic and environmental factors motivated the move to gas. Environmental improvements were urgently needed in the energy industry—the issue was too long ignored in the state sector. Regulations, emanating from both London and Brussels, were becoming increasingly stringent—and were making coal increasingly unattractive. Despite the availability of technology designed to reduce sulphur-dioxide emissions from coal-fired stations (the primary cause of acid rain), for example, it was often more economically advantageous to simply replace these stations with CCGT plants. The exception during this time was Drax, National Power's massive North Yorkshire coal-fired power station, which supplied approximately ten percent of England and Wales's electricity. In the biggest project of its kind in the world, National Power was cleaning up the plant through the implementation of flue gas desulphurization (FGD) retrofits, designed to significantly reduce sulphur dioxide emissions. The effort was begun even before privatization, was not expected to be completed until 1996. Costing an estimated £65.8 billion, the station was expected to result in a 90 percent reduction in harmful emissions.

To the dismay of the beleaguered British coal industry, National Power, like the other electricity generators, continued to look at the import of foreign coal for use in its stations. Foreign-mined coal was not only potentially cheaper but in general had a significantly lower sulphur content than its British counterpart, thus obviating the need for expensive desulphurization equipment.

With gas an increasingly popular and sensible option for the energy industry, National Power also took steps to ensure its own reliable and cost-effective supply; in 1991 alone the company arranged to buy the entire output from the Caister field in the North Sea, made a 15-year deal with Norwegian suppliers, and made another deal with Ranger Oil (UK). The company was also involved in gas exploration, having a 25 percent stake in a consortium led by Total Oil Marine, which was exploring a block in the southern North Sea. Even wind power was being investigated and employed, though on a very small scale as of the mid-1990s. The subsidiary National Wind Power Ltd. was established in 1991 and was expected to be producing 250MW by the end of the century.

National Power was also moving into the field of combined heat and power generation (CHP), another wave of the future for the energy industry. One of National Power's business units, National Power Cogen, was responsible for the development of schemes for such clients as Lancaster University, the chemical manufacturers Albright & Wilson Ltd., the paper manufacturers SCA, and Sterling Organics Ltd., makers of paracetemol.

National Power branched out into the industrial property business in 1993, leasing land at its Eggborough power station to an air separation plant, Air Gas Products. The mutually profitable idea behind the arrangement was that new factories, conveniently located, could tap directly into their power source, therefore rendering unnecessary the need for a middleman in the form of a regional electricity company.

National Power also looked to the international arena for its future growth. The CEBG's overseas activities in its state sector days were restricted almost exclusively to consulting projects carried out by the subsidiary British Electricity International Ltd. After privatization, with its share of the home market dwindling, National Power substantially boosted its international profile. The creation, via a 1993 internal restructure, of a full-fledged division within National Power devoted to researching and developing overseas business strategies and opportunities is indicative of the company's vision of its future. In 1993 the company moved into the United States with the purchase of American National Power for £103 million. A well-established and successful enterprise, American National Power operated in Virginia, Georgia, and New Jersey. National Power's other major foreign ventures included Portugal's Pego power station, owned by a consortium led by National Power, and a £64 million investment in an oil-fired power station project in Pakistan. While National Power's international presence was still young, the company was confident of its prospects. Independent financial commentators tended to agree. Blessed as the company was with healthy cash reserves, and

clearly aware of the tremendous potential of the international market, National Power could expect to be well compensated through such wise investments.

A look at National Power's 1995 sales figures showed a mixed but on the whole optimistic prospect. On one hand, the company's market share was much reduced and electricity prices were down. Furthermore, capital expenditure was up, due to investments in new plants and environmental improvements. Nevertheless, costs to the company were dramatically reduced, due to a rigorous, some might say ruthless, cost-cutting program implemented since privatization. Under the plan, rationalization and increased efficiency measures decisively chopped operational costs, fuel supply expenses were pared, and staff costs were drastically slashed (the pre-privatization work force of 17,000 was just over 5,000 in 1995). As a result, National Power saw consistently rising profits despite continually falling market share.

Controller of nearly half of Britain's electricity market at the end of 1990, National Power had only a third of that market four years later, and the company's share was expected to diminish still more as competition increases. Nonetheless, National Power would likely remain a significant force in U.K. power generation, as the company continued to improve and adapt to meet changing conditions in the energy industry. Furthermore, with a strong cash base to support an avowed and active interest in overseas projects, National Power was poised for international expansion.

Principal Subsidiaries: British Electricity International Ltd.; National Power International Holdings Ltd.; National Power International Ltd.; National Power (North) Ltd.; National Wind Power Ltd.; Seafield Resources PLC.

Further Reading:
''Bills Will Rise for Clean Electricity,'' *Guardian,* January 14, 1994.
''Customers Set to Benefit by up to £500m,'' *Financial Times,* February 12, 1994.
''Generators in Deal to Sell Plant and Reduce Prices,'' *Financial Times,* February 12, 1994.
''Investors Chronicle Survey: Electricity,'' *Investors Chronicle,* April 22, 1994.
''The Lex Column: Power Play,'' *Financial Times,* February 12, 1994.
Mortished, Carl, ''Regulator Forces Power Prospectus Rewrite,'' *The Times,* January 28, 1995, p. 25.
''National Power Beats Forecasts,'' *Lloyds List,* May 19, 1994.
''National Power Breathes Life into Factories,'' *Yorkshire Post,* March 11, 1994.
''National Power to Close Five Plants,'' *Independent,* April 1, 1994.
''National Power to Consider Job Cuts,'' *Independent,* May 19, 1994.
''No Stampede in Power Station Sale,'' *Financial Times,* February 12, 1994.
''Power Generators Meet Offer to Head off MMC Enquiry,'' *The Times,* January 24, 1994.
''Special Report on Competitive Power,'' *Daily Telegraph,* March 11, 1994.
''Survey of Drax—the Big Clean-Up,'' *Financial Times,* January 14, 1994.
''Tough Package of Not Much,'' *Independent,* February 12, 1994.
Waller, Martin, ''Options Row Mars Power Launch,'' *The Times,* February 7, 1995, p. 23.

—Robin DuBlanc

National Steel Corporation

4100 Edison Lakes Parkway
Mishawaka, Indiana 46545
U.S.A.
(219) 273-7000
Fax: (219) 273-7379

Majority Owned Subsidiary of Nippon Kokan K.K.
Incorporated: 1929
Employees: 9,711
Sales: $2.7 billion
Stock Exchanges: New York
SICs: 3312 Blast Furnaces & Steel Mills

The fourth largest steel producer in the United States, National Steel Corporation produces hot and cold rolled steel sheet and steel strip, tin mill products, and galvanized coated products. Selling its steel primarily to the automotive, container, construction, and pipe and tube industries, National Steel grew to become one the country's largest, most efficient steel producers in the mid-1990s.

Exactly two weeks after "Black Thursday" sent the American stock market plummeting, precipitating a decade-long depression that would cripple industrial production and impoverish much of the country's population, three steel companies banded together to form National Steel Corporation. In the two weeks bridging the stock market crash of October 24, 1929 and the merger of Weirton Steel Company, Great Lakes Steel Corporation, and certain subsidiaries of M.A. Hanna Company, United States securities were stripped of more than $40 billion of their value, sending the economy in a tailspin. In the coming three years, unemployment would swell from 1.5 million to 13 million persons—roughly one-third of the nation's work force—while industrial production of primary products such as steel would plunge 50 percent during the same period. Such was the deleterious economic climate pervading National Steel's birth, giving the $120 million steel producer an inauspicious start to its tenure as one of the largest steel producers in the country.

Difficult times were ahead, to be sure, but the amalgamation of the three steel operations gave National Steel a broad foundation from which to begin its climb into the upper echelon of the steel industry. Upon formation, the *New York Times* hailed National Steel as "a complete unit in the steel industry, [owner of] ore lands, vessels, coke ovens, and blast furnaces in addition to mills," giving praise to the steel company's complementary operations. Largest of the company's facilities was Weirton Steel's main steel plant which covered 295 acres of the company town created by Weirton Steel's founder and president, Ernest T. Weir, in Weirton, West Virginia. Befitting the prodigious size of his steel plant and its sizeable contribution to National Steel's operations, Ernest T. Weir was named National Steel's chairperson, with the president of Great Lakes Steel Corporation, George R. Finch, selected as the new steel concern's president, and George M. Humphrey, president of M. A. Hanna Company, selected to chair the company's executive committee. Organized as such, National Steel embarked on its roller-coaster ride in the frequently capricious steel industry, supported initially by facilities in Detroit, Cleveland, and Pittsburgh.

Financially, the company's first decade of existence was less than spectacular. From its formation in 1929 through 1932, National Steel's annual earnings slipped from $17.3 million to $6.6 million, falling as the severity of the nationwide economic slump intensified. Nevertheless, National Steel's management began expanding the steel concern's operations with decided fervor from the outset, strengthening the company's complementary and interdependent operations. By the beginning of 1930, the extensive expansion undertaken by one of M. A. Hanna Company's subsidiaries, Hanna Ore Mining Company, had boosted National Steel's iron ore holdings considerably, making National Steel the second largest holder of ore reserves in the country, trailing only the country's preeminent steel company, U.S. Steel. Before the year was through, National Steel acquired the Michigan Steel Corporation, a $10 million steel concern organized in 1922 by National Steel's president, George R. Finch. The acquisition of Michigan Steel, the first steel manufacturing company to be located in the Detroit area, bolstered National Steel's role as a provider of steel to the automobile industry, a relationship on which the steel company would rely for over the next 60 years.

By the time America's entrance into World War II in 1941 had formally put an end to the Great Depression, National Steel was generating roughly $140 million in annual sales. By the end of the 1940s, National Steel's annual sales volume would be considerably larger, reaching nearly $450 million. This growth was largely attributable to the great discrepancy between the economic conditions characterizing the 1930s and 1940s: the 1930s were disastrous years for many businesses; the 1940s, in contrast, were exceptionally robust. During the war, the U.S. War Production Board exhorted the steel industry to step up production to meet increasing war-time demand, and, after the war, President Harry S. Truman appealed to the industry to increase production capacity, making for a decade of encouraging growth for National Steel. By the end of the 1940s, the scope of National Steel's operations included nearly 400 coke ovens, six blast furnaces producing more than 3.25 million net tons of pig iron, steel mills, and sizeable iron ore and coal producing properties.

Over the course of its first two decades, National Steel had gained the reputation as one of the most profitable and efficient steel producers in the country, attributes National Steel's management sought to strengthen further in the steel industry's new, postwar era. The 1950s and the decades to follow, however, would bring increasing competition from foreign steel producers, as their production methods first equaled those of U.S. producers then eclipsed them in efficiency, and the new era would also witness the introduction of aluminum as a popular substitute for tin plate in the container industry. This latter development had direct ramifications for a company like National Steel, whose production of tin plate for the container industry ranked as its second largest source of income next to supplying the automobile industry with steel. To overcome both the insurgence of foreign steel producers and the emergence of aluminum as container material, National Steel would increase the efficiency of its operations and diversify into other business areas.

Although the company had spent substantial time and money to assure its facilities were the most modern and efficient, capital expenditures increased dramatically beginning in 1959 when National Steel initiated a four-year, $400 million expansion and modernization program. When the program was begun, National Steel ranked as the fifth largest steel producer in the United States; when the program ended in 1963, National Steel ranked as the fourth largest steel producer, accounting for seven percent of total finished steel shipments in the United States and generating nearly $850 million in annual sales. Up to this point, the company had never failed to show a profit during its 35 years of existence, and it had paid dividends without interruption for the same span, a remarkable record in the cyclical steel industry and a record no other major U.S. steel producer had achieved. In 1965 National Steel eclipsed the $1 billion dollar sales plateau, recording $1.1 billion in sales and producing 8.5 million tons of raw steel, prodigious sums for a prodigious force in the U.S. steel industry.

By this point, National Steel was no longer regarded as merely one of the most efficient steel companies in the nation; it stood alone as the industry's most efficient operator. Consistent attention to capital expansion and modernization had greatly contributed to the company's ascension, but much of its success was also attributable to the strategic location of it plants. The company's Detroit plant, which made sheet and strip steel for the city's auto industry, used its prime location to generate 40 percent of the company's total sales. The company's Weirton, West Virginia, plant produced tin plate for the container industry, accounting for 25 percent of sales volume, and the company's Chicago plant served the appliance and packing industries in Illinois and Indiana.

With these facilities supporting National Steel's solid position in the steel market, plus additional iron ore and coal holdings giving the company a vertically integrated approach to steel production, the company represented one of the leading forces in the industry. By the late 1960s, however, it had become apparent to the company's management that no matter how efficient its production facilities were, they could no longer flourish in the face of the steel industry's new challenges. Tin cans were rapidly losing ground to aluminum cans by this point, and, in response, National Steel joined the competition rather than directly opposing it. In May 1967 National Steel acquired 20 percent of Southwire Company's common stock as part of an agreement between the two companies to jointly build an aluminum smelter. Southwire, a pioneer in the production of wire, was seeking to vertically integrate its production processes but

lacked the financial wherewithal to build a smelter on its own, so National Steel footed much of the construction bill, and, through the jointly formed National-Southwire Aluminum Company, an aluminum plant was constructed. Located in Hancock County, Kentucky, the aluminum plant was completed in 1970, giving National Steel a foothold in the burgeoning market for aluminum.

That year, National Steel agreed to acquire Pittsburgh Aluminum Alloys Inc. and its sales affiliate, S & S Sales, for an undisclosed sum, further strengthening the company's stake in aluminum production. However, the diversification begun in the late 1960s never supplanted the company's production of tin plate nor its manufacture of steel for the automobile industry. A decade later, when National Steel embarked on a much more divergent diversification program, the company only derived a modest seven percent of its total sales from non-steel products, which included its interests in aluminum. Instead, the production of steel continued to be the company's mainstay business, and in 1971 that business became appreciably larger. With the acquisition of Granite City Steel Company in August 1971, National Steel surpassed Republic Steel Corporation to become the third largest steel producer in the United States and a secure member of the industry's elite.

Being one of the steel industry's largest companies also meant National Steel inherited some of the industry's ills. Mounting foreign competition, particularly from Japanese steel producers, had eroded the profit margins of domestic steel producers, making survival in the industry a difficult task. National Steel was not excluded from this debilitative development, positioned, ironically enough, as the most efficient U.S. producer yet dogged by shrinking profits. During this time, other major producers sought relief by diversifying into non-steel businesses, hoping to insulate their exposure to the contentious and cyclical industry forces. Armco Inc., for example, diversified into insurance, oil equipment, and engineering services, while another enormous steel concern, U.S. Steel, moved into petrochemicals. National Steel elected to enter into the financial services business. In 1979, when National Steel reported $4.2 billion in sales and earnings of $126.5 million, the company spent $241 million to acquire San Francisco-based United Financial Corporation, the seventh largest savings and loan holding company in the nation and parent of the 88-branch Citizens Savings & Loan. Two years later, National Steel increased its interests in the savings and loan industry, acquiring two troubled East Coast institutions, New York's $2.6 billion West Side Federal and Florida's $1.3 billion Washington Savings & Loan.

Although National Steel's diversification away from steel had followed a pattern established by other leading U.S. steel producers, the manner in which it had done so was markedly different than the company's competitors. In diversifying into non-steel businesses, Armco and U.S. Steel also withdrew a portion of their presence in the steel market. National Steel, on the other hand, did not retreat. The company coupled its move into financial services with an intensified reinvestment in steel production. Already the most mechanized domestic steel producer, National Steel boosted its capital spending in steel-related businesses 50 percent in 1980, pumping money into steel production automation to ensure a stable foundation from which to diversify.

Concurrent with its expansion and modernization program, National Steel also made a strategic shift, moving away from the steel market for cans and cars and into the markets for appliances, construction, railroad, and agricultural building products. Shortly after funnelling money into its steel businesses, however, National Steel's management initiated talks in March 1982 with the employees and management of its Weirton steel division about selling the division to the employees. National Steel's directors had decided to limit its future investment in the Weirton facility and instead invest in areas that offered a higher rate of return. Eight months later, in November 1982, Weirton Steel Corporation was organized to facilitate the spin-off of the division, and in May of the following year the Weirton employees acquired the division for $194.2 million.

After the sale, in September 1983, National Steel reorganized, becoming a wholly owned subsidiary of a holding company it had formed named National Intergroup, Inc. After restructuring, National Steel ranked as the sixth largest steel producer in the nation, having spun off the Weirton steel division, which had contributed 24 percent of the company's total sales and 12 percent of its net income. Five months after forming National Intergroup, National Steel began attracting suitors intent on acquiring the company's steel operations. First to bid for the company was industry giant U.S. Steel, which announced in February 1984 that it was willing to pay $575 million for the steel producing assets of National Intergroup. The following month, however, U.S. Steel abandoned the plan, withdrawing when it became clear that the federal government would attack the acquisition and perhaps nullify it on antitrust grounds. Next came a Japanese steel manufacturer, Nippon Kokan K. K. (NKK), which announced in April 1984 that it was in the process of purchasing a 50 percent stake in National Steel for $292 million. The deal was completed in August, giving NKK and National Intergroup dual control over National Steel.

Soon after NKK completed its acquisition of National Steel, however, business conditions soured and profitability plunged at National Steel. The mid- and late 1980s proved to be tumultuous years for the steel maker, as it struggled to combat production problems and low employee morale. Compared to NKK's steel mills in Japan, National Steel, which had once rivaled the Japanese in efficiency and quality, recorded ten times as many unexpected shutdowns and rejected ten to 12 percent more steel.

During this time, National Intergroup decided to sell a 20 percent interest in National Steel and would eventually divest the remaining shares, as it began to focus on building its newly formed wholesale drug distribution business. Although National Steel continued to struggle in the early 1990s, it had retaken its fourth place position in the U.S. steel industry by 1993.

In 1990 and 1992, joint ventures with Dofasco Inc., in Windsor, Ontario, and with Bethlehem Steel Corporation in Jackson, Mississippi, to build steel coating facilities were expected to help the steel maker begin its turnaround. Despite its laggard performance during the 1980s and early 1990s and increasing competition from highly efficient steel mini-mills, National Steel was firmly established as one of the steel industry's leaders, its long tenure in the industry providing encouragement that its future held more profitable times in store.

Principal Subsidiaries: American Steel Corporation; NSL, Inc.; National Coal Mining Company; National Acquisition Corporation; Mathies Coal Company (86%); NS Land Company; Natland Corporation; Natcoal, Inc.; National Steel Pellet Company; National Caster Acquisition Corporation; National Caster Operating Corporation; National Casting Corporation; Hanna Furnace Corporation; National Mines Corporation; Delray Connecting Railroad Company; Mid-Coast Minerals Corporation; National Ontario Corporation.

Further Reading:

Ansberry, Clare, "National Steel's Troubleshooter Aims to Revive the Firm's Lagging Fortunes," *Wall Street Journal,* July 30, 1990, p. B8.
Chakravarty, Subrata, "Blast Furnace Banker," *Forbes,* October 26, 1981, p. 95.
"Companies Take Merger Action," *New York Times,* November 3, 1970, p. 55.
"Michigan Steel to Go to National," *New York Times,* November 26, 1930, p. 31.
"National Steel Adds Ore," *New York Times,* January 2, 1930, p. 46.
"National Steel: Building a Base Inside and Outside the Industry," *Business Week,* March 3, 1980, p. 43.
"National Steel Charter," *New York Times,* November 9, 1929, p. 28.
"National Steel Corporation," *Wall Street Transcript,* July 9, 1973, p. 33,740.
"National Steel Initiates Talks on Selling Weirton Unit in West Virginia to Workers," *Wall Street Journal,* March 3, 1982, p. 16.
"National Steel Profits Display Solid Strength," *Barron's,* June 1, 1964, p. 24.
O'Boyle, Thomas F., "U.S. Steel Corp., National Cancel Plan to Merge," *Wall Street Journal,* March 12, 1984, p. 2.
Schellhardt, Timothy D., "Japan Firm Buying Half National Steel Seeks Orders From Foreign Auto Makers," *Wall Street Journal,* August 23, 1984, p. 7.
"Steel," *Forbes,* July 1, 1963, p. 30.

—Jeffrey L. Covell

Neiman Marcus Co.

1618 Main St.
Dallas, Texas 75201
U.S.A.
(214) 741-6911

Wholly Owned Subsidiary of Neiman Marcus Group, Inc.
Incorporated: 1907
Employees: 10,600
Sales: $1.56 billion
SICs: 5311 Department Stores; 5961 Catalog and Mail-Order
  Houses

The name Neiman Marcus is practically synonymous with upscale retailing in the United States. In the mid-1990s, Neiman Marcus Co. operated as a division of the Neiman Marcus Group, which included Bergdorf Goodman, another high-end retail operation, and Contempo Casuals, a 247-store chain catering to the needs of younger working women. The Neiman Marcus division included both the 27 stores bearing the famous Neiman Marcus name, and NM Direct, which sells through the Neiman Marcus and Horchow specialty catalogs. For much of the twentieth century, Neiman Marcus has been the clothing store of choice for many of the nation's most fashion-conscious people.

From the very beginning, the founders of Neiman Marcus aimed high. The original store was opened in Dallas in 1907. Its proprietors were Herbert Marcus, his sister Carrie, and Carrie Neiman's husband, A. L. Neiman. All three were working in various retail positions in the Dallas area around the turn of the century. Frustrated by their dead-end jobs, Marcus and Neiman decided to strike out on their own. The pair moved to Atlanta in 1905 to start a sales promotion and advertising business. The venture was quite successful, and they were offered a lucrative buy-out deal after only two years of operation. Given the choice between $25,000 cash or the Missouri franchise for Coca-Cola and some stock in that young company, they opted for the cash. In retrospect, that decision cost them a fortune, as Coke went on to become the Real Thing. In taking the cash, however, they acquired the seed money to launch the first Neiman Marcus store.

Neiman and Marcus returned triumphantly to Dallas in 1907, and immediately set out to open a store that sold the finest women's clothing money could buy. The store was lavishly furnished and stocked with clothing of a quality that was not commonly found in Texas. Within a few weeks, the store's initial inventory, mostly acquired on a buying trip to New York made by Carrie, was completely sold out. Oil-rich Texans, welcoming the opportunity to flaunt their wealth in more sophisticated fashion than was previously possible, flocked to the new store. In spite of a nationwide financial panic set off only a few weeks after its opening, Neiman Marcus was instantly successful, and its first several years of operation were quite profitable.

In 1913 the original Neiman Marcus store, and most of its merchandise, was destroyed by a fire, the first of several in the company's history. Within about two weeks, however, the store re-opened at a temporary site nearby, and construction was quickly begun on a new permanent location. With capital raised through the sale of stock to a handful of manufacturing companies, the new building was ready for business by the autumn of 1914. In its first year at the new building, Neiman Marcus recorded a profit of $40,000 on sales of $700,000, nearly twice the totals reached in its last year at the original location.

Business at Neiman Marcus got better and better over the next several years, as money from oil, cattle, and cotton continued to flow into Texas. Throughout this period, the store maintained its commitment to extravagance, lining the aisles with the fanciest merchandise that could be found. Gradually, the store's reputation expanded beyond the borders of Texas, and soon glamorous types from Hollywood, New York, and even Europe were making special trips to Dallas to shop at Neiman Marcus.

In 1926 Al and Carrie Neiman were divorced, and Neiman's interest in the store was bought out by the Marcus family. The Marcuses remained at the top of the company's management for the next sixty years. Stanley and Edward Marcus, two of Herbert's sons, joined the company in 1926. A big expansion project at the store was completed in 1927, following the acquisition of some property next door. As a result, the store's capacity was nearly doubled. Neiman Marcus added men's clothing to its offerings with the 1928 opening of the Man's Shop. By 1929, the store's net sales had reached $3.6 million.

The onset of the Depression forced Neiman Marcus to shift its strategy. During the 1930s, the company began to include less expensive clothing lines in its inventory in hopes of keeping customers whose fortunes had taken a turn for the worse. At the same time, the store continued to stock the pricier, high-end items that made it famous and it continued to attract wealthy Texans. Company lore from this era tells of a barefoot teenage girl walking confidently into the store and ordering thousands of dollars worth of merchandise. Her father had just struck oil, and her first impulse was to head straight for Neiman Marcus. By striking a balance between upper-crust fashions and more moderate ones, Neiman Marcus was able to maintain its elite reputation while also broadening its customer base. This successful transition to a more democratic clientele enabled the company to sustain its impressive growth rate, and by 1938 annual sales had broken the $5 million mark. Along the way, the store's Man's Shop was expanded, first in 1934 and again in 1941.

The move to include lower-priced merchandise accelerated during the 1940s. World War II brought hundreds of high-paying defense manufacturing jobs to the Dallas area. To the female workers and the wives of their male counterparts, shopping at Neiman Marcus was like a dream come true. The Marcuses were quick to stock their store with merchandise that was affordable to this new wave of middle class customers. Between 1942 and 1944, sales at Neiman Marcus grew from $6 million to $11 million. Still, the company was able to cultivate its special relationship with the super-rich, and the store took on a sort of split personality. This trend increased even further at the war's end, as more companies opened offices in Dallas, and young families with junior executive salaries settled in.

The immediate postwar years saw many changes at Neiman Marcus. Shortly after the war's end Marcus's two other sons, Herbert, Jr. and Lawrence, joined the company. In 1946 Neiman Marcus suffered the second major fire in its history. Despite substantial damage to both the building and its merchandise, the store was closed for only five days. Even with the loss of those peak Christmas shopping days, the store recorded its best season to date that year. Herbert Marcus, Sr. died in 1950, and Carrie Neiman died just two years later, leaving Stanley Marcus in charge of the company's operations.

Stanley Marcus led the company in a period of rapid expansion during the 1950s. In 1951 a second store was opened at Preston Center in the suburbs of Dallas. In 1952 a new service building was opened to handle merchandise for both stores. And in 1953 a major renovation project added a fifth and a sixth floor to the Dallas store. In 1955 Neiman Marcus made its move into the Houston market. Rather than take on the expense of a new building, the company merged an existing store, Ben Wolfman's, into its operation. The company's reputation for lavish display grew along with its stores, as the company inaugurated the annual Neiman Marcus Fortnight in 1957. The Fortnight was a presentation of fashions and culture from a particular country, held in late October and early November of each year. Another popular annual publicity stunt was launched in 1959. Beginning that year, an extraordinary His and Hers gift selection was included in each Neiman Marcus Christmas catalog. His and Hers gifts over the years have included such spectacular items as submarines, dirigibles, and robots.

Another generation of Marcuses came on board in 1963, when Stanley's son Richard Marcus joined the company as a buyer. The following year, fire devastated the main Dallas store, again during the peak Christmas shopping season. Once again, the store was reopened quickly, and the repair work included improvements to the store's appearance. In 1965, with the population of suburban Dallas growing by leaps and bounds, the Preston Center store was closed, and a new store, more than twice as big, was opened at NorthPark Center, also in the Dallas suburbs. Another branch was opened in nearby Fort Worth around that time as well. By 1967 the four Neiman Marcus stores in operation were generating annual sales of $58.5 million, and the company's profit for that year was in excess of $2 million.

Neiman Marcus ceased being a family business in 1968, when the company was merged into Broadway-Hale Stores, Inc., a West Coast retail chain with 46 stores and revenue of $457 million. The merger enabled Neiman Marcus to expand at a much faster pace than would have been possible as an indepen-

dent entity. Over the next decade-and-a-half, the chain grew at a rate of about one store a year. With the opening of stores in California, Florida, and several other states during the 1970s, Neiman Marcus became a coast-to-coast operation. Atlanta; St. Louis; Northbrook, Illinois; Washington, D.C.; and White Plains, New York were among the other places to receive new Neiman Marcus stores during this period. Although this quick proliferation lessened Neiman Marcus's exclusive image in the eyes of some customers, the major loss of lustre that some feared would accompany its marriage to a less ritzy chain did not occur.

Meanwhile, changes and expansion were taking place at Neiman Marcus's Texas strongholds, too. The Dallas service center was dramatically enlarged in 1973, and in 1977 a new store at Ridgmar Mall replaced the previous Fort Worth location. In 1975 Stanley Marcus became executive vice president of Carter Hawley Hale Stores, Inc. (formerly Broadway-Hale), in charge of its specialty store division, which included Neiman Marcus. Son Richard was named chairman and CEO of Neiman Marcus in 1979. By 1980, the year the company opened its first store in the Northeast, annual sales were in the neighborhood of $350 million.

The nationwide expansion of Neiman Marcus proceeded most quickly between 1979 and 1984, when the chain doubled in size to 21 stores. By 1984, however, it was clear that not all of the new stores were performing as well as expected against rivals like Bloomingdale's and Sak's Fifth Avenue. At that point parent Carter Hawley Hale pulled in the reins on the chain's growth. In 1984 a hostile takeover bid for Carter Hawley was launched by retail chain The Limited, which offered to buy the company for $1.1 billion. In battling against the takeover, Carter Hawley found a white knight in General Cinema Corporation, a company whose $1 billion in revenue came from soft drink bottling and movie theaters. General Cinema bailed Carter Hawley out by purchasing 38.6 percent of the company's voting stock.

Two years later, The Limited teamed up with shopping center magnate Edward DeBartolo to launch a second attempt at Carter Hawley. This time, the defense involved a corporate restructuring that included spinning off Carter Hawley's specialty store division into an independent, publicly traded entity called Neiman Marcus Group. In exchange for its Carter Hawley stock, General Cinema was awarded 60 percent interest in the new company, which consisted of not only the Neiman Marcus stores, but also of exclusive New York retailer Bergdorf Goodman and the 200-store Contempo Casuals chain. Neiman Marcus stores contributed about three-fourths of the Group's sales power.

As General Cinema sought to return Neiman Marcus to its dominant position among upper end specialty retailers, Allen Questrom was named president and CEO of Neiman Marcus Stores, replacing Richard Marcus and drawing the final curtain on the Marcus dynasty. By 1990, the Neiman Marcus Group, led by Neiman Marcus Stores, was General Cinema's most important money-maker, contributing about 90 percent of GC's $92 million in operating profit. Questrom resigned his position in February of that year and was succeeded as president and CEO of Neiman Marcus stores by Terry Lundgren.

A new round of expansion began at Neiman Marcus under Lundgren. New stores were opened in Denver in 1990; Minneapolis and Scottsdale, Arizona in 1991; and Troy, Michigan (a Detroit suburb) in 1992. In 1993 Lundgren was given the title of chairman, while remaining CEO. Gerald Sampson, formerly with The May Department Stores Company, was named president and chief operating officer of Neiman Marcus Stores. For that year, the company recorded revenues of $1.45 billion, a 12.7 percent jump over the previous year. Part of this success during a tough retail climate resulted from an increased emphasis on big-name designer labels, such as Calvin Klein, Georgio Armani, and Donna Karan.

As the 1990s rolled on, Neiman Marcus continued its attempts to attract new, younger customers, while maintaining its commitment to meet the needs of its core, upscale clientele. Toward this end, NM Workshop boutiques that focused on career wardrobes were added at several Neiman Marcus locations. In addition, construction was begun on a new Neiman Marcus store in Short Hills, New Jersey, in 1994, and other stores in New Jersey and Pennsylvania were planned. 1994 also brought another reshuffling among executives. Lundgren left the company for a position at Federated Department Stores Inc. in February. The vacated chairman and CEO spots at Neiman Marcus were filled by Burton Tansky, who formerly held those titles at Bergdorf Goodman.

In his 1974 book *Minding the Store,* Stanley Marcus asserted that a company's quality standards inevitably decrease as its number of branches increases. Since that time, Neiman Marcus has managed to thwart its longtime leader's axiom through both good and bad economic periods. Despite its geographic spread and the more populist range of its merchandise, Neiman Marcus's reputation as the store of choice for America's elite remains more or less intact.

Further Reading:

"Big Deal in Big D," *Newsweek,* November 4, 1968, p. 94.

Deutsch, Claudia H., "Neiman-Marcus Minds the Store," *New York Times,* September 4, 1988, p. F4.

Ferry, John William, *A History of the Department Store,* New York: MacMillan, 1960, pp. 161–168.

Haber, Holly, "Winning Big in Designer," *Women's Wear Daily,* October 27, 1993, pp. 8–9.

Harris, Roy J., and Stipp, David, "Carter Hawley Blocks Takeover Attempt With Plan to Spin Off Its Specialty Stores," *Wall Street Journal,* December 9, 1986, p. 3.

"History of Neiman Marcus," Dallas: Neiman Marcus Co., 1992.

Lohr, Steve, "Neiman-Marcus Testing Northeast," *New York Times,* September 4, 1980, p. D1.

Marcus, Stanley, *Minding the Store: A Memoir,* Boston: Little Brown, 1974.

Mason, Todd, "That Neiman-Marcus Mystique Isn't Traveling Well," *Business Week,* July 8, 1985, pp. 44–45.

"The Merchant Prince of Dallas," *Business Week,* October 21, 1967, pp. 115–118.

Montgomery, Leland, "General Cinema: The Value of Camouflage," *Financial World,* September 1, 1992, p. 17.

Pereira, Joseph, "Neiman-Marcus Names Questrom to Head Chain," *Wall Street Journal,* August 15, 1988, p. 21.

"A Store that Serves Two Markets," *Business Week,* September 19, 1953, p. 136.

Strom, Stephanie, "New Neiman Marcus Head Is Named," *New York Times,* April 22, 1994, p. D4.

Tolbert, Frank X., *Neiman-Marcus, Texas,* New York: Henry Holt and Co., 1953.

—Robert R. Jacobson

News America Publishing Inc.

1211 Avenue of the Americas
New York, New York 10036
U.S.A.
(212) 852-7000
Fax: (212) 852-7147

Wholly Owned Subsidiary of The News Corp. Ltd.
Incorporated: 1973
Employees: 700
Sales: $120 million
SICs: 2711 Newspapers; 2721 Periodicals

News America Publishing Inc. was established in 1973 as the American arm of The News Corp. Ltd., Rupert Murdoch's multinational network of newspapers. At one time Murdoch's News America Publishing holdings included tabloid newspapers in New York, Chicago, and Boston, a weekly national tabloid newspaper, and a stable of magazines and other periodicals. During the 1980s Murdoch's attention turned from print journalism towards the establishment of a global communications and entertainment empire. He sold almost all of his American publications to finance television and film enterprises and to reduce the News Corp.'s burdensome debt. By the spring of 1994 there were only two publications left in News America Publishing: the *New York Post,* a daily newspaper, and *Mirabella,* a women's magazine. (*TV Guide* was being held in another Murdoch subsidiary, News America Publications Inc.) And, in early 1995, the *Mirabella* magazine was sold off.

By the time Murdoch turned his attention to the United States, he owned 80 newspapers and 11 magazines, television and radio stations, and printing, paper, and shipping companies in Great Britain, Australia, and New Zealand. Most of his newspapers fed the public a steady diet of sensationalism, heavily loaded with sex and crime stories.

One of Murdoch's first American purchases took place in 1973, when he bought the morning *San Antonio Express* and afternoon *San Antonio News* for $19.7 million. The *Express* had no direct competition, but the *News* had a bigger, more popular afternoon rival in the *San Antonio Light,* a Hearst Corp. paper. Using the formula he had employed in the past, Murdoch crammed the *News* with lurid stories and heavily promoted puzzles and contests. One headline, "Killer Bees Move North," came to be considered a classic example of the Murdoch brand

of journalism. He also introduced Wingo, a form of bingo that distributed prizes and demanded daily readership; it also became a feature of Murdoch newspapers in New York, Boston, and Chicago.

In two years Murdoch lifted *News* daily circulation from 61,000 to 76,000. However, he learned that in the United States circulation did not necessarily translate into profit, because advertising accounted for an average of 75 percent of gross revenues, and analysts contended that most advertisers were looking for customers more affluent than the typical Murdoch reader. Murdoch then redirected the *News* toward the higher end of the market and eventually outstripped the *Light* in circulation as well. The San Antonio papers were profitable by 1983. In 1992 Murdoch sold them to the Hearst Corp., which then closed the *Light,* for $185 million.

Murdoch invested $9 million to launch the *National Star* (later abbreviated to the *Star)* in 1974 as a rival to the established weekly tabloid the *National Enquirer.* Bringing in seasoned Australian and British associates, Murdoch filled the *Star* with the kind of raunchy stories that were a feature of his Sunday London paper *News of the World.* The *Enquirer,* though, once a specialist in articles that prominently featured elements of sex and gore, had toned down its stories to find a lucrative niche in supermarkets. The *Star,* too, shifted its emphasis to features about Hollywood personalities and dieting, and columns by psychics and astrologers, in order to challenge the *Enquirer's* market. By the early 1980s the *Star* had a weekly circulation of four million—almost as high as that of the *Enquirer*—and was recording a profit of about $12 million a year. It was sold to G.P. Group, publisher of the *Enquirer,* in 1990 for $200 million and an 80 percent stake in the newly formed Enquirer/Star Group, which brought about $400 million in a 1991 public offering of stock.

Murdoch bought the *New York Post* in 1976 in order to establish a presence in a city that was not only the nation's media capital but also the principal residence for himself and his wife and children. Founded in 1801 by Alexander Hamilton, the *Post* (originally the *Evening Post)* is the oldest continuously operating daily newspaper in the United States. Although its editors in chief included the poet William Cullen Bryant (1829–78) and the German-American political leader Carl Schurz (1881–83), the *Evening Post* was overshadowed by other newspapers and never achieved circulation of more than 20,000 in the nineteenth century. It later became a supporter of the Democratic Party and had Franklin D. Roosevelt among its stockholders. Dorothy Schiff, heiress to a banking fortune, bought the *Post* in 1939, when its daily circulation was 250,000. She turned the *Post* into a tabloid and kept it the voice in New York City for liberal politics, but was unable to make it profitable.

Murdoch bought the *Post* from her for about $30 million and began emphasizing stories like the notorious "Son of Sam" murder case. Another Murdoch-inspired front-page headline, "Headless Boy in Topless Bar," found its way into journalistic legend. Murdoch also began dabbling in politics, with immediate success. He endorsed Jimmy Carter in 1976 and backed him against Ted Kennedy's 1980 attempt to deny him renomination. An Australian airline partly owned by Murdoch received a $290-million loan from the U.S. Export-Import Bank four days after the *Post* endorsed Carter in the New York Democratic Party primary. Murdoch, however, swung his support to Ronald Reagan in the general election that year. Murdoch also endorsed Edward Koch's campaign to become mayor of New York in 1977 and consequently had a friend in city hall for 12 years.

A political writer said in 1984 that "Murdoch doesn't just endorse you, he campaigns for you." According to a *Wall Street Journal* article, the *Post* "was blatantly supportive" of New York governor Hugh Carey's successful 1978 bid for reelection, after which Carey's administration granted a multimillion-dollar contract to run the state's keno and lottery operations to Leisure System Inc., whose chairman was Murdoch. After Mario Cuomo was elected governor in 1982 despite the *Post*'s opposition, the contract was withdrawn.

Soon after he bought the *Post* Murdoch also acquired the weekly newspaper *Village Voice* and his first two American magazines, *New York* and *New West,* for about $10 million. Murdoch did not interfere with the political viewpoint of the profitable *Village Voice*; sold in 1985, it brought $55 million. *New West,* a California regional magazine, was sold for $3.5 million in 1980. *New York* remained in the Murdoch stable until 1991, when it was sold in a package with other magazines.

In 1977 Murdoch's Australian-based holding company, then called News Ltd., held 48 percent of his British combine News International Ltd. The News Ltd. and News International Ltd. companies each held half of News America Publishing and The City Post Publishing Corp., publisher of the *Post.* Ownership of New York Magazine Co. was split between City Post Publishing and News America Publishing. In a *New York Times* interview, Murdoch explained, "It's like a partnership. In this way, a central bank in London or in Australia can't order you to pay dividends, since you don't have control stock [i.e., majority control]. It means you can plow back profits."

Donald Kummerfeld became president and chief operating officer of News America Publishing in 1978. He mandated stricter budgets, quarterly budget reviews, and a computerized system for dealing with all the currencies in which the company traded. Although it lost money until 1983, largely because of the *Post,* the worth of News America Publishing grew from about $300 million when he became president to nearly $2 billion when he left in 1985. Much of this sum was due to the success of the *Star,* whose annual profits exceeded those of any other Murdoch publication in the United States.

News America Publishing's success did not extend to reviving the *Post,* which lost about $150 million in its first decade of operation under Murdoch. In the first two years its circulation rose from 485,000 to 960,000, but it could not displace the *Daily News* as the city's chief tabloid. It had difficulty attracting advertisers as well. In 1983 the *Post*'s share of advertising in New York newspapers fell to 7.6 percent from 11.3 percent in 1977.

According to Murdoch biographer William Shawcross, the press baron finally decided that the kind of journalism he practiced in Australia and Britain would not work in New York because there was no "cheeky working class" to buy papers. He concluded, "This is a middle-class city. Everybody in this country wants to get ahead, get a piece of the action. That's the

fundamental difference between the Old World and the New World." Nevertheless, the *Post* remained his pet project. He ran his global operations from an office at the newspaper and, according to an editor, often would "critique the paper the next morning picture by picture, headline by headline."

In 1982 News America Publishing bought the barely breathing Boston *Herald-American* from the Hearst Corp. for $1 million plus an additional $7 million out of future profits, if any. Shortening the name of the newspaper to the *Herald,* Murdoch took dead aim at the city's dominant paper, the *Globe.* The *Herald* became known for its aggressive local reporting of politics and crime and its relentless criticism of Senator Ted Kennedy, a target of Murdoch's increasingly right-wing political views. Circulation rose by 150,000 in two years and reached a peak of 365,000 in 1988. The *Herald* became profitable in 1986 but was unable to remain so.

News America Publishing bought the Chicago *Sun-Times* for about $90 million in 1983. It was the kind of acquisition Murdoch relished, a tabloid pitted against the established local newspaper, the *Chicago Tribune.* Sent to oversee the paper, Charles Wilson, deputy editor of the *Times of London,* was met by fierce hostility from the editorial staff. "It was a classic Murdoch-monster-myth situation," he later told Shawcross. "I spent my time trying to convince the staff that Murdoch was not Satan, that we were not going to make the *Sun-Times* into the *National Enquirer.*" A later study found that under Murdoch management news about government affairs was cut, while space given to local stories and coverage of celebrities, entertainment, accidents, disasters, and "*Sun-Times* self-promotion" increased. Annual profits rose from $3 million to $9 million before the *Sun-Times* was sold in 1986 for $145 million.

In 1984 News America Publishing acquired a group of 13 business publications related to travel and aviation from the Ziff-Davis Publishing Co. for $350 million. The aviation group was sold to McGraw-Hill Inc. in 1987 for more than $50 million. The travel and hotel publications were sold in 1989 for $825 million to Reed International P.L.C.

Other Murdoch magazine acquisitions included *New Woman,* purchased in 1984 for $23 million. News America also joined with the French publisher Hachette S.A. to launch *Elle,* a women's magazine, in 1985. It became a hit, reaching a circulation of 825,000; Murdoch's sold his half-interest in the magazine for $160 million in 1988. Other start-ups included *Premiere, European Travel & Life, Automobile,* and *Mirabella,* a women's magazine. *In Fashion* and *Sportswear International* were acquired for an undisclosed sum in 1988, while *Soap Opera Digest* was purchased for about $70 million in 1989. Shortly thereafter, News America commenced publication of *Soap Opera Weekly.* In October 1988 News Corp. bought Triangle Publications, Inc. from Walter Annenberg for a whopping $2.83 billion. This acquisition brought with it *TV Guide, The Daily Racing Form,* and *Seventeen.*

A 1986 News Corp. disclosure document listed not only various publishing properties as subsidiaries of News America Publishing but also Skyband, Inc., Murdoch's satellite-television venture and Fox, Inc., a media giant that included the recently-acquired Twentieth Century Fox and the Fox television network. This subordination of Fox to News America Publishing—also listed in a 1992 company prospectus—appears to have been made for accounting convenience, for it is unlikely that a Hollywood mogul as powerful as Barry Diller (Fox chairman and chief executive officer, 1985–92) reported to the president of News America Publishing. These corporate relationships created some interesting conflicts; Diller was said to have complained that movie stars were not prepared to work for Fox while simultaneously being abused by the tabloid mentality that dominated some of News America Publishing's properties.

In News Corp.'s annual reports, these enterprises were listed separately in a breakdown of profit-and-loss figures. News America Publishing (excluding the Boston and Chicago papers and *New York*) made a profit of $72.2 million in 1986 and $70.2 million in 1987 in Australian dollars ($48.5 million and $49.1 million in U.S. dollars). The 1988 profit was given as A$45 million (U.S. $35.2 million), but in the 1989 annual report the 1988 profit was retrospectively converted into a loss of A$50.4 million (U.S. $39.4 million). The 1989 News America Publishing figure, which did not include recently acquired Triangle Publications, indicated a loss of A$240.8 million (U.S. $191.1 million). With the Triangle publications included in News America Publishing, however, there was a 1990 profit of A$299.5 million (U.S. $234 million). In the 1991 annual report, Triangle's profits were again listed separately, and News America Publishing incurred a loss of A$238.7 million (U.S. $186.5 million). This loss was increased in the 1992 annual report to a retrospective A$423.4 million (U.S. $330.8 million).

Meanwhile pressure in Congress—much of it from Senator Ted Kennedy—forced Murdoch to comply with a Federal Communications Commission rule that made him choose between his Boston and New York newspapers and his Boston and New York television stations. Murdoch eventually was allowed to place his Boston station in an independent trust but sold the *Post* to Peter Kalikow, a real-estate developer, in 1988 for $37 million. Later Murdoch decided to buy back the Boston station. To do so, he sold the *Herald* in 1994 for an undisclosed sum to Patrick J. Purcell, publisher of the *Post* and chief of News America Publishing's newspaper division.

During 1990 News Corp. approached meltdown as a sizable part of the company's debt of $7.6 billion came due. The *Daily Racing Form* and nine Murdoch magazines, including *New York, Premiere, New Woman, European Travel and Life, Seventeen, Soap Opera Digest,* and *Soap Opera Weekly,* were purchased by K-III Holdings for $650 million in a 1991 fire sale. Murdoch refused to include *TV Guide,* and K-III rejected *Mirabella.* Two start-ups, *Men's Life* and *Married Woman,*

were discontinued in 1990 and 1994, respectively, after only a single issue.

By 1993 News Corp. had recovered its financial health, although the *Post* was still experiencing severe problems. Murdoch was given a waiver to the FCC rule in order to enable him to take possession again. In October he paid $25 million to acquire the *Post* in bankruptcy court, but only after extracting labor concessions intended to save $6.2 million a year. In 1994 the newspaper's publisher said Murdoch would invest millions of dollars in new press equipment to produce a full-color newspaper. *Post* daily circulation was 405,300 in October 1994.

Aimed at sophisticated, affluent, and mature women interested in fashion, *Mirabella,* the only remaining unit of the Murdoch magazine stable, was still operating at a loss in 1994. Circulation had risen to 613,000 in 1994, but advertising pages fell from 1,088 in 1990 to only 516 in 1993. And, in early 1995, the company sold its *Mirabella* magazine to Hachette Filipacchi Magazines for an undisclosed price.

News America Publishing registered losses of $184.8 million in 1992, $110.4 million in 1993, and $19.7 million in 1994. It was listed as a unit of News America Holdings, Inc., a subsidiary of News Publishing Australia Ltd. The latter company was a subsidiary of News Corp. and was, despite its name, incorporated in the United States. N.Y.P. Holdings Inc., publisher of the *Post,* was a subsidiary of News America Publishing.

Further Reading:

Cox, Meg, " 'How Do You Tame a Global Company?' Murdoch Does It Alone," *Wall Street Journal,* February 14, 1994, pp. A1, A6.
Garneau, George, "It's Baack," *Editor & Publisher,* October 9, 1993, pp. 12, 35.
Mayer, Jane, "Australia's Murdoch Is Getting His Kicks in U.S. Political Parties," *Wall Street Journal,* November 2, 1984, pp. 1, 18.
Mirabella, Alan, "Mirabella's New Chief Embodies Magazine," *Crain's New York Business,* May 2, 1994, p. 16.
Nevins, Allen. *The Evening Post: A Century of Journalism,* New York: Russell & Russell, 1968.
Potter, Jeffrey, *Men, Money and Magic: The Story of Dorothy Schiff,* New York: Coward, McCann & Geohagen, 1968.
"Sale Is Set for Boston Newspaper," *New York Times,* February 5, 1994, p. 39.
Shawcross, William, *Murdoch,* New York: Simon & Schuster, 1992.
Tuccille, Jerome, *Rupert Murdoch,* New York: Donald I. Fine, Inc., 1989.
Vartan, Vartanig G., "How Murdoch Mobilized His Money," *New York Times,* January 7, 1977, pp. D1, D5.

—Robert Halasz

THE NORTH WEST COMPANY

The North West Company, Inc.

77 Main Street
Winnipeg, Manitoba R3C 2R1
Canada
(204) 934-1502
Fax: (204) 934-1317

Public Company
Incorporated: 1783
Employees: 4200
Sales: C$548.7 million
Stock Exchanges: Toronto Winnipeg
SICs: 5399 Miscellaneous General Merchandise Stores; 5411 Grocery Stores; 5599 Automotive Dealers Not Elsewhere Classified; 5611 Men's & Boys' Clothing Stores; 5621 Women's Clothing Stores; 5641 Children's & Infants' Wear Stores; 5661 Shoe Stores; 5699 Miscellaneous Apparel & Accessory Stores

The North West Company, Inc., is the leading seller of food and other general merchandise in small towns across the northern territories of Canada and Alaska. The company runs general stores in more than 100 locations, providing local populations with a wide variety of services. Boasting an illustrious history that began in the colonial era, the North West Company was split off from a larger retailer in the late 1980s.

The North West Company is part of a long tradition closely linked to the development of the North American continent. The company traces its roots to a trading post at Fort Charles, which was built on the southeast corner of James Bay by Sieur des Groseillier in 1668. Two years later, on May 2, 1670, King Charles II of England granted a royal charter to the Governor and Company of Adventurers of England Trading into Hudson's Bay. This group became the legendary Hudson's Bay Company, with rights to conduct trade over a vast swath of the North American continent. The Hudson's Bay Company, which maintained its headquarters in London, concentrated its efforts on the enormously lucrative fur trade. Its merchant adventurers set out for the new world in a ship called the Nonsuch in the wake of their receipt of the king's charter.

The Hudson's Bay Company got its first real competition in 1779, when Simon McTavish and 15 other men formed a partnership which they called the North West Company. This company was created to trade furs, and its base of operations was established in the new world, in Montreal. In addition to its rivalry with the Hudson's Bay Company, North West faced stiff competition from American fur traders.

In 1783, the North West Company was formerly incorporated. Ten years later, an exploratory expedition sponsored by the company and led by Alexander Mackenzie reached the Pacific by an overland route on July 22, 1793, near the present-day town of Bella Bella. In this and other expeditions across Canada, traders for the North West Company established a reputation as daring risk-takers who often beat their rivals in the Hudson's Bay Company to new locations and engaged them in bloody feuds and running gun battles to protect their turf.

In the late eighteenth century and early nineteenth century, at the height of the rivalry between the two companies, the North West Company established a major trading hub on the western shore of Lake Superior, deep in Indian territory. In addition, the company owned hundreds of fur trading posts, where pelts were bought, sold, and distributed. These were located throughout British colonial North America and the far northern reaches of Rupert's Land. Moreover the company had facilities in London to distribute furs to the European market.

In 1795, the fur trade entered a boom period, and the North West Company pushed its activities further west, building fortified trading posts along the North Saskatchewan River, and making Edmonton a new hub of activities. Intense competitive trading with the Hudson's Bay Company and American fur sellers continued into the early nineteenth century. In 1813, for instance, the North West Company captured Astoria, a fur trading post owned by the American John Jacob Astor, for which he was reimbursed $44,000.

Despite these aggressive and enterprising activities, by the early 1820s the North West Company was in shaky financial shape, its fortunes damaged by an overall decline in the fur trade. In 1821, in a deal brokered in London, the North West Company was absorbed by its longtime rival, the Hudson's Bay Company. Many of the North West Company's partners were not fully informed of the nature of their company's merger until months after the arrangements had been completed. "This is not amalgamation, this is submersion!," one of them was reported in *Maclean's* to have protested. "We are drowned men." In the wake of this merger, which caused the activities of the North West Company to be conducted under the banner of the Hudson's Bay Company, the combined enterprise began to regain some of its former primacy in its old trading domains. The combined companies controlled a fur-trading monopoly that covered one-quarter of North America.

Throughout the rest of the nineteenth century, and into the twentieth, the activities of the North West Company continued under the guise of the Northern Department, which later became the Northern Stores Division, of the Hudson's Bay Company. This arm of the firm ran retail outlets in small communities located in Canada's northern territories. Over time, the Northern's corporate parent evolved into a Canadian department store chain.

In 1979, the Hudson's Bay Company was sold to Thomson International, a newspaper publishing conglomerate. Eight years later, on May 2, 1987, the Hudson's Bay Company sold its

Northern Stores Division to a group of investors, which included 415 of the division's employees. This move came after the price of the stock of the Hudson's Bay Company dropped dramatically, and the company found itself awash in C$2.5 billion of debt.

The transfer of ownership of the Northern Stores division took place in a ceremony that paid homage to the company's historical significance for Canada. At the Manitoba Museum of Man and Nature in Winnipeg, aboard a replica of the Nonsuch, 317 years after the Hudson's Bay Company was chartered, the governor's flag was lowered and presented to the leader of Manitoba, who also received one symbolic share in the company. These gestures were designed to placate the residents of the 178 northern communities served by the Northern Stores division, who had been wholly dependent on the Hudson's Bay Company for many years, and were disturbed by turmoil within the company. For small, isolated towns, the Northern stores were not only a sole source of groceries, but their managers often acted as unofficial legal, financial, social, and sometimes even spiritual and medical advisors to the residents of the communities.

Investors in the holding company, called the North West Company, Inc., paid $215 million for the Northern Division. Among the chief investors were the Mutual Trust Company of Toronto, the Mutual Life Assurance Company of Canada, the Toronto Dominion Bank Capital Group, the Royal Trust Corporation of Canada, the Teacher's Retirement Allowance Fund Board, along with the Hudson's Bay Company.

The new enterprise, temporarily renamed "Hudson's Bay Northern Stores," included 178 retail outlets, two airplanes, and a 3,000-ton freighter, named the Kanguk, which was used to supply Northern stores in Labrador and on the eastern Arctic shore. In addition, the Northern had 3,845 employees, making it the second largest employer in the northern territories after the Canadian government. In keeping with its history, it continued to buy furs at 50 different locations.

All of the senior executives of the Northern Stores stayed with the company, and purchased stock in the new enterprise. On July 17, 1987, the company shortened its name to Northern Stores, Inc., dropping the reference to the Hudson's Bay Company altogether, as stipulated in the sale agreement. The first order of business for the new managers of the Northern Stores was to reduce the company's level of debt, which had originally been taken on to finance the buy-out from Hudson's Bay. Within two years, the company's finances had been greatly strengthened. In 1988, the Northern Stores reported sales of C$436 million, followed in 1989 by sales of C$441 million.

These strong returns were derived from the company's Northern Stores outlets, despite the presence of competition in several key markets. In the City of Thompson, in northern Manitoba, for instance, co-ops, independent stores, and a Woolworth's competed for the dollars of the company's clientele, which was largely made up of Natives. Because of the presence of satellite televisions, demand among this remote population for up-to-date goods remained steady. To meet this demand, the Northern Stores offered goods as diverse as bananas, kiwi fruit, videos, outerwear, furniture, household appliances, satellite dishes, hockey equipment, hunting equipment, and all-terrain vehicles.

In marketing all of these goods, the Northern Stores faced the challenge of transporting them to remote locations. Transporting a 10-kilogram bag of potatoes to some of the company's stores cost as much as the bag of potatoes itself. In order to guarantee service to its customers, the Northern Stores ran its own transportation system, with multi-use cargo vessels that could cut ice, transport barges, and unload goods at ports where there were no docking facilities. Every year, the company sent tons of goods up the St. Lawrence Seaway to remote warehouses for distribution in the arctic. Trucks traveled winter roads between warehouses and stores.

Because of the transportation factor, the job of managing the company's stock and picking suppliers who offered the proper merchandise at a competitive price became even more important. "We have to be told what is selling well, such as Ninja Turtles, or fashion colors," the company's president told *Manitoba Business* in 1990. "That's the job of our suppliers and buyers." In addition, the Northern Stores moved to computerize its control of inventory, to cut interest costs on unsold goods.

In addition to the activities of its Northern Stores, the company ran several other related lines of business. The Inuit Art Marketing Service was the largest marketer of Inuit stone carvings in North America. The Fur Marketing Division and Hudson's Bay Blanket Division harked back to the company's past. Transport Nanuk, Inc., an off-shoot of the Northern Stores' own shipping activities, offered a leading means of transporting goods in the eastern Arctic.

In order to solidify the company's identity as an independent retailer, the Northern Stores company changed its name one final time on March 16, 1990. At that time, it became The North West Company, and its retail operations took the trading name Northern. In order to assume this identity, the company had to gain control of the name from another company, Imperial Oil Limited, which owned the rights to it for one of its exploration subsidiaries. However, this company relinquished rights to the historic label, and the North West Company, long ago subsumed into its rival, took on new life.

With profits again steady, the Northern Stores started to contemplate expansion through the acquisition of other companies. In order to raise capital for such a move, the company made plans to offer stock to the public in the near future, at a time when financial markets were strong. But in the fall of 1990, despite a slow summer, the North West Company went ahead with its planned stock offering, selling shares to the public on the Winnipeg and Toronto Stock Exchanges. With this capital, the company set out to acquire complementary retail operations.

In the early 1990s, the North West Company began a process of shaping its long-range planning and operations. In 1991, the company completed "Enterprise '95," a strategic plan governing the next four years, which focused the company's activities on retailing food, family apparel, and general merchandise in small, northern communities. As part of this plan, the North West Company moved to modernize its stores, and streamline its distribution network. In addition, the company instituted a training program for Native Canadians, to promote their hiring within its stores. The company's 79 percent Native employment rate remained second only to that of the Canadian government.

In addition, the North West Company took steps to consolidate its operations in Winnipeg. In 1992, the company centralized its national warehousing in Winnipeg, purchasing a $12.2 million 350,000-square-foot modern Retail Service Center facility. After extensive technological improvements, this distribution center opened in April of 1993. In addition, the company closed its Montreal buying office and moved it to Winnipeg. With these moves, the company left the city of the historic North West Company, choosing instead a location much closer to its current operations. By 1993, the North West Company's sales had reached C$452.1 million, making it the twelfth largest earner in Manitoba.

On November 20, 1992, the North West Company completed a year-long process of negotiation, and purchased the Alaska Commercial Company for $6.5 million. This company, which was the state's oldest enterprise, dated its founding to 1776, when the Russia-America Trading Company was established. As part of this deal, the North West Company also acquired Frontier Expeditors, Inc., a wholesale grocery firm. With this purchase, the company added ACC's chain of 20 rural stores in Alaska, which held 15 percent of the market, to its own Canadian holdings, which boasted half of the retail market in remote northern territories.

Together, the North West Company's two new properties had $75 million in annual sales. As it had already partially done in its Canadian operations, the company moved to introduce the techniques of modern retailing—from bar-code scanners to in-store pizza restaurants—to its new Alaskan outlets, which had long been starved for capital. The North West Company pledged to infuse $30 million in cash into improvements and to add 15 to 25 new stores over a five year period.

In addition to its retail operations in Canada and Alaska, the North West Company also developed a catalogue to stimulate mail order sales. Called *Selections,* this brochure featured items stored and shipped from the company's Winnipeg warehouse. In a further geographical expansion, the North West Company arranged for this catalogue to be translated into the language of Greenland, and distributed there by KNI Retail A/S, the island's largest retail chain.

In August of 1994, the North West Company further expanded the scope of its activities when it bought six stores located on Kodiak Island from O. Kraft & Sons, a company based in Lake Oswego, Oregon. These stores, which generated $15 million in annual sales, consisted of two grocery stores, two liquor stores, a convenience store, and a combination liquor and grocery store. The company planned to add these units to its AC Value Center line, the name it used for the stores it had acquired from ACC. In addition, the North West Company planned to spend $1 million renovating one of the grocery stores, called the City Market, to add 10,000 square feet of selling space. By the end of 1994, the North West Company's combined operations had yielded C$548.7 million in sales. With an illustrious history stretching back centuries, and a solid record in retailing in northern territories, it seemed certain that the North West Company would continue to thrive in the coming years of the 1990s and beyond.

Principal Subsidiaries: Alaska Commercial Company; Transport Igloolik.

Further Reading:

Carroll, Ed, "Canadian Giant Invades Alaska's Bush," *Alaska Business Monthly,* January 1993, p. 31.

Gage, Ritchie, "Trott at a Gallop," *Manitoba Business,* October 1990, p. 6.

Newman, Peter C., "The NorWesters' Revenge," *Maclean's,* May 11, 1987, p. 42.

—Elizabeth Rourke

Novacor Chemicals Ltd.

645 Seventh Avenue, S.W.
P.O. Box 2535
Postal Station M
Calgary, Alberta T2P 2N6
Canada
(403) 290-8977
Fax: (403) 264-6012

Wholly Owned Subsidiary of NOVA Corporation
Incorporated: 1981
Employees: 3,200
Sales: C$2.65 billion
Stock Exchanges: Alberta Montreal New York Toronto
SICs: 2821 Plastics Materials, Nonvulcanizable Elastomers &
    Synthetic Resins; 2822 Synthetic Rubber (Vulcanizable
    Elastomers); 2865 Cyclic Organic Crudes & Intermediates,
    Organic Dyes & Pigments; 2869 Industrial Organic
    Chemicals, Not Elsewhere Classified; 3083 Laminated
    Plastics, Plate, Sheet & Profile Shapes; 3084 Plastic Pipe;
    3089 Plastic Products, Not Elsewhere Classified

Novacor Chemicals Ltd. is Canada's largest chemicals company as measured in sales. A subsidiary of NOVA Corporation, a worldwide natural gas services and petrochemicals company headquartered in Calgary, Alberta, Canada, Novacor is a major manufacturer and distributor of petrochemicals and plastics. With production facilities in Canada and the United States, Novacor produces primary and basic petrochemicals, such as ethylene, styrene, and propylene, which are used to make plastic resins and other products. The company's broad range of plastic resins, including polyethylene, polystyrene, and styrene/ acrylics, go into the manufacture of rigid and flexible packaging, industrial containers, multi-purpose bags, and a wide variety of consumer and industrial goods such as food packaging, toys, and medical devices.

By the mid-1990s, Novacor was North America's second largest producer of ethylene, the third largest producer of polystyrene, and the fifth largest producer of polyethylene in North America. The company's six petrochemical facilities in Canada and two plants in the United States sold eight billion pounds of petrochemicals worth C$2.65 billion in 1994. Major markets for Novacor's products included over 21 countries in North America, the Pacific Rim, and Europe.

The history of Novacor is closely allied with that of its parent company. NOVA Corporation was originally incorporated as the Alberta Gas Trunk Line Company Ltd. (AGTL) in 1954 by Ernest Manning, the premier of the Province of Alberta. The company was formed to gather natural gas within the province and expanded its scope over the next 20 years to also include operations involved in the exploration and exportation of natural gas.

AGTL also began to invest in chemicals during the 1970s, forming several subsidiaries, including Alberta Gas Chemicals Ltd and Alberta Gas Ethylene Company Ltd. In 1975, AGTL began to explore the possibilities of producing ethylene, and entered into a joint venture with Dow Chemical Co. and Dome Petroleum Ltd. In the agreement, AGTL was to build an ethylene plant near Red Deer, Alberta. Dow would be supplied with the ethylene the plant produced, and Dome would transport the surplus chemical to eastern Canada and the United States.

Under President and CEO S. Robert Blair, AGTL continued expanding its operations, acquiring companies and expanding its pipeline network. By 1977, AGTL's net income had grown to nearly US$58 million. In 1979, AGTL acquired a major share of the stock of Husky Oil Ltd., a prominent gas and oil producer and marketer, through an aggressive and expensive takeover initiative. Also that year, the company's first ethylene plant started operations at Joffre, Alberta. In 1980, AGTL changed its name to NOVA, an Alberta Corporation, to reflect its expanded activities outside of natural gas transportation. The following year, Novacor Chemicals Ltd was incorporated to manage and operate NOVA's growing petrochemical concerns.

By 1982, economic recession, severe price restrictions, and higher taxes from Canada's national energy program put pressure on the profitability of NOVA's oil and chemical concerns. Stock prices fell from C$14.38 a share in 1981 to C$6 a share at the end of 1983. In 1984, NOVA shored up its financial situation by selling some of Husky's assets for a US$505 million profit and another subsidiary. In the same year, NOVA brought into operation a second ethylene plant and started up a polyethylene plant at the Joffre facility. By the end of 1984, things were looking up and NOVA reported a net income of C$203.4 million, five times that of the year before. In 1987, the company was renamed NOVA Corporation of Alberta.

In 1987, the polyethylene plant at Moore Township, Ontario, was added to the petrochemical holdings. The following year, Novacor made a share acquisition and gained control of Polysar Energy & Chemical Corporation of Toronto at a cost of nearly C$1.92 billion. Debt from this purchase prompted NOVA to sell four of its non-chemical subsidiaries the following year in 1989. In the same year, Novacor acquired a polypropylene facility in Marysville, Michigan, and began construction on a polystyrene plant in Alabama. In 1990, the Polysar rubber operations were sold to Bayer AG of Germany for C$1.25 billion. NOVA's net income that year was C$185 million, considerably lower than expected due to volatile prices in the plastics and petrochemicals industries and continued debt from the Polysar purchase.

The chemicals and plastics business proved cyclical and volatile, depending on demand for products, capacity utilization of production facilities, and the cost of feedstocks such as crude oil, condensates, and natural gas liquids. Novacor and all chemical manufacturers faced difficulty in the early 1990s because of rising feedstock costs, low growth in demand for chemical products due to the recession in North America, and production overcapacity of chemicals. Excess production capacity in the chemicals industry depressed selling prices for chemical products. Nevertheless, higher prices for methanol offset the higher cost of feedstocks somewhat and producers looked forward to the full implementation of the United States Clean Air Act, which was expected to increase demand for methanol.

Performance for 1991 was disappointing for Novacor and NOVA Corporation in general. In April, NOVA considered spinning off Novacor Chemicals to finance a pipeline expansion for the gas transmission division. Blair left NOVA that year and was replaced by DuPont Canada president and CEO, J.E. (Ted) Newall. Newall overhauled the balance sheet by writing down C$675 in assets. Moreover, 80 million shares were issued for C$574 million to finance the expanded distribution of natural gas outside of Alberta. Novacor's debt load and the persistence of unfavorable market conditions for petrochemicals at the end of the year scuttled the company's plan to spin off the chemicals division. NOVA reported a loss of C$937 million for 1991 and Novacor Chemicals reported a loss of C$108 million.

The depressed prices and demand for petrochemical products during 1991 and the expectation that these conditions would continue led NOVA to perform a comprehensive strategic review of its petrochemical businesses. NOVA determined that the shape and direction of the organization would have to be modified to keep pace with changing trends in the industry. NOVA reduced and decentralized senior management, sold its interest in Husky for C$325 million, and closed some petrochemical plants that it considered to be non-competitive. The company then realigned its businesses under four major divisions: Alberta Gas Transmission Division, NOVA Gas Services Ltd., Novacorp International Inc., and Novacor Chemicals Ltd. At the same time, the company created a plan for future strategic investment and expansion. NOVA's new corporate mission focused on investments compatible with the company's existing businesses and expertise, especially in areas of potential growth.

Despite continued depressed prices and industry production overcapacity, Novacor's performance improved in 1992 with year-end earnings of C$2 million. At the end of its reorganization, NOVA had cut 300 positions. Novacor was recognized for its innovative and extensive re-employment program for the 60 employees displaced by the closing of its West Haven, Connecticut, plant. Rather than receiving criticism over the closing, the company was cited for its sensitive and realistically helpful transition management techniques. Novacor announced the closing five months ahead of time and announced the re-employment program at the same time. The company provided free consulting, job retraining, and aid in finding open positions at area companies.

In 1992, Novacor fully implemented its Responsible Care environmental program at all of its Canadian facilities. Responsible Care was a comprehensive environmental, health, and safety (EHS) management and improvement program that was volun-

tarily adopted by members of the chemical industry in over 30 countries. Novacor put the initiative in place after five years of preparation for the program's requirements. In 1993, Novacor put identical practices in place at its United States operations. In 1992, Novacor was ranked in the second quartile among comparable companies for environmental performance. The company then set its goal at first quartile performance and took steps to reach that level of performance, including developing a cross-functional team to set standards for EHS policy and an expanded EHS audit program. Novacor and other Canadian chemicals companies also initiated the National Emissions Reduction Master Plan in 1993. The plan required participants to set baseline measures for emissions and wastes, create reduction plans, and make this information public.

1993 saw the expansion of NOVA's chemical concerns with investments in Methanex Corporation and in new technology from DuPont Canada. In July 1994, Novacor acquired DuPont Canada's polyethylene business for C$45 million plus working capital of about C$35 million. The deal included DuPont Canada's 500 million pound per year polyethylene facility at Sarnia, its proprietary SCLAIRTECH technology, and the company's worldwide SCLAIRTECH licensing business. The purchase increased Novacor's production capacity by 30 percent and moved the company into the fifth position in polyethylene production in North America. The purchase in July 1994 also brought complementary technology and product lines to Novacor. After the purchase, the majority of Novacor's ethylene production was used internally for polyethylene and styrene production or sold under long-term cost-of-service agreements that allowed price increases or reductions according to fluctuations in the cost of production and delivery plus a specified after-tax return on Novacor's investment. The DuPont acquisition, along with a $50 million investment in expanding and improving Novacor's ethylene production facilities, made the company's ethylene and polyethylene businesses leaders in cost-competitiveness in North America. In late 1994, Novacor bought a specialty high-density polyethylene business from DuPont's U.S. operations. While the purchase did not include personnel or assets, it added seven new product types to Novacor's offerings, grouped under the heading of the SCLAIRCOAT polyethylene line.

Also in December 1993, NOVA sold three methanol plants to Methanex Corp. of Vancouver, British Columbia, and invested an additional US$185 million to purchase 24 percent of the company, the largest methanol producer and marketer in the world. These plants were among the lowest cost suppliers to the northern United States and western Canada. Through Methanex, Novacor gained a global position in methanol, in keeping with its strategy of investing in expected growth areas compatible with existing businesses and expertise. The investment in Methanex allowed both businesses to realize savings from economies derived from lower logistics costs.

NOVA's profits increased dramatically in 1994, with a record net income of C$575 million. The C$400 million increase over 1993 was attributed to increased prices for petrochemicals and the sale of non-core assets. Polyethylene prices played a large role in the increase due to increased demand, as the recession eased in Novacor's major markets, and reduced supply due to competitor operating problems and lack of production capacity.

The price per pound for polyethylene rose from US$0.26 in January 1994 to US$0.49 by January 1, 1995. For sales to third party markets, Novacor sold more polyethylene than all its other petrochemical products combined.

Methanol prices tripled in 1994, significantly increasing the value of NOVA's investment in Methanex. Methanex's contribution to net income for 1994 was C$134 million, or 33 percent of total net income from petrochemicals. Petrochemicals contributed over 70 percent to total net income for the corporation in 1994.

Since Novacor's products were priced in U.S. dollars, and its costs were established in Canadian dollars, the declining value of the Canadian dollar benefited NOVA's bottom line. Also in 1994, Newall moved to rename the company NOVA Corporation to reflect the increasingly global nature of the company's activities. During this time, John Feick resigned as head of Novacor and was replaced by Dan Boivin, a former DuPont executive, as president and chief operating officer.

In May 1994 Novacor Chemicals Ltd., started along a path of "Business Transformation" (BT), a framework to help companies become more efficient, effective, and competitive in every aspect of their businesses. Dan Boivin, president of Novacor Chemicals, said, "During BT we focused on NOVA's vision. That means we had to develop ways to be the lowest cost producer of what we sell by designing the best business processes, organizational structure and systems to make it all fit together. The end result will allow us to more effectively provide customers with what they need."

As a result of BT, 300 Novacor positions and 200 contract positions were eliminated across the company. NOVA designed an innovative Employee Transition and Continuity Program to be used even after BT to provide those employees leaving the company with educational and business opportunities. While Novacor spent between C$30 and C$40 million on the project, it hoped to save in excess of C$130 million annually because of the changes brought about by BT.

For the future, pressure on the Canadian dollar and the U.S. dollar, rising interest rates, the uncertain outcome of the Quebec referendum, investor disappointment with 1994 equity returns, and the approaching end of some long-term cost-of-production supply agreements presented major challenges to the company. Nevertheless, NOVA's technology acquisitions, strategic production expansions, and new management structure seemed to provide a good foundation for going forward.

Further Reading:

Bores, Alan, "Newall & Nova: Chief Sets Multi-Faceted Company on Straight and Narrow Path," *Wall Street Journal,* April 30, 1994, p. E7.

Burton, Bruce, "Methanex Corp. Announces Changes in Management Team," *PR Newswire,* September 12, 1994.

Jaremko, Gordon, "Nova's Fortunes Rebound," *Calgary Herald,* January 29, 1993, p. F7.

McGee, Susan, "Nova Cancels Petrochemicals Spin-off Proposal, *Wall Street Journal,* December 3, 1991.

Wensky, Arnold, "Turning Crisis into Opportunity," *HRMagazine,* March, 1993, pp. 84–85.

—Katherine Smethurst

OMNI ❧ HOTELS®

Omni Hotels Corp.

500 Lafayette Road
Hampton, New Hampshire 03842
U.S.A.
(603) 926-8911
Fax: (603) 926-6613

Wholly Owned Subsidiary: Wharf Holdings Limited, Hong
  Kong
Incorporated: 1958 as Dunfey Hotels Corporation
Employees: 8,000
Sales: $500 million
SICs: 7011 Hotels & Motels

Omni Hotels Corp. operates a group of unique, upscale, full-service hotels located mostly in urban centers. The company is a subsidiary of Hong Kong-based Wharf Holdings Limited. In 1994, Omni operated about 47 hotels with over 15,000 rooms in the United States, Mexico, and Asia. Backed by its well-heeled parent, Omni began expanding rapidly in the early 1990s.

Omni Hotels's history traces back to the five Dunfey brothers' clam stand. In 1945, the five Dunfey brothers started a clam stand in Hampton Beach, New Hamspshire. The success of their clam stand enabled the brothers to purchase and open other businesses. Most notable among the Dunfeys' purchases was Lamie's Tavern, a combination restaurant and motor inn located not far from their clam stand. The Dunfeys primarily wanted the restaurant, but the owner insisted that the adjoining 32-room hotel be part of the deal. The brothers adopted a theme of "Good old New England hospitality" for their hotel and touted the restaurant as a "cracker barrel lounge."

The success of the Lamie Motor Inn convinced the Dunfeys that they could make more money as innkeepers than they could running restaurants. They purchased their first real hotel (332 rooms) in 1958 and founded the Dunfey Hotels Corporation. During the late 1950s and early 1960s the brothers, under the guidance of company president Jack Dunfey, bought several other properties throughout New England. The Dunfeys became some of the first pioneers of hotel franchising in 1964 when they obtained several existing hotels and motor inns that bore the Sheraton name. With their Sheraton inns acquisition, the Dunfey Hotels Corporation became the largest hotel franchise holder in the world with a total of 14 inns.

By the mid 1960s, the Dunfeys had hotels and operating offices scattered throughout Massachusetts, Maine, and New Hampshire. The properties were successful partly as a result of the Dunfeys' marketing and management strategies. For example, they retained their original New England hospitality slogan and integrated the cracker barrel lounge into many of their hotels. They consolidated their acquisitions's management into the Dunfey Hotels Corporation's New England headquarters to maintain control over their growing operation. The Dunfeys also devised a strategy of targeting struggling hotels in need of renovation that they could buy inexpensively. In 1968, for instance, they bought the financially ailing Parker House in Boston, renovated the facility, and returned it to profitability.

Success with the Parker House served as an incentive for the Dunfeys. Although they wanted to continue expanding, they lacked capital. So, in 1971 they sold all 18 of their hotel and motor inn properties to Aetna Life Insurance Company. Aetna became the owner but retained the Dunfeys to operate them. The Dunfeys were successful at managing the hotel chain and earned the company a reputation for innovation. In 1968, for instance, they started a "Wayfarers Club" that gave perks like free travel insurance, coffee, and newspapers to their most frequent patrons. That successful program became a model for the frequent traveler programs that became commonplace by the 1980s. The Dunfeys also initiated the "Colleen Club," or secretaries club, which provided benefits to both the traveler and the person that made the reservations.

In 1976, Aer Lingus, an Irish airline company, purchased Dunfey Hotels from Aetna. Under Aer Lingus, Dunfey Hotels stepped up its efforts to penetrate the upscale hotel market through the company's Classic Hotel Division, which included only one property in 1976. The Classic Hotel Division was the foundation upon which the Omni Hotels would be built. In 1977, the company added a second holding to its Classic Hotel Division, the Ambassador East Hotel in Chicago. Still under the management of the Dunfey brothers, that property was renovated and its profitability improved. In 1978, Dunfey Hotels purchased the renowned Berkshire Place Hotel in New York. Following a major renovation in 1979 that jewel became the centerpiece of all Dunfey properties. The Berkshire Place would later undergo another complete renovation in the mid-1990s and was expected to reopen in the fall of 1995 as the top four star hotel in New York. Also in 1979, Dunfey Hotels bought the Shoreham Hotel in Washington, D.C.

By 1980, Dunfey Hotels Corporation owned or managed about 9,000 rooms in hotels mostly on the East Coast. Throughout the 1980s the corporation sought to expand its Classic Hotel Division. In 1981, it acquired New Orleans's Royal Orleans Hotel and the Biltmore Plaza Hotel in Providence, Rhode Island. Those purchases brought the number of properties in the Classic Hotel Division to five. Importantly, in 1983 Dunfey Hotels acquired Omni International Hotels, a company that operated three hotels in Atlanta, Norfolk, and Miami. Dunfey Hotels also added the once esteemed Netherland Plaza Hotel in Cincinnati, which it soon restored to its original art deco grandeur.

After the 1983 Omni acquisition Aer Lingus decided to adopt a new business strategy. It chose to develop a hotel chain called Omni Hotels. The new group of hotels would consist of more upscale properties and would be built from the existing Classic Hotel Division holdings. To that end, the company was reorganized into two separate operating divisions: Dunfey Hotels and Omni International Hotels. Omni consisted of nine hotels. Dunfey Hotels was a conglomeration of 14 hotels and motor inns that were operated under independent or franchise names, or under the Dunfey name.

During the 1980s, Aer Lingus gradually liquidated its Dunfey holdings jettisoning its last property in 1992. The Dunfeys sold all of their interests in the company that they had founded. They formed a new company, the Dunfey Brothers Capital Group, a venture capital company oriented toward socially responsible companies. Aer Lingus used cash from the sale of its Dunfey properties to fund the expansion and improvement of Omni. It opened the Baltimore Omni International Hotel in 1984 and the Omni Sagamore Resort in 1985. It also added two properties in Detroit, Michigan, and Charlottesville, Virginia.

To speed up expansion, Omni's management elected to begin franchising the Omni brand to selected hoteliers in 1986. Subsequently, in that same year, the Omni International Hotel in Orlando, Florida, and the Omni Charleston Place in South Carolina were opened. Omni Hotels' strategy during the early and mid-1980s was to buy, create, and manage unique, upscale hotels, mostly in downtown areas. Rather than creating a chain of identical inns, as did many of its industry peers, Omni focused on creating a group of independent, unique properties that would still add value to the Omni name. The effort worked; by the mid-1980s, Omni was recognized as a leading operator of upscale hotels.

Omni thrived during the 1980s, but so did many other hoteliers. The 1980s was an era of explosive growth for the hotel industry. As demand by travelers surged, the hotel industry embarked on an aggressive building spree. The expansion was possible largely because of favorable tax laws and an influx of investment capital into the real estate development sector. By the end of the decade, more than three million hotel rooms existed in the United States, most of which had been constructed since 1980.

The difference in Omni's expansion during the 1980s and that of many other upscale hotel chains was that Omni's growth was slower. Although it had built its chain to 36 by 1987, it had simultaneously divested other of its holdings through the Dunfey Hotels Division. Furthermore, Omni had been very selective about the properties that it added to its portfolio, buying hotels that it felt were undervalued and keeping its total debt low in relation to many of its highly leveraged competitors. Because of its comparatively cautious stratagem, Omni would be positioned to take advantage of the nasty hotel industry shakeout that would lambaste its rivals in the 1990s.

Ownership of Omni Hotels changed hands again in 1987. World International Holdings Limited and its associate Wharf Holdings Limited of Hong Kong bought the company from Aer Lingus for $135 million. World International was a massive diversified conglomerate, with annual revenues of over $5.6 billion, which represented ten percent of the entire Hong Kong stock market. World International was known as a very conservative, savvy organization with a reputation for buying undervalued companies that it could finance and turn into long-term

performers. Omni's new parent company already owned a small chain of upscale hotels in Hong Kong and Singapore called Marco Polo International Hotels. It changed those properties to Omni Hotels. Also in 1987, Omni added its first hotel in Mexico, the Omni Cancun Hotel.

Omni continued to expand during the late 1980s, but escalating property prices slowed its progress. In addition, Omni dealt with two failed properties in the late 1980s. In 1988, a project involving the restoration of a historic mission in Riverside, California, failed when the developer went bankrupt. A year later another California property, which was franchised by Omni, failed as a result of bad dealings by the owner that were outside of Omni's control. Despite modest setbacks, Omni added nine new holdings to its portfolio between 1987 and 1991, boosting its total number of properties to 45.

By 1991, the hotel industry was in the depths of a downturn that had started in the late 1980s. Changed tax laws, a dearth of new investment capital, and an overbuilt market combined to force the hotel industry into a depression of historic proportions. As demand decreased, the average pretax profit gleaned from a U.S. hotel room dropped from a profit of over $1,500 per year in the late 1980s to a loss of $719 by 1991 As industry revenues plunged, the average market value of a hotel room plummeted from $23,600 in 1988 to a $18,400 by 1992, representing a devaluation of industry assets of more than 20 percent in just four years. The average hotel built after 1985 had lost $5,000 per room by 1991. Many hotel owners and operators were forced out of business and had to forfeit their properties to lenders, or to the federally backed Resolution Trust Corporation.

In 1991, Wharf Holdings Limited purchased World International's share of Omni Hotels. Wharf installed a new management team headed by Jerry Best. Best replaced William Sheehan, who had piloted the company since Aer Lingus sold it in 1988. Best recognized opportunities in the industry despite industry woes. Because of property devaluation, a number of premier hotels were being sold for a fraction of their original value. Omni had resisted the temptation to expand irresponsibly during the industry heyday, so it was now in a position to build a portfolio of superior properties by paying rock-bottom prices.

Backed by Wharf's massive base of capital, Best and his team launched an aggressive five-year growth plan. The strategy included three primary goals: 1) to increase the number of North American properties from 39 to 60 by 1997; 2) to scrap any properties that did not complement Omni's market position; and 3) to seek ownership or management contracts with four-star properties in the top ten or 12 U.S. markets. Omni added just one more hotel in 1991, the Omni Houston Hotel. In 1992, though, Omni contracted three new franchises, acquired full equity in two of its properties, purchased a hotel in Dallas, and entered into a management contract for a property in Austin, Texas.

Although Omni was able to take advantage of cut-rate property prices during 1992, the industry began to show signs of recovery. The average U.S. hotel room generated a meager profit of $159 in 1992, which served to buoy property prices in 1993. In 1993, Omni secured a flagship hotel in Chicago, the Chicago Hyatt Regency, which became the Omni Chicago Hotel. It also broadened its presence in Mexico with the addition of a franchise in Juatulco. Additional purchases early in 1994 boosted Omni's worldwide holdings (in operation or under development) to 45 hotels comprising 17,000 rooms. Thirty-six of the hotels were in the United States, two in Mexico, three in Hong Kong, and two in Singapore and Vietnam. Two more properties were scheduled to open in 1995, one in China and another in Indonesia, and several other negotiations were in progress.

By 1994, Omni generated approximately $500 million in annual revenues and employed a work force of more than 8,000. Its upscale and luxury hotels averaged 300 to 400 rooms and were generally oriented to corporate business travelers and business groups and associations. Going into the mid 1990s, Omni was focusing on continued U.S. expansion, particularly on the West Coast, through acquisition, franchising, and management contracts. It was also targeting selected regions in the Far East and Mexico.

Further Reading:

Albertini, Steve, *Omni Hotels History,* Hampton, New Hampshire: Omni Hotels, 1994.
Albertini, Steve, *Omni Hotels Follows Strategic Growth Initiative,* Hampton, N.H.: Omni Hotels, 1994.
McClain, Tim, "Bigger Presence in West still Sought by Omni," *San Diego Daily Transcript,* November 19, 1991, p. 1.
Miller, Leslie, "Once Dunfey-Owned Omni Hotels Seek Bargains as Other Chains Divest Properties," *New Hampshire Review,* August 7, 1992, p. 2.
Moskowitz, Daniel B., "Challenges on Trademarks Are Everywhere for Omni Hotels," *Washington Post,* September 21, 1992, p. E11.

—Dave Mote

Oscar Mayer Foods Corp.

910 Mayer Avenue
Madison, Wisconsin 53704-4256
U.S.A.
(608) 241-3311
Fax: (608) 242-6108

Wholly Owned Subsidiary of Kraft General Foods Inc.
Incorporated: 1911 as Oscar F. Mayer & Bro.
Employees: 11,000
Sales: $2.3 billion
SICs: 2013 Sausages and Other Prepared Meat Products;
    2015 Poultry Slaughtering and Processing; 2035 Pickled
    Vegetables, Vegetable Sauces and Seasonings, and Salad
    Dressings; 2092 Prepared Fresh or Frozen Fish and
    Seafoods; 4731 Arrangement of Transportation of Freight
    and Cargo; 4213 Trucking, Except Local

Oscar Mayer Foods Corp. is the maker of one of the most venerable and successful food brands currently available on supermarket shelves. The company's sliced meats and other products are sold across North America and in parts of South America and Asia. Oscar Mayer's product line includes a wide range of popular meats, including hot dogs, bacon, and prepackaged lunch combinations. In the early 1990s, the company also tried its hand at the restaurant business, in an attempt to find additional outlets for its food products. Oscar Mayer, now part of the Kraft General Foods empire, grew from a modest family business into an international food giant, maintaining a firm presence in both the American refrigerator and the American consciousness.

Oscar F. Mayer, the company's founder, arrived in America from Bavaria in 1873 at the age of 14. Settling in Detroit, his first job was as a butcher boy in a meat market. Mayer moved to Chicago three years later, where he continued his apprenticeship in the meat industry, working in the stockyards of Armour & Co., as well as in a series of retail meat operations over the next few years. By 1880, Mayer had learned the meat business from top to bottom. In hopes of starting a family business, he wrote home suggesting that his brother Gottfried learn the art of sausage-making as an apprentice in Germany. Gottfried followed his older brothers advice, and in 1883 the two Mayers rented the failing Kolling Meat Market on the north side of

Chicago and opened a shop of their own. On its first day of operation, the store sold $59 worth of meat.

When their lease expired in 1888, the Kollings refused to renew it, hoping to get back into business themselves by exploiting the solid reputation the Mayers had secured for the store. Learning from this experience, the Mayer brothers borrowed $10,000 and bought their own building, with room for living quarters, just a few blocks away and reopened without much delay. The new market was an immediate success, and neighborhood residents flocked to the shop for its old world sausages and traditional meat cuts. By this time, a third brother, Max, had joined the operation.

By the turn of the century, Oscar Mayer's reputation had spread well beyond the immediate neighborhood, and the company had at least 40 employees. Salesman were delivering Mayer sausages and other meats to every part of Chicago and even out to the suburbs. In 1904, the company adopted the "Edelweiss" trademark for some of its products, including bacon, linked sausage, and lard. Although branding was not a common industry practice at the time, the Mayers reasoned that a name and logo would help customers notice the difference between their meat and the lower quality products sold by others. Two years later, the company became part of the federal meat inspection program. Another Mayer, Oscar's son Oscar G. Mayer, joined the team in 1909 following his graduation from Harvard. By this time, the company had about 70 employees on its payroll.

In 1911, the company was incorporated as Oscar F. Mayer & Bro., with assets totaling $300,000. Every phase of the operation expanded at a brisk pace over the next several years. Production was decentralized into different departments, and the sales territory grew to include areas well outside of Chicago. By 1912, the company was using its first automobile, a Ford Model T, on one of its 20 sales routes. Cardboard cartons for packaging sausages were also introduced around that time. Gottfried Mayer died in 1913, and the remaining family members continued to press forward, as sales reached $2.69 million that year. The company began spending significant sums on advertising around 1915, when $2,000 was spent on materials for a window display. Newspaper advertising was added two years later.

Sales at Oscar Mayer grew to $11 million by 1918. About a third of that total represented sales to the government for feeding World War I troops. That year the Edelweiss brand name was discontinued, and a new one, "Oscar Mayer Approved Meat Products," took its place. The company was producing and selling 93 different meat products by this time. A major expansion project was begun in 1919, when the company purchased a farmers' cooperative meat packing plant in Madison, Wisconsin, at a bankruptcy auction. This gave Oscar Mayer a reliable source of raw materials for the Chicago plant. Now a two-plant operation, the company's corporate name was changed that year to Oscar Mayer & Co.

Oscar Mayer continued to be a marketing innovator over the next couple of decades. In 1924, the company introduced packaged sliced bacon under the Oscar Mayer brand name. A Milwaukee branch was also opened that year. By 1928, the company had 25 different varieties of "Approved Brand" sausages on the market. That year, Oscar F. Mayer was elected to chair the board, and Oscar G. Mayer was named company president. The company's biggest marketing coup came the following year, when it began placing yellow paper bands bearing the Oscar Mayer brand name on every fourth hot dog. Along the way, the tag line "Meats of Good Taste" was also added to the company's brand identifiers.

By the early 1930s, Oscar Mayer had staked out sales territories reaching all the way to the East Coast, including Cleveland, Detroit, Buffalo, and Rochester, New York. Developments over the next few years included the introduction of the skinless wiener and the unionization of the company's employees. In 1936, Little Oscar and his Wienermobile—a minute chef in a hot dog-shaped vehicle—made their first appearance. They would be a part of Oscar Mayer promotions for decades, appearing at parades and openings or giving cooking demonstrations. 1936 also marked the introduction of the "Yellow Band" trademark on certain Oscar Mayer products.

During World War II, Oscar Mayer was again a major provider of food for the armed forces. The 1940s were also a period of technological innovation at the company. A formal research program was initiated in 1941, and the following year quality control departments were added. Beginning in 1943, the company unveiled a series of technological breakthroughs in the areas of packaging and distribution. The first of these, launched in 1944, was the "Kartridg-Pak," a way of automatically banding hot dogs together in bunches resembling cartridge belts. Kartridg-Pak was so successful that a subsidiary was soon formed to market the machinery to the rest of the industry. In 1946, "Sack-O-Sauce," a separate package of sauce to be used with canned meats, was introduced. Two years later, the company brought out its "Slice-Pak" line, lunch meats sold in vacuum-sealed clear plastic packages with metal bases. Meanwhile, the company was expanding its production capabilities and geographic scope with the 1946 leasing and subsequent purchase of the Kohrs Packing Company in Davenport, Iowa, and the acquisition of F. G. Vogt & Sons, a Philadelphia meat processor, in 1948.

By the beginning of the 1950s, Oscar Mayer's annual sales were over $150 million. In 1951, the Southern California Meat Packers plant in Los Angeles was purchased, giving the company a coast-to-coast presence for the first time. Further technological progress and territorial growth followed. The company began intensive research on Saran vacuum packaging around 1953, and by the middle of the decade its Slice-Pak line of products was a familiar sight on grocery store shelves. Oscar F. Mayer died in 1955 at the age of 95. His son, Oscar G. Mayer succeeded him as chairperson, and grandson Oscar G. Mayer, Jr. was elected company president. In 1957, a new nine-story building was completed in Madison, and this became the company's corporate headquarters. By 1958, the company's seventy-fifth anniversary, Oscar Mayer was producing over 200 varieties of sausages, lunch meats, and smoked and canned meat products.

The early 1960s were boom years for Oscar Mayer. The company continued to improve its packaging techniques through the decade, with the introduction of Saran vacuum-seal packs for wieners and Smokie Links in 1960, and for bacon two years

later. Oscar Mayer's entry into international business came in 1961, when it purchased a Venezuelan meat processor, Venezolana Empacadora. By this time, the company's U.S. distribution network included facilities in Tampa, Dallas, Kansas City, and Denver, and sales had grown to $260 million. In 1963, Oscar Mayer's famous "Wiener Jingle" made its first appearance. The song, which began, "Oh, I wish I were an Oscar Mayer wiener. That is what I'd truly like to be," went on to become one of the longest-running and most popular jingles in advertising history.

During the 1960s, over 30 Oscar Mayer sales distribution centers were opened throughout the United States, and capital spending averaged $8.5 million a year during that period. Among the company's major investments were the 1965 acquisition of a pork processing plant in Perry, Iowa, and the construction of a pork processing plant in Beardstown, Illinois, begun the same year. Oscar Mayer also began buying national network television advertising around that time, and in 1968 the company put its ads on prime time, sponsoring the "Gentle Ben" television series. Meanwhile, another change in leadership accompanied the 1965 death of Oscar G. Mayer. Oscar G. Mayer, Jr. was elected to the chairmanship, and P. Goff Beach was named company president. Before the decade was over, a new subsidiary, Scientific Protein Laboratories, was created to manufacture chemicals and pharmaceuticals using the animal byproducts of Oscar Mayer's processing operations.

Oscar Mayer sustained its momentum into the 1970s. In 1970, the company acquired the 100-year-old Claussen Pickle Co., and the following year a new processing plant was opened in Nashville. The company's common stock was listed on the New York Stock Exchange for the first time in 1971 as well. Around this time, Oscar Mayer began to increase its role in international business. A 25 percent interest in Prima Meat Packers, Ltd. of Tokyo was purchased in 1972, and four years later, the company bought into General De Matederos, a Spanish meat operation that was subsequently renamed Oscar Mayer, S.A. Another leadership change took place in 1973, when Beach was elected chairperson. Harold M. Mayer became vice-chairperson, and Robert M. Bolz took over the company's presidency. That year, the second of Oscar Mayer's wildly popular commercial jingles—"My bologna has a first name, it's O-s-c-a-r. My bologna has a second name, it's M-a-y-e-r," made its initial appearance in a television ad called "Fisherman."

Sales at Oscar Mayer topped the $1 billion mark for the first time in 1975. In 1977, the company launched a major advertising blitz that included a return to print advertising, tied in with a variety of promotions involving premiums, coupons, and other gimmicks. Another reshuffling of executive titles took place that year as well, in which Jerry M. Hiegel was named president, Bolz vice-chair, and Harold M. Mayer chairperson of the executive committee. Along the way, several new products were introduced, some more successfully than others. 1978's entry was "The Big One," a quarter-pound hot dog marketed across the United States. Oscar Mayer went into the restaurant business in 1979, opening the first of its "Rocky Rococo" chain of pizza parlors near Minneapolis.

As the 1970s closed, Hiegel, now CEO, led a diversification program that resulted in the acquisitions of processed turkey leader Louis Rich, Inc., and of Chef's Pantry Inc., a food service company with mainly industrial customers. In 1981, Oscar Mayer was bought by General Foods Corporation, and its name was changed to Oscar Mayer Foods Corp. After Philip Morris Companies, Inc. acquired both General Foods in 1985 and Kraft Inc. in 1988, Oscar Mayer became part of Kraft General Foods, Inc., the subsidiary created by combining the two food giants. For much of the 1980s, Oscar Mayer was the star performer for General Foods, largely on the strength of its Louis Rich business, whose revenue doubled to $600 million between 1979 and 1987.

After a series of product flops, however, sales began to slow up a bit by 1988. The company even trotted out the old Wiener-mobile in an attempt to rev up publicity. In 1989, Oscar Mayer broke out of its slump with the introduction of Lunchables, prepackaged lunch combinations that included meats, cheeses, and crackers. Lunchables were awarded a Sial d'Or medal by the industry press and were so successful that imitations by other companies quickly hit the stores. In spite of the waves the Lunchables were making, Oscar Mayer's sales remained sluggish into the 1990s. Although revenue reached $2.5 billion in 1991, this fell short of the company's stated goal for the year. Turkey products remained popular, but an increasingly health-conscious American public was becoming wary of fatty meat products containing preservatives. Oscar Mayer countered by introducing low-fat and low-sodium products, such as its Healthy Favorites line. Unfortunately, even turkey sales began to decline in 1992.

As the 1990s continued, Oscar Mayer continued searching for ways to stoke the American appetite for processed meat. In 1992, the company launched Hot Dog Construction Co., a chain of fast food establishments operated at transit stations, turnpike stops, amusement areas, and other such sites. A new subsidiary, Branded Restaurant Group, Inc., oversaw the operations. In 1993, the company introduced Oscar Mayer Big & Juicy, a line of extra large hot dogs available in five flavors, including Hot n' Spicy and Smokie Links. Later that year, Robert A. Eckert was named president of Oscar Mayer, replacing John D. Bowlin, who had left to join Miller Brewing Co. as president and chief operating officer.

With over more than a century in the meat business, Oscar Mayer has consistently ranked among the industry's leaders in product, packaging, and marketing innovation. Although the meat industry as a whole has faced enormous challenges in the mid-1990s, the company had a remarkable record when it came to generating big ideas at crucial moments. As long as packaged meat continued to find its way into America's lunchboxes, a large share of that meat was likely to be Oscar Mayer's.

Principal Subsidiaries: Branded Restaurant Group Inc.

Further Reading:

Dolan, Carrie, "If You Really Cut the Mustard, You Will Relish This Job," *Wall Street Journal,* July 7, 1992, p. 1A.
Ginsberg, Stanley, "The Wurst is Yet to Come," *Forbes,* March 2, 1981, p. 40.
Links with the Past: A History of Oscar Mayer & Co., Madison, Wis.: Oscar Mayer & Co., 1979.
Mayer, Oscar G., Jr., *Oscar Mayer & Co.: From Corner Store to National Processor,* New York: The Newcomen Society in North America, 1970.
"Nothing If Not Resourceful," *Forbes,* April 14, 1980, p. 77.
Ruggless, Ron, "Oscar Mayer Expands Hot Dog Construction Co.," *Nation's Restaurant News,* August 22, 1994, p. 7.

—Robert R. Jacobson

Outback Steakhouse, Inc.

550 North Reo Street
Suite 204
Tampa, Florida 33609
U.S.A.
(813) 282-1225
Fax: (813) 282-1209

Public Company
Incorporated: 1987
Employees: 8,850
Sales: $271 million
Stock Exchanges: NASDAQ
SICs: 5812 Eating Places; 6794 Patent Owners Lessors

Outback Steakhouse, Inc., runs a chain of casual restaurants with and Australian theme based in the South and the Midwest, and owns substantial interest in a second chain, Carrabba's Italian Grill, which serves Italian food in a casual atmosphere.

The enterprise was founded in Florida in 1987 by three partners, Tim Gannon, Bob Basham, and Chris Sullivan, all of whom had experience in the restaurant industry. Both Sullivan and Basham had worked at the Steak & Ale restaurant chain, which pioneered the salad bar and other popular concepts in the American restaurant industry. Following this experience, the two moved to a Steak & Ale's competitor, Bennigan's, and then returned to work with Steak & Ale's founder to open outlets of his new chain, Chili's, in Florida. Gannon also worked at Steak & Ale and in other restaurants in New Orleans.

By the late 1980s, all three men were anxious to launch a new endeavor. "Here are three guys who have always worked for other people and always said, 'God, if we had our own, we would do it a little bit different," Gannon later recounted to *Restaurants and Institutions* magazine.

Despite conventional wisdom, which said that Americans were moving away from meat and toward healthier, lighter food, Gannon, Sullivan, and Basham observed that restaurants specializing in steak, from inexpensive eateries like Ponderosa to high-priced restaurants like Ruth's Chris, were doing well. "Our research had really showed us that beef and prime rib were still the No. 1 thing people went out to eat," Basham remarked to *Restaurants and Institutions* magazine. He and his partners decided to open a steak restaurant that served the middle of the market, featuring high-quality food, a casual atmosphere, and an average dinner bill of $15 to $20.

All the partners needed was a theme that would give their restaurant concept a memorable identity. At the time, the 1986 movie *Crocodile Dundee* had recently been released and become a big hit. Despite the fact that none of the restaurant's founders had ever been to Australia, the trio decided to give their venture an Australian theme. In this way, they would be tapping into the traditional "western" association with steak, but with a twist. "Most Australians are fun-loving and gregarious people, and very casual people," Basham later told *F&B Magazine.* "We thought, 'That's exactly the kind of friendliness and atmosphere we want to have in our restaurants.' Then it was just a matter of coming up with an Australian name that worked for us. The Outback was kind of the wild, wild west of Australia. So there you go for the western theme. But instead of United States western, it's Australian western."

Initially, the group had modest plans for their venture. Rather than planning nationwide expansion, they hoped to open half a dozen outlets, and earn a nice living. "We figured if we divided up the profits with what we thought we could make out of five or six restaurants, we could have a very nice lifestyle and play a lot of golf," Basham told *F&B.*

However, opening night for the first Outback restaurant, in March 1988, did not look promising. In keeping with the Australian theme, the restaurant's decor featured boomerangs hung on paneled walls, kangaroo posters, shark jaws, stuffed koalas, and surfboards. The menu, however, was free of Australian influence, containing all American food, with specially seasoned steaks as its centerpiece. This split was deliberate, as was the group's refusal to visit Australia in the course of developing the restaurant's theme. "I might have tried to bring back authentic Australian food, which Americans don't generally like," Sullivan told *Fortune.* "Our company sells American food and Australian fun."

The company wasn't selling either on Outback's debut night. "We opened our doors, and it was very quiet," Gannon later told *F&B.* "Hardly anybody came. We had to call people over for dinner. No one had ever heard of Outback except our friends. And they were our only customer base."

Business began to pick up as the partners increased promotion—including cooking at radio stations and other local events—and as they received favorable reviews from restaurant critics. Outback's timing coincided with growing interest in more traditional, so-called "comfort" foods such as beef. Within 15 months, five more restaurants had been opened, and the chain was off to a fast start.

Outback's quick takeoff attracted the notice of other people in the restaurant industry. "We had guys who came to us and said: 'Listen—we're either going to franchise from you or we're going to rip you off. Take your choice.' Their point was they really loved our concept and they wanted to be a part of it," Gannon related to *F&B.* Faced with this kind of interest, Outback's founding partners agreed to an expansion of their concept.

Through franchise agreements and joint ventures, Outback's founders introduced their restaurant idea to areas outside Tampa in the late 1980s and early 1990s. After takeover talks with Chili's petered out in late 1989, Outback opened locations in Orlando and Jacksonville, Florida; Louisville, Kentucky; Houston and Dallas, Texas; Indianapolis, Indiana; and Washington, D.C. By the end of 1990, the company was operating 23 restaurants. In the following year 26 more locations opened for business, for a total of 49 restaurants.

Late in 1991, Outback's three founders, whose ownership stakes totaled 40 percent each for Sullivan and Basham, with the remaining 20 percent held by Gannon, decided to go public. With the capital raised by Outback's offering on the NASDAQ stock exchange, the company began a gradual process of consolidating its ownership of the Outback locations.

The number of Outback restaurants continued to expand in 1992, as a total of 36 new restaurants were opened. Overall, the company had 52 outlets that it owned outright, 15 joint-venture operations, and 18 franchised locations, for a total of 85 Outback restaurants. In May 1992, Outback was named the third best small company by *Business Week* magazine.

Outback's rapid growth was fueled by several key tenets held by the company's founders. As a result of their extensive experience in the restaurant industry, Outback's owners believed in decentralized management. "We've been in their shoes as regional supervisors," Gannon remarked to *F&B*. "We've worked for companies and said, 'If you guys would just leave us alone and let us do our jobs, we would be so much more efficient.' We know that." Outback required that certain standards be met and retained final approval over plans for expansion, but otherwise let local managers run things as they saw fit.

Outback also gave its managers a stake in the company's overall well-being by allowing them to purchase a ten percent interest in their stores, and other employees had the right to purchase stock in the company. In addition, the company took steps to maintain positive working conditions for its employees, so that they would provide cheerful service to the restaurant's patrons. "If you worry about your employees and their environment and their ability to do the job, and you make sure they're happy, you don't have to worry about the guest," Gannon said. Accordingly, wait staff were responsible for only three tables apiece, and the company devoted 40 percent of the space at each location to the kitchen so food preparers would not be crowded. "We understand from having been managers, waiters, cooks, what they feel like," Gannon told *F&B*. "We know what the heat of the kitchen is like—personally."

The Outback menu featured items such as "Kookaburra Wings," "Aussie Cheesefries," and "Jackaroo Chops," and the company's signature appetizer, the "Bloomin' Onion." This item, which Gannon co-developed with a chef in New Orleans, was a Spanish onion with its center removed, which had been sliced into wedges so that it fanned out like a flower, and deep-fried. The onion was served on a plate with a bowl of sauce at the center for dipping, as an alternative to onion rings. "We had to figure how to get the center out, how to fry it, how to make it work as an appetizer where each petal could be pulled

out individually," Gannon recounted to *F&B*. "Then the idea was to apply New Orleans seasonings to the onion, so that not only did you have something pretty, but you also had something with an exciting flavor profile. And the recipe for the seasoning on ours, that's my recipe."

Outback's steaks, the centerpiece of its menu, also featured a New Orleans flavor, being seasoned with 18 herbs and spices. To help them cope with the enormous cuts of meat that the restaurant served, Outback gave its diners over-sized flatware as well, including a steak knife that more closely resembled a saber.

While American food ruled Outback's menu, the Australian theme reasserted itself at the bar, where each restaurant typically earned 17 percent of its revenues. About three-fifths of the company's beer sales, and four-fifths of its wine sales, were generated by Australian brands, including Foster's, Rosemount, and Black Opal. Much of the bar business came from customers waiting for tables—the restaurants were so popular that there was typically a 30-minute wait for dinner. To meet this demand, Outback began to build larger restaurants in the early 1990s, expanding from its prototype 160-seat design to a 200-seat design. The company also switched from paging waiting customers to a quieter beeper system, which helped cut down on the tumult that came to characterize the Outback experience.

In marketing its concept, Outback targeted people between the ages of 35 and 54 with annual incomes exceeding $50,000. To distinguish its restaurants, Outback developed a huge red neon sign that fronted its buildings. In addition, the company signed on to sponsor the nationally televised college football Gator Bowl, which was played each year in Jacksonville, Florida. Outback also devised a "No Rules" advertising campaign, focusing on the theme that diners could get what they wanted— good food and prompt, cheerful service—at Outback. Customers were assured that they could order items not on the menu and that the kitchen would strive to fulfill their wishes.

One wish Outback did not set out to fulfill, however, was a diner's desire to eat there for lunch. Because a lunch shift complicated restaurant operations, and rarely brought in profits, the company opened only for dinner. "There's not much money in lunch, and it burns out employees," Sullivan explained to *Fortune*. This policy also allowed Outback to save on real estate for the restaurants it built, since locations near where people worked were more expensive than areas where people lived.

By the end of 1992, these policies had pushed Outback's system-wide restaurant sales to $195 million. Rapid growth both in revenues and number of restaurants continued in the following year. Outback added 35 company-owned outlets and 26 new franchised restaurants in 1993. The chain passed the 100-restaurant mark in March of that year, having expanded into 15 states. Overall, Outback had reported 147 percent annual growth over its first three years as a public company.

Outback began to test a second restaurant concept in March 1993, entering into a joint venture with a Houston restaurant group to develop Carrabba's Italian Grill restaurants, which featured Italian cuisine in a casual setting. For $2 million, Outback acquired a half interest in two existing restaurants, and the company agreed to invest an additional $8 million in the construction of new restaurants. The company added two new locations in Houston in 1993, and laid plans to add six to eight more in Texas and Florida in the following year.

The Carrabba's concept was similar to the original Outback restaurant in many ways. Its average diner's check was somewhat higher, and alcohol made up nearly one quarter of sales, versus 17 percent at Outback. Overall, however, food costs at Carrabba's were lower. By opening this second front in the restaurant wars, Outback hoped to guarantee continued growth as the market for Outback steakhouses became saturated.

Outback continued its brisk pace of expansion in 1994. The company opened 68 new Outback steakhouses and eight new Carrabba's Italian Grill locations. Financial returns also remained robust, as the company continued to report increasing sales and revenues. The company was making steady progress in its transformation from a regional restauranteur to a national presence in the hospitality industry.

"It's not a real complicated formula," Basham told *F&B*. "You just have to give great service and great food, and have a great price value in a comfortable atmosphere." With this philosophy, the group that had once wanted simply to guarantee itself ample time for golf had adjusted its sights a little higher. "We want to be the major player in the casual dining segment," Sullivan told *Restaurants and Institutions*. "We're headed in that direction. We understand our business. We don't have to go out and beat our chests. We just quietly want to win."

Principal Subsidiaries: Carrabba's Italian Grill.

Further Reading:

Chaudhry, Rajan, "Outback's Bloomin' Success," *Restaurants & Institutions,* December 15, 1993, pp. 34–55.

George, Daniel P., "Australia, American-style," *F&B Magazine,* November/December 1993, pp. 20–24.

Janofsky, Michael, "On the Menu, Steak Bucks Trend," *New York Times,* January 25, 1993.

Kronsberg, Jane, "Outback's Specialties Outsized," *Charleton Post and Courier,* May 5, 1994, p. 14-D.

McLaughlin, Mary-Beth, "Toledo says 'G'day mate' to new Outback Steakhouse," *Toledo Blade,* March 13, 1993.

Michels, Antony J., and John Wyatt, "Managing," *Fortune,* August 9, 1993, p. 40.

"The Best Small Companies," *Business Week,* May 25, 1992, p. 97.

—Elizabeth Rourke

Packaging Corporation of America

1603 Orrington Ave.
Evanston, Illinois 60201-3853
U.S.A.
(708) 492-5713
Fax: (708) 481-2271

Wholly Owned Subsidiary of Tenneco Inc.
Incorporated: 1959
Employees: 13,400
Sales: $2.04 billion
SICs: 2631 Paperboard Mills; 2653 Corrugated & Solid Fiber
   Boxes; 2657 Folding Paperboard Boxes; 2656 Sanitary
   Food Containers

Packaging Corporation of America (PCA) is one of the world's
leading manufacturers of packaging products. PCA leads all
U.S. producers in the manufacture of styrenic plastic, aluminum
foil, and molded fiber. The company is also among the largest
makers of recycled paperboard, containerboard, and corrugated
boxes. PCA's containers are used in a huge assortment of
industries. Its shipping container products are used in the transport of food, paper products, metal products, rubber and plastics, and automotive products. Soap, detergent, food, and other
consumer goods are among the items commonly packaged in
folding cartons made by PCA. Industries related to food service
are regular users of PCA's disposable plastic and aluminum
containers. Products manufactured by PCA are sold under a
variety of names, including "Packaging Corporation of America," "EZ POR," "Revere Foil Containers," "Dixie Container," and "Agri-Pak." The company operates 55 shipping
container plants, six carton plants, and various other manufacturing facilities, totaling 93 plants in all, including seven overseas. PCA is based in Evanston, Illinois (a suburb of Chicago),
and is a subsidiary of Tenneco Inc..

PCA was formed in 1959 through the merger of three established packaging companies. Each of those companies, Central
Fiber Products Company, American Box Board Company, and
Ohio Boxboard Company, was already a major entity in the
packaging industry by the time of the merger. Both Ohio Boxboard Company, of Rittman, Ohio, and American Box Board
Company (originally called American Paper Box Company),
located in Grand Rapids, Michigan, were founded in 1903. Each
had enjoyed half a century of steady growth prior to the merger.

Central Fiber Products Company, based in Quincy, Illinois, had
itself been assembled through the consolidation of several
smaller packaging firms. It was formed in 1931 upon the merger
of North Star Mill, North Star Egg Case Company, Carey Straw
Mill, H. T. Cherry Company, and Indiana Board and Filler
Company.

By forming PCA, the merger instantly created a major force in
the paperboard and packaging industry. The combined company brought together under one corporate umbrella a network
of over 50 plants and 7,000 employees, with facilities sprawling
from the East Coast out to the Rockies. Within the first few
years of PCA's existence, it was the sixth-largest paperboard
producer, the fourth-largest maker of cartons or folding boxes,
and the tenth-largest manufacturer of corrugated containerboard
in the United States. One of its facilities, a plant located in
Rittman, Ohio, was the largest integrated carton factory in the
world.

In the first years after the merger, PCA took steps to cut costs by
eliminating redundant operations. Corporate airplanes and other
unnecessary assets were sold off, and production was reallo-
cated to take advantage of the company's most efficient facilities. Operations were organized into four divisions: Paperboard,
Carton, Container, and Molded Pulp. For 1960 PCA had sales
of $138 million. The following year, the company made a move
toward self-reliance by purchasing a 52 percent interest in
Tennessee River Pulp & Paper Co. Thereafter, Tennessee River
provided PCA with most of the kraft linerboard it would need to
supply its corrugated container plants. Also in 1961 PCA was
listed on the New York Stock Exchange.

Throughout the early 1960s, PCA struggled to improve its
profitability as sales remained flat and profits became more
elusive, largely due to depressed prices and stiff competition
among container companies. The company was also impaired
by a lengthy strike at its Rittman plant. Nevertheless, the company pressed forward with its expansion plans, and in 1962
PCA acquired container plants in Baltimore, San Antonio, and
the Dallas-Fort Worth area. In 1963 PCA president U. S. Good-
speed was elected vice-chairman of the company's board of
directors. He was replaced as president by J. N. Andrews, who
had joined Ohio Boxboard as a salesman in 1936. At the same
time, W. D. P. Carey, PCA's chairman and its first president,
was named chief executive officer.

Paperboard prices stabilized somewhat in 1964, and PCA was
able to gain ground, posting its best earnings in nearly a decade.
By this time, the company accounted for about 3 percent of all
the paperboard produced in the United States. Of its $145
million in sales that year, 45 percent came from corrugated and
solid fiber containers, 24 percent from folding cartons, 22 percent from paperboard mill products, and the rest from molded
pulp and molded plastic products. Nearly three-fourths of
PCA's paperboard output was converted into containers. The
rest was sold to other companies for use in their manufacturing
operations.

In 1965 PCA was acquired in a stock deal by Tennessee Gas
Transmission Corporation, now known as Tenneco Inc. As a
subsidiary of Tenneco, PCA continued to expand throughout
the 1960s. By 1970 the company was operating 55 U.S. facili-

ties. That year, PCA gained full ownership of Tennessee River Pulp & Paper by buying out the interest formerly held by partners Bell Fibre Products, St. Regis Paper Co., and Tennessee River's former president, G. W. E. Nicholson. The purchase gave PCA full access to Tennessee River's cutting rights on 300,000 acres of timberland in Tennessee, Alabama, and Mississippi. PCA also opened its 34th corrugated container plant, located in Burlington, Wisconsin, that year.

By 1972 PCA had annual revenues of $286 million, which represented about nine percent of Tenneco's total. In early 1973, the company announced that it would begin a $40 million expansion program to boost capacity at its existing paperboard and container plant facilities. The bulk of the spending was to take place at Tennessee River's Counce mill in Counce, Tennessee. Later that year, S. F. Allison, PCA's president and chief executive officer, announced a reorganization of both the company's product line divisions and its management structure. The number of divisions within the company was reduced from four to the following three: the containerboard products division, including the container plants and the company's Filer City, Michigan, containerboard mill; the paperboard products division, including its carton plants and five paperboard mills; and the general products division, newly formed to include the company's plastics and molded products operations as well as facilities involved in the production of storage units. Each division was led by a senior vice-president reporting to Allison.

The entire boxboard container industry was rocked in 1976 when a federal grand jury indicted twenty-three companies and fifty of their executives for price-fixing between 1960 and 1974. PCA was one of the companies found to be in violation of antitrust laws. George V. Bayly, senior vice-president of PCA's general products division, and J. A. Neuman, one of the company's plant managers, were among the group of executives to plead no contest and receive short jail terms and fines. Most of the corporations involved, including PCA, also received fines in the case, which was one of the largest of its kind at that time.

From 1983 into the mid-1990s PCA made sizable acquisitions each year, transforming itself into a true powerhouse in the container industry. In 1983 PCA acquired much of Diamond International Corporation's molded fiber products operation. The purchase included both domestic and foreign properties, including plants in Red Bluff, California, and Plattsburgh, New York; a Portland, Maine research and development facility; an idle Ohio factory; Omni-Pac of West Germany; and Hartmann Fibre, a British firm.

The following year, PCA bought Ekco Products Inc., a manufacturer of aluminum and plastic products, many of them for kitchen use. Based in Wheeling, Illinois, Ekco had facilities in New Jersey, California, England, Denmark, Belgium, and Japan. The Ekco purchase, according to PCA president and CEO Monte R. Haymon, enabled the company to fill out its product line with a greater number of specialized items. In 1985 PCA purchased A&E Plastics, a major producer of rigid plastic containers for use in the food service industry. The following year PCA formed a new division, the PCA Disposable Packaging Group, as an umbrella for the newly added Ekco and A&E operations.

PCA continued to make the kitchen its favorite room over the next few years. In 1986 the company acquired EZPor Corporation, a company specializing in convenience cookware and disposable baking pans for the retail market. In 1987 PCA acquired Kaiser Packaging, the foodservice foil and foil container operation of Kaiser Aluminum & Chemical Corporation. That acquisition brought with it a manufacturing plant in Wanatah, Indiana; equipment and other assets from a plant in Permanente, California; and a specialty operation in Bensenville, Illinois. More aluminum operations were brought into the fold in 1988. That year, PCA acquired the Ekco Group, Inc.'s Canadian aluminum foil and plastic foodservice container unit, and subsequently renamed it PCA Canada, Inc. The company also bought Revere Foil Containers, Inc., a manufacturer of aluminum foil containers and clear plastic domes. Middleton Packaging was also purchased that year. Middleton's specialty was molded fiber filler flats for egg packaging. With the addition of these operations, PCA's annual revenue reached $1.3 billion for the year.

In 1989 PCA acquired Carenes, SA, a Spanish molded fiber operation; and Dahlonega Equipment and Supply Company, an East Coast supplier of egg, produce, and seafood packaging. Carenes was renamed Omni-Pac Embalajes, SA, and Dahlonega's name was shortened to Dahlonega Packaging. Among the company's 1990 additions were Polbeth Packaging Limited, a Scottish foodservice thermoformed container firm; and Alupak, A.G., a Swiss company whose products included sterilizable smoothwall aluminum containers. PCA also purchased two important U.S. companies: Pressware International, which was the largest manufacturer of pressed paperboard food containers in the United States, and Dixie Container Corporation, which was the biggest independent corrugated company in the Southeast, producing recycled corrugating medium.

In 1991 PCA made its largest acquisition to date, assuming the operation of 19 corrugated container plants and two containerboard mills and acquiring the cutting rights to about 650,000 acres of timberland from Georgia-Pacific. Some of these properties were purchased outright, while others were operated through lease arrangements. Another 1991 acquisition, the Ellington Recycling Center, supplied secondary fiber to PCA's Counce linerboard mill. In 1992 the company launched a joint venture in partnership with a Hungarian state-owned packaging company. The newly created firm, PCA-Budafok Paperboard Ltd., was formed to operate a recycled paperboard mill and a folding carton plant outside Budapest.

During 1993 PCA focused on improving productivity rather than continuing to expand, returning a profit of $139 million despite a slight drop in revenues. Over the course of the year, 32 new products were introduced by PCA's Domestic Aluminum and Plastics Packaging Group; at the same time, the company's Molded Fibre unit was merged into this group to form a new division called Specialty Packaging.

In 1994 PCA continued to expand both internally and through international development under President Paul Stecko. Plans were announced late in the year for a $73 million project to upgrade the company's Counce, Tennessee, linerboard mill. The project would enable the mill to produce grades of linerboard that were lighter but stronger than had previously been possible. In Europe, the company increased its ownership in the Budapest mill from 30 to 100 percent. The company also began construction of a folding carton plant in Bucharest. That facility, a 50–50 joint venture with a Romanian company, was to operate using paperboard supplied by the Hungarian plant. Negotiations were also underway during 1994 for a joint venture in China. Conditions for the packaging industry remained solid, and PCA continued to seek out acquisitions that would complement its growing and profitable assortment of operations and products.

Further Reading:

"Come-Back for Packager," *Financial World,* September 16, 1964, p. 7.

Facts about Packaging Corporation of America, Evanston, Illinois: Packaging Corporation of America, 1994.

"Packaging Corp. Unfolds a Recovery in Earnings," *Barron's,* March 23, 1964, p. 36.

"PCA Realigns Mgmt. and Product Line Functions," *Paper Trade Journal,* September 17, 1973, p. 32.

Rolland, Louis J., "Packaging by 'PKG'," *Financial World,* April 18, 1962, p. 24.

Solomon, Caleb, "Tenneco Packaging Subsidiary Weighs Making Acquisitions as Big as $1 Billion," *Wall Street Journal,* October 11, 1994, p. B10.

"Tennessee Gas Plans to Acquire Packaging Corp.," *Wall Street Journal,* March 29, 1965, p. 26.

Thompson, Morris S., "Aides of Box-Making Concerns Sentenced to Prison, Fined in Price-Fixing Case," *Wall Street Journal,* December 1, 1976, p. 4.

—Robert R. Jacobson

Pan American World Airways, Inc.

Pan Am Building
New York, New York 10017
U.S.A.

Incorporated: 1927
Dissolved: December 1991

Over the course of its over six decades in operation, Pan American World Airways, Inc. was one of America's most widely recognized airlines. The firm's pioneering flights to Europe, Asia, and South America helped earn it an important role in aviation history. Under the direction of Juan Trippe, the firm encouraged long distance air travel and secured the technology necessary to achieve international flights. At one time, the company moniker was one of the most recognized trademarks in the world, second only to Coca-Cola. But after eluding total financial ruin several times in the 1970s and 1980s, a combination of bad management, high debt, poor employee relations, and just plain bad luck brought the airline's demise in December of 1991.

The architect of Pan Am's prominence, and ironically of its later decline, was a man named Juan Terry Trippe. Upon graduation from Yale in 1920 Trippe worked for a year in his father's bank. Soon thereafter he left the bank in order to pursue a career in the airline business. When his father died suddenly, Trippe used his inheritance to purchase nine Navy "Jennys" for a new endeavor, Long Island Airways. Unable to generate enough business, the company failed.

Trippe and two wealthy friends from Yale then organized a second airline after the passage of the Kelly Air Mail Act. Their company, Colonial Air Transport, won the first airmail contract route between New York and Boston. They purchased two three-engine Fokker airplanes the following year which enabled them to transport passengers as well as mail. A dispute among stockholders soon resulted in the sale of the company to what later became known as American Airlines. Trippe and his partners were excluded from both the decision and their airline.

Undaunted, Trippe's group purchased Aviation Corporation of the Americas with the intention of bidding on the Key West-Havana mail route. In 1928 the company merged with Pan American Airways and Atlantic, Gulf and Caribbean Airways. The new company retained the Pan American name and insti-

tuted the first scheduled international commercial destination, to Havana, Cuba.

Passengers' often well-founded fears of flying high above 90 miles of open water made it difficult for Pan Am to book all eight seats on each flight. The bravado of the airline's pilots didn't help: some were known to enter Cuban bars and dare American tourists to fly back to Florida. In Miami the company tried a more subtle tack: "Fly with us to Havana, and you can bathe in Bacardi rum four hours from now." One of Pan Am's three Fokker airplanes was, in fact, lost in the ocean in 1928. Nonetheless, Pan Am's embrace of such new technologies as directional radio, navigational instruments, and meteorological measurement helped make long-distance air travel safer and more popular.

Trippe was now planning Pan Am's expansion in the Caribbean. Due to a lack of airports in the region he supported the development of the water-landing Sikorsky S-38 "flying boat." Pan Am purchased 25 of the five-ton airplanes, which could travel 100 miles an hour and had a range of 300 miles. In anticipation of the U.S. Postal Service opening several new routes, Trippe had his flying boats make survey flights beyond Cuba over routes that, at his insistence, were to be selected for airmail contracts. He also dispatched advance men to secure landing rights, mail contracts, and other concessions so that when the post office finally invited airmail bids Pan Am would be the preferred choice. In this way the company secured routes to Puerto Rico, Panama, and other points throughout the Caribbean.

In 1930 Postmaster General Walter Brown compelled the merger of Pan Am and its biggest airmail contract competitor, the New York, Rio and Buenos Aires airlines. The union doubled Pan Am's fleet and earned it the extremely lucrative South American East Coast airmail contract. These routes served as a springboard for future business and promoted Pan Am to the world's largest airline and the "chosen instrument" for flying the U.S. flag abroad.

Pan Am's use of flying boats helped consolidate its coverage of the Caribbean and turned its attention to traversing the oceans. The airline used the newly developed China Clipper (a Martin M-130), with a range of 2500 miles, to transport passengers and mail from California to the Orient. Overcoming huge obstacles of diplomacy, financing, and engineering, Pan Am established service to Europe in June of 1939 using the larger and faster "Dixie Clipper" aircraft.

Pan Am's aeronautical pioneering was quite costly. Trippe was said to have been obsessed with the idea of "having a plane in every airport in the world." This left little money for dividends and, as a result, the stockholders voted to replace him with his old friend and associate "Sonny" Whitney in March of 1939. Whitney, however, was an ineffective manager and proved unable to maintain control of the company. Less than a year later Trippe was asked to return.

As the only established American international airline, Pan Am played a major role in the war effort when it placed itself at the disposal of the U.S. government in the early 1940s. In November of 1940, the company signed a contract with the War Department providing for the construction of airbases and remote supply, radio, and weather stations. In October of 1942 the airline established a war transport service from the United States across the South Atlantic to West Africa and from there to points in the Middle East. Pan Am was rewarded handsomely for having devoted up to three-quarters of its resources to the armed forces during World War II. When the war ended the company's hegemony over international air routes was at its peak.

Trippe hoped to maintain the profitable relationship forged during the war between Pan Am and the federal government through the creation of one official airline that would compete with foreign carriers. His proposal that Pan Am be made a regulated monopoly (not unlike utility companies) was rejected by Congress, however. Furthermore, the government opened the door for the competition Pan Am had never previously experienced. With an eroding market share Pan Am looked to the future, commissioning the development of Boeing's first jetliner, the 707. The delivery of the first 15 of these airplanes precipitated the jet age and propelled Pan Am once again to an enviable competitive advantage.

In the early 1950s Pan Am expanded its transportation holdings through the acquisition of American Overseas Airlines. The company also diversified into hotels, real estate, and corporate jet aircraft, and contracted with the National Aeronautics and Space Administration (NASA). These extracurriculars proved profitable, particularly a New York real estate deal involving the construction and leasing of the Pan Am building, which was dedicated in 1963.

But as the 1960s wore on, the company again lapsed into poor performance as a result of overextension. By the time Juan Trippe announced his plans to retire in the latter years of the decade, his goal of having a plane in every airport in the world had brought about a sprawling 81,430-mile route system. Competition from government-subsidized overseas airlines intensified. Trippe chose Najeeb Halaby, former head of the Federal Aviation Administration, to succeed him in 1969. Halaby found himself presiding over a firm so decentralized that he characterized it as ''an airline without a country.'' Worse, Pan Am was nearly bankrupt. Some thought the system could not be maintained without the award of a government subsidy or a compensatory monopoly, neither of which were likely. The fuel crises of the 1970s only exacerbated existing problems. Pan Am chalked up losses of $364 million from 1969 through 1976, and accumulated over $1 billion in debt.

With the help of tax-loss credits, Pan Am made its first profit in nearly a decade in 1977. The man responsible for this was William Seawell, who was brought in to replace Halaby in 1972. Unable to obtain subsidy relief from either the Civil Aeronautics Board or the White House in 1974 and 1975, or possible funding from the Shah of Iran, Seawell instituted austerity measures in 1976 and renegotiated the company's debt. Abandoning Trippe's grand strategy, he reduced the system 25 percent by severing money losing services. He reduced personnel by approximately 30 percent and approved an offer by employees to accept a wage cut. By these measures complete financial ruin was averted.

Late in 1979 Pan Am received approval for the $437 million acquisition of National Airlines, with which Seawell hoped to bolster Pan Am's relatively weak domestic operations. But the purchase, later criticized as too expensive, was also poorly timed. The early 1980s ratification of Airline Deregulation Act triggered sometimes cutthroat competition from new domestic and foreign carriers. The company was once again on the brink of financial ruin, this time as a result of fiscal overextension. Only by selling a large portion of its assets, including the Pan Am building headquarters, was it able to avoid bankruptcy.

Edward Acker became chairman of Pan Am in September of 1981. This cautious but optimistic manager continued to divest Pan Am's assets. On September 14, 1984, Pan American Airways created a holding company called Pan Am Corporation to assume ownership and control of the airline and the services division. Although the fast-growing Pacific market was one of the few profitable areas Pan Am could rely on, the company was so strapped for cash that it sold its Asian routes to United Airlines for $715.5 million in 1985.

In spite of the divestment of most of the firm's most important assets, Pan Am's domestic division alone lost over $1 billion from 1980 to 1987 and accumulated $914 million in long-term debt at the same time. Several groups—including Kirk Kerkorian, a Beverly Hills financier; Chicago's Pritzker family; and a group of investors led by former Navy Secretary John Lehman—made takeover overtures, but a new chairman, Thomas G. Plaskett, turned them away. In 1988, Plaskett negotiated $180 million in concessions from Pan Am's five unions—enough to get the airline through what would become the harshest winter of its history.

On December 21 of that year, Pan Am's flight 103 en route from London to New York, was demolished by the blast from a terrorist-planted bomb over the town of Lockerbie, Scotland. All 243 passengers and 16 crew members were killed and another eleven people on the ground were crushed by debris. This human tragedy soon began to make a significant impact on the already-struggling airline. Lawsuits on behalf of the victims' relatives found Pan Am and its subsidiary, Alert Management Systems Inc., guilty of willful misconduct in 1992. Damages, which would be assumed by the airline's insurer (the United States Aviation Insurance Group), totaled hundreds of millions. But Pan Am's insurers continued to appeal the decision into late 1994 and refused to make any compensation to the victims' families.

In the meantime, rising fuel costs and increasing competition in the United States and abroad forced Plaskett to layoff 2,500. To raise the cash necessary for continued operation, Plaskett and the board of directors decided to sell the firm's only consistently profitable subsidiary, Pan Am World Services, as well as an important German route, in 1990.

That fall, Plaskett worked to open all Pan Am's options. Although he was, by this time, actively seeking a merger partner, he also optimistically announced an eight-point plan to improve service, marketing, liquidity, and employee relations with the ultimate goal of turning a profit in 1990. The divestment of hubs at Heathrow Airport in London and Washington, D.C.'s Dulles International Airport brought in $290 million, but were not enough to keep the company from seeking bankruptcy protection on January 8, 1991.

After decades of struggling to survive, let alone prosper, Pan Am was by this time left with few options. Having sold most of its assets, opportunities for divestments were seriously limited. In spite of his weakened bargaining position, Chairman Plaskett resolved to sell all the airline, including its employees, or none of it. But after months of negotiations involving most of the industry's largest players, Pan Am's creditors lost patience with Plaskett's pace. Midway through 1991, they voted to accept an offer of $621 million in cash and the assumption of $668 million of Pan Am's liabilities from third-ranking Delta Air Lines Inc.

Delta's acquisition of the majority of Pan Am's international route system catapulted it from a 1990 ranking of 23rd among the world's airlines to a position among the top ten. The addition of most of Pan Am's North Atlantic routes as well as its American and German hubs gave Delta more European destinations than any other American carrier. The purchase also gave Delta a serious case of "corporate indigestion:" it posted a $500 million loss that year. Still, Delta chairman and chief executive officer Ronald Allen stood behind the decision. In August of 1992, he told Terry Maxon of the *Journal of Commerce and Commercial* that "A lot of people may point to the Pan Am acquisition and say, 'Oh, that's why Delta's having so many problems.' That's not true. We had some surprises with that, but overall that's gone very well."

Instead, Allen blamed the same industry forces that brought about Pan Am's December 4, 1991 demise: high costs, fare wars, and inadequate traffic due in part to economic recession and fear of terrorism. By the time Pan Am filed for bankruptcy protection, two other major competitors, Eastern and Continental (both subsidiaries of Continental Airlines Holdings) were also in the midst of Chapter 11 reorganizations, and Trans World Airlines, Inc. joined that list early in 1992. United Airlines, American Airlines, and Delta were able to take advantage of their competitors' weaknesses and together amassed over half of the U.S. market in the early 1990s. Some analysts surmised that Pan Am's failure even benefited struggling carriers like TWA and Continental by reducing industrywide overcapacity.

Pan Am's creditors auctioned off its famous logo, a blue globe, for $1.325 million in 1993. The buyer, Charles Cobb, hoped to license the well-known symbol to travel companies or airlines.

Although Pan Am's dissolution was perceived by some observers as just another business failure, others mourned the airline as they would a respected colleague. In a February 1992 editorial for *Air Transport World,* James P. Woolsey called for "a moment of respect" and praised Pan Am's pioneering spirit, charismatic leadership, and extraordinary perseverance.

Further Reading:

Bender, Marglin, and Selig Altschul, *The Chosen Instrument,* New York: Simon and Schuster, 1982.

Brock, Horace, and Jason Aronson, *Flying the Oceans: A Pilot's Story of Pan Am,* New York, 1978.

Davies, R. E. G., *Pan Am: An Airline and Its Aircraft,* Orion Books, 1987.

Flint, Perry, "Airlines: Playing for Time," *Air Transport World,* March 1991, pp. 50–52.

Gandt, Robert L., *Skygods: The Fall of Pan Am,* Morrow, 1995.

Halaby, Najeeb E., *Crosswinds: An Airman's Memoir,* New York: Doubleday, 1978.

Josephson, Mathew, *Empire of the Air: Juan Trippe and the Struggle for World Airways,* New York: Harcourt Brace, 1944.

Maxon, Terry, "Burdened by Expense of Pan Am Move, Delta Air Lines Adjusts to Lean Times," *Journal of Commerce and Commercial,* August 19, 1992, p. 3B.

McKenna, James T., "Pan Am Creditors, Executives Scramble for Cash as Carrier Shutdown Looms," *Aviation Week & Space Technology,* August 5, 1991, pp. 280.

——, "Former Rivals Poised to Pluck Prime Remnants of Pan Am," *Aviation Week & Space Technology,* December 9, 1991, pp. 18–20.

Newton, Wesley Philips, *The Perilous Sky: U.S. Aviation Diplomacy and Latin America, 1919–1931,* Coral Gables, Fla.: University of Miami Press, 1978.

Ott, James, "D-Day Due for Delta Takeover of Most Pan Am Operations, *Aviation Week & Space Technology,* October 14, 1991, pp. 44–49.

——, "Inability to Adapt in New Era of Aviation Doomed Pan Am," *Aviation Week & Space Technology,* December 16, 1991, pp. 28–29.

——, "Pan Am Filing a Sign of Consolidation, Not an Indication of Competition's End," *Aviation Week & Space Technology,* January 14, 1991, p. 29.

Stern, Richard L., "Pan Am: The End of an Empire," *Forbes,* February 4, 1991, pp. 74, 76.

Taylor, Barry, *Pan American's Ocean Clippers,* AERO, 1991.

Van Doren, Carlton S., "Pan Am's Legacy to World Tourism," *Journal of Travel Research,* Summer 1993, pp. 3–12.

Woolsey, James P. "A Moment of Respect, Please," *Air Transport World,* February 1992, p. 5.

—updated by April Dougal Gasbarre

The Paul Revere Corporation

18 Chestnut Street
Worcester, Massachusetts 01608-0828
U.S.A.
(508) 799-4441
Fax: (508) 793-1415

Public Company
Incorporated: 1895 as The Masonic Protective Association
Employees: 3,353
Total Assets: $5.9 billion
Stock Exchanges: New York
SICs: 6321 Accident and Health Insurance

The Paul Revere Corporation ranks as North America's top provider of individual non-cancelable disability income insurance (DI), holding a market share of 18.4 percent at the end of 1993. The company, which had over a half-million individual DI policies in force in the early 1990s, is the only firm with a primary concentration on individual disability insurance, accounting for over two-thirds of total premiums and nearly three-fourths of income before income taxes in 1993. The remainder of Paul Revere's business is in annuities, individual life and group business, which are employed to complement disability products while contributing to earnings. The firm celebrates its centennial in 1995, having emerged as a publicly traded company after operating as a wholly-owned subsidiary of Textron Inc. from 1985 to 1993. Textron still held a majority (83 percent) stake in Paul Revere in 1993.

The corporation traces its history to the 1895 establishment of the Masonic Protective Association (MPA) in Worcester, Massachusetts. This fraternal accident, disability, and life insurance company was formed by James E. Farwell, Frank M. Heath, and Francis A. Harrington, who was named president. Groups like the secretive Freemasons proved vital to the insurance industry in these early years, helping to diffuse the hardships associated with loss. The MPA operated as a mutual cooperative owned by the policyholding members and was exempt from state insurance legislation due to its fraternal affiliation.

In 1909, however, mounting suspicion of such groups' business dealings spawned legislation that discouraged fraternal insurance organizations in Massachusetts. Thus, MPA reincorporated as a stock company owned by shareholders, all of whom, not coincidentally, were Freemasons. In 1918, Francis Harring-

ton and his family won exclusive ownership of the MPA in what the company called a landmark legal case. The founder controlled the MPA for four more years, until his death, when son Charles Harrington succeeded him; the Harrington family would continue to lead the company for the next 50 years. In spite of its corporate reorganization and a 1922 name change to the more generic Massachusetts Protective Association, the MPA continued to sell policies exclusively to Masons until the formation of Paul Revere in 1930.

The MPA launched its first non-cancelable, guaranteed-renewable disability income product in 1918, and the concept of insurance companies offering disability insurance became popular in the 1920s. There were generally two types of disability protection, both of which were linked to life insurance benefits. One allowed the waiver of premiums without the cancellation of the life insurance, while the other, a more expensive plan, offered a premium waiver as well as a predetermined monthly income to disabled policyholders. The face value of the life insurance was often not reduced by such amendments and was payable in accordance with the original contract provisions at maturity. The policies usually designated a waiting period before disability benefits would be distributed, while providing for the termination of benefits if recovery from disability occurred. While many of these terms endured, contemporary disability insurance is often bound to income and/or earning power. MPA also pioneered non-medical life insurance, which did not require a physician's examination, through the creation of its Massachusetts Protective Life Assurance Company (MPLA) in 1924.

Although losses during the Great Depression and the 1935 creation of Social Security drove many companies out of the disability segment, MPA stayed with it. During this time, the company supplemented its income by offering life insurance products to the general public through a new subsidiary, The Paul Revere Life Insurance Company, which was formed in 1930. Insurance companies initially lost business during the Depression era, and insurance in force declined slightly to below $100 billion in 1933. Moreover, many insurance companies experienced decreased interest earnings and stock losses during this period. Nevertheless, premium income began to recover beginning in 1934, as life insurance emerged as a safe investment (especially in comparison to the volatile stock market), and "life insurance" became a synonym for absolute security and safety.

After World War II, Frank L. Harrington, Sr., nephew of Charles Harrington, succeeded to the leadership of the company. The new president brought sweeping change to the firm, merging MPLA with The Paul Revere Life Insurance Company and assuming the more easily recognized latter name in 1946. The company branched out into the nearly $30 billion group insurance industry that year. Group insurance covered a large number of people, usually the work force of a common employer, under a blanket policy without requiring medical examination and at a very low cost. This type of business grew rapidly in the postwar era. Paul Revere applied its investment expertise more broadly with the 1949 establishment of a brokerage organization. The company established a Canadian office in 1950 and soon became that country's largest disability insurer.

The 1960s brought new business activities, corporate consolidation, and a reorganization. The insurer established the Paul Revere Variable Annuity Company, which was awarded Massachusetts' first variable annuity charter, in 1965. This retirement benefit product differed from standard annuities in that its return fluctuated with the economy. The yield of variable annuities was linked to either the stock market or cost of living indices, and this investment vehicle grew more popular as inflation set in during the 1970s. The company established the Paul Revere Corporation in 1966 to direct a expanded program of investment activities.

The MPA was retired in 1966 after over 70 years in business through a reinsurance agreement with Paul Revere that called for the former subsidiary to assume all of the liabilities and obligations of the original company. That year, Frank L. Harrington, Jr. succeeded his father as leader of the company and directed a "reverse merger" with Avco Corporation. Avco, a nationally-recognized financial services company, was actually acquired by Paul Revere, but the new entity assumed the better-known Avco name, while Paul Revere became a subsidiary. The Harrington family leadership ended shortly thereafter, when Frank Jr. resigned and George L. Hogeman was elected to replace him as president.

Paul Revere's services grew in proportion to increasing complexity of the insurance industry and the general economy in the twentieth century. The company founded a reinsurance division in 1972 to provide supplemental coverage to other insurance companies and created the Paul Revere Protective Life Insurance Company the following year. During the decade, the company began offering disability insurance to groups, including employee groups. In 1974, career Paul Revere associate and top salesman Aubrey K. Reid, Jr. became the company's sixth president. Reid worked to loosen up the traditionally conservative, regimented corporate culture by putting everyone on a first-name basis and espousing a delegative leadership style. Just over a decade after he assumed the top role at Paul Revere, the company and its parent, Avco, were acquired by Textron Inc., an international multi-industry corporation.

Reid lead the mid-1980s implementation of a Total Quality Management (TQM) program adapted from the Japanese manufacturing industry. Paul Revere was one of the first companies in the insurance industry to embrace TQM, a trend that later swept the financial services sector. Paul Revere's adaptation of the theories, dubbed the "Quality Has Value Process," stressed efficiency and customer service in all functions. Tangible results credited by the company to its quality process included a near doubling of annual premium revenues from 1987 to 1992. This growth far outpaced the industry average of 47 percent over the same period.

Paul Revere ended its involvement in the group health insurance sector in 1992, as health care reform became an important issue in that year's presidential campaigns. However, while disability insurance was often discussed in conjunction with health and medical coverage, Paul Revere's primary business was not threatened by the health care reform proposals proffered during the Clinton administration. In fact, the administration heralded an era of unprecedented potential for Paul Revere, as over 80 million workers entered their peak earning years, when their need for disability insurance also peaked. The insurer hoped to maintain its share of the disability market and increase it through the continued introduction of innovative products and policies.

From 1970 into the mid-1990s, Paul Revere emerged as North America's premier disability insurer, and its competitors exited the segment in droves. Out of 1970's top five disability insurers, only Paul Revere remained in the segment, and, from 1988 to 1993, numerous competitors closed their individual disability lines. Paul Revere stepped in to fill the void by forming a National Accounts Program to sell its disability products through other companies. As a pioneer of such strategic alliances, Paul Revere was able to maintain its competitive edge. By 1993, around 30 companies in the United States and Canada sold Paul Revere products through their own distribution systems. By that time, National Accounts constituted over half of annual premiums and was the company's fastest-growing segment.

In 1993, an eventful year for the Paul Revere Insurance Group, Textron sold 17 percent of its insurance subsidiary in an initial public offering on the New York Stock Exchange, an infused an estimated $100 million in capital into Paul Revere. Moreover, the firm, touting its near 100-year history in its first annual report, became the first American insurer to top $100 million in new disability premium in a single year.

Principal Subsidiaries: The Paul Revere Life Insurance Co.

Further Reading:

Connolly, Jim, "Joint Ventures Can Prove Lucrative," *National Underwriter,* March 1, 1993, pp. 45–46.

Crosson, Cynthia, "$100 Million Capital Infusion Seen From Paul Revere IPO," *National Underwriter,* September 13, 1993, pp. 21–22.

Faugno, Rachel, *Paul Revere Insurance Group: 100 Years of Leadership,* Worcester, Mass.: The Paul Revere Corporation, 1995.

Stone, Mildred F., *A Short History of Life Insurance,* Indianapolis: The Insurance Research & Review Service, 1942.

Townsend, Patrick L., "Quality Circles Done Right," *Managing,* 1986, pp. 6–8, 28.

—April Dougal Gasbarre

Pella Corporation

102 Main Street
Pella, Iowa 50129
U.S.A.
(515) 628-1000
Fax: (515) 628-6070

Private Company
Incorporated: 1925 as Rolscreen
Employees: 2,000
Sales: $400 million
SICs: 2431 Millwork

Pella Corporation was the second largest manufacturer of wood windows and doors in the United States in 1995. Based in Pella, Iowa, the company operated three manufacturing plants in its home state. It sold its premium building products primarily through a chain of about 80 independent distributors throughout North America, but was expanding into national retail outlets. Pella changed its name from Rolscreen in 1992.

Rolscreen was founded by P.H. "Pete" Kuyper and his wife Lucille. They purchased a small company in 1925 that, one year earlier, had started manufacturing unique roll-up windows. In 1926 they moved the company to Pella, their home town, and set up shop. The original operation consisted of a three-person work force headed by Kuyper. The company was soon forced to expand as a result of surging demand for its "Rolscreen" window screens. Kuyper's manufacturing operations more than doubled by the end of the 1920s.

Despite economic hardship during the Depression era, Rolscreen continued to grow. In 1934, in fact, Kuyper introduced his second product; high-quality venetian blinds. Three years later he started selling his patented deluxe casement window, a steel-framed casement with a wood interior, divided windowpanes, exterior wash feature, and removable insulating glass. As demand for all of Rolscreen's premium products swelled, the company expanded nationwide. By the mid-1930s Rolscreen had established sales offices in 24 U.S. cities and 15 foreign countries. During the late 1930s Kuyper's sales were particularly brisk, mostly because of orders for its unique casement windows. Rolscreen eventually sold more than one million of those units.

Rolscreen shifted gears beginning in the early 1940s, switching from private-sector manufacturing to building windows for defense-related construction. Government purchases during World War II proved a significant boon to the company, and the postwar housing shortage kept its factories running at full tilt. Demand was so great, in fact, that a temporary mill was established in Pella during 1948 and 1949 to process raw lumber. As the postwar economy and population boomed during the 1950s and 1960s, company sales climbed rapidly as architects and builders increasingly turned to the manufacturer for high-quality building components.

Rolscreen met surging markets with a flurry of new products. In 1950, for example, the company created the Pella multi-purpose window, which could be used as either a casement or awning. Likewise, Kuyper introduced the Pella wood folding door in 1952. That was followed in 1957 by the Pella twinlite window, one of the first window systems to offer efficient, insulating glass as an option. Among other new products, Pella introduced the first removable wood windowpane divider in 1958, the first of many new industry products for the company.

Also during the late 1950s, the popular Pella wooden sliding glass doors were introduced. By the early 1960s those items emerged as a popular design element in many newer homes. Significant product introductions during the 1960s included: folding wood partitions; patented double-hung windows that pivoted for easy washing; wood casement windows; and the first low-maintenance aluminum clad window, which enjoyed immediate acceptance in the homebuilding industry. One of Rolscreen's most important innovations was its "Slimshade" blinds—which featured blinds positioned between the exterior and removable interior glass panes, thus reducing cleaning and maintenance requirements.

The company's growth—even during the Great Depression—was due to a steady stream of product innovations as well as Kuyper's quality strategy. Indeed, from the company's inception Kuyper displayed a commitment to his goal of producing the highest quality products available. Although Pella windows and doors were often more expensive than competing brands, Kuyper found a ready market amongst designers and builders of quality homes. The company eventually earned a reputation as one of the top window and door producers in the United States. "Our philosophy was, if you built a better product, then somebody would come buy it," explained a company representative in *Fortune* in 1993.

The Pella brand sustained its reputation for quality while the company continued to broaden its distribution network and introduce new products. In 1970, for example, Rolscreen introduced its successful line of low-maintenance clad casement windows, which included later add-ons like pivoting windows and clad sliding glass doors. The organization also introduced popular French sliding glass doors in 1979 and a line of sunrooms and skylights in 1980, reflecting a trend toward more openness and natural lighting in homes.

As a result of savvy innovation and quality strategies, Rolscreen enjoyed solid long-term profit gains. Following World War II and through the most of the 1980s, the company increased sales at an average rate of nine percent annually while relying on internal financing and a minimal debt load. The company's employees were rewarded with a generous profit-sharing plan and virtually no layoffs. Although a downturn in construction hampered growth in the late 1970s, housing markets recovered in the 1980s and the Pella brand continued to boost revenues.

Pella's gains were also a result of its strong distribution network. It focused on the high-margin, top-end of the construction industry. Through its network of about 80 distribution centers, the company focused on upscale homeowners, professional designers, and builders of high-quality homes, rather than on the lower-profit mass consumer market. Pella profited from the support of independent distributors that were motivated to sell its products, and Pella distributors benefited from being the primary local suppliers for some of the best products available.

Pella continued to benefit from its established distribution network during the 1980s. In addition, it opened the first Pella Window Store to sell its products to upscale retail buyers. The chain proved extremely successful and spiraled to about 370 in number by the early 1990s. The company also continued to introduce new products and to improve internal operations. It expanded its production facilities with a new plant in Carroll, Iowa, and brought out new products such as: vented skylights; specially coated, energy efficient windows; and stronger wooden doors that closely simulated solid wood.

With thousands of workers churning out windows and doors in high volume, Pella's manufacturing plants in the 1980s barely resembled its shops of the 1930s and 1940s. But the company's goal was to ensure that every component that left the factory had a handcrafted look. Pella continued to manufacture most of its own hardware and fittings, and even manufactured many of its production machines. Quality and productivity were achieved with high-tech manufacturing and quality control systems. For example, new designs were tested with optical (laser) equipment to ensure that they matched perfectly with blueprints.

Because of its superior quality, Pella had firmly established itself as a top producer in the door and window industry by the late 1980s. The U.S. economy began to slow in 1988, however, and the high-end market tailed off. Pella's profits flattened. The company had experienced market downturns before, but management—Kuyper had since retired—sensed that this slowdown was different. Indeed, the building supplies distribution market began shifting during the 1980s to favor producers that could market lower-priced products geared for the larger mass consumer market. As a result, Pella's customer base became increasingly narrow compared to the overall building supply market.

Of paramount concern to Pella management was the rapidly proliferating market comprised of home renovators, small contractors, and do-it-yourselfers. Those segments had grown rapidly, particularly during the late 1980s, and were expected to supply the majority of growth in home construction markets through the end of the century. Most of those customers didn't buy through Pella Window Stores or through Pella's chain of independent distributors. Instead, they often bought from various low-cost suppliers, including the many rapidly growing home and hardware supercenters that were opening up around the nation. Even many of those that were familiar with Pella viewed its products as unaffordable.

Recognizing the need for a major change in its strategy, Pella hired a consulting firm to study its dilemma and make suggestions. The analysis contended that Pella had become too complex, and that it was manufacturing too many products for too small a market niche. The study suggested that the company broaden its target market to include the giant middle-market. To do that, it would have to reduce the complexity of its offerings and focus on reducing production costs so that it could compete with other manufacturers on price.

Between 1990 and 1993 Pella spent $35 million restructuring its operations and reshaping its marketing and distribution strategy. The company reevaluated each of its products and jettisoned those that didn't contribute significantly to the bottom line. Pella also redesigned many of its major products in an effort to make them simpler and more cost-effective to manufacture. It rearranged the products into three groups, or series: Designer, Architect, and Proline. The Designer Series consisted of Pella's more contemporary offerings, while the more expensive Architect Series was comprised of traditionally styled items. Both were sold through Pella Window Stores and wholesale distributors.

The Proline series represented Pella's attempt to penetrate the blooming renovation/do-it-yourself market. Proline windows and doors were designed to be marketed through the proliferating giant home-supply chains such as Builder's Square and Home Depot. Proline components offered fewer options and were designed to be easier to understand and install. They were generally priced at about 10 percent to 20 percent less than components sold in the designer series. Although they were less expensive, the company said that the components were similar in quality. To ease distributor's fear of competition from the Proline Series, Pella gave them a percentage of all Proline products sold in their territory. Pella also trained them in servicing and installing Proline goods.

In addition to reorganizing its product lines, Pella instituted a number of measures aimed at further improving productivity—Pella's Carroll plant had already been recognized as one of the nation's most efficient manufacturing facilities by *Industry Week Magazine*. For example, Pella adopted a Japanese worker-management process known as Kaizen events. Among other benefits, the process served to quickly and continually reconfigure areas of the shop floor to achieve maximum efficiency. It also broke some of the work force down into crews of 12 in hopes of increasing communication and cooperation. The fallout of the efficiency efforts was that the time necessary to fill orders at the company dropped from ten to five days, while productivity in some areas increased 25 percent.

Partially as a result of strong home construction markets, Pella's Proline series was extremely successful. The line generated twice as much revenue as Pella had expected. Between 1990 and 1993, in fact, Pella's sales vaulted from $250 million to

$400 million. "We've virtually redefined who we are and what we are about," explained Pella Chief Executive J. Wayne Bevis in *Fortune* in 1993. Going into the mid-1990s, Pella maintained its status as the second largest player in its industry and continued its legacy of product innovation, particularly with new goods geared for the renovation markets.

Further Reading:

Henkoff, Ronald, "Moving up by Downscaling," *Fortune,* August 9, 1993, p. 72.

Kasler, Dale, "Pella Corp. Takes Goods from Boutiques to Payless," *Des Moines Register,* March 21, 1993.

Koenig, Karen Malamud, "Pella Pulls the Shades Over Poor Quality," *Wood & Wood Products,* October 1991, p. 71.

—Dave Mote

Perrigo Company

117 Water Street
Allegan, Michigan 49010
U.S.A.
(616) 673-8451
Fax: (616) 673-9122

Public Company
Incorporated: 1892
Employees: 3,879
Sales: $669 million
Stock Exchanges: NASDAQ
SICs: 2844 Toilet Preparations; 2834 Pharmaceutical
   Preparations

The Perrigo Company is the largest manufacturer of over-the-counter pharmaceuticals and personal care products for store brands in the United States. Perrigo produces approximately 15 billion pills per year and manufactures more than 850 products—most of them pharmaceuticals such as analgesics, cough and cold remedies, antacids, and laxatives, or personal products such as toothpaste, mouthwash, deodorants, and anti-perspirants. Perrigo supplies 2,200 different retailers with these products under the retailer's own label so that they can be promoted as house brands.

Perrigo has enjoyed continuous growth since the end of World War II. The company's stock was one of the hottest items on the market when Perrigo went public in 1991; it increased in value by 100 percent by 1993. Perrigo's growth can be partly attributed to the mass acceptance of generic and store brand pharmaceutical and personal care products. Perrigo has become the leading supplier of these products to such large drug store chains as Walgreen, Eckerd, CVS, Perry, and Arbor. Other key customers include grocery chains such as Kroger, Albertson's, and Food Lion, and bulk retail outlets such as Wal-Mart, Target, and K-Mart. Perrigo also has its own labels—Swan and Good Sense—but these have historically accounted for less than five percent of all company sales.

The company was founded by Luther and Charles Perrigo in 1887. The Perrigo brothers had moved to Allegan County, Michigan, a few years earlier from New York. Once in Michigan the brothers established a modest business. Luther Perrigo ran a country general store and apple drying business, while Charles helped with sales. Luther decided to package generic

home remedies and sell them to other small country stores like his own. The first packaging plant for these medicines was run out of Charles Perrigo's home, but Charles soon moved to Ohio, leaving the business entirely to his brother. Luther became president of the firm when it incorporated in 1892. Perrigo remained a family-owned business for 90 years. Five of the company's seven presidents were descendants of Luther Perrigo, who died in 1902. His son Harry became president at that time. He held the position for the next 49 years before handing over the reins to his brother Ray.

After World War II, while still under the leadership of Ray Perrigo and future president William L. Tripp Sr., management made a crucial decision. The company shifted its focus from that of a repackager of generic drugs and supplier to mainly small country stores to a manufacturer of quality drugs and beauty aids.

William L. Tripp, one of Luther Perrigo's grandchildren, became president in 1967. During Tripp's tenure as president the company began to reap the rewards of the change from repackager to manufacturer. The company's income and the number of Perrigo employees quadrupled. When Tripp died in 1969 his son Bill Tripp Jr. took over the presidency. By the time of his death in a boating accident in 1980 at the age of 45, Perrigo was the leading private label manufacturer of health and beauty products in the United States. William C. Swaney had been named president of the company two years before the accident, becoming the first leader of the company who was not a member of the Perrigo family.

Swaney's presidency lasted from 1978 until 1983. In those five years Perrigo sales tripled and the company became a much larger operation all around. Swaney acquired new companies, set up distribution centers in three states, and expanded and refurbished existing plants. Before leaving as president Swaney oversaw the sale of the company from the Perrigo family to the management. After almost 100 years of family operation the company was sold.

Michael Jandernoa, who had joined the company in 1979 as vice-president for finance, became the seventh president of Perrigo in 1984, while Swaney took over as chairman of the board and chief executive officer. Swaney instituted a style of management at Perrigo that his successor Jandernoa admitted he probably would have tried to block had he been in a position to do so at the time. Yet Jandernoa came to appreciate the open style of administration that Swaney initiated. The company contends that the different disciplines interact in the decision-making process much more than in traditional American businesses.

Jandernoa continued the policy of expansion started by Swaney. Perrigo acquired Bell Pharmacal Labs of South Carolina in 1984. Early in the Jandernoa presidency, however, the board of directors began entertaining offers from larger companies that might want to acquire Perrigo itself. In 1986 Perrigo became the largest single company in Grow Group, Inc., a publicly held group of 23 manufacturing companies. Jandernoa was named chief executive officer of Perrigo; he continued to serve as president. Perrigo represented about a third of Grow Group, Inc. As the largest component in a conglomerate with access to funds through the New York Stock Exchange (NYSE), Perrigo was able to raise new funds for more expansion.

Perrigo celebrated the company's centenary with two ambitious building projects. It built a $1.5 million plant for the manufacture of effervescent tablets and a $3.5 million graphics art complex to house all of the company's printing needs. Since Perrigo supply many different retailers with the same house brand product, their printing facilities are an important part of their production system. The graphics and printing department employed about 290 people and produced almost 70 percent of the company's labels and 44 percent of their cartons in the early 1990s. The construction of the graphics department, coupled with other expenses, totals approximately $12.6 million in outlays to the company's printing and graphics department since the Grow purchase in 1986.

After only two years as a part of Grow Group, Inc., however, Perrigo was sold back to its management in 1988. That year the company posted sales of $146 million, but by 1994 company sales had ballooned to $669 million. Three years after the sale by Grow to Perrigo management, Jandernoa took the company public. The stock proved popular, though the value has dropped and risen significantly over time. The market value of the company in July 1994 based on a closing price of $14 a share was $1 billion, for instance. But this price was down from a value of $32 a share in January 1994.

The drop in the value of Perrigo shares was attributed to a drop in sales growth. The company, in fact, had another year of record sales and continued to expand, but stock speculators felt that the market had overreacted to the Perrigo stock offering and had inflated the value beyond its true market worth. Some analysts have predicted that the drop in growth is a sign that the national brands will win back bargain-hunting customers in a healthy economy.

Other problems that Perrigo faced in its competition with national brands in the mid-1990s concerned finding the right price range for its products. While Perrigo has long wielded its ability to offer lower prices than national brand competitors, sometimes the price difference can be so dramatic—more than 50 percent in some cases—that it may have a reverse effect on the consumer. The consumer weighs the relative cost savings with a judgment on efficacy equivalence. If the price difference is too dramatic, some observers contend, the consumer becomes suspicious of the Perrigo brand and turns to the national brand. Perrigo therefore developed a system whereby some of the money that it saved from advertising was spent on market research to determine exactly how its products are accepted by the consumer, which products are worth developing, and which have limited potential due to brand allegiance.

One reason for Perrigo's enormous dominance over the store brand market was its ability to work closely with retailers to promote consumer allegiance to store brands. Beginning in the 1980s Perrigo began a major campaign to help retailers design labels, manage inventory, and develop promotions. Perrigo utilized its' house printing and graphics department to ensure accuracy and reliability in labeling and packaging, permitting rapid new product introductions. Perrigo also enjoys an advantage over many of its competitors because retail stores have a

real incentive to give Perrigo's product prominence on their shelves. Profit margins for store brand products are considerably greater than for national brands. The store's public image can be enhanced as well, provided the product sold under their name is satisfactory.

Most of Perrigo's products are packaged to be readily identifiable with the national brand equivalents. There is a fine line between taking advantage of the competitor's advertising and carving out a niche that is independently recognized by the consumer. As reported in the *OTC Market Report* in 1995, the company is threatened with lawsuits "once or twice a year," but the vast majority of them are settled in a short period of time. Most of the disputes focus on product dress rather than the actual content of the product. While Perrigo management has become accustomed to lawsuits from competitor companies, in July 1994 Perrigo found itself faced with a lawsuit from closer to home. Their former parent company, Grow Group, Inc., filed suit against the company. The Grow Group, valued at less than half of Perrigo, demanded the return of Perrigo stock or a sizable settlement in lieu thereof. Grow claimed that Perrigo management did not act in good faith at the time of the 1988 sale and asked for $2 billion in actual damages and $2 billion in punitive damages. Perrigo's response to the summons from their previous partners was sanguine. They reported the news of the summons to shareholders in the 1994 annual report saying that "based on the limited information set forth in the summons, the outcome of this matter is not currently determinable," but that "the Company believes the allegations are totally without merit and intends to oppose the action vigorously."

One of the reasons that many analysts believe that Perrigo is a safe bet for future growth regardless of recession is the fact that the company faces little legitimate competition. In December 1994 the company purchased VI-Jon Laboratories, Inc., a leading manufacturer of store brand personal care products, thereby expanding Perrigo's sales and eliminating a potential competitor at the same time. Perrigo's own assessment of their competition is that it is fragmented both geographically and in terms of product categories. Perrigo is less concerned with competitors who presently manufacture store brand products than the national brands. Those companies still have substantially greater resources than Perrigo. If they decided to offer their products at a drastically lower price, or offered their products to retailers as store brands themselves, the threat to Perrigo would be significant. Companies with national brands have eschewed this strategy entering the mid-1990s, however, preferring to keep their national brand image intact.

Perrigo also believes that other market factors could be beneficial. The OTC (over-the-counter) drug market is due to increase enormously in the next few years as the patents on dozens of prescription drugs run out. Estimates of what this market may be worth vary from $4 billion to $10 billion by the year 2000. Perrigo has been preparing for this boom in potential products throughout the early 1990s by increasing investment in research and development and by entering into joint ventures with generic prescription drug manufacturers such as Sandoz Pharmaceuticals. Once a prescription drug is reclassified as OTC the patent holder has two years of exclusivity. During this period Perrigo watches the success of the product and decides whether it should produce an equivalent version, letting the national brand pick up the tab for advertising the product to the consumer. New products accounted for $45 million of the company's net sales in fiscal year 1994.

The final frontier for Perrigo is the international market. Perrigo is investing in its recently formed subsidiary Perrigo International in hopes of spreading its domestic success overseas and increasing profits accordingly.

Principal Subsidiaries: L. Perrigo Company; Perrigo Company of South Carolina, Inc.; Cumberland-Swan, Inc.; Perrigo International, Inc.

Further Reading:

Benson, Tracy, "Industry's Unsung Heroes: Michael Jandernoa," *Industry Week,* December 7, 1992, pp. 31–32.
Gold, Howard R., "High Priced Brand?" *Barron's,* January 31, 1994, pp. 36–37.
Liscio, John, "No Go for Perrigo," *Barron's,* March 21, 1994, pp. 14–15.
Morris, Kathleen, "No-Name Power," *Financial World,* March 16, 1993, pp. 28–33.
"Perrigo Profile," *OTC Market Report,* January 1994, pp. 1–6.
Prince, Ted, "Plagiarism-Driven Business Strategy," *Journal of Business Strategy,* September/October 1993, pp. 16–17.
Rohan, Barry, "Pain into Profit," *Detroit Free Press,* January 20, 1993, p. 1E.
Shellum, Bernie, "Perrigo is Sued by Former Owner," *Detroit Free Press,* July 29, 1994, p. 2E.

—Donald C. McManus and Hilary Gopnik

Phar-Mor Inc.

20 Federal Plaza W.
Youngstown, Ohio 44501-0400
U.S.A.
(216) 746-6641
Fax:

Private Company
Incorporated: 1982
Employees: 9,800
Sales: $1.5 billion (est.)
SICs: 5912 Drug Stores & Proprietary Stores

Phar-Mor Inc. is one of the top ten deep discount drug store chains in the United States. The company rose to national prominence when, just seven years after it was founded, it catapulted to leadership of the deep discount drug retail segment. At its most prosperous, the chain boasted more than 300 locations in 34 states. In 1992, however, one of the largest corporate frauds in American history was perpetrated against Phar-Mor. As a result, the chain declared bankruptcy, cut its store locations by more than half, and was only beginning to show signs of emerging from the crisis in early 1995.

Phar-Mor came into existence as an affiliate of Pittsburgh-based Giant Eagle, Inc., a $1 billion, family-owned grocery chain with 50 locations. In 1981 Giant Eagle acquired Tamarkin Co., a privately owned grocery chain and distribution firm (later renamed Tamco Distributors Co.). Within a year, Giant Eagle heir David S. Shapira and former Tamarkin vice-president Michael J. "Mickey" Monus established Phar-Mor, Inc., an entry into the fast-growing deep discount drug segment.

The two businessmen seemed to confirm the adage that "opposites attract." The charismatic Monus developed a reputation for flamboyancy in the otherwise stuffy drug store industry—he reportedly traveled with an entourage by white limousine, for example. Shapira, on the other hand, was described as "a member of Pittsburgh's establishment" in an article appearing in *Business Week* in August 1992. Monus served as president of the new venture and Shapira as chief executive officer. Giant Eagle owned 50 percent of Phar-Mor, and real estate mogul Edward J. Debartolo, Sr., reportedly held a substantial equity interest in the new enterprise.

The deep discount segment of the drug store industry traces its history back to close-out shops that appeared during the Great Depression. The popularity of the concept waned when prosperity returned, but saw a resurgence during the recession of the 1970s. Consumers wanted quality goods at low prices, and they were willing to forgo ambiance, convenience, and selection to get them. Discount druggists kept overhead low and used specialized purchasing techniques to achieve economies that they then passed on to their bargain-hungry customers. Discounters rented older—and usually cheaper—retail spaces than their traditional drug store counterparts. They saved advertising dollars by making their own signs and product displays by hand. Most of these operations were led by independent owner/managers.

Purchasing techniques were key to the concept. In the late 1970s and early 1980s, deep discounters obtained merchandise strictly "on deal" from manufacturers, often settling for limited quantities of a product in exchange for discounts of 12 to 20 percent off wholesale prices. Buying stock "on deal" meant that these retailers carried a limited, often erratic, merchandise mix, but customers did not seem to mind, since deep discounters passed savings of 25 to 40 percent off suggested retail prices on to their customers. The retailers made up for their own lean margins with high volume, often achieving six to seven times more sales per square foot than their conventional counterparts. By the early 1980s, the competitive pressures brought by deep discounters, warehouse clubs, and other off-price concepts had begun to capture the attention of traditional retailers, including Giant Eagle, which launched Phar-Mor in 1982.

Phar-Mor used many of the techniques established by deep discounters, and additionally adopted a strategy that had helped make Wal-Mart a national phenomenon: "power buying," or placing the largest possible orders for merchandise in order to secure the best possible terms. Phar-Mor earned a reputation for hiring shrewd purchasing agents who were proficient at negotiating the best wholesale deals from vendors. Their high-pressure tactics sometimes strained supplier relations as well.

Competition intensified dramatically during the mid-1980s, as many mass marketers and independent entrepreneurs joined the deep discount segment. From 1985 to 1990, the overall number of deep discount drug stores in the United States and Canada more than doubled, from 313 to 700. Although a relative latecomer to the segment, Phar-Mor more than kept pace with the industry's rate of growth. By 1987 the chain had nearly 70 stores, and a year later it opened its 100th store. In 1990 Phar-Mor surpassed the 200-store mark, becoming the leader in the industry. As it grew, its merchandise mix expanded from prescription and over-the-counter drugs and health and beauty aids to include more general merchandise, including office equipment, sporting goods, apparel, videos, music, and frozen foods.

Writing for *Discount Store News,* analyst Arthur Markowitz noted the "symbiotic relationship" between power buying and rapid growth. In 1991, he asserted that "Phar-Mor needs an expanding base of stores to sell the huge quantities of merchandise it purchases. At the same time, the increasing number of stores has generated the growing need for vast amounts of goods purchased at the lowest possible cost." The company won financial support for this strategy from Corporate Partners, the investment arm of Lazard Freres & Co., when it sold the firm a 17 percent stake for $200 million in 1991.

In July 1992, chain President Michael Monus hosted what Tony Lisanti of *Discount Store News* called "an uncharacteristically high profile grand opening" of the 300th Phar-Mor store. While there, Monus announced a corporate goal of 340 store openings over the next five years. Even retail giant Sam Walton admitted that, of all his competitors, he feared the Phar-Mor juggernaut the most. But before the month had ended, the fears harbored by many of Phar-Mor's retail rivals evaporated in scandal.

To the shock of most observers and to the dismay of Phar-Mor creditors, investors, and suppliers, on July 31, CEO David Shapira accused Monus, Chief Financial Officer Patrick B. Finn, and two other high-ranking officials of plotting to defraud the chain of $10 million in cash and exaggerate the chain's earnings and inventories by hundreds of millions of dollars over the course of three years. A flurry of firings and finger-pointing ensued. Shapira fired Monus, his protege Finn, two other executives, and the chain's outside auditor, Coopers & Lybrand. Phar-Mor subsequently accused the accounting firm of a "grossly negligent, intentional or reckless failure to uncover a massive fraud perpetrated on Phar-Mor." The lawsuit—one of several scandals that tarnished the accounting firm's reputation in the late 1980s and early 1990s—sought compensatory and punitive damages. Coopers & Lybrand, in turn, sued CEO Shapira "for not catching the fraud," as well as Monus, Finn, Monus's father, and Jeffrey Walley and Stanley Cherelstein (two former Coopers & Lybrand accountants who had transferred to Phar-Mor). For their part, Finn and Walley confessed to the fraud, but implicated Monus as the ringleader.

His accusers traced Monus's problems to the 1987 foundation of the World Basketball League (WBL), a professional association for players under 6′7″ tall. Monus owned at least 60 percent of each of the WBL's ten teams, and was therefore responsible for that fraction of each team's expenses and losses. Milton Kantor, a fellow investor in the WBL, told *Plain Dealer* reporter James F. McCarty that each of the league's games averaged a $13,000 loss. Former Phar-Mor CFO Finn, federal investigators, and even Monus's co-owners in the WBL alleged that Monus had embezzled millions to cover the league's costs, and had conspired to inflate the value of Phar-Mor's inventory in order to garner executive bonuses and other financial advantages. *Business Week* characterized the WBL as "doomed from the start." Its August 1992 collapse coincided with revelations of the multi-million-dollar sham at Phar-Mor.

By mid-August, when anxious vendors began detaining shipments, Phar-Mor filed for bankruptcy protection under Chapter 11. By the end of the month, Shapira laid off over 1,000 employees and wrote off what he hoped were the total damages: $350 million.

At the same time, it became apparent that the entire deep discount drug category was in trouble. Aggressive pricing from conventional drug chains, supermarkets, and mass merchandisers undercut the discounters' price advantage. Over-expansion by the leading chains had saturated key markets. In an article in *Progressive Grocer* in February 1994, reporter Glenn

Snyder placed the blame on strategies that had formerly been recognized as some of the keys to Phar-Mor's success: "excessive inventory, oversized new stores, and straying far beyond core merchandise into such areas as computers and sporting goods."

The company brought in Antonio C. Alvarez as interim chief financial officer and "turnaround chief" in August 1992. Alvarez, who prescribed efficiency, contraction, and a focus on profitable stores to cure the drug chain's ills, was promoted to president and chief operating officer that September. He quickly closed more than one-fourth of Phar-Mor's stores, reduced the payroll by about 20 percent, and negotiated with creditors to save the company $233 million. In February 1993, he was promoted to the chief executive office vacated by David Shapira, who moved on to the chief executive office at Giant Eagle. Alvarez brought in David Schwartz, who had recent experience revitalizing the Smitty's SuperValu grocery chain, based in Phoenix, as president early in 1993. Phar-Mor's new management team was able to win the financial support of creditors and convince suppliers to ship merchandise, but these measures did little to reverse declining sales and low morale.

In January 1993, a federal grand jury indicted Michael Monus on 129 counts of fraud. He was charged with one of the biggest swindles in the history of U.S. business: the suit accused him of defrauding Phar-Mor's investors of $1.1 billion and the chain itself of $11.1 million. A hung jury forced the presiding judge to call a mistrial in June 1994. A second grand jury brought more than 100 new charges against Monus within a month, but as of January 1995, the new case had not yet come to trial.

CEO Alvarez's operational reorganization continued apace with Phar-Mor's financial reorganization. By the end of 1993, the chain had closed or sold 167 of its 310 stores, slashed its employee rolls from over 25,000 to 9,800, and shed superfluous merchandise lines to concentrate on health and beauty aids, drugs, and food. The chain automated inventory procedures and expanded advertising and promotions to raise awareness that Phar-Mor was still in business.

In January 1995 Phar-Mor submitted a financial reorganization plan that proposed taking the chain public. Under the plan, Phar-Mor's senior secured creditors would receive 85 percent of the chain's common stock, up to $107 million cash (or more, depending on the outcome of litigation with Coopers & Lybrand and other parties), and $100 million in variable-rate notes. Unsecured creditors would receive up to $30 million cash and 15 percent of the chain's common stock. With this plan, the company expected that Alvarez would be elected chair and that David Schwartz would advance from president to CEO. An alternative plan was filed in April of that year, however, under which an investor group led by drugstore magnate Robert Haft would purchase 30 percent of Phar-Mor. Haft and his associates would purchase five million shares of the new company's stock from creditors, as well as 2.5 million shares directly from the company. Alvarez remained committed to Phar-Mor's potential to become a strong, financially healthy company. In a press release he noted "under either plan, Phar-Mor will aggressively pursue strategic new store openings.... We believe it is time for the company to emerge from Chapter 11 and focus solely on building a stronger company."

Further Reading:

Brookman, Faye, "Deep-Discounter Phar-Mor Declares Bankruptcy," *Drug Topics,* September 7, 1992, pp. 84–85.

——, "Deep-Discounters Ending Up in Deeper Trouble," *Drug Topics,* March 8, 1993, pp. 74–79.

"Deep Discount Drug Store Waters Run Still: Many Chains Adjust Strategies as Growth of Market Segment Slows," *Chain Store Age Executive,* March 1988, pp. 102–9.

Fitzgerald, Kate, "Retailers Prescribe Pharmacies," *Advertising Age,* March 15, 1993, pp. 3, 51.

Gerdel, Thomas W., "Phar-Mor Moves to End Bankruptcy," *Plain Dealer,* January 19, 1995, p. 1C.

Greene, Jay, "Monus Stays Busy Battling Lawsuits," *Plain Dealer,* December 20, 1992, pp. 1F, 3F.

——, "Monus Indicted for Fraud," *Plain Dealer,* January 30, 1993, pp. 1A, 8A.

Hoffman, Jeff, "The Drug Store Industry in Transition," *Chain Store Age Executive,* August 1993, pp. 30–32A.

King, James, "Phar-Mor Files 2 Plans to Exit Chapter 11," *Plain Dealer,* April 25, 1995, p. C1.

Lisanti, Tony, "Phar-Mor Opens No. 300," *Discount Store News,* August 3, 1992, p. 1.

Markowitz, Arthur, "There's Phar-Mor to 'Drug' Chain Than Meets the Eye," *Discount Store News,* September 2, 1991, p. 1.

McCarty, James F., "Drugstore, Sport Empire Unravels," *Plain Dealer,* August 6, 1992, p. 1A.

Pellet, Jennifer, "Much Ado About Food," *Discount Merchandiser,* Vol. 33, November 1993, pp. 82–85, 95.

"Phar-Mor Is Seeking FBI Probe of Ousted Execs," *Plain Dealer,* August 4, 1992, p. 1G.

Phillips, Stephen, and Jay Greene, "Phar-Mor Collapse—Pointing the Finger of Blame," *Plain Dealer,* August 27, 1992, p. 1A.

——, "Jury Deadlocked on Monus," *Plain Dealer,* June 24, 1994, p. 1C.

Schiller, Zachary, "Wait a Minute—Phar-Mor Is Still Kicking," *Business Week,* March 8, 1993, pp. 60–61.

Schroeder, Michael, "A Scandal Waiting to Happen," *Business Week,* August 24, 1992, pp. 32–33, 36.

Snyder, Glenn, "They've Had Their Day," *Progressive Grocer,* Vol. 73, February 1994, pp. 81–83.

Vachon, Michael, "Phar-Mor Disaster Shakes Private Market Investors," *Investment Dealers Digest,* August 10, 1992, pp. 15–16.

Woolley, Suzanne, "These White Shoes Are Splattered with Mud," *Business Week,* September 7, 1992, p. 32.

—April Dougal Gasbarre

Pier 1 imports®

Pier 1 Imports, Inc.

301 Commerce St.
Fort Worth, Texas 76102
U.S.A.
(817) 878-8000
Fax: (817) 334-0191

Public Company
Incorporated: 1962 as Cost Plus
Employees: 8,000
Sales: $685 million
Stock Exchanges: New York
SICs: 5719 Miscellaneous Home Furnishings Stores; 5947
   Gift, Novelty & Souvenir Shops

Pier 1 Imports, Inc. is the parent company of Pier 1 Imports, a leading specialty retailer of decorative home furnishings, housewares, accessories, gifts, and related items. It sells mostly imported specialty items through a chain of more than 600 stores in North America. Pier 1 has grown quickly and sporadically since its founding in 1962.

Charles Tandy and Luther Henderson opened the precursor to Pier 1 shops in 1962 under the name Cost Plus. Henderson was serving as treasurer for Tandy's burgeoning Tandy Corporation, which became best known for its Radio Shack chain. Pier 1 was inspired by the owner of a rattan furniture importer and wholesaler in San Mateo, California, that was having credit problems. To help liquidate costly inventory, the shop owner opened a liquidation outlet in 1958 called Cost Plus. Impressed by the shop's success, Tandy offered the owner of Cost Plus a loan to start a retail Cost Plus outlet. At the same time, Tandy secured the rights to open and operate additional stores under the Cost Plus name.

The concept behind Tandy's Cost Plus chain plan was relatively simple: a strong U.S. dollar would allow him to import items, including rattan furniture, brass candlesticks, specialty textiles, and other items, at rock bottom prices from countries like Mexico, India, and Thailand. Even with large mark-ups the goods would seem relatively cheap in the United States. Furthermore, items that did not sell well could be easily liquidated by cutting their price to near cost. Although most of the merchandise was second-rate in comparison to U.S. or European-made goods, it was popular with the large baby-boom generation, most of whom were first-time buyers of furnishings.

Tandy opened 16 Cost Plus retail outlets between 1962 and 1965. By 1966, though, Tandy's growing Radio Shack enterprise began to take much of his attention away from his Cost Plus venture. On February 10, 1966, a group of 30 investors lead by Henderson bought the Cost Plus operation. They changed the name to Pier 1 Imports to reflect the stores's import emphasis and embarked on a mission to expand the concept nationally.

By 1967, Pier 1's sales had already reached $4.5 million annually, and growth accelerated throughout the remainder of the decade. By 1969, the chain had grown to 42 stores and demand for Pier 1's goods was increasing. Pier 1 went public in 1969 to raise money for continued expansion. Pier 1 had multiplied its chain to 123 stores by 1971, which represented sales growth of more than 100 percent since 1968. Among Pier 1's shops were stores that had been opened in Australia and England in 1971. During the following two years the chain also branched out into France, West Germany, the Netherlands, and Belgium.

Pier 1 prospered during the late 1960s and early 1970s by focusing on the baby boom generation who were looking for interesting, exotic goods like love beads, incense, leather sandals, and serapes. "You could characterize a lot of our customers as flower children," recounted Pier 1 chief executive officer Clark Johnson in the *Dallas-Fort Worth Business Journal*. "Our stores had the look of an old grocery store . . . and, at that time, the appeal was heavily toward cost." As the "flower children" rushed to Pier 1 to decorate their dormitory rooms, bedrooms, and apartments, by 1973 company sales rose to $68 million and earnings to $3.8 million.

After an explosive decade of growth, Pier 1's fortunes began to change in the mid 1970s. Importantly, global inflation and exchange rate fluctuations exposed Pier 1's unique vulnerability to worldwide financial changes. Foreign goods became much more expensive, thus diminishing Pier 1's important cost advantage. Furthermore, other retail chains and department stores began to vie for some of Pier 1's market share by offering many of the same imported goods. To make matters worse, the core group of customers upon which Pier 1 had focused its energy was changing; baby boomers were becoming more sophisticated by the mid- and late 1970s and were increasingly interested in more mainstream goods. Pier 1 lost touch with its patrons and failed to change its inventory to meet market demands.

In an attempt to buoy sales and profits, Pier 1 mounted several reorganization campaigns and new marketing strategies during the mid-1970s. It even tested different types of stores, including specialty retail outlets, art supply centers, rug stores, and fabric shops. Pier 1 also diversified into several wholesale operations such as Singapore Candle Company, Southwestern Textile Company, Rug Corporation of America, and Pasha Pillows. Many of its retail and wholesale experiments languished and Pier 1 eventually jettisoned most of them.

Although it failed to sustain the rampant growth it had achieved during its first ten years, Pier 1's balance sheet had improved slightly by the late 1970s. By 1979, the chain included approximately 300 stores worldwide and sales and profits had stabilized. Pier 1 merged with Cousins Mortgage and Equity Investments (CMEI) in 1979 in an effort to boost its capital. Then, in

1980, the board of directors brought in Robert Camp to help improve the company's performance.

Camp had successfully operated his own chain of Pier 1 stores in Canada and had a knack for retailing. Camp forced Pier 1 to reevaluate its buying operations and store location strategies. He also focused on improving visual merchandising techniques. During 1981 and 1982, Pier 1 consolidated its retail import operations, closed marginal stores, opened larger outlets in more profitable locations, and shifted from novelty items to higher quality goods. Investors were impressed by Camp's initiatives. Within two years, sales increased 41 percent to $165 million and operating income jumped 66 percent, to $6 million. Pier 1's stock price quickly rose from about $1 in 1980 to more than $7 by 1982.

Just as Pier 1 began to build momentum under the direction of Camp, control of the company changed hands. Under the leadership of Charles (Red) Scott, La Jolla, California-based Intermark, Inc., a billion-dollar holding company with a reputation for turning ailing companies around, bought Pier 1. Camp eventually left and Scott hired Clark Johnson to run Pier 1 in 1985. Johnson, who was known as an aggressive and sociable business man, had a varied background that included experience in both the furniture and sporting goods industries. He had also managed lumberyards and had partnered with Jack Nicklaus to run MacGregor Golf Co. As president of Wickes Furniture he engineered the turnaround of that company during the mid 1970s. Likewise, he boosted sales at MacGregor from $17 million to $50 million in just five years.

Like Camp, Johnson initiated numerous changes within the Pier 1 organization. He immediately sold Pier 1's two major subsidiaries, Sunbelt Nursery Group Inc. and Ridgewood Properties Inc. He also jettisoned the mail-order business, which lost more than $1 million in 1985 alone. In addition, Johnson developed plans to modernize Pier 1's computer information systems, upgrade advertising and marketing programs, and consolidate its North American management offices. Furthermore, between 1985 and 1989 he closed more than 60 marginal stores and refurbished most of the company's existing outlets at an average cost of $190,000 each. More aggressive managers were brought in and given the autonomy to make critical decisions.

Perhaps Johnson's most notable strategic contribution during the mid-1980s was improving Pier 1's attentiveness to its customer base. "It was clear that their was a huge audience out there which had once felt a tremendous allegiance to Pier 1," recalled Johnson in *Adweek's Marketing Week.* "I believed we could rekindle that allegiance if we showed them that we were in tune with their new values." Johnson retained New York PR agency Makovsky & Company to conduct what it termed "the most comprehensive study of the American home ever undertaken."

The study was designed with two goals in mind: 1) to determine whether or not Pier 1 was on track with the values it was emphasizing in its stores; and 2) to generate publicity as the sponsor of the study. Among other statistics, survey findings indicated that 92 percent of college-educated Americans were satisfied with their homes; 86 percent decorated their homes themselves; 57 percent believed that their homes were nicer

than what they grew up in; and an overwhelming majority described their home interior as casual. As hoped, the media reported the survey's findings and brandished Pier 1's name on the cover of major national newspapers and on television screens.

Confident of his strategy to win back Pier 1's customer base and re-position the company, Johnson embarked on an aggressive program of growth in 1986. He set of goal of doubling the total number of Pier 1 outlets by 1990 and increasing the average floor space and annual sales of the stores. Pier 1 achieved its goal one year early. By 1989 the company had doubled its chain to include more than 550 outlets worldwide. In addition, profit margins increased and the average ticket value of store items rose to $25 (from just $5 in the early 1980s). As a result, sales leapt from $173 million in 1985 to $517 million by 1990. More importantly, profits soared from $60 million to $210 million during the same time period.

Encouraged by Pier 1's success, Johnson boldly proposed expansion plans for the next decade. "The best way to predict the future is to create it," Johnson stated in *Adweek's Marketing Week.* "Pier 1 Imports has a vision of the kind of company it would like to become. By the year 2000 Pier 1 will operate more than 1,000 stores, producing more than $1.25 billion in sales and serving more than 10 million customers."

Despite grandiose plans, Johnson was forced to slow Pier 1's pace in 1990 after seven years of expansion. Economic sluggishness in the United States forced the slowdown. Although sales swelled to $562 million in 1991, net income shrunk as retail markets became increasingly competitive. Pier 1 repurchased Sunbelt Nursery Group late in 1990 in an effort to diversify and reduce its total dependence on retail markets. By early 1991, its chain included more than 650 stores, but Johnson planned to open only a few new stores during 1991 and to close several as part of a company consolidation plan. Pier 1 trimmed its home office staff, reorganized management, and brought its advertising activities in-house to save money. Johnson explained that the company was shifting its focus from growth to more acute management of its existing operations.

Pier 1 stumbled in the early 1990s. But, unfortunately for its parent company, Pier 1 was the bright spot on its list of company holdings. Intermark's other major holdings consisted of many different kinds of companies including Dynamark (a manufacturer of mag wheels), Liquor Barns, and Western Sizzlin. Intermark's stock price plunged during 1990 from $12 to $1.37 per share as the company posted a loss of $67 million (on the heels of a $10 million loss in 1990). To avert disaster, CEO Scott was forced to sell Pier 1, making Pier 1 a truly public company. Scott's responsibilities at Intermark were reduced as the company slid into debt-induced jeopardy.

Economic sluggishness continued to hurt Pier 1 during 1992 and 1993. Although its growth in comparison to the late 1980s was meager, it managed to sustain moderate revenue gains and to stabilize profits. Net income surged to about $25 million annually during 1992 and 1993 as sales climbed to $629 million. Unfortunately, Pier 1's long-term debt obligations also increased, from about $92 million in 1990 to $147 million by 1993. As part of its reorganization strategy, Pier 1 repositioned itself as ''The Place to Discover'' in 1992. It also decentralized operations to better serve its 600 stores. In an effort to generate capital, Pier 1 again sold its interests in Sunbelt Nursery.

Although Johnson's efforts at Pier 1 were often lauded by outside observers as exemplary, critics cited drawbacks of his management style and derided Pier 1's financial condition. Of concern to some analysts was Pier 1's excessive debt, which had multiplied five-fold since Johnson's arrival. In addition, Pier 1's operating costs had increased, significantly reducing the company's overall profitability compared to leaner retailers competing in the same market. Other criticisms related to Pier 1's selection of inventory and marketing strategy. Johnson himself had been derided for his high-flying, glad-handing management style as well as his high compensation.

Buffeting criticism, though, was a history of strong growth and relatively steady earnings. In addition, Pier 1 had boosted its image through charitable donations, which included a $785,000 gift to UNICEF in 1992. Pier 1 had started donating to UNICEF after Johnson's arrival in 1982 and had supplied over $3.3 million to the organization between 1985 and 1992 from the sale of greeting cards in Pier 1 outlets. The extremely successful fund raiser was established by Marvin J. Girourd, a Pier 1 veteran and the president and chief operating officer of the company in the mid 1990s.

Pier 1's sales surged to $685 million in 1994, an increase of about eight percent over the previous year, which helped diminish doubts about the validity of Pier 1's overall approach. The company opened 48 new stores and closed 17 during 1994, bringing the total size of its international chain to 636. Pier 1's reach extended into most of the United States, with an emphasis on Florida, California, New York, Texas, and Ohio. It operated 30 stores in Canada and was active in several joint ventures, particularly in Mexico and the United Kingdom.

Pier 1 continued to emphasize imports from low-cost producers in the mid 1990s. China, its largest supplier, contributed about one-third of its inventory in the early 1990s. Other major suppliers included India, Indonesia, Thailand, and the Philippines. Sales of furniture and kitchen goods each represented about one-quarter of the company's revenues in 1994. Textiles and jewelry each comprised about 13 percent of sales, and the remainder was attributable to miscellaneous gifts and accessories.

As revenues continued to increase in early 1995, Johnson reaffirmed his intent to pursue the ambitious growth plans he had proffered in 1989. He still wanted to build the Pier 1 chain to more than 1,000 stores by the turn of the century and to push

sales past the $1 billion mark. Pier 1 was pursuing growth through a multi-faceted strategy in the mid 1990s that highlighted international expansion. Johnson hoped to open 100 foreign stores by the end of the decade by buying into existing retail chains or setting up joint ventures. Pier 1 was already operating two stores in Mexico through a joint-venture with Sears and was involved with a chain of ten stores in England that were called ''The Pier.'' The company focused future expansion efforts on South American countries.

Pier 1 was also striving to boost sales through its credit card, which was used in ten percent of store purchases in 1994, and through the creation of smaller, more conveniently located stores. To that end, Pier was bucking the retail trend toward giant warehouse stores and was initiating a program of building multi-store locations that provided a better shopping experience (e.g. better parking, customer service, and a more pleasant atmosphere). In addition, it was experimenting with new advertising media, including television, in an effort to lure more young buyers. While expansion reminiscent of Pier 1's late 1980s growth was unlikely going into the mid 1990s, long-term annual growth potential of 15 percent or more through the 1990s according to one major securities analyst suggested a bright future for the retailer.

Principal Subsidiaries: Pier 1 Imports.

Further Reading:

''A 60's Store Passes Pier Review; Pier 1 Imports Plays Catch Up with Its Customers,'' *Adweek's Marketing Week,* May 29, 1989, p. S8.

Chatham, Laura, ''Pier 1 Inc. Well-Positioned to Appeal to Baby Boomers,'' *Dallas-Fort Worth Business Journal,* April 21, 1986, p. 2A.

Feldman, Amy, ''But Who Is Minding the Store?,'' *Forbes,* November 22, 1993, p. 47.

''Intermark's CEO Actually Thrives on Failure,'' *San Diego Business Journal,* January 19, 1987, sec. 1, p. 1.

Johnson, Clark A., ''Pier 1 Imports Names Clark A. Johnson Chairman and Marvin J. Giroud President,'' *Business Wire,* August 31, 1988.

Lockwood, Herbert, ''Has Intermark Bottomed Out? Scott Says So,'' *San Diego Daily Transcript,* July 30, 1991, sec. A, p. 1.

Narum, Beverly, ''Pier 1 Imports Set to Spend $100 Million on Major Expansion and Renovation Program,'' *Dallas-Fort Worth Business Journal,* sec. 1, p. 1.

The Pier 1 Imports Story, Fort Worth, TX: Pier 1 Imports, Inc., 1992.

Purcell, Joy, ''Pier 1 Imports Presents More Than $785,000 to UNICEF,'' *Business Wire,* April 28, 1992.

Sain, Ariane, ''Pier 1's Ship Has Finally Come in as Baby Boomers Mature,'' *Adweek's Marketing Week,* January 9, 1989, p. 43.

—Dave Mote

Ply Gem Industries Inc.

777 Third Avenue
New York, New York 10017
U.S.A.
(212) 832-1550
Fax: (212) 888-0472

Public Company
Incorporated: 1943
Employees: 4,000
Sales: $796 million
Stock Exchanges: New York
SICs: 2431 Millwork; 2435 Hardwood Veneer & Plywood;
2436 Softwood Veneer & Plywood; 3564 Blowers & Fans

Ply Gem Industries Inc. is a leading national manufacturer and distributor of specialty products for the home improvement industry. Its products, which include wood and vinyl windows and doors, vinyl siding and accessories, vacuum cleaner bags, and numerous specialty products, are sold primarily in home stores. Ply Gem is actually an amalgam of several independent, incentive-driven operating companies that produce complimentary goods and services. The company has grown dramatically since 1982, allowing it to report net income, before nonrecurring charge, of $17.2 million on sales of $796 million by 1994.

Ply Gem was founded in 1944, during World War II, by 27-year-old Bernard Hewitt. Hewitt started the company in New York by purchasing plywood crates for twenty-five cents and then reselling the wood for a profit. Hard work and determination allowed him to save enough money to get into the plywood manufacturing business. Postwar economic growth during the 1950s and 1960s generated a massive demand for plywood and other building products. As sales of plywood products increased, Hewitt diversified his business into paneling and other wall covering products.

In 1969, Hewitt purchased Studley Products Inc., a major manufacturer of vacuum cleaner bags. During the 1970s the company continued to expand its operations by serving mostly regional markets in the northeastern United States and Canada. Demand for wood paneling products leveled during the late 1970s as housing starts declined and new building materials continued to supplant wood paneling. In fact, the total number of U.S. companies still manufacturing significant amounts of paneling had dropped since the 1960s to about 40 by the late 1970s. That

number would continue to fall to only seven by the mid-1980s. Nevertheless, Ply Gem had grown its revenue base to about $55 million annually by 1980 and it boasted a healthy balance sheet.

In the early 1980s, Ply Gem caught the eye of savvy Wall Street investment specialist Jeffrey Silverman. Silverman believed that the solid, sleepy little paneling and vacuum cleaner bag manufacturer was undervalued and possessed vast potential for growth. In 1982 he purchased a controlling share in Ply Gem and in 1983 was named president of the company. Hewitt stayed on as chairman of the board and chief executive but gradually transferred his duties and title to Silverman. Silverman's arrival signaled the commencement of fervid growth and expansion that would hike Ply Gem's sales more than ten-fold by the end of the decade.

Silverman may have seemed like an odd match for Ply Gem. With a background in finance, the 35-year-old Silverman had no experience in building supply or manufacturing industries; he once told *Fortune,* "I don't invest in anything that a mad scientist has to explain to me." What Silverman had, however, was a knack for spotting potentially successful businesses—and investing in them. His interest in investments dated back to high school when he started an investment club. By age 21 he had collared the distinction of being the youngest member ever on the New York Stock Exchange.

While Silverman studied the ins and outs of the paneling and vacuum cleaner bag business under CEO Hewitt, he also launched his growth strategy for Ply Gem. Silverman recognized that Ply Gem had a solid product line and good regional distribution channels. However, he believed that the company was failing to capitalize on opportunities. His plan was to use Ply Gem's access to capital to purchase manufacturers with complementary products and/or distribution channels. He would select companies that would benefit from Ply Gem's competencies and also help Ply Gem expand its core products. The end result, he anticipated, would be an overall positive synergy, with the financial rewards of the whole organization becoming greater than the sum of the individual parts.

Silverman initiated his buying binge in 1983 with the purchase of Goldenberg Group, Inc. and Hoover Treated Wood Products, Inc. Goldenberg was a West Coast manufacturer and distributor of furniture components, laminates, and board products. Its primary customers were furniture manufacturers, building material retailers, and wholesalers. Hoover produced treated wood products, including fire retardant and insect- and moisture-resistant lumber. It sold to home center chains, lumberyards, and building material retailers and wholesalers. Both acquisitions gave Ply Gem a stronger national presence and broadened its product line.

In addition to his expansion strategy, Silverman also worked to shore up Ply Gem's original product lines, particularly vacuum cleaner bags and plywood paneling. In 1983, for example, Ply Gem conducted a study of women who redecorate their homes. The results showed that women generally view wood paneling as masculine and useful only for dens and basements. So, Ply Gem began manufacturing paneling that did not have a wood grain appearance. The product, which combined the benefits of wallpaper and paneling, was well received by the market and actually cost less to produce than conventional paneling. "We take inexpensive wood and give it the look of a fine precious wood," Ply Gem president Howard Steinberg told the *Philadelphia Business Journal*. Within three years the new product represented more than 50 percent of Ply Gem's paneling sales.

As a result of product innovations and new acquisitions, Ply Gem's revenues rocketed from the $55 million mark in the early 1980s to $160 million by 1984, and net income grew to $4.5 million. Although the company's debt load also swelled, a surge in Ply Gem's stock price reflected the enthusiasm of analysts. Silverman added another company to his fold in 1985 with the buyout of Allied Plywood Corporation. Allied was a national distributor of various specialty wood and wood-related products, including hardwood plywood and lumber, laminated board products, solid surface materials, and cabinet hardware. It was also a major importer of Russian wood products. Its customer base consisted of industrial wood processors such as mills and store furniture manufacturers.

Silverman engineered the acquisition of two more companies in 1986; Variform, Inc. and Great Lakes Window, Inc. Variform allowed Ply Gem to assume a leading role in the U.S. vinyl siding industry. Its products were sold to major home centers and lumber yards as well as to wholesale distributors. Great Lakes Window was a manufacturer of high-quality, energy-efficient, maintenance-free replacement windows and glass doors. It sold its products through a highly-trained sales force to window distributors, and was recognized as an industry innovator. Both acquisitions broadened Ply Gem's product offerings and offered new potential distribution channels for its other goods.

Ply Gem's sales surged to $286 million in 1986, $312 million in 1987, and then $384 million in 1988, when net income reached $16 million. As a result of investor zeal, the company's stock price shot up from just $2 before Silverman took the reins to around $13 by 1989. Subsequently, the value of Silverman's controlling stock had ballooned to $23 million. The gains were partially attributable to the 1989 purchase of Sagebrush Sales, Inc. and Continental Wood Preservers, Inc. The former was a manufacturer and distributor of specialty lumber and building products serving the home improvement and building materials markets in the Southwest. Continental was a midwest manufacturer of pressure-treated wood products.

Silverman did relatively little to combine his acquisitions into a cohesive unit during the 1980s. Instead, he managed the company by allowing each separate subsidiary to operate largely autonomously. In fact, he encouraged management to stay on board and continue to operate their business. He enticed them to stay and to do a good job managing the companies by offering financial incentives, including stock options, based on performance. "We try to encourage all our people to be as innovative and entrepreneurial as possible, then reward them for their good ideas," Silverman explained in *Equities*. The end result of the strategy during the 1980s was strong revenue growth, though comparatively weaker income gains.

Spurred by the success of its buyout strategy, Silverman executed Ply Gem's largest acquisition ever with the 1989 purchase of SNE Enterprises, Inc. SNE was a Wausau, Wisconsin-based manufacturer of windows, doors, skylights, and related products. The company started in 1978 and had grown quickly to comprise more than 1,000 workers. It was an industry leader in production and distribution efficiency, as evidenced by its steady growth during the housing downturn of the late 1980s. Mostly as a result of that acquisition, Ply Gem's sales rose to $545 million during 1990, thus boosting the holding company's growth rate during most of the 1980s to 25 percent annually.

Despite continued revenued growth, however, net income plummeted to $3.2 million in 1992 and then edged upward to about $9.7 million by 1993. Silverman had temporarily backed away from his expansion plans in 1990, concentrating instead on improving his existing operations and cutting Ply Gem's debt load. Toward that end, he launched TEAMWORK 90's, a strategic growth plan focusing on internal development designed to increase Ply Gem sales to the national home center chains.

By 1990 Ply Gem had accrued long-term debt of more than $100 million in its effort to buy new companies. It slashed that burden to just $58 million one year later. That move made it easier to finance the purchase of Richwood Building Products, Inc. in 1992. Richwood was a producer of siding accessories that sold to both remodeling and new construction markets. That purchase rounded out Ply Gem's offerings related to siding and outdoor home fixtures. It was a neat fit because it was the only major manufacturer of vinyl siding in North America that matched colors offered by almost all other siding/accessory companies.

In addition to shoring up Ply Gem's balance sheet in the early 1990s, Silverman engineered a plan to consolidate and streamline the Ply Gem organization to take advantage of its subsidiary's complementary competencies. To accomplish this feat he brought in Monte R. Haymon late in 1993 to serve as president of the company. Haymon had most recently served as president of Packaging Corp. of America. There, he increased earnings seven-fold and built it from a small paperboard company into a $2 billion international packaging corporation. The 59-year-old Haymon was a chemical engineer, a Harvard M.B.A., and a native New Yorker. Although he had no experience in the home or building supplies industries, he was undaunted by the task: "I'm a quick study," he said in *Crain's New York Business*. "I was brought in to add value . . . I wasn't brought in for my technical expertise in doors."

Haymon had his work cut out for him at Ply Gem. By 1994 the company had become a major supplier to the building supply retail market, which included warehouse stores like Home Depot and Builders' Square. The warehouse store market, in fact, accounted for about two-thirds of Ply Gem's sales. The company had also retained its presence in the more volatile professional builders' markets. However, Ply Gem had failed to take advantage of huge opportunities to cut costs and unify its operations. During Haymon's first year he initiated a $41 million restructuring program designed to streamline manufacturing, cut redundancies at the 11 operating divisions, and add $12 million to the company's net income over a period of only 12 months.

Even before the October 1994 announcement of the major restructuring, Haymon's presence was being felt at the company. He had already started eliminating managers who did not subscribe to his new corporate creed of efficiency and conformity to standards. In addition, he had slated a consolidation of Ply Gem's 4,000-member work force and its 50 offices spread across the United States and Canada. The response by Wall Street to Haymon's efforts was dramatic. Despite a rise in interest rates (which suggested a rocky short-term future for the housing industry), Ply Gem's stock price rose to nearly $23 by the end of 1994, nearly double that of the prior year.

As it entered the mid-1990s, Ply Gem was striving to position itself as a leading manufacturer and distributor of high-margin, home-related products for sale to home improvement superstores. Ply Gem's revenues soared to a record $722 million in 1993, making it one of the top 500 companies in the United States (based on sales). Furthermore, because of the anticipated boom in home improvement and renovation spending through at least the year 2000, long-term expectations for growth were positive. As Haymon worked to strengthen Ply Gem's internal operations, Silverman continued to pursue new acquisitions and focus on increasing sales to the national home center giants. In April 1995, Haymon resigned his positions as president and chief operating officer, opting to continue serving in the capacity of consultant, particularly on matters involving the restructuring initiatives implemented the year before. Involved in a search for a new company president, Silverman affirmed in a company press release that management had "assembled a team of capable managers to lead Ply Gem in its next stage of growth and development," and noted that "new executives appointed in 1994 at both the corporate and subsidiary levels will continue to implement 'best practices' in manufacturing, quality and procurement across the Ply Gem companies and to generate strong revenue and profit improvements.''

Principal Subsidiaries: Allied Plywood Corporation; Continental Wood Preservers, Inc.; Goldenberg Group, Inc.; Great Lakes Window, Inc.; Hoover Treated Wood Products, Inc.; Ply Gem Manufacturing; Richwood Building Products, Inc.; Sagebrush Sales, Inc.; Studley Products, Inc.; SNE Enterprises, Inc.; Variform, Inc.

Further Reading:

Cady, Diane M., "Ply Gem Names Monte R. Haymon President and COO," *PR Newswire,* December 6, 1993.

Crompton, Kim, "SNE Plant Here Finds Its Niche in Wood Parts," *Journal of Business-Spokane,* April 25, 1991, sec. 1, p. 7.

"Gems of the Amex," *Equities,* January 1994.

McNatt, Robert, "Gem in the Rough," *Crain's New York Business,* October 17, 1994.

——, "Getting Its House in Order," *Crain's New York Business,* September 28, 1992, sec. 1, p. 3.

Moss, Linda, "New Ply Gem Chairman's Acquisitions Put Life in Sleepy Wood Products Firm," *Crain's New York Business,* March 10, 1986, sec. 1, p. 11.

Piccari, Teresa, "Gloucester's Ply Gem Hopes to Change the Face of Paneling," *Philadelphia Business Journal,* February 24, 1986, p. 12B.

Ramirez, Anthony, "Ply Gem Industries," *Fortune,* August 14, 1989, p. 76.

—Dave Mote

Polaris Industries Inc.

1225 Highway 169 N.
Minneapolis, Minnesota 55441-5078
U.S.A.
(612) 542-0500
Fax: (612) 542-0599

Public Company
Founded: 1954 as Hetteen Hoist & Derrick
Employees: 2,400
Sales: $826.28 million
Stock Exchanges: New York
SICs: 3799 Transportation Equipment, Not Elsewhere
 Classifed; 3732 Boat Building and Repairing; 2329 Men's
 and Boy's Clothing, Not Elsewhere Classified; 2339
 Women's and Misses' Outerwear, Not Elsewhere
 Classified

Polaris Industries Inc. is the largest manufacturer of snowmobiles in the world and the largest U.S. manufacturer of all-
terrain vehicles (ATVs) and personal watercraft (PWC). Appropriately, Polaris's operations remained centered where they
began, in Minnesota—a state that boasts 60 percent of all
snowmobile production worldwide (Polaris being responsible
for 35 percent, and Arctic Cat for the remaining 25 percent). A
pioneering force in the American snowmobile industry, Polaris
has since its inception enjoyed a strong reputation for quality
and innovation. In 1989, for instance, *MacNeil-Lehrer News
Hour* called Polaris America's version of Mercedes-Benz.

The snowmobile industry leader has had its share of troubles
during its history, however. In 1964 it nearly went bankrupt
with the failure of the Comet, its first front-engine sled. And
during the late 1970s and early 1980s—a period of flagging
sales and selloffs that shook the industry as a whole—Polaris's
future looked just as grim. A mid-1981 leveraged buyout that
took the form of a limited partnership prevented an otherwise
imminent plant shutdown, but it was several years before Polaris was again running smoothly, this time as a revitalized company uniquely situated in a far leaner industry. A decade later,
on December 23, 1994, Polaris completed its transformation
from a limited partnership to a corporation, just as the company
was ending its sixth straight year of record sales and earnings.
Headquartered in Minneapolis, Polaris operated manufacturing
facilities in Roseau, Minnesota, Osceola, Wisconsin, and Spirit

Lake, Iowa, and sold its products through approximately 1,900
North American dealers and a network of international distributors that marketed Polaris products in 65 countries around
the world.

Polaris Industries was born in Roseau, a small community
within a few miles of the northernmost point in the contiguous
48 states. This relatively remote area, located closer to Winnipeg, Manitoba, than to Minneapolis, inspired a climate of
persistent innovation. But Hetteen Hoist & Derrick, the forerunner of Polaris, was established in 1945 not for the manufacture
of snowmobiles, but as a problem-solving job shop that became
known for its fabrication of one-of-a-kind machinery for
farmers in the region. Metal supply was at a premium at the end
of World War II, and Edgar Hetteen was a skilled and inventive
metal worker who could help people make do with what they
had. Close friend David Johnson bought into the company while
he was still serving in the navy, and Edgar's brother Allan
Hetteen became a partner in the early 1950s. The company
produced farm equipment, including straw choppers, portable
grain elevators, and sprayers, but also depended on welding,
grinding, and general repair work in the off-season.

Given the area's climate, the seasonal nature of the original
business, and the fact that the founders were avid outdoorsmen,
it was perhaps inevitable that the idea of snowmobile production would eventually transform the company. At the time, trips
to fishing, hunting, and trapping areas in the winter had to be
navigated by cross-country skis or snowshoes. Although inventors had been toying with the concept of snow machines since
the 1920s, no reliable machine was readily available that could
be used for such utilitarian purposes. Not until the 1950s,
largely due to the work of Johnson, did the general notion of
creating a snow-going vehicle steered by skis begin to take
shape as an industry in the United States. The company sold its
first machine, a rough, virtually untested model, to an eager
Roseau lumberyard owner in 1954. There was then no clear
development plan to guide the company in this new area.
Indeed, Edgar Hetteen was focused principally on selling the
company's mainstay straw choppers and was lukewarm on the
idea of snow machines until he saw the considerable interest
generated when the company's first snowmobile customer demonstrated his powered sled.

Other orders followed that year and the company, which renamed itself Polaris Industries after the Latin name for "north
star," worked on improving the original concept with each
consecutive model. Five machines were built in the winter of
1954–55 (all of which sold for less than $800), 75 in the winter
of 1956–57, and more than 300 in 1957–58. The earliest
models were called Sno-Cats, then Sno-Travelers, and were
purchased primarily by outdoorsmen and utility companies. The
sleds, propelled by a rear-end 4-cycle engine, featured a tobog-
gan-style front with a steering wheel and control levers. The
early production line yielded one-of-a-kind machines, with
components varying from one vehicle to the next. Skis were
fabricated from bumpers of Chevrolets and steering wheels
were appropriated from cars and trucks. Not surprisingly, the
early machines were heavy and utilitarian. The Ranger rear-
engine prototype and the Ranger model, manufactured between
1956 and 1964, formed the basis for Polaris snowmobile development.

When the bulk of the business shifted from fabricating farm equipment to designing, building, and testing snowmobiles, Edgar Hetteen was faced with a marketing problem. The company needed to broaden interest in the machine beyond utilitarian to recreational use. In short, Polaris had to convince people it would be fun to ride around in the middle of winter in a small, open-air vehicle. As Jerry Bassett wrote in *Polaris Partners,* ''Edgar Hetteen, as the first president, had to establish a sales network for a product that could only be sold in places which got snow to people who weren't totally certain that they needed his product.'' During a promotional trip Hetteen made in 1958, according to C. J. Ramstad in *Legend: Arctic Cat's First Quarter Century,* ''Hetteen got a real taste of the enormity of the problem that year when he set up an exhibit at a sport and travel show. Full of enthusiasm, he hustled show goers into his booth and eagerly showed them his new 'snow machine.' The curious public thought the machine somehow produced snow. They wanted to know which end the snow came out!''

Then, inspired by a friend's suggestion, Hetteen decided to make a snowmobile trip across Alaska to demonstrate both the durability and recreation his company's product offered. In March 1960 Hetteen and three others covered more than a thousand miles in about three weeks on one Trailblazer and two Rangers. The adventure yielded national publicity, but Hetteen was shocked to find that it had also created dissension at home. The negative response of some of the company's backers to Hetteen's trip, viewed by them as unnecessary, even frivolous, resulted in his selling out his controlling interest in Polaris. After a trip back up to Alaska he returned to Minnesota, this time west of Roseau to Thief River Falls, where he started the company that became Arctic Enterprises and later Arctco Inc., producer of Arctic Cat snowmobiles. His younger brother Allan, 31 at the time, became president of Polaris.

Running a nearly parallel course to Polaris was another company that contributed to the early industry history. In Canada, Joseph-Armand Bombardier developed and patented the sprocket-and-track assembly in 1937 and developed a one-piece molded rubber track in 1957. In 1958, the first year of Ski-Doo brand manufacturing, his company produced 240 snowmobiles, while Polaris manufactured about 300 that same year. The early 1960s marked the beginning of snowmobiling as a sport with the front-engined Bombardier Ski-Doo. Such vehicles were used for recreation as well as competitive racing. The testing of the first Polaris front-engined machine, the Comet, looked promising, but the 1964 model failed in production. The company's very survival was suddenly at stake.

Polaris co-founder David Johnson later joked, ''We made 400 machines and got 500 back.'' But it was the value of his word and reputation at the time that convinced the creditors to give the company breathing room and a second chance. Johnson and Hetteen redoubled their efforts by converting the Comets to rear-engined machines while they worked on a new front-end model. They hit pay dirt with the front-engined Mustang, which enjoyed successful production from 1965 to 1973 and brought the company into the sporty racing vehicle arena.

After its one stumble, the company grew rapidly in the boom years of the 1960s. So pronounced was the growth that it outstripped the management skills of the owners, who had to decide whether to hire professional managers or sell the company. In 1968 Polaris was sold to Textron, a diversified company holding E-Z Go golf carts, Bell helicopters, Talon zippers, and Schaefer pens. The company kept Polaris in Roseau and continued snowmobile manufacturing, but also began limited research and development on watercraft and wheeled turf vehicles. Herb Graves of Textron became president and Johnson stayed on as vice-president to oversee production.

During the 1970s Polaris began to solidify its reputation for high-performance snowmobiles. In pre-Textron years, Polaris had purchased its snowmobile engines from a number of suppliers. With the entry of Textron, Polaris was able to bring on Fuji Heavy Industries as its sole supplier. Fuji engineers went to Roseau to work on building a high-quality engine specifically for Polaris. Increasingly, the Polaris product lines were being noticed. The TX Series set a standard for power and handling in racing and gained popularity with recreational riders. Introduced in 1977, the liquid-cooled TX-L was a strong cross-country racing competitor. Polaris also introduced the RX-L in the mid-1970s, which carried the first Independent Front Suspension (IFS) and produced winners on the racing circuits shortly after its debut. The 1970s also marked the opening of corporate offices in Minneapolis, with product development and production staying up north.

The sport of snowmobiling grew by leaps and bounds in the early 1970s; enthusiasts in the snowbelts of the United States and Canada now numbered more than a million. And the growth rate for the industry was 35 percent per year, versus 20 percent for other recreation industry manufacturers. In 1970, 63 companies manufactured snowmobiles in the United States, Canada, Europe, and Japan. Bombardier held 40 percent of the market, with an additional 40 percent shared by Arctic Cat, Polaris, Scorpion, and Sno Jet. About one-third of the machines manufactured in North America in the early 1970s were made in Minnesota.

Factory-backed racing teams found Polaris support in the days of Allan Hetteen and Textron, but the death of a Polaris team member in 1978 effectively ended the program. From 1981 on the company sponsored a modified racing program with independent racers. Hill climbs, stock and modified oval racing, snow and grass drag racing, and cross-country endurance racing tested the limits of the machines and appealed to customers. Racing was an important part of engineering research and development as well as public relations and product marketing.

Yet in the late 1970s, despite everything that favored the industry—including regular improvements in safety and an expanding trail system that would eventually rival the U.S. Interstate Highway System in total miles—the snowmobiling boom was about to go bust. Companies began shutting down or selling off their snowmobile divisions in the face of declining sales. Names such as Scorpion, AM, Harley-Davidson, Johnson & Evinrude, Chaparral, and Suzuki would no longer be seen on snowmobile nameplates. By 1980 even Arctic Enterprises, the number one manufacturer, was in trouble. High energy costs, economic recessions, snowless winters, and overexpansion eventually drove all but three manufacturers of snowmobiles out of business. Industry sales slid downhill from 500,000 units annually in the early 1970s to 316,000 in 1975; 200,000 in 1980; 174,000 in 1981; and 80,000 in 1983.

Textron wanted out of the snowmobile business, too. Textron president Beverly Dolan, who had been president of Polaris during its first years with Textron, told Polaris's then-president W. Hall Wendel, Jr. to sell off the company. However, a deal to sell the Polaris division to Canada's Bombardier fell through due to the threat of antitrust action by the U.S. Department of Justice. Liquidation was on the horizon. This opened the door for a management group leveraged buyout led by Wendel, who believed there was a market for snowmobiles and that seasonal snowfalls would rise again. Polaris Industries was created in July 1981, and a shutdown of the Roseau plant was avoided. Also at this time, plant workers voted the union out and the company proceeded to establish a Japanese labor model of worker participation, with a crew that had first-hand knowledge of the machines and their capabilities. Times were still tough, though: the 1982 product line consisted of the 1981 model with some detail changes, and just over 5,000 machines were built that season. The same year as the buyout, Polaris attempted to purchase Arctic Cat. When the deal failed, Arctic Cat shut down, leaving Polaris, at least for awhile, as the only American snowmobile manufacturer.

The first years following the management buyout from Textron were lean and characterized by a skeleton factory crew and tight budgets. But the Textron debt was paid off ahead of schedule and the snowmobile line was expanded and improved. The company also expanded into Canada in order to become more price competitive and to create a stronger dealer network. Five years after the buyout the company had reached sales of $40 million and employed 450 people. A Polaris innovation of the early 1980s was the "Snow Check" early deposit program. Polaris encouraged its dealers with incentives to make spring deposits on machines for preseason delivery. For the first time snowmobiles were built to dealer orders rather than manufacturer forecasts, which had been resulting in excess inventory. Other factors helping the industry along at the time were advancements in clothing technology, winter resorts welcoming snowmobilers on winter vacations, and new engineering on the machines producing quieter, more reliable vehicles. By 1984 there were 20 million snowmobilers in the northern snowbelt and mountain regions using the vehicles for rescue and outdoor work as well as recreational and sporting events.

One of the highlights of the 1980s was the introduction of the Indy line of snowmobiles, which became so popular that other high-quality Polaris sleds, such as the Cutlass, were phased out. Good suspension, special features (such as handwarmers and reverse drive), powerful engines, and reliability all pushed Polaris into the number one position in the market. The Indy 500 was named the "sled of the decade" by *Snowmobile* magazine.

Into the 1990s Polaris continued to improve the performance, ride, and reliability of its machines by introducing such features as the triple-cylinder and high-displacement engines, extra-long travel suspensions, and specialized shock absorbers. The machines of the 1990s were a long way from the industry's early noisy, pull-start models, with uncertain braking and questionable reliability. In 1990 Polaris held 30 percent of the snowmobile market, manufacturing 165,000 units. Arctco, Inc. held 25 percent of the total market, followed by Yamaha and Ski-Doo (Bombardier, Inc.), both at 22.5 percent.

Just as the snow outside Polaris's doors had provided a proving ground for snowmobiles, the summertime swampland of the far north provided a place for testing wheeled turf vehicles. The company built and sold two-wheel tractor-tired bikes in the mid- to late-1960s as it was testing diversification into such areas as lawn and garden products, single and two-person watercraft, and snowmobile-engined go-karts. The Textron acquisition and merger with E-Z Go golf carts ended formal ATV product development, so testing stayed underground until after the buyout. The company then tried but failed to sell private-label ATVs to other large companies. Still hoping to better utilize its manufacturing facilities, the company brought out two ATV designs, a three-wheel and a four-wheel with automatic shifting, which caught the interest and commitment of distributors. Added features such as racks and trailers appealed to farmers, ranchers, and lawn maintenance workers. ATVs made perfect sense for Polaris in that they shared engines and clutches with snowmobiles, could be marketed through the same dealers, and represented a seasonal line manufactured in fall and winter months for sale in the summer, just the opposite of snowmobiles.

When Polaris entered the ATV market all the major manufacturers were Japanese, led by Honda. Polaris ATVs, a combination recreation-utility vehicle, avoided direct competition with the leaders. The majority of the 2 million ATVs in use in the mid-1980s were in the United States and Canada. The first production run of the Polaris ATVs was a resounding success and quickly sold out to dealers. Eventually production of three-wheel vehicles would be curtailed by all manufacturers, in response to reports of rising accidents and deaths and action by the Consumer Product Safety Commission. Polaris ceased manufacture of its three-wheel adult version after its first year of ATV production. In 1990 the retail cost of a four-wheel ATV ranged from $2,400 to $4,000 and Polaris controlled about 7 percent of a shrinking market. But by the end of 1993 ATV sales made up 26 percent of entire sales by product line. ATV manufacture was now year-round, with a dedicated production line, and had the potential to surpass snowmobile production. Due to marketing and distribution that now extended beyond the snowbelt to tractor, lawn and garden, used car, and motorcycle dealers, Polaris had become a key national as well as international player in the broader market of recreational vehicles.

Polaris introduced its first personal watercraft (PWC) in 1990, becoming the first major U.S. company to enter that industry. The recreational vehicle started off with a splash due to its speed and handling. Just as it had in snowmobiles and ATVs, Polaris emphasized machine stability, coming up with an entry in the market that was wider than most and was a sit-down rather than stand-up model, which by then was declining in popularity. In the late 1980s personal watercraft was the growth segment of the marine industry and the trend was toward machines requiring less athletic ability and targeting a broader age range. The recreational vehicle was similar to the snowmobile and the ATVs in terms of engine type and channels of distribution. By testing competitors' products Polaris identified the qualities it wanted in its entry: a machine that was fast and fun to drive, with good handling and stability, as well as better boarding in deep water than the competitors'. The company's first model was a success and drew high-income, first-time buyers. By the end of 1993 PWC made up 9 percent of total Polaris sales.

In 1994 Polaris employed 2,400 people company-wide, had a sister plant in Osceola, Wisconsin, and was planning another plant in Iowa. Polaris Canada, a wholly owned subsidiary, provided 25 percent of total sales, or about $100 million. Since 1991, $70 million had been spent in plant improvements and new product development. David Johnson, the only person to see Polaris through all its incarnations, commented in Bassett's retrospective, "The biggest strength of Polaris is the people. . . . Everybody who's involved at Polaris, whether it's with the watercraft, or with the ATVs or the snowmobiles, they want to make the best machine they know how." Polaris's partnership with its employees meant not only sharing in making the best product possible, but sharing in the benefits. Profit sharing began in 1982 with an average of $200 per employee. By 1993 employees shared $6.8 million.

In December 1994 Polaris converted from a limited partnership to a public corporation for several reasons, including its desire to maximize shareholder value, its need for greater flexibility, and the approaching 1997 deadline for relinquishing its partnership tax status. The small company that began up along the Canadian border 40 years earlier had since transformed itself, through a series of rebirths, into a worldwide leader, with annual sales of more than $800 million.

Further Reading:

"All-Terrain Vehicle Makers Accused of Not Enforcing Safety Agreement," *Wall Street Journal,* April 16, 1992, p. B5.

Bassett, Jerry, *Polaris Partners,* St. Paul, Minnesota: Recreational Publications, Inc., 1994.

Beal, Dave, "Can Roseau County Keep It Up?" *St. Paul Pioneer Press,* March 4, 1991.

——, "For Snowmobile Makers, Storm of Century Timely," *St. Paul Pioneer Press,* November 11, 1991.

Dapper, Michael, "Snow Pioneers," *Snowmobile,* November 1994, pp. 74–93.

Foster, Jim, "Polaris Now a Public Corporation," *Minneapolis Star Tribune,* December 23, 1994, p. 3D.

Harris, John, "Noisemakers," *Forbes,* October 29, 1990, pp. 104–06.

Hendricks, Dick, "Snowmobiling: The Next Generation," *Snowmobile,* January 1995, p. 13.

McCartney, Jim, "Polaris Will Dive into Water Scooter Market Next Year," *St. Paul Pioneer Press,* August 2, 1991.

Opre, Tom, "Snowmobiles at 25," *Outdoor Life,* January 1984, pp. 18–20.

"Polaris Snowmobile Celebrates Birthday," *St. Paul Pioneer Press,* July 17, 1989.

Poole, Wiley, "Built in the U.S.A.," *Trailer Boats,* September 1992, pp. 60–61.

Ramstad, C. J., *Legend: Arctic Cat's First Quarter Century,* Deephaven, Minnesota: PPM Books, 1987.

Rubenstein, David, "Wheels of Fortune," *Corporate Report Minnesota,* March 1986, pp. 58–62.

"The Ruckus over Snowmobiles," *Changing Times,* January 1980, p. 16.

Skorupa, Joe, "Ski-Doo: 50 Years on Snow," *Popular Mechanics,* January 1992, pp. 94–95.

"Splendor in the Snow," *Corporate Report Minnesota,* April 1977, pp. 10–12.

"Those Wild Snowmobilers—Expensive Fun in More Ways Than One," *Corporate Report Minnesota,* February 28, 1970, pp. 8–10.

"Those Wild Snowmobilers—Where Do They Go from Here?" *Corporate Report Minnesota,* March 14, 1970, pp. 8–10.

—Jay P. Pederson

POLO RALPH LAUREN

Polo/Ralph Lauren Corporation

650 Madison Avenue
New York, New York 10022
U.S.A.
(212) 318-7000
Fax: (212) 888-5780

Private Company
Incorporated: 1968 as Polo Fashions, Inc.
Employees: 2,700
Sales: $450 million
SICs: 2311 Men's and Boys' Suits and Coats; 2321 Men's
and Boys' Shirts; 2323 Men's and Boys' Neckwear

The Polo/Ralph Lauren Corporation has become one of the most successful fashion design and licensing houses in the world. Founded by American designer Ralph Lauren in the late 1960s, the company boomed in the 1980s as Lauren's designs came to be associated with a sophisticated and distinctly American attitude. The company's first products were wide ties, but it soon designed and manufactured an entire line of menswear before entering the more lucrative women's fashion market as a designer and licenser. By the 1980s, the Polo/Ralph Lauren name helped sell a wide array of products, including fragrances and accessories for men and women, clothing for young boys and infants, and a variety of housewares, shoes, furs, jewelry, leather goods, hats, and eyewear. By the mid 1990s, Polo had a stake in retail sales that topped $3.9 billion, though industry analysts were unable to ascertain the exact value of the company.

The Polo empire began in the late 1960s, when clothing salesman Ralph Lauren got sick of selling other people's neckties and decided to design and sell his own. Lauren had no experience in fashion design, but he had grown up in the New York fashion world, selling men's gloves, suits, and ties. In 1967, he went to his employer, Abe Rivetz, with a proposal to design a line of ties, but Rivetz told him, "The world is not ready for Ralph Lauren." Lauren decided that it was, and he convinced clothier Beau Brummel to manufacture his Polo line of neckwear. "I didn't know how to make a tie," Lauren confessed to *Vogue* in 1982. "I didn't know fabric, I didn't know measurements. What did I know? That I was a salesman. That I was honest. And that all I wanted was quality." Lauren's ties were wider and more colorful than other ties on the market and they soon found a niche, first in small menswear stores and later in the fashionable Bloomingdale's department store.

Within a year, Lauren decided to form his own company with help from his brother Jerry and $50,000 in backing from Norman Hilton, a Manhattan clothing manufacturer. The company, Polo Fashions, Inc. (which changed its name to Polo/Ralph Lauren Corporation in 1987), expanded the Polo menswear collection to include shirts, suits, and sportswear, as well as the trademark ties. The company designed, manufactured, and distributed the Polo collection, which met with the approval of both the department stores that featured the clothes and the fashion critics who praised their style. Fashion critic Bernadine Morris was quoted in *Time* as saying, "He's acquired a certain reputation for clothes that are, you know, with it. But not too with it. Not enough to shock the boys at the bank." In 1970, Lauren received the coveted Coty Award for menswear. In a rare move, Lauren then began designing clothes for women as well as for men. His first designs—men's dress shirts cut for women—met with great success in 1971, and soon sales topped $10 million.

The rapid growth of Polo Fashions, Inc. proved hard to manage for the young entrepreneur, who had succeeded in crafting a brand identity but not in managing his business. By 1972, according to *Time,* "Lauren suddenly discovered that his enterprise was almost bankrupt because of poor financial management and the costs of headlong expansion." "I almost blew my business," Lauren told *Forbes.* "I wasn't shipping on time and had problems delivering." "It was probably . . . one of the darkest moments in my life," he remembered in *New York.* Scrambling to survive, Lauren invested $100,000 of his savings in the business and convinced Peter Strom to leave his job with Norman Hilton and become his partner. The arrangement gave Lauren 90 percent and Strom 10 percent ownership. Strom described their duties to the *New York Times Magazine:* "We divide the work this way: I do everything Ralph doesn't want to do; and I don't do anything he likes to do. He designs, he does advertising, public relations; I do the rest." The Lauren brothers and Strom soon made changes in the structure of the company that set the stage for over two decades of unparalleled success.

During its first four years, Polo Fashions, Inc. had controlled each stage in the clothes making process, from design, to manufacture, to distribution. Their first step in reorganization was to concentrate on what they did best—design—and leave the rest to other companies. With this in mind, Polo Fashions, Inc. licensed the manufacture of Ralph Lauren brand womenswear to Stuart Kreisler, an experienced manufacturer who set out to build the reputation of the Lauren brand name. Under licensing agreements, the designer got a cut of wholesale revenues—usually between five and eight percent for Polo, according to *Forbes*—and shared in advertising costs. Such agreements would be the basis for Polo's future business. Moreover, Strom insisted that those retailers who sold the company's clothes make a commitment to selling the entire line, which meant they had to carry the $350 Polo suit. "That eliminated two-thirds of our accounts," Strom told *Vogue.* "But those who stayed with us experienced our commitment to them, and it wasn't long before we felt their loyalty in return." With business once again secure, the company was able to turn its attention to crafting a brand image as distinctive as any in America.

Beginning in the mid 1970s, Polo Fashions, Inc. entered a period of phenomenal growth that carried it through the late 1980s. From being a designer and licenser of limited lines of men's and women's clothing, the company expanded its products to include fragrances, eyewear, shoes, accessories, housewares, and a range of other products. Yet even as the number of products bearing the brand names "Polo" or "Ralph Lauren" expanded, the image of the company became more secure and more singular. Soon, people were speaking of the "Laurenification of America," crediting Ralph Lauren with creating a unique American aesthetic, and calling the 1980s the "decade of Ralph Lauren." The company's success in this period can be credited to the design skills of Ralph Lauren and to the astute image-making and marketing skills of Lauren and his principal partner, Peter Strom.

Fashion critics and journalists used words like integrity, elegance, tradition, sophistication, WASPy, mannered, pseudo-English, and sporty to describe Lauren's many designs. Yet no single word could encompass the many themes—from the famous English Polo Club designs to the distinctly American western designs—with which Lauren experimented. Some critics complained that Lauren was a relentless borrower, possessed of no unique vision. Lauren himself stated in *New York* that he was interested in "style but not flamboyance, but sophistication, class, and an aristocratic demeanor that you can see in people like Cary Grant and Fred Astaire." And, as Lauren pointed out, "The things I do are not about novelty. They're things I love and can't get away from. There are some things in life that, no matter what the times are, keep getting better and better. That's really my philosophy."

Polo excelled at getting Lauren's distinctive design image across to consumers. From its very first advertisements in New York City newspapers in 1974, the company attempted to portray its products as part of a complete lifestyle. Polo pioneered the multi-page lifestyle advertisement in major magazines. These ads presented a world lifted out of time, where wealthy, attractive people relaxed in Polo products during a weekend at their country estate or on safari in Africa. *Vogue* described the ads as a kind of "home movie," with a cast of "faintly sorrowful but wildly attractive people. The women are always between childhood and thirty; the men are sometimes old." Polo lavished huge amounts of money on these ads, as much as $15 and $20 million a year, though its licensees shared some of the cost by returning two to three percent of sales into the advertising budget. An ad director for a major fashion magazine told *Time:* Polo "has some of the best advertising in the business because it sets a mood, it evokes a life-style."

Lauren's intuitive design sense and the company's ability to create an idealized image for its products provided the base for the company to expand the variety of products it marketed and attain greater control over retailing. From its first product lines—Polo by Ralph Lauren menswear and Ralph Lauren womenswear—the company introduced a variety of products: Polo by Ralph Lauren cologne and boys' clothing in 1978; a girlswear line in 1981; luggage and eyeglasses in 1982; home furnishings in 1983. Later brand extensions included shoes, furs, and underwear. The company expected to introduce its collection of apparel for newborns, infants, and toddlers in 1994. These new product lines were accompanied by continual updating of the older brand names.

Though Polo retained control over the design and advertising of its products, the success or failure of Polo product expansion often depended upon its licensees, as Polo's experience with fragrances and its home collection indicated. Polo's fragrances became a major income producer only when it found a licensee who was willing to help develop and promote the products. Though Polo had marketed its fragrances—Polo by Ralph Lauren for men and Lauren for women—since 1978, they were not major sellers until the mid 1980s, when the company licensed fragrance production to Cosmair, Inc. In 1990, Cosmair introduced Polo Crest for men and Safari for women, made to accompany a new line of clothing also bearing the Safari name. *Cosmetic Insiders' Report* called Safari the "Fragrance of the Year" after it recorded sales as high as $11,000 a day at Bloomingdale's flagship stores. Cosmair hoped to sell between $25 and $30 million wholesale by the end of the fragrance's first year. Two years later Polo and Cosmair launched Safari for Men, which they promoted in an uncharacteristic television commercial in which Ralph Lauren rode a horse bareback on a beach. According to *Women's Wear Daily,* Cosmair hoped to sell $28 million in wholesale at the end of six months, and to top $50 million by the end of two years.

Not all licensing arrangements worked so well. In 1983, Polo began to promote the introduction of its "Home Collection," a line of products that Lauren had designed for the home. *House & Garden* called the collection, which numbered over 2,500 items and included everything from sheets to furniture to flatware, "the most complete of its kind conceived by a fashion designer." But the collection soon ran into serious trouble as the licensee, the J. P. Stevens Company, experienced difficulties getting the products to retail outlets on time. J. P. Stevens also had trouble maintaining quality control, having themselves licensed elements of the line to other companies. In addition, Stevens demanded that stores that wanted to show the collection construct $250,000 free-standing, wood-paneled boutiques to display the items—and stores balked at the price tag. Polo/Ralph Lauren vice-chairman Peter Strom told *Time* that the introduction was "A disaster! Disaster!" It took several years for Polo to get the collection back on track.

Over the years, Polo used a number of techniques to exert control over the way its merchandise was distributed and sold. Early on, the company insisted that retailers offer the entire product line instead of simply selecting items it wanted to carry, arguing that the lines had to stand as a coherent whole. Beginning in 1971, the company began to offer franchises as well, and it has franchised over 100 Polo/Ralph Lauren stores worldwide since that time. Instead of charging a franchise fee, the company made money as the wholesaler for the clothing. These franchises allowed an entire store to concentrate on the Polo image. In 1982, Polo opened the first of its 50 outlet stores in Lawrence, Kansas. The outlet stores allowed the company to control the distribution of irregulars and items that had not sold by the end of each season, thereby preventing the company's products from appearing in discount stores. These outlet stores were placed at a significant distance from the full-price retailers to ensure that they did not steal business. Such expansion occurred not only in America but around the world, as Polo opened shops in London, Paris, and Tokyo.

The flagship of the Polo/Ralph Lauren retail enterprise was the refurbished Rhinelander mansion on Madison Avenue in New York City. Opened in 1986, the 20,000-square-foot mansion featured mahogany woodwork, hand-carved balustrades lining marble staircases, and sumptuous carpeting. "While men who look like lawyers search for your size shirt and ladies who belong at deb parties suggest complementary bags and shoes, you experience the ultimate in lifestyle advertising,'' wrote Lenore Skenazy in *Advertising Age.* Naomi Leff, who designed the interior of the Polo palace, called it "a marker in retailing history. It tells manufacturers that if they're willing to put out, they'll be able to make their own statement, which is not being made in the department stores.''

Establishing brand-focused retail outlets made perfect sense for Polo/Ralph Lauren, for it allowed the company to increase profits by eliminating the middleman as well as to control the environment in which the products appeared. In fact, other designers have since followed Polo/Ralph Lauren's lead, including Calvin Klein, Liz Claiborne, Adrienne Vittadini, and Anne Klein. But the move caused tension between the designer and his traditional retailers, the large department stores. A *Forbes* feature on Lauren's strategy claimed that "a lot of people in business think it is in bad taste to compete with your own customers. Lauren clearly does not agree. And such is his pull at the cash register that he may get away with this piece of business heresy.''

The Polo/Ralph Lauren Corporation rode its expertly crafted brand image and astute retailing strategies to remarkable heights in the 1980s, as sustained economic growth and America's fascination with Lauren's image fueled an unparalleled expansion in products bearing the Ralph Lauren name. But retail expansion slowed dramatically with the economic downturn in the early 1990s, and some stores that once thrived on the sales of Ralph Lauren's high-priced products complained that the company was unable to adjust to changes in the market. Robert Parola, writing in the *Daily News Record* in 1990, noted that many clothing manufacturers had lifted their designs from Ralph Lauren and begun selling them for less.

Polo/Ralph Lauren was hardly a company to be counted out in the 1990s, however. Successful fragrance introductions and the development of the popular Polo Sport active-sportswear and Double RL jeanswear lines promised to keep money rolling into the company coffers. The 1994 sale of 28 percent of the company to a Goldman Sachs & Co. investment fund for $135 million prompted speculation about the future of the company. *Wall Street Journal* reporter Teri Agins remarked that "the company is at a crossroads as it embarks on a strategy to improve its retail operations and lure a younger generation'' to its products. In the short term, industry observers expected the company to use the cash influx to expand its retail stores. But observers also wondered whether this sale, the first in the company's history, indicated that the company would eventually go public or that Ralph Lauren was beginning to look toward life after designing. If either of the latter speculations were to prove correct, the nature of Polo/Ralph Lauren would certainly change, for it is hard to imagine a design house controlled by a board of directors. What remained to be seen in the mid 1990s was whether Polo/Ralph Lauren's continued entrance into retailing would complement or supplant the company's role as designer of choice for the upwardly mobile of the world.

Principal Licensees: Ralph Lauren Womenswear, Bidermann Industries; Ralph Lauren Fragrances, Cosmair, Inc.; Ralph Lauren Home Collection.

Further Reading:

Agins, Terry, "Clothing Makers Don Retailers' Garb, Manufacturers Open Stores, Irk Main Outlets,'' *Wall Street Journal,* July 13, 1989.
——, "Izod Lacoste Gets Restyled and Repriced,'' *Wall Street Journal,* July 22, 1991, p. B1.
——, "Ralph Lauren Sells 28 Percent Stake in Polo Concern,'' *Wall Street Journal,* August 24, 1994, pp. A3, A10.
——, "Retailing Executive Farah Is Said to be Discussing a Post with Ralph Lauren,'' *Wall Street Journal,* October 7, 1994, p. B10.
Aronson, Steven M. L., "High Style in Jamaica,'' *House & Garden,* October 1984, pp. 127–137, 230.
Barns, Lawrence, "J. P. Stevens Takes the Designer Route,'' *Business Week,* September 19, 1983, pp. 118–119.
"A Big Time Safari for Ralph Lauren,'' *Women's Wear Daily,* October 27, 1989, pp. 1, 14.
Born, Pete, "Polo Crest Takes Fashion Approach to Fragrance,'' *Daily News Record,* July 26, 1991, p. 3.
——, "Lauren Hits TV Trail for Men's Safari,'' *Women's Wear Daily,* August 21, 1992, p. 5.
Donaton, Scott, and Pat Sloan, "Hearst, Lauren at Work on Lifestyle Magazine,'' *Advertising Age,* April 27, 1992, pp. 1, 54.
——, "Ralph Lauren Sets Magazine Test,'' *Advertising Age,* November 2, 1992, p. 3.
Ettorre, Barbara, " 'Give Ralph Lauren All the Jets He Wants,' '' *Forbes,* February 28, 1983, pp. 102–103.
Ferretti, Fred, "The Business of Being Ralph Lauren,'' *New York Times Magazine,* September 18, 1983, pp. 112–113, 124–133.
Gross, Michael, "The American Dream,'' *New York,* December 21–28, 1992, pp. 71–72.
Koepp, Stephen, "Selling a Dream of Elegance and the Good Life,'' *Time,* September 1, 1986, pp. 54–61.
Kornbluth, Jesse, "Ralph Lauren: Success American Style,'' *Vogue,* August, 1982, pp. 263–265, 306–307.
Lafayette, Jon, "Ralph Lauren Drops WRG,'' *Advertising Age,* September 18, 1989, pp. 1, 84.
"Lauren,'' *New York,* October 21, 1985, pp. 40–47.
"Lauren Price Cuts Don't Spark a Trend,'' *Women's Wear Daily,* June 14, 1991, p. 17.
Ling, Flora, "Ralph Lauren's Polo Game,'' *Forbes,* June 26, 1978, p. 88.
Lockwood, Lisa, "Ralph Lauren's Sales Go Up as Prices Fall,'' *Women's Wear Daily,* June 11, 1991, p. 1.
Mander, Lois, "Safari for Men by Ralph Lauren Off to a Powerful Start,'' *PR Newswire,* September 18, 1992.
McHugh, David, and Joanne Miller, "Sales Team Had Designs on $1.4 Million,'' *Detroit Free Press,* September 12, 1991.
Parola, Robert, "Polo/Ralph Lauren,'' *Daily News Record,* October 17, 1990, p. 3.
——, "Polo/Ralph Lauren: At the Crossroads,'' *Daily News Record,* October 29, 1990, p. 10.
"Polo/Ralph Lauren Adding Store in California,'' *Women's Wear Daily,* October 29, 1990, p. 11.
"Ralph Lauren: The Dream Maker,'' *U.S. News & World Report,* February 8, 1988, p. 78.
"Ralph Lauren, the Seventh Avenue Designer Known for His Sportswear, Is Taking a Major Swing at the Golf Market,'' *Golf Pro Merchandiser,* 1989, p. 37.
Rosen, Pat, "Phony Pony?: Polo Player Rides to Court in Logo Lawsuit,'' *Houston Business Journal,* May 6, 1991, p. 1.
Skenazy, Lenore, "Lauren Gets Honorable Mansion,'' *Advertising Age,* October 20, 1986, p. 56.
Sohng, Laurie, "Polo Partners Ralph Lauren Footwear Always Plays to Win,'' *Footwear News,* October 14, 1991, p. S4.
Spevack, Rachel, "Polo and Izod: Adding New Luster to Knit Logos,'' *Daily News Record,* March 12, 1991, p. 5.
Talley, Andre Leon, "Everybody's All-American,'' *Vogue,* February 1992, pp. 203–210, 284.
Trachtenberg, Jeffrey A., "You Are What You Wear,'' *Forbes,* April 21, 1986, pp. 94–98.

—Tom Pendergast

POPE & TALBOT, INC.

Pope and Talbot, Inc.

1500 S.W. First Avenue
Portland, Oregon 97201
U.S.A.
(503) 228-9161

Public Company
Incorporated: 1852 as Puget Mill Company
Employees: 3,100
Sales: $628.9 million
SICs: 2421 Sawmills & Planing Mills General; 2611 Pulp
   Mills; 2676 Sanitary Paper Products

Pope and Talbot, Inc., is one of America's oldest and most successful wood-fiber products companies. The firm makes and markets wood pulp, softwood lumber, consumer tissue, and disposable diaper products. Pope and Talbot serves a variety of markets, including the housing industry, newsprint manufacturers, printing and writing paper manufacturers, supermarkets, mass merchandisers, food and drug distributing firms, and drugstores. The company's Ultra Thin disposable diaper has become one of the leading products in the consumer tissues market.

Andrew Jackson Pope and Frederick Talbot, two ambitious young men from Maine, arrived in San Francisco on December 1, 1849, after a grueling 51-day journey around South America on a number of different steam ships. Although they were exhausted when they stepped ashore, the excitement of San Francisco, which had grown from a population of 6,000 to 20,000 in just six months, overwhelmed the two Easterners. Pope and Talbot immediately recognized the potential for starting a new business, and on the following day, they joined with partners Lucius Sanborn and J. P. Keller to establish a company to operate barges in San Francisco bay.

A short two months later, the partners were able not only to pay for the cost of their new barges and boats, but also to turn a profit of more than $800. After buying out Sanborn's interest, Pope, Talbot, and Keller decided to enter the lumber business. A number of disastrous fires in San Francisco had convinced the partners that demand for lumber would remain high. Soon they opened a lumber yard and began transporting consignments of the product from one area to another. A stroke of good fortune occurred when Frederick Talbot's older brother, W. C. Talbot, arrived in California with his brig, the *Oriental*. A large, sea-worthy vessel, the *Oriental* provided the firm with a greater range of transport. When Frederick Talbot decided to permanently return to the East Coast and open a business in New York, his older brother replaced him as a partner in the company.

For a short time, the partners shipped lumber from Maine to California through arrangements with Pope's relatives. They found this impractical as a long-term strategy, however, especially given the enormous demand for lumber in and around the San Francisco area. They built their own mill in the Oregon Territory on Puget Sound, on a site that Native Americans called Teekalet, or "Brightness of the Noonday Sun"; settlers renamed it Port Gamble. By 1853 the partners' mill was producing nearly 2,000 board feet of lumber per day. Four years later production had jumped to a total of eight million board feet for the year, and the company was known as the largest and most successful business on Puget Sound.

The late 1850s brought an Indian war, a gold rush that destabilized the labor market, and a short period of overproduction as a result of new lumber mills established on Puget Sound. Yet the mill at Port Gamble, now called the Puget Mill Company, continued to prosper. In response to a growing demand for lumber during and after the Civil War, the Puget Mill Company added new equipment and began to acquire smaller mills in the area, including important mills on Camano Island and Port Ludlow. By 1879 the company was producing more than 200,000 board feet per day and nearly 70 million feet per year.

As the nineteenth century progressed, leadership of the firm changed hands. J. P. Keller died in June 1862, and was replaced as a partner of the firm by mill superintendent Cyrus Walker. Andrew Pope died in September 1878, and Captain Talbot in August 1881. William H. Talbot, the son of Captain Talbot, had been groomed by his father in every aspect of the lumber business, and when the elder Talbot died, the son quickly became the driving force behind the company, relying heavily on Cyrus Walker's 28 years of experience in the mill. In 1882 the total capacity of all the Puget Mill operations amounted to 99,000,000 board feet of lumber per year. In 1885 the number of cargoes of lumber shipped from the mill at Port Gamble alone reached 49; by 1888, the number had risen to 78. The company also owned one of the largest shipping fleets for the transportation of its lumber, with fourteen ships carrying lumber to customers in Japan, Hawaii, Australia, South America, China, Korea, India, and South Africa. During this same period, the Puget Mill Company was also purchasing enormous tracts of timberland in order to maintain a reliable source of wood for its mills; by 1892, the firm reported ownership of 186,000 acres.

During the 1890s and the years immediately following the turn of the century, Puget Mill Company expanded its marketing operations and opened three new offices in San Francisco. The development of railroad traffic heralded even greater prosperity for the company, since it transformed the isolated state of Washington into America's largest distributor of lumber. As timberlands in Wisconsin, Michigan, and Minnesota were depleted, demand for Washington's lumber skyrocketed. The number of mills in Washington had grown from 46 in 1870 to 310 by 1890. By 1906 there were more than 900 lumber mills in the state producing 4,305,000,000 board feet of lumber.

Beginning in 1907, however, the Puget Mill Company suffered a series of setbacks. When the state of Washington levied a tax increase on the acreage of timberland held by the company, Puget Mill's extensive holdings nearly became a liability. In addition, equipment used in the company's mills had become antiquated, and Puget Mill's operations were running inefficiently. In 1908 the company sold the last of its aging fleet of schooners, once the largest lumber armada on the West Coast. The company joined an organization that chartered the tonnage for shipment, thus relieving Puget Mill Company of the burden of maintaining its own fleet. By the end of World War I, the company had grown large, diverse, and somewhat cumbersome, with some 15 corporations under the direct management of Puget Mill. Labor unrest, which occurred throughout the Northwest region during this time, affected all of the company's holdings.

In July 1925, William Talbot, exhausted and in ill health, decided to sell Puget Mill Company to the Charles R. McCormick Lumber Company. McCormick, a native of Michigan, had arrived in Portland, Oregon, in 1901. He renovated a dilapidated millsite at St. Helens on the Columbia River, and from there he created a lumber empire that grew to become one of the largest on the Pacific Coast. McCormick purchased all of Puget Mill Company, including mills and timberlands, at a price of $15,000,000. Talbot, known as a shrewd businessman, made McCormick agree to build a new mill at Port Gamble, with Puget Mill Company holding a mortgage on all the mills, timberlands, and logging camps operated by McCormick.

From the beginning of the takeover, McCormick's management team made serious errors and miscalculations. Modernizations and improvements at Port Ludlow and St. Helens, as well as the new mill at Port Gamble, were plagued by cost overruns. McCormick soon faced rising interest rates, amortization payments, and annual taxes of more than $1 million. As his debts steadily increased, McCormick devised a strategy of expansion, hiring a larger sales staff and increasing production. Costs continued to outrun revenues, however, and by the start of the Depression in 1930 the company had posted a loss of $858,587. The company's situation only worsened with the economic problems brought on by the Depression.

After William Talbot died, George Pope, Sr., assumed the position of president of Puget Mill Company and began to pressure McCormick to resign. When McCormick's expansion strategy failed to revitalize the company, he vacated his position in December 1931. Pope was then elected chairman of the board of Charles R. McCormick Lumber Company, with the intention of protecting the interests of the Puget Mill Company. He immediately appointed managers who exemplified his own financially conservative viewpoint, and began to reduce the debt incurred by McCormick. By 1937 all the bank loans and a significant portion of the mortgage bonds were retired. In 1938 the Puget Mill Company brought a suit of foreclosure against the Charles R. McCormick Lumber Company. Unable to pay its obligations of over $7 million, the McCormick Company was forced to cede all of its holdings to the owners of Puget Mill. The principals of the foreclosure suit, George Pope, Sr.; George Pope, Jr.; Frederic C. Talbot; and Talbot Walker, all descendants of the original owners, reacquired the company their forefathers had labored to build.

George Pope, Sr., became president of the company, which was renamed Pope & Talbot, Inc. Before any analysis and reorganization of the lumber operations and steamship activities could take place, however, World War II began. George Pope, Sr., became chairman of the board, allowing his son, George Pope, Jr., to assume the position of president and deal with the demands of the war years.

Pope & Talbot mills operated at full capacity during the entire war. The company produced lumber for panel bridges used in the invasion of Europe, tent poles, and Signal Corps material for communication lines. Company lumber was used for the construction of naval housing, and the company's fleet of steamships made vital contributions to the American war effort. Pope & Talbot vessels transported the supplies necessary for waging war in every area of conflict, and stopped at ports including Murmansk, Bizerte, Salerno, Guadalcanal, and Okinawa. The company also suffered casualties: four ships were sunk during the war, including the *S.S. West Ivis*, which lost its entire crew. During the height of worldwide hostilities, Pope & Talbot was responsible for more than 75 ships. The war helped improve the financial position of the company, which was one of the three largest lumber producers in the entire Northwest by the end of the war.

The future appeared especially promising for the company's steamship operations during the postwar years: industry along the Pacific Coast needed large quantities of bulk materials, while the East Coast needed lumber and other products from the western United States. However, volatile labor relations plagued the company. In 1948 a three-month strike by dock workers cost the firm more than $1,250,000, and a series of strikes in 1954 caused Pope & Talbot to lose a significant portion of its steamship cargoes. By 1958 the company was down to one shipping route, and another year of strikes in the maritime industry during 1959 brought its vessels to a standstill. Competition from the railroad industry also began to take business away from shipping. As a result, in 1963 Pope & Talbot decided to terminate shipping operations by selling the four remaining vessels in its once-proud fleet.

In contrast to its shipping activities, the company's lumber operations were highly successful. Having purchased a large tract of timberland near Oakridge, Oregon, in 1946, management assured itself of adequate timber holdings for the foreseeable future. By 1950 the company owned over one billion board feet of timber ready for cutting, and during the next decade it opened new mills in the United States and Canada. Pope & Talbot also implemented a diversification strategy which included building a particleboard plant, a veneer mill, and a wood treatment facility, and in 1961 the company purchased a plywood plant. These moves brought the company closer to fulfilling its goal of a fully integrated wood products program.

In 1963 George Pope, Jr., resigned as president of the company and was replaced by Cyrus T. Walker, a descendant of one of the company's early partners. In 1966 Pope & Talbot reported that its lumber division provided 61.6 percent of its revenues, plywood 13.9 percent, veneer 7.1 percent, particleboard 6.2 percent, and hardboard 6.2 percent. Net earnings increased from $717,000 in 1965 to $1,203,000 in 1966. In 1968 sales increased an astronomical 73 percent over the previous year, totaling $3,025,238. The company's success lay in the fact that management was moving quickly to take advantage of growing markets for new wood products. In 1969 the firm continued its expansion strategy by purchasing another mill in Canada, procuring cutting rights to more than a million acres of timberland in Canada, and constructing a new log utilization plant.

The company changed leadership in 1971 when Cyrus Walker retired and the fourth generation of Popes and Talbots assumed control. Peter T. Pope was elected chairman of the board, and Guy B. Pope was appointed president and chief operating officer. Under their tenure, the firm continued to grow. In 1972 Pope & Talbot was listed on the New York Stock Exchange, and the following year the company surpassed $100 million in revenues. When the housing and construction industry was hit hard by a recession during the mid-1970s, Pope & Talbot made plans to enter the pulp and paper industry, which would allow the company to utilize all of the yield from its timberlands. Consequently, in March 1978, the firm invested $24 million in a joint venture with American Can Company to operate a bleached kraft pulp mill near Halsey, Oregon.

During the 1980s, Pope & Talbot insulated itself as much as possible from the cyclical nature of the housing and construction industry. The pulp mill at Halsey took the company into a entirely new, and highly profitable, direction. Pulp is made from softwood chips, hardwood chips, and sawdust, and is used to manufacture newspaper and printing and writing grade paper.

Soon the company had major contracts throughout the Pacific Northwest to sell its pulp. Not content with just pulp production, Pope & Talbot began to diversify into the consumer products market by either acquiring or building diaper and tissue plants. By the early 1990s, Pope & Talbot listed two tissue plants and six diaper plants as part of its holdings. Manufacturing an entire line of napkins, paper towels, and facial and bath tissues from 100 percent recycled paper for private label customers became highly profitable. The Ultra Thin disposable diaper developed into the company's most lucrative product. By 1993 Pope and Talbot's wood products were bringing in approximately 48 percent of revenues, while its pulp, tissue, and diaper products were generating 52 percent.

Throughout its history, Pope & Talbot has demonstrated the ability to divest itself of unprofitable operations and diversify into growing, productive markets. Led by new generations of Popes and Talbots, the company is heading into the future with strong leadership and the expectation of continued prosperity.

Further Reading:

Coman, Edwin T., Jr., and Helen T. Gibbs, *Time, Tide & Timber: Over a Century of Pope & Talbot,* Portland, Ore.: Pope & Talbot, Inc., 1978.
Marcial, Gene G., "This Papermaker Could Crash out of the Woods," *Business Week,* January 20, 1992, p. 80.

—Thomas Derdak

Quaker Oats Company

Quaker Tower
321 North Clark Street
Chicago, Illinois 60604-9001
U.S.A.
(312) 222-7111
Fax: (312) 222-8392

Public Company
Incorporated: 1901
Employees: 31,000
Sales: $5.95 billion
Stock Exchanges: New York Midwest Pacific Toronto
London Amsterdam
SICs: 2043 Cereal Breakfast Foods; 2037 Frozen Fruits &
Vegetables; 2047 Dog & Cat Food

The product of a rocky union between three 19th-century millers, Quaker Oats Company maintains a portfolio of strong branded products within the food business. Long considered closed and old-fashioned, Quaker Oats now has one of the most dynamic and respected CEOs in the food industry. The company has also drawn consistent praise for its community involvement and social conscience.

Ferdinand Schumacher undertook an ambitious project in 1856 when he organized his German Mills American Oatmeal Factory in Akron, Ohio. His mission was to introduce steel-cut oats to the American table at a time when oats were considered an inappropriate food for anything but horses. German and Irish immigrants were his initial customers, since they were accustomed to eating oats and unused to the high cost of American meat. Oat milling was a low-cost operation, and competitors quickly appeared as oats gained acceptance as a food.

One competitor with an innovative approach to business was Henry Parsons Crowell of nearby Ravenna, Ohio. Crowell purchased the Quaker Mill in Ravenna, gave his oats the Quaker name, and packed them in a sanitary, two-pound paper package with printed cooking directions. He also advertised in newspapers with German, Scottish, and Irish readers, a practice which was at that time associated with disreputable showmen. Crowell became the first marketer to register a trademark for cereal, registering his Quaker symbol in 1877. Soon Crowell's success impinged on Schumacher's business, with urban customers often specifically requesting Quaker brand oats.

Another competitor, Robert Stuart, emigrated with his father from Embro, Ontario, to establish a mill in Cedar Rapids, Iowa, in 1873. Eventually he helped finance the building of a new oatmeal mill in Chicago and expanded the original mill. Under the same label the two mills established markets throughout the Midwest, especially in Chicago, Milwaukee, and Detroit, carefully avoiding territories dominated by Schumacher or Crowell.

In 1885 Crowell and Stuart joined forces in a price war against Schumacher's larger operation. An attempt to form the Oatmeal Millers Association that year failed when Schumacher refused to join. One year later Schumacher's largest mill burned to the ground; Crowell reacted by immediately raising his prices. Because Schumacher had been uninsured, he finally agreed to join Stuart and Crowell in their venture. Crowell became president of the Consolidated Oatmeal Company, Stuart was vice-president, and Schumacher, the former oatmeal king, was treasurer.

Consolidated, however, only made up half of the trade, and the other half was determined to destroy it. Competitors built mills they didn't want, knowing Consolidated would purchase them simply to keep them out of production. Half of Consolidated's earnings were spent this way, and in 1888, under financial and legal pressure, it collapsed.

A third and finally successful attempt at consolidation came that same year, when seven of the largest American oat millers united as the American Cereal Company. Schumacher ended up with a controlling interest, and he appointed himself president and Crowell vice-president. The company doubled production in two years by consolidating production into the two major mills at Cedar Rapids and Akron, Ohio. The concentration of facilities gave them the strength to survive the depression of the 1890s.

Crowell promoted Quaker Oats aggressively during the decade. However, Schumacher insisted that his own brand, F. S. Brand, be sold alongside Quaker, blunting the success of the better-selling Quaker.

As treasurer, Stuart crossed Schumacher by purchasing two food companies at bargain prices and investing in machinery for the Cedar Rapids mill. Opposed to both actions, Schumacher requested and secured Stuart's resignation in 1897. The following year the president also voted Crowell out of the organization.

Crowell and Stuart, who together owned 24 percent of American Cereal, quietly began to buy available shares. In 1899, after a proxy fight, Schumacher lost control of the company to Stuart and Crowell. Stuart immediately built new facilities and diversified the product line while Crowell increased promotion. Quaker now produced wheat cereals, farina, hominy, corn meal, baby food, and animal feed.

In 1901 American Cereal became the Quaker Oats Company, with sales of $16 million. Twenty years of growth followed, including a wartime peak of $123 million in sales in 1918. With the 1911 acquisition of Mother's Oats, Quaker owned half of all milling operations east of the Rocky Mountains. (The federal government filed a suit against the purchase, but eventually withdrew its last appeal in 1920, when national interest in trust-busting had faded.)

An interest in finding a use for discarded oat hulls led to the establishment of a chemical division in 1921. Although a profitable use for furfural (a chemical produced from oat hulls that has solvent and other properties) did not appear until World War II, postwar sales of the product exceeded oatmeal sales into the 1970s.

Also in 1921 the company weathered a grain-surplus crisis; dealers had been caught with an oversupply and prices fell rapidly, leading that year to the company's first reported loss. Stuart's eldest son John became president of Quaker the following year. John Stuart immediately changed Quaker's retail sales strategy to one of optimum, rather than maximum, sales. The growth of the grocery chains helped to encourage a system of fast turnover rather than bulk purchasing.

Early in the century Crowell and Stuart invested in foreign markets by establishing self-supporting overseas subsidiaries. These subsidiaries operated mills in Europe and sold oats in South America and Asia. Under John Stuart's company reorganization in 1922, foreign operations became a corporate division. Then, as now, approximately 25 percent of Quaker's sales were abroad.

During John Stuart's 34 years as CEO, the company increased its toehold on the growing market of ready-to-eat cereals with Puffed Wheat and Puffed Rice. Quaker further diversified its product line by purchasing name brands that were already established, such as Aunt Jemima pancake flour in 1925. Similarly, the company entered the pet-food industry through the purchase of Ken-L-Ration in 1942. Internal attempts to develop a cat food failed, and the company purchased Puss 'n Boots brand cat food in 1950.

In 1942 sales reached $90 million. Wartime demand for meat and eggs pumped new life into the sagging animal-feed division as well as boosting sales of the company's grains and prepared mixes. Quaker's furfural became important in the manufacture of synthetic rubber, and during the war Quaker built and ran a bomb-assembly plant for the government.

During the war and in the years that followed, Quaker's sales grew to $277 million generated by 200 different products, a broad product line requiring heavy promotion. John Stuart's younger brother, R. Douglas Stuart, studied under Crowell and assumed control of promotions when John became CEO. After World War II he adopted the then-radical policy of using more than one advertising agency. The Stuart brothers recognized that the grocery industry would continue to expand into pet foods, convenience products, and ready-to-eat cereals, and matched the company's product line and promotions accordingly.

The company's first outside manager, Donald B. Lourie, rose to CEO in 1953. Under Lourie, Quaker retained the atmosphere of a family company with personal leadership; however, the company needed external support for its increasingly complex marketing decisions. National advertising for the Aunt Jemima brand came at a price of $100,000. The cost of introducing Cap'n Crunch in 1963 was $5 million.

For many food companies, the 1960s were a period of automatic growth as consumer demand for convenience increased and brand recognition grew. For Quaker, however, sales rose just 20 percent and profits only 10 percent as long-term development absorbed earnings. Quaker expanded in the industry's fastest-growing areas: pet foods, convenience foods, and ready-to-eat

cereals. By the end of the decade growth rates had increased, but not as much as hoped.

Robert D. Stuart, Jr., became CEO in 1966. The decade's slow growth and a general corporate trend toward diversification prompted him to make acquisitions outside the food industry for the first time since 1942. Many of these acquisitions were eventually sold, but Fisher-Price Toy Company, purchased in 1969, was held and grew beyond expectations. Within ten years, it made up 25 percent of Quaker's total sales.

Late in 1970 Stuart restructured Quaker's organization around four decentralized businesses: grocery products, which now included cookies and candy; industrial and institutional foods, which contained the newly acquired Magic Pan restaurants; toys and recreational products; and international. Sales in 1968 had been frustratingly low at $500 million, but with Stuart's acquisitions, the company reported $2 billion in sales by 1979.

Economic recession during the 1970s kept sales down. A second toy company, Louis Marx Toys, was purchased in 1972. During 1974 and 1975, Marx, which was purchased as a "recession-proof" company, drove earnings per share from $2.04 to $1.45. Magic Pan Restaurant's profits fell for four consecutive years. The chemical division reported a net loss of $7 million when a cheaper substitute for furfural came onto the market. This introduction took the company by surprise, as it expected earnings from that division to climb steadily.

Looking to expand its foreign market in grocery and pet foods, Quaker made seven acquisitions of foreign companies during the decade. But while the company focused on diversification, product development slipped. Between 1970 and 1978, only one new major product, 100 Percent Natural Cereal, was introduced. Shelf space in major grocery chains did not increase. Stuart had successfully lessened the company's dependence on grocery products, but profits also dropped, to a low of $31 million in 1975.

By the end of the decade, however, a turnaround was in sight. Quaker's least profitable areas were limited to its smallest divisions, and since the entire industrial and restaurant industries had been weakening, the company was already preparing to divest its holdings in that field.

William D. Smithburg replaced Stuart as CEO in late 1979. Smithburg aggressively increased Quaker's sales force and advertising budget, improvements that were badly needed. The company also refocused on its core food business. Quaker had two new successes as the 1980s dawned: Ken-L-Ration's Tender Chunks became the second-best-selling dog food in its first year, and Corn Bran had a commendable 1.2 percent share of the ready-to-eat cereal market. In addition, Fisher-Price sales had increased tenfold since 1969, to $300 million. Quaker planned to expand the division by building plants in Europe, raising its target age group, and lowering unit selling prices.

By 1979 Quaker had a return on invested capital of 12.3 percent—higher than the industry average, but well below competitor Kellogg's 19.4 percent. The company still needed to divest its interests in companies that absorbed profits.

In the first half of the decade, Quaker sold Burry, a cookie maker; Needlecraft; Magic Pan restaurants; its Mexican toy operations; and its chemical division. During the same period, the company made several acquisitions. Like many food companies at the time, Quaker entered specialty retailing, with purchases like Jos. A. Bank Clothiers, the Brookstone mail order company, and Eyelab, all purchased in 1981. All would be sold in late 1986. By then, Smithburg had decided that the price for retail chains was inflated and that Quaker could get a better return on food. He proved himself right. By 1987 Quaker's return on shareholder equity matched Kellogg's. Quaker confirmed its new path with its 1983 bid on Stokely-Van Camp, the maker of Gatorade sports drink and Van Camp pork and beans. By expanding Gatorade's geographic market, Quaker made the drink its top seller in 1987.

Quaker's revival came about through the strong potential of its low-cost acquisitions. Golden Grain Macaroni Company, the maker of Rice-a-Roni, gave the company a base to expand further into prepared foods. Anderson Clayton & Company, purchased in late 1986, gave Quaker a 15 percent share of the pet-food market with its Gaines brand, effectively challenging Ralston Purina's lead in that market.

With the purchase of Anderson Clayton, financed by the sale of its unwanted divisions, Smithburg managed to strengthen Quaker's position in existing markets and improve its product mix without overloading the company with specialty products. Products with leading market shares made up 75 percent of 1987 sales, and over half came from brands that Quaker hadn't owned six years earlier.

The late 1980s tempered that success, however. Pet food sales were flat throughout the industry and Quaker took $112 million in charges related to its recently expanded pet division. The corporation was a rumored takeover candidate because of its high volume of shares outstanding and its strong branded products. In response, the company announced in April, 1989 that it would purchase seven million of its nearly 80 million outstanding shares, and that July, Smithburg reassigned some managerial duties. The company also decreased its advertising and marketing expenses.

Despite these minor setbacks, Quaker entered the 1990s with 14 years of unbroken sales growth. The company concentrated on three major divisions: American and Canadian grocery products; international grocery products; and Fisher-Price Toys. Quaker continued to streamline its operations into the early 1990s, spinning off Fisher-Price Toys in 1991, a move which made Quaker solely a packaged-food company for the first time in over 20 years. Sales that year hit a record $5.5 billion, and over 70 percent of the products in Quaker's portfolio held either the first- or second-share position in their segments. Quaker's international sales continue to be a significant percentage of the company's total, and in 1991, the company restructured both its European and Latin American operations to focus marketing on a continental, as opposed to a country-by-country, basis.

As it divested itself of its non-grocery products, Quaker continued to expand its packaged foods portfolio. Its concentration was on healthful food brands, such as Near East rice and pasta products, Chico-San rice cakes, and Petrofsky's bagels, all acquired in 1993. The buying spree continued through 1994 and into 1995 with the acquisitions of Proof & Bake frozen bagels,

Maryland Club coffee, Arnie's Bagelicious Bagels, and Nile Spice Foods, a maker of dried soups, pasta and beans. Quaker's largest acquisition was its 1994 purchase of Snapple Beverage Corp., a maker of ready-to-drink juice beverages and teas, for $1.7 billion. Some industry experts considered the price too high for this upstart company with annual sales just below $1 billion, but the purchase boosted Quaker's share of the non-alcoholic beverage market significantly. With combined sales of over $2 billion, Quaker was now the nation's third-largest producer of non-alcoholic beverages.

On the international front, Quaker continued its aggressive Gatorade marketing drive, and by 1994 the beverage was available in 25 countries across Latin America, Asia, and Europe. The company also strengthened its foothold in the Latin American food products market with the 1994 acquisition of Adria Produtos Alimenticos, Ltd., Brazil's top pasta manufacturer. Although much of Quaker's expansion was through acquisitions, the company also sought to grow its products portfolio internally, especially in its historically strong rice and grains category. Between 1992 and 1995, volume in that category tripled with the addition of new products such as Quaker chewy granola bars and flavored rice cakes. Company-wide sales in 1994 hit $5.95 billion, a record high for the nineteenth consecutive year.

Despite its record sales figures, Quaker's overall financial outlook was not so bright as it entered 1995. Due to the acquisition of Snapple, Quaker held a high debt to total capitalization ratio and felt it necessary to divest itself of a number of businesses in early 1995. In February, its European pet foods division was sold to Dalgety PLC for $700 million. Soon later, H. J. Heinz acquired Quaker's U.S. and Canadian pet foods operations for $725 million. The company also instituted what may prove to be an ongoing series of "efficiency moves," eliminating a total of 300 positions worldwide.

As it nears its 100th anniversary, Quaker is once again a food company with a well-balanced portfolio of products. Many of Quaker's products have strong potential for continued growth, both in the U.S. and overseas. Its ability to continue to deliver investor profits depends entirely on marketing and management. Maintaining market share, introducing successful new products, and streamlining operations are all essential in the years to come.

Principal Subsidiaries: The Quaker Oats Co. of Canada Ltd.; Quaker Oats Ltd. (U.K.); Quaker Oats, N.V. (Belgium); Quaker Oats, B.V. (the Netherlands); Quaker Produtos Alimenticos Ltda. (Brazil); Quaker France; OTA A/S (Denmark); Chiari & Forti, S.p.A. (Italy) (97.2%); Elaboradora Argentina de Cereales, S.A.; Quaker Products Australia Ltd.; Herrschners, Inc.; Snapple Beverage Corp., Nile Spice Foods, Inc., Adria Produtos Alimenticos, Ltd.

Further Reading:

Marquette, Arthur F., *Brands, Trademarks and Good Will: The Story of the Quaker Oats Company,* New York: McGraw-Hill, 1967.
McManus, John, "Quaker Matrix Managment Models for Turbulent Future," *Brandweek,* May 23, 1993, p. 16.

—updated by Maura Troester

QUEBECOR INC.

Quebecor Inc.

612 Rue St. Jacques
Montréal, Quebec H3C 4M8
Canada
(514) 877-9777
Fax: (514) 877-9757

Public Company
Incorporated: 1965
Employees: 25,307
Sales: C$3.08 billion
Stock Exchanges: Montréal New York Toronto
SICs: 2711 Newspapers: Publishing, or Publishing &
   Printing; 2731 Books: Publishing, or Publishing &
   Printing; 2752 Commercial Printing, Lithographic; 2754
   Commercial Printing, Gravure; 2759 Commercial Printing
   Not Elsewhere Classified

Quebecor Inc. is a vertically integrated company specializing in publishing and distribution, printing, and forest products. The publishing and distribution arm, Quebecor Group Inc., produces daily and weekly newspapers, as well as magazines, books, and print advertisements. It is Quebec's largest publishing firm and largest magazine and newspaper distributor. Quebecor Group also distributes books, musical recordings, and photographic equipment. The company's printing division, Quebecor Printing Inc., is the largest diversified commercial printing concern in Canada and the second largest in the United States and North America. Quebecor Printing also has holdings in France and Mexico. Subsidiaries of Quebecor Printing make advertising insets and circulars, catalogues, telephone directories, magazines, books, checks, money, and passports. Quebecor Printing customers include Bloomingdale's, L.L. Bean, Radio Shack, Sears, and the magazines *People, Sports Illustrated, Time,* and *TV Guide.* Donohue Inc., Quebecor's forestry products subsidiary, manages forest tracts, operates mills, and produces newsprint, pulp and lumber.

Pierre Péladeau, Quebecor's founder, president, and chief executive officer, bought his first newspaper in 1950 when he was 25 years old. His father had been successful in business, but lost his fortune by the time of his death when his son was only ten. His mother managed to send Péladeau to an exclusive school and he continued his education at elite universities. At an early age, Péladeau decided he would control his own financial destiny.

"I always created my own jobs," Péladeau told *Forbes.* A graduate of McGill University with a degree in law and of the University of Montreal with a Master's degree in Philosophy, Péladeau borrowed C$1,500 from his mother to buy the ailing weekly *Le Journal de Rosemont,* and worked hard to make the paper a success. In 1953 Péladeau bought his first printing press. More dailies and printing presses followed, until Péladeau had built the beginnings of his empire.

A 1964 strike at Quebec's leading French language daily, *La Presse,* gave Péladeau a big opportunity. In *La Presse*'s absence, Péladeau launched his own daily, *Le Journal de Montréal.* The tabloid, which featured graphic pictures of crime scenes, heavy sports coverage, pin-up girl photos, and no editorials, met with immediate success. *La Presse*'s return to the stands seven months later slowed but did not halt that success. In fact, circulation rose during the following years until *Le Journal* became Quebec and North America's leading French language daily in the late 1970s, a status it maintained into the 1990s.

After an entrepreneurial beginning and incorporation in 1965, Quebecor Inc. pursued a decades long course of acquisition and expansion that aimed to consolidate the company's leading position in the fields of publishing and printing in Canada and the United States. Since 1965, over 100 subsidiaries have been added to the Quebecor empire. The location and business activity of Quebecor's subsidiary purchases indicates the success of the company's stated strategic objective: "[To] Broaden its reach across North America and overseas; to acquire additional product market share and diversity; to target and acquire underperforming assets that are geographically well situated and improve their performance; and to achieve a size that maximizes the benefits of economies of scale."

In 1967, Péladeau founded *Le Journal de Quebec,* and later added an entertainment magazine and *The Winnipeg Sun* to his newspaper holdings. Labor lawyer Brian Mulroney, eventually to become Canada's prime minister, worked out *Le Journal*'s first labor agreement. Péladeau's generous dealings with labor cemented his positive reputation with the public. In 1972, Péladeau offered shares in Quebecor.

In 1977, Péladeau gambled in the U.S. newspaper market by launching the *Philadelphia Journal.* But this venture turned out to be one of Péladeau's few misjudgments of the market and the competition. He thought the extensive sports coverage and tabloid format used in *Le Journal* would be a big hit in Philadelphia. Yet the paper's competition simply increased its sports coverage and cut advertising rates to squeeze Péladeau out of the market. Five years later, at a loss of US$14 million, the paper closed its doors.

In the next several years, Péladeau undertook a more aggressive campaign to establish a presence in the U.S. market and to take the number one position in Canada. He saw that technology and economies of scale were becoming increasingly important to success in the printing and publishing industries due to changes in technology and a more competitive world economy. His strong customer orientation and grasp of client needs, both in business-to-business and consumer markets, were great assets in the strategic expansion of Quebecor. Quebecor invested in emerging technologies, allowing retailers and advertisers to regionalize product offerings and prices. Bar code technology allowed the creation of large databases from which computers could determine demographic buying patterns, making it possible to tailor publications to specific regions, neighborhoods, or even individuals. These technologies required specialized capabilities such as special binding techniques to allow customized compilation of pages destined for different markets.

Péladeau and British publishing magnate Robert Maxwell teamed up in 1987 to form Mircor Inc., a joint subsidiary created to purchase—for C$320 million—a 54 percent stake in Donohue Inc., a leading forest products company in Quebec. Quebecor took a 51 percent share of the newly-formed Mircor. The Donohue acquisition gave Quebecor its status as one of the most vertically integrated communications companies in the world, for it allowed the company to do everything from cutting the tree to distributing the printed product. Donohue supplied paper for Quebecor's journals and magazines and for direct mail advertising for its retail clients.

In 1988, Quebecor bought almost all of the printing assets of BCE Inc., the owner of Bell Canada, for C$161 million and a 21 percent share of Quebecor capital stock. The acquisition expanded Quebecor's printing capabilities and brought in lucrative contracts for printing telephone directories, currency, and passports. This acquisition made Quebecor first in printing in Canada and gave the company significant economies of scale, positioning it well for success in the increasingly competitive and technology-driven industry.

In 1990, Quebecor bought Maxwell Communication Corp.'s 14 U.S. printing operations, forming the basis of Quebecor Printing. The US$510 million deal included a non-competition agreement and the purchase by Maxwell of a 25.8 percent interest in Quebecor Printing for US$100 million. According to Michael Crawford in *Canadian Business,* the purchase gave Quebecor access to a C$744 million customer list and rotogravure presses tailored to U.S. advertisers and catalogue companies. Only a year later, Robert Maxwell's death revealed his holdings to be in a financial mess. Quebecor bought back its shares from Maxwell for US$94.8 million dollars, US$5.2 million less than Maxwell had paid for it, giving Quebecor 100 percent ownership of Quebecor Printing.

Quebecor was not immune from the recession in the early 1990s. Plummeting newsprint prices in 1991 created heavy losses at Donohue, substantially eating into Quebecor's revenues. Advertising was down as well, putting pressure on the publishing and printing segments. In anticipation of the North American Free Trade Agreement, Quebecor established a foothold in Mexico by buying Mexican printer Graficas Monte Alban S.A. The move was another step forward in Quebecor's determination to become a truly North American company and gave Quebecor a presence in all three North American countries. Graficas prints books for Mexican and South American publishers. With about 200 employees and annual sales of US$4.5 million, Graficas was not a large acquisition. Nevertheless, it provided a starting point from which to learn the Mexican market and expand holdings in the fast growing market of 80 million people.

Quebecor expanded further in 1992 as it made large investments in its printing facilities and took Quebecor Printing Inc. public with an initial public offering that left the parent company with a 67.57 percent share of its printing subsidiary. Proceeds from the offering were used to reduce bank debt. In the same year, Quebecor won two lucrative five year contracts to print and bind Canadian telephone directories. The value of the contracts over five years was estimated at a combined total of C$505 million.

In 1992 and 1993, Quebecor Printing acquired Arcata Graphics, San Jose, and three major Arcata Corporation printing plants, bringing in clients such as *Reader's Digest, Parade,* and *TV Guide.* The acquisition of these plants substantially expanded Quebecor's market share and capacity in producing catalogues, magazines, and books. Advanced web offset publication, special binding, ink jet printing, and shorter run production capabilities were some of the technologies enhanced by the purchase. In 1994, Quebecor completed its buyout of Arcata when it exercised its option to buy the company's outstanding shares. The final acquisition added five book manufacturing plants and a distribution facility to Quebecor, making the company the second largest book fabricator in the United States.

The strategic importance of Quebecor's expansion of its printing operations and move into the United States market was apparent from financial figures. By the end of 1993, U.S. sales represented more than 73 percent of Quebecor Printing's revenues and 64 percent of Quebecor Inc.'s revenues.

Quebecor's launch of *Le Magazine Provigo* with Provigo supermarkets in early 1993 was another example of Quebecor management's insight into consumer trends and changing markets. Four years before the magazine was introduced, Quebecor had approached the supermarket chain with the idea of differentiating itself from competitors by producing a monthly magazine on nutrition and health, with bits about local sports and entertainment celebrities. Quebecor hoped the magazine would join its information and distribution networks with Provigo's large target market to produce an effective advertising vehicle. Though Provigo wasn't ready to make the investment at the time, increased competition increased and narrowing profit margins in the retail grocery business eventually compelled Provigo to embrace the more upscale image offered by the magazine.

Quebecor Printing continued its international expansion with purchases and contracts in France, India, and Lebanon. Quebecor chose France because it is strategically situated to serve the European market, the world's second largest market for printed products after the United States. In 1993, Quebecor acquired 70 percent of the shares of commercial printer Groupe Fécomme for about US$12 million. The concern was renamed Imprimeries Fécomme-Quebecor S.A. The operation included three printing plants that made magazine covers, advertising inserts and circulars, and direct mail. Quebecor signed a letter of intent a few months after the Fécomme purchase to buy 49 percent of the shares of Groupe Jean Didier, the largest printer in France, for US$27.6 million. The deal was completed in early 1995. The company produced magazines, catalogues, and inserts. With the two acquisitions, Quebecor established a significant foothold in Europe.

A partnership was formed in 1993 with Tej Bandhu Group in India to construct a printing plant, called Tej Quebecor Printing Ltd., for printing the majority of telephone directories in India. With a population of 850 million, the establishment of a subsidiary in India provided great potential for future expansion. In 1994, Quebecor was awarded a contract to produce bank notes for the central bank of Lebanon. The job specifies at least 29 million large denomination pound notes. The new issue is the first time Lebanon has printed its currency outside of England since its independence in 1943.

On the domestic front, 1994 saw the loss of one of Quebecor's major contracts, the printing of the U.S. edition of *Reader's Digest,* the largest paid monthly circulation magazine in the United States. Quebecor lost the US$20 million-a-year, ten-year contract to its major U.S.-based competitor, R. R. Donnelley & Sons Co. Donnelley was the largest commercial printer in North America and the world, with three times the revenues of Quebecor Printing. The contract was apparently awarded to Donnelley because of the company's technological capabilities in targeting advertising to specific subscriber groups. Another factor in the loss of the contract may have been the refusal of some unionized workers at Quebecor Printing of Buffalo Inc., where the magazine was printed, to accept a ten year no-strike/no-lockout amendment to the contract. Quebecor planned to make up the lost volume with growth in book printing.

While Quebecor appeared to be well positioned strategically and financially to meet the changing demands of its industries going into the twenty-first century, several management and business issues will have to be handled carefully to ensure future success. The ever-increasing competition and costly technological changes in Quebecor's main business sector will continue to present strategic challenges. The other main issue facing the company was the succession of founder Pierre Péladeau, whose flamboyant entrepreneurial style was an integral part of the company's development. Péladeau, 70 years old in 1995, planned to relinquish his position as president and CEO and take the slot of chairman of the board of directors "soon," though he had not specified what soon means. Two sons, Pierre Karl and Érik, held executive positions in the company and were considered likely candidates for the top slot.

Principal Subsidiaries: Donohue Inc. (63.6%); Quebecor Printing Inc. (75.4%); Imprimeries Fécomme-Quebecor SA (70%; France); Quebecor Printing (USA) Corp.; Tej Quebecor Printing Ltd. (40%; India).

Further Reading:

Bomberger, Paul, "Donnelley Planning Big Expansion Here," *Intelligencer Journal,* September 15, 1994, p. A1.
"Business Brief—Quebecor Inc.: Mexican Printer Is Acquired by a Unit of the Company," *Wall Street Journal,* January 7, 1992, p. 2.
Coles, Alex, "Quebecor Inc.—Sanford Evans Communications Ltd. Restructures Its Direct List Brokerage Services," *Business Wire,* February 22, 1993.
Crawford, Michael, "Prey for the Paper Tiger," *Canadian Business,* November 1993, p. 22.
Dougherty, Kevin, "The Powerful World of the Péladeaus," *Financial Post,* March 21, 1992, p. 2S16.
Dunn, Brian, "Provigo and Quebecor Launch Magazine for Grocery Shoppers," *Montreal Gazette,* March 1, 1993, p. C15.
Gray, Alan, "Quebecor Makes Paper, Prints on It and Distributes the Published Product," *Montreal Gazette,* March 22, 1993, p. F8.
McIntosh, Andrew, "Pierre Péladeau to quit Quebecor—Next Year," *Monteal Gazette,* April 29, 1994, p. 1.
Palmeri, Christopher, "Nietzsche's Out God's In," *Forbes,* December 10, 1990, pp. 40–41.
"Quebecor Earnings Fell 89 Percent in Quarter, Revenue Declined 9 Percent," *Wall Street Journal,* February 13, 1992.
"Quebecor Finalizes Arcata Deal," *Graphic Arts Monthly,* August 1994, p. 21.
"Quebecor Printing Gets Contract," *Wall Street Journal,* September 29, 1992, p. B8.
"Quebecor Printing Gets 5-Year Contract to Print Directories," *Wall Street Journal,* July 6, 1992, p. 27.
"Quebecor Unit Acquires Plant," *Wall Street Journal,* January 23, 1992, p. 4.
"Quebecor Unit Sets Initial Public Offering of 14 Million Shares," *Wall Street Journal,* April 13, 1992, p. C11.
"Reader's Digest Selects Donnelley as Printer for Its U.S. Edition," *Wall Street Journal,* September 14, 1994, p. A4.
Rojo, Oscar, "Canadian High-Tech Firms Heading Overseas," *Toronto Star,* April 4, 1994, p. F3.

—Katherine Smethurst

Remington Arms Company, Inc.

1007 Market Street
Wilmington, Delaware 19898
U.S.A.
(302) 774-1000
Fax: (302) 774-5776

Wholly Owned Subsidiary of Clayton, Dubilier & Rice
Incorporated: 1816
Employees: 2,300
Sales: $400 million
SICs: 3399 Primary Metal Products; 3484 Small Arms; 2329
   Men's/Boy's Clothing

Remington Arms Co. Inc. is one of the oldest manufacturers of firearms in the United States and the largest U.S. producer of rifles. A worldwide supplier of small arms, Remington holds a special place in American popular culture, its name having grown synonymous with the taming of the American west in the 19th century. In addition, the company is known for its long history of innovation, and counts the famous breach-loading rifle among its many advancements in technology.

Eliphalet Remington, Jr., the progenitor of Remington Arms, was born in 1793 to Eliphalet and Elizabeth Remington. The family moved west—from Connecticut to New York—in 1800 to find land and start a farm. They settled in what is now Ilion, New York. In addition to the farm, Eliphalet set up a forge and blacksmith shop to help him build his farm equipment. Eliphalet Jr. was drawn to the shop early, and displayed a canny Yankee ingenuity. For example, when the Remington family wanted some silver spoons for Eliphalet Jr.'s sister, Mary, they sent the young Eliphalet to a silversmith with pieces of rough silver. After watching the silversmith for a day, Eliphalet Jr. returned with the silver pieces. He then proceeded to make the spoons himself, to everyone's satisfaction, in the family's blacksmith shop.

Remington acted similarly when he decided to make his own hunting rifle. Unable to afford the purchase price of a new rifle, he fashioned his own from scrap iron. Locals were so impressed with Remington's homemade firearm that they began paying him to make rifles for them. Within a few years Remington's skills were recognized throughout the region and he was deluged with orders for custom-made firearms. Throughout the 1820s Eliphalet Jr. and his father shipped rifles to customers

throughout New England by way of the Erie Canal. In 1828 he expanded the business by purchasing 100 acres of land closer to the canal. With financial backing from friends, he set up a new forge and blacksmith shop. Unfortunately, Eliphalet Sr. was accidentally killed while transporting equipment to the new location.

Remington's operation continued to blossom during the 1830s as his guns became known for their high-quality craftsmanship. The company received a major boost in 1845 when it landed its first government contract. Also in 1845, Remington crafted the first gun barrel in America to be fashioned from solid steel. Remington's steel rifles quickly garnered a reputation for precision. Orders poured in. Beginning in the 1850s, Remington started designing and manufacturing revolvers. For several years the company sold its popular Beal revolver. It followed that model with the Rider revolver, one of the first self-cocking revolvers. In 1856 Eliphalet and his three sons officially joined forces to form E. Remington and Sons.

Not surprisingly, E. Remington and Sons experienced explosive growth during the Civil War and contributed to the Union victory. Even before the war started the Remington armory was churning out rifles by the thousands for various government contracts. After the War began, though, production boomed. The company filled one order, for example, for 40,000 rifles priced at $16 each. To keep up with skyrocketing demand, the company built a temporary production facility to make army revolvers and installed a steam generation system to produce power. At times, every man and boy in the town of Ilion worked day and night for periods of weeks to meet contract deadlines. Remington produced nearly $3 million worth of rifles during the war. Importantly, Remington developed its famous breach-loading gun at this time to replace the conventional muzzle-loading rifle.

The demands of war-time production proved to be too much for the 68-year-old Remington. He died during the first few months of the conflict, leaving his three sons to fill his shoes. Philo, the oldest of the three and the best craftsmen, became president of the company. Younger brother Samuel, who was known as a savvy business man, became responsible for finding new contracts. He is credited with extending Remington's reach overseas. In fact, Samuel eventually made his home in Paris and London, and later assumed the title of president of the company in order to enhance his prestige (and ability to get new business) in Europe. Eliphalet, the youngest, was placed in charge of the office and day-to-day operating activities.

Business dropped after the War, but orders surged within a few years as a result of Remington's increasingly popular breach-loading rifles. Besides new orders by the U.S. Army, Remington shipped hundreds of thousands of rifles overseas to countries such as Sweden, France, Egypt, Spain, and Denmark. Samuel eventually secured more than $11 million in contracts with the French government alone, largely as a result of that country's war with Germany. By the 1870s Remington's gun production capacity had surpassed that of the entire nation of England. It employed 1,850 people and, at times, churned out an average of 1,400 rifles and 200 revolvers daily.

International orders slowed during the late 1800s. To keep its workers busy, Remington diversified into a number of unique industries where its penchant for innovation was rewarded. For example, it contracted to build the first 100 Baxter steam cars (streetcars capable of producing 25 horsepower and traveling at speeds of more than 15 miles per hour). Remington was later the first company to manufacture a Baxter steam canal boat. Similarly, the Remington armory manufactured the first 100 velocipedes (vehicles that sported two wooden wheels with attached crank pedals) made in the United States, thus giving birth to the domestic bicycle industry. Remington even shipped a special tandem, or two-seater, model. Other innovations manufactured by Remington beginning in the late 1880s included specialized sewing machines and devices, the typewriter, electric lighting systems, pill- and tablet-making equipment, gasoline-powered engines, deep-well pumps, lathes, burglar alarms, and cigar-making machines.

After development by the armory, most of Remington's inventions were contracted out for manufacture or set up as separate operating companies under the constantly unfolding Remington corporate umbrella. Soon, Remington became known as a haven for inventors. At times during the 1870s and 1880s, Remington secured an average of four new patents each week. Inventors were welcomed into Philo Remington's home, where they would present their ideas. If Philo approved, Remington's armory would assist in patenting and producing the device. Meanwhile, the company continued to innovate in the firearms industry. It introduced the James P. Lee military rifle, for example, a type of bolt-action gun that was followed by more advanced Remington models. Remington also developed a rapid-fire naval gun, one of the earliest precursors to the modern machine gun, and a popular double-barreled shotgun. Among other unique novelties was Remington's ''gun cane,'' a gun that looked like a walking stick, and a portable gun designed to project 200 yards of lifeline to the upper floors of burning buildings.

By the mid-1880s Remington had established itself as a pillar of American ingenuity. Unfortunately, the Remington brothers's (Samuel had died in 1882) strategy of diversification had failed to bear fruit and the company was financially troubled. Problems were exacerbated by untimely setbacks, such as the infamous Chicago fire of 1874, which destroyed Remington's sewing machine company. Remington went bankrupt in 1886 and was bought out in 1888 by a private investor who was also a Remington salesman. The town of Ilion was stunned as the Remington family endured its darkest hour. Philo died in 1889, but Eliphalet III lived until 1924. Although he was removed from the company's operations, Eliphalet lived to see the resurgence of E. Remington and Sons as the Remington Arms Company. As the company's performance continued to wane during the 1890s, the new owners shed Remington's non-performing operations, including its long-running farm implements business. Nevertheless, Remington's legacy of innovation continued. It was particularly recognized for its inventions related to the bicycle and the typewriter.

Although Remington experienced financial problems, the company never lost its reputation as the inventor and producer of some of the finest firearms in the world. While Remington became a major player in the northeastern U.S. industrial community, its firearms helped to tame the American West. In fact, many of Remington's rifles and revolvers achieved legendary status. Wild Bill Hickock, for example, was known for carrying a Remington double-barreled Derringer pistol in his vest pocket. Likewise, infamous bank robber Frank James and renowned riverboat gambler Bat Masterson both publicly endorsed Remington firearms in newspaper advertisements. Remington's role in the settling of the country would be recounted endlessly in the Hollywood westerns of the 20th century.

Remington's fortunes began to improve following a government order in 1898 for 100,000 guns during the Spanish-American War. As its firearms business healed, the company bailed out of less successful endeavors, including its large bicycle operation. It kept its typewriter division, the Remington Standard Typewriter Company (renamed Remington Typewriter Company in 1903)—In 1927 it folded that company into an affiliated office equipment company called Remington Rand, Inc. Sales were again buoyed with the onset of World War I, first by orders from English and French governments and later by the United States when it finally entered the conflict. During World War I Remington spent about $1 million dollars on new land, buildings, and equipment necessary to meet ballooning demand. After the United States entered the War in 1917, Remington's work force swelled from about 900 to more than 11,000. That figure eventually climbed as high as 15,000, many of whom were women. Daily output reached a record 3,000 rifles daily.

Remington was better prepared to deal with the post-war sales slide following World War I than it had been after previous conflicts. Specifically, Remington introduced its first cash register in 1918. Sales of the patented device were swift during most of the 1920s. But even that business slumped following the Great Depression. Remington sold the operation to National Cash Register Company in 1931 in an effort to buoy lagging gun sales. By the early 1930s Remington employed only 300 workers at its core Ilion plant. In need of a facelift, Remington sold a major interest to E.I. du Pont de Nemours & Company in 1933. Under Du Pont's direction, Remington tore down several unneeded buildings and refurbished some of its aging facilitates. By the late 1930s Remington was well-positioned for the impending World War II production boom.

Du Pont's interest in Remington was both well-timed and appropriate. Founded in 1802, the company had started as a manufacturer of gunpowder and explosives. By the early 1900s Du Pont controlled the lion's share of the U.S. gunpowder market. Because Remington had augmented its firearms operations with extensive munitions manufacturing, the companies complemented one another. The partnership was particularly beneficial during World War II, when demand for both gunpowder and firearms soared. Remington again shifted into overdrive during that War, hiring more than 9,000 workers to produce its renowned Springfield rifle. The U.S. government accepted delivery from Remington of more than one million rifles during the early 1940s. Remington's factories ran 24 hours each day, seven days per week. The company celebrated the sale of its two-millionth rifle in 1942.

Following the war, Remington again focused on developing and producing firearms for sport. Its payroll was quickly reduced to about 1,500 workers and business was expectedly sluggish. To boost sales from its core firearms and munitions segments, Remington diversified into new arenas. Notable was its entrance into the industrial tool field. Remington developed and began manufacturing a "Cartridge-powered Stud Driver," a device that fired stud fasteners into various structural materials. The model 450, as it was labeled, used cartridges similar to bullet cartridges. The product enjoyed success during the massive postwar housing and construction boom.

Remington continued to glean profits from military contracts and to sell its sporting rifles and shotguns during the mid-1900s. In addition, it branched out into a number of new markets. It continued to produce sewing machines and office equipment through its affiliation with Remington-Rand, for example, although that unit was eventually sold. Remington began producing goods ranging from hunting knives and mens' accessories (such as Remington shavers) to household utensils and tools. As its offerings and sales expanded, Remington's manufacturing infrastructure extended throughout the United States, with both corporate and government-owned plants spreading to Delaware, Connecticut, Arkansas, Ohio, and Oklahoma, among other places.

By 1980, Remington was generating approximately $300 million in sales, most of which was attributable to its firearms and munitions divisions. When Du Pont completed its purchase of Remington Arms in 1980 as part of its strategy to diversify out of its core chemical business, which was suffering from a savage petrochemical industry downturn, however, the investment proved a big disappointment. Remington experienced major setbacks during the early and mid-1980s, especially in the face of strong foreign competition. Low-cost gunmakers, particularly in emerging Asian economies, inundated U.S. markets with inexpensive firearms. At the same time, Remington's strongest demographic market segment, midwestern farmers, fell on hard times.

By 1986, Remington's annual revenues had plummeted to a discouraging $200 million. Distressed by the failure of the division, Du Pont initiated a reorganization at Remington that was designed to streamline operations, improve research and development, and ultimately improve profitability. Du Pont closed some of Remington's facilities, among other cost-cutting measures, and made plans to broaden Remington's product line. Items introduced during 1986 included a line of hunting apparel and a high-tech deer rifles made with kevlar (a light-weight synthetic material that is five times stronger than steel). Providing the foundation for those innovations were proven Du Pont performers, including: the Model 700 line of hunting rifles; the XP-100 pistols, which were considered among the most accurate in the world; and popular shotgun models 11-87, 1100, and 870.

During the late 1980s and early 1990s, Remington's financial performance improved significantly, largely as a result of successful product line extensions and new introductions. By 1992, in fact, Remington had nearly doubled its sales over 1986 levels to about $400 million annually. In 1993, Du Pont announced that it had reached an agreement to sell Remington to leveraged-buyout specialist Clayton, Dubilier & Rice, a private investment group. Remington enthusiasts were fearful that Remington's legacy of quality and innovation might be trammeled by the private investment group. Those concerns were allayed shortly after the new owner announced its long-term plans for Remington. For example, under the direction of Remington's new chief executive, Tommy Milner, Remington planned to open a new research and development center in Kentucky to be staffed with 60 employees. Remington also announced its intent to consolidate operations, lower operating costs, and to more actively support legislation related to gun-owner's and hunter's rights.

Further Reading:

James, Frank W., "Remington Answers Shooter's Needs," *Shooting Industry,* October 1991, p. 18.

Schulz, Warren E., *Ilion—The Town Remington Made,* Hicksville, N.Y.: Exposition Press, 1977.

Shaw, Donna, "Legendary Remington Gunmaker Sold to Manhattan Investment Firm," *Knight-Ridder/Tribune Business News,* October 21, 1993, p. 102.

Slutsker, Gary, "The Name Game," *Forbes,* December 15, 1986, p. 187.

Sundra, Jon R., "Following a Year Under New Ownership, Remington Proves to be in Good Hands," *Shooting Industry,* January 1995, p. 20.

—Dave Mote

Resorts International, Inc.

1133 Boardwalk
Atlantic City, New Jersey 08401
U.S.A.
(609) 344-6000
Fax: (609) 340-6284

Public Company
Incorporated: 1958 as Mary Carter Paint Company
Employees: 7,200
Sales: $436.9 million
SICs: 7011 Hotels & Motels; 6719 Holding Companies, Not
  Elsewhere Classified

Resorts International, Inc., operates a hotel and casino in Atlantic City, New Jersey, and a vacation destination on Paradise Island in the Bahamas. The company opened the first casino allowed on the East Coast in the late 1970s and watched its profits soar. However, in an effort to capitalize on the potential of the Atlantic City market, Resorts amassed large debts, which eventually jeopardized its financial stability. In the mid-1980s, the company changed hands twice, in a series of controversial deals, and eventually wound up in bankruptcy. Less ambitious in the 1990s, Resorts has sought to consolidate its financial standing.

The company that evolved into Resorts started in 1958 as the Mary Carter Paint Company, which was itself the successor of a company founded in 1908. Initially, Mary Carter Paint grew by acquiring other paint companies, such as the Victor Paint Company, purchased in 1962, and the Atlantic Paint Company, purchased in 1963.

That year, Mary Carter Paint made another acquisition that would have a more significant impact on its future: Bahamas Developers Ltd. To this new interest in properties the company soon added property on the resort of Paradise Island. In December 1967, Mary Carter Paint completed construction of the Paradise Island Hotel and Villas, which would be operated by the Loews Corporation until 1981, and also opened the Paradise Island Casino. Clearly, this property development sideline soon became the company's main focus, and, accordingly, in May 1968, Mary Carter Paint sold its paint division to Delafield Industries for just over $10 million. As part of the purchase price, Delafield gained the right to the Mary Carter name. Thus, on June 24, 1968, what had been the Mary Carter Paint Com-

pany became Resorts International, Inc., a corporation engaged in developing property, as well as owning and operating casinos and resorts.

Six months after the completion of this corporate transformation, Resorts finished a second hotel on Paradise Island, the Britannia Beach Hotel. The following year, the company expanded its geographic scope, establishing Resorts International N.V., based in the Netherlands. At the same time, Resorts also founded International Intelligence, Inc., known as Intertel, as part of its efforts to ensure security in its gaming operations.

In the early 1970s, Resorts further expanded its holdings in the vacation destination industry when it purchased Marine World and Africa U.S.A., two theme parks, for $3.4 million. Two years later, the company also bought Tennis United, Inc., a new facility where tennis was taught in New York City. To consolidate its vacation operations on Paradise Island, Resorts bought Chalk's International Airline, Inc., in April 1974. This carrier brought patrons for the company's casino and hotel to the island from the mainland United States.

Resorts next made its first move into what would become its major arena of business, when the company acquired Leeds & Lippincott Company, which owned Chalfont-Haddon Hall, an ocean-front hotel in Atlantic City, New Jersey, with 1,000 rooms, built in 1917. Resorts purchased 67 percent of Leeds & Lippincott in August 1976, and completed the acquisition the following month, paying a total of $2.489 million. In doing so, Resorts, the casino owner, was engaging in a little gambling of its own. The rundown Haddon Hall Hotel would only become a valuable property if casino gambling was legalized in Atlantic City. Although a previous state-wide referendum to legalize gambling in New Jersey had failed in 1974, on November 2, 1976, after heavy lobbying by casino operators like Resorts, a second referendum, which permitted casinos but restricted them to Atlantic City, passed by a large margin.

Thus, Resorts possessed a potential gold mine, since it would have the right to operate a casino in the only area in the United States, outside Las Vegas, Nevada, where gambling was legal. The company announced plans for a $50 million renovation of the Haddon Hall Hotel, as well as the construction of a new casino. Resorts planned to import 150 pit bosses and other casino workers from its operations in the Caribbean to train New Jersey workers for jobs in its new casino. In addition, the company announced that it would name the new gaming complex "The Palace." After local objection, however, the company decided simply to name it Resorts International.

By April 1978, Resorts had officially applied for a permit to open its new casino in Atlantic City. The company vowed, publicly, that it would open the doors to the gaming hall by Memorial Day. On May 17, 1978, Resorts was granted a six-month permit to operate a gambling casino in Atlantic City by the New Jersey gaming control board, and on May 26, 1978, Resorts opened the doors of the first casino on the East Coast. Customers who had travelled from around the country waited in line for hours on the Atlantic City boardwalk to try their hands at the slots and the gaming tables after the governor of New Jersey cut a ribbon to commemorate the opening of this facility.

With a temporary monopoly on gambling on the East Coast, Resorts' revenues soared in the second half of 1978. After just one month of operation, the casino reported that it had taken in $16 million. To enhance its holdings in the gaming industry, Resorts used some of the money earned in its new casino to buy a one-half stake in the slot machine manufacturing operations of Williams Electronics in June 1978.

In the following months, Resorts also increased its holdings of Atlantic City real estate. In July, the company bought the Steel Pier, a long-time site of amusements on the beach, and in August, it purchased the Ramada Inn Hotel in Atlantic City for $7.5 million. This property was eventually converted to the Resorts International Hotel-North.

At the end of August 1978, Resorts reported a profit of $10.2 million for the first half of the year. As gamblers continued to flock to the only casino open, the company's profits soared. At the end of September, 1978, Resorts reported third quarter profits of $23.9 million, a level higher than the company's net income for the whole first six months of the year, and more than twice the earnings from that period, which had lasted twice as long. Resorts had, indeed, struck gold in Atlantic City. The company reported overall profits for 1978 of $51 million.

The company entered 1979 with its monopoly intact, although other casinos were under construction up and down the Boardwalk. The company's take for January 1979 dropped eight percent from its level of the previous month, but the casino operation still reported profits far higher than those of Las Vegas properties. In February, Resorts won a permanent permit to operate casinos in Atlantic City. At that time, the company also banned card counters from its casinos, despite objections that the practice was legal.

In May 1979, Resorts added 32 gaming tables and increased the size of the minimum bets in its Atlantic City casino, and two months later, the company announced the construction of its second New Jersey hotel and casino, a project slated to cost $120 million. During this time, the company shed its amusement park operations, the Marine World/Africa U.S.A. theme park, for $3.6 million. Resorts also bought more Atlantic City real estate, purchasing the 300 room Seaside Hotel and the adjoining 150 room Terrace Motel.

By the end of 1979, Resorts' monopoly in New Jersey had come to an end, as first Caesar's World, and then Bally's Park Place Casino Hotel opened on the Boardwalk. Nevertheless, the company reported profits for the year of $91.1 million, nearly twice the level of the previous year. By the start of the following year, however, Resorts had started to feel the pinch of competition, as first quarter earnings dropped 25 percent, to $14.2 million. In addition, the company faced dissent among its shareholders, for its failure to pay dividends, despite the vast increase in its earnings. In its efforts to capitalize on the booming casino market in New Jersey, Resorts had spent heavily, running up large debts, a circumstance which left the company in perilous financial shape, despite the runaway success of its casino on the boardwalk.

Late in the spring of 1980, Resorts took several steps to manipulate its financial situation. First, it tried to pay off some debts with stock, and also tried to buy back some of its own shares, an

effort which was abandoned in June. Also at that time, Resorts faced charges by the New Jersey Gaming Enforcement Division that it had been lax in its operation of its casino, and had extended credit to gamblers too freely. In July, the company paid a $225,000 fine for 7,500 credit law violations.

Resorts' financial difficulties continued in 1981, as the company laid off 400 employees at its Atlantic City casino and reported a $27 million loss in the third quarter of the year, due to a drop in investment markets, in which the company was heavily exposed. Nevertheless, the company went ahead with plans to construct a second $100 million 1,500 room hotel and convention center in Atlantic City.

Resorts continued its aggressive activity in the financial markets in 1982, despite a shareholder suit aimed at preventing it from doing so, and in August the company reported that a risky investment in interest rate futures contracts had paid off handsomely. However, the company remained burdened by debts, as it pushed ahead with development of its second casino project, dubbed the Taj Mahal. A year later, Resorts increased its holding of Atlantic City real estate yet again when it bought yet another parcel of land for development, this one located at the entrance to the city.

In the mid-1980s, Resorts' identity and fate as a casino operator was thrown into question, as it earnings steadily sank. By 1984, the company's debts had grown so great that its diminishing earnings were insufficient to cover interest payments on the money it owed. Over the course of 1985, Resorts acquired a large stake in Pan American World Airways, and rumors began to circulate that it would sell its New Jersey casino and hotel operations.

Late in 1985, word came that Resorts would sell its Atlantic City properties to U.S. Capital, a group of private investors, for $325 million. This offer was rejected, however, and a long series of moves and countermoves between Resorts and another suitor, Pratt Hotel, took place over the course of 1986. Throughout this time, the company's financial condition worsened steadily. At the end of 1985, Resorts reported earnings of $6.1 million, down from $22 million two years earlier. Worse, Resorts closed out 1986 with a loss of $30.64 million.

After Pratt Hotel's final offer for Resorts collapsed in December 1986, New York real estate investor Donald J. Trump stepped into the fray, offering $101 million for 78 percent of the company held by the estate of the recently deceased Resorts chairman. Although this offer was contested by a group of private investors led by a top Resorts executive, Trump had taken control of the company by July 1987. Immediately following the change-over in ownership, the company sold off its interest in Pan Am for $61 million.

In winning Resorts, Trump had taken over the company's troubled Taj Mahal casino project, which was still under construction and suffering from heavy cost overruns, which had pushed its cost to three times initial estimates, causing Resorts to run up $700 million in debt. Shortly after taking control of the company, Trump appointed himself chairman of Resorts and told its board of directors that he wanted to be paid fees equivalent to all of the company's income for the foreseeable future. Stockholders in Resorts were reportedly not informed of this deal until after it had taken place, at which point the price of their stock dropped from $62 to $12, in December 1987.

Trump then announced, in February 1988, that he would take Resorts private by buying the company's now nearly worthless outstanding stock. Then, in March 1988, entertainer and hotel owner Merv Griffin made a bid for Resorts. When the deal finally closed in November 1988, Trump earned $68 million for his shares from Griffin, and took full possession of the Taj Mahal, still under construction. Griffin took control of Resorts, which consisted of the aging Resorts International casino and hotel in Atlantic City and vacation properties on Paradise Island in the Bahamas. With these assets, Griffin also assumed all of the financial obligations Resorts had amassed in trying to build the Taj Mahal, while giving away the pay-off for those expenditures, the casino itself, which was located next door to the worn Resorts operations. According to Richard L. Stern, writing for *Forbes,* "Griffin didn't realize it at the time, but he was doing Donald trump a tremendous favor. In over his head, Trump was bailed out when Griffin made an offer Trump couldn't refuse."

In August 1989, Griffin stopped paying interest on Resorts' $925 million worth of debts, amassed through his purchase of the company from Trump, as Resorts neared a point of total insolvency. In November, Resorts was forced into Chapter 11 bankruptcy by its bondholders, as shareholders filed suit in the wake of the deal between Griffin and Trump. Reports charging impropriety and even Mafia ties in the deal concerning Griffin and Trump surfaced in business magazines, as Griffin maintained that he had been unaware of any irregularities in the deal.

In the wake of Resorts' bankruptcy, the company reorganized its finances, with Griffin turning over 78 percent of Resorts to its bondholders. In addition, the company sold off its airline subsidiary, Chalk's International Airlines, and began to seek a buyer for its properties in the Bahamas. In April 1990, the company suffered another blow when the Taj Mahal casino finally opened next door to Resorts. The newer gaming hall siphoned off bettors from Resorts' casino and also offered employment to many of the best workers at the older hotel.

By the spring of 1991, Resorts had officially exited bankruptcy, and the company's future appeared to be brightening somewhat, as losses at the Atlantic City casino and hotel started to slow. Griffin, who had initially become wealthy through his interests in television game shows, had discovered that holding contestant searches at his Atlantic City hotel was a good way to fill the casino. Resorts also invested $50 million in efforts to refurbish and brighten the New Jersey properties, using an Art Deco "Hollywood" theme to lend distinction to hotel rooms for high rollers. The company also inaugurated an employee retraining program to enhance hospitality at the hotel and casino.

In October 1993, after similar renovations at its property in the Bahamas, Resorts sold 60 percent of its Paradise Island properties to Sun International Hotels, Limited, for $75 million. With this move, the company came closer to the firm financial footing it had enjoyed in the late 1970s. Nevertheless, as Resorts moved into the mid-1990s, the company faced a daunting task, given its turbulent history and its shaky financial standing. Whether it would ultimately survive the monetary turmoil of the industry that it had helped to pioneer remained to be seen.

Principal Subsidiaries: P. I. Resorts, Limited; Paradise Island Airlines, Inc.; GGRI, Inc.; Resorts International Hotel, Inc.

Further Reading:

Butler, Charles, "Merv Bounces Back," *Successful Meetings,* April 1991, pp. 40–49.
Connolly, John, and Richard L. Stern, "How Merv Griffin Got Taken to the Cleaners," *Forbes,* June 11, 1990, pp. 38–41.
Davis, Ed, *Atlantic City Diary,* Atlantic City: Atlantic City News Agency, 1989.
Mahar, Maggie, "Wheel of Misfortune," *Barron's,* September 24, 1990, pp. 10+.
Mahar, Maggie, "Wheel of Misfortune: More on the Saga of Resorts International," *Barron's,* May 6, 1991, p. 18–19.
Wolf, Carlo, "Merv Griffin's Magic Theater," *Lodging Hospitality,* February 1993, pp. 30–33.

—Elizabeth Rourke

The Royal Bank of Scotland

The Royal Bank of Scotland Group plc

42 St. Andrew Square
Edinburgh EH2 2YE
United Kingdom
(031) 556 8555
Fax: (031) 557 6565

Public Company
Incorporated: 1727
Employees: 23,299
Sales: £293 million
Stock Exchanges: London
SICs: 6711 Holding Companies; 6012 Recognized Banks

Established in 1727, the Royal Bank of Scotland was the second bank started in Scotland. One of the largest banks in Scotland, the Royal Bank of Scotland also holds a significant position in the United Kingdom's banking industry. Since the 1980s the bank has successfully diversified both in terms of product line and geography, having established a popular and profitable insurance business, Direct Line, and a growing American banking subsidiary, Citizens Financial Group.

After one failed attempt, the Royal Bank of Scotland was established on May 31, 1727. The first attempt to establish the bank came in the late seventeenth century when Scotland tried to improve its economic position with the so-called Darien scheme. The Darien scheme was a plan to establish a Scots trading colony, designed along the lines of England's London East India Company, in Panama. With a population of only around 1,100,000 at the end of the seventeenth century, Scotland could not hope to raise the requisite capital alone, so the scheme's architects relied on England for the bulk of their subscriptions. English investors, however, withdrew their money at the last minute when the English government realized that a successful Scottish venture could jeopardize the position of the London East India Company. Forced to finance the venture alone, the Scots raised £238,000 for the enterprise. Unfortunately, the entire sum was lost when the venture collapsed in 1699 due to difficulties with the heat, the Spanish, and outbreaks of fever.

The failure was devastating to Scotland, which had lost a quarter of its liquid assets in the disaster. Feelings ran so high

against England for its lack of support that when the two countries were joined by the 1707 Act of Union, the English government deemed it wise to agree to pay compensation. The government provided for an "Equivalent" of £398,085 (and ten shillings) to cover the Darien losses and other debts, and allowed for an "Arising Equivalent," which would be a percentage of tax revenue. Because only £150,000 of the promised money was actually available in cash, many Scottish creditors were given debentures bearing interest at five percent. Little of this interest actually materialized, however, until 1719, when an act was passed establishing an annual fund of £10,000 to be raised by Scotland's customs and excise.

Organizations such as the Society of the Subscribed Equivalent Debt arose in both Scotland and England to aid in collecting the interest due, to buy more debenture stock, and to issue loans to members based on the value of their holdings. In 1724 these organizations were joined and regularized by Parliament to create the Equivalent Company. By 1727 this company, which was essentially acting as a bank to its members, chose to take the next logical step and officially become a bank. It was impossible to do so in England, where the Bank of England's monopoly was firmly fixed, but the field was open in Scotland, where the monopoly of the Bank of Scotland, established by an act of the Scots Parliament in 1695, had expired in 1716. The Equivalent Company was granted a charter for banking on May 31, 1727, and was incorporated as the Royal Bank of Scotland.

The new bank opened in Edinburgh on December 8, 1727, with an authorized capital of £111,347 and a governor, a court of directors, and a staff of eight: a cashier, a secretary and his clerk, an accountant and his clerk, two tellers, and a messenger. It was a modest beginning but the new bank received a welcome boost in the form of £20,000 from the government, which chose that occasion to finally honor a commitment undertaken as part of the 1707 Act of Union, which provided for that sum to be lent out at interest for the development of Scottish fisheries and general manufacturing.

The Royal Bank learned to compete well against the Bank of Scotland and other banks as they were subsequently established. Circulation wars were an especially popular way of discomfiting the competition. At the time official government-backed banknotes did not exist; each bank issued its own, and a favorite ploy was to amass as many of a rival's banknotes as possible and present them for payment all at once, causing frequent embarrassment and occasional temporary closures. Before long, however, an efficient counter-tactic was mounted when competitors demanded redemption of banknotes be paid entirely with sixpences. Eventually the practice died out.

Although the tricks may have been discontinued, the rivalry among competing banks remained. By the later eighteenth century the struggle for dominance shifted to Glasgow, Scotland's second largest city, which was rapidly gaining prominence as a center for industry and commerce. Smaller banks had already sprung up there to satisfy new demand, and the big two, the Royal Bank and the Bank of Scotland, both Edinburgh-based, soon reacted to the threat of more competition. The Royal's first Glasgow branch opened in 1783 and the bank became deeply involved in the city's booming industries: the cotton trade, steam ships, sugar, and tobacco. Before long the Royal dominated the financial market in Glasgow; indeed, by the 1810s the bank's Glasgow trade eclipsed its business in Edinburgh.

By the early nineteenth century a new threat faced the Royal and its arch-rival the Bank of Scotland. As large banking institutions whose clients tended to be big companies and very wealthy individuals, the two were perceived—and accurately so—as being removed from the interests of the general public. The average small customer's banking needs were served by small private banks which in turn banked with the Royal or the Bank of Scotland. The system, which struck many as unsatisfactory, was changed with the arrival in 1810 of the new Commercial Bank of Scotland, which billed itself as "the Bank of the Citizens." The new bank did well, having built up a branch network in Scotland of 30 banks by 1831, when it was granted a Royal Charter of Incorporation. The Commercial's success was watched with interest, and other, similar banks soon appeared, most notably the National Bank of Scotland, incorporated in 1825.

Increased competition notwithstanding, the Royal continued to thrive as the nineteenth century progressed. As its success in Glasgow had proved, the bank was keenly aware of the opportunities afforded by the expansion of industry: in 1826 it financed Scotland's first steam-powered railway, the first of several successful transport ventures. As the bank prospered it also expanded. By 1836 five new outlets had been established in Dundee, Paisley, Perth, Rothesay, and Dalkeith. The Royal Bank began a policy of aggressive acquisition, taking over many new branches after the 1857 failure of the Western Bank of Scotland and in 1864 acquiring the Dundee Banking Company. The Royal Bank also expanded its operations into England in 1874.

The Scottish banking community was shocked in 1878 when the City of Glasgow Bank spectacularly crashed: although the incident worked to the big banks' advantage (they divided the unfortunate bank's branches between them), it highlighted the need for limited liability and for a bank's accounting practices to be audited by independent, professional accountants. The Royal Bank was already protected on the first score under the terms of its charter, but the Commercial and the National made haste to register under the Companies Act to prevent a similar misfortune befalling them.

The Royal increased its presence in England in the early twentieth century. In 1924 the bank acquired Drummonds' Bank, a small but highly regarded London bank (whose clients had included George III and Beau Brummel) originally founded in 1717 by an expatriate Scotsman. Six years later the Royal acquired the Bank of England's West End Branch and also Williams Deacon's Bank, whose branch network in Manchester and the northwest provided the Royal with its first English presence outside the capital. The trend toward acquisition continued in 1939 with the addition of another private London bank, Glyn, Mills & Co. This bank and Williams Deacon's continued to operate under their own names as subsidiaries, and together with their parent the Royal Bank were known as the Three Banks Group. As the bank grew it took advantage of technology. At this time the Royal Bank introduced telephones, typewriters, adding machines, and teleprinters. After World War II the bank founded a residential banking college to train staff for an increasingly sophisticated financial world.

By 1959 banking trends clearly favored consolidation. Scottish banks needed to match the financial might of their English counterparts if they were to be able to accommodate the needs of growing Scottish industry and commerce. Accordingly, the National and Commercial banks merged to form the National Commercial Bank, and in 1966 further strengthened their position by acquiring the English and Welsh branches of the National Bank. Three years later, however, the National Commercial Bank merged with the Royal Bank. The Scottish components of the new group were organized under a holding company, the National and Commercial Banking Group Ltd., and the English concerns, Glyn, Mills & Co., Williams Deacon's, and the National Bank, came together as Williams & Glyn's Bank Ltd., trading as such until 1985 when they adopted the name of the Royal Bank.

Greatly strengthened by the amalgamation, the group was ideally placed to take full advantage of the two watershed economic events of the 1970s. In 1971 the regulatory Bank of England eased restrictions on Scottish banks operating in England, allowing the royal Bank to compete freely for the first time. The range of financial services that banks could provide was also substantially broadened. Perhaps even more significantly, the rise of the North Sea oil industry in the 1970s proved an unprecedented boom to the Scottish economy and especially to banks, like the Royal, which were quick to recognize the tremendous potential of the new industry. Taking advantage of its new found strength, the bank expanded its foreign interests, establishing branches in New York and Hong Kong and opening representative offices in Chicago, Houston, Los Angeles, and San Francisco.

The 1980s began a time of expansion and diversification for the Royal Bank. In 1985 the bank created Direct Line, a telephone-based general insurance business. The subsidiary proved a runaway success, becoming the largest motor insurer in the United Kingdom. It soon offered household and life insurance. In 1988 the Royal acquired the Rhode Island-based Citizens, the fifth largest bank in New England, and promptly set upon a course of aggressive expansion in the region: as of 1994 Citizens Financial Group had added eight further acquisitions to its portfolio.

The tremendous success of Direct Line and Citizens led to speculation that the Royal would sell one or both of these subsidiaries, but there had been no indication that the bank had any intention of letting go of either profitable sideline in the early 1990s. In fact the subsidiaries played a fundamental role not only in keeping profits high but in protecting the group from fluctuations: if one sector of the Royal Bank's business were to suffer a reverse, the others could carry the group for a time.

Although the bank describes itself as "conservative," it is by no means fearful of creating and exploiting new opportunities. Its innovative use of technology is second to none in U.K. banking. Indeed, the Royal is, according to a commentator in the *Herald,* "setting a fast pace for the competition to follow these days." In 1994 the bank introduced a 24-hour, seven-days-a-week telephone banking service, Direct Banking. Perhaps the bank's biggest coup, however, is its creation of the

Inter-Bank On-Line System (IBOS), a sophisticated cross-border banking system whereby funds can by transferred nearly instantaneously from the United Kingdom to IBOS member banks in Europe. The project grew out of a 1988 alliance with the Spanish Banco Santander and as of 1994 there were 3,500 IBOS branches in five countries, with many more planned.

With astonishing rapidity the Royal has been diversifying into new financial services, products, and initiatives. In 1994 the bank pioneered its new "finance shops," which offered an extensive realm of mortgage and savings products to customers. The bank has also placed a new emphasis on credit card services, making this an independent operation. Also, the Royal established a specialist group to finance public sector projects in 1994. This innovative scheme has the blessing of the government and could include projects in transport and water management. The bank was also capturing an increasing share of the U.K. mortgage lending market, traditionally the province of the building societies. Indeed, in 1994 there was much speculation—confirmed by the Royal—that the bank intended to buy a U.K. building society when the right opportunity arose.

The bank's successes were supported by its continual attention to its internal structure. In 1992 the Royal launched an ongoing Operation Columbus program, an initiative dedicated to streamlining operations through staff cuts and an increasing and more efficient use of automation. Simultaneously, in a bid to return to an older tradition of more personalized banking, managers throughout the branches have been freed from administrative tasks to allow them time to attend to their base of clients.

Clearly the Royal Bank of Scotland, old and venerable institution though it is, is far from moribund with age, as it enthusias-tically entered a new era of its history. The bank's aim for the future was an ambitious one; according to the company's 1994 interim report: "We are on track to reach our goal of becoming the best performing financial services group in the United Kingdom by 1997." Given the Royal's historical and present record, this might not be an impossible dream.

Principal Subsidiaries: Citizens Financial Group, Inc. (U.S.A.); Direct Line Insurance plc; Royal Bank of Scotland plc; RoyScot Financial Services Ltd.

Further Reading:

"Growth in Mortgage Lending Helps Royal Bank Double to Pounds 201m" *Financial Times,* May 12, 1994.
"RBS Doubles Profits and Weighs Purchase," *Independent,* May 12, 1994.
"Royal Bank Is Set to Expand IBOS System," *Herald,* January 21, 1994.
The Royal Bank of Scotland: A Short History, Edinburgh: Royal Bank of Scotland, 1993.
The Royal Bank of Scotland, 1727–1977, Edinburgh: Royal Bank of Scotland, 1977.
"Royal Bank's Profits More than Double," *Scotsman,* May 12, 1994.
"Royal Takes Over Another US Bank," *Scotsman,* July 6, 1994.
"Royal to Drop Axe on More Managers," *Herald,* March 2, 1994.
"Royal to Fund Public Sector," *Herald,* April 14, 1994.
"UK Company News: Royal Bank Expands in US with Dollars 140m Buy," *Financial Times,* June 14, 1994.
"UK Company News: Where Diversity Helps Balance the Books," *Financial Times,* May 11, 1994.

—Robin DuBlanc

Russ Berrie and Company, Inc.

111 Bauer Drive
Oakland, New Jersey 07436
U.S.A.
(201) 337-9000
Fax: (201) 337-9634

Public Company
Incorporated: 1963
Employees: 2,600
Sales: $444.4 million
SICs: 2771 Greeting Cards; 3942 Dolls & Stuffed Toys;
    2499 Wood Products, Not Elsewhere Classified; 3999
    Manufacturing Industries, Not Elsewhere Classified

Russ Berrie & Company, Inc. sells a wide variety of gift items, including stuffed animals, mugs, picture frames, figurines, greeting cards, and stationery, through retailers located around the world. The company has grown and prospered by appealing to the impulses of shoppers, seeking always to offer fresh merchandise, which reflects current trends and fads. Founded by a New Jersey toy salesman, the company saw its sales escalate dramatically after it went public in the early 1980s and began to acquire other gift makers.

The company that bears Russ Berrie's name was founded in 1963. Berrie himself had always had entrepreneurial leanings. As a child in the East Bronx he worked delivering Sunday newspapers, and selling scorecards at baseball games. After attending the University of Florida, Berrie worked as a salesman and as a manufacturer's representative, and in 1963, he decided to strike out on his own. With $500, he rented a garage in Palisades Park, New Jersey, and launched his own firm, named after himself. Berrie intended to design, market, and distribute "impulse" gift items.

Berrie believed that the market for impulse gift market was ripe for expansion. Impulse gifts, items that shoppers did not seek specifically but noticed while in a store and purchased on a whim, were designed to be affordable and evoke an emotional response in the shopper. The classic impulse gift was an object such as a stuffed animal, a mug, or a cute figurine found in a gift and card store. Demand for these items had been growing in the early 1960s, and Berrie believed that they could be sold in all sorts of retail outlets, not just stationery and gift stores.

Berrie also chose this field because he felt that his experience in the toy industry would serve him well. He knew which products sold well, and, through the contacts he had made, was able to purchase his merchandise directly from manufacturers. In his first year of business, Berrie himself was Russ Berrie and Company's sole employee. He handled all tasks, from selling products, to putting them in packages, to typing up invoices. At the end of the year, he had racked up $60,000 in sales.

In 1964, Berrie created his first line of manufactured novelty items. Working with a designer, he came up with a line of stuffed animals and dubbed them "Fuzzy Wuzzies." In the following year, he supplemented the Fuzzy Wuzzie franchise with the "Bupkis Family," a group of soft, rubbery dolls. On the basis of the popularity of these products, sales for Russ Berrie & Company continued to grow throughout the company's first two years.

In 1966, Berrie formally incorporated his enterprise. Also that year, the company moved locations, trading up to a larger facility in Palisades Park, New Jersey, and adding to its work force. In 1968, as the company shifted quarters again, moving to Elmwood Park, New Jersey, Berrie introduced Sillisculpts, small statues with messages inscribed on them, and these, too, became popular sellers.

Berrie used the capital generated by sales of his first three product lines to finance further expansion of the company. Among his chief goals was the creation of a national sales force to sell his products to retailers. In 1968, the company hired its first full-time salesperson. This step allowed Russ Berrie & Company to promote its own products, rather than rely on manufacturers' representatives, who carried the goods of a several different firms.

In 1971, as sales passed the $7 million mark, Russ Berrie & Company moved again, to a new corporate headquarters facility in Oakland, New Jersey. This location would become the center of the company's worldwide marketing and distribution businesses. In the following year, Russ Berrie & Company opened a second new facility, when a distribution center, in Santa Rosa, California, came on line. This was the first of a planned network of regional centers, each designed to fulfill warehousing, order processing, customer service, credit, and collections functions for accounts in a separate part of the country.

For its first ten years in business, Russ Berrie & Company concentrated on creating and designing its own products, and then contracted with manufacturers in the United States and abroad to produce them. Key to the company's success was the maintenance of a steady flow of ever-changing merchandise. Stores that sold Russ Berrie products needed a constant stream of seasonal, holiday, and everyday items to continually appeal to customers. In order to create these products and ensure that they tapped into current trends, Berrie inaugurated a product development department.

By 1973, however, dealings with manufacturers in Asia had become difficult, and Berrie decided to have his company take over the manufacturing of its products. Over the course of the next two years, the company purchased several manufacturing facilities, adding a stuffed animal factory in California, an injection molding factory in Florida, and another factory in

Haiti. In addition, the company established a plastics factory in New Jersey and acquired a second plant in Florida. By 1977, Russ Berrie & Company had become a diversified producer and marketer of novelty goods, with a large number of different operations being run under the company's umbrella.

Such dramatic expansion in Russ Berrie & Company's activities, however, presented problems, as the company had, according to some critics, lost its focus. Berrie's expertise lay in sales and marketing, and he made sure to offer a wide variety of carefully selected products. As a manufacturer, however, Russ Berrie & Company was forced to abandon careful selection of products to market, in favor of keeping the machines in its factories running. As a result of its rapid expansion into manufacturing, Russ Berrie & Company found itself on the brink of bankruptcy. When Berrie realized that what his company did best was come up with ideas for novelty items, and market and sell them, not actually manufacture them, the company decided to withdraw from the production end of its business. In the mid-1970s, it began to shut down and sell off its factories.

Following this decision, Berrie flew to the Far East and began to put into place structures for the manufacture of Russ Berrie products by others. In 1977, in Korea, the company set up the first of several satellite offices it would eventually open to facilitate production. Employees in this office were responsible for keeping tabs on items being manufactured for Russ Berrie & Company in the Far East. In this way, by hiring its own direct employees, the company hoped to avoid the difficulties of dealing with agents. Two years later, a second office, in Taiwan, was opened. Workers there oversaw the production of Russ Berrie goods in Taiwan and also took part in product development, helping to produce seasonal catalogues.

Also in 1979, Russ Berrie & Company established a subsidiary in the United Kingdom to serve customers there, as well as in the wider European market. The company set up a distribution center in Southhampton, England, which had a sales and support staff mirroring that of the company's American operations. With time, this facility was replaced with a larger one and distribution was expanded to cover Ireland, Holland, and Belgium. Russ Berrie & Company also set up agreements with independent distributors in other countries throughout Europe, guaranteeing that its products would achieve wide penetration of this market.

In the early 1980s, Russ Berrie & Company's sales continued to grow, and the company continued to expand its line of products. In fact, in 1982, the company was listed as one of the 500 fastest growing privately held firms in the United States by *Inc.* magazine. At this time, Russ Berrie & Company's sales force had grown to include 200 people. In a reorganization of company activities, the firm split its operations into two units: Plush & Stuff, which sold stuffed animals, fabric dolls, and other soft items; and Gift/Expression, which was responsible for figurines, picture frames, greeting cards, magnets, mugs, and holiday ornaments and designs. With this new structure, each retail account was serviced by two salespeople, one from each division. In order to make this possible, Russ Berrie & Company hired a large number of new salespeople, doubling the size of its domestic sales force.

By 1983, annual sales of Russ Berrie & Company products had exceeded $100 million. To keep track of the increased volume of products, the company installed a new computer system to oversee inventory and sales. Moreover, the company's MIS department was created for providing accurate data to managers, so that they could make decisions about which merchandise to select or discontinue.

Also in 1983, Russ Berrie & Company opened its Tri Russ International office in Hong Kong. Employees at this location were responsible for overseeing manufacturing in Hong Kong and also for providing sales and product support to all Russ Berrie & Company distributors around the world who did not have their own direct sales representative.

In 1984, Russ Berrie & Company sold stock to the public for the first time, as it was listed on the New York Stock Exchange. In the wake of this move, sales of the company's products started to grow rapidly. As a sign of this growth, Russ Berrie & Company opened two new warehouses to distribute its goods. One, in South Brunswick, New Jersey, serviced the eastern part of the United States. Another, in Petaluma, California, was designed to help move products from the Far East to other locations within the country most efficiently. Together, these two new facilities boasted 700,000 square feet of space, making the company's worldwide total of property owned more than 1.5 million square feet of space.

By 1985, Russ Berrie & Company sales had reached $204.6 million, and revenues more than doubled in just two years. At this time, the company embarked upon a program of rapid growth through acquisitions. In that year, Russ Berrie & Company bought Amram's Distributing Limited, which already functioned as the distributor for the company's products in Canada. Under the umbrella of the parent company, Amram's quickly expanded, until it had more than 60 salespeople peddling Russ Berrie & Company products to over 6,300 retailers.

The following year, the company purchased two more firms in its industry: Freelance, Inc. and the Effanbee Doll Company. In 1987, the company also bought Phil Papel Imports, Inc. The Freelance and Papel operations were amalgamated into one subsidiary, called Papel/Freelance, which was served by more than 100 salespeople. This division of the company distributed seasonal and everyday gifts, and was particularly well known for its beverage mugs. More than 20,00 retailers sold these goods throughout the United States, Canada, and the United Kingdom.

Also in 1987, Russ Berrie & Company entered the retail business for the first time, when it bought Fluf N'Stuf, a chain of 21 gift stores. Fluf N'Stuf outlets were located in regional malls throughout the East Coast of the United States. In this way, Russ Berrie & Company was able not only to sell its own goods, but to get an accurate picture of where demand for gift items was moving.

Also in 1987, Russ Berrie & Company became a licensee of the National Football League, with the right to sell products marked with the insignia of various NFL teams. At the end of the year, the company was given an award for its high sales of NFL products. Later, the company also began to market Major League Baseball merchandise.

As a result of its steady expansion through acquisition, Russ Berrie & Company reported pre-tax profits of $56 million in 1987. This figure was also enhanced by a boom in the demand for stuffed animals. The following year, however, the market for stuffed animals crashed, as the fad passed, and Russ Berrie & Company's profits plummeted to $23 million. Consequently, the price of the company's stock fell as well.

In the late 1980s, the company opened additional manufacturing supervision offices in Indonesia and Thailand, as these areas became locations of production for the company. In addition, Russ Berrie & Company expanded its distribution to areas of the former Soviet Union after the fall of the Berlin Wall in 1989. In time, its products and dolls were even featured in the Moscow airport gift shop.

Russ Berrie & Company continued its expansion through the acquisition in the early 1990s. In 1991, the company bought Bright of America, which produced place mats and stationary products sold primarily through big mass marketers, such as Wal-Mart and Kmart. In the wake of this purchase, Russ Berrie & Company began to utilize this company's manufacturing facility, located in West Virginia, to manufacture greeting cards and other paper products. Bright also ran a school fund-raising operation, in which schools purchased gift items for the students to resell in order to earn money for clubs and trips. During this time, Russ Berrie & Company also bought Weaver Werks, another gift producer, which specialized in popular and trendy items, such as cleverly packaged jelly beans and candy. The products of this subsidiary were added to the company's Papel/ Freelance division.

In 1992, Russ Berrie & Company's fortunes got a lift, when the popularity of one of its oldest products, Trolls, first introduced in the 1960s, escalated dramatically. Although they had not been a big seller for many years, suddenly the company's trolls—squishy dolls with rubbery faces and hair that stood on end—were experiencing wild demand. To meet this clamor, Russ Berry & Company's designers began to churn out hundreds of different troll products, and the company's Far Eastern suppliers raced to keep output high. By the end of the year, pushed by the troll fad, the company's earnings had soared to $300 million.

Flush with this success, Russ Berrie & Company expanded its product line even further in 1993, when it purchased Cap Toys, Inc., a Cleveland distributor of toys and candies. With this move, the company hoped to diversify its activities. Cap Toy products included the Stretch Armstrong and Spin Pops candies, which were supported through heavy advertising and were sold through many large retailers. With the addition of these products, the company's product line grew to more than 8,000. With a strong record of success over the previous three decades and a solid franchise in the gift market, the company seemed assured of continued success as it moved into the late 1990s.

Principal Subsidiaries: Amram's Distributing, Limited (Canada); Bright of America, Inc.; Cap Toys, Inc.; Fluf N' Stuf, Inc.; Papel/Freelance, Inc.; Russ Berrie, Limited (UK); Tri Russ International, Limited (Hong Kong).

Further Reading:

Berrie, Russell, ''Concentrate on Doing What You Do Best,'' *Baylor Business Review,* Fall 1994, pp. 2–5.
Toplis, Maggie, ''Awakenings,'' *Financial World,* July 7, 1992, p. 66.

—Elizabeth Rourke

Russell Stover Candies Inc.

1000 Walnut Street
Kansas City, Missouri 64106
U.S.A.
(816) 842-9240
Fax: (816) 842-5593

Private Company
Incorporated: 1923
Employees: 4,400
Sales: over $300 million
SICs: 2064 Candy & Other Confectionery Products; 2066
Chocolate & Cocoa Products; 5441 Candy, Nut &
Confectionery Stores

Russell Stover Candies Inc. is considered one of the largest manufacturers of boxed chocolates in the United States. It sold its candies primarily through about 40,000 accounts (drug stores, card and gift shops, and mass merchandisers) in the mid-1990s, but also through 50 Russell Stover Candies retail shops and various department stores.

Russell William Stover and his wife Clara started the company that would bear their name in 1923. According to company annals, they began the business in their Colorado bungalow home, experimenting with new recipes and concocting new confections in their kitchen. They soon started selling their candies locally under the name ''Mrs. Stover's Bungalow Candies.'' It was during the start-up of the enterprise that they established the tenets that guided the company throughout the twentieth century: quality, service, and value.

Legend connotes an enthusiastic couple starting a candy company in their kitchen and building it into what would become one of the largest confectioners in the country. But the Stovers were not neophytes to the candy industry. By the time Russell and Clara Stover began experimenting with their own recipes, Russell Stover had spent several years working for other candy manufacturers and had gained a strong grip on the business side of the candy industry.

Russell Stover's ancestors came to the United States from Prussia in 1728. John and Sarah Stover, Russell's parents, settled in Alton, Kansas. Russell Stover was born on May 6, 1888, in a sod house. The Stover family soon moved to an Iowa farm, where Russell Stover was raised and attended Iowa City

Academy. Russell Stover studied chemistry at Iowa State University after high school. After only a year of college, he left to take a job as a sales representative for the American Tobacco Co. In 1911, one year after taking his first job, he married Clara Lewis, a farmer's daughter. The newlyweds settled on a 580-acre farm in Saskatchewan, Canada, that they had received as a wedding gift.

Russell and Clara Stover tried their hand at raising wheat and flax for less than a year. But bad weather and a rotten crop convinced Russell Stover that his future would not be in farming. The couple moved to Winnipeg and Russell Stover accepted a job with a Minnesota candy company. He gained four years of experience with the confectioner before they had a falling out. Russell Stover had received some faulty inventory and wanted the company to replace it with high-quality goods. Headquarters refused. Frustrated, Russell Stover resigned and accepted a position with candy maker A.G. Morris in Chicago, Illinois.

Russell Stover worked with A.G. Morris for one year before getting a better offer from Bunte Candy. He gained three more years of experience at Bunte before switching jobs again. This time, Russell Stover moved back to his native state, Iowa, where the Des Moines-based Irwin Candy Co. was floundering. Russell Stover went to work at Irwin in 1918 and was eventually able to turn the operation around. The Stovers had settled in nearby Omaha, Nebraska, by that time. While Russell Stover worked at Irwin, Clara began experimenting with her own creations at home.

At the same time that Clara was trying to fashion some new confectionery sensations, another inventor, Christian Nelson, was at work in the nearby town of Onawa, Iowa. His creation would soon become famous, and would also lead to the founding of Russell Stover Candies. Nelson was a part-time Latin teacher in Onawa who moonlighted as a soda jerk. One day in 1919 a local schoolboy entered the shop. With only a nickel to spare, the boy agonized over whether he should buy chocolate or ice cream. Nelson was intrigued by the dilemma. His solution?—the ''I-Scream Bar,'' a sandwich with vanilla ice cream filling and a coating comprised of chocolate and cocoa butter.

Nelson introduced his treat at the Onawa Fireman's Tournament. It was well received. Confident that his idea was a winner, Nelson approached several confectioners about the possibility of making and selling his I-Scream Bar. Seven companies rejected the concept as implausible, citing the bar's propensity to melt, lack of long-term consumer interest in such novelty items, and other potential flaws. Finally, Nelson presented his treat to Russell Stover in Omaha on July 31, 1921.

Nelson's proposal piqued Russell Stover's interest. He was also inspired by the 25-year-old entrepreneur's enthusiasm. Russell Stover went into partnership with the aspiring inventor. Russell Stover made several changes to the I-Scream Bar, changing its name to Eskimo Pie and removing the superfluous stick which Nelson had inserted at the base of the bar to hold it. Nelson patented the Eskimo Pie on January 24, 1922. The patent documented the creation as ''an ice cream confection containing normally liquid material frozen to a substantially hard state and encased in a chocolate covering to maintain its original form during handling.''

Nelson and Stover's venture was an instant success. To even Nelson's surprise, people rushed to buy the Eskimo Pie. In Omaha, a quarter of a million pies were sold in a single 24-hour period. As an Eskimo Pie craze swept the nation, the excited partners scrambled to keep up with the demand. Unable to serve the entire market themselves, Russell Stover opened a Chicago office and began licensing other companies to produce the treat. Within a year more than 1,500 manufacturers had been licensed to make and sell Eskimo Pies. In return, they agreed to pay Russell Stover and Nelson four cents for every dozen pies that they sold.

Russell Stover and Nelson initially profited handsomely from their flourishing enterprise. Unfortunately, many other companies began making their own versions of the Eskimo Pie without the originator's permission. As the market became overwhelmed with Eskimo Pie look-alikes, Russell Stover and Nelson struggled to protect their patent. They were soon doling out more than $4,000 daily in legal fees. In 1923, moreover, jealous competitors succeeded in having the patent declared invalid, thus placing Russell Stover and Nelson's operation at a distinct disadvantage to more established manufacturers. Disillusioned by the whole ordeal, the Stovers sold their interest to a lawyer for $30,000 and moved to Denver.

As soon as the Stovers were situated in their Denver bungalow, Clara was again busy in the kitchen working on her candy recipes. Meanwhile, Russell Stover began devising plans to launch the family's own candy business. Despite the fiasco which eventually plagued his Eskimo Pie undertaking, Russell Stover was still eager to run his own company. In 1924, the Stovers began selling boxes of their ''Mrs. Stover's Bungalow Candies.'' The interest of nearby residents had already been kindled by the inebriating bouquets emanating from the Stover kitchen. So, before the Stovers even began selling their candies an eager audience awaited.

Mrs. Stover's Bungalow Candies were an instant local success. Within a few months they had opened two stores and by the end of the year they were selling their candies in seven local shops. In addition, they purchased a specially equipped motorcycle with a sidecar to make deliveries. Early in 1925 they opened their first factory in Denver. To keep pace with mushrooming sales they had to open a second factory later that year, in Kansas City, where the company would eventually be headquartered. Russell Stover named himself president of the corporation and Clara served as vice president. Sales boomed during the remainder of the 1920s.

Despite widespread hardship during the Depression years, Mrs. Stover's Bungalow Candies remained profitable, though growth stalled. Strong demand for the hand-dipped chocolates eventually resumed, however, and the Stovers opened a third factory in 1942 near Omaha in Lincoln, Nebraska. The Stovers shortened their company's name to Russell Stover Candies in 1943. Reflecting his growing stature in the industry, Russell Stover chaired the Washington Committee of the National Confectioners Association during World War II. In 1946, moreover, he

was awarded the confectionery industry's highest honor, the Candy Kettle Award.

Russell Stover's achievements in the confectionery industry went beyond sheer dollar volume sales. Besides introducing the Eskimo Pie, he had also patented dipping tables and a candy manufacturing process he termed the ''Zephyr Freeze.'' Russell Stover continued to run the company until his death at age 66 on May 11, 1954. By the time he died, his Kansas City-based company was selling 11 million pounds of candy annually through 40 Russell Stover shops and in about 2,000 department stores. The Stover family and their partners continued to operate Russell Stover Candies until 1960, when the partnership was terminated and the venture was sold to Louis Ward.

Under Ward's leadership, Russell Stover Candies evolved from a regional to a national supplier of boxed chocolates and candies. The company opened a fourth factory in 1969 in Clarksville, Virginia, which complemented Ward's efforts to expand sales on the East Coast. Throughout the 1970s Russell Stover Candies grew rapidly, carving out a niche in the second-tier boxed chocolates market.

A common distinction between premium chocolates and Russell Stover's products is that the former usually contains no preservatives. As a result, top-tier chocolates usually have a shorter shelf-life and are often much more expensive. Despite its emphasis on the mid-priced market, Russell Stover Candies prided itself on quality and taste. Even through the 1980s and into the 1990s the company continued to cook its candies in small batches, often using the same basic recipes that it had been following since the 1940s.

Russell Stover Candies boosted its sales during the 1970s and 1980s through innovative marketing techniques. For example, the company achieved stellar gains with its heart-shaped chocolate boxes, which were especially popular during the Valentine's Day season. In fact, many customers came to associate Russell Stover Candies with its heart-shaped box. It achieved similar gains with its popular boxes of cherry cordials and its ''Little Ambassadors,'' or miniature chocolates.

By the early 1980s, Russell Stover Candies was generating sales of about $150 million annually and profits of approximately $17 million. It was distributing its candies nationally and had assumed a dominant leadership role in the boxed chocolates market. During the 1980s Russell Stover Candies stepped up its expansion efforts, largely through product line diversification. It initiated a broad line of Easter items, for example, including Easter basket gift packs and its renowned chocolate-covered creme eggs. It also strengthened it presence in drug store and card shop distribution channels.

As Russell Stover Candies boosted sales during the 1980s, it continued to observe the tenets of quality, service, and value originated by the company's founders. Evidencing these maxims was Russell Stover Candies's Clarksville, Virginia factory. The plant was completely renovated in 1986. Many of its old-fashioned hand-dipping lines were replaced with advanced, automated enrobers, which improve consistency and cut production costs. It retained its small batch cooking processes though, despite cost savings that it could have achieved by converting to large-batch manufacturing processes. It also maintained its own truck fleet so that it could ensure timely delivery of raw materials from suppliers, thus reducing the risk of ingredients losing their freshness.

In addition, the plant began roasting its own nuts to improve quality control. "There's much better control," explained plant manager Mike Rowlands in *Candy Industry.* "There's such a fine line between that deep color and a scorch . . . In everything we do there are several reasons why we do it to get a better product." Russell Stover Candies also established a school to continuously educate all employees, from executives to line workers, about the importance of adhering to old, proven procedures. The school was started in 1987 following the retirement of several of its senior candy makers.

Though the Virginia plant was the smallest of Russell Stover Candies's four production facilities, it was set up to operate 24 hours daily. It often processed 20,000 pounds of chocolate, 13,000 pounds of sugar, and 4,000 pounds of milk and cream in a single day. Reflecting the company's treatment of its workers, many of the plant's employees had worked there since it opened in 1969. "You get here and you just stay," related a line worker in *Candy Industry.* "Every day is a challenge." Eight of the plant's supervisors had been with the plant since it had opened.

By the early 1990s, Russell Stover Candies was generating sales of an estimated $250 million. It had since closed some of its original production facilities, and was operating four factories in Tennessee, Colorado, Virginia, South Carolina. A fifth facility was scheduled to open in Abilene, Kansas, in 1995. It also owned several distribution centers scattered around the United States and maintained a fleet of refrigerated delivery trucks.

In 1993 Russell Stover Candies strengthened its position in the boxed chocolates market when an affiliate acquired the Pennsylvania-based Whitman's Candies. The 150-year-old confectioner was generating about $60 million in sales annually in the early 1990s. Critics unsuccessfully contested the merger in court, claiming that the resultant market share would give Russell Stover Candies an unfair advantage. With the addition of Whitman's Chocolates, Russell Stover Candies and affiliates had estimated sales of over $300 million by 1994.

By 1994, Russell Stover Candies was selling its candies in 50 company owned retail outlets, department stores, mass merchandisers, drug stores, and card and gift shops. It employed a work force of 4,400. Consumption of boxed chocolates surged at double-digit rates throughout the early 1990s, sustaining the legacy of growth initiated by Clara and Russell Stover in 1923.

Further Reading:

Candy Man "Russell Stover" Found Sweet Smell of Success in Denver. Kansas City, MO: Russell Stover Candies Inc., 1994.
Moyle, Mike, "Preat Files Antitrust Suit to Block Chocolate Company Merger," *PR Newswire,* April 15, 1993.
Tiffany, Susan, "Russell Stover: A Paragon of Excellence," *Candy Industry,* October 1994, p. 26.
Washington, Barbara A., "Candy Company Molds Chocolate to Client's Needs," *Kansas City Business Journal,* September 17, 1990, sec. 1, p. 8.

—Dave Mote

Salant Corporation

1114 Avenue of the Americas
New York, New York 10036
U.S.A.
(212) 221-7500
Fax: (212) 354-3467

Public Company
Incorporated: 1919 as Salant & Salant, Incorporated
Employees: 4,200
Sales: $419.28 million
Stock Exchanges: New York
SICs: 2321 Men's/Boys' Shirts; 2325 Men's/Boys' Trousers
& Slacks; 2323 Men's/Boys' Neckwear; 2337 Women's/
Misses' Suits & Coats

A leading apparel company in the United States, Salant Corporation designs, manufactures, imports, and markets clothing products under several brand names, including Perry Ellis, Dr. Denton, JJ. Farmer, John Henry, Manhattan, Thomson, Vera, Osh Kosh B'Gosh, and Peanuts. Among its several divisions, Salant's men's and boys' shirt business was ranked second in the apparel industry by *Ward's Business Directory 1995*. Salant's 1993 introduction of its Thomson brand wrinkle-free dress shirt also brought the first branded wrinkle-free dress shirt to market and came at a time when men's clothing was the fastest growing segment of the apparel industry. Apart from its focus on men's wear, the company's other activities include the manufacture and sale of children's wear and women's wear.

Salant Corporation, incorporated in 1987, is the successor business to Salant & Salant, Incorporated, originally a manufacturer of work shirts. Solomon Salant founded the original company as a partnership with his son, Gabriel, and a third partner in 1893. The partner soon left the company, leaving no mark on its history. Gabriel stayed and the company became a father and son operation, incorporated in 1919. Though the company first became public in 1959 when it was listed on the NASDAQ supplemental, in 1971 Salant distributed enough shares through a primary and a secondary offering to be listed on the New York Stock Exchange. The Salant family decided to offer company shares publicly to diversify the family investments and reorganize equity.

In the beginning, the company's major business was selling to wholesalers and large customers like Montgomery Ward, which

maintained a long and substantial account with the company. When the Spanish-American war broke out in 1898, the company also supplied uniforms for the military. Though the army account dried up upon the war's completion, the company maintained its small customer base of wholesalers and large firms well into the twentieth century.

The face of the company changed as it began to diversify in the 1930s. The biggest change occurred in 1938 when the company began to manufacture utility pants made out of twill. The pants were predecessors to the khakis of World War II. Utility pants became one of Salant's principal products by the 1950s.

Though the company's primarily manufactured slacks, jeans, and utility pants between the 1950s and 1970s, it diversified into many other areas, among them sportswear, with sport shirts in 1949, jackets in 1954, and casual slacks in 1955. It started selling children's wear in 1962 and jeans in 1967. Acquisitions in 1964 and 1966 brought coveralls, men's and boys' outerwear, suits and sport jackets, and a higher priced line of men's and boys' slacks to the company's product mix. In 1964, the company also became one of the first to introduce permanent press apparel, which contributed a substantial amount to company sales until the early 1970s.

As clothing styles changed, the company moved away from the production of chambray work shirts and twill pants, favoring the manufacture of popularly-priced jeans and sport and western shirts. This shift in focus by the company's original and largest division allowed it to retain its profitability and position as Salant's mainstay until the demand for jeans slowed and competition, especially from overseas, grew in the mid-1970s.

These market changes adversely affected the Salant & Salant division's profitability beginning in 1976. The business, which Donald Hamilton of Furman Selz noted in *Forbes* was "barely profitable when the jeans business was booming . . . had to cut prices below breakeven" when the jeansmaker Levi Strauss lowered its prices. At the same time, rising interest costs and customer demands strained Salant's ability to provide "mostly low-margin private label goods" to retailers like Sears, Roebuck & Co. and Kmart, according to *Forbes*. Between 1977 and 1980 the division's cumulative losses amounted to $4 a share or about half of Salant's reported earnings during that period. Believing the basic jeans business was no longer a growing market, the company closed the Salant & Salant division in 1981 and began to focus on menswear, specifically its branded apparel in its large and successful Thomson division. By 1993, the company's product mix was 82 percent men's apparel and accessories, eight percent women's apparel and accessories, and ten percent children's apparel and accessories.

As Salant diversified its products it also added to its distribution. In the 1930s and early 1940s, the company might have had 50 customers. In the 1950s, the company continued to sell to national chains and mail-order houses, but gradually wholesalers disappeared by either going out of business or becoming retail chains. As its traditional customer base changed, Salant's management decided to increase volume by selling to smaller retailers and regional chains. By 1972, the company had widened its customer base to about 20,000 accounts, which represented about 37,000 separate stores. At that time, the company sold to most types of retailers, including national chains, mail-order houses, discount stores, regional chains, department stores, smaller independent retailers, and golf pro shops. Wholesalers had become an insignificant part of the company's business.

Though Salant began to broaden its customer base, some of its customers continued to make up significant portions of company sales. Sears, Roebuck & Co. remained one of Salant's largest customers for nearly three decades. Two of Salant's subsidiaries held agreements (one started in 1960 and the other in 1967) with Sears to buy a set amount of its requirements. In 1971 Sears was the company's biggest customer, accounting for 17 percent of sales. By 1980, Sears accounted for 34 percent of net sales, J. C. Penney Co. Inc. for 16 percent, and Kmart for 12 percent of net sales. In 1985, Sears accounted for 31 percent of sales and J. C. Penney for 18 percent. Salant's efforts to diversify its customer base had succeeded to such a point by 1993, however, that the no one customer made up more than six percent of the company's net sales.

Salant's financial difficulties, stemming from the drop in demand for jeans in the mid-1970s, continued into the 1980s. When Salant declared its first bankruptcy in 1985, it reported a net loss of $8.08 million, which compared with a net loss of $21.2 million the previous year. In an effort to return to profitability the company discontinued several of its clothing divisions, including its Salvation sportswear and Thomson women's wear product lines, terminated the operations of its United Pioneer Company outerwear division (which had made ski jackets and parkas part of the company's principal products line for about a decade), closed its retail outlet stores, and closed several production facilities. Also between 1980 and 1985, Salant had reduced the number of its employees from 9,200 to 2,700. Salant emerged from its first bankruptcy in 1987 with its debt almost halved to $48 million.

In 1988, Salant acquired Manhattan Industries, an apparel company with three times Salant's annual volume. To finance the acquisition, the company raised its debt to $270 million. Two years later, the company became bankrupt a second time. The company was not alone, however, and joined about 25 other companies who between 1985 and 1994 had fallen into second bankruptcy. Though some of the other companies eventually liquidated, Salant got its balance sheet in order, reducing its debt to a manageable amount.

Salant had help deleveraging from one of the most successful corporate empire builders of the 1990s, Leon Black, and one of his companies, Apollo Apparel Partners, L.P. In 1991, Leon Black bought a significant number of defaulted Salant bonds. When Salant came out of bankruptcy in September 1993, Apollo Apparel traded its Salant bonds for company stock. The swap allowed Salant to discharge claims of $64.8 million in principal of some bonds due in 1995 and gave Apollo Apparel 43.8 percent ownership of Salant. Salant's financial position in 1994 led *Financial World* to use it as an example of a "potential winner," noting that Salant had more than halved its debt.

As Salant emerged from its second bankruptcy, it concentrated on its largest business, menswear. Salant's purchase of Manhattan Industries, which lead in part to its second bankruptcy filing,

turned into one of the company's smartest decisions. Manhattan Industries brought a large international sourcing business to Salant and, more importantly, a license agreement with Perry Ellis. The Perry Ellis business "was so strong it continued to thrive despite Salant Corp.'s 1990 bankruptcy filing," according to *Crain's New York Business.* The *Daily News Record* reported that in 1993 the Perry Ellis name was "three times as strong" as when Salant assumed control in 1988. By 1994, it accounted for 26 percent of Salant's net sales, compared with Salant's Manhattan trademark, which accounted for 12 percent, the John Henry trademark (nine percent, and the Thomson trademark (eight percent of net sales). No other of Salant's more than a dozen trademarks made up more than five percent of Salant's 1994 sales.

Salant's acquisition of Manhattan significantly increased its international business. Before the 1970s, Salant owned a Canadian subsidiary that designed, manufactured, and sold slacks, jeans, utility pants, and shirts in Canada, and in 1972, Salant built its first of several production facilities in Mexico. But by the 1990s, over half of the company's products were produced abroad. Though the company continued to operate its Mexican plants and a Canadian subsidiary (the first was sold and another purchased in the meantime), much of the company's imported products and materials came from Manhattan's extensive international sourcing business. In 1994, Salant's facilities accounted for 84 percent of its domestic-made products and 28 percent of its foreign-made products.

As it did after its first bankruptcy, Salant sought to improve its competitive strength by buying a better product mix. The second time, however, Salant kept a keener eye on its balance sheet. With its limited resources, Salant acquired Canadian-based JJ. Farmer Clothing Inc. in June of 1994. The acquisition was notable, however, because it left Salant's financial position almost unchanged. Salant retained its financial flexibility by making the acquisition on an earnout basis, which links the purchase price of JJ. Farmer to its performance over a certain (as yet unspecified) period of time. JJ. Farmer quickly helped boost Salant's sales, accounting for approximately one-third of Salant's $13.6 million net sales increase in the third quarter of 1994.

In addition to its acquisition, Salant added to its dress shirt business through a license agreement with Crystal Brands, Inc. in 1994. Salant agreed to produce dress shirts and furnishings under the Salty Dog and Gant trademarks. Salant president Nicholas P. DiPaolo noted the strong consumer following enjoyed by the Gant brand and remarked, "with our marketing and manufacturing expertise we will be able to build on an already solid base. The addition of the Gant and Salty Dog brands to our existing well-known labels insures our continued growth and leadership role in the dress shirt and furnishings categories."

Salant's focus on menswear in the 1990s was on track with trends in the apparel industry. Men's clothing, which accounted for 36 percent of all apparel sales, outperformed all other apparel categories in 1992, according to *Standard & Poor's Industry Surveys.* The sale of men's sportswear benefitted from wrinkle-resistant textiles, which followed a "trend toward more casual attire in the office." Though Salant's start-up costs for entering the wrinkle-resistant shirt business lowered operating earnings in 1994, the company was "encouraged by sales of Perry Ellis sportswear and wrinkle resistant dress shirts and slacks," according to the *Daily News Record.*

Salant's corporate operations have remained centered in its New York headquarters. But by the 1990s the company's production had become dispersed, mainly throughout the South. In 1994, Salant owned six U.S. manufacturing facilities located in Alabama, Georgia, New York, Tennessee, and Texas, three manufacturing facilities in Mexico, and five distribution centers located in Georgia, New York, South Carolina, and Texas. The company also leased space for 57 factory outlet stores and one retail store.

Salant looked toward a solid future in 1994. Despite a declining dress shirt market, Salant had increased its sales and market share in that category "to benefit from any improvement in market conditions," according to the company. The company's Manhattan label had become the Wal-Mart chains best-selling brand of dress shirt while both the Perry Ellis and John Henry brands enjoyed increased sales in department and specialty stores. As Salant took steps to maintain the strength of its position in men's dress wear, it planned to expand into the fastest growing area of menswear, casual apparel. Supported by its profitable Children's Apparel Group, which makes sleepwear under brands including Dr. Denton, Barney, Disney characters, and Osh Kosh B'Gosh, and sales of it women's wear brands, including Vera and Made in the Shade, Salant's menswear business seemed capable of maintaining its solid and prosperous position in the 1990s market.

Further Reading:

Furman, Phyllis, "Without Its Founder, Perry Ellis Thrives," *Crain's New York Business,* October 26, 1992, p. 3.
Hart, Elena, "Perry Ellis Men's Stronger Than Ever," *Daily News Record,* February 19, 1993, p. 5.
Light, Larry, "Trouble Outfits that Turn into Two-Time Losers," *Business Week,* April 26, 1993, pp. 81–82.
"Salant Acquires JJ. Farmer, Canadian Sportswear Maker," *Daily News Record,* June 16, 1994.
"Salant Operating Earnings Plummet 62% in Second Period," *Daily News Record,* August 9, 1994, p. 7.
Schifrin, Matthew, and Riva Atlas, "Hocus-Pocus," *Forbes,* March 14, 1994, pp. 81–83.
Taub, Stephen, "Market Watch: Double-Dippers, Bankruptcy Style," *Financial World,* March 29, 1994, p. 14.

—Sara Pendergast

Sauder Woodworking Co.

502 Middle St.
Archbold, Ohio 43502
U.S.A.
(419) 446-2711
Fax: (419) 446-2980

Private Company
Incorporated: 1940
Employees: 3,200
Sales: $415 million
SICs: 2426 Hardwood Dimension & Flooring; 2511 Wood
    Household Furniture

Sauder Woodworking Co. is the tenth largest furniture manufacturer in the United States and the largest producer of ready-
to-assemble (RTA) furniture. Sauder Woodworking expanded
rapidly during the 1980s and early 1990s by focusing on its
RTA lines, which are sold primarily through Sears, K-Mart, and
other discount retailers. Still 60 percent family owned, the company generated sales of about $415 million in 1994 and em-
ployed more than 3,000 workers.

Sauder Woodworking is the progeny of Erie Sauder, a devout
Mennonite cabinetmaker. Erie Sauder had worked at Archbold
Ladder Co. in Archbold, Ohio, before he decided to start working for himself in 1934. He initially found work making kitchen
cabinets around Archbold. One of his first large orders came
from a local hatchery that needed sticks to insert between
incubator cages. Erie Sauder and his wife Leona worked together in a small, weather-beaten barn; she sawed the boards
while he finished the sticks. Although they earned only $5 per
week, it was enough to feed their family.

A few years after he started his business a nearby church burned
down. Erie Sauder won the job of building new pews, thus
expanding his business into church furniture; Sauder Woodworking eventually become a leading manufacturer of church
furniture in the United States. Erie Sauder kept his workers busy
during down times by making custom cabinets and taking on
other miscellaneous work. For example, he began making
small, inexpensive tables from the precious oak, maple, and
walnut scraps left on his shop floor at the end of the day, low-
priced "leftovers" as he called them.

One day in 1940 a traveling salesman stopped by Sauder's shop.
They were intrigued by his low-priced tables and asked Erie

Sauder if they could take some samples to a furniture show in
Chicago. They later returned with an order for 25,000 tables.
Erie Sauder was stunned by the request and doubted the ability
of his modest shop to produce so many pieces. But he was able
to secure a loan from a nearby bank that he used to incorporate
his business, expand his production facilities, and hire more
workers. With the help of friends and relatives, as well as "a lot
of luck," according to Erie Sauder, he was able to fill the order.
"It's amazing what you can do when you don't know it can't
be done," became Erie Sauder's motto.

Erie Sauder continued to make his custom cabinets, church
pews, and tables throughout the 1940s and 1950s. Sauder
Woodworking, like many other manufacturers of the time, benefitted from the post-World War II economic expansion that
began in the late 1940s. Of import to Sauder Woodworking's
success was a request from a furniture retailer in Detroit in
1951. A buyer from the Federal Department Store determined
that if he could devise a way to make furniture lay flat in a box,
he could significantly reduce shipping and inventory storage
costs. He envisioned a sort of snap-together table that customers
could set up at home. Erie Sauder designed such a table, and
with it the ready-to-assemble industry. The inexpensive tables
sold rapidly and strengthened Sauder Woodworking's business.

Erie Sauder retired in 1974, when the company's sales had
reached $12 million annually. With only an eighth grade educa-
tion, Sauder had built his company from a simple shop in a
weatherbeaten barn to a multi-million-dollar furniture manufacturer. Erie Sauder's sons, Maynard and Myrl, took over the company's management. At age 42, Maynard Sauder assumed the
chief executive slot when his father stepped aside, and his younger
brother, Myrl, was placed in charge of engineering, research, and
development. The combination of Myrl Sauder's engineering
expertise and Maynard Sauder's business savvy would prove to be
a powerful combination during the next two decades.

The majority of Sauder Woodworking's sales in 1974 came
from the sale of church furniture and ready-to-assemble pieces.
Most of the company's furniture sold through a distributor, who
branded the product Foremost Furniture. Although Sauder
Woodworking was generally pleased with the distributor's efforts, Sauder Woodworking decided to take on its own sales and
marketing efforts in 1974, and continued to sell its products
under the Foremost name until it had completely phased in the
Sauder Woodworking brand name by the mid-1980s.

Sauder Woodworking emphasized technology during the late
1970s and 1980s as it shifted the focus of its operations to the
growing market for ready-to-assemble (RTA) furniture. RTA
furniture is usually comprised of panels made of particle board
(boards fashioned from glue and wood chips or tiny wood
particles). The boards are usually laminated to simulate either a
real wood finish, or covered with some other colored protective
coating that improves the panel's appearance. The boards are
typically pre-drilled and routed to accept accompanying screws,
fasteners, and other hardware. The customer assembles the
furniture at home, usually needing only a screwdriver and/or
hammer to finish the job. Maynard Sauder sought to make
Sauder Woodworking's production facilities state-of-the-art,
thus improving both quality and productivity. Sauder Woodworking engineers introduced advanced chemical etching techniques, for example, which allowed them to carve ridges into

simulated wood grain. They also incorporated new cutting methods to create curved molding and bracket feet from particle-board. Importantly, Sauder Woodworking worked to improve assembly instructions and provided consumers with a toll-free number that they could call to get help. As a result, returns to merchants were reduced and the retailer's perceived value of the product increased.

At the same time Sauder Woodworking improved its operations during the 1970s and 1980s, demand for RTA furniture increased. Consumers began to realize the value of RTA furniture; they could purchase an RTA table, desk, dresser, or other furnishing for 25 percent to 50 percent less than they might have to pay for conventional furniture. In addition, because it was easy to ship and store, RTA goods became extremely popular with discount retailers and mass merchandisers. Those distribution channels far outpaced expansion of conventional furniture sales channels throughout the 1980s and early 1990s.

Largely because of the efforts of Sauder Woodworking and its competitors, the public perception of RTA improved significantly during the 1980s and early 1990s. New high-tech laminating processes were developed that made particle board panels nearly indistinguishable from natural wood. Etched paper laminates, for example, closely mimicked both the look and feel of real wood. Improved epoxies eliminated moisture problems and new joints and connections increased the rigidity of RTA pieces. As RTA furniture improved, consumers began using it for everything from kitchen tables and office furniture to living room shelves and stereo cabinets. In fact, Sauder Woodworking sold RTA pieces that were priced as high as $400.

Sauder Woodworking's technological edge made it the United States's largest RTA manufacturer. Myrl Sauder had invented or adapted from other industries a variety of highly efficient machinery that made Sauder Woodworking more efficient than most of its competitors and far more cost effective than traditional furniture makers. For example, hardwood furniture makers often lost about 50 percent of the raw material during the production process. In contrast, Sauder Woodworking used high-tech saw lines to cut parts precisely with minimal waste. Scraps were collected for reuse, and even the sawdust was sold as composting material.

To manufacture its RTA furniture, Sauder Woodworking would take raw particle board and fiber board sheets, laminate both sides with veneer-like paper, and then cut the panels and parts to suit the product being made. The company typically produced different products in lots of 6,000 to 10,000 and stored them until time for packaging. By the early 1990s, Sauder Woodworking was processing 50 truckloads of particle board daily in its Ohio factories. It boasted more than 70 acres of production and warehouse facilities and a work force of 2,500, about 1,850 of which were engaged in building RTA furniture.

Indeed, because of Sauder Woodworking's strong growth during the 1980s, the shift changes had become the major event in Archbold, a town with a population of 3,500. Sauder Woodworking's production facilities had expanded to employ the large majority of the local residents, and most of those that were not employed at Sauder Woodworking were directly dependent on its workers. The work force, which was all non-union, operated in three shifts, 24 hours per day, up to six days per week.

During the late 1980s and early 1990s, the U.S. economy dipped into a recession, stifling revenue growth and profits for much of the furniture industry. In contrast, Sauder Woodworking continued to post solid sales gains in excess of 15 percent annually throughout the early 1990s. Sales topped $300 million in 1992 and reached the $415 million mark by 1994. By that time, the company was employing more than 3,000 workers. To keep pace with demand, Sauder Woodworking had invested tens of millions of dollars in production facilities during the early 1990s, including work on a planned facility that would use the wood scraps it generated for its own energy.

Despite the capital required by rampant growth, Sauder Woodworking remained a family owned and operated company during the 1980s and into the 1990s. During this time, Maynard and Myrl Sauder were gradually passing control of the operation to a new generation of Sauders.

Although family members were welcome into the business, they were expected to meet certain standards. "We've got three rules for family members who want to work here," Maynard Sauder told Forbes. "A good education, success working someplace where the family name means nothing, and interest in a real opening at the company." Maynard Sauder's son, Kevin, became vice-president of marketing and sales in the early 1990s. He had worked at Northern Telecom after receiving his M.B.A. from Duke University. Similarly, Maynard Sauder's son-in-law, Garrett Tinsman, was hired to oversee Sauder Woodworking's new production facility scheduled to open in 1994.

At 89 years of age, Erie Sauder continued to return to Archbold every spring from his winter home in Florida. He oversaw Sauder Woodworking's nonprofit Sauder Farm and Craft Village, where visitors could watch craftspeople at work and attend fiddle contests and quilt fairs. "It draws 120,000 people to Archbold a year and still loses money," Maynard Sauder noted in Forbes.

Going into the mid-1990s, Sauder Woodworking benefitted from continued domestic growth in the demand for RTA. Although church furniture represented an increasingly small percentage of Sauder Woodworking's sales, the company remained a leading manufacturer of church pews. Sauder Woodworking also enjoyed solid success overseas. After only a few years in the export business, by 1994 Sauder Woodworking was exporting $40 million worth of product to more than 60 countries worldwide. In 1993, Sauder Woodworking was named the Ohio Exporter of the Year. The company launched a national RTA advertising campaign in 1994, with a goal of doubling company sales by the turn of the century.

Further Reading:

Amatos, Christopher A., "Sawdust Not Gathering at Sauder," *Columbus Dispatch,* September 13, 1992, Bus. Sec.

A History of Sauder Woodworking Co. Archbold, Ohio: Sauder Woodworking Co., 1994.

Waldon, George, "More Home Work: Office Product Sales Are Booming as Workers Stay Home for a Living," *Arkansas Business,* June 8, 1992, p. 14.

Weinberg, Neil, "Old-Fashioned Ways Still Work," *Forbes,* March 14, 1994.

—Dave Mote

Scott Fetzer Company

28800 Clemens Road
Westlake, Ohio 44145
U.S.A.
(216) 892-3000
Fax: (216) 892-3060

Wholly Owned Subsidiary of Berkshire Hathaway Inc.
Incorporated: 1914
Employees: 14,000
Sales: $905 million
SICs: 3635 Household Vacuum Cleaners; 3421 Cutlery

The best-known of Scott Fetzer Company's businesses in the mid-1990s included World Book encyclopedias and Kirby vacuum cleaners. Vacuum cleaners were the company's mainstay until it went on an acquisition spree in the 1960s and emerged with 31 businesses. A new CEO later trimmed Scott Fetzer back to concentrate on its core products. Conglomerate Berkshire Hathaway acquired the company in 1986, and its earnings have been steady since then.

Founded in 1914, Scott Fetzer manufactured flare pistols through World War I. During the 1920s, it entered the vacuum cleaner business. This product was the company's staple for the next 40 years. It began diversifying between 1964 and 1973, broadening its manufacturing range to include chain saws and trailer hitches.

Ralph E. Schey became president in 1974. Schey was a noted venture capitalist who quickly applied himself to trimming and restructuring the company. By 1976, Schey also held the posts of chairman and chief executive officer of Scott Fetzer. Within four years, Schey reduced Scott Fetzer from 31 to 20 divisions. He concentrated the remaining divisions in brand name goods for consumer markets, based upon his belief that such goods were more recession-proof. In addition, the company's senior managers at that time were primarily marketers rather than manufacturers, and this goal suited their strengths.

Scott Fetzer Company's new direction was the home improvement market. Schey's first large acquisition was Wayne Home Equipment, a maker of oil and gas burners and pumps. As a subsidiary of Scott Fetzer, Wayne went from supplying manufacturers to becoming a retail competitor, issuing branded products into mass merchandise stores. By the mid-1980s, Wayne

was forming a new operating group—known as Environmental Products & Services—to sell a broad line of air- and water-treatment products, as well as heating, cooling, and home-security products.

While these changes were taking place, Schey was also working on expanding the direct sales arm of Scott Fetzer. The retail arena was experiencing fluctuations at the time due to rising overhead costs, which led to clerk cutbacks, and an increase in double-income households, which gave consumers less time to shop. Direct selling, also known as door-to-door, avoided both of these obstacles. For $50 million, Schey purchased World Book from Field Enterprises in 1978. At the time, World Book was the market leader in direct sales. The company came with a profitable mail-order business in books and various consumer goods. Encyclopedia buyers proved to be ideal mail-order customers: they had already been found credit worthy—as most encyclopedias were purchased on credit—and were willing to receive products through the mail. World Book's only ostensible competitor was Encyclopaedia Britannica.

After the purchase, Schey spent two years revising World Book by selling off the Japanese division and trimming domestic operations in much the same way as he had tightened Scott Fetzer. Preschool and elementary school lines were expanded so that customers could start buying sooner and then trade up into other sets of encyclopedias as their children grew older. By 1984, World Book had more than 30,000 sales representatives. Scott Fetzer's other prime product, Kirby vacuum cleaners, was also sold door-to-door by dealers who bought the machines for cash. As these sales representatives worked strictly on commission, Scott Fetzer's profit margins grew plump enough to attract attention.

As the sales force of World Book was reorganized in 1981, Scott Fetzer also revised its traditional selling strategies. Instead of attaching salaries only to sales, sales managers were given greater responsibility for expenses and profits. Recruiting, training, motivational, and compensation strategies were all updated, and the sales force was increased by 50 percent in 1984. Around the same time, other direct-selling giants, like Avon and Mary Kay, were unable to get the number of sales representatives they needed. Direct selling was honed to a science by Scott Fetzer during the early 1980s. Sales people no longer wandered through neighborhoods, knocking on doors and applying charm like a vise to the random housewife. Sales representatives now contacted potential buyers first by phone, at fairs, or in shopping malls, and set up appointments. From there, the sales challenges were the same, but Kirby sales representatives in the 1980s boasted one sale out of every three pitches—a good record for a purchase that then ran up to $900, with accessories.

Just as World Book had undergone reconstruction, Kirby too was overhauled between 1977 and 1981. A dramatic change came in 1980, when Kirby eliminated half of its distributors. For the most part, these distributors were independent contractors who recruited their own sales staffs. At the time, a practice called bojacking was in vogue. Bojacking by distributors referred to the practice of buying vacuums from Kirby and jacking up the price, then reselling them with a price tag that undercut Kirby salesmen. This prompted Scott Fetzer to write a new dealer agreement that mandated that Kirby vacuum cleaners be sold in the home. The roughly 700 distributors who disagreed with this new policy were eventually dismissed. Between 1971 and 1981, unit sales plunged by one-third. The company, instead of panicking, concentrated on training its key salespeople to run their own dealerships. This strategy inspired other direct sellers to turn their attention to training as a way to increase productivity.

It also culled compliments from competitors. And it worked. Direct sales traditionally pepped up when the economy dragged, with revenues reflecting the number of available representatives rather than market size. A slowed economy meant cutbacks, which translated to more people looking for work such as direct selling. The sales force thinned as the company recovered. This was not the case, though, during the down-cycle of the late 1970s and early 1980s. Those who usually entered direct sales to help meet family bills went looking for part-time company work instead. The sales force dipped during this time, and when the recovery arrived, there were even fewer candidates. Avon and Mary Kay Cosmetics were especially bruised by this trend; in fact, Avon had to give up on its goal for an increased sales force. Scott Fetzer had already streamlined its sales force and unleashed the highly trained group on consumers. It was so successful that by the mid-1980s, World Book and Kirby vacuum cleaners accounted for more than half the company's sales and operating profits, while direct sales titans like Avon and Mary Kay were wobbling.

Up to this point, Scott Fetzer was prospering quite quietly. In the four quarters leading up to December 1984, sales had risen 17 percent and earnings were up 45 percent. In the takeover craze of the 1980s, Scott Fetzer could not go unnoticed. Financier Ivan Boesky began accumulating shares of the company before the spring of 1984, when Schey announced a plan by a group he led to take the company private in a leveraged buyout. Kelso & Company, a New York investment firm, entered the fray with a $61-a-share bid. Kelso's specialty was corporate buyouts through employee stock ownership plans (ESOP). An ESOP would have taken over up to 60 percent of the company within five years, had Kelso's deal gone through. The bid was raised to $62 a share in January 1985, but ultimately the sale was made to Berkshire Hathaway for roughly $320 million in early 1986.

Berkshire was an Omaha-based holding company managed by CEO and part-owner Warren E. Buffett. Buffett became something of a hero in investor circles, with a good record of finding companies whose stock prices did not reflect their intrinsic worth. Using this for a guide, Berkshire acquired interests as diverse as insurance, publishing, candy, and furniture. At the time of the sale, Scott Fetzer was considered well-managed and a good earner, two of Buffett's favorite green lights for a purchase. Berkshire Hathaway specifically sought companies with consistent earnings that it would not have to micromanage, in industries that were not so technical that board members could not comprehend the business.

Scott Fetzer, with 17 businesses at the time, had sales of about $700 million. In addition to World Book, which then accounted for about 40 percent of Scott Fetzer's sales, other businesses included Kirby, Campbell Hausfeld air compressors, and Wayne burners and water pumps. World Book was then selling more sets of encyclopedias in the United States than its four largest competitors combined. After the ESOP plan was scuttled, Buffett wrote to Ralph Schey saying he admired the company's record. Just a week after their first dinner together, the acquisition contract had been signed.

In 1986, World Book's unit volume increased for the fourth consecutive year. Encyclopedia sales were up 45 percent over 1982. The Childcraft unit sales were also growing significantly. Success was in part attributed to good prices and editing and a sales force that was strongly identified as educators. More than half of the active sales force in the mid-1980s were teachers and another 5 percent were librarians. Kirby sales were also strong, with unit sales worldwide growing 33 percent between 1982 and 1986. In Kirby's case, the product was more expensive than most competing cleaners, but it was known for its longevity. Some homes boasted 35-year-old Kirbys still on duty. Campbell Hausfeld, Scott Fetzer's largest unit, was the nation's leading producer of small and medium-sized air compressors. Its earnings more than doubled in 1986.

Pre-tax earnings for Scott Fetzer rose 10 percent in 1987. At the close of that year, World Book introduced its most extensively revised edition since 1962. The number of color photos had nearly doubled, more than 6,000 articles were revised, and these changed helped unit sales to increase for the fifth year in a row. The company's export business was particularly strong in 1988, when World Book became available in the Soviet Union. World Book had begun a costly decentralization into four locations in anticipation of having to leave its Chicago Merchandise Mart location. At the same time, Kirby's overseas sales more than doubled in two years.

If Scott Fetzer had been an independent company, it would have ranked close to the top of the Fortune 500 in 1990 in terms of return on equity. Despite costs of moving and a small decrease in unit volume, World Book earnings improved. A new Kirby vacuum cleaner was introduced and did very well. However, earnings overall for Kirby did not grow as quickly as sales because of start-up and learning curve costs for the new product. Northland, a division of Scott Fetzer based in Watertown, New York, also kept the company tradition of quiet excellence. It won a design award in 1990 for a redesigned bypass cover that cut production costs by up to $8,000 annually, while producing a more consistent product. International business remained strong, with another 20 percent sales gain in 1990. Campbell Hausfeld had record sales of $109 million that same year, most of which came from products introduced within the past five years.

In 1991, pre-tax earnings declined for World Book and the rest of Scott Fetzer, except Kirby. The following year, Kirby remained steady while World Book and the rest of Scott Fetzer's units increased again. All units again increased earnings in 1993. From the time of its purchase by Berkshire Hathaway in 1986, Scott Fetzer had consistently increased its earnings while reducing its investment in both inventory and fixed assets— using minor amounts of borrowed money outside of its finance subsidiary. It seemed healthy indeed, and Berkshire's continued parenting was proof.

Principal Subsidiaries: Adalet; Campbell Hausfeld; Carefree; Cleveland Wood Products; Douglas Products; ECM; France; Halex; Kirby; Meriam Instrument; Northland; Powerwinch; Quikut; ScottCare; Scot Labs; Stahl; United Consumer Financial Services; Wayne Home Equipment; Western Enterprises; Western Plastics; World Book Group.

Further Reading:

"Mastering the Process," *Chief Executive,* May 1991, p. 46.

"Personality Clashes," *Development Journal,* September 1989, p. 17.

"A Sale for Scott Fetzer," *Fortune,* January 7, 1985, p. 11.

Saporito, Bill, "A Door-to-Door Bell Ringer," *Fortune,* December 10, 1984, pp. 83–88.

"Scott Fetzer Inc.," *Insiders' Chronicle,* September 30, 1985, p. 2.

"Vacuum-Cleaner Motor Now 84 Percent Quieter," *Appliance Manufacturer,* December 1990, p. 35.

—Carol I. Keeley

Sealy Inc.

1228 Euclid Avenue
Cleveland, Ohio 44115
U.S.A.
(216) 522-1310
Fax: (216) 522-1366

*Wholly Owned Subsidiary of Zell/Chilmark Fund Limited
    Partnership*
Incorporated: 1912 as Ohio Mattress Co.
Employees: 4,500
Sales: $623.9 million (est.)
SICs: 2515 Mattresses & Bedsprings; 6719 Holding
    Companies Nec

Sealy Inc. evolved from a loose amalgamation of licensees into
the world's largest mattress manufacturer during the mid-twentieth century. In 1993 Sealy commanded nearly 23 percent of
the bedding market, almost as much as its next two competitors
combined. Of Sealy's three main rivals in the $2.3 billion
industry, Serta and Spring Air are licensee groups and Simmons
is a national manufacturer.

Sealy was established as a licensing organization in Chicago in
1882. The company's licensees owned all the Sealy Inc. stock,
and leaders of the individual affiliates comprised Sealy's board
of directors. Sealy's decentralized organizational structure
evolved from the nature of mattress production and distribution,
with the size and weight of mattresses inhibiting both shipping
and storage. Sealy licensees agreed to limit themselves to exclusive territories of 200 miles in radius, which were contractually
protected from competition with other dealers. (The territories
were later expanded to 300 miles as transportation methods
improved.) Sealy affiliates gave the Chicago company royalties
in exchange for national and cooperative brand advertising,
access to research and development undertaken by the central
organization, and quality control guidelines. The decentralized
organizational structure used by Sealy in the 1880s was still in
use by the majority of mattress companies in the United States
in the late twentieth century.

In 1907 Morris Wuliger, a Hungarian immigrant, established
Ohio Mattress Co. in an abandoned church. The company
bought its first Sealy license in 1924, when Frank Wuliger, son
of the founder, inherited the presidency of Ohio Mattress. The
Sealy name gave the Ohio company permission to use what had

become the most recognized name in the industry. In 1939
Frank called his son, Ernest, home from his second year of
classes at the University of Chicago to help run the family
business. Ernie Wuliger—who once told an interviewer that he
was "born to sell mattresses"—was soon recognized as an
authority in the bedding industry. By the time he was 35, he was
serving as chairman of Sealy's national advertising committee.

From 1951 to 1955, the annual sales of Ohio Mattress quadrupled from $1.5 million to over $6 million, and by 1956, the
company was the largest of Sealy affiliates in the United States
and Canada, which numbered more than 30. In 1956 Ohio
Mattress acquired the Sealy Mattress Co. of Houston, Texas,
signaling the start of Wuliger's push to dominate the Sealy
organization and the mattress industry.

Ernest Wuliger succeeded his father as president of Ohio Mattress in 1963, and dedicated his $7-million-a-year company to
several ambitious goals: surpassing $100 million in annual
sales, national expansion, and a listing on the New York Stock
Exchange. The declaration launched a quarter-century battle
that stretched from the Sealy territories to the United States
Supreme Court.

In defiance of the exclusive territory clauses, the maverick
licensee launched intra-brand competition within other Sealy
licensees' territories, undercutting their prices and squeezing
their profit margins until they sold out to him. Very often,
however, the threatened licensees appealed to Sealy to invoke
and exercise a "right to first refusal." The clause allowed Sealy
to acquire several endangered affiliates, thereby blocking
Wuliger and gaining additional revenues. In 1960 the Justice
Department had charged Sealy Inc. with two antitrust violations
related to price fixing and the exclusive territories. Seven years
of appeals brought the case before the Supreme Court in 1967,
when justices ultimately found Sealy in violation of the Sherman Antitrust Act. Rather than changing their illegal business
practices, Sealy simply renamed the offending clauses, retaining their content and requirements.

In 1970 Ohio Mattress became the only publicly held mattress
manufacturer in the United States. Its initial public offering
raised money for further expansion, and Wuliger changed the
growing company's name to Ohio-Sealy Mattress Mfg. Co. One
year later, Ohio-Sealy brought its first lawsuit against the licenser, charging that it had not stopped its anti-competitive
practices. The case came to court in 1974, and within four
months, a jury ruled in favor of Ohio-Sealy and awarded it triple
damages of $20.4 million. Appeals and a 1975 settlement with
Sealy Inc. earned Ohio-Sealy $13 million, but its battle had
just begun.

Wuliger tenaciously fought Sealy for over a decade, winning a
final judgment of $77 million in 1986. He forgave the damages
in exchange for the right to acquire eight remaining licenses,
and thereby gain full control of Sealy Inc. One holdout, Sealy
Mattress Co. of New Jersey, filed suit to block Ohio Mattress,
but gave in before the end of 1987. Wuliger borrowed $250
million to finance his purchases, then pared that debt down to
about $75 million with the proceeds of an offering of four
million new shares.

In the meantime, Wuliger had also shored up Ohio-Sealy's position in the larger bedding industry with the 1983 purchases of Monterey Mfg. Co., a leading waterbed manufacturer based in Los Angeles, and Lifetime Foam Products, a bedding manufacturer previously owned by Sears, Roebuck & Co. Ohio-Sealy also acquired a furniture and waterbed frame manufacturer, TrendWest furniture.

In December 1983 Wuliger also acquired Stearns & Foster, a prominent mattress brand, helping him to achieve two of his coveted goals. The Cincinnati-based firm cost Ohio-Sealy $52 million in cash and stock, but gave Wuliger complete control of a prestigious national brand and helped catapult his company (which subsequently reassumed its traditional Ohio Mattress Co. name) over the $100 million mark. Sales more than doubled, from $98 million in 1983 to $251 million in 1984, earning Ohio Mattress a spot on the New York Stock Exchange. Wuliger set out immediately to energize the 136-year-old Stearns & Foster brand, launching the label's first national advertising campaign since 1909. The $4 million budget was largely spent on ads in such high-end shelter magazines as *Bon Appetit, Metropolitan Home, Gourmet, Town & Country, Architectural Digest, House Beautiful,* and others. The brand's slogan, ''You've earned a Stearns & Foster,'' was targeted toward the prosperous consumer.

In 1989, less than two years after gaining control of the world's largest mattress brand, 67-year-old Ernest Wuliger suffered a heart attack and subsequently announced his intention to sell Ohio Mattress. Some observers maintained that ''the vision of his own mortality caused the decision,'' but according to Barbara Solomon of *Management Review,* Wuliger said he was motivated by the realization that ''people would pay exorbitant amounts for companies with consumer franchises.'' Indeed, although Ohio Mattress was valued at $427 million late in 1988, merchant banker Gibbons Green van Amerongen paid more than twice that amount, $965 million, to take the company private in 1989.

The new owners kept Wuliger on as chair and CEO, and appointed Malcolm Candlish as chief operating officer and president. But Wuliger—along with many of his top managers—resigned less than three months after the deal was completed, ''angrily proclaiming he was being ignored,'' as *Plain Dealer* analyst Marcus Gleisser reported in 1993. Wuliger's abrupt exit—as well as the company's 1990 assumption of the Sealy Corp. name—signaled the firm's shift from an entrepreneurial operation to a modern, consolidated corporation. Nonetheless, Candlish vowed in a 1990 interview with Barbara Solomon for *Management Review* ''to retain as much as we can of what is good about being an organization of licensees, and we will complement it with all the advantages of being a national company.''

Unfortunately, Gibbons Green van Amerongen's highly leveraged (and overpriced) buyout was also rather poorly timed. The firm tried to float $475 million in unsecured debentures, or junk bonds, just as that market collapsed under the weight of numerous defaults and bankruptcies. While the new owners scrambled to finance their purchase, they relied on a high-interest ''bridge loan'' from First Boston Corp. to pay for the privatization. This sticky financial situation earned Sealy the nickname ''the burn-

ing bed,'' according to a May 1990 article in *Business Week.* Without a market for its junk bonds, Gibbons Green van Amerongen was soon compelled to exchange First Boston's debt (which was held by an affiliate, the Clipper Group) for a 40 percent equity stake in Sealy.

In spite of this overarching financial predicament, CEO Candlish was able to prune corporate expenses, keep up with interest payments, and increase revenue by 6.2 percent to $702.3 million. The new leader closed more than one-third of Sealy's 38 plants and opened three new, more efficient plants in strategic locations. Candlish standardized production and centralized some purchasing to take advantage of the company's new-found national buying power. He hoped to save $30 million annually through these cost-cutting measures. The divestment of surplus real estate and a subsidiary helped pay down some debt as well. In mid-1990, Sealy also invested in its biggest advertising campaign ever. The national effort spent about $11 million on prime-time television spots prepared by Leo Burnett Co.

In 1991 the Clipper Group swapped its $400 million in Sealy junk bonds for an additional 53.6 percent of the mattress-maker's equity, effectively buying out Gibbons Green van Amerongen. The deal cut Sealy's debt from $890 million to $490 million (mostly bank debt), and reduced the company's annual interest expense by half, to $56 million. This ownership transition soon led to a leadership transition. In 1992 Candlish announced that he would leave Sealy by year's end, citing conflicts with the new board, dominated by First Boston. In August 1992, Candlish told the *Plain Dealer* that ''since a change of boards following the financial restructuring, there has been a change in management philosophy that has not sat with me as well as the previous philosophy.''

Sealy brought in Lyman M. (John) Beggs to succeed Candlish before the end of the month. Beggs's experience included work with such global consumer products companies as Procter & Gamble Co., Del Monte Corp., Tambrands, Inc., and Norelco Consumer Products Group. The Clipper Group's ownership of Sealy was generally viewed as a transitional investment scheme, and in 1993, the firm sold its 94 percent stake for $250 million to Zell/Chilmark Fund Limited Partnership of Chicago.

Principal Subsidiaries: Sealy Inc.; Stearns & Foster Bedding Co.; Stearns & Foster Upholstery Furniture Co.; Advanced Sleep Products; International Monterey S.A. de C.V. (97.3%); Woodstuff Manufacturing Inc.; Sealy Mattress Company of San Diego; Sealy Mattress Co.; Sealy Mattress Company of Puerto Rico; Ohio-Sealy Mattress Manufacturing Co., Inc.; Ohio-Sealy Mattress Manufacturing Co., Fort Worth; Ohio-Sealy Mattress Manufacturing Co.; Ohio-Sealy Mattress Manufacturing Co., Houston; Sealy Mattress Company of Michigan Inc.; Sealy Mattress Company of S.W. Virginia; Sealy Connecticut Inc.; Sealy Mattress Company of Kansas City Inc.; Sealy of Maryland & Virginia; A. Brandwein & Co.; Sealy Mattress Company of Albany Inc.; Sealy of Minnesota Inc.; Sealy Mattress Company of Memphis; Ohio Mattress Company Licensing & Components Group; Sealy Mattress Manufacturing Company Inc.; Sealy Canada Ltd.; Gestion Centurion Inc.; Matelas Centurion Inc.

Further Reading:

Andresky, Jill, "Mattress Wars," *Forbes,* Vol. 139, June 15, 1987, p. 41.

Brunton, David, "Mattress-Making Company Is Anything but Somnolent," *Plain Dealer,* January 27, 1985, p. 4C.

Gerdel, Thomas W., "Mattress Maker Is on Top," *Plain Dealer,* October 3, 1987, p. 10A.

Gleisser, Marcus, "Sealy Chairman Trying to Liven up Old Family Firm," *Plain Dealer,* June 12, 1990, pp. 1D, 9D.

——, "First Boston Taking Control of Sealy," *Plain Dealer,* September 20, 1991, p. 1F.

——, "New Chief Executive Named at Sealy Inc.," *Plain Dealer,* August 25, 1992, p. 1G.

——, "Chicago Partners Buy Stake in Sealy," *Plain Dealer,* January 28, 1993, p. 1F.

Mallory, Maria, "Ohio Mattress Gets the Lumps Out at Last," *Business Week,* May 7, 1990, pp. 127–128.

Sabath, Donald, "Mattress Company Financially Firm," *Plain Dealer,* November 9, 1980, p. 1E.

——, "No Sagging for Ohio Mattress," *Plain Dealer,* September 25, 1984, p. 1D.

"Sealy Here Acquires Operation in Texas," *Plain Dealer,* 1956.

Solomon, Barbara, "Bed Wars: A Sealy Licensee Causes Sleepless Nights," *Management Review,* Vol. 79, December 1990, pp. 50–53.

—April Dougal Gasbarre

Severn Trent PLC

2308 Coventry Road
Birmingham
West Midlands B26 3JZ
United Kingdom
(0121) 722 6000
Fax: (0121) 722 6150

Public Company
Incorporated: 1989
Employees: 6,757
Sales: £998 million
Stock Exchanges: London
SICs: 6711 Holding Companies; 4941 Water Supply

As the fourth largest privately owned water company in the world, Severn Trent PLC supplies water and sewerage services to eight million domestic and industrial consumers across the British Midlands. In the mid-1990s, its service area encompassed 8,000 square miles, reaching from Gloucestershire to Humberside, mid-Wales to Rutland. Water supply became the primary activity of Severn Trent, the successor company to the state-owned Severn Trent Water Authority, when it was privatized—along with the rest of the water industry—in 1989. Privatization improved the company's profits, but also exposed it to controversy over such issues as executive salaries and environmental stewardship. Since becoming a PLC, Severn Trent has also diversified into several related areas, including waste management, water technology services, and the creation of software systems for a variety of industrial applications. The company has also reached beyond the boundaries of its home market, becoming involved in a number of consulting and operational activities abroad.

The harnessing of water resources in Britain began during the Industrial Revolution, when rapidly expanding urban centers demanded more water than local rivers and lakes could provide. In the Severn Trent region, the principal city of Birmingham was among the first to develop modern water management. In the nineteenth century water was brought to the city via an aqueduct dependent on gravity from the Elan Valley reservoirs in rural Wales. Other cities in the region, notably Derby, Nottingham, and Leicester, brought water from the Peak District in Derbyshire.

Water projects in these early days—the province of either private companies or local authorities—were regulated in the sense that each project required an act of parliamentary approval to proceed. Since each proposal was considered in isolation of the others, however, water supply across the nation was haphazard and inefficient. The major cities were comparatively well served, as were smaller settlements lucky enough to lie along the route from a water source to a city, but many areas had no water provision at all. As early as 1869 the problems inherent in such an unplanned system were recognized, and the Royal Commission on Water Supply raised the suggestion of regional planning. No action was taken, however, until 1924, when the Ministry of Health established Regional Advisory Water Committees to coordinate development and operation.

Successive acts of Parliament solidified the central government's involvement with water supply, culminating in the Water Act of 1973, which put an end to the network of individual suppliers and created 10 regional Water Authorities in England and Wales. The far-reaching act also encompassed river management and sewage disposal, operations hitherto entirely separate from water supply, bringing all three related operations under common management.

During the 1980s Britain's Conservative government instituted a wide-ranging policy of privatizing public utilities and services. This policy soon affected the water industry, and as a result the Severn Trent Water Authority became Severn Trent PLC in 1989. After privatization, however, the former water authorities, as monopoly providers of an essential utility, remained subject to government regulatory control. The Office of Water Services (Ofwat) set a ceiling on the rates the water companies could charge their customers. Severn Trent and the other providers were also required to meet standards regarding water purity and pollution control stipulated by both the United Kingdom and the European Community. It would be difficult to determine which issue—pricing or environmental quality—has attracted more controversy since Severn Trent was privatized.

The privatized water industry as a whole has come under attack for its pricing policies, and Severn Trent has certainly taken its share of the criticism. It was frequently alleged that Severn Trent's profits were disproportionately benefiting shareholders rather than being recycled back to customers. The cost of water to the average domestic consumer in the Severn Trent region increased 69 percent from 1989 to 1994—during a period when Severn Trent's profits were steadily rising. The company stoutly defended its policies, however, citing the vast capital outlay required to achieve environmental standards mandated by both London and Brussels.

Environmental issues certainly did not receive adequate attention when the industry was in the public sector: Severn Trent and the other former authorities inherited an antiquated, ecologically hazardous infrastructure in urgent need of upgrading. Severn Trent invested heavily in improvements to the system, and continued to do so through a 10-year program, begun at privatization, that was estimated to cost £5 billion. Critics maintained, however, that the investment burden was being unfairly shouldered by consumers when it should have been borne by Severn Trent, whose healthy profits proved it perfectly capable of doing so. Further, it was alleged that the required capital outlay, much of which was expended in the first few years after privatization, was mitigated in the company's favor by two factors. First, the government's debt write-off was designed to ease the water authorities' financial obligations. Second, the cost of improvements was substantially lower than expected due to very favorable deals made during the economic recession of the early 1990s. Furthermore, critics argued that Severn Trent's financial commitments were actually significantly lower than those of the other former authorities. Because the Severn Trent region is landlocked, the company was thus saved the formidable expense of cleaning up beaches and treating sewage disposed of in the sea.

The company responded to such criticism by stating that the costs of necessary improvements were so onerous that they had to be shared by the consumer. Severn Trent also claimed that its charges were the second-lowest among the country's water companies, and that it had not raised water rates beyond the maximum allowed by the industry regulator, Ofwat. Finally, the company attributed its higher profits at least partially to the rigorous and successful cost-cutting program it had initiated since privatization.

Nevertheless, one outraged journalist at the *Birmingham Post* responded: "If the commercial minds at Severn Trent were to be troubled by conscience, they would be asking themselves this: how the financial rewards can have been reaped so richly from privatization and the environmental responsibilities so grossly neglected." Severn Trent pointed to several improvements it had made since privatization in response to environmental concerns, including the reservoir Carsington Water and a complete overhaul, at a cost of £70 million, of the Frankley Water Treatment Works. The company also cited encouragingly high compliance rates with quality standards: 99.8 percent in drinking water purity, and 99.0 percent with effluent standards. However, Severn Trent was convicted of six pollution offenses in 1993, making it the fourth-worst offender in the United Kingdom for dumping waste into rivers.

The company was widely suspected of incompetence if not malfeasance in a 1994 incident in Worcestershire, for example, when a pollution scare left 35,000 homes without water for a few days. A Shropshire waste disposal firm known as Vitalscheme dumped—without, Severn Trent emphasized later, the knowledge or permission of the water company—a chemical cocktail of industrial solvents into its sewerage works. The pollutant flowed 80 miles down the River Severn, undetected for several days, until it reached drinking water supplies and consumers reported evil-smelling, foul-tasting water. Several people became ill. Severn Trent reacted quickly to the complaints, warned consumers against drinking the water, traced the pollution to its source, took steps to remedy the situation, and subsequently voluntarily paid £25 compensation to each household affected. Nonetheless, the incident damaged Severn Trent's reputation. Some alleged that the company, even if not actually compliant in the original dumping, was deficient in detecting the pollutant and reckless in precipitately assuring consumers that the water was again safe to drink. Severn Trent set up its own independent enquiry into the affair, led by Professor Kenneth Ives, and decided to prosecute Vitalscheme. The Ives report found that, "Severn Trent responded with great speed and efficiency to the emergency, thanks to well prepared emergency planning." The long-term health effects of the chemicals, if any, were unknown.

Severn Trent's image also suffered from the financial arrangements surrounding Chairman John Bellak's early retirement in 1994. Most customers and some shareholders were already disgruntled with the massive increases in executive salaries post-privatization. Severn Trent was by no means unique in boosting its top executives' pay—it was a common practice among Britain's privatized industries—but critics questioned the necessity for raising the chairman's salary a total of 241 percent, from a 1989 level of £51,000 to the opulent 1994 figure of £174,000. The controversy came to a head when Bellak (who had enjoyed some very lucrative share options in addition to his increased salary) received £500,000 in compensation for being requested to retire a few years early. Severn Trent's customers and shareholders and a group of 50 MPs condemned the deal and repeatedly demanded an explanation for Bellak's departure. Tempers were not improved by the subsequent revelation that Richard Ireland, Bellak's replacement, was garnering £100,000 for a work schedule that equated to attending less than one meeting per week. Ireland responded that he would, in fact, be devoting two days a week to his job.

Severn Trent's non-core business activities were by contrast free from controversy. The company became a major player in the waste management industry with its 1991 purchase, for £212 million, of Biffa Waste Services, the fourth-largest firm of its kind in Britain and the tenth-largest in Europe. Biffa operated a threefold business in the United Kingdom and Belgium: collection, whereby it disposed of other companies' waste materials; landfills, a rapidly growing area; and liquid waste management, handled through liquid treatment plants. Biffa's financial returns were somewhat disappointing, but this was due not to the subsidiary's actual performance—its productivity and potential were sound—but rather to the financing scheme by which it was purchased. Severn Trent bought Biffa through Eurobonds with an extremely high interest rate (the annual interest bill was some £24 million) and this adversely affected profits. Independent financial commentators agreed with Severn Trent that once it came out from under its financing cloud, Biffa should prove a credit to the company.

Severn Trent Systems was the computer software arm of the company. The business arose almost tangentially from Severn Trent's own need to process the volumes of information necessary for running a major utility. Customers' needs and specifications, billing, costs of labor and materials, resource management, regulatory and environmental requirements—all such data needed to be processed quickly and accurately. At first in conjunction with IBM and later on its own—after it had purchased the U.S.-based Computer Systems and Applications— Severn Trent developed systems appropriate to its needs. Having established the groundwork, it was a logical next step to market the experience to other, similar organizations. Severn Trent Systems offered a highly complex and sophisticated range of computer services encompassing work management systems, customer information and complaints systems, systems specific to industry types, and professional consulting services in an array of procedural and technical areas. The company's clients in the utility industries have included Western Reserves, which supplied Kansas City, Missouri, with gas and electricity; London Electricity; Houston Lighting and Power Co.; Sydney Electricity; and the City of Seattle Water Department.

Severn Trent Technologies developed and marketed purification technology. The subsidiary Capital Controls was in the chlorine, ozone, and ultraviolet disinfection business, while Stoner Associates specialized in pipe network computer modeling and served the water, gas, and oil industries. Severn Trent Technologies operated in the U.S. and European markets, and was investigating opportunities in China.

Severn Trent Water International Ltd. operated on numerous levels: as a water management consultant, a provider of water and wastewater technology, an operations contractor, and a water utility manager/operator. The company's most significant operations were centered in the United States, Mexico, and Belgium. In the United States, Severn Trent had contracts to operate more than 150 water and wastewater treatment plants. The recent acquisitions of the American companies AM-TEX and McCullough Environmental Services helped to increase Severn Trent's penetration of the market.

In 1994, Severn Trent received a 10-year contract to provide an array of water and wastewater services to a quarter of Mexico City. Included in the project were the installation of 250,000 water meters, the development of customer billing services, and operation and maintenance of secondary water distribution and sewerage systems.

In Belgium, Severn Trent operated through its 20 percent interest in Aquafin, a designer and builder of sewers and wastewater treatment facilities whose influence was spreading throughout the northern part of the country. The Belgian arm of Biffa provided extensive waste management services. In addition, Severn Trent acquired Cotrans in 1994, through which the company entered the municipal contracts market, responsible for the collection of domestic and industrial waste. Severn Trent Water International was also actively pursuing interests in Germany, Puerto Rico, Swaziland, Mauritius, and India.

Severn Trent's post-privatization diversification program has already proved more successful than many such programs initiated by the other former water authorities. Expansion seemed likely and promising for the company. For the foreseeable future, however, the majority of Severn Trent's profits were expected to derive from its primary function as a U.K. supplier of water and wastewater services. And in this area of its business, Severn Trent has been hounded by controversy. As a monopoly supplier of an essential utility, Severn Trent's position was in some ways an unenviable one: struggling to balance the sometimes conflicting needs of the environment, customers, and shareholders.

Nevertheless, in late 1994, the company announced that its operating performance and profits continued to improve and

that it remained committed to achieving, in the words of chairperson Ireland, "the right balance between the interests of our shareholders and our customers." Toward that end, the company allocated a total of £47.5 million for improving customer service and reducing the impact of tariffs on customers. As a result, Severn Trent's domestic customers received a £4 reduction in their bills during 1995–96. Moreover, a similar reduction was expected for 1996–97.

Principal Subsidiaries: AM-TEX Corp., Inc. (U.S.A.); Aquafin N.V. (Belgium; 20%); Biffa Waste Services Ltd.; Biffa Waste Services S.A. (Belgium); Capital Controls Co., Inc. (U.S.A.); Centrale Verzorgingsdienst Cotrans N.V. (Belgium); Computer Systems and Applications Inc. (U.S.A.); Severn Trent Industries Ltd.; Severn Trent Systems Ltd.; Severn Trent Water Ltd.; Stoner Associates (U.S.A.).

Further Reading:

Butler, Daniel, "A Chance They Mustn't Waste," *Accountancy,* June 1993, pp. 34–35.
"500,000 Pounds Severn Trent Payoff to Ex-chairman Infuriates Shareholders," *Independent,* July 30, 1994.
"Homes and Trade Hit as MP Demands Action on River Pollution," *Birmingham Post,* April 19, 1994.
Leathley, Arthur, "Labour Steps Up Campaign over Utility Chiefs' Pay," *Times (London),* January 7, 1995, p. 2.
"The Lex Column: Severn Trent," *Financial Times,* June 15, 1994.
"Outrage as Water Bills Rise 9pc," *Birmingham Post,* February 24, 1994.
"Pollution Scare Hits Water for Thousands," *Birmingham Post,* April 16, 1994.
"Public Left to Clean Up the Mess," *Birmingham Post,* July 8, 1994.
"Severn's Clear Message of Commitment," *Investors Chronicle,* February 4, 1994.
"Severn Trent Hunting for Chemical Cocktail Solution," *Birmingham Post,* May 5, 1994.
"Severn Trent in the Top Four of River Polluters," *Birmingham Post,* March 7, 1994.
"Severn Trent Managers Attacked over Profits," *Birmingham Post,* December 18, 1993.
"Severn Trent's Dirty Washing," *Birmingham Post,* July 6, 1994.
"Severn Trent Takes Legal Action over Chemical Spillage," *Times (London),* June 15, 1994.
"Severn Water 'Approved' Contamination," *Independent,* April 24, 1994.
"Tapping a Well of Riches," *Birmingham Post,* February 24, 1994.
Turncocks to Ozone: A Brief History of Severn Trent Water, Birmingham, England: Severn Trent Water Ltd., 1994.
"UK Company News: Severn Trent Held to 4 Percent Rise," *Financial Times,* June 15, 1994.
"Water Boss Earns Pounds 100,000 for One Meeting a Week," *Birmingham Post,* July 8, 1994.
"Water Company's List of Shame," *Birmingham Post,* July 26, 1994.
Wilsher, Peter, "British Water Makes Waves Overseas," *Management Today,* October 1993, pp. 86–90.

—Robin DuBlanc

Shaklee Corporation

444 Market Street
San Francisco, California 94111
U.S.A.
(415) 954-3000
Fax: (415) 986-0808

Wholly Owned Subsidiary of Yamanouchi Pharmaceutical
Incorporated: 1956
Employees: 600
Sales: $650 million
SICs: 5963 Direct Selling Establishments; 5961 Catalog &
   Mail Order Houses

Shaklee Corporation, currently a subsidiary of Japanese pharmaceutical manufacturer Yamanouchi Pharmaceutical, is a major producer and distributor of nutritional supplements, personal care products, and household products. Shaklee products are largely in-house inventions and have traditionally been sold door-to-door by a team of fiercely loyal independent contractors. In recent years the company has also begun to sell through the mail-order catalog produced by its Bear Creek subsidiary.

Shaklee bears the name of its founder, chiropractor Dr. Forrest Shaklee. Shaklee was born in Iowa in 1894. After a vigorous youth, part of which he spent as a traveling carnival performer, he studied chiropractic and established a practice of his own in Rockwell City, Iowa, in 1915. Nine years later he moved to Mason City and opened a health care facility which he named the Shaklee Clinic. During this time he came to believe that conventional chiropractic wisdom was too narrow, and that diet and nutrition were crucial to overall good health. "Too many of the people who came in for treatment appeared to me to be overfed and undernourished," he would later say. He began studying current scientific research on nutrition and experimented with developing his own nutritional supplements.

In 1929 however, a fire destroyed the Shaklee Clinic. Instead of rebuilding, Shaklee moved to the West Coast with his wife, Ruth, and their two sons. They eventually settled in Oakland, California, where Shaklee opened a new practice. In 1941 Ruth Shaklee died after being struck by an automobile, and shortly thereafter Shaklee's sons both enlisted in the armed forces. Left alone, Shaklee closed his practice and retired to a ranch in an isolated part of northern California.

Shaklee emerged from this self-imposed exile in 1945, selling his ranch and returning to Oakland. He resumed part-time practice as a chiropractor and nutritionist, but also began a second career as a motivational speaker. In personal appearances, local radio broadcasts, and four books published in 1951, he expounded a philosophy based on the power of positive thinking, which he called "Thoughtsmanship."

In 1955 Shaklee resolved to combine his motivational philosophy with his years of experience as a nutritionist. Together with his two sons, Forrest Jr. and Raleigh, he founded Shaklee Products, which was officially launched in 1956. Drawing on talents they had developed in their previous careers, Forrest Jr. handled the accounting and managed the day-to-day operations of the company, while Raleigh, a former insurance salesman, took charge of marketing operations. Their father directed research and development. The company's first product was a protein-lecithin supplement of Dr. Shaklee's own invention, which they sold under the name Pro-Lecin Nibblers. Later in 1956, it added Herb-lax, a herbal laxative. The next year, it introduced Vita-Lea, a multivitamin, multimineral supplement in tablet form that would quickly become one of the company's mainstays.

Dr. Shaklee's concept of "Thoughtsmanship" entered Shaklee Product's operations through its sales force. Rather than hire a permanent sales staff, the company decided from the outset to recruit independent contractors and offer them a series of lucrative incentives that would reward them in proportion to the sales that they generated. It was a system that one loyal Shaklee saleswoman later described as "unstructured" and requiring highly self-motivated participants—a system that was wholly in keeping with Dr. Shaklee's belief in self-motivation and his own persuasive powers. In their first attempt to recruit a sales force, the Shaklees placed an ad in the *Oakland Tribune* asking interested readers to attend an introductory meeting. Six people answered, and all six signed on as distributors.

Shaklee distributorships spread quickly, so that the company was well established throughout California by the end of the decade. This required a gruelling travel schedule from all three Shaklees, father and sons, who wanted their distributors to meet all of them personally. At the same time, the company continued to introduce new products and to branch out from the field of dietary supplements. In 1960 Basic-H Concentrated Organic Cleaner, a soap-free, biodegradable cleaning solution, made its debut after Dr. Shaklee experimented with ways to help the wife of a distributor with sensitive skin. Soon thereafter, the company introduced a line of skin care products made from natural ingredients.

In the early 1960s, the Shaklee gospel began to find an even larger audience. In 1962 a Shaklee customer who had moved from San Diego to Minnesota established the company's first distributorship outside of California, selling mostly Basic-H. Shortly thereafter, a Massachusetts family whose grown son had discovered Basic-H while living in Minnesota established the first Shaklee distributorship on the East Coast. In the early 1970s Shaklee recruited its first Spanish-speaking distributors.

The 1970s saw astounding growth for Shaklee. Annual sales skyrocketed from $20 million to more than $300 million by decade's end. In 1971 the company opened a new research facility, the Forrest C. Shaklee Research Center, in Hayward, California. The company changed its name to its current form in 1972 and went public the next year. In 1976 Shaklee established two subsidiaries, Shaklee Japan and Shaklee Canada, to handle some of its foreign distributorships. During this time, the Shaklees themselves began to play less important roles in the company as it evolved from a family-run organization into a major corporation. Even so, the Shaklee family continued to own a substantial portion of the company's stock. Dr. Shaklee himself continued to be wildly popular among his salespeople—a company staff attorney once attested that "if we didn't have a bodyguard around him (at company conventions), they'd tear his clothes off"—and was still vigorous enough at the age of 85 to break ground on the company's new manufacturing facility in Norman, Oklahoma, in 1979. The next year, the company moved its headquarters to a new complex in San Francisco.

At about the same time, however, Shaklee found itself at the center of a nasty and highly publicized controversy. In 1978 the company sued former distributors Franklin and El Marie Gunnell for more than $1.6 million, charging that the Utah couple had illegally defamed Shaklee's products and interfered with its business relationships after signing on with a rival company. The dispute was made all the more bitter by the fact that the competitor in question was Enhance, a health food company that had been founded by Robert J. Wooten shortly after he resigned as chairman and president of Shaklee in 1976.

In 1981 a Salt Lake city jury decided in favor of Shaklee after a six-week trial, but awarded it a judgement so small that it did not even cover the company's legal fees. The evidence showed that the Gunnells had indeed made outrageous claims about Shaklee's products, but also revealed information about one Shaklee product that the company had hitherto concealed. Company documents subpoenaed for the trial showed that in 1973 Shaklee discovered that the alfalfa it was using to make alfalfa tablets—then something of a fad in health food circles—was tainted with salmonella bacteria. The company then began treating its alfalfa with ethylene oxide (ETO), despite the fact that the fumigant, used mainly to sterilize medical instruments, had been banned by the U.S. Department of Agriculture as a suspected carcinogen. In 1977 the Shaklee finally burned its alfalfa supply and stopped making alfalfa tablets. However, it had never revealed that it had treated its alfalfa with ETO. After the trial, the jury foreman said that "most of the jurors felt that Shaklee had lied about its products."

The first half of the 1980s proved to be a difficult time for Shaklee, and not just because of the negative publicity that came out of the Gunnell case. Profits declined as, ironically, economic prosperity in the United States drew many Shaklee distributors who preferred secure employment back into the conventional job market. At the same time, changing demographics affected the company's sales force: as the female homemakers who had used Shaklee distributorships as a second household income began to seek careers outside the home, the company turned more and more to men to distribute their products. In 1985 the company suffered a great loss when Dr. Forrest Shaklee died at the age of 91.

Shaklee soon began to pull out of its difficulties, however. In 1984 it received a publicity boost when it was named Official Nutrition Consultant to the United States ski team that competed at the Winter Olympics in Sarajevo. In 1986 it found a way around its distribution problems when it acquired Bear Creek Corporation, which was well known for the luxury fruit baskets and confections sold through its Harry and David mail order catalogue. By the end of the decade, Shaklee began selling its own products through the Harry and David catalogue.

Sales turned back up in the second half of the 1980s, drawing the attention of the investment community. In March 1989 Minneapolis-based investor Irwin Jacobs launched a $40-per-share tender offer for Shaklee in March 1989. Jacobs's bid was not entirely welcome, especially among Shaklee salespeople, who feared that a hostile takeover would bring radical changes in corporate culture and destroy the intimate, family-like feeling between the company and its sales force that had bred their loyalty. Some distributors even considered making a counteroffer.

Two weeks after Irwin Jacobs began acquiring Shaklee stock, however, a white knight appeared in a rather unlikely form. In mid-March Shaklee agreed to be acquired by Yamanouchi Pharmaceutical, a large Japanese drug company with a substantial presence in that country's competitive market for anti-ulcer medication. Yamanouchi's offer came as a surprise to Shaklee management and industry analysts, as Yamanouchi had acquired Shaklee Japan in February but had given no sign of being interested in acquiring its parent company. Yamanouchi's financial package was valued at $395 million, or $28 per share plus a $20 per share one-time dividend to Shaklee shareholders. As part of the deal Yamanouchi also bought out Raleigh and Forrest Shaklee, Jr., who owned 28 percent of Shaklee stock between them.

Yamanouchi's move was part of a general trend affecting Japanese pharmaceutical companies. Faced with worldwide consolidation in the pharmaceutical industry, Japanese companies began to expand overseas in the late 1980s, entering into joint sales, production, and research ventures with foreign drug companies. Acquisition of smaller American and European companies was seen by analysts and Japanese drug executives alike as a way of gaining quick access to important foreign markets. Nonetheless, some analysts familiar with the Japanese pharmaceutical industry questioned the wisdom of Yamanouchi's move, saying that Shaklee offered the company few obvious strategic advantages, neither strengthening its research operations nor building its overseas distribution network. Whatever the wisdom of Yamanouchi's move, Shaklee continued to grow and to expand its overseas operations. In 1992 it created Shaklee Mexico, and in 1994 it established Shaklee Taiwan.

1994 was also a year to look back and reflect, as the company sprinkled its calendar with events commemorating the 100th anniversary of the birth of Dr. Forrest Shaklee. The company had surmounted a number of challenges over the years—not just the alfalfa scandal of 1981 and Irwin Jacobs's hostile takeover bid in 1989, but also continual skepticism from different sectors of the scientific community about the efficacy of high-dosage nutritional supplements. Throughout it all, Shaklee has survived and continues to survive, thanks in large part to the loyalty and enthusiasm of its sales force, which are unusual even by the standards of direct sales. Shaklee distributors are not just salespeople; they are true believers, famous for using the products that they sell with an exclusivity that borders on fanaticism. Before her falling out with the company, El Marie Gunnell used Basic-H, the company's organic cleaning solution, in her baking, because she believed it would help her homemade bread rise. With salespeople like that, how could Shaklee possibly fail?

Principal Subsidiaries: Bear Creek Corporation; Shaklee Mexico; Shaklee Japan; Shaklee Mexico; Shaklee Taiwan.

Further Reading:

Brenner, Nancy, *Shaklee: The Enduring Dream,* San Francisco: Shaklee Corporation, 1995.

Chase, Marilyn, ''For Shaklee Faithful, Selling Is Believing,'' *Wall Street Journal,* March 9, 1989.

Hill, G. Christian, ''Japan's Yamanouchi to Acquire Shaklee for $395 Million, Thwarting Jacobs' Bid,'' *Wall Street Journal,* March 14, 1989.

Zonana, Victor F., ''Health Products Firm Used Toxic Substance, Ex-Distributor Claims,'' *Wall Street Journal,* January 21, 1982.

—Douglas Sun

Sharp Corporation

22-22 Nagaike-cho
Abeno-ku
Osaka 545
Japan
+81-6-621-1221
Fax: +81-6-628-1667

Public Company
Incorporated: 1935 as Hayakawa Metal Industrial Laboratory
Employees: 60,000
Sales: ¥1.49 billion ($13.3 billion)
Stock Exchanges: Tokyo Osaka Nagoya Paris Luxembourg
   Zurich Basel Geneva
SICs: 3631 Household Cooking Equipment; 3651 Household
   Audio & Video Equipment; 3579 Office Machines, Not
   Elsewhere Classified; 3661 Telephone & Telegraph
   Apparatus

The Sharp Corporation is one of the largest and oldest Japanese consumer goods manufacturers. Founded on a business creed reminiscent of the ancient trading houses—Sincerity and Creativity—and built largely on the hard work and determination of one man, Sharp is in many ways Japan's most "traditional" modern electronics manufacturer. Sharp remains an outward-looking, international corporation, as dedicated in each of its foreign markets to assimilation as to overall success.

The company was founded as a small metal works in Osaka in 1912 by an inventor and tinkerer named Tokuji Hayakawa. After three years in business, earning a modest income from gadgets and repair jobs, Hayakawa engineered a mechanical pencil he called the "Ever-Sharp." Consisting of a retractable graphite lead in a metal rod, the Ever-Sharp pencil won patents in Japan and the United States. Demand for this simple and durable instrument was immense. To facilitate greater production, Hayakawa first adopted an assembly line and later moved to a larger factory.

Hayakawa's business, as well as his life, were ruined on September 1, 1923. On that day, the Great Kanto Earthquake caused a fire which destroyed his factory and took the lives of his wife and children. Hayakawa endured severe depression; it was a year before he re-established his factory. The Hayakawa Metal Industrial Laboratory, as the company was called, re-

sumed production of the Ever-Sharp pencil, but Hayakawa became interested in manufacturing a new product: radios.

The first crystal radio sets were imported into Japan from the United States in the early 1920s. Hearing one for the first time, Hayakama immediately became convinced of its potential. With little understanding of radios, or even electricity, he set out to develop Japan's first domestically-produced crystal radio. After only three months of study and experimentation, Hayakawa succeeded in receiving a signal from the broadcasting service which had begun programming—to a very small audience—only a few months before, in 1925.

The radio entered mass production shortly afterward, and sold so well that facilities had to be expanded. Crystal radios, however, are passive receivers whose range is limited. Hayakawa felt that powered radios, capable of amplifying signals, should be the subject of further development. While competitors continued to develop better crystal sets, Hayakawa began work on an AC vacuum tube model. When the company introduced a commercial model, the Sharp Dyne, in 1929, Sharp was firmly established as Japan's leading radio manufacturer. The company expanded greatly in the following years, necessitating its reorganization into a corporation in 1935.

The laboratory, for all its success, was not a leader in a wide range of technologies; it led only in a narrow section of the market. In addition, the company did not have the benefit of financial backing from the *zaibatsu* conglomerates or the government. It was, in the realm of the national modernization effort, an outsider. This may have been its saving grace, however, as the government had become dominated by a group of right-wing imperialists within the military. Whatever their political opinions, the leaders of Japan's largest corporations were compelled to cooperate with the militarists in their quest to establish Japanese supremacy in Asia. Hayakawa, on the other hand, was for the most part left alone.

During World War II, Hayakawa and his company were forced to produce devices for the military, and even to restructure, as new industrial laws intended to concentrate industrial capacity were passed. Renamed Hayakawa Electrical Industries in 1942, the company emerged from the war damaged but not destroyed. While other industrialists were purged from public life for their support of the militarists, Hayakawa was permitted to remain in business. His biggest concerns were rebuilding his company and surviving Japan's postwar recession.

By 1950 more than 80 of Hayakawa's competitors were bankrupt. But Hayakawa's officials personally guaranteed the company's liabilities when the company suffered a critical drop in sales, and Hayakawa Electric was able to obtain the cooperation of major underwriters until the first major expansion in the Japanese economy occurred in 1952.

Hayakawa considered television, a field that had not yet proved commercially successful, a highly promising new area. The company began development of an experimental TV set in 1951, even before plans had been made to begin broadcasting in Japan. Two years later, when television broadcasting started, Hayakawa Electric introduced its first commercial television set under the brand name "Sharp," in honor of the pencil. Hayakawa's good timing was essential in allowing the company to establish and maintain a significant and profitable market share.

The company started development of a color television in the mid-1950s. In 1960, with the advent of color broadcasting in Japan, Hayakawa introduced a line of color sets. This was followed in 1962 by a commercial microwave oven, and in 1964 by a desk-top calculator. The Compet calculator, which looked like an adding machine, was the first in the world to use transistors. In 1966 the microwave oven received a rotating plate and calculators shrank with the use of integrated circuits.

Hayakawa recognized the great sales potential of the United States; a sales subsidiary was established in 1962. It served the dual purpose of facilitating sales and observing the market. By the late 1960s, the Sharp brand name had become well-established in North America. Sales in the United States provided the company with a large and increasing portion of its income. In addition, subsidiaries were established in West Germany in 1968 and Britain in 1969.

Hayakawa Electric made two major breakthroughs in 1969. That year the company introduced the Extra Large Scale Integration Calculator, a device now reduced to the size of a paperback book. The other new product was the gallium arsenide light-emitting diode (LED)—in effect, a tiny computer light. Like the radio and television before them, improved versions of both the calculator and LED were subsequently introduced in future years.

Tokuji Hayakawa retired from the day-to-day operations of his company in 1970, assuming the title of chairman. He was replaced as president by Akira Saeki, a former executive director. Saeki oversaw an important reorganization of the company intended to establish a new corporate identity and unify product development efforts. That year, Hayakawa Electric Industries also adopted its new name: Sharp Corporation.

Saeki, who witnessed the Apollo moon landing while in America, decided that the company's future efforts should center on the development of semiconductors, the electronic components which had made the lunar mission possible. He initiated construction of a massive research complex called the Advanced Development and Planning Center. The project was a significant investment for Sharp, since its budget was already seriously strained by the construction of an exhibit for Expo '70. Nevertheless construction was begun on a 55-acre research complex in Tenri, Nara Prefecture.

During the 1970s, Sharp consolidated its position in consumer goods by broadening its product line to include refrigerators, washers, portable stereos, copiers, desk-top computers, video equipment, and Walkman-type headsets. Profit generated from consumer goods sales was largely invested in the Tenri facility. When completed, the research complex cost ¥7.5 billion, representing about 70 percent of Sharp's capitalization.

Perhaps the most important product to come out of the Tenri research facility was the Very Large Scale Integration (VLSI) factory automation system. Building upon existing integration technologies, VLSI production lines enabled manufacturers to reduce defects and raise productivity through the use of industrial robots and other mechanical apparatus.

In an effort to head off impending protectionist trade legislation, Sharp built new factories in its largest overseas markets, principally the United States. The company's decision to build a plant in Memphis, Tennessee was criticized at first. RCA had closed a plant in Memphis in 1966, favoring production in Taiwan. Sharp maintained that RCA had merely suffered from inept management and went ahead with the plant. By pushing its American suppliers for parts with zero defects and incorporating the Japanese concept of full worker involvement, the Memphis plant proved highly successful.

President Saeki retired in 1986, continuing to serve the company as an advisor. He was succeeded by Haruo Tsuji, a "numbers man" with an exemplary record in middle and upper management. Through its 18 divisions, Sharp had diversified during Saeki's tenure into a wide range of consumer products. By the time of his retirement, Sharp operated 12 research laboratories and 34 plants in 27 countries and its employees were equally divided between Japan and foreign countries. The logistics of running a truly international corporation took their toll on Sharp's earnings, however. Largely due to a strong appreciation in the value of the yen, Sharp's earning for the year plunged 42 percent to ¥20.78 billion ($137.5 million). Nevertheless, Saeki had left his company poised for a future of vigorous growth.

While rivals Sony and Matsushita expanded through acquiring a number of Hollywood-based entertainment companies during the 1980s, Sharp focused on research and development. In consumer electronics and appliances, the company engaged in a measured effort to move upmarket, offering more expensive, but higher-quality, products. By the late 1980s, Sharp had offered a number of innovations in its product line such as a video disc player capable of reproducing three-dimensional images, a cordless telephone with a 100-meter range, and Zarus, a highly successful computerized personal organizer, capable of reading handwritten Japanese text.

Most fruitful, however, was Sharp's continual development of liquid crystal display (LCD) technology. By the mid-1980s, Sharp was the market leader in LCD technology, which it had parried into a number of high-definition color televisions. In 1989, Tsuji appointed Kiyoshi Sakashita, a board member and an expert in industrial design, to lead a team of 50 engineers to further exploit its LCD technology. Three years and countless brainstorming sessions later, Sharp unveiled ViewCam, an ingeniously redesigned video camcorder that presented the image on a four-inch LCD screen as it was being recorded. First shown at Japan's prestigious consumer electronics show in Osaka, Sharp's ViewCam "set the industry abuzz," according to the *Far Eastern Economic Review*. The ViewCam competed heavily against Sony's best-selling Handycam. Within two years, over 1.6 million ViewCam units were sold, at an average price of ¥223,000 ($2,275).

In the early 1990s, the company completed two new research and development centers: the Makuhari Building in Tokyo, which focused on multimedia, networking, and software for advanced information systems; and Sharp Laboratories of Europe Ltd. in Oxford, United Kingdom, which focused on areas of artificial intelligence such as pan-European translation technology and opto-electronics. In 1992 alone, the company spent over ¥100 billion on research and development. Sharp also fortified its television manufacturing operations in the United States, Spain, Thailand, and Malaysia, and entered into key relationships with Intel Corporation and Apple Computer, Inc. to jointly develop flash memory chips and personal information equipment.

As it celebrated its 60th anniversary, Sharp's continuous focus on research and development was beginning to pay mightily. Fueled by the success of ViewCam, Zarus (and its American counterpart Newton, which Sharp manufactured and Apple Computers developed and marketed), Sharp's 1993 profits outpaced those of its Japanese rivals, although its sales were considerably smaller. By mid-1994, *Far Eastern Economic Review* announced that Sharp was "poised to usurp Sony as the electronics maker to watch in the 1990s—providing it can keep churning out goods products." Given its strong and continuous commitment to finding new technologies, Sharp was in an excellent position to do just that.

Principal Subsidiaries: Sharp Electronics Corporation (U.S.); Sharp Manufacturing Company of America; Sharp Microelectronics Technology Inc. (U.S.); Hycom Inc. (U.S.); Sharp Electronics of Canada Ltd.; Sharp Electronics (Europe) GmbH (West Germany); Sharp Electronics (Svenska) AB (Sweden); Sharp Electronics (U.K.) Ltd.; Sharp Precision Manufacturing (U.K.) Ltd.; Sharp Electronics GmbH (Austria); Sharp Electronics (Schweiz) AG (Switzerland); Sharp Electronica Espana S.A.; Sharp Corporation of Australia Pty. Ltd.; Sharp Manufacturing France S.A.; Sharp-Roxy Sales (Singapore) Pte. Ltd.; Sharp Electronics (Singapore) Pte. Ltd.; Sharp Electronics (Taiwan) Company Ltd.; Sharp Appliances (Thailand) Ltd.; Sharp-Roxy (Hong Kong), Ltd., Sharp Thebnakorn (Thailand) Co. Ltd. (STLC), Sharp-Roxy Electronics (Maliysia) Corporation (M) Sdn. Bhd. (SREC), Sharp Laboratories of Europe (England) Ltd.

Further Reading:

Eisenstodt, Gale, "Unidentical Twins," *Forbes,* July 5, 1993, p. 42.
Friedland, Jonathan, "Sharp's Edge: Prowess in LCD Screens Puts it Ahead of Sony," *Far Eastern Economic Review,* July 28, 1994, p. 74.
Gross, Neil, "Sharp's Long-Range Gamble On its Innovation Machine," *Business Week,* April 29, 1991, pp. 84–85.
Morris, Kathleen, "The Town Watcher," *Financial World,* July 19, 1994, pp. 42–45.
Teresko, John, "Japan: Reengineering vs. Tradition," *Industry Week,* September 5, 1994, pp. 62–70.

—updated by Maura Troester

Solectron Corp.

777 Gibraltar Drive
Milpitas, California 95035
U.S.A.
(408) 957-8500
Fax: (408) 956-6075

Public Company
Incorporated: 1977
Employees: 6,700
Sales: $1.46 billion
Stock Exchanges: New York
SICs: 3674 Semiconductors; 3679 Electronic Components
   NEC

Solectron Corp. is a leading worldwide independent provider of manufacturing services to electronics equipment manufacturers, including IBM, Apple Computer, and Hewlett Packard. Examples of equipment for which Solectron manufactures circuit boards and other assemblies include computers, telecommunications gear, medical electronics, avionics, and various industrial devices. Recognized as a global leader in service and quality, Solectron has achieved stellar growth, particularly during the early 1990s.

Roy Kusumoto started Solectron in 1977, and was joined about one year later by Dr. Winston Chen. Kusumoto and Chen formed the company to take advantage of an opportunity that they saw opening up in the burgeoning solid state electronics market. They noted that many manufacturers of electronic equipment were often burdened by temporary periods of work overflow, during which they had trouble making or acquiring enough circuit boards or other assemblies to complete their components. Through Solectron, Kusumoto and Chen hoped to provide manufacturing services to companies that were experiencing shortages.

Most of Solectron's growth and success during the 1980s has been credited to Chen. During Solectron's first full year of operation Kusumoto lost $150,000. Then a friend put him in touch with Chen. Chen, a manufacturing expert with doctorates from Harvard, was employed at International Business Machines (IBM) at the time. Kusumoto, also a former IBM employee, became interested in Chen's ideas and asked for his help. Chen joined the tiny Solectron as executive vice president in 1978 and was named president twelve months later. The

company generated a profit of $400,000 during the first year under his leadership. From that point forward Solectron's earnings grew steadily. In 1984, Chen succeeded Kusumoto as chief executive.

By the time Chen joined Solectron, the 36-year-old already had acquired a reputation within his industry peer group as a highly intelligent, hard-working innovator. Chen was born and raised in a middle class family in Taiwan. His father owned and managed a construction firm and impressed a strong work ethic on his children. Influenced by his family's construction background, Chen studied civil engineering at National Chang Kung University in Taiwan. He finished first in his class of 130 and earned a fellowship to study at Harvard in 1965.

Chen's chance to travel to the United States came at an opportune time because he had become dissatisfied with the political climate in Taiwan. Specifically, Chen was frustrated by barriers to economic and social mobility that existed in the country. "We were one of the lucky families in Taiwan," Chen recalled in the *Business Journal-San Jose.* ". . . but that just made me realize how unfair the political system could be. It was terribly self-perpetuating." Chen had become one of the more outspoken students at his college and had seen some of his friends arrested. After studying at Harvard Chen decided to remain in the United States while most of his family stayed in Taiwan.

Chen earned two doctorates, one in applied mechanics and the other in applied physics, in less than five years at Harvard. "There's no secret to success in school or business: Hard work," explained Chen in the *Business Journal-San Jose.* Chen's accomplishments are additionally impressive because of the hurdles posed by learning the English language. An amusing episode related to a thesis Chen wrote on the theories of the relative strengths of certain materials illustrates Chen's struggles. He titled the piece "Necking in a Bar" before a professor suggested changing the name to "Necking of a Bar." Despite Chen's difficulty with word choice, his paper became influential in his field of study; he had utilized a new computer program that was subsequently adopted by many other researchers. Also while at Harvard, Chen discovered billiards, which became his hobby and escape as a student, and he married another Taiwanese doctoral student.

IBM recruited the 27-year-old Chen upon his graduation in 1969. He worked in New York for three years before he was transferred to San Jose, California. During his nearly ten years at IBM, Chen was exposed to both the manufacturing and marketing sides of the computer business. He was involved in several major projects, including the development of IBM's ink-jet printers and creation of various tape-head technologies. Also, Chen had developed an intense interest in the teachings of W. Edwards Deming, whose ideologies and techniques related to manufacturing and quality were being widely embraced in Japan and other parts of Asia. He believed in Deming's methods but was frustrated by IBM's failure to recognize their validity. So Chen was already open to the idea of starting and running a new company before Kusumoto asked for his help in 1978.

During the early and mid 1980s, Solectron found a willing market for its manufacturing services. Because of the founders's ties to IBM, much of their work came from that company. But

Solectron slowly diversified and was able to parlay its experience serving IBM into manufacturing contracts with several other major electronics companies. Furthermore, as its clients became familiar with its service and style, Solectron began to shift away from its early emphasis on overflow, production-oriented jobs. Eventually, customers started coming to Solectron for help with entire manufacturing programs and development projects.

Solectron's quick success during the early and mid 1980s stemmed from Chen's management techniques, many of which were grounded in Deming's philosophies. Deming is generally credited with inspiring the Total Quality Management philosophy that was adopted during the mid 1900s in Japan and became popular in the United States during the 1980s. Deming, an American, was sent to Japan to help rebuild that economy after World War II. His ideas were generally ignored in the United States until Japan began to pose a serious threat to the American manufacturing sector. In short, Deming developed a people-focused management strategy designed to achieve continual increases in customer satisfaction and quality at continually lower costs. He advocated the use of comprehensive quality management techniques that saturated an organization, involving all departments and employees and extending backward and forward to envelop both the supply and customer chains.

"Dr. Deming's philosophy is simple: improvement doesn't happen by itself," Chen told the *Business Journal-San Jose*. "It must be a well-thought-out process, with everyone participating." Indeed, Solectron was among the first U.S. companies to truly implement Deming's basic philosophies into its environment. Deming's works became required reading for all Solectron managers. In addition, the company set up an elaborate computerized quality control system that could track every stage of a project. Furthermore, when other companies later rejected some popular quality initiatives, such as quality circles, as unworkable trends, Solectron continued to tinker the programs until they produced measurable results.

Chen's quality focus permeated Solectron from the start. For example, Chen had rules about the number of times that a telephone could ring before it was answered. He even set the example by answering his own telephone. And he required all Solectron managers to wear beepers so that their customers could access them at all times. Most importantly, Solectron tried to hire only the best people, paying them the best wages and treating them with respect. Although he set strict standards, Chen allowed his managers to operate autonomously and to make key decisions on their own. That independence and autonomy was a welcome change for the many Solectron managers who had been hired away from IBM. "IBM hires the cream of the crop and trains people better than anybody else, but they underutilized their people and micro-managed them," Koichi Nishimura, a Solectron employee since 1988, noted in the *Los Angeles Times*. As a result of its personnel policies, Solectron enjoyed one of the lowest employee turnover rates in the industry throughout the 1980s and early 1990s.

In addition to its innovative management philosophy, Solectron benefitted from Chen's and his fellow managers marketing strategies. Chen focused the firm's long-term efforts on the surface-mount style of circuit board manufacturing early in the mid 1980s before most of Solectron's peers recognized the importance of the technology. Surface-mount circuit boards represented an improvement over more conventional through-hole boards because they were (eventually) less expensive to produce, lighter in weight, smaller, and could be printed on both sides of the board, among other advantages. Solectron's decision to emphasize surface-mount technology would pay off handsomely in the early and mid 1990s, when demand for that technology exploded.

Solectron prospered as a result of its sound management and marketing initiatives during the 1980s. But the company also benefitted from a strong trend toward outsourcing by major manufacturers. Indeed, many producers learned that they could benefit significantly by hiring outside manufacturers, like Solectron, to handle specialty manufacturing activities. The potential benefits were numerous. As electronics markets became increasingly competitive during the 1980s, original equipment manufacturers (OEMs) were faced with constantly shrinking product life cycles, which meant that they had to reduce the amount of time they took to bring a new product from the concept stage to market. Specialists like Solectron were able to drastically reduce that time span.

In addition to "reduced time to market," another benefit that Solectron offered to its customers was reduced capital investments. Rather than having to invest the large sums of money necessary to develop production facilities for a particular type of circuit board, a company could pay a much smaller fee to have Solectron build the board. The OEM could then invest its resources in other activities. Solectron's technological advantage allowed it to produce circuit boards and other electronic assemblies for its customers at a much lower cost and at a much higher level of quality than its customers could achieve themselves given their limited resources and technological know-how.

By the end of the 1980s, Solectron was generating more than $100 million in annual revenues—1989 profits topped $4.5 million from sales of about $130 million, up from sales of just $88 million in 1988. Although the company had realized momentous growth since its inception not much more than ten years earlier, it was about to experience a five-year growth spurt that would outstrip even Chen's expectations. The expansion started in late 1989 when Chen took Solectron public in an effort to generate capital for expansion. Solectron sold stock for six dollars per share in November. By July of 1990 the stock price had nearly doubled to ten dollars. Chen considered his success at taking Solectron public the achievement of his life.

At the same time that Solectron went public, the company began to benefit from extremely strong demand for its services related to surface-mount technology. As orders and contracts poured in from manufacturers around the globe, Solectron began to leave its two major competitors, Flextronics Inc. and SCI Systems Inc., behind. Surface-mount work represented 22 percent of Solectron's billings in 1988 before rising to 36 percent during 1989. As surface-mount sales soared, Solectron's revenues passed $200 million in 1990 and then rose to $265 million in 1991. Solectron's growth was largely the result of more then five years worth of large capital investments in new surface-mount equipment.

Awards bolstered Solectron's public image as a quality manufacturer. In 1991, it received the coveted Malcolm Baldridge National Quality Award in recognition of its system of ensuring customer satisfaction and quality products. Solectron had won more than 35 other quality awards since the early 1980s, including ten in 1990. But the Baldridge Award, which is awarded to a maximum of two companies annually in the manufacturing category, was a crowning achievement. It reflected Solectron's incredible quality and service advantage over its industry peers. By the early 1990s, Solectron had surpassed even its Japanese competitors in most award categories.

Solectron's quality of customer service could be seen when comparing its performance to a good Japanese outsourcing company. While a good Japanese outsourcing company typically took six weeks to create a prototype of a circuit board for a new disk drive in 1991, Solectron could handle the task in 13 days. Likewise, most Japanese companies would not permit any schedule changes 30 days prior to delivery. In contrast, Solectron would often accept changes the day before production. Furthermore, Solectron delivered the highest quality product available. Indeed, by the early 1990s Solectron had become a global model for manufacturing quality and service. Although the company was already an industry leader in quality by the mid 1980s, it had reduced it defects-per-shipment by more than 50 percent between 1987 and 1992, to less than 233 defects per million parts manufactured. And its on-time delivery rate was nearly 98 percent.

As Solectron's customers began to rely on its services, the company's sales rose. To keep up with increasing demand, Solectron drew on its large capital base and began acquiring other production facilities. Early in 1992, Solectron purchased a circuit board assembly operation in North Carolina from IBM. The acquisition fit neatly into Solectron's organization because Solectron's managers, many of whom had worked at or with IBM, were already familiar with the new company's existing labor and production environment. Solectron even retained the plant's president, Hank Ewert. Ewert was known as a hard driving, resourceful manager. He welcomed the chance to leave IBM's shrinking organization, and to participate in Solectron's plans to build the facility into one of its major production arms. Solectron nearly doubled the plant's work force in one year to about 300, and planned to eventually add as many as 2,500 more workers.

Encouraged by the success of its North Carolina plant acquisition, Solectron went on a buying spree between 1993 and 1994, acquiring facilities from Hewlett-Packard, Phillips, Apple and other major electronics producers in locations ranging from Scotland and Malaysia to France and Washington state. Although many of the plants incorporated leading edge technology, they had failed to generate profits in the increasingly competitive electronics market. Solectron, with its proven management and production techniques, was able to move into the facilities and return them to profitability. In addition, Solectron would usually benefit by getting contracts from the previous owners of the facilities to produce circuit boards and related assemblies for their televisions, computers, and other goods.

Solectron's sales rose to $406 million in 1992, $836 million in 1993, and then to a $1.46 billion in 1994, making Solectron one of the fastest growing companies in the nation. Profits paralleled sales growth as net income almost quadrupled from $14.5 million in 1992 to $55.5 million in 1994. All the while, Solectron's debt load remained sparse as cash poured into the manufacturer's coffers. Hopeful observers heralded the success as a example of America's renewed manufacturing prowess. And Solectron's rise did reflect a general trend toward increased U.S. competitiveness in high-tech industries. But Solectron's success also mirrored the efforts of a vastly diverse, multicultural, multilingual work force representing more than 20 foreign cultures.

Solectron entered the 1990s without the guidance of Chen. Since 1991, Chen had been gradually removed himself from command of the company, and, by 1994, he had ceded his chairmanship of Solectron's board to Charles A. Dickinson, who had served as director of the company since 1984. Prior to that, Chen had handed off his president and chief executive positions to Kiochi Nishimura, who had been hired away from IBM in 1988. The still-young Chen left the company to spend more time with his family and to pursue other interests. The management team he left in charge was committed to the same initiatives that had built the company from a fledgling start-up with a few hundred thousand dollars in sales to a leading, billion-dollar-plus global contender. Analysts expected Solectron's growth to persist throughout the mid 1990s, though at a slower pace than that achieved between 1991 and 1994, when sales nearly doubled every year.

Principal Subsidiaries: Solectron Asia; Solectron California Corp.; Solectron Europe; Solectron France, S.A.; Solectron Japan, Inc.; Solectron Scotland Limited (United Kingdom); Solectron Technology, Inc.; Solectron Technology SDN. BHD (Malaysia); Solectron Washington, Inc.

Further Reading:

Byrne, Joe, "Solectron Reports Financial Reports," *Business Wire,* April 16, 1989.

Fralix, David, "The Guy at the Top," *Business Journal-Charlotte,* December 21, 1992, p. 12.

Helm, Leslie, "Solectron's Mantra for Success," *Los Angeles Times,* April 26, 1994, Sec. 2, p. 13.

Krey, Michael, "Winston Chen; He Believes in Lots of Hard Work and a Little Meditation," *Business Journal-San Jose,* July 2, 1990, p. 12.

"Solectron Corp.," *Business America,* October 21, 1991, p. 5.

—Dave Mote

SONY

Sony Corporation

7-35 Kitashinagawa 6-chome
Shinagawa-ku
Tokyo 141
Japan
+81-3-5448-2111
Fax: +81-3-5448-2244

Public Company
Incorporated: 1946 as Tokyo Tsushin Kogyo K.K.
Employees: 23,560
Sales: ¥63.48 billion (US $11.2 billion)
Stock Exchanges: Tokyo Osaka Nagoya New York London
  Amsterdam Pacific Hong Kong Paris Frankfurt Zurich
SICs: 3651 Household Audio & Video Equipment; 3661
  Telephone & Telegraph Apparatus; 5064 Electrical
  Appliances—Television & Radio.

The Sony Corporation is one of the best-known names in consumer electronics. Since it was established shortly after World War II, Sony has introduced a stream of revolutionary products, including the transistor radio, the Trinitron television, the Betamax VCR, and the Walkman portable cassette player.

Sony maintains a number of joint ventures, including one with Union Carbide to manufacture Eveready batteries in Japan. The company also operates a life-insurance company in association with the Prudential Life Insurance Company and, with PepsiCo, runs a company that imports and markets Wilson sports equipment. Sony has also established a joint venture with the Chinese government to produce television sets in the People's Republic of China.

Sony was founded by a former naval lieutenant named Akio Morita and a defense contractor named Masaru Ibuka. Morita, a weapons researcher, first met Ibuka during World War II while developing a heat-seeking missile-guidance system and a night-vision gun scope. After the war Ibuka worked as a radio repairman for a bomb-damaged Tokyo department store. Morita found him again when he read in a newspaper that Ibuka had invented a shortwave converter. In May of 1946 the two men established a partnership with $500 in borrowed capital, and registered their company as the Tokyo Tsushin Kogyo (Tokyo Telecommunications Engineering Corporation, or TTK). Morita and Ibuka moved their company to a crude facility on a hill in southern Tokyo where they developed its first consumer product: a rice cooker which failed commercially. In its first year TTK registered a profit of $300 on sales of less than $7,000.

But as the Japanese economy grew stronger, demand for consumer goods increased. Morita and Ibuka abandoned the home-appliance market and, with injections of capital from Morita's father, concentrated on developing new electronic goods. Ibuka developed a tape recorder fashioned after an American model he had seen at the Japan Broadcasting Corporation. Demand for the machine remained low until Ibuka accidentally discovered a U.S. military booklet titled *Nine Hundred and Ninety-Nine Uses of the Tape Recorder*. Translated into Japanese, the booklet became an effective marketing tool. Once acquainted with its many uses, customers such as the Academy of Art in Tokyo purchased so many tape recorders that TTK was soon forced to move to a larger building in Shinagawa.

Norio Ohga, an opera student at the academy, wrote several letters to TTK criticizing the sound quality of its recorder. Impressed by the detail and constructive tone of the criticisms, Morita invited Ohga to participate in the development of a new recorder as a consultant. Ohga accepted, and subsequent models were vastly improved.

Constantly searching for new technological advances, Masaru Ibuka heard of a tiny new capacitor called a transistor in 1952. The transistor, developed by Bell Laboratories, could be used in place of larger, less-durable vacuum tubes. Western Electric purchased the technology in order to manufacture transistorized hearing aids. Ibuka acquired a patent license from Western Electric for $25,000 with the intention of developing a small tubeless radio.

TTK began mass production of transistor radios in 1954, only a few months after they were introduced by a small American firm called Regency Electronics. The TTK radio was named Sony, from *sonus,* Latin for "sound." The Sony radio had tremendous sales potential, not only in the limited Japanese market, but also in the United States, where the economy was much stronger.

Traditionally, international sales by Japanese companies were conducted through trading houses such as Mitsui, Mitsubishi, and Sumitomo. Although these trading companies were well represented in the United States, Morita chose not to do business with them because they were unfamiliar with his company's products and did not share his business philosophy. Morita traveled to New York, where he met with representatives from several large retail firms. Morita refused an order from Bulova for 100,000 radios when that company required that each carry the Bulova name. Morita pledged that his company would not manufacture products for other companies and eventually secured a number of more modest orders that assured his company's growth at a measured pace.

The rising popularity of the Sony name led Morita and Ibuka to change the name of their company to Sony Kabushiki Kaisha (Corporation) in January of 1958. The following year Sony announced that it had developed a transistorized television. In 1960, after a business dispute with Delmonico International, the company Morita had appointed to handle international sales,

Sony established a trade office in New York City and another in Switzerland called Sony Overseas.

A subsidiary called Sony Chemicals was created in 1962 to produce adhesives and plastics to reduce the company's dependence on outside suppliers. And in 1965 a joint venture with Tektronix was established to produce oscilloscopes in Japan.

During the early 1960s Sony engineers continued to introduce new, miniaturized products based on the transistor, including an AM/FM radio and a videotape recorder. By 1968 Sony engineers had developed new color-television technology. Using one electron gun, for more-accurate beam alignment, and one lens, for better focus, the Sony Trinitron produced a clearer image than conventional three-gun, three-lens sets. In what has been described as its biggest gamble, Sony, confident that technology alone would create new markets, invested a large amount of capital in the Trinitron.

Also in 1968, Sony Overseas established a trading office in England, and entered into a joint venture with CBS to produce phonograph records. The venture was under the direction of Norio Ohga, the art student who had complained about Sony's early tape recorder, whom Morita had persuaded in 1959 to give up opera and join Sony. The company, called CBS/Sony, later became the largest record manufacturer in Japan. In 1970 Sony Overseas established a subsidiary in West Germany to handle sales in that country.

After a decade of experience in videotape technology, Sony introduced the U-matic three-quarter-inch video-cassette recorder (VCR) in 1971. Intended for institutions such as television stations, the U-matic received an Emmy Award for engineering excellence from the National Academy of Television Arts and Sciences. In 1973, the year Sony Overseas created a French subsidiary, the academy honored the Trinitron series with another Emmy.

Sony developed its first VCR for the consumer market, the Betamax, in 1975. The following year the Walt Disney Company and Universal Pictures filed a lawsuit against Sony, complaining that the new machine would enable widespread copyright infringement of television programs. A judgment in favor of Sony in 1979 was reversed two years later. Litigation continued, but by the time the matter reached the U.S. Supreme Court the plaintiffs' original case had been severely undermined by the proliferation of VCRs, making any legal restriction on copying television programs for private use nearly impossible to enforce.

During the mid 1970s, competitors, such as the American RCA and Zenith and the Japanese Toshiba and Victor Company of Japan (JVC), effectively adopted and improved upon technologies developed by Sony. For the first time, Sony began to lose significant market share, often in lines that it had pioneered. Strong competition, however, was only one factor that caused Sony's sales growth to fall (after growing 166 percent between 1970 and 1974, it grew only 35 percent between 1974 and 1978).

Like many Sony officials, Akio Morita lacked formal management training. Instead, he relied on his personal persuasive skills and his unusual ability to anticipate or create markets for new products. In typical fashion, Sony introduced the Betamax VCR well before its competitors, in effect creating a market in which it would enjoy a short-term monopoly. At this stage, however, Morita failed to establish the Betamax format as the industry standard by inviting the participation of other companies.

Matsushita Electric (which owned half of JVC) developed a separate VCR format called VHS (video home system), which permitted as many as three additional hours of playing time on a tape, but which was incompatible with Sony's Betamax. When the VHS was introduced in 1977, Morita was reported to have felt betrayed that Sony's competitors did not adopt the Betamax format. He appealed to 81-year-old Konosuke Matsushita, in many ways a patriarch of Japanese industry, to discontinue the VHS format in favor of Betamax. When Matsushita refused, many believed it was because he felt insulted by Morita's failure to offer earlier collaboration.

Matsushita launched a vigorous marketing campaign to convince customers and other manufacturers not only that VHS was superior, but that Betamax would soon be obsolete. The marketing war between Matsushita and Sony was neither constructive nor profitable; both companies were forced to lower prices so much that profits were greatly depressed. Although Betamax was generally considered a technically superior product, the VHS format grew in popularity and gradually displaced Betamax as a standard format. Despite its falling market share (from 13 percent in 1982 to five percent in 1987), Sony refused to introduce a VHS line until the late 1980s.

In 1979 Morita personally oversaw the development of a compact cassette tape player called the Walkman. Inspired by Norio Ohga's desire to listen to music while walking, Morita ordered the development of a small, high-fidelity tape player, to be paired with small, lightweight headphones that were already under development. The entire program took only five months from start to finish, and the product's success is now legendary—Walkman even became the generic term for similar devices produced by Sony's competitors.

During the 1970s, Masaru Ibuka, 12 years Morita's senior, gradually relinquished many of his duties to younger managers such as Norio Ohga, who was named president of Sony in 1982. Ohga became president shortly after a corporate reorganization that split Sony into five operating groups (marketing and sales, manufacturing, service, engineering, and diversified operations). While not formally trained in business, Ohga nonetheless understood that Sony was too dependent on an unstable consumer-electronics market. In one of his first acts, he inaugurated the 50–50 program to increase sales in institutional markets from 15 to 50 percent by 1990.

During this time, Sony's research-and-development budget consumed approximately nine percent of sales (Matsushita budgeted only four percent). Another groundbreaking result of Sony's commitment to research and development was a machine that used a laser to reproduce music recorded digitally on a small plastic disk. The compact disk (or CD) player eliminated much of the noise common to conventional, analog phonograph records. Sony developed the CD in association with the Dutch electronics firm Philips, partly in an effort to ensure broad format standardization. Philips, which had developed the most advanced laser technology, was an ideal partner for Sony, which led in the pulse-code technology that made digital sound reproduction possible. Soon the CD format was adopted by competing manufacturers; by the mid-1990s it had virtually replaced phonograph systems as the recording medium of choice.

Early in the 1980s, Morita began ceding some of his duties to Sony's president, Norio Ohga, the young opera student hired 30 years earlier to improve Sony's tape recorders. Under Ohga, Sony entered into a new acquisitions phase with intent of protecting itself from the costly mistake it had made with Betamax. One example of the changes Ohga brought about was Sony's video camera, introduced in 1985. Lighter, less expensive, and more portable than VHS cameras, the camera used 8mm videotape, and was incompatible with both Betamax and VHS machines. The key difference between this and earlier Sony products was that Sony developed the new 8mm video format in conjunction with over 100 competitors. While the camera may have been incompatible with the older Betamax and VHS technologies, Sony ensured that it would be compatible with the next generation of video cameras. Within three years of its introduction, the camera captured over 50 percent of the European, 30 percent of the Japanese, and 20 percent of the North American markets.

In May 1984 Sony purchased Apple Computer's hard-disk-technology operations. As a result of this acquisition, Sony was able to capture about 20 percent of the Japanese market for "work stations," personal computers used in business offices, thus helping to increase the proportion of its sales derived from institutional customers. Ohga also broke a decades-old tradition in 1984 when he established a division to manufacture and market electronics components for other companies. By 1988, fueled by strong sales of semiconductors (once manufactured only for Sony products), the components division had grown to represent about 11 percent of Sony's total sales.

Sony also sought to gain control of the software end of the electronics/entertainment industry. On November 29, 1985 the Sony Corporation of America, which operated several assembly plants in the United States, purchased the Digital Audio Disk Corporation from its affiliate CBS/Sony. Two years later, Sony purchased CBS Records for $2 billion. CBS Records, whose labels included Epic and Columbia, was during this time the largest producer of records and tapes in the world.

Sony had learned through its Betamax experience that a superior product alone wouldn't ensure market dominance; had Sony been able to flood the market with exclusively Beta-formatted movies, the VCR battle might have turned out differently. Looking towards the future development of audio equipment, including digital audio tape (DAT), Sony bought the record manufacturer with an eye toward guaranteeing that the products it manufactured to play music would remain compatible with the medium used to record music. The acquisition marked less of a diversification for Sony than an evolution toward dominance in a specific market.

Sony sought further diversification in U.S. entertainment companies. In 1988, the company considered an acquisition of MGM/UA Communications Company, but decided the price

was too high. Then in 1989 Sony made headlines around the world when it bought Columbia Pictures Entertainment from Coca-Cola for $3.4 billion. Columbia provided Sony with an extensive film library and strong U.S. distribution system. It also carried a $1 billion debt, which almost tripled Sony's short-term debt to around 8 billion yen. Industry analysts applauded the move; however, when a recession hit the film industry shortly after Sony's purchase, some began to question Sony's ability to deliver its traditionally strong profits.

Sony did deliver, however, posting record earnings in 1990 of 58.2 billion yen ($384 million), a 38.5 percent increase over 1989. In 1992, Columbia Pictures and its subsidiary TriStar jointly captured 20 percent of the U.S. market share, far above the shares held by competing studios.

However, the complexities of operating a truly multinational corporation began taking their toll on Sony. Most of the world's largest economies (Europe, Japan, and the United States) were experiencing a slowdown in the early 1990s. This factor created what Sony called "an unprecedentedly challenging operating environment." Although sales in most of Sony's businesses increased in 1992, operating income dropped 44 percent to 166 billion yen ($1.2 billion). Net income increased slightly to 120 billion yen.

The ongoing appreciation of yen against most major currencies had an even more adverse effect on Sony's bottom line in 1993: net income fell a dramatic 70 percent to $36 billion yen ($313 million) on sales of 3,993 billion yen ($34.4 billion). Had the yen's value held steady at 1992 figures, Sony's net income would have totaled about 190 billion yen ($1.3 billion).

During that year, Ohga assumed the duties of chief executive in addition to his role as president. He and Morita responded to Sony's tough economic situation by bolstering marketing, reducing inventory levels, streamlining operations, and keeping a watchful control of capital investments. The company also embarked on an extensive reorganization effort with the goal of decentralizing operations and reducing unnecessary management. Despite these measures, Sony was unable to stem the slide. Net income plummeted another 50 percent in 1994 to 15 billion yen, on sales of 3,734 billion yen.

By this time Morita had relinquished virtually all his duties in the company, having suffered a stroke in late 1993. In Sony's 1994 annual report, his picture and signature were conspicuously absent from the letter to shareholders, implicitly announcing Ohga's new leadership position. Under Morita's leadership, Sony's rise to preeminence in the world consumer-electronics market was almost entirely self-achieved; Sony outperformed not only its Japanese rivals, among them associates of the former *zaibatsu* (conglomerate) companies, but also larger American firms, which by 1995 had all but abandoned the consumer-electronics market.

In the late 1980s Morita told *Business Week* that he regarded the Sony Corporation as a "venture business" for the Morita family, which had produced several generations of mayors and whose primary business remained the 300-year-old Morita & Company. Under the direction of Akio Morita's younger brother Kuzuaki, Morita & Company produced sake, soy sauce, and Ninohimatsu brand rice wine in Nagoya. The company, whose initial $500 investment in TTK was worth $430 million in 1995, owned a 9.4 percent share of Sony.

In April 1995, Ohga ascended to the chairmanship of Sony, and Morita was made an honorary chairman. The company's new president was Nobuyuki Idei, a 34-year veteran of the company, who had founded Sony's French subsidiary in 1970 and had since played a role in many of the company's major accomplishments, including audio CD technology, computer workstations, and the 8-mm video camcorder.

Sony's success had been a direct result of the wisdom of its founders, who had the talent to anticipate the demands of consumers and to develop products to meet those demands; Idei's presidency, some suggested, signalled a new era for the company.

Immediate among Idei's concerns were helping Sony become an integral player in the information highway industry. He also hoped to help the company establish an industry standard for DVDs, or digital videodisks, larger CD-like disks containing full-length films for play on television screens via videodisk players, which were becoming increasingly popular among electronics buffs. According to one writer in *Fortune* magazine, Idei also sought to "reinforce the open-minded and cooperative ideals of Sony's founders—which he calls Sony Spirit—companywide."

Principal Subsidiaries: Sony Precision Magnetics Corp., Sony Shiroshi Semiconductor Inc., Sony Digital Porducts Inc., Sony Asco Inc., Sony Finance International, Sony Music Entertainment (Japan) Inc., Sony Creative Products Inc., Sony Pictures (Japan) Inc., Sony Chemicals Corp., Sony Magnascale Inc., Sony Plaza Co. Ltd., Aiwa Co. Ltd., Sony Life Insurance Co. Ltd., Sony/Tektronix Corp., Sony Corporation of America, Sony Music Entertainment Inc. Sony Pictures Entertainment, Sony of Canada Ltd., magneticos de Mexico, S.A. de C.V., Sony Corporation of Panama S.A., Cony Comerico e Industria Ltd. (Brazil), Sony Chile Ltda., Sony de Venezuela S.A., Sony Austria GmbH, Sony Belgium N.V., Sony Nordic (Denmark), Sony France S.A. Sony Europa GmbH (Germany), Sony Production Technology Division, Sony Italia SpA, Sony Nederland B.V., Sony Portugal Limitada, Sony Espana, S.A., Sony (Schweitz) AG (Switzerland), Sony Overseas S.A. (Switzerland), Sony United Kingdom Ltd., Sony Gulf FZE (United Arab Emrites) Sony Electronics of Korea Corp., Taiwan Toyo Radio Co. Ltd., Sony Corporation of Hong Kong Ltd., Sony Magnetic Products (Thailand) Ltd., Sony (Malaysia) Sales and Service Sdn. Bhd., Sony International (Singapore) Ltd., Sony Precision Engineering Center (Singapore) Pte. Ltd., P.T. Sony Electronics Indonesia, Sony Australia Ltd., Sony New Zealand, Ltd.

Further Reading:

Landro, Luar, Ono, Yumiko, Rubinfein, Elizabeth, "A Changing Sony Aims to Own the 'Software' That Its Products Need," *Wall Street Journal,* December 30, 1988, p. 1.

Lyons, Nick. *The Sony Vision,* New York: Crown, 1976.

Morita, Akio. *Made in Japan, Akio Morita and Sony,* New York: Dutton, 1986.

"Media Colossus: Sony Is Out To Be the World's One-Stop Shop for Entertainment," *Business Week*, March 25, 1991, p. 64.

Schlender, Brent, "Sony's New President: Here's the Plan, *Fortune,* April 17, 1995, pp. 18–19.

—updated by Maura Troester

Starter Corp.

370 James Street
New Haven, Connecticut 06513
U.S.A.
(203) 781-4000
fax: (203) 776-3689

Public Company
Incorporated: 1971
Employees: 619
Sales: $282.7 million
Stock Exchanges: New York
SICs: 2329 Men's/Boys' Clothing Not Elsewhere Classified;
  2339 Women's/Misses Outerwear Not Elsewhere
  Classified; 3089 Plastics Products Not Elsewhere
  Classified

Starter Corp. designs, manufactures, and markets insignia clothing for professional athletic organizations and retail markets. Known as a "pioneer in the fusion of fashion with athletic clothing," Starter holds the top share of the $7 billion licensed sports apparel market. Its licensed sports apparel division is divided into two lines: "official apparel" which incorporates the names and logos of teams in the National Basketball Association, the National Football League, the National Hockey League, and over 150 colleges and universities; and "authentic apparel," which is a virtual copy of the clothing worn by professional players and coaches during games. The company recently ventured into the highly competitive sportswear market, taking on giants such as Champion, Inc. with a line of basic athletic clothing, casual sportswear, non-athletic footwear and young men's fashion. Starter goods are sold through sporting goods stores, specialty stores and department stores. The majority of its sales are in North America; however, the company has recently expanded into Europe and South East Asia and plans to increase its presence in both regions.

Starter was founded in 1971 by David A. Beckerman, a former basketball player for Southern Connecticut State University, to manufacture team uniforms for high school athletic programs. In 1976, the company entered into non-exclusive licensing agreement with a number of professional sports league, paying royalties of eight to ten percent for the right to manufacture and market copies of professional athletic apparel. Its first retail product was a line of jackets emblazoned with the insignias of Major League Baseball teams. Soon the company expanded its licensed apparel line to include into headgear, activewear and accessories. In 1979, the company became one of the first licensees to supply clothing worn on the field by professional teams through an agreement to manufacture satin jackets for players on Major League baseball teams. Starter incorporated this design into streetwear, and was, in the words of *Business Week* reporter Tim Smart, the "first to make team jackets out of satin, instead of the usual cheap nylon."

Attention to quality drove Starter's tremendous growth in the 1980s. By 1983, the company had entered licensing agreements with the National Basketball Association, the Canadian Football League, the National Football League, and the National Hockey League. As coverage of national sports leagues on cable television expanded, Starter's bright, flashy team jackets became status symbols among kids. But the company's growth during this decade can also be attributed to an aggressive marketing strategy. Not only had the company made licensed sports apparel a fashion status symbol, it also created brand loyalty by making its "S and Star" logo a prominent part of the apparel's design. Starter innovatively placed its embroidered logo on jacket sleeves and on the back of baseball caps. Often, when people wore their baseball hats backwards, a person saw the Starter logo before they even saw the insignia of the team it represented.

Behind the company's marketing program was the desire to represent a connection between the fan and the team, and then, according to Starter's 1993 annual report, "translate the fans' enthusiasm for sports into a demand for sports-related products." To this end, Starter sought maximum exposure on the field, and in the locker rooms. In 1986, the company became the first to create NBA locker room t-shirts, first worn on television by the Boston Celtics, and later worn by millions of kids across the United States and Canada. In a similar way, Starter won a contract to create the parkas that coaches wore on NFL sidelines. For the retail market, Starter designed the "breakaway jacket," a pullover jacket that closely resembled the coach's parka and soon became an important wardrobe element of fashion conscious teenagers. The rage for Starter clothing was so strong that some children owned as many as 20 baseball caps; others would pay over $150 for a Starter jacket. Sales in 1989 were $58.9 million. By 1990, they had more than doubled to $124.6 million.

Starter also aggressively pursued "promotional exposure," cultivating relationships with players, managers, and coaches in all sports in order to enhance the company's image as an authentic sportswear manufacturer. In 1991 it launched the "Starter Tip-off Classic," a college basketball exhibition game benefitting the Basketball Hall of Fame. On the non-athletic front, the company secured placements of its clothing on popular television shows such as *The Fresh Price of Bel Air, Seinfeld, In Living Color,* and *Roseanne,* and in the films *Sleepless in Seattle* and *White Men Can't Jump.* Using sports figures such as Florence Griffith Joyner, Don Shula, and Emmitt Smith, Starter advertised heavily on the ESPN sports channel and MTV, as well as in trade publications, magazines, newspapers, and outdoor advertising.

Within two years, Starter's net sales nearly doubled to $356 million. The company went public on the New York Stock Exchange in April of 1993, earning an estimated $98 million. Profits increased 24 percent in its first period after going public, and stock prices leapt from $21 to $28 dollars a share before stabilizing around $24 a share. Proceeds from the initial pubic offering were used to expand sales to Europe and the Pacific Rim and also to launch ''Brand Starter,'' the company's own sportswear line minus team logos. ''We built the brand alongside of the team logos and now our awareness is up dramatically,'' said Beckerman in 1993. Capitalizing on the high recognizability of its name, Starter went head-to-head against such formidable brands as Champion and Russell. Basic athletic clothing was offered under the name Starter Sport, casual active clothing was marketed under the name S2, young men's fashion was introduced under the brand name Flipside, and a line of non-athletic footwear was launched under the name Rugged Terrain. Retail prices ranged from $12.99 for headgear to $200 for a vintage style jacket.

Brand Starter was launched in February 1993, supported by a $10 million national television advertising campaign and a $2 million bus and shelter advertising campaign in 12 to 14 metro markets. The $10 million TV campaign was geared to the youth market. Styled after music videos and highlighting the lives of well known athletes, the campaigns narrate the inspirational tales of Emmitt Smith and Karl Malone, athletes who were once told they would fail, yet ultimately achieved tremendous success. ''This business is about selling fantasy,'' Stuart Crystal told *Brandweek* in 1993, ''If you put on the jacket Dennis Eckersley wore, you can share his dreams and build your own.'' Other campaigns relied heavily on celebrity spokespeople such as college basketball star Christian Laettner, MTV veejay Karen ''Duff'' Duffy, and NFL player Doug Flutie (for ads airing on the East Coast and Canada). In its first year, Brand Starter netted sales of nearly $30 million.

Starter also strengthened its international distribution network in 1993, covering over 25 countries in North America, Europe, and the Pacific Rim. Promotional exposure in Europe and Asia was gained through sponsoring exhibition games such as the McDonald's Open basketball series in Europe and the NFL's American Bowl in Japan and Europe. In a move to further strengthen its European market position, Starter signed licensing agreements with the Juventus and Manchester United soccer teams of Italy and England, as well as the D.E.G. hockey team of Germany and the Australian Football League. All of this was supported by advertising on the Eurosport and MTV Europe networks. In North America, Starter continued expanding its professional sports apparel line, supplying outerwear to the Toronto Blue Jays and Philadelphia Phillies during the 1993 World Series. 1993 sales totaled $356 million, up 26 percent over 1992.

Starter's competition in the licensed sports apparel business intensified in 1994 when Logo 7 Inc., the number two licensed sports apparel manufacturer, won a much coveted NFL Pro Line license and beefed up its advertising budget in an attempt to knock Starter from its number one position. Overall, the boom in the licensed sports apparel market began to slacken in early 1994, slowing from an average of 38 percent annual growth to 15 percent annual growth. Starter moved into new markets with its licensed sports apparel, focusing on sales to young children and youth, and signed a new contract to manufacture the Center Ice Jersey for the National Hockey League. The company purchased a retail chain, First Pick Stores, for $5 million of new stock in March of 1994, and also established a Hong Kong office to better coordinate relations with manufactures. Beckerman stepped down as president, although he retained the posts of chairman and chief executive. John Tucker, former president and chief executive of a sporting goods and sportswear concern, assumed the position of president.

Although Starter began 1994 with a 23 percent increase over the first quarter 1993, it suffered a loss of $2.2 million in the second quarter. Second quarter 1994 sales were flat: $57.8 million, slightly lower than second quarter sales from 1992. Starter had predicted the loss, which it blamed on late deliveries from vendors, shipping delays to retailers, additional advertising and personnel costs, as well as start-up costs for a new Memphis distribution facility. Despite the licensed sports apparel slump, Starter seems to be in a healthy position for future growth. Management seems cognizant of the fact that the licensed apparel market is saturated, and its move to sell its own sportswear line is perhaps a proactive moved based on that understanding. Its decision to closely control manufacturing relations and to diversify its holdings into the retail arena can be taken as a healthy sign that Starter is ready to move from a maverick seller of trendy clothing into an established apparel manufacturer.

Further Reading:

David, Gregory E., ''Starter Corp.: The Perils of Fashion,'' *Financial World,* January 4, 1994, p. 19.
Gaffney, Andrew, and Greg Pesky, ''The SGB Interview: David Beckerman, President and CEO, Starter Corp.'' *Sporting Goods Business,* July 1994, p. 62–63.
Lefton, Terry, ''Starter Throws Its Own Hat into Branded Apparel Ring,'' *Brandweek,* June 21, 1993, p. 23.
Smart, Tim, and Irene Recio, ''A Sportswear House with Major-League Dreams,'' *Business Week,* April 5, 1993, p. 62.

—Maura Troester

Sun Distributors L.P.

1 Logan Square
Philadelphia, Pennsylvania 19103
U.S.A.
(215) 665-3650
Fax: (215) 665-3662

Public Company
Incorporated: 1987
Employees: 3,600
Sales: $612 million
Stock Exchanges: New York
SICs: 5084 Industrial Machinery & Equipment; 5039
   Construction Materials, Not Elsewhere Classified; 6719
   Holding Companies, Not Elsewhere Classified

Sun Distributors L.P. is a leading industrial distribution firm. The company sells more than 100,000 products and related services in three main areas of operation: fluid power, glass, and maintenance items. Sun's customers are located throughout the United States, Canada, and Mexico. Founded as a subsidiary of an oil company, the company was spun off into a limited partnership in the late 1980s, commencing a period of strong growth through acquisitions of other businesses in its industry.

Sun got its start in 1975, when the Sun Company, Inc., an oil company perhaps best known for its Sunoco gas stations, purchased a distributing business, which supplied equipment and other materials to a wide variety of industrial customers. With this move, Sun hoped to create a financial counter-balance to its highly cyclical petroleum businesses. Sun established Sun Distributors as a subsidiary, and the company began to acquire other properties in the distribution field.

In entering the distribution field, Sun moved into an industry in a state of flux. In the years before World War II, most industrial distribution businesses had emerged as very small "mom and pop" organizations, which resold equipment to a very small segment of one industry. Because they were tied to the single narrow market that they served, distributors saw their financial fates rise and fall with those of their customers. In the wake of World War II, however, many of these businesses started to grow and diversify their product offerings and target customer bases. With time, larger companies started to buy up smaller ones, as the industry consolidated, and Sun became part of that process.

In August 1976, Sun bought Walter Norris, a distributor of hydraulic and pneumatic controls. During this time, the company also announced that it would acquire Kar Products, Inc., a distributor of fastening systems. This purchase was completed in February 1977, when Sun paid $31.5 million for the property. In November of that year, Sun paid $10 million for Unibraze. At the end of 1977, Sun had sales of $20 million.

Sun's steady string of acquisitions continued in March 1978, when the company paid $3.6 million for the Atlas Screw & Specialty company. At the end of that year, Sun also bought the J.N. Fauver Company, a Canadian enterprise in the fluid power field.

In putting together a group of different companies, Sun sought to become a major player in the "value-added reseller" field, making the parts it provided to manufacturers more valuable and competitive through the level of service that went along with them. Traditionally, competitors in the distribution business had focused on price as the sole selling point for their goods, and the only way in which one company was differentiated from another. As manufacturing became more complex, however, the demands that customers made upon distributors also became more sophisticated, and service, which allowed industrial customers to work more effectively and efficiently, became just as important as price.

Although the products that Sun offered were relatively commonplace, the level of expertise that the company's various subsidiaries offered in addition to the parts themselves helped the company's offerings stand out in the marketplace. "They take over activities or functions performed by either the manufacturer or the customer and charge for them," one industry analyst explained to *Forbes*. In this way, Sun's operations strived to bridge the gap between the manufacturing economy and the service economy.

Sun continued to grow through acquisitions and diversify its operations in the early 1980s. In 1981, the company purchased the Special-T-Metals Company of Lawrence, Kansas. In late May 1985, Sun bought the Keathley-Patterson Electric Company, Inc.

By 1985, Sun Distributors had come to account for three percent of its parent company's revenues. In the following year, the Sun oil company decided to sell off its non-energy businesses, and the company announced that it was seeking a buyer for Sun Distributors in the late spring of 1986. Shortly after that, Sun augmented its holdings again, when the company bought the Air Draulics Company.

In August 1986, Sun announced that it would sell off its distributor business to a group of the subsidiary's executives, who joined with the investment bank Shearson Lehman Brothers to purchase the company in a leveraged buyout. In October, Shearson Lehman Brothers Holdings, Inc. bought Sun Distributor's capital stock for $199 million.

At that time, Sun also withdrew from one of the market segments in which it had been operating at a loss. The company sold its pipe and steel business, the Federal Pipe and Steel Corporation, taking a $1.5 million pretax loss in the process.

After Sun Distributors was acquired by Shearson Lehman Brothers, in January 1987, the company was reorganized as a master limited partnership. Shearson reportedly chose this corporate structure to take advantage of a temporary loophole in tax laws. At the time, tax rates for individuals were much lower than those for corporations. By setting up Sun Distributors as a master limited partnership, the investment bank enabled investors to apply losses against the company's profits, a practice otherwise impossible as a conventional corporation. At the end of ten years, Sun would be required to convert to a regular corporation and start paying corporate income taxes, or be sold.

In February 1987, all but one percent of the operating partnership of Sun Distributors was sold, in units priced at $10 each. Each unit consisted on one share of class A stock and one share of class B stock. Roughly 40 thousand of these units, or a quarter of the equity shares, were held by Sun's management, and more than ten million were sold to the general public. Because of Sun's status as a master limited partnership, and its two-tiered structure of stock offerings, investing in Sun became a complicated process for many potential stockholders.

Nevertheless, in the wake of its successful stock offering, Sun once again began to acquire companies. In July 1987, the company purchased the Warren Engineering Corporation, and by the end of the year, Sun's annual revenues had risen to $426 million, which generated nearly $19 million of operating income. However, because of costs associated with its separation for its parent company, and its establishment as a master limited partnership and initial offering of stock, the company posted a loss for the year of $6.6 million.

In February 1988, Sun also purchased the assets of Glass Related Products, Inc. By this time, Sun's string of acquisitions had made it one of the ten largest industrial distributors in the country. The company sought out entrepreneurial enterprises with strong management that put an emphasis on customer service. In addition, Sun had focused its activities on four fields: electrical supplies, such as light fixtures and cables; fluid power equipment for pneumatic and hydraulic systems; glass materials, for cars and mirrors; and maintenance products, such as cleaners, chemicals, nuts, and bolts. Within these areas, which encompassed 15 subsidiaries, Sun sold more than 100,000 different products.

Sun's customers ranged from original equipment manufacturers and users of replacement parts, to construction firms and maintenance companies. Increasingly, in the late 1980s, these operations turned to "just-in-time" processes, a more efficient method of manufacturing which sought to reduce the amount of money spent on inventory and replacement parts. In order to implement just-in-time processes, manufacturers relied on quick delivery of parts and special services. This created a market niche for Sun to fill, and the company worked to develop the capacity to make specialized production runs at short notice. Big manufacturers, Sun's chairperson, Donald Marshall, explained to Forbes, "can't make a pump and a motor with 20 valves out of 1,000 coming out sideways. They can't have salesmen running down to St. Joe to make a call on a guy who's going to spend $1,000 a year or wants a little design help. This creates an opening for us." All in all, Sun sought to sell the engineering and repair services that made its products better than those of its competitors.

Although, on the whole, Sun's strategy proved effective, there were some areas of operation that proved weak. For instance, the company found it difficult to make a profit on its sales of electrical supplies, and was also struggling in the sheet glass market, where it was consistently undercut by low-cost competitors. In an effort to alleviate this problem, Sun cut back on its operations in this area, concentrating instead on tinted, beveled, or mirrored glass. As part of this process, Sun purchased Glass Related Products, Inc., in February 1988.

In managing its constellation of 15 subsidiaries, Sun adopted a hands-off approach. Because the company only sought to buy well-managed companies, it refrained from tampering with operations that were doing well already. Instead, Sun provided capital for expansion and expertise in the systems needed to run a distribution business. Because of this low-interference policy, Sun was able to keep the size of its central headquarters staff quite low, and the company was overseen from Philadelphia by just 13 people: the company's chairman, four vice-presidents, four accountants, and four secretaries. Each of Sun's four operating groups was administered by a vice-president, accountant, and secretary.

To further emphasize the decentralized structure of Sun's corporate philosophy, managers of the company's subsidiaries were not summoned to Philadelphia to report to their superiors, but were visited at the site of their businesses by the company's president, who spent more than half of his year on the road. According to The Service Edge: 101 Companies that Profit from Customer Care, a book in which Sun Distributors was featured, Marshall told one Philadelphia business magazine that "behind our nearly half-billion in annual sales are thousands of employees who've built years-long relationships with thousands of customers. The surest way to destroy all of that would be for corporate-level staff to travel out there imposing a 'generic' model of the distribution business on each of the divisions."

After establishing its corporate independence and raising capital through its stock offering, Sun moved aggressively to further expand its business through the acquisition of successful companies in its four areas of concentration. In 1988, Sun purchased the Gem City Electric Company, Air-Dreco, Inc., E & B Electric Supply, Inc., and E & B Electric Supply of Crosset, Inc. Over the next two years, Sun also acquired the A & H Bolt and Nut Company, Limited, Edwards Engineering Corporation, and Industrial Air and Hydraulics, Inc. In July 1990, Sun divested itself of an asset, selling the property of the Atlas Screw & Specialty Company. As a result of its steady growth through mergers with small suppliers, Sun's revenues had grown to exceed $500 million by the time the company entered the 1990s.

At the start of the 1990s, however, Sun confronted a sharp drop in demand for many of the products it offered, as the industries it served felt the effects of economic recession. In response to these conditions, the company embarked upon a two-year program of cutting costs, adjusting the size of its operations, and maximizing its assets.

In addition, the company continued to make strategic acquisitions. In 1991, Sun purchased Hydra Power Systems, Rogers Wholesale Electric, Inc., and Activation, Inc. The following year, Sun's leaders sought to renegotiate the debt that the company had amassed through its acquisition spree and agreed to a moratorium on further acquisitions for the next two years.

By 1992, Sun's expectations for market recovery had proved overly optimistic. Therefore, management reassessed its plans and shifted the company's focus, in hopes of promoting further growth. Specifically, the company decided to become more proactive in seeking growth, rather than responding to fluctuating conditions within the market as a whole. Accordingly, Sun made some major changes in its traditional operations. In 1992, the company changed the way it paid presidents of its subsidiaries, setting up incentive programs for meeting sales goals. In addition, the company's headquarters staff became more involved in running the operations of its previously highly independent subsidiaries, to the extent that some operations were combined. Finally, Sun replaced the leaders of four troubled units, bringing in new managers.

In September 1992, frustrated by the restrictions imposed by the company's high debt load, and the financial constraints of its status as a master limited partnership, Sun's management announced that it had hired financial advisors to explore ways that the company's value could best be maximized. The options under consideration included a restructuring of the company, sale of certain selected assets, or liquidation of the entire company. The announcement that this process was being undertaken contributed immediately to a rise in the price of the company's stock.

By the start of 1993, Sun's efforts to restructure had helped to contribute to a record of steady growth. Net profits had grown 14 percent a year for the last five years, despite the fact that sales had only increased by six percent. Although the company's sales flattened somewhat in the first half of 1993, and earnings dipped, Sun's fortunes had revived by the end of the year, and sales reached $656 million, a new high. The company's managers attributed this growth to a re-emphasis on service and the exploration of new markets, a necessary alternative to growth through acquisition, banned until 1995.

Sun's returns remained strong in the first half of 1994, as innovative operations, like repair centers in the company's fluid power group, made strong contributions. In the fall of 1994, Sun announced that it had completed the process of internal re-evaluation of its assets and options. The company's managers stated that they had decided not to liquidate Sun's assets, but to shift the company's emphasis somewhat, shedding operations in one of its four main business areas. In October, the company announced that it would sell its three electrical group divisions, long a source of poor returns. The concerns to be sold included the American Electric Company, the Keathley-Patterson Electric Company, and Philips & Company. Sun also divested itself of Dorman Products, a subsidiary of its maintenance group.

With the proceeds of the this sale, which totaled $73 million, the company planned to pay down debts and finance further acquisitions. Sun also hoped to move away from the period of financial stricture which had governed its operations in the early 1990s. In November 1994, Sun appointed a new president and executive vice-president, John McDonnell, as the company readied itself for an aggressive policy of expansion in its remaining core businesses: fluid power, glass, and maintenance. "Our strategy has been to acquire well-managed distributors where the present ownership has reached an age to go on to retirement, or on to something else, and there is no apparent succession in the family," McDonnell told the *Philadelphia Enquirer.*

In addition, Sun planned to step up its burgeoning operations in Mexico. The company did a brisk business supplying manufacturing plants that had sprung up just over the border, and also planned to begin operations in central Mexico. As Sun moved into the late 1990s, its three remaining operating units appeared strong, and its status as a major player in the distribution field appeared secure.

Principal Subsidiaries: S.D.I. Operating Partners, L.P.

Further Reading:

Byrnes, Nanette, "Sun Distributors B: Out of the Partnership Trap," *FW,* October 12, 1993, p. 18.

Simon, Ruth, "We Sell Service, Not Products," *Forbes,* March 7, 1988, p. 98.

"The Man Behind the Power Is in the President's Chair," *Philadelphia Enquirer,* December 5, 1994.

Zemke, Ron, *The Service Edge: 101 Companies that Profit from Customer Care,* pp. 486–88.

—Elizabeth Rourke

Swedish Match S.A.

P.O. Box 222
Chemin du Canal 5
CH-1260 Nyon 1
Switzerland
(41) 22 363 93 93
Fax: (41) 22 363 9191

Holding Company
Founded: 1917 as The Swedish Match Company
Employees: 25,600
Sales: $1.3 billion
SICs: 2434 Wood Kitchen Cabinets; 2819 Industrial
    Inorganic Chemicals Not Elsewhere Classified; 3996 Hard
    Surface Floor Coverings; 3999 Manufacturing Industries

Based in Stockholm, Swedish Match S.A. is a leading global manufacturer of matches, disposable cigarette lighters, floor coverings, cabinets, doors, and packaging materials. During the early 1900s Swedish Match became one of the first companies to achieve a truly global presence. The company employed more than 25,000 workers around the world in the early 1990s and garnered more than two-thirds of its revenues from international operations.

Swedish Match was founded by Ivar Kreuger, an internationally renowned industrial magnate and a controversial figure who was regarded as a scoundrel by some. Kreuger was born in 1880 in Kalmar, a city in southern Sweden. His family owned and operated a match factory that had been started by Ivar's grandfather. The match industry was relatively young at the time that Ivar's grandfather started the business. Matches had been produced commercially only since the early 1800s, but a large market had developed since matches were commonly used at that time to light kerosene lamps and gas stoves. By the late 1800s the Swedish match industry was employing 7,000 workers and producing about 40,000 tons of matches annually.

The early Swedish match industry was dependent on international suppliers and buyers. Aspen wood, for example, was supplied primarily by Russia. Chemicals like potassium chlorate, phosphorus, and paraffin were purchased mostly from Great Britain and Germany. Likewise, Germany and England were the greatest export markets for Swedish matches. In fact, Sweden exported about 85 percent of the matches it produced. World War I disturbed the import and export dynamics because

supplies were cut and some countries imposed restrictive trade barriers. Nevertheless, by the time Ivar Kreuger entered the business the foundation for his international empire had been laid.

When Ivar Kreuger began his operations in the early 1910s, Sweden had assumed a global leadership role in the match industry. That lead was largely attributable to technological breakthroughs. In 1884 Gustaf Eric Pasch of the Swedish Royal Academy of Science invented the safety match. It utilized red phosphorus (instead of more toxic yellow phosphorus), which was applied to a striking surface rather than the match head. The result was a much safer match. Early match-making machines had emerged as well.

Kreuger exhibited little interest in his family's enterprise as a young man. His business cunning and penchant for overseas adventure, however, were evident from an early age. As a boy Kreuger stole final term papers from the principal's office and sold copies to students for the equivalent of five cents apiece. After his schooling, in which he studied engineering, Ivar traveled the globe, taking jobs in South Africa, Canada, Germany, and the United States. His brother, meanwhile, operated the family's struggling match business. Unfortunately, the match industry at the time suffered from the growing popularity of electric lighting at the time. Only the cigarette smoker market, a major purchaser of matches, prevented further damage to the industry.

Kreuger returned to Sweden when he was 28 years old. He and a fellow engineer, Paul Toll, started a real estate and construction company. Kreuger & Toll was successful, but Kreuger was soon sidetracked by opportunities related to the family business.

The Swedish match industry was highly consolidated by that time. One giant company, Jonkoping & Vulcan, controlled 75 percent of the market and the Kreugers were one of a few small players still competing. Kreuger was intrigued by the challenge of overcoming Jonkoping's dominance. But he also had greater designs—he believed that he could parlay Sweden's technological advantages into global dominance of the match industry.

Kreuger's business savvy, although ethically questionable, was undeniable. During the early 1910s he managed to bring together most of the remaining Swedish match companies, including his family's, into a single organization called United Match Factories. Kreuger artificially inflated the value of United, making it look as though his company had much more capital that it actually possessed. He used that artificial value to back his takeover of Jonkoping in 1917, thus effectively establishing a monopoly in his home country. When World War I ended a year later, he shifted the focus of his newly formed holding company, The Swedish Match Company, to the European mainland.

During the 1920s Kreuger embarked on an aggressive acquisition campaign, striking deals and snapping up match factories all over Europe. Although his business acumen was revered at the time, his bid for industry dominance would later earn him a reputation for chicanery. For example, it was discovered that he sent secret agents to companies in which he had an interest. The undercover proxies made extremely low offers to buy the enterprises. Kreuger followed these agents in and offered a higher—though still low—price. The practice allowed him to snag new factories at deflated prices. In addition, he often secretly purchased interests in competitors in an effort to avoid national restrictions related to monopolies and foreign ownership.

By the late 1920s the industrious Kreuger had amassed a huge match manufacturing network. He controlled a significant share of the match business in Hungary, Yugoslavia, and other East European countries and acquired major stakes in leading British and American match companies. Kreuger also built new factories in countries like India. More importantly, Swedish Match effectively claimed control of the match industries in Norway, Denmark, Holland, Finland, and Switzerland. The company also diversified into other business areas during this time. By the end of the 1920s, in fact, Kreuger controlled a telecommunications company, a pulp and paper enterprise, and a mining company that owned the third largest gold deposit in the world.

Kreuger's empire churned out 2.8 million cases of matches annually by 1929, making up about 40 percent of total world match output. But leadership in the match industry was only part of the Swedish Match story to that point, for Ivar Kreuger's international reputation grew significantly after the conclusion of World War I. Kreuger used part of his massive fortune to make loans to needy national governments battered by the war. Although many of the loans were used to secure permission for Swedish Match to develop a monopoly in the borrower's country, Kreuger's post-war lending to financially troubled governments was viewed by many as magnanimous. By 1930 Kreuger had doled out more than $350 million in loans to a dozen different countries.

In less than a decade, Kreuger had built one of the largest international companies ever created. His business acumen had achieved legendary status. Hundreds of millions of dollars flowed through his diverse holdings of companies, which were organized under four divisions: Swedish Match; Kreuger & Toll; International Match (New York); and Continental Investment (Liechtenstein). Kreuger's enviable reputation as a socially conscious business leader continued to grow, particularly after he made a celebrated $30 million loan to Germany to help it pay war reparations. That move earned him the title of "the savior of Europe" from some politicians at the time.

Kreuger shocked the global financial community when he shot and killed himself on March 12, 1932. His suicide in his Paris bachelor apartment capped the end of his two-year effort to keep his collapsing empire glued together. The previously hidden weaknesses of Kreuger's mammoth enterprise were exposed following the global financial meltdown spurred by stock market crashes around the world. As the value of his companies plunged, Kreuger's personal liabilities ballooned past the $250 million mark and his companies were unable to meet their obligations. Kreuger took desperate measures, even going so far as to forge $142 million worth of Italian government bonds and promissory notes. Kreuger himself forged the signatures needed on the notes, but misspelled the names. The ruse failed and Kreuger's reputation was damaged.

It was later discovered that Kreuger's dynasty was built partially on overvalued assets and deceptive accounting practices. Although his business acumen was undeniable, Kreuger had consistently engaged in questionable reporting practices in an effort to expand his holding company. "Throughout his bizarre career," wrote Robert Shaplen, author of the 1960 biography *Kreuger,* "Kreuger alone supplied the figures for the books of his various companies, and he mostly kept them in his head." Backing that assertion was Allen Churchill's *The Incredible Ivar Kreuger,* who noted that a former secretary of Kreuger's claimed that Kreuger once dictated the text of the annual reports for his four companies in a single afternoon—"I accounted for it by the fact that I had often been told that he was a genius," she explained.

To Kreuger's credit, he was a highly intelligent business man and financier. Many of his defenders contend that, while his dealings may appear shady in retrospect, at the time many of his activities were representative of the norm. Shaplen's biography related the following excerpt from a statement made by Kreuger to Bjorn Prytz, a Swedish tycoon and diplomat: "In olden times, the princes and everyone would go to confession because it was the thing to do, whether they believed it or not. Today the world demands balance sheets, profit-and-loss statements once a year. But if you're really working on great ideas, you can't supply these on schedule and expose yourself to view. You've got to tell the public something, and so long as it's satisfied and continues to have faith in you, it's really not important what you confess."

Teams of attorneys, bankers, and accountants labored for four years sorting out Kreuger's affairs and divvying up the remains of his companies after his death. The Price, Waterhouse accounting firm finally calculated that Kreuger had inflated the earnings of his companies by more than $250 million between 1917 and 1932. Millions of dollars were never accounted for, and Ivar's brother, Tortsen, was sent to jail for one and a half years. After his release, Tortsen spent much of the remainder of his life trying to prove that Ivar was murdered. Tortsen's story fell on deaf ears and the company was wrested from Kreuger-family control.

The Wallenberg family of Sweden came to the rescue of Swedish Match. In an agreement that involved a transfer of $15 million from Stockholm to New York, Jacob Wallenberg was able to gain control of the injured enterprise. The company lost its monopoly contracts with foreign governments and was diminished in size and strength. Nevertheless, Kreuger had amassed massive holdings in the match industry that allowed Swedish Match to sustain its market leadership.

Following World War II and throughout the mid-1900s, Swedish Match tried to expand its match business. Swedish Match purchased the Cricket disposable cigarette lighter division of Gilette in the mid-1980s, a purchase that—combined with its own Feudor and Poppell lighter brands—gave Swedish Match a hefty 15 percent of that global market. The company's entrance into the cigarette lighter business illustrated how much Swedish Match had changed since Kreuger's reign. Indeed, in an effort to squelch competition from lighter manufacturers, Kreuger had succeeded in getting some countries to ban the use of lighters in public—those laws lingered on the books for several years in a few nations.

By the late 1980s matches made up less than 25 percent of Swedish Match's global sales. Still, the company remained the largest manufacturer of matches in the world and continued to improve its position in the world market. In 1980, for example, Swedish Match bought out Universal Match, the largest producer of matches in the United States. In 1987 it acquired Britain's second-largest match manufacturer, Wilkinson Sword. The latter purchase gave Swedish Match control of a leading 25 percent world match markets. Going into the early 1990s, Swedish Match employed more than 25,000 workers globally and generated annual revenues of more than $17 million, about $250 million of which were attributable to U.S. sales.

The company also diversified into several other arenas. Swedish Match company purchased Tarkett, making it the second largest manufacture of floor coverings in the world by the late 1980s. Swedish Match also acquired cabinet makers Marbodal and HTH, and door maker Sweedor, which made it the biggest producer of doors in Sweden. Other acquisitions included forays into packaging material and razor blade industries.

In 1988, Swedish Match was acquired by Stora Kopparbergs Bergslags AB, a diversified company and among the largest forestry companies in Europe. Stora reportedly paid SKr 5.9 billion for Swedish Match, in its efforts to enhance its line of raw materials with consumer products businesses. Stora's parentage was short-lived, however, as Swedish Match was sold to Volvo in 1990. As Swedish Match entered the mid-1990s, another change of ownership seemed imminent, as Barings Bank plc entered final negotiations to purchase Swedish Match in 1995.

Further Reading:

Abrose, Jules, "Swedish Match Again Strikes Out in New Directions," *International Management,* October 1987, pp. 87–90.

Hassbring, Lars, *The International Development of the Swedish Match Company, 1917–1924,* Stockholm: Swedish Match Company, 1979.

Kapstein, Jonathan, and Charles Gaffney, "Peter Wallenberg is Rebuilding a Dynasty," *Business Week,* November 2, 1987, pp. 158–159.

Loeffelhyolz, Suzanne, "Global Report: Fore Products—Outside Looking In," *Financial World,* February 20, 1990, pp. 66–67.

Moskowitz, Milton, *The Global Marketplace,* New York: Macmillan, 1987.

Wikander, Ulla, *Kreuger's Match Monopolies, 1925–1930,* Stockholm: Swedish Match Company, 1980.

—Dave Mote

Synovus Financial Corp.

P.O. Box 120
Columbus, Georgia 31902-0129
U.S.A.
(706) 649-5220
Fax: (706) 649-2342

Public Company
Incorporated: 1972
Employees: 5,300
Total Assets: $7.3 billion
Stock Exchanges: New York
SICs: 6021 National Commercial Banks; 6022 State
   Commercial Banks; 6211 Securities Brokers and Dealers;
   6712 Bank Holding Companies

Synovus Financial Corp. is a major bank holding company with banking operations in Georgia, Florida, and Alabama. In addition to operating more than 30 community banks, Synovus is a leading provider of diversified financial services through its fee-based subsidiary, Total System Services, Inc. Synovus achieved stellar growth throughout the 1980s and early 1990s, increasing its assets more than seven-fold to $7.3 billion.

Columbus Bank and Trust, a relatively small regional institution headquartered in Columbus, Georgia, changed its structure to a bank holding company to take advantage of new state and federal laws related to the banking industry in the early 1970s. Columbus Bank and Trust created CB&T Bancshares as a subsidiary in 1972. Through Synovus, Columbus could expand its operations more easily within the state of Georgia. It could also begin participating in a number of non-banking-related financial markets.

Prior to the formation of Synovus, James W. Blanchard led Columbus Bank and Trust. He was highly regarded by his fellow managers and employees. Under Blanchard's guidance, Columbus's assets more than tripled between the late 1950s and late 1960s. Blanchard, unfortunately, died of lung cancer in 1969, leaving the bank without a chief executive. Columbus had a seasoned banking staff from which it could have drawn Blanchard's successor, but the bank's board hired Blanchard's son, James H. (Jimmy) Blanchard. The board's decision was startling because the younger Blanchard was only 28 years old and a practicing attorney with no banking experience. "We already had executives who knew banking, but what we needed

was dynamic leadership," said Synovus chairman William B. Turner in *Georgia Trend.* "We had watched Jimmy grow up; we had seen his success at school. He was a very, very capable, involved person who we felt would make a good choice."

Doubting his ability to lead Columbus, Blanchard rejected the bank's offer. But three months later, realizing that it was a tremendous opportunity, he changed his mind. "I wouldn't have been asked to do it if my last name had not been Blanchard," he told *Georgia Trend.* "It was a radical decision. I wasn't really equipped to do it. But I decided to do it, and I'm glad I did." Blanchard took Columbus's helm in 1970 and spent several years getting acclimated to the industry and environment at Columbus.

Although Blanchard lacked banking experience, he later considered that deficiency an advantage because his mind was more open to emerging opportunities. "I think not being a banker was a real plus," he said in *Forbes.* An example of Blanchard's enlightened opportunism was his interest in fee-based financial services. Blanchard's intrigue with fee-based financial services was piqued in 1974 when a Florida banker told him about the huge fees he was having to pay for credit card processing. Blanchard thought Columbus could combine its computerized operations (that it had installed in 1966) with the advancements in telecommunications that were occurring at the time, to provide credit card processing and other services. Moreover, because Columbus had access to inexpensive labor, Blanchard thought that Columbus could undercut the competition and still enjoy large profit margins. Under Blanchard's direction, Synovus was among the first banks to enter the financial services boom that would proliferate throughout the 1980s and early 1990s.

By the late 1970s Synovus had become a regional bank holding company with more than $500 million in assets and annual income of about $5 million. Although Synovus had established itself as a major player in its core regional markets, during the next decade the holding company would far exceed the pace of growth it had achieved in any previous period. The expansion would result largely from continued state and federal deregulation. Notably, the legislation Congress passed in the mid 1980s that allowed holding companies like Synovus to begin expanding their operations across state lines. More importantly, though, Synovus's keen and aggressive management would help it to overcome many of its peers, making it one of the fastest growing banks and financial service providers in the nation.

Synovus launched an ambitious growth program in 1983 when it acquired one banking systems in Florida and two in Georgia: Buena Vista Loan & Savings (Florida); Bank of Hazlehurst; and Citizens Bank & Trust, a relatively large banking chain based in Carrollton. In 1984, Synovus added just one institution, Citizens Bank of Colquitt, Georgia. That acquisition boosted Synovus's asset base to nearly $1 billion and its annual net income to nearly $12 million.

Augmenting the company's profits during that period was its subsidiary, Total System Services, Inc. Synovus had spun off its growing financial services operations in 1983, creating Total System Services. As a part of Columbus, Total System had generated fees of about $15 million in 1982, but by 1985 and as a subsidiary Total System had sales of $28 million, of which $4.3 million was netted as profit.

Blanchard increased Synovus's expansion effort in 1985, and acquired a total of seven new Georgia-based banks. During 1986 and 1987 the company acquired six more institutions, bringing its total asset base going into 1988 to nearly $2 billion. Furthermore, following interstate banking deregulation, Synovus bought three Florida banks in 1988, and two Alabama banks and one more Georgia institution in 1989. As a result of its aggressive acquisition strategy and keen management of its existing assets, Synovus's assets grew to $2.4 billion by the end of the 1980s as its net income rose to a record $31.4 million. Synovus had boosted both its holdings and profits more than four-fold since the start of the decade.

Though Synovus grew rapidly during the 1980s (and during the early 1990s), its growth reflected a dominant banking industry trend toward consolidation that had been occurring since the late 1970s. Banks had increasingly been under pressure since the late 1970s from less-regulated financial sectors that were quickly stealing market share. In an effort to compete in the competitive environment, bank holding companies had been purchasing smaller competitors. The owners and managers of those holding companies typically benefitted from economies of scale. In addition, the better managed banks were able to improve the performance of the acquisitions by restructuring their operations and improving their margins. Synovus was one of more than 1,300 bank holding companies that emerged by the end of the 1980s. It was also among the most successful.

Although Synovus's general growth strategy was reflective of overall trends, its specific tactics represented a departure from industry norms. Most bank holding companies completely integrated the banks that they acquired into the parent organization. Integrating acquisitions usually entailed changing the name of the bank and its branches to reflect the parent's name, making the bank look and feel like the other banks throughout the holding company's chain, and sometimes installing an entirely new management team. The general idea was to reduce costs, such as those related to advertising and administration, by creating an integrated chain of similar banks.

Synovus adopted a unique, decentralized approach. It allowed the banks that it purchased to retain their name and management. One result was that Synovus had higher operating costs. However, Blanchard believed that the strategy resulted in overall greater returns because the banks retained their local image and appeal. To the surprise of some critics, Synovus significantly outperformed industry averages with the strategy throughout the 1980s and early 1990s.

As Synovus swelled its asset base through merger and acquisition during the 1980s, it also continued to post solid gains with its Total System subsidiary. In fact, Total System benefitted greatly from banking industry trends during the decade. Indeed, when bank holding companies acquired new banks they were often faced with the task of processing as many as twice the number of credit card accounts that they had previously managed. Rather than scramble to expand their own processing facilities, they turned to companies like Total System, paying them a fee to service the accounts for them. At the same time, several non-banking entities sought Total System's services.

Total System's competitive advantage over similar service companies was a technical orientation. Indeed, Synovus had invested heavily in top-notch technology to make its subsidiary one of the most efficient, low-cost credit card account processors in the nation. As a result of its efforts, Total System had quickly become one of the largest contenders in that industry, second only to American Express. By 1990, Total System was processing 16 million accounts, generating fees of about $84 million annually, and capturing annual profits of nearly $12 million. It was the processor of choice for several major creditors, including General Electric Capital Corp. and Prudential. In 1990, moreover, the company scored a major victory when it landed a five-year contract to service the newly created AT&T Universal Card. Within three years that huge client added ten million new accounts and was contributing nearly 30 percent of Total System's entire revenue base.

After achieving growth during the 1980s, Synovus aggressively increased its expansion efforts during the early 1990s. After a depression in real estate and construction markets in the late 1980s, a string of bank and savings and loans failed. As banks failed at a rate unparalleled since the Great Depression, still-healthy banks were selling at an apparent discount. Synovus took advantage of the bargains. During the first three years of the 1990s, it bought 20 new banks that were scattered throughout Georgia, Alabama, and North Florida. By 1992, Synovus's asset base had risen to $5.2 billion as its net income had increased to $61 million.

Synovus tempered its acquisition activity during 1993, choosing instead to focus on streamlining its existing operations. The company added one new bank to its fold; Birmingham Federal Savings Bank, its largest acquisition ever. Synovus's 1993 gains, however, were largely attributable to Synovus's fast-growing Total System subsidiary. In 1993, the fee-based service provider announced a string of successes, including a new seven-year contract with its biggest customer, AT&T, and negotiations to acquire the card-processing business of Bank of America, one of the largest credit card issuers in the nation. Most importantly, Total System designed and implemented a $33 million software system designed to place it at the forefront of the industry in terms of service and cost. "It is the single biggest event in the history of this company," Blanchard said about the new system in the *Atlanta Constitution*. "This is like a rocket ship to the moon in terms of technology."

The value of Synovus's strategy and long-term potential was evidenced in its stock price, which increased more than 20 percent in 1993. At the same time, Total System Services's stock price rose nearly 50 percent. Any doubts about Blanchard's ability to lead the company had long ago been put to rest. "In my first ten years here, I probably had 1,000 people tell me I'd never measure up to my daddy," Blanchard recalled in the *Atlanta Constitution*. "He was always used as a club to bang me over the head . . . but he was a great banker." Still under the direction of the 52-year-old Blanchard, Synovus managed to boost its assets to $5.6 billion in 1993 and to bolster its income about 18 percent to a record $74 million. Synovus continued to pursue its proven growth tactics going into 1994.

Principal Subsidiaries: Columbus Bank and Trust Company; Total System Services, Inc. (82%).

Further Reading:

Crockett, Barton, "Synovus at Crossroads after Decade of Growth," *American Banker,* February 16, 1993, p. 1A.

Fleming, John, "James Blanchard: Is It Time to Deregulate Banking?," *Georgia Trend,* February 1991, sec. 1, p. 72.

King, Jim, "Synovus CEO Putting Hope on 'Rocket Ship,' " *Atlanta Constitution,* October 3, 1993, sec. H, p. 1.

Lindsey, Kelly, "Big Profits from Small Banks: Like Other Regional Banks, Synovus Has Been on a Buying Spree," *Georgia Trend,* October 1993, sec. 1, p. 28.

Novack, Janet, "Backwater Bliss," *Forbes,* August 20, 1990.

Seward, Christopher, "Synovus to Merge with Bank in S.C.," *Atlanta Constitution,* October 6, 1994, sec. E, p. 1.

"Synovus Financial: Does its Price Fully Reflect its Performance?," *Better Investing,* May 1994, p. 58.

—Dave Mote

Tandy Corporation

800 One Tandy Center
Fort Worth, Texas 76102
U.S.A.
(817) 390-3700
Fax: (817) 390-3500

Public Company
Incorporated: 1960
Employees: 37,000
Sales: $4.1 billion
Stock Exchanges: New York
SICs: 5731 Radio, Television & Electronics Stores; 6794
    Patent Owners & Lessors; 3651 Household Audio &
    Video Equipment; 3571 Electronic Computers

Tandy Corporation is one of the world's leading computer and electronics retailers. The transformation of Tandy from a small family owned leather store into an electronics giant was primarily due to the two strong CEOs who have been in charge since the company was incorporated in 1960. Charles Tandy made the company a giant in electronic retailing. His successor, John Roach, spearheaded a move to make the corporation a force to be reckoned with in the personal computer industry.

Charles Tandy's talent for marketing became evident when he took over the leather store his family had operated since 1919. He began to expand into the hobby market. Subsidiary locations had to be found as mail order and direct sales increased. In 1960, as Scouts and campers all over America made moccasins and coin purses from Tandy leathercraft and hobby kits, the Tandy Corporation began trading on the New York Stock Exchange.

As good as business was, it couldn't satisfy Tandy's passion for retailing. By the early 1960s, he began looking for a way to diversify. In 1963, Tandy purchased Radio Shack, a virtually bankrupt chain of electronics stores in Boston. Within two years, Tandy was making a profit on a company that had nearly $800,000 in uncollectibles when he took over. Ten years after starting with nine Boston outlets, the Tandy Corporation was opening two Radio Shack stores every working day. By 1988, there were more than 7,000 Radio Shack stores, and, according to Tandy estimates, one out of every three Americans was a Tandy customer.

By all accounts, Charles Tandy was an modest man from Fort Worth, who stayed in his original office and answered his own phone until the day he died. While his CB radio moniker was ''Mr. Lucky,'' Tandy's success was, according to analysts, due to more than just luck. They gave much more credit to three key marketing strategies that Charles Tandy developed and implemented.

First, Tandy stressed the importance of gross profit margins. Popular wisdom said a chain store's profits lay in cutting prices to yield a high sales volume. Tandy thought differently. As far as he was concerned, cutting the profit margin cut the profit. So he maintained market prices but reduced Radio Shack's 20,000 item inventory to the 2,500 best-selling items.

Second, Tandy kept Radio Shack prices competitive. He eliminated a whole spectrum of middleman costs by limiting stock to private label items. At first, the company established exclusive contracts with manufacturers, but as Radio Shack grew, more and more items were designed and manufactured by associates or subdivisions of the Tandy Corporation. In the late 1980s, Tandy still manufactured about half of the products sold in its Radio Shack stores. Twenty-five North American and six overseas manufacturing plants produced everything from simple wire to sophisticated microchips, and Radio Shack's ''Realistic'' brand name had achieved nationwide recognition.

Charles Tandy's strategy of pairing high profit margin with high turnover and of in-house marketing and distribution more than proved itself. The gross profit margin on sales for Radio Shack division has been consistently above 50 percent.

Even as he consolidated his inventory, Tandy was keenly aware that buyers must be aware of a company's presence. ''If you want to catch a mouse,'' Tandy was fond of saying, ''you have to make a noise like a cheese.'' So another Tandy strategy was to go all out on advertising. Especially in the early years, as much as nine percent of the corporation's gross profits went straight back into advertising. For years, Radio Shack's newspaper ads and flyers were not only frequent but also flamboyant. Bold type and huge letters proclaimed a never-ending series of ''super sales.'' In more recent times, as Radio Shack and Tandy worked on strengthening their Fortune 500 image, the ads were toned down.

The third arm of Charles Tandy's strategy was, in the words of one company official, to ''institutionalize entrepreneurship.'' Tandy Corporation and Radio Shack employees were living testimony that hard work and impressive sales earn their own rewards. Store managers, division vice-presidents, and Charles Tandy himself regularly earned eight or ten times their relatively modest salaries through bonuses based on a percentage of the profits they had a direct hand in creating; this policy spawned some 60 home-grown millionaires.

As Radio Shack's electronics line grew increasingly central to Tandy, the family leather business became more and more of an anomaly. Finally, in 1975, the leather line and a related wall and floor-covering business were spun off into separate companies.

When Charles Tandy died suddenly in 1978, at the age of 60, pundits and insiders alike wondered if the corporation could survive without its workaholic director and his individualistic marketing philosophy. Philip North, a director of the company and Tandy's administrative assistant and boyhood friend, stepped in as interim president and CEO of Tandy Corporation.

By his own admission, North knew virtually nothing about the technical side of Radio Shack's product line. "All I know about electronics is that the funny end of the battery goes into the flashlight first," he told *Fortune* magazine. However, North knew plenty about his late friend's retailing style. Analysts credited him with keeping the corporation's strong management team together during the adjustment period after Tandy's death.

During these years, North called more and more on the expertise of John Roach, a man whose scientific and computer background had already attracted Charles Tandy's attention. Within a few years of hiring Roach as the manager of Tandy Data Processing, Tandy had made Roach vice-president of distribution for Radio Shack. Two years later, in 1975, Roach became vice-president of manufacturing. Roach was then appointed Radio Shack's executive vice-president immediately after Tandy died, became the Radio Shack division's president and chief operating officer in 1980, and CEO in 1981. When North retired in July 1982, Roach became chairman as well.

Roach's major contribution was in masterminding Tandy's entry into the computer market. Before Charles Tandy's death, Roach had talked him into venturing into the preassembled computer market. The sale of 100,000 computers between September 1, 1977 and June 1, 1979 kept Radio Shack comfortably in the black even as the bottom dropped out of the CB radio market.

As Roach moved up the corporate structure, he intensified investment in computers. In 1982, less than a year after becoming CEO, Roach was singled out as "the best of the best" by *Financial World,* which lauded Roach as "the driving force at the front-running company in the red-hot personal computer race."

Within a short time, however, there were rumblings that the driving force in this hot race might have been burned. By 1984, Radio Shack's impressive 19 percent market share had plummeted to under nine percent. According to some critics, one of Tandy's problems resulted from Charles Tandy's policy of limiting Radio Shack to private label items, preferably manufactured by one of Tandy's subsidiary divisions. As software and applications software poured out for Apple and IBM-compatible systems, fewer and fewer serious computer users were willing to limit themselves to software designed exclusively for Radio Shack's TRS-80, or "Trash-80", as some sneeringly referred to it. In fact, Tandy found that even a superior machine couldn't overcome the software handicap. Officials at the company were shaken to find they simply couldn't sell their 1983 Model 2000, even though it was three times as fast as IBM's own PC, because it couldn't run half of the available IBM software.

In addition, Radio Shack's marketing strategies had a vulnerable side. Company policy was to let other retailers test the waters with items like stereos, CB radios, and "fuzz buster" radar detectors. Then Tandy would take over a significant part of the market by introducing a house brand it advertised intensively. However, it's not always possible to know what will boom and when, and when Radio Shack simply did not have stock on hand when the VCR market exploded in the mid-1980s—the same time the computer market was drying up—both sales and revenues fell at an alarming rate.

That crisis lead Tandy to modify its policy. In 1984, the company introduced two new computers that were fully IBM-compatible and exchanged the TRS label for Tandy. Radio Shack management then set about underselling its Big Blue competitor. Such price competition was a departure from previous marketing strategy, but because Tandy's own in-house manufacturing divisions still produced virtually all the components, from wire to plastic boards to microchips, Tandy was able to keep profits up.

While it never regained its initial share of the PC market, Tandy consistently held first place among IBM-compatibles since it entered the field from 1985 to 1990. Tandy regained its place in the computer market by offering the buyer significant savings over IBM and other compatibles. At the same time, Roach also oversaw a wholesale revamping of the company's image. Ordinary Radio Shack stores were given a face-lift. To overcome the reluctance of serious business customers to take a computer shelved next to a CB or electronic toy seriously, Roach established a series of specialized Radio Shack Computer Centers, providing a level of support and service that earned a "Hall of Fame" award from *Consumer's Digest* in 1985.

Tandy continued to pour money into research and development to assure that they wouldn't be left behind again by new developments in the computer field. In 1988 it acquired GRiD Systems Corporation, an innovator in the burgeoning laptop computer market. GRiD's ability to manufacture and market field automation systems using laptop computers opened a whole new area of expansion into government and *Fortune* 1000 marketing companies. Sales in GRiD's first year as a Tandy subsidiary exceeded expectations and helped underscore Tandy's image as a leader in personal computer technology by introducing innovations such as hand writing recognition and removable hard disc drive cartridges. In 1989, Tandy acquired the European marketing operations of Victor Microcomputer and Micronic, two respected microcomputer manufacturers. Merged under the name Victor Technologies Group, Tandy used the subsidiary to market GRiD products throughout Europe.

Tandy continued to maintain a high profile in the consumer electronics market outside of computers. In the late 1980s, the company put special emphasis on becoming a major force in both manufacturing and retailing cellular telephones and home computers, which it saw as a major consumer product of the 1990s. Extensive efforts also went into the development of more business-oriented technology, including multimedia applications and digital recording. The latter resulted in the development of an erasable and recordable compact disc that commanded a great deal of interest in the electronics industry.

In many ways, during the 1980s, the Tandy Corporation had simply expanded on Charles Tandy's philosophies. The company centered its manufacturing and marketing firmly around computers and consumer electronics which it retailed primarily through its Radio Shack outlets. Nonetheless, there were some significant deviations from Charles Tandy's views during the late 1980s. In 1985 the company entered the name brand retail market with the acquisitions of Scott-McDuff and Videoconcepts, two electronic equipment chain stores. The 290 stores organized under the Tandy Brand Name Retail Group did not follow the Radio Shack policy of selling exclusively private label brands. Other subsidiaries in the Tandy Marketing Companies also began to develop broader distribution channels. Memtek products, which included the Memorex brand of audio and video tapes, became available virtually everywhere such products were sold.

Tandy also made a push to sell its computers outside of Radio Shack stores. In 1985, the company edged into broader markets by offering its computers on college campuses, military bases, and through special offers to American Express cardholders. In 1988, Tandy test-marketed its 100SX computer line through 50 Wal-Mart stores. The company also announced plans to develop new computers with Digital Equipment Corporation (reselling the finished product under the DEC name) and to supply personal computers to Panasonic (which would be sold under the Panasonic name).

Some Radio Shack dealers saw Tandy's move to broaden its computer distribution as a potentially lethal threat. Many Radio Shack dealers depended on their computer business for a significant portion of sales and doubted whether they could survive if customers began to shop around, looking for the same Tandy products for less elsewhere. In August 1988, a small group of dealers formed the Radio Shack Dealers Association and began considering a class action suit against Tandy.

Tandy's foundation at the time was its retail outlets. But beyond remodeling its 7,000 Radio Shack stores and refining retail strategies, by the late 1980s, Tandy's own success had left its retail divisions with little room for growth. In 1989, Tandy posted record earnings. Business at Radio Shack Stores, however, continued to decline, while sales in Tandy's subsidiaries GRiD, Memtek, Lika, and O'Sullivan Industries grew by over 50 percent.

In the early 1990s, with its non-retail segment growing steadily, Tandy turned its attention to boosting its retail division. Leading the way were its McDuff and Video Concept Stores, which experienced an average of 14 percent same-store sales growth in 1989 and 1990. Tandy began a rapid expansion project, more than doubling the number of stores to 380 by fall of 1991.

However, Radio Shack continued to feel the effects of a soft consumer electronics market. Tandy responded by closing its Radio Shack Computer Center chain and by instituting an extensive marketing strategy that emphasized the high quality of both Radio Shack products and service. In June 1991, Tandy announced plans to open Computer City, a new chain of computer superstores that was the first to offer IBM, Hewlett-Packard, Apple, Compaq, and Tandy computers, accessories, and software all under one roof. With its new 1000RL, a home computer system developed specifically for family use, Tandy went head-to-head against IBM for the home computer market, betting that this industry segment would grow by ten percent annually in the 1990s.

Tandy also opened The Edge in Electronics, a chain of upscale consumer electronics "boutiques" designed to complement Radio Shack's moderately priced goods. However, its biggest new foray into consumer electronics retail came with the 1992 launch of Incredible Universe, an elaborate 160,000 square-foot consumer electronics mini-mall, complete with child care centers, karoke contests, a recycling center, and a restaurant. According to Tandy literature, Incredible Universe was patterned after "Disney's famous theme-park style of customer service. The store experience is called 'the show,' employees are known as 'cast members' and customers are the 'guests'." Its $9 million inventory included everything from ten brands of computers to 300 different television sets and over 40,000 music and video movie titles.

The company took an enormous risk with opening Incredible Universe. Industry analysts predicted that each new store would have to turn over a volume of $100 million annually to remain profitable. Tandy committed itself entirely to the new venture. In 1993, it restructured its entire operations to focus on retailing and, in a bold move, sold all its manufacturing operations. Victor, Tandy, and GRiD were sold to AST Research, Inc. for $201 million. O'Sullivan Industries, its successful furniture manufacturing arm, was spun-off to raise $350 million. Memtek Products was sold to Hanny Magnetics for $128 million, and plans were made to sell Lika's manfacturing facilities for cash and notes.

Tandy then devoted its energies to polishing its image and expanding is base as an electronics retailer. Incredible Universe became a separate division and plans were announced to open 50 units by the year 2000. Computer City, which posted over $600 million in annual sales in its second year of operation, announced plans to open 20 new stores by the end of 1994. Radio Shack improved merchandising and service in its 6,500 locations and hired the agency Young & Rubicam to design a new advertising campaign. For the first time since the early 1980s, Radio Shack posted eight straight months of in-store sales growth. The Tandy Brand Name Retail Group's McDuff's and Video Concepts stores grew to become two of the biggest home appliance and electronics appliance retailers in southeastern and south central United States.

In less than two years, Tandy transformed itself from a long-standing supplier and retailer of consumer electronics into a high-image conglomeration of electronics "superstore" chains. Merchandising and marketing became the company's primary focuses. While marketing had been the cornerstone of Tandy's early corporate philosophy, success in new ventures—particularly Incredible Universe—would depend on the skills of Tandy's traditionally strong management team. While no one can say how Charles Tandy would regard the changes his company has seen or the challenges it faces, it seems fair to guess that he would have no quarrel with the outcome so far.

Principal Subsidiaries: Radio Shack; Computer City; Incredible Universe; Tandy Name Brand Retail Group.

Further Reading:

Anderson Forest, Stephanie, "Thinking Big—Very Big—at Tandy," *Business Week,* July 20, 1992, pg. 85–86.

Biesada, Alexandra, "Incredible Gamble," *Financial World,* June 9, 1992, pp. 49–51.

Faison, Seth, " 'Incredible Universe' Seeks a Big New York Bang," *New York Times,* November 17, 1994, p. D1.

Miller, Annetta, "Shufflin' at the Shack," *Newsweek,* June 7, 1993, p. 44.

"Tandy Plans Huge Store," *New York Times,* February 27, 1995, p. D4.

"Tandy Will Close 233 Stores in Its Revamping," *New York Times,* January 4, 1995, p. D3.

—updated by Maura Troester

TAYLOR

PUBLISHING COMPANY

Taylor Publishing Company

P.O. Box 597
Dallas, Texas 75221
U.S.A.
(214) 637-2800
Fax: (214) 637-2800

Wholly Owned Subsidiary of Insilco Corporation
Incorporated: 1943
Employees: 2,000
Sales: $250 million
SICs: 2741 Miscellaneous Publishing

Taylor Publishing Company is the leading publisher of year-books in the United States, selling primarily to middle schools and senior high schools. Taylor also produces a range of specialty publications. It has weathered considerable storms since its inception, including a World War, recessions, declining student enrollment, and the bankruptcy of its parent company, Insilco Corporation.

Founded in 1938, Taylor Publishing was built on the combined experiences of the three Taylor brothers, Herbert C. (known as H. C.), Edgar M. (E. M.), and J. W., Jr. (Bill). Working on his high school yearbook, H. C. had learned about book production and grown intrigued with engraving. In 1923, he and E. M., who had been working as a salesman, joined with engraving sales-man Roy Beard to buy a Houston company called Star Engrav-ing. Star was restructured to produce diplomas, invitations, and announcements, and to sell class rings. Business thrived, and Bill, the youngest Taylor brother, joined Star as a traveling salesman in 1929, just before the Depression pulled the rug out from under the American economy. Luckily the Taylors' busi-ness stayed afloat, for even in hard times people valued school memorabilia.

While his brothers insisted on producing their goods using the costly photoengraving process, Bill began experimenting with a more affordable process called photo offset lithography. Mean-while, differences had caused the brothers to dissolve their partnership with Roy Beard. The Taylors sold their shares of the company and, in 1938, launched Taylor Engraving Company in Houston. Along with several lines of school jewelry, the com-pany offered steel and copper plate engraving for diplomas and invitations. They had no equipment of their own, relying on Caudle Engraving in Dallas for production. The arrangement proved a good marriage.

In 1939, Taylor Engraving moved to Dallas and reorganized as a partnership of H. C. and E. M. The brothers opened a tiny 12′-by-12′ office and all three hit the road to woo customers. Soon E. M. tried peddling one of Bill's lithography yearbooks and was stunned at the positive response. All three brothers saw a new future for the business. Taylor Engraving slowly withdrew from announcements and jewelry and focused on lithographed yearbooks. Their first year in business, the com-pany produced small cardboard-cover yearbooks and sold them to 35 schools. It was a modest but admirable beginning.

Buoyed by the success of their new product, the brothers took out a $1,500 loan, made a down payment on a Davidson press, rented a new office, and hired their first employee. The new employee labored as hard over the press as the brothers did at selling. The coming of World War II war brought hard times again, plus the rationing of paper and ink. Then E. M. had a brainstorm. If the company pitched memory books to the mili-tary, they could requisition paper and ink for military projects. These yearbooks for graduating cadets became a huge hit. By 1943, the company was prosperous enough to require another move. That same year, the brothers filed incorporation papers and became Taylor Publishing Company. They had ten busy employees.

By the end of the war, Taylor was selling $500,000 in cadet books a year. But peacetime meant shifting their focus again. As a transition they launched county military books, collecting the photos and military stories of servicemen within a given county radius, and publishing them. The books were popular and the blooming post-war economy gave them a push. At the same time, Taylor concentrated on building its school yearbook busi-ness. To this end, a full-time salesman was dispatched to the Southeast.

Bill Taylor returned home from the Air Corps and joined Taylor full-time in 1945. He hired and trained the growing sales force and, in 1946, hatched the company's next great innovation, called the ''Blue Book.'' The Blue Book was simply a step-by-step storyboard that walked customers through the production of a yearbook. This powerful sales tool proved so useful that by 1959 it was the centerpiece of Taylor's new business of con-ducting seminars for student yearbook staffs. These seminars eventually became the core of an entire division of the com-pany, the Seminar Division, and were still used in the 1990s.

Taylor grew quickly—sometimes too quickly—in the late 1940s and into the 1950s. By 1947 plant expansion had eaten up all the space at their existing location, so they bought land for a new plant. The operation was under one roof again by October of 1948, but two years later facilities had more than doubled again. Despite the expanding production facilities, Taylor strug-gled to keep up with demand. Spring was invariably hell for the company, as graduation day deadlines pushed production. Eventually, Taylor devised a summer delivery which helped take pressure off of production and allowed the yearbooks to include year-end pictures such as proms, athletics, and gradua-tion. Naturally, this idea was popular all around.

By the 1950s, growth necessitated innovation. In 1952, Taylor linked with L. G. Balfour Company, then a leader in the class jewelry business. Balfour began pitching Taylor yearbooks along with its product line, using its national sales force to introduce Taylor from New England to California. In 1953, typesetting replaced hand-lettering and freed up the art staff, who had been laboriously setting every ad by hand.

By its third decade, Taylor was ready to go public. Its first shareholders meeting as a publicly held company took place in the summer of 1960. Response was as strong as the company's sales, for Taylor was the leader in U.S. yearbook publishing. Capital infusions allowed acquisitions, including the Joe Alexander Press of Austin, Texas, and Newsfoto Publishing Company of San Angelo, Texas, and Yearbooks, Inc. of Monrovia, California. Newsfoto was an especially important acquisition, for it had been a fierce competitor, known for quality and affordability.

Joe Alexander Press and Newsfoto operated as separate companies under Taylor's management. Yearbooks Inc. was made a branch of the parent company and provided a bridge into California's market. Yearbooks Inc. was renamed and struggled through peaks and busts until operations were shut down in 1982. In 1962, Taylor acquired American Beauty Cover Company (ABC), of Dallas, which had long supplied Taylor with yearbook covers. Sales volumes climbed to an all-time high in 1963, but Taylor was creaking from its own sudden growth. The order backlog was daunting and plant equipment and staff were severely taxed. Spring production in 1965 broke more records, and a new plant was slated for a 1967 opening.

The mid-1960s saw crucial changes in the company's leadership and direction: Herbert C. Taylor stepped down as company chairman in 1965, though he remained on the board; E. M. moved from president to chairman; and Bill became president. At this time, the bulk of Taylor's business was school yearbooks, while the remaining 10 percent of sales came from reprinting rare books and cattle sale catalogs, and miscellaneous commercial printing jobs like specialty advertising brochures. By the late 1960s, Taylor had all the requisite charms of a prime acquisition target, and had been approached by corporate giants such as RCA and Times-Mirror. Then the Connecticut-based International Silver Company—later Insilco—approached Taylor and proved compatible. The merger agreement went through in 1967. Randy Marston, a financial wizard with Insilco who helped hammer out the deal, went on to form a bond with Bill Taylor so close that Taylor named Marston his executive heir. Marston and his family moved to Dallas in 1969.

After the boom of the mid-1960s, Taylor was startled by sagging profits in 1968 and 1969. By 1970, Taylor had hit a low point. The company's problems were widespread and long-standing, a result of growth without modernization. One dominating crisis was in typesetting, where the company employed antiquated hot metal linotype machines. When the head of this production walked out one day, unable to bear the hard work and his chronically revolving staff, the company was forced to switch to the still-revolutionary cold type process within five months in order to make production. In order to cope with their backlog, Taylor brought in outside management consultants who worked for more than eight months to overhaul the production system. By 1972, Taylor's efforts were paying off and the company celebrated its best production season ever.

Business boomed between 1972 and 1976, and annual profits passed the $2 million mark for the first time in the early 1970s. The yearbook field had changed enough that Taylor's association with Balfour's sales force needed revising. Yearbooks had become a specialty, sufficiently complex that they needed a sales force of their own. In 1970, 80 percent of Taylor's yearbook sales came from combined sales offices. By 1989, it was less than 20 percent. Both delivery and sales were stable enough for Bill Taylor to retire in 1976. The baby boom had peaked, though, and student enrollments were already declining, a trend that would continue through the 1980s. Fifteen of Taylor's yearbook competitors went under. Taylor revved up its sales team and moved to even more high-tech solutions to production problems, to save on labor and time. The company managed to hang on to its market share and increase profits even though school enrollment declined 26 percent. In 1977, Taylor opened the doors of its first manufacturing venture in the north, a plant based in Pennsylvania. A Fine Books Division and a Publishing Division were created, growing by 1989 to account for 12 percent of Taylor's annual sales.

With the 1980s, technology brought its own revolutions. The company was offering videotaped "yearbooks" as supplements to printed volumes and employing four-color scanners, continuous tone processors, and other new technologies. Taylor had broken ground in the mid-1970s by paginating its yearbooks with a computerized copy preparations system, which had yet to become the new wave in publishing. New on-line laser color scanners improved the quality of photos and Taylor also led the pack by using lithographed hard covers, broadening customer's creative choices. So Taylor was well-poised to take advantage of the almost daily innovations in computer-assisted publishing.

Taylor was also honing its specialty publications and began to focus on four topics: gardening, sports, cooking, and self-help/health books. This division produced such titles as *Spirits of the Sky: The Airplanes of World War II* and *Antique Roses of the South* in the fall of 1990. Taylor was also donating a portion of net proceeds from some of its self-help titles to relevant organizations, such as the National Coalition Against Domestic Violence, which received money from sales of *The Battered Woman's Survival Guide*. At the same time, Taylor was moving aggressively into distribution, representing 17 different presses and publishers in 1990, including Cybourg Communications, Story Line Press, and Mississippi River Publishing Company.

While Taylor was trotting to keep up with the technological changes in publishing, Insilco—which had changed its name in 1969—had continued a buying blaze through the 1970s and 1980s, acquiring Rolodex Corporation, Signal Transformer, ESCOD Industries, and General Thermodynamics, among others. Its interests ranged from publishing to cable and wire assemblies, specialized connector systems, power transformers, and the metal tubing used in heat transfer applications and radiators. Insilco was growing at a speed that might have stunned the Taylor brothers.

The growth proved too much to manage, however, and in January of 1991, Insilco filed for Chapter 11 bankruptcy. The company's troubles seemed not to impact Taylor Publishing too much. By April of 1993, Insilco emerged from Chapter 11; by November of that same year, it was trading stock on NASDAQ. During that same period, Taylor was implementing a new system for scanning photos and line graphics. Taylor was printing more than 10 million pictures a year in its yearbooks, and paginating more than 150,000 pages a week. Automated pagination and other new technologies that saved labor without sacrificing quality were key to Taylor's lead in the industry. The scanning system cut pagination costs by roughly half, improved image quality, reduced the annual consumption of film, and nearly eliminated the need for a copy camera and stripping department, so lessened money spent for skilled labor. The new system hit a few bumps before running smoothly, but the benefits were immense.

In 1993, Insilco's balance sheet was much improved, it had a new board of directors, and its net sales had increased from $578.5 million in 1992, to $615.1 million. Just more than a quarter of those sales were in Insilco's Technologies Group, mostly serving the telecommunications and electronic components end markets; another quarter were due to the Metal Parts Group, which includes the two operating units Thermal Components and Steel Parts; and nearly 33 percent of its sales were in Office Products/Publishing Group. Taylor alone contributed about 16 percent of 1993 sales. In the summer of 1994, Taylor was awarded a patent for its Electronic Yearbook Publication System, which covered the digital processing of pictures for yearbooks. It had best-selling books about the Dallas Cowboys, Green Bay Packers, and Detroit Lions. Seeing that commemo-

rative sports books were so popular, Taylor began negotiations with other teams. The digital picture publishing gave Taylor an edge over competitors and the company reported an increase in yearbook orders in 1994.

Insilco had maintained market position even during its bankruptcy and reorganization. Taylor did likewise, throughout its parent company's troubles. By 1994, it was marketing its yearbooks through 250 exclusive, commissioned sales representatives and producing about 30 percent of the country's yearbooks annually.

Further Reading:

Aucoin, Patsi, "Feeling at Home at Work: Taylor Publishing's 450 'In-Homes' Enjoy Answering to Themselves," *Dallas Business Journal,* January 23, 1989, p. 16.
"Pagination Costs Cut in Half," *Graphics Arts Monthly,* September 1993, p. 84.
Raley Borda, Laura, "Largest Dallas-Fort Worth-area Commercial Printing Companies," *Dallas Business Journal,* December 17, 1993, p. 10.
Steinberg, Don, "Publisher Installs DECnet," *PC Week,* July 28, 1987, p. C8.
Summer, Bob, "Sleuthing Around," *Publishers Weekly,* September 20, 1993, p. 22.
——, "Taylor Publishing: Building Identity," *Publishers Weekly,* October 19, 1990, p. 39.
Wasowksi, Andy, *Never An Easy Spring: A History of Taylor Publishing Company, The First 50 Years: 1930–1989,* Dallas, Tex.: Taylor Publishing Company, 1989.

—Carol I. Keeley

Thomasville

Thomasville Furniture Industries, Inc.

Box 339
401 E. Main Street
Thomasville, North Carolina 27360
U.S.A.
(910) 472-4000
Fax: (910) 472-4071

Wholly Owned Subsidiary of Armstrong World Industries, Inc.
Incorporated: 1904 as Thomasville Chair Company
Employees: 7,000
Sales: $526 million
SICs: 2511 Wood Household Furniture; 2512 Upholstered Household Furniture

Thomasville Furniture Industries, Inc. is a leading manufacturer of upper medium to higher-priced dining room, bedroom, upholstered, and occasional furniture. Into the 1990s, the company remained the economic keystone of Thomasville, North Carolina, operating 11 plants and employing more than half the population there. The landmark Big Chair—an 18-foot reproduction of a Duncan Phyfe design first erected in 1922 and rebuilt in 1951—remained in the town square as a symbol of the company's long-standing (and well-seated) success. The chair's size also remained a tribute to the company's growth: by the 1990s, Thomasville Furniture had become a subsidiary of a Fortune 500 parent, Armstrong World Industries, Inc., and displayed its wares in more than 550 Thomasville Galleries and 100 Thomasville stores nationwide. Through one of the furniture industry's most aggressive marketing campaigns, the company's brand name continued to work itself into the American mindset—in order to better position its products for the nation's living-room set of the future.

Founded in 1904 with $10,000 and a turnover of 180 chairs a day, Thomasville Chair Company was one of many small chair manufacturers in the region. By 1907, the fledgling enterprise owed $2,000 in lumber fees to T.J. Finch and his brother, D.F. Finch. The brothers had already distinguished themselves as prominent entrepreneurs by farming timber, producing and selling lumber, and helping found a telephone company and two banks. In addition, T.J. Finch was the sheriff of Randolph County. Within a year of reluctantly accepting payment in stock

in the place of the young company's scarce cash, the brothers moved to "protect their investment" by buying out the remaining shares. By the end of that year, T.J. Finch occupied the company's presidential seat.

True to their nature, the Finch family didn't sit still for long. By 1908, the company reported profits on sales of $91,522. A year later, total assets were nearly doubled by the acquisition of Bard Lumber and Manufacturing Company. Moreover, T.J. Finch positioned the growing company for vertical integration, starting a machine shop, a three-story building for wrapping and upholstery operations and inventory, and one of the largest veneer plants in the South. The 1914 acquisition of Cramer Furniture Co. more than doubled the company's size once again, and by 1917 sales topped $1 million. Meanwhile, T.J. Finch had begun delegating key responsibilities to his son, T. Austin Finch, with an eye on the next generation of success.

Following World War I, new emphasis was placed on diversification of product line to accommodate customer demand. The first in-house designers were hired in 1925. Alliances were formed with other furniture manufacturers so that Thomasville chairs could be marketed as integral parts of furniture sets. Chairs were crafted by Thomasville, tables by St. Johns Table Co. of Michigan, and buffets by B.F. Huntley Furniture Co. of Winston-Salem. These wares, peddled by the first national sales force in the furniture industry, proved so successful that T. Austin Finch positioned the company to produce them on its own. By 1927, Thomasville offered a complete line of dining room furniture, distinguishing itself as the most diversified producer in the industry.

After T. Austin Finch ascended to the Thomasville presidency in 1927, he positioned the company for higher quality products and trendsetting innovation. Rather than cut wages, prices, and quality during the strain of the Depression years, the company stepped up to a higher grade of furniture—a move that involved immediate risks, but that set Thomasville apart from its competitors when the economic storm clouds cleared later that decade. Initiative in automation helped the company produce its higher-end products more efficiently, as well. In 1937, the company installed one of the first conveyor systems in the industry and retrofitted its equipment for automated processes. Meanwhile, T. Austin's brother, Doak Finch, played a growing role in the company's operations. For example, he contracted a manufacturer of automatic nail machines for shoemaking to design the first such machines for the furniture industry. Following T. Austin's death in 1943, the younger brother continued the lineage of Finch company presidents.

During the second world war, 65 percent of Thomasville's efforts were geared toward government orders. From army double deck bunk beds to wood plugs for bombs, tent stakes, and spatulas, the company's products had moved from domestic sitting rooms to overseas battle fields. Stores of consumer furniture were sold exclusively to customers who had bought from Thomasville before the war.

The postwar era was marked by strong economic recovery on all domestic fronts, with a prominent share of the furniture market moving to the South. Large, biannual exhibits—in April and October—served as forums for furniture makers to showcase their products. Thomasville launched marketing campaigns designed to get potential consumers right into the factory, and in 1958, the company opened a massive, four-story showroom that dwarfed those of virtually all its competitors.

The 1960s ushered in a period of unprecedented growth, spurred by a series of mergers that changed not only the scope of the company's client base, but its name. In 1961, Thomasville Chair Company merged with B.F. Huntley Co., continuing a 35-year alliance in marketing and developing complete furniture packages. The new entity, renamed Thomasville Furniture Industries, went public in April 1962 and began selling shares on the New York Stock Exchange in 1964. With greater resources at hand, the company broadened both its product line and its client base, moving decisively into contemporary styles and forging strong ties with business clients, such as hotels, in the contract furniture market.

Starting in the late 1960s, the company took great strides in quality control by pioneering the industry's first Environmental Simulation Package Testing Laboratory. Using climatized chambers and specialized machines to simulate variable conditions, these facilities helped assure the durability of packaging and, ultimately, the condition of Thomasville's delivered goods.

In 1968, Thomasville Furniture became a subsidiary of Armstrong Cork Company, a leading industrial firm with a history dating back to 1860, when Thomas M. Armstrong and John D. Glass began producing cork bottle stoppers in a one-room shop. By the time Armstrong acquired Thomasville, it had become a major industrial manufacturer. Shortly thereafter, its name was changed to Armstrong World Industries to better reflect its diversified product line, which ultimately ranged from industrial floor coverings to carpets, wood products, furniture, adhesives and sealants, and gaskets by the 1990s.

Under Armstrong's parentage, Thomasville continued to pattern of growth through acquisitions that had started in the early 1960s. Indeed, the 1960s were fruitful years for mergers with a number of valuable companies: Phoenix Chair Company in 1964; Founders Furniture Company in 1965; Western Carolina Furniture Company in 1966; and Caldwell Furniture Company in 1968. During the 1970s, the company continued to expand its operations with the start up of the Armstrong furniture line, a lower priced line of bedroom furniture. Under the leadership of Frederick Starr, who became president and CEO in 1982, that growth continued. Key mergers and facility developments included Gilliam Furniture Inc. in May 1986; construction of a new plant at Carysbrook, Virginia, in June 1986; the Westchester Group of Companies in November 1987; Gordon's Inc. in August 1988; and construction of a 40,000 square-foot addition to one of its Thomasville dining room furniture plants in late 1988.

With recessionary trends in the early 1990s, Thomasville lost some of the growth momentum that it had enjoyed during the boom of the mid- to late 1980s. The furniture industry was particularly recession-prone for two key reasons: most consumers were quick to put off furniture purchases in bad times; and furniture sales were highly dependent on real estate, which was hit hard by recession. Moreover, as analyst Wallace Eppeson Jr. noted in a January 1994 *Business-North Carolina*

article, furniture sales historically remained stalled long after recessions were over—reflecting in large part the deferrable nature of the product. Still, Starr took few draconian measures to curtail the ambitious plans he had begun on the crest of the 1980s. Drawing on the expertise of financial officers running complex computer programs in late 1990, Thomasville calculated its likely profits if the company were to suffer ten, 15, or 20 percent reductions in sales. Concluding that medium-term growth might be flat, but not detrimental, Starr and his team positioned the company for continued growth in the not-to-distant future. "We really do not want to close plants. . . . We've got great plants, great people. You can't get them back if you close them," Starr told John Burgess in a November 25, 1990 article for *The Washington Post.*

Rather than close plants or severely cut back on operations, therefore, Thomasville moved to lighten its financial burden with a series of effective cost reduction measures in the early 1990s. The company stepped up programs to reduce production and distribution time, to improve quality, and to restructure its salaried and hourly organizations. The company also shifted production toward lower-cost items that would perform better in hard times, such as upholstered and non-assembled furniture. In addition, in 1991 Thomasville moved into a key, new market that promised exceptional growth: furniture equipped with electronic components. In an October 25, 1993 article for *Investor's Business Daily,* Kathleen M. Berry reported that sales of such furniture designs were expected to reach $3 billion by 1995. To tap that potential, Thomasville struck an alliance with Holland's Philips Electronic NV, collaborating on new entertainment centers or home theater systems with price tags between $10,000 and $12,000. The company also made cross-merchandising arrangements in 1993 with Eastman House to sell mattresses and quilted bedsets with its beds and also began to develop its international business.

In an effort to maximize its share of a stagnant market, Thomasville redoubled marketing and advertising efforts that it had started aggressively pursuing in the 1980s. Such a strategy provided an appreciable advantage in an industry that tended to neglect consumer advertising. Although furniture makers shipped $18 billion in products each year, manufacturers spent only $170 million annually on consumer advertising, the Home Furnishing Council estimated in *Advertising Age* on January 10, 1994. (Furniture manufacturers traditionally spent their marketing money on trade ads, leaving the task of consumer advertising to retailers.) Thomasville was among a small minority of exceptions. As early as 1989, the company initiated a $10 million-plus television ad campaign. Moreover, Thomasville forged ahead in its "galleries" program, consisting of free-standing stores that displayed only the company's products, as well as fully furnished displays in retailing stores. By 1990, Thomasville had already established more than 500 such galleries, with many more on the drawing board. The push was a success: between 1982 and 1988, Thomasville saw its sales double to $360 million.

Along with their advantages, Thomasville's marketing efforts caused some troubles for the company. In April 1988, a group of North Carolina discount retailers filed two antitrust federal court challenges against Thomasville. In May, the retailers pressed for a bill in the General Assembly that would permit them to sell furniture by mail and toll-free telephone. They claimed that the furniture manufacturer was placing excessive restrictions on retailers by forbidding them from selling Thomasville goods over the phone to customers who had never set foot in the showroom or to solicit business outside the local area. Thomasville argued that it was merely protecting the rights of furniture manufacturers to draw customers into the showroom, where they could see a broad complement of furniture. The company also intended to stop "free riding" customers who shopped at their local galleries and then ordered goods from afar, often at lower prices. In June 1989, Thomasville amended its distribution policy by which retailers could sell to any client in the state and to any mail or telephone customers they had prior to June 8. By the end of November 1989, this compromise had prompted the retailers to drop the suit.

In mid-1994, Thomasville consolidated the lessons of all its past marketing efforts. The company combined direct mail, TV, and print advertising for a nationwide image campaign developed by Pascale & Associates, a Greensboro, North Carolina, agency. Promotion of a new product line, Country Inns & Back Roads, was directed at a target audience of upscale women interested in antiques, museum art, cooking, and gardening. Pascale started the campaign by issuing three separate direct mail postcards, taking out billboards, and placing three newspaper ads, all of which aroused consumer interest without showing the actual product line. Capitalizing on the anticipation from that first phase, the campaign depended on a second phase: a combination of mini-catalog mailers, retailer brochures, newspaper ads, and radio and TV spots that actually described the furniture products.

Such sophisticated marketing campaigns, in conjunction with general initiatives to improve performance, lead to record sales and earnings in 1994, and boded well for the company's ongoing success. Thomasville could boast an impressive ascent since its origins as a small-town manufacturer of chairs, and, despite the ongoing rigors of the furniture industry of the 1990s, it seemed unlikely that Thomasville would stand—or sit—still for a moment before going forward.

Further Reading:

Berry, Kathleen M., "Furniture and Electronics Makers Form Alliances," *Investor's Business Daily,* October 25, 1993, p. 4.

Brown, Nicholas, "Furniture Discounters Drop Suit Against Thomasville," *Greensboro News & Record,* November 29, 1989, p. B5.

Brown, Nicholas, "Thomasville Gallery Program a Success," *Greensboro News & Record,* November 6, 1989, p. C3.

Burgess, John, "Fighting to Stay Fit: Economy's Failing Vital Signs Force Firms to Find Cures," *The Washington Post,* November 25, 1990, p. H1.

Gattuso, Greg, "The Advertising Road Less Travelled; Marketing Technique of Thomasville Furniture Industries, Inc.," *Direct Marketing Magazine,* June 1994, p. 20.

Gault, Ylonda, "Traditional Furniture Seeks City Market," *Crain's New York Business,* July 8, 1991, p. 28.

"Have a Seat and Wait: That's What the Furniture Industry is Doing," *Business Dateline; Business-North Carolina,* January 1994, p. 73.

Johnson, Bradley, "A Dispute in the Gallery," *Greensboro News & Record,* April 10, 1989, p. C10.

Kelt, Deborah, "Thomasville Lenox: Double Date," *HFD–The Weekly Home Furnishings Newspaper,* April 19, 1993, p. M2.

Schancupp, Pam, "Matching Linen for Restonic, Thomasville Beds," *HFD–The Weekly Home Furnishings Newspaper,* May 3, 1993, p. 26.

Sloan, Pat, "Furniture Maker Builds on TV Ads," *Advertising Age,* December 5, 1988, p. 12.

Steenhuysen, Julie, "Finally, Furniture Makers Fashion Ads," *Advertising Age,* January 10, 1994, p. S2.

—Kerstan Cohen

Thrifty PayLess, Inc.

9275 Southwest Peyton Lane
Wilsonville, Oregon 97070
U.S.A.
(503) 682-4100
Fax: (503) 685-6194

Private Company
Incorporated: 1994
Employees: 33,000
Sales: $4.65 billion
SICs: 5912 Drug Stores and Proprietary Stores

Thrifty PayLess, Inc., is the second-largest drug store chain in America. It was formed in 1994 when TCH Corporation, controlled by an investment group managed by Leonard Green & Partners, agreed to purchase the PayLess Drug Stores subsidiary of the giant retailer Kmart. Green's group already owned Thrifty Corporation, which it had purchased from Pacific Enterprises in 1992. The Green partnership merged the companies, and Thrifty PayLess was born.

Thrifty Corporation

Thrifty began as Borun Bros., a wholesaling business in sundries and proprietary drugs that was incorporated in 1919. The Borun brothers, Harry and Robert, and their brother-in-law Norman Levin opened their first retail drug store in Los Angeles in 1929, and in 1935 they reorganized the business as Thrifty Drug Stores Co., Incorporated. By 1945, the year it went public, Thrifty had 63 drug stores in southern California, principally in the Los Angeles area. Thrifty's stores offered broad selection— stocked items included liquor, electrical appliances, and sporting goods—and also had extensive soda fountain and restaurant facilities. Some of the merchandise was marketed under trade names that Thrifty owned, and some was manufactured by Borun Bros., now a subsidiary.

In the postwar period, Thrifty continued to thrive. In 1964, when the company had grown to 238 stores, sales and earnings had risen for each of the past ten years; in nine of those years, the dividend was increased. At that point, 75 percent of Thrifty's sales volume came from southern California, 20 percent from northern California, and the remainder from 12 units in Idaho, Oregon, Nevada, Utah, and Arizona. Most stores were

profitable during their first year of operation, as the company continued to capitalize on the growth in the California market. The stores were also getting bigger: in the late 1950s and early 1960s they averaged 16,000 feet, but in the second half of the 1960s the mean was 20,000 feet, with a few as big as 27,000 feet. By 1970, the company was reporting annual sales of more than $325 million and earnings of more than $7 million.

After generating nearly all of its growth internally, in 1971 Thrifty bought the Big 5 chain from United Merchandising Corp. of Los Angeles; the chain had 18 stores, most of which were in California. Thrifty's profits plunged 58 percent in 1974 as the result of a 19-day strike and a change in inventory accounting, but the company quickly recovered and continued to post higher sales and earnings in the late 1970s. Thrifty also remained relatively unaffected by the economic slowdown of the early 1980s. At that point, Thrifty had begun to shift its emphasis from opening new stores to refurbishing existing units, which produced sales increases of up to 50 percent per store within 18 months of remodeling. The company was also continuing to expand the number of Big 5 Sporting Goods stores, operating 62 units in 1982 versus 48 in 1978.

In 1986 Thrifty was purchased in an exchange of stock by Pacific Lighting, a natural gas distributor in southern California that was seeking to diversify its operations. The drug retailer initially performed well for Pacific Lighting, and in 1988 Thrifty added the 147-store Pay 'n Save chain through a purchase for stock. Soon afterward, however, significant problems emerged. Competition grew fierce, as nationwide discount chains like Phar-Mor and Drug Emporium entered the southern California market, and older rivals like Sav-On picked up steam. Moreover, pharmacies were becoming a common feature in supermarkets, warehouse clubs, and discount superstores like Wal-Mart and Kmart. By most accounts, Thrifty did not respond well to the challenge. Industry observers found its stores dirty, employees lackadaisical, information systems outdated, and inventory shrinkage excessive. The company was also heavily unionized, while most of its key competitors were not. In 1990 Pacific took a $100 million charge for inventory adjustments and the planned closing of marginal stores. In 1991 Thrifty reported a loss of $164 million on sales of $3.3 billion, and in the first quarter of 1992, Pacific took an after-tax writeoff of $475 million to reflect the reduced value of its Thrifty assets.

That May, Thrifty suffered another jolt. As one of the earliest of the retail drug chains in southern California, Thrifty had numerous stores in older, inner-city neighborhoods. When Los Angeles was struck by riots after the Rodney King trial, the retailer was hit hard. Four of its stores burned to the ground, and some 19 others were looted. At Thrifty headquarters in Los Angeles, 1,750 employees were evacuated. Later, a crowd of 300 surrounded the building; a fire was started but soon extinguished.

These events capped Pacific's ill-starred venture in the drugstore field. A month later, in June 1992, the company announced that it would sell Thrifty Corporation to two different buyers. The Thrifty chain and five other smaller retail operations were sold to the L.A.-based investor group of Leonard Green & Partners. The Pay 'n Save business went to Kmart's PayLess subsidiary. After six years of dealing with the problems of a drug retailer, Pacific announced that it intended to refocus on its natural gas business.

PayLess Drug Stores

The first PayLess Drug Store was opened in La Grande, Oregon, in 1939. By 1945, under the leadership of Peyton Hawes, PayLess Drug Stores had opened nine stores in Oregon, Washington, and Idaho. PayLess expanded rapidly during the 1960s—between 1959 and 1967, sales increased by more than 400 percent. By that time, PayLess was operating 25 stores through 22 separate companies in which Peyton Hawes held varying degrees of ownership. In 1967 these companies were amalgamated as PayLess Drug Stores Northwest Inc., and the firm went public. Two years later, PayLess began trading on the New York Stock Exchange.

PayLess operated under an unusually high degree of decentralization, with each manager responsible for selecting merchandise, pricing, purchasing, and advertising and managers' compensation tied closely to the pre-tax profits of the store. Seeking to provide one-stop shopping for people living in smaller communities, PayLess served as a general merchandise store, with its product mix including refrigerators and washing machines. Part of its success stemmed from offering consistently lower prices than its competitors.

PayLess continued to prosper in the 1970s. In 1976 it acquired 22 Value Giant Stores located in northern California and the Pacific Northwest. PayLess also continued to grow internally. When a distribution center that opened in 1976 was pinched for space just two years later, the company built a huge, 500,000-square-foot distribution facility in Wilsonville, Oregon (outside Portland), and also established its corporate headquarters there. The company achieved significant efficiencies by purchasing merchandise in volume; while in some respects this limited the autonomy of store managers, they still enjoyed a high degree of independence. Between 1973 and 1978, the company's sales grew from $128 million to $298 million, and earnings rose from $3.5 million to $8.3 million. By that time, PayLess operated a total of 77 stores, including 31 in Oregon, 27 in Washington, 16 in California, and three in Idaho.

In 1980 PayLess acquired the 61 stores of PayLess Drug Stores of Oakland, California, which made a good fit with PayLess because their stores were the same size, they carried the same merchandise, and the geographic distribution of their stores was complementary—in addition to the fact that their names were virtually identical. In 1981 PayLess's sales nearly doubled, rising to some $750 million, while earnings were up 15 percent to $14.3 million. The company discontinued the major appliance business, which was unprofitable, but otherwise continued to display its wide range of offerings. Indeed, no merchandise category, including prescription drugs, represented more than 10 percent of PayLess sales.

In 1985 Kmart purchased PayLess for $500 million. PayLess was allowed a high degree of autonomy and continued to do well, benefitting from the solid financial backing of Kmart. A second 500,000 foot distribution center was opened in Woodland, California, in 1986, and PayLess picked up 24 stores from the Osco chain in 1987. PayLess also continued to grow inter-

nally, and in 1990 celebrated its 300th store opening. The company became more efficient by implementing a computerized purchasing system in the early 1990s, which helped the unit increase its inventory by 26 percent and cut inventory investment per store from $302,000 in 1990 to $224,000 in 1992.

In 1991, when Kmart began breaking out the results of its large subsidiaries in an effort to attract buyers, it became clear that PayLess (as it was now spelled) was among its star performers. Sales were up 15 percent from 1990 levels to $1.89 billion, and operating margins were a healthy 4.8 percent. The company had substantially raised the share of higher-margin prescription drugs in its merchandise mix, from below 10 percent in the mid-1980s to over 30 percent. It had acquired 52 more stores from the Osco chain and now operated more than 400 stores. In 1992 PayLess made another leap when it acquired the 124 Pay 'n Save stores from Thrifty, which by that time was experiencing significant problems.

Thrifty PayLess, Inc.

After buying Thrifty in 1992, Leonard Green installed new management that stemmed the string of losses and appeared to turn the company around. Losses fell from $324 million for fiscal 1992 (ended in October) to $3.2 million in fiscal 1993. In the first fiscal quarter of 1994 (ended January 2, 1994) the company made a small profit. Meanwhile, Kmart was seeking to dispose of assets, and PayLess was one of its most attractive properties. With Thrifty apparently on the way to recovery, Green tried to sell Wall Street on a merger of Thrifty with PayLess. Some analysts noted that two of Green's recent acquisitions—Almac supermarkets in Rhode Island and Florida-based Kash N'Karry—had performed poorly, but Green countered that the two flops were minor blemishes on a record of 33 successful deals.

Eventually Green was able to complete the merger, and Thrifty PayLess, Inc., was formed. Several analysts were still unconvinced that the two chains could be easily integrated. Management styles differed sharply—the company's new CEO, Tim McAlear, who had previously been head of PayLess and had worked for Kmart for almost 30 years, described the Thrifty management philosophy as "almost dictatorial." Some departments at Thrifty had as many as seven layers of management; PayLess, in contrast, had operated under much more of a "bottom up" style.

The new company also faced the more mundane problems of merging two large organizations. Neither had a computer that would be able to track the new company's inventory, and Thrifty and PayLess had maintained their books under different accounting methods. Thrifty PayLess also had to decide how and where to put its people (most industry observers thought that the company would eventually be based in the spacious, well-equipped Wilsonville, Oregon, office rather than Los Angeles). Relocations can produce disorder: when the company started to coordinate all purchasing from its Wilsonville office, 70 confused vendors called in one day to find out what was going on. And, of course, many employees wondered whether they would be needed at all in the new organization.

Nevertheless, Thrifty PayLess had notable strengths. The company was certain to realize economies of scale through merging functions from purchasing to accounting. It had decided to leave the names of the stores in the two chains intact, and it would thus benefit from the name recognition they commanded. While Thrifty had had its problems, it still enjoyed a very strong identity in California. According to industry analysts, the company also had an unusually talented and experienced chief executive in Tim McAlear.

Further Reading:

Campbell, N. John, "Thrifty Corporation," *Wall Street Transcript,* January 4, 1983, pp. 68,529.
Gebhart Fred, "Buyers Found for Thrifty, Pay'n Save Drug Chains," *Drug Topics,* June 22, 1992, p. 89.
Gordon, Mitchell, "Thrifty Drug Stores Head for Healthy Earnings Gain," *Barron's,* November 6, 1972, p. 31.
——, "L.A.-Based Thrifty Drug Stores to Ring up Nifty Profits Advance," *Barron's,* July 26, 1976.
Halverson, Richard, "PayLess Good Candidate for Spinoff," *Discount Store News,* May 4, 1992, p. 1.
Parrish, Michael, "Pacific Enterprises Sheds Thrifty Corp," *Los Angeles Times,* May 23, 1992, p. D1.
"PayLess Drug Stores Northwest, Inc.," *Wall Street Transcript,* July 8, 1968, p. 13,819.
Picker, Ida, "A Gala Spring Sale," *Institutional Investor,* July 1994.
Rose, Michael, "When Corporate Cultures Collide," *Business Journal-Portland,* July 22, 1994, pp. 1, 17.
Ross, Dennis, "PayLess Drugs Northwest," *Wall Street Transcript,* April 3, 1978, p. 50,193.
Symons, Allene, "Drug Chains Torched, Looted in L.A. Rioting," *Drug Store News,* May 18, 1992.
——, "PE Selling Thrifty Corp. Units," *Drug Store News,* June 8, 1992.
Wilson, Marianne, "PayLess-Thrifty: Putting the Pieces Together," *Chain Store Executive Age,* April 1994, pp. 43–45.
Zitnick, Louis, "Thrifty Drug Stores, Inc.," *Commercial and Financial Chronicle,* January 7, 1963, p. 2.

—Bob Schneider

Tootsie Roll Industries Inc.

7401 S. Cicero Ave.
Chicago, Illinois 60629
U.S.A.
(312) 838-3400
Fax: (312) 838-3564

Public Company
Incorporated: 1922 as Sweets Company of America
Employees: 1,500
Sales: $297 million
Stock Exchanges: New York
SICs: 2060 Candy and Other Confectionery Products

Tootsie Roll Industries Inc. is one of the largest candy companies in the United States, with headquarters in Chicago and operations in Massachusetts, New York, Tennessee, Mexico, and Canada, as well as licenses in countries such as Colombia and the Philippines. The company is, of course, best known for producing the candies that bear the company name—the chewy, chocolate cylinders in the distinctive brown, white, and red wrappers. In addition to the famous Tootsie Rolls—which can still be purchased in some varieties at their original cost of one penny—the company manufactures lollipops and hard candy under the brand names Tootsie Roll Pops, Charms, Blow Pops, Blue Razz, and Zip-A-Dee-Doo-Da-Pops; chocolate covered cherries under the Cella's trademark; and various confectionery products under the names Mason Dots and Mason Crows. In 1993, the company made the largest acquisition in its history, taking over the chocolate and caramel brands of the Warner-Lambert Company, expanding its product line to include the Sugar Daddy, Sugar Babies, Junior Mints, Charleston Chew, and Pom Poms brands. Although Tootsie Roll maintained a two percent share of the $8 billion total candy market, which was dominated by such corporate giants as Nestlé and Hershey, it has been a longtime leader in the non-chocolate and lollipop segment of the industry, enjoying a 50 percent market share.

The genesis of the company that has been a familiar part of the American cultural landscape for nearly a century can be traced to the Brooklyn kitchen of a newly arrived immigrant from Austria, Leo Hirshfeld. In 1896, after having already developed such successful products as Bromangelon, a jelling powder that would later serve as the prototype for modern day gelatins, Hirshfeld concocted a thick, chewy chocolate mixture, which he

divided into bite-size rolls, wrapping each piece with paper to keep it clean and sanitary. The hand wrapping—believed to be an industry first—enabled Hirshfeld's product, named "Tootsie Roll" after his daughter Clara "Tootsie" Hirshfeld, to stand out among the competitor's candy-counter offerings, which were sold by the scoop out of large barrels or jars. The new penny candy was an instant success with the children in Hirschfeld's Brooklyn neighborhood. He soon realized that he would need more capital to promote and expand his candy business to meet the growing demand. To that end, he merged his operation with a local candy manufacturer, Stern & Staalberg, just a year later. Sales continued to boom, and by 1922 the company, renamed Sweets Company of America, was listed on the New York Stock Exchange.

The Great Depression put a temporary halt to the remarkable growth of the young company. It was during this period, though, that William Rubin, a box manufacturer whose family would control Tootsie Roll for the better part of the century, quietly began purchasing shares in the Sweets Company of America. As the nation's economy improved, Tootsie Roll began to receive more orders; by 1938, the company was ready to expand again, opening up a modern, 120,000-square-foot in Hoboken, New Jersey. With the help of such innovations as the conveyor belt, which ushered in the era of mass production, the company again enlarged its operating facilities, adding 40,000 square feet to the plant in 1941.

While the World War II economy forced many candy companies to suspend production, it proved quite a boon for Tootsie Roll. Highly valued for its "quick energy" properties and its ability to stay fresh for long periods of time, Tootsie Rolls were included in G.I. rations. While the company's involvement in the war effort, to be sure, resulted in gains on its balance sheet, it also contributed largely to the company's enduring status as an American icon. Frederick Arnold, in his autobiography of his days as a World War II fighter pilot, *Doorknob Five Two,* told, for instance, how he carried Tootsie Rolls with him on every mission, rewarding himself with a segment after each completed stage. This ritual proved a lifesaver when his plane was shot down over the Sahara; stranded in a stone quarry for three days, he sustained his energy with his Tootsie Rolls, and after he was taken in by a native tribe who shared their raw dog meat with him, he returned the favor by giving them a Tootsie Roll segment and a cigarette.

With the postwar boom in the United States economy and the increased availability of raw materials such as sugar and cocoa, Tootsie Roll was able to take full advantage of the competitive edge it had gained. Under the direction of William Rubin—who by 1948 had worked his way up to the post of company president—Tootsie Roll continued to expand. With Rubin's appointment came a stronger focus on the marketing and advertising efforts of the company. In 1950, he came up with a *Life* magazine ad that became a rich part of company lore; surrounded by the words *Sweet!*, *Popular!* and *Wholesome!* was pictured a beaming 18-year-old woman who embodied those adjectives, Rubin's daughter and future company president, Ellen Gordon. In the 1950s, while continuing to advertise in magazines, newspapers, and on the radio, the company also put some of its advertising dollars into the fledgling medium of television, becoming the first regular advertiser on classic children's programs such as the ''Howdy Doody Show'' and the ''Mickey Mouse Club.''

Under Rubin's leadership, the company experienced 15 consecutive years of record growth and opened up a second operating plant in Los Angeles to accommodate the ever increasing demand of its customers. In 1962, Melvin Gordon took over chief executive duties, and the company continued along this pattern of growth, with net earnings nearly tripling during the first six years of the decade. In 1966, the company changed its name to Tootsie Roll Industries, Inc. and opened a large Midwest plant in Chicago's South Side, which would later become company headquarters. By 1970, both the Hoboken and Los Angeles operations had been consolidated in Chicago to facilitate both distribution and production. From this more central location, goods could be shipped more efficiently throughout the United States, and such fundamental commodities as corn syrup, a product of the midwestern corn refineries, could be more easily obtained. Starting in the late 1960s, the company also began exploring foreign markets, establishing a subsidiary in Mexico, where the candy became known as ''Tutsi.'' Encouraged by its success south of the border, Tootsie Roll, after negotiating a licensing agreement in the Philippines in 1969, branched into Canada in 1971.

Tootsie Roll also looked towards acquisitions as a means of expanding. In 1972, the company purchased the Mason and Bonomo division of the Candy Corporation of America, adding such established brand names as Mason Dots, Mason Licorice Crows, Mason Mints, as well as Bonomo Turkish Taffy and Bonomo Sour Balls, to its repertoire. The decade was not without its hardships, though. In 1974, a 600 percent increase in sugar prices, combined with a similar rise in cocoa prices, forced the company to reexamine the size and price of some of its products. ''We had to take a hard look at things,'' Ellen Gordon—Melvin's wife and, at the time, a company director—explained in a *Chicago Tribune* article, noting that ''we had to make some pieces smaller and increased the price of other items, but that was true of the entire industry.'' While Nestlé raised its prices that year, Hershey reduced the size of its chocolate bars.

Having proven her business savvy in her ten years with the company, serving as a director responsible for managing outside investments and the pension fund, Ellen Gordon joined her husband at the top of the management team, taking over as president in 1978. The Gordons, who controlled 47 percent of the company's stock in 1994, proved a formidable duo. After guiding the company through the cocoa-sugar crisis, they were faced with a challenge that would again test their management skills: the Tylenol crisis of 1982. At the outset of that year's Halloween candy-buying season, traditionally the company's most profitable period, seven Chicago area people died after taking Extra Strength Tylenol capsules, causing many parents throughout the country to worry that their children's trick-or-treat candy might be poisoned. While sales for the candy industry as a whole suffered in the wake of the Tylenol scare, Tootsie Roll—already known for its public service announcements to the media to promote safe Halloween candy giving—recorded a slight increase in sales, and, just two years later, sales jumped almost 20 percent. The Gordons, in a 1985 *Chicago Tribune* article, cited two primary factors behind the rebounding sales

figures: first, an increase in distribution through the sale of more products in stores that already carried the Tootsie Roll line and the introduction of products in stores that did not; and second, the development of new products, such as the ''foot of Tootsie,'' a larger version of the original Tootsie Roll.

The company's success did not go without notice in the candy industry. In May 1984, Ellen Gordon was awarded *Candy Industry* magazine's Kettle Award for outstanding achievement in candy manufacturing. The first woman to receive the award, Mrs. Gordon stated in her acceptance speech that ''the kettle confirms that a woman's place is still in the kitchen, but also confirms that her place is in the wrapping room.'' As one of the founding members and president from 1987 through 1989 of the Committee of 200, an elite organization of high-level women executives and entrepreneurs, Gordon was recognized as a success story and role model among women, in particular, during this time, but her leadership abilities and industry expertise were equally respected by men and women in the business community as a whole. *Working Woman* magazine's Stephen Wilkinson, for example, commented: ''Certainly Ellen Gordon is an executive who has used her skills as a business person rather than relied on her role as a 'woman president'.''

During the 1980s, Tootsie Roll strengthened its position in the candy market through key acquisitions. In 1985, the company purchased Cella's Confections, Inc., a New York based manufacturer of chocolate-covered cherries, putting ''Tootsie squarely into an adult market,'' according to the *Chicago Tribune* writer Gormon, by adding ''changemakers''—the small, foil-wrapped candies often offered at check-out counters—to their product line. Three years later, the company invested another $65 million on the acquisition of the Charms Company, a purchase which enabled Tootsie Roll to gain a virtual lock on the lollipop market. Such additions, according to *Candy Industry* Pat Magee of *Working Woman*, were successful due to the Gordons' focus on acquiring companies ''that will fit well into their own philosophy of candy making, their own marketing methodology.'' Magee noted that the company added ''snap and pizzazz to the companies that they buy,'' primarily by ''upgrad[ing] the packaging.'' Also during this time, Ellen Gordon invested $10 million in a manufacturing modernization program and a new, sophisticated computer system was installed.

As the company moved into the late 1980s and early 1990s, ''Tootsie on Roll,'' became a familiar phrase within business circles, aptly describing the company's continued growth in spite of the recessionary environment. Net sales rose more than 80 percent between 1987 and 1990, while net profits increased 75 percent during the same period. As Malcolm Berko stated in a *Akron Beacon Journal* column, the company appeared ''nearly impervious to economic cycles.'' Berko noted that ''since 1979, Tootsie Roll's dividends have increased threefold, sales have tripled, book value has jumped five-fold, net profit margins have doubled while sales sweetened from $60 million to $220 million'' in 1991.

One of the primary factors behind the success of Tootsie Roll was undoubtedly the distinctive quality of its products. While customers were inundated with the multitude of shapes, sizes, and colors of the various chocolate bars and other sweets offered in the candy aisle, the trademark packaging of Tootsie Roll products stood as something of an American classic. That the company's products achieved the status of a "national institution" was due in no small part to the creativity of its television advertising. One especially successful commercial initiated in the 1970s featured a young boy asking a venerable Mr. Owl, "How many licks does it take to get to the center of a Tootsie Pop?" After taking three licks, Mr. Owl bit into the candy and concluded that three licks was all it took. Tens of thousands of children, however, actually wrote the company with their own answers—usually between 800 to 2,000 licks, according to company reports. The ad was still prompting responses in the 1990s, when two American soldiers, stationed in the Middle East during Operations Desert Shield and Desert Storm, concluded that it took a little over 1,600 licks to reach the Tootsie Roll center.

Noting that the company was a mainstay on *Forbes*' honor roll of small companies and *CFO* magazine's list of America's strongest companies, analysts pointed to Tootsie Roll's efficient style of management. "People ask us how we can compete against the giant candy corporations," stated Melvin Gordon in an interview with *Midway* reporter Jack Klobucar. Gordon explained, "we wonder how they can compete against us. We can make decisions on the spot; we have hands-on management that's impossible in most billion-dollar companies." One of the strategies behind the Gordons' successful company was their hands-on, "vertical" style of management. As Melvin Gordon explained in an interview with *Compass Readings*' Jane Ammeson, "We try to be vertical wherever we can. We have our own sugar refinery, probably the only candy manufacturer in the world with its own. We have our own printing press and rebuild our own machinery in-house. We bought our own advertising agency. We even make the sticks for the Tootsie Roll Pops." By maintaining control over these services, *Midway*'s Klobucar observed, "they not only reduce operating costs but also reinforce their independence—a commodity almost as precious as chocolate."

Many analysts expected Tootsie Roll to continue its consistent pattern of growth through the 1990s, based on the company's plans for further acquisitions and more foreign expansion. In 1993, the company made the largest purchase in its history, obtaining Warner-Lambert's chocolate and caramel brands— Junior Mints, Charleston Chew, Pom Poms, Sugar Babies and Sugar Daddy's—for an estimated $81 million. The new brands "were a natural to join the Tootsie family," Ellen Gordon told *Snack Food*'s Wendy Kimbrell. "We have, while keeping the nostalgia and general look of the products, designed new packaging for the some of the Warner-Lambert products, so they fit better with our existing line," Gordon noted. Analysts regarded the strategy as successful: sales from the new brands contributed to the company's six percent increase in total sales for 1993. Moreover, Tootsie Roll's record sales figures for the first nine months of 1994 were achieved principally as a result of the Warner-Lambert brands.

With the 1993 passage of the North American Free Trade Agreement (NAFTA), which promised to relax trade restrictions between the United States and its neighboring countries of Canada and Mexico, Tootsie Roll was expected to place more emphasis on its operations to the north and south. In an interview for *Snack Food* magazine, Ellen Gordon predicted more intense competition as a result of NAFTA, commenting, "there's no doubt about it—Mexican candies will come into the U.S. and American candies will go down into Mexico." Nevertheless, as her husband was quick to add, Tootsie Roll had "unique products down there. Tutsi has been advertised in a major way ever since it started in Mexico in 1968 on Televisa, the nation's largest TV network." The Gordons planned to bolster their Canadian operations as well, while they settled on the location of a new overseas plant, possibly in the Far East or Europe, where the demand for confectionery was reportedly higher than in the United States. With the Gordon management team leading these developments and the added advantage of a healthy balance sheet, Tootsie Roll was expected to enlarge its niche in the candy industry and continue to add to its 17 consecutive years of growth.

Principal Subsidiaries: Cella's Confections, Inc.; Charms Company; Cambridge Brands Inc.

Further Reading:

Ammeson, Jane, "Tootsie Roll's Sweet Taste of Success," *Compass Readings,* December 1989, pp. 32–37.

Barko, Malcolm, "A Sweet Deal for Long-Term Investors," *Akron Beacon Journal,* August 4, 1991.

Bettner, Jill, "Sticky Business," *Forbes,* February 13, 1984, p. 112.

Blades, John, "Tootsie's on a Roll," *Chicago Tribune,* December 6, 1990.

Boas, Nancy, "How Sweet It Is," *Across the Board,* December 1984.

Driscoll, Mary, and Maile Hulihan, "America's Strongest Companies," *CFO,* April 1991, p. 17

Gorman, John, "Tootsie Roll Turns Chocolate into Gold," *Chicago Tribune,* June 24, 1985, sec. 4, p. 1.

Kichen, Steve, "The Best Small Company Honor Roll," *Forbes,* November 11, 1994, p. 264.

Kimbrell, Wendy, "Way to Grow," *Snack Food,* May 1994, p. 22.

Klobucar, Jack, "How Sweet It Is: Tootsie Roll Industries Posts Record Sales," *Midway,* May 1986, p. 24.

Lappen, Alyssa A., "Tootsie Rolling in Money," *Forbes,* January 21, 1991.

Magee, Patricia, "Ellen Gordon Reaches 'Top of the Mountain'," *Candy Industry,* September 1985.

Merrion, Paul, "Tootsie Rolling Downhill," *Crain's Chicago Business,* May 23, 1994, p. 46.

Morris, Kathleen, "Tootsie Roll: Cashing in on Closet Candy Eating," *Financial World,* January 21, 1992, p. 16.

Ryan, Nancy, "Tootsie on a Roll in Forbes Magazine Survey," *Chicago Tribune,* October 29, 1991.

Tiffany, Susan, "Tootsie Roll Keeps Rolling in the Riches," *Candy Industry,* June 1993.

Wilkinson, Stephen, "The Practical Genius of Penny Candy," *Working Woman,* April 1989.

—Jason Gallman

TOSHIBA

Toshiba Corporation

1-1 Shibaura 1-chome
Minato-ku, Tokyo 105
Japan
(03) 457 2104
Fax: (03) 456-4776

Public Company
Incorporated: 1896
Employees: 175,000
Sales: ¥4.63 trillion (US$44.96 billion)
Stock Exchanges: Tokyo Osaka Nagoya Kyoto Hiroshima
   Fukuoka Sapporo Niigata London Paris Amsterdam
   Düsseldorf Frankfurt Luxembourg
SICs: 3500 Industrial Machinery & Equipment; 3571
   Electronic Computers; 3800 Instruments & Related
   Products; 5040 Professional & Commercial Equipment;
   5060 Electrical Goods; 5080 Machinery, Equipment &
   Supplies; 7373 Computer Integrated Systems Design

Toshiba Corporation is one of Japan's oldest and largest producers of consumer and industrial electric products. The company also ranks as the world's largest manufacturer of DRAM (dynamic random access memory) computer chips. Toshiba, a family of over 200 consolidated and affiliated businesses, is one of Japan's second-tier *keiretsu* or conglomerates. These corporate groups are linked through history and tradition, as well as cross-shareholdings, interlocking directorates, and personal contacts. With a history that dates back to the nineteenth century and a product line that extends from semiconductors to nuclear power plants, Toshiba has played an active role in Japan's rise to the forefront of international business.

Toshiba was formed through the 1939 union of two manufacturers of electrical equipment, Shibaura Seisakusho Works and Tokyo Electric Company, Ltd. The older of the two, Shibaura, traced its roots to Japan's first telegraph equipment shop, Seizo-sha. Hisashige Tanaka, who has been called the "Edison of Japan," established the business in 1875. The business climate in which the company began, however, was far from the atmosphere in which it later operated. During the late nineteenth century, Japan lagged far behind Britain, France, Germany and the United States in industrial development. Besieged with economic problems resulting from the overthrow of the Tokugawa government in 1869 and a tremendous influx of imported goods

and machinery which threatened her fledgling industries, Japan was vulnerable to colonization. Confronted with the task of strengthening its faltering industries, the new government was quick to respond.

In October of 1870 the Ministry of Industry (Kobusho) was formed and subsequently acted as a catalyst for the country's industrial development. In its attempt to integrate contemporary technologies into Japan, the government concentrated on hiring foreign engineers, technicians, and scientists to instruct domestic engineers in operating imported machinery; the government also sent its own engineers abroad to inspect manufacturing techniques with the intent of selecting machinery and manufacturing techniques for use in Japanese industries.

The integration of foreign technologies was first put into practice by Seizo-sha, which had adopted the name Shibaura Seisakusho Works in 1893. The company's 1,300 horsepower steam engine, copied from blueprints of an English counterpart, was successfully constructed in a plant in Kanebo, Japan. This venture convinced Japanese industrialists of their potential for technological advancement through the adoption of foreign technology and its adaptation to domestic skills and resources.

Shibaura embraced this concept in the 1880s, determining that paying outright for technological knowledge was the most expedient means to upgrade its technological capabilities. This strategy helped the company expand into the manufacture of transformers, electric motors, and other heavy electric equipment in the 1890s.

Shibaura made its own discoveries as well during this period, originating Japan's first hydroelectric generators in 1894. By 1902 Shibaura's own technological capabilities had produced a 150-kilowatt 3-phase-current dynamo for the Yokosuka Bay Arsenal, marking one of the initial transformations from foreign to Japanese-based technology, and the beginning of the company's rise to the forefront of international business. The company developed Japan's first X-ray tubes in 1914.

While Shibaura and other Japanese corporations were growing in strength and increasing their capabilities, they were deeply debilitated by the advent of World War I. As the war began, Japanese manufacturers were cut off from Germany, England, and the United States, major suppliers of machines, industrial materials, and chemicals, forcing them to turn to one another for necessary materials and machinery to keep their fledgling industries alive. The hardships experienced during this period had long-term advantages however, for they forced Japanese industry into self-sufficiency and paved the way for the country's industrial advancement.

Shibaura continued to grow in the interim between world wars, and merged with the Tokyo Electric Company, Ltd. in 1939. Tokyo Electric had also been established before the turn of the twentieth century. Originally known as Hakunetsusha & Company, the firm was founded by Dr. Ichisuke Fujioka and Shoichi Miyoshi. Hakunetsusha had distinguished itself as Japan's first manufacturer of incandescent lamps. The newly merged company, named Tokyo Shibaura Electric Company, Ltd., soon became widely known as Toshiba. The company's pre-World War II Japanese innovations included fluorescent lamps and radar.

During the late 1940s, Japan rapidly passed from a period of self-isolation and self-reliance into a period of largely benevolent occupation and advocacy. With the assistance of the Japanese government and its citizens, the American Occupation Authority instituted social and economic reforms, and poured resources into post-war financial markets. Japan's readmittance into the international trading community gave it access to overseas markets for manufactured goods and raw materials. The glut of raw materials available at the time enabled Japan to obtain necessary commodities in large quantities at favorable prices and, consequently, to regain its financial and industrial strength.

In this more favorable climate, Toshiba once again began to flourish. The company's shares were first listed on the Tokyo Stock and Osaka Securities Exchanges in 1949. Backed by the powerful trading house of the Mitsui Group, the company's financial status was well secured. Starting in the 1950s, Toshiba began a program to strengthen its competitiveness in both the domestic and international markets. The company produced Japan's first broadcasting equipment in 1952, and launched digital computers in 1954.

Yet it would be some time before modern business policies affected the company in any fundamental way. Toshiba executives were criticized for their rigid adherence to a feudal system of hierarchy and status. Top officials maintained lax working hours and were far removed from any operational business. An indisputable separation between a superior and his subordinates made the exchange of ideas virtually impossible. To reduce the burden of responsibility on any one executive, numerous signatures were needed to approve a document. Thus innovation was easily stymied in a chain of bureaucracy.

In the early 1960s, these internal problems were compounded by an economic recession. In one year Toshiba's pre-tax profits slid from $36 million to $13 million. To halt any further erosion, a radical change was in order. For only the second time in Toshiba's history the company sought an outsider to aid the ailing business. The company's board hired Toshiwo Doko to take charge of the company. Doko had won acclaim as the architect of the 1960 merger of Ishikawajima Heavy Industries and Harima Shipbuilding & Engineering Company, which formed the world's largest shipbuilder, IHI.

When he joined Toshiba as president in 1965, Doko retained his title as chairman of IHI. The combined status ranked Doko as Japan's leading industrialist. These two companies had shared interests prior to Doko's appointment at Toshiba; IHI owned over ten million shares in Toshiba and Toshiba controlled over four million shares in IHI. After Doko became president, Toshiba raised its stake in IHI as both companies shared executives on their boards and established trade agreements. This exchange, a *keiretsu* hallmark, strengthened Toshiba's financial standing.

Doko's other corrective measures included the reduction of Toshiba's dependence on borrowed capital. This was aided by the U.S.-based General Electric Company's agreement to purchase all of Toshiba's capital issue. General Electric's interest in Toshiba dated back to before World War II, but had declined in the intervening years. The infusion of capital enabled Toshiba to expand and modernize its operations.

The new company president also initiated a comprehensive campaign to export Toshiba products around the world. By establishing independent departments, the company could better facilitate the export of consumer and industrial goods. Major contracts were finalized with U.S. companies to export generators, transformers, and motors, as well as televisions and home appliances.

Other streamlining efforts took the form of expanding the sales force, hiring new management, and consolidating operations. By 1967 Toshiba controlled 63 subsidiaries and employed upward of 100,000 people; the company ranked as the largest electronic manufacturer in Japan and the nation's fourth largest company. But in light of the dramatic expansion of domestic competitors like Sony and Hitachi in the 1970s, Toshiba's performance was generally considered mediocre.

In 1980, a new president, Shoichi Saba, brought renewed vigor to the company. Trained as an electrical engineer, Saba funneled vast resources into research and development, especially in the areas of semiconductors, computers and telecommunications. In October of 1984, Toshiba formed an Information and Communications Systems Laboratory to develop and integrate office automation products. That same year, Toshiba was responsible for the world's first direct broadcast satellite. The company's R&D investment paid off handsomely in 1985, when Toshiba won the global race to develop the first one-megabyte DRAM memory chip. By 1987 the company was producing almost half of the world's one-megabyte chips.

Utilized in equipment from stereos to computers, semiconductors soon became an important part of Toshiba's portfolio. In 1986 alone, Toshiba's semiconductor facilities experienced a 55 percent increase due to contracts in France and West Germany, as well as burgeoning domestic demand. For the first time in its history, Toshiba surpassed its closest competitor, Hitachi, Ltd., to become the second largest semiconductor manufacturer in the world, behind NEC Corporation.

Joint ventures and agreements with both Japanese and foreign corporations facilitated technology exchange. In 1986 Toshiba entered into a joint venture with Motorola for its Japanese production of computer memories and microprocessors. The two companies became involved in the collective development of microcomputer and memory chips based on the exchange of technology, and also developed a manufacturing facility in Japan. Efforts of this type facilitated the development of voice recognition systems and digital private branch exchange systems (PBXs), which transmit telephone calls within private buildings. Through a 1986 agreement with AT&T, Toshiba began marketing these systems throughout Japan, as well as assisting that corporation with technological insight.

In the same year, Toshiba entered into an agreement with IBM-Japan to market their general purpose computers domestically. Through this arrangement, Toshiba marketed its own communications equipment with IBM-Japan's computers, selling to governmental agencies, local governments, and other institutions to which IBM (as a foreign interest) had previously been blocked. An additional marketing contract with IBM introduced the first

PC-compatible laptop computer, the TJ3100, to Japan, and met with great success. By 1991, Toshiba had garnered over one-fifth of the laptop market.

The area for which Toshiba is best known remains its consumer products division, which grew at a rapid pace in the 1980s through acquisition and innovation. In April of 1984 Toshiba reorganized the production, marketing, and research and development sections of its video and audio products, incorporating them into one centralized location. While sales of standard consumer products such as VCRs, compact disc players, televisions, and personal cassette recorders continued to grow, Toshiba was quick to capitalize on new markets as well. In 1986 the company entered the home video market, creating a wholly-owned subsidiary and introducing 110 new video titles to the Japanese market. That same year, it inked an agreement to supply cable equipment to American Television and Communications Corporation.

Although Toshiba is best known in America for its computer-related and consumer products, it has a wide range of additional business ventures. Among Japanese corporations, Toshiba is a leader in the production of advanced medical electronic equipment. In 1986 the corporation initiated the supply of blood chemical analyzers, used to detect liver and kidney disease, to Allied Corporation, a leading U.S. chemical manufacturer. Other accomplishments suggested Toshiba's technological foresight in solving global and domestic problems. Toshiba has begun production of equipment for uranium fuel enrichment for use in nuclear power plants, marking an important step towards Japan's acquisition of a domestic nuclear fuel supply.

These many successes realized under Shoichi Saba were overshadowed by a 1987 scandal involving Toshiba Machine, a subsidiary half-owned by Toshiba. According to Washington sources, the subsidiary sold submarine sound-deadening equipment to the then-communist Soviet Union. The equipment made detection more difficult and forced NATO to modernize its antisubmarine detection equipment. While Toshiba claimed that it was not able to control the subsidiary's daily operations, the sale broke a Western law concerning the sale of technologically advanced equipment to Communist countries. Two executives at the subsidiary under investigation were arrested and four top-ranking officials resigned. The Japanese government prohibited the subsidiary from exporting products to the Soviet Union for one year and repealed its right to sponsor visas for visiting personnel from Eastern-bloc countries. Amid growing protests in both Japan and the United States, Toshiba President Sugichiro Watari issued a public apology to the United States. Then, on July 1, 1987, both Watari and Chairman Shoichi Saba tendered their resignations from the Toshiba Corporation in the wake of a U.S. Senate vote to ban the import of Toshiba products for three years. Joichi Aoi, a former senior executive vice-president, assumed Toshiba's presidency.

Ironically, the anti-Japan mood roused by this episode may have revitalized morale at Toshiba. Perhaps to compensate for the loss of the U.S. market, Chairman Joichi Aoi led the company's energetic expansion into global markets. In the latter years of the 1980s, Toshiba began offering its integrated circuit technology to the Chinese Electronics Import and Export Corporation to assist in development of television production. A 1991 joint venture with General Electric furthered this effort, with a special emphasis on large home appliances. The company also won a contract worth ¥12 billion to build a color television assembly plant in Russia, marking Moscow's first agreement of this nature with a Japanese company. Thus, in spite of losing up to ¥5 billion as a result of the U.S. embargo, the company's net income nearly doubled, from ¥61 billion in 1987 to ¥121 billion in 1990. Toshiba's fiscal triumphs were capped with the 1991 naming of chairman Joichi Aoi as Asia's CEO of the Year.

But with the new decade came new economic imperatives, especially those created by a global recession and the rising value of the yen. While Toshiba's annual revenues remained essentially flat from 1990 to 1994, the electronics giant's profits declined over 90 percent to ¥12 billion, their lowest level in well over a decade.

Toshiba Chairman Aoi and President Fumio Sato employed a variety of strategies in the hopes of reversing this downward course. A 1993 reorganization focused on fostering interaction between and flexibility among the company's hundreds of operations. In line with industry trends, the leaders worked to shorten product development cycles, lower production expenses, and more closely monitor consumer demands. They also moved to further diversify Toshiba's consumer product line, 50 percent of which was still in color televisions. The company worked to shift its emphasis to such high-potential products as cellular communications, multimedia, and mobile electronics. Amid all these changes, however, the company planned to continue its liberal use of strategic alliances for mutual benefit.

Principal Subsidiaries: Iwate Toshiba Electronics Co., Ltd.; Kaga Toshiba Electronics Co., Ltd.; Kitashiba Electric Co., Ltd.; Kyodo Building Corporation; Marcon Electronics Co., Ltd.; Nishishiba Electric Co., Ltd.; Nogata Toshiba Electronics Co.; Onkyo Corp.; Shibaura Engineering Works Co., Ltd.; TIM Electronics Sdn. Bhd.; Tokyo Electric Co., Ltd.; Toshiba Air Conditioning Co., Ltd.; Toshiba America Consumer Products, Inc.; Toshiba America Electronic Components, Inc.; Toshiba America Entertainment, Inc.; Toshiba America, Inc.; Toshiba America Information Systems, Inc.; Toshiba America Medical Systems, Inc.; Toshiba America MRI Inc.; Toshiba Automation Co., Ltd.; Toshiba Battery Co., Ltd.; Toshiba Builders Appliance Co., Ltd.; Toshiba Building Corporation; Toshiba Ceramics Co., Ltd.; Toshiba Chemical Corporation; Toshiba Compressor (Taiwan) Corp.; Toshiba Consumer Products (Thailand) Co., Ltd.; Toshiba Consumer Products Europe GmbH; Toshiba Consumer Products (France) S.A.; Toshiba Consumer Products (UK) Ltd.; Toshiba Credit Corporation; Toshiba Dalian Co., Ltd.; Toshiba Device Corporation; Toshiba Display Devices (Thailand) Co., Ltd.; Toshiba Display Devices Inc.; Toshiba East Japan Life Electronics Co., Ltd.; Toshiba Electric Appliances Co., Ltd.; Toshiba Electronics Europe GmbH; Toshiba Electronics (UK) Ltd.; Toshiba Elevator Technos Co., Ltd.; Toshiba Engineering & Construction Co., Ltd.; Toshiba Engineering Corporation; Toshiba Europe (I.E.) GmbH; Toshiba Glass Co., Ltd.; Toshiba Home Technology Corporation; Toshiba Information Equipments Co., Ltd.; Toshiba Information Systems (Japan) Corporation; Toshiba International Corporation; Toshiba International Finance (Netherlands) B.V.; Toshiba International Finance (UK) Plc.; Toshiba Lighting &

Technology Corporation; Toshiba Logistics Corporation; Toshiba (UK) Ltd.; Toshiba Medical Systems Co., Ltd.; Toshiba Medical Systems Europe B.V.; Toshiba Nishi Nihon Life Electronics Co., Ltd.; Toshiba (Australia) Pty, Ltd.; Toshiba Semiconductor (Thailand) Co., Ltd.; Toshiba Semiconductor GmbH; Toshiba Silicone Co., Ltd. TAE Holding, Inc.; Vertex Semiconductor Corporation. The company also lists 53 other domestic and 21 other international subsidiaries.

Further Reading:

Abrams, Judith, "Toshiba Eyes New Media Frontier," *Dealerscope Merchandising,* July 1994, pp. 24–25.
Johnstone, Bob, "Industry: Quick as a Flash," *Far Eastern Economic Review,* January 7, 1993, p. 57.
Meyer, Richard, "Power Surge," *Financial World,* April 3, 1990, pp. 42–46.
——, "Asia's CEO of the Year: Joichi Aoi of Toshiba—'We Just Stay With It,'" *Financial World,* October 15, 1991, pp. 50–54.
Sato, Kazuo, ed., *Industry and Business in Japan,* New York: Croom Helm, 1980.
Schlender, Brenton R., "How Toshiba Makes Alliances Work," *Fortune,* October 4, 1993, pp. 116–120.
Tanzer, Andrew, "The Man Toshiba Hung Out to Dry," *Forbes,* September 7, 1987, pp. 96–98.
Uchida, Michio, "Toshiba Bounces Back," *Tokyo Business Today,* June 1989, pp. 14–19.
Young, Lewis H., "Why Toshiba Likes the Component Business," *Electronic Business Buyer,* December 1994, pp. 52–56.

—updated by April Dougal Gasbarre

Trans World Airlines, Inc.

605 Third Avenue
New York, New York 10158
U.S.A.
(314) 589-3000
Fax: (314) 589-3000

Public Company
Incorporated: 1928 as Transcontinental Air Transport
Employees: 20,871
Sales: $3.15 billion
Stock Exchanges: New York
SICs: 4512 Air Transportation, Scheduled

In the early 1990s Trans World Airlines, Inc. ranked as the United States' seventh-largest airline company. The firm's near seventy-year history has been influenced by such well-known personalities as Charles Lindbergh, Amelia Earhart, Jack Frye, and Howard Hughes. But under the late 1980s and early 1990s stewardship of corporate raider Carl Icahn, the company widely known as TWA squandered its reputation for innovation and plunged into bankruptcy. Icahn took the airline private in 1988, then sold it to its employees and creditors as part of a 1992 bankruptcy reorganization. While TWA returned to public ownership in the mid-1990s, it had not recorded a full year of profitability since 1987.

TWA was established through the merger of several small airline companies in the 1920s. One of those small companies was Maddux Air Lines, which began a luxury passenger service between Los Angeles and San Diego on July 21, 1927. Maddux and a number of other carriers were organized by a group of investors who sought to establish a transcontinental passenger line using a combination of airplane flights and railroads. The group, Transcontinental Air Transport, hired Charles Lindbergh to survey the route. On July 7, 1929, TAT inaugurated the "Lindbergh Line," offering coast-to-coast transportation in about 48 hours. The journey departed New York in the evening and crossed the eastern U.S. by the Pennsylvania Railroad. The next morning passengers flew from Columbus, Ohio to Waynoka, Oklahoma. From there the Santa Fe Railroad took them overnight to Clovis, New Mexico. From Clovis the passengers flew on to either Los Angeles or San Francisco.

In those early days of commercial aviation, airlines made most of their money hauling mail for postal services. The United States Postmaster, Walter Folger Brown, was responsible for assigning three transcontinental airmail routes. American Airlines won the southern route, Northwest Airlines won the northern route, and TAT was awarded the central route, but only on the condition that the company merge with Western Air Express. In 1930, the two companies joined to form Transcontinental and Western Air Lines, or TWA. That October the new company covered the coast-to-coast route completely with airplanes, in light of the failure of the previous scheme. The trip was reduced to 36 hours and then later to 24.

Bill Boeing manufactured what were generally regarded as the best airplanes of the day; however, he refused to sell them to any air transport company except his own. Excluded from the Boeing market, TWA's general manager Jack Frye solicited designs from a number of manufacturers. A small California operation run by Donald Douglas proposed an impressive design which outperformed Frye's basic specifications. TWA accepted Douglas's offer, and the first DC-1 was built. The DC-1, however, became obsolete before it could be mass produced, so it was lengthened and otherwise improved. The new plane, the DC-2, was every bit as practical as the DC-1, but more difficult to fly.

Air travel was a risky business in the 1930s. Breaches in pilot discipline and frequent equipment failures caused a number of TWA airplane crashes. At one point, the airline was losing 5 percent of its personnel annually to such accidents. The company was further troubled when the Roosevelt administration decided to cancel all government airmail contracts with private carriers in 1934. Many airlines, including TWA, depended on mail contracts for their profitability. During this crisis TWA was sold to a group led by the Lehman Brothers and John Hertz of the Yellow Cab Company. The government decided to restore the airmail contracts a few months later and reopened the bidding. Curiously, companies that had held contracts before were barred from bidding. In order to get around this stipulation, the company responded by merely adding "Incorporated" to its name. It was re-awarded 60 percent of its original airmail system and, over a period of a few years, recovered the rest.

Under the new owners, Jack Frye, a vice-president and former Hollywood stunt pilot, was promoted to president. The new management instituted major improvements in TWA's training and flight efficiency and also upgraded its airport facilities. The airline employed directional "homing" radar and installed runway lights to facilitate night flying. The DC-3 became the company's new workhorse while business improved significantly.

In the 1930s airline companies became especially vulnerable to buyouts. General Motors Corp. acquired Eastern Airlines in 1933 and American Airlines was taken over by the auto magnate E. L. Cord. When General Motors purchased stock in TWA, the airline worried that it would be forcibly merged with some other GM interest. In 1938, when TWA had fully recovered from the airmail fiasco, the Lehman/Hertz group sold the airline to another group of investors. During this time Frye personally convinced millionaire Howard Hughes to invest in TWA. It is very likely that Frye wanted Hughes's interest in the company so that he could help to defend it from any hostile takeover bids, especially from GM.

At the outset, Frye and Hughes respected each other as aviators and businessmen. Frye was a daredevil flier, a man totally enthralled with aviation and its possibilities. Hughes was an equally eccentric young man who was devoted to breaking aviation records. From his father he inherited ownership of the extremely lucrative Hughes Tool Company, the primary supplier of oil well drilling bits. Using this large fortune Hughes purchased 25 percent of TWA's stock. In 1941 he gained a controlling interest in the airline and later increased his share to 78 percent.

One of Hughes's first activities at TWA was to begin development of a new airplane, the L-049 Constellation, in association with Lockheed. While the Constellation was still being developed, Hughes approved Frye's proposal to buy another new airplane, Boeing's 307 Stratoliner, for the interim. The Stratoliner had a pressurized cabin and was able to reach an altitude of 20,000 feet. As a result, it could fly over bad weather rather than be forced to navigate through it.

TWA was one of the first American airline companies to serve during the Battle of Britain in 1940. Even before the U.S. government had committed itself to the war effort, TWA was helping the Army Air Corps assist the British. When the U.S. became fully involved in 1941, TWA was assigned two military supply routes: the North Atlantic route to Prestwick, Scotland, and the South Atlantic route from Brazil to Liberia and points east.

The airline had the distinction of flying President Roosevelt and a number of other government personnel to and from various meeting places during the war, most notably, Casablanca. The war gave TWA the opportunity to upgrade and expand its facilities worldwide in anticipation of the allied victory. The U.S. War Department actively supported the airline's activities during the war. It would be fair to say that TWA served the country well and that it also profited handsomely. When TWA's military service was over it had flown 40 million miles for the Army, and was exposed to hundreds of new destinations.

The major overseas carriers after the war were Pan Am, American, and TWA. All these airlines requested licensing for commercial use of much of their wartime network. TWA was granted two transatlantic routes to Europe, one via the "great circle" near the Arctic, and the other via the Azores to the Mediterranean. From there TWA flew on to India, Southeast Asia, and Japan. The company also enjoyed a government subsidy in the immediate postwar years.

Hughes and Frye had grandiose, but divergent, plans for their company, whose name they had changed to Trans World Airlines. The Constellation they helped to develop first flew in 1944, served briefly during the war, and entered wide commercial use in the postwar era. However, it was at this time that the two men began to disagree. Hughes, who was injured in the crash of a test plane during the war, had developed a very difficult personality and was known to hold up major business decisions for weeks while he agonized over minute details. He even disappeared for several days with a Constellation, only to turn up in Bermuda making endless test landings.

TWA soon found that it did not have enough business on its 21,000 miles of postwar international routes to generate a profit.

Frye's efforts to rectify the problem collided with the plans of Hughes's financial manager, Noah Dietrich. Dietrich charged that Frye had mismanaged the airline into a financial crisis and dangerous overexpansion. Hughes offered to provide money for TWA from the Hughes Tool Company, but only on the condition that Frye resign. Thus in January of 1947 Frye left TWA.

TWA suspended many of its plans for further expansion. The headquarters was moved from Kansas City to New York. Ralph Damon, who had previously been with American Airlines, was brought in to replace Jack Frye. Damon was an old-school engineer and airplane manufacturer known for his careful attention to detail. Damon's numerous successes at the airline, however, were shrouded by Hughes's continued interference and manipulation. Hughes insisted that the company reduce its advertising and promotion at a time when it was probably most needed. Regardless, TWA went off its postwar government subsidy in 1952, and a year later was healthy enough to declare a 10 percent stock distribution. Two years later Damon died at work, a victim of pneumonia and exhaustion. Doctors suggested that his poor health was exacerbated by the unrelenting pressure of running an airline for Howard Hughes.

Damon's successor was Carter Burgess, a former Assistant Secretary of Defense. Burgess lasted only 11 months, during which time he had never even met Hughes. TWA's next president was Charles Thomas. Thomas kept a low profile, followed all of Hughes's orders, and kept the company in good financial condition. When Thomas took over in the mid-1950s, all of the airlines were competing to be the first to have jetliners in their fleets. While the other leading companies were laying their plans and placing orders, TWA's order was delayed by Hughes's indecision over which airplane to buy, the Boeing 707 or the DC-8. Weeks later he finally decided to order 76 airplanes from Boeing and Convair. The jetliners would cost $500 million, much more than TWA could afford. Hughes's plan was to have his successful tool company purchase the planes and lease them to the airline. He wanted to keep TWA's profits low, channel money out of the Tool Company, and thereby avoid paying large penalty taxes.

Unfortunately, a world oil glut hurt the Hughes Tool Company so badly that it was unable to pay for the new airplanes. As a result, TWA was forced to turn to a group of Wall Street investment bankers for financial support. The bankers were aware of Hughes's reputation as a successful tycoon, but also recognized that his interests were probably not the same as those of the airline. As a condition for their financial assistance, they required that Hughes's majority voting interest in TWA be placed in a trust under their control. Negotiations lasted until the bankers' deadline, when Hughes finally conceded.

One of the investment group's first actions was to install Charles Tillinghast as president of TWA. Tillinghast, a lawyer, promptly filed an antitrust suit against Hughes, alleging violations of the Sherman Act and the Clayton Anti-Monopoly Act, and accusing him of monopolizing aircraft purchases for his own benefit and to the detriment of TWA. Hughes responded with a countersuit, charging that they swindled him out of his airline. The litigation continued for many years and cost TWA over $10 million. In the end, the courts returned no clear decision.

Tillinghast reorganized the airline quickly and completely. Management was restructured and pared down. TWA placed orders for newer B-727s and French-built Caravelles. In addition, Tillinghast attempted to change the company's public image. In light of its association with Hughes, TWA was regarded as being overly concerned with speed, glamour, and style, and not enough with dependability, efficiency and safety. TWA emerged from its troubles with stable and consistent profits through 1966, largely due to the direction of Charles Tillinghast. Ironically, the chief beneficiary of TWA's improvement was Howard Hughes. In 1966 he sold his stock in the airline for $546.5 million, or $86 per share. Three years earlier TWA stock had sold for a paltry $7.50.

Aside from the large profits and the Hughes fiasco, the 1960s were important in another way. It was at this time that Tillinghast made perhaps his most important contribution. Hoping to provide the company with protection against the unpredictable and unstable airline business, he initiated a diversification program aimed at strengthening the airline's capital structure and cash flow.

TWA's diversification began in 1964 with a contract to provide base support services to the National Aeronautics and Space Administration at Cape Kennedy. In 1967 TWA purchased Hilton International, the operator of all Hilton Hotels outside the United States. Later, TWA acquired the Canteen Corporation, Spartan Food Services, and Century 21, a real estate firm. The company was the first to diversify into non-airline businesses, and its timing was auspicious, as the industry was suffering from the recession of the early 1970s. TWA's B-747s and L-1011's were flying with nearly empty passenger cabins. The original decision to purchase the jetliners was made in response to Pan Am's huge orders, and not based on TWA's needs. As a result, the airline was plagued with overcapacity; it owned too many big, inefficient planes.

To make matters worse, TWA suffered a crippling six-week flight attendants' strike in 1973. By 1975 several payrolls could only be met with the immediate sale of six 747s to the Iranian Air Force. It was an unfortunate financial transaction for TWA (which sold the jetliners for about one-sixth their actual value), but the airline was desperate for cash. TWA was also losing money on its trans-Pacific route, which had been awarded during Lyndon B. Johnson's presidency. For the first time in its history, TWA's network stretched around the world, but even this would soon come to an end.

Tillinghast retired amid these numerous crises. He was succeeded in January of 1976 by Carl Meyer. Meyer navigated the airline through a series of changes in the airline passenger market. Costs were reduced as international traffic expanded. The Airline Deregulation Act of 1978 allowed TWA to establish a more efficient dual hub system: St Louis for domestic traffic and New York for international traffic. Moreover, under Carl Meyer TWA reduced its fleet and its staff. The company purchased more fuel-efficient airplanes while selling the "gas-guzzlers" as soon as their value had completely depreciated.

On January 1, 1979, TWA created a holding company called the Trans World Corporation, which assumed ownership of the airline and the various subsidiaries. Several years later, facing financial difficulties, Trans World Corporation decided to sell its airline. Thus TWA was acquired by the "corporate raider" Carl Icahn early in 1986. Icahn's style of "raiding" usually involved buying up enough of a company's stock to threaten the other stockholders with a controlling interest or takeover. This drives the price of the stock up to a point where the raider decides to sell, usually at a large profit. In his battle with Texas Air Corporation (parent of Eastern Airlines) for control of TWA, Icahn enlisted the support of the target airline's labor unions with pledges to honor their numerous demands. With their support, Icahn was able to hold out with a bid of $18.17 per share and ultimately took over. Icahn fired the airline's popular president, Richard Pearson, and replaced him with Joseph Corr.

Icahn's apparent commitment to TWA and hands-on approach surprised many observers. He launched a new subsidiary, the Travel Channel, acquired Ozark Airlines, pared expenses to the industry's lowest cost-per-available-seat-mile (8.5¢), and turned 1986's $106 million loss into a $106 million profit for 1987. That success, however, was fleeting. A number of intractable problems—including an insufficient number of hubs and feeder lines, a rapidly declining market presence, heavy debt load, and price wars—plagued the airline.

By the end of 1988, when Icahn took TWA private, the firm's nearly $4 billion debt load gave it a negative net worth and contributed to the growing dissatisfaction of TWA's labor unions. Both the Air Line Pilots Association and the Independent Federation of Flight Attendants filed suits against Icahn alleging poor management. The financier in turn threatened to liquidate the airline in a long, drawn out bankruptcy if he didn't get wage concessions from the unions and cooperation from creditors.

From 1985 until January 1992, when TWA declared Chapter 11 bankruptcy, its share of the domestic market had slipped from 7 percent to 5.5 percent and its slice of the international market was halved from 20.9 percent to 10 percent. The company's bankruptcy reorganization plan called for its 28,000 employees to make 15 percent ($660 million) wage and work rule concessions in exchange for an additional 35 percent stake in the company, raising their share of TWA's equity to 45 percent. Creditors forgave $1 billion of the airline's $1.5 billion debt in exchange for the remaining equity. Icahn gave up his entire 90 percent share of the company, left it $200 million in cash, and paid the federal government's Pension Benefit Guaranty Corporation $240 million to prop up TWA's pension plan, which was underfunded by an estimated $1.2 billion. About 2,000 jobs were eliminated, domestic capacity was reduced by 13 percent, and international volume was cut by 38 percent. The company even relocated its headquarters from Mt. Kisco, New York, to the more centrally-located St. Louis, Missouri.

Robin H. H. Wilson and Glenn A. Zander were selected to run the company on an interim basis in the fall of 1992. Wilson had been with TWA for most the 1960s and 1970s, and Zander was a 28-year veteran of the company. In February of 1993, the joint chief executives traveled around the United States to explain their plan to bring the company out of bankruptcy, which included a major image overhaul, from low-budget to quality-conscious. A new advertising campaign launched TWA's "Comfort Class" seating, with more legroom than any other leading airline. Although the effort raised customer satisfaction, TWA continued to lose money in 1992 and 1993.

TWA emerged from bankruptcy protection months later than it had hoped to, in November of 1993, after the peak summer season. Wilson and Zander became executive vice-presidents of operations and finance, respectively, and former Piedmont Airlines chief William R. Howard took the airline's helm. Within just two months, however, Howard and Zander resigned after a dismal winter season, leaving TWA with yet another dilemma. Although board member Donald F. Craib, Jr. had no airline experience (he was formerly chairman and CEO of Allstate), he was selected to succeed Howard.

As new owners, TWA's employees made heroic efforts to sustain their company, improving service and timeliness and donating their own pay to fund advertising and capital expenses. Yet they watched the value of their shares decline by over one-third in the first six months of 1994. That June, two of the airline's three largest unions agreed to another $200 million in concessions to help the company survive yet another harsh winter. The company also started post-bankruptcy negotiations with creditors, including the Pension Benefit Guaranty Corp., offering a swap of about 15 percent in equity for about $800 million of debt. Late in 1994, when the plan was unveiled, Anthony L. Velocci, Jr. of *Aviation Week & Space Technology,* who had long followed the saga, related analysts' general skepticism that the offer would be accepted.

TWA's continuing problems have raised the question of its ability to continue as an independent airline. Throughout this difficult period in the firm's history, mergers with Eastern Airlines, America West, USAir, and British Airways have been speculated on and reportedly negotiated.

Principal Subsidiaries: Trans World Express, Inc.; WORLD-SPAN (50%).

Further Reading:

Biederman, Paul, *The U.S. Airline Industry: End of an Era,* New York: Praeger, 1982.

Donlan, Thomas G., "Super Pilot or Predator? Zeroing In on What Carl Icahn Has Wrought at TWA," *Barron's,* September 26, 1988, pp. 8–9.

Driscoll, Lisa, " 'Carl Has 9 Lives, But He's Getting Up to 8½,' " *Business Week,* February 24, 1992, pp. 56–57.

Flint, Perry, "Return the Company to Profitability," *Air Transport World,* January 1994, p. 88.

Icahn, Carl C., "It's Your Captain Speaking: TWA's Corporate Pilot States His Case," *Barron's,* October 31, 1988, pp. 35–38.

Kelly, Kevin, "Can a 'Labor of Love' End TWA's Tailspin?," *Business Week,* April 19, 1993, pp. 80–82.

Laing, Jonathan R., "What's the Next Chapter?" *Barron's,* January 3, 1994, pp. 17–19.

Serling, Robert J., *Howard Hughes' Airline: An Informal History of TWA,* New York: St. Martin's Press, 1983.

"TWA: The End of the Raid," *Economist,* September 12, 1992, pp. 89–90.

"TWA: Phoenix Arises," *Economist,* February 27, 1993, pp. 70–72.

Underwood, Elaine, "Up, Up and Away," *Brandweek,* September 20, 1993.

Velocci, Anthony L., Jr., "TWA Employees Near Goal of Ending Icahn's Reign, Leaving Chapter 11," *Aviation Week & Space Technology,* August 10, 1992, pp. 30–31.

——, "TWA Plea to Creditors: Take More Equity," *Aviation Week & Space Technology,* October 17, 1994, p. 35.

——, "TWA Taps 'Outsider' to Head Ailing Carrier," *Aviation Week & Space Technology,* January 10, 1994, p. 30.

—John Buckvold
—updated by April Dougal Gasbarre

TSB Group plc

P.O. Box 260
60 Lombard Street
London EC3V 9DN
United Kingdom
(0171) 398 3980
Fax: (0171) 398 3988

Public Company
Incorporated: 1810
Employees: 33,484
Assets: £31.42 billion
Stock Exchanges: London
SICs: 6711 Holding Companies; 6111 Financial Institutions;
  6311
Life Insurance

TSB Group plc is the holding company for the TSB—Trustee Savings Bank—and has a history of banking service stretching back to the early nineteenth century. Until the 1980s, the history of what is called the TSB is really the history of individual TSBs: small, independent trustee savings banks formed by members of a community to serve that community. TSBs then evolved from a confederation of separate banks to a corporate whole, a process culminating in 1986, when TSB was sold to the public and became a recognized corporate structure like any other bank. Plunging almost immediately into a period of difficulty following its flotation, the bank subsequently found its fortunes reviving; in 1994 TSB, as the sixth largest bank in the United Kingdom, served some 7.5 million customers and was a profitable and popular member of Britain's banking community.

The first trustee savings bank was established in 1810 in Ruthwell, Scotland, by the Rev. Dr. Henry Duncan. The purpose of the institution was to provide incentive and encouragement to financial responsibility among those of smaller income, who did not patronize the big, established joint stock banks. The idea proved immensely popular, and more TSBs sprouted quickly, most operated as a local public service run by trustees who were often area businessmen, clergy, or landowners. Such were the banks' popularity and proliferation that by 1817 Parliament began enacting a series of laws designed to provide a regulatory framework. The legislation established that no trustee could receive financial benefit from his position and the banks' depos-

its were to be invested with the government body, the Commissioner for the Reduction of the National Debt.

By 1860 there were as many as 600 separate trustee savings banks, spread throughout Britain but with a high concentration in Scotland and northern England. During World War I they became associated with National Savings, a government-backed savings scheme. The number of TSBs began to fall steadily, as individual institutions amalgamated, shifted operations to the Post Office Savings Bank, or simply closed. At the time of World War II there were only about 100 trustee savings banks, and their number continued to dwindle. At the same time, however, the TSB movement as a whole became stronger, as individual operations continued a trend of mergers: in 1945 the banks served more customers than any other bank in the United Kingdom.

During the 1960s it became apparent to the various TSBs that they must broaden their portfolio of customer service if they were to remain competitive in an increasingly complex and sophisticated financial world. Traditionally, the banks had offered only savings accounts and special investment accounts; in 1965 they began to provide checking accounts and in 1968 unit trusts. The banks were still in a disadvantageous position vis-a-vis other financial institutions, however, as they were prevented by statute from lending to their customers, restricted in allowable investments of customers' deposits, and regulated in the returns they could pay to their depositors.

Enter the Page Committee in 1971, formed by the chancellor of the exchequer to assess the future direction of National Savings and the role of the TSBs. Published in 1973, the committee's report recommended sweeping changes to the way TSBs were allowed to operate. The results were the Trustee Savings Acts of 1976 and 1978, which permitted the banks freer rein to offer their customers the full range of financial services and products. The banks eagerly put their new powers into practice, developing a thriving business in credit services: personal loans, overdrafts, home improvement loans, mortgages, bridging facilities, and Trustcard, a Visa credit card.

Simultaneously, the TSBs were inexorably moving from a loose alliance of separate organizations to a more unified entity. In the early 1970s the banks pooled their computer facilities, in retrospect a significant sign of eventual centralization. In the mid-1970s the TSBs restructured operations, trimming their numbers from 72 to 20. (By 1983 these had been further reduced to a core of four: TSB England and Wales, TSB Scotland, TSB Northern Ireland, and TSB Channel Islands.) Meanwhile, the Trustee Savings Bank Central Board was formed to coordinate and regulate the banks' activities.

Although now substantially enabled to operate in the competitive financial market, the TSBs were still on unequal footing with recognized banks, subject as they were to a different supervisory framework. The banks' plans to change their status through flotation were threatened by an odd circumstance arising from their unusual evolutionary history: it was unclear who could be said to actually own the TSBs. The government agreed to the flotation, enacting legislation in 1985 to put the banks' standing in line with that of other financial institutions, and the assets and obligations of the banks were vested in new

TSB banking companies. But some customers in Scotland, claiming that the banks' assets were owned by depositors, took the matter to court to prevent flotation. Their case was rejected, however, as a 1986 House of Lords decision permitted the flotation to proceed.

A massive marketing campaign was thereafter launched to attract shareholders. Mindful of the objections of some customers to the proposed sell-off, the new company set aside priority shares for customers, aiming for half of the new shareholders to be current clients. Individuals rather than institutions were sought, and the once-disputed ownership of TSB passed into the hands of some 3.1 million shareholders.

Aside from the wish to regularize the bank's status, there were other reasons the flotation was desirable: to raise capital for growth and to unify what had hitherto been allied but basically separate entities into a coherent, centrally driven corporate organization. This was achieved with the 1986 flotation and the loose confederation of TSBs completed the process of becoming the corporate whole, TSB Group plc.

Thus poised to make its entry into the financial world proper, with the announced intention of becoming a producer of a wide array of financial services to most financial markets, TSB faltered almost immediately and landed itself in serious trouble. Part of this was due simply to unfortunate timing: all of Britain's banks were hit hard by the recession in the late 1980s and TSB suffered along with the rest. Another factor was TSB's own reaction to its flotation success. "TSB has been a rather dozy institution for 150 years," explained an unnamed analyst quoted in the *Independent on Sunday.* "It suddenly got an extra £1.5 billion of capital and went mad."

In its marketing blitz prior to flotation, TSB had proudly hailed itself as "the fastest moving bank in Britain"; much of its subsequent trouble arose from moving rather too fast. Eager— in retrospect perhaps too eager—to expand, TSB used a substantial portion of its flotation proceeds to finance acquisitions which quickly proved unwise: Target Group, in the business of life insurance, unit trusts, and pensions, and Hill Samuel, a provider of financial services primarily involved with merchant banking. Nursing great plans for the latter acquisition, TSB set out to transform the merchant bank into a corporate bank; "in hindsight," as the company itself later remarked, "this was exactly the wrong time to make such a move. With an increased capital base Hill Samuel Bank increased its corporate lending to a sector about to experience the worst recession in living memory."

"The bank that likes to say yes," as TSB's slogan ran at the time, was soon proved to have said it too often. Plagued by a mountain of bad debts, watching helplessly as several of its new diversified business ventures failed, and hampered still by its legacy of a haphazard and inefficient corporate structure, TSB hit bottom in 1991 with a loss of £47 million.

Clearly a change in strategy—and in chief executives—was in order. TSB launched a substantial reorganization of its operations, shedding, in the process, hundreds of branches and thousands of jobs. From 1991 to 1993 some 18 businesses—most not central to TSB's primary functions—were disposed of, including TSB Northern Ireland, Swan National, and Noble Lowndes. Others, such as Mortgage Express and the life insurance and pensions aspects of Hill Samuel, were retained but closed to new business. Indeed, that subsidiary pulled in its grandiose horns and concentrated solely on its former specialty of merchant banking and on investment management. In short, TSB's ambitions of the late 1980s, when the company sought to become a diversified supplier of financial services, narrowed in the early to mid-1990s to a determination to focus on its core activities of U.K. retail banking and insurance.

TSB's new strategies are working. The results of the company's efforts are perhaps best expressed numerically: from 1991's loss of £47 million, TSB moved to a modest profit of £5 million in 1992 and soared upwards to a profit of £301 million the following year. By 1994 this had risen to £504 million. The decline of bad debt played a crucial role in this turnaround, as did improved performance brought about by the bank's reforms.

"Back from a dalliance with every mistake in the Eighties' book," according to the *Independent,* "the one-time boring old savings bank that tried to play with the big boys is beginning to find a role." Arguably the most important aspect of that role is TSB's dominance in the newish field of "bankassurance." The 1992 merger of TSB Retail Bank with its insurance business, TSB Trust Co., created the U.K.'s first real bankassurance organization. TSB has been very successful in selling insurance products and services to its own retail banking customers. Here it is helped by the socioeconomic profile of its customers, who tend to be at the lower levels and thus, statistically, less likely to have already made insurance arrangements.

As of the mid-1990s, TSB's record here was very good. The bank's growth in the mortgage market is well outpacing that of the industry as a whole. Sales of life insurance, pension products, and unit trusts are also healthy. The bank's scheme of luring customers with high deposit rates (thus sacrificing some banking income) in order to sell them insurance products has proved very profitable. Further, TSB attracts a significant percentage of young people opening their first bank account— surely a good omen for the future.

In 1994 the bank introduced TSB PhoneBank, a 24-hour telephone banking service. Begun in Wales, the new service looked a promising area for growth, prompting TSB to plan expansion: a big center for TSB PhoneBank was slated to open in Glasgow in the summer of 1995.

Hill Samuel is still regarded with some suspicion. Martin Hughes, banking analyst at Credit Lyonnais Laing, expressed the opinion of many when he commented: "In the 1980s, Hill Samuel wasn't a very good merchant bank. It has stayed a not very good merchant bank." TSB itself hinted strongly in 1993 that it was looking for a buyer for the subsidiary, but subsequently decided to retain it. Recently, however, the company's performance has improved somewhat and it has even scored a few coups, having won the contracts to advise the government on the National Lottery and the Channel Tunnel Rail Link.

While acknowledging the undoubted success of TSB's decision to scale down its ambitions and focus on its strengths of retail banking and insurance, financial analysts question where the bank will go from here. Its growth in bankassurance is impressive, but how long can it last? Most commentators believe that the next step to expansion is likely to be through acquisition. Indeed, the bank has publically expressed interest in acquiring a building society, probably one based in the south to counteract TSB's northern bias, but as of early 1995 the issue remained speculative. One thing is certain: the bank will tread very carefully in making any such decision, for, as the *Daily Telegraph* commented, the prospect of TSB making a new purchase is "an idea to send shivers down shareholders' spines after Hill Samuel and Target."

Once derided as a "banking basket case" (by the *Evening Standard*) and described (by the *Herald*) as "a disaster prone institution," TSB is now viewed as a "sensibly and tightly run bank" (the *Herald* again). The earliest TSBs arose to meet the needs of the communities they served. For years they prospered by continuing to answer those demands. Having made some unfortunate decisions at an unpropitious time, TSB found itself floundering in the late 1980s and early 1990s. Pulling back from expansion in a wider financial market, TSB is in a sense returning to its roots, as it focuses once more on the tradition of service to individuals, clearly its strong point: the bank attracted a record 300,000 new customers in 1994. For the future, a judgment of cautious optimism seems to be the consensus, well expressed by the *Daily Telegraph*: "TSB's renaissance . . . has been little short of staggering, but the real challenge is to take the group forward from here."

Principal Subsidiaries: TSB Bank plc; TSB Bank Channel Islands Limited; TSB Bank Scotland plc; TSB Life Limited; TSB Pensions Limited; TSB General Insurance Limited; TSB Unit Trusts Limited; Hill Samuel Bank Limited; Hill Samuel Bank Limited; Hill Samuel Asset Management Group Limited; Investment advisers Inc. (U.S.); Atlanta Capital Management Company (U.S.); Hill Samuel Investment Services Group Lim-ited; Mortgage Express Holdings Limited; TSB Property Services Limited; United Dominions Trust Limited.

Further Reading:

"Allied Dunbar to Take Over Hill Samuel's Life Sellers," *Financial Times,* March 24, 1994.
Bennett, Neil, "TSB Profits Leap as Bad Debts Recede," *The Times,* January 13, 1995, p. 23.
"Confident TSB Eyes Expansion," *Herald,* March 23, 1994.
"The Lex Column: TSB's Tough Task," *Financial Times,* January 14, 1994.
Meller, Paul, "TSB—Counting on a Two Pronged Attack," *Marketing,* November 28, 1991, pp. 18–19.
Miller, Robert, "Axe Falls Again as TSB Closes a Further 200 Branches," *The Times,* October 5, 1994.
"New-Look TSB Is Well Placed for Growth," *Independent,* January 14, 1994.
"Popular Shares: Mixed Views on TSB," *Investors Chronicle,* December 16, 1994.
"Proof There's Life after Death for the Banks," *Guardian,* January 14, 1994.
"Small Business Customers Say No to the TSB," *Sunday Times,* November 20, 1994.
"Soaring TSB Takes an Axe to Its Staff," *Guardian,* January 14, 1994.
"TSB Forced to Rely on Loyalty of Investors," *Independent on Sunday,* January 9, 1994.
"TSB Keeps Powder Dry for Big Game," *Daily Telegraph,* January 14, 1994.
"TSB Says Yes to 500 Glasgow Bank Jobs," *Scotsman,* November 25, 1994.
"TSB's Big Jump in Profits Brings Smiles to the City," *Herald,* January 14, 1994.
"TSB Strides to £301m Recovery," *Daily Telegraph,* January 14, 1994.
"TSB to Close 200 More Branches," *Daily Telegraph,* October 5, 1994.

—Robin DuBlanc

Tyco Toys, Inc.

6000 Midlantic Drive
Mount Laurel, New Jersey 08054
U.S.A.
(609) 234-7400
Fax: (609) 273-2885

Public Company
Incorporated: 1926 as Mantua Inc.
Employees: 2,500
Sales: $753.1 million
Stock Exchanges: New York Philadelphia
SICs: 3944 Games, Toys & Children's Vehicles; 3942 Dolls
& Stuffed Toys

Tyco Toys, Inc. ranks as the third largest toy manufacturer in the United States. Having undertaken a ten-year program of diversification, Tyco grew from a maker of toy trains and electric racing sets into a corporation distributing a broad range of toys throughout the world. In the mid-1990s, Tyco produced over a thousand different toys, making it one of the most diversified toy companies in the world. The company has never relied upon or become identified with one overwhelming hit toy. Rather, it has used good management and a diverse product line to lift it to the top ranks of this extremely lucrative industry.

Tyco was founded in 1926 by John N. Tyler. Tyler named the company Mantua Metal Products, after the town of Mantua, New Jersey, where he ran his small business out of his home. Tyler's company built H-O model trains, track, and other accessories. H-O model trains were half the size of the O standard, hence the name H-O. Tyler initially produced products that would be compatible with existing model train sets built by other companies. Model train building was as old as trains themselves, so Tyler's little company had a guaranteed market if he could produce a good product. In the 1930s he took the first step toward the present-day company when he started producing and marketing his own brand of complete toy train kits.

During this period Tyler's company was as much a part of the hobby industry as a toy manufacturer. While there was some crossover between these two sectors, the hobby industry targeted both adult and child consumers, whereas the toy industry attempted to gauge the changing tastes of children. As the company shifted its focus to toys, the marketing strategy, and

indeed the company philosophy, changed dramatically. From a middle-of-the-pack competitor in a fringe sector for over 30 years, Tyco went on to become the third largest toy manufacturer in America.

The first step in this transition occurred in the late 1940s, when Mantua's marketing director, Milt Grey, convinced Tyler to produce a ready-to-run H-O train set rather than continue with model kits. Pre-assembled train sets had been on the market for years, but they were almost always sold in the O scale. Grey argued that the smaller scale would be attractive to kids as well as take up less space on retailers' shelves and stockrooms. With the increase in profit per unit of shelf space, the toys would also be attractive to buyers from the increasingly popular discount chain stores.

The change was risky. It meant marketing a product that was pre-assembled rather than a product whose whole appeal lay in the fact that the purchaser was to assemble it himself. The production and assembly line had to be completely altered to produce assembled sets rather than specific parts. Despite these difficulties, Mantua's preassembled sets were a runaway hit, and industry leaders Lionel and Marx were suddenly forced to take notice of the small New Jersey firm. This success was largely due to the fact that the small pre-assembled sets retained the accuracy of hobby sets, but they could be liberated from hobby stores and therefore reach a much wider potential market. Model manufacturers quickly followed Mantua's lead and competition for this new market became fierce. Several manufacturers were put out of business by the price wars that followed, but Mantua survived and thrived.

Although for years Mantua had been commonly referred to as Tyco after its charismatic owner John Tyler, the company name was finally officially changed from Mantua to Tyco in the 1960s. It was during this decade that the company expanded its line to include electric race-car sets, a logical extension of the already-established niche of preassembled train sets. The addition of electric race-car sets accentuated Tyco's subtle move away from the hobby sector and toward toys. Race cars continued to be a staple of Tyco's product line in the 1990s, and the company would also eventually capture the largest market share in radio control toys.

Tyco remained a private, relatively small-scale company producing model trains and racing sets until the Tyler family sold the company to Consolidated Foods in 1970. Like many large food industry corporations at that time, Consolidated Foods, a subsidiary of the Sara Lee Corporation, was looking to diversify. The large corporation placed one of its top executives in charge of the small toy company, only to discover that selling model trains and race cars had very little in common with selling frozen cake. Tyco earnings began to drop at an alarming rate, and Sara Lee eventually realized that it needed a management team with experience in the toy industry to make Tyco profitable once again.

The most significant development during the Consolidated Foods/Sara Lee era at Tyco was the decision in 1973 to hire Richard Grey as president and Harry Pearce as chief financial officer. Grey had been familiar with Tyco products since the late 1940s, when his father, Milt Grey, had convinced Tyler to market ready-to-run train sets. The young Grey had since graduated from the University of California at Los Angeles and become a manufacturer's representative for Tyco, and he understood the toy business like few others could. Grey and Pearce, who joined the company from Arthur Anderson & Co., improved Tyco's performance dramatically and quickly. Despite Grey's success in turning Tyco around, however, the company was sold when Sara Lee streamlined its own operations. The new owners, Savoy Industries, decided to keep both Grey and Pearce in their management positions at Tyco, where they remained into the mid-1990s.

Savoy Industries was a publicly owned investment group run by financier Benson Selzer when it acquired Tyco from Sara Lee in 1981. Savoy specialized in leveraged buyouts of troubled companies, which the firm would restructure and then take public. The two main figures at Tyco during the 1980s were Grey and Selzer, who eventually became chairman of the board. Although Selzer gave Grey free reign in the day-to-day management of Tyco, the two men had differing ideas on the long-term goals of the company. Selzer wanted to use Tyco's assets to build a diversified conglomerate, whereas Grey felt that Tyco could only be successful if it remained firmly rooted in the toy industry. As Grey stated to *Business Week* in 1992, "Not everything they [Selzer's board] did was terrible but a couple of things were absolutely self-serving."

The matter came to a head after Savoy took Tyco public in 1986. Tyco, under Selzer's chairmanship, began to lend money to and make acquisitions from other Selzer companies—deals often completely unrelated to the toy business. It was in 1988, when Tyco purchased a struggling Puerto Rican underwear maker indirectly controlled by the Selzer family, that shareholders finally cried foul. A group of shareholders brought a suit against the company, and even members of Tyco's board began to feel that the value of the company would suffer a serious blow if something was not done to control the Selzer family's power. Under Grey's persuasion, the board named two more outsiders as members, and in 1991 the Selzer family agreed to sell their stake in the company.

Not all of Tyco's legal battles in the 1980s involved Selzer's control of the company, however. Under Grey's leadership, part of Tyco's approach to product development was to see what was working for other companies and copy it. It seemed that the cost of litigation surrounding these imitations was simply factored into Tyco's plans. The most striking example of this strategy came when the company marketed Tyco Super Blocks, a building block set designed to be interchangeable with the multi-million dollar selling Lego brand. Referring to Lego, Tyco president Richard Grey told *Forbes* in 1988 that "we knew they had a reputation for being litigious." Soon, Lego did sue on both trademark and copyright infringement grounds. After an expensive three-year legal battle, Tyco won the case. The $3 million in legal fees proved to be well worthwhile, as Tyco Super Blocks became a stable $20 million product line for Tyco. Tyco had similar success with its own version of Kenner's Play-doh molding clay, the Tyco formulation of which was called Tyco Super Dough. Tyco's product was ex-

tremely popular and, as in the Lego case, suits were filed but successfully defended by Tyco.

Tyco began television advertising of its toy trains and cars in the 1960s, when television advertising aimed at children began to be a major force in the toy industry. Although originally prohibited by government regulation, the deregulation of the 1980s saw a new and very powerful phenomenon enter the toy industry—the toy-driven children's television program. This phenomenon saw toy companies becoming television producers, as they wrote and produced kids' shows featuring animated versions of their products. Instead of toys being created from popular kids' culture, the culture was actually created to sell the toy.

Hoping to capitalize on this new trend, Tyco launched a set of action figures called Dino-Riders that were designed to cash in on the dinosaur craze of the late 1980s. A television series, comic books, and even a national Dino-Riders club were all part of the grand scheme. Although initial sales of Dino-Riders were well above expectations, the cost of producing the detailed figures became prohibitive. The market could not absorb an increase in the price of the units, so the Dino-Riders line was retired. The descendants of Dino-Riders were Cadillacs & Dinosaurs, which aired as a television series in 1993 and were introduced as toys the following year. However, these new dinosaur-based action figures failed to capture the fickle taste of American boys.

Convinced that hit toys were the ones that entered the deep structure of kids' culture through media support, in the late 1980s and early 1990s Tyco also entered into a series of licensing agreements to produce toys based on characters with already-proven kid appeal. In 1993, for example, Tyco signed an exclusive master toy license with Warner Bros. to produce toys based on such popular Looney Tunes characters as Bugs Bunny, Daffy Duck, and Road Runner. This deal was a considerable coup for Tyco because it was the first of its kind for Warner's. The Warner's deal followed contracts with the Children's Television Workshop to produce Sesame Street characters and with The Walt Disney Company for the rights to The Little Mermaid character. Tyco produced an Ariel The Little Mermaid doll to capitalize on the success of the hit Disney movie, but the strategy proved to have a built-in flaw. After impressive sales in 1992, its first year on the market, sales fell considerably the following season as children's interests gravitated to newer items.

The late 1980s and 1990s witnessed a tremendous consolidation of the toy industry, as acquisition after acquisition concentrated a large percentage of the toy market into the hands of the top two toy companies, Hasbro and Mattel. In order to bolster its position in the industry, Tyco also took an active part in growth through acquisitions. By the early 1990s Tyco had purchased seven smaller toy companies, helping it climb from 22nd in the industry in 1986 to become the third-largest toy manufacturer by 1992. Tyco's biggest acquisition was its 1992 purchase of Universal Matchbox Group at a cost of $106 million.

The acquisition of Matchbox was a return, in some respects, to Tyco's roots in the miniature diecast car and train sector. Tyco's purchase of Matchbox was also designed to increase its international presence, as Matchbox already had a well-established international distribution system. It was also hoped that the Matchbox cars would provide a direct challenge to Mattel's perennial mega-hit Hotwheels brand. Other purchases included the View-Master/Ideal Group, makers of the kid-friendly 3-D Viewer and the very popular Magna Doodle drawing toy (with worldwide sales reaching 40 million units), as well as other successful toys, dolls, and games. Tyco's Sesame Street license developed as the result of its June 1992 acquisition of Illco Toy Co. USA, at a cost of $52.1 million, which had already developed the rights to the popular characters extensively in pre-school toys. Tyco's many acquisitions helped to catapult it into the upper echelon of the industry, but they also contributed to Tyco's huge losses in 1993 and 1994.

In November 1992, Tyco acquired a 75 percent interest in Croner-Tyco Toys Pty., Ltd., an Australian company, and in April 1993 acquired a 75 percent interest in EnsueÑo-Tyco Toys, S.A. de C.V., the company's Mexican subsidiary. The company acquired the remaining 25 percent interest in EnsueÑo-Tyco in early 1995. In addition, a 50 percent interest was held in Rivergate Partnership L.P., an operator of warehousing space in Portland, Oregon.

As reported in *Business Week* in 1992, analysts worried that Tyco had bitten off more than it could chew with its major spate of acquisitions, but Grey remained sanguine. After all, Grey had brought Tyco to the number three position in the American toy industry without a single runaway hit product. His strategy had always been essentially conservative. Grey was convinced that the company could grow quickly without becoming unmanageable due to overextension. Along with his chief financial officer, Harry Pearce, Grey had kept the operation as sleek as possible, with as small a staff as they could manage. With the new acquisitions, Tyco consolidated warehouses and eliminated redundant staff so that its total employment remained under 3,000, including foreign subsidiaries. Despite this basic philosophy, however, Tyco was unable to avoid the pitfalls that analysts had predicted.

The year 1993 proved to be a disastrous one for Tyco. After recording an impressive operating income of $44 million in 1992, Tyco posted an operating loss of $57 million in 1993. These losses were due partly to the disappointing performance of key products—such as The Incredible Crash Test Dummies and The Little Mermaid—and partly to large price tags for major acquisitions. By far the greatest problem for Tyco, however, was poor timing and execution of its European operations. Now even Grey admitted that Tyco had taken on too much too quickly. "We just had too much on our plate," Grey stated in a 1994 article in *Business Week,* though he remained optimistic that the large number of new products Tyco was developing would turn the dismal figures around in 1994. In an effort to reign in costs, in July 1993, Tyco consolidated its Tyco Preschool and Playtime direct import companies into a single unit, transferring all promotional products to the company's domestic segment and eliminating duplicate functions expecting to result in increased operating efficiencies.

In 1994, Tyco took steps to combine the operations of Tyco Germany into the Matchbox Germany facility in Hoesbach,

eliminating duplicated functions and overlapping staff to result in substantial operating efficiencies. Tyco also closed its Italian subsidiary that year. At home Tyco reduced its work force by five percent. The company also retained Allen & Company, Incorporated as financial adviser to assist the company in raising additional private equity to strengthen its financial position. In April 1994, Tyco issued $50 million in six percent Convertible Exchangeable Preferred Stock to a group led by Corporate Partners, L.P., and investment adviser and affiliate of Lazard Freres & Co. The company also announced that it was consolidating certain European operations in Belgium in order to streamline its activities, reduce operating expenses, and enhance its customer service.

Rumors of a Tyco takeover abounded. In an industry that was consolidating at a rapid rate, the troubled Tyco looked like a prime candidate for acquisition. Grey put on a staunch public face about the possibility, telling *Business Week* in February of 1994 that shareholders "were better served by Tyco remaining an independent toy company," but he also did not entirely rule out an acquisition. In an interview with the *Wall Street Journal* later that year, Grey hedged his bets, stating that a deal where "the synergies are right and where two and two make six" would be attractive, but adding that Tyco had not had serious discussions with anyone concerning a sale.

Although income improved in 1994 with domestic sales rising approximately ten percent, Tyco still posted a net loss of $35 million, much of it associated with the European restructuring. Sales rose slightly to $753 million, but none of Tyco's new toys became the hit that would have been required to bring the company back into the black. Despite the poor timing of European ventures and the lackluster performance of some of Tyco's new products, however, several factors pointed to a recovery entering the late 1990s, including the exclusive master license with Warner Bros. for Looney Tunes plush characters, continued associations with Disney and Sesame Street, its number one position in radio-control toys, the expanded line of Matchbox diecast cars, its successful line of large dolls and the number one selling drawing toy, Magna Doodle. Tyco's international subsidiaries also offered such popular product lines as Mighty Morphin Power Rangers, X-Men, and Gund plush toys. The international subsidiaries accounted for approximately 40 percent of 1994 consolidated sales.

Principal Subsidiaries: Tyco Industries, Inc.; Tyco (Hong Kong) Ltd.; Matchbox; Tyco Manufacturing Corp.; Tyco Distribution Corp.; Tyco Manufacturing (Europe), Inc.; Tyco Toys (U.K.) Ltd.; Tyco Toys (France) S.A.; Tyco Toys (Canada) Inc.; Tyco Distribution (Europe) N.V.; Tyco Toys (Benelux) N.V.; Tyco Matchbox (Deutschland) GmbH; Tyco Toys (Espana) S.A.; Tyco Playtime, Inc.; Tyco Toys (Switzerland) A.G.; Tyco Toys (Austria) GmbH; Tyco Toys (New Zealand) Pty., Ltd.; Croner-Tyco Toys Pty., Ltd. (50%); Rivergate Partnership L.P. (50%).

Further Reading:

Busch, Anita M., *Hollywood Reporter,* January, 29, 1993, p. 3.
Fitzgerald, Kate, "Toyland's Elusive Goal: Win Over Both Sexes," *Advertising Age,* February 8, 1993, pp. S2, S18.
Galarza, Pablo, "In Control," *Forbes,* May 11, 1992, p. 204.

Hackney, Holt, ''Tyco: Picking Up the Pieces,'' *Financial World,* March 1, 1994, p. 20.

Hebel, Sara, ''Toy Merger Makes for 2-Player Game,'' *Advertising Age,* September 29, 1993, p. 34.

Lesly, Elizabeth, ''Will Tyco End Up in a Rival's Toybox?'' *Business Week,* February 28, 1994, pp. 78–9.

Levy, Richard, and Ronald Weingartner, *Inside Santa's Workshop,* New York: Henry Holt and Company, 1990.

Meeks, Fleming, ''So Sue Me,'' *Forbes,* November 28, 1988, p. 72.

Pereira, Joseph, ''Tyco Toys Looks to New Lineup to Rediscover Itself,'' *Wall Street Journal,* April 1, 1994, p. B4.

Stern, Sydney, and Ted Schoenhaus, *Toyland: The High-Stakes Game of the Toy Industry,* Chicago: Contemporary Books, 1990.

Touby, Laurel, ''Suddenly Tyco Is Playing with the Big Kids,'' *Business Week,* June 15, 1992, pp. 124–6.

Warner, Fara, *Brandweek,* May 10, 1993, p. 12.

—Donald C. McManus and Hilary Gopnik

UGI Corporation

460 North Gulph Road
P.O. Box 858
Valley Forge, Pennsylvania 19482
U.S.A.
(610) 337-1000
Fax: (610) 768-7696

Public Company
Incorporated: 1882 as United Gas Improvement Co.
Employees: 5,789
Total Assets: $2.1 billion
Stock Exchanges: New York Philadelphia
SICs: 4911 Electric Services; 4924 Natural Gas Distribution;
5984 LP Gas (Propane) Dealer

UGI Corporation is a holding company with two principal subsidiaries. UGI Utilities, Inc. owns and operates natural gas and electric utilities in 14 counties of eastern and central Pennsylvania. AmeriGas Partners, L.P. distributes propane gas in 43 states. Between 1987 and 1991, UGI was the nation's tenth most profitable energy-gas distributor, averaging an annual return of 11.7 percent on equity.

UGI is the oldest public-utility holding company in the United States, having been incorporated in 1882 as the United Gas Improvement Co. The company was founded by Philadelphia businessmen to introduce a new process for the manufacture of "water gas"—made by combining air and steam with coal—in place of the older method of making illuminating gas from the distillation of coal. The new Lowe process exposed water-gas vapors to a thin stream of petroleum naphtha, enriching the gas with hydrocarbons from the oil and producing almost twice the candle power of coal gas at less cost. United Gas Improvement manufactured, sold, and installed equipment needed for the Lowe process. The company also leased the production and distribution facilities of existing gas works, operated the plants, and sold the gas.

Within its first year of operation, United Gas Improvement began acquiring interests in local gas works in various parts of the country, in what was perhaps the first attempt to bring several independent and geographically separated public utilities under one management. United Gas Improvement (or UGI, as it became known) also acquired extensive interests in electric utilities and electric street railways, particularly in New York, Connecticut, northern New Jersey, and eastern Pennsylvania.

The establishment of UGI initially required some rather complex business transactions; the stocks of the gas companies acquired were placed in the hands of a trustee, since Pennsylvania law did not allow one corporation to hold the securities of another. To simplify this cumbersome process, UGI's founders acquired the charter of the Union Co. Formerly known as the Union Contract Co., this company had been granted a charter in 1870 by a special act of the Pennsylvania legislature and was thereby allowed to purchase and own the securities of other corporations. The name of the Union Co. was changed to The United Gas Improvement Co. in 1888, and, the following year, the new company acquired the assets of the old United Gas Improvement Co. By 1902, the company held interests in 45 firms providing gas, electric, and railway service across the country.

In 1897, UGI secured a 30-year lease from Philadelphia to run the city gas works. UGI would continue to lease and manage Philadelphia's gas works until the early 1970s, when it was replaced by a city-owned nonprofit corporation. By that time, the works was the largest municipally owned gas operation in the United States.

In 1925, UGI merged with the American Gas Co., and, two years later, it acquired the Philadelphia Electric Co. The company diversified into heavy construction during this time, forming, through United Engineers & Constructors, Inc., the largest general engineering and construction firm in the United States. UGI also held a minority interest in Samuel Insull's Midland Utilities, which operated in more than 5,000 communities in over 32 states. By the end of 1934, UGI directly or indirectly had interests in 55 subsidiary companies, stretching from New Hampshire to Arizona. Most of these companies were fully owned by UGI.

Thanks to conservative management, the utility holding company suffered relatively little from the Great Depression. Dividends paid by its utility subsidiaries fell only 10.6 percent between 1931 and 1938. However, according to some critics at the time, UGI was doing too well. Writing in *The Nation,* Isidor Feinstein alleged that "The same group sits on both sides of the table in fixing management fees, construction costs, and financing charges," and that without federal regulation the consumer was paying "a premium on inefficient operation, costly management, and a bloated capital structure." UGI's various subsidiaries, Feinstein noted, were providing the parent company with average annual returns ranging from 11 percent to as high as 84 percent.

In 1935, the U.S. Congress passed the Public Utility Holding Company Act, which required utility holding companies to register with the Securities and Exchange Commission (SEC). The act also gave the Federal Power Commission and the Federal Trade Commission authority to regulate interstate transmission of electric power and gas, respectively, and restricted electric and gas holding companies to single and concentrated systems confined to a single area. Contending that the act was unconstitutional, UGI management sought injunctions to restrain the government from enforcing it.

Although UGI eventually lost its court battle, the company continued to grow and, by the end of 1940, was at the peak of its power. Operating in 11 states, UGI held investments in four sub-holding companies, 38 gas and electric utilities, and 48 nonutility companies, including water, transit, ice, and cold-storage firms. It had 120,000 stockholders and assets of $846 million.

In 1941, the SEC directed UGI to divest itself of properties in Arizona, Connecticut, Illinois, Indiana, Michigan, New Hampshire, New Jersey, Ohio, and Tennessee. As a result, UGI was restricted to one compact property largely intrastate in character. In 1943, UGI's subsidiaries were selling electricity or gas to more than five million customers in seven states, but, by the end of 1953, these operations were limited to eastern Pennsylvania. Ironically, when the company's government-mandated divestiture plan was filed in 1942, investors decided that less was more; UGI's common stock jumped from $4 to $6 per share and reached $9.88 in 1943, before UGI distributed to shareholders stock representing some two-thirds of its assets.

In 1952, the SEC approved a plan to reorganize UGI by dissolving the holding company structure, merging its remaining subsidiaries into UGI, which became a Pennsylvania public-utility operating company, dissolving its nonutility subsidiaries, and disposing of its stock in nonsubsidiary companies. On the last day of 1952, seven Pennsylvania public-utility subsidiaries, including management of the city-owned Philadelphia Gas Works Co., were merged into the new UGI. The company's assets of $75 million were less than one-tenth of its prewar total; even its Philadelphia Electric subsidiary had been stripped. The name of the parent company was officially changed to UGI Corporation on July 1, 1968.

The UGI system converted from manufactured gas to natural gas during the 1950s. Most of UGI's customers were residential, with industrial sales accounting for only 15 percent of gas consumption in 1955. To promote greater industrial use of natural gas, the company instituted a special summer industrial rate to drum up business during the slack season. At the same time, UGI was striving to convince homeowners to convert to gas heat as well as to win business from buyers of new homes. Only 11 percent of all homeowners in the company's area of operation had gas heat in 1956, excluding the territory of the Philadelphia gas works, where most households were cooking and heating with manufactured gas. UGI's efforts were so successful that between 1955 and 1971 its gas sales increased fivefold.

A majority-owned UGI subsidiary called Ugite Gas, Inc. entered the unregulated liquefied petroleum (LP) gas business in 1959 by acquiring three companies serving communities in eastern Pennsylvania and Maryland. Operations soon were extended to western Pennsylvania and eastern Ohio as well. By 1973, Ugite had expanded its "bottled gas" service to 35 locations in eight states, including Kentucky and Tennessee. Between 1974 and 1976, the subsidiary acquired more LP-gas properties in Florida, Alabama, and Georgia, adding annual volume of nine million gallons to its propane sales.

The principal LP gases, propane and butane, were separated from natural gas at processing plants and from crude oil at refineries. Stored and transported in a liquid state, propane vaporized to a clean-burning gas with properties similar to natural gas. The retail segment of the propane business was attractive to UGI because it was a distribution business similar to that of a local natural gas company and one with the same types of customers, who used the fuel primarily for heating. Moreover, unlike a natural-gas utility, the retail sale of propane was unregulated and free to spread geographically. Perhaps most importantly, however, it required only small capital investment. In 1977, additional propane distribution and storage facilities in New York, Pennsylvania, and North Carolina brought sales up to approximately 78 million gallons of propane.

During this time, Ugite was the company's LP-Gas Division and a holding company for UGI's expansion in compressed gases. Newly acquired SEC Corp. of El Paso, Texas, a producer and distributor of carbon dioxide and other gases in 16 states, became the Carbon Dioxide Division. In 1977, a new subsidiary, AmeriGas, was established, succeeding Ugite as the parent of the LP-Gas and Carbon Dioxide Divisions. A year later, AmeriGas acquired Northern Gases and Manitowoc Gases, the only producers of industrial gases in Wisconsin; this acquisition formed the new Industrial Gases Division, a producer and distributor of oxygen, nitrogen, argon, and acetylene. AmeriGas also produced and sold welding equipment and supplies.

UGI responded to the energy crisis by forming a division to explore for natural gas. It acquired oil and gas rights on 75,000 acres in western and central Pennsylvania and began exploratory drilling in 1974. Three years later, UGI formed a joint venture with Amoco Production Co. to search for oil and gas on more than a million acres of southwestern Pennsylvania. In 1979, all of the company's oil and gas activities were transferred to a new wholly owned subsidiary, UGI Development Co., the consolidation of which was completed in 1981. Gas production began in 1977, and four drilling rigs were operating in 1980.

By 1980, UGI was shifting its focus from its core gas and electric distribution to substantial interests in a half-dozen energy-related activities. Company president Thomas Lefevre related that UGI intended to shift its income ratio from three-fourths regulated utility business to half utility and half nonutility business within three to four years. Propane and industrial gases appeared to be a lucrative field for expansion, with operating income from AmeriGas having risen 48 percent during the period between mid-1979 and mid-1980, compared to eight percent from natural gas and electric utilities.

By the end of 1981 UGI was the leading supplier of carbon dioxide to the nation's oilfields, where it was used to stimulate well production. AmeriGas was producing carbon dioxide from eight production plants and two natural wells. The company also expected other industrial gases to enjoy rapid growth in the upcoming years. It completed an air-separation plant in 1981 to produce nitrogen for oilwell stimulation and had begun construction on a second plant.

The early 1980s were a period of rapid expansion for UGI, as it acquired several companies that serviced oilfields. However, by the mid-1980s the oil and gas drilling activity stimulated by the hikes in energy prices during the 1970s had collapsed, forcing UGI to make cuts. In 1983, UGI sold half of its LP-Gas Division and formed AP Propane, Inc., a joint venture with the Prudential Insurance Company. In mid-1986 only five UGI oil and gas drilling and supplying companies in three markets were still operating, as compared to 12 in seven markets at the end of 1985. Moreover, UGI's oil and gas work force was cut from 1,130 to less than 500. The company took a $45.7 million writedown of oil and gas assets and other investments in 1985 and reported a rare annual loss.

Between 1986 and 1987 UGI Development Co. discontinued all its oil and gas activities, including selling a significant portion of its oilfield service operations to UTI Energy Corp. In 1987, as part of UGI's strategy of focused growth in propane, AmeriGas, through the AP Propane joint venture, acquired Cal Gas Corporation and instantly became the nation's fourth largest propane marketer. At the time, Cal Gas was three times the size of the AmeriGas propane operations. Over the next few years, AmeriGas withdrew from the industrial gases industry in a series of seven transactions, selling practically all the operating assets of its industrial gases and carbon dioxide divisions to the BOC Group, Inc. for about $146 million. James A. Sutton, chair and chief executive officer, told shareholders at UGI's 1990 annual meeting that its divestiture of oil and gas and industrial gases businesses since 1986 had "transformed the company from one operating in four distinct industries through over 20 separate businesses into a company focused in two industries with three businesses."

In 1990 AmeriGas took total control of the joint venture established with Prudential in 1983, buying Prudential's 49 percent stake in AP Propane Inc. for $63 million. This company was then merged into AmeriGas Propane. The following year, UGI was reincorporated in Pennsylvania, emerging as a restructured holding company by the same name. The former UGI Corporation was renamed UGI Utilities, Inc. This subsidiary operated the regulated Pennsylvania electric and gas utilities, while AmeriGas, Inc. conducted propane distribution through AmeriGas Propane, Inc., its wholly owned subsidiary.

In 1993, UGI acquired a significant interest in and management of debt-laden Petrolane, Inc., one of the nation's largest marketers of propane, through a prepackaged plan of reorganization under Chapter 11 of the U.S. Bankruptcy Code. The company hoped to turn Petrolane around financially and to combine it with its AmeriGas Propane operations. By early 1994 Amerigas and UGI had acquired 35 percent of Petrolane. UGI also announced plans to acquire the remaining 65 percent in 1995 and to form a master limited partnership in which AmeriGas would hold a majority interest.

During fiscal 1994, 48 percent of UGI's revenue and 57 percent of its operating income came from propane. Forty-four percent and eight percent of revenues, and 47 percent and seven per-

cent of operating income came from gas and electric utilities, respectively. The electric utility was serving 60,000 customers in parts of two northeastern Pennsylvania counties (Luzerne and Wyoming), from a generating plant near Kingston, Pennsylvania, in operation since 1959. The natural gas utility was serving 14 counties in eastern and south-central Pennsylvania, with about 238,000 customers receiving natural gas in 1994 through a distribution system of 3,965 miles of gas mains. Moreover, AmeriGas and Petrolane constituted the nation's largest propane marketing network, serving 890,000 customers from 572 district locations in 43 states. Propane Transport, Inc., an AmeriGas subsidiary, also transported ammonia and propane for other companies.

In April 1995 UGI completed the acquisition of the remaining 65 percent of Petrolane and combined the operations of Petrolane and AmeriGas Propane into one entity—AmeriGas Partners, L.P., a master limited partnership—owner and operator of the nation's largest retail propane marketing organization. AmeriGas then owned 59 percent of the partnership. The remaining partnership units were publicly held and traded on the New York Stock Exchange under the symbol APU. The purchase of the unowned equity in Petrolane, the initial public offering of the partnership units and related financings had an aggregate value of $1.2 billion.

James A. Sutton, UGI's chairperson and chief executive officer, stated that the UGI- and AmeriGas-led transactions had strengthened the balance sheet of the combined propane business by reducing its debt from approximately 76 percent of total capital to 53 percent. Sutton also noted that consolidation of AmeriGas Partners's assets with UGI's made UGI a $2 billion company with approximately 70 percent of its assets in the unregulated propane industry.

Principal Subsidiaries: AmeriGas Inc.; UGI Utilities, Inc.; AmeriGas Partners, L.P. (59%).

Further Reading:

Bemis, Samuel, "Some Recent Municipal Gas History," *Forum,* March 1898, pp. 72–75.
Campanella, Frank W., "UGI Sweetens Mix," *Barron's,* June 30, 1990, pp. 36–37, 41.
Commins, Kevin, "UGI Strategy for the 1980s: Diversification of Operations," *Journal of Commerce,* July 25, 1980, p. 3.
"Death Sentence," *Business Week,* February 1, 1941, pp. 14–15.
"Design for Dying?" *Business Week,* March 1, 1941, pp. 14–15.
Feinstein, Isidor, "Corporate Tammany Halls," *The Nation,* December 18, 1935, p. 710.
Pratt, Tom, "Smith Barney Unveils LP for UGI's Petrolane Deal," *Investment Dealers' Digest,* November 14, 1994, pp. 10–11.
"Resignation to Revolt," *Time,* December 2, 1935, pp. 62–63.
UGI Corporation: The First 100 Years, Valley Forge, Penn.: UGI Corp., 1982.

—Robert Halasz

Unifi, Inc.

7201 W. Friendly Road
Greensboro, North Carolina 27410
U.S.A.
(910) 294-4410
Fax: (910) 294-4410

Public Company
Incorporated: 1969
Employees: 6,000
Sales: $1.38 billion
Stock Exchanges: New York
SICs: 2282 Throwing & Winding Mills

Unifi, Inc. is one of the largest manufacturers of textured polyester and nylon in the world. The company also produces various natural and blended materials. From its high-tech production facilities in the United States and Ireland, Unifi exports its output to more than 40 different countries. Unifi increased its revenues more than three-fold during the early 1990s by merging with several other companies to form Unifi Spun Yarns, Inc. Sales in 1994 (fiscal year ended July 26) were $1.38 billion.

The Unifi (rhymes with butterfly) story is one of spectacular triumph over adversity. The company started its operations 1971, manufacturing polyester yarn that was popular with the textile industry at the time. When Unifi opened its doors, there were already more than 50 other companies competing in the United States. Unfortunately, demand for Unifi's product collapsed during the 1970s and 1980s. Indeed, the industry's production capacity plummeted during those two decades from 2.5 billion pounds to only 700 million pounds as the number of competitors shrank to only three by the late 1980s. Despite the shakeout, Unifi prospered. Through grit, determination, and savvy business strategies, Unifi's management team was able to grow the company's revenues from $21 million in 1971 to $300 million by 1988, and then to more than $1 billion a few years later. "Unifi is one of the great American success stories," observed analyst Michael Hopwood in the April 5, 1988 *Financial World,* noting that "through that entire bloodbath, it never posted a loss once."

Unifi's miraculous success is largely attributable to Allen Mebane, chairperson and founder of Unifi. Mebane was born in 1924 and raised in Greensboro, North Carolina. Although his father was an insurance salesman, Mebane's great-great-grand-

father had owned a cotton mill, and Mebane himself was intrigued with the textile industry. His father sent him to Davidson College, but Mebane transferred to the Philadelphia College of Textiles and Science to learn more about the industry. Immediately after graduating in 1950, he went to work with Sale Knitting Co. in Martinsville, Virginia.

Mebane started in manufacturing, working long hours and gaining valuable knowledge about the production side of the business. But it didn't take him long to realize that he was in the wrong place. "I was there at six o'clock in the morning, and I was there at eight or nine at night," Mebane recalled in the November 1993 *Business North Carolina,* "and the fellows selling the yarn would come in and they'd have a suit on and they'd have a car and could take people out to lunch and have an expense account, and I said 'I'm doing the wrong thing here.' " Mebane left his job to serve in the Army during the Korean War, and when he returned in 1954, he took a job as a sales trainee at American & Efird Inc., a fiber manufacturer.

Mebane soon left American & Efird for a better job. Between 1957 and 1964, he sold yarn for Burlington Industries. At Burlington, Mebane benefitted from being able to meet and talk with the people who owned and ran the textile companies. By observing their different strategies and styles, he was able to determine which methods did and didn't work. "The ones that were successful were the ones that were innovative, moving all the time," he noted in the *Business North Carolina* article. "The ones that weren't successful were the status-quo boys." By that time, the 40-year-old Mebane was eager to make his mark on the industry with his own textile operation.

He got his chance to run a textile company in 1964, when he was hired by Throwing Corporation of America to serve as the manufacturer's president. Confident in his ability to improve Throwing's performance, Mebane bought 20 percent of the company for $10,000. He was only at Throwing for a short time, though, before becoming a partner at Universal Textured Yarns. Mebane made his move to Universal at an opportune time. Universal was getting in on the ground floor of the burgeoning polyester texturing industry. Through the texturing process, producers like Universal were able to heat raw polyester fibers and manipulate them to generate different characteristics and qualities. Because the polyester could be converted into stronger fibers with the look and feel of natural materials, polyester was viewed as a breakthrough, wonder fabric. Not only was it was durable, inexpensive, and versatile, but it never had to be ironed.

As the popularity of textured polyester surged, Universal thrived. Mebane and his fellow top managers sold their shares in the company for $1 million in 1971. They immediately invested that money, along with a $6 million dollar bank loan, into their own operation—Unifi. The strategy employed by Mebane and his fellow managers during Unifi's start-up was one that they would continue to employ throughout the 1970s, 1980s, and into the mid-1990s; they invested in cutting edge manufacturing equipment that would give them a long-term cost and quality advantage over competitors. They first purchased 32 high-tech English machines, which were considered state-of-the-art in the early 1970s. As their competitors adopted similar technology in the mid-1970s, Unifi upped the ante. In

1975, the company invested heavily in new German-built equipment that could make better yarn and at a faster rate.

Unifi prospered during the early and mid-1970s and quickly established itself as a low-cost provider of high-quality polyester yarns. Although Unifi's business strategy was impressive, the same couldn't be said for the popularity of polyester by the late 1970s. Dismissed by many retailers and consumers as a fad, polyester's appeal waned as markets renewed their desire for natural fibers like cotton, silk, and wool. While polyester leisure suits and dresses, for example, had been a hit in the mid-1970s, they had become a joke by the late 1970s and early 1980s. As a result, domestic polyester production plunged. Manufacturing overcapacity quashed price growth, and many producers were forced out of business.

In order to stay afloat, Mebane and company knew that they were going to have to either find new markets for their polyester or vastly increase their share of the market. They did both. At home, Unifi benefitted from its manufacturing prowess. Because its operations were so advanced, it was able to undercut its less efficient competitors and rapidly steal market share. Unifi management understood early that it was operating in a commodity business; if one of its competitors was forced to charge even a slightly higher price, Unifi knew that it was only a matter of time until that company folded. So, despite dying demand, Unifi continued to risk hefty capital investments in new production facilities and techniques. And it was able to keep its selling and administrative costs to an industry low of three percent throughout the late 1970s and 1980s. As its rivals struggled and failed to keep up, Unifi bought them out or simply took on their customers when they went out of business.

But leadership in U.S. markets wasn't enough to keep Unifi profitable during the lean late 1970s and early 1980s. To buoy profits, Unifi aggressively pursued foreign business. Importantly, Unifi was among the first U.S. companies to begin selling to China when the People's Republic opened its doors to exports in 1980. The emerging, yet massive, Chinese market proved a boon for Unifi during the early 1980s. As demand soared, so did Unifi's overseas sales. At one point, Unifi trucks were literally blocking the road to the port as they waited to unload tons of commodity yarns for export to China. By 1983, Unifi was garnering about one-quarter of its $176 million in annual revenues from sales in China, and shipments to the country were topping one million pounds per week.

Unfortunately, the China boom was short-lived. China and several other Asian countries, particularly Taiwan, soon built their own texturing facilities. Besides costs related to shipping, Asian producers also benefitted from advantages like cheap labor and loose environmental regulations. Asian demand for U.S. polyester faded quickly after 1983, but Mebane and his fellow executives were undaunted. They mimicked their domestic strategy by purchasing the polyester operations of another major U.S. polyester supplier to China, Macfield Inc., in 1986. More importantly, Unifi continued to search for new international customers in Latin America, South America, Australia, Israel, Africa, and the Far East.

Integral to Unifi's international strategy was its 1980 entrance into Europe. After only two years of exporting to that region,

Unifi had captured a healthy six percent share of the Western European polyester market. However, Unifi's success in that region was hampered by European Economic Community charges that the company was dumping polyester into Europe at prices below cost. Unifi was eventually cleared of the allegations, and it elected to pursue a different strategy in that heavily protected market. In 1984, it purchased a manufacturing plant in Ireland and spent $50 million making the plant into one of the most efficient and technologically advanced in the world. By the early 1990s, Unifi's Irish operations were supplying 20 percent of European demand (measured in sales volume).

As Unifi expanded globally, the U.S. polyester markets continued to deteriorate. Demand for filament poly (used to make polyester yarn) collapsed from 1.4 billion pounds in 1975 to 650 million in 1985. "The market went to hell in a handbasket," Mebane confirmed in the January 24, 1994, *Fortune*. But Unifi continued to boost domestic market share during the mid- and late 1980s through its aggressive high-tech, low-cost operating strategy. In addition, Unifi diversified into nylon and began cultivating new markets for its polyester fibers. Most notably, Unifi was successful in marketing its polyester and nylon products to the automobile industry for the production of seat covers and vehicle interiors. The company also developed a large niche in the hosiery business. One of its largest customers, in fact, became Sara Lee, a leading supplier of women's hosiery.

By 1988, Unifi had become one of the largest manufacturers of polyester and nylon in the world. It was controlling about 40 percent of the U.S. market and had a strong toehold in Europe and several other export regions. Unifi's total revenues had swelled to $275 million in 1987, up from $248 million the previous year. Similarly, net income had grown steadily from $5.6 million in 1985, to $10.4 million in 1986, and then to $12 million during 1987. Moreover, Unifi achieved those gains as it steadily shrunk its long-term debt to $1 million by early 1988.

Unifi's long-term outlook seemed bright. Domestic demand for polyester seemed to have stabilized, and the company was making massive capital investments in cutting edge technology, including the purchase of new Japanese texturing equipment in 1988. Much of Unifi's success during the late 1980s was credited to William Kretzer, who had assumed the president slot in 1985. Kretzer controlled day-to-day operations, while chairperson Mebane retained his strategic role.

While Unifi's gains throughout the 1980s had wowed observers, the company experienced even greater expansion and profitability during the early 1990s. Unifi's success during that period was simply more evidence of Mebane's emphasis on long term growth. For example, since deciding to go global in the late 1970s, Unifi's managers had determined that they would stick with the markets that they entered, even when performance in a particular region waned. By contrast, many of Unifi's competitors had simply bailed out of ailing markets, ceding their share to Unifi. As a result, Unifi was invariably positioned to take advantage of different recovering markets. "They are the first in the gate when the rebound starts," explained industry specialist Bill Dawson in the November 1993 *Business North Carolina*.

Unifi's gains during the early 1990s were also the result of major acquisitions. In 1991, for example, Unifi acquired the remaining operations of Macfield, as well as a company called Vintage Yarns. Macfield had been Unifi's largest competitor, and the two mergers literally doubled Unifi's size. The buyouts gave Unifi a dominant presence in the U.S. nylon industry and extended its reach into profitable market niches like hosiery and vehicle interiors. By 1993, Unifi was employing 5,000 workers in its various manufacturing plants, increasing its work force while also working to make operations more efficient. For example, Unifi's major Pennsylvania facility generated about 3.2 million pounds of nylon per week in 1981 with about 1,300 employees. In 1993, the same plant was pumping out about twice as much material with only 1,000 workers.

Due largely to the mergers, Unifi's sales suddenly escalated past the $1 billion mark in 1992, and net income leapt to a record $63 million. Then, in 1993, Unifi merged again. This time it effectively absorbed Pioneer Yarn Mills, Pioneer Spinning, Edenton Cotton Mils, and Pioneer Cotton Mill—companies merged into a single entity, the Pioneer Corporations, and subsequently acquired by Unifi. Unifi formed a subsidiary for the division called Unifi Spun Yarns, Inc. The acquisition was important because it represented Unifi's move into the natural fibers industry; the former Pioneer companies' primary products were spun yarns made of cotton, but also some cotton/synthetic blends. During 1994 (fiscal year ended June 26), Unifi achieved sales of $1.38 billion, about $76.5 million of which was netted as income.

Going into the mid-1990s, Unifi was controlling a full 70 percent of the U.S. polyester market and was selling about $500 million worth of nylon annually. It was serving 20 percent of demand in Europe and planned to boost that share to at least 30 percent by the late 1990s. As a result of the mergers, its work force had grown to 6,000 employees in 15 U.S. production facilities, one plant in Ireland, and sales offices in England, France, and Japan. The company spent nearly $400 million between 1991 and 1993 to ensure that its plants would continue to be amongst the most advanced in the world.

Furthermore, Unifi's three most influential executives—Mebane, Kretzer, and William J. Armfield, all of whom had been with Unifi since the early 1970s—were still at the helm, suggesting continued innovation and dominance of Unifi's key markets throughout the decade. "Its hard to bet against Unifi," said textile industry analyst Lorraine Miller in the *Business North Carolina* article, who added that "come hook or by crook, whether it's through acquisition or by adding on to their own facilities, they're going to be positioned to take market share."

Principal Subsidiaries: Unifi Spun Yarns, Inc.

Further Reading:

Bailey, David, "Getting His Irish Up: Faced with EC Protectionism, Unifi's Allen Mebane Decided the Way to Beat the Europeans Was to Join Them," *Business North Carolina,* November 1993, p. 26.

McAllister, Isaacs III, "Unifi Tops the Sales Yarn Market and Is Still Moving," *Textile World,* August 1993, p. 33.

Serwer, Andrew S., "Business is Bad? It's Time to Grow!," *Fortune,* January 24, 1994, p. 88.

"Synthetics Prove to Be the Real Thing for Unifi," *Business North Carolina,* January 1988, p. 57.

Wrubel, Robert, "Unifi: The Next Textile Takeover," *Financial World,* April 5, 1988, p. 16.

—Dave Mote

varian ⓋⒶ

Varian Associates Inc.

3050 Hansen Way
Palo Alto, California 94304-1000
U.S.A.
(415) 493-4000
Fax: (415) 424-5994

Public Company
Incorporated: 1948
Employees: 8,500
Sales: $1.5 billion
Stock Exchanges: New York
SICs: 3671 Electron Tubes; 3674 Semiconductors; 3826
   Analytical Instruments; 3841 Surgical and Medical
   Instruments

Varian Associates Inc. is a diversified, international electronics company that designs, manufactures, and markets high-technology systems and components. Varian's major product lines include radiation equipment for cancer therapy; analytical instruments for science and industry; semiconductor manufacturing equipment; and electron devices for advanced applications in defense, industry, and research. Recognized as a global technological leader, Varian was a pioneer of the renowned high-tech hotbed of Silicon Valley, California.

Varian Associates was started in 1948 by brothers Russell (Russ) and Sigurd (Sig) Varian. Although they started with only $22,000 and a handful of employees, the Varian team was brimming with technical know-how. In fact, the Varian story dates back to at least the late 1930s, when the Varian brothers put their heads together to develop the famed klystron tube. The United States was faced with the need for improved navigational aids for its fledgling aviation industry as well as the possibility of war. The Varians's idea won them $100 for materials and part-time use of a laboratory at Stanford University. The goal of the project was to create the electron tube, a device that is capable of directing a beam of electrons and could, therefore, be utilized in a number of new applications.

The klystron was invented in the summer of 1937 and formally introduced in 1939 in the *Journal of Applied Physics*. European scientists were feverishly trying to develop similar technology at the time, so the announcement was welcomed in England. In fact, the United Kingdom wasted no time in adapting klystron technology to provide a lightweight source of microwaves for

their radar receivers. By 1940 the Royal Air Force had equipped its night fighters with klystron radar receivers, which helped England defend its shores and claim victory in the Battle of Britain.

The Klystron Project team continued to advance its new technology during World War II. Later, team members would recall not only the Project's scientific achievements, but also its contribution to technology management. Because of the war, team members were forced to couple their discoveries with real social needs rather than simply advancing technology for its own sake. Besides playing a role during World War II, the klystron was credited with initiating the microwave industry. Among other distinctions, microwave technology made commercial air navigation safe, allowed the development of worldwide communications satellites, and spawned numerous breakthrough devices, such as high-energy particle accelerators, that were integral to the advancement of medicine and nuclear physics.

After the war, the Varians and some of their Klystron Project peers decided to start their own company in California. They suspected that klystron technology was too expensive for them to get into on their own, but they felt that other emerging technologies, such as nuclear magnetic resonance, offered potential. So, with $22,000 and no real plan for exactly what they were going to do, the group started Varian Associates. The original company consisted of the Varians, Fred Salisbury, Myrl Stearns, and Russell's wife, Dorothy.

Although they were dwarfed in terms of size and capital by their competitors, smallness turned out to be their greatest advantage. When the government solicited bids for a klystron development project after the War, few manufacturers were interested because it offered an unrealistically low allowance for overhead. But Varian, with negligible overhead, decided to take on the project and soon developed the R-1 klystron. Its success with that project helped it earn several other government and private sector jobs, and attract top scientific talent. During the following ten years, in fact, the Varian think tank produced a string of major breakthroughs related to various electronic technologies.

Among Varians's most recognized early achievements was its development of nuclear induction, or nuclear magnetic resonance (NMR), technology. NMR revolutionized chemistry by allowing chemists to quickly determine the structure of molecules. Russ Varian had tracked the development of NMR at Stanford and Harvard during World War II, and he hired Martin Packard, a key NMR researcher, to head Varian's project. "Prior to the use of NMR . . . you could spend literally months and years trying to determine the structure of a molecule," Packard explained in Varian archives. "With NMR, infrared, mass spectrometry, and other such tools, the same problems can often be solved in hours, and the whole field of chemistry has been able to undergo a much more rapid advance and expansion." Varian and Packard applied for a U.S. patent on their ideas related to NMR in 1948.

Varian soon built upon its successful development of klystron and NMR technologies. The company eventually integrated klystron technology into a range of new applications for the telephone, radio, television broadcast, satellite, radar, and related communications industries. Likewise, Varian used NMR technology to develop a line of scientific instruments used in chemistry, physics, biology, medicine, and other fields. Varian opened its Palo Alto Microwave Tube Division in 1953 in Building 1 of the Stanford Industrial Park. The facility became known as the first high-tech industrial park in the United States and signaled the beginning of Silicon Valley.

Another major technological breakthrough ascribed to Varian in the 1950s was the medical linear accelerator. A linear accelerator is a machine used to produce x-rays, electrons, and other high-energy particles. It was invented by Bill Hansen and Ed Ginzton, both of whom had worked on the Klystron Project, joined Varian early on as directors, and served as consultants to the company. Varian's goal for its medical linear accelerator project was to take the large, clumsy linear accelerator, or linac, and shape it into a compact, agile device that doctors could use to accurately distribute dosages of particles to the human body.

In collaboration with Stanford Medical Center, Ginzton led the evolution of klystron technology to create the Varian Linac accelerator, the first practicable medical accelerator. The device soon became an important tool in the research of cancer treatment with radiation. Although implementation of the device in the private sector took several years, Varian used technology developed in the Linac project in other ventures and was eventually able to parlay the breakthrough into a marketable line of medical apparatuses. Considered one of Varian's crowning achievements, the resulting Varian Clinac line of radiotherapy systems would become Varian's most successful product line.

Besides the klystron, NMR, and linear accelerator, a fourth major breakthrough for Varian was its electronic vacuum pump. Until the mid-1950s a major hurdle to the manufacturing of vacuum tubes was contaminants that attached themselves to the tubes' innards and shortened tube life. Part of the problem was debris from oil diffusion pumps that were used to create the vacuum in the tubes. Varian began experimenting with gas discharge "sputtering," which lead to the sputter-ion pump. It turned out that, in addition to creating cleaner vacuum tubes, the pump was more portable, required no cooling water, and had a number of other beneficial attributes.

Varian developed a marketable pump called the VacIon Pump in 1958, and in 1959 launched an entire business division based on the new technology. Varian delivered some of its first pumps to RCA, the Atomic Energy Commission, and NASA. The division flourished during the 1960s as the VacIon Pump spawned several product lines for a variety of different applications. Most importantly, Varian's vacuum pump technology later provided ingress into the burgeoning semiconductor industry. Varian gradually honed important technology related to ion implantation and thin-film coating that became integral to the semiconductor fabrication process.

Because of its technological prowess, Varian earned a reputation as a leading technological innovator during the 1950s and 1960s. The same praise could not be applied to its business accomplishments, however. Despite a flurry of highly marketable product introductions, Varian's financial performance was spotty. Indeed, the company was so intently focused on the exciting science and engineering game that it sometimes ignored the bottom line. That resulted in part from the fact that

most of the company's workers and managers had formerly been (and often continued to be) associated with academia. One well-known story within the company is of an engineer that invented a computer printer capable of printing enough data to cover a football field. When asked who in the world would want such a device, the engineer replied, "Lawrence Livermore Laboratory. They'll buy one of everything."

To Varian's credit, the academic environment had allowed its scientists to innovate and achieve. Nevertheless, the company suffered from erratic profit performance because of its lack of business savvy. Business boomed in the late 1950s. In the early 1960s, though, its government contracting business dried up and the company nearly went bust. The company staged a comeback in the mid-1960s by emphasizing nonmilitary markets. But by the late 1960s Varian was in financial trouble again. Varian brought in a new, business-oriented manager in 1971 who made several seemingly smart moves. Varian purchased a minicomputer company, for example, and eventually grabbed about ten percent of that growing market. Indicative of the overall company performance, however, Varian scientists had trouble adapting to fast-changing markets and the company was unable to control manufacturing costs. The computer division languished and was jettisoned in 1977.

Varian had about $640 million in sales in 1981 from its growing and diversified high-tech product lines. Unfortunately, it also lost $3.6 million. In another bid to bring its balance sheet in line with its technological ability, Varian brought in a new president in 1982, Thomas Sege. Sege was a 55-year-old former Yugoslavian who had escaped from the country in 1940, shortly before Hitler invaded. Sege believed that Varian's problems stemmed from its loose, splintered environment. "The name 'Varian Associates' is significant," he noted in *Forbes*. "It means a loose association of people doing their own thing. . . . We had a number of small shops with small objectives."

In an effort to rectify the situation, Sege quickly established tight controls over inventories and receivables and tied manager pay and incentives to financial performance. He also started selling or closing marginal operations that were losing money, and diversifying into new businesses that promised to complement existing technologies. Although some researchers and managers resisted the change in the working environment, others welcomed the new direction and the feeling of an overall corporate focus. The changes seemed to work. In 1982 Varian announced the first of what would be three years of consecutively improved results, ending with record sales ($973 million) and earnings ($69.7 million) in 1984. During the mid-1980s, moreover, recovering defense markets boosted revenues over $800 million.

Although Varian's financial performance improved during the early and mid-1980s, its successes were short-lived. Varian's sales continued to surge, but profits were spotty and the company failed to become integrated. Under Sege's direction, Varian made a number of acquisitions, many of which it later dumped. By the late 1980s Varian was generating more than $1 billion in sales from its diversified, global operations. But it had also become an unwieldy, barely profitable techno-behemoth with 20 decentralized divisions. "They are not very well managed and have a history of problems," noted industry analyst Carolyn A. Rogers in the *Los Angeles Times.*

Despite Varian's business shortcomings, the company continued to be recognized as a leader in electronic-related technology. For example, Varian had introduced several major innovations in the semiconductor industry and had become a major player in specific segments of the health care industry, particularly those related to cancer treatment. In fact, by the early 1990s Varian had captured more than half the global market for radiation therapy equipment. Varian also retained a leadership role in instrument and electron device markets.

However, Varian had been criticized for being too focused on technology and for offering only ultra-high-end, premium products and ignoring the sometimes larger middle market. Likewise, the company had acquired a reputation for investing heavily in questionable new technologies. For example, Varian developed a system that could be used to irradiate produce, thus killing bugs and extending shelf life. The product never made it to market, though, because of glitches related to federal approval. "You just can't experiment without thinking about the bottom line," analyst Stephen Balog told *Fortune.*

In an effort to capitalize on Varian's strong product and market position, Varian called Tracy O'Rourke to the helm in 1990 and Sege stepped aside and became vice-chairman. The 54-year-old O'Rourke boasted a track record of management successes. Most notably, he was credited with turning around the Allen-Bradley division of Rockwell International, a major high-tech defense contractor. He had taken that company from $450 million to $1.4 billion in sales, all the while improving profits and margins. O'Rourke was known as a visionary with a knack for international expansion. At the time of his arrival, Varian was similar to Allen-Bradley in both size and markets served, with $1.3 billion in 1989 sales and an international work force of 12,000.

Immediately after his arrival O'Rourke designed and began to implement a three-phase restructuring program aimed at whipping the technological giant into financial health. "Like a hummingbird, we were going from opportunity to opportunity, only to abandon them when the competition got too hot. We were simply spreading ourselves too thin," O'Rourke explained in *Industry Week.* During the first phase of O'Rourke's program, which Varian completed during the early 1990s, Varian sold 11 languishing divisions and product lines for $60 million, closed nonperforming units, and initiated a massive labor reduction designed to eventually pare about one-third of Varian's 12,400-member work force.

That effort alone allowed Varian to post a record profit of $58 million in 1991 following a depressing loss in 1990. Phase two of the process, which was started in 1992, was a long-term goal of significantly improved quality and service. O'Rourke wanted to consolidate and streamline the entire organization, reduce the amount of time required to take new ideas to market, and develop a customer-oriented culture. "People had fallen into the habit that it was o.k. to be late," O'Rourke recalled in *Industry Week.* "As a result, customer shipments from some of our core businesses would lag, sometimes by several months." Finally, O'Rourke's third phase entailed the development of a long-term profit and growth strategy designed to take Varian into the 21st century.

By 1994, the effects of O'Rourke's efforts were already apparent. Although sales hovered around the $1.3 billion mark, sales per employee jumped more than 50 percent and earnings ranged between $45 million and $60 million during 1991, 1992, and 1993. Order backlogs were reduced significantly, and quality control improved. Furthermore, Varian slashed its total corporate debt from about $110 million in 1989 to almost zero in 1993. Importantly, Varian boosted research and development spending, reflecting O'Rourke's intent to sustain Varian's legacy of technological leadership.

Going into the mid-1990s, Varian operated its subsidiaries through four core businesses: health care systems (30 percent of 1993 sales); instruments (27 percent); semiconductor equipment (22 percent); and electron devices (21 percent). In 1994, Varian was the world's leading supplier of cancer radiation equipment, the top developer and producer (by sales volume) of analytical instrumentation for studying chemical composition of matter, one of the largest manufacturers of semiconductor fabrication equipment, and a leading U.S. supplier of microwave-related equipment, particularly for satellite communications. Varian operated more than 50 sales offices outside of the United States (and about 40 domestically), with about 43 percent of revenues coming from foreign shipments. A steadily rising stock price in the first half of the 1990s suggested market confidence in Varian's long-term potential, as the company's share price climbed to an all-time high ($46 per share) and it posted record sales and earnings in 1994–95.

Principal Subsidiaries: Oncology Systems; X-Ray Tube Products; Nuclear Magnetic Resonance Instruments; Vacuum Products; Ion Implantation Systems; Thin Film Systems; Power-Grid Tube Products; Microwave Equipment Products; Microwave Power Tube Products.

Further Reading:

Bates, James, "Varian Finds Itself Tangled in Pentagon Scandal," *Los Angeles Times,* July 2, 1988, Sec. 4, p. 1.

Goldman, James S., "Intevac Arises from Varian's Restructuring," *Business Journal-San Jose,* April 13, 1992, p. 1.

Krey, Michael, "Varian's Laying It on the (Bottom) Line," *Business Journal-San Jose,* December 4, 1989, p. 1.

Nickel, Karen, "Will a Disciplinarian Shake up Varian?," *Fortune,* May 7, 1990, p. 26.

Privett, Cyndi, "Mired in Slump, Varian Struggles to Snap Free," *Business Journal-San Jose,* July 28, 1986, p. 1.

Simpson, Gary, "Varian Associates Inc. Named O'Rourke Chairman, Chief Executive Officer," *Business Wire,* February 28, 1990.

Teresko, John, "Varian," *Industry Week,* October 19, 1992, p. 55.

Varian Associates: An Early History, Palo Alto, Calif.: Varian Associates, Inc.

Weigner, Kathleen K., "It's About Time," *Forbes,* April 25, 1983, p. 41.

—Dave Mote

Venture Stores Inc.

2001 E. Terra Lane
O'Fallon, Missouri 63366-0110
U.S.A.
(314) 281-5500
Fax: (314) 281-5152

Public Company
Incorporated: 1970
Employees: 18,000
Sales: $2 billion
Stock Exchanges: New York
SICs: 5311 Department Stores

Venture Stores Inc. is a leading regional discount store chain in the midwestern and southwestern United States. Venture was operating 114 stores in nine states in 1995, concentrating in the Texas, Illinois, and Missouri, areas. Despite fiercely competitive markets, Venture has grown rapidly since its parent company spun it off in 1990.

Venture Stores was started in 1970 by The May Department Stores Company. May was a leading upscale department store operator based in St. Louis, Missouri. It was known at the time for its popular Famous Barr department stores. The upscale department store chain, as well as other department store companies that May operated, including Kaufman's and Woodward & Lothrop, continued to be May's primary focus during the 1970s and 1980s. However, by 1970 May felt pressure from the increasingly popular discount retailers. Although many of the most popular discount chains had originated in the Northeast and West, they had begun expanding into the Midwest by the late 1960s and were threatening to erode the retail market share of May and other traditional retailers.

In an effort to profit from the discount store boom and to diversify its holdings, May decided to start its own discount retail division, and created Venture. It patterned its Venture division after other discount retail houses such as Korvette, Kmart, and Wal-Mart. May's strategy was relatively straight forward. Venture would purchase inventory in bulk at reduced prices. It would sell the goods in a store environment that, compared to department stores, was austere and low-budget. By emphasizing self-service, volume sales, and a small operating budget, the store would be able to appeal to consumers by offering low prices.

The first Venture store opened in St. Louis in 1970. During the 1970s, Venture opened several stores in its chosen core St. Louis and Chicago markets, and eventually branched out into other major Midwest metropolitan areas. Venture soon dominated some metropolitan areas. Venture's quick start-up and success hinged largely on May's support. May was known as a savvy, aggressive, profitable retailer. Its large capital base allowed it to finance the construction and stocking of large stores, and then aggressively market them to regional shoppers. In Chicago, May acquired some existing stores and converted them into Venture stores. In addition, Venture benefitted from May's proven expertise and infrastructure related to important retail elements like purchasing, distribution, and promotion.

May expanded the Venture division relatively slowly during the early and mid-1970s and remained focused on its core upscale department store operations. Importantly, in 1978 May selected Julian Seeherman to serve as Venture's vice chairman. The 49-year-old Seeherman would eventually be credited with building the Venture chain to more than 100 stores by the early 1990s. Seeherman had only been with May since 1977. A retail industry veteran, he had been hired to serve as president and chief executive of Consumers Distributing, May's catalog showroom operation. Prior to joining May, he had spent more than 25 years with Abraham and Strauss, rising through the ranks of sales clerk and department manager, and finally executive vice-president.

Seeherman, a native of Pennsylvania, was known as a hard worker and shrewd merchant. As a boy he had pumped gas and checked oil at the service station that his father managed. He later worked as a busboy at Summer resorts in the Catskill Mountains to pay his way through college. After graduating from the Syracuse University School of Business Administration, he entered the retailing industry as an executive trainee. "Nothing was given to him on a silver platter," said Seeherman's cousin, Steve Seeherman, in the *St. Louis Business Journal.* "His father was a hard worker and believed everyone else should be a hard worker."

Also taking credit for Venture's rise during the 1980s and 1990s was the man that would eventually serve as president of Venture, Philip G. Otto. Otto joined May in 1969, one year before the start-up of the Venture division. He served at various finance-related posts during the early 1970s before joining Venture as senior vice president of finance and operations in 1976. He jockeyed within Venture's upper-level management before becoming chairman in 1986 and president in 1990. He succeeded Seeherman as president when Seeherman became CEO in 1990. Otto was known as a detailed businessman with retail expertise in finance and operations. In contrast, Seeherman excelled at the merchandising end of the business. So Seeherman and Otto complemented each other at Venture.

Although Venture enjoyed a relative dearth of discount competition during the early and mid-1970s, the retail discount industry became increasingly competitive during the late 1970s. Industry consolidation was one result. Retailers scrambled to increase economies of scale by buying up smaller competitors, and a few discounters like Kmart and Wal-Mart emerged as national discount powerhouses. That trend was intensified during the early 1980s by a slowdown in consumer spending during the U.S. economic recession of the period. The smaller regional discount chains like Venture and Korvette began facing fierce competition in some metropolitan areas.

Though competition forced the discount store pioneer, Korvette, into failure, Venture thrived. Venture became one of the lowest cost retailers in the nation and was recognized for its ability to deter rivals in its dominant Chicago market. Competition did force Venture to accept smaller profit margins. In St. Louis and Chicago, Venture mainly competed with Kmart and Target.

Venture vied for customers by expanding its number of stores and its offerings. After Seeherman had been named president of the Venture chain in 1982, Venture's growth excelled. By 1985, Venture consisted of more than 50 stores, most of which were in Chicago and St. Louis. During the next five years, Venture added approximately six stores per year. Though many of Venture's early stores were located in urban centers, Venture began emphasizing the construction of discount superstores in suburbs during the mid-1980s. At the same time, Venture broadened its offerings to include more clothing and other soft goods.

May bought another discount chain in 1985 and drew on the talents of two of Venture's top executives to run it. Caldor, the discount chain May acquired when it bought Associated Dry Goods (ADG), consisted of more than 100 stores throughout the Northeast, but lacked Venture's financial strength. May replaced Caldor's leaders with Don R. Clarke, who became chief executive, and Marc Balmuth, who was named president. May significantly improved Caldor's performance during the late 1980s.

Venture did not suffer without Clarke or Balmuth, achieving steady gains. The chain consisted of nearly 80 stores by 1990, and had expanded into new markets. Venture opened its first Kentucky outlet in 1985 and by 1990 was operating in eight states: Missouri, Illinois, Kentucky, Iowa, Oklahoma, Kansas, Arkansas, and Indiana. Though operating results continued to improve into the late 1980s, the pace of the improvements had slowed. Sales rose from $1.2 billion in 1988, to $1.3 billion in 1989, and then to $1.4 billion in 1990.

To the surprise of many observers, May decided to sell all its discount operations in 1989. May executives had become disenchanted with the discount divisions. Besides the nagging recession, they were also discouraged by the increasingly combative nature of the discount industry. May jettisoned Caldor in 1989 and then spun-off Venture in 1990. Seeherman was named CEO of the independent Venture chain and Otto became president.

Despite Venture's proven management team, some analysts doubted the company's ability to thrive away from its parent. Part of the doubt stemmed from the fact that May had increased the company's debt prior to spinning it off. Nevertheless, others were optimistic. In fact, some observers felt that Venture had languished under May's umbrella, unable to take advantage of growth opportunities that it could have pursued had its parent not been focused on its department stores. Indeed, the results of Seeherman's efforts during the early 1990s supported that appraisal. Under Seeherman's direction, Venture added five more stores onto its chain during 1991 and added another nine in 1992. In 1993, moreover, Seeherman aggressively entered

Texas markets. Venture opened a total of 12 new stores, 11 of which were in Texas. That boosted Venture's total number of outlets to 104 by the end of the year. In 1992, *Discount Store News* awarded Venture the "Discounter of the Year Award."

In addition to assuming a more aggressive growth strategy, Seeherman streamlined the company. He outlined four goals Venture would need to achieve to remain competitive: 1) to improve customer service; 2) to drive costs down with new technology and upgrade warehouse and distribution operations; 3) to increase sales-per-square-foot; and 4) to continue to project an image of social responsibility. "No matter how good we are today, we must get better," Seeherman declared in *Discount Store News*. "It won't get any easier." Seeherman's and Otto's efforts paid off during the early 1990s as Venture flourished. Sales rose to $1.5 billion in 1991 and to $1.8 billion in 1992. Likewise, net earnings increased to $41.5 million in 1991 and to $47.5 million the next year.

Unfortunately, competition threatened Venture's success in 1993. Wal-Mart, Kmart, and Target had all entered Venture's largest market, Chicago. Although consumer surveys indicated that Venture was still the preferred discount store for most buyers in that city, relative newcomers Wal-Mart and Target were gradually eroding Venture's dominance. Kmart was already operating more than 60 stores in the region going into 1994, compared to Venture's 39.

As competition proliferated, Venture's sales fell short of projections in 1993. It generated revenues of $1.9 billion during the year, about $23 million short of its goals. Net earnings slipped to $41 million. Furthermore, the company reported dismal profits early in 1994, suggesting a downward trend in the company's performance. "If you look at a lot of the retailers's margins, it was a blood bath last year in terms of competitive pricing," Seeherman said in the *St. Louis Post Dispatch*. While markets soured and profits fell, Otto announced his resignation late in 1994, effective in May 1995. Otto's resignation came just as the 62-year-old Seeherman was looking for a successor to pilot the Venture chain. Otto had been the logical replacement.

During this time, Venture entered its ninth state, opening ten stores and Dallas and Houston in July 1993. By 1995, the company was operating 20 stores in the new Texas market. Despite short term disappointments, Venture remained a dominant player in its major markets and continued to pursue an ambitious growth strategy going into the mid-1990s. The discounter had earmarked about $450 million for new store construction and about $50 million to renovate existing locations. It opened nine new outlets in 1994 and planned to open an average of ten new stores annually throughout the mid-1990s, most of which would be located in Texas. That would bring the size of the Venture chain to about 150.

Further Reading:

"Caldor, Venture Survive as Chains; Proceeds from Spin-Offs Fall Short of Expectations," *Discount Store News,* October 30, 1989, p. 1.

Darks, Sarah A., "Venture's Seeherman Comes Far from Days of Pumping Gas for Dad," *St. Louis Business Journal,* August 31, 1992, sec. 1, p. 1.

Donaldson, Rob, "Venture Spins Off to Terrific First Year," *St. Louis Business Journal,* June 15, 1992, sec. 2, p. 5.

Flannery, William, "Venture's Chief Sees Competitive Market," *St. Louis Post Dispatch,* May 21, 1994, sec. A, p. 8.

Halverson, Richard C., "May to Raise Seed Money to Hasten Sale of Venture," *Discount Store News,* July 2, 1990, p. 1.

Lisanti, Tony, "Seeherman: A Quintessential Merchant," *Discount Store News,* September 21, 1992, p. 133.

Ludington, Callaway, "Venture Stock Could Be Good Value, Analysts Say," *St. Louis Business Journal,* June 25, 1990, p. 9A.

"Otto Bids Venture Good-Bye," *Discount Store News,* October 3, 1994, p. 1.

Quick, Julie, "Venture to Open 40 Stores, Spend $450 Million in 5 years," *St. Louis Business Journal,* sec. 1, p. 3.

Stroud, Jerri, "Changing Trends Hurt Venture," *St. Louis Post-Dispatch,* July 16, 1994, sec. A, p. 9.

—Dave Mote

VICORP

Restaurants, Inc.

VICORP Restaurants, Inc.

400 West 48th Avenue
Denver, Colorado 80216
U.S.A.
(303) 296-2121
Fax: (303) 672-2668

Public Company
Incorporated: 1959 as Village Inn Pancake House, Inc.
Employees: 14,300
Sales: $418.1 million
Stock Exchanges: NASDAQ
SICs: 5812 Eating Places; 6794 Patent Owners & Lessors

VICORP Restaurants, Inc., is a U.S. operator and franchiser of more than 400 Village Inn and Bakers Square family restaurants. The Village Inn chain consists of both corporate-operated and franchised restaurants, which are located primarily in the Central and Rocky Mountain regions of the United States. The smaller Bakers Square chain, concentrated in California and the upper Midwest, is entirely operated by the corporation. The two chains are purveyors of pies and other fresh-baked products as well as in-restaurant meals.

The origins of VICORP lie with two Coloradans, James Mola and Mertin Anderson, who in the late 1950s opened the first Village Inn restaurant in Colorado Springs. In 1959 the partners sold this original location and moved north to Denver, where they opened a new Village Inn at the corner of East Colfax Avenue and Yosemite Street. In December of that year Mola and Anderson incorporated under the name Village Inn Pancake House, Inc. New buildings and acquisitions in the 1960s and 1970s allowed the corporation to grow steadily, with several Village Inn locations added in the Midwest and Mountain regions.

During the 1980s VICORP acquired restaurants from competitors and expanded its business into new sectors. The May 1983 buyout of Poppin' Fresh Pies, Inc., a subsidiary of the Pillsbury Corporation, provided VICORP with 59 new restaurant locations in the Midwest and a baking facility outside Chicago. These restaurants were to become the nucleus of a new VICORP chain, Bakers Square. Emerson B. Kendall, who had served as president of Poppin' Fresh Pies since 1975, was kept on as president of the new Bakers Square division, which was operated out of an existing office in Matteson, Illinois.

1984 was a huge growth year for VICORP in terms of restaurant acquisition, but rapid expansion also saddled the company with many unforeseen problems. In February the company acquired 71 restaurants from the Continental Restaurant Systems division of Ralston Purina and incorporated them into its growing specialty restaurant group. In October the corporation made another large acquisition, this time of 175 restaurant locations in California, Florida, and Arizona operated under the name Sambo's. The restaurants, which were slated for conversion either to Village Inn or Bakers Square establishments, proved be a huge headache for the company. Long-range plans called for a relatively smooth conversion process to be completed within two years of the buyout. Instead, the process dragged on for almost four years and resulted in an overall decline in management quality as midlevel managers were relocated to far flung and struggling establishments that were already experiencing falling levels of food and service quality. Management also cited the smaller size of many Sambo's locations—some as much as 20 percent smaller than the average Village Inn, which seats approximately 150 and covers 5,000 square feet—as another roadblock to quick conversion. The net effect for VICORP was a serious drop in profits that extended well into the 1980s.

VICORP experienced its greatest problems in Florida, where the acquisition and conversion of several Sambo's locations seriously depleted the company's resources in that region. In 1989, after closing 15 of the converted restaurants and threatening to do the same to the remaining ones, President and Chief Operating Officer Robert S. Benson summed up the situation in the *Nation's Restaurant News:* "We shot ourselves in the foot in 1985, pushing too many people into outlying Sambo's locations, which proved non-viable. . . . Then we compounded this judgment error by papering over these problems, sometimes recycling failed units to new franchises." Benson had joined the company in the fall of 1987 and hoped to slow its rapid expansion by instead focusing resources on existing units, as well as more clearly defining a market strategy to combat sluggish sales.

The following year, Benson named James Carter president of Village Inn, hoping to provide renewed leadership for the foundering company. With one third of its Florida establishments closed and put up for sale, VICORP cut its operating losses in that division to $1.3 million in 1989 (down from $2 million the previous year) and also tightened the reins on franchises, with the corporation taking at least temporary control of nearly 20 restaurants in the same period. Elsewhere, Village Inn West, which included all of the Village Inn locations outside of Florida, demonstrated sales gains of 5.6 percent in 1988 and continued strength into 1990.

The other side of VICORP's holdings, the still-young Bakers Square restaurant group, proved to be a mirror image of its sibling, Village Inn. Like Village Inn–Florida, the Bakers Square–West division, consisting of approximately 80 former Sambo's establishments spread throughout California, suffered in the late 1980s, particularly feeling the effects of labor shortages and high costs in the West. Under the leadership of Benson, VICORP reacted with a new emphasis on personnel and management training in an effort to stem high employee turnover in the region. The initiative showed some tangible success, but California, like Florida, continued to be carried by the company's strongest division, Bakers Square–Midwest. In the late 1980s the 62 restaurants of the Great Lakes region provided the company with an average annual gross of $1.9 million, nearly double the volume of similar units in California. At the same time VICORP also drew profits from its six Taste of Bakers Square establishments, which provided the same fresh pies and baked goods as Bakers Square restaurants, but for carry-out only.

Financial turnaround for VICORP was also promoted in the 1980s with the help of a long-term plan to cut company debt and spending. Operating margins for the corporation had peaked in 1984 at 14.5 percent, and, after a low in 1986 of 4.8 percent, hovered around 9.8 percent for 1988. The sale of 15 Village Inn restaurants in Florida also provided VICORP with a substantial write-off for 1988. Capital expenditures were curtailed by 62 percent between 1986 and 1988, reflecting VICORP's initiative to control growth and focus on better management. This allowed the company to cut its long-term debt from $110.5 million in 1986 to $40.6 million at the end of 1988.

In 1990 VICORP was the object of a class-action suit. On November 1, 1990, the company became aware of what it called accounting "irregularities" and disclosed a statement reassessing its earnings for the year at a value $4 million less than had been expected. The resulting plunge in VICORP stock, a dive from 13½ to 6¾, led to a shareholder outcry spearheaded by Florida stockholder Martin Kaplan. Kaplan had spoken with VICORP treasurer Peter Doane on October 30 and was assured by him that the company's financial position was sound. Soon after, Kaplan filed a lawsuit in the U.S. District Court of Denver. The case was settled in the spring of 1992, with Kaplan and approximately 3,500 other investors receiving a total of $6.5 million in damages from the company. VICORP, however, denied that it had intentionally mislead its shareholders. Doane stated that he was unaware of the problem at the time he spoke with Kaplan, and had revealed the information as soon as it was made available to him. The accounting problem itself was traced to two accountants, both of whom were fired. As Doane explained in *Restaurant Business,* "They were hiding costs in inventory accounts, and yes, the effect was to make the company appear to be doing better than it was. There was no theft involved." Doane also argued that "the market overreacted to the news." He added, "It took our net income down a total of $4 million over two fiscal years, but we were still a very healthy and profitable company in those years, and the market quickly came around to that. The stock was back up to $9 the next day, and within two months it was back to where it was."

Despite the brief setback of the Kaplan suit and with the financial outlook looking brighter after the mid-1980s slump, VICORP moved aggressively into the 1990s. The company carried on with, and improved, many of its capital and employee investment plans and devised several inventive renovation and advertising strategies for the new decade. Perhaps the single most important individual in overseeing these plans was James Caruso, named president of Village Inn in 1991. Caruso had brought 15 years of experience with Denny's restaurants to VICORP in 1990, when he was hired as vice-president of company operations. In an interview with the *Nation's Restaurant News* Caruso explained his outlook on the company after his first year, "We have some very talented people here," he remarked. "We've demonstrably improved operations over the past year and are now concentrating our efforts into our management programs and maintaining consistent levels of service." Caruso solidified these management training efforts in the new Village Inn Training and Leadership Program, or VITAL, which put each management trainee through an 8-week, hands-on rotation of every employee station in the restaurant. In addition, the program was designed to focus on individual career paths for restaurant managers in hopes of keeping employees at the management level with the company over the long term.

Caruso also had his hand in another change undertaken in the early 1990s, the large-scale renovation of the Village Inn chain, including interior and exterior remodeling. Outside upgrades were designed to make each unit more visible and visually appealing, and included neon lighting and signage, as well as the construction of green mansard roofs. Inside, decorators provided each restaurant with a lighter color scheme and new carpeting. The cost for the remodeling ranged between $200,000 and $300,000, but showed some positive effects in terms of sales and served to project a new and more vital image for the Village Inn.

In terms of marketing and advertising, the early 1990s proved an exciting period of experimentation and change for VICORP. Village Inn, attempting to strengthen its lunch and dinner business, offered several new salad and sandwich choices on its menu and tested other dinner possibilities such as lasagna and pot roast. In 1994 the chain also expanded its line of hamburgers, hoping to take a portion of the lunch market from fast-food competitors. With the tagline "Open Wide," Village Inn launched its All-World Double Cheeseburger and an assortment of other specialty burgers. The slogan was devised by the Denver-based Henry Gill Silverman advertising agency, which took the Village Inn account from the Minneapolis firm of McElligott Wright Morrison and White in mid-1992.

In the ensuing years, Silverman was allowed to break Village Inn out of its purely traditional image. The firm produced adds promoting the restaurant's line of healthy foods. Spandex-clad chickens on treadmills in one television ad, for instance, demonstrated a new and humorous approach for the chain. Silverman also wrote the song "Drop on In. How Ya Been? Village Inn," which won an International Broadcast Award in 1992. He summed up his agency's contributions to Village Inn in the *Nation's Restaurant News* as follows: "We've managed to capture the kind of neighborly, folksy image they already have in the eye of the consumer. . . . We've contrasted this warm, sincere music," he continued, "against some wacko humor and great food photography. Those three things add up to a very human, memorable kind of place." The results of this approach continued to be positive, with the campaign increasing sales by an estimated $20 million between the years 1991 and 1993, to a level of approximately $240 million.

Bakers Square, likewise, made some advertising and marketing adjustments in the 1990s. In 1992 the chain launched its "Square Deal Meals" as a response to relatively lower prices among competitors in the mid-range lunch and dinner market. The company also hoped to muster more broad-based appeal and create a marketing edge with a new slogan, "Nobody goes further than fresh," devised by CME KHBB Advertising of Chicago in 1993. The chain continued to struggle, however, in the 1990s. Declining sales—not only in California, but also in the Midwest division—culminated in the firing of President Emerson B. Kendall and Executive Vice-President of Marketing J. D. "Jim" Fisher in November 1993. Kendall was replaced with James Caruso, whose success with Village Inn had put the chain back on the expansion track by mid-1993, with plans to open 30 new stores over the next two years.

Placing Caruso at the head of the struggling Bakers Square, however, had little effect over the short term. Continued declines in profits for the division, which fell an estimated $1 million over the course of 1993, brought about the resignation of VICORP president Robert Benson in July 1994. Benson, who had been with the company for seven years, explained to the *Nation's Restaurant News* soon after his departure, "Our results have been disappointing, and in an organization where we stress accountability, I'll live up to those principles." Meanwhile, the company as a whole undertook a reassessment of its position, with its board of directors authorizing the repurchase of 500,000 shares of common stock, bringing the number of outstanding shares of VICORP stock to approximately 9.5 million.

Despite these problems, 1994 also saw a new innovation for VICORP, a concept called Angel's Diner & Bakery. Essentially a converted Village Inn restaurant decorated with neon and stainless steel to resemble a postwar diner, the first Angel's location saw a near tripling of weekly sales in its first few months of operation. The Angel's Diner appeared to be a promising investment for the company, especially as an alternative to sluggish sales in the Bakers Square–West division. Still, VICORP remained cautious about the Diner, opening only a handful in 1994 and waiting to see if the conversion paid off in the long-term. The company saw modest overall growth in the early 1990s and, though still plagued with financial troubles in Florida and California, continued to focus its attention on innovation, renewal, and—with the help of Angel's Diner—growth.

Further Reading:

"Bakers Square Corners 'Fresh' in New Ads," *Nation's Restaurant News,* July 5, 1993, p. 12.

Carlino, Bill, "Bakers Square, Village Inn on the Prowl for New Ad Agencies," *Nation's Restaurant News,* May 4, 1992, p. 12.

——, "New Prexy Caruso Steers Village Inn Back to Value Track," *Nation's Restaurant News,* December 16, 1991, p. 3, 61.

——, "VICORP Fires Bakers Square President, Marketing Head: Headquarters to be Consolidated as Parent Plans 'Fresh Start' for Struggling Chain," *Nation's Restaurant News,* November 29, 1993, p. 1, 4.

——, "VICORP Ponders Future of Angel's Diner," *Nation's Restaurant News,* March 21, 1994, p. 3, 72.

——, "VICORP President, COO Benson Resigns Post," *Nation's Restaurant News,* July 11, 1994, p. 1, 119.

Chaudhry, Rajan, "VICORP Gives Florida Units Last Chance," *Nation's Restaurant News,* January 23, 1989, p. 1, 82.

——, "VICORP Looks to Prosperous '89: Cuts Debt, Raises Earnings, and Trims Spending," *Nation's Restaurant News,* January 30, 1989, p. 64.

Howard, Theresa, "Village Inn Joins Fast-Food Fray with Hamburger Line," *Nation's Restaurant News,* April 11, 1994, p. 12.

Sokolove, Michael, "Phone Call Costs VICORP $6.5 Million: Angry Florida Shareholder Spurs Call-Action Suit," *Restaurant Business,* July 1, 1992, p. 22.

Van Warner, Rick, "VICORP Hitting Comeback Trail: 'Samboless' Company Getting Back to Basics," *Nation's Restaurant News,* April 24, 1988, p. 87.

"Village Inn Says, 'How Ya Been?' to Dinner Daypart," *Nation's Restaurant News,* August 30, 1993, p. 14.

"Village Inn to Open 15 Units in 1 Year," *Nation's Restaurant News,* August 9, 1993, p. 18.

—S. Thomas McCready

Virgin Group PLC

120 Campden Hill Road
London, Greater London W8 7AR
United Kingdom
71 2291282
Fax: 71 7278200

Private Company
Founded: 1973 as Virgin Records
Employees: 7,900
Sales: $1.2 billion
SICs: 4512 Air Transportation, Scheduled; 5735 Record and
  Prerecorded Tape Stores; 7372 Prepackaged Software;
  7929 Entertainers and Entertainment Groups

Virgin Group PLC is a privately owned holding company primarily involved with airline, music, video, publishing, and retail ventures. Based in Great Britain, Virgin has operations in more than 20 other countries, including the United States. Virgin Group was the creation of British entrepreneur Richard Branson, who had dropped out of boarding school at the age of 17, in 1967, to start his own magazine. That venture was an immediate success, establishing the foundation for what would become a billion dollar conglomerate during the 1980s. Along the way, Branson would attain cult status in his home country— the result of his business exploits, quests for adventure, and unique personal style.

Branson's entrepreneurial bent emerged during his childhood. "The fact that we never had any money was a very good thing," explained Branson's mother, Eve, in the November 1987 *Inc.* Eve Branson went on to suggest that her son "wanted to help the family." A friend cited Branson's love for sports and competition as another major ingredient of his success; "He likes playing the game for the sake of playing he game. He competes hard because he enjoys the competition," noted Simon Draper in the *Inc.* article.

Although Branson loved sports as a youngster, he was forced to rechannel that energy following a serious knee injury. He decided, instead, to focus on establishing a business. Branson embarked on his first venture, in fact, when he was around 11 years old, planting 1,000 seedlings, which he hoped to eventually sell as Christmas trees. When rabbits ate the seedlings, Branson tried a different scheme a year later. His plan this time was to breed and sell a type of small, highly reproductive parrot. That effort fell through when, according to Branson, rats ate the

parrots; Branson's mother, however, contended that she released the birds.

Branson was undaunted by early failures. With the same enthusiasm that would characterize his entry into new endeavors as an adult, he initiated his first major success at the age of 15, when he started a magazine called *Student*. His parents reportedly were under the impression that Branson had been working on a simple school newspaper, but they learned that he intended to launch a magazine for the general public after he travelled to London to sell advertising space. Branson's father, Edward, had his doubts, but he didn't want to quash his son's excitement. Besides, Edward reasoned, Richard only had 100 pounds (about $150) to his name, and it would be good for him to learn a lesson about the difficulty of making it on his own.

To the surprise of his parents, Branson sold 50,000 copies of the first issue of *Student*. In fact, the venture was so successful that Branson dropped out of school when he was 17 to run his business full time. Soon thereafter, he launched his second major undertaking, a company called Virgin. Virgin started out as a mail-order record company. A new law had just been passed that allowed people to sell records at discounted prices, and Branson was among the first to take advantage. Like his magazine, Branson's new company was an immediate success. Sales skyrocketed, and Branson scrambled to find workers to keep up with the tremendous order load. When a postal strike crushed the mail-order endeavor, the resilient Branson responded by changing his strategy. He opened a small, discount record shop that was also a hit. A string of Virgin Record stores followed.

Early setbacks, such as the postal strike, were representative of the great obstacles that Branson would be forced to overcome in Britain's anti-business climate of the 1970s and even 1980s. Indeed, during the 1970s, the country was mired in economic malaise. Tax rates on unearned income were as high as 98 percent, and labor strikes like the one that nearly destroyed Virgin were the norm. Furthermore, a general disdain for entrepreneurs and "new money" permeated the business and social environment, making it more difficult for would-be capitalists to get their ideas off the ground. A mid-1980s survey, for example, showed that 29 percent of the executives in the United Kingdom viewed business owners as having the lowest status in the country, while only 13 percent thought they had the highest status.

Nevertheless, Britain's political, social, and economic environments were perfect for Branson; a rebel by nature, he loved a good challenge and enjoyed bucking convention. That characteristic was most conspicuously evidenced by the name that he chose for his company. He used Virgin to signify his lack of knowledge about the businesses into which he entered. While convention demanded that entrepreneurs have experience in the ventures they began, Branson elected to enter businesses that interested him, regardless of his background; he would ask questions and invent his own route to success. Having no preconceived ideas about an industry, he was able to identify unnecessary hurdles that his competitors took for granted, as well as to recognize hidden opportunities.

Branson demonstrated his unique style again when he entered the recording business in 1973. By then, the 23-year-old entrepreneur was becoming bored with his publishing and record store endeavors, Still, he was fascinated by the recording business and wanted to take a crack at running his own studio. Snubbed by the British financial establishment, Branson was able to get friends and relatives to contribute start-up capital for the project. The first act he signed was an unknown artist named Mike Oldfield. They cut a unique album, Virgin Record's first, titled "Tubular Bells." The record sold five million copies, became one of the biggest selling albums of the decade, and was used as the soundtrack for the movie blockbuster, "The Exorcist."

While Branson enjoyed success with Virgin Records during the mid-1970s, by the end of the decade, the company was trying to shake its image as an outmoded "hippie" label. To that end, Branson signed a popular band known as the Sex Pistols. A crude, irreverent, hard-core punk band with a flair for the obscene, the Sex Pistols had become popular during the mid-1970s and were credited with spawning the entire hard-core punk movement. Branson had tried unsuccessfully to sign the band before. Then, in 1976, the Pistols were dumped by the company that held their recording contract, following a particularly offensive display by the band on national television.

Although another company was quick to sign the Pistols, within hours of signing that contract, the band trashed that firm's offices and found themselves once again in need of a sponsor. Then, Branson moved in to sign a band that would bring the youth market back to Virgin with a vengeance. Under Virgin, the Pistols continued to shock the world—some of their songs were even banned by the British Broadcasting Company (BBC)—and thereby helped Virgin achieve notoriety in the industry. More importantly, though, the Pistols attracted other major talent to Virgin's studios. Other major stars, including Steve Winwood, Boy George, Phil Collins, Genesis, and the Rolling Stones, signed onto the Virgin roster.

Branson's burgeoning operations prospered during the early 1980s. Still, the entrepreneur was restless and continued to seek new opportunities. In 1984, he came across another industry that interested him and about which he knew relatively little: the airline industry. Critics effectively laughed off Branson's proposal to begin providing long-haul air service between the United States and London. Nevertheless, he purchased a Boeing 747 and began flying people back and forth between London and New Jersey, offering improved service and unique features. Virgin Atlantic Airways wowed observers by posting a profit in its second year. "It's not so divorced from the music business," Branson pointed out in the November 14, 1988 Forbes, noting that "if people are traveling for ten hours, they want to be entertained."

Entertainment was, indeed, an important element of Virgin Atlantic's success during the 1980s and early 1990s. Passengers were entertained with videos and, in some cases, live performances from mimes or musicians like cellist Julian Lloyd Webber. In addition, first-class travelers enjoyed perks like round-trip limousine service to and from the airport. Furthermore, Branson kept costs low by growing his airline slowly and focusing on low costs and high profit margins. By 1988, the airline consisted of only two planes, but was boasting the highest occupancy rate and greatest profit margins in the industry. Virgin Atlantic expanded during the early 1990s to include routes to several U.S. cities, Tokyo, Hong Kong, and Greece.

By 1985, Branson's Virgin companies were generating a hefty $25 million in profits from more than $225 million in sales. His holdings included a string of 60 retail stores, a budding videocassette and television operation, the recording studio, and the airline. Hungry for expansion capital, Branson formed Virgin Group PLC in 1985, which consisted of all of his holdings except the airline company and some miscellaneous businesses. He put the airline and the other ventures, which included a night club business and airfreight operations, into a separate company called Voyager Ltd.

Branson took Virgin Group PLC public in a 1986 stock offering that generated more than $56 million. In typical Branson style, the offering was promoted through a media blitz that included a television commercial with a pinstriped executive dancing on his desk and the ad slogan: "From the rock market to the stock market." By 1987, Virgin Group PLC's sales had risen to more than $230 million; when combined with sales at Virgin Atlantic, Branson's companies were pulling in over $350 million annually. Interestingly, Branson took the company private again in 1988, restructured his companies, and sold 25 percent of his Virgin Music Group for $170 million.

Virgin's success during the 1970s and 1980s was a tribute to Branson's unusual management style, which was a radical departure from corporate norms at the time. Branson abandoned the traditional suit and tie in favor of a sweater and slacks. And he operated his unwieldy holding company from the bow of his private barge, relying on telephones, fax machines, and a personal secretary to keep him in touch with his managers. The barge, named Duende, was located in the industrial Regents Canal. Branson's logic behind his remote office was that it gave his subordinates, spread out in more than 25 London buildings, greater autonomy. "People always want to deal with the top person in a building," he explained in the November 1987 Inc., "so somebody besides me takes complete responsibility. He becomes chairman of that company . . . and I can be left to push the group forward into new areas."

Indeed, one of Branson's greatest virtues was his ability to delegate authority and allow managers to take control of the pet projects that he conceived and started. He relied heavily on a small group of hand-picked executives that he could trust. Allowing them to operate their divisions with minimal interference, Branson also offered them high-value incentives based on performance. For example, distant relative Simon Draper ran the profitable music division. He joined Virgin in 1971 after emigrating from South Africa, and had become a multimillionaire by the late 1980s.

Another of Branson's innovative techniques involved breaking his operations up into multiple units, rather than allowing them to grow into large, less personal organizations. For example, he had broken his record enterprise into five separate companies by the late 1980s, each of which concentrated on different bands and artists. His collection of companies had swelled to an assemblage of more than 100 loosely connected enterprises by the late 1980s, each of which was run by a small, streamlined staff. Importantly, he encouraged his employees to innovate and take risks without the fear of failure. "You fail if you don't try things," Branson explained in the November 1991 Florida Trend. "If you run a company based on fear, then you're not going to get the best out of people. They won't make bold decisions. They won't make any decisions,'' he stated.

Another important, and perhaps the most intriguing, aspect of Branson's leadership was his penchant for peril. His wild, sometimes daredevil stunts earned him a reputation in Britain and the United States as an adventurer and risk-taker. His first publicized stunt was a speed boat crossing of the Atlantic Ocean. The previous speed record of 30 hours was held by an American boat, and when a sailor told Branson that the record could be beat, Branson became hooked on the idea. In 1985, Branson set out in a speedboat that struck submerged debris just three hours short of finishing. Predictably, Branson tried again in 1986 and succeeded in setting a new world record.

Branson's second major stunt was a 1987 attempt to cross the Atlantic in a hot air balloon. He combined the adventure with a public relations effort to market his airline, which included television documentaries that aired both before and after the flight. The project was riddled with mishaps. For example, Branson spiraled out of control on his first parachute jump and was barely rescued, mid-air, by his instructor. The televised misadventure sent Virgin Group's stock price tumbling the day after it was broadcast. Although the harrowing balloon trip succeeded in getting Branson and his copilot across the Atlantic in less than two days, the passenger capsule failed to disengage from the balloon when it landed, and Branson nearly died in the Irish Sea.

Despite brushes with death, Branson's exploits succeeded in boosting Virgin's image and improving the Virgin Group's bottom line. Branson even decided to start a new company that manufactured balloons, provided balloon flight training, and sold balloon vacations. Branson secured rights to fly over the Taj Mahal and the Pyramids. In addition, he wanted the venture to design and build small balloon airships that would carry observers up for traffic reports, or simply for entertainment, at a fraction of the price that a helicopter operator would charge.

At the same time that Branson was risking his life over the Atlantic, he continued to grow his Virgin Group at an astonishing rate. During the late 1980s, Virgin was reporting over $1 billion in annual sales and was comprised of more than 150 different companies operating in 20 countries. Going into the 1990s, Branson was overseeing holdings related to broadcasting, entertainment, air travel, real estate development, publishing, and other industries. His original Virgin Records enterprise alone had branched into 14 different companies.

The giant, privately held Virgin Group generated estimated sales of more than $2 billion in 1991, and the 41-year-old Branson continued to deal. He signed pop star Janet Jackson, for example, in a contract valued at $30 million, and was rapidly expanding his Virgin Atlantic airline operations. He also purchased an airline company in Florida. In fact, the buy reflected the company's increasing emphasis on the U.S. market, particularly in Florida, beginning in the early 1990s. Branson planned to build a 40,000-square-foot music superstore there, as he had at 20 other international locations, and was considering making Florida the home office for Virgin Records. Back in Britain, Branson relocated his barge-based office to a three-story Victorian villa backing up to London's Holland Park.

Branson's office move reflected the immense growth and complexity of Virgin Group. Despite his monstrous financial gains, however, the entrepreneur was generally respected by his fellow capitalist-wary countrymen—he was even selected as the third most popular Brit in a late 1980s poll. ''People can recognize him in a very English sort of sense of fair play and decency and modesty and good manners,'' explained Mick Brown in an *Inc.* article. ''He's that unusual combination, really, of all the things that people expect success and money to corrupt out of people,'' Brown wrote. Backing that assertion was the fact that Branson drove a 1959 Bristol automobile, for which he paid $5,900, and continued to wear casual clothing.

Virgin Group expanded during the early 1990s, despite a global economic downturn that started in the United States and spread to Europe. Branson diminished his holdings significantly when he sold Virgin Records for about $1 billion early in 1992, evidencing his intent to focus on his airline operations. He also began to engage in various interactive media ventures. Late in 1992, for example, Virgin announced a joint venture with Florida tycoon and entrepreneur H. Wayne Huizenga of Blockbuster Video. The two decided to combine their knowledge of record store and video store retailing to create mega-media outlets that offered a full range of entertainment products. They opened their first Blockbuster Virgin store in December 1992 in Los Angeles.

Among other innovative ventures during the early 1990s, Branson fired up an airline charter service connecting Key West and Orlando, using refurbished DC-3 planes and requiring the flight attendants to wear 1940s attire. And in 1994 Virgin launched an AM radio station aimed at music listeners in the 25 to 44 age group. In addition to building new businesses, Branson continued to seek adventure. Most notable was his hair-raising attempt to cross the Pacific Ocean in a balloon. The craft floated into the jet stream and was blown into the Yukon territory in Canada. After crashing on a frozen lake, Branson was tracked by radar and rescued before he froze to death.

Principal Subsidiaries: Virgin Atlantic Airways; Virgin Communications.

Further Reading:

Beale, Claire, ''Virgin Turns the Dial,'' *Marketing,* April 29, 1993, p. 22.
Benson, Diane, ''Think Small to Score Big,'' *Florida Trend,* November 1991, p. 19.
Brent, Paul, ''Virgin Tunes in to Canada: British Retail Group Plans Chain of Music Stores,'' *Financial Post,* November 10, 1994, p. 1.
Fuhrman, Peter, and Peter Newcomb, ''A British Original,'' *Forbes,* December 9, 1991, p. 43.
Gubernick, Lisa, ''If at First You Don't Succeed . . . ,'' *Forbes,* November 14, 1988, p. 82.
Larson, Erik, ''Then Came Branson,'' *Inc.,* November 1987, p. 84.
Sambrook, Clara, ''Virgin/IMP's Freeway Drive,'' *Marketing,* March 22, 1990, p. 15.
Stackel, I. M., ''An Interview with Richard Branson,'' *South Florida Business Journal,* January 22, 1993, p. A9.
Wada, Isae, ''Soulful Music, Boxer Underwear, Champagne Liven Up 'V' Debut,'' *Travel Weekly,* May 23, 1994, p. 78.

—Dave Mote

Wachovia Corporation

301 N. Main Street, Box 3099
Winston-Salem, North Carolina 27150
U.S.A.
(910) 770-5000
Fax: (910) 770-7021

Public Company
Incorporated: 1968
Employees: 15,600
Total Assets: $39.2 billion
Stock Exchanges: New York Boston Philadelphia
SICs: 6712 Bank Holding Companies; 6021 National
   Commercial Banks; 6153 Short-Term Business Credit
   Institutions, Except Agriculture; Mortgage Bankers and
   Loan Correspondents; 6211 Security Brokers, Dealers and
   Flotation Companies; 6311 Life Insurance

Wachovia Corporation is a southeastern interstate bank holding company with dual headquarters in Atlanta, Georgia, and Winston-Salem, North Carolina. Wachovia's principal subsidiaries are Wachovia Bank of Georgia, Wachovia Bank of North Carolina, and Wachovia Bank of South Carolina. Each of those principal banks boasts a heritage dating back more than a century. Together the corporation's member companies operate approximately 500 banking offices in more than 200 cities and communities and offer personal, corporate, trust, and institutional financial services for regional, national, and international markets.

While the banking industry was marked by fierce competition and volatility in the early 1990s, Wachovia managed to maintain its prominence in both size and reputation. In 1994, Wachovia was listed by *Financial World* magazine as the most financially stable of the nation's largest bank companies holding assets greater than $30 billion. A September 15, 1992 article in *The American Banker* attributed the bank's "enviable performance record" to "one of the lowest loss experiences in the industry and [its place as] one of the highest and most stable earners."

In addition to its size and financial stability, Wachovia is characterized by its diversification and balance of business lines, geographic markets, and credit exposures. Major corporate and institutional relationships of the company's banks outside the southeast are managed by Wachovia Corporate Ser-

vices. Through its banking subsidiaries, Wachovia also has international representative offices in New York, London, and Tokyo, representative offices at Grand Cayman, and an Edge Act bank branch and domestic corporate service offices in Chicago and New York City. The company operates residential mortgage offices in Florida, Georgia, North Carolina, and South Carolina; a major credit card operation in Delaware; and a credit life and accident insurance company in Georgia. Other financial services that help diversify the company include underwriting for state and local government securities, discount brokerage, sales and trading, foreign exchange, corporate finance, and other money market services.

Several specialized divisions help Wachovia manage its diverse array of financial services. Wachovia Trust Services, Inc. provides fiduciary, investment management, and related financial services for corporate, institutional, and individual clients throughout the total organization. (The three main bank divisions serve corporate customers in their home markets, as well.) Wachovia Operational Services Corporation provides centralized information processing and systems development services for Wachovia's subsidiaries.

Wachovia's preeminence in the banking industry and its broad range of services was secured by a strategic merger in the mid-1980s. Within a week of the June 10, 1985 Supreme Court decision to uphold regional reciprocal interstate banking, Wachovia and First Atlanta Corp. merged their respective strengths and market coverage into a new company, First Wachovia Corporation. In May 1991, the organization moved to employ a single identity for all its constituent parts: The First National Bank of Atlanta became Wachovia Bank of Georgia; Wachovia Bank and Trust Company became Wachovia Bank of North Carolina; and the parent company, First Wachovia Corporation, was renamed Wachovia Corporation. Then on December 6, 1991, South Carolina National Corporation joined the bandwagon and added its member bank, South Carolina National Bank (SCN) to the Wachovia family. Following the trend toward a common corporate identity, SCN changed its name to Wachovia Bank of South Carolina in May 1994.

Though its three principal subsidiaries were secured under one common parent company by the mid-1990s, each bank remained a separate legal entity with its own board of directors, management, and staff. Moreover, each of the three principal banks was invested with a long history of its own, adding yet another layer of complexity—and interest—to Wachovia's past.

Wachovia Bank of Georgia traces its history to the Civil War, the subsequent financial rebuilding of Atlanta, and the determination of one prominent civic leader, General Alfred Austell, who gained banking experience at Atlanta's Bank of Fulton. After this bank closed at the end of the war, Austell played a significant role in both redeeming the Bank of Fulton's Confederate notes and in plying influential contacts in Washington D.C. toward securing a national bank charter for Atlanta. On September 14, 1865, a federal charter was granted to the Atlanta National Bank making it the first national bank in the Southeast. Austell became president.

Other Georgia entrepreneurs made the best of reconstruction and formed banks that would eventually branch into the Wachovia tree. Joining forces with his father, Colonel Robert J. Lowry founded the state-chartered Lowry Banking Company. Changing to a national charter, that bank became the Lowry National Bank in 1900.

Colonel Robert Flournoy Maddox and his partner, Jett Rucker, established a planters' warehouse that eventually became a lending business, using tobacco and cotton as collateral. In 1879, the partners moved exclusively into banking with the establishment of a private bank, Maddox-Rucker & Company, which obtained a National Charter and changed its name to American National Bank in 1908. Their enterprise continued to grow over the next several decades, converting to a state-chartered bank—the Maddox-Rucker Banking Company—in 1891, and finally obtaining a national charter and changing its name to American National Bank in 1908.

From his post as mayor of Atlanta in 1880, Captain James W. English was well connected to start yet another influential Georgia bank. By 1889, he had become one of the founders and in 1890 was named the president of state-chartered American Trust and Banking Company. By 1896, the bank had adopted a federal charter as the Fourth National Bank of Atlanta.

Though these early Georgia banks continued to prosper beyond the turn of the century, they were constrained by a state law prohibiting banks from expanding beyond their city limits. A series of mergers that began just before World War I, however, provided an alternative means of growth. In 1916, Atlanta National Bank merged with American National and kept the Atlanta National name. In 1923, Lowry National Bank merged with Trust Company of Georgia to become the Lowry Bank and Trust Company of Georgia; a year later, the new entity merged with Atlanta National to become the Atlanta and Lowry National Bank. Finally, in 1929, the Atlanta and Lowry National Bank merged with the Fourth National Bank to become The First National Bank of Atlanta—making it the largest and the oldest national bank in the Southeast.

While banking in postbellum Georgia was undergoing rapid change and consolidation, important predecessors to Wachovia were also evolving in North Carolina. In 1804, the state's General Assembly chartered North Carolina's first two banks—the Bank of Cape Fear and the New Bern Bank. Though organized banking came relatively late to North Carolina, its charter offered one main advantage over other state banking charters: statewide branch banking was permitted. By 1847, with Israel Lash as cashier, the bank had its first full-time branch in Salem.

Although the Bank of Cape Fear, like many of its peers, didn't survive the Civil War, Lash used it as the groundwork for the First National Bank of Salem, which opened in 1866 with Lash as president and his nephew, William Lemly, as cashier. When Lash died in the late 1870s, Lemly helped implement new growth and change at the bank. After choosing a new site in the adjoining town of Winston and signing a new charter, he established Wachovia National Bank on June 16, 1879. Wyatt Bowman served as the bank's first president until his death in 1882, when Lemly took the helm.

Meanwhile, economic growth in the Piedmont region precipitated the development of trust companies. In 1891, a group of local financiers proposed legislation to permit the new innova-

tive combination of banking services with the responsibilities of trust management. The North Carolina General Assembly voted favorably, and on June 15, 1893 Wachovia Loan and Trust Company became the state's first chartered trust company.

The Loan and Trust Company's early success was largely attributable to the unusual perseverance and innovation of its chief management; Francis Henry Fries served as president, and his nephew, Henry Fries Shaffner, served as secretary-treasurer. Fries and Shaffner distinguished Wachovia Loan and Trust as a financial innovator.

The new bank's name reflected its regional bent. Salem and Winston were situated in the Piedmont region, primarily settled by Moravian colonists of German descent in the 1750s. Their benefactor, Count Zinzendorf, traced his ancestral roots to a region along the Danube known as Der Wachau. In deference to that lineage, the Moravians called their new home and many of its businesses "Wachovia."

In 1910, that name was again put to use, this time to describe a third Wachovia, the merger between Wachovia National Bank and Wachovia Loan and Trust Company. The new institution, Wachovia Bank and Trust Company, opened its doors for business on January 1, 1911.

With deposits of $4 million and a total capital base of $7 million, the consolidated bank stood out as the largest bank in the South and one of the largest trusts in the East. Management of the institutions also merged: Francis Fries was elected president, and James Gray—former president of Wachovia National Bank—became vice-president. The new bank distinguished itself with innovations across the financial board. Over the next several decades, the bank continued to grow, joining the Federal Reserve System in 1918; opening a second Winston-Salem office in 1919 (the two towns had merged in 1913); and merging with Forsyth Savings to establish a third Winston-Salem location in 1930.

While the turn-of-the-century predecessors to Wachovia Corp. were taking shape in Georgia and North Carolina, South Carolina saw the development of other financial institutions that would eventually join Wachovia. In 1792, the Bank of the United States opened a branch bank in the port city of Charleston. The branch also served as a depository for federal taxes and duties. On December 17, 1834, the state approved an act chartering the Bank of Charleston. In July, the stockholders appointed James Hamilton Jr. president, and, by late November, the Bank of Charleston had replaced the public Branch Bank of the United States as a major new private financial institution in the region.

Early growth of the Bank of Charleston was attributable to Henry Workman Conner, who became president in 1841 and who became known for his hard work and initiative. Under Conner, the bank instituted an early interstate banking venture by creating a network of financial agencies from Augusta, Georgia, to New Orleans, Louisiana, and beyond. By 1848, the agency department accounted for $7.5 million in transactions, up from $300,000 only seven years earlier. As Charleston became an even more important trading hub, the bank's operations continued to grow until the Civil War. After Gordon Rose was elected president in 1850, the bank consistently managed to declare dividends that averaged eight to ten percent of its capital stock per year, while keeping total assets well ahead of liabilities.

The Civil War temporarily interrupted the Bank of Charleston's upward trajectory. In fact, by 1869, the bank was insolvent. Nevertheless, under the guidance of president Archibald S. Johnson, the Bank of Charleston became the only antebellum South Carolina bank to revive itself during Reconstruction. After stockholders approved the conversion to a national charter, the bank reopened its Broad Street office in 1872; and even though its national charter prohibited branch banking, it remained a strong presence in the industry for decades.

In 1914, as Europe became embroiled in war, the Bank of Charleston joined the newly formed Federal Reserve System, designed to stabilize the national banking system. In 1922, the Comptroller of the Currency authorized two branch banks, allowing for greater volume of accounts for small businesses and individuals, and paving the way for further expansion.

The bank's development reached a new plateau in 1926, when its 12th president, Robert S. Small, oversaw the consolidation of the Carolina National Bank of Columbia and the Norwood National Bank of Greenville with the Bank of Charleston to form The South Carolina National Bank. By the early 1930s, The South Carolina National Bank was present in 19 cities and communities across the state and provided a broad range of services.

From World War I to the 1980s, The South Carolina National Bank, The First National Bank of Atlanta, and Wachovia Bank and Trust Company responded to industry-wide trends in ways that would influence their eventual alliance. As the banking industry grew at unprecedented rate, one major problem faced by all banks—including Wachovia's ancestors—was that of currency control. The result was a boom-and-bust trend: panics in 1837, 1873, 1893, 1903, 1907, for example, undermined credit stability and set both banks and their clients on edge—if not in the red.

In 1912, Congressman Carter Glass proposed a system to improve mobility of bank reserves and provide a standard for controlling checking deposits. On December 24, 1913, the Federal Reserve Act was signed into law. Creating a system of regional Federal Reserve Banks, the law required all national banks to become members and keep a portion of their reserves on deposit in a Federal Reserve branch. State banks were given the option of joining the system. Incentives were introduced to entice national banks into keeping their federal charters: banks holding such charters were permitted, for the first time, to offer trust services, real estate loans, and mortgage loans. Passage of the McFadden Act of 1927 further empowered existing banks to engage in intrastate branch banking.

After the Great Depression mandated a national bank holiday that forced all banks to close, the federal government outlined new standards to assess the readiness of banks to reopen. Wachovia Bank and The First National Bank of Atlanta were among the first banks to pass the test. Shortly thereafter, the Banking Act of 1933 established more permanent controls. Strict federal insurance of deposits became the rule, and state-chartered banks were strongly encouraged to participate. More-

over, commercial banking was separated from most securities underwriting and trading—an area that was thereafter regulated by the new Securities and Exchange Commission.

Just as the effects of the Depression began to subside, World War II began, launching Wachovia's precursors into an all-out campaign to help finance the Treasury Department by selling defense bonds and providing other financial services. Wachovia, The First National Bank of Atlanta, and SCN all helped finance the war effort.

The postwar era saw a surge in economic growth, spurring new and expanded bank services. New term installment loans replaced the more volatile "call-loan" approach. No longer permitted to underwrite stocks or bonds of private enterprise, banks joined a massive "T-loan" program to implement corporate lending. And a sweeping Social Security system introduced in the 1930s began manifesting itself in the growing number of retirement and pension plans, many of which were funded by trust institutions and the trust departments of banks. Wachovia and SCN offered new financial services to accommodate these changes.

With the advent of heightened competition in the 1960s, banks introduced more flexible financial products and services. More and more savings were flowing out of banks and into other institutions—so-called nonbank banks—that were not controlled by such restrictions as interest-rate ceilings or reserve requirements. To compete with these investment firms, insurance companies, and retailers with financial subsidiaries, banks called for regulatory reform. After 1962, interest rate ceilings were slightly relaxed, giving banks a bit more competitive ground, especially with the development of such products as negotiable certificates of deposit and variable-rate mortgages linking rates on loans to the prime rate, reserve-free foreign investments and Eurodollar investing. The First National Bank of Atlanta, SCN and Wachovia Bank—like many others—established formal international departments in the 1960s.

Banks also found other creative solutions to existing regulations. The Bank Holding Company Act of 1956, for example, prohibited bank holding companies from expanding across state lines. However, that provision did not apply to holding companies with only one bank, and, consequently, many commercial banks established themselves as subsidiaries of "one-bank holding companies." Not surprisingly, Wachovia's three relatives established their own holding companies: The Wachovia Corporation in 1968; First National Holding Corporation in 1969; and South Carolina National Corporation in 1972.

The 1970s were marked by further bank deregulation, permitting greater diversification in the industry. In 1970, an amendment to the Bank Holding Company Act permitted bank holding companies to engage in a far wider range of banking-related businesses. Diversification became the order of the day. First Atlanta established an overseas office in London and, at home, capitalized on new statewide banking privileges to acquire 13 banks across Georgia. In the 1970s, Wachovia introduced its Personal Banker program to augment retail customer banking using computerized account management and in 1980 forged ahead in its introduction of adjustable mortgages. SCN's Common Trust Fund reflected a new rise in trust services, also carried out by Wachovia's master trust service and First Atlanta's Timberland Fund.

Nevertheless, overall economic malaise in the United States strained financial markets. Factors such as inflation and foreign oil dependency—culminating in the Arab oil embargoes of 1973 and 1978—prompted Congress to consider revisions of federal fiscal policy. Wachovia's conservative policies—such as high loan loss reserves and low loan-to-deposit ratios—helped the bank weather the recession almost unscathed, while its largest competitor in the Southeast, NCNB Corp., suffered significant losses. "We are going back to a more purist view of banking," CEO John G. Medlin Jr. told *Business Week* magazine on November 1, 1976.

Legislation passed in 1980 continued the trend toward bank deregulation. That year, the Financial Institutions Deregulation and Monetary Control Act lifted interest-rate ceilings on savings accounts linked to transaction accounts, phasing out regulation Q and interest-rate ceilings within two years. Banks were thus better able to compete head-on with the likes of money market mutual funds.

Bank holding companies gained still greater freedom to compete more equitably with the U.S. Supreme Court passage, in June 1985, of legislation upholding their right to reciprocal interstate banking. Within days of the court ruling, leading financial institutions moved to realize the mutual benefits of a new era in banking. Wachovia Corporation merged with First Atlantic on December 5, 1985, and on December 6, 1991, they were joined by SCN.

A concerted effort was made to establish a joint identity for the growing holding company. On May 31, 1994, SCN began operating as Wachovia Bank of South Carolina. A campaign of advertisements and celebrations heralded the common name, embodied by the blue Wachovia sign and logo. The program to adopt a unifying corporate identity—which had begun in 1990—was completed in just under four years.

Much of Wachovia's success could be attributed to the corporation's use of technology to connect its widespread network of members and to provide new, sophisticated services. As early as the 1970s, automated teller machines provided 24-hour-a-day account information and cash. Tape-driven computers were eventually replaced by electronic machines capable of unprecedented processing power.

By the 1980s and 1990s, new technologies helped Wachovia achieve a whole new level of information management and service delivery. First Atlanta and Wachovia were early leaders in highly automated lockbox centers to process receivables and provide cash management services to corporations. SCN helped pioneer debit card electronic transaction banking, while First Atlanta contributed to anti-fraud systems designed for merchants using VISA or MasterCard. In tandem with state-of-the-art operational centers to coordinate general operations across all three states, Wachovia collaborated with the Federal Reserve to develop date encryption systems to maximize transmission security. In addition, from 1991 to 1993, Wachovia spent more than $3 million on computer-aided software engineering, known as CASE, to set the groundwork for a competitive edge in the design and maintenance of new banking products. "If CASE delivers even a fraction of what we feel comfortable it will do," Walter E. Leonard Jr., president of Wachovia Operational Services Inc., told *The American Banker* on July 6, 1993, "this is a very important thing for us over the long haul."

On January 1, 1994, L. M. Baker, Jr. stepped up as CEO of Wachovia, succeeding John G. Medlin, Jr., who remained the board's chairperson. Along with Baker, a new management team set ambitious goals for the corporation's transition into the 21st century. Following an industry trend toward increased centralization, Wachovia Corp. created a General Banking Division to manage retail and home market commercial operations across its three states. The new division was headed by G. Joseph Prendergast. "All we've done here is taken the three banks and put me in the position of trying to facilitate the coordination of an agenda," Mr. Prendergast told *The American Banker* on November 14, 1994. That agenda included a number of measures, including scaling back the branch networks in all three states; consolidating Wachovia's back office; and automating processes for greater efficiency.

Indeed, efficiency was a key factor for a corporation that had grown out of a myriad of banks to become one of the Southeast's largest financial institution in the 1990s. One risk of consolidation and closing branches would be a loss of customers to competitors. The proper implementation of technological systems, on the other hand, could enable the corporation to reach a far wider client base with fewer conventional branches. In this regard, Wachovia's aggressive investment in CASE technology could pay off handsomely in the long term. Still, Wachovia's complexity remained somewhat daunting. In the *Winston-Salem Journal* of March 21, 1994, Mr. Baker summarized a jocular exchange with his recent predecessor: "John Medlin came in the other day and said, 'How are things going,' and I said, 'I haven't the slightest idea.'" As the leader of one of the world's most reputable banks, Baker epitomized the sort of humor derived from deep-set confidence—but that also acknowledges uncertainty in a volatile and quickly changing industry.

Principal Subsidiaries: Wachovia Bank of North Carolina, N.A.; Wachovia Mortgage Co.; Wachovia Bank of Georgia, N.A.; The First National Bank of Atlanta (Delaware); Wachovia Bank Card Services, Inc.; Financial Life Insurance Co. of Georgia; Wachovia Investments Inc.; Wachovia Bank of South Carolina, N.A.; South Carolina National Corp.; Southern Provident Life Insurance Co.; Atlantic Savings Bank, FSB; Wachovia Corporate Services, Inc.; Wachovia Operational Services Corp.

Further Reading:

"Caution Works At Wachovia," *Business Week,* November 1, 1976, p. 57.

Cline, Kenneth, "Q and A: Wachovia's Medlin: Buying Branches May Mean Investing in Obsolescence," *The American Banker,* September 2, 1993, p. 5.

Cline, Kenneth, "The Back Office: Systems Development—Wachovia Puts Its Money on Automated Software Development," *The American Banker,* July 6, 1993, p. 12A.

Cline, Kenneth, "Wachovia Creates General Banking Division," *The American Banker,* November 14, 1994, p. 5.

Cope, Debra, "Wachovia Launching a Fund that Invests in Forests," *The American Banker,* April 14, 1994, p. 20.

Epper, Karen, "Wachovia Deploys New Software to Automate Its Indirect Lending," *The American Banker,* May 10, 1994, p. 14.

A History of Banking and Wachovia, A Course Well Charted, Winston Salem: Wachovia Corp., 1994.

Moore, Pamela, "Wachovia's New CEO is a Man of Many Interests," *Winston-Salem Journal,* March 21, 1994, p. 13.

Svare, Christopher J., "Entry Into South Carolina Strengthens Wachovia's Base," *The Magazine of Bank Management,* January, 1992, p. 16.

"Wachovia Announces Major Cash Management Technology Investment," *Business Wire,* December 3, 1992.

Zack, Jeffrey, "Seems Like a Seamless Transition at Wachovia," *The American Banker,* January 9, 1995, p. 8A.

—Kerstan Cohen

The Warnaco Group Inc.

90 Park Avenue
New York, New York 10016
U.S.A.
(212) 661-1300
Fax: (212) 370-0832

Public Company
Incorporated: 1874
Employees: 13,700
Sales: $703 million
Stock Exchanges: New York
SICs: 2321 Men's/Boy's Shirts; 2341 Women's/Children's
  Underwear; 2342 Bras, Girdles & Allied Garments

With more than 40 manufacturing and distribution facilities throughout the world, The Warnaco Group Inc. is one of the largest international apparel companies. Most of its revenues (approximately 65 percent) derive from intimate apparel sold under popular brand names like Warner's, Olga, and Fruit of the Loom. But it also sells well-known menswear brands including Calvin Klein and Hathaway. In 1994, Warnaco distinguished itself as the only Fortune 500 industrial company with a female chief executive.

Brothers DeVer and Lucien Warner started what would become Warnaco in 1874. Both men had been trained as doctors, but each also had an entrepreneurial bent, as evidenced by their ventures ranging from traveling medical lecture series, to snake-oil remedies. Among the latter was ''Warner's Safe Kidney and Liver Cure,'' a bottled formula prescribed for urinary disorders and malaria, among other afflictions. Another of the brothers' projects was a replacement for the corset, which they felt was hazardous to women's health. They had devised a less constricting ''waist pattern'' in the 1860s, but it did little to shape women's waists. In 1874, though, DeVer invented an improved version that sported shoulder straps. Manufactured samples were met with enthusiasm in New York. The brothers quit their other jobs and, with $2550 in start-up capital, began selling their ''Dr. Warner's Health Corset.''

Problems were numerous during the start-up phase. A competing manufacturer threatened to sue the Warner's for copying its design, and the brothers were forced to change the original name of their corset (Dr. Warner's Sanitary Corset) because somebody else already owned the name. Understandably, they

also suffered from a dearth of pattern-making experience. While DeVer learned the necessary pattern-making skills, Lucien used his contacts in New York City to begin developing distribution channels for their corset. Lucien's wife, Karen, pitched in and the three labored in Lucien's home. Once they got the operation up-and-running, sales were swift. They moved the company out of the Warner abode in 1875, and by 1876 had already outgrown their small manufacturing plant in McGraw, New York.

As word of Warner's comfortable corset spread, sales soared at an astonishing rate. In 1876 the Warner's moved to Bridgeport, where they built a four-story factory. They continued to redesign and improve their corsets with considerable success. They even introduced new products like an innovative folding bustle (used to support the rear of a dress). Particularly successful was the Coraline Corset line, which was manufactured in part with Tampico grass imported from Mexico. In 1883, in fact, *Harper's Bazaar* identified the four most popular corsets in America as Warner corsets, three of which were Coralines. The incredible success of the Coraline and other Warner designs made both brothers millionaires by the early 1880s. By the mid-1880s the Warners employed more than 1,500 workers, most of whom were immigrant women or poor New England farm girls.

During the remainder of the late 1880s, Warner Brothers, as the company was called, continued to flourish. The brothers introduced a steady stream of designs, usually based on European fashions, and began importing products from England for resale. Some ideas languished. Failed efforts included wool underwear, a chemical business, a Florida orange grove operation, and an attempt to manufacture baseballs. But the corset company constantly prospered and both brothers amassed considerable wealth. Besides building opulent homes for themselves and their families, they heaped their fortunes on a number of beneficiaries. For instance, they established the Seaside Institute, a type of boarding house for poor women that served meals at cost and offered a reading and music room, among other amenities. Lucien also donated large sums to his alma matter, Oberlin College.

By the end of the century the Warner brothers had effectively retired from the day-to-day operations of the company. DeVer married a 26-year-old beauty after his wife died in 1895. He then purchased a succession of yachts that he sailed up and down the East Coast. DeVer wintered in Augusta, Georgia, where he established a strong friendship with John D. Rockefeller. Lucien, a frequent White House guest who cultivated friendships with Presidents Cleveland, Taft, Harrison, and Roosevelt, became a world traveler after his secession from the business, vacationing in China, Japan, New Zealand, Egypt, and elsewhere throughout the world.

With its originators no longer active in the company, Warner Brothers was legally changed from a partnership to a corporation in 1894. DeVer's son, D.H., took control of the company around that time. D.H. differed from his father and uncle in that he had little formal education. He started working at the company when he was 19 years old (in 1887) and worked as an apprentice in every department in preparation for his father's departure. Despite his lack of education, D.H. was a savvy businessman with multiple talents and a flair for leadership. As a young man, he had been an amateur boxer, flute player, and yachtsman, among other credits. By the time he took over Warner Brothers, he was also acting as the president or director of several other concerns, including the Bridgeport National Bank, a gas company, and a department store. When he finally focused his intensity on Warner, the company profited handsomely.

Between 1894 and 1913, Warner's sales vaulted more than three-fold to $7 million and profits averaged $700,000 annually. The gains were largely the result of ongoing innovation. Warner introduced rust-proof steel boning as a replacement for more expensive whalebone in corsets, and introduced a successful corset that doubled as a hose supporter. The latter innovation is recognized as an important evolutionary step in the development of the brassiere in the 1910s. Indeed, Mary Phelps Jacob patented the bra in 1915, and shortly thereafter sold the invention to Warner. The purchase of the bra proved to be an excellent move at the time, and during the late 1910s Warner achieved steady sales and profit growth, with revenues hitting $12.6 million in 1920.

Contributing to the success of the company during the early 1900s was Lucien's son, L.T. He was very different from D.H. in both background and personality. The two often clashed, but their skills were complementary and their combined efforts were ultimately beneficial to the company. The Warner's fortunes began to change, however, after 1920. Corsets quickly fell out of fashion early in the decade and were replaced with the "wraparound." The company scrambled to adapt its products with only tepid success. Throughout the Roaring Twenties, Warner's performance waned. Sales fell to a pitiful $2.5 million by the end of the decade. During the Great Depression, moreover, Warner began to lose money. By 1932 its balance sheet was bleeding more than $1 million in red ink.

Augmenting the company's downfall was the deterioration of D.H. Although an energetic businessman and leader as a young man, D.H. was a dissolute womanizer throughout his adult life. His decline hastened after his wife died in 1931. He continued to spend lavishly and drink to excess before his death in 1934 at the age of 66. D.H.'s son-in-law, John Field, became the new chief executive and L.T. became chairman of the board. A Yale graduate, Field had worked with D.H. and L.T. at Warner for several years. Under Field's control, Warner tightened its belt and revamped its product line during the 1930s, barely escaping bankruptcy. Vital to Warner's survival were inventions like the "Two-Way-One-Way" girdle, an elastic undergarment that wrapped around the body and flattened the hips yet still allowed full body movement.

By the early 1940s Warner's sales had surged back up to about $4 million, approximately $300,000 of which was retained as profit. The lean war years were followed by solid growth as the U.S. economy boomed. Warner's revenues topped $12 million and profits roared back to $1 million by 1947. John Field's son, John Jr., joined the company and was placed in charge of advertising, among other duties. Warner continued to prosper during the 1950s by selling its popular Warner brand lines of bras, girdles, and "corselettes." Sales rocketed to more than $25 million by 1956, growing at more than three times the industry average. Beginning in the mid-1950s, though, Warner Brothers lost focus and became too unwieldy. Frustrated by his

73-year-old father's authoritative, non-progressive management style, John Field Jr. wrested control of the company from the elder Field by persuading the board of directors to oust him.

New managers worked to whip Warner Brothers Company into shape during the late 1950s. In addition to restructuring, they grew the company at a rapid rate by diversifying, acquiring other companies, and expanding distribution channels. Specifically, Warner broadened its product lines to include menswear and accessories, and both men's and women's sportswear. It expanded distribution by selling through large chain stores like Sears and J.C. Penney, and by opening production facilities in Europe and South America. Importantly, Warner purchased C.F. Hathaway Company, America's oldest shirt manufacturer, and Lady Hathaway, a well-known women's sportswear division. That buyout instantly made Warner a major player in those respective industries. Warner went public in 1961 and by the early 1960s was generating annual revenues in the $100 million range.

During the 1960s Warner Brothers Company continued to grow through acquisition and merger. It purchased the popular Puritan and Thane brands in 1964, and then bought out White Stag, a casual sportswear maker. Sales careened to an impressive $185 million in 1968 and profits reached an all-time high of $77 million, reflecting annual growth since 1960 of more than 25 percent. By the late 1960s the company had unarguably become a leader in the U.S. apparel industry. It stepped up its rampant expansion strategy in the early 1970s. In an effort to keep up with rapidly changing fashions during this period, Warner tried to assemble a diverse group of holdings that would allow it to capitalize on consumer whims as they emerged. Brands accumulated in the 1970s included Speedo, Playmore, Rosanna, Jerry Silverman, and High Tide. Warner also branched into retail stores and launched a more aggressive international agenda.

Warnaco celebrated its 100th anniversary with record sales and profits. By the mid-1970s, though, the company had again grown unwieldy, ballooning into a diversified, international apparel conglomerate with nearly 20 divisions. The aggressive diversification strategy had made Warnaco a big player, but was failing to generate profit growth. In fact, Warnaco's profitability began to slip in the mid-1970s. During 1975 and 1976 the company experienced severe stress as a result of various mishaps. Warnaco's entry into the leisure suit business, for example, brought crushing losses when that short-lived style quickly faded. Its retail store division also suffered, contributing to hefty losses. Distressed by Warnaco's mounting difficulties, Field offered to allow a new, fresh management team to pick up the ball and carry Warnaco into the 1980s.

Warnaco's board brought in two outside managers—Philip Lamoureux and James Walker—to work with Field and eventually assume leadership of the company. They immediately clashed with Field, assuming control of day-to-day operations, but then edging him out of the decision-making process. The situation deteriorated to the point where Field, like his father, had to be forced out of his leadership role. Warnaco's balance sheet improved significantly under the new management. Walker and Lamoureux jettisoned several of Warnaco's nonperforming units, restructured management, and labored to improve the profitability of its successful core apparel lines. Profits soon recovered to record levels during the late 1970s. Even during the recession of the early 1980s Warnaco's sales and profits boomed.

After successfully reviving the embattled Warnaco, Lamoureux left Warnaco in 1982. The following year, Walker died unexpectedly from a kidney-related virus. The company itself, however, remained healthy to most appearances, and in 1983 hit a record net income of $28.3 million. Furthermore, the company's balance sheet was strong, with relatively little debt and a vigorous cash flow. But Warnaco's balance sheet failed to reflect some underlying problems. During the late 1970s and early 1980s Warnaco had reduced spending on research and development and cut back on its marketing efforts. These moves reduced costs, but boded poorly for Warnaco's long-term growth. In 1984 the company's profits again started to slide. Performance continued to slip into the mid-1980s, despite the purchase of the successful Olga Co. in 1984. Warnaco began to review its alternatives.

Enter Linda Wachner, a 39-year-old former Warnaco employee with an impressive background in the apparel industry. Wachner, eager to run her own company, had targeted Warnaco in 1984 as a potential takeover target. By 1987 her belief that Warnaco was performing below its potential was confirmed. She joined forces with Los Angeles investor Andrew Galef in a month-long battle for control of the company. Wachner and Galef, through their newly-formed W. Acquisition Corp., won the bid and Wachner stepped in as chief executive in April of 1987—Galef became chairman. Wachner quickly replaced Warnaco management with her own team and reorganized the company. Her strategy was to streamline the corporation, pay down the debt incurred as a result of the leveraged buyout, and build Warnaco into a dominant force in its key market niches.

Wachner, one of just a few women heading Fortune 500 companies, was a force to be reckoned with. She had known since her childhood in Forest Hills, New York, that she wanted to run something. She came to that conclusion at the age of 11, lying in a full-body cast after undergoing surgery to correct severe scoliosis. Facing the possibility that she may never walk again, she became determined to take charge of whatever she did in her life. "The focus I have today comes from when I was sick," she explained in the June 15, 1992 *Fortune*. "When you want to walk again, you learn how to focus on that with all your might, and you don't stop until you do."

Wachner translated her intensity into career success beginning in 1966. She graduated from the University of Buffalo in that year at the age of 20 and went to work in the retail industry with a division of Federated Department Stores. She immediately began telling her superiors how they could improve the operation, earning a reputation as an aggressive business woman. Wachner accepted a position in Warnaco's marketing department in 1974. Within less than a year she was promoted to vice-president. In 1978 she was recruited to head the sagging Max Factor division of Norton Simon, and in two years turned the operation from a $16 million loss to a $5 million profit. Wachner unsuccessfully attempted a leverage buyout of Max Factor in 1984, after which she resigned. She tried to buy Revlon in 1986 before setting her sights on Warnaco.

Wachner assumed an aggressive stance at Warnaco. She pared the company's 15 divisions down to two main categories: intimate apparel and menswear. She dumped other units, including the large women's apparel and sportswear businesses, and initiated widespread cost-cutting programs. She brought a new customer and cash-flow focus to Warnaco that resulted in significant gains. In addition, she broadened Warnaco's core product lines with new ventures, such as a deal to supply the popular Victoria's Secret retail chain. She also raised capital with a successful public offering. By 1992, Wachner had slashed Warnaco's burdensome debt load by 40 percent, boosted the company's stock price by a hefty 75 percent, and increased cash flow from $50 million to $90 million annually. The only criticism of her performance came from former employees who derided her tough, hard-nosed management style.

Few people were able to criticize Warnaco's financial performance during the early 1990s. Despite a recession during much of that time, Warnaco's sales steadily grew from $518 million in 1989 to more than $700 million by 1993. Warnaco experienced losses during the late 1980s, but was netting income of about $50 million by 1992. More importantly, the company had reduced its long-term debt from more than $500 million in the late 1980s to less than $250 million by 1993. And the company was positioned for future growth. Warnaco had plowed capital into its important Warner and Olga brands, allowing it to cash in on the growing upscale lingerie market in the mid-1990s. And its Speedo division was enjoying solid gains. Furthermore, in 1993 Warnaco purchased the underwear business of Calvin Klein. Following these successes, the company is projecting sales growth of at least 15 percent annually between 1995 and the turn of the century.

Principal Subsidiaries: Warnaco Inc.

Further Reading:

Cainiti, Susan, "America's Most Successful Businesswoman," *Fortune,* June 15, 1992, p. 102.

Donlon, J.P., "Queen of Cash Flow," *Chief Executive,* January/February 1994, p. 38.

Field, John W., *Fig Leaves and Fortunes: A Fashion Company Named Warnaco,* West Kennebunk, Maine: Phoenix Publishing, 1990.

Furman, Phyllis, "Refocusing Warnaco Paying off for Wachner," *Crain's New York Business,* November 21, 1994, p. 51.

Govoni, Steve, "Garment Centered," *Financial World,* June 10, 1986, p. 8.

Jaffe, Thomas, "What's in a Label," *Forbes,* September 24, 1984, p. 238.

Lunzer, Francesca, "Big Shoes to Fill," *Forbes,* December 5, 1983, p. 264.

Taylor, Alex, "New Outfit for a Queen of Beauty: Linda Wachner," *Fortune,* January 5, 1987, p. 56.

—Dave Mote

Washington National Corporation

300 Tower Parkway
Lincolnshire, Illinois 60069
U.S.A.
(708) 793-3000
Fax: (708) 793-3700

Public Company
Incorporated: 1923 as Washington Fidelity National
    Insurance Co.
Employees: 971
Sales: $628.5 million
Stock Exchanges: New York Chicago
SICs: 6311 Life Insurance; 6321 Accident & Health
    Insurance; 6719 Holding Companies, Not Elsewhere
    Classified

Through its two primary operating companies, Washington National Insurance Company and United Presidential Life Insurance Company, Washington National Corporation operates as an insurance holding company involved in marketing and underwriting life insurance, annuities, and health insurance for individuals and groups. After undergoing several years of extensive restructuring during the late 1980s and early 1990s, Washington National was poised to compete in the volatile market for individual and group health insurance, banking on its more than 60 years of experience as an underwriter of accident and health insurance to guide it through one of the most turbulent, yet potentially lucrative, periods in the health insurance industry's history.

The first link in the chain of events that led to Washington National's formation was the establishment of Washington Life and Accident Insurance Company of Chicago in 1911. This company, the earliest predecessor to Washington National, was organized as an assessment insurance organization, or an insurer with the authority to assess or charge its policyholders for losses the company incurs, rather than being restricted to a fixed premium for a specific type of insurance coverage. Assessment companies, occasionally referred to as stipulated premium companies, were relatively common during the 19th and early 20th centuries, but many later exited the business, a course Washington Life and Accident Insurance Company of Chicago took in 1923 when it was reorganized and incorporated as Washington Fidelity National Insurance Company. When this latter com-

pany was incorporated, it merged with two insurance companies, Fidelity Life & Accident Insurance Company of Louisville and United States National Life & Casualty Company, although the merger transaction was not completed until three years later, in 1926.

In 1931, Washington Fidelity National Insurance Company, the insurance concern created in 1923, changed its name to Washington National Insurance Company (WNIC), a name the company would keep for the rest of the century. Thirty-seven years after adopting its new and permanent name, WNIC formed Washington National Corporation as a holding company, but during the intervening years, WNIC developed into an insurance company specializing in group accident and health insurance. WNIC entered the group accident and health insurance market, which comprised insurers writing accident and health insurance to groups of people sharing common characteristics, in 1930, when the company began writing loss of time insurance for teachers. In the years leading up to the formation of Washington National by WNIC, WNIC's stake in group accident and health insurance for teachers remained substantial, accounting for roughly 25 percent of the company's group accident and health business, the largest segment of WNIC's insurance business.

As WNIC's accident and health insurance business grew, taking on other groups of policyholders in addition to teachers, the company grew in other areas as well, acquiring Des Moines, Iowa-based Great Western Insurance Company in 1938 and Chicago, Illinois-based Hercules Life Insurance Company the following year. In conjunction with the acquisition of Hercules Life, WNIC also assumed the insurance business formerly belonging to National Life Insurance Company, which operated as a separate operation from WNIC until 1948.

By the mid-1960s, WNIC was one of the 25 largest insurance underwriters in the country, writing a full-line of life and accident and health insurance. Assets in 1966 totaled $437 million, capital funds amounted to $101 million, and insurance in force equalled $3.2 billion, figures that had doubled during the previous decade. The company by this point conducted business in every state except Hawaii, Alaska, and New York, employing a sales force nearly 4,000 strong. With two-thirds of the company's business derived from accident and health premiums and the remaining third generated by life insurance business, WNIC occupied an enviable position in the insurance industry, boasting a 35-year record of never registering an underwriting loss. Dramatic changes were in the offing, however, not because WNIC's operations required significant readjustment—the company's market position was sound—but because of the substantial benefits a corporate reorganization would engender. The reorganization that ensued led to the formation of Washington National Corporation.

During the late 1960s, the trend among insurance companies was to form holding companies, a corporate maneuver that then permitted insurance companies to diversify—something WNIC's chairman at the time, G. Preston Kendall, wanted to pursue. Preston, whose father, George Kendall, and uncle, Harry Kendall, had founded WNIC, announced in late 1967 that WNIC was organizing a holding company to enable WNIC's diversification into variable annuities (policies that provide income payments of varying amounts depending on the earnings of the investments supporting the annuity). Washington National Corporation was incorporated early the following year as a holding company to acquire all of the outstanding stock of WNIC through a share-for-share exchange, marking the beginning of Washington National's existence and ushering in a period of dramatic growth for WNIC and its new holding company.

Washington National spent the next decade taking full advantage of its classification as a holding company by branching out into other fields in the insurance business. By either forming subsidiary companies or acquiring companies, the newly formed holding company broadened the scope of its operations and evolved into a well-rounded insurance entity. The first step toward the company's decade-long diversification was taken in early 1969, slightly more than a year after Washington National was incorporated, when Washington National announced its intentions to acquire Anchor Corporation, one of the largest and oldest mutual fund organizations in the world, and its life insurance subsidiary, Anchor National Life Insurance Company. The acquisition of Anchor, the largest mutual manager ever absorbed by an insurance company, aped another insurance industry trend of the period that saw a rash of affiliations between mutual fund companies and insurance companies, as insurance carriers fought to keep pace with each other in the race toward diversification. Later that year, Washington National added another subsidiary company to its corporate umbrella when it formed Washington National Equity Company as a broker-dealer to enable the sale of mutual funds and variable annuities by the holding company's sales force. Along with its equity company, the holding company formed Washington National Corporation Development Company to engage in equity-related real estate investments.

The following year, in 1970, Washington National acquired Washington National Trust Company, a non-banking trust company that added trust services to Washington National's growing list of business lines. By the time this deal was concluded, however, Washington National was in the midst of dealing with a potentially debilitating problem that required the concerted attention of the company's management and temporarily halted the formation and acquisition of additional subsidiaries.

The company's unblemished record of underwriting accident and health insurance without a loss came to an end in 1969, when a rise in hospitalization costs and an increase in the number of accident and health insurance claims impaired Washington National's ability to generate profits, making for disappointing losses in 1969 and 1970. The losses incurred by the company during the two-year slide, however, reflected deeper-rooted problems than an unexpected increase in accident and health claims and the sudden escalation of hospitalization costs, both of which were typical occurrences in the insurance industry. Instead, the losses were attributable to the manner in which Washington National salespeople were compensated, a system that was based on the volume of group business written by a salesperson, rather than on the profitability of business written. Accordingly, salespeople could generate more business and get paid more money if they offered the lowest premiums possible, and they could retain that business if they avoided raising premiums for existing business. For the customer and the sales-

person this system of remuneration had its obvious advantages, but for the company itself the focus on volume rather than profitability sent its earnings into a tailspin and sent the company's management scurrying to correct the problem in 1970.

To ameliorate Washington National's future profitability, the company's management adjusted the company's rate structure to reflect the rising cost of hospital care and established new premium rates to protect it from continued cost increases. A profit center accounting system was established to determine the profitability of each of the company's lines of business, insurance premiums were adjusted according to specific geographic areas and, perhaps most importantly, the company's compensation system was amended to reward profitability of business written and not volume. With these changes, and the concurrent rise of a new generation of corporate managers, Washington National was able to arrest the retrogressive slide its earnings had experienced in 1969 and 1970 and return to the more robust financial performance characterizing its past.

Once headed in the right direction, the company resumed its diversification efforts, forming Anchor National Financial Services in 1971, which was created to market a full range of financial services, including mutual funds, life, accident and health insurance, as well as trust services, to Anchor Corporation clients. The following year, Washington National acquired Nathan Hale Life Insurance Company of New York, later renaming it Washington National Life Insurance Company of New York. The purchase of Nathan Hale Life extended Washington National's geographic presence into the New York state market, one of the few places where none of the holding company's subsidiaries were involved. Despite the number of subsidiaries Washington National had either formed or acquired since being established in 1969, WNIC continued to be the primary engine driving Washington National's growth, accounting for 85 percent of the holding company's revenues, earnings, and total assets. The importance of WNIC to Washington National's existence would increase as the 1970s progressed and Washington National began divesting properties instead of acquiring them.

Two more subsidiaries were formed after the acquisition of Nathan Hale Life—Washington National Trust Company, a non-banking trust company, in 1974, and Washington National Financial Services, Inc., a subsidiary created for insurance brokerage sales purposes, in 1977—but in 1978 the holding company reversed its direction, shedding one of its subsidiaries rather than adding one, when it sold Anchor Corporation. Anchor Corporation's life insurance subsidiary, Anchor National Life Insurance Company, was sold eight years later, in 1986, but its divestiture and the sale of Anchor Corporation did not reflect Washington National's strategy to downsize. Instead, during the span separating the sale of Anchor Corporation and the sale of Anchor National life, the holding company was setting the foundation for an acquisition that would be an integral contributor to its operations in the 1990s. During the late 1980s and into the 1990s, there were two chief operating companies that constituted the essence of Washington National; one was WNIC and the other was a company Washington National slowly began to acquire in 1981.

Founded in 1965, United Presidential Life Insurance Company initially sold whole life endowment policies, typically the most expensive type of life insurance sold, under which a policy-holder receives the value of the policy if he or she survives the endowment period. The company did not begin to record its exponential growth until it switched to selling term insurance in the early 1970s. Term insurance, a cheaper alternative to en-dowment insurance that covers the policyholder for a limited, specified duration, became widely popular during the early 1970s and United Presidential Life benefitted accordingly. The company moved into the brokerage market in 1974, using inde-pendent agents instead of company employees to sell its poli-cies and earned the reputation as a quick, reliable insurer, garnering business from larger insurance carriers because it issued policies more expeditiously.

The next milestone in United Presidential Life's growth oc-curred in 1981, when the company's core insurance product switched from term insurance to universal life insurance, a type of insurance under which premiums were flexible, protection was adjustable, and insurance company expenses and other charges were disclosed to the policyholder. Universal life insur-ance had been developed in the late 1970s and by 1981 had just been approved by governing insurance regulatory bodies, clearing all obstacles barring United Presidential Life's move into selling the newly developed insurance except one: The company needed additional capital. Washington National re-moved this last barrier in 1981, when it purchased 23.5 percent of United Presidential Life's unissued stock and thereby pro-vided United Presidential Life with more than $3 million.

Once United Presidential Life began selling universal life insur-ance, success was immediate. The company's annualized new premium leapt from $800,000 to three million dollars and Washington National's stake in the company increased as well, rising to 30.3 percent by 1984, when Washington National was given 25 percent representation on United Presidential Life's board. At the time, United Presidential Life officials claimed Washington National was merely a silent partner, while Wash-ington National officials stated the company's interest in United Presidential Life was solely for investment purposes, but three years later, Washington National, through WNIC, paid $19 a share for the 2.6 million United Presidential Life shares it did not already own, giving Washington National a new subsidiary company and one of the two primary operating companies that would carry the holding company into the 1990s.

As Washington National entered the 1990s, it stripped itself of one more subsidiary acquired during its acquisitive spree in the 1970s, selling Washington National Life Insurance Company of New York (formerly Nathan Hale Life Insurance Company of New York) to Columbian Mutual Life Insurance Company, based in Binghamton, New York. The divestiture of this subsid-iary was made against the backdrop of declining revenues, as Washington National recorded successive decreases in its an-nual revenue between 1989 and 1992. The company's annual revenue total had flirted with the one billion dollar mark the

year after the acquisition of United Presidential Life was com-pleted, reaching $963.7 million, but by 1992 the company's revenues had slipped to $570.4 million. After divesting some unprofitable businesses, Washington National recorded a ten percent increase in revenues in 1993, when the holding com-pany collected $628.5 million. Late that year, Washington Na-tional's Individual Health and Employee Benefits Division were combined into a single Health Division, as the company pre-pared to contend with impending nationwide health care reform.

As Washington National planned for the future, two business areas (later combined in 1993) were targeted to carry the com-pany forward: individual health care and group employee bene-fits. With a focus on these two business segments, the company moved away from life insurance and annuities, gearing itself for a larger stake in the accident and health insurance field "outside of big cities in areas farther away from the major players," as the company's chairman related to *Crain's Chicago Business*. Much of the company's success in this volatile arena depended on its ability to respond to whatever legislative changes the country's health care industry underwent, the extent and manner of which remained undetermined as Washington National en-tered the mid-1990s.

Principal Subsidiaries: Washington National Insurance Com-pany; United Presidential Life Insurance Company

Further Reading:

Cartwright, Levering, "Washington National Insurance Co.," *Invest-ment Dealer's Digest,* April 19, 1965, pp. 40–41.

Con, Brian, "Wash. Nat'l Divests Another Unit in Restructure," *Na-tional Underwriter—Life & Health Financial Services,* April 1, 1991, p. 36.

Frisby, Kent J., "Washington National Corporation," *Wall Street Tran-script,* December 10, 1973, p. 35, 249.

"An Insurer Turns to a Bank for a Loan," *Business Week,* April 18, 1972, p. 58.

"Merger Is Slated by Anchor Corp., Insurance Firm," *Wall Street Journal,* March 12, 1969, p. 6.

Nieman, Janet, "Washington National Shifts Gears," *Crain's Chicago Business,* June 8, 1992, p. 46.

"Tight Operating Policy Benefits Washington National Insurance," *Barron's,* April 3, 1967, p. 37.

"Washington National Corp.," *Wall Street Journal,* July 18, 1988, p. 25.

"Washington National Corp.," *Wall Street Transcript,* April 5, 1971, p. 23,713.

"Washington National Insurance to Set Up a Holding Company," *Wall Street Journal,* December 13, 1967, p. 16.

"Washington National Sees 'Substantially Better' 1971 Profit," *Wall Street Journal,* May 13, 1971, p. 17.

"Washington National Unit Increases Stake in United Presidential," *Wall Street Journal,* August 14, 1984, p. 4.

"Washington National's Unit," *Wall Street Journal,* March 10, 1987, p. 15.

"United Presidential Life," *Indiana Business Magazine,* October 1990, pp. 29–33.

—Jeffrey L. Covell

Waterford Wedgwood Holdings PLC

Barlaston
Stoke-on-Trent
Staffordshire
ST129ES
England
78 220 4141
Fax: 78 220 4402

Public Company
Incorporated: 1947 as Waterford Crystal Limited
Employees: 7,606
Sales: IR£319.2 million (US$450.1 million)
Stock Exchanges: Irish London NASDAQ
SICs: 3250 Structural Clay Products; 5719 Glassware; 3262
   Vitreous China Table & Kitchenware; 3263 Semivitreous
   Table & Kitchenware; 3220 Glass & Glassware, Pressed
   or Blown

Waterford Wedgwood Holdings PLC serves as the parent company for two of the world's most highly respected names in tableware: Waterford Crystal, which is the world's leading manufacturer of premium cut-glass crystal and one of the most important exporters in Ireland, and Josiah Wedgwood and Sons Limited, a British producer of bone china and fine ceramics that is best known for its distinctive and long-lived patterns. Both branches of the company draw upon traditions of craftsmanship that date back to the eighteenth century.

Waterford Crystal

Although the present company was founded in 1947, the firm traces its heritage to the 1780s, when a relaxation of trade restrictions on the Irish glass industry ushered in a 40-year period known as the "Age of Exuberance." Hopeful entrepreneurs established many new glasshouses during this time, among them Quaker brothers George and William Penrose. The partners invested a then-hefty IR£10,000 in a crystal factory named for the port county of Waterford in southeast Ireland. They hired more than 50 employees to carry out the extremely labor-intensive crystal-making process.

The operation first involved mixing the "batch" of heavy flint or crystal glass, which contained 35 percent lead to make the highest grade crystal. This batch of glass was then heated for more than 36 hours to 1400 °C, where it reached the consistency necessary for forming. Each piece was hand-blown into a water-soaked wooden mold, forming thick glass walls to accommodate the deep, intricate cuts that came to characterize Waterford crystal. After a period of controlled cooling known as "annealing," teams of glass cutters created the complex geometric patterns for which Waterford soon became recognized around the world. Waterford employees have used essentially the same tools and techniques throughout the company's history.

The Waterford Glass Works' first foreman was John Hill, a highly respected craftsman who had brought some of his best craftsmen from England to Ireland to escape excessive glass taxes. Hill was credited with setting up the Waterford factory, but his career there was short-lived. Personal clashes with owner William Penrose's wife led to his premature exit from the company. Before he left, however, Hill passed on valuable technical information to a clerk, Jonathan Gatchell.

The Penrose family sold its enterprise to Gatchell in 1799. In spite of rising taxes and a changing roster of partners, Gatchell was able to pass the Waterford legacy on to his brothers, James and Samuel, and his son-in-law Joseph Walpole, upon his death in 1823. In accordance with Gatchell's will, these three ceded the works to his son, George, upon his twenty-first birthday in 1835. Unfortunately, a new excise tax had been enacted just two years after Gatchell's death. George found a partner in one of the works' employees, George Saunders, but Saunders sold out by 1850, as heavy taxation eliminated any profits. Gatchell entered a Waterford piece in the Great Exhibition of 1851 (held, ironically, in London's Crystal Palace), then closed the business later that year.

Nearly a century elapsed before the Waterford tradition was revived in 1947 by Joseph McGrath and Joseph Griffin. They established their glass company less than two miles from the site of the original Waterford Glass Works, and hired talented employees from Czechoslovakia to staff the operation. Following the lead set by their eighteenth-century antecedents, their chief designer, Miroslav Havel, adopted historical patterns that had been documented by the National Museum of Ireland. McGrath and Griffin focused their sales efforts on the massive and prosperous postwar American market. By the late 1960s, Waterford had captured the largest share of the fine glassware market.

Maintaining dominance of the industry was effortless throughout the 1970s: Waterford didn't introduce any new patterns or revise its advertising from 1972 to 1982. In the early 1980s, however, Waterford began to face challengers; while the market for fine lead crystal tripled from 1979 to 1983, Waterford's sales grew by only about one-fifth, and its market share slid by five points to 25 percent. The company added new patterns, enlisted a new advertising agency, and, in 1986, acquired Josiah Wedgwood and Sons Ltd. in the hopes of finding retail and distribution synergies.

Wedgwood

The roots of Wedgwood ceramics are most often traced to Josiah Wedgwood, himself the descendant of four generations of potters. Josiah embarked on his life's work at the age of nine, when he left school to work under his eldest brother at the family pottery works. An outbreak of smallpox left the youngster physically impaired at the age of eleven. (The disease left a lingering infection in his leg, which eventually lead to its amputation.) Unable to continue throwing pottery as a result, he turned instead to design and formulation of ceramics and glazes. When Josiah's apprenticeship ended at the age of 19, his brother inexplicably refused to take him on as a partner.

For the next ten years, the young potter cast about for a business associate; during this period his longest partnership, with Thomas Whieldon, lasted for five years. Wedgwood struck out on his own in 1759. Not content to imitate the generally substandard wares on the market, Wedgwood achieved his first important innovation, No. 7 green glaze, shortly thereafter. The potter used his new glaze to produce rococo-style teapots, plates, compotes, and other practical pieces shaped like fruits, vegetables and leaves. Wedgwood created demand for his pottery by offering innovative products, including asparagus pans, egg spoons and baskets, sandwich sets, and even special plates for "Dutch fish."

By 1765, word of Wedgwood's elegant yet durable wares had reached Britain's royal family. That year, Queen Charlotte ordered a tea service made of Wedgwood's second important development, a uniquely cream-colored earthenware. Through this, the first of many "command performances," Wedgwood earned the right to call his ivory-colored pottery "Queen's Ware." Needless to say, the endorsement added to the potter's prestige, popularity, and sales.

Such successes allowed Wedgwood to purchase an estate, which he named Etruria, in 1766. A factory on the site was completed three years later, just in time to accommodate an order from Catherine the Great of Russia for a 952-piece service for fifty. The amazing set featured more than 1,200 hand-painted scenes of the English countryside. Wedgwood named a pattern with maroon flowers after Catherine. That style, as well as the Queen's Ware and Shell Edge styles, exemplified the enduring nature of the founder's designs: all were still in production in the twentieth century.

Wedgwood capitalized on the popularity of his wares by expanding his line in the 1770s. With the help of an amicable partner, Thomas Bentley, Wedgwood began producing wall tiles and such ornamental wares as plaques, vases, busts, candlesticks, medallions, and even chess sets. Many early decorative pieces were made of a proprietary ceramic called Black Basalt. Although Wedgwood was sure that Black Basalt would enjoy an enduring popularity, it was his Jasper ware, introduced in 1774, that would symbolize Wedgwood for centuries of consumers and collectors. Jasper, an unglazed, translucent stoneware that assimilated colors well, was produced in green, yellow, maroon, black, white, and the shades of blue Jasper that became known as "Wedgwood blue." Historian Alison Kelly, author of The Story of Wedgwood, asserted that "Connoisseurs of pottery since [Wedgwood's] day have valued [Jasper] both as a technical triumph and as an ornament perfect of its kind."

Wedgwood worked alone for ten years after Bentley died in 1780. He went into semi-retirement in 1790, taking his three sons and a nephew into partnership that year. In addition to his

artistic achievements, the founder had invented a pyrometer to measure the heat of his kilns and implemented steam-driven potters' wheels and some principles of mass production. Upon his death in 1795, his second son, also named Josiah, shared management of the works with his cousin, Thomas Byerley. Josiah II assumed full control when Byerley died in 1810.

The Napoleonic Wars, which made trade with continental Europe all but impossible, were followed by economic slowdown that made the early years of the nineteenth century difficult for Josiah II. In 1828 financial shortfalls compelled him to close the company's London showrooms and sell the bulk of Wedgwood's stock, molds, and models for £16,000. Still, the Etruria works survived both hardship and Josiah II's often-criticized management. His third son, Francis, succeeded him upon his death in 1843. Francis had joined the company in 1827, and would control it for 27 years. He revived the founder's legacies of innovation and modernization, adding machines that mixed and dried the clay, as well as new colored ceramics in the tradition of Jasper. His celadon, a pale gray-green ceramic, a lavender clay, and Parian Ware, which featured marbled effects, appealed to Victorian tastes. By 1875, Francis was able to reopen the London showrooms. He also reinstituted production of bone china, which had briefly been offered in the early 1800s. This line would later form the foundation of Wedgwood's export trade.

Successive generations of Wedgwoods took the company into the twentieth century, which witnessed a revival of interest in the company's classical designs, both among collectors and consumers. The Wedgwood Museum was opened in 1906, the same year that the company established an American sales office. Overseas trade expanded dramatically during the early decades of the 1900s: by 1920, the U.S. office had grown sufficiently to justify a new subsidiary.

Even the Great Depression did not slow Wedgwood's growth. In 1938 the company laid plans to build a modern facility near Barlaston. The plant, which featured the first electric pottery kilns used in Britain, began production in 1940. Since 80 percent of Wedgwood's production was for export, the company was allowed to continue production throughout World War II. At war's end, Wedgwood was poised for expansion. During the late 1940s and early 1950s, the company incorporated Canadian and Australian subsidiaries, expanded its factory, and inaugurated special "Wedgwood Rooms" in upscale department stores. By the end of the 1950s, the company employed more than 2,000 people at the Barlaston plant.

In 1963, Sir Arthur Bryan became Wedgwood's managing director, marking the first time in the company's history that an individual who was not related to Josiah Wedgwood held that position. Bryan was named chairman five years later.

Wedgwood's first public offering on the London Stock Exchange in the late 1960s marked the beginning of an eight-year acquisition spree. The company acquired four competitors in 1966 and 1967, including Coalport, manufacturers of high-quality bone china figurines. Wedgwood doubled in size with the acquisition of Johnson Brothers, which included five tableware factories as well as overseas plants. The company entered the glass market with the 1969 purchase of King's Lynn Glass, then began the 1970s with the acquisition of J & G Meakin and Midwinter companies, manufacturers of fine china and earthenware. These purchases gave Wedgwood access to broader markets without compromising the reputation of their premier brand. Additions in the ensuing years helped Wedgwood integrate vertically. They included Precision Studios, a producer of decorative materials for the ceramics industry, and Gered, a retailer and longtime customer of Wedgwood. By 1975, Wedgwood had nearly 9,000 employees in twenty factories.

The company's growth came to an abrupt halt in the early 1980s, when recession forced Wedgwood to lay off nearly half its workforce. As the company struggled, threats of hostile takeover necessitated Wedgwood's amicable union with Waterford.

Waterford Wedgwood PLC

Waterford and Wedgwood merged in 1986, when the crystal manufacturer executed a "white knight" takeover of the china producer for £252.6 million. A recession in the late 1980s and early 1990s brought the premium crystal market's growth to a halt, as price-conscious consumers traded down. From 1989 to 1992, sales in the premium market in the United States (then the world's largest market) dropped by 25 percent, while sales of second-tier crystal increased by half. At the same time, employment costs for both Waterford and Wedgwood had soared: Waterford's labor expenses, which accounted for more than two-thirds of the company's overhead, grew three times faster than inflation in the late 1980s. From 1987 to 1990, Waterford Crystal alone lost more than £60 million, and total corporate debt had swelled to £150 million.

In 1988 Anthony J. F. "Tony" O'Reilly (chairman, president, and CEO of H. J. Heinz Company, as well as "the wealthiest man in Ireland") offered Waterford Wedgwood chairman Howard Kilroy a buyout. His first attempt was refused, but by early 1990, the struggling company was ready to deal. O'Reilly formed a coalition of investors, including his own Fitzwilton Public Limited Company and New York investment house Morgan Stanley Group Inc. Together, they exchanged an estimated £80 million for about one-third of the tableware firm's equity. Morgan Stanley took 15 percent, 9.4 percent went to Fitzwilton, and O'Reilly personally acquired 5 percent. The deal valued Waterford Wedgwood at £230 million—less than it had paid for Wedgwood alone just three years earlier.

The company's problems were deeper than O'Reilly had surmised. When Waterford Wedgwood lost IR£1.2 million on IR£71 million sales in 1991, Don Brennan of Morgan Stanley replaced Kilroy as chairman. The new managers traced their financial woes to expensive labor, especially at Waterford. The company trimmed some of its labor costs and simultaneously countered the contraction of the premium crystal market with the 1991 introduction of the "Marquis by Waterford" line, which retailed at about 30 percent less than traditional Waterford. This new offering was manufactured in Germany and Slovenia, where wages averaged 10 percent less than in Ireland. Stylistically, Marquis featured less elaborately cut designs than Waterford patterns. Company executives were careful to assert that they were not reaching "down-market," but that the elegant new designs appealed to more modern, youthful, "continental" tastes. The launch was an unquestionable success: from 1992 to 1993, sales of Marquis increased by 24 percent, and the brand captured the number-six spot among premium crystal brands sold in the United States.

At the same time, the company was beset by confrontations with its domestic workforce, including strikes and even a shutdown. In 1992, after management threatened to move more of Waterford's production to Eastern Europe, the unions agreed to a wage freeze and job cuts. In return, the company pledged to keep its Waterford operations in Ireland as long as it could remain competitive.

Although Waterford Wedgwood's share price sank as low as 12p. in 1992, the company recorded its first operating profit (IR£500,000) since 1987 that year, with sales 4.5 percent higher than in 1991. In 1993 profits increased again, to £10 million, and Waterford Wedgwood's share price grew to 60p. The turnaround was credited to O'Reilly, who advanced from deputy chairman to chairman in 1994. O'Reilly was confident that his stalwart brands would regain their steady and strong profitability. Future growth was targeted for the mature markets of Japan and the United Kingdom.

Principal Subsidiaries: Waterford Crystal Limited (Ireland); Josiah Wedgwood and Sons Limited (United Kingdom); Waterford Crystal Gallery Limited (Ireland); Waterford Wedgwood Australia Limited; Waterford Wedgwood Japan Limited; Waterford Wedgwood Retail Limited (United Kingdom); Josiah Wedgwood & Sons (Exports) Limited; Waterford Wedgwood Trading Singapore Pte. Limited; Wedgwood G.m.b.H. (Germany); Waterford Wedgwood U.K. plc; Wedgwood Limited; Waterford Glass Research and Development Limited (Ireland).

Further Reading:

Craig, Carole, "Home Truths for Ireland: Mixed Fortunes at Waterford Crystal," *International Management,* May 1993, p. 34.
Dunlevy, Mairead, *Waterford Crystal: The History,* Waterford, Ireland: Waterford Crystal Ltd., 1990.
Kelly, Alison, *The Story of Wedgwood,* London: Viking Press, 1975.

—April Dougal Gasbarre

Weight Watchers ®

Weight Watchers International Inc.

500 N. Broadway
Jericho, New York 11753
U.S.A.
(516) 939-0400
Fax: (516) 949-0699

Wholly Owned Subsidiary of H.J. Heinz Co.
Incorporated: 1963
Employees: 7,500
Operating Revenues: $1.6 billion
SICs: 7299 Miscellaneous Personal Services

Weight Watchers International is the largest and most successful weight-loss program in the world. The company has grown from the dream of one woman into a worldwide franchise that has captured more than 40 percent of the weight-control market, with over one million members in 24 countries; more than a half million people attend 15,000 weekly seminars in the United States alone. With a complete line of portion-control breakfasts, snacks, entrees, and desserts, numerous cookbooks, exercise videos, and a national magazine, all in addition to carefully organized support groups, Weight Watchers is one of the most stunning entrepreneurial success stories ever recorded.

In 1961 Jean Nidetch was an overweight, 40-year old homemaker living in Queens, New York. At 214 pounds and wearing a size 44 dress, Nidetch was always on a diet but never lost any weight. Thoroughly discouraged by dieting fads that didn't help her, she attended a diet seminar offered by the City Board of Health in New York City. Although she lost 20 pounds following the advice provided, she soon discovered her motivation diminishing. Determined to stay on her diet and lose weight, she phoned a few overweight friends and asked them to come to her apartment. When her friends arrived, Nidetch confessed that she had an obsession for eating cookies. Her friends not only sympathized but also began to share their own obsessions about food. Soon Nidetch was arranging weekly meetings for her friends in her home. The women shared stories about food and offered each other support. Most importantly, they all began to lose weight.

Within a short time, Nidetch was arranging meetings for more than 40 people in her small apartment. Not long afterward, she began to arrange support group meetings at other people's homes. As more and more people attended the meetings,

Nidetch realized that losing weight was not merely adhering to a diet, but encouraging people to support each other and change their eating habits. One couple, Felice and Al Lippert, invited Nidetch to speak to a group of overweight friends at their house in Baldwin Harbor. After meeting every week for four months, Al lost 40 pounds and Felice lost nearly 50. Al Lippert, a merchandise manager for a women's apparel chain, began to give Nidetch advice on how to organize and expand her activities, and soon a four-person partnership was formed among Nidetch and her husband, Marty, and Al and Felice Lippert. In May 1963, Weight Watchers was incorporated and opened for business in Queens, New York.

The company's first public meeting was held in a space located over a movie theater. Although the meeting wasn't advertised, more than 400 people waited in line to hear Nidetch speak. Nidetch divided the crowd into groups of 50 and spent the entire day addressing the overwhelming guilt and hopelessness that many people felt about being overweight, as well as providing advice about shedding pounds effectively. Nidetch began to hold meetings three times a day, seven days a week. When she started to show signs of fatigue, Al Lippert suggested that she pick key people who had lost weight themselves and had strong communication skills to help her expand the program. The first 100 people chosen to run meetings throughout New York City shared their personal stories and helped people gain control over their eating habits. Nidetch's extraordinary speaking skills and Al Lippert's genius for organization helped raise Weight Watchers to the level of an evangelical movement.

From 1963 to 1967, Lippert organized training programs, expanded the number of company locations throughout the United States, and implemented a franchising system. By 1968, Weight Watchers had 102 franchises in the United States, Canada, Great Britain, Israel, and Puerto Rico. It was relatively easy for a person to get a franchise for Weight Watchers programs. Lippert sold the territory for a minimal fee, then charged the franchisee a royalty rate of 10 percent on the gross income. The most important requirement was that the franchisee had graduated from the company's programs and kept off the weight that he or she had lost. Most of the franchisees were women from New York City who were willing to travel to establish a Weight Watchers franchise. This group was emotionally involved in the program and had a great deal of faith in its principles; as a result, their commitment to the franchise sometimes bordered on religious fervor.

The mid and late 1960s saw a boom for the company. In 1965 Lippert contracted various food companies in the United States to produce Weight Watchers food lines for supermarkets and grocery stores, including low-calorie frozen entrees and dry and dairy low-calorie foods. Lippert was also creative in other ways. He designed a billfold that held small packets of sugar substitutes, skimmed milk, and bouillon that enabled adherents of the Weight Watchers program to more easily control their diet when away from home. Lippert began to sell items for use in the Weight Watchers classroom, such as postal scales to weigh food; established a joint venture with *National Lampoon* to publish *Weight Watchers Magazine;* and opened a summer camp for children with weight problems.

One of the company's most successful ideas, created under the direction of Felice Lippert, was the publication of a Weight Watchers cookbook. Since the inception of the company, Felice Lippert had been in charge of new recipe development, nutrition, and food research. Her first Weight Watchers cookbook catapulted to the top of the best-seller lists and sold more than 1.5 million copies. In 1968 the company made its first stock offering to the public. Although some financial analysts on Wall Street were skeptical of the offering, the general public was overwhelmingly enthusiastic. The first day of trading saw Weight Watchers stock shoot up from an initial price of $11¼ to $30.

In 1973 Weight Watchers held its 15th anniversary celebration in Madison Square Garden in New York City. Host of past Republican and Democratic party presidential conventions, legendary boxing matches, and other historic national events, the Garden was filled to the rafters with admirers of the Weight Watchers program. It was a far cry from the 10th anniversary celebration held just five years earlier, which was held in a high school auditorium. Although celebrities in attendance included Bob Hope and Pearl Bailey, people had really come to see Jean Nidetch. She spoke until 1:30 a.m., with the crowd captivated by her inspiring stories.

With the company's rapid growth, in 1973 Nidetch decided to resign from her position as president of Weight Watchers to devote herself entirely to public relations. She traveled the world granting an endless number of radio, newspaper, and magazine interviews and speaking to huge audiences about the success of Weight Watchers programs. Al Lippert continued to organize the operation, hiring Dr. Richard Stuart, an expert in behavioral psychology, to helped the company create a training department and design the first guides and manuals for the Weight Watchers program. Lippert also hired Carol Morton, a Weight Watchers graduate and German teacher, to begin operations in Europe. From 1974 to 1976 Lippert, along with a growing list of professional staff members in the areas of marketing, advertising, licensing, and nutrition, began to formalize a strategy for continued growth. Weight Watchers was not only an inspirational program that helped people lose weight, but a highly successful business venture. Lippert and his staff focused on the best way to attract people to Weight Watchers meetings and to sell them food, cookbooks, magazines, camps, spas, and various other weight-loss products.

By the late 1970s, however, Al Lippert had experienced two heart attacks and recognized that the phenomenal growth of Weight Watchers was much too rapid for his small management group to handle. Annual revenues had grown to approximately $50 million, and it was at this point that Lippert started searching for a larger corporate partner to help Weight Watchers achieve the next level of organization and success. H. J. Heinz Company approached Lippert about purchasing Foodways National, one of Weight Watchers' frozen food licensees. Heinz initially sought to merge Foodways with Ore-Ida, its own frozen food and controlled-portion entree producer. Heinz management, however, soon realized that it was the Weight Watchers International brand name that was valuable, not its licensee. As a result, Heinz acquired Weight Watchers and Foodways National in 1978 for approximately $100 million. Lippert re-

mained chief executive officer and chairman of the board at Weight Watchers.

Between 1978 and 1981, management at Heinz assimilated Weight Watchers into its corporate organization. Heinz divided the company into three parts: Foodways National's frozen food business was subsumed under Ore-Ida; Camargo Foods, a condiments, dry snacks, and dairy producer, and a licensee of Weight Watchers which was also purchased by Heinz, was merged with Heinz U.S.A.; and Weight Watchers' meeting service business remained Weight Watchers International. Heinz's strategy was to incorporate the food business of Weight Watchers into its own food operations, while allowing the meeting service business to continue functioning separately.

Chuck Berger, the new president of Weight Watchers International, initiated an aggressive strategy that included an innovative program for weight loss, an improved meeting service, and a plan to buy back the company's franchise territories. In 1983 Berger became CEO of Weight Watchers International and, along with Andrew Barrett and Dr. Les Parducci, laid the foundation for a brand new weight-loss diet. Dubbed ''Quick Start,'' the diet aimed to quicken the rate of weight loss during the first two weeks. Launched with a well-conceived media blitz, the new program helped to double the company's revenues within two years. Barrett, as executive vice-president, improved marketing, added new food product lines, and concentrated on the lifestyle needs of people with weight control problems. One of his most successful ideas was the ''At Work Program,'' which organized meetings for professional women at their place of work.

Between 1982 and 1989, Weight Watchers International experienced unprecedented growth in product sales. In 1982 the Weight Watchers brand name food items switched from aluminum-tray to fiberboard packaging, and introduced one of the world's first lines of microwaveable frozen-food entrees. Foodways National also introduced low-calorie dessert products, and by 1988 the company's desserts had a larger market share than Sara Lee and Lean Cuisine. In 1982 Weight Watchers Magazine had a circulation of approximately 700,000 readers; by 1986, circulation had increased to over one million. The magazine had changed its focus and was marketed to women committed to ''self-improvement.'' Collaborating with Time-Life's books division, Weight Watchers International developed a series of highly successful fitness tapes for the video market and started additional projects for books, audiotapes, and videos in the areas of exercise, weight loss, and health awareness.

By 1988, each of the three separate business units of Weight Watchers was recording skyrocketing revenues. When combined, sales for the Weight Watchers businesses amounted to over $1.2 billion. Even as these figures were released, however, the weight control business was changing dramatically. In 1989 and 1990, numerous competitors like Jenny Craig, Slim Fast, Healthy Choice, and NutriSystem began to challenge Weight Watchers for a share of the market. During 1990 and 1991, after nearly seven years of increasing market share, the company suddenly stopped growing. Sales of Weight Watchers brand food products declined precipitously, and even the renowned support group meetings began to fall in attendance.

In 1991 Brian Ruder, a vice-president in marketing at Heinz, was hired as the president of a newly reconstituted Weight Watchers Food Company. Ruder immediately embarked on a comprehensive reorganization strategy, implementing new sales, marketing, finance, manufacturing, and research and development procedures. Within 15 months of the new company's formation, Ruder had redesigned almost half of its products. New product development time amounted to a mere 14 weeks, down from the 22-month cycle previously adhered to. One product line, low-fat, low calorie entrees called ''Smart Ones,'' was an immediate success. During the same time, Dr. Les Parducci was appointed by Heinz management as the head of Weight Watchers International. Parducci revamped the company's strategy for meeting services by simplifying the contents of programs, relocating meetings to more attractive surroundings, introducing more fun and interesting materials for members, and developing an entire new line of convenience food products.

In 1994 Michael McGrath replaced Ruder as the president of Weight Watchers Food Company. McGrath's background in-cluded experience as vice-president of Kraft's Budget Gourmet. The new president continued to focus on food product introduction, with an emphasis on nutrition and taste. Weight Watchers International, with Parducci in charge, focused on sophisticated and innovative techniques that helped meet the needs of customers seeking to lose weight. Although the weight-loss market as a whole has suffered from strong ''anti-diet'' public sentiment in the early and mid-1990s, Weight Watchers is still the program of choice among those people who want to control their weight.

Further Reading:

Dienstag, Eleanor Foa, ''The Weight Watchers Story,'' *In Good Company: 125 Years at the Heinz Table,* Warner Books, 1994, pp. 211–43.
The History of Weight Watchers, Jericho, N.Y.: Weight Watchers International Inc., 1995, pp. 1–2.
Schroeder, Michael, ''The Diet Business Is Getting a Lot Skinnier,'' *Business Week,* June 24, 1991, p. 132.

—Thomas Derdak

WELLS FARGO & CO.

Wells Fargo & Company

420 Montgomery Street
San Francisco, California 94163
U.S.A.
(415) 477-1000
Fax: (415) 396-7664

Public Company
Incorporated: 1968
Employees: 15,400
Total Assets: $52.16 billion
Stock Exchanges: New York Pacific London Frankfurt
SICs: 6022 State Commercial Banks; 6711 Offices of Bank
  Holding Companies

Wells Fargo & Company is a multibillion-dollar regional bank holding company, the second largest in California and the seventh largest in the United States in 1995. Wells traces its origins to a banking and express business formed in 1852 to exploit the economic opportunities created by the California gold rush. Throughout its colorful history, the company has provided innovative services to its customers and has demonstrated an ability to weather economic conditions that have ruined its competitors.

Soon after gold was discovered in early 1848 at Sutter's Mill near Comona, California, financiers and entrepreneurs from all over North America and the world flocked to California, drawn by the promise of huge profits. Vermont native Henry Wells and New Yorker William G. Fargo watched the California boom economy with keen interest. Before either Wells or Fargo could pursue opportunities offered in the West, however, they had business to attend to in the East. Wells, founder of Wells and Company, and Fargo, a partner in Livingston, Fargo and Company, were major figures in the young and fiercely competitive express industry. In 1849 a new rival, John Butterfield, founder of Butterfield, Wasson & Company, entered the express business. Butterfield, Wells, and Fargo soon realized that their competition was destructive and wasteful, and in 1850 they decided to join forces to form the American Express Company.

Soon after the new company was formed, Wells, the first president of American Express, and Fargo, its vice-president, proposed expanding their business to California. Fearing that American Express's most powerful rival, Adams and Company (later renamed Adams Express Company), would acquire a

monopoly in the West, the majority of the American Express Company's directors balked. Undaunted, Wells and Fargo decided to start their own business while continuing to fulfill their responsibilities as officers and directors of American Express.

On March 18, 1852, they organized Wells, Fargo & Company, a joint-stock association with an initial capitalization of $300,000, to provide express and banking services to California. Financier Edwin B. Morgan was appointed Wells Fargo's first president. The company opened its first office, in San Francisco, in July, 1852. The immediate challenge facing Morgan and Danforth N. Barney, who became president in 1853, was to establish the company in two highly competitive fields under conditions of rapid growth and unpredictable change. At the time, California regulated neither the banking nor the express industry, so both fields were wide open. Anyone with a wagon and team of horses could open an express company and all it took to open a bank was a safe and a room to keep it in. Because of its late entry into the California market, Wells Fargo faced well established competition in both fields.

From the beginning, the fledgling company offered diverse and mutually supportive services: general forwarding and commissions; buying and selling of gold dust, bullion, and specie; and freight service between New York and California. Under Morgan's and Barney's direction, express and banking offices were quickly established in key communities bordering the gold fields and a network of freight and messenger routes was soon in place throughout California. Barney's policy of subcontracting express services to established companies, rather than duplicating existing services, was a key factor in Wells Fargo's early success.

In 1855, Wells Fargo faced its first crisis when the California banking system collapsed as a result of overspeculation. A run on Page, Bacon & Company, a San Francisco bank, began when the collapse of its St. Louis, Missouri, parent was made public. The run soon spread to other major financial institutions, all of which, including Wells Fargo, were forced to close their doors. The following Tuesday Wells Fargo reopened in sound condition, despite a loss of one-third of its net worth. Wells Fargo was one of the few financial and express companies to survive the panic, partly because it kept sufficient assets on hand to meet customers' demands rather than transferring all its assets to New York.

Surviving the Panic of 1855 gave Wells Fargo two advantages. First, it faced virtually no competition in the banking and express business in California after the crisis; second, Wells Fargo attained a reputation for dependability and soundness. From 1855 through 1866, Wells Fargo expanded rapidly, becoming the West's all-purpose business, communications, and transportation agent. Under Barney's direction, the company developed its own stagecoach business, helped start and then took over the Overland Mail Company, and participated in the Pony Express. This period culminated with the "grand consolidation" of 1866 when Wells Fargo consolidated under its own name the ownership and operation of the entire overland mail route from the Missouri River to the Pacific Ocean and many stagecoach lines in the western states.

In its early days, Wells Fargo participated in the staging business to support its banking and express businesses. But the character of Wells Fargo's participation changed when it helped start the Overland Mail Company. Overland Mail was organized in 1857 by men with substantial interests in four of the leading express companies—American Express, United States Express, Adams Express, and Wells Fargo. John Butterfield, the third founder of American Express, was made Overland Mail's president. In 1858, Overland Mail was awarded a government contract to carry the U.S. mail over the southern overland route from St. Louis to California. From the beginning, Wells Fargo was Overland Mail's banker and primary lender.

In 1859 there was a crisis when Congress failed to pass the annual post office appropriation bill and left the post office with no way to pay for the Overland Mail Company's services. As Overland Mail's indebtedness to Wells Fargo climbed, Wells Fargo became increasingly disenchanted with Butterfield's management strategy. In March, 1860 Wells Fargo threatened to foreclose. As a compromise. Butterfield resigned as president of Overland Mail and control of the company passed to Wells Fargo. Wells Fargo, however, did not acquire ownership of the company until the consolidation of 1866.

Wells Fargo's involvement in Overland Mail led to its participation in the Pony Express in the last six of the express's 18 months of existence. Russell, Majors & Waddell launched the privately owned and operated Pony Express. By the end of 1860, the Pony Express was in deep financial trouble; its fees did not cover its costs and, without government subsidies and lucrative mail contracts, it could not make up the difference. After Overland Mail, by then controlled by Wells Fargo, was awarded a $1 million government contract in early 1861 to provide daily mail service over a central route (the Civil War had forced the discontinuation of the southern line), Wells Fargo took over the western portion of the Pony Express route from Salt Lake City to San Francisco. Russell, Majors & Waddell continued to operate the eastern leg from Salt Lake City to St. Joseph, Missouri, under subcontract.

The Pony Express ended when transcontinental telegraph lines were completed in late 1861. Overland mail and express services were continued, however, by the coordinated efforts of several companies. From 1862 to 1865 Wells Fargo operated a private express line between San Francisco and Virginia City, Nevada; Overland Mail stagecoaches covered the route from Carson City, Nevada, to Salt Lake City; and Ben Holladay, who had acquired Russell, Majors & Waddell, ran a stagecoach line from Salt Lake City to Missouri.

By 1866, Holladay had built a staging empire with lines in eight western states and was challenging Wells Fargo's supremacy in the West. A showdown between the two transportation giants in late 1866 resulted in Wells Fargo's purchase of Holladay's operations. The ''grand consolidation'' spawned a new enterprise that operated under the Wells Fargo name and combined the Wells Fargo, Holladay, and Overland Mail lines and became the undisputed stagecoach leader. Barney resigned as president of Wells Fargo to devote more time to his own business, the United States Express Company; Louis McLane, Wells Fargo's general manager in California, replaced him.

The Wells Fargo stagecoach empire was short lived. McLane had reached an agreement with a railroad group that failed. Although the Central Pacific Railroad, already operating over the Sierra Mountains to Reno, Nevada, carried Wells Fargo's express, the company did not have an exclusive contract. Moreover, the Union Pacific Railroad was encroaching on the territory served by Wells Fargo stagelines. Ashbel H. Barney, Danforth Barney's brother and cofounder of United States Express Company, replaced McLane as president in 1868. The transcontinental railroad was completed in the following year, causing the stage business to dwindle and Wells Fargo's stock to fall.

Central Pacific promoters, led by Lloyd Tevis, organized the Pacific Express Company to compete with Wells Fargo. The Tevis group also started buying up Wells Fargo stock at its sharply reduced price. In October, 1869 William Fargo, his brother Charles, and Ashbel Barney traveled to Omaha, Nebraska, to confer with Tevis and his associates. There Wells Fargo agreed to buy the Pacific Express Company at a much-inflated price and received exclusive express rights for ten years on the Central Pacific Railroad and a much-needed infusion of capital. All of this, however, came at a price: control of Wells Fargo shifted to Tevis.

Ashbel Barney resigned in 1870 and was replaced as president by William Fargo. In 1872 William Fargo also resigned to devote full time to his duties as president of American Express. Lloyd Tevis replaced Fargo as president of Wells Fargo, and the company expanded rapidly under his management. The number of banking and express offices grew from 436 in 1871 to 3,500 at the turn of the century. During this period, Wells Fargo also established the first transcontinental express line, using more than a dozen railroads. The company first gained access to the lucrative East Coast markets beginning in 1888; successfully promoted the use of refrigerated freight cars in California; had opened branch banks in Virginia City, Carson City, and Salt Lake City by 1876; and expanded its express services to Japan, Australia, Hong Kong, South America, Mexico, and Europe. In 1885 Wells Fargo also began selling money orders.

In 1905 Wells Fargo separated its banking and express operations. Edward H. Harriman, a prominent financier and dominant figure in the Southern Pacific and Union Pacific railroads, had gained control of Wells Fargo. Harriman reached an agreement with Isaias W. Hellman, a Los Angeles banker, to merge Wells Fargo's bank with the Nevada National Bank, founded in 1875 by the Nevada silver moguls James G. Fair, James Flood, John Mackay, and William O'Brien to form the Wells Fargo Nevada National Bank.

Wells Fargo & Company Express had moved to New York City in 1904. In 1918 the government forced Wells Fargo Express to consolidate its domestic operations with those of the other major express companies. This wartime measure resulted in the formation of American Railway Express (later Railway Express Agency). Wells Fargo continued some overseas express operations until the 1960s.

The two years following the merger tested the newly reorganized bank's, and Hellman's, capacities. In April, 1906 the San Francisco earthquake and fire destroyed most of the city's business district, including the Wells Fargo Nevada National

Bank building. The bank's vaults and credit were left intact, however, and the bank committed its resources to restoring San Francisco. Money flowed into San Francisco from around the country to support rapid reconstruction of the city. As a result, the bank's deposits increased dramatically, from $16 million to $35 million in 18 months.

The Panic of 1907, begun in New York in October, followed on the heels of this frenetic reconstruction period. The stock market had crashed in March. Several New York banks, deeply involved in efforts to manipulate the market after the crash, experienced a run when speculators were unable to pay for stock they had purchased. The run quickly spread to other New York banks, which were forced to suspend payment, and then to Chicago and the rest of the country. Wells Fargo lost $1 million in deposits a week for six weeks in a row. The years following the panic were committed to a slow and painstaking recovery.

In 1920, Hellman was very briefly succeeded as president by his son, I. W. Hellman II, who was followed by Frederick L. Lipman. Lipman's management strategy included both expansion and the conservative banking practices of his predecessors. In late 1923, Wells Fargo Nevada National Bank merged with the Union Trust Company, founded in 1893 by I. W. Hellman, to form the Wells Fargo Bank & Union Trust Company. The bank prospered during the 1920s and Lipman's careful reinvestment of the bank's earnings placed the bank in a good position to survive the Great Depression. Following the collapse of the banking system in 1933, the company was able to extend immediate and substantial help to its troubled correspondents.

The war years were prosperous and uneventful for Wells Fargo. In the 1950s, Wells Fargo President I. W. Hellman III, grandson of Isaias Hellman, began a modest expansion program, acquiring two San Francisco Bay-area banks and opening a small branch network around San Francisco. In 1954 the name of the bank was shortened to Wells Fargo Bank, to capitalize on frontier imagery and in preparation for further expansion.

In 1960, Hellman engineered the merger of Wells Fargo Bank with American Trust Company, a large northern California retail-banking system and the second-oldest financial institution in California, to form the Wells Fargo Bank American Trust Company, renamed Wells Fargo Bank again in 1962. This merger of California's two oldest banks created the eleventh-largest banking institution in the United States. Following the merger, Wells Fargo's involvement in international banking greatly accelerated. The company opened a Tokyo representative office and, eventually, additional branch offices in Seoul, Hong Kong, and Nassau, as well as representative offices in Mexico City, São Paulo, Caracas, Buenos Aires, and Singapore.

In November, 1966, Wells Fargo's board of directors elected Richard P. Cooley president and CEO. At 42, Cooley was one of the youngest men to head a major bank. Stephen Chase, who planned to retire in January, 1968, became chairman. Cooley's rise to the top had been a quick one. From a branch manager in 1960 he rose to become a senior vice-president in 1964, an executive vice-president in 1965 and in April, 1966 a director of the company. A year later Cooley enticed Ernest C. Arbuckle, the former dean of Stanford's business school, to join Wells Fargo's board as chairman.

In 1967 Wells Fargo, together with three other California banks, introduced a Master Charge card (now MasterCard) to its customers as part of its plan to challenge Bank of America in the consumer lending business. Initially 30,000 merchants participated in the plan. Credit cards would later prove a particularly profitable operation.

Cooley's early strategic initiatives were in the direction of making Wells Fargo's branch network statewide. The Federal Reserve had blocked the bank's earlier attempts to acquire an established bank in southern California. As a result, Wells Fargo had to build its own branch system. This expansion was costly and depressed the bank's earnings in the later 1960s. In 1968 Wells Fargo changed from a state to a federal banking charter, in part so that it could set up subsidiaries for businesses like equipment leasing and credit cards rather than having to create special divisions within the bank. The charter conversion was completed August 15, 1968. The bank successfully completed a number of acquisitions during 1968 as well. The Bank of Pasadena, First National Bank of Azusa, Azusa Valley Savings Bank, and Sonoma Mortgage Corporation were all integrated into Wells Fargo's operations.

In 1969 Wells Fargo formed a holding company and purchased the rights to its own name from the American Express Corporation. Although the bank always had the right to use the name for banking, American Express had retained the right to use it for other financial services. Wells Fargo could now use its name in any area of financial services it chose (except the armored car trade—those rights had been sold to another company two years earlier).

Between 1970 and 1975 Wells Fargo's domestic profits rose faster than those of any other U.S. bank. Wells Fargo's loans to businesses increased dramatically after 1971. To meet the demand for credit, the bank frequently borrowed short-term from the Federal Reserve to lend at higher rates of interest to businesses and individuals.

In 1973 a tighter monetary policy made this arrangement less profitable, but Wells Fargo saw an opportunity in the new interest limits on passbook savings. When the allowable rate increased to five percent, Wells Fargo was the first to begin paying the higher rate. The bank attracted many new customers as a result, and within two years its market share of the retail savings trade increased more than two points, a substantial increase in California's competitive banking climate. With its increased deposits, Wells Fargo was able to reduce its borrowings from the Federal Reserve, and the one-half percent premium it paid for deposits was more than made up for by the savings in interest payments. In 1975 the rest of the California banks instituted a 5 percent passbook savings rate, but they failed to recapture their market share.

In 1973, the bank made a number of key policy changes. Wells Fargo decided to go after the medium-sized corporate and consumer loan businesses, where interest rates were higher. Slowly Wells Fargo eliminated its excess debt, and by 1974 its balance sheet showed a much healthier bank. Under Carl Reichardt, who later became president of the bank, Wells Fargo's real estate lending bolstered the bottom line. The bank focused on California's flourishing home and apartment mortgage business and left risky commercial developments to other banks.

While Wells Fargo's domestic operations were making it the envy of competitors in the early 1970s, its international operations were less secure. The bank's 25 percent holding in Allgemeine Deutsche Credit-Anstalt, a West German bank, cost Wells Fargo $4 million due to bad real estate loans. Another joint banking venture, the Western American Bank, which was formed in London in 1968 with several other American banks, was hard hit by the recession of 1974 and failed. Unfavorable exchange rates hit Wells Fargo for another $2 million in 1975. In response, the bank slowed its overseas expansion program and concentrated on developing overseas branches of its own rather than tying itself to the fortunes of other banks.

Wells Fargo's investment services became a leader during the late 1970s. According to *Institutional Investor,* Wells Fargo garnered more new accounts from the 350 largest pension funds between 1975 and 1980 than any other money manager. The bank's aggressive marketing of its services included seminars explaining modern portfolio theory. Wells Fargo's early success, particularly with indexing—weighting investments to match the weightings of the Standard and Poor's 500—brought many new clients aboard.

By the end of the 1970s Wells Fargo's overall growth had slowed somewhat. Earnings were only up 12 percent in 1979 compared with an average of 19 percent between 1973 and 1978. In 1980 Richard Cooley, now chairman of the holding company, told *Fortune,* "It's time to slow down. The last five years have created too great a strain on our capital, liquidity, and people."

In 1981 the banking community was shocked by the news of a $21.3 million embezzlement scheme by a Wells Fargo employee, one of the largest embezzlements ever. L. Ben Lewis, an operations officer at Wells Fargo's Beverly Drive branch, pleaded guilty to the charges. Lewis had routinely written phony debit and credit receipts to pad the accounts of his cronies and received a $300,000 cut in return.

The early 1980s saw a sharp decline in Wells Fargo's performance. Richard Cooley announced the bank's plan to scale down its operations overseas and concentrate on the California market. In January of 1983, Carl Reichardt became chairman and CEO of the holding company and of Wells Fargo Bank. Cooley, who had led the bank since the late 1960s, left to revive a troubled rival. Reichardt relentlessly attacked costs, eliminating 100 branches and cutting 3,000 jobs. He also closed down the bank's European offices at a time when most banks were expanding their overseas networks.

Rather than taking advantage of banking deregulation, which was enticing other banks into all sorts of new financial ventures, Reichardt and Wells Fargo President Paul Hazen kept things simple and focused on California. Reichardt and Hazen beefed up Wells Fargo's retail network through improved services like an extensive automatic teller machine network, and through active marketing of those services.

In 1986, Wells Fargo purchased rival Crocker National Corporation from Britain's Midland Bank for about $1.1 billion. The

acquisition was touted as a brilliant maneuver by Wells Fargo. Not only did Wells Fargo double its branch network in southern California and increase its consumer loan portfolio by 85 percent, but the bank did it at an unheard of price, paying about 127 percent of book value at a time when American banks were generally going for 190 percent. In addition, Midland kept about $3.5 billion in loans of dubious value.

Crocker doubled the strength of Wells Fargo's primary market, making Wells Fargo the tenth-largest bank in the United States. Furthermore, the integration of Crocker's operations into Wells Fargo's went considerably smoother than expected. In the 18 months after the acquisition, 5,700 jobs were trimmed from the banks' combined staff and costs were cut considerably.

Before and after the acquisition, Reichardt and Hazen aggressively cut costs and eliminated unprofitable portions of Wells Fargo's business. During the three years before the acquisition, Wells Fargo sold its realty-services subsidiary, its residential-mortgage service operation, and its corporate trust and agency businesses. Over 70 domestic bank branches and 15 foreign branches were also closed during this period. In 1987, Wells Fargo set aside large reserves to cover potential losses on its Latin American loans, most notably to Brazil and Mexico. This caused its net income to drop sharply, but by mid-1989 the bank had sold or written off all of its medium- and long-term Third World debt.

Concentrating on California was a very successful strategy for Wells Fargo. But after its acquisition of Barclays Bank of California in May of 1988, few targets remained. One region Wells Fargo considered expanding into in the late 1980s was Texas, where it made an unsuccessful bid for Dallas's FirstRepublic Corporation in 1988. In early 1989 Wells Fargo expanded into full-service brokerage and launched a joint venture with the Japanese company Nikko Securities. Also in 1989, the company divested itself of its last international offices, further tightening its focus on domestic commercial and consumer banking activities.

Wells Fargo & Company's major subsidiary, Wells Fargo Bank, was still loaded with debt, including relatively risky real estate loans, in the late 1980s. However, the bank had greatly improved its loan-loss ratio since the early 1980s. Furthermore, Wells continued to improve its health and to thrive during the early 1990s under the direction of Reichardt and Hazen. Much of that growth was attributable to gains in the California market. Indeed, despite an ailing regional economy during the early 1990s, Wells Fargo posted healthy gains in that core market. Wells slashed its labor force—by more than 500 workers in 1993 alone—and boosted cash flow with technical innovations. The bank began selling stamps through its ATM machines, for example, and in 1995 was partnering with CyberCash, a software startup company, to begin offering its services over the Internet.

After dipping in 1991, Wells' net income surged to $283 million in 1992 before climbing briskly to $841 million in 1994. At the end of 1994, after 12 years of service during which Wells Fargo & Co. investors enjoyed a 1,781 percent return, Reichardt stepped aside as head of the company. He was succeeded by Hazen. Wells Fargo Bank entered 1995 as the second largest bank in California and the seventh largest in the United States. Under Hazen, the bank continued to improve its loan portfolio, boost service offerings, and cut operating costs, suggesting a bright long-term future for one of California's oldest financial institutions.

Principal Subsidiaries: Wells Fargo Bank, N.A.

Further Reading:

Acello, Richard, "The Boy Wonder Banker Relaxes—Just Briefly," *San Diego Daily Transcript,* January 6, 1995, p. 1.

Beebe, Lucius M., and Charles M. Clegg, *U.S. West: The Saga of Wells Fargo,* New York: E. P. Dutton, 1949.

Carlsen, Clifford, "Wells Fargo Hitches Wagon to Commerce on the Net," *San Francisco Business Times,* December 16, 1994, p. 6.

"Corporate Profiles 1995: Wells Fargo Leads San Diego with 73 Branches, 2,500 Staff," *San Diego Daily,* January 23, 1995, p. S77.

Hungerford, Edward, *Wells Fargo: Advancing the American Frontier,* New York: Random House, 1949.

Kellogg, Kim, "Wells Fargo Reports Fourth Quarter Earnings of $215 Million," *Business Wire,* January 17, 1995.

Loomis, Noel M., *Wells Fargo: An Illustrated History,* New York: Clarkson N. Potter, 1968.

Moody, Ralph, *Wells Fargo,* Boston: Houghton Mifflin, 1961.

"Waving Good-bye to Wells Fargo," *Business Week,* August 1, 1994, p. 36.

Wells Fargo Since 1852, San Francisco: Wells Fargo & Company, 1988.

Wilson, Neill C., *Treasure Express: Epic Days of the Wells Fargo,* New York: Macmillan, 1936.

Winther, Oscar O., *Via Western Express and Stagecoach,* Stanford, Calif.: Stanford University Press, 1945.

—updated by Dave Mote

Western Atlas Inc.

P.O. Box 1407
Houston, Texas 77251
U.S.A.
(713) 963-2224
Fax: (713) 952-9837

Public Company
Incorporated: 1933 as Western Geophysical Company
Employees: 18,000
Sales: $2.1 billion
Stock Exchanges: New York
SICs: 1389 Oil and Gas Field Services, Not Elsewhere
   Classified; 1382 Oil and Gas Exploration Services

Providing oil field and factory automation services around the globe, Western Atlas Inc. is the world's largest provider of seismic data to the oil industry and is the leading designer of assembly lines for U.S. vehicle manufacturers. The company was spun off from Litton Industries late in 1993. Sales during 1994, its first year of operation as an independent, topped $2 billion. About 75 percent of those receipts were garnered from foreign operations.

The precursor to Western Atlas was founded during the Great Depression by Henry Salvatori, who established the Western Geophysical Company in 1933 in a small Los Angeles facility. Salvatori hoped to profit in the burgeoning western U.S. oil industry using a recording truck that he and his two employees built. The truck used seismic surveying technology to find underground oil reserves. In short, seismic surveying was accomplished by penetrating the earth's surface (or ocean floor) with precisely timed sound waves. Sound waves reflected back to the earth's surface were detected by sensitive receivers and translated into readable media. Geophysicists and geologists used the data to help them identify promising structural features into which they could drill for oil and gas.

As oil companies scrambled to uncover new reserves during the 1930s, Western's business boomed. Within 18 months, the company was fielding ten seismic crews in California, Colorado, Kansas, Texas, and Louisiana. Less than five years after starting operations, Western Geophysical expanded overseas, initiating a legacy of international growth that the company would sustain throughout the twentieth century. Western sent a crew to Italy in 1937 and began searching for oil in Canada soon

thereafter. Demand for Western's high-tech seismic services became so great in those two regions that management decided to start a Canadian subsidiary in 1952, Western Geophysical Company of Canada, Ltd., and an Italian subsidiary in 1957, Western Riserche Geofisiche.

At the same time that Western was growing its foreign and U.S. land-based seismic operations, its was also pioneering the search for oil below the ocean floor. Western began its marine geophysical activity in 1938 when a crew tethered one of its high-tech instrument trucks to a barge and began surveying bays along the Texas coast. Although the effort was a success, progress of its marine operations was hampered by a dispute about boundaries between state and federal waters. The boundary issue was finally resolved in 1952, and Western immediately set up marine operations in California. By 1955, Western was maintaining ten marine crews and had assumed the lead in the burgeoning marine geophysics industry.

Western's rampant growth during the 1930s, 1940s, and 1950s was partially attributable to a generally strong demand for seismic services by the oil and gas industries. Importantly, though, Western was able to surpass most of its peers during the period through technological leadership. Western was one of the few companies in its industry—not only in the early 1900s, but also into the 1990s—that used only seismic equipment that it had designed and built. Its advanced equipment research and development operations helped Western's crews throughout the world cultivate a reputation for being among the most effective in the industry.

Western's technological leadership was evidenced by its early innovations related to marine geophysics, and it became even more obvious in the 1950s, when Western invented the first practicable system for processing analog data on a large scale. At the time, crews would detonate explosives and then record the resultant seismic data on analog tape. Several different channels (analogous to frequencies) were processed individually to determine if their characteristics suggested the existence of recoverable oil and gas. Western developed a device that could simultaneously process 24 seismic channels. Meanwhile, its competitors were still handling each channel individually.

Western Geophysical continued to lead industry innovation in the 1960s, when it became one of the first companies to convert to digital recording and processing. Western also developed its breakthrough AQUAPULSE and MAXIPULSE systems, for which it was granted several patents. Those systems eventually eliminated the time-consuming and troublesome use of large explosives to generate seismic data, relying instead on safer generation techniques and much more sophisticated data processing methods. Similarly, in the 1970s, Western introduced the first reliable high-pressure air gun, which was used to generate seismic data. Later in the decade, the company was granted a patent for its KILOSEIS systems, which could receive and record seismic information more efficiently than any other device in the industry.

In 1960, the company was acquired by Litton Industries, a leading manufacturer of high-tech defense equipment. Litton had purchased Western Geophysical in an attempt to diversify and diminish its dependence on government contracts. Western benefitted from Litton's deep pockets and technological resources and was able to remain relatively autonomous from an operating standpoint. Shortly after the merger, Booth B. Strange took the reins at Western and moved the company from Los Angeles to Houston. During the late 1960s and 1970s, Western achieved dramatic growth and established itself as the leading global provider of seismic services.

Western's strategic success during the 1970s resulted from the efforts of several managers. John R. Russell, for example, joined Litton's Western Geophysical division in 1969, and by 1993 had worked his way up to vice-president of finance in the division. In 1990, he earned the president and chief executive slot. Russell succeeded M. Howard Dingman, Jr., who had been with the company for 42 years. Russell was joined at the helm by vice-president Thomas B. Hix, Jr., who had also started at Western Geophysical in 1969. The man who would have, perhaps, the greatest influence on Western Atlas during the 1980s and 1990s was Alton J. Brann. Brann, who joined Litton Industries in 1974 when he was 31 years old, would eventually oversee Western's transition to an independent company again and would become the company's chief executive.

Intelligent and hard working, Brann had overcome several challenges before rising to the position of CEO at Wester. Raised primarily by his grandparents in the Boston tenement district of East Cambridge, Brann began working at a young age, taking a part-time job at the Boston Museum of Science while in the seventh grade. He was paid $10 per weekend to supervise a group of young people who volunteered at the museum; "ten dollars a weekend was $40 a month—our rent was only $30," Brann recalled in the July 11, 1994 *Los Angeles Business Journal*. Soon after Brann started high school, his grandfather died from a prolonged illness, and, as his grandmother was unable to find a job, Brann began supplementing his weekend income by giving $100 science lectures at such organizations as the Kiwanis Club, and he also served as a counselor at a posh New Hampshire boys camp. Besides providing much-needed income, such work experiences helped him become more articulate and cultured.

Brann left the museum in 1963 at the age of 22, taking a job with Dynamics Research Corp. as a data technician. Working under project managers with doctoral degrees, Brann developed a desire for more formal education. In 1966, he enrolled in University of Massachusetts' new Boston campus, while continuing his work at Dynamics. Brann graduated with a B.S. in mathematics in 1969, and shortly thereafter was appointed department head at Dynamics. In 1973, he was offered a better position in Los Angeles with Litton, which hired him to supervise 170 workers in its Guidance and Control Systems division. "My first day on the job, we had a meeting at 6:30 in the morning," Brann recalled in the *Los Angeles Business Journal* article. "I was instantly in the middle of work. People were yelling at me, 'I'm behind schedule and what are you going to do about it? You're in charge now.' It was a very rough and tumble environment . . . that suited me just fine."

Brann's talent and hard work were rewarded at Litton, and, as Brann progressed through the ranks of the defense contracting side of the business, Litton's Western Geophysical division continued to prosper. In addition, Litton became active in an-

other industry during this time, factory automation, having begun designing and building factory assembly lines and related equipment for companies throughout the world. Litton's extension into the factory automation arena signified ongoing efforts to diversify during the 1980s and to maximize the effectiveness of Litton's technological resources. The diversification strategy was generally successful. As defense contracts escalated beginning in the mid-1980s, Western was able to offset the effects of a concurrent slump in the oil industry.

Indeed, during the early and mid-1980s the oil exploration industry fell on relatively hard times. Total worldwide expenditures on geophysical exploration tumbled to about $2.9 billion in 1985 and then plummeted 37 percent during the following two years to about $1.8 billion. As a result, the total number of exploration crews operating globally shrunk to just 329 land-based and only 59 marine crews by 1987. Although about 40 percent of those crews were operating in the United States, the companies that endured the shakeout with the least difficulty were those with extensive overseas operations. Western Geophysical fell into that category.

In addition to geographic diversification, Western Geophysical buoyed its financial performance during the early and mid-1980s by sustaining its technological edge over competitors. The company refined a high-tech, low-pressure air gun—the Litton Low-Pressure gun—that was capable of achieving deeper measurements than high-pressure guns. Western also introduced a "sleeve gun" in the late 1980s. The sleeve gun became a popular energy source for marine exploration and was eventually installed aboard most of Western's seismic vessels. With Litton's help, Western was also able to construct or revamp its computer processing centers, where seismic information was processed, to make them the most advanced in the world. By the early 1990s, Western was operating ten computer centers on several continents. Furthermore, Western made large strides in the area of three-dimensional seismography, which generated views of geophysical structures in three dimensions as opposed to a flat plane.

In 1987, Litton entered into a joint venture with Dresser Industries to form Western Atlas International, Inc. The resultant Western Atlas International offered clients a full service package, including: reservoir description services, whereby the characteristics of oil reserves were tested and specifically detailed; seismic services; core and fluid analyses; and wireline logging, which entailed dropping sensors down oil wells to measure rock porosity, chemical content of fluids in the well, and other factors. Western Geophysical became the largest division of Litton's new Western Atlas International, Inc. As exploration markets recovered slightly, Western Atlas's annual revenues surged toward the $1 billion mark in the late 1980s.

Litton's oil and gas services and its factory automation division posted steady gains during the early 1990s. In fact, each of the divisions were drawing sales of about $1 billion annually, accounting for roughly 40 percent of Litton's entire revenue base. Unfortunately, however, Litton's core defense contracting business was in a serious slump as a result of massive federal cutbacks in defense spending. By 1992, Brann, who had been named president and CEO of Litton, decided that Litton's best course would be to sell its seismic and automation divisions and invest the cash into its struggling, though still healthy, defense-related operations.

In preparation for the split, Litton bought back Dresser Industries' share of the Western Atlas joint venture and then combined all of the factory automation and seismic operations into a division named Western Atlas Inc. On December 31, 1993, Western Atlas was officially freed from Litton's control and began 1994 as an independent. Brann assumed the chief executive position at the newly formed company. Having prepared for the move—studying literature about the oil and gas industry and visiting factories from Detroit to Russia to push the company's automation systems—Brann was looking forward to the challenge of building Western into a successful independent corporation.

In 1994, Western Atlas had about $1.2 billion in sales from its seismic operations and about $900 million in revenues from its automation operations. Its seismic division was the largest in the world, with operations scattered throughout the globe. Moreover, the company was still considered the technological and profit leader, with operating margins at least 25 percent higher than the industry average. Likewise, Western was designing and building automated assembly lines in China, Russia, India, and Mexico, among other places. About 75 percent of the company's sales, in fact, were coming from countries other than the United States and Canada. Under Brann's direction, the company was focused on a strategy of long-term growth through acquisition going into the mid-1990s.

Principal Subsidiaries: Western Geophysical.

Further Reading:

A Brief History of Western Geophysical, Houston, Tex.: Western Atlas Inc., 1983.

Berger, Robin, "Carving Out a New Identity," *Los Angeles Business Journal,* July 11, 1994, p. 12.

Deady, Tim, "The Reconfiguring of Litton Gets Down to the Wire as Deadline Looms," *Los Angeles Business Journal,* December 20, 1993, p. 1.

Drummond, Jim, "Seismic Struggling for the Moment: Future Outlook May be Brighter," *The Oil Daily,* August 12, 1987.

Knapp, Robert S., "Litton's Oilfield Services Subsidiary Two More Seismic Survey Ships as Productivity, Quality Prove Value," *Business Wire,* July 15, 1992.

Knapp, Robert S., "Litton's Western Atlas International Completes Multimillion-Dollar Upgrade of Marine Exploration Data Center," *Business Wire,* October 19, 1989.

Knapp, Robert S., "Litton's Western Atlas Subsidiary Elects Russell Chief Operating Officer, Hix Chief Financial Officer," *Business Wire,* May 11, 1990.

Knapp, Robert S., "Russell Elected President, CEO of Litton's Western Atlas Oil Services Subsidiary and a Senior V.P. of Litton," *Business Wire,* December 13, 1990.

Knight, Jennifer, "Planning, Teamwork, Get the Job Done," *Corporate Cashflow Magazine,* August 1994, p. 44.

Koerber, Dirk, "Litton Western Atlas Acquires Halliburton Seismic Activities," *Business Wire,* December 14, 1993.

Palmieri, Christopher, "Divide and Prosper," *Forbes,* November 21, 1994, p. 118.

—Dave Mote

Western Resources, Inc.

P.O. Box 889
Topeka, Kansas 66601
U.S.A.
(913) 575-6300
Fax: (913) 575-6399

Public Company
Incorporated: 1992
Operating Revenues: $1.9 billion
Employees: 5,192
Stock Exchanges: New York
SICs: 4939 Combination Utility

Western Resources, Inc., is the result of a 1992 merger between the Kansas Power and Light Company (KPL) and the Kansas Gas and Electric Company (KG&E). The company is one of the largest combination utilities in the Midwestern United States, providing natural gas and electric utility service to customers in Kansas, Missouri, and Oklahoma. Of its three operating groups, KG&E and KPL provide electrical service to over 550,000 retail customers in the area, while the company's third operating group, Gas Service, provides over 500,000 customers with natural gas service.

The history of Western Resources is a story of nearly 370 mergers and acquisitions of various utility companies. Electric lighting was first introduced in the United States in Cleveland, Ohio, on April 29, 1879. Natural gas, which was also used for lighting, had already been introduced in Fredonia, New York, in 1821. The prospect of providing lighting for businesses and homes inspired a wave of entrepreneurs to establish small companies across America. However, many of the small companies were unable to overcome the technological and financial difficulties that accompanied the growing demand for electrical and natural gas services. Thus the smaller companies were taken over by larger firms with professional management, more capital, and the resources to develop innovative technologies.

The Kansas Power and Light Company was incorporated on March 6, 1924, for the purpose of acquiring, financing, constructing, and equipping a electrical generator plant located in Tecumseh, Kansas. The firm was also responsible for building electrical transmission lines from Tecumseh to Topeka and Atchison in order to provide service for new customers. KPL was financed by its ultimate parent company, North American

Light and Power Company. North American, which controlled a large number of utility companies throughout Kansas, Illinois, Iowa, and Missouri, was a holding company. At that time, a holding company such as North American didn't directly operate utilities, but owned and directed them through outstanding voting securities. The most important function for a utility holding company was to provide the financing necessary for its subsidiaries to expand and develop technological improvements.

During the time the power plant at Tecumseh was under construction, KPL completed the Neosho facility, with 15,000 kilowatts—later 40,000 kilowatts—generated by coal. KPL also moved quickly to reach new customers by acquiring the Union Power Company, which including numerous smaller utilities in Kansas, and the entire generating facility, electrical transmission lines, and distribution system in Douglas, Wyoming. When the Tecumseh plant was finished, it started operations with a 6,000 kilowatt generator. Soon power for electricity was generated for the utilities serving Topeka and Atchison. In 1927 KPL acquired the Kansas Public Service Company, which encompassed all the utilities in Topeka and Atchison, Kansas.

KPL's major acquisition during the 1930s was the United Power and Light Corporation. Established in 1898 by Jacob Brown in a grist mill in Abilene, United Power and Light initially used the mill machinery to produce electrical power for the city. Brown's son, C. L. Brown (who founded United Life Insurance Company and was instrumental in laying the groundwork for what are now known as United Telecom and U.S. Sprint) expanded the operation to include 12 other Kansas utilities. This single acquisition brought most of central Kansas under the service of KPL.

During the 1940s, KPL made another extremely important acquisition with its purchase of the Kansas Electric Power Company. Founded in 1922, the Kansas Electric Power Company provided natural gas and electric service to a large area of Eastern Kansas. KPL extended its customer base due to Kansas Electric's involvement in Franklin D. Roosevelt's rural electrification program, and the construction of natural gas pipelines and gas-generated power plants that served the burgeoning demand for electricity. In 1949 the North American Light and Power Company, the holding company for KPL, was liquidated; KPL stock was first listed on the New York Stock Exchange that same year.

Until the 1950s, much of the area serviced by KPL was farmland. However, as the population increased the area became more urban and attractive to manufacturing companies. By 1959, KPL was providing electricity and natural gas to flour mills, chemical companies, oil refineries, iron and steel manufacturers, cement firms, and clothing stores. In 1959 the sale of electricity generated nearly two-thirds of company revenues, while the sale of natural gas generated about one-third. The number of industrial customers increased by more than 125 percent, and individual domestic customers doubled in number. Total gas revenues during the period between 1950 and 1959 increased 112 percent.

During the 1960s, KPL continued to upgrade its technology and expand its customer base. In 1962 the Tecumseh plant installed a 142,000 kilowatt unit. In 1965 the company began work on the first 345 kV electrical transmission line in the state of Kansas. KPL completed construction of the line, which operated from Kansas City all the way to the Oklahoma state line, one year later. Around the same time, KPL joined 16 other electrical utility companies to build the Southwest Experimental Fast Oxide Reactor (SEFOR). In 1968 one of the larger generators at the company's Lawrence Generating Station was fitted with a limestone wet scrubber system, designed to reduce the amount of sulfur emissions into the atmosphere. This system was the first of its kind in the world.

Over the next two decades, KPL grew rapidly. The company opened a number of new utility power plants with state-of-the-art technology. Coal-fired power units, combustion turbines, and nuclear reactors formed the core of KPL's utility plants. During this period the Wolf Creek Generating Station, a nuclear reactor providing electrical service to a huge number of customers in the state of Kansas, began commercial operations with a capacity of 1,150,000 kilowatts. The Jeffrey Energy Center, with one of KPL's largest coal-fired units, began commercial operations at approximately the same time. When KPL merged with Kansas Gas and Electric Company in 1992, the firm was one of the largest and most successful utilities in the United States.

The Kansas Gas and Electric Company was established in 1909 by the holding company American Power and Light to operate utility services in Wichita, Pittsburg, and Frontenac, Kansas. The company built a coal-burning generating station in Wichita with an 8,750 kilowatt capacity in 1912. In 1925 the company sold KG&E's natural gas service to Hutchinson, Newton, Pittsburg, and Wichita in order to concentrate exclusively on electrical power. In 1910 KG&E served only three small communities and 5,525 customers; however, by 1925 the company had extended its services to over 50 communities and a much larger number of customers.

Continuing to expand during the 1930s and 1940s, KG&E added numerous coal-fired power plants to provide a growing customer base with electricity. In 1948 American Power and Light, the holding company for KG&E, sold 150,000 shares of company stock to the public. One year later, KG&E's remaining 450,000 shares of company stock were offered to the public. In 1954 the Murray Gill Station began operations with a 124,000 kilowatt capacity; it was the company's first use of natural gas as the primary fuel for a utility plant. In 1955 KG&E was listed on the New York Stock Exchange; at the same time, the company was adding more generating power to its Murray Gill Station and other utility operations. By 1959, the Murray Gill Station alone had a capacity of 609,000 kilowatts. During the late 1960s and early 1970s, KG&E entered the field of nuclear energy and began to plan a nuclear power plant in Coffey County. In the 1980s, like most other utility companies, KG&E continued to upgrade its technology and expand its services to customers. When KG&E combined with the Kansas Power & Light Company to form Western Resources, the company was financially stable and well managed, but in need of the resources of a larger utility firm to help it weather rising costs and increasing competition.

Western Resources' third operating group, Gas Service, was established in August 1925 by Henry L. Doherty. From the turn of the century, Henry L. Doherty & Company worked as the financial agent for various utility companies operating in Kansas, Missouri, and Oklahoma. Doherty's firm also represented Cities Service Company, one of the large holding companies for both utility and non-utility businesses. Doherty was contracted by Cities Service to organize the Gas Service Company in order to develop new markets for the natural gas resources that Cities Service owned, produced, and transmitted, and also to take control of and operate Cities Service's extensive distribution systems. The Gas Service Company grew slowly but steadily. Its stock was initially traded in 1971 on the New York Stock Exchange. By the time Gas Service was acquired by KPL in 1983, the company served over one million customers in Kansas, Missouri, Oklahoma, and Nebraska. (The company's Nebraska interests were later sold.)

In July 1990, Kansas City Power & Light Company (KCP&L) attempted a hostile takeover of KG&E at $27 per share. Management and the board of directors at KG&E rejected the proposal and filed a lawsuit challenging the takeover attempt. Within one month, KG&E began to search for an alternative transaction that management regarded as more beneficial for both the company and the stockholders. In October, management at KG&E announced that the company would merge with KPL at a mutually agreed upon $32 per share in stock and cash. At first, KCP&L refused to withdraw its offer; however, by December KCP&L recognized the futility of its takeover attempt and announced a halt to any further negotiations.

When the merger of KPL and KG&E became public, there was an immediate opposition to the proposal. Public hearings in Independence, Wichita, Overland Park, and various other locations served by the two utilities focused on the possibility of a rate increase to fund the costs of the merger. The Kansas House of Representatives even introduced legislation to "protect customers in a merger." With significant revisions after much debate, the Kansas House passed a bill prohibiting any rate increase that would result from the costs incurred during the merger of utility companies. On February 5, 1992, the U.S. Securities and Exchange Commission approved the merger application. By March, KG&E had merged with KPL as a wholly owned subsidiary of the latter, and in May the shareholders approved the new name of Western Resources, Inc., for the company.

By 1993, management had fully integrated the merger between KG&E and KPL, and located its corporate office in Topeka, Kansas. Western Resources' total net generating capability amounted to 4,985,000 kilowatts in 1993. Total operating revenues were reported at $1.9 billion. During that year, Western Resources produced nearly 80 percent of its electricity from low sulfur coal, 17 percent from nuclear generators, and the rest from natural gas. The company sold almost all of its natural gas properties located in Missouri to the Southern Union Company, operating out of Austin, Texas. This sale led to a decrease in the number of natural gas customers to 637,000 from a high of 1,093,000. Nonetheless, Western Resources owned and operated an extensive natural gas transmission pipeline system throughout Kansas, and owned underground storage facilities for natural gas in south central Kansas.

During its brief existence, Western Resources has made two significant additions to its operations. The company created a subsidiary, Astra Resources, to conduct its non-regulated business interests, searching for investment opportunities in the areas of pipeline compression services, natural gas gathering and processing, and natural gas marketing. Western Resources also established a Power Technology Center in Wichita to address the growing number of customers requiring technical assistance. Engineers from Western Resources' Power Technology Center resolve problems for customers that arise in providing electrical power for sensitive electronic equipment. The Power Technology Center also tests experimental vehicles that use electricity or natural gas; in 1993 as part of the National Consortium for Emission Reduction in Lawn Care, the company distributed 100 battery powered lawn mowers.

Western Resources has planned carefully for the vagaries of a highly competitive marketplace. The company intends to create new market opportunities in non-regulated areas closely tied to its core business, while continuing to profitably service customers in its traditional markets.

Principal Subsidiaries: Astra Resources.

Further Reading:

Cook, James, "When 2 Plus 2 Equals 5," *Forbes,* June 8, 1992, p. 128.
"Western Resources: Special Merger Edition," *Stars,* May 5, 1992, pp. 1–31.

—Thomas Derdak

Westinghouse Electric Corporation

Westinghouse Building
Gateway Center
Pittsburgh, Pennsylvania 15222
U.S.A.
(412) 244-2000
Fax: (412) 256-5266

Public Company
Incorporated: 1886
Employees: 120,000
Sales: $10 billion
Stock Exchanges: New York Midwest Boston Philadelphia
    Pacific Cincinnati
SICs: 3612 Transformers Except Electronic; 3632 Household
    Refrigerators & Freezers; 3812 Search & Navigation
    Equipment

Westinghouse Electric Corporation is among the country's largest electronics companies, with units committed to serving the U.S. defense industry, as well as interests in power generation and manufacturing. The company also maintains an office furniture subsidiary, The Knoll Group, and a broadcasting subsidiary, Westinghouse Broadcasting.

George Westinghouse, who invented the air-brake as a 22 year-old engineer with little formal education, founded the Westinghouse Electric Company in Pittsburgh in 1886 as a way of entering the infant electrical industry. He began by trying to develop an economical system of transmission using alternating current (AC). At that time direct current (DC), championed by Thomas Edison, was the only form of electrical power in common use. Edison and his Edison General Electric Company responded to the challenge by sponsoring a smear campaign aimed at convincing the public that AC was unsafe. Despite this effort, Westinghouse Electric installed the nation's first AC power system in 1891 in Telluride, Colorado, and scored two major victories in 1893 when it provided the generating system that powered the World's Fair in Chicago and won a contract to provide generators for the new hydroelectric power station at Niagara Falls.

During these years both Edison General Electric and Westinghouse spent small fortunes accumulating patents, with the result that neither company could market new products without fear of patent infringement litigation. After a series of expensive legal battles in the early 1890s, the two companies called a truce in 1896 and set up a patent control board to avoid all such disputes (in fact, they established a virtual duopoly in electric railway equipment during the 1890s). It marked the beginning of the odd relationship between the two largest electrical companies in the United States, a relationship that has ranged over the years from illegal collusion to fierce competition. The infancy of the electrical industry was dominated by inventor-entrepreneurs like George Westinghouse and Thomas Edison, but their professional rivalry would continue long after both men had died and the Edison General Electric Company had dropped its founder's name.

Westinghouse's association with the company that he founded ended in 1910. After years of expansion, Westinghouse Electric found itself unable to produce the necessary cash to pay $14 million worth of debt that was about to come due because a stock panic had depressed the financial markets and made it impossible to raise money through them. The company was placed in receivership and the bankers who reorganized it appointed a new board of directors. From January, 1909 to July, 1910, when he was ousted, Westinghouse continued as president, with limited authority. He died in 1914 at the age of 67.

But if Westinghouse Electric missed the guiding hand of its founder, it didn't show. During the 1910s the company accumulated patents in the area of wireless communication. In 1919 and 1920, it joined RCA, General Electric (GE), United Fruit, American Telephone & Telegraph Company, and Wireless Specialty Company in a series of cross-licensing agreements that paved the way for the commercial introduction of radio. Under these agreements, Westinghouse and GE carved up the exclusive right to manufacture radio receivers between them, with RCA as the selling organization.

Westinghouse had also become a pioneer in radio broadcasting when it realized that continuous service would help receiver sales. In 1920 it set up radio station KDKA, which broadcast from the roof of the Westinghouse plant in East Pittsburgh. Over the next five years it opened several more stations across the country, and broadcasting has remained a substantial part of Westinghouse's business ever since.

Westinghouse, however, missed a chance to get in on the ground floor of television manufacturing. Vladimir Zworykin, the inventor of the electronic picture tube, began his research at Westinghouse in the early 1920s. But his superiors showed indifference to his work, and when RCA acquired the manufacturing and sales rights for radio and TV receivers and tubes, David Sarnoff was able to woo him to RCA. While at RCA, Zworykin filed the patent that would form the basis for the modern television set.

The first electrical appliances for consumers were also introduced in the 1920s and Westinghouse was in the forefront. The company offered a variety of products, from electric ranges to smaller household appliances. It introduced a line of electric refrigerators in 1930 and later added washing machines to its repertoire. It also entered the elevator business in 1927 when it acquired Kaestner & Hecht Company.

Westinghouse did not expand very much during the 1930s, as the Depression cast a pall over American industry. All of that changed, however, in 1941, when Westinghouse entered the military electronics business. It became one of the leading contractors for radar, which was invented before World War II. In fact, Westinghouse radar had provided a warning signal of the advance of Japanese planes on Pearl Harbor, but it was assumed that the planes were American. During the war years, Westinghouse grew at a frenetic pace and its defense business became so large that CEO A. W. Robertson hired banker Gwilym Price in 1943 just to handle financial negotiations on military contracts. Price succeeded Robertson as CEO in 1946.

Westinghouse's performance during the postwar economic boom shows a mixture of successes and difficulties. Its longtime connections with electrical utilities enabled it to move quickly into the burgeoning field of nuclear power, and the company has remained a leading producer of nuclear-generating equipment ever since. The company also became the leading supplier of reactors for the U.S. Navy's nuclear submarine fleet. And during the Korean War, it scored what *Fortune* called "a brilliant coup" by developing the axial-flow jet engine, which became the prototype for jet engines for the rest of the decade. But following a change in weight specifications for navy airplanes the navy canceled millions of dollars worth of contracts for Westinghouse's J-40 and J-46 engines.

Westinghouse also moved slowly in targeting other branches of the armed forces, with the result that from 1955 to 1957 it ranked only 25th in sales among defense contractors. Rival GE, by comparison, ranked third. Adding to its troubles, poor marketing plagued its consumer-appliance operations and it all but conceded the foremost place in this business to GE. Beginning in October, 1955 Westinghouse suffered through a five-month electrical-workers strike, the longest walkout against an American corporation since the Depression. And in the early 1950s, the three principal manufacturers of heavy electrical machinery—Westinghouse, GE, and Allis-Chalmers—waged a devastating price war that cut into revenues.

As a result of that price war those three companies, along with 26 smaller manufacturers who did business with electrical utilities, entered into a bid-rigging scheme in 1955 in hopes of securing their profit margins. Under the plan, each of the participants agreed beforehand on the amount of each bid and on who would win the contract. In the area of power switchgear, for instance, it was agreed that Westinghouse would win 35 percent of the contracts, GE 39 percent, I-T-E Circuit Breaker 11 percent, Allis-Chalmers eight percent and Federal Pacific Electric seven percent. In 1957 the Justice Department began to investigate possible violations of the Sherman Antitrust Act, and two years later a grand jury was called into session after the Tennessee Valley Authority complained of collusion among the manufacturers. Forty-five executives from 29 companies were indicted and all pleaded guilty. In the wake of the scandal Mark Cresap, who had succeeded Gwilym Price as CEO in 1958, announced that a section of the company's legal department would devote itself solely to compliance with antitrust laws.

Cresap resigned in 1963 because of ill health and died later that year. He left a Westinghouse that had, according to *Fortune,* "reached a low ebb in its corporate life." Still reeling from the bid-rigging scandal, the company was also plagued by stagnant sales, eroding prices, and declining profits. Into this unenviable

position stepped engineer Donald Burnham. It was said of the affable and unpretentious Burnham that when he wanted to rearrange the paintings in the CEO's office, he asked his secretary for a hammer and started pounding nails into the wall himself.

One of Burnham's top priorities as chief executive was to reorganize the corporate chain of command, decentralizing authority and giving individual division heads more freedom. Along with shaking up the bureaucracy, he sought ways to cut costs and use incentives to improve managerial performance. Westinghouse also embarked on a remarkable program of diversification under Burnham, buying into businesses as divorced from its core operations as soft-drink bottling, car rental, motels, transport refrigeration, land development, and mail-order record clubs. One of its most unusual ventures was Urban Systems Development Corporation, which Westinghouse set up in 1968 to respond to the need for low-cost housing by building pre-fabricated residential units. It was a venture consistent with Burnham's belief that social responsibility and corporate profitability were not necessarily incompatible.

In 1964 Westinghouse recorded record sales of $2.1 billion, but profits were sharply lower than in the previous year because of continued depressed prices in its major product lines. In 1966, however, profits reached $119.7 million, nearly a threefold increase from 1963. By the late 1960s the company's financial outlook had brightened considerably, and Burnham was hailed as a hero of corporate America.

By the time he retired in 1974, however, Westinghouse was once again in trouble. Decentralization of corporate authority had allowed overzealous division managers to stretch the company's resources to the breaking point. As vice-chairman Marshall Evans told *Fortune* in 1976, "we learned to our horror that these companies had gone totally hog-wild in committing the corporation to very substantial projects that were costly to complete." A prime example of this was Urban Systems Development. Although Robert Kirby, Burnham's successor, blamed its failure on lack of cooperation from the federal government, Urban Systems also expanded far too quickly for its own good and wound up posting after-tax losses of $45 million from 1972 through 1975. And although some of the unfamiliar businesses into which Westinghouse diversified turned a profit, like the Seven-Up Bottling Company of Los Angeles (purchased in 1969), many others did not. The acquisition of Longines-Wittenauer Watch Company, undertaken in 1970 mainly for its mail-order record operations, turned sour immediately, as discount record shops began to give mail-order businesses unwelcome competition. By the time Westinghouse divested its mail-order business in 1975 it had lost $65 million after taxes.

Westinghouse was also hurt by the continued lackluster performance of its consumer-appliance business and the high inflation of the early 1970s, which reduced revenues from fixed-price heavy-equipment contracts that it had signed years earlier. Wall Street analysts continued to downgrade the company, despite the fact that in April, 1974 it received an order for twelve nuclear power systems from France's state-run nuclear power agency, with options for four more units—the largest single order for nuclear equipment in history. One analyst told the *New York Times* that Burnham's decision to continue manufacturing appliances was "greeted with horror." Later that year Westinghouse stock dropped to $8 a share, from a high of $55 several years earlier. In late 1974, it sold its appliance business to White Consolidated Industries, leaving a field it had helped to pioneer, although White continued to market its products under the name White-Westinghouse.

When Robert Kirby became CEO he immediately declared that Westinghouse would get back to basics and in 1975 the company began to spin off its other unprofitable businesses. But the major event of the first half of Kirby's watch came about as a consequence of Westinghouse's decision in the early 1960s to become a uranium supplier. It had agreed to supply utilities that purchased its reactors with a total of 65 million pounds of uranium concentrate over a period of 20 years, at an average of $9.50 a pound. In 1973, however, the price of uranium skyrocketed, eventually exceeding $40 a pound. Westinghouse was caught with scanty reserves and found itself unable to buy enough uranium to meet its commitments. The 27 utilities with which it had uranium contracts sued to force Westinghouse to live up to those contracts. This would have cost the company $2 billion, the entire worth of its shareholder assets at the time. Westinghouse settled the last of these lawsuits in 1980, having paid a total of $950 million in damages, and managed to recoup some of those losses by suing a number of foreign and domestic uranium producers, charging that they had formed a cartel to drive up uranium prices unfairly. Some of these lawsuits were thrown out of court, but others were eventually settled for cash damages.

With its uranium problems mostly out of the way as it entered the 1980s, Westinghouse once again gave thought to expansion. As early as 1980 it had declared its intention to enter the field of robotics. In 1982 it acquired Unimation, a leading robot manufacturer. Westinghouse Broadcasting also expanded its cable television operations, acquiring cable giant Teleprompter Corporation in 1981 in the largest merger between communications companies in U. S. history. In 1982, a proposed joint cable venture with the Walt Disney Company fell through, but Westinghouse did join with NLT Corporation, a Nashville-based entertainment concern, to form The Nashville Network.

Reduced demand and utility overcapacity in the late 1970s and growing anxiety in the 1980s over the safety of nuclear power hurt Westinghouse's nuclear-equipment business, but the Reagan administration's massive military buildup added life to its defense operations. During the 1980s, Westinghouse received major contracts on such weapons as the F-16 and F-4E fighters, the B-52 and B-1B strategic bombers, the AWACS radar plane, the Mk 48 torpedo, the Trident nuclear submarine, and the MX missile. In 1985 the *Wall Street Journal* ranked Westinghouse as the nation's 13th-largest defense contractor. And in 1988 Westinghouse's electronic systems business, which is comprised almost entirely of military projects, accounted for roughly one-fifth of sales.

Douglas Danforth succeeded Robert Kirby as CEO in 1983. Also in that year, Westinghouse Broadcasting sold its Satellite News Channel to rival Cable News Network after the two had exchanged antitrust and unfair-competition lawsuits. Westinghouse sold its cable television operations in 1986 to a consortium of cable companies for $1.7 billion as part of a major restructuring program.

The mid- and late 1980s were marked by a number of divestitures of small- and medium-sized companies. Westinghouse also entered a series of joint ventures with foreign firms, most of them reflecting the growing dominance of Japanese companies in the electronics industry. In 1982 and 1985, it joined with Mitsubishi Electric to produce and market circuit breakers. In 1984 it formed a joint venture, subsequently dissolved, with Toshiba to manufacture high-resolution color picture tubes for computers and televisions. It also formed a joint venture with the Korean company Hyundai in 1984 to manufacture elevators and escalators, and with Siemens of West Germany to manufacture automation products in 1988.

Between 1985 and 1987 Danforth sold 70 less-profitable businesses, replacing them with 55 acquisitions that complement existing Westinghouse spheres of operation. In early 1989, Westinghouse also sold off two of its businesses to Swiss concerns: its elevator operations were acquired by Schindler Holdings and, after several years of disappointing performance, Unimation was purchased by Staubli International.

By 1990 Westinghouse's focus was no longer on manufactured goods for the consumer. Rather, the company focused on producing such technology as turbines for power generators and radar for the F-16 fighter plane, earning around $11 billion a year in sales. Westinghouse's Paul Lego assumed the chairmanship in 1990 and set a goal of 8.5 percent annual revenue growth for the company. Under Lego, Westinghouse briefly enjoyed a period of fiscal stability that was stronger than at any other time in its history. Its defense business pulled in annual revenues of $2.5 billion through developing products that would survive U.S. defense department cuts. Its financial service department was also quite strong, with annual earnings over $115 million.

Once Westinghouse was streamlined into a handful of core businesses, the company began to expand on its existing expertise. One venture, Westinghouse Government & Environmental Services, employed the company's knowledge of nuclear materials to operate hazardous, nuclear and municipal waste sites. This helped offset Westinghouse's declining sales in the nuclear power industry, which would soon become a thorn in its side. Another new undertaking successfully used Westinghouse's military technology to develop civilian products such as air traffic control equipment and home and office security systems. Westinghouse's broadcasting division also ventured into new arenas, handling the lucrative distribution rights and advertising for such popular television programs as "Teen-Age Mutant Ninja Turtles" and the "Cosby Show."

Westinghouse's financial stability was short-lived, however. It's restructuring was largely financed by the success of Westinghouse Credit Corp., a unit in its Financial Services division. During the 1980s, Credit Corp.'s assets grew from $2 billion to $10 billion due to a strategy of investing in high-interest real estate and commercial loans. When the bottom fell out of the real estate market in the early 1990s, a large number of Credit Corp. customers defaulted. The division posted a $1.6 billion loss in the second quarter of 1991, and by 1993, the company had amassed over $5 billion in debt. The company's reputation among financial analysts was further damaged when Westinghouse, at the recommendation of Lazard Freres & Co., put $1 billion worth of junk bonds up for sale. According to *Business Week,* the bonds were dumped at the bottom of the market, and Westinghouse filed suit against Lazard, charging that the brokerage firm was siphoning off some of Westinghouse's profits.

With its enormous new debt load, the company sought to trim its operations once again. In 1992, Westinghouse exited the rough and tumble financial service business and also announced plans to sell its office furniture, residential real estate, electric-supply, and electric distribution and control subsidiaries. In 1993, Westinghouse sold its electric distribution and control unit to Eaton Corp. for $1.1 billion. After the sale, Westinghouse realigned its operations into five units: broadcasting, electronic systems, environmental, industries, and power systems. It continued to seek buyers for its electric-supply, residential real estate, and office furniture subsidiaries.

In the mid-1990s, Westinghouse suffered a number of public relations setbacks. It successfully fought a suit filed by the Philippine government charging that Westinghouse conspired to bribe former president Ferdinand Marcos to win a $2.1 billion nuclear power contract. In 1993 a U.S. jury absolved Westinghouse of the charges, but the Philippine government vowed to appeal the case. More threatening to the company's bottom line was a series of lawsuits stemming from allegations that Westinghouse sold faulty equipment to a group of five utilities companies in the late 1960s. *Business Week* estimated that—should Westinghouse lose the hotly contested suit—the company could pay up to $1 billion in damages and potentially face a number of "copycat" suits from other utilities companies.

Despite these problems as well as cuts in the defense industry, Westinghouse's core businesses in broadcasting, electronic systems, environmental, industries, and power systems remained strong in the mid-1990s. The company continued to retrench, focusing on paying down debt and fortifying its existing businesses.

Principal Subsidiaries: Westinghouse Broadcasting Company; Thermo King Corporation; The Knoll Group; Aptus, Inc.; Resource Energy Systems; WCI Communities; Westinghouse Government and Environmental Services Company; Westinghouse Savannah River Company.

Further Reading:

Baker, Stephen, "Can Westinghouse Dodge a Nuclear Knockdown Punch?," *Business Week,* October 3, 1994, p. 58.

Berg, Eric N., "Westinghouse Seeks Growth in Old Lines," *New York Times,* June 19, 1990, pp. D1, D5.

Novack, Janet, "What's a Westinghouse?," *Forbes,* April 4, 1988, pp. 34–36.

Nulty, Peter, "Behind the Mess at Westinghouse," *Fortune,* November 4, 1991, pp. 92–99.

Passer, Harold C., *The Electrical Manufacturers 1875–1900,* Cambridge, Mass.: Harvard University Press, 1953.

—updated by Maura Troester

Whirlpool Corporation

2000 M-63 North
Benton Harbor, Michigan 49022
U.S.A.
(616) 926-5000
Fax: (616) 923-5486

Public Company
Incorporated: 1929 as Nineteen Hundred Corporation
Employees: 35,500
Sales: $8.10 billion
Stock Exchanges: New York Midwest London
SICs: 3630 Appliances; 6141 Personal Credit Institutions

From its beginning as a manufacturer of electrically powered clothes washers, Whirlpool Corporation has become a leading producer of a complete line of household appliances. The company is the number-one source of home laundry equipment in the United States, and also markets appliances such as dishwashers, refrigerators, ovens, ranges, and air conditioners worldwide under the Whirlpool, KitchenAid, and Roper brand names.

The company that preceded Whirlpool was founded in 1911 by Lou Upton and his uncle, Emory Upton, who lent their family name to the machine shop they opened in Saint Joseph, Michigan. Lou Upton, a life insurance salesman, had recently lost his investment in a small appliance dealership that had failed. In an attempt to compensate Upton for his loss, the dealer gave him the patent for a manually operated clothes washer. Emory Upton was able to outfit the machine with an electric motor, and—with a $5,000 stake from L. C. Bassford, a Chicago retailing executive—the Upton Machine Company began producing electric wringer washers. The company soon snared its first customer, the Federal Electric division of Chicago-based Commonwealth Edison.

The relationship lasted three years, until Federal Electric began manufacturing its own washers. Although losing this customer was a major blow, the company stayed afloat by manufacturing toys, camping equipment, and automobile accessories until it rebounded in 1916 with an agreement to produce two types of wringer washers for Sears, Roebuck and Company, which at that time operated exclusively through mail order. Sales of Upton's washers through the Sears catalog grew rapidly during and after World War I. In order to avoid total dependence on the Sears account, however, Upton also launched a washer under its own brand name in the early 1920s.

During the 1920s, Sears's expansion into retailing and its selection of Upton as its sole supplier of washing machines forced the company to find a way to increase its manufacturing capacity and distribution efficiency. This was accomplished through a merger, in 1929, with the Nineteen Hundred Washer Company of Binghamton, New York. The post-merger company, known as the Nineteen Hundred Corporation, survived the Great Depression without any lasting damage and even expanded and modernized its production facilities during this time to handle increasing sales volume.

During World War II the company manufactured weapons parts and related products needed for the war effort. The company also focused on the development of an automatic, spinner-type washer during the 1940s. This machine, nicknamed the "Jeep," was introduced by Sears in 1947 under that company's Kenmore brand name, and then under Nineteen Hundred's own newly introduced Whirlpool brand one year later.

In 1949 Elisha "Bud" Gray II succeeded retiring Lou Upton as president and led the company through the postwar period, which was characterized by heavy consumer demand for convenience products. The Nineteen Hundred Corporation aggressively launched a complete line of Whirlpool home laundry appliances, including wringer and automatic clothes washers, electric and automatic clothes dryers, and irons. In 1950 the company changed its name to Whirlpool Corporation.

Although sales continued to climb, it became clear by the mid-1950s that the company's emphasis on laundry equipment made it vulnerable to increasing competition from more diversified manufacturers. In 1955 Whirlpool merged with the Seeger Refrigerator Company and added a line of refrigerators. The company also began to make air conditioners and cooking-range products in 1955. The two lines had formerly been produced by Radio Corporation of America (RCA), and were marketed under the RCA-Whirlpool name. The company itself operated under the name of Whirlpool-Seeger Corporation until 1957. Between 1955 and 1957 the company introduced its first full line of home appliances under the RCA-Whirlpool brand. The line consisted of 12 types of machines and 150 models. The 1957 merger with Chicago's Birtman Electric Company brought a vacuum cleaner line under Whirlpool's expanding product umbrella.

As its product line grew, Whirlpool's network of independent dealers and distributors assumed an increasingly important role in the company's marketing and sales efforts. A subsidiary called Appliance Buyers Credit Corporation was formed in 1957 to provide financing to these distributors and to help strengthen Whirlpool's position as an industry leader. Also in 1957, the company broadened its reach beyond the United States by initiating the first of several acquisitions of major Brazilian appliance manufacturers.

Intensifying consumerism in the 1960s created growing pressure on appliance manufacturers to offer better quality and service. As a result, Whirlpool launched new support services, as well as a continuing stream of new products, such as the home trash compactor. Its toll-free Cool-Line service enabled

Whirlpool appliance owners to obtain immediate information on subjects like installation and repair. At the same time, however, price reductions, caused by the softening demand for appliances, and growing competition led the company to institute a series of measures designed to streamline production and decrease manufacturing costs. Since the Whirlpool name itself had gained wide acceptance, the company also reached a friendly agreement with RCA during the mid-1960s to drop RCA's brand name from the company's products.

Further attempts to diversify yielded mixed results. The company's purchase of Heil-Quaker Corporation in 1964 enlarged Whirlpool's scope beyond consumer appliances to central heating and cooling equipment. But this subsidiary was sold to Inter-City Gas Corporation of Canada in 1986 as Whirlpool refocused its attention on home appliances. Its 1966 entry into the consumer-electronics market with the acquisition of Warwick Electronics ended in failure ten years later, at which time the business was sold to Sanyo Electric Company. To close out the decade, the company penetrated the Canadian market for the first time with its 1969 purchase of Inglis, a home appliance manufacturer. Inglis has since served as Whirlpool's Canadian arm.

Continued emphasis on consumerism combined with the 1973 energy crisis, a slump in the housing industry, and an economic recession increased pressure on the appliance industry to produce more energy-efficient products and to improve manufacturing efficiency. Faced with sluggish retail sales, Whirlpool dealers and Sears, still the company's largest customer, liquidated their inventories, a move which forced Whirlpool to lay off over one-third of its workforce. A 1974 strike at its Evansville, Indiana, plant, which produced refrigeration and air conditioning equipment, further tested the company's ability to weather the downturn in the appliance market. Although the strike ended after four months, the plant's compressor facilities closed permanently in 1983 as part of a companywide initiative to reduce manufacturing costs. These developments stood in marked contrast to the period between 1967 and 1973, when manufacturers had built, delivered, and sold one appliance every 3.2 seconds.

By 1977 the market cycled upward, and Whirlpool and its competitors were again experiencing strong demand for labor-saving devices from first-time buyers of the postwar generation, from households replacing existing appliances, and from the military post exchanges with which the company had established a buying arrangement in 1967. As Whirlpool grew, however, traditional appliance retailers struggled against the increasing sales strength of mass merchandisers.

Whirlpool's progress during the 1970s was guided by chairman John H. Platts, who had started his career with the company in 1941 on the assembly line and was hand-picked to succeed Elisha Gray II in 1971. Improvement of products for residential use remained an important priority for Whirlpool during this period. In 1977 it introduced the first automatic clothes washer with solid-state electronic controls and a line of microwave ovens. The company had originally entered the microwave market in the late 1950s and quickly withdrew due to limited potential.

A move toward vertical integration was also initiated in 1977, when the company started producing its own appliance motors to reduce its dependence on outside suppliers. One of Whirlpool's few failures during the decade involved the launch of a commercial ice-making system for use in hotels and motels and by food purveyors. The product never met sales goals and the business was sold in 1982.

In 1980 Whirlpool was found guilty of discrimination in a suit brought by the Department of Labor, alleging that Whirlpool had taken inappropriate disciplinary action against two employees who had refused to perform what they considered to be hazardous work in the company's Marion, Ohio, plant. After several years of litigation, the Supreme Court ruled in the employees' favor, stating that the act of placing letters of reprimand in their personnel files was discriminatory.

Upon Platts's retirement in November 1982, vice chairman Jack D. Sparks became chairman and CEO, and set about broadening the company's focus. Sparks's sales and marketing experience was felt important as Whirlpool faced an environment of increasing foreign competition in the United States, industry consolidation, and changing consumer preferences. Under Sparks's leadership, Whirlpool embarked upon a major capital spending program to increase manufacturing productivity and instituted a five-year plan to address industry trends.

One result of this planning process was the expansion of the company's product line beyond appliances and into related consumer durable goods. In 1985 Whirlpool entered the lucrative kitchen-cabinet market by acquiring Mastercraft Industries Corporation, followed by the purchase of another cabinet manufacturer, St. Charles Manufacturing Company, the next year. The cabinet business did not produce the hoped for results—Whirlpool was unable to capture a satisfactory share of the residential-construction market—and the cabinet operation was sold in 1989.

Sparks also oversaw the acquisition of the KitchenAid division of Hobart Corporation, which added a popular line of higher-priced dishwashers, ovens, and other kitchen appliances to the Whirlpool product line. Initiated in 1985, the transaction's completion was delayed for a year as White Consolidated Industries alleged antitrust violations. White's suit eventually proved unsuccessful and the acquisition was finalized in 1986.

Sparks also emphasized growth in the company's international markets and formed Whirlpool Trading Company in 1984, to explore overseas opportunities. Two years later the company attempted to forge a joint venture with Dutch company N. V. Philips to manufacture and market household appliances overseas. The project fell through due to unstable currency and market conditions.

In 1987 David R. Whitman, succeeding Jack Sparks as president and CEO, took over the direction and implementation of the company's five-year global strategy. The company continued to focus on increasing manufacturing productivity and reducing costs, while applying new technology to appliance production. Whirlpool contracted with McDonnell Douglas Astronautics Company to develop prototypes of appliances for use in U.S. space stations.

Until 1988 the company operated under a centralized structure, with decision-making concentrated at the senior management level. In 1988 Whirlpool reorganized its activities into seven units in order to maximize efficiency and market responsiveness. These units were: the Kenmore, KitchenAid, and Whirlpool appliance groups; Whirlpool International; Inglis Limited; Whirlpool Finance Corporation; and the company's export group.

Shortly thereafter, the company attempted to acquire Roper Corporation, another major manufacturer and supplier of appliances to Sears. This move was hoped to strengthen Whirlpool's cooking-appliance product line with electric and gas ranges and open new opportunities in the outdoor-equipment market Roper served with its lawn mowers and garden tractors. The Roper purchase was stymied, however, by General Electric Company (GE), which alleged that Roper had not solicited competitive bids upon receiving the Whirlpool offer as it was required to do so by the Securities and Exchange Commission. As the controversy intensified, Whirlpool withdrew its tender offer and reached a settlement with GE in which GE would acquire Roper's manufacturing facilities while Whirlpool would obtain the rights to the Roper name. The rivals also forged a two-year agreement under which GE would supply Whirlpool with appliance motors and gas and electric ranges.

In 1988 the company successfully revived its proposed joint venture with N. V. Philips. This effort was spurred primarily by Whirlpool's desire to participate in the post-1992 European market for home appliances. The ensuing agreement cleared the way for Whirlpool to market a full line of major home appliances in Europe. Philips's appliances were more appropriately designed for European customers than Whirlpool's models. The following year, the Whirlpool name was added to the Philips product line to strengthen recognition in the European market.

Whirlpool's initiatives in Europe reflected the company's aggressive international strategy, which earned it a reputation as one of the most globally diversified companies in the world during the early 1990s. Indeed, during this period Whirlpool expanded its overseas operations at a steady pace and lengthened its lead as the largest producer of appliances in the world. By late 1994, Whirlpool was manufacturing in 11 countries and marketing its products under ten brand names in 120 nations. The company enjoyed hefty sales gains in its giant European market in the early and mid-1990s. But it was pinning its hopes for greatest growth on Asia. Whirlpool shipped 700,000 units in Asia in 1994, was hoping to sell three million in that region in 1995, and expected similar growth to continue through at least the late 1990s. Similarly, sales in Latin America leapt 40 percent in 1994.

Besides surging global sales, Whirlpool worked to improve its operations in the flattening North American appliance market by restructuring. In 1994 it announced plans to cut about nine percent of its global work force, primarily through plant closures in Canada and the United States. Similar restructuring during the early 1990s resulted in a restructuring charge that cut 1994 profits by 32 percent, to about $158 million. During the same year, though, Whirlpool's total revenues jumped more than eight percent and profits were growing at record levels in 1995. Massive untapped global markets, combined with Whirlpool's combative global tactics under Whitman's command, suggested healthy long-term performance for the appliance maker.

Principal Subsidiaries: KitchenAid, Inc.; North American Appliance Group; Whirlpool Financial Corporation; Whirlpool Asia; Whirlpool Europe.

Further Reading:

Heinrich, Erik, "Ontario Jobs Lost in Whirlpool Shakeup," *Financial Post,* November 16, 1994, p. 8.
Maurer, Mitch, "Whirlpool Cuts 3,200; Tulsa Plans Unchanged," *Tulsa World,* November 16, 1994, p. B1.
——, "Whirlpool Income Rises," *Tulsa World,* October 14, 1994, p. B2.
Reid, T. R., "Whirlpool Enters China with Joint Ventures in Microwave Ovens and Refrigerators," *Business Wire,* December 7, 1994.
——, "Whirlpool's Full-year 1994 Operating Results are Best Ever," *Business Wire,* January 26, 1995.
Whirlpool Corporation 1911–1986: Progressing Toward the 21st Century, Benton Harbor, Mich.: Whirlpool Corporation, 1986.

—Sandy Schusteff
—updated by Dave Mote

White Castle

White Castle Systems, Inc.

P.O. Box 1498
Columbus, Ohio 43216-1498
U.S.A
(614) 228-5781
Fax: (614) 464-0596

Private Company
Incorporated: 1924 as the White Castle System of Eating
   Houses Corporation
Employees: 9,700
Sales: $307 million
SICs: 5812 Eating Places; 3444 Sheet Metal Work

White Castle Systems, Inc. operates the ninth largest hamburger chain in the United States, with 287 restaurants located primarily in urban areas throughout the Midwest and Northeast, as well as a small number of restaurants in Japan and other Pacific Rim countries. Unlike most hamburger chains, White Castle's U.S. restaurants are not franchised; all units are owned and operated by White Castle Systems, of which the E.W. Ingram family has been sole proprietor since 1933. In the mid-1990s, E.W. Ingram III—grandson of founder E.W. Ingram—directed the company as chairperson, president, and CEO, while his father, E.W. Ingram Jr., held the position of chairman emeritus.

White Castle Systems also owns and operates its own bakeries and meat processing plants. Its subsidiary, Porcelain Steel Building Company, manufactures White Castle restaurant equipment. Another subsidiary, White Castle Distributing, markets and distributes frozen White Castle hamburgers to supermarkets nationwide. The company prides itself on its generous employee benefit plans and a turnover rate that is unusually low for the fast food industry.

Although primarily known for its square hamburgers, White Castle also offers cheeseburgers, chicken sandwiches, french fries, onion rings, breakfast meals, and dessert pastries. In its 75 years of operation, White Castle hamburgers have developed an image that sets them apart from other fast-food burgers. The pop music group The Beastie Boys sang an ode to the sandwiches in the 1980s, and the Canadian pop group The Smithereens wrote "White Castle Blues" several years later. According to a *Columbus Monthly* story on the seventieth anniversary of the company, "Public opinion about the hamburgers [which sell at a rate of 480 million a year] seems to fall into three

categories: Those who swear by the things, those who detest them, and those who haven't tried them out of fear or lack of opportunity and are waiting to be included in the first two categories."

White Castle hamburgers have such nicknames as Sliders, Gut Bombs, Castles, Whitey-One-Bites and Belly Busters, and in recent years, the company's marketing team has capitalized on this image. Company publicity refers to the hamburgers as "Sliders" and has even stated that "the full impact of eating White Castle hamburgers normally isn't felt until the day after." The company also sponsors contests for recipes incorporating White Castle hamburgers and sells clothing emblazoned with the White Castle logo or its "Slider" nickname.

The distinctive taste of White Castle hamburgers is attributed to one of the restaurant's co-founders, Walter Anderson. Anderson worked in a Wichita, Kansas, restaurant and had perfected a unique way of cooking hamburger patties, adding shredded onions and placing both halves of the bun over the sizzling meat. In 1916, he rented a remodeled streetcar, bought a griddle plate and refrigerator, and opened his own hamburger stand. Using the slogan "buy 'em by the sack," Anderson sold a good number of hamburgers.

By 1921, he had three hamburger stands in operation and was looking to finance the opening of a fourth. That year, he met E.W. "Billy" Ingram, a real-estate and insurance broker. With a $700 loan, the two founded the first White Castle restaurant, an 11- by 16-foot cement block structure that resembled a small castle, complete with turrets and battlements.

At that time, hamburgers were a relatively novel food item, sold at fairs, amusement parks, carnivals, and some restaurants. Very few hamburger stands were in operation, and the ones that were had reputations as unclean purveyors of products that were less than 100 percent pure beef. According to a speech by Ingram at a 1964 Newcomen Society meeting in Columbus, Ohio, his and Anderson's goal was to "break down a deep-rooted prejudice against the hamburger by constantly improving its quality and serving it in clean and sanitary surroundings." He added that the two chose the name White Castle, because " 'White' signifies purity and cleanliness and 'Castle' represents strength, permanence and stability."

The two established a motto: "Serve the finest products, for the least cost, in the cleanest surroundings, with the most courteous personnel." The two also had another motto: "He who owes no money will never go broke." Within 90 days of opening its first restaurant, the firm of Anderson and Ingram repaid its debt. Profits were fueled back into the organization, and more restaurants were opened. In 1924, Anderson and Ingram incorporated their company as the White Castle System of Eating Houses Corporation. Competing hamburger stands inspired by the success of White Castle popped up all over Wichita, run by theater operators, real-estate brokers, and even Ingram's own dentist.

Between 1923 and 1931, White Castle Systems established 100 restaurants in cities across the Midwest. In his speech to the Newcomen Society, Ingram claimed that in each city where they opened a restaurant, "We searched carefully but did not find any places specializing in the sales of hamburger sandwiches.'' He went on to add that White Castle created its own competition.

In its early years, White Castle also focused on the quality of its coffee. ''We try to serve the best coffee in town'' signs were hung in each restaurant, earnestly stating a company goal during the first 30 years of business. Indeed, White Castle took this statement seriously, setting uniform standards throughout its restaurant system. Adherence was maintained using a hydrometer created especially for White Castle coffee.

In keeping with trends in the burgeoning foodservice industry, White Castle was also concerned about the nutritional value of its hamburgers. The company hired the head of the physiological chemistry department at a Big 10 university to spend a summer studying the food value of its burgers. The chemist hired a student as test subject, asking him to eat nothing but White Castle hamburgers for the entire summer. At the end of the period, the student was found to be in good health, despite the fact that he was ''eating 20 to 24 hamburgers a day during the last few weeks.'' The professor recommended that calcium be added to the flour used in the buns and suggested a specific weight ratio of meat to bun to provide a more nutritious balance of proteins, carbohydrates, and fat. White Castle complied, and altered its recipe only slightly since that time.

In 1931, White Castle became the first fast food restaurant to advertise in a newspaper. Ingram and Anderson chose to concentrate on generating new carry-out business, as counter space inside the restaurant was limited to under 20 seats. Using Anderson's ''buy 'em by the sack'' slogan, White Castle ran a quarter-page ad in two St. Louis evening newspapers. Included in the advertisement was a coupon offering five hamburgers for a dime between two o'clock p.m. and midnight on the following Saturday. The advertisement was a success. By two p.m. that Saturday, most White Castles had lines forming outside their take-out windows. Within an hour, some operations had run out of buns. Supply houses had to work overtime to produce buns and burgers to meet the demand. Buoyed by the achievements of their original advertisement, Ingram and Anderson continued the practice, making coupons valid for 24-hour periods, to prevent the flood of customers they experienced the first time.

1931 was a year of innovations for the company. While there was no doubt that Anderson's ''buy 'em by the sack'' slogan was successful, a problem arose in that the burgers at the bottom of a sack full of hamburgers would often be crushed by the time a customer arrived at his destination. To prevent this from happening, White Castle developed cardboard cartons with heat-resistant linings—the first paper cartons used in the food industry. The company then expanded this concept to include cardboard containers for hot and cold drinks, french fries, and pie.

Other innovations introduced during this time included improving the quality and safety of beef through the use of frozen hamburger patties, as well as a patented coffee mug design and exhaust systems and specially designed griddles in the restaurants. In 1932, White Castle incorporated its first subsidiary, the Paperlynen Company, to manufacture paper hats worn by White Castle employees. Company engineers had developed a machine that manufactured paper hats so quickly that one machine could make enough hats in two weeks to supply the entire White Castle chain for a year. Realizing they had a potentially profitable business on their hands, the company began marketing the paper caps to other foodservice establishments. By 1964, Paperlynen was selling over 54 million caps worldwide a year.

As part of its marketing drive in the early 1930s, White Castle also began a campaign ''to upgrade the image of the hamburger'' in the minds of housewives. In each city where White Castles were located, the company hired hostesses who went by the name of ''Julia Joyce.'' Julia Joyce would guide housewives on tours of their local White Castle, allowing them to examine the cleanliness of White Castle kitchens and the sanitary manner in which hamburgers were cooked. After the housewives finished their tour, the hostess presented each with a coupon offering five carry-out hamburgers for ten cents redeemable immediately, as well a coupon for children, valid the following Saturday. Julia Joyce also set up meetings with local women's clubs where she served hamburgers, coffee, soft drinks, and pie in carryout containers and then went on to explain how White Castle's carry-out service could be used for families or club outings.

Perhaps one of White Castle's most unusual innovations was the design and construction of semi-permanent restaurants that could be easily transported from one location to another. Because White Castles were relatively small (15 feet by 11 feet), many landlords refused to lease such a scant parcel of land for over 30 days. Ingram came up with idea of developing a building that could be moved, thus preventing the loss of a building when landlords refused to renew the restaurant's lease. In 1928, Ingram hired L.W. Ray to patent a movable restaurant unit. Modeled after Chicago's Water Tower landmark, the restaurant consisted of a metal frame with siding, battlements, and turrets made of white porcelain. White Castle incorporated another subsidiary, the Porcelain Steel Building Company to manufacture Ray's unique White Castle buildings and also most of the company's kitchen equipment. Porcelain Steel constructed 55 of these restaurants, although only two ultimately had to be moved.

In 1934, Ingram bought out his partner's interest in the operation and moved to Columbus, Ohio, purchasing a ten-acre track of land on which the company set up corporate headquarters and its Porcelain Steel manufacturing operations. Despite the severe economic effects of the Great Depression, White Castle's business grew steadily during the 1930s, from 59 million burgers sold during its first decade of operation to 294 million by the end of its second.

World War II, however, had a somewhat negative impact on White Castle's growth. Due to shortages of beef caused by rationing, the number of restaurant units shrunk from 100 to 70. White Castle's subsidiaries stopped making restaurant equipment and devoted their efforts to supporting the war. At the close of the war, when the restaurant business remained in a slump, Porcelain Steel began supplying fertilizer spreaders to the O.M. Scoot & Sons Company.

In 1949, a White Castle employee made the discovery that broken hamburger patties cooked faster. This led to the development of White Castle's signature five-holed hamburger, a process that allowed the burger to cook more quickly and eliminated the time-consuming task of flipping the burger. The economy resumed its growth in the 1950s, and White Castle expanded into high-traffic urban areas in the Northeast, such as Detroit, Minneapolis/St. Paul, Cleveland, and New York City. During that time, the company began the practice of selling frozen burger patties to customers who wanted to cook them at home. In 1957, the company hired Simpson Marketing of Chicago to handle advertising, and the number of hamburgers sold reached 846 million.

By 1963, White Castle was operating 100 restaurants in 11 metropolitan areas and owned 34 prime properties and two manufacturing subsidiaries. Growth continued steadily throughout the 1960s with little change in menu—with the exception of its 1965 decision to use all-vegetable oil for french fries, onion rings, and other fried foods (another industry first). When founder Billy Ingram died in 1966, his son E.W. (Edgar) Ingram, Jr., subsequently assumed the post of president.

White Castle's expansion remained conservative and modest, supported by internal funding and very few loans. Growth of the fast food industry exploded in the 1970s and 1980s, led by the expansion of McDonald's, Burger King, and Wendy's restaurant chains. From 1970 to the late 1980s, however, White Castle grew slowly but steadily, collecting stories about customers who "would do anything to get their hands on [White Castle] hamburgers." These included tales of a man who rented a silver Rolls Royce to take his wife to dine at White Castle in honor of their fiftieth wedding anniversary, as well as the story of a family who moved to a western state and missed White Castle hamburgers so much they had another family member drop bags of burgers down by parachute as he flew his plane over their farm. In 1977, E.W. (Bill) Ingram III took over as president of the company, the third generation of Ingrams to hold that post. Two years later, in response to changes in the fast food industry, the company opened its first drive-through establishment, in Indianapolis. The number of White Castle hamburgers sold topped 2.3 billion.

From 1977 to 1987, the number of restaurants grew by over 100, and White Castle entered the second most productive period of its history. In 1981, the company instituted its innovative "Hamburgers to Fly" program, a service that provided a toll-free number through which people could order frozen White Castle burgers and have them delivered anywhere in the United States within 24 hours. The service, according to company officials, was "an overnight success." During the 1980s, frozen White Castle hamburgers virtually created their own supermarket niche as private entrepreneurs purchased frozen

burgers from restaurants and resold them to grocery stores at a profit. In 1987, White Castle decided to get in on its own game. The company discontinued its "Hamburgers to Fly," program, incorporated White Castle Distributing, Inc., and began an intensive campaign to market its frozen burgers at supermarkets across the United States. Sales grew by an average of 15 to 20 percent annually. By 1990, White Castle frozen hamburgers had captured the number three position in the frozen sandwich category with annual sales of $27.2 million.

1986 gross sales exceeded $268.5 million, with per unit sales averaging $1.3 million, near the best in the industry. In 1987, White Castle ended its 30-year relationship with Simpson Marketing of Chicago and hired Gunder & Associates, a Columbus agency, to handle its $5 million advertising account. Soon thereafter, the company instituted several new marketing strategies, including breakfast meals, children's meals, and a chicken sandwich.

While new store openings in the United States continued at a rate of 25 units a year, the company also expanded overseas in the 1980s, granting its first franchise rights to a Japanese firm in 1986. Soon, four White Castle units were operating in Kyoto, and other franchises were established in Thailand, Malaysia, Indonesia, and Singapore. By 1989, White Castle had 243 restaurants in operation, with an average volume per store second only to McDonald's.

In 1991, White Castle celebrated its seventieth anniversary with the slogan, "After 70 years, it's like nothing else. Nothing." The company took out a full-page color advertisement in *USA Today,* detailing the history of White Castles and previewing its coupons for 70 cent value meals. Sales that year hit $305 million; in 1993, gross sales topped $307 million. As it neared its seventy-fifth anniversary, White Castle Systems continued to grow in much the same manner it had throughout its history: conservatively, thoughtfully, and with a good dose of Billy Ingram's homespun wisdom.

Further Reading:

Ingram, E.W., Sr., *All This from a 5-Cent Hamburger!,* New York: Newcomen Society in North America, 1975.
Meinhold, Nancy M., "From 'Doggy Bag' to Shopping Bag," *Food Processing,* October 1991, p. 14.
Oliphant, Jim, "White Castle: 70 Years of Sliders," *Columbus Monthly,* February 1991, p. 26.
Wiedrich, Bob, "Every Worker's King at White Castle," *Chicago Tribune,* November 30, 1987, p. C1.

—Maura Troester

World Book, Inc.

525 West Monroe Street
Chicago, Illinois 60661
U.S.A
(312) 258-3700
Fax: (312) 258-3950

Wholly Owned Subsidiary of Scott Fetzer Co.
Founded: 1917
Employees: 5,600
Sales: $200 million
SICs: 2731 Book Publishing; 5963 Direct Selling
   Establishments

World Book, Inc. is a leading publisher of reference materials. Through three of its five divisions, the company markets hundreds of different reference and educational products in more than 50 countries and in more than a dozen languages. Its *World Book* is the largest selling print encyclopedia in the world by numerical volume. World Book is owned by Scott Fetzer Co., which is, in turn, held by Berkshire Hathaway Inc.

World Book, Inc. is the progeny of entrepreneurs J.H. Hanson and John Bellows. In the early 1900s, through their publishing house, Hanson-Bellows Company, the two Chicago businessmen published *The New Practical Reference Set,* a general purpose reference tool. Hanson and Bellows soon found that their set of encyclopedias, like many other works at the time, were ill-suited to the needs of children. Indeed, finding the content and format of encyclopedias too rigid and technical for children, Hanson and Bellows believed that a market existed for reference materials geared specifically toward young people.

In 1915, Hanson and Bellows sought the help of Wisconsin academic Michael Vincent O'Shea. O'Shea was full of ideas about how *The New Practical Reference Set* could be adapted for a younger audience. In essence, O'Shea thought that the text, while still accurate and informative, should be more engaging and easier to read. He also believed that illustrations could be used with the entries to capture the reader's attention and to provide important visual information. O'Shea spent two years editing the book and molding it to fit his vision.

In 1917, Hanson and Bellows published the results of O'Shea's work, a set of encyclopedias entitled *World Book.* The first *World Book* series consisted of eight volumes with 6,300 pages.

The text was accompanied by thousands of detailed illustrations and photographs. The Hanson-Roach-Fowler Company was listed as the publisher of the encyclopedia, and O'Shea was its editor in chief. "As a rule, encyclopedias are apt to be quite formal and technical," O'Shea wrote in the preface to the first edition, noting that "a faithful effort has been made in the *World Book* to avoid this common defect."

The World Book was well received in the marketplace. In fact, the company published a revised edition in 1918 that added two new volumes to the set. Intrigued by the potential of the concept, publisher W.F. Quarrie & Company purchased *World Book* in 1919. Quarrie would guide and oversee *World Book*'s development over the next 25 years, publishing a revised edition almost every year. The first major revision of the text occurred in 1929, when Quarrie added hundreds of pages of text and illustrations and boosted the number of volumes to 13. As demand for the encyclopedia swelled, Quarrie continued to add new information, and, in 1933, another revised edition was published with 19 volumes.

During the 1930s, Quarrie assembled an editorial advisory board to guide the project's development. Comprised of several distinguished educators, the *World Book* board conducted a thorough analysis of typical school curriculums to determine exactly what material was being taught in classes from kindergarten through high school. Such ongoing curriculum analysis programs became the foundation of *World Book*'s editorial success during the mid- and late 1900s. The information was used to make *World Book* more relevant to the school environment and to eventually facilitate the introduction of many other reference volumes and sets geared at school-age kids.

Quarrie launched one of its most successful children's reference sets in the late 1930s—*Childcraft—The How and Why Library.* The seven-volume *Childcraft* was created as a sort of encyclopedia for young children. With an emphasis on simple text and illustrations, the books were designed to make learning fun and to give schools an alternative to more traditional published materials. Each volume addressed different subjects, including literature, such as short stories and poetry, as well as mathematics and the sciences. Like *World Book,* the project was welcomed in the marketplace, particularly by schools and other institutions.

In addition to looking for new markets, Quarrie continued to improve *World Book* by making it easier to read and more informative. In the 1930s, for example, *World Book* adopted the "unit-letter" system of arrangement, which allowed readers easier access to the information they sought. *World Book* gradually became recognized as a leader in the field in terms of ease-of-use and readability. In addition to successfully marketing its books to schools and institutions, Quarrie also prospered by establishing a large direct sales force. Salespeople pitched the encyclopedia as a family learning tool that was more usable than the expensive, formal encyclopedias, such as those published by Encyclopedia Britannica, Inc.

In 1945, Chicago magnate Marshall Field III purchased Quarrie (which had changed its name to The Quarrie Corporation in 1936), and Quarrie became a division of Field Enterprises, Inc. In 1958, Field grouped *World Book* and *Childcraft* into a separate operation, which he named Field Enterprises Educational Corporation. Although the operation changed ownership, it sustained its business strategy and continued to improve its texts. Two years after the buyout, in fact, a major revision of *World Book* was published that increased the number of volumes to 19. Similarly, *Childcraft* was completely revised in 1949, being expanded to include 14 volumes, about twice the size of the original set.

During the 1950s and 1960s, Field Enterprises enjoyed strong demand for its reference books. The nation was experiencing a postwar population and economic boom, and Field's youth-oriented encyclopedias were in high demand. To take advantage of surging markets, the company launched several new initiatives. In 1955, for example, "The Classroom Research Program" was introduced. The program represented an extension of the efforts of *World Book*'s editorial advisory board. Students in classrooms across the nation were asked to fill out cards describing the subjects they had looked for in reference books. This data then informed the encyclopedia's content. By the early 1990s, students were submitting more than 100,000 cards annually.

In 1960, Field completed the third major revision of *World Book*. In addition to boosting the size of the collection to 20 volumes, the company introduced enhanced graphics to the revised encyclopedia. In 1962, moreover, the *World Book Year Book* program was started, whereby owners of the *World Book* could receive an annual volume that updated the information in their set. One year later, the company introduced the *World Book Dictionary*. The dictionary was similar to the encyclopedia in that it was designed to be very easy to read and contained a large amount of graphics. The two-volume dictionary had grown to resemble a compact encyclopedia by the early 1990s, with nearly 225,000 entries and about 3,000 illustrations.

In 1965, the company published the first edition of *Science Year,* created in response to the rapidly changing field of science and developed for use with the *World Book.* Like the *Year Book, Science Year* represented the beginning of a series designed to generate follow-up sales from existing *World Book* customers. Also that year, Field began publishing *The Childcraft Annual,* the *Childcraft* analogue of the *World Book Year Book.*

In addition to boosting profit centers, Field continued to improve its reference books during the 1970s. Importantly, *World Book* added a research guide/index volume to its revised 1972 edition. The new encyclopedia consisted of 22 volumes, and the in-depth index provided readers with an easy means of conducting independent research and cross-referencing different subjects. In 1975, moreover, *World Book* hopped on the metric bandwagon, adding metric equivalents to virtually all of the measurements in the *World Book.*

Three years later, Field's reference book operations were purchased by the Scott Fetzer Company, which renamed the division World Book-Childcraft International before changing the name to World Book, Inc. in 1983. A diversified conglomerate, Fetzer was founded in 1914 as a manufacturer of automobile parts. In 1919, the company switched to producing vacuum cleaners and remained a single-product firm until the mid-

1960s, when it started to diversify. In the 1980s, another diversified conglomerate, Berkshire Hathaway Inc., purchased Scott Fetzer. By the early 1990s, Fetzer was operating more than 20 different companies organized in five business groups, ranging from industrial equipment and vacuum cleaners to encyclopedias.

Although growth in sales of reference books to schools had begun to slow by the late 1970s as the baby boom generation aged, the World Book operations had become one of the largest general encyclopedia publishers in the world by the time Fetzer acquired it. And, by the time the baby boom generation started sending their own kids to school in the 1980s, *World Book* was the most popular encyclopedia in the world, outselling the venerable *Encyclopedia Britannica* by a margin of three-to-one. The company also boasted the world's largest educational direct sales force, with more than 60,000 people, many of whom worked part-time. Moreover, the company was publishing its *Childcraft* series in about a dozen languages and shipping to more than 50 countries around the globe.

Under Fetzer's direction, World Book continued to innovate and improve its publications. Between the mid-1980s and early 1990s, the company introduced several new publications and related educational products. In 1987, for example, World Book started selling an international edition of *Childcraft.* The following year, an extensively revised *World Book* was introduced with 22 volumes and more than 10,000 new color illustrations. In 1992, moreover, World Book launched an international edition of *World Book,* targeted toward English-speaking nations outside of North America.

In addition to bolstering its core publications, World Book brought out some completely new books. In 1990, for example, it introduced *Young Scientist,* a multi-volume set of science-oriented books for children. The set was based on the principles that had guided *World Book* and *Childcraft* for so many years: ease-of-use and accuracy. World Book also began publishing *World Book Encyclopedia of Science,* an eight-volume encyclopedia for young readers in both the institutional and home markets. Other World Book products included: *The World Book Atlas*; *The World Book of People and Places*; the *Early World of Learning* books and products designed for young children; and a range of complementary learning books, videos, and products designed for the youth educational market.

World Book's product diversification during the 1980s and early 1990s reflected a response to slow growth in core encyclopedia markets. Encyclopedia sales had begun to decline in the late 1980s. In fact, domestic encyclopedia sales at both World Book and Britannica, the two industry leaders, plunged about 50 percent during the late 1980s and early 1990s according to some industry sources. Analysts disagreed as to the cause of the drop-off, but many speculated that the rise of the personal computer had something to do with it. Indeed, rather than purchasing encyclopedia sets, segments of both the home and school markets were choosing to funnel money into electronic learning devices, namely computers, which offered more flexibility and were of increasing interest to young people.

In response to surging markets for electronic information, both World Book and Britannica introduced computer products in the late 1980s and early 1990s. Among other CD-ROM products, World Book introduced its *Illustrated Information Finder,* which contained the entire *World Book* text, 3,000 pictures and 260 maps, as well as thousands of definitions from *The World Book Dictionary.* In 1995, an enhanced *Information Finder* was renamed *The World Book Multimedia Encyclopedia,* which, in addition to the existing features, included animation, video, and audio to make research more informative and exciting. While emerging computer technologies represented an obvious threat to World Book's traditional print business, they also offered potential opportunities. In fact, multimedia systems offered the same advantages that World Book had striven to perfect through its books; multimedia made the reference works easier to access and, because of video and sound, were much more informative and interesting to the user.

Although the company was entering a transition period into an industry environment more focused on electronic technology, World Book nevertheless remained dedicated to its original intent: providing useful, interesting educational tools to young people. Entering the mid-1990s, the company was shipping over one-and-a-half million printed annuals and updates each year and selling its books in over a dozen languages in more than 50 countries on six continents.

Principal Subsidiaries: World Book Direct Marketing; World Book Educational Products; World Book Financial Services; World Book International; World Book Publishing.

Further Reading:

Goerne, Carrie, ''Publishers Offer Novels, Encyclopedias in Computer Versions,'' *Marketing News,* February 17, 1992, p. 6.

Harris, Roger, ''World Book Encyclopedia Campaign Targets Employers,'' *Business First-Louisville,* September 5, 1994, p. 12.

Langberg, Mike, ''CD-ROM Technology Poses Challenge for Encyclopedia Industry,'' *Knight-Ridder/Tribune Business News,* June 26, 1994.

Toney, Ellen, ''Pam Picou's World is World Book,'' *Morning Advocate,* August 22, 1993.

Trivette, Don, ''Electronic Encyclopedias Merge Text, High-Res Visuals, and Sound,'' *PC Magazine,* September 25, 1990, p. 537.

—Dave Mote

World Color Press Inc.

101 Park Avenue
New York, New York 10178
U.S.A.
(212) 986-2440
Fax: (212) 455-9266

Wholly Owned Subsidiary of Printing Holdings L.P.
Incorporated: 1903 as World Color Printing Company
Employees: 6,454
Sales: $838 million
SICs: 2721 Periodicals; 2741 Miscellaneous Publishing; 2754
   Commercial Printing Gravure; 2759 Printing, Not
   Elsewhere Classified

World Color Press Inc. is the largest printer of consumer magazines in the United States and the third largest commercial printer in North America. Headquartered in New York, World Color Press operates 17 production, distribution, and sales facilities throughout the country and is recognized as a leader in various segments of the printing industry. The company's core business is magazine printing; contracts with hundreds of leading periodicals, including *U.S. News & World Report, Cosmopolitan, Rolling Stone,* and *Forbes,* accounted for approximately half of the company's 1993 revenues. While fostering its long-term relationships with most of the major publication companies in the United States, the printing giant—second only to R.R. Donnelley & Sons in the United States—has expanded its operations into a number of specialty services. Catalog printing contracts, from Sears to Victoria's Secret, generated more than a fifth of total revenues in 1993 and represented the company's fastest growing division. World Color Press and its subsidiaries are also engaged in the business of printing various commercial products, including annual reports, brochures, direct mail and newspaper inserts, and directories, while also providing customers with a broad range of pre-press services, such as desktop production and assembly.

World Color Press was founded in 1903 when the owners of the St. Louis *Star* formed a company to handle the color printing for the Louisiana Purchase Exposition, the World's Fair to be held in their city the following year. They named their wholly owned subsidiary World's Fair Color Printing, expecting to disband operations at the conclusion of the event. After the fair closed, however, they shortened the company name to World Color

Printing and continued to do business as a commercial printer, focusing on a new and unique product, the color "funnies" section of the Sunday newspaper. Under the leadership of Robert Grable and Roswell Messing Sr., two senior employees from the *Star* who purchased the company in 1922, the fledgling organization grew steadily over the next two decades as the popularity of the Sunday color comic section increased. By the early 1930s, the company's profitable niche business had grown to include printing contracts with papers from Florida to Hawaii.

While the demand for Sunday comics sustained the company in its early years, the funnies were quickly evolving into a virtual institution in American popular culture, and more and more large metropolitan papers began printing their own comic supplements. For World Color to continue to grow, it had to diversify. To that end, the company made its first major acquisition in 1928, purchasing another St. Louis-based printer, Commercial Color Press, which specialized in printing weekly newspapers and circulars. The addition of these products helped the company to survive the Great Depression years of the early 1930s.

World Color Press did not, however, abandon its interest in Sunday comic strips; rather, it sought to present them in a new form. Company management attempted to maximize profits by reprinting the funnies in magazine format, creating the prototype for the first comic book. While the initial comic books were simply collections of previously published editions of the Sunday funnies, by 1936 they contained original material. World Color Press, in creating its first specialty market, had invented the modern day comic book. The company made the most of the idea and quickly emerged as the leading printer in this new field. Comic book sales boomed during World War II and the postwar period; comic magazines were easily the most popular form of newsstand magazine on the market. To keep up with the ever increasing demand for comic books, the company began construction on a satellite plant in Sparta, Illinois. The state-of-the-art production facility opened in 1948 and was designed to be the most technologically advanced plant in the industry devoted solely to the printing of comic magazines. "The success of this undertaking," stated Robert Ynostroza in *Graphic Arts Monthly,* "might be measured by the fact that within five years World Color Press became the largest producer of comic magazines in the industry."

While maintaining its position as the nation's leading producer of comic books through the 1940s and 1950s, World Color Press took advantage of monumental developments in printing and distribution technology. In 1956, the company helped lead the industry into the modern era of print technology by installing one of the first web-offset presses in its Sparta plant. This innovative printing process, in which rolls or "webs" of paper were fed through rubber-blanketed cylinders producing tens of thousands of impressions an hour, enabled the company to diversify into another relatively new and untested product line: the web-offset printed newsstand and special interest magazine.

Equally important to the company's growth during the 1950s was its development of the pool shipping concept—a method of distribution in which publications from different customers going to the same destination were shipped together, reducing freight costs and increasing the timeliness of deliveries. By establishing the first major pool shipping network to newsstands, the company was able to expand its customer base by offering the lowest distribution costs in the industry—a claim which continued to be a major selling point for the company.

Several additions to the Sparta plant underscored the success of the company's marketing strategy and suggested the need for a new production facility. In 1969, the company started construction at Effingham, Illinois, approximately 120 miles northeast of Sparta. The new web-offset facility was designed initially to produce newsstand and special interest magazines printed on coated paper with extensive use of "four-color," or multicolor, technology. The higher quality product line proved successful, leading to a 1971 expansion of the Effingham plant that nearly doubled its original size. With the addition came another transition for the company: the capability to produce large-circulation monthly magazines printed on letter-press equipment.

The 1960s also saw the company continue to lead the industry in technological advancement by initiating the computerization of many aspects of its business. With the advent of the computer age came not only more efficient production and distribution, but the capability to perform more complicated printing procedures and reproduce more complex data. Implementing the new technology, of course, required large amounts of capital, which was supplied by City Investing, a large New York-based diversified company that purchased World Color Press in 1968. With the strong financial backing needed to support equipment purchases and plant expansion, World Color had succeeded in capturing the majority share of the comic and newsstand special-interest publication market by the early 1970s.

With the added emphasis on higher quality publications came the need to increase the company's flexibility in scheduling presses. In 1970, the company decided to standardize the make and type of its presses. While the rest of the industry relied largely on the services of 23 ⁹/₁₆″ presses with combination folders, World Color Press opted for the 23 ¾″ cutoff and double former folders. The shorter cutoff gave the company's production managers the option to perform printing or binding jobs on any of several comparable lines of equipment. In the short term, though, the new production philosophy meant that the company was unable to bid on many magazines. Nevertheless, the bold decision—96 percent of presses the company purchased during the 1970s had the shorter cutoff—paid off in the long term. "Publishers soon reacted favorably to the paper savings, consistent quality, schedule flexibility and the economies of a standard lineup of presses with two-former folders and common auxiliaries," according to a 1986 *Graphic Arts Monthly* article.

The switch to the shorter cutoff presses enabled the company to become a stronger competitor in the four-color, high quality magazine market. To facilitate this shift of focus, the company purchased Fawcett Printing of Louisville, Kentucky, in 1974. The acquisition enabled World Color Press to add another printing process to its repertoire of services: rotogravure, a method in which the printing image was recessed and filled with ink while its surroundings remained free from ink. Shortly after the

purchase, company management decided to bring the gravure plant closer to its letterpress facility, moving the Fawcett plant's personnel and equipment to southern Illinois. In 1975, the company expanded its gravure division with the construction of Salem Gravure, located approximately half-way between Effingham and Sparta. Several additions to the 610,000 square-foot plant in the late 1970s enabled the company to handle more complex gravure printing tasks. As the company continued to attract more magazine publishers, it again expanded its operations to keep up with the growing demand, adding a new plant in Des Plaines, Illinois, in 1980.

By the beginning of the 1980s, the company had emerged as the recognized leader in the printing and distribution of consumer publications. By 1982, sales had reached more than $371 million. "World Color's rapid climb to success," wrote *Graphic Arts Monthly*'s Jody Estabrook, can be traced "to several bold management decisions involving a customer-oriented market strategy backed by sophisticated printing equipment." Just as the company distinguished itself from the competition by changing the size of its presses a few years earlier, it also predicted yet another downsizing trend in magazine trim sizes and changed its presses accordingly, installing shorter cutoff presses in 1983. During this time, the company also broadened its revenue base by expanding its product line to include telephone directories, weekly magazines, coupon inserts, and freestanding inserts. By 1985, the corporation's sales team had added 1,000 printing contracts for other-than-monthly publications to its still growing list of more than 200 monthly titles, such as *Good Housekeeping, McCalls,* and *TV Guide.* That year, World Color Press was listed as the fourth largest printer in North America, with sales totalling $544 million, more than a 29 percent jump from the previous year.

During the 1980s, the company also added seven state-of-the-art plants to service the printing needs of its rapidly expanding customer base. The facilities, strategically located throughout the United States, were equipped to offer its customers improvements on its existing printing and binding capabilities, as well as improvements in pre-press services and pool mailing and shipping services. World Color Press also continued to lead the industry in implementing computer technology into its machinery. For instance, in the mid-1980s, the company developed an automatic magazine collating system driven by programmable control technology. Joseph A. Hattrup, an electrical engineer writing for *Graphic Arts Monthly,* summarized some of the features of the technology at the company's Sparta, Illinois plant: "The system is designed to automatically do the job of counting magazines, assembling them into various count bundles, affixing mail labels, wrapping the bundles with heat-shrinkable plastic, and sorting the bundles according to zip code regions for mailing purposes." Each collator, Hattrup added, "has the capability of discharging over 500 magazines per minute, or more than 175,000 per eight-hour shift." With this innovative system in use, World Color Press was able to strengthen its reputation for providing low distribution costs.

As the company moved into the 1990s, it continued to follow its strategy of diversified growth through acquisitions and grew to become a top competitor in several new markets. In January 1993, the company purchased widely respected catalog/direct mail printer Alden Press for an estimated $110 million. Having contracts with such mail order giants as Victoria's Secret, Coach Leatherware, and Sundance, Alden was expected to boost revenues significantly. As Robert Burton, who took over as World Color's chief executive in 1991, stated in the *Delaney Report,* "We're $650 million in revenues now, and we're shooting to be $2 billion in a couple of years." Another step towards that goal was taken in December of that year when World Color Press acquired California's third largest printer, George Rice & Sons, for $86 million. This purchase, combined with the acquisition of Chicago's Bradley Printing two years earlier, bolstered the company's revenue base in the commercial printing industry. As Burton explained in *Printing Impressions* magazine, "This acquisition will add to World Color's already formidable capabilities in the printing of annual reports, advertising and marketing materials, automotive and travel destination brochures."

Equally important to World Color's growth strategy in the 1990s was its renewed commitment to printing technology. With the financial backing of its parent company since 1984, Kohlberg Kravis Roberts & Co.—an investments giant that maintained a significant interest in such well-known companies as Duracell, RJR Nabisco, and Safeway Stores—World Color Press invested $500 million in technology and training in the early 1990s. One of the more notable expenditures was for installing the Opti-Copy RegiStar digital registration system. In 1990, World Color's Salem division became one of the first publication printers to utilize the innovative prepress process in which digital technology and computer memory were used to match, or "register and punch," the colors from a full-color negative. "The obvious benefit to having this built-in quality control system," suggested Estabrook, "is the fact that identifying and correcting for problems in color registration does not have to wait till a plate or cylinder is already on the press." By identifying problems at the beginning of the prepress operation, the RegiStar system saved the company time, material, and money.

Advertising itself as "the printer with ideas that go beyond the printed page," World Color has also garnered a reputation for utilizing the most environmentally conscious printing techniques available. The company's telephone directories division, for instance, pioneered the use of the flexographic printing process. This unique application of flexography—a rotary letterpress process utilizing flexible plates and fast-drying inks—enhanced the vibrancy of color in yellow page advertisements, while reducing ink rub and eliminating the harmful VOC emissions in both white and yellow page sections. In a similar fashion, the company's publication and catalog divisions ushered in the industry's use of a special bimetal printing plate that, while providing greater flexibility in processing and increased control over variables on the press, offered fully recy-

clable chemistry. Long noted for its professionalism as well as its attention to environmental concerns, World Color Press came to the aid of one of its major competitors, R.R. Donnelley & Sons, in January 1995, printing 300,000 issues of *People* magazine for the printing giant after flood waters had forced the closing of a Donnelley plant near Los Angeles.

Under Burton's direction, World Color Press positioned itself favorably in several markets within the printing industry. With services ranging from desktop publishing and digital imaging to computerized marketing and distribution, the company hoped to strengthen its hold on the magazine publications market. Its most promising area of growth, however, was expected to be in catalog and commercial publishing, where in just a few years the company became a major competitor. With such reputable companies as Bradley, Alden, and George Rice under the World Color umbrella, revenues were expected to surpass the $1 billion milestone sometime in the mid-1990s. Furthermore, according to one analyst quoted in *Buyouts* magazine, the possibility that World Color would soon go public is "a pretty good bet." Regardless of this potential development, the company planned to continue expanding its operations. As Burton stated in the *Delaney Report,* "We're going to continue to look to diversify our revenue lines. We want to increase our business in catalogs and directories. And we'll continue our focus on magazines. When contracts come up, we'll go after them aggressively."

Principal Subsidiaries: Alden Press; Bradley Printing; George Rice & Sons; Midwest Litho Arts; Network Color Technology; Universal Graphics; Web Inserts.

Further Reading:

Estabrook, Jody, "Market Strategy is Client-Oriented," *Graphic Arts Monthly,* May 1990, pp. 126–130.
"Forgiving Plate Aids Processing," *Graphic Arts Monthly,* December 1993, p. 64.
Hattrup, Joseph A., "Programmable Controllers in the Magazine Bindery," *Graphic Arts Monthly,* June 1985, pp. 91–92.
"Hot Presses," *Delaney Report,* January 25, 1993.
"KKR's World Color Sets Another Acquisition," *Buyouts,* December 6, 1993.
"To Our Readers," *People,* January 23, 1995, p. 4.
"The Top Printing Companies in North America," *Graphic Arts Monthly,* October 1983 and December 1985.
"World Color Shortens Cutoff," *Graphic Arts Monthly,* May 1986, p. 54.
"World Color to Buy George Rice & Sons," *Printing Impressions,* January 1994, p. 5.
Ynostroza, Roger, "The Colorful World of World Color Press," *Graphic Arts Monthly,* June 1978, pp. 56–58.

—Jason Gallman

Ziff Communications Company

1 Park Ave.
New York, New York 10016
U.S.A.
(212) 503-3500
Fax: (212) 503-4599

Private Company
Incorporated: 1927
Employees: 2,573
Sales: $925 million
SICs: 2721 Periodicals; 2731 Book Publishing; 2741
   Miscellaneous Publishing

Ziff Communications Company was a major force in American magazine publishing for more than 65 years. The company initially prospered through the publication of specialty consumer magazines, then branched out into business niche publications. After selling 24 of these titles at the peak of their popularity in two separate 1985 deals for more than $700 million, Ziff Communications successfully refocused itself on the burgeoning computer magazine niche, including such landmark titles as *PC Magazine.* The company also diversified into computer trade shows and exhibits through its Ziff-Davis Exhibitions subsidiary, database and CD-ROM publishing through the acquisition of Information Access Company and other companies, and the emerging online publishing realm with Ziffnet and the Interchange Online Network. With the family owners wishing to pursue other interests, the company was sold in 1994 in four separate deals totaling more than $2 billion.

Although the name Ziff Communications Company was not used until much later, the company was effectively founded in 1927—initially as Popular Aviation Company, becoming Ziff-Davis Publishing Company shortly thereafter. Founded by majority partner William B. Ziff, World War I flyer, author, and lecturer, and minority partner Bernard Davis, the company launched a line of hobby and leisure magazines with *Popular Aviation* (still published today as *Aviation*). During the early years, the company grew at a tremendous rate (32 times its initial size in its first ten years), publishing a combination of reference, trade, and juvenile books; "pulp" magazines such as *Amazing Stories, Air Adventures, Mammoth Detective, Mammoth Mystery,* and *Mammoth Western;* and specialty consumer magazines such as *Modern Bride, Popular Aviation,*

Popular Electronics, and *Radio News.* Although the company was successful with most of its various publishing ventures, William Ziff never devoted his full attention to the business, preferring to focus on his writing, flying, and other interests, so Davis effectively handled day-to-day operations. By the early 1950s, the company was losing money.

When Ziff died of a heart attack in 1953, his share in the company passed to his son, William B. Ziff, Jr., then 24 and a student of philosophy. He surprised his family by deciding to give up his promising academic career to run Ziff-Davis. Unlike his father, he immediately immersed himself in the business, buying out Davis in 1956. He concentrated on expanding the company's specialty consumer line by aggressively acquiring additional niche magazines. His timing was perfect in that the arrival of television as *the* medium for mass communication spelled the downturn for general-interest magazines like *Life* and *Saturday Evening Post.* Ziff's response to television was to focus on publications that were tightly focused on narrow topics, giving readers specialized information they could obtain nowhere else and providing advertisers an audience tailored for their products. Over the next 30 years, Ziff-Davis acquired such titles as *Car and Driver, Popular Mechanics, Psychology Today,* and *Stereo Review,* identifying each as the market leader in its particular field or one that Ziff-Davis could move into that position.

Meanwhile Ziff recognized another lucrative area for growth through the acquisition of what *Newsweek* called "obscure but highly profitable trade publications." Similar to Ziff's consumer titles, these business journals were each targeted at a narrow audience, primarily people in the travel and aviation industries for whom the titles became must-reading. The titles included *Business & Commercial Aviation, Hotel & Travel Index, Travel Weekly, World Aviation Directory,* and the flagship of the group, *Meetings & Conventions,* which by 1983 generated $12 million in annual revenues.

In 1969 Ziff formed the Ziff Communications Company and made Ziff-Davis one of its divisions. At this time, he transferred ownership through trust funds to his three sons, who held a 90 percent interest, and three nephews, who held the remaining 10 percent. Ziff himself remained in firm control of the company throughout this period as chairman, with a hands-on management style criticized by some insiders and outside observers as autocratic but difficult to question given the company's continued profitability.

Besides innovation in developing special interest magazines, Ziff Communications also pioneered in its approaches to market research and advertising. Through heavy expenditures on market research, the company gathered detailed profiles of who was reading each magazine, the content they sought, and the advertising to which they might respond. This data helped each editor tailor his or her magazine to the readership and enabled the advertising salespeople to precisely target potential clients. The market research data was also shared with the advertisers themselves to design campaigns in what was known as "consultative selling." Another advertising innovation was offering clients discounts for placing the same ad in a group of related magazines. By 1984, these strategies had fueled the company's continuing growth, with the group of Ziff consumer magazines alone posting estimated annual revenues of $140 million.

According to many observers, Ziff had become bored with the business and with his success when in the early 1980s he began to take Ziff Communications into new territory. In 1979 he spent $89 million to purchase Rust Craft Greeting Cards Incorporated for its six television stations, but within a few years he sold them for $100 million, saying that television was not the "turn-on" he had hoped for. A longer-lasting and eventually more successful foray was into a new area of specialty publishing: computer magazines. The initial titles in this line, such as *PCjr,* were developed in-house beginning in 1981, but Ziff soon returned to its acquisition strategy, most notably through the purchase of *PC Magazine* in 1982. The beginning years for these magazines were difficult, however, as the boom in the computer industry spawned a boom in the publication of specialty computer magazines. Although most of these titles were losing money in the early 1980s, the losses eventually represented an investment that was recouped many times over. Similarly, another new Ziff venture at this time was a "bleeding edge" 1980 acquisition of Information Access Company (IAC), a pioneer in electronic publishing and one of the first companies to produce databases on CD-ROM, including *Magazine Index, National Newspaper Index,* and *Trade and Industry Index.* IAC designed its InfoTrac workstations that accessed these databases to be user-friendly and offered full text on some of them, providing a competitive advantage over other indexes that offered only article abstracts.

Meanwhile, Ziff's consumer and business publications were reaching their peak of success. By 1984, many of these magazines were the circulation and/or revenue leaders in their respective markets. *Car & Driver* outpaced *Road & Track, Popular Photography* was the top choice for photographers, and *Cycle* lead *Cycle World* for motorcyclists. Annual revenue for the most part was increasing. For example, *Car & Driver* posted $33 million in revenue in 1983, a gain of 18.6 percent over the previous year. The business publications were in similarly strong positions as market leaders—with $12 million in 1983 revenue for *Meetings & Conventions,* an increase of 20.5 percent—and enjoyed particularly high margins. Many in the industry were surprised, then, by the October 1984 announcement that Ziff was placing 24 magazines up for sale, 12 in its consumer group and 12 in its business group. Rumors soon began to circulate that William Ziff, Jr., was becoming progressively more ill with prostate cancer and wished to simplify his estate and protect his family's future. His three sons were 14, 18, and 20.

After much speculation about possible purchasers, receipt of a variety of bids (for the whole lot, for one group or the other, and for individual magazines), and estimates that Ziff would receive between $300 million and $750 million for all 24 titles, CBS Inc. announced on November 20, 1984, that it had reached agreement with Ziff to purchase the complete consumer group for $362.5 million, thought to be a record at the time for the sale of a group of magazines. The very next day, Rupert Murdoch announced that he had bought the entire business group for $350 million. Following these sales, Ziff Communications was essentially reduced to its computer magazines and IAC—none

of which were offered in the auction, in part because their financial situations were less robust.

William Ziff, Jr., reduced his role in the operation of Ziff Communications for the next few years as he successfully battled against cancer. How closely the fortunes of the company were tied to his involvement is evident from the company's struggles during these years: 1985 saw the company post a loss of $10 million on $100 million in revenue. With his cancer in remission, he returned to full-time leadership of the company in 1987 and oversaw a second application of the Ziff formula for special interest publishing, this time fueling a growth spurt through the computer magazines left out of the 1984 sale. Like the business niche publications so recently sold, the computing publications developed and acquired by Ziff targeted a specific audience needing help with their purchase decisions—buyers of personal computers in the business world. Such magazines as *PC Magazine* and *MacUser* thus focused tightly on product specifications, evaluations, and recommendations from the editors. Using similar market research and advertising techniques honed through the company's decades of innovative magazine publishing, Ziff's line of computer magazines soon began to dominate the industry. By 1991, *PC Magazine* boasted a circulation of more than 800,000, more than $160 million in advertising revenue, and a ranking as the tenth-largest U.S. magazine.

There were some failures along the way as well. Contributing to them was the development of significant competitors in the computer magazine industry, notably International Data Group (IDG), publisher of *InfoWorld* and *PC World,* and CMP Publications, publisher of *VAR Business* and *Windows Magazine.* Ziff had acquired *Government Computer News* in 1986 and invested heavily in it, but finally surrendered to IDG and its competitive title when it sold the magazine to Cahners Publishing. Among Ziff's start-ups that failed were *PCjr*—one of the first Ziff computer magazines—and *Corporate Computing.* The latter was launched with great fanfare early in 1992 and positioned as the one magazine for executives needing to make computer purchases. To meet its objective, it had to cover all bases from personal computers to networks to mainframes. At the time, however, the business market was shifting toward personal computers and thus right back to the strength of Ziff's other magazines. Feeling that *Corporate Computing* was beginning to compete with the flagship *PC Magazine,* as well as *PC Week,* the company folded the title just over one year after launch, having invested $10 million in it.

With the increasing competition leading to a slowing of the growth in advertising revenue generated by the magazines, Ziff Communications reacted with three strategies. First, to lessen reliance on the U.S. market, Ziff launched an ambitious line of European computer magazines early in 1991. The second response was to move beyond the corporate computing world, said by some observers to be maturing, into home computing, which was viewed as the next big growth area. In another combination of organic and acquired growth, the company purchased *Computer Gaming World* and launched two new titles in 1994—*Computer Life* and *Family PC,* the latter in a joint venture with Walt Disney. The third area was a recommitment to electronic publishing through IAC and the development of online systems.

From the mid-1980s IAC had continued to expand, and by 1992 the company was the leader in full text with more than two million articles culled from more than one thousand sources. The sheer amount of information offered through the products spun out of its databases began about this time to run up against the limits of CD-ROM technology. One option—almost a stop-gap measure—offered to large libraries having large enough mainframes was to mount the database directly on it for patrons to access via the terminals used to access the library's catalog. The longer-term solution that IAC began to implement in 1993 was dubbed InfoTrac Central 2000 and allowed libraries to have their patrons access the IAC databases directly via the Internet.

IAC, whose strength had traditionally rested in the library market, now sought ways to achieve a longstanding goal of lessening the company's dependence on its main market. It formed a new Consumer/Educational division to target the home market, and it increased its presence in the corporate market through acquisitions. In 1991 it acquired Predicasts Inc., whose databases included *PROMT*—a competitor of IAC's *Trade and Industry Index*. In 1994 IAC acquired Sandpoint, which had developed a software application called Hoover designed to run on Lotus Notes, a groupware application that was becoming increasing popular with corporations. Hoover was an interface like InfoTrac, but a much more powerful one since it allowed a user to access information from many different types of platforms, from CD-ROMs to online systems to broadcast news sources (the name was derived from its being a vacuum cleaner for information). Users of Hoover would also find a system more flexible in the different ways it allowed users to access information. By 1994, there were 16,000 users of Hoover at 70 companies.

Further electronic publishing initiatives in the early 1990s were highlighted by the development of the Interchange Online Network. The company had successfully tested the online services market over several years with Ziffnet, which was an online extension of its computer magazines offered through such services as CompuServe and Prodigy. Interchange was designed as an online service of its own and promised to be the first one to fully implement a graphical-user interface (GUI). True to Ziff tradition, it was designed to be a special interest service as opposed to the existing general-interest services. The first interest area to be developed was, predictably, computers, but plans were made to develop areas including sports, health, and personal finance. Interchange would offer more than simply electronic text of magazines, adding such features as discussion groups, product information, and reference sources. As the Internet and the "information superhighway" became household names in the early 1990s, Interchange represented Ziff's claim to its piece of the multi-billion dollar digital information market.

Late in 1993, as revenue for Ziff Communications approached $1 billion, William Ziff, Jr., announced that he was retiring as chairman of the company and would have only an advisory role in the future as chairman emeritus. Eric Hippeau, who had already been in charge of all operations except corporate finance as chairman and CEO of Ziff-Davis Publishing, now assumed full control of Ziff Communications as chairman. That an outsider was placed in charge of what had always been a family-run business was telling to some observers who predicted that the company would either be sold or go public, but such rumors were denied for several months, with Ziff pointing out that two of his sons and one nephew were vice presidents at the company. Nevertheless, within months, in June 1994, the company announced that it had hired Lazard Freres & Company to handle the sale of the company, seeking $2 billion or more. The decision to sell stemmed from William Ziff's sons wishes not to make the company their career. The two brothers who had been vice presidents at the company, Dirk and Robert, wished to invest the proceeds from the sale in their investment company, Ziff Brothers Investments. The third brother, Daniel, was a college student at this time.

At the time of the sale, the company was the unquestioned leader in computer magazine publishing and a leading electronic information provider through IAC. In 1994 the company expected a profit of $160 million on $950 million in revenue. Still, some observers thought that William Ziff was again selling out at a time when the company's most prized possessions—the computer publications—were past their peak. Others, however, pointed to numbers showing that the business magazine group (all the U.S. computer magazines except those aimed at consumers) alone was expecting revenues of $505 million and $146 million in operating income in 1994. The figures did show that Ziff's other units were either marginally profitable or losing money, in many cases from heavy investing in new ventures like the new consumer magazines and the Interchange system. In the end, these variances in the divisions, perhaps coupled with the enormity of the company, forced the sellers to accept a piecemeal sale rather than a sale of the whole company as they hoped for. First, the New York investment firm of Forstmann Little & Co. purchased Ziff-Davis Publishing Co.—the business and consumer computer magazines, the international magazine group, a market research division, and the Ziffnet online service—for $1.4 billion. Ziff-Davis Exhibitors, a unit that managed computer trade shows, was bought by Softbank of Japan for $202 million, and the Thomson Corporation, a huge Canadian publisher, purchased Information Access Company for $465 million. Finally, in December 1994 AT&T purchased the Interchange Online Network, at the time still undergoing final testing, for $50 million. All told, the sales totaled more than $2.1 billion.

While a final chapter was thus concluded in the fascinating history of Ziff Communications Company, the legacy of William Ziff, Jr., and his innovative approaches to magazine publishing and information distribution, were certain to continue to influence the operation of the now-scattered Ziff units. Ziff-Davis in particular seemed positioned to continue to follow the Ziff practice of special-interest publishing, as Forstmann Little said it would continue with the same management team, including chairman Eric Hippeau, and unaltered editorial content.

Further Reading:

Carmody, Deirdre, "Forstmann to Acquire Ziff-Davis," *New York Times,* October 28, 1994, pp. D1–D2.

Churbuck, David C., "Motivated Seller," *Forbes 400,* October 17, 1994, pp. 350–54.

Fabrikant, Geraldine, "For a Ziff Sale, Spit and Polish and Good Timing," *New York Times,* September 9, 1994, pp. D1–D2.

——, "For Ziffs, Sale Is a Family Affair," *New York Times,* June 10, 1994, pp. 37, 46.

Johnson, Bradlye, "Wm. Ziff Retires, but His Company Stays in Family," *Advertising Age,* November 23, 1993, p. 22.

Kleinfield, N. R., "The Big Magazine Auction," *New York Times,* November 16, 1994, pp. D1, D3.

——, "CBS to Buy 12 of Ziff's Magazines," *New York Times,* November 21, 1984, pp. D1, D3.

Landler, Mark, "Auctioning off an Empire," *Business Week,* June 27, 1994, p. 27.

Levison, Andrew, "Ziff-Davis: For Sale," *Online,* September/October 1994, pp. 31–38.

Palmeri, Christopher, " 'The Idea that Print Is Dead Is Preposterous'," *Forbes,* June 10, 1991, pp. 42–44.

Wayne, Leslie, "Murdoch Buys 12 Ziff Publications," *New York Times,* November 22, 1984, pp. D1, D13.

Weber, Jonathan, "Mogul for a New Age: Bill Ziff's Media Empire Is Built on High Tech—and High Standards," *Los Angeles Times,* October 10, 1993, p. D1.

"Ziff Announces New Online Service and Next-Generation Publishing Platform," *Business Wire,* January 24, 1944.

—David E. Salamie

ZIONS BANCORPORATION

Zions Bancorporation

1380 Kennecott Bldg.
Salt Lake City, Utah 84133
U.S.A.
(801) 524-4787
Fax: (801) 524-2129

Public Company
Incorporated: 1955 as Keystone Insurance and Investment
   Co.
Employees: 2,574
Total Assets: $4.4 billion
Stock Exchanges: NASDAQ
SICs: 6021 National Commercial Banks; 6022 State
   Commercial Banks; 6712 Bank Holding Companies

Zions Bancorporation is the second largest multibank holding
company in Utah. Through its various subsidiaries, the Salt
Lake City-based Zions provides a full range of banking and
related services primarily in Utah, Arizona, and Nevada. Its
primary holding is Zions First National Bank based in Salt Lake
City. The company has grown quickly since the early 1990s by
acquiring other banks and expanding existing operations.

Keystone Insurance and Investment Co., the precursor to Zions
Bancorporation, was incorporated in Utah in 1955 by a group of
investors for the purpose of acquiring the Lockhart Corporation.
In addition to Lockhart's financial holdings, during the next few
years Keystone purchased an insurance agency and about 120
acres of land in an industrial park. When Keystone went public
in 1960, it was worth about $2 million.

In 1960, a group of investors, the chief of which was Keystone,
purchased a controlling share of Zions First National Bank. A
holding company, Zions First National Investment Co., was
incorporated in Nevada to own the bank. The holding company's name was changed to Zions Utah Bancorporation in
1965. The holding company went public in 1966 when existing
stockholders sold their shares. In 1971 Zions Utah Bancorporation merged into Keystone, with Keystone becoming the surviving company. Keystone subsequently changed its name to
Zions Utah Bancorporation.

Zions chief holding, Zions First National Bank, was a leading
local bank in Salt Lake City. Prior to the buyout by Keystone
and its associates, the bank was principally owned by the Latter-

day Saints Church. Renowned Mormon leader Brigham Young
had started the bank in 1873 to serve the church and local
community. Throughout the late 1800s and through the mid-
1900s Zions had close ties to the Mormon Church, taking
deposits from, and providing loans to, church members, and
handling many of the church's financial transactions.

The group of investors that bought out the church's ownership
interest in First National in 1960 was Roy W. Simmons.
Simmons was a Mormon with a strong banking background.
Both his father and grandfather had worked in banking and had
served as officers of the competing First National Bank of
Layton, near Salt Lake City. Under Simmons's direction, First
National prospered during the 1960s and 1970s. Besides emphasizing its core Salt Lake City market, the bank expanded
into rural Utah and eventually amassed a regional network of
branches throughout the northern part of the state.

By the 1980s, First National had cemented a position as the
second largest banking organization in the state of Utah, earning
Simmons a reputation as a savvy banker and businessman.
"Roy has an uncanny knack for figures and sizing up a situation," Lawrence Adler, president of the Utah Bankers Association, told *Knight-Ridder/Tribune Business News.* "He's a
banker from the old school."

In addition to running one of the region's most successful banks
during the 1960s and 1970s, Simmons successfully helped raise
his family, sending four sons to Harvard. One of his sons,
Harris, would follow in the footsteps of the three generations
before him. Harris Simmons was born in 1955, about five years
before his father lead the buyout of First National and assumed
leadership of the bank. He began his banking career at age 16 as
a teller filing canceled checks. When he returned from Harvard,
he went to work with First National and was named assistant
vice president at Zions Utah Bancorporation in 1981.

Although Zions achieved steady gains during the 1960s and
1970s, it was during the 1980s that the bank would realize its
heady expansion. Zions' success was due in part to management
strategies and in part to trends in the banking industry. By the
late 1970s, banks began to feel competition from nonbank
financial institutions. The new competitors were vying for consumer dollars that had traditionally gone to bank deposits, and
were also competing as lenders and financiers. Because of
restrictive bank industry regulations passed through Congress in
the wake of a flurry of bank failures during the Depression era,
banks had been functioning at a disadvantage to their competitors. But during the mid 1960s and early 1970s, Congress
eliminated some of the restrictions and created a variety of
favorable tax incentives for specific banking activities. During
that period, a number of Bank holding companies like Zions
were created to take advantage of deregulation and to begin
participating in a number of nonbanking-related financial
markets.

Nevertheless, Zions and other banks suffered because of interstate banking restrictions. For example, General Motors was
free to offer consumer financing for its vehicles throughout the
United States, thus benefitting from various economies of scale.
In contrast, most of the activities of Zions and other bank
holding companies were confined to a single state or region. In

the mid 1980s, Congress allowed bank holding companies to engage in interstate banking. That legislation, combined with other banking industry dynamics, set the stage for a period of rampant growth that would double Zions's size by the mid-1990s.

By the time interstate banking regulations were loosened, the industry was already experiencing rapid consolidation. The new legislation only served to intensify the trend. The percentage of U.S. assets held by commercial banks dropped from about 37 percent in the late 1970s to 25 percent by the late 1980s. That reduction left many competitors scrambling for business. To survive, banks began merging to achieve economies of scale. The number of independent banking entities in the United States dropped from about 13,000 in 1983 to less than 10,000 by 1990. Meanwhile, the number of multi-bank holding companies like Zions grew from about 300 to around 1,000.

Augmenting the consolidation trend was the fact that computers and electronic banking devices were increasingly making it easier for banks like Zions to operate across broad regions. Thus, Zions's growth strategy in the 1980s was relatively straight forward. It wanted to acquire smaller competitors and integrate them in the Zions Utah Bancorporation system. Besides working to improve the performance of the banks it purchased, Zions's managers would reduce aggregate operating costs by amassing a large network of branches in a multi-state region. The savings would result from economies of scale related to marketing, reporting, and management overhead at the executive level.

Harris Simmons assumed his father's position of president of Zions Bancorporation in 1986. Roy Simmons became chairman of the company and retained his chief executive title. In January of 1986, Zions entered the Arizona banking market by opening a commercial loan branch of its Zions First National Bank in Phoenix. The branch started out with one man, Clark Hinckley, in a hotel room and expanded rapidly with Zions's financial backing. In October of 1986, Zions purchased Mesa Bank and changed the name of its Arizona operations to Zions First National Bank of Arizona. Zions added a third branch to its Arizona operations with the 1987 acquisition of Camel Bank. Also in 1987, the holding company shortened its name to Zions Bancorporation reflecting expansion efforts outside of Utah.

After adding millions of dollars of assets to its portfolio in Utah, Nevada, and Arizona, Zions Bancorporation seemed to be growing at a healthy clip going into the late 1980s. Unfortunately, souring commercial real estate markets and general economic malaise in the late 1980s hurt Zions and many other banks. But problems at Zions were compounded by a downturn in the local copper industry.

Though some of Zions's properties remained profitable, the company struggled through the late 1980s. Zions's Nevada and Arizona operations sustained profitability, generating combined earnings of about $1.8 million in 1986 and $2 million in 1987. In contrast, Zions of Utah stumbled. It posted a profit of $24 million in 1986, but then reported a loss of $14.1 million in 1987. The next year brought a loss of $17.9 million. The losses were so bad that Roy Simmons suspended his $191,000 chair-

man's salary in 1988 and cut his officer's pay. Nevertheless, Zions continued to pay dividends to its shareholders throughout the slump.

As many of its competitors became mired in nonperforming real estate loans, Zions recovered in 1989 as local markets perked up and its loan portfolio improved. Zions's net income rose to nearly $18 million, and the company stepped up its acquisition efforts. Because the banking industry was in such a slump during the early 1990s and capital was hard to come by, Zions was presented with several good investment opportunities. Harris Simmons became chief executive in 1991. Under his direction, the bank cautiously took advantage of several of those opportunities.

Among Zions's most notable acquisitions during the early 1990s was National Bancorp of Arizona, a $435 million institution based in Tuscon. That purchase made Zions the seventh largest banker operating in the state. Zions moved up a notch in the rankings with the subsequent purchase of $107 million Rio Salado Bancorp. That purchase gave Zions a total asset base of about $630 million in Arizona by 1993 and extended its reach into Phoenix, Tuscon, and Flagstaff. Although it emphasized expansion in Arizona, Zions added holdings in Utah, as well. Similarly, Zions expanded its Nevada State Bank in Las Vegas, increasing its total number of branches to 19 by early 1994.

Perhaps Zions's most interesting purchase during the early 1990s was Discount Corporation of New York, a dealer in U.S. government securities. Observers questioned the deal, but Simmons believed it was a shrewd move. ''I spent a couple of days explaining to analysts and stockholders that we weren't crazy,'' Simmons told *Knight-Ridder/Tribune Business News.* The subsidiary allowed Zions to begin repackaging and securitizing the loans that it made, rather than selling them in secondary markets. Most banks sell the home mortgages that they make to an investment house, which packages several mortgages and sells them as securities. The investment house makes money on the sales and the originating banks continue to make money servicing the loans. By bringing the securitizing process in-house, Zions was able to reap profits from both sides of the business. Discount Corporation made Zions one of only two primary dealers in government securities headquartered in the western United States. And it complemented Zions's expanding lending operations related to student loans, mortgages, credit card receivables, and other consumer financing.

The Discount Corporation acquisition revealed Simmons's penchant for innovation. For example, Zions was one of only a few lenders that had chased the accounts receivable lending business. Zions would extend credit to customers that was backed by the accounts receivables of their business. Viewing it as labor intensive, most banks shunned the niche. But Zions set up a separate division to serve the market, and found much new business in the mid-1990s. Another area where Zions was a recognized innovator was in opening branch offices in grocery stores. The bank was one of the first to begin securitizing small business loans.

Although Zions changed radically during the 1980s and early 1990s, one part of its business that did not change was its tie to the Mormon Church. Many people still thought of Zions as the

''Mormon Bank'' in the mid-1990s because of its long-time affiliation with the church. The church continued to be one of Zions's largest single customers. Zions had a separate ''missionary remittance office'' that handled electronic transfer funds to missionaries at the Mormon Church's 285 worldwide missions.

Besides expanding through acquisition, increasing its fee services, and innovating new profit centers, Zions achieved significant gains during the early 1990s by streamlining internal operations and tightening controls. The combined results of Zions's strategy was strong revenue growth and even greater profit gains, suggesting a bright future for the holding company. As Zions Bancorporation's asset base grew from $3 billion in 1989 to nearly $4.5 billion in 1993, the company's net income surged to $26.6 million in 1990 and to $53 million in 1993. By 1994, Zions was operating about 125 branches in its three states and was involved in negotiations to acquire other banks in Arizona and Utah. In addition, it provided insurance, data processing, credit, and consumer lending services through several subsidiaries.

Principal Subsidiaries: Nevada State Bank; Zions First National Bank; Zions First National Bank of Arizona.

Further Reading:

Anderson, Gary L., ''Corporate Profile for Zions Bancorporation,'' *Business Wire,* June 24, 1994.
Deters, Barbara, ''Salt Lake City, Utah, Bank Finds Plenty of Opportunity,'' *Knight-Ridder/Tribune Business News,* February 6, 1994.
Max, Jarman, ''Zions Pushing Receivables Loans,'' *Arizona Business Gazette,* November 22, 1991, sec. 1, p. 6.
O'Brien, Pat, ''Zions First Finds Niche Among Big Banks in Local Marketplace,'' *Business Journal-Phoenix & the Valley of the Sun,* July 18, 1988, sec. 1, p. 9.
Zions Bancorporation History, Salt Lake City: Zions Bancorporation, 1994.

—Dave Mote

INDEX TO COMPANIES AND PERSONS _____

Listings are arranged in alphabetical order under the company name; thus Eli Lilly & Company will be found under the letter E. Definite articles (The) and forms of incorporation that precede the name (A.B. and N.V.) are ignored for alphabetical purposes. Company names appearing in bold type have historical essays on the page numbers appearing in bold. Updates to entries that appeared in earlier volumes are signified by (upd.). The index is cumulative with volume numbers printed in bold type.

Agrico Chemical Company, **IV** 82, 84, 576; **7** 188
Agricultural Insurance Co., **III** 191
Agricultural Minerals Corp., **IV** 84
Agrifan, **II** 355
Agrigenetics Corp., **I** 361
Agrippina Versicherungs AG, **III** 403, 412
Agroferm Hungarian Japanese Fermentation Industry, **III** 43
AGTL. *See* Alberta Gas Trunk Line Company, Ltd.
Aguila (Mexican Eagle) Oil Co. Ltd., **IV** 657
Aguilo, Miguel, **6** 97
Agway, Inc., 7 17–18
Ahlman, Einar, **IV** 300
Ahman, Fritiof, **6** 87
Ahmanson. *See* H.F. Ahmanson & Company.
Ahmanson Bank, **II** 182
Ahmanson Bank and Trust Co., **II** 181
Ahmanson, Howard Fieldstead, **II** 181; **10** 342
Ahmanson Mortgage Co., **II** 182; **10** 343
Ahmanson Trust Co., **II** 182
Ahmanson, William A., **II** 181
Ahold's Ostara, **II** 641
AHP. *See* American Home Products.
Ahronovitz, Joseph, **II** 204
AHSC Holdings Corp., **III** 9–10
AIC. *See* Allied Import Comapny.
Aichi Bank, **II** 373
Aichi Kogyo Co., **III** 415
Aichi Steel Works, **III** 637
Aida Corporation, **11** 504
Aidekman, Alex, **II** 672–74
Aidekman, Ben, **II** 672
Aidekman, Sam, **II** 672
AIG Data Center, Inc., **III** 196
AIG Energy, **III** 197
AIG Entertainment, **III** 197
AIG Financial Products Corp., **III** 197
AIG Oil Rig, Inc., **III** 196–97
AIG Political Risk, **III** 197
AIG Risk Management, Inc., **III** 196
AIG Specialty Agencies, Inc., **III** 197
AIG Trading Corp., **III** 198
AIGlobal, **III** 197
Aiken, Edmund, **II** 284
Aikoku Sekiyu, **IV** 554
AIM Create Co., Ltd., **V** 127
Ainslie, Michael L., **9** 344
Air & Water Technologies Corporation, 6 441–42
Air Afrique, **9** 233
Air BP, **7** 141
Air Brasil, **6** 134
Air Canada, 6 60–62, 101; **12** 192
Air Co., **I** 298
Air Compak, **12** 182
Air France, **I** 93–94, 104, 110, 120; **II** 163; **6** 69, 95–96, 373; **8** 313; **12** 190
Air Inter, **6** 92–93; **9** 233
Air Lanka Catering Services Ltd., **6** 123–24
Air Liberté, **6** 208
Air Micronesia, **I** 97
Air Midwest, Inc., **11** 299
Air Nippon Co., Ltd., **6** 70
Air Products and Chemicals, Inc., I 297–99, 315, 358, 674; **10 31–33 (upd.); 11** 403
Air Reduction Co., **I** 297–98; **10** 31–32

Air Southwest Co. *See* Southwest Airlines Co.
Air Spec, Inc., **III** 643
Air-India, 6 63–64
Airborne Accessories, **II** 81
Airborne Express. *See* Airborne Freight Corp.
Airborne Express Japan, **6** 346
Airborne Freight Corp., 6 345–47 345
Airbus, **10** 164
Airbus Industrie, **6** 74; **7** 9–11, 504; **9** 418. *See also* G.I.E. Airbus Industrie.
AirCal, **I** 91
Aircraft Marine Products, **II** 7
Aircraft Services International, **I** 449
Aircraft Transport & Travel Ltd., **I** 92
Airlease International, **II** 422
Airmec-AEI Ltd., **II** 81
Airport Ground Service Co., **I** 104, 106
Airstream, **II** 468
Airtel, **IV** 640
AirTouch Communications, 10 118; **11 10–12**
Airtours International GmbH. and Co. K.G., **II** 164
Airways Housing Trust Ltd., **I** 95
Airwick, **II** 567
Airwork. *See* AirEgypt.
Aisin (Australia) Pty. Ltd., **III** 415
Aisin (U.K.) Ltd., **III** 415
Aisin America, Inc., **III** 415
Aisin Asia, **III** 415
Aisin Deutschland, **III** 415
Aisin do Brasil, **III** 415
Aisin Seiki Co., Ltd., III 415–16
Aisin U.S.A. Manufacturing Co., **III** 415
Aisin-Warner Ltd., **III** 415
Aitken, W. Max (Lord Beaverbrook), **III** 704; **IV** 208; **6** 585
AITS. *See* American International Travel Service.
Aivaz, Boris, **IV** 260
Aizu-Toko K.K., **II** 62
Ajax, **6** 349
Ajax Iron Works, **II** 16
Ajinomoto Co., Inc., II 463–64, 475; **III** 705
Ajinomoto Frozen Foods, **II** 463
Ajisaka, Mutsuya, **I** 636
Ajman Cement, **III** 760
Ajroldi, Paolo, **6** 47–48
Akane Securities Co. Ltd., **II** 443
Akashi, Teruo, **II** 325
Akashic Memories, **11** 234
Akema, Terayuki, **V** 727
Akerman, Jack, **IV** 685
Akers, John, **III** 149; **6** 252
Akiyama, Takesaburo, **II** 67
Akiyama, Tomiichi, **11** 477
AKO Bank, **II** 378
Akron Brass Manufacturing Co., **9** 419
Akron Corp., **IV** 290
Akseli Gallen-Kallela, **IV** 314
Aktiebolaget Aerotransport, **I** 119
Aktiebolaget Electrolux, **III** 478–81
Aktiebolaget SKF, III 622–25; IV 203
Aktiengesellschaft für Berg- und Hüttenbetriebe, **IV** 201
Aktiengesellschaft für Maschinenpapier-Zellstoff-Fabrikation, **IV** 323
Aktiv Placering A.B., **II** 352
Akzo, **I** 674; **II** 572; **III** 44
Al Copeland Enterprises, Inc., **7** 26–28
al Sulaiman, Abd Allah, **IV** 536

al-Badri, Abdallah, **IV** 455
al-Banbi, Hamdi, **IV** 413
al-Marri, Jaber, **IV** 525
al-Mazrui, Sohal Fares, **IV** 364
al-Thani, Abdulaziz bin Khalifa (Sheikh), **IV** 524
al-Thani family, **IV** 524
al-Thani, Khalifa bin Hamad (Sheikh), **IV** 524
Alaadin Middle East-Ersan, **IV** 564
Alabaster Co., **III** 762
Aladdin's Castle, **III** 430, 431
Alais et Camargue, **IV** 173
Alamito Company, **6** 590
Alamo Engine Company, **8** 514
Alamo Rent A Car, Inc., 6 348–50
Alarm Device Manufacturing Company, **9** 413–15
Alascom, **6** 325–28
Alaska Air Group, Inc., 6 65–67; 11 50
Alaska Airlines. *See* Alaska Air Group, Inc.
Alaska Co., **III** 439
Alaska Commercial Company, **12** 363
Alaska Hydro-Train, **6** 382; **9** 510
Alaska Natural Gas Transportation System, **V** 673, 683
Alaska Pulp Co., **IV** 284, 297, 321
Alba, **III** 619–20
Albany and Susquehanna Railroad, **II** 329
Albany Assurance Co., Ltd., **III** 293
Albany Felt Company. *See* Albany International Corp.
Albany Felt Company of Canada, **8** 13
Albany International Corp., 8 12–14
Albarda, Horatius, **I** 108
Albeck, Andy, **II** 148
Albee, Mrs. P.F.E., **III** 15
Albemarle Paper Co., **I** 334–35; **10** 289
Albers Brothers Milling Co., **II** 487
Albers, William, **II** 643
Albert, Carl, **9** 205, 207
Albert E. Reed & Co. Ltd., **7** 343
Albert Heijn NV, **II** 641–42
Albert, King (Belgium), **I** 395
Albert, Kurt, **I** 392
Albert Nipon, Inc., **8** 323
Alberta Distillers, **I** 377
Alberta Gas Trunk Line Company, Ltd., **V** 673–74
Alberta Sulphate Ltd., **IV** 165
Alberthal, Lester M., **III** 138
Alberto, **II** 641–42
Alberto-Culver Company, 8 15–17
Alberts, Robert C., **II** 507
Albertson, Joe, **II** 601–04; **7** 19–21
Albertson's Inc., II 601–03, 604–05, 637; **7 19–22 (upd.); 8** 474
Albi Enterprises, **III** 24
Albion, **III** 673
Albion Reid Proprietary, **III** 673
Albrecht, R.A., **I** 254
Albright & Friel, **I** 313; **10** 154
Albright & Wilson Ltd., **I** 527; **IV** 165; **12** 351
Albright, Joseph, **IV** 683
Albright, Josephine, **IV** 683
Albu, George, **IV** 90
Albu, Leopold, **IV** 90
Albuquerque Gas & Electric Company. *See* Public Service Company of New Mexico.
Albuquerque Gas, Electric Light and Power Company, **6** 561–62

The Brush Electric Light Company, **11** 387
Brush Electrical Machines, **III** 507–09
Brush Moore Newspaper, Inc., **8** 527
Bruson, Herman, **I** 392
Bryan, Arthur, **12** 528
Bryan Bros. Packing, **II** 572
Bryan, John H., **II** 572–73
Bryan, Joseph, **12** 302
Bryan, William Jennings, **IV** 625
Bryant, George A., **8** 42
Bryant Heater Co., **III** 471
Bryant, William Cullen, **12** 358
Bryce & Co., **I** 547
Bryce Brothers, **12** 313
Bryce Grace & Co., **I** 547
Brydges, Charles J., **6** 359
Brymbo Steel Works, **III** 494
Brynner, Yul, **12** 228
Bryson, John, **V** 717
Bryson, Vaughn D., **11** 91
BSB, **IV** 653; **7** 392
BSC (Industry) Ltd., **IV** 42
BSkyB, **IV** 653; **7** 392
BSN Groupe S.A., II 474–75, 544
BSN-Gervais-Danone, **II** 474–75
BSR, **II** 82
BT. *See* British Telecommunications, plc.
BT Credit Co., **II** 230
BT New York Corp., **II** 230
BT Securities Corp., **12** 209
BTI Services, **9** 59
BTM. *See* British Tabulating Machine Company.
BTR plc, I 428–30; **III** 185, 727; **8** 397
Buccleuch (Duke of), **III** 358
Bucerius, Gerd (Dr.), **IV** 592
Buchan, Carl, **V** 122
Buchanan, **I** 239–40
Buchanan Electric Steel Company, **8** 114
Buchner, Edouard, **I** 391
Buck, Pearl S., **IV** 671
Buckeye Union Casualty Co., **III** 242
Buckingham Corp., **I** 440, 468
Buckler Broadcast Group, **IV** 597
Buckley, Peter, **I** 246, 279
Buckley, R.M. (Mike), **IV** 342
Buckley, Robert J., **8** 19; **9** 484
Bucknell, Earl, **III** 329
Bucy, J. Fred, **II** 114; **11** 507
Bucyrus-Erie Company, **7** 513
The Budd Company, IV 222; **8** 74–76
Budd, Edward, **8** 74–75
Budd, Edward G., Jr., **8** 75
Budd, Edward H., **III** 389
Budd, Ralph, **V** 427, 428
Budd Wheel, **III** 568
Buderus AG, **III** 692, 694–95
Buderus, Georg, **III** 694
Buderus, Georg, II, **III** 694
Buderus, Georg, III, **III** 694
Buderus, Hugo, **III** 694
Buderus, Johann Wilhelm, I, **III** 694
Buderus, Johann Wilhelm, II, **III** 694
Buderus'sche Eisenwerke, **III** 694–95
Budge, Alexander G., **II** 491
Budget Rent a Car Corporation, I 537; **6** 348–49, 393; **9** 94–95
Buegler, Larry, **8** 490
Buell, Margaret, **III** 40
Buena Vista Distribution, **II** 172; **6** 174
Buetow, Herbert, **I** 500
Buffalo Forge Company, **7** 70–71
Buffalo Insurance Co., **III** 208
Buffalo Mining Co., **IV** 181

Buffets, Inc., 10 186–87
Buffett Partnership, Ltd., **III** 213
Buffett, Warren, **III** 29, 190, 213–15
Buffett, Warren E., **12** 436
Buffington, A.L., **7** 496
Buhler, Hans, **I** 410
Buick, David, **I** 171; **10** 325
Buick Motor Co., **I** 171; **III** 438; **8** 74; **10** 325
Builders Square, **V** 112; **9** 400; **12** 345, 385
Buitoni SpA, **II** 548
Buley, R. Carlyle, **III** 266
Bulgarian Oil Co., **IV** 454
Bulkeley, Eliphalet, **III** 180, 236
Bulkeley, Morgan G., **III** 180–81
Bull. *See* Compagnie des Machines Bull S.A.
Bull, Frank, **10** 378
Bull, Fredrik Rosing, **III** 122
Bull HN Information Systems, **III** 122–23
Bull, M.W.J., **I** 288
Bull Motors, **11** 5
Bull S.A., **III** 122–23
Bull, Stephen, **10** 377
Bull Tractor Company, **7** 534
Bull-GE, **III** 123
Bulldog Computer Products, **10** 519
Bullis, Henry, **II** 501; **10** 322
Bullock, L.C., **I** 714
Bullock, Thomas A., **6** 142, 144
Bullock's, **III** 63
Bulolo Gold Dredging, **IV** 95
Bulova Watch Co., **I** 488; **II** 101; **III** 454–55; **12** 316–17, 453
Bulova-Citizen, **III** 454
Bumble Bee Seafoods, Inc., **II** 491, 508, 557
Bumkor-Ramo Corp., **I** 539
Bumpus, James N., **6** 560
Bumstead, Albert, **9** 367
Bunawerke Hüls GmbH., **I** 350
Bund, Karlheinz, **IV** 195
Bunker, Arthur H., **IV** 18
Bunker, George, **I** 67–68
Bunker, Gerald, **III** 228
Bunker Ramo Info Systems, **III** 118
Bunte Candy, **12** 427
Buntrock, Dean, **11** 436
Buntrock, Dean L., **V** 752
Bunyan, John, **I** 293
Bunzl & Biach, **IV** 260–61
Bunzl & Biach (British) Ltd., **IV** 260
Bunzl family, **IV** 260–61
Bunzl, G.G., **IV** 261
Bunzl, Hugo, **IV** 260
Bunzl PLC, IV 260–62; **12** 264
Bunzl Pulp & Paper Ltd., **IV** 260
Burbank, James C., **III** 355
Burberry's Ltd., **V** 68; **10** 122
Burbidge, Frederic, **V** 430
Burbridge, F. B., **6** 539
Burda family, **11** 292
Burda, Franz, **IV** 590–91
Burda, Frieder, **IV** 590–91
Burden, John, III, **V** 27
Burdines, **9** 209
Bureau de Recherches de Pétrole, **IV** 544–46, 559–60; **7** 481–83
Burger Boy Food-A-Rama, **8** 564
Burger Chef, **II** 532
Burger King Corporation, I 21, 278; **II** 556–57, **613–15**, 647; **7** 316; **8** 564; **9** 178; **10** 122; **12** 43, 553

Burger, Ralph, **II** 637
Burger, Warren, **9** 368
Burgess, Carter, **I** 126; **12** 488
Burgess, Ian, **III** 688
Burgess, Ray, **8** 238
Burgin, Robert A., Jr., **12** 309
Burill, William, **II** 424
Burke, Daniel, **II** 131
Burke Dowling Adams Advertising Agency, **I** 29
Burke, Edmund S., **8** 291
Burke, Frank, **12** 6
Burke, James, **III** 36–37; **8** 282–83
Burke, John J., **12** 254
Burke, Richard, **9** 524
Burke Scaffolding Co., **9** 512
BURLE Industries Inc., **11** 444
Burlesdon Brick Co., **III** 734
Burlington, **8** 234
Burlington Air Express, Inc., **IV** 182
Burlington Coat Factory Warehouse Corporation, 10 188–89
Burlington Industries, Inc., V 118, **354–55**; **9** 231; **12** 501
Burlington Mills Corporation, **12** 117–18
Burlington Northern Air Freight, **IV** 182
Burlington Northern, Inc., V 425–28; **10** 190–91; **12** 145, 278
Burlington Northern Railroad, **11** 315
Burlington Resources Inc., 10 190–92; **11** 135; **12** 144
Burmah Castrol PLC, IV 381–84
Burmah Engineering, **IV** 382
Burmah Industrial Products, **IV** 382
Burmah Oil Company, **IV** 378, 381–83, 440–41, 483–84, 531; **7** 56
Burmah-Castrol Co., **IV** 382
Burmah-Shell, **IV** 440–41, 483
Burmeister & Wain, **III** 417–18
Burn & Co., **IV** 205
Burn Standard Co. Ltd., **IV** 484
Burnards, **II** 677
Burnett, Clinton Brown, **III** 707; **7** 292
Burnett, Leo, **I** 22, 36
Burnett, Robert, **11** 292–93
Burnham and Co., **II** 407–08; **6** 599; **8** 388
Burnham, Daniel, **II** 284
Burnham, Donald, **II** 121; **12** 545
Burnham, Duane L., **11** 9
Burnham, I.W. "Tubby", **II** 407–08; **8** 388–89
Burns & Wilcox Ltd., **6** 290
Burns, C.F., **7** 104
Burns Cos., **III** 569
Burns, Ed, **7** 104
Burns Fry Ltd., **II** 349
Burns, George, **II** 133, 151
Burns International, **III** 440
Burns, John, **IV** 392
Burns, John, Jr., **10** 45
Burns, M. Anthony, **V** 505
Burns, Robin, **9** 203
Burns, Thomas S., **I** 464
Burpee Co. *See* W. Atlee Burpee Co.
Burr & Co., **II** 424
Burr, Aaron, **II** 217, 247
Burr, Donald C., **I** 117–18, 123–24
Burr, Robert, **11** 135
Burrill & Housman, **II** 424
Burritt, Arthur W., **II** 252
Burritt, Henry, **12** 158–59
Burroughs Adding Machine Co., **III** 165–66

Drayton Corp., **II** 319
Drayton, Harold Charles (Harley), **IV** 686
Drennen, Michael, **II** 417
Dresden Bankhaus, **II** 281
Dresdner Bank A.G., **I** 411; **II** 191,
    238–39, 241–42, 256–57, 279–80,
    281–83, 385; **III** 201, 289, 401; **IV** 141
Dresdner Feuer-Versicherungs-Gesellschaft,
    III 376
Dresser Industries, Inc., **I** 486; **III** 429,
    470–73; 499, 527, 545–46; **12** 539
Dresser Manufacturing Co., **III** 471
Dresser Manufacturing Co., Ltd., **III** 471
Dresser, Paul, **8** 104
Dresser Power, **6** 555
Dresser, Solomon, **III** 470
Dresser Vaduz, **III** 472
Dresser-Rand, **III** 473, 527
Drever, Thomas, **7** 30
Drew, Daniel, **II** 395; **10** 59
Drew, William, **II** 593
Drewry Photocolor, **I** 447
Drews, Rudolph, **I** 496; **12** 332
Drexel and Company, **II** 329–30, 407; **8**
    388
Drexel, Anthony J., **II** 329, 407
Drexel Burnham, **9** 346
Drexel Burnham and Company, **II** 407; **8**
    388
Drexel Burnham Lambert Incorporated,
    II 167, 330, **407–09**, 482; **III** 10, 253,
    254–55, 531, 721; **IV** 334; **6** 210–11; **7**
    305; **8** 327, 349, 388–90, 568; **12** 229.
    See also New Street Capital Inc.
Drexel Firestone Inc., **II** 407; **8** 388
Drexel, Francis Martin, **II** 407; **8** 388
Drexel, Harjes & Co., **II** 329
Drexel Heritage, **11** 534
Drexel Heritage Furnishings Inc., **12**
    129–31
Drexel Heritage Furniture, **III** 571
Drexel Morgan & Co., **II** 329, 430
Drexler, Millard Mickey, **V** 60–62
Dreyer's Grand Ice Cream, Inc., **10**
    147–48
Dreyfus, Camille E. (Dr.), **I** 317–18
Dreyfus, Henri (Dr.), **I** 317
Dreyfus Interstate Development Corp., **11**
    257
Dreyfus, Ludwig, **II** 414
Dreyfus, Pierre, **I** 189–90
DRI. *See* Dominion Resources, Inc.
Dribeck Importers Inc., **9** 87
Drinkwater, Terrell, **I** 96
Driscoll, Alfred, **I** 710–11; **10** 549–50
Drohan, Thomas E., **I** 497; **12** 332
Drohan, Thomas P., **12** 332
Dromer, Jean, **III** 393
Drott Manufacturing Company, **10** 379
Drouot Group, **III** 211
Drown, L.M., **III** 91
Drug City, **II** 649
Drug Emporium, Inc., **12 132–34**, 477
Drug House, **III** 9
Drug, Inc., **III** 17
Drumheller, Roscoe, **9** 531
Drummond, Gerard K., **7** 376–77
Drummond Lighterage. *See* Puget Sound
    Tug and Barge Company.
Drummonds' Bank, **12** 422
Druout, **I** 563
Dry Milks Inc., **I** 248
Dryden and Co., **III** 340
Dryden, Forrest, **III** 337–38

Dryden, John F., **III** 337–38
Dryfoos, Orvil E., **IV** 648
Drysdale Government Securities, **10** 117
DSC Communications Corporation, **12**
    135–37
DSC Nortech, **9** 170
DSM N.V., **I 326–27**; **III** 614
DST Systems Inc., **6** 400–02
Du Bain, Myron, **I** 418
Du Bouzet, **II** 233
Du Mont Company, **8** 517
Du Pont. *See* E.I. du Pont de Nemours &
    Co.
Du Pont, Alfred I., **I** 328; **IV** 311
Du Pont Chemical Company, **11** 432
Du Pont, Coleman, **III** 247
Du Pont de Nemours, Alfred, **I** 328
Du Pont de Nemours, Eleuthàre Irenée, **I**
    328
Du Pont de Nemours, Henry, **I** 328
Du Pont, Eugene, **I** 328
Du Pont Fabricators, **III** 559
Du Pont family, **11** 431
Du Pont Glore Forgan, Inc., **III** 137
Du Pont Photomask, **IV** 600
Du Pont, Pierre S., **I** 328
Du Pont, Richard C., **I** 131; **6** 131
Du Pont Walston, **II** 445
Dubin, Ronald N., **10** 235
Dublin and London Steam Packet
    Company, **V** 490
Dubose, Lori, **I** 117
Dubreuil, Audouin, **7** 35–36
Dubreuil, Haardt, **7** 35–36
Dubrule, Paul, **10** 12–14
Ducat, D., **I** 605
Ducatel-Duval, **II** 369
Duck Head Apparel Company, Inc., **8**
    141–43
Ducon Group, **II** 81
Dudley, Alfred E., **8** 180
Duebel, George, **12** 175–76
Duerden, Peter, **III** 350
Duerksen, Christopher J., **I** 325
Duff Bros., **III** 9–10
Duff, Tom, **8** 561
Duffield, Edward D., **III** 338
Duffy, Ben, **I** 28–29
Duffy, Edward W., **III** 763
Duffy-Mott, **II** 477
Dugan, Allan E., **6** 290
Duisberg, Carl, **I** 305, 309
Duke, James, **8** 24; **12** 108
Duke, James Buchanan (Buck), **I** 300, 425;
    IV 10; **V** 395, 408, 417, 600; **9** 312, 533
Duke Power Company, **V 600–02**
Duke, William Meng, **I** 544
Dulles, John Foster, **I** 507
Dumaine, F.C. "Buck", Jr., **8** 32; **9** 213
Dumaine, Frederic C., Sr., **8** 32–33; **9** 213
Dumas, Roland, **12** 252
Dumez, **V** 655–57
Dumont Broadcasting Corporation, **7** 335
Dumont, Francois, **IV** 226
Dumont, Victor, **IV** 226
Dun & Bradstreet Corporation, **I** 540;
    IV 604–05, 643, 661; **8** 526; **9** 505; **10**
    4, 358
Dun & Bradstreet Cos. Inc., **IV** 605
Dun & Bradstreet, Inc., **IV** 605
**Dun & Bradstreet Software Services
    Inc.**, **11 77–79**
Dun, Robert Graham, **IV** 604
Dunbar, Michael, **I** 427

Duncan, Alexander E., **8** 117
Duncan, Daniel, **III** 96–97
Duncan, Dr. Henry, **12** 491
Duncan Foods Corp., **I** 234; **10** 227
Duncan, James H., **8** 188
Duncan, James S., **III** 651
Duncan, John C., **7** 107–08
Duncan, John W., **6** 446
Duncan Mackinnon, **III** 521
Duncan Macneill, **III** 522
Duncan, Sherman & Co., **II** 329
Duncan, Val, **IV** 191–92
Duncan, William (Sir), **I** 83
Duncan, William A., Jr., **11** 237
Duncanson, Thomas S., **IV** 645
Dundee Cement Co., **III** 702; **8** 258–59
Dunfey Brothers Capital Group, **12** 368
Dunfey Hotels Corporation, **12** 367
Dunfey, Jack, **12** 367
Dunham, Sylvester, **III** 387–88
Dunhams Stores Corporation, **V** 111
Dunhill, **IV** 93
Dunhill Holdings, **V** 411
Dunkin' Donuts, **II** 619
Dunlevy, George, **6** 348
Dunlop, **V** 250, 252–53
Dunlop Holdings, **I** 429; **III** 697
Dunlop Japan, **V** 252
Dunlop, John Boyd, **10** 444
Dunlop, Robert G., **IV** 549–50; **7** 414
Dunlop Tire (USA), **I** 429
Dunn, Frank H., Jr., **10** 299
Dunn, Henry, **IV** 604
Dunn, J.H., **IV** 409; **7** 309
Dunn Paper Co., **IV** 290
Dunn, Vincent B., **11** 281
Dunn, Warren, **12** 338
Dunne, James E., **III** 216
Dunnett, Peter J.S., **I** 196
Dunnigan, T. Kevin, **11** 516
Dunning, Harrison, **IV** 330
Dunning Industries, **12** 109
Dunoyer, **III** 675
Dupar, Frank A., **9** 547
Dupar, Harold E., **9** 547
Dupil-Color, Inc., **III** 745
Dupol, **III** 614
duPont, Alfred I., **8** 151, 485–86
DuPont Canada, **12** 365
Dupont Chamber Works, **6** 449
DuPont Chemical Company, **7** 546
duPont de Nemours, Éleuthère Irenée, **8**
    151
duPont, Pierre S., **8** 151
Duquesne Enterprises, **6** 484
Duquesne Light Company, **6** 483–84
Duquesne Systems, **10** 394
Dura Corp., **I** 476
Dura-Vent, **III** 468
Duracell International Inc., **9 179–81**; **12**
    559
Durand & Huguenin, **I** 672
Durant, Ariel, **IV** 671
Durant, Don, **11** 522
Durant, Thomas C., **V** 529
Durant, Will, **IV** 671
Durant, William, **I** 171; **10** 325
Durante, Jimmy, **II** 151
Duray, Inc., **12** 215
Durban Breweries and Distillers, **I** 287
Dureau, David Henry, **IV** 248
DuRell, Benjamin M., **11** 552–53
Durfee, Dorothy, **IV** 252

Magdeburger Versicherungsgruppe, **III** 377
Magee, Frank, **IV** 15
Maggin, Daniel, **7** 145
Magic Chef, **8** 298
Magic Chef Co., **III** 573
Magic Pan, **II** 559–60; **12** 410
Magic Pantry Foods, **10** 382
MagicSoft Inc., **10** 557
Maginness, George, **I** 696
Magirus, **IV** 126
Maglificio di Ponzano Veneto dei Fratelli
  Benetton. *See* Benetton.
Magma Copper Company, **7 287–90**,
  385–87
Magma Electric Company, **11** 271
Magma Energy Company, **11** 270
Magma Power Company, **11 270–72**
Magna Computer Corporation, **12** 149
Magnaflux, **III** 519
Magne Corp., **IV** 160
Magnesium Metal Co., **IV** 118
Magness, Bob, **II** 160
Magnet Cove Barium Corp., **III** 472
Magnetic Controls Company, **10** 18
Magnolia Petroleum Co., **III** 497; **IV** 82,
  464
Magnus Co., **I** 331
Magnus Eriksson, King (Sweden), **IV** 335
La Magona d'Italia, **IV** 228
Magoon, Robert, Jr., **9** 272
Magor Railcar Co., **I** 170
Magowan, Peter, **II** 655–56
Magowan, Robert, **II** 655
Magraw, Lester A., **6** 469–70
MAGroup Inc., **11** 123
Maguire, John J., **I** 312; **10** 154
Maguire, William G., **V** 691
Maharam Fabric, **8** 455. *See also* Design/
  Craft Fabrics.
Maher, James R., **11** 334
Mahir, **I** 37
Mahone, William, **V** 484
Mahoney, Richard J., **I** 366; **9** 356
Mahoney, Terah, **I** 47
Mahou, **II** 474
MAI Basic Four, Inc., **10** 242
MAI Inc., **11** 486
Mai Nap Rt, **IV** 652; **7** 392
MAI Systems Corporation, **11 273–76**
Maier, Cornell C., **IV** 123
Maier, Gerald, **V** 738
Maier, Russell W., **7** 446–47
Mailson Ferreira da Nobrega, **II** 200
MAIN. *See* Mid-American Interpool
  Network.
Main Event Management Corp., **III** 194
Main Street Advertising USA, **IV** 597
Mainline Travel, **I** 114
Mair, Alex, **7** 461–62
Mairs, Samuel, **I** 419; **11** 21–22
Maison Bouygues, **I** 563
Maizuru Heavy Industries, **III** 514
Majestic Contractors Ltd., **8** 419–20
Majestic Wine Warehouses Ltd., **II** 656
Major League Baseball, **12** 457
Major Video Concepts, **6** 410
Major Video, Inc., **9** 74
MaK Maschinenbau GmbH, **IV** 88
Mak van Waay, **11** 453
Makhteshim, **II** 47
Makihara, Minoru "Ben", **12** 342
Makita Electric Works, **III** 436
Makita, Jinichi, **I** 579–80
Makita, Shinichiro, **I** 580

Makiyama, **I** 363
Makkonen, Veikko, **II** 303
Mako, B.V., **8** 476
Makovsky & Company, **12** 394
Malama Pacific Corporation, **9** 276
Malamud, Bernard, **IV** 622
Malapai Resources, **6** 546
Malayan Airways Limited, **6** 117
Malayan Breweries, **I** 256
Malayan Motor and General Underwriters,
  III 201
Malaysia LNG, **IV** 518–19
Malaysia-Singapore Airlines, **6** 117. *See
  also* Malaysian Airlines System BHD.
Malaysian Airlines System BHD, **6** 71,
  100–02
Malaysian Airways Ltd., **6** 100, 117
Malaysian International Shipping Co., **IV**
  518
Malaysian Sheet Glass, **III** 715
Malbak Ltd., **IV** 92–93
Malcolm's Diary & Time-Table, **III** 256
Malcolmson, Alexander, **I** 164; **11** 136
Malcus Industri, **III** 624
Malec, John, **10** 358
Malenick, Donald H., **7** 599
Malheur Cooperative Electric Association,
  12 265
Maljers, Floris A., **7** 544
Malkin, Judd, **IV** 702–03
Malleable Iron Works, **IV** 34
Mallinckrodt Inc., **III** 16; **IV** 146; **8** 85
Mallon, Henry Neil, **III** 471–72
Malmö Flygindustri, **I** 198
Malmsten & Bergvalls, **I** 664
Malnik, Alvin, **6** 200–01
Malone & Hyde, Inc., **II** 625, 670–71; **9**
  52–53
Malone, John, **II** 160–61, 167
Malone, Thomas F., **III** 389
Malone, Wallace D., Jr., **11** 455
Maloney, George T., **9** 98
Maloney, Martin, **11** 387
Maloon, James, **9** 297
Malott, Robert H., **I** 443; **11** 134–35
Malozemoff, Plato, **7** 288, 386–87
Malrite Communications Group, **IV** 596
Malt-A-Milk Co., **II** 487
Maltby, Harold E., **9** 547
Maltby, John, **IV** 383
Malthus, Thomas, **7** 165
Mameco International, **8** 455
Mamlock, Max, **I** 64
Mamroth, Paul, **I** 410
Man Aktiengesellschaft, **III** 301, **561–63**
MAN B&W Diesel, **III** 563
MAN Gutehoffnungshütte, **III** 563
MAN Nutzfahrzeuge, **III** 563
MAN Roland, **III** 563
MAN Technologie, **III** 563
Management Decision Systems, Inc., **10**
  358
Management Engineering and Development
  Co., **IV** 310
Management Recruiters International, **6**
  140
Management Science America, Inc., **11** 77
Manbré and Garton, **II** 582
Manchester and Liverpool District Banking
  Co., **II** 307, 333
Manchester Commercial Buildings Co., **IV**
  711
Mancuso, Frank, **II** 156
Mandabach & Simms, **6** 40

Mandai, Junshiro, **II** 325
Mandarin Oriental International Ltd., **I**
  471; **IV** 700
Mandel Bros., **IV** 660
Mandel, Evan William, **III** 55
Mandel, Jack, **9** 419
Mandel, Joseph, **9** 419
Mandel, Morton, **9** 419–20
Mange, John I., **V** 629
Manhattan Co., **II** 217, 247
Manhattan Electrical Supply Co., **9** 517
Manhattan Fund, **I** 614
Manhattan Trust Co., **II** 229
Mani, Ravi, **6** 64
Maniatis, Thomas, **8** 215
Manifatture Cotoniere Meridionali, **I** 466
Manistique Pulp and Paper Co., **IV** 311
Manitoba Bridge and Engineering Works
  Ltd., **8** 544
Manitoba Paper Co., **IV** 245–46
Manitoba Rolling Mill Ltd., **8** 544
Manley, L.B., **III** 282
Manley, Marshall, **III** 263
Mann, Donald, **6** 360
Mann Egerton & Co., **III** 523
Mann, Ellery, **8** 511, 513
Mann, Horace, **III** 312
Mann, Jack, **8** 385
Mann Theatres Chain, **I** 245
Manne Tossbergs Eftr., **II** 639
Mannerheim, Carl Gustav Emil (Baron),
  IV 299, 348
Mannerheim, Carl Robert (Count), **IV** 299
Manners, Arthur, **I** 223
Mannesmann AG, **I** 411; **III 564–67**; **IV**
  222, 469
Mannesmann Anlagenbau AG, **III** 565
Mannesmann Comercial S.A., **III** 566
Mannesmann, Max, **III** 564
Mannesmann Mobilfunk GmbH, **III** 566;
  11 11
Mannesmann, Reinhard, **III** 564
Mannesmann Tube Co., **III** 565
Mannesmannröhren-Werke, **III** 566
Mannheimer Bank, **IV** 558
Mannheimer, Theodor, **II** 351
Manning, Ernest, **12** 364
Manning, Selvage & Lee, **6** 22
Mannstaedt, **IV** 128
Manoff, Tom, **7** 462
Manoogian, Alex, **III** 568–69
Manoogian, Charles, **III** 568
Manoogian, George, **III** 568
Manoogian, Richard, **III** 569–70
Manor Care, Inc., **6 187–90**
Manor Healthcare Corporation, **6** 187–88
Manorfield Investments, **II** 158
Manpower, Inc., **6** 10, 140; **9 326–27**
Manpower Southampton, **9** 326
Mansager, Felix N., **12** 251
Manship, Paul, **III** 275
Mantua Metal Products. *See* Tyco Toys,
  Inc.
Manuel, Moses, **12** 243
Manufacturers & Merchants Indemnity Co.,
  III 191
Manufacturers and Traders Trust Company,
  11 108–09
Manufacturers Hanover Consumer Credit
  Division, **11** 16
Manufacturers Hanover Corporation, **II**
  254, **312–14**, 403; **III** 194; **9** 124
Manufacturers Hanover Investment Corp.,
  II 446

Northern Indiana Public Service Company, **6** 532–33

Northern Joint Stock Bank, **II** 303

Northern Natural Gas Co., **V** 609–10

Northern Pacific Railroad, **II** 278, 329; **III** 228, 282

Northern Paper, **I** 614

Northern States Life Insurance Co., **III** 275

Northern States Power Company, **V** **670–72**

Northern Stores, Inc., **12** 362

Northern Sugar Company, **11** 13

Northern Telecom Canada Ltd., **6** 310

Northern Telecom Inc., **11** 69

Northern Telecom Limited, **II** 70; **III** 143, 164; **V** 271; **V 308–10**; **6** 242, 307; **9** 479; **10** 19, 432; **12** 162

Northern Trust Company, **III** 518; **9** **387–89**

Northern Trust Corporation, **9** 389

Northern Trust International Banking Corporation, **9** 388

Northfield Metal Products, **11** 256

Northland. *See* Scott Fetzer Company.

Northrop Corporation, **I** 47, 49, 55, 59, **76–77**, 80, 84, 197, 525; **III** 84; **9** 416, 418; **10** 162; **11** 164, 166, 266, 269, **363–65 (upd.)**

Northrop, Jack, **9** 12

Northrop, Jack Knudsen, **11** 266, 363

Northrop, John Knudson, **I** 64, 76–77

Northrup King Co., **I** 672

NorthStar Computers, **10** 313

Northwest Airlines, **12** 191, 487

Northwest Airlines Inc., **I** 42, 64, 91, 97, 100, 104, **112–14**, 125, 127; **6** 66, 74, 82 **103–05 (upd.)**; **9** 273; **11** 266, 315

Northwest Benefit Assoc., **III** 228

Northwest Engineering Co. *See* Terex Corporation.

Northwest Industries, **I** 342, 440; **II** 468 **8** 367. *See also* Chicago and North Western Holdings Corporation.

Northwest Instruments, **8** 519

Northwest Orient, **6** 123. *See also* Northwest Airlines, Inc.

Northwest Paper Company, **8** 430

Northwest Telecommunications Inc., **6** 598

Northwestern Bell Telephone Co., **V** 341

Northwestern Benevolent Society, **III** 228

Northwestern Engraving, **12** 25

Northwestern Expanded Metal Co., **III** 763

Northwestern Financial Corporation, **11** 29

Northwestern Industries, **III** 263

Northwestern Manufacturing Company, **8** 133

Northwestern Mutual Life Insurance Company, **III 321–24**, 352; **IV** 333

Northwestern National Insurance Co., **IV** 29

Northwestern Public Service Company, **6** 524

Northwestern States Portland Cement Co., **III** 702

Northwestern Telephone Systems, **6** 325, 328

Norton, Charles H., **8** 396

Norton Company, **III** 678; **8 395–97**

Norton Emery Wheel Company, **8** 395

Norton, Eugene, **IV** 81; **7** 185

Norton, Frank, **8** 395

Norton Healthcare Ltd., **11** 208

Norton Opax PLC, **IV** 259

Norton, Peter, **10** 508

Norton Simon Inc., **I** 446; **IV** 672; **6** 356

Norton Stone Ware, F.B., **8** 395

Norwales Confectionery Ltd., **11** 239

Norwales Development Ltd., **11** 239

Norwegian Assurance, **III** 258

Norwegian Globe, **III** 258

Norwegian Petroleum Consultants, **III** 499

Norwest Mortgage Inc., **11** 29

Norwest Publishing, **IV** 661

Norwich Pharmaceuticals, **I** 370–71; **9** 358

Norwich Union Fire Insurance Society, Ltd., **III** 242, 273, 404; **IV** 705

Norwich Winterthur Group, **III** 404

Norwich Winterthur Reinsurance Corp. Ltd., **III** 404

Norwich-Eaton Pharmaceuticals, **III** 53; **8** 434

Nottingham Manufacturing Co., **V** 357

Nourse, Alexandra "Aagje," **10** 167

Nourse, Robert E.M., **10** 166–68

Nouvelles Galeries, **10** 205

Nouvelles Messageries de la Presse Parisienne, **IV** 618

Nova, an Alberta Corporation, **V** 674

Nova Corporation of Alberta, **V 673–75**; **12** 364–66

NovaCare, Inc., **11 366–68**

Novacor Chemicals Ltd., **12 364–66**

Novak, William, **I** 145

Novalta Resources Inc., **11** 441

Novell, **12** 335

Novell Data Systems. *See* Novell, Inc.

Novell, Inc., **6** 255–56, 260, **269–71**; **9** 170–71; **10** 232, 363, 473–74, 558, 565; **11** 59, 519–20

Novello and Co., **II** 139

Novo Industri A/S, **I 658–60**, 697

Nowell Wholesale Grocery Co., **II** 681

Nox Ltd., **I** 588

Noxell Corporation, **III** 53; **8** 434

Noyce, Robert, **II** 44–46; **10** 365–66

Noyes, John Humphrey, **7** 406

Noyes, Pierrepont Burt, **7** 406–07

Nozaki, Hirota, **IV** 655

NRG Energy, Inc., **11** 401

NS. *See* Norfolk Southern Corporation.

NS Petites Inc., **8** 323

NSG America, Inc., **III** 715

NSG Foreign Trade, **III** 715

NSG Information System Co., **III** 715

NSG Materials Service Co., **III** 715

NSG-Taliq, **III** 715

NSK. *See* Nippon Seiko K.K.

NSK Bearings Europe, **III** 589

NSK Corp., **III** 589

NSK do Brasil Industria e Comercio de Rolamentos, **III** 589

NSK Kugellager, **III** 589

NSK-Torrington, **III** 589

NSMO. *See* Nederlandsche Stoomvart Maatschappij Oceaan.

NSP. *See* Northern States Power Company.

NSU Werke, **10** 261

NTCL. *See* Northern Telecom Canada Ltd.

NTN Bearing Corp. of America, **III** 595

NTN Bearing Corp. of Canada, **III** 595

NTN Bearing Manufacturing Corp., **III** 595

NTN Bearings-GKN, **III** 595

NTN Bower Corp., **III** 596

NTN Corporation, **III 595–96**, 623

NTN de Mexico, **III** 596

NTN Driveshaft, **III** 596

NTN France, **III** 595

NTN Kugellagerfabrik, **III** 595–96

NTN Manufacturing Canada, **III** 595

NTN Manufacturing Co., Ltd., **III** 595

NTN Sales, **III** 595

NTN Suramericana, **III** 596

NTN Toyo Bearing Co., **III** 595–96

NTN Trading-Hong Kong, **III** 595

NTN Wälzlager Europa, **III** 595

NTRON, **11** 486

NTT. *See* Nippon Telegraph and Telephone Corp.

NTT International Corporation, **V** 305–06

NTTI. *See* NTT International Corporation.

NTTPC. *See* Nippon Telegraph and Telephone Public Corporation.

NU. *See* Northeast Utilities.

Nuclear Electric, **6** 453; **11** 399–401; **12** 349

Nucoa Butter Co., **II** 497

Nucor Corporation, **7 400–02**

Nucorp Energy, **II** 262, 620

NUG Optimus Lebensmittel-Einzelhandelgesellschaft mbH, **V** 74

Nugent, D. Eugene, **7** 420

Nugent, Frank, **III** 738

Nugget Polish Co. Ltd., **II** 566

Numerax, Inc., **IV** 637

Nunn, Sam, **10** 161

Nuovo Pignone, **IV** 420–22

NUR Touristic GmbH, **V** 100–02

Nurad, **III** 468

Nursefinders, **6** 10

Nusbaum, Aaron, **V** 180

NutraSweet Company, **II** 463, 582; **8** **398–400**

Nutrena, **II** 617

Nutri/System Inc., **10** 383

Nutrilite Co., **III** 11–12

NutriSystem, **12** 531

Nutt, Roy, **6** 227

NVH L.P., **8** 401. *See also* NVR L.P.

NVHomes, Inc., **8** 401–02. *See also* NVR L.P.

NVR Finance, **8** 402–03

NVR L.P., **8 401–03**

NVRyan L.P., **8** 401. *See also* NVR L.P.

NWA Aircraft, **I** 114

NWK. *See* Nordwestdeutsche Kraftwerke AG.

NWL Control Systems, **III** 512

NWS BANK plc, **10** 336–37

Nya AB Atlas, **III** 425–26

Nybom, F.K., **II** 302

Nydqvist & Holm, **III** 426

Nye, David E., **I** 168

Nye, Gerald, **I** 57; **10** 315

Nyers, Howard, **IV** 673; **7** 527

Nyhamms Cellulosa, **IV** 338

NYK. *See* Nihon Yusen Kaisha.

NYK. *See* Nippon Yusen Kabushiki Kaisha *and* Nippon Yusen Kaisha.

Nylex Corp., **I** 429

Nyman & Schultz Affarsresbyraer A.B., **I** 120

NYNEX Corporation, **V 311–13**; **6** 340; **11** 87

NYNEX Mobile Communications, **11** 19

Nyrop, **I** 113

Nyrop, Donald, **6** 104

Nysco Laboratories, **III** 55

NYSEG. *See* New York State Electric and Gas Corporation.

NZI Corp., **III** 257

Perusahaan Tambang Minyak Negara Republik Indonesia, **IV** 491
Perusahaan Tambang Minyak Republik Indonesia, **IV** 491
Peruvian Corp., **I** 547
Pesatori, Enrico, **10** 563–64
Pesch, LeRoy, **III** 74
Pesenti, Carlo, **III** 347
Peskin, Kenneth, **II** 674
Pestalozzi, Martin O., **6** 9–11
Pestche, Albert, **V** 655–56
de Pesters, Jonkheer C.A., **I** 257
Pet Company, **10** 554
Pet Dairy Products Company, **7** 428
Pet Incorporated, **I** 457; **II** 486–87; **7** 428–31; **10** 554; **12** 124
Pet Milk Co. See Pet Incorporated.
Petain, Henri, **II** 12
Peter Bawden Drilling, **IV** 570
Peter, Cailler, Kohler, Chocolats Suisses S.A., **II** 546; **7** 381
Peter Gast Shipping GmbH, **7** 40
Peter J. Schweitzer, Inc., **III** 40
Peter Jones, **V** 94
Peter Kiewit Sons' Inc., **I** 599–600; **III** 198; **8** 422–24
Peter Norton Computing Group, **10** 508–09
Peter Paul, **II** 477
Peter Paul/Cadbury, **II** 512
Peter, Thomas J., **6** 233
Peterbilt Motors Co., **I** 185–86
Peters, Bob, **I** 584–85
Peters, Donald C., **I** 584–85
Peters, J.F.M., **III** 179
Peters, Jon, **II** 137, 149; **12** 75
Peters Shoe Co., **III** 528
Peters, Thomas J., **I** 501; **III** 132
Petersen, Alfred, **IV** 140–41
Petersen, Donald, **I** 167
Petersen, George, **II** 504
Peterson, Duane, **V** 496
Peterson, Ethel, **II** 634
Peterson, Howell & Heather, **V** 496
Peterson, P.A., **III** 438
Peterson, Peter, **II** 451
Peterson, Peter G., **9** 63
Peterson, Roger, **12** 8
Peterson, Rudy, **II** 228
Peterson Soybean Seed Co., **9** 411
Peterson, W.E. "Pete", **10** 556
Petite Sophisticate, **V** 207–08
Petitjean, Armand, **8** 129
Petito, Frank, **II** 432
Petrello, Anthony G., **9** 364
Petrie, Milton, **V** 203
Petrie, Milton J., **8** 425–27
Petrie Stores Corporation, **8** 425–27
Petrini's, **II** 653
Petro/Chem Environmental Services, Inc., **IV** 411
Petro-Canada, **IV** 367, 494–96, 499
Petro-Canada Inc., **IV** 496
Petro-Canada Limited, **IV** 494–96
Petro-Coke Co. Ltd., **IV** 476
Petro-Lewis Corp., **IV** 84; **7** 188
Petroamazonas, **IV** 511
Petrobel, **IV** 412
Petrobrás. See Petróleo Brasileiro S.A.
Petrobrás Distribuidora, **IV** 501–02
Petrobrás Fertilizantes S.A., **IV** 503
Petrobrás Mineracao, **IV** 503
Petrobrás Quimica S.A., **IV** 503
Petrocarbona GmbH, **IV** 197–98
Petrochemical Industries Co., **IV** 451

Petrochemie Danubia GmbH, **IV** 486–87
Petrochim, **IV** 498
Petrocomercial, **IV** 511
Petroecuador. See Petróleos del Ecuador.
Petrofertil, **IV** 501
Petrofina, **IV** 455, **497–500**, 576
Petrofina Canada Inc., **IV** 495, 499
Petrofina S.A., **IV** 497; **7** 179
Petrogal. See Petróleos de Portugal.
Petroindustria, **IV** 511
Petrol, **IV** 487
Petrol Ofisi Anonim Sirketi, **IV** 564
Petróleo Brasileiro S.A., **IV** 424, **501–03**
Petróleo Mecânica Alfa, **IV** 505
Petróleos de México S.A., **IV** 512
Petróleos de Portugal S.A., **IV** **504–06**
Petróleos de Venezuela S.A., **II** 661; **IV** 391–93, **507–09**, 571
Petróleos del Ecuador, **IV** **510–11**
Petróleos Mexicanos, **IV** **512–14**, 528
Petróleos Mexicanos Internacional Comercio Internacional, **IV** 514
Petroleum and Chemical Corp., **III** 672
Petroleum Authority of Thailand, **IV** 519
Petroleum Co. of New Zealand, **IV** 279
Petroleum Development (Oman and Dhofar) Ltd., **IV** 515
Petroleum Development (Qatar) Ltd., **IV** 524
Petroleum Development (Trucial States) Ltd., **IV** 363
Petroleum Development Corp. of the Republic of Korea, **IV** 455
Petroleum Development Oman LLC, **IV** **515–16**
Petroleum Projects Co., **IV** 414
Petroleum Research and Engineering Co. Ltd., **IV** 473
Petrolgroup, Inc., **6** 441
Petroliam Nasional Bhd. See Petronas.
Petrolube, **IV** 538
Petromex. See Petróleos de Mexico S.A.
Petronas, **IV** **517–20**
Petronas Carigali, **IV** 518–19
Petronas Carigali Overseas Sdn Bhd, **IV** 519
Petronas Dagangan, **IV** 518
Petronas Penapisan (Melaka) Sdn Bhd, **IV** 520
Petronor, **IV** 514, 528
Petropeninsula, **IV** 511
Petroproduccion, **IV** 511
Petroquímica de Venezuela SA, **IV** 508
Petroquimica Española, **I** 402
Petroquisa, **IV** 501
PETROSUL, **IV** 504, 506
Petrotransporte, **IV** 511
Petry, Thomas, **8** 158
Peugeot, Armand, **I** 187
Peugeot, Roland, **I** 187–88
Peugeot S.A., **I** 163, **187–88**; **II** 13; **III** 508; **11** 104
Pew, Arthur E., **IV** 549; **7** 413
Pew family, **I** 631
Pew, J. Howard, **IV** 548–49; **7** 413–14
Pew, James Edgar, **IV** 548; **7** 413
Pew, Joseph Newton, **IV** 548–49; **7** 413
Pew, Joseph Newton, Jr., **IV** 549; **7** 414
Pew, Robert Cunningham, **IV** 548; **7** 413, 494
Pew, Robert, III, **7** 494
Pew, Walter C., **7** 413
Peyrelevade, Jean, **III** 393–94
Pezim, Murray "The Pez," **9** 281–82

The Pfaltzgraff Co., **8** 508. See also Susquehanna Pfaltzgraff Company.
Pfaltzgraff, George, **8** 508–09
Pfaltzgraff, Henry, **8** 508
Pfaltzgraff, Johann George, **8** 508
Pfaltzgraff, John B., **8** 508
Pfaudler Vacuum Co., **I** 287
PFCI. See Pulte Financial Companies, Inc.
Pfeiffer, Eckhard, **III** 125; **6** 222
Pfeiffer, Gustave A., **I** 710; **10** 549
Pfeiffer, Robert, **10** 42
Pfister, Robert K., **I** 700
Pfizer, Charles, **I** 661; **9** 402
Pfizer, Hoechst Celanese Corp., **8** 399
Pfizer Inc., **I** 301, 367, **661–63**, 668; **9** 356, **402–05 (upd.)**; **10** 53–54; **11** 207, 310–11, 459; **12** 4
Pflaumer, Robert, **III** 704
PGE. See Portland General Electric.
PGH Bricks and Pipes, **III** 735
Phar-Mor Inc., **12** 209, **390–92**, 477
Pharaon, Gaith, **6** 143
Pharma Plus Drugmarts, **II** 649–50
Pharmacia A.B., **I** 211, **664–65**
Pharmaco Dynamics Research, Inc., **10** 106–07
Pharmaco-LSR, **10** 107
Pharmacom Systems Ltd., **II** 652
PharmaKinetics Laboratories, Inc., **10** 106
Pharmaprix Ltd., **II** 663
Pharmazell GmbH, **IV** 324
Pharmedix, **11** 207
Pharos, **9** 381
Phelan & Collender, **III** 442
Phelan Faust Paint, **8** 553
Phelan, Michael, **III** 442
Phelps, Anson, **IV** 176
Phelps, Anson, Jr., **IV** 176
Phelps, Dodge & Co., **IV** 176–77
Phelps, Dodge & Co., Inc., **IV** 177
Phelps Dodge Aluminum Products Corp., **IV** 178
Phelps Dodge Copper Corp., **IV** 177
Phelps Dodge Copper Products Corp., **IV** 178
Phelps Dodge Corporation, **IV** 33, **176–79**, 216; **7** 261–63, 288
Phelps Dodge Industries, Inc., **IV** 176, 179
Phelps Dodge Mining Co., **IV** 176, 179
Phelps Dodge Products de Centro America S.A., **IV** 178
Phelps, Douglas, **III** 726
Phelps, Ed, **IV** 171
Phelps, Guy Rowland, **III** 225, 236–37
Phenix Bank, **II** 312
Phenix Cheese Corp., **II** 533
Phenix Flour Ltd., **II** 663
Phenix Insurance Co., **III** 240
Phenix Mills Ltd., **II** 662
PHF Life Insurance Co., **III** 263; **IV** 623
PHH Corporation, **V** **496–97**
PHH Group, Incorporated, **6** 357
Phibro Corp., **II** 447–48; **IV** 80
Phibro Energy Inc., **II** 447
Phibro-Salomon Inc., **II** 447–48
Philadelphia and Reading Corp., **I** 440; **II** 329; **6** 377
Philadelphia Carpet Company, **9** 465
Philadelphia Coke Company, **6** 487
Philadelphia Company, **6** 484, 493
Philadelphia Drug Exchange, **I** 692
Philadelphia Electric Company, **V** **695–97**; **6** 450
Philadelphia Life, **I** 527

Takashimaya Iida Limited, **V** 193
Takashimaya Shoji Limited, **V** 195
Takatoshi, Suda, **III** 637
Takayama, Fujio, **II** 392
Takayanagi, Kenjiro, **II** 118–19
Takeda Abbott Products, **I** 705
**Takeda Chemical Industries Ltd., I
    704–06**; **III** 760
Takeda Food Industry, **I** 704
Takeda, Haruo, **III** 386
Takeda, Ohmiya Chobei, VI, **I** 704–05
Takeda Riken, **11** 504
Takei, Takeshi, **II** 109
Takeoka, Yoichi, **V** 719
Takeuchi, Keitaro, **I** 183
Takeuchi, Masahiko, **IV** 475
Takeuchi Mining Co., **III** 545
Takeuchi, Yasuoki, **IV** 479
Takimoto, Seihachiro, **III** 715
Takkyubin, **V** 537
Tako Oy, **IV** 314
Talbot, Frederic C., **12** 407
Talbot, Frederick, **12** 406
Talbot, Harold, **I** 48
Talbot, J. Thomas, **9** 272
Talbot, Matthew, **7** 538
Talbot, Nancy, **11** 497
Talbot, Rudolf, **11** 497
Talbot, W.C., **12** 406
Talbot,-William H., **12** 406–07
Talbot's, **II** 503; **10** 324; **12** 280
Talbots Canada, Inc., **11** 498
The Talbots, Inc., 11 497–99
Talbott, H.E., **III** 151; **6** 265
Talbott, Harold, **II** 33
Talbott, W.H., **I** 265
Talcott National Corporation, **11** 260–61
Taliafero, Paul, **IV** 550
Taliaferro, W.C., **7** 450
Taliq Corp., **III** 715
Talisman Energy, 9 490–93
Talley Industries, Inc., **10** 386
Talmadge, Norma, **II** 146
TAM Ceramics, **III** 681
Tamar Bank, **II** 187
Tamarkin Co., **12** 390
Tambrands Inc., 8 511–13; **12** 439
Tamco Distributors Co., **12** 390
TAMET, **IV** 25
Tamm, Peter, **IV** 591
Tampa Electric Company, **6** 582–83
Tampax, **III** 40
Tampax Inc., **8** 511–12. *See also*
    Tambrands Inc.
Oy Tampella Ab, **II** 47; **III** 648; **IV** 276
Tampere Paper Board and Roofing Felt
    Mill, **IV** 314
Tampereen Osake-Pankki, **II** 303
Tampimex Oil, **11** 194
Tamuke, Jyuemon, **I** 518
Tamura Kisan Co., **II** 552
Tan, Thomas S., **9** 297
Tanabe, Masaru, **III** 742
Tanabe Seiyaku, **I** 648; **9** 328
Tanaka, **6** 71
Tanaka, Hisashige, **12** 483
Tanaka, Kakuei, **I** 66, 494; **IV** 728; **11** 268
Tanaka Kikinzoku Kogyo KK, **IV** 119
Tanaka, Kyubei, **II** 326
Tanaka Matthey KK, **IV** 119
Tanaka, Tadao, **II** 68
Tanaka, Taro, **III** 593
Tanaka, Tukujiro, **III** 385

Tandem Computers, Inc., 6 278–80; **10**
    499; **11** 18
Tandem Telecommunications Systems,
    Inc., **6** 280
Tandy Brands, Inc., **10** 166
Tandy, Charles, **II** 106–08; **12** 393, 468
Tandy Corporation, II 70, **106–08**; **6**
    257–58; **9** 43, 115, 165; **10** 56–57,
    166–67, 236; **12 468–70 (upd.)**
Tandy Marketing Cos., **II** 107
Tang, Jack, **III** 705
Tang, Shiu-kin (Sir), **IV** 717
Tangent Systems, **6** 247–48
Tanii, Akio, **II** 56
Tanjong Pagar Dock Co., **I** 592
Tanks Oil and Gas, **11** 97
Tanner, Mikko, **IV** 469
Tanner, Nathan Eldon, **V** 738
Tansky, Burton, **12** 357
TAP Air Portugal. *See* Transportes Aereos
    Portugueses.
Tapiola Insurance, **IV** 316
Taplin, Frank E., **7** 369
Tappan, Arthur, **IV** 604
Tappan, David S., Jr., **I** 571; **8** 192
Tappan, Lewis, **IV** 604
Tara Exploration and Development Ltd.,
    IV 165
Tara Foods, **II** 645
Tarbox, Richard C., **11** 485
Target Stores, V 35, 43–44; **10** 284,
    515–17; **12** 508
Tariki, Sayyid Abdullah H., **IV** 537
Tarkenton, Fran, **9** 309–10
Tarkett, **12** 464
Tarkington, Andrew W., **IV** 401
Tarmac America, **III** 753
Tarmac Civil Engineering, **III** 752
Tarmac Ltd., **III** 751–53
Tarmac PLC, III 734, **751–54**
Tarmac Roadstone, **III** 752
Tarmac Vinculum, **III** 752
TarMacadam (Purnell Hooley's Patent)
    Syndicate Ltd., **III** 751
Tarr, Robert J., **I** 245
Tarslag, **III** 752
Tartikoff, Brandon, **6** 165; **10** 288
Tasco, Frank J., **III** 283
Tashima, Hideo, **III** 575
Tashima, Kazuo, **III** 574–75
Tashima Shoten, **III** 574
Tashiro, Shigeki, **V** 384
Tasman Pulp and Paper (Sales) Ltd., **IV**
    279
Tasman Pulp and Paper Co. Ltd., **IV**
    278–79
Tasman U.E.B., **IV** 249
Tasmanian Fibre Containers, **IV** 249
Tata Airlines. *See* Air-India.
Tata, Dorabji (Sir), **IV** 217–18
Tata Electric Co., **IV** 219
Tata Engineering and Locomotive Co., **IV**
    218–19
Tata Enterprises, **III** 43
Tata family, **IV** 217–19
Tata Group, **IV** 218–19
Tata Hydro-Electric Power Supply Co., **IV**
    218
Tata Industries Ltd., **IV** 218–19
Tata Iron and Steel Company Ltd., IV
    48, 205–07, **217–19**
Tata, J.R.D., **6** 63
Tata, Jamsetji, **IV** 205, 218
Tata, Jamsetji Nusserwanji, **IV** 217–19

Tata, Jehangir Ratanji Dadabhoy, **IV** 219
Tata, Ratan Naval, **IV** 219
Tata, Ratanji, **IV** 217–19
Tata Services, **IV** 219
Tataka, Masao, **III** 546
Tate & Lyle PLC, II 514, **580–83**; **7**
    466–67
Tate, Alfred, **II** 580
Tate, Caleb, **II** 580
Tate, Edwin, **II** 580
Tate, Ernest, **II** 580–81
Tate, Henry, **II** 580
Tate, Sidney B., **10** 299
Tate, Toyoo, **9** 350
Tate, Vernon, **II** 581
Tate, William, **II** 581
Tate, William Henry, **II** 580
Tatebayashi Flour Milling Co., **II** 554
Tateisi Electric Manufacturing, **II** 75
Tateisi Medical Electronics Manufacturing
    Co., **II** 75
Tateisi, Kazuma, **II** 75–76
Tateisi, Takao, **II** 76
Tatian, Marie, **III** 568
Tatò, Franco, **IV** 587
Tatsumi, Sotoo, **II** 361
Tatum, John, **11** 538
Tatung Co., **III** 482
Taub, Henry, **III** 117; **9** 48–49
Taub, Joe, **III** 117; **9** 48
Taubman, A. Alfred, **11** 454
Taurus Programming Services, **10** 196
Tavoulareas, William, **IV** 465; **7** 353
Taylor, Allan, **II** 345
Taylor, Andrew, **6** 393
Taylor, Arthur, **II** 133; **6** 158
Taylor, Bernard D., **9** 264
Taylor, Bill, **12** 471–72
Taylor, Charles G., **III** 292
Taylor, Charles H., **7** 13–14; **9** 133
Taylor, Charles H., Jr., **7** 14
Taylor, Claude I., **6** 61
Taylor, David, **II** 262
Taylor Diving and Salvage Co., **III** 499
Taylor, E.M., **12** 471
Taylor, Edgar M. *See* Taylor, E.M.
Taylor, Elizabeth, **II** 176
Taylor Engraving Company, **12** 471
Taylor, Ernest, **II** 586
Taylor, Frank, **I** 590–91; **11** 61
Taylor, Frederick, **IV** 385
Taylor, Frederick W., **IV** 252
Taylor, George C., **II** 397; **10** 61
Taylor, Graham D., **I** 330
Taylor, H.C., **12** 471
Taylor, Herbert C. *See* Taylor, H.C.
Taylor, J.W., Jr. *See* Taylor, Bill.
Taylor, Jack Crawford, **6** 392
Taylor, James, **II** 306
Taylor, James B., **8** 315
Taylor, James E., **11** 356–57
Taylor, James W., **10** 174
Taylor, John, **II** 306
Taylor, John, Jr., **II** 306
Taylor, John M., **III** 237–38
Taylor, John R., **III** 330
Taylor, Moses, **II** 253; **9** 123
Taylor, Myron C., **IV** 573; **7** 550
Taylor, Nathan A., **6** 161
Taylor Publishing Company, 12 471–73
Taylor, R.J., **III** 240
Taylor, Reese, **IV** 570
Taylor Rental Corp., **III** 628
Taylor, S. Blackwell, **III** 602

INDEX TO INDUSTRIES

Index to Industries

ACCOUNTING

Deloitte & Touche, 9
Ernst & Young, 9
Price Waterhouse, 9

ADVERTISING & OTHER BUSINESS SERVICES

Ackerley Communications, Inc., 9
Adia S.A., 6
Advo, Inc., 6
Aegis Group plc, 6
American Building Maintenance Industries, Inc., 6
Chiat/Day Inc. Advertising, 11
D'Arcy Masius Benton & Bowles, Inc., 6
Dentsu Inc., I
Equifax, Inc., 6
Foote, Cone & Belding Communications, Inc., I
Grey Advertising, Inc., 6
Hakuhodo, Inc., 6
Interpublic Group Inc., I
Japan Leasing Corporation, 8
JWT Group Inc., I
Katz Communications, Inc., 6
Kelly Services Inc., 6
Ketchum Communications Inc., 6
Leo Burnett Company Inc., I
The Ogilvy Group, Inc., I
Olsten Corporation, 6
Omnicom Group, I
Pinkerton's Inc., 9
Saatchi & Saatchi PLC, I
ServiceMaster Limited Partnership, 6
Sotheby's Holdings, Inc., 11
TBWA Advertising, Inc., 6
Wells Rich Greene BDDP, 6
WPP Group plc, 6
Young & Rubicam, Inc., I

AEROSPACE

Aerospatiale, 7
Avions Marcel Dassault-Breguet Aviation, I
Beech Aircraft Corporation, 8
The Boeing Company, I; 10 (upd.)
British Aerospace PLC, I
Cessna Aircraft Company, 8
Fairchild Aircraft, Inc., 9
G.I.E. Airbus Industrie, I; 12 (upd.)
General Dynamics Corporation, I; 10 (upd.)
Grumman Corporation, I; 11 (upd.)
Gulfstream Aerospace Corp., 7
N.V. Koninklijke Nederlandse Vliegtuigenfabriek Fokker, I
Learjet Inc., 8
Lockheed Corporation, I; 11 (upd.)
Martin Marietta Corporation, I
McDonnell Douglas Corporation, I; 11 (upd.)
Messerschmitt-Bölkow-Blohm GmbH., I
Northrop Corporation, I; 11 (upd.)

Pratt & Whitney, 9
Rockwell International, I
Rockwell International Corporation, 11 (upd.)
Rolls-Royce plc, I; 7 (upd.)
Sundstrand Corporation, 7
Textron Lycoming Turbine Engine, 9
Thiokol Corporation, 9
United Technologies Corporation, I; 10 (upd.)

AIRLINES

Aeroflot Soviet Airlines, 6
Air Canada, 6
Air-India, 6
Alaska Air Group, Inc., 6
Alitalia—Linee Aeree Italiana, SPA, 6
All Nippon Airways Company Limited, 6
America West Airlines, 6
American Airlines, I; 6 (upd.)
British Airways PLC, I
Cathay Pacific Airways Limited, 6
Continental Airlines, I
Delta Air Lines, Inc., I; 6 (upd.)
Deutsche Lufthansa A.G., I
Eastern Airlines, I
EgyptAir, 6
Finnair Oy, 6
Garuda Indonesia, 6
Groupe Air France, 6
HAL Inc., 9
Iberia Líneas Aéreas de España S.A., 6
Japan Air Lines Company Ltd., I
Koninklijke Luchtvaart Maatschappij, N.V., I
Korean Air Lines Co. Ltd., 6
Malaysian Airlines System BHD, 6
Mesa Airlines, Inc., 11
Northwest Airlines, Inc., I; 6 (upd.)
Pan American World Airways, Inc., I; 12 (upd.)
People Express Airlines, Inc., I
Philippine Airlines, Inc., 6
Qantas Airways Limited, 6
Saudi Arabian Airlines, 6
Scandinavian Airlines System, I
Singapore Airlines Ltd., 6
Southwest Airlines Co., 6
Swiss Air Transport Company, Ltd., I
Texas Air Corporation, I
Thai Airways International Ltd., 6
Trans World Airlines, Inc., I; 12 (upd.)
Transportes Aereos Portugueses, S.A., 6
United Airlines, I; 6 (upd.)
USAir Group, Inc., I; 6 (upd.)
VARIG, SA, 6

AUTOMOTIVE

Adam Opel AG, 7
American Motors Corporation, I
Arvin Industries, Inc., 8
Automobiles Citroen, 7
Bayerische Motoren Werke A.G., I; 11 (upd.)

Bendix Corporation, I
The Budd Company, 8
Chrysler Corporation, I; 11 (upd.)
Cummins Engine Co. Inc., I; 12 (upd.)
Daihatsu Motor Company, Ltd., 7
Daimler-Benz A.G., I
Dana Corporation, I; 10 (upd.)
Eaton Corporation, I; 10 (upd.)
Echlin Inc., I; 11 (upd.)
Federal-Mogul Corporation, I; 10 (upd.)
Fiat Group, I
Fiat S.p.A, 11 (upd.)
Ford Motor Company, I; 11 (upd.)
Fruehauf Corporation, I
General Motors Corporation, I; 10 (upd.)
Genuine Parts Company, 9
Harley-Davidson Inc., 7
Hino Motors, Ltd., 7
Honda Motor Company Limited (Honda Giken Kogyo Kabushiki Kaisha), I; 10 (upd.)
Isuzu Motors, Ltd., 9
Kelsey-Hayes Group of Companies, 7
Kia Motors Corp., 12
Mack Trucks, Inc., I
Mazda Motor Corporation, 9
Midas International Corporation, 10
Mitsubishi Motors Corporation, 9
Navistar International Corporation, I; 10 (upd.)
Nissan Motor Company Ltd., I; 11 (upd.)
Oshkosh Truck Corporation, 7
Paccar Inc., I
The Pep Boys—Manny, Moe & Jack, 11
Peugeot S.A., I
Regie Nationale des Usines Renault, I
Robert Bosch GmbH., I
Rolls-Royce Motors Ltd., I
Rover Group plc, 7
Saab-Scania A.B., I; 11 (upd.)
Saturn Corporation, 7
Sealed Power Corporation, I
Sheller-Globe Corporation, I
SPX Corporation, 10
Superior Industries International, Inc., 8
Suzuki Motor Corporation, 9
Toyota Motor Corporation, I; 11 (upd.)
Volkswagen A.G., I; 11 (upd.)
AB Volvo, I; 7 (upd.)
Winnebago Industries Inc., 7

BEVERAGES

Adolph Coors Company, I
Allied-Lyons PLC, I
Anheuser-Busch Companies, Inc., I; 10 (upd.)
Asahi Breweries, Ltd., I
Bass PLC, I
Brauerei Beck & Co., 9
Brown-Forman Corporation, I; 10 (upd.)
Carlsberg A/S, 9
Carlton and United Breweries Ltd., I
Cerveceria Polar, I
Coca Cola Bottling Co. Consolidated, 10

Longview Fibre Company, 8
Metal Box PLC, I
National Can Corporation, I
Owens-Illinois, Inc., I
Primerica Corporation, I
Sonoco Products Company, 8
Toyo Seikan Kaisha, Ltd., I

DRUGS

A.L. Pharma Inc., 12
Abbott Laboratories, I; 11 (upd.)
ALZA Corporation, 10
American Home Products, I; 10 (upd.)
Amgen, Inc., 10
A.B. Astra, I
Baxter International Inc., I; 10 (upd.)
Becton, Dickinson & Company, I
Block Drug Company, Inc., 8
Carter-Wallace, Inc., 8
Chiron Corporation, 10
Ciba-Geigy Ltd., I; 8 (upd.)
Eli Lilly & Company, I; 11 (upd.)
F. Hoffmann-Laroche & Company A.G., I
Fisons plc, 9
Fujisawa Pharmaceutical Company Ltd., I
G.D. Searle & Company, I; 12 (upd.)
Genentech, Inc., I; 8 (upd.)
Genetics Institute, Inc., 8
Glaxo Holdings PLC, I; 9 (upd.)
Johnson & Johnson, III; 8 (upd.)
Marion Merrell Dow, Inc., I; 9 (upd.)
McKesson Corporation, 12
Merck & Co., Inc., I; 11 (upd.)
Miles Laboratories, I
Mylan Laboratories, I
Novo Industri A/S, I
Pfizer Inc., I; 9 (upd.)
Pharmacia A.B., I
R.P. Scherer, I
Rorer Group, I
Roussel Uclaf, I; 8 (upd.)
Sandoz Ltd., I
Sankyo Company, Ltd., I
Sanofi Group, I
Schering A.G., I
Schering-Plough, I
Sigma-Aldrich, I
SmithKline Beckman Corporation, I
Squibb Corporation, I
Sterling Drug, Inc., I
Syntex Corporation, I
Takeda Chemical Industries, Ltd., I
The Upjohn Company, I; 8 (upd.)
Warner-Lambert Co., I; 10 (upd.)
The Wellcome Foundation Ltd., I

ELECTRICAL & ELECTRONICS

ABB ASEA Brown Boveri Ltd., II
Acuson Corporation, 10
Advanced Technology Laboratories, Inc., 9
Alps Electric Co., Ltd., II
AMP, Inc., II
Analog Devices, Inc., 10
Andrew Corporation, 10
Arrow Electronics, Inc., 10
Atari Corporation, 9
Autodesk, Inc., 10
Avnet, Inc., 9
Bicoastal Corporation, II
Cabletron Systems, Inc., 10
Compagnie Générale d'Électricité, II
Cooper Industries, Inc., II
Digi International Inc., 9
E-Systems, Inc., 9
Emerson Electric Co., II
Fuji Electric Co., Ltd., II
General Electric Company, II; 12 (upd.)

General Electric Company, PLC, II
General Instrument Corporation, 10
General Signal Corporation, 9
GM Hughes Electronics Corporation, II
Goldstar Co., Ltd., 12
Harris Corporation, II
Honeywell Inc., II; 12 (upd.)
Hubbell Incorporated, 9
Intel Corporation, II; 10 (upd.)
Itel Corporation, 9
KitchenAid, 8
KnowledgeWare Inc., 9
Koor Industries Ltd., II
Kyocera Corporation, II
Loral Corporation, 9
Lucky-Goldstar, II
Matsushita Electric Industrial Co., Ltd., II
Mitsubishi Electric Corporation, II
Motorola, Inc., II; 11 (upd.)
National Semiconductor Corporation, II
NEC Corporation, II
Nokia Corporation, II
Oki Electric Industry Company, Limited, II
Omron Tateisi Electronics Company, II
N.V. Philips Gloeilampenfabrieken, II
Pittway Corporation, 9
The Plessey Company, PLC, II
Potter & Brumfield Inc., 11
Premier Industrial Corporation, 9
Racal Electronics PLC, II
Raychem Corporation, 8
Raytheon Company, II; 11 (upd.)
RCA Corporation, II
Read-Rite Corp., 10
Reliance Electric Company, 9
Sanyo Electric Company, Ltd., II
Schneider S.A., II
SCI Systems, Inc., 9
Sensormatic Electronics Corp., 11
Sharp Corporation, II; 12 (upd.)
Siemens A.G., II
Silicon Graphics Incorporated, 9
Solectron Corp., 12
Sony Corporation, II; 12 (upd.)
Sumitomo Electric Industries, Ltd., II
Sunbeam-Oster Co., Inc., 9
Tandy Corporation, II; 12 (upd.)
TDK Corporation, II
Tektronix, Inc., 8
Telxon Corporation, 10
Teradyne, Inc., 11
Texas Instruments Incorporated, II; 11 (upd.)
Thomson S.A., II
Varian Associates Inc., 12
Victor Company of Japan, Ltd., II
Vitro Corp., 10
Westinghouse Electric Corporation, II; 12 (upd.)
Zenith Data Systems, Inc., 10
Zenith Electronics Corporation, II

ENGINEERING & MANAGEMENT SERVICES

Analytic Sciences Corporation, 10
The Austin Company, 8
CDI Corporation, 6
CRSS Inc., 6
Day & Zimmermann Inc., 9
EG&G Incorporated, 8
Foster Wheeler Corporation, 6
Jacobs Engineering Group Inc., 6
JWP Inc., 9
McKinsey & Company, Inc., 9
Ogden Corporation, 6
The Parsons Corporation, 8
Rust International Inc., 11

Susquehanna Pfaltzgraff Company, 8
United Dominion Industries Limited, 8
VECO International, Inc., 7

ENTERTAINMENT & LEISURE

AMC Entertainment Inc., 12
Asahi National Broadcasting Company, Ltd., 9
Blockbuster Entertainment Corporation, 9
British Broadcasting Corporation, 7
Cablevision Systems Corporation, 7
Capital Cities/ABC Inc., II
CBS Inc., II; 6 (upd.)
Central Independent Television plc, 7
Cineplex Odeon Corporation, 6
Columbia Pictures Entertainment, Inc., II
Columbia TriStar Motion Pictures Companies, 12 (upd.)
Comcast Corporation, 7
Continental Cablevision, Inc., 7
Gaylord Entertainment Company, 11
Granada Group PLC, II
Home Box Office Inc., 7
Japan Broadcasting Corporation, 7
King World Productions, Inc., 9
Ladbroke Group PLC, II
Lucasfilm Ltd., 12
MCA Inc., II
Media General, Inc., 7
MGM/UA Communications Company, II
National Broadcasting Company, Inc., II; 6 (upd.)
Orion Pictures Corporation, 6
Paramount Pictures Corporation, II
Promus Companies, Inc., 9
Rank Organisation PLC, II
Sega of America, Inc., 10
Tele-Communications, Inc., II
Television Española, S.A., 7
Thomas Cook Travel Inc., 9
The Thomson Corporation, 8
Touristik Union International GmbH. and Company K.G., II
Turner Broadcasting System, Inc., II; 6 (upd.)
Twentieth Century Fox Film Corporation, II
Vail Associates, Inc., 11
Viacom International Inc., 7
Walt Disney Company, II; 6 (upd.)
Warner Communications Inc., II

FINANCIAL SERVICES: BANKS

Abbey National PLC, 10
Algemene Bank Nederland N.V., II
American Residential Mortgage Corporation, 8
AmSouth Bancorporation, 12
Amsterdam-Rotterdam Bank N.V., II
Anchor Bancorp, Inc., 10
Australia and New Zealand Banking Group Ltd., II
Banc One Corporation, 10
Banca Commerciale Italiana SpA, II
Banco Bilbao Vizcaya, S.A., II
Banco Central, II
Banco do Brasil S.A., II
Bank Brussels Lambert, II
Bank Hapoalim B.M., II
Bank of Boston Corporation, II
Bank of Montreal, II
Bank of New England Corporation, II
The Bank of New York Company, Inc., II
The Bank of Nova Scotia, II
Bank of Tokyo, Ltd., II
BankAmerica Corporation, II; 8 (upd.)
Bankers Trust New York Corporation, II

FINANCIAL SERVICES: NON-BANKS

FOOD PRODUCTS

Southern New England
 Telecommunications Corporation, 6
Southwestern Bell Corporation, V
Sprint Communications Company, L.P., 9
Swedish Telecom, V
SynOptics Communications, Inc., 10
Telecom Australia, 6
Telecom Eireann, 7
Telefonaktiebolaget LM Ericsson, V
Telefónica de España, S.A., V
Telephone and Data Systems, Inc., 9
Tellabs, Inc., 11
U S West, Inc., V
United States Cellular Corporation, 9
United Telecommunications, Inc., V
Vodafone Group plc, 11

TEXTILES & APPAREL

Albany International Corp., 8
Amoskeag Company, 8
Benetton Group S.p.A., 10
Birkenstock Footprint Sandals, Inc., 12
Brown Group, Inc., V
Burlington Industries, Inc., V
Charming Shoppes, Inc., 8
Coach Leatherware, 10
Coats Viyella Plc, V
Cone Mills Corporation, 8
Courtaulds plc, V
Crystal Brands, Inc., 9
Danskin, Inc., 12
Delta Woodside Industries, Inc., 8
Dominion Textile Inc., 12
Edison Brothers Stores, Inc., 9
Esprit de Corp., 8
Fieldcrest Cannon, Inc., 9
Fruit of the Loom, Inc., 8
The Gitano Group, Inc. 8
Guilford Mills Inc., 8
Hartmarx Corporation, 8
Interface, Inc., 8
J. Crew Group Inc., 12
Jockey International, Inc., 12
Kellwood Company, 8
L.A. Gear, Inc., 8
L.L. Bean, Inc., 10
Lee Apparel Company, Inc., 8
The Leslie Fay Companies, Inc., 8
Levi Strauss & Co., V
Liz Claiborne, Inc., 8
Milliken & Co., V
Mitsubishi Rayon Co., Ltd., V
Nike, Inc., V; 8 (upd.)
OshKosh B'Gosh, Inc., 9
Oxford Industries, Inc., 8
Polo/Ralph Lauren Corporation, 12
Reebok International Ltd., V; 9 (upd.)
Russell Corporation, 8
Springs Industries, Inc., V
Starter Corp., 12
Stride Rite Corporation, 8
Teijin Limited, V
Toray Industries, Inc., V
Unifi, Inc., 12
Unitika Ltd., V
VF Corporation, V
Walton Monroe Mills, Inc., 8
The Warnaco Group Inc., 12
Wellman, Inc., 8
West Point-Pepperell, Inc., 8

TOBACCO

American Brands, Inc., V
Dibrell Brothers, Incorporated, 12
Gallaher Limited, V
Imasco Limited, V
Japan Tobacco Incorporated, V

Philip Morris Companies Inc., V
RJR Nabisco Holdings Corp., V
Rothmans International p.l.c., V
Tabacalera, S.A., V
Universal Corporation, V
UST Inc., 9

TRANSPORT SERVICES

Airborne Freight Corp., 6
Alamo Rent A Car, Inc., 6
Alexander & Baldwin, Inc., 10
Amerco, 6
American President Companies Ltd., 6
Anschutz Corp., 12
Avis, Inc., 6
BAA plc, 10
British Railways Board, V
Budget Rent a Car Corporation, 9
Burlington Northern Inc., V
Canadian National Railway System, 6
Canadian Pacific Limited, V
Carlson Companies, Inc., 6
Carnival Cruise Lines, Inc., 6
Carolina Freight Corporation, 6
Chargeurs, 6
Chicago and North Western Holdings
 Corporation, 6
Compagnie Générale Maritime et
 Financière, 6
Consolidated Freightways, Inc., V
Consolidated Rail Corporation, V
Crowley Maritime Corporation, 6
CSX Corporation, V
Danzas Group, V
Deutsche Bundesbahn, V
DHL Worldwide Express, 6
East Japan Railway Company, V
Emery Air Freight Corporation, 6
Enterprise Rent-A-Car Company, 6
Federal Express Corporation, V
Fritz Companies, Inc., 12
GATX, 6
Hankyu Corporation, V
Hapag-Lloyd AG, 6
The Hertz Corporation, 9
Illinois Central Corporation, 11
J.B. Hunt Transport Services Inc., 12
Kansas City Southern Industries, Inc., 6
Kawasaki Kisen Kaisha, Ltd., V
Keio Teito Electric Railway Company, V
Kinki Nippon Railway Company Ltd., V
Koninklijke Nedlloyd Groep N.V., 6
Kuhne & Nagel International A.G., V
La Poste, V
Leaseway Transportation Corp., 12
London Regional Transport, 6
Mayflower Group Inc., 6
Mitsui O.S.K. Lines, Ltd., V
National Car Rental System, Inc., 10
NFC plc, 6
Nippon Express Co., Ltd., V
Nippon Yusen Kabushiki Kaisha, V
Norfolk Southern Corporation, V
Ocean Group plc, 6
Odakyu Electric Railway Company
 Limited, V
Österreichische Bundesbahnen GmbH, 6
Overseas Shipholding Group, Inc., 11
The Peninsular and Oriental Steam
 Navigation Company, V
Penske Corporation, V
PHH Corporation, V
Post Office Group, V
Preston Corporation, 6
Roadway Services, Inc., V
Ryder System, Inc., V
Santa Fe Pacific Corporation, V

Schenker-Rhenus AG, 6
Seibu Railway Co. Ltd., V
Seino Transportation Company, Ltd., 6
Société Nationale des Chemins de Fer
 Français, V
Southern Pacific Transportation Company,
 V
Stinnes AG, 8
The Swiss Federal Railways
 (Schweizerische Bundesbahnen), V
Tidewater Inc., 11
TNT Limited, V
Tobu Railway Co Ltd, 6
Tokyu Corporation, V
Totem Resources Corporation, 9
Transnet Ltd., 6
TTX Company, 6
Union Pacific Corporation, V
United Parcel Service of America Inc., V
Yamato Transport Co. Ltd., V
Yellow Freight System, Inc. of Delaware,
 V

UTILITIES

The AES Corporation, 10
Air & Water Technologies Corporation, 6
Allegheny Power System, Inc., V
American Electric Power Company, Inc., V
American Water Works Company, 6
Arkla, Inc., V
Associated Natural Gas Corporation, 11
Atlanta Gas Light Company, 6
Atlantic Energy, Inc., 6
Baltimore Gas and Electric Company, V
Bayernwerk A.G., V
Big Rivers Electric Corporation, 11
Boston Edison Company, 12
British Gas plc, V
British Nuclear Fuels plc, 6
Brooklyn Union Gas, 6
Carolina Power & Light Company, V
Cascade Natural Gas Corporation, 9
Centerior Energy Corporation, V
Central and South West Corporation, V
Central Hudson Gas and Electricity
 Corporation, 6
Central Maine Power, 6
Chubu Electric Power Company,
 Incorporated, V
Chugoku Electric Power Company Inc., V
Cincinnati Gas & Electric Company, 6
CIPSCO Inc., 6
Citizens Utilities Company, 7
City Public Service, 6
CMS Energy Corporation, V
Cogentrix Energy, Inc., 10
The Coleman Company, Inc., 9
The Columbia Gas System, Inc., V
Commonwealth Edison Company, V
Consolidated Edison Company of New
 York, Inc., V
Consolidated Natural Gas Company, V
Consumers' Gas Company Ltd., 6
Destec Energy, Inc., 12
The Detroit Edison Company, V
Dominion Resources, Inc., V
DPL Inc., 6
DQE, Inc., 6
Duke Power Company, V
Eastern Enterprises, 6
El Paso Natural Gas Company, 12
Electricité de France, V
Elektrowatt AG, 6
ENDESA Group, V
Enron Corp., V
Enserch Corporation, V
Ente Nazionale per L'Energia Elettrica, V

WASTE SERVICES

NOTES ON CONTRIBUTORS

Notes on Contributors

CANIPE, Jennifer Voskuhl. Free-lance writer and researcher.

COHEN, Kerstan. Free-lance writer and French translator; editor for *Letter-Ex* poetry review.

COLLINS, Cheryl L. Free-lance writer and researcher.

COVELL, Jeffrey L. Free-lance writer and corporate history contractor.

DERDAK, Thomas. Free-lance writer and adjunct professor of philosophy at Loyola University of Chicago; former executive director of the Albert Einstein Foundation.

DUBLANC, Robin. Free-lance writer and copyeditor in Yorkshire, England.

FIERO, John W. Free-lance writer, researcher, and consultant; Professor of English at the University of Southwestern Louisiana in Lafayette; director of creative writing and the Deep South Writers Conference.

GALLMAN, Jason. Free-lance writer and graduate student in English at Purdue University.

GASBARRE, April Dougal. Archivist and free-lance writer specializing in business and social history in Cleveland, Ohio.

GOPNIK, Hilary. Free-lance writer.

HALASZ, Robert. Former editor-in-chief of *World Progress* and *Funk & Wagnalls New Encyclopedia Yearbook;* author, *The U.S. Marines* (Millbrook Press, 1993).

HECHT, Henry. Editorial consultant and retired vice-president, editorial services, Merrill Lynch.

HUGHES, Terry W. Educator and free-lance writer with special interests in education, home video, home audio, motion pictures, woodworking, and historic preservation.

JACOBSON, Robert R. Free-lance writer and musician.

KEELEY, Carol I. Free-lance writer and researcher; columnist for *Neon;* researcher for *Ford Times* and *Discovery.* Contributor to *Oxford Poetry,* 1987, and *Voices International,* 1989.

McCREADY, Sean. Free-lance writer and copyeditor.

McMANUS, Donald. Free-lance writer.

MONTGOMERY, Bruce P. Curator and director of historical collection, University of Colorado at Boulder.

MOTE, Dave. President of information retrieval company Performance Database.

PEDERSON, Jay P. Free-lance writer and editor.

PENDERGAST, Sara. Free-lance writer and copyeditor.

PENDERGAST, Tom. Free-lance writer and graduate student in American studies at Purdue University.

PFALZGRAF, Taryn Benbow. Free-lance editor, writer, and consultant in the Chicago area.

ROURKE, Elizabeth. Free-lance writer.

SALAMIE, David E. Part owner of InfoWorks Development Group, a reference publication development and editorial services company.

SCHNEIDER, Bob. Free-lance writer and translator.

SMETHURST, Katherine. Free-lance writer.

SUN, Douglas. Assistant professor of English at California State University at Los Angeles.

TROESTER, Maura. Free-lance writer based in Chicago.